ADDICTION PROBLEMS

- **EXPANDED CATEGORY** Substance Use Disorder (Chapter 12)

  ▶ Combines past categories *substance abuse* and *substance dependence*.

- **POSSIBLE FUTURE CATEGORY** Caffeine Use Disorder (Chapter 12)

  ▶ Features maladaptive pattern of caffeine use leading to significant impairment or distress.

- **REORGANIZATION** Gambling Disorder (Chapter 12)

  ▶ Grouped with *addictive disorders,* not *impulse-control disorders.*

- **POSSIBLE FUTURE CATEGORY** Internet Gaming Disorder (Chapters 5, 19)

  ▶ Features excessive need for online gaming and/or other online activities.

PROBLEMS OF SEX AND GENDER

- **NEW NAME** Delayed Ejaculation (Chapter 13)

  ▶ Replaces past term *male orgasmic disorder.*

- **EXPANDED CATEGORY** Female Sexual Interest/Arousal Disorder (Chapter 13)

  ▶ Combines past categories *female hypoactive sexual desire disorder* and *female sexual arousal disorder.*

- **NEW NAME** Gender Dysphoria (Chapter 13)

  ▶ Replaces *gender identity disorder.*

PROBLEMS OF PSYCHOSIS

- **POSSIBLE FUTURE CATEGORY** Attenuated Psychosis Syndrome (Chapter 14)

  ▶ Features psychotic symptoms that are milder and less problematic than those found in schizophrenia.

PROBLEMS OF PERSONALITY

- **POSSIBLE FUTURE MODEL** Alternative Model for Personality Disorders (Chapter 16)

  ▶ Features a dimensional model in which diagnosticians rate the degree of impairment caused by one or more problematic traits (e.g., impulsivity, suspiciousness, or hostility).

LIFESPAN PROBLEMS

- **EXPANDED CATEGORY** Autism Spectrum Disorder (Chapter 17)

  ▶ Combines past categories *autistic disorder, Asperger's disorder,* and *childhood disintegrative disorder.*

- **NEW NAME** Intellectual Developmental Disorder (Intellectual Disability) (Chapter 17)

  ▶ Replaces past term *mental retardation.*

- **EXPANDED CATEGORY** Specific Learning Disorder (Chapter 17)

  ▶ Combines past categories *reading disorder, mathematics disorder,* and *disorder of written expression.*

PROBLEMS OF COGNITION AND AGING

- **NEW NAME** Major Neurocognitive Disorder (Chapter 18)

  ▶ Replaces past term *dementia.*

- **NEW CATEGORY** Mild Neurocognitive Disorder (Chapter 18)

  ▶ Features mild cognitive impairments such as those found in early stages of Alzheimer's disease.

* Based on the APA (2013).

Abnormal Psychology

EIGHTH EDITION

Ronald J. Comer

Princeton University

WORTH PUBLISHERS

A Macmillan Higher Education Company

Senior Vice President, Editorial and Production: Catherine Woods
Publisher: Kevin Feyen
Acquisitions Editor: Rachel Losh
Senior Development Editor: Mimi Melek
Marketing Manager: Lindsay Johnson
Marketing Coordinator: Julie Tompkins
Supplements Editor: Katherine Garrett
Associate Managing Editor: Lisa Kinne
Media Editor: Elizabeth Block
Project Editor: Jennifer Bossert
Permissions Manager: Jennifer MacMillan
Photo Department Manager: Ted Szczepanski
Art Director and Interior/Cover Designer: Babs Reingold
Chapter Opener Photo Researcher: Lyndall Culbertson
Layout Designer: Paul Lacy
Cover Photo: Lukasz Laska/Getty Images
Production Manager: Sarah Segal
Composition: Northeastern Graphic, Inc.
Printing and Binding: RR Donnelley

Credits for chapter opening photos: p. xxvi: © 2009 Alex Haas; p. 24: francois Brunelle/agefotostock; p. 46: Peter Jackson/LensModern; p. 82: Karim Parris; p. 112: Anna Fabroni/Wildcard Images/Glasshouse Images; p. 152: Quavondo Nguyen/www.quavondo.com; p. 188: Larry Hamill/age footstock; p. 222: Jonathan Barkat; p. 256: Jamie MacFadyen/Gallery Stock; p. 284: Link Image/Glasshouse Images; p. 316: Ross Honeysett/Gallery Stock; p. 346: Tim Georgeson/Gallery Stock; p. 386: plainpicture/Glasshouse Images; p. 424: Wildcard Images/Glasshouse Images; p. 448: Erin Mulvehill; p. 474: Gareth Munden/LensModern; p. 516: Clare Park/LensModern; p. 560: Bastienne Schmidt/Gallery Stock; p. 588: Kelvin Hudson/LensModern.

Credits for timeline photos, inside front cover (by date): 1893, Sigmund Freud Copyrights/Everett Collection; 1901, W. H. Freeman and Company; 1907, Stephane Audras/REA/Redux; 1929, AJ Photo/Science Source; 1963, LHB Photo/Alamy; 1981, Pallava Bagla/Corbis; 1998, Tony Cenicola/*New York Times*/Redux; 2006, Pool photo by Getty Images.

Credits for *MediaSpeak* photos: children playing "musical chairs" in yard, image100/Corbis; young couple showing intimacy, Corbis; traditional peat bog in County Galway, The Irish Image Collection/Design Pics/Corbis; businessmen standing by window, Getty Images; mother and daughter shopping, Corbis; woman's face with eyes closed, Michael Stewart/Corbis; bean on grid, Getty Images; aerial of bridge, Brand X Pictures; children with fireman's helmets and balloons, Getty Images; young friends toasting, Randy Faris/Corbis; senior woman at computer, Getty Images; upset woman sitting on bed, UpperCut/MediaBakery; dog, Corbis; man and woman laughing, Getty Images; children in choir, Digital Stock; seal, Eyewire Images; oil drilling rig, Corbis; paramedics, Corbis.

Credits for miscellaneous text excerpts: p. 287, Dennis Yusko, "At Home, but Locked in War," *Times Union* (Albany) Online. Copyright © 2008 by *Times Union*/Albany. Reproduced with permission via Copyright Clearance Center; pp. 479–480, case study excerpt from Bernstein et al., *Personality Disorders.* Copyright © 2007 by Sage Publications Inc. Books. Reproduced with permission via Copyright Clearance Center; pp. 496–497, case study excerpts from Meyer, *Case Studies in Abnormal Behavior,* 6th edition. Copyright © 2005. Reprinted by permission of Pearson Education, Inc.; p. 504, case study excerpt reprinted with permission from the DSM IV-TR Casebook. Copyright © 2002 American Psychiatric Association.

Library of Congress Control Number: 2013936019

ISBN-13 978-1-4641-3719-8
ISBN-10 1-4641-3719-6

Second Printing

Worth Publishers
41 Madison Ave
New York, NY 10010
www.worthpublishers.com

To Delia Sage Comer
—Welcome to the World

ABOUT THE AUTHOR

RONALD J. COMER has been a professor in Princeton University's Department of Psychology for the past 38 years, serving also as Director of Clinical Psychology Studies. In addition, he is chair of the university's Institutional Review Board (IRB). His courses—Abnormal Psychology, Theories of Psychotherapy, Childhood Psychopathology, Experimental Psychopathology, and Controversies in Clinical Psychology—have been among the university's most popular offerings.

Professor Comer has received the President's Award for Distinguished Teaching at the university. He is also a practicing clinical psychologist and serves as a consultant to the Eden Institute for Persons with Autism and to hospitals and family practice residency programs throughout New Jersey.

In addition to writing *Abnormal Psychology*, Professor Comer is the author of the textbook *Fundamentals of Abnormal Psychology*, now in its seventh edition; co-author of the introductory psychology textbook *Psychology Around Us*, now in its second edition; and co-author of *Case Studies in Abnormal Psychology*. He is the producer of various educational videos, including *The Higher Education Video Library Series*, *Worth Video Anthology for Abnormal Psychology*, *Video Segments in Neuroscience, Introduction to Psychology Video Clipboard*, and *Developmental Psychology Video Clipboard*. He also has published journal articles in clinical psychology, social psychology, and family medicine.

Professor Comer completed his undergraduate studies at the University of Pennsylvania and his graduate work at Clark University. He lives in Lawrenceville, New Jersey, with his wife, Marlene. From there he can keep a close eye on the Philadelphia sports teams with which he grew up.

Paul L. Bree

CONTENTS IN BRIEF

CONTENTS

CHAPTER : 4

Clinical Assessment, Diagnosis, and Treatment

83

CHAPTER : 5

Anxiety, Obsessive-Compulsive, and Related Disorders

113

CHAPTER :6

CHAPTER :7

CHAPTER :8

CHAPTER : 9

CHAPTER : 10

CHAPTER : 11

CHAPTER : 12

Substance Use and Addictive Disorders — 347

CHAPTER : 13

Disorders of Sex and Gender — 387

CHAPTER : 14

Schizophrenia 425

CHAPTER : 15

Treatments for Schizophrenia and Other Severe Mental Disorders 449

CHAPTER : 16

Personality Disorders 475

PREFACE

I have been writing my textbooks, *Abnormal Psychology and Fundamentals of Abnormal Psychology,* for more than three decades—approximately half of my life. The current version, *Abnormal Psychology,* Eighth Edition DSM-5 UPDATE, represents the sixteenth edition of one or the other of the textbooks. I feel deeply privileged to have had the opportunity to help educate more than a half-million readers over the years.

This textbook journey truly has been a labor of love, but I also must admit that each edition has required enormous effort, ridiculous pressure, and too many sleepless nights to count. I mention these labors not only because I am a world-class whiner but also to help emphasize that I have approached each edition as a totally new undertaking rather than as a cut-and-paste revision of past editions. My goal each time has been that the new edition is a fresh, comprehensive, and exciting presentation of the current state of this ever-changing field and that it includes enlightening and innovative pedagogical techniques. This "new book" approach to each edition is, I believe, the key reason for the continuing success of the textbooks.

That said, the current edition includes even more changes than in any of the textbook's previous editions, for several reasons: (1) A significantly changed, new edition of the field's classification and diagnostic system, DSM-5, has now been introduced, the first such revision in 19 years; (2) the field of abnormal psychology has had a dramatic growth spurt over the past several years; (3) the field of education has produced many new pedagogical tools; (4) the world of publishing has developed new, striking ways of presenting material; and (5) the world at large has changed dramatically, featuring a monumental rise in technology's impact on our lives, growing influence by the media, and near unthinkable economic, political, and societal events, including apparent increases in mass killings and other kinds of violence. Changes of this kind certainly should find their way into a book about the current state of human functioning, and I have worked hard to include them here in a meaningful way.

I believe I have produced a new edition of *Abnormal Psychology* that will once again excite readers and speak to them and their times. I have again tried to convey my passion for the field of abnormal psychology, and I have built on the generous feedback of my colleagues in this undertaking—the students and professors who have used this textbook over the years.

New and Expanded Features

In line with the enormous changes that have occurred over the past several years in the fields of abnormal psychology, education, and publishing and in the world, I have brought the following new features and changes to the current edition.

•NEW• DSM-5: A FIELD IN TRANSITION With the publication of DSM-5, abnormal psychology is clearly a field in transition. To help students appreciate the field's current status and new directions, I present, integrate, and critique DSM-5 material throughout the textbook. Controversy aside, this is now the field's classification and diagnostic system, and it is important that readers understand and master its categories and criteria, appreciate its strengths and weaknesses, and recognize its assumptions and implications, just as past readers learned about the categories, quality, and implications of previous DSM editions. DSM-5 offers at least six kinds of changes, all of which are integrated into *Abnormal Psychology,* Eighth Edition DSM-5 UPDATE:

•**Name changes:** DSM-5 has changed the names of many disorders in order to overcome disparaging or misleading connotations. *Intellectual disablility (intellectual developmental disorder)* (page 546), *neurocognitive disorder* (page 570), *illness anxiety disorder* (page 199), and *gender dysphoria* (page 416) have replaced, respectively, terms like mental retardation, dementia, hypochondriasis, and gender identity disorder.

•**New categories:** A number of new categories—some quite controversial—have been added to DSM-5, including *hoarding disorder* (page 148), *binge eating disorder* (page 324), *excoriation (skin-picking) disorder* (page 148), *mild neurocognitive disorder* (page 570), *disruptive mood dysregulation disorder* (page 525), and *premenstrual dysphoric disorder* (page 228).

•**New criteria:** The criteria for many disorders have been changed in DSM-5, and some of the changes have also produced controversy in the field. Certain people experiencing bereavement, for example, may now qualify for a diagnosis of *major depressive disorder* (page 227). Such individuals were usually excluded from this diagnosis in the past.

•**Consolidation of categories:** DSM-5 has merged certain past categories. The previous categories of substance abuse and substance dependence have been combined into *substance use disorder* (page 348). Autistic disorder, Asperger's disorder, and childhood disintegrative disorder have merged into the single category of *autism spectrum disorder* (page 539). And reading disorder, mathematics disorder, and disorder of written expression have been fused into *specific learning disorder* (page 547).

•**Expansion of boundaries:** DSM-5 has expanded the boundaries of certain categories. *Gambling disorder,* which used to be considered an impulse problem, is now viewed as a "behavioral addiction," much like repeated substance misuse is considered to be an addiction (page 382). And a diagnosis of *somatic symptom disorder,* a variation of past disorders called somatoform disorders, may now be assigned to people with significant medical problems, if those individuals are judged to be psychologically overreacting to their physical ailments (pages 193–194).

•**Future categories:** DSM-5 has designated certain categories for further study for possible inclusion in upcoming revisions of DSM-5, to be called DSM-5.1, DSM-5.2, and so on. These future possibilities include *personality disorder trait specified* (page 512), *attenuated psychosis syndrome, Internet use gaming disorder* (page 383), *non-suicidal self-injury* (page 289), and *suicidal behavior disorder* (page 286).

These important changes—as well as critiques and presentations of their logic, implications, and controversial nature—are offered in various ways throughout my textbook. First and foremost, the new categories, criteria, and the like are woven smoothly into the narrative of each and every chapter. Second, reader-friendly pedagogical tools, including numerous short, enlightening features located in margins throughout the book, called *DSM-5 Checklist* and *DSM-5 Controversy,* help students fully grasp the DSM-5 material. Third, periodic *PsychWatch* boxes highlight special DSM-5 issues and controversies, such as *Premenstrual Dysphoric Disorder: Déjà Vu All Over Again* (page 230) and *What Happened to Asperger's Disorder?* (page 540).

•**NEW**• **THE IMPACT OF TECHNOLOGY** The breathtaking rate of technological change that characterizes today's world has had significant effects—both positive and negative—on the mental health field, and it will undoubtedly affect the field even more in coming years. In this edition I cover this impact extensively, including numerous discussions in the book's narrative, boxes, photographs, and figures. The book examines, for example, how the Internet, texting, and social networks have become convenient tools for those who wish to bully others or pursue pedophilic desires (pages 519 and 412); how social networking sites may provide a new source for social anxiety (page 614); and how today's technology has helped create new psychological disorders such as Internet addiction (page 614). It also looks at troubling and dangerous new trends such as the posting of self-cutting videos on the Internet (page 492), live Web suicides (page 311), and pro-anorexia and pro-suicide Web sites (page 108). And it brings to life for the reader the growth of *cybertherapy* in its ever-expanding forms—from long-distance therapy using Skype to therapy enhanced by video game avatars and other virtual reality experiences to Internet-based support groups (pages 614–615).

•NEW• ADDITIONAL SECTIONS Over the past several years, a number of topics in abnormal psychology have received special and intense attention. In this edition, I have provided new sections on such topics, including *the psychology of mass killings* (page 487); *the use of psychological debriefing at disaster scenes* (pages 168–169); *dialectical behavior therapy* (pages 494–496); *dimensional views of abnormal functioning* (pages 100, 509–513); *the overuse of diagnoses such as PTSD, ADHD, and childhood bipolar disorder* (pages 185, 524–525, 533); and *sexism in the clinical field* (page 404).

•NEW• ADDITIONAL "CUTTING-EDGE" BOXES In this edition, I have grouped the various boxes into two categories to better orient the reader. *PsychWatch* boxes examine text topics in more depth, emphasize the effect of culture on mental disorders and treatment, and explore examples of abnormal psychology in movies, the news, and the real world. *MediaSpeak* boxes offer provocative pieces by news, magazine, and Web writers on current issues and trends in abnormal psychology. In addition to updating the *PsychWatch* and *MediaSpeak* boxes that have been retained from past editions, I have added many new ones, including:

•*PsychWatch:* Mass Murders: Where Does Such Violence Come From? (Chapter 16)

•*MediaSpeak:* A Rorschach Cheat Sheet on Wikipedia? (Chapter 4)

•*PsychWatch:* Adjustment Disorders: A Category of Compromise? (Chapter 6)

•*MediaSpeak:* The Poverty Clinic (Chapter 6)

•*MediaSpeak:* The Crying Game: Male Versus Female Tears (Chapter 8)

•*MediaSpeak:* Live Web Suicides: A Growing Phenomenon (Chapter 10)

•*MediaSpeak:* A Mother's Loss, a Daughter's Story (Chapter 11)

•*MediaSpeak:* The Sugar Plum Fairy (Chapter 11)

•*MediaSpeak:* Enrolling at Sober High (Chapter 12)

•*MediaSpeak:* A Different Kind of Judgment (Chapter 13)

•*MediaSpeak:* "Alternative" Mental Health Care (Chapter 15)

•*MediaSpeak:* Videos of Self-Injury Find an Audience (Chapter 16)

•*MediaSpeak:* The Patient as Therapist (Chapter 16)

•*MediaSpeak:* Targets for Bullying (Chapter 17)

•*PsychWatch:* The Oldest Old (Chapter 18)

•*MediaSpeak:* Focusing on Emotions (Chapter 18)

•NEW• HIGHLIGHTED CRITICAL THINKING The eighth edition of *Abnormal Psychology* DSM-5 UPDATE has been redesigned strikingly to give it an open, clean, and modern look—one that helps readers better learn, enjoy, and think about the topics under discussion. In a new feature of this design, "critical thought questions" pop up within the text narrative, asking students to pause at precisely the right moment and think critically about the material they have just read. At the same time, the design retains a fun and thought-provoking feature from past editions that has been very popular among students and professors—reader-friendly elements called "Between the Lines," consisting of text-relevant tidbits, surprising facts, current events, historical notes, interesting trends, enjoyable lists, and stimulating quotes.

•NEW• THOROUGH UPDATE In this edition I present current theories, research, and events, including more than 2,000 new references from the years 2010–2013, as well as hundreds of new photos, tables, and figures.

•EXPANDED COVERAGE• KEY DISORDERS AND TOPICS In line with the field's (and college students') increased interest in certain psychological problems and treatments, I have added or expanded the coverage of topics such as the psychology of mass killings (page 487); torture, terrorism, and psychopathology (pages 160–162); club drugs such as Ecstasy (page 365), crystal meth (pages 361–362), and salvia (page 364); binge drinking (page 352); postpartum depression (page 229) and postpartum psychosis (page 436); cyber-therapy and virtual reality treatments (page 69); the pill versus Viagra (page 404); race and eating disorders (pages 332–334); fashion, media, and eating disorders (pages 330–33?); medical use of marijuana (pages 368–369); fatal drug use among celebrities (pages 370–372); transgender issues (pages 415–420); self-cutting (pages 289–290, 490–492); antidepressant drugs and suicide risk (page 304); race and suicide (pages 291–292); music and suicide (page 294); live Web suicides (page 311); dark sites on the Internet (page 108); gay bullying (page 529); jailing people with mental disorders (pages 470–471); Facebook and mental health (pages 613–614); serial murderers (page 608); and more.

•EXPANDED COVERAGE• PREVENTION AND MENTAL HEALTH PROMOTION In accord with the clinical field's growing emphasis on prevention, positive psychology, and psychological wellness, I have increased significantly the textbook's attention to these important approaches (for example, pages 17–19, 309–313, and 583–584).

•EXPANDED COVERAGE• MULTICULTURAL ISSUES Over the past 25 years, clinical theorists and researchers increasingly have become interested in ethnic, racial, gender, and other cultural factors, and my previous editions of *Abnormal Psychology* certainly have included these important factors. In the twenty-first century, however, the study of such factors has, appropriately, been elevated to a broad perspective—the *multicultural perspective,* a theoretical and treatment approach to abnormal behavior that is, or should be, considered across all forms of psychopathology and treatment. Consistent with this clinical movement, the current edition includes broad *multicultural perspective* sections within each chapter (for example, pages 76–78), numerous boxes emphasizing multicultural issues (pages 272, 333, and 459), and numerous photographs, art, and case presentations that reflect our multicultural society. A quick look through the pages of this textbook will reveal that it truly reflects the diversity of our society and of the field of abnormal psychology.

•EXPANDED COVERAGE• "NEW-WAVE" COGNITIVE AND COGNITIVE-BEHAVIORAL THEORIES AND TREATMENTS The traditional focus and treatment approaches of cognitive and cognitive-behavioral clinicians have been joined in recent years by "new-wave" cognitive and cognitive-behavioral theories and therapies that help clients "accept" and objectify those maladaptive thoughts and perspectives that are resistant to change. The current edition of *Abnormal Psychology* has expanded its coverage of these "new-wave" theories and therapies, including *mindfulness-based cognitive therapy* and *Acceptance and Commitment Therapy* (ACT), presenting their propositions, techniques, and research in chapters throughout the text (for example, pages 64, 121–122).

•EXPANDED COVERAGE• NEUROSCIENCE The twenty-first century has witnessed the continued growth and impact of remarkable brain-imaging techniques, genetic mapping strategies, and other neuroscience approaches, all of which are expanding our understanding of the brain. Correspondingly, the new edition of *Abnormal Psychology* has expanded its coverage of how biochemical factors, brain structure, brain function, and genetic factors contribute to abnormal behavior (for example, pages 49–51 and 228–234). It also offers more revealing descriptions of the neuroimaging techniques themselves and their role in the study of abnormal psychology (for example, pages 94–96), using a stimulating array of *brain scan* photos (for example, page 94) and enlightening anatomical art (for example, pages 49 and 147).

Continuing Strengths

In this edition I have also retained the themes, material, and techniques that have worked successfully and been embraced enthusiastically by past readers.

BREADTH AND BALANCE The field's many theories, studies, disorders, and treatments are presented completely and accurately. All major models—psychological, biological, and sociocultural—receive objective, balanced, up-to-date coverage, without bias toward any single approach.

INTEGRATION OF MODELS Discussions throughout the text, particularly those headed "Putting It Together," help students better understand where and how the various models work together and how they differ.

EMPATHY The subject of abnormal psychology is people—very often people in great pain. I have tried therefore to write always with empathy and to impart this awareness to students.

INTEGRATED COVERAGE OF TREATMENT Discussions of treatment are presented throughout the book. In addition to a complete overview of treatment in the opening chapters, each of the pathology chapters includes a full discussion of relevant treatment approaches.

RICH CASE MATERIAL I integrate numerous and culturally diverse clinical examples to bring theoretical and clinical issues to life. More than 25 percent of the clinical material in this edition is new or revised significantly.

MARGIN GLOSSARY Hundreds of key words are defined in the margins of pages on which the words appear. In addition, a traditional glossary is available at the back of the book.

"PUTTING IT TOGETHER" A section toward the end of each chapter, "Putting It Together," asks whether competing models can work together in a more integrated approach and also summarizes where the field now stands and where it may be going.

FOCUS ON CRITICAL THINKING The textbook provides tools for thinking critically about abnormal psychology. As I mentioned earlier, in this edition, "critical thought" questions appear at carefully selected locations within the text discussions. The questions ask readers to stop and think critically about the material they have just read.

STRIKING PHOTOS AND STIMULATING ILLUSTRATIONS Concepts, disorders, treatments, and applications are brought to life for the reader with stunning photographs, diagrams, graphs, and anatomical figures. All of the figures, graphs, and tables, many new to this edition, reflect the most up-to-date data available. The photos range from historical to today's world to pop culture. They do more than just illustrate topics: they touch and move readers.

ADAPTABILITY Chapters are self-contained, so they can be assigned in any order that makes sense to the professor.

Supplements

I have been delighted by the enthusiastic responses of both professors and students to the supplements that accompany my textbooks. This edition offers those supplements once again, revised and enhanced, and adds a number of exciting new ones.

FOR PROFESSORS

•NEW• *WORTH VIDEO ANTHOLOGY FOR ABNORMAL PSYCHOLOGY* (previously called *Abnormal Psychology Video Segments*). *Produced and edited by Ronald J. Comer, Princeton University, and Gregory Comer, Princeton Academic Resources. Faculty Guide included.* This incomparable video series offers 120 clips—more than one-third of them new to this edition—that depict disorders, show historical footage, and illustrate clinical topics, pathologies, treatments, experiments, and dilemmas. Videos are available within the Instructor Flash Drive for *Abnormal Psychology,* Eighth Edition DSM-5 UPDATE or on DVD. I also have written an accompanying guide that fully describes and discusses each video clip, so that professors can make informed decisions about the use of the segments in lectures.

•NEW• INTERACTIVE PRESENTATION SLIDES FOR *ABNORMAL PSYCHOLOGY* by *Karen Clay Rhines, American Public University System*. This extraordinary series of "next-generation" Interactive Presentation Lectures gives instructors a dynamic, yet easy-to-use, new way to engage students during classroom presentations of core abnormal psychology topics. Each lecture provides opportunities for discussion and interaction and enlivens the psychology classroom with an unprecedented number of embedded video clips and animations. Each *Interactive Presentation Lecture* features:

• Embedded videos

• A number of activities

• Ready-to-use clicker questions

• Vivid images

Worth's Interactive Presentation Slides for *Abnormal Psychology* is available on a flash drive.

•NEW• INSTRUCTOR FLASH DRIVE FOR *ABNORMAL PSYCHOLOGY*, EIGHTH EDITION DSM-5 UPDATE This flash drive includes prebuilt PowerPoint presentations for each chapter; a digital library of photographs, figures, and tables from the text; an electronic version of the Instructor's Resources and Lecture Guides; and the 125 video clips contained in the *Worth Video Anthology for Abnormal Psychology*.

CLINICAL VIDEO CASE FILE FOR *ABNORMAL PSYCHOLOGY* *Produced and edited by Ronald J. Comer and Gregory Comer. Faculty guide is available on the book companion Web site at www.worthpublishers.com/comer under Video Case File Faculty Guide.* I have also produced a set of 10 longer *video case studies* that bring to life particularly interesting forms of psychopathology and treatment. These in-depth and authentic videos are available on DVD.

THE BOOK COMPANION WEB SITE FOR *ABNORMAL PSYCHOLOGY*, EIGHTH EDITION DSM-5 UPDATE, offers cutting-edge online activities that facilitate critical thinking and learning, as well as tools to help monitor student progress, create interactive presentations, and explore course management solutions. This password-protected instructor site includes a quiz gradebook, links to additional tools for campus course management systems, and a full array of teaching resources, including:

• **PowerPoint® Slides** *available at www.worthpublishers.com/comer.* These PowerPoint® slides featuring all chapter photos and illustrations can be used as is or customized to fit a professor's needs.

• **Digital Photo Library** *available at www.worthpublishers.com/comer.* This collection gives professors access to all the photographs from *Abnormal Psychology,* Eighth Edition DSM-5 UPDATE.

• ***Instructor's Resource Manual*** *by Karen Clay Rhines, American Public University System.* This comprehensive guide ties together the ancillary package for professors and teaching assistants. The manual includes detailed chapter outlines, lists of principal learning objectives, ideas for lectures, discussion launchers, classroom activities, extra credit projects, word searches, and crossword puzzles, and DSM criteria for each of the disorders discussed in the text. It also offers strategies for using the accompanying media, including the video segments series, and the companion Web site. Finally, it includes a comprehensive set of valuable materials that can be obtained from outside sources—items such as relevant feature films, documentaries, teaching references, and Internet sites related to abnormal psychology.

ASSESSMENT TOOLS

PRINTED TEST BANK *by John H. Hull, Bethany College, and Debra B. Hull, Wheeling Jesuit University.* A comprehensive test bank offers more than 2,200 multiple-choice, fill-in-the-blank, and essay questions. Each question is graded according to difficulty, identified as factual or applied, and keyed to the topic and page in the text where the source information appears.

DIPLOMA COMPUTERIZED TEST BANK This *Windows and Macintosh dual-platform CD-ROM* guides professors step-by-step through the process of creating a test and allows them to add an unlimited number of questions, edit or scramble questions, format a test, and include pictures and multimedia links. The accompanying grade book enables them to record students' grades throughout the course and includes the capacity to sort student records and view detailed analyses of test items, curve tests, generate reports, add weights to grades, and more. The CD-ROM also provides tools for converting the Test Bank into a variety of useful formats as well as Blackboard-formatted versions of the Test Bank for *Abnormal Psychology,* Eighth Edition DSM-5 UPDATE.

ONLINE QUIZZING *Accessed via the Book Companion Site at www.worthpublishers.com/comer.* Professors can quiz students online easily and securely using the multiple-choice questions provided for each chapter (note that these questions are not from the Test Bank). Students receive instant feedback and can take the quizzes multiple times. Professors can view results by quiz, student, or question or can get weekly results via e-mail.

FOR STUDENTS

PSYCHPORTAL *Available at www.yourpsychportal.com.* Created by psychologists for psychologists, PsychPortal is an innovative, customizable online course space that combines a complete e-Book, powerful quizzing engine, and unparalleled media resources.
    PsychPortal for *Abnormal Psychology,* Eighth Edition DSM-5 UPDATE, contains:

• NEW *LearningCurve* Combining adaptive question selection, personalized study plans, and state-of-the-art question analysis reports, *LearningCurve* provides students with a unique learning experience. *LearningCurve* quizzing activities have a gamelike feel that keeps students engaged in the material while helping them learn key concepts.

• NEW Sixteen *Web-Based Case Studies* in *PsychPortal* by Elaine Cassel, Marymount University and Lord Fairfax Community College; Danae L. Hudson, Missouri State University; and Brooke L. Whisenhunt, Missouri State University. These case studies offer realistic, contemporary examples of individuals suffering from various disorders. Each case describes the individual's history and symptoms and is accompanied by a set of guided questions that point to the precise DSM-5 criteria for the disorder and suggest a course of treatment.

• UPDATED *Abnormal Psychology Video Tool Kit, produced and edited by Ronald J. Comer, Princeton University, and Gregory Comer, Princeton Academic Resources.* Updated with new videos from the *Worth Video Anthology for Abnormal Psychology,* this Student Tool Kit offers intriguing video cases running three to seven minutes each. The video cases focus on persons affected by disorders discussed in the text. Students first view a video case and then answer a series of thought-provoking questions about it. Additionally, the Student Tool Kit contains multiple-choice practice test questions with built-in instructional feedback for every option.

• *Interactive e-Book* In addition to being integrated into *PsychPortal,* the *Abnormal Psychology,* Eighth Edition DSM-5 UPDATE e-Book is available in a stand-alone version that can either complement a text or serve as a low-cost alternative. The e-Book fully integrates the entire text and all student media resources, plus a range of study and customization features, including a powerful notes feature that allows instructors and students to customize any page; Google-style full-text search; text highlighting; a bookmark function; and a full, searchable glossary.

ABNORMAL PSYCHOLOGY COMPANION WEB SITE *by Nicholas Greco, College of Lake County, and Jason Spiegelman, Community College of Baltimore County, accessible at www.worthpublishers.com/comer.* This Web site provides students with a virtual study guide 24 hours a day, seven days a week. These resources are free and do not require any special access codes or passwords. The tools on the site include chapter outlines, annotated Web links, quizzes, interactive flash cards, research exercises, and frequently asked questions about clinical psychology.

STUDENT WORKBOOK *by Ronald J. Comer, Princeton University, and Gregory Comer, Princeton Academic Resources.* The engaging exercises in this student guide actively involve students in the text material. Each chapter includes a selection of practice tests and exercises, as well as key concepts, guided study questions, and section reviews.

CASE STUDIES IN ABNORMAL PSYCHOLOGY *by Ethan E. Gorenstein, Behavioral Medicine Program, New York-Presbyterian Hospital, and Ronald J. Comer, Princeton University.* This casebook provides 20 case histories, each going beyond DSM diagnoses to describe the individual's history and symptoms, a theoretical discussion of treatment, a specific treatment plan, and the actual treatment conducted. The casebook also provides three cases without diagnoses or treatment, so that students can identify disorders and suggest appropriate therapies. In addition, case study evaluations by Ann Brandt-Williams, Glendale Community College, are available at www.worthpublishers.com/comer. Each evaluation accompanies a specific case and can be assigned to students to assess their understanding as they work through the text.

THE SCIENTIFIC AMERICAN READER TO ACCOMPANY ABNORMAL PSYCHOLOGY *Edited by Ronald J. Comer, Princeton University.* Upon request, this reader is free when packaged with the text. Drawn from *Scientific American,* the articles in this full-color collection enhance coverage of important topics covered by the course. Keyed to specific chapters, the selections provide a preview of and discussion questions for each article.

SCIENTIFIC AMERICAN EXPLORES THE HIDDEN MIND: A COLLECTOR'S EDITION On request, this reader is free when packaged with the text. In this special edition, *Scientific American* provides a compilation of updated articles that explore and reveal the mysterious inner workings of our wondrous minds and brains

iCLICKER RADIO FREQUENCY CLASSROOM RESPONSE SYSTEM *Offered by Worth Publishers in partnership with iClicker.* iClicker is Worth's polling system, created by educators for educators. This radio frequency system is the hassle-free way to make your class time more interactive. Among other functions, the system allows you to pause to ask questions and instantly record responses, as well as take attendance, direct students through lectures, and gauge students' understanding of the material.

COURSE MANAGEMENT

•ENHANCED• **COURSE MANAGEMENT SOLUTIONS: SUPERIOR CONTENT, ALL IN ONE PLACE** *Available for Blackboard, Desire2Learn, Moodle, Sakai, and Angel at* www.bfwpub. com/lms. As a service for adopters, Worth Publishers is offering an enhanced turnkey course for *Abnormal Psychology,* Eighth Edition DSM-5 UPDATE. The enhanced course includes a suite of robust teaching and learning materials in one location, organized so that you can quickly customize the content for your needs, eliminating hours of work. For instructors, the enhanced course cartridge includes the complete Test Bank and all PowerPoint slides. For students, we offer interactive flash cards, quizzes, crossword puzzles, chapter outlines, annotated Web links, research exercises, case studies, and more.

Acknowledgments

I am very grateful to the many people who have contributed to writing and producing this book. I particularly thank Marlene Comer and Marlene Glissmann for their outstanding work on the manuscript. In addition, I am indebted to Marlene Glissmann for her fine work on the references. And I sincerely appreciate the superb work of the book's assistants—Linda Chamberlin, Keisha Craig, Emily Graham, and Tina McCoy—and research assistants—Greg Comer and Jamie Hambrick.

I am indebted greatly to those outstanding academicians and clinicians who have provided feedback on this new edition of *Abnormal Psychology,* along with that of its partner, *Fundamentals of Abnormal Psychology,* and have commented with great insight and wisdom on its clarity, accuracy, and completeness. Their collective knowledge has in large part shaped the current edition: Christopher Adams, Fitchburg State University; Alisa Aston, University of North Florida; Stephanie Baralecki, Chestnut Hill College; Stephen Brasel, Moody Bible Institute; Conrad Brombach, Christian Brothers University; Daniel Chazin, Rutgers University; Patrick J. Courtney, Central Ohio Technical College; Dennis Curtis, Metropolitan Community College; Lauren Doninger, Gateway Community College; Anne Duran, California State University Bakersfield; Daniella K. C. Errett, Pennsylvania Highlands Community College; William Everist, Pima Community College; Jennifer Fiebig, Loyola University Chicago; Kathryn E. Gallagher, Georgia State University; Rosemarie B. Gilbert, Brevard Community College; RaNae Healy, Gateway Community College; Art Hohmuth, The College of New Jersey; Art Houser, Fort Scott Community College; Ashleigh E. Jones, University of Illinois at Urbana-Champaign; Ricki E. Kantrowitz, Westfield State University; Barbara Kennedy, Brevard Community College; Tricia Z. King, Georgia State University; Toby Marx, Union County College; Tara McKee, Hamilton College; Michele Metcalf, Coconino Community College; John Mitchell, Lycoming College; Jeri Morris, Roosevelt University; Susan A. Nolan, Seton Hall University; Ryan O'Loughlin, Nazareth College; Dominic J. Parrott, Georgia State University; Edie Sample, Metropolitan Community College; Jackie Sample, Central Ohio Technical College; Shalini Sharma, Manchester Community College; Caroline Stanley, Wilmington College; Wayne Stein, Brevard Community College; David Steitz, Nazareth College; Jaine Strauss, Macalester College; Terry Trepper, Purdue University Calumet; Arthur D. VanDeventer; Thomas Nelson, Community College; Maggie VandeVelde, Grand Rapids Community College; Jennifer Vaughn, Metropolitan Community College; Jamie Walter, Roosevelt University; Steve Wampler; Southwestern Community College; Eleanor M. Webber, Johnson State College; Justin Williams, Georgia State University; Lucinda E. Woodward, Indiana University Southeast; Kim Wright, Trine University; and Anthony M. Zoccolillo, Rutgers University.

Earlier I also received valuable feedback from academicians and clinicians who reviewed portions of the previous editions of *Abnormal Psychology* and *Fundamentals of Abnormal Psychology.* Certainly their collective knowledge has also helped shape this new edition, and I gratefully acknowledge their important contributions: Dave W. Alfano, Community College of Rhode Island; Kent G. Bailey, Virginia Commonwealth University; Sonja Barcus, Rochester College; Marna S. Barnett, Indiana University of Pennsylvania; Jillian Bennett, University of Massachusetts Boston; Otto A. Berliner, Alfred State College; Allan Berman, University of Rhode Island; Douglas Bernstein, University of Toronto, Mississauga; Sarah Bing, University of Maryland Eastern Shore; Greg Bolich, Cleveland Community College; Barbara Brown, Georgia Perimeter College; Jeffrey A. Buchanan, Minnesota State University, Mankato; Gregory M. Buchanan, Beloit College; Laura Burlingame-Lee, Colorado State University; Loretta Butehorn, Boston College; Glenn M. Callaghan, San Jose State University; E. Allen Campbell, University of St. Francis; Julie Carboni, San Jose College and National University; David N. Carpenter, Southwest Texas University; Marc Celentana, The College of New Jersey; Edward Chang, University of Michigan; Sarah Cirese, College of Marin; June Madsen Clausen, University of San Francisco; Victor B. Cline, University of Utah; E. M. Coles, Simon Fraser University; Michael Connor, California State University, Long Beach; Frederick L. Coolidge, University of Colorado, Colorado Springs; Charles Cummings, Asheville-Buncombe Technical Community College; Timothy K. Daugherty, Winthrop University; Mary Dozier, University of Delaware; S. Wayne Duncan, University of Washington, Seattle; Morris N. Eagle, York University; Miriam Ehrenberg, John Jay College of Criminal Justice; Jon Elhai, University of Toledo; Carlos A. Escoto, Eastern Connecticut State University; David M. Fresco, Kent State University; Anne Fisher, University of Southern Florida; William F. Flack Jr., Bucknell University; John Forsyth, State University of New York, Albany; Alan Fridlund, University of California, Santa Barbara; Stan Friedman,

Southwest Texas State University; Dale Fryxell, Chaminade University; Lawrence L. Galant, Gaston College; Karla Gingerich, Colorado State University; Nicholas Greco, College of Lake County; Jane Halonen, James Madison University; James Hansell, University of Michigan; Neth Hansjoerg, Rensselaer Polytechnic Institute; David Harder, Tufts University; Morton G. Harmatz, University of Massachusetts; Jinni A. Harrigan, California State University, Fullerton; Jumi Hayaki, College of the Holy Cross; Anthony Hermann, Kalamazoo College; Paul Hewitt, University of British Columbia; David A. Hoffman, University of California, Santa Cruz; Danae Hudson, Missouri State University; William G. Iacono, University of Minnesota; Lynn M. Kemen, Hunter College; Audrey Kim, University of California, Santa Cruz; Guadalupe Vasquez King, Milwaukee Area Technical College; Bernard Kleinman, University of Missouri, Kansas City; Futoshi Kobayashi, Northern State University; Alan G. Krasnoff, University of Missouri, St. Louis; Robert D. Langston, University of Texas, Austin; Kimberlyn Leary, University of Michigan; Harvey R. Lerner, Kaiser-Permanente Medical Group; Arnold D. LeUnes, Texas A&M University; Michael P. Levin, Kenyon College; Barbara Lewis, University of West Florida; Mary Margaret Livingston, Louisiana Technical University; Karsten Look, Columbus State Community College; Joseph LoPiccolo, University of Missouri, Columbia; L. F. Lowenstein, Southern England Psychological Services; Jerald J. Marshall, University of Central Florida; Janet R. Matthews, Loyola University; Robert J. McCaffrey, State University of New York, Albany; Rosemary McCullough, Ave Maria University; F. Dudley McGlynn, Auburn University; Lily D. McNair, University of Georgia; Mary W. Meagher, Texas A&M University; Dorothy Mercer, Eastern Kentucky University; Joni L. Mihura, University of Toledo; Andrea Miller, Georgia Southwestern State University; Antoinette Miller, Clayton State University; Regina Miranda, Hunter College; Robin Mogul, Queens University; Linda M. Montgomery, University of Texas, Permian Basin; Karen Mottarella, University of Central Florida; Maria Moya, College of Southern Nevada; Karla Klein Murdock, University of Massachusetts, Boston; Sandy Naumann, Delaware Technical & Community College; David Nelson, Sam Houston State University; Paul Neunuebel, Sam Houston State University; Ryan Newell, Oklahoma Christian University; Katherine M. Nicolai, Rockhurst University; Fabian Novello, Purdue University; Mary Ann M. Pagaduan, American Osteopathic Association; Crystal Park, University of Connecticut; Daniel Paulson, Carthage College; Paul A. Payne, University of Cincinnati; David V. Perkins, Ball State University; Julie C. Piercy, Central Virginia Community College; Lloyd R. Pilkington, Midlands Technical College; Harold A. Pincus, chair, DSM-IV, University of Pittsburgh, Western Psychiatric Institute and Clinic; Chris Piotrowski, University of West Florida; Debbie Podwika, Kankakee Community College; Norman Poppel, Middlesex County College; David E. Powley, University of Mobile; Laura A. Rabin, Brooklyn College; Max W. Rardin, University of Wyoming, Laramie; Lynn P. Rehm, University of Houston; Leslie A. Rescorla, Bryn Mawr College; R. W. Rieber, John Jay College, CUNY; George Esther Rothblum, University of Vermont; Vic Ryan, University of Colorado, Boulder; Randall Salekin, Florida International University; A. A. Sappington, University of Alabama, Birmingham; Martha Sauter, McLennon Community College; Laura Scaletta, Niagara County Community College; George W. Shardlow, City College of San Francisco; Roberta S. Sherman, Bloomington Center for Counseling and Human Development; Wendy E. Shields, University of Montana; Sandra T. Sigmon, University of Maine, Orono; Susan J. Simonian, College of Charleston; Janet A. Simons, Central Iowa Psychological Services; Jay R. Skidmore, Utah State University; Rachel Sligar, James Madison University; Katrina Smith, Polk Community College; Robert Sommer, University of California, Davis; Jason S. Spiegelman, Community College of Baltimore County; John M. Spores, Purdue University, South Central; Amit Steinberg, Tel Aviv University; B. D. Stillion, Clayton College and State University; Deborah Stipp, Ivy Tech College; Joanne H. Stohs, California State University, Fullerton; Mitchell Sudolsky, University of Texas at Austin; John Suler, Rider University; Sandra Todaro, Bossier Parish Community College; Thomas A. Tutko, San Jose State University; Norris D. Vestre, Arizona State University; Lance L. Weinmann, Canyon College; Doug Wessel, Black Hills State University; Laura Westen, Emory University; Brook Whisenhunt, Missouri

State University; Joseph L. White, University of California, Irvine; Amy C. Willis, Veterans Administration Medical Center, Washington, DC; James M. Wood, University of Texas, El Paso; Lisa Wood, University of Puget Sound; David Yells, Utah Valley State College; Jessica Yokely, University of Pittsburgh; and Carlos Zalaquett, University of South Florida.

A special thank you to the authors of the book's supplements package for doing splendid jobs with their respective supplements: Debra B. Hull, Wheeling Jesuit University, and John H. Hull, Bethany College (*Test Bank*); Karen Clay Rhines, American Public University System (*Instructor's Resource Manual*); Gregory Comer, Princeton Academic Resources (*Student Workbook*); Nicholas Greco, College of Lake County, and Jason Spiegelman, Community College of Baltimore County (Book Companion Site); and Ann Brandt-Williams, Glendale Community College; Elaine Cassel, Marymount University and Lord Fairfax Community College; Danae L. Hudson, Missouri State University; John Schulte, Cape Fear Community College and University of North Carolina; and Brooke L. Whisenhunt, Missouri State University (additional Web site materials).

I also extend my deep appreciation to the core team of professionals at Worth Publishers and W. H. Freeman and Company who have worked so closely with me to produce this edition and many previous editions. This team consists of truly extraordinary people—each extremely talented, each committed to excellence, each dedicated to the education of readers, each bound by a remarkable work ethic, and each a wonderful person. It is accurate to say that they were once again my co-authors and co-teachers in this enterprise, and I am in their debt. They are Kevin Feyen, publisher; Lisa Kinne, associate managing editor; Tracey Kuehn, director of print and media development; Paul Lacy, layout designer; Rachel Losh, acquisitions editor; Mimi Melek, senior development editor; Jennifer Bossert, project editor, and Jane O'Neill, senior project editor; Babs Reingold, art director; Lyndall Culbertson, senior designer; Sarah Segal, production manager; Ted Szczepanski, photo department manager; and Catherine Woods, senior vice president, editorial and production.

Elizabeth Widdicombe, president of Worth and Freeman, has continued to lead the companies superbly, to create a very supportive environment for my books, and to be a good friend. I also am indebted to Elizabeth Block, media editor, and Katherine Garrett, editorial assistant, who, along with Stacey Alexander, production manager, have so skillfully developed and guided the production of the extraordinary and innovative supplements package that accompanies the text. Still other professionals at Worth and at Freeman to whom I am indebted are Todd Elder, director of advertising; Michele Kornegay, copy editor; Robert Swanson, indexer; and John Philp, for his outstanding work on the video supplements for professors and students. Not to be overlooked are the superb professionals at Worth and at Freeman who continuously work with great passion, skill, and judgment to bring my books to the attention of professors across the world: Kate Nurre, executive marketing manager; Lindsay Johnson, marketing manager; Julie Tompkins, marketing coordinator; Craig Bleyer, national sales manager; and the company's wonderful sales representatives. Thank you so much.

One final note. As I mentioned in the preface of the previous edition, I have become increasingly aware of just how fortunate I am with each passing year. So, at the risk of sounding like a walking cliché, let me say once again, with a clarity that at the age of 66 is sharper and better informed than at earlier points in my life, how appreciative I am that I have the opportunity each day to work with so many interesting and stimulating students during this important and exciting stage of their lives. Similarly, I am grateful beyond words that I have a number of wonderful friends and an extraordinary family, particularly my terrific sons, Greg and Jon; my fantastic daughters-in-law, Emily and Jami; my perfect granddaughter, Delia; and my truly magnificent wife, Marlene.

Ron Comer
Princeton University
April 2013

ABNORMAL PSYCHOLOGY: PAST AND PRESENT

Johanne cries herself to sleep every night. She is certain that the future holds nothing but misery. Indeed, this is the only thing she does feel certain about. "I'm going to suffer and suffer and suffer, and my daughters will suffer as well. We're doomed. The world is ugly. I hate every moment of my life." She has great trouble sleeping. She is afraid to close her eyes. When she does, the hopelessness of her life—and the ugly future that awaits her daughters—becomes all the clearer to her. When she drifts off to sleep, her dreams are nightmares filled with terrible images—bodies, decay, death, destruction.

Some mornings Johanne even has trouble getting out of bed. The thought of facing another day overwhelms her. She wishes that she and her daughters were dead. "Get it over with. We'd all be better off." She feels paralyzed by her depression and anxiety, overwhelmed by her sense of hopelessness, and filled with fears of becoming ill, too tired to move, too negative to try anymore. On such mornings, she huddles her daughters close to her and sits away the day in the cramped tent she shares with her daughters. She feels she has been deserted by the world and left to rot. She is both furious at life and afraid of it at the same time.

During the past year Alberto has been hearing mysterious voices that tell him to quit his job, leave his family, and prepare for the coming invasion. These voices have brought tremendous confusion and emotional turmoil to Alberto's life. He believes that they come from beings in distant parts of the universe who are somehow wired to him. Although it gives him a sense of purpose and specialness to be the chosen target of their communications, the voices also make him tense and anxious. He does all he can to warn others of the coming apocalypse. In accordance with instructions from the voices, he identifies online articles that seem to be filled with foreboding signs, and he posts comments that plead with other readers to recognize the articles' underlying messages. Similarly, he posts long, rambling YouTube videos that describe the invasion to come. The online comments and feedback that he receives typically ridicule and mock him. If he rejects the voices' instructions and stops his online commentary and videos, then the voices insult and threaten him and turn his days into a waking nightmare.

Alberto has put himself on a sparse diet as protection against the possibility that his enemies may be contaminating his food. He has found a quiet apartment far from his old haunts, where he has laid in a good stock of arms and ammunition. After witnessing the abrupt and troubling changes in his behavior and watching his ranting and rambling videos, his family and friends have tried to reach out to Alberto, to understand his problems, and to dissuade him from the disturbing course he is taking. Every day, however, he retreats further into his world of mysterious voices and imagined dangers.

Most of us would probably consider Johanne's and Alberto's emotions, thoughts, and behaviors psychologically abnormal, the result of a state sometimes called *psychopathology, maladjustment, emotional disturbance,* or *mental illness* (see *PsychWatch* on the next page). These terms have been applied to the many problems that seem closely tied to the human brain or mind. Psychological abnormality affects the famous and the unknown, the rich and the poor. Celebrities, writers, politicians, and other public figures of the present and the past have struggled with it.

PsychWatch

Verbal Debuts

We use words like "abnormal" and "mental disorder" so often that it is easy to forget that there was a time not that long ago when these terms did not exist. When did these and similar words (including slang terms) make their debut in print as expressions of psychological dysfunctioning? The *Oxford English Dictionary* offers the following dates.

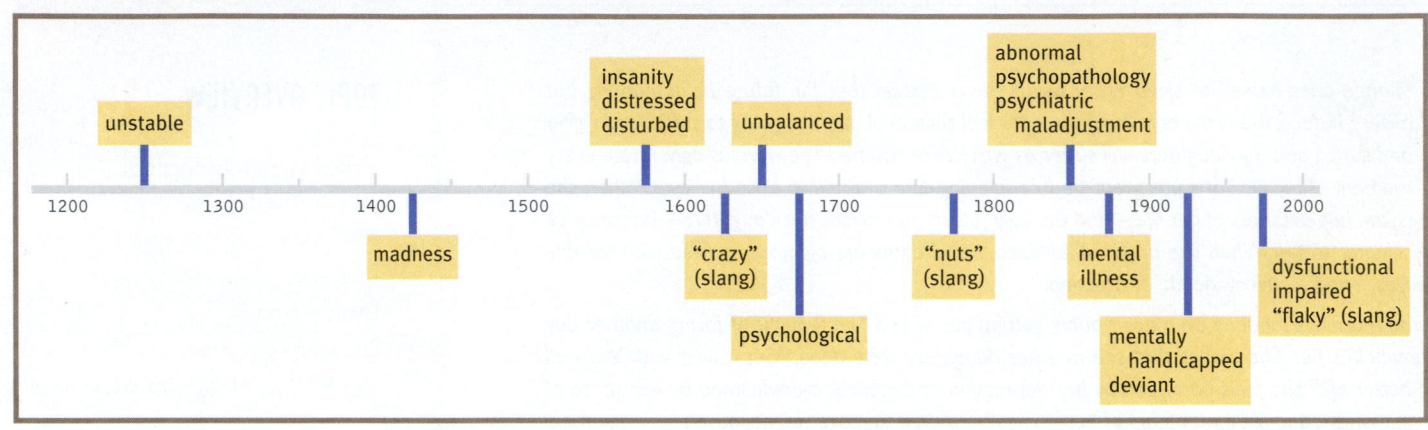

Psychological problems can bring great suffering, but they can also be the source of inspiration and energy.

Because they are so common and so personal, these problems capture the interest of us all. Hundreds of novels, plays, films, and television programs have explored what many people see as the dark side of human nature, and self-help books flood the market. Mental health experts are popular guests on both television and radio, and some even have their own shows, Web sites, and blogs.

Why do actors and actresses who portray characters with psychological disorders tend to receive more awards for their performances?

The field devoted to the scientific study of the problems we find so fascinating is usually called **abnormal psychology.** As in any science, workers in this field, called *clinical scientists,* gather information systematically so that they may describe, predict, and explain the phenomena they study. The knowledge that they acquire is then used by *clinical practitioners,* whose role is to detect, assess, and treat abnormal patterns of functioning.

What Is Psychological Abnormality?

Although their general goals are similar to those of other scientific professionals, clinical scientists and practitioners face problems that make their work especially difficult. One of the most troubling is that psychological abnormality is very hard to define. Consider once again Johanne and Alberto. Why are we so ready to call their responses abnormal?

While many definitions of abnormality have been proposed over the years, none has won total acceptance (Pierre, 2010). Still, most of the definitions have certain features in common, often called "the four Ds": deviance, distress, dysfunction, and danger. That is, patterns of psychological abnormality are typically *deviant* (different, extreme, unusual, perhaps even bizarre), *distressing* (unpleasant and upsetting to the person), *dysfunctional* (interfering with the person's ability to conduct daily activities in a constructive way), and possibly *dangerous.* This definition offers a useful starting point from which to explore the phenomena of psychological abnormality. As you will see, however, it has key limitations.

•**abnormal psychology**•The scientific study of abnormal behavior in an effort to describe, predict, explain, and change abnormal patterns of functioning.

•**norms**•A society's stated and unstated rules for proper conduct.

•**culture**•A people's common history, values, institutions, habits, skills, technology, and arts.

Deviance

Abnormal psychological functioning is *deviant,* but deviant from what? Johanne's and Alberto's behaviors, thoughts, and emotions are different from those that are considered normal in our place and time. We do not expect people to cry themselves to sleep each night, hate the world, wish themselves dead, or obey voices that no one else hears.

In short, abnormal behavior, thoughts, and emotions are those that differ markedly from a society's ideas about proper functioning. Each society establishes **norms**—stated and unstated rules for proper conduct. Behavior that breaks legal norms is considered to be criminal. Behavior, thoughts, and emotions that break norms of psychological functioning are called abnormal.

Judgments of abnormality vary from society to society. A society's norms grow from its particular **culture**—its history, values, institutions, habits, skills, technology, and arts. A society that values competition and assertiveness may accept aggressive behavior, whereas one that emphasizes cooperation and gentleness may consider aggressive behavior unacceptable and even abnormal. A society's values may also change over time, causing its views of what is psychologically abnormal to change as well. In Western society, for example, a woman seeking the power of running a major corporation or indeed of leading the country would have been considered inappropriate and even delusional a hundred years ago. Today the same behavior is valued.

Judgments of abnormality depend on *specific circumstances* as well as on cultural norms. What if, for example, we were to learn that Johanne is a citizen of Haiti and that her desperate unhappiness began in the days, weeks, and months following the massive earthquake that struck her country, already the poorest country in the Western hemisphere, on January 12, 2010? The quake, one of history's worst natural disasters, killed 250,000 Haitians, left 1.5 million homeless, and destroyed most of the country's business establishments and educational institutions. Half of Haiti's homes and buildings were immediately turned into rubble, and its electricity and other forms of power disappeared. Tent cities replaced homes for most people. In the coming months, a devastating hurricane, outbreak of cholera, and violent political protests brought still

Deviance and abnormality
Along the Niger River, men of the Wodaabe tribe put on elaborate makeup and costumes to attract women. In Western society, the same behavior would break behavioral norms and probably be judged abnormal.

Context is key
On the morning after Japan's devastating earthquake and tsunami in 2011, Reiko Kikuta, right, and her husband Takeshi watch workers try to attach ropes to their home and pull it ashore. Anxiety and depression were common and seemingly normal reactions in the wake of this extraordinary disaster, rather than being clear symptoms of psychopathology.

more death and destruction to the people of Haiti. Even today, more than two years after the earthquake, relatively little rebuilding has taken place, over 1 million Haitians remain homeless, and hundreds of thousands still live in the country's 1,200 tent cities (MCEER, 2011; Wilkinson, 2011).

In the weeks and months that followed the earthquake, Johanne came to accept that she wouldn't get all of the help she needed and that she might never again see the friends and neighbors who had once given her life so much meaning. As she and her daughters moved from one temporary tent or hut to another throughout the country, always at risk of developing serious diseases, she gradually gave up all hope that her life would ever return to normal. The modest but happy life she and her daughters had once known was now gone, seemingly forever. In this light, Johanne's reactions do not seem quite so inappropriate. If anything is abnormal here, it is her situation. Many human experiences produce intense reactions—financial ruin, large-scale catastrophes and disasters, rape, child abuse, war, terminal illness, chronic pain (Kolassa et al., 2010). Is there an "appropriate" way to react to such things? Should we ever call reactions to such experiences abnormal?

Distress

Even functioning that is considered unusual does not necessarily qualify as abnormal. According to many clinical theorists, behavior, ideas, or emotions usually have to cause *distress* before they can be labeled abnormal. Consider the Ice Breakers, a group of people in Michigan who go swimming in lakes throughout the state every weekend from November through February. The colder the weather, the better they like it. One man, a member of the group for 17 years, says he loves the challenge of man against nature. A 37-year-old lawyer believes that the weekly shock is good for her health. "It cleanses me," she says. "It perks me up and gives me strength."

Certainly these people are different from most of us, but is their behavior abnormal? Far from experiencing distress, they feel energized and challenged. Their positive feelings must cause us to hesitate before we decide that they are functioning abnormally.

Should we conclude, then, that feelings of distress must always be present before a person's functioning can be considered abnormal? Not necessarily. Some people who function abnormally maintain a positive frame of mind. Consider once again Alberto, the young man who hears mysterious voices. Alberto does experience distress over the coming invasion and the life changes he feels forced to make. But what if he enjoyed listening to the voices, felt honored to be chosen, loved sending out warnings on the Internet, and looked forward to saving the world? Shouldn't we still regard his functioning as abnormal?

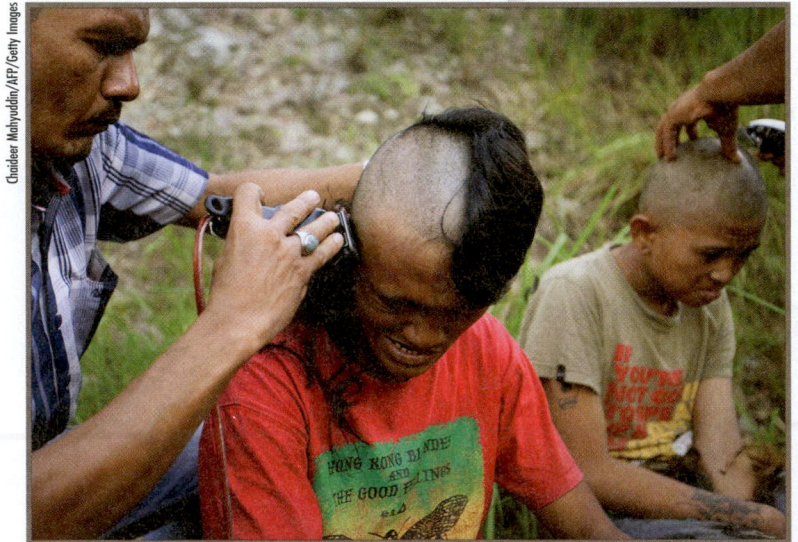

Dealing with deviance
Each culture identifies and deals with deviant behavior in its own way. For example, uncomfortable with the deviant appearances of young punk rockers—mohawks, tattoos, nose piercings, tight jeans, and chains—sharia police in Aceh province on Sumatra Island in Indonesia arrested 60 such individuals in 2011 and forced them to undergo a 10-day "moral rehabilitation" camp. There the rockers were forced to have their heads shaved, bathe in a lake, wear traditional clothes, remove their piercings, and pray.

Dysfunction

Abnormal behavior tends to be *dysfunctional;* that is, it interferes with daily functioning. It so upsets, distracts, or confuses people that they cannot care for themselves properly, participate in ordinary social interactions, or work productively. Alberto, for example, has quit his job, left his family, and prepared to withdraw from the productive life he once led.

Here again one's culture plays a role in the definition of abnormality. Our society holds that it is important to carry out daily activities in an effective manner. Thus Alberto's behavior is likely to be regarded as abnormal and undesirable, whereas that of the Ice Breakers, who continue to perform well in their jobs and enjoy fulfilling relationships, would probably be considered simply unusual.

Then again, dysfunction alone does not necessarily indicate psychological abnormality. Some people (Gandhi or Cesar Chavez, for example) fast or in other ways deprive themselves of things they need as a means of protesting social injustice. Far from receiving a clinical label of some kind, they are widely viewed as admirable people—caring, sacrificing, even heroic.

Danger

Perhaps the ultimate in psychological dysfunctioning is behavior that becomes *dangerous* to oneself or others. Individuals whose behavior is consistently careless, hostile, or confused may be placing themselves or those around them at risk. Alberto, for example, seems to be endangering both himself, with his diet, and others, with his buildup of arms and ammunition.

Although danger is often cited as a feature of abnormal psychological functioning, research suggests that it is actually the exception rather than the rule (Hiday & Burns, 2010). Despite powerful misconceptions, most people struggling with anxiety, depression, and even bizarre thinking pose no immediate danger to themselves or to anyone else.

The Elusive Nature of Abnormality

Efforts to define psychological abnormality typically raise as many questions as they answer. Ultimately, a society selects general criteria for defining abnormality and then uses those criteria to judge particular cases.

One clinical theorist, Thomas Szasz (1920–2012), placed such emphasis on society's role that he found the whole concept of mental illness to be invalid, a *myth* of sorts (Szasz, 2010, 2006, 1963, 1960). According to Szasz, the deviations that society calls abnormal are simply "problems in living," not signs of something wrong within the person. Societies, he was convinced, invent the concept of mental illness so that they can better control or change people whose unusual patterns of functioning upset or threaten the social order.

Even if we assume that psychological abnormality is a valid concept and that it can indeed be defined, we may be unable to apply our definition consistently. If a behavior—excessive use of alcohol among college students, say—is familiar enough, the society may fail to recognize that it is deviant, distressful, dysfunctional, and dangerous. Thousands of college students throughout the United States are so dependent on alcohol that it interferes with their personal and academic lives, causes them great discomfort, jeopardizes their health, and often endangers them and the people around them (Hingson & White, 2010). Yet their problem often goes unnoticed and undiagnosed. Alcohol is so much a part of the college subculture that it is easy to overlook drinking behavior that has become abnormal.

Conversely, a society may have trouble separating an abnormality that requires intervention from an *eccentricity*, an unusual pattern with which others have no right to interfere. From time to time we see or hear about people who behave in ways we consider strange, such as a man who lives alone with two dozen cats and rarely talks to other people. The behavior of such people is deviant, and it may well be distressful and dysfunctional, yet many professionals think of it as eccentric rather than abnormal (see *PsychWatch* on the next page).

What behaviors might fit the criteria of deviant, distressful, dysfunctional, or dangerous but would not be considered abnormal by most people?

In short, while we may agree to define psychological abnormalities as patterns of functioning that are deviant, distressful, dysfunctional, and sometimes dangerous, we should be clear that these criteria are often vague and subjective. In turn, few of the current categories of abnormality that you will meet in this book are as clear-cut as they may seem, and most continue to be debated by clinicians.

Changing times
Just decades ago, a woman's love for race car driving would have been considered strange, perhaps even abnormal. Today, Danica Patrick (right) is one of America's finest race car drivers. The size difference between her first-place trophy at the Indy Japan 300 auto race and that of second-place male driver Helio Castroneves symbolizes just how far women have come in this sport.

Marching to a Different Drummer: Eccentrics

▶ Writer **James Joyce** always carried a tiny pair of lady's bloomers, which he waved in the air to show approval.

▶ **Benjamin Franklin** took "air baths" for his health, sitting naked in front of an open window.

▶ **Alexander Graham Bell** covered the windows of his house to keep out the rays of the full moon. He also tried to teach his dog how to talk.

▶ Writer **D. H. Lawrence** enjoyed removing his clothes and climbing mulberry trees.

(ASIMOV, 1997; WEEKS & JAMES, 1995)

These famous persons have been called eccentrics. The dictionary defines an *eccentric* as a person who deviates from common behavior patterns or displays odd or whimsical behavior. But how can we separate a psychologically healthy person who has unusual habits from a person whose oddness is a symptom of psychopathology? Little research has been done on eccentrics, but a few studies offer some insights (Stares, 2005; Pickover, 1999; Weeks & James, 1995).

Researcher David Weeks studied 1,000 eccentrics and estimated that as many as 1 in 5,000 persons may be "classic, full-time eccentrics." Weeks pinpointed

15 characteristics common to the eccentrics in his study: *nonconformity, creativity, strong curiosity, idealism, extreme interests and hobbies, lifelong awareness of being different, high intelligence, outspokenness, noncompetitiveness, unusual eating and living habits, disinterest in others' opinions or company, mischievous sense of humor, nonmarriage, eldest or only child,* and *poor spelling skills.*

Weeks suggests that eccentrics do not typically suffer from mental disorders. Whereas the unusual behavior of persons with mental disorders is thrust upon them and usually causes them suffering, eccentricity is chosen freely and provides pleasure. In short, "Eccentrics know they're different and glory in it" (Weeks & James, 1995, p. 14). Similarly, the thought processes of eccentrics are not severely disrupted and do not leave these persons dysfunctional. In fact, Weeks found that eccentrics in his study actually had fewer emotional problems than individuals in the general population. Perhaps being an "original" is good for mental health.

Musical eccentric Pop superstar Lady Gaga is known far and wide for her eccentric behavior, outrageous sense of fashion, and unusual performing style. Her millions of fans enjoy her unusual persona every bit as much as the lyrics and music that she writes and sings.

What Is Treatment?

Once clinicians decide that a person is indeed suffering from some form of psychological abnormality, they seek to treat it. *Treatment,* or *therapy,* is a procedure designed to change abnormal behavior into more normal behavior; it, too, requires careful definition. For clinical scientists, the problem is closely related to defining abnormality. Consider the case of Bill:

February: *He cannot leave the house; Bill knows that for a fact. Home is the only place where he feels safe—safe from humiliation, danger, even ruin. If he were to go to work, his co-workers would somehow reveal their contempt for him. A pointed remark, a quizzical look—that's all it would take for him to get the message. If he were to go shopping at the store, before long everyone would be staring at him. Surely others would see his dark mood and thoughts; he wouldn't be able to hide them. He dare not even go for a walk alone in the woods—his heart would probably start racing again, bringing him to his* *knees and leaving him breathless, incoherent, and unable to get home. No, he's much better off staying in his room, trying to get through another evening of this curse called life. Thank goodness for the Internet. Were it not for his reading of news sites and postings to blogs and online forums, he would, he knows, be cut off from the world altogether.*

July: *Bill's life revolves around his circle of friends: Bob and Jack, whom he knows from the office, where he was recently promoted to director of customer relations, and Frank and Tim, his weekend tennis partners. The gang meets for dinner every week at someone's house, and they chat about life, politics, and their jobs. Particularly special in Bill's life is Janice. They go to movies, restaurants, and shows together. She thinks Bill's just terrific, and Bill finds himself beaming whenever she's around. Bill looks forward to work each day and his one-on-one dealings with customers. He is taking part in many activities and relationships and more fully enjoying life.*

Therapy . . . not
Recently, a hotel in Spain that was about to undergo major renovations invited members of the public to relieve their stress by destroying the rooms on one floor of the hotel. This activity may indeed have been therapeutic for some, but it was not *therapy*. It lacked, among other things, a "trained healer" and a series of systematic contacts between healer and sufferer.

Bill's thoughts, feelings, and behavior interfered with all aspects of his life in February. Yet most of his symptoms had disappeared by July. All sorts of factors may have contributed to Bill's improvement—advice from friends and family members, a new job or vacation, perhaps a big change in his diet or exercise regimen. Any or all of these things may have been useful to Bill, but they could not be considered treatment, or therapy. Those terms are usually reserved for special, systematic procedures for helping people overcome their psychological difficulties. According to clinical theorist Jerome Frank, all forms of therapy have three essential features:

1. A *sufferer* who seeks relief from the healer.
2. A trained, socially accepted *healer,* whose expertise is accepted by the sufferer and his or her social group.
3. A *series of contacts* between the healer and the sufferer, through which the healer . . . tries to produce certain changes in the sufferer's emotional state, attitudes, and behavior.

(Frank, 1973, pp. 2–3)

Despite this straightforward definition, clinical treatment is surrounded by conflict and confusion. Carl Rogers, a pioneer in the modern clinical field (you will meet him in Chapter 3), noted that "therapists are not in agreement as to their goals or aims. . . . They are not in agreement as to what constitutes a successful outcome of their work. They cannot agree as to what constitutes a failure. It seems as though the field is completely chaotic and divided."

Some clinicians view abnormality as an illness and so consider therapy a procedure that helps *cure* the illness. Others see abnormality as a problem in living and therapists as *teachers* of more functional behavior and thought. Clinicians even differ on what to call the person who receives therapy: those who see abnormality as an illness speak of the "patient," while those who view it as a problem in living refer to the "client." Because both terms are so common, this book will use them interchangeably.

Despite their differences, most clinicians do agree that large numbers of people need therapy of one kind or another. Later you will encounter evidence that therapy is indeed often helpful.

How Was Abnormality Viewed and Treated in the Past?

In any given year as many as 30 percent of the adults and 19 percent of the children and adolescents in the United States display serious psychological disturbances and are in need of clinical treatment (Lopez-Duran, 2010; Kessler et al., 2009, 2007, 2005; Narrow et al., 2002). The rates in other countries are similarly high. Furthermore, most people

AP Photo/FBI

PsychWatch

Modern Pressures: Modern Problems

The twenty-first century, like each of the centuries before it, has spawned new fears and concerns that are tied to its unique technological advances, community threats, and environmental dangers. These new fears have received relatively little study. They may or may not reflect abnormal functioning. Nevertheless, they have caught the attention of the media and clinical observers. Such fears include *terrorism terror, crime phobia,* and *cyber fear.*

"Terrorism Terror"

Global terrorism is a major source of anxiety in contemporary society, particularly since the September 11, 2001, attacks on the World Trade Center in New York City and the Pentagon in Washington, DC. Moreover, everyday hassles of the past have been turned into potential threats by their association with the actions of terrorists (Aly & Green, 2010; Furedi, 2007). When boarding planes, subway cars, or buses, for example, travelers who formerly worried only about the low risks of flying, the possibility of being late for work, or the repercussions of missing an appointment may now find themselves worrying that the transporting vehicles are about to become targets or tools of terrorist actions. Indeed, for some individuals, such concerns have become a terrifying and obsessive preoccupation that transforms normal travel into a truly anxiety-provoking experience.

"Crime Phobia"

People today have become increasingly anxious about crime (Morrall et al., 2010; Scarborough et al., 2010). Some observers note that the fear of crime—predominantly armed violence—has restructured the lives

It could have happened This powerful explosion was staged by the FBI in 2010 to show what would have resulted had a terrorist car bombing attempt succeeded in crowded Times Square a few months earlier. The attempted destruction of this famous commercial intersection in New York City was foiled when two street vendors spotted smoke coming from the car.

of Americans. Political scientist Jonathan Simon says, "[F]ear of crime can have a more powerful effect on people and neighborhoods than crime itself. Fear of crime governs us in our choices of where to live, where to work, where to send our children to school. And these choices are made with increasing reference to crime" (quoted in Bergquist, 2002). Many theorists point to disproportionate media coverage of violent crimes as a major cause of crime phobia, particularly given that crime anxiety seems to keep rising even while actual crime rates are falling (Bean, 2011; Stearns, 2006).

"Cyber Fear"

Many people live in fear of computer crashes, server overloads, or computer viruses (FBI, 2010; Casey, 2008). And some, stricken by a combination of crime phobia and cyber fear, worry constantly about *e-crimes,* such as computer hoaxes or scams, theft of personal information by computer, computer-identity theft, or cyberterrorism (Whittle, 2010). Several treatment programs have, in fact, been developed to help individuals deal with such anxieties and return to carefree keyboarding (Wurman et al., 2000).

have difficulty coping at various times and go through periods of extreme tension, dejection, or other forms of psychological discomfort.

It is tempting to conclude that something about the modern world is responsible for these many emotional problems—perhaps rapid technological change, the growing threat of terrorism, or a decline in religious, family, or other support systems (North, 2010; Comer & Kendall, 2007) (see *PsychWatch* above). Although the pressures of modern life probably do contribute to psychological dysfunctioning, they are hardly its primary cause (Wang et al., 2010). Every society, past and present, has witnessed psychological abnormality. Perhaps, then, the proper place to begin our examination of abnormal behavior and treatment is in the past.

Ancient Views and Treatments

Historians who have examined the unearthed bones, artwork, and other remnants of ancient societies have concluded that these societies probably regarded abnormal behavior as the work of evil spirits. People in prehistoric societies apparently believed that all events around and within them resulted from the actions of magical, sometimes sinister, beings who controlled the world. In particular, they viewed the human body and mind as a battleground between external forces of good and evil. Abnormal behavior was typically interpreted as a victory by evil spirits, and the cure for such behavior was to force the demons from a victim's body.

This supernatural view of abnormality may have begun as far back as the Stone Age, a half-million years ago. Some skulls from that period recovered in Europe and South America show evidence of an operation called **trephination,** in which a stone instrument, or *trephine,* was used to cut away a circular section of the skull. Some historians have concluded that this early operation was performed as a treatment for severe abnormal behavior—either hallucinations, in which people saw or heard things not actually present, or melancholia, characterized by extreme sadness and immobility. The purpose of opening the skull was to release the evil spirits that were supposedly causing the problem (Selling, 1940).

In recent decades, some historians have questioned whether Stone Age people actually believed that evil spirits caused abnormal behavior. Trephination may instead have been used to remove bone splinters or blood clots caused by stone weapons during tribal warfare (Maher & Maher, 2003, 1985). Either way, later societies clearly did attribute abnormal behavior to possession by demons. Egyptian, Chinese, and Hebrew writings all account for psychological deviance this way. The Bible, for example, describes how an evil spirit from the Lord affected King Saul and how David feigned madness to convince his enemies that he was visited by divine forces.

The treatment for abnormality in these early societies was often *exorcism.* The idea was to coax the evil spirits to leave or to make the person's body an uncomfortable place in which to live. A *shaman,* or priest, might recite prayers, plead with the evil spirits, insult the spirits, perform magic, make loud noises, or have the person drink bitter potions. If these techniques failed, the shaman performed a more extreme form of exorcism, such as whipping or starving the person.

Expelling evil spirits
The two holes in this skull recovered from ancient times indicate that the person underwent trephination, possibly for the purpose of releasing evil spirits and curing mental dysfunctioning.

John W. Verano

? In addition to exorcism, what other demonological explanations or treatments are still around today, and why do they persist?

Greek and Roman Views and Treatments

In the years from roughly 500 B.C. to 500 A.D., when the Greek and Roman civilizations thrived, philosophers and physicians often offered different explanations and treatments for abnormal behaviors. Hippocrates (460–377 B.C.), often called the father of modern medicine, taught that illnesses had *natural* causes. He saw abnormal behavior as a disease arising from internal physical problems. Specifically, he believed that some form of brain pathology was the culprit and that it resulted—like all other forms of disease, in his view—from an imbalance of four fluids, or **humors,** that flowed through

•**trephination**•An ancient operation in which a stone instrument was used to cut away a circular section of the skull, perhaps to treat abnormal behavior.

•**humors**•According to the Greeks and Romans, bodily chemicals that influence mental and physical functioning.

Bettmann/Corbis

Humors in action
Hippocrates believed that imbalances of the four humors affected personality. In these depictions of two of the humors, yellow bile (left) drives a husband to beat his wife, and black bile (right) leaves a man melancholic and sends him to bed.

Bewitched or bewildered?
A great fear of witchcraft swept Europe beginning in the 1300s and extending through the "enlightened" Renaissance. Tens of thousands of people, mostly women, were thought to have made a pact with the devil. Some appear to have had mental disorders, which caused them to act strangely (Zilboorg & Henry, 1941). This individual is being "dunked" repeatedly until she confesses to witchery.

Corbis-Bettmann

the body: *yellow bile, black bile, blood,* and *phlegm* (Zuckerman, 2011). An excess of yellow bile, for example, caused *mania,* a state of frenzied activity; an excess of black bile was the source of *melancholia,* a condition marked by unshakable sadness.

To treat psychological dysfunctioning, Hippocrates sought to correct the underlying physical pathology. He believed, for instance, that the excess of black bile underlying melancholia could be reduced by a quiet life, a diet of vegetables, temperance, exercise, celibacy, and even bleeding. Hippocrates' focus on internal causes for abnormal behavior was shared by the great Greek philosophers Plato (427–347 B.C.) and Aristotle (384–322 B.C.) and by influential Greek and Roman physicians.

Europe in the Middle Ages: Demonology Returns

The enlightened views of Greek and Roman physicians and scholars were not enough to shake ordinary people's belief in demons. And with the decline of Rome, demonological views and practices became popular once again. A growing distrust of science spread throughout Europe.

From 500 to 1350 A.D., the period known as the Middle Ages, the power of the clergy increased greatly throughout Europe. In those days the church rejected scientific forms of investigation, and it controlled all education. Religious beliefs, which were highly superstitious and demonological, came to dominate all aspects of life. Once again behavior was usually interpreted as a conflict between good and evil, God and the devil. Deviant behavior, particularly psychological dysfunctioning, was seen as evidence of Satan's influence. Although some scientists and physicians still insisted on medical explanations and treatments, their views carried little weight in this atmosphere.

The Middle Ages were a time of great stress and anxiety—of war, urban uprisings, and plagues. People blamed the devil for these troubles and feared being possessed by him. Abnormal behavior apparently increased greatly during this period (Henley & Thorne, 2005). In addition, there were outbreaks of *mass madness,* in which large numbers of people apparently shared *delusions* (absurd false beliefs) and *hallucinations* (imagined sights or sounds). In one such disorder, *tarantism* (also known as *Saint Vitus' dance*), groups of people would suddenly start to jump, dance, and go into convulsions (Waller, 2009; Sigerist, 1943). Some dressed oddly; others tore off their clothing. All were convinced that they had been bitten and possessed by a wolf spider, now called a tarantula, and they sought to cure their disorder by performing a dance called a tarantella. In another form of mass madness, *lycanthropy,* people thought they were possessed by wolves or other animals. They acted wolflike and imagined that fur was growing all over their bodies.

Not surprisingly, some of the earlier demonological treatments for psychological abnormality reemerged during the Middle Ages. Once again the key to the cure was to rid the person's body of the devil that possessed it. Exorcisms were revived, and clergymen, who generally were in charge of treatment during this period, would plead, chant, or pray to the devil or evil spirit (Sluhovsky, 2007). If these techniques did not work, they had others to try, some indistinguishable from torture.

?
How might Twitter, Facebook, text messages, the Internet, cable television, or other technologies facilitate current forms of mass madness?

It was not until the Middle Ages drew to a close that demonology and its methods began to lose favor. Towns throughout Europe grew into cities, and government officials gained more power and took over nonreligious activities. Among their other responsibilities, they began to run hospitals and direct the care of people suffering from mental disorders. Medical views of abnormality gained favor once again, and many people with psychological disturbances received treatment in medical hospitals, such as the Trinity Hospital in England (Alldridge, 1979).

The Renaissance and the Rise of Asylums

During the early part of the Renaissance, a period of flourishing cultural and scientific activity from about 1400 to 1700, demonological views of abnormality continued to decline. German physician Johann Weyer (1515–1588), the first physician to specialize in mental illness, believed that the mind was as susceptible to sickness as the body was. He is now considered the founder of the modern study of psychopathology.

The care of people with mental disorders continued to improve in this atmosphere. In England such individuals might be kept at home while their families were aided financially by the local parish. Across Europe religious shrines were devoted to the humane and loving treatment of people with mental disorders. Perhaps the best known of these shrines was at Gheel in Belgium. Beginning in the fifteenth century, people came to it from all over the world for psychic healing. Local residents welcomed these pilgrims into their homes, and many stayed on to form the world's first "colony" of mental patients. Gheel was the forerunner of today's *community mental health programs,* and it continues to demonstrate that people with psychological disorders can respond to loving care and respectful treatment (Guarnieri, 2009; Aring, 1975, 1974). Many patients still live in foster homes there, interacting with other residents, until they recover.

Unfortunately, these improvements in care began to fade by the mid-sixteenth century. Government officials discovered that private homes and community residences could house only a small percentage of those with severe mental disorders and that medical hospitals were too few and too small. More and more, they converted hospitals

Bedlam
In this eighteenth-century work from *The Rake's Progress,* William Hogarth depicted London's Bethlehem Hospital, or Bedlam, as a chaotic asylum where people of fashion came to marvel at the strange behavior of the inmates.

BETWEEN THE LINES

Historical Notes

During the Middle Ages, there was, on average, one church for every 200 people (Asimov, 1997). ‹‹

From the Middle Ages through the 1800s, *barbers* sometimes performed the treatments, including *bloodletting,* for both medical and mental disorders. Today's striped barber poles originated back then, when they were staffs that patients would grip while being bled by a barber. ‹‹

Most of the patients in asylums, from all classes and circumstances, were women (Barton, 2004; Gold, 1998). ‹‹

Doctors who treated people with mental disorders in the eighteenth century were called "mad-doctors." ‹‹

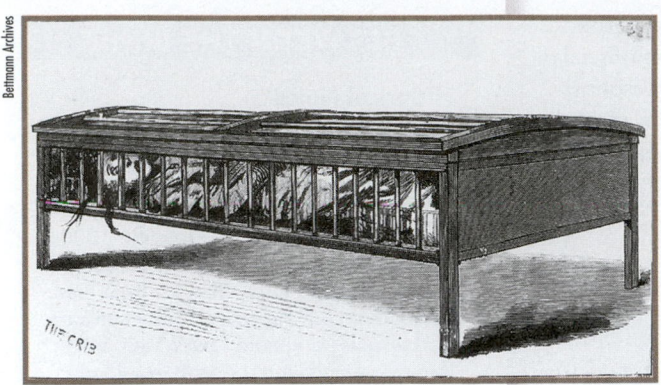

Bettmann Archives

THE CRIB

The "crib"

Outrageous devices and techniques, such as the "crib," were used in asylums, and some continued to be used even during the reforms of the nineteenth century.

and monasteries into **asylums,** institutions whose primary purpose was to care for people with mental illness. These institutions began with every intention of providing good care. Once the asylums started to overflow, however, they became virtual prisons where patients were held in filthy conditions and treated with unspeakable cruelty.

In 1547, for example, Bethlehem Hospital was given to the city of London by Henry VIII for the sole purpose of confining the mentally ill. In this asylum patients bound in chains cried out for all to hear. The hospital even became a popular tourist attraction; people were eager to pay to look at the howling and gibbering inmates. The hospital's name, pronounced "Bedlam" by the local people, has come to mean a chaotic uproar (Selling, 1940). Such asylums remained a widely used form of "care" until the late 1700s.

The Nineteenth Century: Reform and Moral Treatment

As 1800 approached, the treatment of people with mental disorders began to improve once again (Maher & Maher, 2003). Historians usually point to La Bicêtre, an asylum in Paris for male patients, as the first site of asylum reform. In 1793, during the French Revolution, Philippe Pinel (1745–1826) was named the chief physician there. He argued that the patients were sick people whose illnesses should be treated with sympathy and kindness rather than chains and beatings (Davidson, Rakfeldt, & Strauss, 2010). He unchained the patients and allowed them to move freely about the hospital grounds; replaced the dark dungeons with sunny, well-ventilated rooms; and offered support and advice. Pinel's approach proved remarkably successful. Many patients who had been shut away for decades improved greatly over a short period of time and were released. Pinel later brought similar reforms to a mental hospital in Paris for female patients, La Salpetrière.

Meanwhile, an English Quaker named William Tuke (1732–1819) was bringing similar reforms to northern England. In 1796 he founded the York Retreat, a rural estate where about 30 mental patients lived as guests in quiet country houses and were treated with a combination of rest, talk, prayer, and manual work (Raad & Makari, 2010; Charland, 2008, 2007).

Dance in a madhouse

A popular feature of moral treatment was the "lunatic ball." Hospital officials would bring patients together to dance and enjoy themselves. One such ball is shown in this painting, *Dance in a Madhouse,* by George Bellows.

The Spread of Moral Treatment The methods of Pinel and Tuke, called **moral treatment** because they emphasized moral guidance and humane and respectful techniques, caught on throughout Europe and the United States. Patients with psychological problems were increasingly perceived as potentially productive human beings whose mental functioning had broken down under stress. They were considered deserving of individual care, including discussions of their problems, useful activities, work, companionship, and quiet.

Dance in a Madhouse, 1917 (litho), Bellows, George Wesley (1882–1925)/ San Diego Museum of Art, USA/Museum Purchase/The Bridgeman Art Library.

The person most responsible for the early spread of moral treatment in the United States was Benjamin Rush (1745–1813), an eminent physician at Pennsylvania Hospital who is now considered the father of American psychiatry. Limiting his practice to mental illness, Rush developed humane approaches to treatment (Rush, 2010; Whitaker, 2002). For example, he required that the hospital hire intelligent and sensitive attendants to work closely with patients, reading and talking to them and taking them on regular walks. He also suggested that it would be therapeutic for doctors to give small gifts to their patients now and then.

Rush's work was influential, but it was a Boston schoolteacher named Dorothea Dix (1802–1887) who made humane care a public and political concern in the

United States. From 1841 to 1881, Dix went from state legislature to state legislature and to Congress speaking of the horrors she had observed at asylums and calling for reform. Dix's campaign led to new laws and greater government funding to improve the treatment of people with mental disorders (Davidson et al., 2010; Zilboorg & Henry, 1941). Each state was made responsible for developing effective public mental hospitals, or **state hospitals,** all of which intended to offer moral treatment. Similar hospitals were established throughout Europe.

The Decline of Moral Treatment By the 1850s, a number of mental hospitals throughout Europe and America reported success using moral approaches. By the end of that century, however, several factors led to a reversal of the moral treatment movement (Cautin, 2011; Bockoven, 1963). One factor was the speed with which the movement had spread. As mental hospitals multiplied, severe money and staffing shortages developed, recovery rates declined, and overcrowding in the hospitals became a major problem. Another factor was the assumption behind moral treatment that all patients could be cured if treated with humanity and dignity. For some, this was indeed sufficient. Others, however, needed more effective treatments than any that had yet been developed. An additional factor contributing to the decline of moral treatment was the emergence of a new wave of prejudice against people with mental disorders. As more and more patients disappeared into large, distant mental hospitals, the public came to view them as strange and dangerous. In turn, people were less open-handed when it came to making donations or allocating government funds. Moreover, many of the patients entering public mental hospitals in the United States in the late nineteenth century were poor foreign immigrants, whom the public had little interest in helping.

By the early years of the twentieth century, the moral treatment movement had ground to a halt in both the United States and Europe. Public mental hospitals were providing only custodial care and ineffective medical treatments and were becoming more overcrowded every year. Long-term hospitalization became the rule once again.

The Early Twentieth Century: The Somatogenic and Psychogenic Perspectives

As the moral movement was declining in the late 1800s, two opposing perspectives emerged and began to compete for the attention of clinicians: the **somatogenic perspective,** the view that abnormal psychological functioning has physical causes, and the **psychogenic perspective,** the view that the chief causes of abnormal functioning are psychological. These perspectives came into full bloom during the twentieth century.

The Somatogenic Perspective The somatogenic perspective has at least a 2,400-year history—remember Hippocrates' view that abnormal behavior resulted from brain disease and an imbalance of humors? Not until the late nineteenth century, however, did this perspective make a triumphant return and begin to gain wide acceptance.

Two factors were responsible for this rebirth. One was the work of an eminent German researcher, Emil Kraepelin (1856–1926). In 1883 Kraepelin published an influential textbook arguing that physical factors, such as fatigue, are responsible for mental dysfunction. In addition, as you will see in Chapter 4, he developed the first modern system for classifying abnormal behavior. He identified various syndromes, or clusters of symptoms; listed their physical causes; and discussed their expected course (deVries et al., 2008; Engstrom et al., 2006).

New biological discoveries also triggered the rise of the somatogenic perspective. One of the most important discoveries was that an organic disease, *syphilis,* led to *general paresis,* an irreversible disorder with both physical and mental symptoms, including paralysis and delusions of grandeur (Kaplan, 2010). In 1897 Richard von Krafft-Ebing (1840–1902), a German neurologist, injected matter from syphilis sores into patients suffering from general paresis and found that none of the patients developed symptoms of syphilis. Their immunity could have been caused only by an earlier case of syphilis. Since

•asylum• A type of institution that first became popular in the sixteenth century to provide care for persons with mental disorders. Most became virtual prisons.

•moral treatment• A nineteenth-century approach to treating people with mental dysfunction that emphasized moral guidance and humane and respectful treatment.

•state hospitals• State-run public mental institutions in the United States.

•somatogenic perspective• The view that abnormal psychological functioning has physical causes.

•psychogenic perspective• The view that the chief causes of abnormal functioning are psychological.

The more things change . . .
Patients at a modern-day mental hospital in Bangladesh eat their lunch off of the floor of their ward. Such conditions are similar to those that existed in some state hospitals throughout the United States well into the twentieth century.

all patients with general paresis were now immune to syphilis, Krafft-Ebing theorized that syphilis had been the cause of their general paresis. Finally, in 1905, Fritz Schaudinn (1871–1906), a German zoologist, discovered that the microorganism *Treponema pallida* was responsible for syphilis, which in turn caused general paresis.

The work of Kraepelin and the new understanding of general paresis led many researchers and practitioners to suspect that physical factors were responsible for many mental disorders, perhaps all of them. These theories and the possibility of quick and effective medical solutions for mental disorders were especially welcomed by those who worked in mental hospitals, where patient populations were now growing at an alarming rate.

Despite the general optimism, biological approaches yielded mostly disappointing results throughout the first half of the twentieth century. Although many medical treatments were developed for patients in mental hospitals during that time, most of the techniques failed to work. Physicians tried tooth extraction, tonsillectomy, hydrotherapy (alternating hot and cold baths), and lobotomy, a surgical cutting of certain nerve fibers in the brain. Even worse, biological views and claims led, in some circles, to proposals for immoral solutions such as *eugenic sterilization,* the elimination (through medical or other means) of individuals' ability to reproduce (see Table 1-1). Not until the 1950s, when a number of effective medications were finally discovered, did the somatogenic perspective truly begin to pay off for patients.

The Psychogenic Perspective The late nineteenth century also saw the emergence of the psychogenic perspective, the view that the chief causes of abnormal functioning are often psychological. This view, too, had a long history, but it did not gain much of a following until studies of *hypnotism* demonstrated its potential.

table: 1-1

Eugenics and Mental Disorders

Year	Event
1896	Connecticut became the first state in the United States to prohibit persons with mental disorders from marrying.
1896–1933	Every state in the United States passed a law prohibiting marriage by persons with mental disorders.
1907	Indiana became the first state to pass a bill calling for people with mental disorders, as well as criminals and other "defectives," to undergo sterilization.
1927	The U.S. Supreme Court ruled that eugenic sterilization was constitutional.
1907–1945	Around 45,000 Americans were sterilized under eugenic sterilization laws; 21,000 of them were patients in state mental hospitals.
1929–1932	Denmark, Norway, Sweden, Finland, and Iceland passed eugenic sterilization laws.
1933	Germany passed a eugenic sterilization law, under which 375,000 people were sterilized by 1940.
1940	Nazi Germany began to use "proper gases" to kill people with mental disorders; 70,000 or more people were killed in less than two years.

Source: Whitaker, 2002.

Hypnotism is a procedure that places people in a trance-like mental state during which they become extremely suggestible. It was used to help treat psychological disorders as far back as 1778, when an Austrian physician named Friedrich Anton Mesmer (1734–1815) established a clinic in Paris. His patients suffered from *hysterical disorders,* mysterious bodily ailments that had no apparent physical basis. Mesmer had his patients sit in a darkened room filled with music; then he appeared, dressed in a colorful costume, and touched the troubled area of each patient's body with a special rod. A surprising number of patients seemed to be helped by this treatment, called *mesmerism* (Dingfelder, 2010; Lanska & Lanska, 2007). Their pain, numbness, or paralysis disappeared. Several scientists believed that Mesmer was inducing a trancelike state in his patients and that this state was causing their symptoms to disappear. The treatment was so controversial, however, that eventually Mesmer was banished from Paris.

Hypnotism update
Hypnotism, the procedure that opened the door for the psychogenic perspective, continues to influence many areas of modern life, including the fields of psychotherapy, entertainment, and law enforcement. Here a forensic clinician uses hypnosis to help a witness recall the details of a crime. Recent research has clarified, however, that hypnotic procedures are as capable of creating false memories as they are of uncovering real memories.

It was not until years after Mesmer died that many researchers had the courage to investigate his procedure, later called *hypnotism* (from *hypnos,* the Greek word for "sleep"), and its effects on hysterical disorders. The experiments of two physicians practicing in the city of Nancy in France, Hippolyte-Marie Bernheim (1840–1919) and Ambroise-Auguste Liébault (1823–1904), showed that hysterical disorders could actually be induced in otherwise normal people while they were under the influence of hypnosis. That is, the physicians could make normal people experience deafness, paralysis, blindness, or numbness by means of hypnotic suggestion—and they could remove these artificial symptoms by the same means. Thus they established that a *mental* process—hypnotic suggestion—could both cause and cure even a physical dysfunction. Leading scientists concluded that hysterical disorders were largely psychological in origin, and the psychogenic perspective rose in popularity.

Among those who studied the effects of hypnotism on hysterical disorders was Josef Breuer (1842–1925) of Vienna. This physician discovered that his patients sometimes awoke free of hysterical symptoms after speaking candidly under hypnosis about past upsetting events. During the 1890s Breuer was joined in his work by another Viennese physician, Sigmund Freud (1856–1939). As you will see in Chapter 3, Freud's work eventually led him to develop the theory of **psychoanalysis,** which holds that many forms of abnormal and normal psychological functioning are psychogenic. In particular, he believed that *unconscious* psychological processes are at the root of such functioning.

Freud also developed the *technique* of psychoanalysis, a form of discussion in which clinicians help troubled people gain insight into their unconscious psychological processes. He believed that such insight, even without hypnotic procedures, would help the patients overcome their psychological problems.

Freud and his followers offered psychoanalytic treatment primarily to patients suffering from anxiety or depression, problems that did not typically require hospitalization. These patients visited therapists in their offices for sessions of approximately an hour and then went about their daily activities—a format of treatment now known as *outpatient therapy.* By the early twentieth century, psychoanalytic theory and treatment were widely accepted throughout the Western world (Cautin, 2011).

Current Trends

It would hardly be accurate to say that we now live in a period of great enlightenment about or dependable treatment of mental disorders. In fact, surveys have found that 43 percent of respondents believe that people bring mental disorders on themselves, and 35 percent consider such disorders to be caused by sinful behavior (Stanford, 2007; NMHA, 1999). Nevertheless, the past 50 years have brought major changes in the ways clinicians

•psychoanalysis•Either the theory or the treatment of abnormal mental functioning that emphasizes unconscious psychological forces as the cause of psychopathology.

understand and treat abnormal functioning. More theories and types of treatment exist, as do more research studies, more information, and, perhaps for these reasons, more disagreements about abnormal functioning today than at any time in the past. In some ways the study and treatment of psychological disorders have made great strides, but in other respects clinical scientists and practitioners are still struggling to make a difference.

From Julliard to the streets

Nathaniel Ayers, subject of the book and movie *The Soloist*, plays his violin on the streets of Los Angeles while living as a homeless person in 2005. Once a promising musical student at the Julliard School in New York, Ayers developed schizophrenia and eventually found himself without treatment and without a home. Tens of thousands of people with severe mental disorders are currently homeless.

How Are People with Severe Disturbances Cared For?

In the 1950s researchers discovered a number of new **psychotropic medications**—drugs that primarily affect the brain and reduce many symptoms of mental dysfunctioning. They included the first *antipsychotic drugs,* which correct extremely confused and distorted thinking; *antidepressant drugs,* which lift the mood of depressed people; and *antianxiety drugs,* which reduce tension and worry.

When given these drugs, many patients who had spent years in mental hospitals began to show signs of improvement. Hospital administrators, encouraged by these results and pressured by a growing public outcry over the terrible conditions in public mental hospitals, began to discharge patients almost immediately.

Since the discovery of these medications, mental health professionals in most of the developed nations of the world have followed a policy of **deinstitutionalization,** releasing hundreds of thousands of patients from public mental hospitals. On any given day in 1955, close to 600,000 people were confined in public mental institutions across the United States (see Figure 1-1). Today the daily patient population in the same kinds of hospitals is less than 40,000 (Althouse, 2010).

In short, outpatient care has now become the primary mode of treatment for people with severe psychological disturbances as well as for those with more moderate problems. Today when severely disturbed people do need institutionalization, they are usually given *short-term* hospitalization. Ideally, they are then given outpatient psychotherapy and medication in community programs and residences (McEvoy & Richards, 2007).

Chapters 3 and 15 will look more closely at this recent emphasis on community care for people with severe psychological disturbances—a philosophy called the *community mental health approach.* The approach has been helpful for many patients, but too few community programs are available to address current needs in the United States (Lieberman, 2010; Rosenberg & Rosenberg, 2006). As a result, hundreds of thousands of persons with severe disturbances fail to make lasting recoveries, and they shuttle back and forth between the mental hospital and the community. After release from the hospital, they at best receive minimal care and often wind up living in decrepit rooming houses or on the streets. In fact, only 40 to 60 percent of persons with severe psychological disturbances currently receive treatment of any kind (Gill, 2010; NIMH, 2010). At least 100,000 individuals with such disturbances are homeless on any given day; another 135,000 or more are inmates of jails and prisons (Kooyman & Walsh, 2011; Althouse, 2010). Their abandonment is truly a national disgrace.

Figure 1-1

The impact of deinstitutionalization The number of patients (fewer than 40,000) now hospitalized in public mental hospitals in the United States is a small fraction of the number hospitalized in 1955. (Adapted from Althouse, 2010; Torrey, 2001; Lang, 1999.)

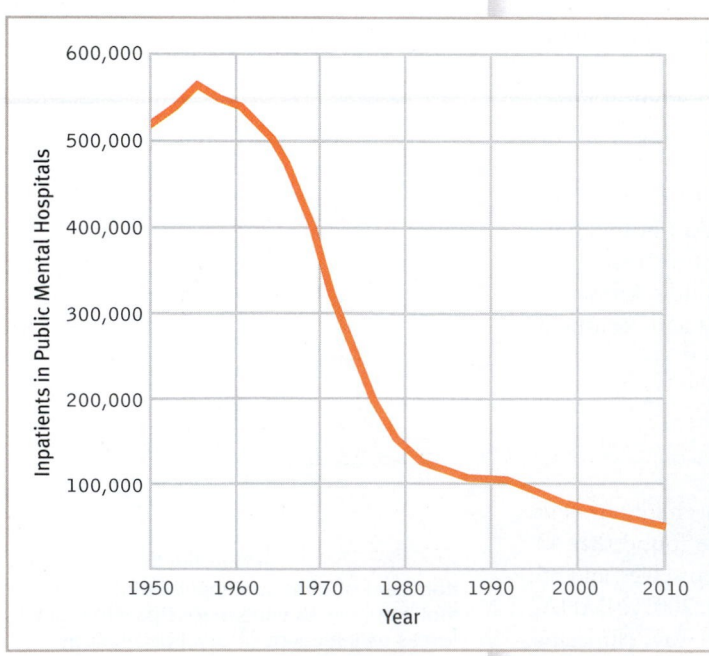

How Are People with Less Severe Disturbances Treated?

The treatment picture for people with moderate psychological disturbances has been more positive than that for people with severe disorders. Since the 1950s, outpatient care has continued to be the preferred mode of treatment for them, and the number and types of facilities that offer such care have expanded to meet the need.

Before the 1950s, almost all outpatient care took the form of **private psychotherapy,** an arrangement by which an individual directly pays a psychotherapist for counseling services. This tended to be an expensive form of treatment, available only to the wealthy. Since the 1950s, however, most health insurance plans have expanded coverage to include private psychotherapy, so that it is now also widely available to people with more modest incomes. In addition, outpatient therapy is now offered in a number of less expensive settings, such as community mental health centers, crisis intervention centers, family service centers, and other social service agencies. The new settings have spurred a dramatic increase in the number of persons seeking outpatient care for psychological problems. Surveys suggest that nearly one of every six adults in the United States receives treatment for psychological disorders in the course of a year (NIMH, 2010). The majority of clients are seen for fewer than five sessions during the year.

Outpatient treatments are also becoming available for more and more kinds of problems. When Freud and his colleagues first began to practice, most of their patients suffered from anxiety or depression. Almost half of today's clients suffer from those same problems, but people with other kinds of disorders are also receiving therapy. In addition, at least 20 percent of clients enter therapy because of milder problems in living—problems with marital, family, job, peer, school, or community relationships (Druss et al., 2007).

Yet another change in outpatient care since the 1950s has been the development of programs devoted exclusively to one kind of psychological problem. We now have, for example, suicide prevention centers, substance abuse programs, eating disorder programs, phobia clinics, and sexual dysfunction programs. Clinicians in these programs have the kind of expertise that can be acquired only by concentration in a single area.

A Growing Emphasis on Preventing Disorders and Promoting Mental Health

Although the community mental health approach has often failed to address the needs of people with severe disorders, it has given rise to an important principle of mental health care—**prevention** (Eckenrode, 2011; Janzen et al., 2010). Rather than wait for

•psychotropic medications• Drugs that mainly affect the brain and reduce many symptoms of mental dysfunctioning.

•deinstitutionalization• The practice, begun in the 1960s, of releasing hundreds of thousands of patients from public mental hospitals.

•private psychotherapy• An arrangement in which a person directly pays a therapist for counseling services.

•prevention• Interventions aimed at deterring mental disorders before they can develop.

The availability of therapy
Therapy for people with mild to severe psychological disturbances is widely available in individual, group, and family formats.

•**positive psychology**•The study and enhancement of positive feelings, traits, and abilities.

•**multicultural psychology**•The field of psychology that examines the impact of culture, race, ethnicity, gender, and similar factors on our behaviors and thoughts and focuses on how such factors may influence the origin, nature, and treatment of abnormal behavior.

•**managed care program**•A system of health care coverage in which the insurance company largely controls the nature, scope, and cost of medical or psychological services.

psychological disorders to occur, many of today's community programs try to correct the social conditions that underlie psychological problems (poverty or violence in the community, for example) and to help individuals who are at risk for developing emotional problems (for example, teenage mothers or the children of people with severe psychological disorders). As you will see later, community prevention programs are not always successful and they often suffer from limited funding, but they have grown in number throughout the United States and Europe, offering great promise as the ultimate form of intervention.

Prevention programs have been further energized in the past few years by the field of psychology's ever-growing interest in **positive psychology** (Azar, 2011; Seligman & Fowler, 2011; Seligman, 2007). Positive psychology is the study and enhancement of positive feelings such as optimism and happiness, positive traits like hard work and wisdom, positive abilities such as social skills and other talents, and group-directed virtues, including altruism and tolerance (see *PsychWatch* below).

In the clinical arena, positive psychology suggests that practitioners can help people best by *promoting* positive development and psychological wellness. While researchers study and learn more about positive psychology in the laboratory, clinicians with this

Why do you think it has taken psychologists so long to start studying positive behaviors?

PsychWatch

Positive Psychology: Happiness Is All Around Us

Judging from many Web sites, TV news shows, and the spread of self-help books, you might think that happiness is rare. But there's good news. Research indicates that people's lives are, in general, more joyful than we think. In fact, most people around the world say they're happy—including most of those who are poor, unemployed, elderly, and disabled (Bakalar, 2010; Becchetti & Santoro, 2007; Pugno, 2007). Men and women are equally likely to declare themselves satisfied or very happy. Wealthy people appear only slightly happier than those of modest means (Diener et al., 2010; Easterbrook, 2005). Overall, only 1 person in 10 reports being "not too happy" (Myers, 2000; Myers & Diener, 1996), and only 1 in 7 reports waking up unhappy (Wallis, 2005).

Happiness is everywhere As the joy in the faces of these Tibetan women illustrates, happiness is tied to factors beyond a person's economic plight, age, residence, or health.

Of course, some people are indeed happier than others. Particularly happy people seem to remain happy from decade to decade, regardless of job changes, moves, and family changes (Holder & Klassen, 2010; Diener et al., 2000). Such people adjust to negative events and return to their usual cheerful state within a few months. Conversely, unhappy people are not cheered in the long term even by positive events.

Some research indicates that happiness is linked to personality characteristics and interpretive styles. Happy people are, for example, generally optimistic, outgoing, curious, and tender-minded; they also tend to persevere, have several close friends, possess high self-esteem, be spiritual, and have a sense of control over their lives (Fisher, 2010; Peterson et al., 2007; Sahoo et al., 2005).

A better understanding of the roots of happiness is likely to emerge from the current flurry of research. In the meantime, we can take comfort in the knowledge that the human condition isn't quite as unhappy as news stories (and textbooks on abnormal psychology) may make it seem.

orientation teach people coping skills that may help protect them from stress and adversity and encourage them to become more involved in personally meaningful activities and relationships (Bond & Hauf, 2007). In this way, the clinicians are trying to promote mental health and prevent mental disorders.

Multicultural Psychology

We are, without question, a society of multiple cultures, races, and languages. Members of racial and ethnic minority groups in the United States collectively make up 35 percent of the population, a percentage that is expected to grow to more than 50 percent in the coming decades (Arroyos-Jurado et al., 2010; Santa-Cruz, 2010; U.S. Census Bureau, 2010). This change is partly because of shifts in immigration trends and partly because of higher birth rates among minority groups in the United States (NVSR, 2010).

In response to this growing diversity, a new area of study called **multicultural psychology** has emerged. Multicultural psychologists seek to understand how culture, race, ethnicity, gender, and similar factors affect behavior and thought and how people of different cultures, races, and genders may differ psychologically (Matsumoto & van de Vijer, 2011; Alegria et al., 2010, 2007, 2004). As you will see throughout this book, the field of multicultural psychology has begun to have a powerful effect on our understanding and treatment of abnormal behavior.

The Growing Influence of Insurance Coverage

So many people now seek therapy that private insurance companies have changed their coverage for mental health patients. Today the dominant form of coverage is the **managed care program**—a program in which the insurance company determines such key issues as which therapists its clients may choose, the cost of sessions, and the number of sessions for which a client may be reimbursed (Glasser, 2010).

At least 75 percent of all privately insured persons in the United States are currently enrolled in managed care programs (Deb et al., 2006; Kiesler, 2000). The coverage for mental health treatment under such programs follows the same basic principles as coverage for medical treatment, including a limited pool of practitioners from which patients can choose, preapproval of treatment by the insurance company, strict standards for judging whether problems and treatments qualify for reimbursement, and ongoing reviews and assessments. In the mental health realm, both therapists and clients typically dislike managed care programs (Merrick & Reif, 2010; Schneid, 2010). They fear that

Matthew S. Gunby/AP Photo

Positive psychology in action
Often positive psychology and multicultural psychology work together. Here, for example, two young girls come together as one at the end of a "slave reconciliation" walk by 400 people in Maryland. The walk was intended to promote racial understanding and to help Americans overcome the lasting psychological effects of slavery.

Marilynn K. Yee/The New York Times/Redux Pictures

An ounce of prevention
The clinical field's growing emphasis on prevention has affected how employers address the problem of stress in the workplace. About 20 percent of corporate employers now offer some kind of stress reduction program, such as this regular yoga class at Armani (the fashion company) in New York City. Corporate spending has helped fuel the $12 billion stress-management industry.

the programs inevitably shorten therapy (often for the worse), unfairly favor treatments whose results are not always lasting (for example, drug therapy), pose a special hardship for those with severe mental disorders, and result in treatments determined by insurance companies rather than by therapists (Glasser, 2010).

A key problem with insurance coverage—both managed care and other kinds of insurance programs—is that reimbursements for mental disorders tend to be lower than those for medical disorders. This places persons with psychological difficulties at a distinct disadvantage. In 2011, a federal **parity** law went into effect in the United States a law that directs insurance companies to provide equal coverage for mental and medical problems (Clay, 2011). It is not yet clear, however, whether this law is indeed leading to better coverage or better treatment for people with psychological problems.

What Are Today's Leading Theories and Professions?

One of the most important developments in the clinical field has been the growth of numerous theoretical perspectives that now coexist in the field. Before the 1950s, the *psychoanalytic* perspective, with its emphasis on unconscious psychological problems as the cause of abnormal behavior, was dominant. Then the discovery of effective psychotropic drugs inspired new respect for the somatogenic, or *biological,* view. As you will see in Chapter 3, other influential perspectives that have emerged since the 1950s are the *behavioral, cognitive, humanistic-existential,* and *sociocultural* schools of thought. At present no single viewpoint dominates the clinical field as the psychoanalytic perspective once did. In fact, the perspectives often conflict and compete with one another, yet in some instances they complement each other and together provide more complete explanations and treatments for psychological disorders.

In addition, a variety of professionals now offer help to people with psychological problems. Before the 1950s, psychotherapy was offered only by *psychiatrists,* physicians who complete three to four additional years of training after medical school (a *residency*) in the treatment of abnormal mental functioning. After World War II, however, with millions of soldiers returning home to countries throughout North America and Europe, the demand for mental health services expanded so rapidly that other professional groups had to step in to fill the need (Humphreys, 1996).

Among those other groups are *clinical psychologists*—professionals who earn a doctorate in clinical psychology by completing four to five years of graduate training in abnormal functioning and its treatment and also complete a one-year internship at a mental health setting. Psychotherapy and related services are also provided by *counseling psychologists, educational* and *school psychologists, psychiatric nurses, marriage therapists, family therapists,* and—the largest group—*psychiatric social workers* (see Table 1-2). Each of these specialties has its own graduate training program. Theoretically, each conducts therapy in a distinctive way, but in reality clinicians from the various specialties often use similar techniques.

table: **1-2**

Profiles of Mental Health Professionals in the United States

	Degree	Began to Practice	Current Number	Percent Female
Psychiatrists	M.D., D.O.	1840s	40,904	25
Psychologists	Ph.D., Psy.D., Ed.D.	Late 1940s	170,200	52
Social workers	M.S.W., D.S.W.	Early 1950s	430,300	77
Counselors	Various	Early 1950s	379,700	90

Source: AMA, 2011; Carey, 2011; U.S. Bureau of Labor Statistics, 2011, 2002; Weissman, 2000.

Everybody's problems are better than mine.

One final key development in the study and treatment of mental disorders since World War II has been a growing appreciation of the need for effective research (Goodwin, 2011; NIMH, 2011). *Clinical researchers* have tried to determine which concepts best explain and predict abnormal behavior, which treatments are most effective, and what kinds of changes may be required. Today well-trained clinical researchers conduct studies in universities, medical schools, laboratories, mental hospitals, mental health centers, and other clinical settings throughout the world. Their work has produced important discoveries and has changed many of our ideas about abnormal psychological functioning.

PUTTING IT ... together

A Work in Progress

Since ancient times, people have tried to explain, treat, and study abnormal behavior. By examining the responses of past societies to such behaviors, we can better understand the roots of our present views and treatments. In addition, a look backward helps us appreciate just how far we have come—how humane our present views are, how impressive our recent discoveries are, and how important our current emphasis on research is.

At the same time we must recognize the many problems in abnormal psychology today. The field has yet to agree on one definition of abnormality. It is currently made up of conflicting schools of thought and treatment whose members are often unimpressed by the claims and accomplishments of the others. And clinical practice is carried out by a variety of professionals trained in different ways.

As you travel through the topics in this book, keep in mind the field's current strengths and weaknesses, the progress that has been made, and the journey that lies ahead. Perhaps the most important lesson to be learned from our look at the history of this field is that our current understanding of abnormal behavior represents a work in progress. The clinical field stands at a crossroads, with some of the most important insights, investigations, and changes yet to come.

How, then, should you proceed in your study of abnormal psychology? To begin with, you need to learn about the basic tools and perspectives that today's scientists and practitioners find most useful. This is the task we turn to in the next several chapters. Chapter 2 describes the research strategies that are currently informing our knowledge of abnormal functioning. Chapter 3 then examines the range of views that influence

BETWEEN THE LINES

Famous Psych Lines from the Movies

"I opened up to you and you judged me." (*Silver Linings Playbook*, 2012) ‹‹

"Be aggressive, passive aggressive!" (*The Perks of Being a Wallflower*, 2012) ‹‹

"Don't let the beard fool you. He's a child!" (*The Hangover*, 2009) ‹‹

"You know, your mood swings are kinda giving me whiplash." (*Twilight*, 2008) ‹‹

"Take baby steps." (*What About Bob?* 1991) ‹‹

"Rosebud." (*Citizen Kane*, 1941) ‹‹

"I see dead people." (*The Sixth Sense*, 1999) ‹‹

"Dave, my mind is going. . . . I can feel it." (*2001: A Space Odyssey*, 1968) ‹‹

"All right, Mr. DeMille, I'm ready for my close-up." (*Sunset Boulevard*, 1950) ‹‹

"I love the smell of napalm in the morning." (*Apocalypse Now*, 1979) ‹‹

"Snakes, why does it always have to be snakes?" (*Raiders of the Lost Ark*, 1981) ‹‹

today's clinical theorists and practitioners. Finally, Chapter 4 examines how abnormal behaviors are currently being assessed, diagnosed, and treated. Later chapters present the major categories of psychological abnormality as well as the leading explanations and treatments for each of them. In the final chapter, you will see how the science of abnormal psychology and its professionals address current social issues and interact with legal, social, and other institutions in our world.

Summing Up

- **WHAT IS PSYCHOLOGICAL ABNORMALITY?** Abnormal functioning is generally considered to be *deviant, distressful, dysfunctional,* and *dangerous.* Behavior must also be considered in the context in which it occurs, however, and the concept of abnormality depends on the *norms* and *values* of the society in question. *pp. 2–5*

- **WHAT IS TREATMENT?** *Therapy* is a systematic process for helping people overcome their psychological difficulties. It typically requires a *patient,* a *therapist,* and a *series of therapeutic contacts. pp. 5–6*

- **HOW WAS ABNORMALITY VIEWED AND TREATED IN THE PAST?** The history of psychological disorders stretches back to ancient times.

PREHISTORIC SOCIETIES Prehistoric societies apparently viewed abnormal behavior as the work of evil spirits. There is evidence that Stone Age cultures used *trephination,* a primitive form of brain surgery, to treat abnormal behavior. People of early societies also sought to drive out evil spirits by *exorcism. p. 9*

GREEKS AND ROMANS Physicians of the Greek and Roman empires offered more enlightened explanations of mental disorders. Hippocrates believed that abnormal behavior was caused by an imbalance of the four bodily fluids, or *humors:* black bile, yellow bile, blood, and phlegm. Treatment consisted of correcting the underlying physical pathology through diet and lifestyle. *pp. 9–10*

THE MIDDLE AGES In the Middle Ages, Europeans returned to demonological explanations of abnormal behavior. The clergy was very influential and held that mental disorders were the work of the devil. As the Middle Ages drew to a close, such explanations and treatments began to decline, and people with mental disorders were increasingly treated in hospitals instead of by the clergy. *pp. 10–11*

THE RENAISSANCE Care of people with mental disorders continued to improve during the early part of the Renaissance. Certain religious shrines became dedicated to the humane treatment of such individuals. By the middle of the sixteenth century, however, persons with mental disorders were being warehoused in *asylums. pp. 11–12*

THE NINETEENTH CENTURY Care of those with mental disorders started to improve again in the nineteenth century. In Paris, Philippe Pinel started the movement toward *moral treatment.* Similar reforms were brought to England by William Tuke. In the United States Dorothea Dix spearheaded a movement to ensure legal rights and protection for people with mental disorders and to establish state hospitals for their care. Unfortunately, the moral treatment movement disintegrated by the late nineteenth century, and mental hospitals again became warehouses where inmates received minimal care. *pp. 12–13*

THE EARLY TWENTIETH CENTURY The turn of the twentieth century saw the return of the *somatogenic perspective,* the view that abnormal psychological functioning is caused primarily by physical factors. Key to this development were the work of Emil Kraepelin in the late 1800s and the finding that *general paresis* was caused by the organic disease syphilis. The same period saw the rise of the *psychogenic perspective,* the view that the chief causes of abnormal functioning are psychological. An important factor in its rise was the use of *hypnotism* to treat patients with *hysterical disorders*. Sigmund Freud's psychogenic approach, *psychoanalysis*, eventually gained wide acceptance and influenced future generations of clinicians. *pp. 13–15*

■ **CURRENT TRENDS** The past 50 years have brought significant changes in the understanding and treatment of abnormal functioning. In the 1950s, researchers discovered a number of new *psychotropic medications,* drugs that mainly affect the brain and reduce many symptoms of mental dysfunctioning. Their success contributed to a policy of *deinstitutionalization,* under which hundreds of thousands of patients were released from public mental hospitals. In addition, *outpatient treatment* has become the primary approach for most persons with mental disorders, both mild and severe; *prevention programs* are growing in number and influence; the field of *multicultural psychology* has begun to influence how clinicians view and treat abnormality; and *insurance coverage* is having a significant impact on the way treatment is conducted. Finally, a variety of *perspectives* and *professionals* have come to operate in the field of abnormal psychology, and many well-trained *clinical researchers* now investigate the field's theories and treatments. *pp. 15–21*

PsychPortal

Visit **PsychPortal**
www.yourpsychportal.com
to access the e-book, videocases, and other case materials and activities, as well as study aids including flashcards, crossword puzzles, quizzes, FAQs, and research exercises.

BETWEEN THE LINES

In Their Words

"I became insane, with long intervals of horrible sanity." ‹‹
Edgar Allen Poe

"Everyone is more or less mad on one point." ‹‹
Rudyard Kipling

"I can calculate the motion of heavenly bodies but not the madness of people." ‹‹
Sir Isaac Newton

RESEARCH IN ABNORMAL PSYCHOLOGY

"Next Christmas, the iPod will be dead, finished, gone, kaput."

Amstrad (electronics company), 2005

"The brain is an organ of minor importance."

Aristotle, Greek philosopher, fourth century B.C.

"Guitar music is on the way out."

Decca Recording Company, 1962

"There is no reason for any individual to have a computer in their home."

Ken Olson, Digital Equipment Corp., 1977

"640K ought to be enough for anybody."

Bill Gates, 1981

"Woman may be said to be an inferior man."

Aristotle

"The cloning of mammals . . . is biologically impossible."

James McGrath and Davor Solter, genetic researchers, 1984

"The 'telephone' has too many shortcomings to be seriously considered as a means of communication."

Western Union, 1876

Each of these statements was once accepted as gospel. Had their accuracy not been tested, had they been judged on the basis of conventional wisdom alone, had new ideas not been proposed and investigated, human knowledge and progress would have been severely limited. What enabled thinkers to move beyond such misperceptions? The answer, quite simply, is research, the systematic search for facts through the use of careful observations and investigations.

Research is the key to accuracy in all fields of study; it is particularly important in abnormal psychology because a wrong belief in this field can lead to great suffering. Consider, for example, schizophrenia and the treatment procedure known as the lobotomy. *Schizophrenia* is a severe disorder that causes people to lose contact with reality. Their thoughts, perceptions, and emotions become distorted and disorganized, and their behavior may be bizarre and withdrawn. For the first half of the twentieth century, this condition was attributed to poor parenting. Clinicians blamed *schizophrenogenic* ("schizophrenia-causing") mothers for the disorder—women they described as cold, domineering, and unresponsive to their children's needs. As you will see in Chapter 14, this widely held belief turned out to be wrong.

During the same era, practitioners developed a surgical procedure that supposedly cured schizophrenia. In this procedure, called a *lobotomy,* a pointed instrument was inserted into the frontal lobe of the brain and rotated, destroying much brain tissue. Early clinical reports described lobotomized patients as showing near-miraculous improvement. This impression, too, turned out to be wrong, although the mistake wasn't discovered until tens of thousands of persons had been lobotomized. Far from

My lobotomy

After undergoing a lobotomy at age 12 to "cure" his psychological problems, Howard Dully experienced decades of misery and psychological pain—a journey that he recounts in his recent memoir *My Lobotomy*. Only after Dully and tens of thousands of other people received lobotomies did properly conducted research reveal that this form of brain surgery caused irreversible brain damage that left many patients withdrawn and even stuporous.

curing schizophrenia, lobotomies caused irreversible brain damage that left many patients withdrawn and even stuporous.

These errors underscore the importance of scientific research in abnormal psychology. Theories and treatments that seem effective in individual instances may prove disastrous to other people in different situations. Only by fully testing a theory or technique on representative groups of individuals can clinicians evaluate the accuracy, effectiveness, and safety of their ideas and techniques. Until clinical researchers conducted properly designed studies, millions of parents, already heartbroken by their children's schizophrenia, were additionally labeled as the primary cause of the disorder, and countless people with schizophrenia, already debilitated by their symptoms, were made permanently apathetic and spiritless by a lobotomy.

Clinical researchers face certain challenges that make their work very difficult. They must, for example, figure out how to measure such elusive concepts as unconscious motives, private thoughts, mood changes, and human potential. They must consider the different cultural backgrounds, races, and genders of the people they choose to study. And, as we are reminded in *PsychWatch* on the next page, they must always ensure that the rights of their research participants, both human and animal, are not violated (Hobson-West, 2010). Despite such difficulties, research in abnormal psychology has taken giant steps forward, especially during the past 40 years. In the past, most clinical researchers were limited by a lack of training and by less-than-useful techniques. Now graduate clinical programs train large numbers of students to design and conduct proper studies on clinical topics. Moreover, the development of new research methods has greatly improved our understanding and treatment of psychological dysfunction. It may even help to prevent psychological disorders.

Can you think of beliefs that were once accepted as gospel but, as a result of scientific research, eventually were proven to be false?

What Do Clinical Researchers Do?

Clinical researchers, also called clinical scientists, try to discover universal laws, or principles, of abnormal psychological functioning. They search for a general, or **nomothetic,** understanding of nature, causes, and treatments of abnormality ("nomothetic" is derived from the Greek *nomothetis,* "lawgiver") (DeMatteo et al., 2010). They do not typically assess, diagnose, or treat individual clients; that is the job of clinical practitioners, who seek an *idiographic,* or individualistic, understanding of abnormal behavior. You will read about the work of practitioners in later chapters.

To gain a nomothetic understanding of abnormal psychology, clinical researchers, like scientists in other fields, use the **scientific method**—that is, they collect and evaluate information through careful observations. These observations in turn enable them to pinpoint and explain relationships between *variables.* Simply stated, a variable is any characteristic or event that can vary, whether from time to time, from place to place, or from person to person. Age, sex, and race are human variables. So are eye color, occupation, and social status. Clinical researchers are interested in variables such as childhood upsets, present life experiences, moods, social functioning, and responses to treatment. They try to determine whether two or more such variables change together and whether a change in one variable causes a change in another. Will the death of a parent cause a child to become depressed? If so, will a given treatment reduce that depression?

Such questions cannot be answered by logic alone because scientists, like all human beings, frequently make errors in thinking. Thus clinical researchers must depend mainly on three methods of investigation: the *case study,* which typically focuses on one individual, and the *correlational method* and *experimental method,* approaches that usually gather information about many individuals. Each is best suited to certain kinds of circumstances and questions. As a group, these methods enable scientists to form and

PsychWatch

Animals Have Rights

For years researchers have learned about abnormal human behavior from experiments with animals. Animals have been shocked, prematurely separated from their parents, and starved. They have had their brains surgically changed and have even been killed, or "sacrificed," so that researchers could autopsy them. It is estimated that medical animal research (for example, cardiovascular research) has helped increase the life expectancy of humans by almost 24 years. Similarly, animal research has been key to the development of many medications for psychological disorders, leading to a savings of hundreds of billions of dollars every year in the United States alone (Shields, 2010; Lasker Foundation, 2000). Nevertheless, concerns remain: Are such actions always ethically acceptable?

Animal rights activists say no (McCance, 2011; Fellenz, 2007). They have called such undertakings cruel and unnecessary and have fought many forms of animal research with legal protests and demonstrations. Some have even harassed scientists

and vandalized their labs (Conn & Rantin, 2010). In turn, some researchers have accused activists of caring more about animals than about human beings. In response to this controversy, a number of state courts, government agencies, and the American Psychological Association have issued rules and guidelines for animal research. But the battle still goes on.

Where does the public stand on this issue (Hobson-West, 2010)? In one survey, 64 percent of the respondents said that

they dislike animal research, but 75 percent said they can "accept" it as long as it is for medical purposes (MORI, 2005, 1999). People in such surveys tend to approve of experiments that use mice or rats more than those that use monkeys. Most of them disapprove of experiments that bring pain to animals, except when the investigations are seeking a cure for childhood leukemia, AIDS, or other life-threatening problems.

Paul Sakuma/AP Photo

Making a point Members of an organization called *In Defense of Animals* wear monkey outfits and sit in locked cages in front of the University of California, San Francisco, to protest the use of monkeys in research.

---

test **hypotheses,** or hunches, that certain variables are related in certain ways—and to draw broad conclusions as to why. More properly, a hypothesis is a tentative explanation offered to provide a basis for an investigation.

The Case Study

A **case study** is a detailed description of a person's life and psychological problems. It describes the person's history, present circumstances, and symptoms. It may also speculate about why the problems developed, and it may describe the person's treatment (Lee, Mishna, & Brennenstuhl, 2010).

In his famous case study of Little Hans (1909), Sigmund Freud discusses a 4-year-old boy who developed a fear of horses. Freud gathered his material from detailed letters sent to him by Hans' father, a physician who had attended lectures on psychoanalysis, and from his own limited interviews with the child. Freud's study runs 140 pages in his *Collected Papers,* so only key excerpts are presented here.

One day while Hans was in the street he was seized with an attack of morbid anxiety. . . . [Hans's father wrote:] "He began to cry and asked to be taken home. . . . In the evening he grew visibly frightened; he cried and could not be separated from his mother. . . .

•**nomothetic understanding**•A general understanding of the nature, causes, and treatments of abnormal psychological functioning in the form of laws or principles.

•**scientific method**•The process of systematically gathering and evaluating information through careful observations to gain an understanding of a phenomenon.

•**hypothesis**•A hunch or prediction that certain variables are related in certain ways.

•**case study**•A detailed account of a person's life and psychological problems.

[When taken for a walk the next day], again he began to cry, did not want to start, and was frightened. . . . On the way back from Schönbrunn he said to his mother, after much internal struggling: 'I was afraid a horse would bite me.' . . . In the evening he . . . had another attack similar to that of the previous evening. . . ."

But the beginnings of this psychological situation go back further still. . . . The first reports of Hans date from a period when he was not quite three years old. At that time, by means of various remarks and questions, he was showing a quite peculiarly lively interest in that portion of his body which he used to describe as his "widdler" [his word for penis]. . . .

When he was three and a half his mother found him with his hand to his penis. She threatened him in these words: "If you do that, I shall send for Dr. A. to cut off your widdler. And then what'll you widdle with?" . . . This was the occasion of his acquiring [a] "castration complex." . . .

[At the age of four, Hans entered] a state of intensified sexual excitement, the object of which was his mother. The intensity of this excitement was shown by . . . two attempts at seducing his mother. [One such attempt, occurring just before the outbreak of his anxiety, was described by his father:] "This morning Hans was given his usual daily bath by his mother and afterwards dried and powdered. As his mother was powdering round his penis and taking care not to touch it, Hans said: 'Why don't you put your finger there?' . . ."

. . . The father and son visited me during my consulting hours. . . . Certain details which I now learnt—to the effect that [Hans] was particularly bothered by what horses wear in front of their eyes and by the black round their mouths—were certainly not to be explained from what we knew. But as I saw the two of them sitting in front of me and at the same time heard Hans's description of his anxiety-horses, a further piece of the solution shot through my mind. . . . I asked Hans jokingly whether his horses wore eyeglasses, to which he replied that they did not. I then asked him whether his father wore eyeglasses, to which, against all the evidence, he once more said no. Finally I asked him whether by "the black round the mouth" he meant a moustache; and I then disclosed to him that he was afraid of his father, precisely because he was so fond of his mother. It must be, I told him, that he thought his father was angry with him on that account; but this was not so, his father was fond of him in spite of it, and he might admit everything to him without any fear. Long before he was in the world, I went on, I had known that a little Hans would come who would be so fond of his mother that he would be bound to feel afraid of his father because of it. . . .

By enlightening Hans on this subject I had cleared away his most powerful resistance. . . . [T]he little patient summoned up courage to describe the details of his phobia, and soon began to take an active share in the conduct of the analysis.

. . . It was only then that we learnt [that Hans] was not only afraid of horses biting him—he was soon silent upon that point—but also of carts, of furniture-vans, and of buses . . . , of horses that started moving, of horses that looked big and heavy, and of horses that drove quickly. The meaning of these specifications was explained by Hans himself: he was afraid of horses falling down, and consequently incorporated in his phobia everything that seemed likely to facilitate their falling down.

It was at this stage of the analysis that he recalled the event, insignificant in itself, which immediately preceded the outbreak of the illness and may no doubt be regarded as the exciting cause of the outbreak. He went for a walk with his mother, and saw a bus-horse fall down and kick about with its feet. This made a great impression on him. He was terrified, and thought the horse was dead; and from that time on he thought that all horses would fall down. His father pointed out to him that when he saw the horse fall down he must have thought of him, his father, and have wished that he might fall down in the same way and be dead. Hans did not dispute this interpretation. . . . From that time forward his behavior to his father was unconstrained and fearless, and in fact a trifle overbearing.

It is especially interesting . . . to observe the way in which the transformation of Hans's libido into anxiety was projected on to the principal object of his phobia, on to horses.

Horses interested him the most of all the large animals; playing at horses was his favorite game with the older children. I had a suspicion—and this was confirmed by Hans's father when I asked him—that the first person who had served Hans as a horse must have been his father. . . . When repression had set in and brought a revulsion of feeling along with it, horses, which had till then been associated with so much pleasure, were necessarily turned into objects of fear.

[Hans later reported] two concluding phantasies, with which his recovery was rounded off. One of them, that of [a] plumber giving him a new and . . . bigger widdler, was . . . a triumphant wish-phantasy, and with it he overcame his fear of castration. . . . His other phantasy, which confessed to the wish to be married to his mother and to have many children by her . . . corrected that portion of those thoughts which was entirely unacceptable; for, instead of killing his father, it made him innocuous by promoting him to a marriage with Hans's grandmother. With this phantasy both the illness and the analysis came to an appropriate end.

(Freud, 1909)

Most clinicians take notes and keep records in the course of treating their patients, and some, like Freud, further organize such notes into a formal case study to be shared with other professionals. The clues offered by a case study may help a clinician better understand or treat the person under discussion (Lee et al., 2010; Stricker & Trierweiler, 1995). In addition, case studies may play nomothetic roles that go far beyond the individual clinical case (Goodwin, 2011).

How Are Case Studies Helpful?

Case studies can be a source of *new ideas* about behavior and "open the way for discoveries" (Bolgar, 1965). Freud's theory of psychoanalysis was based mainly on the patients he saw in private practice. He pored over their case studies, such as the one he wrote about Little Hans, to find what he believed to be broad psychological processes and principles of development. In addition, a case study may offer *tentative support* for a theory. Freud used case studies in this way as well, regarding them as evidence for the accuracy of his ideas. Conversely, case studies may serve to *challenge a theory's assumptions* (Hinshelwood, 2010; Elms, 2007).

Case studies may also show the value of *new therapeutic techniques* or unique applications of existing techniques. The psychoanalytic principle that says patients may benefit from discussing their problems and discovering underlying psychological causes, for example, has roots in the famous case study of Anna O., presented by Freud's collaborator Josef Breuer, a case you will read about in Chapter 3. Similarly, Freud believed that the case study of Little Hans demonstrated the therapeutic potential of a verbal approach for children as well as for adults.

Finally, case studies may offer opportunities to study *unusual problems* that do not occur often enough to permit a large number of observations (Goodwin, 2011). For years information about multiple personality disorders was based almost exclusively on case studies, such as a famous case popularly referred to as *The Three Faces of Eve,* a clinical account of Chris Sizemore, a woman who displayed three alternating personalities, each having a separate set of memories, preferences, and personal habits (Thigpen & Cleckley, 1957).

Both: Armando Gallo/Retna Ltd./Corbis

Case studies, Hollywood style
Case studies often find their way into the arts and capture the public's attention, as witnessed by the success of the HBO series *In Treatment.* Each episode of this series focuses on one case, treated by relentless therapist Paul Weston (played by Gabriel Byrne, right). For example, the patient April (played by Alison Pill, left) is an architecture student with lymphoma who is in denial about the severity of her illness. She has been hiding her condition from everyone but her therapist.

•**internal validity**•The accuracy with which a study can pinpoint one of various possible factors as the cause of a phenomenon.

•**external validity**•The degree to which the results of a study may be generalized beyond that study.

•**correlation**•The degree to which events or characteristics vary along with each other.

•**correlational method**•A research procedure used to determine how much events or characteristics vary along with each other.

Does mental dysfunctioning run in families?
One of the most celebrated case studies in abnormal psychology is a study of identical quadruplets dubbed the "Genain" sisters by researchers (after the Greek term for "dire birth"). All of the sisters developed schizophrenia in their twenties.

What Are the Limitations of Case Studies?

Case studies also have limitations (Girden & Kabacoff, 2011; Lee et al., 2010). First, they are reported by *biased observers,* that is, by therapists who have a personal stake in seeing their treatments succeed. These therapists must choose what to include in a case study, and their choices may at times be self-serving. Second, case studies rely on *subjective evidence.* Is a client's problem really caused by the events that the therapist or client says are responsible? After all, those are only a fraction of the events that may be contributing to the situation. When investigators are able to rule out all possible causes except one, a study is said to have internal accuracy, or **internal validity** (Lee et al., 2010). Obviously, case studies rate low on that score.

Why do case studies and other anecdotal offerings influence people so much, often more than systematic research does?

Another problem with case studies is that they provide *little basis for generalization.* Even if we agree that Little Hans developed a dread of horses because he was terrified of castration and feared his father, how can we be confident that other people's phobias are rooted in the same kinds of causes? Events or treatments that seem important in one case may be of no help at all in efforts to understand or treat others. When the findings of an investigation can be generalized beyond the immediate study, the investigation is said to have external accuracy, or **external validity** (Lee et al., 2010). Case studies rate low on external validity, too (Goodwin, 2011).

The limitations of the case study are largely addressed by two other methods of investigation: the *correlational method* and the *experimental method.* They do not offer the rich detail that makes case studies so interesting, but they do help investigators draw broad conclusions about abnormality in the population at large. Thus they are now the preferred methods of clinical investigation.

Three features of the correlational and experimental methods enable clinical investigators to gain general, or nomothetic, insights: (1) The researchers typically observe many individuals (see *MediaSpeak* on the next page). That way, they can collect enough information, or data, to support a conclusion. (2) The researchers apply procedures uniformly. Other researchers can thus repeat, or *replicate,* a particular study to see whether it consistently gives the same findings. (3) The researchers use *statistical tests* to analyze the results of a study. These tests can help indicate whether broad conclusions are justified.

The Correlational Method

Correlation is the degree to which events or characteristics vary with each other. The **correlational method** is a research procedure used to determine this "co-relationship" between variables (Girden & Kabacoff, 2011). This method can, for example, answer the question, "Is there a correlation between the amount of stress in people's lives and the degree of depression they experience?" That is, as people keep experiencing stressful events, are they increasingly likely to become depressed?

To test this question, researchers have collected life stress scores (for example, the number of threatening events experienced during a certain period of time) and depression scores (for example, scores on a depression survey) from individuals and have correlated these scores. The people who are chosen for a study are its subjects, or *participants,* the term preferred by today's investigators. The participants in a given study are collectively called its *sample.* A sample must be representative of the larger population that the researchers wish to understand. Otherwise the relationship found in the study may not apply elsewhere in the real world—it may not have external validity.

MediaSpeak

On Facebook, Scholars Link Up with Data

By Stephanie Rosenbloom, *New York Times*

Each day about 1,700 juniors at an East Coast college log on to Facebook.com to accumulate "friends," compare movie preferences, share videos and exchange cybercocktails and kisses. Unwittingly, these students have become the subjects of academic research.

To study how personal tastes, habits and values affect the formation of social relationships (and how social relationships affect tastes, habits and values), a team of researchers from Harvard and the University of California, Los Angeles, are monitoring the Facebook profiles of an entire class of students at one college, which they declined to name because it could compromise the integrity of their research. . . .

In other words, Facebook—where users rate one another as "hot or not," play games like "Pirates vs. Ninjas" and throw virtual sheep at one another—is helping scholars explore fundamental social science questions.

"We're on the cusp of a new way of doing social science," said Nicholas Christakis, a Harvard sociology professor who is also part of the research. "Our predecessors could only dream of the kind of data we now have." . . .

Social scientists at Indiana, Northwestern, Pennsylvania State, Tufts, the University of Texas and other institutions are mining Facebook to test traditional theories in their fields about relationships, identity, self-esteem, popularity, collective action, race and political engagement. . . . In a few studies, the Facebook users do not know they are being examined. A spokeswoman for Facebook says the site has no policy prohibiting scholars from studying profiles of users who have not activated certain privacy settings. . . .

. . . The site's users have mixed feelings about being put under the microscope. [One student] said she found it "fascinating that professors are using [Facebook]," but [another] said, "I don't feel like academic research has a place on a Web site like Facebook." He added that if it was going to happen, professors should ask students' permission.

Although federal rules govern academic study of human subjects, universities, which approve professors' research methods, have different interpretations of the guidelines. "The rules were made for a different world, a pre-Facebook world," said Samuel D. Gosling, an associate professor of psychology at the University of Texas, Austin, who uses Facebook to explore perception and identity. "There is a rule that you are allowed to observe public behavior, but it's not clear if online behavior is public or not." . . .

Photo Illustration by Chris Jackson/Getty Images

If researchers were to find a correlation between life stress and depression in a sample consisting entirely of children, for example, they could not draw clear conclusions about what, if any, correlation exists among adults.

Describing a Correlation

Suppose you were to use the correlational method to conduct a study of depression. You would collect life stress scores and depression scores for 10 people and plot the scores on a graph, as shown in Figure 2-1, on the next page. As you can see, the participant named Jim has a recent life stress score of 7, meaning seven threatening events over the past three months; he also has a depression score of 25. Thus he is "located" at the point on the graph where these two scores meet. The graph provides a visual representation of your data. Here, notice that the data points all fall roughly along a straight line that slopes upward. You would draw the line so that the data points are as close to it as possible. This line is called the *line of best fit*.

Erik Lesser/ZUMA Press/Corbis

Stress and depression

In Norcross, Georgia, friends and workers bring all of this family's possessions to the curb after their bank has foreclosed on their mortgage, another casualty of the subprime loan crisis and economic downturn. Researchers have found that the stress produced by the loss of one's home is often accompanied by the onset of depression and other psychological symptoms.

The line of best fit in Figure 2-1 slopes upward and to the right, indicating that the variables under examination are increasing or decreasing together. That is, the greater someone's life stress score, the higher his or her score on the depression scale. When variables change the same way, their correlation is said to have a positive *direction* and is referred to as a *positive correlation.* Most studies of life stress and depression have indeed found a positive correlation between those two variables (Gutman & Nemeroff, 2011).

Correlations can have a negative rather than a positive direction. In a *negative correlation,* the value of one variable increases as the value of the other variable decreases. Researchers have found, for example, a negative correlation between depression and activity level. The greater one's depression, the lower the number of one's activities. When the scores of a negative correlation are plotted, they produce a downward-sloping graph, like the one shown in Figure 2-2.

There is yet a third possible outcome for a correlational study. The variables under study may be *unrelated,* meaning that there is no consistent relationship between them. As the measures of one variable increase, those of the other variable sometimes increase and sometimes decrease. The graph of this outcome looks like Figure 2-3. Here the line of best fit is horizontal, with no slope at all. Studies have found that depression and intelligence are unrelated, for example.

In addition to knowing the direction of a correlation, researchers need to know its *magnitude,* or strength (see Figure 2-4). That is, how closely do the two variables correspond? Does one *always* vary along with the other, or is their relationship less exact? When two variables are found to vary together very closely in person after person, the correlation is said to be high, or strong.

Look again at Figure 2-1. In this graph of a positive correlation between depression and life stress, the data points all fall very close to the line of best fit. Researchers can

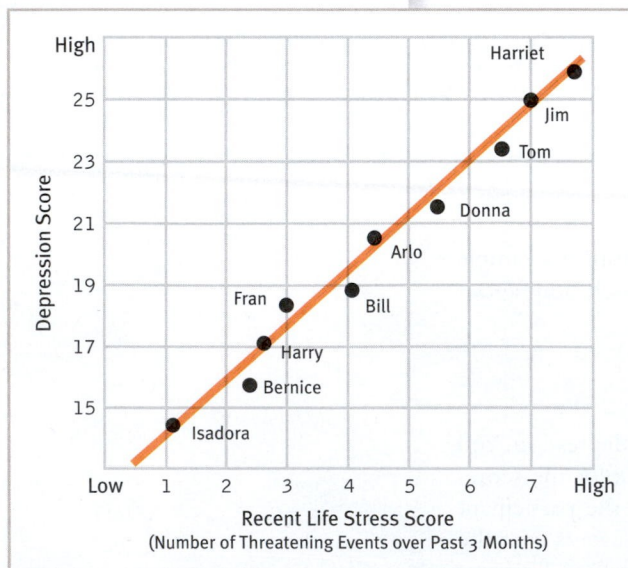

Figure 2-1

Positive correlation The relationship between amount of recent stress and feelings of depression shown by this hypothetical sample of 10 participants is a near-perfect "positive" correlation.

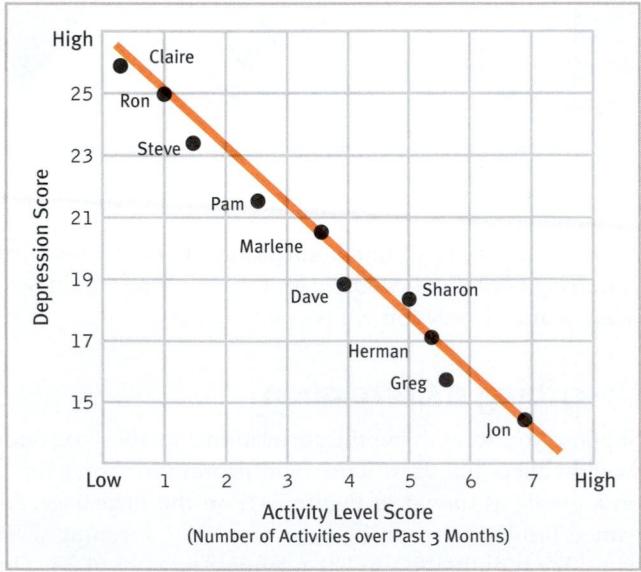

Figure 2-2

Negative correlation The relationship between number of activities and feelings of depression shown by this hypothetical sample is a near-perfect "negative" correlation.

predict each person's score on one variable with a high degree of confidence if they know his or her score on the other. But what if the graph of the correlation between depression and life stress looked more like Figure 2-4? In this figure the data points are loosely scattered around the line of best fit rather than hugging it closely. In this case, researchers could not predict with as much accuracy an individual's score on one variable from his or her score on the other variable. The correlation in Figure 2-1 is stronger, or greater in magnitude, than that in Figure 2-4.

The direction and magnitude of a correlation are often calculated numerically and expressed by a statistical term called the *correlation coefficient,* symbolized by the letter *r.* The correlation coefficient can vary from +1.00, which indicates a perfect positive correlation between two variables, down to −1.00, which represents a perfect negative correlation. The *sign* of the coefficient (+ or −) signifies the direction of the correlation; the *number* represents its magnitude. An *r* of .00 reflects a zero correlation, or no relationship between variables. The closer *r* is to .00, the weaker, or lower in magnitude, the correlation. Thus correlations of +.75 and −.75 are of equal magnitude and equally strong, whereas a correlation of +.25 is weaker than either.

Everyone's behavior is changeable, and many human responses can be measured only approximately. Most correlations found in psychological research, therefore, fall short of a perfect positive or negative correlation. For example, one early study of life stress and depression, with a sample of 68 adults, found a correlation of +.53 (Miller, Ingham, & Davidson, 1976). Although hardly perfect, a correlation of this magnitude is considered large in psychological research.

When Can Correlations Be Trusted?

Scientists must decide whether the correlation they find in a given sample of participants accurately reflects a real correlation in the general population. Could the observed correlation have occurred by mere chance? Scientists can never know for certain, but they can test their conclusions with a *statistical analysis* of their data, using principles of probability. In essence, they ask how likely it is that the study's particular findings have occurred by chance. If the statistical analysis indicates that chance is unlikely to account

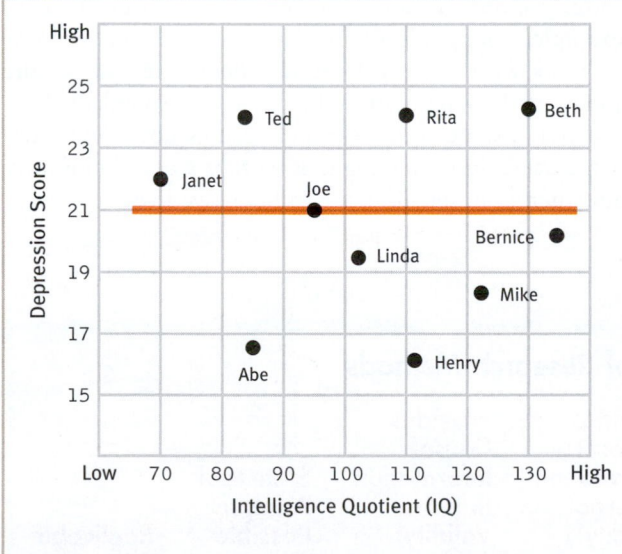

Figure 2-3
No correlation The relationship between intelligence and feelings of depression shown by this hypothetical sample is a "near-zero" correlation.

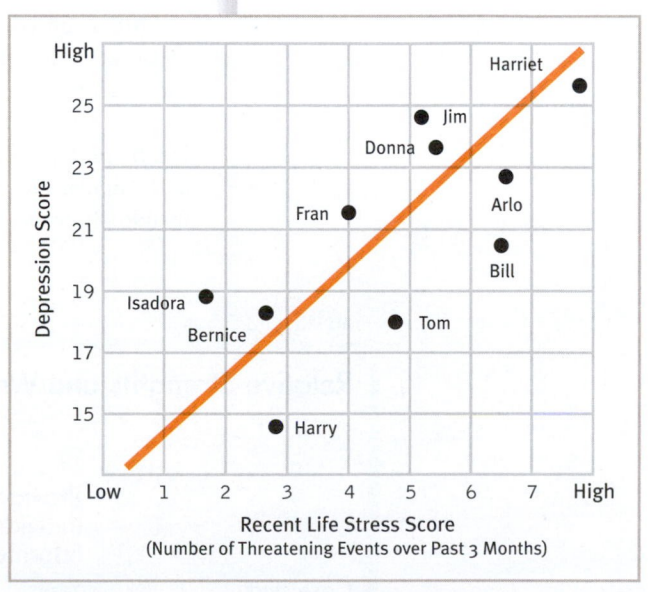

Figure 2-4
Magnitude of correlation The relationship between amount of recent stress and feelings of depression shown by this hypothetical sample is a "moderately positive" correlation.

BETWEEN THE LINES

Psychological Disorders Linked to Life Stress

Depression ‹‹

Anxiety disorders ‹‹

Eating disorders ‹‹

Posttraumatic stress disorder ‹‹

Schizophrenia ‹‹

Substance abuse ‹‹

Dissociative disorder ‹‹

Sleep disorders ‹‹

Sexual dysfunction ‹‹

Suicide ‹‹

(Hollander & Simeon, 2011; Bernert et al., 2007; Hartley et al., 2007)

for the correlation they found, researchers may conclude that their findings reflect a real correlation in the general population.

A cutoff point helps researchers make this decision. By convention, if there is less than a 5 percent probability that a study's findings are due to chance (signified as $p < .05$), the findings are said to be *statistically significant* and are thought to reflect the larger population. In the life stress study described earlier, a statistical analysis indicated a probability of less than 5 percent that the $+.53$ correlation found in the sample was due to chance. Therefore, the researchers concluded with some confidence that among adults in general, depression does tend to rise along with the amount of recent stress in a person's life. Generally, our confidence increases with the size of the sample and the magnitude of the correlation. The larger they are, the more likely it is that a correlation will be statistically significant.

What Are the Merits of the Correlational Method?

The correlational method has certain advantages over the case study (see Table 2-1). First, it possesses high *external validity*. Because researchers measure their variables, observe large samples, and apply statistical analyses, they are in a better position to generalize their correlations to people beyond the ones they have studied. Furthermore, researchers can easily repeat correlational studies using new samples of participants to check the results of earlier studies.

On the other hand, correlational studies, like case studies, lack *internal validity* (Remler & Van Ryzin, 2011). Although correlations allow researchers to describe the relationship between two variables, they do not *explain* the relationship. When we look at the positive correlation found in many life stress studies, we may be tempted to conclude that increases in recent life stress cause people to feel more depressed. In fact, however, the two variables may be correlated for any one of three reasons: (1) Life stress may cause depression. (2) Depression may cause people to experience more life stress (for example, a depressive approach to life may cause people to perform poorly at work or may interfere with social relationships). (3) Depression and life stress may each be caused by a third variable, such as financial problems (Gutman & Nemeroff, 2011).

Can you think of other correlations in life that are interpreted mistakenly as causal?

Although correlations say nothing about causation, they can still be of great use to clinicians. Clinicians know, for example, that suicide attempts increase as people become more depressed. Thus, when they work with severely depressed clients, they stay on the lookout for signs of suicidal thinking. Perhaps depression directly causes suicidal behavior, or perhaps a third variable, such as a sense of hopelessness, causes both depression and suicidal thoughts. Whatever the cause, just knowing that there is a correlation may enable clinicians to take measures (such as hospitalization) to help save lives.

table: **2-1**

Relative Strengths and Weaknesses of Research Methods

	Provides Individual Information	Provides General Information (External Validity)	Provides Causal Information (Internal Validity)	Statistical Analysis Possible	Replicable
Case study	Yes	No	No	No	No
Correlational method	No	Yes	No	Yes	Yes
Experimental method	No	Yes	Yes	Yes	Yes

Of course, in other instances, clinicians do need to know whether one variable causes another. Do parents' marital conflicts cause their children to be more anxious? Does job dissatisfaction lead to feelings of depression? Will a given treatment help people to cope more effectively in life? Questions about causality call for the experimental method, as you will see later.

Special Forms of Correlational Research

Epidemiological studies and longitudinal studies are two kinds of correlational research used widely by clinical investigators. **Epidemiological studies** reveal the incidence and prevalence of a disorder in a particular population (Kasl & Jones, 2011). **Incidence** is the number of new cases that emerge during a given period of time. **Prevalence** is the total number of cases in the population during a given time period; prevalence includes both existing and new cases. Many researchers also refer to epidemiological studies as "descriptive studies" because the goal of such investigations is largely to *describe* the incidence or prevalence of a disorder "without trying to predict or explain when or why it occurs" (Compas & Gotlib, 2002, p. 69).

Over the past 35 years, clinical researchers throughout the United States have worked on one of the largest epidemiological studies of mental disorders ever conducted, called the Epidemiologic Catchment Area Study (Maulik et al., 2010). They have interviewed more than 20,000 people in five cities to determine the prevalence of many psychological disorders and the treatment programs used. Two other large-scale epidemiological studies in the United States, the National Comorbidity Survey and the National Comorbidity Survey Replication, have questioned more than 9,000 individuals (Nierenberg et al., 2010; Druss et al., 2007). All of these studies have been further compared with epidemiological studies of specific groups, such as Hispanic and Asian American populations, or with epidemiological studies conducted in other countries, to see how rates of mental disorders and treatment programs vary from group to group and from country to country (Jimenez et al., 2010; Alegria et al., 2007, 2004, 2000).

Such epidemiological studies have helped researchers identify groups at risk for particular disorders. Women, it turns out, have a higher rate of anxiety disorders and depression than men, while men have a higher rate of alcoholism than women. Elderly people have a higher rate of suicide than young people. Hispanic Americans experience posttraumatic stress disorder more than other racial and ethnic groups in the United States. And persons in some countries have higher rates of certain mental disorders than those in other countries. Eating disorders such as anorexia nervosa, for example, appear to be more common in Western countries than in non-Western ones. These trends may lead researchers to suspect that something unique about certain groups or settings is helping to cause particular disorders. Declining health in elderly people, for example, may make them more likely to commit suicide. Similarly, the pressures or attitudes common in one country may be responsible for a rate of mental dysfunctioning that differs from the rate found in another. Yet, like other forms of correlational research, epidemiological studies alone cannot confirm such suspicions.

In **longitudinal studies** (also called *high-risk* or *developmental studies*), correlational studies of another kind, researchers observe the same individuals on many occasions over a long period of time (Girden & Kabacoff, 2011). In several such studies, investigators have observed the progress over the years of normally functioning children whose mothers or fathers suffered from schizophrenia (Donatelli et al., 2010; Schiffman et al., 2006; Mednick, 1971). The researchers have found, among other things, that the children of the parents with the most severe cases of schizophrenia were particularly likely to develop a psychological disorder and to commit crimes at later points in their development. Because longitudinal studies report the order of events, their correlations

•epidemiological study• A study that measures the incidence and prevalence of a disorder in a given population.

•incidence• The number of new cases of a disorder occurring in a population over a specific period of time.

•prevalence• The total number of cases of a disorder occurring in a population over a specific period of time.

•longitudinal study• A study that observes the same participants on many occasions over a long period of time.

Twins, correlation, and inheritance
Correlational studies of many pairs of twins have suggested a link between genetic factors and certain psychological disorders. Identical twins (who have identical genes) display a higher correlation for some disorders than do fraternal twins (whose genetic makeup is not identical).

Kris Timken/Blend Images/Corbis

•**experiment**•A research procedure in which a variable is manipulated and the effect of the manipulation is observed.

•**independent variable**•The variable in an experiment that is manipulated to determine whether it has an effect on another variable.

•**dependent variable**•The variable in an experiment that is expected to change as the independent variable is manipulated.

•**confound**•In an experiment, a variable other than the independent variable that is also acting on the dependent variable.

provide clues about which events are more likely to be causes and which are more likely to be consequences. Certainly, for example, the children's problems did not cause their parents' schizophrenia. But longitudinal studies still cannot pinpoint causation. Did the children who developed psychological problems inherit a genetic factor? Or did their problems result from their parents' inadequate coping behaviors, their parents' long absences because of hospitalization, or some other factor? Only experimental studies can supply an answer.

The Experimental Method

An **experiment** is a research procedure in which a variable is manipulated and the manipulation's effect on another variable is observed. In fact, most of us perform experiments throughout our lives without knowing that we are behaving so scientifically. Suppose that you go to a party on campus to celebrate the end of midterm exams. As you mix with people at the party, you begin to notice many of them becoming quiet and depressed. It seems the more you talk, the more subdued the other guests become. As the party falls apart before your eyes, you decide you have to do something, but what? Before you can eliminate the problem, you need to know what's causing it.

Your first hunch may be that something you're doing is responsible. Perhaps your remarks about academic pressures have been upsetting everyone. You decide to change the topic to skiing in the mountains of Colorado and to watch for signs of depression in the next round of conversations. The problem seems to clear up; most people now smile and laugh as they chat with you. As a final check of your suspicions, you could go back to talking about school with the next several people you meet. Their dark and dismal reaction would probably convince you that your tendency to talk about school was indeed the cause of the problem.

You have just performed an experiment, testing your hypothesis about a causal relationship between your topic of conversation and the depressed mood of the people around you. You manipulated the variable that you suspected to be the cause (the topic) and then observed the effect of that manipulation on the other variable (the mood of the people around you). In scientific experiments, the manipulated variable is called the **independent variable** and the variable being observed is called the **dependent variable**.

To examine the experimental method more fully, let's consider a question that is often asked by clinicians (Abramowitz & Braddock, 2011): "Does a particular therapy relieve the symptoms of a particular disorder?" Because this question is about a causal relationship, it can be answered only by an experiment (see Table 2-2). That is, experimenters must give the therapy in question to people who are suffering from a disorder and then observe whether they improve. Here the therapy is the independent variable, and psychological improvement is the dependent variable.

If the true cause of changes in the dependent variable cannot be separated from other possible causes, then an experiment gives very little information. Thus, experimenters must try to eliminate all **confounds** from their studies—variables other than the independent variable that may also be affecting the dependent variable. When there are confounds in an experiment, they, rather than the independent variable, may be causing the observed changes.

For example, situational variables, such as the location of the therapy office (say, a quiet country setting) or soothing

table: 2-2

Most Investigated Questions in Clinical Research

Most Common *Correlational* Questions

Are stress and onset of mental disorders related?

Is culture (or gender or race) generally linked to mental disorders?

Are income and mental disorders related?

Are social skills tied to mental disorders?

Is social support tied to mental disorders?

Are family conflict and mental disorders related?

Is treatment responsiveness tied to culture?

Which symptoms of a disorder appear together?

How common is a disorder in a particular population?

Most Common *Causal* Questions

Does factor X cause a disorder?

Is cause A more influential than cause B?

How does family communication and structure affect family members?

How does a disorder affect the quality of a person's life?

Does treatment X alleviate a disorder?

Is treatment X more helpful than no treatment at all?

Is treatment A more helpful than treatment B?

Why does treatment X work?

Can an intervention prevent abnormal functioning?

background music in the office, may have a therapeutic effect on participants in a therapy study. Or perhaps the participants are unusually motivated or have high expectations that the therapy will work, factors that thus account for their improvement. To guard against confounds, researchers include three important features in their experiments—a *control group, random assignment,* and a *blind design* (Remler & Van Ryzin, 2011).

The Control Group

A **control group** is a group of research participants who are not exposed to the independent variable under investigation but whose experience is similar to that of the **experimental group,** the participants who are exposed to the independent variable. By comparing the two groups, an experimenter can better determine the effect of the independent variable.

To study the effectiveness of a particular therapy, for example, experimenters typically divide participants into two groups after obtaining their consent to participate in the experiment (see *PsychWatch* below). The experimental group may come into an office and receive the therapy for an hour, while the control group may simply come into the office for an hour. If the experimenters find later that the people in the experimental group improve more than the people in the control group, they may conclude that the therapy was effective, above and beyond the effects of time, the office setting, and any other confounds. To guard against confounds, experimenters try to provide all participants, both control and experimental, with experiences that are identical in every way—except for the independent variable.

Of course, it is possible that the differences observed between an experimental group and control group have occurred simply by chance. Thus, as with correlational studies, investigators who conduct experiments must do a statistical analysis on their data and find out how likely it is that the observed differences are due to chance. If the likelihood is very low—less than 5 percent ($p < .05$)—the differences between the two groups are considered to be statistically significant, and the experimenter may conclude with some confidence that they are due to the independent variable. As a general rule, if the sample of participants is large, if the difference observed between groups is great, and if the range of scores within each group is small, the findings of an experiment are likely to be statistically significant.

An additional point is worth noting with regard to clinical treatment experiments. It is always important to distinguish between *statistical significance* and a notion called *clinical significance.* As you have just read, *statistical significance* indicates whether a participant's

•**control group**•In an experiment, a group of participants who are not exposed to the independent variable.

•**experimental group**•In an experiment, the participants who are exposed to the independent variable under investigation.

Is laughter a good medicine?
Members of this laughter club in Chandigarh, India, practice therapeutic laughing, or *Hasyayog,* a relatively new group treatment based on the belief that laughing at least 15 minutes each day will drive away depression and other ills. As many as 400 kinds of therapies are currently used for psychological problems. An experimental design is needed to determine whether this or any other form of treatment actively causes clients to improve.

•**random assignment**•A selection procedure that ensures that participants are randomly placed either in the control group or in the experimental group.

•**blind design**•An experiment in which participants do not know whether they are in the experimental or the control condition.

•**placebo therapy**•A sham treatment that the participant in an experiment believes to be genuine.

•**double-blind design**•Experimental procedure in which neither the participant nor the experimenter knows whether the participant has received the experimental treatment or a placebo.

improvement in functioning—large or small—occurred because of treatment. *Clinical significance* indicates whether the amount of improvement is meaningful in the individual's life. Even if the moods of depressed participants improve because of treatment, the individuals may still be too unhappy to enjoy life. Thus, although experimenters can determine *statistical* significance, only individuals and their clinicians can fully evaluate *clinical* significance.

Random Assignment

Researchers must also watch out for differences in the *makeup* of the experimental and control groups since those differences may also confound a study's results. In a therapy study, for example, the experimenter may unintentionally put wealthier participants in the experimental group and poorer ones in the control group. This difference, rather than their therapy, may be the cause of the greater improvement later found among the experimental participants. To reduce the effects of preexisting differences, experimenters typically use **random assignment**. This is the general term for any selection procedure that ensures that every participant in the experiment is as likely to be placed in one group as the other (Remler & Van Ryzin, 2011). Researchers might, for example, select people by flipping a coin or picking names out of a hat.

Blind Design

A final confound problem is *bias*. Participants may bias an experiment's results by trying to please or help the experimenter (Goodwin, 2011). In a therapy experiment, for example, if those participants who receive the treatment know the purpose of the study and which group they are in, they might actually work harder to feel better or fulfill the experimenter's expectations. If so, *subject,* or *participant, bias* rather than therapy could be causing their improvement.

To avoid this bias, experimenters can prevent participants from finding out which group they are in. This experimental strategy is called a **blind design** because the individuals are blind as to their assigned group. In a therapy study, for example, control participants could be given a *placebo* (Latin for "I shall please"), something that looks or tastes like real therapy but has none of its key ingredients. This "imitation" therapy is called **placebo therapy.** If the experimental (true therapy) participants then improve more than the control (placebo therapy) participants, experimenters have more confidence that the true therapy has caused their improvement.

Why might sugar pills or other kinds of placebo treatments help some people feel better?

An experiment may also be confounded by *experimenter bias*—that is, experimenters may have expectations that they unintentionally transmit to the participants in their studies. In a drug therapy study, for example, the experimenter might smile and act confident while providing real medications to the experimental participants but frown and appear hesitant while offering placebo drugs to the control participants. This kind of bias is sometimes referred to as the *Rosenthal effect,* after the psychologist who first identified it (Rosenthal, 1966). Experimenters can eliminate their own bias by arranging to be blind themselves. In a drug therapy study, for example, an aide could make sure that the real medication and the placebo drug look identical. The experimenter could then administer treatment without knowing which participants were receiving true medications and which were receiving false medications.

While either the participants or the experimenter may be kept blind in an experiment, it is best that both be blind—a research strategy called a **double-blind design.**

In fact, most medication experiments now use double-blind designs to test promising drugs (Wender et al., 2011). Many experimenters also arrange for judges to assess the patients' improvement independently, and the judges, too, are blind to group assignments. This strategy is called a *triple-blind design* (Wheatley, 2004).

Alternative Experimental Designs

It is not easy to devise an experiment that is both well controlled and enlightening. Control of every possible confound is rarely achievable. Moreover, because psychological experiments typically use living beings, ethical and practical considerations limit the kinds of manipulations one can do (Nagy, 2011) (see *PsychWatch* on page 42). Thus clinical researchers must often settle for experimental designs that are less than ideal. The most common such variations are the *quasi-experimental design,* the *natural experiment,* the *analogue experiment,* and the *single-subject experiment.*

Quasi-Experimental Design

In **quasi-experiments,** or **mixed designs,** investigators do not randomly assign participants to control and experimental groups but instead make use of groups that already exist in the world at large (Girden & Kabacoff, 2011; Remler & Van Ryzin, 2011). Consider, for example, research into the effects of child abuse. Because it would be unethical for investigators of this issue to actually abuse a randomly chosen group of children, they must instead compare children who already have a history of abuse with children who do not. Such a humane strategy is, of course, preferable, but, at the same time, it violates the rule of random assignment and so introduces possible confounds into the study. Children who receive excessive physical punishment, for example, usually come from poorer and larger families than children who are punished verbally. Any differences found later in the moods or self-concepts of the two groups of children may be the result of differences in wealth or family size rather than abuse.

Child-abuse researchers often try to address the confound problems of quasi-experiments by using *matched control participants.* That is, they match the experimental participants with control participants who are similar in age, sex, race, number of children in the family, socioeconomic status, type of neighborhood, or other characteristics. For every abused child in the experimental group, they choose a child who is not abused but who has similar characteristics to be included in the control group. When the data from studies of this kind show that abused children are typically sadder and have lower self-esteem than matched control participants who have not been abused, the investigators can conclude with some confidence that abuse is causing the differences (Briggs et al., 2011).

Natural Experiment

In **natural experiments** nature itself manipulates the independent variable, and the experimenter observes the effects. Natural experiments must be used for studying the psychological effects of unusual and unpredictable events, such as floods, earthquakes, plane crashes, and fires. Because the participants in these studies are selected by an accident of fate rather than by the investigators' design, natural experiments are actually a kind of quasi-experiment.

On December 26, 2004, an earthquake occurred beneath the Indian Ocean off the coast of Sumatra, Indonesia. The earthquake triggered a series of massive tsunamis that flooded the ocean's coastal communities, killed more than 225,000 people, and injured and left millions of survivors homeless, particularly in Indonesia, Sri Lanka, India, and Thailand. It was one of the deadliest natural disasters in history. Within months of this disaster, researchers conducted natural experiments in which they collected data from hundreds of survivors and from control groups of people who lived in areas not directly

•**quasi-experiment**•An experiment in which investigators make use of control and experimental groups that already exist in the world at large. Also called a *mixed design.*

•**natural experiment**•An experiment in which nature, rather than an experimenter, manipulates an independent variable.

Christopher Brown/Stock Boston

Natural experiments

A man surveys the damage wrought by a hurricane upon his home and belongings. Natural experiments conducted in the aftermath of such catastrophes have found that many survivors experience lingering feelings of anxiety and depression.

affected by the tsunamis. The disaster survivors scored significantly higher on anxiety and depression measures (dependent variables) than the controls did. The survivors also experienced more sleep problems, feelings of detachment, arousal, difficulties concentrating, startle responses, and guilt feelings than the controls did (Heir, Piatigorsky, & Weisaeth, 2010; Bhushan & Kumar, 2007; Tang, 2007, 2006). Over the past several years, other natural experiments have focused on survivors of the 2010 Haitian earthquake, the 33 Chilean miners who were trapped for months a half mile beneath the desert in 2010, and victims of the massive earthquake and tsunami in Japan in 2011. These studies have also revealed lingering psychological symptoms among survivors of those disasters (Carey, 2011; O'Hanlon, 2010; Ray, 2010).

Because natural experiments rely on unexpected occurrences in nature, they cannot be repeated at will. Also, because each natural event is unique in certain ways, broad generalizations drawn from a single study could be incorrect. Nevertheless, catastrophes have provided opportunities for hundreds of natural experiments over the years, and certain findings have been obtained repeatedly. As a result, clinical scientists have identified patterns of reactions that often occur in such situations. You will read about these patterns—acute stress disorders and posttraumatic stress disorders—in Chapter 6.

Analogue Experiment

There is one way in which investigators can manipulate independent variables relatively freely while avoiding many of the ethical and practical limitations of clinical research. They can induce laboratory participants to behave in ways that seem to resemble real-life abnormal behavior and then conduct experiments on the participants in the hope of shedding light on the real-life abnormality. This is called an **analogue experiment**.

Analogue studies often use animals as participants. Animals are easier to gather and manipulate than humans, and their use poses fewer ethical problems. While the needs and rights of animal subjects must be considered, most experimenters are willing to subject animals to more discomfort than humans. They believe that the insights gained from such experimentation outweigh the discomfort of the animals, as long as their distress is not excessive (Nagy, 2011; Barnard, 2007). In addition, experimenters can, and often do, use human participants in analogue experiments.

Do outside restrictions on research —either animal or human studies— interfere with necessary investigations and thus limit potential gains for human beings?

As you'll see in Chapter 8, in a classic body of work investigator Martin Seligman has used analogue studies with great success to investigate the causes of human depression. Seligman has theorized that depression results when people believe they no longer have any control over the good and bad things that happen in their lives. To test this theory, he has produced depression-like symptoms in laboratory participants—both animals and humans—by repeatedly exposing them to negative events (shocks, loud noises, task failures) over which they have no control. In these "learned helplessness" analogue studies, the participants seem to give up, lose their initiative, and become sad—suggesting to some clinicians that human depression itself may indeed be caused by loss of control over the events in one's life.

It is important to remember that the laboratory-induced learned helplessness produced in Seligman's analogue experiments is not known with certainty to be analogous to human depression. If this laboratory phenomenon is actually only superficially similar to depression, then the clinical inferences drawn from such experiments may

•analogue experiment• A research method in which the experimenter produces abnormal-like behavior in laboratory participants and then conducts experiments on the participants.

•single-subject experimental design• A research method in which a single participant is observed and measured both before and after the manipulation of an independent variable.

Mikel Roberts/Sygma/Corbis

Similar enough?
Celebrity chimpanzee Cheetah, age 59, does some painting along with her friend and trainer. Chimps and human beings share more than 90 percent of their genetic material, but their brains and bodies are very different, as are their perceptions and experiences. Thus, abnormal-like behavior produced in animal analogue experiments may differ from the human abnormality under investigation.

be misleading. This, in fact, is the major limitation of all analogue research: researchers can never be certain that the phenomena they see in the laboratory are the same as the psychological disorders they are investigating.

Single-Subject Experiment

Sometimes scientists do not have the luxury of experimenting on many participants. They may, for example, be investigating a disorder so rare that few participants are available. Experimentation is still possible, however, with a **single-subject experimental design**. Here a single participant is observed both before and after the manipulation of an independent variable (Kazdin, 2011). Single-subject experiments rely first on baseline data—information gathered prior to any manipulations. These data set a standard with which later changes may be compared. The experimenter next introduces the independent variable and again observes the participant's behavior. Any changes in behavior are attributed to the effects of the independent variable.

In one kind of single-subject design, called an *ABAB,* or *reversal, design,* a participant's reactions are measured and compared not only during a baseline period (condition A) and after the introduction of the independent variable (condition B) but also after the independent variable has been removed (condition A again) and after it has been reintroduced one more time (condition B again). If the individual's responses change back and forth along with changes in the independent variable, the experimenter may conclude that the independent variable is causing the shifting responses. Essentially, in an ABAB design a participant is compared with himself or herself under different conditions rather than with control participants. The individual, therefore, serves as his or her own control.

One researcher used an ABAB design to determine whether the systematic use of rewards was helping to reduce a teenage boy's habit of disrupting his special education class with loud talk (Deitz, 1977). He rewarded the boy, who suffered from intellectual developmental disorder (previously called mental retardation), with extra teacher time whenever he went 55 minutes without interrupting the class more than three times. In condition A (baseline period), the student was observed to disrupt the class frequently with loud talk. In condition B, the boy was given a series of teacher reward sessions (introduction of the independent variable); as expected, his loud talk decreased dramatically. Then the rewards from the teacher were stopped (condition A again); and the student's loud talk increased once again. Apparently the independent variable had indeed been the cause of the improvement. To be still more confident about this conclusion,

Humans Have Rights, Too

From 1953 to 1963, in collaboration with the CIA, Army researchers conducted a study called Project MK-ULTRA in which they gave unknowing human participants (usually soldiers) repeated doses of LSD. The goal of this study was to determine the psychological effects of LSD, but at what cost? Participants were uninformed and endangered throughout the project (Goodwin, 2011).

In another long-term study, carried out from 1956 to 1970, medical researchers deliberately infected with hepatitis 1 of every 10 children admitted to the Willowbrook State School in New York City, an institution for persons with mental retardation. The goal of the study was to develop a hepatitis vaccine, but again at what cost? The children were uninformed and endangered throughout the project, their parents were pressured into giving consent, and the goals of the study were not even related directly to the children's disorders (Goodwin, 2011; Streatfeild, 2007; Iacono, 2006).

Soon after these and several other scandalous studies came to light in the 1970s, regulations were established to ensure that the rights of human participants, particularly those with psychological disorders, are protected in research. In the United States, for example, Congress passed a law requiring every research institute to set up a review board to observe and protect participants' well-being in all federally funded studies (Goldman et al., 2010; Bankert & Madur, 2006).

Despite such efforts, the clinical field was rocked just a few years ago by a series of reports that revealed that in recent decades, many patients with severe mental disorders have been harmed by or placed at risk in clinical studies (Whitaker, 2010; Emanuel et al., 2003; Kong, 1998). The studies typically involved antipsychotic drug treatments for patients with psychosis (loss of contact with reality). Many patients in these studies had agreed to change their drug treatments without fully understanding the risks involved. In addition, the drugs

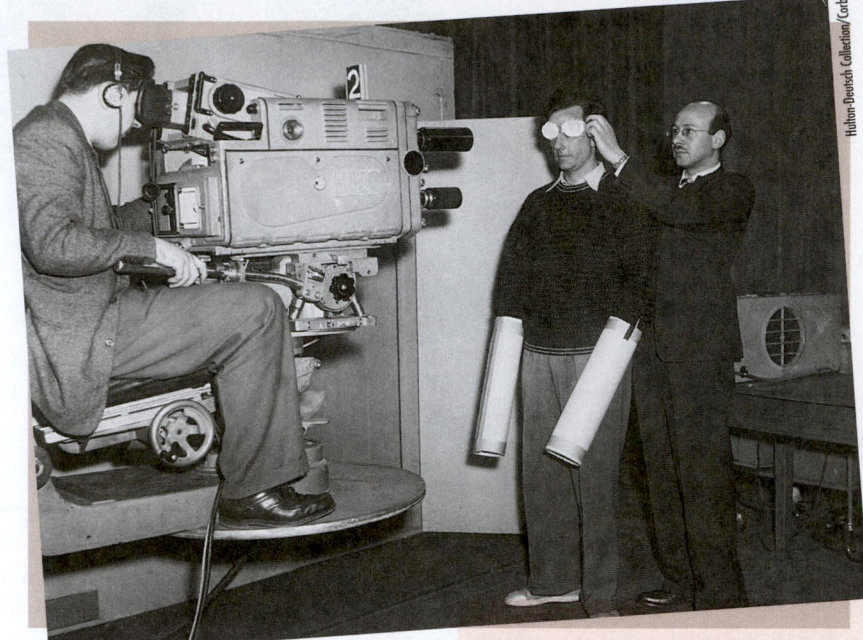

How times have changed In a 1957 study of the psychological effects of complete isolation, participants were placed in a sound-proof box wearing dark goggles, gloves, and cardboard tubes over their hands to deprive them of hearing, sight, and touch. The 25-hour study was actually televised live throughout England, an event that probably would not be permitted today, given current human research safeguards, such as participant confidentiality, informed consent, and research review board approval and monitoring.

used in these studies left some of the participants with more intense psychotic symptoms. Four types of studies have been cited:

▶ **New Drug Studies** Clinical patients are administered an experimental drug to see whether it reduces their symptoms. The patients may be helped, unaffected, or damaged by the new drug.

▶ **Placebo Studies** When a new drug is being tested on a group of experimental participants, researchers may administer a placebo drug to a group of control participants. Unfortunately, the placebo control participants—often people with severe disorders—are receiving no treatment at all.

▶ **Symptom-Exacerbation Studies** Patients are given drugs designed to *intensify* their symptoms so that researchers may learn more about the biology of their disorder. For example, people suffering from psychotic disorders have been given amphetamine, ketamine, and other drugs that lead to more delusions, hallucinations, and the like.

▶ **Medication-Withdrawal Studies** Researchers prematurely stop medications for patients who have been symptom-free while taking their medications. The researchers then follow the patients as they relapse, in the hope of learning more about how and when patients can be taken off particular medications.

Each of these kinds of studies seeks to increase understanding of the biology of certain disorders and to improve treatment, but each carries enormous risks for the studies' participants. As the clinical community and the public have grown more aware of these risks, they have called for still better safeguards to protect research participants with mental disorders. In recent years, for example, the National Institute of Mental Health has suspended some of its symptom-exacerbation studies. Moreover, the Office for Human Research Protection has become much more aggressive in its protection of human participants. Despite such efforts, it is clear to most clinicians and policy makers that this important issue is far from resolved.

the researcher had the teacher apply reward sessions yet again (condition B again). Once again the student's behavior improved.

Obviously, single-subject experiments, such as the ABAB design, are similar to individual case studies in their focus on one participant. In single-subject experiments, however, the independent variable is manipulated systematically so that the investigator can confidently draw conclusions about the cause of an observed effect (Johnston & Smith, 2010; Compas & Gotlib, 2002). The single-subject experiment therefore has greater internal validity than the case study. At the same time, single-subject experiments, like case studies, have only limited external validity. Because only one person is studied, the experimenter cannot be sure that the participant's reaction to the independent variable is typical of people in general (Goodwin, 2011).

PUTTING IT ... together

The Use of Multiple Research Methods

We began this discussion by noting that clinical scientists look for general laws that will help them understand, treat, and prevent psychological disorders. Various obstacles interfere with their progress, however. We have already observed some of them. The most fundamental are summarized here.

1. *Clinical scientists must respect the rights of both human and animal subjects.* Ethical considerations greatly limit the kinds of investigations that clinical scientists can conduct.

2. *The causes of human functioning are very complex.* Because human behavior generally results from multiple factors working together, it is difficult to pinpoint specific causes. So many factors can influence human functioning that it has actually been easier to unravel the secrets of energy and matter than to understand human sadness, stress, and anxiety.

3. *Human beings are changeable.* Moods, behaviors, and thoughts fluctuate. Is the person under study today truly the same as he or she was yesterday? Variability in a single person, let alone from person to person, limits the kinds of conclusions researchers can draw about abnormal functioning.

4. *Human self-awareness may influence the results of clinical investigations.* When human participants know they are being studied, that knowledge influences their behavior. They may try to respond as they think researchers expect them to or to present themselves in a favorable light. Similarly, the attention they receive from investigators may itself increase their optimism and improve their mood. It is a law of science that the very act of measuring an object distorts the object to some degree. Nowhere is this more true than in the study of human beings.

5. *Clinical investigators have a special link to their research participants.* Clinical scientists, too, experience mood changes, troubling thoughts, and family problems. They may identify with the pain of the participants in their studies or have personal opinions about their problems. These feelings can bias an investigator's attempts to understand abnormality.

In short, human behavior is so complex that clinical scientists must use a range of methods to study it. Each method addresses some of the underlying problems, but no one approach overcomes them all. Case studies allow investigators to consider a broader range of causes, but experiments pinpoint causes more precisely. Similarly, correlational studies allow broad generalizations, but case studies are richer in detail. It is best to view each research method as part of a team of approaches that together may shed light on abnormal human functioning. When more than one method has been used to investigate a disorder, it is important to ask whether all the results seem to point in

Bernard Schoenbaum/Cartoonbank.com

"Oh, if only it were so simple."

the same direction. If they do, clinical scientists are probably making progress toward understanding and treating that disorder. Conversely, if the various methods seem to produce conflicting results, the scientists must admit that knowledge in that particular area is still tentative.

Before accepting any research findings, however, students in the clinical field must review the details of these studies with a very critical eye. Were the variables properly controlled? Was the choice of participants representative, was the sample large enough to be meaningful, and has bias been eliminated? Are the investigator's conclusions justified? How else might the results be interpreted? Only after asking these questions can we conclude that a truly informative investigation has taken place.

Summing Up

- **WHAT DO CLINICAL RESEARCHERS DO?** Researchers use the *scientific method* to uncover *nomothetic* principles of abnormal psychological functioning. They attempt to identify and examine relationships between variables and depend primarily on three methods of investigation: the case study, the correlational method, and the experimental method. *pp. 26–27*

- **THE CASE STUDY** A *case study* is a detailed account of a person's life and psychological problems. It can serve as a source of ideas about behavior, provide support for theories, challenge theories, clarify new treatment techniques, or offer an opportunity to study an unusual problem. Yet case studies may be reported by biased observers and rely on subjective evidence. In addition, they tend to have low *internal validity* and low *external validity*. *pp. 27–30*

- **THE CORRELATIONAL METHOD** Correlational studies systematically observe the degree to which events or characteristics vary together. This method allows researchers to draw broad conclusions about abnormality in the population at large.

  A *correlation* may have a *positive* or *negative direction* and may be high or low in *magnitude*. It can be calculated numerically and is expressed by the *correlation coefficient* (*r*). Researchers perform a *statistical analysis* to determine whether the correlation found in a study is truly characteristic of the larger population or due to chance. Correlational studies generally have high external validity but lack internal validity. Two widely used forms of the correlation method are *epidemiological studies* and *longitudinal studies*. *pp. 30–36*

■ **THE EXPERIMENTAL METHOD** In *experiments*, researchers manipulate suspected causes to see whether expected effects will result. The variable that is manipulated is called the *independent variable*, and the variable that is expected to change as a result is called the *dependent variable*.

 Confounds are variables other than the independent variable that are also acting on the dependent variable. To minimize their possible influence, experimenters use *control groups*, *random assignment*, and *blind designs*. The findings of experiments, like those of correlational studies, must be analyzed statistically. *pp. 36–39*

■ **ALTERNATIVE EXPERIMENTAL DESIGNS** Clinical experimenters must often settle for experimental designs that are less than ideal, including the *quasi-experiment*, the *natural experiment*, the *analogue experiment*, and the *single-subject experiment*. *pp. 39–43*

■ **THE USE OF MULTIPLE RESEARCH METHODS** Because research participants have rights that must be respected, because the origins of behavior are complex, because behavior varies, and because the very act of observing an individual's behavior influences that behavior, it can be difficult to assess the findings of clinical research. Also, researchers must take into account their own biases as well as a study's unintended impact on participants' usual behavior. To help address such obstacles, clinical investigators must use multiple research approaches. *pp. 43–44*

PsychPortal

Visit **PsychPortal**
www.yourpsychportal.com
to access the e-book, videocases, and other case materials and activities, as well as study aids including flashcards, crossword puzzles, quizzes, FAQs, and research exercises.

BETWEEN THE LINES

Recent Studies Conducted Online

Attitudes Toward Adoption ‹‹

Self-Presentation on Dating Websites ‹‹

E-mails to Improve Your Mood ‹‹

Causes of Internet Pornography Usage? ‹‹

Do You Have a Positive Personality? ‹‹

Are You a Cyberslacker? ‹‹

You and Your Parents ‹‹

Personality and Computer Game Use ‹‹

(Krantz, 2011)

MODELS OF ABNORMALITY

Philip Berman, a 25-year-old single unemployed former copy editor for a large publishing house, . . . had been hospitalized after a suicide attempt in which he deeply gashed his wrist with a razor blade. He described [to the therapist] how he had sat on the bathroom floor and watched the blood drip into the bathtub for some time before he [contacted] his father at work for help. He and his father went to the hospital emergency room to have the gash stitched, but he convinced himself and the hospital physician that he did not need hospitalization. The next day when his father suggested he needed help, he knocked his dinner to the floor and angrily stormed to his room. When he was calm again, he allowed his father to take him back to the hospital.

The immediate precipitant for his suicide attempt was that he had run into one of his former girlfriends with her new boyfriend. The patient stated that they had a drink together, but all the while he was with them he could not help thinking that "they were dying to run off and jump in bed." He experienced jealous rage, got up from the table, and walked out of the restaurant. He began to think about how he could "pay her back."

Mr. Berman had felt frequently depressed for brief periods during the previous several years. He was especially critical of himself for his limited social life and his inability to have managed to have sexual intercourse with a woman even once in his life. As he related this to the therapist, he lifted his eyes from the floor and with a sarcastic smirk said, "I'm a 25-year-old virgin. Go ahead, you can laugh now." He has had several girlfriends to date, whom he described as very attractive, but who he said had lost interest in him. On further questioning, however, it became apparent that Mr. Berman soon became very critical of them and demanded that they always meet his every need, often to their own detriment. The women then found the relationship very unrewarding and would soon find someone else.

During the past two years Mr. Berman had seen three psychiatrists briefly, one of whom had given him a drug, the name of which he could not remember, but that had precipitated some sort of unusual reaction for which he had to stay in a hospital overnight. . . . Concerning his hospitalization, the patient said that "It was a dump," that the staff refused to listen to what he had to say or to respond to his needs, and that they, in fact, treated all the patients "sadistically." The referring doctor corroborated that Mr. Berman was a difficult patient who demanded that he be treated as special, and yet was hostile to most staff members throughout his stay. After one angry exchange with an aide, he left the hospital without [permission], and subsequently signed out against medical advice.

Mr. Berman is one of two children of a middle-class family. His father is 55 years old and employed in a managerial position for an insurance company. He perceives his father as weak and ineffectual, completely dominated by the patient's overbearing and cruel mother. He states that he hates his mother with "a passion I can barely control." He claims that his mother used to call him names like "pervert" . . . when he was growing up, and that in an argument she once "kicked me in the balls." Together, he sees his parents as rich, powerful, and selfish, and, in turn, thinks that they see him as lazy, irresponsible, and a behavior problem. When his parents called the therapist to discuss their son's treatment, they stated that his problem began with the birth of his younger brother, Arnold, when Philip was 10 years old. After Arnold's birth Philip apparently became [a disagreeable] child who cursed a lot and was difficult to discipline. Philip recalls this period only vaguely. He reports that his mother once was hospitalized for depression, but that now "she doesn't believe in psychiatry."

•model• A set of assumptions and concepts that help scientists explain and interpret observations. Also called a *paradigm*.

•neuron• A nerve cell.

•synapse• The tiny space between the nerve ending of one neuron and the dendrite of another.

•neurotransmitter• A chemical that, released by one neuron, crosses the synaptic space to be received at receptors on the dendrites of neighboring neurons.

•receptor• A site on a neuron that receives a neurotransmitter.

Mr. Berman had graduated from college with average grades. Since graduating he had worked at three different publishing houses, but at none of them for more than one year. He always found some justification for quitting. He usually sat around his house doing very little for two or three months after quitting a job, until his parents prodded him into getting a new one. He described innumerable interactions in his life with teachers, friends, and employers in which he felt offended or unfairly treated, . . . and frequent arguments that left him feeling bitter . . . and spent most of his time alone, "bored." He was unable to commit himself to any person, he held no strong convictions, and he felt no allegiance to any group.

The patient appeared as a very thin, bearded . . . young man with pale skin who maintained little eye contact with the therapist and who had an air of angry bitterness about him. Although he complained of depression, he denied other symptoms of the depressive syndrome. He seemed preoccupied with his rage at his parents, and seemed particularly invested in conveying a despicable image of himself. . . .

Spitzer et al., 1983, pp. 59–61

Philip Berman is clearly a troubled person, but how did he come to be that way? How do we explain and correct his many problems? To answer these questions, we must first look at the wide range of complaints we are trying to understand: Philip's depression and anger, his social failures, his lack of employment, his distrust of those around him, and the problems within his family. Then we must sort through all kinds of potential causes—internal and external, biological and interpersonal, past and present.

Although we may not realize it, we all use theoretical frameworks as we read about Philip. Over the course of our lives, each of us has developed a perspective that helps us make sense of the things other people say and do. In science, the perspectives used to explain events are known as **models,** or **paradigms.** Each model spells out the scientist's basic assumptions, gives order to the field under study, and sets guidelines for its investigation (Kuhn, 1962). It influences what the investigators observe as well as the questions they ask, the information they seek, and how they interpret this information (Sharf, 2012). To understand how a clinician explains or treats a specific set of symptoms, such as Philip's, we must know his or her preferred model of abnormal functioning.

Until recently, clinical scientists of a given place and time tended to agree on a single model of abnormality—a model greatly influenced by the beliefs of their culture. The *demonological model* that was used to explain abnormal functioning during the Middle Ages, for example, borrowed heavily from medieval society's concerns with religion, superstition, and warfare. Medieval practitioners would have seen the devil's guiding hand in Philip Berman's efforts to commit suicide and his feelings of depression, rage, jealousy, and hatred. Similarly, their treatments for him—from prayers to whippings—would have sought to drive foreign spirits from his body.

Today several models are used to explain and treat abnormal functioning. This variety has resulted from shifts in values and beliefs over the past half-century, as well as improvements in clinical research. At one end of the spectrum is the *biological model,* which sees physical processes as key to human behavior. In the middle are four models that focus on more psychological and personal aspects of human functioning: The *psychodynamic model* looks at people's unconscious internal processes and conflicts, the *behavioral model* emphasizes behavior and the ways in which it is learned, the *cognitive model* concentrates on the thinking that underlies behavior, and the *humanistic-existential model* stresses the role of values and choices. At the far end of the spectrum is the *sociocultural model,* which looks to social and cultural forces as the keys to human functioning. This model includes the *family-social perspective,* which focuses on an individual's family and social interactions, and the *multicultural perspective,* which emphasizes an individual's culture and the shared beliefs, values, and history of that culture.

Given their different assumptions and principles, the models are sometimes in conflict. Those who follow one perspective often scoff at the "naive" interpretations, investigations, and treatment efforts of the others. Yet none of the models is complete in itself. Each focuses mainly on one aspect of human functioning, and none can explain all aspects of abnormality.

BETWEEN THE LINES

Whose Brain Has the Most Neurons?

Human	100,000,000,000 neurons ‹‹
Octopus	300,000,000 neurons ‹‹
Rat	21,000,000 neurons ‹‹
Frog	16,000,000 neurons ‹‹
Cockroach	1,000,000 neurons ‹‹
Honey bee	850,000 neurons ‹‹
Fruit fly	100,000 neurons ‹‹
Ant	10,000 neurons ‹‹

The Biological Model

Philip Berman is a biological being. His thoughts and feelings are the results of biochemical and bioelectrical processes throughout his brain and body. Proponents of the *biological model* believe that a full understanding of Philip's thoughts, emotions, and behavior must therefore include an understanding of their biological basis. Not surprisingly, then, they believe that the most effective treatments for Philip's problems will be biological ones.

How Do Biological Theorists Explain Abnormal Behavior?

Adopting a medical perspective, biological theorists view abnormal behavior as an illness brought about by malfunctioning parts of the organism. Typically, they point to problems in brain anatomy or brain chemistry as the cause of such behavior.

Brain Anatomy and Abnormal Behavior
The brain is made up of approximately 100 billion nerve cells, called **neurons,** and thousands of billions of support cells, called *glia* (from the Greek word for "glue"). Within the brain large groups of neurons form distinct areas, or *brain regions.* Toward the top of the brain, for example, is a cluster of regions, collectively referred to as the *cerebrum,* which includes the *cortex, corpus callosum, basal ganglia, hippocampus,* and *amygdala* (see Figure 3-1). The neurons in each of these brain regions control important functions. The cortex is the outer layer of the brain, the corpus callosum connects the brain's two cerebral hemispheres, the basal ganglia plays a crucial role in planning and producing movement, the hippocampus helps regulate emotions and memory, and the amygdala plays a key role in emotional memory. Clinical researchers have discovered connections between certain psychological disorders and problems in specific areas of the brain. One such disorder is *Huntington's disease,* a disorder marked by violent emotional outbursts, memory loss, suicidal thinking, involuntary body movements, and absurd beliefs. This disease has been traced to a loss of cells in the basal ganglia and cortex.

Brain Chemistry and Abnormal Behavior
Biological researchers have also learned that psychological disorders can be related to problems in the transmission of messages from neuron to neuron. Information is communicated throughout the brain in the form of electrical impulses that travel from one neuron to one or more others. An impulse is first received by a neuron's *dendrites,* antenna-like extensions located at one end of the neuron. From there it travels down the neuron's *axon,* a long fiber extending from the neuron's body. Finally, it is transmitted through the *nerve ending* at the end of the axon to the dendrites of other neurons (see Figure 3-2).

But how do messages get from the nerve ending of one neuron to the dendrites of another? After all, the neurons do not actually touch each other. A tiny space, called the **synapse,** separates one neuron from the next, and the message must somehow move across that space. When an electrical impulse reaches a neuron's ending, the nerve ending is stimulated to release a chemical, called a **neurotransmitter,** that travels across the synaptic space to **receptors** on the dendrites of the neighboring neurons. After binding to the

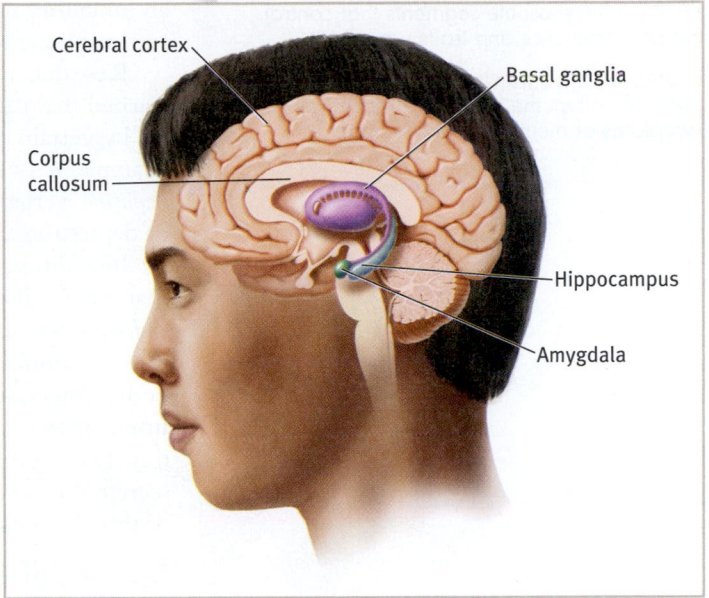

Figure 3-1
The cerebrum Some psychological disorders can be traced to abnormal functioning of neurons in the cerebrum, which includes brain structures such as the basal ganglia, hippocampus, amygdala, corpus callosum, and cerebral cortex.

Figure 3-2
A neuron communicating information A message in the form of an electrical impulse travels down the sending neuron's axon to its nerve ending, where neurotransmitters are released and carry the message across the synaptic space to the dendrites of a receiving neuron.

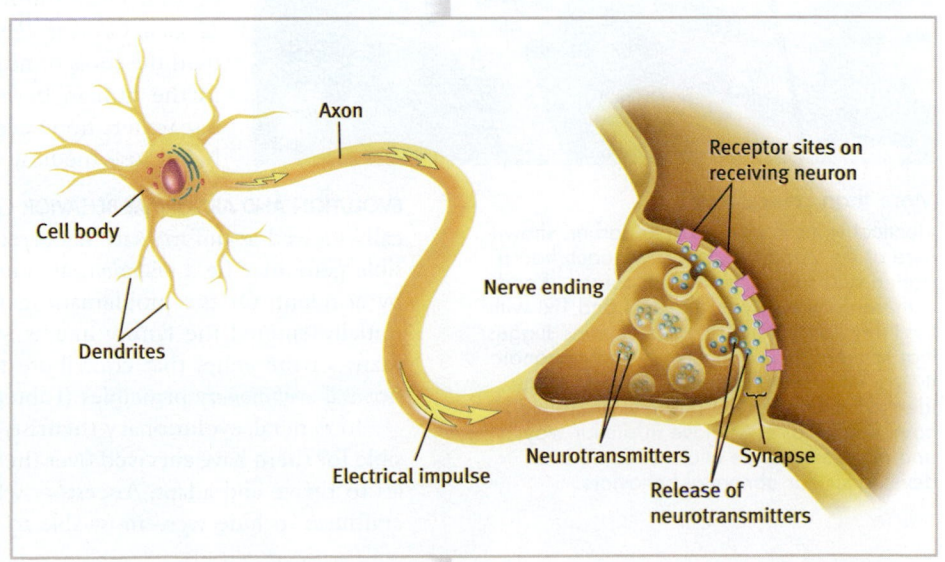

•**hormones**•The chemicals released by endocrine glands into the bloodstream.

•**gene**•Chromosome segments that control the characteristics and traits we inherit.

•**psychotropic medications**•Drugs that primarily affect the brain and reduce many symptoms of mental dysfunctioning.

receiving neuron's receptors, some neurotransmitters give a message to receiving neurons to "fire," that is, to trigger their own electrical impulse. Other neurotransmitters carry an inhibitory message; they tell receiving neurons to stop all firing. As you can see, neurotransmitters play a key role in moving information through the brain.

Researchers have identified dozens of neurotransmitters in the brain, and they have learned that each neuron uses only certain kinds. Studies indicate that abnormal activity by certain neurotransmitters can lead to specific mental disorders. Depression, for example, has been linked to low activity of the neurotransmitters *serotonin* and *norepinephrine.* Perhaps low serotonin activity is partly responsible for Philip Berman's pattern of depression and rage.

In addition to focusing on neurons and neurotransmitters, researchers have learned that mental disorders are sometimes related to abnormal chemical activity in the body's *endocrine system.* Endocrine glands, located throughout the body, work along with neurons to control such vital activities as growth, reproduction, sexual activity, heart rate, body temperature, energy, and responses to stress. The glands release chemicals called **hormones** into the bloodstream, and these chemicals then propel body organs into action. During times of stress, for example, the *adrenal glands,* located on top of the kidneys, secrete the hormone *cortisol* to help the body deal with the stress. Abnormal secretions of this chemical have been tied to anxiety and mood disorders.

Sources of Biological Abnormalities
Why do some people have brain structures or biochemical activities that differ from the norm? Three factors have received particular attention in recent years—*genetics, evolution,* and *viral infections.*

GENETICS AND ABNORMAL BEHAVIOR Abnormalities in brain anatomy or chemistry are sometimes the result of genetic inheritance. Each cell in the human brain and body contains 23 pairs of *chromosomes,* with each chromosome in a pair inherited from one of the person's parents. Every chromosome contains numerous **genes**—segments that control the characteristics and traits a person inherits. Altogether, each cell contains around 30,000 genes (Dermitzakis, 2011; Oskenberg & Hauser, 2010). Scientists have known for years that genes help determine such physical characteristics as hair color, height, and eyesight. Genes can make people more prone to heart disease, cancer, or diabetes, and perhaps to possessing artistic or musical skill. Studies suggest that inheritance also plays a part in mood disorders, schizophrenia, and other mental disorders. It appears that in most cases, several genes combine to help produce our actions and reactions, both functional and dysfunctional.

The precise contributions of various genes to mental disorders have become clearer in recent years, thanks in part to the completion of the *Human Genome Project* in 2000. In this major undertaking, scientists used the tools of molecular biology to *map,* or *sequence,* all of the genes in the human body in great detail. With this information in hand, researchers hope eventually to be able to prevent or change genes that help cause medical or psychological disorders.

More than coincidence?
Identical twins Ronde and Tiki Barber, shown here at the 2006 NFL Pro Bowl, each had a storied and successful football career—Ronde with the Tampa Bay Buccaneers and Tiki with the New York Giants. Studies of twins suggest that some aspects of behavior and personality are influenced by genetic factors. Many identical twins, like the Barbers, are found to have similar tastes, behave in similar ways, and make similar life choices. Some even develop similar abnormal behaviors.

EVOLUTION AND ABNORMAL BEHAVIOR Genes that contribute to mental disorders are typically viewed as unfortunate occurrences—almost mistakes of inheritance. The responsible gene may be a *mutation,* an abnormal form of the appropriate gene that emerges by accident. Or the problematic gene may be inherited by an individual after it has initially entered the family line as a mutation. According to some theorists, however, many of the genes that contribute to abnormal functioning are actually the result of normal *evolutionary* principles (Fábrega, 2010, 2006, 2002).

In general, evolutionary theorists argue that human reactions and the genes responsible for them have survived over the course of time because they have helped individuals to thrive and adapt. Ancestors who had the ability to run fast, for example, or the craftiness to hide were most able to escape their enemies and to reproduce. Thus, the genes responsible for effective walking, running, or problem solving were particularly likely to be passed on from generation to generation to the present day.

Similarly, say evolutionary theorists, the capacity to experience fear was, and in many instances still is, adaptive. Fear alerted our ancestors to dangers, threats, and losses, so that persons could avoid or escape potential problems. People who were particularly sensitive to danger—those with greater fear responses—were more likely to survive catastrophes, battles, and the like and to reproduce and pass on their fear genes. Of course, in today's world pressures are more numerous, subtle, and complex than they were in the past, condemning many individuals with such genes to a near-endless stream of fear and arousal. That is, the very genes that helped their ancestors to survive and reproduce might now leave these individuals particularly prone to fear reactions, anxiety disorders, or related psychological disorders.

The evolutionary perspective is controversial in the clinical field and has been rejected by many theorists. Imprecise and at times impossible to research, this explanation requires leaps of faith that many scientists find unacceptable. Nevertheless, as genetic discoveries and insights have grown, interest in the possible causes of genetic differences and how they relate to current circumstances has grown as well, and evolutionary theories have received considerable attention.

VIRAL INFECTIONS AND ABNORMAL BEHAVIOR Another possible source of abnormal brain structure or biochemical dysfunctioning is *viral infections.* As you will see in Chapter 14, for example, research suggests that *schizophrenia,* a disorder marked by delusions, hallucinations, or other departures from reality, may be related to exposure to certain viruses during childhood or before birth (Arias et al., 2012). Studies have found that the mothers of many individuals with this disorder contracted influenza or related viruses during their pregnancy. This and related pieces of circumstantial evidence suggest that a damaging virus may enter the fetus' brain and remain dormant there until the individual reaches adolescence or young adulthood. At that time, the virus may produce the symptoms of schizophrenia. During the past decade, researchers have sometimes linked viruses to anxiety and mood disorders, as well as to psychotic disorders (Fox, 2010).

Biological Treatments

Biological practitioners look for certain kinds of clues when they try to understand abnormal behavior. Does the person's family have a history of that behavior, and hence a possible genetic predisposition to it? (Philip Berman's case history mentions that his mother was once hospitalized for depression.) Is the behavior produced by events that could have had a physiological effect? (Philip was having a drink when he flew into a jealous rage at the restaurant.)

Once the clinicians have pinpointed physical sources of dysfunctioning, they are in a better position to choose a biological course of treatment. The three leading kinds of biological treatments used today are *drug therapy, electroconvulsive therapy,* and *psychosurgery.* Drug therapy is by far the most common of these approaches.

In the 1950s, researchers discovered several effective **psychotropic medications,** drugs that mainly affect emotions and thought processes. These drugs have greatly changed the outlook for a number of mental disorders and today are used widely, either alone or with other forms of therapy. However, the psychotropic drug revolution has also produced some major problems. Many people believe, for example, that the drugs are overused. Moreover, while drugs are effective in many cases, they do not help everyone (see Figure 3-3).

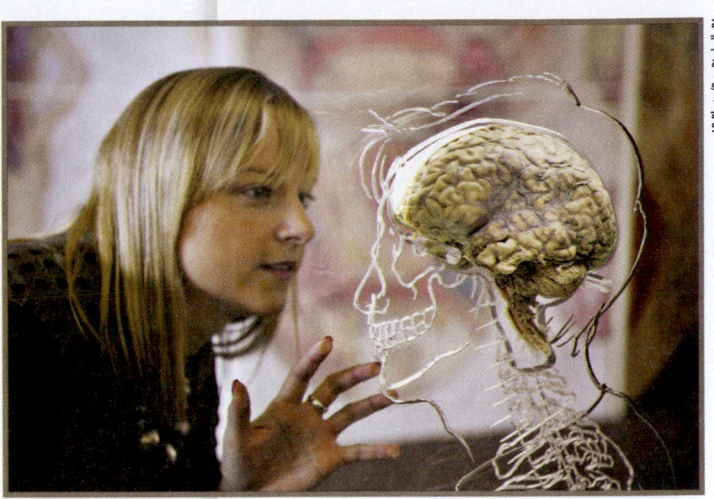

A popular subject
The human brain increasingly has captured the attention not only of neuroscientists but also the public at large. Here, at the "Real Brain" exhibit in the United Kingdom, a patron inspects a real human brain, suspended in liquid and positioned within an impression of a skeleton and nervous system.

BETWEEN THE LINES

In Their Words
"My brain? That's my second favorite organ." ‹‹

Woody Allen

? What might the popularity of psychotropic drugs suggest about coping styles and problem-solving skills in our society?

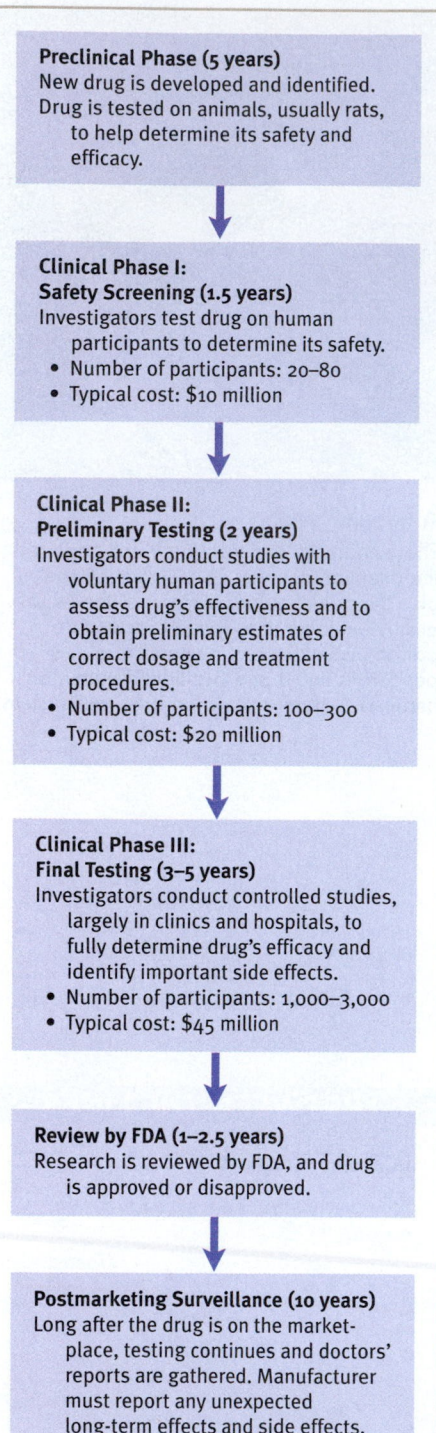

Preclinical Phase (5 years)
New drug is developed and identified. Drug is tested on animals, usually rats, to help determine its safety and efficacy.

Clinical Phase I:
Safety Screening (1.5 years)
Investigators test drug on human participants to determine its safety.
- Number of participants: 20–80
- Typical cost: $10 million

Clinical Phase II:
Preliminary Testing (2 years)
Investigators conduct studies with voluntary human participants to assess drug's effectiveness and to obtain preliminary estimates of correct dosage and treatment procedures.
- Number of participants: 100–300
- Typical cost: $20 million

Clinical Phase III:
Final Testing (3–5 years)
Investigators conduct controlled studies, largely in clinics and hospitals, to fully determine drug's efficacy and identify important side effects.
- Number of participants: 1,000–3,000
- Typical cost: $45 million

Review by FDA (1–2.5 years)
Research is reviewed by FDA, and drug is approved or disapproved.

Postmarketing Surveillance (10 years)
Long after the drug is on the marketplace, testing continues and doctors' reports are gathered. Manufacturer must report any unexpected long-term effects and side effects.

Figure 3-3

How does a new drug reach the marketplace? It takes an average of 12 years and $350 million for a pharmaceutical company in the United States to bring a newly discovered drug to market. The company must carefully follow steps that are specified by law. Only 1 in 1,000 lab-tested compounds even make it to human testing. (Drugs.com, 2011; Benesh, 2010; Dulichand, 2010).

Four major psychotropic drug groups are used in therapy: antianxiety, antidepressant, antibipolar, and antipsychotic drugs. **Antianxiety drugs,** also called *minor tranquilizers* or *anxiolytics,* help reduce tension and anxiety. **Antidepressant drugs** help improve the mood of people who are depressed. **Antibipolar drugs,** also called *mood stabilizers,* help steady the moods of those with a bipolar disorder, a condition marked by mood swings from mania to depression. And **antipsychotic drugs** help reduce the confusion, hallucinations, and delusions of *psychotic disorders,* disorders (such as schizophrenia) marked by a loss of contact with reality.

A second form of biological treatment, used primarily on depressed patients, is **electroconvulsive therapy (ECT).** Two electrodes are attached to a patient's forehead, and an electrical current of 65 to 140 volts is passed briefly through the brain. The current causes a brain seizure that lasts up to a few minutes. After seven to nine ECT sessions, spaced two or three days apart, many patients feel considerably less depressed. The treatment is used on tens of thousands of depressed persons annually, particularly those whose depression fails to respond to other treatments (Perugi et al., 2012).

A third form of biological treatment is **psychosurgery,** or **neurosurgery,** brain surgery for mental disorders. It is thought to have roots as far back as trephining, the prehistoric practice of chipping a hole in the skull of a person who behaved strangely. Modern procedures are derived from a technique first developed in the late 1930s by a Portuguese neuropsychiatrist, Antonio de Egas Moniz. In that procedure, known as a *lobotomy,* a surgeon would cut the connections between the brain's frontal lobes and the lower regions of the brain. Today's psychosurgery procedures are much more precise than the lobotomies of the past. Even so, they are considered experimental and are used only after certain severe disorders have continued for years without responding to any other form of treatment.

Assessing the Biological Model

Today the biological model enjoys considerable respect. Biological research constantly produces valuable new information. And biological treatments often bring great relief when other approaches have failed. At the same time, this model has its shortcomings. Some of its proponents seem to expect that all human behavior can be explained in biological terms and treated with biological methods. This view can limit rather than

"Don't judge me until you've walked a mile on my medication."

enhance our understanding of abnormal functioning. Our mental life is an interplay of biological and nonbiological factors, and it is important to understand that interplay rather than to focus on biological variables alone.

Another shortcoming is that several of today's biological treatments are capable of producing significant undesirable effects. Certain antipsychotic drugs, for example, may produce movement problems such as severe shaking, bizarre-looking contractions of the face and body, and extreme restlessness. Clearly such costs must be addressed and weighed against the drug's benefits.

The Psychodynamic Model

The *psychodynamic model* is the oldest and most famous of the modern psychological models. Psychodynamic theorists believe that a person's behavior, whether normal or abnormal, is determined largely by underlying psychological forces of which he or she is not consciously aware. These internal forces are described as *dynamic*—that is, they interact with one another—and their interaction gives rise to behavior, thoughts, and emotions. Abnormal symptoms are viewed as the result of conflicts between these forces.

Psychodynamic theorists would view Philip Berman as a person in conflict. They would want to explore his past experiences because, in their view, psychological conflicts are tied to early relationships and to traumatic experiences that occurred during childhood. Psychodynamic theories rest on the *deterministic* assumption that no symptom or behavior is "accidental": All behavior is determined by past experiences. Thus Philip's hatred for his mother, his memories of her as cruel and overbearing, the weakness of his father, and the birth of a younger brother when Philip was 10 may all be important to the understanding of his current problems.

The psychodynamic model was first formulated by Viennese neurologist Sigmund Freud (1856–1939) at the turn of the twentieth century. First, Freud worked with physician Josef Breuer (1842–1925), conducting experiments on hypnosis and hysterical illnesses—mysterious physical ailments with no apparent medical cause. In a famous case, Breuer had treated a woman he called "Anna O.," whose hysterical symptoms included paralysis of the legs and right arm, deafness, and disorganized speech. Breuer placed the woman under hypnosis, expecting that suggestions made to her in that state would help rid her of her hysterical symptoms. While she was under hypnosis, however, she began to talk about traumatic past events and to express deeply felt emotions. This expression of repressed memories seemed to enhance the effectiveness of the treatment. Anna referred to it as her "talking cure."

Building on this early work, Freud developed the theory of *psychoanalysis* to explain both normal and abnormal psychological functioning as well as a corresponding method of treatment, a conversational approach also called psychoanalysis. During the early 1900s, Freud and several of his colleagues in the Vienna Psychoanalytic Society—including Carl Gustav Jung (1875–1961) and Alfred Adler (1870–1937)—became the most influential clinical theorists in the Western world.

How Did Freud Explain Normal and Abnormal Functioning?

Freud believed that three central forces shape the personality—instinctual needs, rational thinking, and moral standards. All of these forces, he believed, operate at the *unconscious level,* unavailable to immediate awareness; he further believed these forces to be dynamic, or interactive. Freud called the forces the *id,* the *ego,* and the *superego.*

The Id Freud used the term **id** to denote instinctual needs, drives, and impulses. The id operates in accordance with the *pleasure principle;* that is, it always seeks gratification. Freud also believed that all id instincts tend to be sexual, noting that from the very earliest stages of life a child's pleasure is obtained from nursing, defecating, masturbating, or engaging in other activities that he considered to have sexual ties. He further suggested that a person's *libido,* or sexual energy, fuels the id.

•**antianxiety drugs**•Psychotropic drugs that help reduce tension and anxiety. Also called *minor tranquilizers* or *anxiolytics.*

•**antidepressant drugs**•Psychotropic drugs that improve the moods of people with depression.

•**antibipolar drugs**•Psychotropic drugs that help stabilize the moods of people suffering from a bipolar mood disorder. Also called *mood stabilizers.*

•**antipsychotic drugs**•Psychotropic drugs that help correct the confusion, hallucinations, and delusions found in psychotic disorders.

•**electroconvulsive therapy (ECT)**•A form of biological treatment, used primarily on depressed patients, in which a brain seizure is triggered as an electric current passes through electrodes attached to the patient's forehead.

•**psychosurgery**•Brain surgery for mental disorders. Also called *neurosurgery.*

•**id**•According to Freud, the psychological force that produces instinctual needs, drives, and impulses.

LucasFilm/20th Century Fox/The Kobal Collection

"Luke, I am your father."
This light-saber fight between Luke Skywalker and Darth Vader highlights the most famous, and contentious, father-son relationship in movie history. According to Sigmund Freud, however, all fathers and sons experience significant tensions and conflicts that they must work through, even in the absence of the special pressures faced by Luke and his father in the *Star Wars* series.

The Ego During our early years we come to recognize that our environment will not meet every instinctual need. Our mother, for example, is not always available to do our bidding. A part of the id separates off and becomes the **ego.** Like the id, the ego unconsciously seeks gratification, but it does so in accordance with the *reality principle,* the knowledge we acquire through experience that it can be unacceptable to express our id impulses outright. The ego, employing reason, guides us to know when we can and cannot express those impulses.

The ego develops basic strategies, called **ego defense mechanisms,** to control unacceptable id impulses and avoid or reduce the anxiety they arouse. The most basic defense mechanism, *repression,* prevents unacceptable impulses from ever reaching consciousness. There are many other ego defense mechanisms, and each of us tends to favor some over others (see Table 3-1).

The Superego The **superego** grows from the ego, just as the ego grows out of the id. As we learn from our parents that many of our id impulses are unacceptable, we unconsciously adopt our parents' values. Judging ourselves by their standards, we feel good when we uphold their values; conversely, when we go against them, we feel guilty. In short, we develop a *conscience.*

According to Freud, these three parts of the personality—the id, the ego, and the superego—are often in some degree of conflict. A healthy personality is one in which an effective working relationship, an acceptable compromise, has formed among the three forces. If the id, ego, and superego are in excessive conflict, the person's behavior may show signs of dysfunction.

table: 3-1

The Defense Never Rests: Defense Mechanisms to the Rescue

Defense	Operation	Example
Repression	Person avoids anxiety by simply not allowing painful or dangerous thoughts to become conscious.	An executive's desire to run amok and attack his boss and colleagues at a board meeting is denied access to his awareness.
Denial	Person simply refuses to acknowledge the existence of an external source of anxiety.	You are not prepared for tomorrow's final exam, but you tell yourself that it's not actually an important exam and that there's no good reason not to go to a movie tonight.
Projection	Person attributes own unacceptable impulses, motives, or desires to other individuals.	The executive who repressed his destructive desires may project his anger onto his boss and claim that it is actually the boss who is hostile.
Rationalization	Person creates a socially acceptable reason for an action that actually reflects unacceptable motives.	A student explains away poor grades by citing the importance of the "total experience" of going to college and claiming that too much emphasis on grades would actually interfere with a well-rounded education.
Displacement	Person displaces hostility away from a dangerous object and onto a safer substitute.	After a perfect parking spot is taken by a person who cuts in front of your car, you release your pent-up anger by starting an argument with your roommate.
Intellectualization	Person represses emotional reactions in favor of overly logical response to a problem.	A woman who has been beaten and raped gives a detached, methodical description of the effects that such attacks may have on victims.
Regression	Person retreats from an upsetting conflict to an early developmental stage at which no one is expected to behave maturely or responsibly.	A boy who cannot cope with the anger he feels toward his rejecting mother regresses to infantile behavior, soiling his clothes and no longer taking care of his basic needs.

Freudians would therefore view Philip Berman as someone whose personality forces have a poor working relationship. His ego and superego are unable to control his id impulses, which lead him repeatedly to act in impulsive and often dangerous ways—suicide gestures, jealous rages, job resignations, outbursts of temper, frequent arguments.

Developmental Stages Freud proposed that at each stage of development, from infancy to maturity, new events challenge individuals and require adjustments in their id, ego, and superego. If the adjustments are successful, they lead to personal growth. If not, the person may become **fixated,** or stuck, at an early stage of development. Then all subsequent development suffers, and the individual may well be headed for abnormal functioning in the future. Because parents are the key figures during the early years of life, they are often seen as the cause of improper development.

Freud named each stage of development after the body area that he considered most important to the child at that time. For example, he referred to the first 18 months of life as the *oral stage.* During this stage, children fear that the mother who feeds and comforts them will disappear. Children whose mothers consistently fail to gratify their oral needs may become fixated at the oral stage and display an "oral character" throughout their lives, one marked by extreme dependence or extreme mistrust. Such persons are particularly prone to develop depression. As you will see in later chapters, Freud linked fixations at the other stages of development—*anal* (18 months to 3 years of age), *phallic* (3 to 5 years), *latency* (5 to 12 years), and *genital* (12 years to adulthood)—to yet other kinds of psychological dysfunction.

How Do Other Psychodynamic Explanations Differ from Freud's?

Personal and professional differences between Freud and his colleagues led to a split in the Vienna Psychoanalytic Society early in the twentieth century. Carl Jung, Alfred Adler, and others developed new theories. Although the new theories departed from Freud's ideas in important ways, each held on to Freud's belief that human functioning is shaped by dynamic (interacting) psychological forces. Thus all such theories, including Freud's, are referred to as *psychodynamic.*

Three of today's most influential psychodynamic theories are ego theory, self theory, and object relations theory. **Ego theorists** emphasize the role of the ego and consider it a more independent and powerful force than Freud did (Sharf, 2012). **Self theorists,** in contrast, give the greatest attention to the role of the *self*—the unified personality. They believe that the basic human motive is to strengthen the wholeness of the self (Wolitzky, 2011; Kohut, 2001, 1977). **Object relations theorists** propose that people are motivated mainly by a need to have relationships with others and that severe problems in the relationships between children and their caregivers may lead to abnormal development (Williams, 2012; Kernberg, 2005, 2001, 1997).

Psychodynamic Therapies

Psychodynamic therapies range from Freudian psychoanalysis to modern therapies based on self theory or object relations theory. All seek to uncover past traumas and the inner conflicts that have resulted from them. All try to help clients resolve, or settle, those conflicts and to resume personal development.

According to most psychodynamic therapists, therapists must subtly guide therapy discussions so that the patients discover their underlying problems for themselves. To aid in the process, the therapists rely on such techniques as *free association, therapist interpretation, catharsis,* and *working through.*

Free Association In psychodynamic therapies, the patient is responsible for starting and leading each discussion. The therapist tells the patient to describe any thought, feeling, or image that comes to mind, even if it seems unimportant. This practice is known as **free association.** The therapist expects that the patient's associations will eventually

•**ego**•According to Freud, the psychological force that employs reason and operates in accordance with the reality principle.

•**ego defense mechanisms**•According to psychoanalytic theory, strategies developed by the ego to control unacceptable id impulses and to avoid or reduce the anxiety they arouse.

•**superego**•According to Freud, the psychological force that represents a person's values and ideals.

•**fixation**•According to Freud, a condition in which the id, ego, and superego do not mature properly and are frozen at an early stage of development.

•**ego theory**•The psychodynamic theory that emphasizes the role of the ego and considers it an independent force.

•**self theory**•The psychodynamic theory that emphasizes the role of the self—our unified personality.

•**object relations theory**•The psychodynamic theory that views the desire for relationships as the key motivating force in human behavior.

•**free association**•A psychodynamic technique in which the patient describes any thought, feeling, or image that comes to mind, even if it seems unimportant.

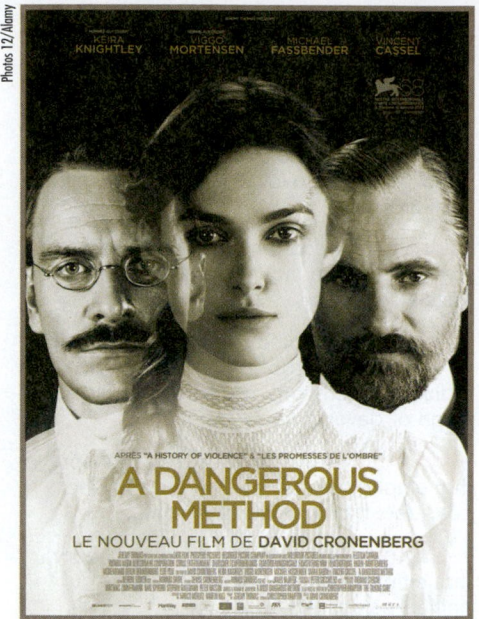

A cultural phenomenon
The history and practice of psychoanalysis has been a very popular subject in the arts over the years. For example, the critically-acclaimed 2011 film *A Dangerous Method* portrays complex personal and professional reasons for the collapse of Sigmund Freud's relationship with his close colleague and friend, Carl Jung.

•**resistance**•An unconscious refusal to participate fully in therapy.

•**transference**•According to psychodynamic theorists, the redirection toward the psychotherapist of feelings associated with important figures in a patient's life, now or in the past.

•**dream**•A series of ideas and images that form during sleep.

•**catharsis**•The reliving of past repressed feelings in order to settle internal conflicts and overcome problems.

•**working through**•The psychoanalytic process of facing conflicts, reinterpreting feelings, and overcoming one's problems.

uncover unconscious events. In the following excerpts from a famous psychodynamic case, notice how free association helps a woman to discover threatening impulses and conflicts within herself:

> *Patient:* So I started walking, and walking, and decided to go behind the museum and walk through [New York's] Central Park. So I walked and went through a back field and felt very excited and wonderful. I saw a park bench next to a clump of bushes and sat down. There was a rustle behind me and I got frightened. I thought of men concealing themselves in the bushes. I thought of the sex perverts I read about in Central Park. I wondered if there was someone behind me exposing himself. The idea is repulsive, but exciting too. I think of father now and feel excited. I think of an erect penis. This is connected with my father. There is something about this pushing in my mind. I don't know what it is, like on the border of my memory. (Pause)
>
> *Therapist:* Mm-hmm. (Pause) On the border of your memory?
>
> *Patient:* (The patient breathes rapidly and seems to be under great tension.) As a little girl, I slept with my father. I get a funny feeling. I get a funny feeling over my skin, tingly-like. It's a strange feeling, like a blindness, like not seeing something. My mind blurs and spreads over anything I look at. I've had this feeling off and on since I walked in the park. My mind seems to blank off like I can't think or absorb anything.
>
> *(Wolberg, 2005, 1967, p. 662)*

Therapist Interpretation Psychodynamic therapists listen carefully as patients talk, looking for clues, drawing tentative conclusions, and sharing interpretations when they think the patient is ready to hear them. Interpretations of three phenomena are particularly important—*resistance, transference,* and *dreams.*

Patients are showing **resistance,** an unconscious refusal to participate fully in therapy, when they suddenly cannot free associate or when they change a subject to avoid a painful discussion. They demonstrate **transference** when they act and feel toward the therapist as they did or do toward important persons in their lives, especially their parents, siblings, and spouses. Consider again the woman who walked in Central Park. As she continues talking, the therapist helps her to explore her transference:

> *Patient:* I get so excited by what is happening here. I feel I'm being held back by needing to be nice. I'd like to blast loose sometimes, but I don't dare.
>
> *Therapist:* Because you fear my reaction?
>
> *Patient:* The worst thing would be that you wouldn't like me. You wouldn't speak to me friendly; you wouldn't smile; you'd feel you can't treat me and discharge me from treatment. But I know this isn't so, I know it.
>
> *Therapist:* Where do you think these attitudes come from?
>
> *Patient:* When I was nine years old, I read a lot about great men in history. I'd quote them and be dramatic. I'd want a sword at my side; I'd dress like an Indian. Mother would scold me. Don't frown, don't talk so much. Sit on your hands, over and over again. I did all kinds of things. I was a naughty child. She told me I'd be hurt. Then at fourteen I fell off a horse and broke my back. I had to be in bed. Mother told me on the day I went riding not to, that I'd get hurt because the ground was frozen. I was a stubborn, self-willed child. Then I went against her will and suffered an accident that changed my life, a fractured back. Her attitude was, "I told you so." I was put in a cast and kept in bed for months.
>
> *(Wolberg, 2005, 1967, p. 662)*

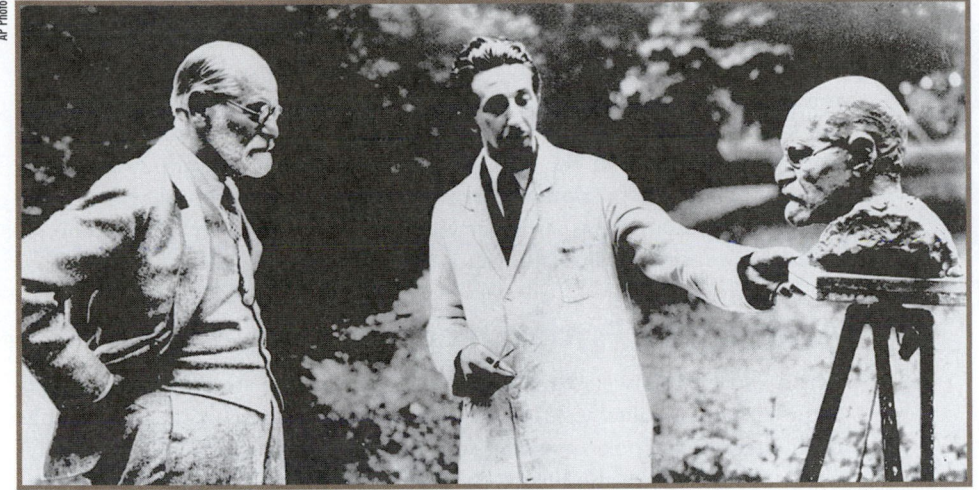

AP Photo

Freud takes a closer look at Freud
Sigmund Freud, founder of psychoanalytic theory and therapy, contemplates a sculptured bust of himself in 1931 at his village home in Potzlein, near Vienna. As Freud and the bust go eyeball to eyeball, one can only imagine what conclusions each is drawing about the other.

Finally, many psychodynamic therapists try to help patients interpret their **dreams** (see Table 3-2). Freud (1924) called dreams the "royal road to the unconscious." He believed that repression and other defense mechanisms operate less completely during sleep and that dreams, if correctly interpreted, can reveal unconscious instincts, needs, and wishes. Freud identified two kinds of dream content—manifest and latent. *Manifest content* is the consciously remembered dream; *latent content* is its symbolic meaning. To interpret a dream, therapists must translate its manifest content into its latent content.

? **Why do you think most people try to interpret and make sense of their own dreams? Are such interpretations of value?**

Catharsis Insight must be an emotional as well as an intellectual process. Psychodynamic therapists believe that patients must experience **catharsis,** a reliving of past repressed feelings, if they are to settle internal conflicts and overcome their problems.

Working Through A single episode of interpretation and catharsis will not change the way a person functions. The patient and therapist must examine the same issues over and over in the course of many sessions, each time with greater clarity. This process, called **working through,** usually takes a long time, often years.

Current Trends in Psychodynamic Therapy The past 35 years have witnessed significant changes in the way many psychodynamic therapists conduct sessions. An increased demand for focused, time-limited psychotherapies has resulted in efforts to make psychodynamic therapy more efficient and affordable. Two current psychodynamic approaches that illustrate this trend are *short-term psychodynamic therapies* and *relational psychoanalytic therapy.*

SHORT-TERM PSYCHODYNAMIC THERAPIES In several short versions of psychodynamic therapy, patients choose a single problem—a *dynamic focus*—to work on, such as difficulty getting along with other people (Wolitzky, 2011). The therapist and patient focus on this problem throughout the treatment and work only on the psychodynamic issues that relate to it (such as unresolved oral needs). Only a limited number of studies have tested the effectiveness of these short-term psychodynamic therapies, but their findings do suggest that the approaches are sometimes quite helpful to patients (Wolitzky, 2011; Present et al., 2008).

table: **3-2**

Percent of Research Participants Who Have Had Common Dreams

	Men	Women
Being chased or pursued, not injured	78%	83%
Sexual experiences	85	73
Falling	73	74
School, teachers, studying	57	71
Arriving too late, e.g., for a train	55	62
On the verge of falling	53	60
Trying to do something repeatedly	55	53
A person living as dead	43	59
Flying or soaring through the air	58	44
Sensing a presence vividly	44	50
Failing an examination	37	48
Being physically attacked	40	44
Being frozen with fright	32	44
A person now dead as living	37	39
Being a child again	33	38

Source: Copley, 2008; Kantrowitz & Springen, 2004.

Pat Byrnes/The New Yorker Collection

"I'm doing a lot better now that I'm back in denial."

RELATIONAL PSYCHOANALYTIC THERAPY Whereas Freud believed that psychodynamic therapists should take on the role of a neutral, distant expert during a treatment session, a contemporary school of psychodynamic therapy referred to as **relational psychoanalytic therapy** argues that therapists are key figures in the lives of patients—figures whose reactions and beliefs should be included in the therapy process (Luborsky et al., 2011). Thus, a key principle of relational therapy is that therapists should also disclose things about themselves, particularly their own reactions to patients, and try to establish more equal relationships with patients.

Assessing the Psychodynamic Model

Freud and his followers have helped change the way abnormal functioning is understood (Wolitzky, 2011). Largely because of their work, a wide range of theorists today look for answers outside of biological processes. Psychodynamic theorists have also helped us to understand that abnormal functioning may be rooted in the same processes as normal functioning (see *PsychWatch* on the next page). Psychological conflict is a common experience; it leads to abnormal functioning only if the conflict becomes excessive.

Freud and his many followers have also had a monumental impact on treatment. They were the first to apply theory systematically to treatment. They were also the first to demonstrate the potential of psychological, as opposed to biological, treatment, and their ideas have served as starting points for many other psychological treatments.

At the same time, the psychodynamic model has its shortcomings. Its concepts are hard to research (Wampold et al., 2011; Nietzel et al., 2003). Because processes such as id drives, ego defenses, and fixation are abstract and supposedly operate at an unconscious level, there is no way of knowing for certain if they are occurring. Not surprisingly, then, psychodynamic explanations and treatments have received limited research support over the years, and psychodynamic theorists rely largely on evidence provided by individual case studies. Nevertheless, recent research evidence suggests that long-term psychodynamic therapy may be helpful for many persons with long-term complex disorders (Leichsenring & Rabung, 2011, 2010), and 15 percent of today's clinical psychologists identify themselves as psychodynamic therapists (Sharf, 2012; Prochaska & Norcross, 2010).

What are some of the ways that Freud's theories have affected literature, film and television, philosophy, child rearing, and education in Western society?

The Behavioral Model

Like psychodynamic theorists, behavioral theorists believe that our actions are determined largely by our experiences in life. However, the *behavioral model* concentrates on *behaviors,* the responses an organism makes to its environment. Behaviors can be external (going to work, say) or internal (having a feeling or thought). In turn, behavioral theorists base their explanations and treatments on *principles of learning,* the processes by which these behaviors change in response to the environment.

Many learned behaviors help people to cope with daily challenges and to lead happy, productive lives. However, abnormal behaviors also can be learned. Behaviorists who try to explain Philip Berman's problems might view him as a man who has received improper training: He has learned behaviors that offend others and repeatedly work against him.

Whereas the psychodynamic model had its beginnings in the clinical work of physicians, the behavioral model began in laboratories where psychologists were running experiments on **conditioning,** simple forms of learning. The researchers manipulated

•**relational psychoanalytic therapy**• A form of psychodynamic therapy that considers therapists to be active participants in the formation of patients' feelings and reactions, and therefore calls for therapists to disclose their own experiences and feelings in discussions with patients.

•**conditioning**•A simple form of learning.

•**operant conditioning**•A process of learning in which behavior that leads to satisfying consequences is likely to be repeated.

•**modeling**•A process of learning in which an individual acquires responses by observing and imitating others.

•**classical conditioning**•A process of learning by temporal association in which two events that repeatedly occur close together in time become fused in a person's mind and produce the same response.

Robert Allison/Contact Press Images

PsychWatch

Maternal Instincts

On an August day in 1996, a 3-year-old boy climbed over a barrier at the Brookfield Zoo in Illinois and fell 24 feet onto the cement floor of the gorilla compound. An 8-year-old 160-pound gorilla named Binti-Jua picked up the child and cradled his limp body in her arms. The child's mother, fearing the worst, screamed out, "The gorilla's got my baby!" But Binti protected the boy as if he were her own.

She held off the other gorillas, rocked him gently, and carried him to the entrance of the gorilla area, where rescue workers were waiting. Within hours, the incident was seen on videotape replays around the world, and Binti was being hailed for her maternal instincts.

When Binti was herself an infant, she had been removed from her mother, Lulu, who did not have enough milk. To make up for this loss, keepers at the zoo worked around the clock to nurture Binti; she was always being held in someone's arms. When Binti became pregnant at age 6, trainers were afraid that the early separation from her mother would leave her ill prepared to raise an infant of her own. So they gave her mothering lessons and taught her to nurse and carry around a stuffed doll.

After the incident at the zoo, clinical theorists had a field day interpreting the gorilla's gentle and nurturing care for the child, each within his or her preferred theory. Many *evolutionary theorists,* for example, viewed the behavior as an expression of the maternal instincts that have helped the gorilla species to survive and evolve. Some *psychodynamic theorists* suggested that the gorilla was expressing feelings of attachment and bonding, already experienced with her own 17-month-old daughter. And *behaviorists* held that the gorilla may have been imitating the nurturing behavior that she had observed in human models during her own infancy or enacting the parenting training that she had received during her pregnancy. In the meantime, Binti-Jua, the heroic gorilla, returned to her relatively quiet and predictable life at the zoo.

stimuli and *rewards,* then observed how their manipulations affected the responses of their research participants.

During the 1950s, many clinicians became frustrated with what they viewed as the vagueness and slowness of the psychodynamic model. Some of them began to apply the principles of learning to the study and treatment of psychological problems. Their efforts gave rise to the behavioral model of abnormality.

How Do Behaviorists Explain Abnormal Functioning?

Learning theorists have identified several forms of conditioning, and each may produce abnormal behavior as well as normal behavior. In **operant conditioning,** for example, humans and animals learn to behave in certain ways as a result of receiving *rewards*—any satisfying consequences—whenever they do so. In **modeling** individuals learn responses simply by observing other individuals and repeating their behaviors.

In a third form of conditioning, **classical conditioning,** learning occurs by *temporal association*. When two events repeatedly occur close together in time, they become fused

Figure 3-4
Working for Pavlov In Ivan Pavlov's experimental device, the dog's saliva was collected in a tube as it was secreted, and the amount was recorded on a revolving cylinder. The experimenter observed the dog through a one-way glass window.

Whispering or conditioning?

In the TV series *Dog Whisperer,* Cesar Millan helps owners to rehabilitate their misbehaving or troubled dogs. Millan suggests that these dogs are responding to "pack leadership" from the owners. But many observers have noted that his techniques often follow basic principles of conditioning, used for years to teach animals various tricks and behaviors.

in a person's mind, and before long the person responds in the same way to both events. If one event produces a response of joy, the other brings joy as well; if one event brings feelings of relief, so does the other. A closer look at this form of conditioning illustrates how the behavioral model can account for abnormal functioning.

Ivan Pavlov (1849–1936), a famous Russian physiologist, first demonstrated classical conditioning with animal studies. He placed a bowl of meat powder before a dog, producing the natural response that all dogs have to meat: They start to salivate (see Figure 3-4). Next Pavlov added a step: Just before presenting the dog with meat powder, he sounded a bell. After several such pairings of bell tone and presentation of meat powder, Pavlov noted that the dog began to salivate as soon as it heard the bell. The dog had learned to salivate in response to a sound.

In the vocabulary of classical conditioning, the meat in this demonstration is an *unconditioned stimulus* (US). It elicits the *unconditioned response* (UR) of salivation, that is, a natural response with which the dog is born. The sound of the bell is a *conditioned stimulus* (CS), a previously neutral stimulus that comes to be linked with meat in the dog's mind. As such, it too produces a salivation response. When the salivation response is produced by the conditioned stimulus rather than by the unconditioned stimulus, it is called a *conditioned response* (CR).

BEFORE CONDITIONING	AFTER CONDITIONING
CS: Tone → No response	CS: Tone → CR: Salivation
US: Meat → UR: Salivation	US: Meat → UR: Salivation

Classical conditioning explains many familiar behaviors. The romantic feelings a young man experiences when he smells his girlfriend's perfume, say, may represent a conditioned response. Initially, this perfume may have had little emotional effect on him, but because the fragrance was present during several romantic encounters, it came to elicit a romantic response.

Abnormal behaviors, too, can be acquired by classical conditioning. Consider a young boy who is repeatedly frightened by a neighbor's large German shepherd dog. Whenever the child walks past the neighbor's front yard, the dog barks loudly and lunges at him, stopped only by a rope tied to the porch. In this unfortunate situation, the boy's parents are not surprised to discover that he develops a fear of dogs. They are stumped, however, by another intense fear the child displays, a fear of sand. They cannot understand why he cries whenever they take him to the beach and screams in fear if sand even touches his skin.

Where did this fear of sand come from? Classical conditioning. It turns out that a big sandbox is set up in the neighbor's front yard for the dog to play in. Every time the dog barks and lunges at the boy, the sandbox is there too. After repeated pairings of this kind, the child comes to fear sand as much as he fears the dog.

Behavioral Therapies

Behavioral therapy aims to identify the behaviors that are causing a person's problems and then tries to replace them with more appropriate ones by applying the principles of classical conditioning, operant conditioning, or modeling (Wilson, 2011). The therapist's attitude toward the client is that of teacher rather than healer.

Classical conditioning treatments, for example, may be used to change abnormal reactions to particular stimuli. **Systematic desensitization** is one such method, often applied in cases of *phobia*—a specific and unreasonable fear. In this step-by-step procedure, clients learn to react calmly instead of with intense fear to the objects or situations they dread (Fishman et al., 2011; Wolpe, 1997, 1995, 1990). First, they are taught the skill of relaxation over the course of several sessions. Next, they construct a *fear hierarchy*, a list of feared objects or situations, starting with those that are less feared and ending with the ones that are most dreaded. Here is the hierarchy developed by a man who was afraid of dogs:

1. Read the word "dog" in a book.
2. Hear a neighbor's barking dog.
3. See photos of small dogs.
4. See photos of large dogs.
5. See a movie in which a dog is prominently featured.
6. Be in the same room with a quiet, small dog.
7. Pet a small, cuddly dog.
8. Be in the same room with a large dog.
9. Pet a big, frisky dog.
10. Play roughhouse with a dog.

Desensitization therapists next have their clients either imagine or actually confront each item on the hierarchy while in a state of relaxation. In step-by-step pairings of feared items and relaxation, clients move up the hierarchy until at last they can face every one of the items without experiencing fear. As you will read in Chapter 5, research has shown systematic desensitization and other classical conditioning techniques to be effective in treating phobias (Olatunji et al., 2011; Kraft & Kraft, 2010).

Assessing the Behavioral Model

The behavioral model has become a powerful force in the clinical field. Various behavioral theories have been proposed over the years, and many treatment techniques have been developed. As you can see in Figure 3-5, approximately 10 percent of today's clinical psychologists report that their approach is mainly behavioral (Sharf, 2012; Prochaska & Norcross, 2010).

Perhaps the greatest appeal of the behavioral model is that it can be tested in the laboratory, whereas psychodynamic theories generally cannot. The behaviorists' basic concepts—stimulus, response, and reward—can be observed and measured. Experimenters have, in fact, successfully used the principles of learning to create clinical symptoms in laboratory participants, suggesting that psychological disorders may indeed develop in the same way. In addition, research has found that behavioral treatments can be helpful to people with specific fears, compulsive behavior, social deficits, mental retardation, and other problems (Wilson, 2011).

At the same time, research has also revealed weaknesses in the model. Certainly behavioral researchers have produced specific symptoms in participants. But are these symptoms *ordinarily* acquired in this way? There is still no indisputable evidence that most people with psychological disorders are victims of improper conditioning. Similarly, behavioral therapies have limitations. The improvements noted in the therapist's office do not always extend to real life. Nor do they necessarily last without continued therapy.

Finally, some critics hold that the behavioral view is too simplistic, that its concepts fail to account for the complexity of behavior. In 1977 Albert Bandura, a leading behaviorist, argued that in order to feel happy and function effectively people must develop a positive sense of **self-efficacy.** That is, they must know that they can master and perform needed behaviors whenever

•**systematic desensitization**•A behavioral treatment in which clients with phobias learn to react calmly instead of with intense fear to the objects or situations they dread.

•**self-efficacy**•The belief that one can master and perform needed behaviors whenever necessary.

Figure 3-5

Theoretical orientations of today's clinical psychologists In one survey, 29 percent of clinical psychologists labeled themselves as "eclectic," 28 percent considered themselves "cognitive," and 15 percent called their orientation "psychodynamic" (Sharf, 2012; Prochaska & Norcross, 2010).

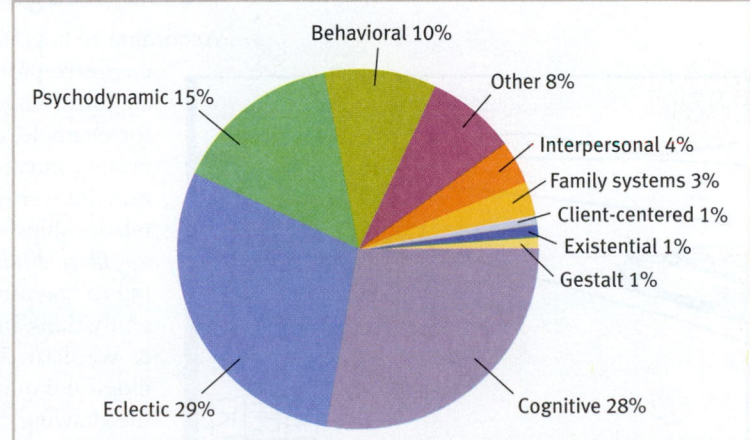

Behavioral 10%
Other 8%
Psychodynamic 15%
Interpersonal 4%
Family systems 3%
Client-centered 1%
Existential 1%
Gestalt 1%
Eclectic 29%
Cognitive 28%

See and do

Modeling may account for some forms of abnormal behavior. A well-known study by Albert Bandura and his colleagues (1963) demonstrated that children learned to abuse a doll by observing an adult hit it. Children who had not been exposed to the adult model did not mistreat the doll.

necessary. Other behaviorists of the 1960s and 1970s similarly recognized that human beings engage in *cognitive behaviors,* such as anticipating or interpreting—ways of thinking that until then had been largely ignored in behavioral theory and therapy. These individuals developed *cognitive-behavioral explanations* that took unseen cognitive behaviors into greater account (Fishman et al., 2011; Meichenbaum, 1993; Goldiamond, 1965) and **cognitive-behavioral therapies** that helped clients to change both counterproductive behaviors and dysfunctional ways of thinking. Cognitive-behavioral theorists and therapists bridge the behavioral model and the cognitive model, the view to which we turn next.

The Cognitive Model

Philip Berman, like the rest of us, has *cognitive* abilities—special intellectual capacities to think, remember, and anticipate. These abilities can help him accomplish a great deal in life. Yet they can also work against him. As he thinks about his experiences, Philip may misinterpret experiences in ways that lead to poor decisions, maladaptive responses, and painful emotions.

In the early 1960s two clinicians, Albert Ellis (1962) and Aaron Beck (1967), proposed that cognitive processes are at the center of behaviors, thoughts, and emotions and that we can best understand abnormal functioning by looking to cognition—a perspective known as the *cognitive model.* Ellis and Beck claimed that clinicians must ask questions about the assumptions and attitudes that color a client's perceptions, the thoughts running through that person's mind, and the conclusions to which they are leading. Other theorists and therapists soon embraced and expanded their ideas and techniques.

How Do Cognitive Theorists Explain Abnormal Functioning?

According to cognitive theorists, abnormal functioning can result from several kinds of cognitive problems. Some people may make *assumptions* and adopt *attitudes* that are disturbing and inaccurate (Beck & Weishaar, 2011; Ellis, 2011). Philip Berman, for example, often seems to assume that his past history has locked him in his present situation. He believes that he was victimized by his parents and that he is now forever doomed by his past. He seems to approach all new experiences and relationships with expectations of failure and disaster.

Illogical thinking processes are another source of abnormal functioning, according to cognitive theorists. Beck, for example, has found that some people consistently think in illogical ways and keep arriving at self-defeating conclusions (Beck & Weishaar, 2011). As you will see in Chapter 8, he has identified a number of illogical thought processes regularly found in depression, such as *overgeneralization,* the drawing of broad negative conclusions on the basis of a single insignificant event. One depressed student couldn't remember the date of Columbus' third

YOUR OWN TEDIOUS THOUGHTS NEXT 200 MILES

BEK

voyage to America during a history class. Overgeneralizing, she spent the rest of the day in despair over her wide-ranging ignorance.

Cognitive Therapies

According to cognitive therapists, people with psychological disorders can overcome their problems by developing new, more functional ways of thinking. Because different forms of abnormality may involve different kinds of cognitive dysfunctioning, cognitive therapists have developed a number of strategies. Beck, for example, has developed an approach that is widely used, particularly in cases of depression (Beck & Weishaar, 2011).

In Beck's approach, called simply **cognitive therapy,** therapists help clients recognize the negative thoughts, biased interpretations, and errors in logic that dominate their thinking and, according to Beck, cause them to feel depressed. Therapists also guide clients to challenge their dysfunctional thoughts, try out new interpretations, and ultimately apply the new ways of thinking in their daily lives. As you will see in Chapter 8, people with depression who are treated with Beck's approach improve much more than those who receive no treatment.

How might your efforts to reason with a depressed friend differ from Beck's cognitive therapy strategies for people with depression?

In the excerpt that follows, a cognitive therapist guides a depressed 26-year-old graduate student to see the link between the way she interprets her experiences and the way she feels and to begin questioning the accuracy of her interpretations:

> *Therapist:* How do you understand it?
> *Patient:* I get depressed when things go wrong. Like when I fail a test.
> *Therapist:* How can failing a test make you depressed?
> *Patient:* Well, if I fail I'll never get into law school.
> *Therapist:* So failing the test means a lot to you. But if failing a test could drive people into clinical depression, wouldn't you expect everyone who failed the test to have a depression? . . . Did everyone who failed get depressed enough to require treatment?
> *Patient:* No, but it depends on how important the test was to the person.
> *Therapist:* Right, and who decides the importance?
> *Patient:* I do.
> *Therapist:* And so, what we have to examine is your way of viewing the test (or the way that you think about the test) and how it affects your chances of getting into law school. Do you agree?
> *Patient:* Right. . . .
> *Therapist:* Now what did failing mean?
> *Patient:* (Tearful) That I couldn't get into law school.
> *Therapist:* And what does that mean to you?
> *Patient:* That I'm just not smart enough.
> *Therapist:* Anything else?
> *Patient:* That I can never be happy.
> *Therapist:* And how do these thoughts make you feel?
> *Patient:* Very unhappy.
> *Therapist:* So it is the meaning of failing a test that makes you very unhappy. In fact, believing that you can never be happy is a powerful factor in producing unhappiness. So, you get yourself into a trap—by definition, failure to get into law school equals "I can never be happy."
>
> *(Beck et al., 1979, pp. 145–146)*

•**cognitive-behavioral therapies**• Therapy approaches that seek to help clients change both counterproductive behaviors and dysfunctional ways of thinking.

•**cognitive therapy**•A therapy developed by Aaron Beck that helps people recognize and change their faulty thinking processes.

BETWEEN THE LINES

In Their Words

"Help! I'm being held prisoner by my heredity and environment." ‹‹

Dennis Allen

Assessing the Cognitive Model

The cognitive model has had very broad appeal. In addition to a large number of cognitive-behavioral clinicians who apply both cognitive and learning principles in their work, many cognitive clinicians focus exclusively on client interpretations, attitudes, assumptions, and other cognitive processes. Altogether approximately 28 percent of today's clinical psychologists identify their approach as cognitive (Sharf, 2012; Prochaska & Norcross, 2010).

The cognitive model is popular for several reasons. First, it focuses on a process unique to human beings—the process of human thought—and many theorists from varied backgrounds find themselves drawn to a model that considers thought to be the primary cause of normal and abnormal behavior.

Cognitive theories also lend themselves to research. Investigators have found that people with psychological disorders often make the kinds of assumptions and errors in thinking the theorists claim (Ingram et al., 2007). Yet another reason for the popularity of this model is the impressive performance of cognitive and cognitive-behavioral therapies. They have proved very effective for treating depression, panic disorder, social phobia, and sexual dysfunctions, for example (Clark & Beck, 2012; Hollon & DiGiuseppe, 2011).

Nevertheless, the cognitive model, too, has its drawbacks. First, although disturbed cognitive processes are found in many forms of abnormality, their precise role has yet to be determined. The cognitions seen in psychologically troubled people could well be a result rather than a cause of their difficulties. Second, although cognitive and cognitive-behavioral therapies are clearly of help to many people, they do not help everyone. Is it enough simply to change cognitions? Can such changes make a general and lasting difference in the way people feel and behave? Moreover, a growing body of research suggests that the kinds of cognitive changes proposed by Beck and other cognitive therapists are not always possible to achieve (Sharf, 2012).

In response to such limitations, a new group of cognitive and cognitive-behavioral therapies, sometimes called the *new wave* of cognitive therapies, has emerged in recent years (Hollon & DiGiuseppe, 2011). These new approaches, such as the widely used *Acceptance and Commitment Therapy (ACT),* help clients to *accept* many of their problematic thoughts rather than judge them, act on them, or try fruitlessly to change them (Hayes & Lillis, 2012). The hope is that by recognizing such thoughts for what they are—just thoughts—clients will eventually be able to let them pass through their awareness without being particularly troubled by them.

As you will see in Chapter 5, ACT and other new-wave cognitive therapies often employ *mindfulness-based* techniques to help their clients achieve such acceptance. These techniques borrow heavily from a form of meditation called *mindfulness meditation,* which teaches individuals to pay attention to the thoughts and feelings that are flowing through their minds during meditation and to accept such thoughts in a nonjudgmental way. Early research indicates that ACT and other new-wave cognitive therapies are indeed often helpful in the treatment of anxiety and depression (Hayes & Lillis, 2012).

A final drawback of the cognitive model is that, like the other models you have read about, it is narrow in certain ways. Although cognition is a very special human dimension, it is still only one part of human functioning. Aren't human beings more than the sum of their thoughts, emotions, and behaviors? Shouldn't explanations of human functioning also consider broader issues, such as how people approach life, what value they extract from it, and how they deal with the question of life's meaning? This is the position of the humanistic-existential model.

The Humanistic-Existential Model

Philip Berman is more than the sum of his psychological conflicts, learned behaviors, or cognitions. Being human, he also has the ability to pursue philosophical goals such as self-awareness, strong values, a sense of meaning in life, and freedom of choice. According to humanistic and existential theorists, Philip's problems can be understood only in the light of such complex goals. Humanistic and existential theorists are often grouped together—in an approach known as the *humanistic-existential model*—because of their common focus on these broader dimensions of human existence. At the same time, there are important differences between them.

Humanists, the more optimistic of the two groups, believe that human beings are born with a natural tendency to be friendly, cooperative, and constructive. People, these theorists propose, are driven to **self-actualize**—that is, to fulfill this potential for goodness and growth. They can do so, however, only if they honestly recognize and accept their weaknesses as well as their strengths and establish satisfying personal values to live by. Humanists further suggest that self-actualization leads naturally to a concern for the welfare of others and to behavior that is loving, courageous, spontaneous, and independent (Maslow, 1970).

Existentialists agree that human beings must have an accurate awareness of themselves and live meaningful—they say "authentic"—lives in order to be psychologically well adjusted. These theorists do not believe, however, that people are naturally inclined to live positively. They believe that from birth we have total freedom, either to face up to our existence and give meaning to our lives or to shrink from that responsibility. Those who choose to "hide" from responsibility and choice will view themselves as helpless and may live empty, inauthentic, and dysfunctional lives as a result.

The humanistic and existential views of abnormality both date back to the 1940s. At that time Carl Rogers (1902–1987), often considered the pioneer of the humanistic perspective, developed **client-centered therapy,** a warm and supportive approach that contrasted sharply with the psychodynamic techniques of the day. He also proposed a theory of personality that paid little attention to irrational instincts and conflicts.

The existential view of personality and abnormality appeared during this same period. Many of its principles came from the ideas of nineteenth-century European existential philosophers who held that human beings are constantly defining and so giving meaning to their existence through their actions (Yalom & Josselson, 2011).

The humanistic and existential theories, and their uplifting implications, were extremely popular during the 1960s and 1970s, years of considerable soul-searching and social upheaval in Western society. They have since lost some of their popularity, but they continue to influence the ideas and work of many clinicians.

Rogers' Humanistic Theory and Therapy

According to Carl Rogers, the road to dysfunction begins in infancy (Raskin, Rogers, & Witty, 2011; Rogers, 1987, 1951). We all have a basic need to receive *positive regard* from the important people in our lives (primarily our parents). Those who receive *unconditional* (nonjudgmental) *positive regard* early in life are likely to develop *unconditional self-regard*. That is, they come to recognize their worth as persons, even while recognizing that they are not perfect. Such people are in a good position to actualize their positive potential.

Unfortunately, some children repeatedly are made to feel that they are not worthy of positive regard. As a result, they acquire *conditions of worth,* standards that tell them they are lovable and acceptable only when they conform to certain guidelines. To maintain positive self-regard, these people have to look at themselves very selectively, denying or distorting thoughts and actions that do not measure up to their conditions of worth. They thus acquire a distorted view of themselves and their experiences. They do not know what they are truly feeling, what they genuinely need, or what values and goals would be meaningful for them. Problems in functioning are then inevitable.

Rogers might view Philip Berman as a man who has gone astray. Rather than striving to fulfill his positive human potential, he drifts from job to job and relationship to relationship. In every interaction he is defending himself, trying to interpret events in ways he can live with, usually blaming his problems on other people. Nevertheless, his basic negative self-image continually reveals itself. Rogers would probably link this problem to the critical ways Philip was treated by his mother throughout his childhood.

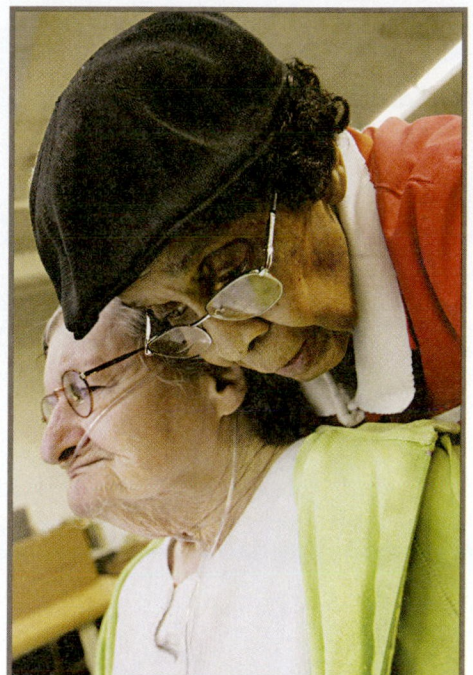

AP Photo/Columbus Daily Dispatch, Eric Albrecht

Actualizing the self
Humanists suggest that self-actualized people show concern for the welfare of humanity. This 89-year-old social services volunteer (right), for example, has participated for the past 20 years as a companion to elderly persons with mental retardation and developmental disabilities. The self-actualized are also thought to be highly creative, spontaneous, independent, and humorous.

•**self-actualization**•The humanistic process by which people fulfill their potential for goodness and growth.

•**client-centered therapy**•The humanistic therapy developed by Carl Rogers in which clinicians try to help clients by conveying acceptance, accurate empathy, and genuineness.

Clinicians who practice Rogers' client-centered therapy try to create a supportive climate in which clients feel able to look at themselves honestly and acceptingly (Raskin et al., 2011). The therapist must display three important qualities throughout the therapy—*unconditional positive regard* (full and warm acceptance for the client), *accurate empathy* (skillful listening and restatements), and *genuineness* (sincere communication). In the following classic case, the therapist uses all these qualities to move the client toward greater self-awareness:

> **Client:** Yes, I know I shouldn't worry about it, but I do. Lots of things—money, people, clothes. In classes I feel that everyone's just waiting for a chance to jump on me.... When I meet somebody I wonder what he's actually thinking of me. Then later on I wonder how I match up to what he's come to think of me.
>
> **Therapist:** You feel that you're pretty responsive to the opinions of other people.
>
> **Client:** Yes, but it's things that shouldn't worry me.
>
> **Therapist:** You feel that it's the sort of thing that shouldn't be upsetting, but they do get you pretty much worried anyway.
>
> **Client:** Just some of them. Most of those things do worry me because they're true. The ones I told you, that is. But there are lots of little things that aren't true.... Things just seem to be piling up, piling up inside of me.... It's a feeling that things were crowding up and they were going to burst.
>
> **Therapist:** You feel that it's a sort of oppression with some frustration and that things are just unmanageable.
>
> **Client:** In a way, but some things just seem illogical. I'm afraid I'm not very clear here but that's the way it comes.
>
> **Therapist:** That's all right. You say just what you think.
>
> *(Snyder, 1947, pp. 2–24)*

In such an atmosphere, clients are expected to feel accepted by their therapists. They then may be able to look at themselves with honesty and acceptance. They begin to value their own emotions, thoughts, and behaviors, and so they are freed from the insecurities and doubts that prevent self-actualization.

Unconditional positive regard
Carl Rogers argued that clients must receive unconditional positive regard in order to feel better about themselves and to overcome their problems. In this spirit, a number of organizations now arrange for individuals to have close relationships with gentle and nonjudgmental animals. Here a Bosnian child hugs her horse during rehabilitation therapy at the Therapeutic and Leisure center Kakrinje near Sarajevo.

AP Photo/Amel Emric

Client-centered therapy has not fared very well in research (Sharf, 2012). Although some studies show that participants who receive this therapy improve more than control participants, many other studies have failed to find any such advantage. All the same, Rogers' therapy has had a positive influence on clinical practice (Raskin et al., 2011). It was one of the first major alternatives to psychodynamic therapy, and it helped open up the clinical field to new approaches (see *PsychWatch* on page 69). Rogers also helped pave the way for *psychologists* to practice psychotherapy, which had previously been considered the exclusive territory of psychiatrists. And his commitment to clinical research helped promote the systematic study of treatment. Approximately 1 percent of today's clinical psychologists, 1 percent of social workers, and 3 percent of counseling psychologists report that they employ the client-centered approach (Sharf, 2012; Prochaska & Norcross, 2010).

Gestalt Theory and Therapy

Gestalt therapy, another humanistic approach, was developed in the 1950s by a charismatic clinician named Frederick (Fritz) Perls (1893–1970). Gestalt therapists, like client-centered therapists, guide their clients toward self-recognition and self-acceptance (Yontef & Jacobs, 2011). But unlike client-centered therapists, they often try to achieve this goal by challenging and even frustrating their clients. Some of Perls' favorite techniques were skillful frustration, role playing, and numerous rules and exercises.

In the technique of *skillful frustration,* gestalt therapists refuse to meet their clients' expectations or demands. This use of frustration is meant to help people see how often they try to manipulate others into meeting their needs. In the technique of *role playing,* the therapists instruct clients to act out various roles. A person may be told to be another person, an object, an alternative self, or even a part of the body. Role playing can become intense, as individuals are encouraged to express emotions fully. Many cry out, scream, kick, or pound. Through this experience they may come to "own" (accept) feelings that previously made them uncomfortable.

Perls also developed a list of *rules* to ensure that clients will look at themselves more closely. In some versions of gestalt therapy, for example, clients may be required to use "I" language rather than "it" language. They must say, "I am frightened" rather than "The situation is frightening." Yet another common rule requires clients to stay in the *here and now.* They have needs now, are hiding their needs now, and must observe them now.

Approximately 1 percent of clinical psychologists and other kinds of clinicians describe themselves as gestalt therapists (Sharf, 2012; Prochaska & Norcross, 2010). Because they believe that subjective experiences and self-awareness cannot be measured objectively, proponents of gestalt therapy have not often performed controlled research on this approach (Yontef & Jacobs, 2011; Strümpfel, 2006, 2004).

Spiritual Views and Interventions

For most of the twentieth century, clinical scientists viewed religion as a negative—or at best neutral—factor in mental health (Van Praag, 2011; Day, 2010). In the early 1900s, for example, Freud argued that religious beliefs were defense mechanisms, "born from man's need to make his helplessness tolerable" (1961, p. 23). This negative view of religion now seems to be ending, however. During the past decade, many articles and books linking spiritual issues to clinical treatment have been published, and the ethical codes of psychologists, psychiatrists, and counselors have each concluded that religion is a type of diversity that mental health professionals must respect (Peteet, Lu, & Narrow, 2011).

Researchers have learned that spirituality does, in fact, often correlate with psychological health. In particular, studies have examined the

? **What various explanations might account for the correlation between spirituality and mental health?**

•gestalt therapy• The humanistic therapy developed by Fritz Perls in which clinicians actively move clients toward self-recognition and self-acceptance by using techniques such as role playing and self-discovery exercises.

Beating the blues
Gestalt therapists often guide clients to express their needs and feelings in their full intensity by banging on pillows, crying out, kicking, or pounding things. Building on these techniques, a new approach, *drum therapy,* teaches clients, such as this woman, how to beat drums in order to help release traumatic memories, change beliefs, and feel more liberated.

mental health of people who are devout and who view God as warm, caring, helpful, and dependable. Repeatedly, these individuals are found to be less lonely, pessimistic, depressed, or anxious than people without any religious beliefs or those who view God as cold and unresponsive (Day, 2010; Loewenthal, 2007; Koenig, 2002). Such individuals also seem to cope better with major life stressors—from illness to war—and to attempt suicide less often. In addition, they are less likely to abuse drugs.

Do such correlations indicate that spirituality helps *produce* greater mental health? Not necessarily. As you'll recall from Chapter 2, correlations do not indicate causation. It may be, for example, that a sense of optimism leads to more spirituality, and that, independently, optimism contributes to greater mental health. Regardless of how the correlation between spirituality and mental health should be interpreted, many therapists now make a point of including spiritual issues when they treat religious clients (Aten, McMinn, & Worthington, 2011; Worthington, 2011), and some further encourage clients to use their spiritual resources to help them cope with current stressors (Galanter, 2010).

Spirituality and science

A few years ago, Tibetan spiritual leader the Dalai Lama (right) met with professor of psychiatry Zindel Segal (left) and other mental health researchers at a conference examining possible ties between science, mental health, and spirituality. Such meetings indicate that the alienation between the clinical field and religion seems to be ending.

Existential Theories and Therapy

Like humanists, existentialists believe that psychological dysfunctioning is caused by self-deception; existentialists, however, are talking about a kind of self-deception in which people hide from life's responsibilities and fail to recognize that it is up to them to give meaning to their lives. According to existentialists, many people become overwhelmed by the pressures of present-day society and so look to others for explanations, guidance, and authority. They overlook their personal freedom of choice and avoid responsibility for their lives and decisions (Yalom & Josselson, 2011). Such people are left with empty, inauthentic lives. Their dominant emotions are anxiety, frustration, boredom, alienation, and depression.

Existentialists might view Philip Berman as a man who feels overwhelmed by the forces of society. He sees his parents as "rich, powerful, and selfish," and he perceives teachers, acquaintances, and employers as oppressing. He fails to appreciate his choices in life and his capacity for finding meaning and direction. Quitting becomes a habit with him—he leaves job after job, ends every romantic relationship, and flees difficult situations.

In **existential therapy** people are encouraged to accept responsibility for their lives and for their problems. Therapists try to help clients recognize their freedom so that they may choose a different course and live with greater meaning (Yalom & Josselson, 2011; Schneider & Krug, 2010). The precise techniques used in existential therapy vary from clinician to clinician. At the same time, most existential therapists place great emphasis on the *relationship* between therapist and client and try to create an atmosphere of honesty, hard work, and shared learning and growth.

•**existential therapy**•A therapy that encourages clients to accept responsibility for their lives and to live with greater meaning and value.

> Patient: I don't know why I keep coming here. All I do is tell you the same thing over and over. I'm not getting anywhere.
> Doctor: I'm getting tired of hearing the same thing over and over, too.
> Patient: Maybe I'll stop coming.
> Doctor: It's certainly your choice.
> Patient: What do you think I should do?
> Doctor: What do you want to do?
> Patient: I want to get better.
> Doctor: I don't blame you.

(continued on p. 70)

Cybertherapy: Surfing for Help

Over the past few decades, computer-based treatment, or *cybertherapy,* has come to complement, and in some instances replace, traditional face-to-face therapy. This growth has closely paralleled advances in computer technology and the growth of digital communication.

The clinical field's first journey into the digital world took the form of *computer software therapy programs* (Harklute, 2010; Tantam, 2006). These programs, which continue to be popular, seek to reduce emotional distress through typed conversations between human "clients" and their computers. The computer software programs try to apply the basic principles of actual therapy. One program, for example, helps people state their problems in "if-then" statements, a technique similar to that used by cognitive therapists.

Advocates of computer software therapy programs argue that many people find it easier to disclose sensitive personal information to a computer than to a therapist, and indeed research indicates that some of the programs are helpful to a degree (Harklute, 2010; Lange et al., 2004). Computer experts currently are working to develop software programs for recognizing clients' faces and emotions. This development will likely increase the versatility and appeal of computer software therapy programs.

Another form of cybertherapy, *e-mail therapy,* has exploded in popularity over the past decade. Thousands of therapists have set up online services that invite people with problems to e-mail their questions and concerns (Mulhauser, 2010; Chester & Glass, 2006). These services can cost as much as $2 to $3 per minute. Services of this kind have raised concerns about the quality of care and about confidentiality (Fenichel, 2011). Many e-mail therapists do not even have advanced clinical training. Nevertheless, the use of e-mail therapy continues to grow by leaps and bounds.

Also on the rise is *visual e-therapy* (Hoffman, 2011; Strong, 2010), which more closely mimics the conventional therapy experience. A client sets up an appointment with a therapist and, with

Treatment of the future? A young man wears electrodes on his scalp to control the actions of his avatar in a virtual environment. Several forms of cybertherapy use avatars to help clients interact with and better relate to key people in their lives.

the aid of Skype or a webcam, the two proceed to have a face-to-face session. The advantage? Clients can receive counseling conveniently while sitting at home or in their offices, and they can have access to a counselor who is located even thousands of miles away. The key disadvantage? Once again, quality control (Fenichel, 2011).

Still more common than either e-mail therapy or visual e-therapies are Internet chat groups and "virtual" support groups. Tens of thousands of these groups are currently "in session" around the clock for everything from depression to substance abuse, anxiety, and eating disorders (Maheu, 2010; Moskowitz, 2008, 2001). Like in-person self-help groups, the online chat groups provide opportunities for people with similar problems to communicate with each other, freely trading information, advice, and empathy. Of course, unlike members of in-person self-help groups, people who choose Internet chat group therapy do not know who is on the other end of the computer connection or whether the advice they receive is well intentioned or at all appropriate.

A relatively new feature in cybertherapy is the use of *avatars,* three-dimensional graphical representations of the users and/or other key persons in their lives (Thomas, 2011; Carey, 2010). Some computer software therapy programs, for example, have users interact not only with printed words

or verbalizations that are being generated by the program but also with on-screen virtual human figures who ask questions such as "What kinds of things do you dislike about yourself?", nod sympathetically when users offer self-criticisms, and reinforce certain user statements with smiles or encouraging words.

In another use of avatars, some real-life therapists now guide their clients to enter virtual environments on their computers, acquire virtual bodies, and interact with animated figures who resemble their parents, bosses, or friends—in situations that can feel very real. Theoretically, experiences in virtual worlds of this kind can help clients change their behaviors or emotional reactions in the real world (Thompson, 2011; Carey, 2010).

The use of avatars in therapy is still being developed and researched, and the actual effectiveness of such approaches has yet to be determined. At the same time, efforts in this direction, along with the other forms of cybertherapy, serve as reminders that digital technology's impact on the mental health field is as powerful and potentially useful as its impact on most other fields in our society.

"Just remember, son, it doesn't matter whether you win or lose—unless you want Daddy's love."

Patient: If you think I should stay, ok, I will.
Doctor: You want me to tell you to stay?
Patient: You know what's best; you're the doctor.
Doctor: Do I act like a doctor?

(Keen, 1970, p. 200)

Existential therapists do not believe that experimental methods can adequately test the effectiveness of their treatments. To them, research dehumanizes individuals by reducing them to test measures. Not surprisingly, then, very little controlled research has been devoted to the effectiveness of this approach (Schneider & Krug, 2010). Nevertheless, around 1 percent of today's clinical psychologists use an approach that is primarily existential (Sharf, 2012; Prochaska & Norcross, 2010).

Assessing the Humanistic-Existential Model

The humanistic-existential model appeals to many people in and out of the clinical field. In recognizing the special challenges of human existence, humanistic and existential theorists tap into an aspect of psychological life that typically is missing from the other models (Watson et al., 2011; Cain, 2007). Moreover, the factors that they say are essential to effective functioning—self-acceptance, personal values, personal meaning, and personal choice—are certainly lacking in many people with psychological disturbances.

The optimistic tone of the humanistic-existential model is also an attraction. Indeed, such optimism meshes quite well with the goals and principles of positive psychology, a current movement described in Chapter 1. Theorists who follow the principles of the humanistic-existential model offer great hope when they assert that, despite past and present events, we can make our own choices, determine our own destiny, and accomplish much. Still another attractive feature of the model is its emphasis on health. Unlike clinicians from some of the other models who see individuals as patients with psychological illnesses, humanists and existentialists view them simply as people who have yet to fulfill their potential.

At the same time, the humanistic-existential focus on abstract issues of human fulfillment gives rise to a major problem from a scientific point of view: These issues are difficult to research. In fact, with the notable exception of Rogers, who tried to investigate his clinical methods carefully, humanists and existentialists have traditionally rejected the use of empirical research. This antiresearch position is just now beginning to change. Humanistic and existential researchers have conducted several recent studies that use appropriate control groups and statistical analyses, and they have found that their therapies can be beneficial in some cases (Schneider & Krug, 2010; Strümpfel, 2006). This newfound interest in research should lead to important insights about the merits of this model in the coming years.

The Sociocultural Model: Family-Social and Multicultural Perspectives

Philip Berman is also a social and cultural being. He is surrounded by people and by institutions, he is a member of a family and a cultural group, he participates in social relationships, and he holds cultural values. Such forces are always operating upon Philip, setting rules and expectations that guide or pressure him, helping to shape his behaviors, thoughts, and emotions.

According to the *sociocultural model,* abnormal behavior is best understood in light of the broad forces that influence an individual. What are the norms of the individual's society and culture? What roles does the person play in the social environment? What

BETWEEN THE LINES

Pressures of Poverty

94 Number of victims of violent crime per 1,000 poor persons ‹‹

50 Number of victims per 1,000 middle-income people ‹‹

40 Number of victims per 1,000 wealthy people ‹‹

(U.S. Bureau of Justice Statistics, 2011)

kind of family structure or cultural background is the person a part of? And how do other people view and react to him or her? In fact, the sociocultural model is comprised of two major perspectives—the *family-social perspective* and the *multicultural perspective*.

How Do Family-Social Theorists Explain Abnormal Functioning?

Proponents of the family-social perspective argue that clinical theorists should concentrate on those broad forces that operate *directly* on an individual as he or she moves through life—that is, family relationships, social interactions, and community events. They believe that such forces help account for both normal and abnormal behavior, and they pay particular attention to three kinds of factors: *social labels and roles, social networks,* and *family structure and communication.*

Social Labels and Roles Abnormal functioning can be influenced greatly by the labels and roles assigned to troubled people (Walker & Shapiro, 2010; Link et al., 2004, 2001). When people stray from the norms of their society, the society calls them deviant and, in many cases, "mentally ill." Such labels tend to stick. Moreover, when people are viewed in particular ways, reacted to as "crazy," and perhaps even encouraged to act sick, they gradually learn to accept and play the assigned social role. Ultimately the label seems appropriate.

A famous study called "On Being Sane in Insane Places" by clinical investigator David Rosenhan (1973) supports this position. Eight normal people, actually colleagues of Rosenhan, presented themselves at various mental hospitals, complaining that they had been hearing voices say the words "empty," "hollow," and "thud." On the basis of this complaint alone, each was diagnosed as having schizophrenia and admitted.

Moreover, the "pseudopatients" had a hard time convincing others that they were well once they had been given the diagnostic label. Their hospitalizations ranged from 7 to 52 days, even though they behaved normally and stopped reporting symptoms as soon as they were admitted. In addition, the label "schizophrenia" kept influencing the way the staff viewed and dealt with them. For example, one pseudopatient who paced the corridor out of boredom was, in clinical notes, described as "nervous." Overall, the pseudopatients came to feel powerless, invisible, and bored.

Social Connections and Supports Family-social theorists are also concerned with the social environments in which people operate, including their social and professional relationships. How well do they communicate with others? What kind of signals do they send to or receive from others? Researchers have often found ties between deficiencies in social networks and a person's functioning (Gask et al., 2011; Vega et al., 2011; Paykel, 2006, 2003). They have observed, for example, that people who are isolated and lack social support or intimacy in their lives are more likely to become depressed when under stress and to remain depressed longer than are people with supportive spouses or warm friendships.

Some clinical theorists believe that people who are unwilling or unable to communicate and develop relationships in their everyday lives will often find adequate social contacts online, using social networking sites like Facebook. Although this may be true for some such individuals, research suggests that persons' online relationships tend to parallel their offline relationships (Dolan, 2011). One survey of 172 college students, for example, found that those students with the most friends on Facebook also were particularly social offline, while those who were less willing to communicate with other people offline also tended to initiate far fewer relationships on Facebook (Sheldon, 2008).

BETWEEN THE LINES

Cultural Oversight

Despite the growing cultural diversity throughout the United States, minority group members are remarkably underrepresented as participants in psychotropic drug treatment studies. A few years back, when UCLA researchers reviewed the best available studies of drugs for mood disorders, schizophrenia, and attention-deficit/hyperactivity disorder, they found that only 8 percent of the patients studied were members of minority groups. Of almost 44,000 patients in antidepressant studies, only 2 were Hispanic; of almost 3,000 patients with schizophrenia, 3 were Asian; and of 825 patients in bipolar disorder drug studies, none were Hispanic or Asian (Vedantam, 2005). ‹‹

"I used to call people, then I got into e-mailing, then texting, and now I just ignore everyone."

•**family systems theory**•A theory that views the family as a system of interacting parts whose interactions exhibit consistent patterns and unstated rules.

•**group therapy**•A therapy format in which a group of people with similar problems meet together with a therapist to work on those problems.

•**self-help group**•A group made up of people with similar problems who help and support one another without the direct leadership of a clinician. Also called a *mutual help group*.

•**family therapy**•A therapy format in which the therapist meets with all members of a family and helps them to change in therapeutic ways.

Family Structure and Communication

Of course, one of the important social networks for an individual is his or her family. According to **family systems theory,** the family is a system of interacting parts—the family members—who interact with one another in consistent ways and follow rules unique to each family (Chabot, 2011; Goldenberg & Goldenberg, 2011). Family systems theorists believe that the *structure* and *communication* patterns of some families actually force individual members to behave in a way that otherwise seems abnormal. If the members were to behave normally, they would severely strain the family's usual manner of operation and would actually increase their own and their family's turmoil.

Family systems theory holds that certain family systems are particularly likely to produce abnormal functioning in individual members. Some families, for example, have an *enmeshed* structure in which the members are grossly overinvolved in each other's activities, thoughts, and feelings. Children from this kind of family may have great difficulty becoming independent in life (Santiseban et al., 2001). Some families display *disengagement,* which is marked by very rigid boundaries between the members. Children from these families may find it hard to function in a group or to give or request support (Corey, 2012, 2004).

How might family theorists react to writer Leo Tolstoy's famous claim that "every unhappy family is unhappy in its own fashion"?

Philip Berman's angry and impulsive personal style might be seen as the product of a disturbed family structure. According to family systems theorists, the whole family—mother, father, Philip, and his brother Arnold—relate in such a way as to maintain Philip's behavior. Family theorists might be particularly interested in the conflict between Philip's mother and father and the imbalance between their parental roles. They might see Philip's behavior as both a reaction to and stimulus for his parents' behaviors. With Philip acting out the role of the misbehaving child, or scapegoat, his parents may have little need or time to question their own relationship.

Family systems theorists would also seek to clarify the precise nature of Philip's relationship with each parent. Is he enmeshed with his mother and/or disengaged from his father? They would look too at the rules governing the sibling relationship in the family, the relationship between the parents and Philip's brother, and the nature of parent-child relationships in previous generations of the family.

Family-Social Treatments

The family-social perspective has helped spur the growth of several treatment approaches, including *group therapy, family* and *couple therapy,* and *community treatment.* Therapists of any orientation may work with clients in these various formats, applying the techniques and principles of their preferred models. However, more and more of the clinicians who use these formats believe that psychological problems emerge in family and social settings and are best treated in such settings, and they include special sociocultural strategies in their work.

Group Therapy Thousands of therapists specialize in **group therapy,** a format in which a therapist meets with a group of clients who have similar problems. Indeed, one survey of clinical psychologists revealed that almost one-third of them devoted some portion of their practice to group therapy (Norcross & Goldfried, 2005). Typically, members of a therapy group meet together with a therapist and discuss the problems of one or more of the people in the group. Together they develop important insights, build social skills, strengthen feelings of self-worth, and share useful information or advice (Burlingame & Baldwin, 2011). Many groups

Why might group therapy actually be more helpful to some people with psychological problems than individual therapy?

Sharing and supporting
Clients often benefit from group therapy or self-help groups. Many such groups focus on particular client populations, such as bereaved persons, abused spouses, or people with social skill deficits.

are created with particular client populations in mind; for example, there are groups for people with alcoholism, for those who are physically handicapped, and for people who are divorced, abused, or bereaved.

Research suggests that group therapy is of help to many clients, often as helpful as individual therapy (Burlingame & Baldwin, 2011). The group format also has been used for purposes that are educational rather than therapeutic, such as "consciousness raising" and spiritual inspiration.

A format similar to group therapy is the **self-help group** (or **mutual help group**). Here people who have similar problems (for example, bereavement, substance abuse, illness, unemployment, or divorce) come together to help and support one another without the direct leadership of a professional clinician (White & Madara, 2010; NSDUH, 2009; Mueller et al., 2007). According to estimates, there are now between 500,000 and 3 million such groups in the United States alone, attended each year by as many as 3 to 4 percent of the population.

Family Therapy **Family therapy** was first introduced in the 1950s. A therapist meets with all members of a family, points out problem behaviors and interactions, and helps the whole family to change its ways (Goldenberg & Goldenberg, 2011; Kaslow, 2011). Here, the entire family is viewed as the unit under treatment, even if only one of the members receives a clinical diagnosis. The following is a typical interaction between family members and a therapist:

Tommy sat motionless in a chair gazing out the window. He was fourteen and a bit small for his age. . . . Sissy was eleven. She was sitting on the couch between her Mom and Dad with a smile on her face. Across from them sat Ms. Fargo, the family therapist.

Ms. Fargo spoke. "Could you be a little more specific about the changes you have seen in Tommy and when they came about?"

Mrs. Davis answered first. "Well, I guess it was about two years ago. Tommy started getting in fights at school. When we talked to him at home he said it was none of our business. He became moody and disobedient. He wouldn't do anything that we wanted him to. He began to act mean to his sister and even hit her."

"What about the fights at school?" Ms. Fargo asked.

•couple therapy•A therapy format in which the therapist works with two people who share a long-term relationship. Also called *marital therapy.*

•community mental health treatment• A treatment approach that emphasizes community care.

This time it was Mr. Davis who spoke first. "Ginny was more worried about them than I was. I used to fight a lot when I was in school and I think it is normal. . . . But I was very respectful to my parents, especially my Dad. If I ever got out of line he would smack me one."

"Have you ever had to hit Tommy?" Ms. Fargo inquired softly.

"Sure, a couple of times, but it didn't seem to do any good."

All at once Tommy seemed to be paying attention, his eyes riveted on his father. "Yeah, he hit me a lot, for no reason at all!"

"Now, that's not true, Thomas." Mrs. Davis has a scolding expression on her face. "If you behaved yourself a little better you wouldn't get hit. Ms. Fargo, I can't say that I am in favor of the hitting, but I understand sometimes how frustrating it may be for Bob."

"You don't know how frustrating it is for me, honey." Bob seemed upset. "You don't have to work all day at the office and then come home to contend with all of this. Sometimes I feel like I don't even want to come home."

Ginny gave him a hard stare. "You think things at home are easy all day? I could use some support from you. You think all you have to do is earn the money and I will do everything else. Well, I am not about to do that anymore." . . .

Mrs. Davis began to cry. "I just don't know what to do anymore. Things just seem so hopeless. Why can't people be nice in this family anymore? I don't think I am asking too much, am I?"

Ms. Fargo . . . looked at each person briefly and was sure to make eye contact. "There seems to be a lot going on. . . . I think we are going to need to understand a lot of things to see why this is happening."

(Sheras & Worchel, 1979, pp. 108–110)

Today's TV families

Unlike television viewers of the 1950s, when problem-free families like the Nelsons (of *Ozzie & Harriet*) and the Andersons (of *Father Knows Best*) ruled the airwaves, today's viewers prefer more complex, sometimes dysfunctional, families, like the Pritchetts, whose trials and tribulations are on display in ABC's popular series *Modern Family.*

Danny Feld/ABC via Getty Images

Family therapists may follow any of the major theoretical models, but many of them adopt the principles of *family systems theory* (Chabot, 2012). Today 3 percent of all clinical psychologists, 14 percent of social workers, and 1 percent of psychiatrists identify themselves mainly as *family systems therapists* (Sharf, 2012; Prochaska & Norcross, 2010).

As you read earlier, family systems theory holds that each family has its own rules, structure, and communication patterns that shape the individual members' behavior. In one family systems approach, *structural family therapy,* therapists try to change the family power structure, the roles each person plays, and the relationships between members (Goldenberg & Goldenberg, 2011; Minuchin, 2007, 1997, 1987, 1974). In another, *conjoint family therapy,* therapists try to help members recognize and change harmful patterns of communication (Sharf, 2012; Satir, 1987, 1967, 1964).

Family therapies of various kinds are often helpful to individuals, although research has not yet clarified how helpful (Goldenberg & Goldenberg, 2011; Kaslow, 2011). Some studies have found that as many as 65 percent of individuals treated with family approaches improve, while other studies suggest much lower success rates. Nor has any one type of family therapy emerged as consistently more helpful than the others (Alexander et al., 2002).

Couple Therapy In **couple therapy,** or **marital therapy,** the therapist works with two individuals who are in a long-term relationship. Often they are husband and wife, but the couple need not be married or even living together. Like family therapy, couple therapy often focuses on the structure and communication patterns occurring in the relationship (Baucom et al., 2012, 2010, 2009; Gurman & Snyder, 2011). A couple approach may also be used when a child's psychological problems are traced to problems in the parents' relationship.

Although some degree of conflict exists in any long-term relationship, many adults in our society experience serious marital discord. The divorce rate in Canada, the United States, and Europe is now close to 50 percent of the marriage rate (U.S. Census Bureau, 2011). Many couples who live together without marrying apparently have similar levels of difficulty (Harway, 2005).

Couple therapy, like family and group therapy, may follow the principles of any of the major therapy orientations. *Cognitive-behavioral couple therapy,* for example, uses many techniques from the cognitive and behavioral perspectives (Baucom et al., 2012, 2010; Gurman, 2003). Therapists help spouses recognize and change problem behaviors largely by teaching specific problem-solving and communication skills. A broader, more sociocultural version, called *integrative couple therapy,* further helps partners accept behaviors that they cannot change and embrace the whole relationship nevertheless (Christensen et al., 2010, 2006). Partners are asked to see such behaviors as an understandable result of basic differences between them.

Couples treated by couple therapy seem to show greater improvement in their relationships than couples with similar problems who fail to receive treatment, but no one form of couple therapy stands out as superior to others (Gurman & Snyder, 2011; Christensen et al., 2010). Although two-thirds of treated couples experience improved marital functioning by the end of therapy, fewer than half of those who are treated achieve "distress-free" or "happy" relationships. One-fourth of all treated couples eventually separate or divorce.

Community Treatment

Community mental health treatment programs allow clients, particularly those with severe psychological difficulties, to receive treatment in familiar social surroundings as they try to recover. In 1963 President John F. Kennedy called for such a "bold new approach" to the treatment of mental disorders—a community approach that would enable most people with psychological problems to receive services from nearby agencies rather than distant facilities or institutions. Congress passed the Community Mental Health Act soon after, launching the community mental health movement across the United States. Community-based treatments, including community day programs and residential services, continue to be a major part of today's efforts to help people with severe mental disorders (Daly, 2010). A number of other countries have launched similar community movements over the past several decades.

As you read in Chapter 1, a key principle of community treatment is *prevention.* Here clinicians actively reach out to clients rather than wait for them to seek treatment. Research suggests that such efforts are often very successful (Cummings & Schatz, 2012; Juhnke et al., 2011; Hage et al., 2007). Community workers recognize three types of prevention, which they call *primary, secondary,* and *tertiary.*

Primary prevention consists of efforts to improve community attitudes and policies. Its goal is to prevent psychological disorders altogether (Heitman et al., 2012). Community workers may, for example, consult with a local school board, offer public workshops on stress reduction, or construct Web sites on how to cope effectively.

Secondary prevention consists of identifying and treating psychological disorders in the early stages, before they become serious. Community workers may work with teachers, ministers, or police to help them recognize the early signs of psychological dysfunction and teach them how to help people find treatment. Similarly, hundreds of mental health Web sites provide this same kind of information to family members, teachers, and the like.

The goal of *tertiary prevention* is to provide effective treatment as soon as it is needed so that moderate or severe disorders do not become long-term problems. Today community agencies across the United States successfully offer tertiary care for millions of people with moderate psychological problems, but, as you read in Chapter 1, they often

The community way
People with mental health challenges or developmental disabilities are taught computer and broader life skills at the Queens Community Center, a program in New York City funded by Catholic Charities.

Najlah Feanny/Corbis

fail to provide the services needed by hundreds of thousands with severe disturbances (Althouse, 2010). One of the reasons for this failure is lack of funding, an issue that you will read about in later chapters (Weisman, 2004).

An unacceptable difference
Dressed in traditional American Indian clothing, a high school student from the Mescalero Apache Reservation in New Mexico testifies before Congress on "The Preventable Epidemic: Youth Suicides and the Urgent Need for Mental Health Care Resources in Indian Country."

How Do Multicultural Theorists Explain Abnormal Functioning?

Culture refers to the set of values, attitudes, beliefs, history, and behaviors shared by a group of people and communicated from one generation to the next (Matsumoto & Hwang, 2012, 2011; Matsumoto, 2007, 2001). We are, without question, a society of multiple cultures. Indeed, by the year 2050, members of racial and ethnic minority groups in the United States will, collectively, outnumber white Americans (Kaiser Family Foundation, 2010; U.S. Census Bureau, 2010).

Partly in response to this growing diversity, the **multicultural,** or **culturally diverse, perspective** has emerged (Comas-Diaz, 2011; Jackson, 2006). Multicultural psychologists seek to understand how culture, race, ethnicity, gender, and similar factors affect behavior and thought and how people of different cultures, races, and genders differ psychologically (Alegria et al., 2012, 2007, 2004; Matsumoto & van de Vijer, 2011). Today's multicultural view is different from past—less enlightened—cultural perspectives: it does not imply that members of racial, ethnic, and other minority groups are in some way inferior or culturally deprived in comparison with a majority population. Rather, the model holds that an individual's behavior, whether normal or abnormal, is best understood when examined in the light of that individual's unique cultural context, from the values of that culture to the special external pressures faced by members of the culture.

The groups in the United States that have received the most attention from multicultural researchers are ethnic and racial minority groups (African American, Hispanic American, American Indian, and Asian American groups) and groups such as economically disadvantaged persons, homosexual individuals, and women (although women are not technically a minority group). Each of these groups is subjected to special pressures in American society that may contribute to feelings of stress and, in some cases, to abnormal functioning. Researchers have learned, for example, that psychological abnormality, especially severe psychological abnormality, is indeed more common among poorer people than among wealthier people (Kim & Evans, 2011; Sareen et al., 2011) (see Figure 3-6). Perhaps the pressures of poverty explain this relationship.

Figure 3-6

Poverty and mental health Recent surveys in the United States find that people with low annual incomes (below $20,000) have a greater risk of experiencing mental disorders than do those with higher incomes (above $70,000). For example, 10 percent of low-income people experience persistent symptoms of anxiety, compared to 6 percent of higher-income people (Sareen et al., 2011).

Of course, membership in these various groups overlaps. Many members of minority groups, for example, also live in poverty. The higher rates of crime, unemployment, overcrowding, and homelessness; the inferior medical care; and the limited educational opportunities typically experienced by poor persons may place great stress on many members of such minority groups (Carlo, Crockett, & Carranza, 2011; Miller et al., 2011).

Multicultural researchers have also noted that the prejudice and discrimination faced by many minority groups may contribute to various forms of abnormal functioning (Guimón,

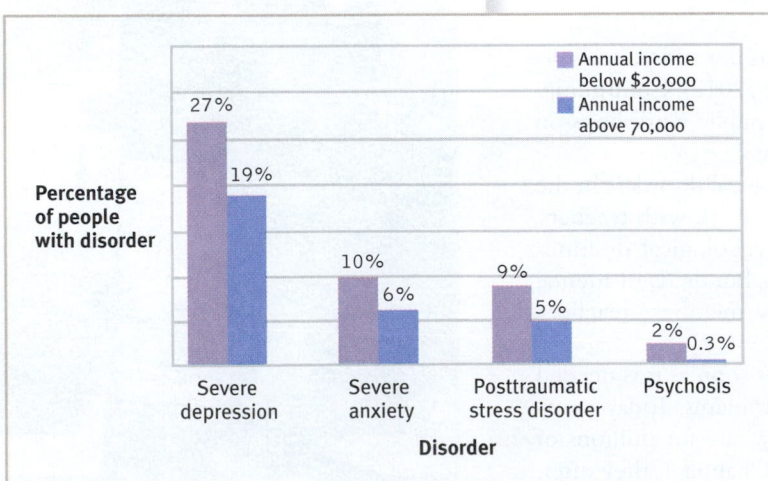

Percentage of people with disorder

Annual income below $20,000
Annual income above 70,000

Severe depression: 27% / 19%
Severe anxiety: 10% / 6%
Posttraumatic stress disorder: 9% / 5%
Psychosis: 2% / 0.3%

Disorder

table: 3-3

Percentage of Ethnic/Minority Populations Experiencing Psychological Difficulties

	"Serious Psychological Distress"	"Extreme Sadness"	"Constant Nervousness"	"Constant Restlessness"
White American Population	2.8%	2.4%	3.8%	5.2%
African American Population	3.7%	3.7%	2.9%	3.7%
Hispanic American Population	3.3%	4.9%	4.5%	5.1%
American Indian Population	4.7%	7.4%	8.8%	15.4%

Source: CDCP, 2011; HHS, 2009.

2010; Carter, 2007; Nelson, 2006). Women in Western society receive diagnoses of anxiety disorders and of depression at least twice as often as men (Jeglic & Murphy-Eberenz, 2012). Similarly, African Americans, Hispanic Americans, and American Indians are more likely than white Americans to experience serious psychological distress or extreme sadness (see Table 3-3). American Indians also display exceptionally high alcoholism and suicide rates (CDCP, 2011; Beals et al., 2005). Although many factors may combine to produce these differences, racial and sexual prejudice and the problems they pose may contribute to abnormal patterns of tension, unhappiness, low self-esteem, and escape (Guimón, 2010).

Multicultural Treatments

Studies conducted throughout the world have found that members of ethnic and racial minority groups tend to show less improvement in clinical treatment, make less use of mental health services, and stop therapy sooner than members of majority groups (Comas-Diaz, 2012, 2011; Ward, 2007; Wang et al., 2006).

A number of studies suggest that two features of treatment can increase a therapist's effectiveness with minority clients: (1) greater sensitivity to cultural issues and (2) inclusion of cultural morals and models in treatment, especially in therapies for children and adolescents (Comas-Diaz, 2012, 2011; Castro, Holm-Denoma, & Buckner, 2007). Given such findings, some clinicians have developed **culture-sensitive therapies,** approaches that seek to address the unique issues faced by members of cultural minority groups. Therapies geared to the pressures of being female, called **gender-sensitive,** or **feminist therapies,** follow similar principles (Calogero, Tantleff-Dunn, & Thompson, 2011).

Culture-sensitive approaches typically include the following elements (Brown, 2011; Prochaska & Norcross, 2010; Wyatt & Parham, 2007):

1. Special cultural instruction of therapists in their graduate training programs
2. Awareness by the therapist of a client's cultural values
3. Awareness by the therapist of the stress, prejudices, and stereotypes to which minority clients are exposed
4. Awareness by therapists of the hardships faced by the children of immigrants
5. Helping clients recognize the impact of both their own culture and the dominant culture on their self-views and behaviors
6. Helping clients identify and express suppressed anger and pain
7. Helping clients achieve a bicultural balance that feels right for them
8. Helping clients raise their self-esteem—a sense of self-worth that has often been damaged by generations of negative messages

•**multicultural perspective**•The view that each culture within a larger society has a particular set of values and beliefs, as well as special external pressures, that help account for the behavior and functioning of its members. Also called *culturally diverse perspective.*

•**culture-sensitive therapies**•Approaches that seek to address the unique issues faced by members of minority groups.

•**gender-sensitive therapies**•Approaches geared to the pressures of being a woman in Western society. Also called *feminist therapies.*

Community mental health: Argentine style
Staff members and patients from Buenos Aires' Neuropsychiatric Hospital set up a laptop and begin broadcasting on the popular radio station Radio La Colifata (*colifa* is slang for "crazy one"). The station was started 15 years ago to help patients pursue therapeutic activities and reach out to the community.

Assessing the Sociocultural Model

The family-social and multicultural perspectives have added greatly to the understanding and treatment of abnormal functioning. Today most clinicians take family, cultural, social, and societal issues into account, factors that were overlooked just 35 years ago. In addition, clinicians have become more aware of the impact of clinical and social roles. Finally, the treatment formats offered by the sociocultural model sometimes succeed where traditional approaches have failed.

At the same time, the sociocultural model has certain problems. To begin with, sociocultural research findings are often difficult to interpret. Indeed, research may reveal a relationship between certain family or cultural factors and a particular disorder yet fail to establish that they are its *cause*. Studies show a link between family conflict and schizophrenia, for example, but that finding does not necessarily mean that family dysfunction causes schizophrenia. It is equally possible that family functioning is disrupted by the tension and conflict created by the psychotic behavior of a family member.

Another limitation of the sociocultural model is its inability to predict abnormality in specific individuals. If, for example, social conditions such as prejudice and discrimination are key causes of anxiety and depression, why do only some of the people subjected to such forces experience psychological disorders? Are still other factors necessary for the development of the disorders?

Given these limitations, most clinicians view the family-social and multicultural explanations as operating in conjunction with the biological or psychological explanations. They agree that family, social, and cultural factors may create a climate favorable to the development of certain disorders. They believe, however, that biological or psychological conditions—or both—must also be present for the disorders to evolve.

PUTTING IT...together

Integration of the Models

Today's leading models vary widely (see Table 3-4), and none of the models has proved consistently superior. Each helps us appreciate a key aspect of human functioning, and each has important strengths as well as serious limitations.

BETWEEN THE LINES

Gender Bias in the Workplace

Women today earn 79¢ for every $1 earned by a man. ❬❬

Around 42 percent of young adult women believe that women have to outperform men at work to get the same rewards; only 11 percent of young adult men agree. ❬❬

Around 19 percent of adults believe women should return to their traditional roles. ❬❬

(Bureau of Labor Statistics, 2011; Pew Research Center, 2009; Yin, 2002)

table: **3-4**

Comparing the Models

	Biological	Psychodynamic	Behavioral	Cognitive	Humanistic	Existential	Family-Social	Multicultural
Cause of dysfunction	Biological malfunction	Underlying conflicts	Maladaptive learning	Maladaptive thinking	Self-deceit	Avoidance of responsibility	Family or social stress	External pressures or cultural conflicts
Research support	Strong	Modest	Strong	Strong	Weak	Weak	Moderate	Moderate
Consumer designation	Patient	Patient	Client	Client	Patient or client	Patient or client	Client	Client
Therapist role	Doctor	Interpreter	Teacher	Persuader	Observer	Collaborator	Family/social facilitator	Cultural advocate/teacher
Key therapist technique	Biological intervention	Free association and interpretation	Conditioning	Reasoning	Reflection	Varied	Family/social intervention	Culture-sensitive intervention
Therapy goal	Biological repair	Broad psychological change	Functional behaviors	Adaptive thinking	Self-actualization	Authentic life	Effective family or social system	Cultural awareness and comfort

With all their differences, the conclusions and techniques of the various models are often compatible. Certainly our understanding and treatment of abnormal behavior are more complete if we appreciate the biological, psychological, *and* sociocultural aspects of a person's problem rather than only one of them. Not surprisingly, then, a growing number of clinicians favor explanations of abnormal behavior that consider more than one kind of cause at a time. These explanations, sometimes called **biopsychosocial theories,** state that abnormality results from the interaction of genetic, biological, developmental, emotional, behavioral, cognitive, social, cultural, and societal influences (Pincus, 2012; Jacofsky et al., 2010). A case of depression, for example, might best be explained by pointing collectively to an individual's inheritance of unfavorable genes, traumatic losses during childhood, negative ways of thinking, and social isolation.

Some biopsychosocial theorists favor a *diathesis-stress* explanation of how the various factors work together to cause abnormal functioning ("diathesis" means a predisposed tendency). According to this theory, people must *first* have a biological, psychological, or sociocultural predisposition to develop a disorder and must *then* be subjected to episodes of severe stress. In a case of depression, for example, we might find that unfavorable genes and related biochemical abnormalities predispose the individual to develop the disorder, while the loss of a loved one actually triggers its onset.

In a similar quest for integration, many therapists are now combining treatment techniques from several models (Norcross & Beutler, 2011). In fact, 29 percent of today's clinical psychologists, 26 percent of social workers, and 53 percent of psychiatrists describe their approach as "eclectic" or "integrative" (Sharf, 2012; Prochaska & Norcross, 2010). Studies confirm that clinical problems often respond better to combined approaches than to any one therapy alone. For example, as you will see, drug therapy combined with cognitive therapy is sometimes the most effective treatment for depression (NIMH, 2011).

Given the recent rise in biopsychosocial theories and combination treatments, our examinations of abnormal behavior throughout this book will take two directions. As different disorders are presented, we will look at how today's models explain each

•**biopsychosocial theories**•Explanations that attribute the cause of abnormality to an interaction of genetic, biological, developmental, emotional, behavioral, cognitive, social, and societal influences.

disorder, how clinicians who endorse each model treat people with the disorder, and how well these explanations and treatments are supported by research. Just as important, however, we will also be observing how the explanations and treatments may build upon and strengthen each other, and we will examine current efforts toward integration of the models.

Summing Up

■ **MODELS OF PSYCHOLOGICAL ABNORMALITY** Scientists and clinicians use *models*, or *paradigms*, to understand and treat abnormal behavior. The principles and techniques of treatment used by clinical practitioners correspond to their preferred models. *pp. 47–48*

■ **THE BIOLOGICAL MODEL** Biological theorists look at the biological processes of human functioning to explain abnormal behavior, pointing to *anatomical* or *biochemical* problems in the brain and body. Such abnormalities are sometimes the result of *genetic inheritance of abnormalities, normal evolution,* or *viral infections.* Biological therapists use physical and chemical methods to help people overcome their psychological problems. The leading ones are *drug therapy, electroconvulsive therapy,* and, on rare occasions, *psychosurgery. pp. 49–53*

■ **THE PSYCHODYNAMIC MODEL** Psychodynamic theorists believe that an individual's behavior, whether normal or abnormal, is determined by underlying psychological forces. They consider psychological conflicts to be rooted in early parent-child relationships and traumatic experiences. The psychodynamic model was formulated by Sigmund Freud, who said that three dynamic forces—the *id, ego,* and *superego*—interact to produce thought, feeling, and behavior. Freud also proposed that individuals who do not make appropriate adjustments in the id, ego, and superego during their early years may become fixated at an early stage of development. Other psychodynamic theories are *ego theory, self theory,* and *object relations theory.* Psychodynamic therapists help people uncover past traumas and the inner conflicts that have resulted from them. They use a number of techniques, including *free association* and interpretations of psychological phenomena such as *resistance, transference,* and *dreams.* The leading contemporary psychodynamic approaches include short-term psychodynamic therapies and relational psychoanalytic therapy. *pp. 53–58*

■ **THE BEHAVIORAL MODEL** Behaviorists concentrate on *behaviors* and propose that they develop in accordance with the *principles of learning.* These theorists hold that three types of conditioning—*classical conditioning, operant conditioning,* and *modeling*—account for all behavior, whether normal or dysfunctional. The goal of the behavioral therapies is to identify the client's problematic behaviors and replace them with more appropriate ones, using techniques based on one or more of the principles of learning. The classical conditioning approach of *systematic desensitization,* for example, has been effective in treating phobias. *pp. 58–62*

■ **THE COGNITIVE MODEL** According to the cognitive model, we must understand human thought to understand human behavior. When people display abnormal patterns of functioning, cognitive theorists point to cognitive problems, such as *maladaptive assumptions* and *illogical thinking processes.* Cognitive therapists try to help people recognize and change their faulty ideas and thinking processes. Among the most widely used cognitive treatments is Beck's *cognitive therapy. pp. 62–64*

■ **THE HUMANISTIC-EXISTENTIAL MODEL** The humanistic-existential model focuses on the human need to confront philosophical issues such as self-awareness, values, meaning, and choice successfully to be satisfied in life.

Humanists believe that people are driven to *self-actualize.* When this drive is interfered with, abnormal behavior may result. One group of humanistic therapists, *client-centered therapists,* tries to create a very supportive therapy climate in which people can look at themselves honestly and acceptingly, thus opening the door to self-actualization. Another group, *gestalt therapists,* uses more active techniques to help people recognize and accept their needs. Recently the role of *religion* as an important factor in mental health and in psychotherapy has caught the attention of researchers and clinicians.

According to existentialists, abnormal behavior results from hiding from life's responsibilities. Existential therapists encourage people to accept *responsibility* for their lives, to recognize their *freedom to choose* a different course, and to choose to live with greater meaning. *pp. 64–70*

■ **THE SOCIOCULTURAL MODEL** The *family-social* perspective looks outward to three kinds of factors. Some proponents of this perspective focus on *social labels* and *roles;* they hold that society calls certain people "mentally ill" and that those individuals in turn follow the role implied by such a label. Others focus on *social connections and supports,* believing that isolation, poor social supports, and the like may contribute to psychological difficulties. Still others emphasize the *family system,* believing that a family's structure or communication patterns may force members to behave in abnormal ways. Practitioners from the family-social model may practice *group, family,* or *couple therapy* or *community treatment.*

The *multicultural* perspective holds that an individual's behavior, whether normal or abnormal, is best understood when examined in the light of his or her unique cultural context, including the values of that culture and the special external pressures faced by members of that culture. Practitioners of this model may practice *culture-sensitive therapies,* approaches that seek to address the unique issues faced by members of cultural minority groups. *pp. 70–78*

PsychPortal

Visit **PsychPortal**
www.yourpsychportal.com
to access the e-book, videocases, and other case materials and activities, as well as study aids including flashcards, crossword puzzles, quizzes, FAQs, and research exercises.

BETWEEN THE LINES

When Humanism and Neuroscience Cross Paths

When participants in a study conducted at the University of Oregon were led to believe that their research money was going to charity, the pleasure centers in their brains—the caudate nucleus and the nucleus accumbens—became more active. When the participants actually *chose* to give the money to charity, brain scans indicated that the pleasure centers were particularly active (Mayr, 2007). ‹‹

CLINICAL ASSESSMENT, DIAGNOSIS, AND TREATMENT

Angela Savanti was 22 years old, lived at home with her mother, and was employed as a secretary in a large insurance company. She . . . had had passing periods of "the blues" before, but her present feelings of despondency were of much greater proportion. She was troubled by a severe depression and frequent crying spells, which had not lessened over the past two months. Angela found it hard to concentrate on her job, had great difficulty falling asleep at night, and had a poor appetite. . . . Her depression had begun after she and her boyfriend Jerry broke up two months previously.

(Leon, 1991, 1984, p. 109)

Feelings of despondency led Angela Savanti to make an appointment with a therapist at a local counseling center. Her clinician's first step was to learn as much as possible about Angela and her disturbance. Who is she, what is her life like, and what are her symptoms? The answers might help to reveal the causes and probable course of her present dysfunction and suggest what kinds of strategies would be most likely to help her. Treatment could then be tailored to Angela's needs and particular pattern of abnormal functioning.

In Chapters 2 and 3 you read about how researchers in abnormal psychology build a general understanding of abnormal functioning. Clinical practitioners apply this broad information in their work, but their main focus when faced with new clients is to gather **idiographic,** or individual, information about them (Kral et al., 2011). To help persons overcome their problems, clinicians must fully understand them and their particular difficulties. To gather such individual information, clinicians use the procedures of *assessment* and *diagnosis.* Then they are in a position to offer *treatment.*

Clinical Assessment: How and Why Does the Client Behave Abnormally?

Assessment is simply the collecting of relevant information in an effort to reach a conclusion. It goes on in every realm of life. We make assessments when we decide what cereal to buy or which presidential candidate to vote for. College admissions officers, who have to select the "best" of the students applying to their college, depend on academic records, recommendations, achievement test scores, interviews, and application forms to help them decide. Employers, who have to predict which applicants are most likely to be effective workers, collect information from résumés, interviews, references, and perhaps on-the-job observations.

Clinical assessment is used to determine how and why a person is behaving abnormally and how that person may be helped. It also enables clinicians to evaluate people's progress after they have been in treatment for a while and decide whether the treatment should be changed. The specific tools that are used to do an assessment depend on the clinician's theoretical orientation. Psychodynamic clinicians, for example, use methods that assess a client's personality and probe for unconscious conflicts he or she may be experiencing. This kind of assessment, called

•**idiographic understanding**•An understanding of the behavior of a particular individual.

•**assessment**•The process of collecting and interpreting relevant information about a client or research participant.

•**standardization**•The process in which a test is administered to a large group of people whose performance then serves as a standard or norm against which any individual's score can be measured.

•**reliability**•A measure of the consistency of test or research results.

•**validity**•The accuracy of a test's or study's results; that is, the extent to which the test or study actually measures or shows what it claims.

a *personality assessment,* enables them to piece together a clinical picture in accordance with the principles of their model (Meersand, 2011). Behavioral and cognitive clinicians are more likely to use assessment methods that reveal specific dysfunctional behaviors and cognitions. The goal of this kind of assessment, called a *behavioral assessment,* is to produce a *functional analysis* of the person's behaviors—an analysis of how the behaviors are learned and reinforced (Cipani & Schock, 2011; O'Brien & Carhart, 2011).

The hundreds of clinical assessment techniques and tools that have been developed fall into three categories: *clinical interviews, tests,* and *observations.* To be useful, these tools must be *standardized* and must have clear *reliability* and *validity.*

Characteristics of Assessment Tools

All clinicians must follow the same procedures when they use a particular technique of assessment. To **standardize** a technique is to set up common steps to be followed whenever it is administered. Similarly, clinicians must standardize the way they interpret the results of an assessment tool in order to be able to understand what a particular score means. They may standardize the scores of a test, for example, by first administering it to a group of research participants whose performance will then serve as a common standard, or norm, against which later individual scores can be measured. The group that initially takes the test must be typical of the larger population for whom the test is intended. If an aggressiveness test meant for the public at large were standardized on a group of Marines, for example, the resulting "norm" might turn out to be misleadingly high.

Reliability refers to the *consistency* of assessment measures. A good assessment tool will always yield the same results in the same situation (Wang et al., 2012). An assessment tool has high *test–retest reliability,* one kind of reliability, if it yields the same results every time it is given to the same people. If a woman's responses on a particular test indicate that she is generally a heavy drinker, the test should produce the same result when she takes it again a week later. To measure test–retest reliability, participants are tested on two occasions and the two scores are correlated. The higher the correlation (see Chapter 2), the greater the test's reliability.

An assessment tool shows high *interrater* (or *interjudge*) *reliability,* another kind of reliability, if different judges independently agree on how to score and interpret it. True–false and multiple-choice tests yield consistent scores no matter who evaluates them, but other tests require that the evaluator make a judgment. Consider a test that requires the person to draw a copy of a picture, which a judge then rates for accuracy. Different judges may give different ratings to the same drawing.

Reliable assessments

Former National Basketball Association stars Clyde Drexler, James Worthy, Brent Barry, Dominique Wilkins, and Julius Erving served as judges at the 2011 All-Star slam dunk contest. Holding up their scores after each dunk, they displayed high interrater reliability and showed that they still know a great dunk when they see one.

Icon SMI/Corbis

Finally, an assessment tool must have **validity**: It must *accurately* measure what it is supposed to measure (Wang et al., 2012). Suppose a weight scale reads 12 pounds every time a 10-pound bag of sugar is placed on it. Although the scale is reliable because its readings are consistent, those readings are not valid, or accurate.

A given assessment tool may appear to be valid simply because it makes sense and seems reasonable. However, this sort of validity, called *face validity,* does not by itself mean that the instrument is trustworthy. A test for depression, for example, might include questions about how often a person cries. Because it makes sense that depressed people would cry, these test questions have face validity. It turns out, however, that many people cry a great deal for reasons other than depression, and some extremely depressed people fail to cry at all. Thus an assessment tool should not be used unless it has high *predictive validity* or *concurrent validity* (Burns, Scholin, & Zaslofsky, 2011; Osman et al., 2011).

Predictive validity is a tool's ability to predict future characteristics or behavior. Let's say that a test has been developed to identify elementary schoolchildren who are likely to take up cigarette smoking in high school. The test gathers information about the children's parents—their personal characteristics, smoking habits, and attitudes toward smoking—and on that basis identifies high-risk children. To establish the test's predictive validity, investigators could administer it to a group of elementary school students, wait until they were in high school, and then check to see which children actually did become smokers.

Concurrent validity is the degree to which the measures gathered from one tool agree with the measures gathered from other assessment techniques. Participants' scores on a new test designed to measure anxiety, for example, should correlate highly with their scores on other anxiety tests or with their behavior during clinical interviews.

How reliable and valid are the tests you take in school? What about the tests you see online and in printed magazines?

Before any assessment technique can be fully useful, it must meet the requirements of standardization, reliability, and validity. No matter how insightful or clever a technique may be, clinicians cannot profitably use its results if they are uninterpretable, inconsistent, or inaccurate. Unfortunately, more than a few clinical assessment tools fall short, suggesting that at least some clinical assessments, too, miss their mark.

Clinical Interviews

Most of us feel instinctively that the best way to get to know people is to meet with them face to face. Under these circumstances, we can see them react to what we do and say, observe as well as listen as they answer, and generally get a sense of who they are. A *clinical interview* is just such a face-to-face encounter (Mohlman et al., 2012; Cepeda, 2010). If during a clinical interview a man looks as happy as can be while describing his sadness over the recent death of his mother, the clinician may suspect that the man actually has conflicting emotions about this loss.

Conducting the Interview The interview is often the first contact between client and clinician. Clinicians use it to collect detailed information about the person's problems and feelings, lifestyle and relationships, and other personal history. They may also ask about the person's expectations of therapy and motives for seeking it. The clinician who worked with Angela Savanti began with a face-to-face interview:

Angela was dressed neatly when she appeared for her first interview. She was attractive, but her eyes were puffy and ringed with dark circles. She answered questions and related information about her life history in a slow, flat tone of voice, which had an impersonal quality to it. She sat stiffly in her chair....

The client stated that the time period just before she and her boyfriend terminated their relationship had been one of extreme emotional turmoil. She was not sure whether she wanted to marry Jerry, and he began to demand that she decide either one way or the other. Mrs. Savanti [Angela's mother] did not seem to like Jerry and was very cold and aloof whenever he came to the house. Angela felt caught in the middle and unable to make a decision about her future. After several confrontations with Jerry over whether she would marry him or not, he told her he felt that she would never decide, so he was not going to see her anymore....

Angela stated that her childhood was a very unhappy period. Her father was seldom home, and when he was present, her parents fought constantly....

Angela recalled feeling very guilty when Mr. Savanti left.... She revealed that whenever she thought of her father, she always felt that she had been responsible in some way for his leaving the family....

•**mental status exam**•A set of interview questions and observations designed to reveal the degree and nature of a client's abnormal functioning.

•**test**•A device for gathering information about a few aspects of a person's psychological functioning from which broader information about the person can be inferred.

Angela described her mother as the "long-suffering type" who said that she had sacrificed her life to make her children happy, and the only thing she ever got in return was grief and unhappiness.... When Angela and [her sister] began dating, Mrs. Savanti ... would make disparaging remarks about the boys they had been with and about men in general....

Angela revealed that she had often been troubled with depressed moods. During high school, if she got a lower grade in a subject than she had expected, her initial response was one of anger, followed by depression. She began to think that she was not smart enough to get good grades, and she blamed herself for studying too little. Angela also became despondent when she got into an argument with her mother or felt that she was being taken advantage of at work....

The intensity and duration of the [mood change] that she experienced when she broke up with Jerry were much more severe. She was not sure why she was so depressed, but she began to feel it was an effort to walk around and go out to work. Talking with others became difficult. Angela found it hard to concentrate, and she began to forget things she was supposed to do.... She preferred to lie in bed rather than be with anyone, and she often cried when alone.

(Leon, 1991, 1984, pp. 110–115)

Joining the mix

In recent years, online mental health questionnaires—a new form of clinical assessment—have increased in number, helping clinicians to identify and assess people with various psychological problems. Here, the Department of Defense reaches out to service members and their families, encouraging them to take an anonymous online questionnaire of this kind.

Beyond gathering basic background data of this kind, clinical interviewers give special attention to whatever topics they consider most important (Segal, June, & Marty, 2010). Psychodynamic interviewers try to learn about the person's needs and memories of past events and relationships. Behavioral interviewers try to pinpoint information about the stimuli that trigger responses and their consequences. Cognitive interviewers try to discover assumptions and interpretations that influence the person. Humanistic clinicians ask about the person's self-evaluation, self-concept, and values. Biological clinicians look for signs of biochemical or brain dysfunction. And sociocultural interviewers ask about the family, social, and cultural environments.

Interviews can be either unstructured or structured (Madill, 2012). In an *unstructured interview*, the clinician asks open-ended questions, perhaps as simple as "Would you tell me about yourself?" The lack of structure allows the interviewer to follow leads and explore relevant topics that could not be anticipated before the interview.

In a *structured interview*, clinicians ask prepared questions. Sometimes they use a published *interview schedule*—a standard set of questions designed for all interviews. Many structured interviews include a **mental status exam,** a set of questions and observations that systematically evaluate the client's awareness, orientation with regard to time and place, attention span, memory, judgment and insight, thought content and processes, mood, and appearance (Daniel & Gurczynski, 2010). A structured format ensures that clinicians will cover the same kinds of important issues in all of their interviews and enables them to compare the responses of different individuals.

Although most clinical interviews have both unstructured and structured portions, many clinicians favor one kind over the other. Unstructured interviews typically appeal to psychodynamic and humanistic clinicians, while structured formats are widely used by behavioral and cognitive clinicians, who need to pinpoint behaviors, attitudes, or thinking processes that may underlie abnormal behavior (Segal & Hersen, 2010).

What Are the Limitations of Clinical Interviews?
Although interviews often produce valuable information about people, there are limits to what they can accomplish. One problem is that they sometimes lack validity, or accuracy (Mohlman et al., 2112; Chang & Krosnick, 2010). Individuals may intentionally mislead in order to present themselves in a positive light or to avoid discussing embarrassing topics (Gold & Castillo, 2010). Or people may be unable to give an

accurate report in their interviews. Individuals who suffer from depression, for example, take a pessimistic view of themselves and may describe themselves as poor workers or inadequate parents when that isn't the case at all (Feliciano & Gum, 2010).

Interviewers too may make mistakes in judgments that slant the information they gather (Clinton, Fernandez, & Alicea, 2010). They usually rely too heavily on first impressions, for example, and give too much weight to unfavorable information about a client (Wu & Shi, 2005). Interviewer biases, including gender, race, and age biases, may also influence the interviewers' interpretations of what a client says (Ungar et al., 2006).

Interviews, particularly unstructured ones, may also lack reliability (Madill, 2012; Davis et al., 2010). People respond differently to different interviewers, providing, for example, less information to a cold interviewer than to a warm and supportive one (Quas et al., 2007). Similarly, a clinician's race, gender, age, and appearance may influence a client's responses (Davis et al., 2010; Springman, Wherry, & Notaro, 2006).

Because different clinicians can obtain different answers and draw different conclusions, even when they ask the same questions of the same person, some researchers believe that interviewing should be discarded as a tool of clinical assessment. As you'll see, however, the two other kinds of clinical assessment methods also have serious limitations.

"I'll say a normal word, then you say the first sick thing that pops into your head."

Clinical Tests

Tests are devices for gathering information about a few aspects of a person's psychological functioning, from which broader information about the person can be inferred. On the surface, it may look easy to design an effective test. Every month, magazines and Web sites present new tests that supposedly tell us about our personalities, relationships, sex lives, reactions to stress, or ability to succeed. Such tests might sound convincing, but most of them lack reliability, validity, and standardization. That is, they do not yield consistent, accurate information or say where we stand in comparison with others.

More than 500 clinical tests are currently in use throughout the United States. Clinicians use six kinds most often: *projective tests, personality inventories, response inventories, psychophysiological tests, neurological and neuropsychological tests,* and *intelligence tests.*

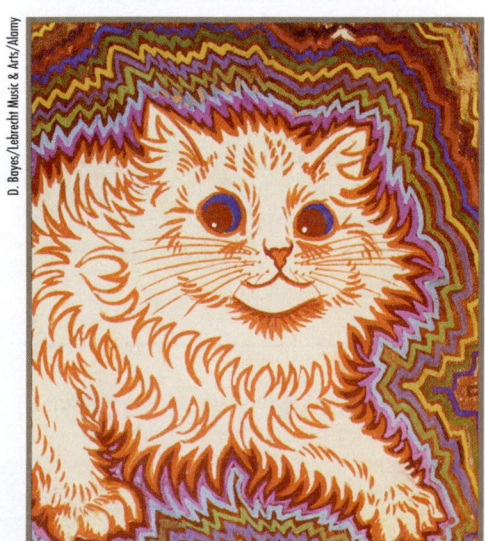

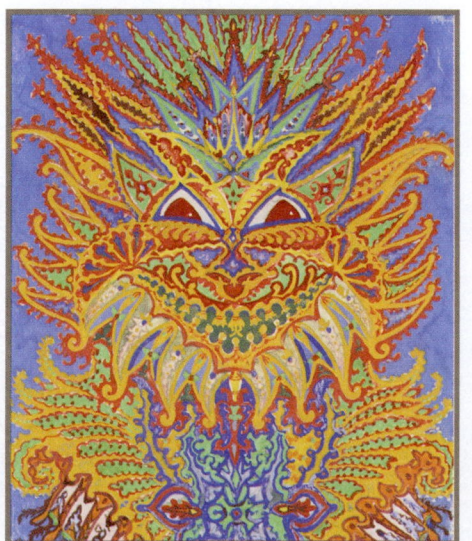

The art of assessment
Clinicians often view works of art as informal projective tests in which artists reveal their conflicts and mental stability. The sometimes bizarre cat portraits of early-twentieth-century artist Louis Wain, for example, have been interpreted as reflections of the psychosis with which he struggled for many years. Others believe such interpretations are incorrect, however, and note that the decorative patterns in some of his later paintings were actually based on textile designs.

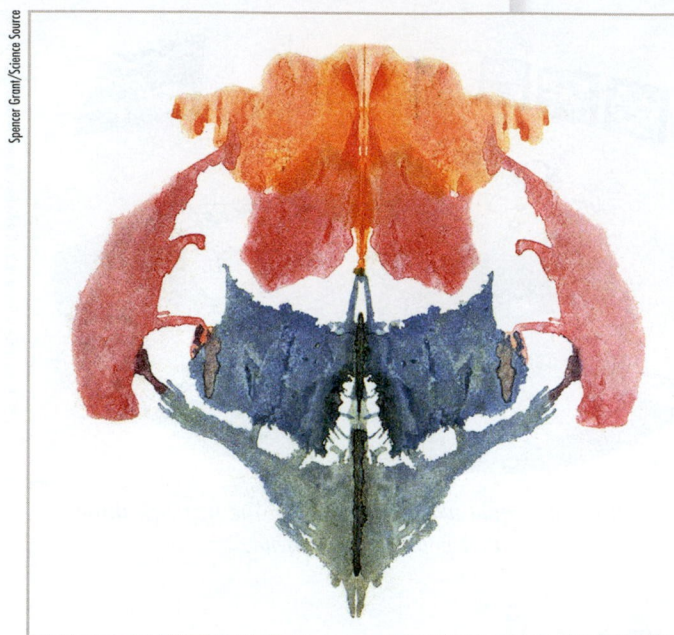

Figure 4-1

An inkblot similar to those used in the Rorschach test. In this test, individuals view and react to a total of 10 inkblot images.

Spencer Grant/Science Source

Projective Tests **Projective tests** require that clients interpret vague stimuli, such as inkblots or ambiguous pictures, or follow open-ended instructions such as "Draw a person." Theoretically, when clues and instructions are so general, people will "project" aspects of their personality into the task. Projective tests are used primarily by psychodynamic clinicians to help assess the unconscious drives and conflicts they believe to be at the root of abnormal functioning (McGrath & Carroll, 2012; Baer & Blais, 2010). The most widely used projective tests are the *Rorschach test,* the *Thematic Apperception Test, sentence-completion tests,* and *drawings.*

RORSCHACH TEST In 1911 Hermann Rorschach, a Swiss psychiatrist, experimented with the use of inkblots in his clinical work. He made thousands of blots by dropping ink on paper and then folding the paper in half to create a symmetrical but wholly accidental design, such as the one shown in Figure 4-1. Rorschach found that everyone saw images in these blots. In addition, the images a viewer saw seemed to correspond in important ways with his or her psychological condition. People diagnosed with schizophrenia, for example, tended to see images that differed from those described by people experiencing depression.

Rorschach selected 10 inkblots and published them in 1921 with instructions for their use in assessment (see *MediaSpeak* on the next page). This set was called the *Rorschach Psychodynamic Inkblot Test.* Rorschach died just eight months later, at the age of 37, but his work was continued by others, and his inkblots took their place among the most widely used projective tests of the twentieth century.

Clinicians administer the "Rorschach," as it is commonly called, by presenting one inkblot card at a time and asking respondents what they see, what the inkblot seems to be, or what it reminds them of. In the early years, Rorschach testers paid special attention to the themes and images that the inkblots brought to mind (Butcher, 2010; Weiner & Greene, 2008). Testers now also pay attention to the style of the responses: Do the clients view the design as a whole or see specific details? Do they focus on the blots or on the white spaces between them?

> **Despite its limitations, just about everyone has heard of the Rorschach. Why do you think it is so famous and popular?**

THEMATIC APPERCEPTION TEST The Thematic Apperception Test (TAT) is a pictorial projective test (Teglasi, 2010; Morgan & Murray, 1935). People who take the TAT are commonly shown 30 black-and-white pictures of individuals in vague situations and are asked to make up a dramatic story about each card. They must tell what is happening in the picture, what led up to it, what the characters are feeling and thinking, and what the outcome of the situation will be.

Clinicians who use the TAT believe that people always identify with one of the characters on each card. The stories are thought to reflect the individuals' own circumstances, needs, and emotions. For example, a female client seems to be revealing her own feelings when telling this story about a TAT picture similar to the image shown in Figure 4-2:

> *This is a woman who has been quite troubled by memories of a mother she was resentful toward. She has feelings of sorrow for the way she treated her mother, her memories of her mother plague her. These feelings seem to be increasing as she grows older and sees her children treating her the same way that she treated her mother.*
>
> *(Aiken, 1985, p. 372)*

Figure 4-2

A picture similar to one used in the Thematic Apperception Test.

Dan Moore/Getty Images

MediaSpeak

A Rorschach Cheat Sheet on Wikipedia?

Noam Cohen, New York Times

The online encyclopedia Wikipedia has been engulfed in a furious debate involving psychologists who are angry that the 10 original Rorschach [inkblot] plates are reproduced online, along with common responses for each. For them, the Wikipedia page is the equivalent of posting an answer sheet to next year's SAT.

What had been a simmering dispute over the reproduction of a single plate reached new heights in June (2009) when . . . an emergency-room doctor from Moose Jaw, Saskatchewan, posted images of all 10 plates to the bottom of the [Wikipedia] article about the test, along with what research had found to be the most popular responses for each. . . .

Psychologists have registered with Wikipedia to argue that the site is jeopardizing one of the oldest continuously used psychological assessment tests. . . . "The more test materials are promulgated widely, the more possibility there is to game it," said Bruce L. Smith, a psychologist . . . . He quickly added that . . . a coached subject could . . . "render the results of [his or her Rorschach test] meaningless."

To psychologists, to render the Rorschach test meaningless would be a particularly painful development because there has been so much research conducted—tens of thousands of papers, by Dr. Smith's estimate—to try to link a patient's responses to certain psychological conditions. Yes, new inkblots could be used, these advocates concede, but those blots would not have had the research—"the normative data," in the language of researchers—that allows the answers to be put into a larger context.

And, more fundamentally, the psychologists object whenever diagnostic tools fall into the hands of amateurs who haven't been trained to administer them. . . .

[A] spokeswoman for Hogrefe & Huber Publishing, . . . publisher of Hermann Rorschach's book, said in an e-mail message last week: "We are assessing legal steps . . . . It is . . . unbelievably reckless and even cynical of Wikipedia . . . to on

one hand point out the concerns and dangers voiced by recognized scientists and important professional associations and on the other hand—in the same article—publish the test material along with supposedly 'expected responses.'". . .

[However, as one might expect, the emergency room doctor who originally posted the Rorschach material on Wikipedia sees things differently.] "Restricting information for theoretical concerns is not what we are here to do," [he] said, adding that he was not impressed by the predictions of harm from those who sought to keep the Rorschach plates secret. "Show me the evidence. . . ."

SENTENCE-COMPLETION TEST The sentence-completion test, first developed in the 1920s (Payne, 1928), asks people to complete a series of unfinished sentences, such as "I wish . . ." or "My father . . . ." The test is considered a good springboard for discussion and a quick and easy way to pinpoint topics to explore.

DRAWINGS On the assumption that a drawing tells us something about its creator, clinicians often ask clients to draw human figures and talk about them (McGrath & Carroll, 2012). Evaluations of these drawings are based on the details and shape of the drawing, solidity of the pencil line, location of the drawing on the paper, size of the figures, features of the figures, use of background, and comments made by the respondent during the drawing task. In the *Draw-a-Person (DAP) Test*, the most popular of the drawing

•**projective test**•A test consisting of ambiguous material that people interpret or respond to.

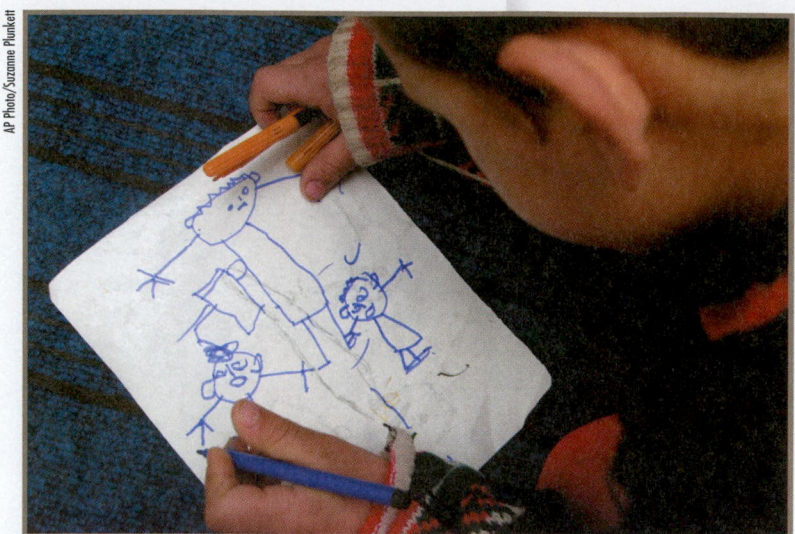

AP Photo/Suzanne Plunkett

Drawing test
Drawing tests are commonly used to assess the functioning of children. A popular one is the Kinetic Family Drawing test, in which children draw their household members performing some activity ("kinetic" means "active").

tests, individuals are first told to draw "a person" and then are instructed to draw another person of the opposite sex.

WHAT ARE THE MERITS OF PROJECTIVE TESTS? Until the 1950s, projective tests were the most common technique for assessing personality. In recent years, however, clinicians and researchers have relied on them largely to gain "supplementary" insights (McGrath & Carroll, 2012; Butcher, 2010). One reason for this shift is that practitioners who follow the newer models have less use for the tests than psychodynamic clinicians do. Even more importantly, the tests have not consistently shown much reliability or validity (Butcher, 2010; Wood et al., 2002).

In reliability studies, different clinicians have tended to score the same person's projective test quite differently. Similarly, in validity studies, when clinicians try to describe a client's personality and feelings on the basis of responses to projective tests, their conclusions often fail to match the self-report of the client, the view of the psychotherapist, or the picture gathered from an extensive case history (Bornstein, 2007).

Another validity problem is that projective tests are sometimes biased against minority ethnic groups (Costantino, Dana, & Malgady, 2007) (see Table 4–1). For example, people are supposed to identify with the characters in the TAT when they make up stories about them, yet no members of minority groups are in the TAT pictures. In response to this problem, some clinicians have developed other TAT-like tests with African American or Hispanic figures (Costantino et al., 2007).

Personality Inventories An alternative way to collect information about individuals is to ask them to assess themselves. The **personality inventory** asks respondents a wide range of questions about their behavior, beliefs, and feelings. In the typical personality inventory, individuals indicate whether each of a long list of statements applies to them. Clinicians then use the responses to draw conclusions about the person's personality and psychological functioning (Watson, 2012; Blais et al., 2010).

By far the most widely used personality inventory is the *Minnesota Multiphasic Personality Inventory* (*MMPI*) (Butcher, 2011). Two adult versions are available—the original test, published in 1945, and the *MMPI-2*, a 1989 revision which was itself revised in 2001. A special version of the test for adolescents, the *MMPI-A*, is also used widely (Williams & Butcher, 2011).

The MMPI consists of more than 500 self-statements, to be labeled "true," "false," or "cannot say." The statements cover issues ranging from physical concerns to mood, sexual behaviors, and social activities. Altogether the statements make up 10 clinical scales, on each of which an individual can score from 0 to 120. When people score above 70 on a scale, their functioning on that scale is considered deviant. When the 10 scale scores are considered side by side, a pattern called a *profile* takes shape, indicating the person's general personality. The 10 scales on the MMPI measure the following:

Hypochondriasis Items showing abnormal concern with bodily functions ("I have chest pains several times a week.")

Depression Items showing extreme pessimism and hopelessness ("I often feel hopeless about the future.")

Hysteria Items suggesting that the person may use physical or mental symptoms as a way of unconsciously avoiding conflicts and responsibilities ("My heart frequently pounds so hard I can feel it.")

Psychopathic deviate Items showing a repeated and gross disregard for social customs and an emotional shallowness ("My activities and interests are often criticized by others.")

•**personality inventory**•A test designed to measure broad personality characteristics, consisting of statements about behaviors, beliefs, and feelings that people evaluate as either characteristic or uncharacteristic of them.

table: 4-1

Multicultural Hot Spots in Assessment and Diagnosis

Cultural Hot Spot	Effect on Assessment or Diagnosis
● Immigrant Client	**● Dominant-Culture Assessor**
Homeland culture may differ from current country's dominant culture	May misread culture-bound reactions as pathology
May have left homeland to escape war or oppression	May overlook client's vulnerability to posttraumatic stress
May have weak support systems in this country	May overlook client's heightened vulnerability to stressors
Lifestyle (wealth and occupation) in this country may fall below lifestyle in homeland	May overlook client's sense of loss and frustration
May refuse or be unable to learn dominant language	May misunderstand client's assessment responses, or may overlook or misdiagnose client's symptoms
● Ethnic-Minority Client	**● Dominant-Culture Assessor**
May reject or distrust members of dominant culture, including assessor	May experience little rapport with client, or may misinterpret client's distrust as pathology
May be uncomfortable with dominant culture's values (e.g., assertiveness, confrontation) and so find it difficult to apply clinician's recommendations	May view client as unmotivated
May manifest stress in culture-bound ways (e.g., somatic symptoms such as stomachaches)	May misinterpret symptom patterns
May hold cultural beliefs that seem strange to dominant culture (e.g., belief in communication with dead)	May misinterpret cultural responses as pathology (e.g., a delusion)
May be uncomfortable during assessment	May overlook and feed into client's discomfort
● Dominant-Culture Assessor	**● Ethnic-Minority Client**
May be unknowledgeable or biased about ethnic-minority culture	Cultural differences may be pathologized, or symptoms may be overlooked
May nonverbally convey own discomfort to ethnic-minority client	May become tense and anxious

Source: Rose et al., 2011; Bhattacharya et al., 2010; Dana, 2005, 2000; Westermeyer, 2004, 2001, 1993; López & Guarnaccia, 2005, 2000; Kirmayer, 2003, 2002, 2001; Sue & Sue, 2003; Tsai et al., 2001; Thakker & Ward, 1998.

Masculinity-femininity Items that are thought to separate male and female respondents ("I like to arrange flowers.")

Paranoia Items that show abnormal suspiciousness and delusions of grandeur or persecution ("There are evil people trying to influence my mind.")

Psychasthenia Items that show obsessions, compulsions, abnormal fears, and guilt and indecisiveness ("I save nearly everything I buy, even after I have no use for it.")

Schizophrenia Items that show bizarre or unusual thoughts or behavior ("Things around me do not seem real.")

Hypomania Items that show emotional excitement, overactivity, and flight of ideas ("At times I feel very 'high' or very 'low' for no apparent reason.")

Social introversion Items that show shyness, little interest in people, and insecurity ("I am easily embarrassed.")

"We're going to run some tests: blood work, a cat-scan, and the S.A.T.'s."

The MMPI-2, the newer version of the MMPI, contains 567 items—many identical to those in the original, some rewritten to reflect current language ("upset stomach," for instance, replaces "acid stomach"), and others that are new. Before being adopted, the MMPI-2 was tested on a more diverse group of people than was the original MMPI. Thus scores on the revised test are thought to be more accurate indicators of personality and abnormal functioning (Butcher, 2011, 2010).

The MMPI and other personality inventories have several advantages over projective tests (Ben-Porath, 2012; Watson 2012). Because they are paper-and-pencil (or computerized) tests, they do not take much time to administer, and they are objectively scored. Most of them are standardized, so one person's scores can be compared to those of many others. Moreover, they often display greater test–retest reliability than projective tests (Zubeidat et al., 2011). For example, people who take the MMPI a second time after a period of less than two weeks receive approximately the same scores (Graham, 2006).

Personality inventories also appear to have greater validity, or accuracy, than projective tests (Butcher, 2011, 2010; Lanyon, 2007). However, they can hardly be considered *highly* valid. When clinicians have used these tests alone, they have not regularly been able to judge a respondent's personality accurately (Braxton et al., 2007). One problem is that the personality traits that the tests seek to measure cannot be examined directly. How can we fully know a person's character, emotions, and needs from self-reports alone?

Another problem is that despite the use of more diverse standardization groups by the MMPI-2 designers, this and other personality tests continue to have certain cultural limitations. Responses that indicate a psychological disorder in one culture may be normal responses in another (Butcher, 2010; Dana, 2005, 2000). In Puerto Rico, for example, where it is common to practice spiritualism, it would be normal to answer "true" to the MMPI item "Evil spirits possess me at times." In other populations, that response could indicate psychopathology (Rogler, Malgady, & Rodriguez, 1989).

Despite such limits in validity, personality inventories continue to be popular. Research indicates that they can help clinicians learn about people's personal styles and disorders as long as they are used in combination with interviews or other assessment tools.

Response Inventories Like personality inventories, **response inventories** ask people to provide detailed information about themselves, but these tests focus on one specific area of functioning (Watson, 2012; Blais & Baer, 2010). For example, one such test may measure affect (emotion), another social skills, and still another cognitive processes. Clinicians can use them to determine the role such factors play in a person's disorder.

Affective inventories measure the severity of such emotions as anxiety, depression, and anger (Osman et al., 2008). In one of the most widely used affective inventories, the Beck Depression Inventory, shown in Table 4–2, people rate their level of sadness and its effect on their functioning. *Social skills inventories*, used particularly by behavioral and family-social clinicians, ask respondents to indicate how they would react in a variety of social situations (Norton et al., 2010; Wilson et al., 2010). *Cognitive inventories* reveal a person's typical thoughts and assumptions and can uncover counterproductive patterns of thinking (Takei et al., 2011; Glass & Merluzzi, 2000). They are, not surprisingly, often used by cognitive therapists and researchers.

Both the number of response inventories and the number of clinicians who use them have increased steadily in the past 30 years (Black, 2005). At the same time, however, these inventories have major limitations. With the notable exceptions of the Beck Depression Inventory and a few others, only some of them have been subjected to careful standardization, reliability, and validity procedures (Blais & Baer, 2010; Weis & Smenner, 2007). Often they are created as a need arises, without being tested for accuracy and consistency.

•**response inventories**•Tests designed to measure a person's responses in one specific area of functioning, such as affect, social skills, or cognitive processes.

•**psychophysiological test**•A test that measures physical responses (such as heart rate and muscle tension) as possible indicators of psychological problems.

table: 4-2

Sample Items from the Beck Depression Inventory

Items	Inventory	
Suicidal ideas	0	I don't have any thoughts of killing myself.
	1	I have thoughts of killing myself but I would not carry them out.
	2	I would like to kill myself.
	3	I would kill myself if I had the chance.
Work inhibition	0	I can work about as well as before.
	1	It takes extra effort to get started at doing something.
	2	I have to push myself very hard to do anything.
	3	I can't do any work at all.
Loss of libido	0	I have not noticed any recent change in my interest in sex.
	1	I am less interested in sex than I used to be.
	2	I am much less interested in sex now.
	3	I have lost interest in sex completely.

Psychophysiological Tests Clinicians may also use **psychophysiological tests,** which measure physiological responses as possible indicators of psychological problems (Rodriguez-Ruiz et al., 2012). This practice began three decades ago after several studies suggested that states of anxiety are regularly accompanied by physiological changes, particularly increases in heart rate, body temperature, blood pressure, skin reactions (*galvanic skin response*), and muscle contraction. The measuring of physiological changes has since played a key role in the assessment of certain psychological disorders.

One psychophysiological test is the *polygraph,* popularly known as a *lie detector* (Boucsein, 2012; Grubin, 2010; Meijer & Verschuere, 2010). Electrodes attached to various parts of a person's body detect changes in breathing, perspiration, and heart rate while the individual answers questions. The clinician observes these functions while the person answers "yes" to *control questions*—questions whose answers are known to be yes, such as "Are your parents both alive?" Then the clinician observes the same physiological functions while the person answers *test questions,* such as "Did you commit this robbery?" If breathing, perspiration, and heart rate suddenly increase, the person is suspected of lying.

Like other kinds of clinical tests, psychophysiological tests have their drawbacks. Many require expensive equipment that must be carefully tuned and maintained. In addition, psychophysiological measurements can be inaccurate and unreliable (see *PsychWatch* on the next page). The laboratory equipment itself—elaborate and sometimes frightening—may arouse a participant's nervous system and thus change his or her physical responses. Physiological responses may also change when they are measured repeatedly in a single session. Galvanic skin responses, for example, often decrease during repeated testing.

Why might an innocent person "fail" a lie detector test? How might a guilty person manage to "pass" the test?

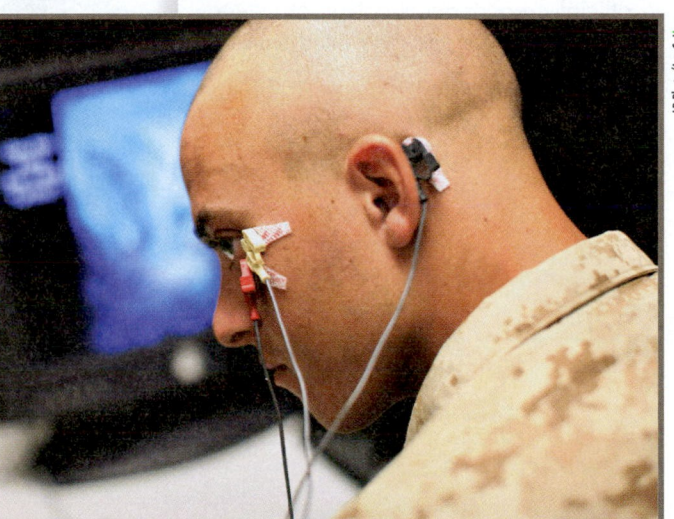

AP Photo/Joe C. Hong

Blink of the eye
Before entering combat duty, this Marine takes an eye blink test—a psychophysiological test in which sensors are attached to the eye lid and other parts of the face. The test tries to detect physical indicators of tension and anxiety and to predict which Marines might be particularly susceptible to posttraumatic stress disorder.

The Truth, the Whole Truth, and Nothing but the Truth

In movies, criminals being grilled by the police reveal their guilt by sweating, shaking, cursing, or twitching. When they are hooked up to a *polygraph* (a lie detector), the needles bounce all over the paper. This image has been with us since World War I, when some clinicians developed the theory that people who are telling lies display systemic changes in their breathing, perspiration, and heart rate (Marston, 1917).

The danger of relying on polygraph tests is that, according to researchers, they do not work as well as we would like (Grubin, 2010; Meijer & Verschuere, 2010; Iacono, 2008; Vrij, 2004). The public did not pay much attention to this inconvenient fact until the mid-1980s, when the American Psychological Association officially reported that polygraphs were often inaccurate and the United States Congress voted to restrict their use in criminal prosecution and employment screening (Krapohl, 2002). Research indicates that 8 out of 100 truths, on average, are called lies in polygraph testing (Grubin, 2010; Raskin & Honts, 2002; MacLaren, 2001). Imagine, then, how many innocent people might be convicted of crimes if polygraph findings were taken as valid evidence in criminal trials.

Given such findings, polygraphs are less trusted and less popular today than they once were. For example, few courts now admit results from such tests as evidence of criminal guilt (Grubin, 2010; Daniels, 2002). Polygraph testing has by no means disappeared, however. The FBI uses it extensively, parole boards and probation offices routinely use it to help decide whether to release convicted offenders, and in public-sector hiring (such as for police officers), the use of polygraph screening may actually be on the increase (Meijer & Verschuere, 2010; Kokish et al., 2005).

AP Photo/Fernando Vergara

All the rage A student learns to administer polygraph exams at the Latin American Polygraph Institute in Bogota, Colombia. Despite evidence that these tests are often invalid, they are widely used by businesses in Colombia, where employee deception has become a major problem.

Neurological and Neuropsychological Tests Some problems in personality or behavior are caused primarily by damage to the brain or changes in brain activity. Head injury, brain tumors, brain malfunctions, alcoholism, infections, and other disorders can all cause such impairment. If a psychological dysfunction is to be treated effectively, it is important to know whether its primary cause is a physical abnormality in the brain.

A number of techniques may help pinpoint brain abnormalities. Some procedures, such as brain surgery, biopsy, and X ray, have been used for many years. More recently, scientists have developed a number of **neurological tests,** designed to measure brain structure and activity directly. One neurological test is the *electroencephalogram (EEG),* which records *brain waves,* the electrical activity taking place within the brain as a result of neurons firing. In this procedure, electrodes placed on the scalp send brain–wave impulses to a machine that records them.

Other neurological tests actually take "pictures" of brain structure or brain activity. These tests, called **neuroimaging,** or **brain scanning, techniques,** include *computerized axial tomography* (*CAT scan* or *CT scan*), in which X rays of the brain's structure are taken at different angles and combined; *positron emission tomography* (*PET scan*), a computer-produced motion picture of chemical activity throughout the brain; and *magnetic resonance imaging* (*MRI*), a procedure that uses the magnetic property of certain hydrogen atoms in the brain to create a detailed picture of the brain's structure.

A more recent version of the MRI, *functional magnetic resonance imaging* (*fMRI*), converts MRI pictures of brain structures into detailed pictures of neuron activity, thus offering a picture of the *functioning* brain. In this procedure, an MRI scanner detects rapid changes in the flow or volume of blood in areas across the brain while an individual is experiencing emotions or performing specific cognitive tasks. By interpreting these blood changes as indications of neuron activity at sites throughout the brain, a computer then generates images of the brain areas that are active during the individual's emotional experiences or cognitive behaviors, thus offering a picture of the functioning brain. Partly because fMRI-produced images of brain functioning are so much clearer than PET scan images, the fMRI has generated enormous enthusiasm among brain researchers since it was first developed in 1990.

Though widely used, these techniques are sometimes unable to detect subtle brain abnormalities. Clinicians have therefore developed less direct but sometimes more revealing **neuropsychological tests** that measure cognitive, perceptual, and motor

•**neurological test**•A test that directly measures brain structure or activity.

•**neuroimaging techniques**•Neurological tests that provide images of brain structure or activity, such as CT scans, PET scans, and MRIs. Also called *brain scans*.

•**neuropsychological test**•A test that detects brain impairment by measuring a person's cognitive, perceptual, and motor performances.

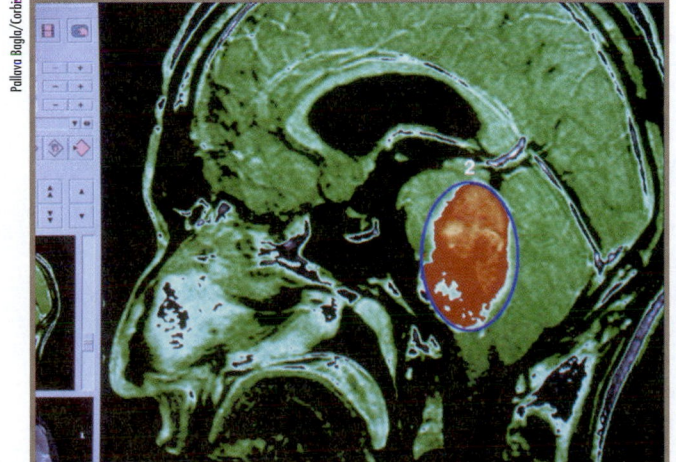
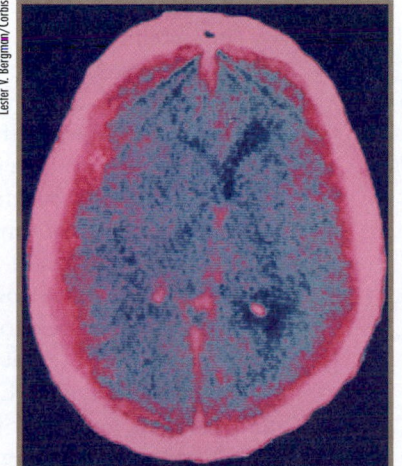
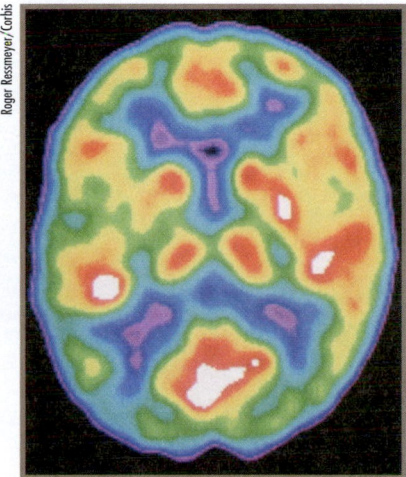
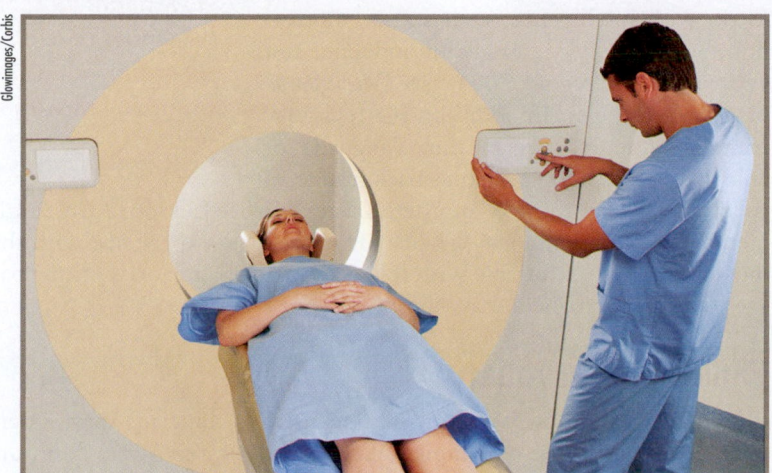

Traditional scanning

The most widely used neuroimaging techniques in clinical practice—the MRI, CAT, and PET scans—take pictures of the living brain. The machinery for each of these techniques is bulky and imposing, much like the MRI machine shown at left. However, the scans produced by the machines are very different. Here, an MRI scan (above left) reveals a large tumor, colored in orange; a CAT scan (above center) reveals a subdural hemotoma, a mass of blood within the brain; and a PET scan (above right) shows which areas of the brain are active (those colored in red, orange, and yellow) when an individual is stimulated.

The EEG
Electrodes pasted to the scalp help measure the brain waves of this baby boy.

performances on certain tasks and interpret abnormal performances as an indicator of underlying brain problems (Summers & Saunders, 2012). Brain damage is especially likely to affect visual perception, memory, and visual–motor coordination, so neuropsychological tests focus particularly on these areas. The famous *Bender Visual-Motor Gestalt Test,* for example, consists of nine cards, each displaying a simple geometrical design. Patients look at the designs one at a time and copy each one on a piece of paper. Later they try to redraw the designs from memory. Notable errors in accuracy by individuals older than 12 are thought to reflect organic brain impairment. Clinicians often use a *battery,* or series, of neuropsychological tests, each targeting a specific skill area (Aas et al., 2012; Reitan & Wolfson, 2005, 1996).

Intelligence Tests An early definition of intelligence described it as "the capacity to judge well, to reason well, and to comprehend well" (Binet & Simon, 1916, p. 192). Because intelligence is an *inferred* quality rather than a specific physical process, it can be measured only indirectly. In 1905 French psychologist Alfred Binet and his associate Theodore Simon produced an **intelligence test** consisting of a series of tasks requiring people to use various verbal and nonverbal skills. The general score derived from this and later intelligence tests is termed an **intelligence quotient,** or **IQ,** so called because initially it represented the ratio of a person's "mental" age to his or her "chronological" age, multiplied by 100.

There are now more than 100 intelligence tests available. As you will see in Chapter 17, intelligence tests play a key role in the diagnosis of intellectual developmental disorder (mental retardation), but they can also help clinicians identify other problems.

Intelligence tests are among the most carefully produced of all clinical tests (Bowden et al., 2011; Kellerman & Burry, 2007). Because they have been standardized on large groups of people, clinicians have a good idea how each individual's score compares with the performance of the population at large. These tests have also shown very high reliability: people who repeat the same IQ test years later receive approximately the same score. Finally, the major IQ tests appear to have fairly high validity: children's IQ scores often correlate with their performance in school, for example.

Nevertheless, intelligence tests have some key shortcomings. Factors that have nothing to do with intelligence, such as low motivation or high anxiety, can greatly influence test performance (Gregory, 2004) (see *MediaSpeak* on the next page). In addition, IQ tests may contain cultural biases in their language or tasks that place people of one background at an advantage over those of another (Tanzer, Hof, & Jackson, 2010; Ford, 2008). Similarly, members of some minority groups may have little experience with this kind of test, or they may be uncomfortable with test examiners of a majority ethnic background. Either way, their performances may suffer.

> How might IQ scores be misused by school officials, parents, or other individuals? Why is society preoccupied with these scores?

Clinical Observations

In addition to interviewing and testing people, clinicians may systematically observe their behavior. In one technique, called *naturalistic observation,* clinicians observe clients in their everyday environments. In another, *analog observation,* they observe them in an

•**intelligence test**•A test designed to measure a person's intellectual ability.

•**intelligence quotient (IQ)**•An overall score derived from intelligence tests.

MediaSpeak

Intelligence Tests Too? eBay and the Public Good

Michelle Roberts, Associated Press

Intelligence tests . . . are for sale on eBay Inc.'s online auction site, and the test maker is worried they will be misused.

The series of Wechsler intelligence tests, made by San Antonio-based Harcourt Assessment, Inc., are supposed to be sold to and administered by only clinical psychologists and trained professionals.

Travis Amos

The Wechsler Adult Intelligence Scale-Revised (WAIS-R) This widely used intelligence test has 11 subtests, which cover such areas as factual information, memory, vocabulary, arithmetic, design, and eye-hand coordination.

Given more than a million times a year nationwide, according to Harcourt, the intelligence tests often are among numerous tests ordered by prosecutors and defense attorneys to determine the mental competence of criminal defendants. A low IQ, for example, can be used to argue leniency in sentencing.

Schools use the tests to determine whether to place a student in a special program, whether for gifted or struggling students. Harcourt officials say they fear the tests for sale on eBay will be misused for coaching by lawyers or parents.

But eBay has denied their request to restrict the sale of the tests. eBay officials say there is nothing illegal about selling the tests, and it cannot monitor every possible misuse of items sold through its network of 248 million buyers and sellers. [The tests continue to be available on eBay as of 2011.] Five of the tests were listed for sale . . . for about $175 to $900. The latest edition of the adult test, which retails for $939, was offered on eBay for $249.99.

"In order for it to maintain its integrity, there needs to be limited availability," said [a] Harcourt spokesman. . . . "Misinterpreting the results [of questions and tasks on the tests], even without malicious intent, could lead to mistakes in assessing a child's intelligence. . . ."

---

artificial setting, such as a clinical office or laboratory. Finally, in *self-monitoring,* clients are instructed to observe themselves.

Naturalistic and Analog Observations Naturalistic clinical observations usually take place in homes, schools, institutions such as hospitals and prisons, or community settings. Most of them focus on parent-child, sibling-child, or teacher-child interactions and on fearful, aggressive, or disruptive behavior (Lindheim, Bernard, & Dozier, 2011; Murdock et al., 2005). Often such observations are made by *participant observers,* key persons in the client's environment, and reported to the clinician.

When naturalistic observations are not practical, clinicians may resort to analog observations, often aided by special equipment such as a video camera or one-way mirror (Lindheim et al., 2011; Haynes, 2001). Analog observations often have focused on children interacting with their parents, married couples attempting to settle a disagreement, speech-anxious people giving a speech, and fearful people approaching an object they find frightening.

Although much can be learned from actually witnessing behavior, clinical observations have certain disadvantages (Norton et al., 2010; Connor-Greene, 2007). For one thing, they are not always reliable. It is possible for various clinicians who observe the same person to focus on different aspects of behavior, assess the person differently, and arrive at different conclusions (Meersand, 2011). Careful training of observers and the use of observer checklists can help reduce this problem.

Similarly, observers may make errors that affect the validity, or accuracy, of their observations (Wilson et al., 2010; Aiken & Groth-Marnat, 2006). The observer may

An ideal observation
Using a one-way mirror, a clinical observer is able to view a mother interacting with her child without distracting the duo or influencing their behaviors.

suffer from *overload* and be unable to see or record all of the important behaviors and events. Or the observer may experience *observer drift,* a steady decline in accuracy as a result of fatigue or of a gradual unintentional change in the standards used when an observation continues for a long period of time. Another possible problem is *observer bias*—the observer's judgments may be influenced by information and expectations he or she already has about the person (Pellegrini, 2011).

A client's *reactivity* may also limit the validity of clinical observations; that is, his or her behavior may be affected by the very presence of the observer (Mowery et al., 2010; Norton et al., 2010). If schoolchildren are aware that someone special is watching them, for example, they may change their usual classroom behavior, perhaps in the hope of creating a good impression (Lane et al., 2011).

Finally, clinical observations may lack *cross-situational validity.* A child who behaves aggressively in school is not necessarily aggressive at home or with friends after school. Because behavior is often specific to particular situations, observations in one setting cannot always be applied to other settings (Kagan, 2007).

Self-Monitoring As you saw earlier, personality and response inventories are tests in which persons report their own behaviors, feelings, or cognitions. In a related assessment procedure, *self-monitoring,* people observe themselves and carefully record the frequency of certain behaviors, feelings, or thoughts as they occur over time (Norton et al., 2010; Wright & Truax, 2008). How frequently, for instance, does a drug user have an urge for drugs or a headache sufferer have a headache? Self-monitoring is especially useful in assessing behavior that occurs so infrequently that it is unlikely to be seen during other kinds of observations. It is also useful for behaviors that occur so frequently that any other method of observing them in detail would be impossible—for example, smoking, drinking, or other drug use. Finally, self-monitoring may be the only way to observe and measure private thoughts or perceptions.

Like all other clinical assessment procedures, however, self-monitoring has drawbacks (Baranski, 2011; Wright & Truax, 2008). Here too validity is often a problem. People do not always manage or try to record their observations accurately. Furthermore, when people monitor themselves, they may change their behaviors unintentionally (Holifield et al., 2010; Otten, 2004). Smokers, for example, often smoke fewer cigarettes than usual when they are monitoring themselves, and teachers give more positive and fewer negative comments to their students.

Diagnosis: Does the Client's Syndrome Match a Known Disorder?

Clinicians use the information from interviews, tests, and observations to construct an integrated picture of the factors that are causing and maintaining a client's disturbance, a construction sometimes known as a *clinical picture* (Kellerman & Burry, 2007). Clinical pictures also may be influenced to a degree by the clinician's theoretical orientation (Garb, 2010, 2006). The psychologist who worked with Angela Savanti held a cognitive-behavioral view of abnormality and so produced a picture that emphasized modeling and reinforcement principles and Angela's expectations, assumptions, and interpretations:

Angela was rarely reinforced for any of her accomplishments at school, but she gained her mother's negative attention for what Mrs. Savanti judged to be poor performance at school or at home. Mrs. Savanti repeatedly told her daughter that she was incompetent,

•**diagnosis**•A determination that a person's problems reflect a particular disorder.

•**syndrome**•A cluster of symptoms that usually occur together.

•**classification system**•A list of disorders, along with descriptions of symptoms and guidelines for making appropriate diagnoses.

and any mishaps that happened to her were her own fault. . . . When Mr. Savanti deserted the family, Angela's first response was that somehow she was responsible. From her mother's past behavior, Angela had learned to expect that in some way she would be blamed. At the time that Angela broke up with her boyfriend, she did not blame Jerry for his behavior, but interpreted this event as a failing solely on her part. As a result, her level of self-esteem was lowered still more.

The type of marital relationship that Angela saw her mother and father model remained her concept of what married life is like. She generalized from her observations of her parents' discordant interactions to an expectation of the type of behavior that she and Jerry would ultimately engage in. . . .

Angela's uncertainties intensified when she was deprived of the major source of gratification she had, her relationship with Jerry. Despite the fact that she was overwhelmed with doubts about whether to marry him or not, she had gained a great deal of pleasure through being with Jerry. Whatever feelings she had been able to express, she had shared with him and no one else. Angela labeled Jerry's termination of their relationship as proof that she was not worthy of another person's interest. She viewed her present unhappiness as likely to continue, and she attributed it to some failing on her part. As a result, she became quite depressed.

(Leon, 1991, 1984, pp. 123–125)

With the assessment data and clinical picture in hand, clinicians are ready to make a **diagnosis** (from the Greek word for "a discrimination")—that is, a determination that a person's psychological problems constitute a particular disorder. When clinicians decide, through diagnosis, that a client's pattern of dysfunction reflects a particular disorder, they are saying that the pattern is basically the same as one that has been displayed by many other people, has been investigated in a variety of studies, and perhaps has responded to particular forms of treatment. They can then apply what is generally known about the disorder to the particular individual they are trying to help. They can, for example, better predict the future course of the person's problem and the treatments that are likely to be helpful.

Classification Systems

The principle behind diagnosis is straightforward. When certain symptoms occur together regularly—a cluster of symptoms is called a **syndrome**—and follow a particular course, clinicians agree that those symptoms make up a particular mental disorder. If people display this particular pattern of symptoms, diagnosticians assign them to that diagnostic category. A list of such categories, or disorders, with descriptions of the symptoms and guidelines for assigning individuals to the categories, is known as a **classification system.**

Why do you think many clinicians prefer the label "person with schizophrenia" over "schizophrenic person"?

In 1883 Emil Kraepelin developed the first modern classification system for abnormal behavior (see Chapter 1). His categories formed the foundation for the *Diagnostic and Statistical Manual of Mental Disorders* (*DSM*), the classification system currently written by the American Psychiatric Association (APA, 2013). The DSM is the most widely used classification system in the United States. Most other countries use a system called the *International Classification of Diseases* (*ICD*), developed by the World Health Organization.

The DSM has been changed significantly over time. The current edition, called DSM-5, was published in 2013. It features a number of changes from the previous edition, DSM-IV-TR, and the editions prior to that.

DSM-5

DSM-5 lists approximately 400 mental disorders (see Figure 4-3). Each entry describes the criteria for diagnosing the disorder and its key clinical features. The system also describes features that are often but not always related to the disorder. The classification system is further accompanied by background information such as research findings; age, culture, or gender trends (see *PsychWatch* on the next page); and each disorder's prevalence, risk, course, complications, predisposing factors, and family patterns.

DSM-5 requires clinicians to provide both categorical and dimensional information as part of a proper diagnosis. *Categorical information* refers to the name of the category (disorder) indicated by the client's symptoms. *Dimensional information* is a rating of how severe a client's symptoms are and how dysfunctional the client is across various dimensions of personality.

Categorical Information
First, the clinician must decide whether the person is displaying one of the hundreds of psychological disorders listed in the manual. Some of the most frequently diagnosed disorders are the anxiety disorders and depressive disorders—problems you will read about later.

ANXIETY DISORDERS People with anxiety disorders may experience general feelings of anxiety and worry (*generalized anxiety disorder*); fears of specific situations, objects, or activities (*phobias*); anxiety about social situations (*social anxiety disorder*); repeated outbreaks of panic (*panic disorder*); or anxiety about being separated from one's parents or other key individuals (*separation anxiety disorder*).

DEPRESSIVE DISORDERS People with depressive disorders may experience an episode of extreme sadness and related symptoms (*major depressive disorder*), persistent and chronic sadness (*persistent depressive disorder*), or severe premenstrual sadness and related symptoms (*premenstrual dysphoric disorder*).

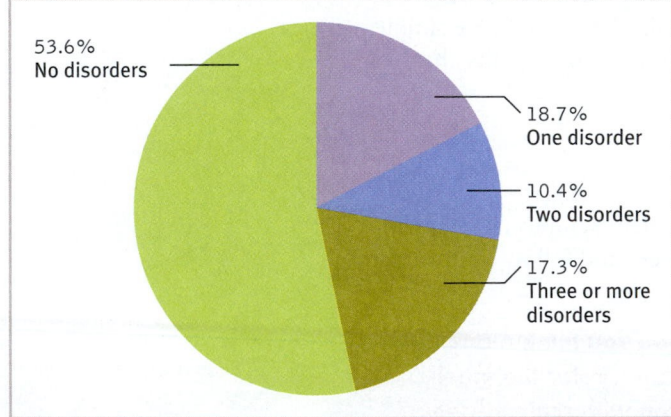

53.6%
No disorders

18.7%
One disorder

10.4%
Two disorders

17.3%
Three or more disorders

Figure 4-3

How many people in the United States qualify for a DSM diagnosis during their lives? Almost half, according to some surveys. Some of them even experience two or more different disorders, an occurrence known as comorbidity. (Adapted from Greenberg, 2011; Kessler et al., 2005.)

Although people may receive just one diagnosis from the DSM-5 list, they often receive more than one. Angela Savanti would likely receive a diagnosis of *major depressive disorder*. In addition, let's suppose the clinician judged that Angela's indecisiveness over marrying Jerry was really but one example of a much broader, persistent pattern of excessive worry, procrastination, and avoidance. She might then also receive a diagnosis of *generalized anxiety disorder*.

Dimensional Information
In addition to deciding what disorder a client is displaying, diagnosticians assess the current severity of the client's disorder—that is, how much the symptoms impair the client. For each disorder, the framers of DSM-5 have suggested various rating scales that may prove useful for evaluating the severity of the particular disorder (APA, 2012). In cases of major depressive disorder, for example, the Severity of Illness Rating Scale may be used. This scale asks clinicians to indicate where the client falls on a 7-point scale ranging from "normal, not at all ill" (rating of 1) to "among the most extremely ill patients" (rating of 7). Based on her clinical interview, tests, and observations, Angela might warrant a rating of 5 ("markedly ill") from her therapist. DSM-5 is the first edition of the DSM to consistently seek both categorical and dimensional information as part of the diagnosis, rather than categorical information alone.

Additional Information
Clinicians also have the opportunity to provide other useful information when making a diagnosis. They may, for example, specify relevant medical conditions and special psychosocial problems the client has. If Angela Savanti had diabetes, the clinician might indicate that. Similarly, Angela's recent breakup with

Culture-Bound Abnormality

Red Bear sits up wild-eyed, his body drenched in sweat, every muscle tensed. The horror of the dream is still with him; he is choked with fear. Fighting waves of nausea, he stares at his young wife lying asleep on the far side of the wig-wam, illuminated by the dying embers.

His troubles began several days before, when he came back from a hunting expedition empty-handed. Ashamed of his failure, he fell prey to a deep, lingering depression. . . . The signs of windigo were all there: depression, lack of appetite, nausea, sleeplessness and, now, the dream. Indeed, there could be no mistake.

He had dreamed of the windigo—the monster with a heart of ice—and the dream sealed his doom. Coldness gripped his own heart. The ice monster had entered his body and possessed him. He himself had become a windigo, and he could do nothing to avert his fate.

Suddenly, the form of Red Bear's sleeping wife begins to change. He no longer sees a woman, but a deer. His eyes flame. Silently, he draws his knife from under the blanket and moves stealthily toward the motionless figure. . . . A powerful desire to eat raw flesh consumes him.

With the body of the "deer" at his feet, Red Bear raises the knife high, preparing the strike. Unexpectedly, the deer screams and twists away. But the knife flashes down, again and again. Too late, Red Bear's kinsmen rush into the wigwam. . . . [T]hey drag him outside into the cold night air and swiftly kill him.

(LINDHOLM & LINDHOLM, 1981, P. 52)

Red Bear was suffering from *windigo*, a disorder once common among Algonquin Indian hunters. They believed in a supernatural monster that ate human beings and had the power to bewitch them and turn them into cannibals. Red Bear was among the few afflicted hunters who actually did kill and eat members of their households.

Windigo is but one of numerous unusual mental disorders discovered around the world, each unique to a particular

Do Western abnormalities follow? A culture clash is on display as this woman with a head scarf walks past a Western billboard upon leaving a metro stop in Turkey (religious Muslim women cover their hair). The spread of Western values, fashions, and ads to eastern European and Asian countries appears to have more than a political and cultural impact. According to research, such changes are often accompanied by a rise in the rates of anorexia nervosa and other psychological disorders that once seemed to be found strictly in Western society.

culture, each apparently growing from that culture's pressures, history, institutions, and ideas (Flaskerud, 2009; Draguns, 2006). Such disorders remind us that the classifications and diagnoses applied in one culture may not always be appropriate in another.

Susto, a disorder found among members of Indian tribes in Central and South America and Hispanic natives of the Andean highlands of Peru, Bolivia, and Colombia, is most likely to occur in infants and young children. The symptoms are extreme anxiety, excitability, and depression, along with loss of weight, weakness, and rapid heartbeat. The culture holds that this disorder is caused by contact with supernatural beings or with frightening strangers or by bad air from cemeteries.

People affected with *amok,* a disorder found in Malaysia, the Philippines, Java, and some parts of Africa, jump around violently, yell loudly, grab knives or other weapons, and attack any people and objects they encounter. Within the culture, amok is thought to be caused by stress, severe shortage of sleep, alcohol consumption, and extreme heat.

Koro is a pattern of anxiety found in Southeast Asia in which a man suddenly becomes intensely fearful that his penis will withdraw into his abdomen and that he will die as a result. Cultural lore holds that the disorder is caused by an imbalance of "yin" and "yang," two natural forces believed to be the fundamental components of life. Accepted forms of treatment include having the individual keep a firm hold on his penis until the fear passes, often with the assistance of family members or friends, and clamping the penis to a wooden box.

Latah is a disorder found in Malaysia. Certain circumstances (hearing someone say "snake" or being tickled, for example) trigger a fright reaction that is marked by repeating the words and acts of other people, uttering obscenities, and doing the opposite of what others ask.

Carolyn Drake/The New York Times/Redux Pictures

her boyfriend might be noted as a special psychosocial problem. Altogether, Angela might receive the following diagnosis:

> **Diagnosis:** Major depressive disorder
> **Severity rating:** 5 ("markedly ill")
> **Additional information**
> *Medical problem:* Diabetes
> *Psychosocial problem:* Termination of relationship

Is DSM-5 an Effective Classification System?

A classification system, like an assessment method, is judged by its reliability and validity. Here *reliability* means that different clinicians are likely to agree on the diagnosis when they use the system to diagnose the same client. Early versions of the DSM were at best moderately reliable (Regier et al., 2011; Malik & Beutler, 2002). In the early 1960s, for example, four clinicians, each relying on DSM-I, the first edition of the DSM, independently interviewed 153 patients (Beck et al., 1962). Only 54 percent of their diagnoses were in agreement. Because all four clinicians were experienced diagnosticians, their failure to agree suggested deficiencies in the classification system.

The framers of DSM-5 followed certain procedures in their development of the new manual to help ensure that DSM-5 would have greater reliability than the previous DSMs (APA, 2013, 2012; Hyman, 2011). For example, they conducted extensive reviews of research to pinpoint which categories in past DSMs had been too vague and unreliable. In addition, they gathered input from a wide range of experienced clinicians and researchers. They then developed a number of new diagnostic criteria and categories, expecting that the new criteria and categories were in fact reliable. Despite such efforts, some critics continue to have concerns about the procedures used in the development of DSM-5 (Freedman et al., 2013; Frances, 2013, 2012; Robbins, 2012). They worry, for example, that the framers failed to run a sufficient number of their own studies—in particular, *field studies* that test the merits of the new criteria and categories. In turn, the critics fear that DSM-5 has retained several of the reliability problems that were on

"Am I a happy man or just an asymptomatic one?"

AP Photo/Keystone/Martial Trezzini

display in the past DSMs. It may be, for example, that, as DSM-5 is used over the coming years, many clinicians will have difficulty distinguishing one kind of DSM-5 anxiety disorder from another. The disorder of a particular client may be classified as generalized anxiety disorder by one clinician, agoraphobia (fear of traveling outside of one's home) by another, and social anxiety disorder (fear of social situations) by yet another.

The *validity* of a classification system is the accuracy of the information that its diagnostic categories provide. Categories are of most use to clinicians when they demonstrate *predictive validity*—that is, when they help predict future symptoms or events. A common symptom of major depressive disorder is either insomnia or excessive sleep. When clinicians give Angela Savanti a diagnosis of major depressive disorder, they expect that she may eventually develop sleep problems even if none are present now. In addition, they expect her to respond to treatments that are effective for other depressed persons. The more often such predictions are accurate, the greater a category's predictive validity.

DSM-5's framers tried to also ensure the validity of this new edition by conducting extensive reviews of research and consulting with numerous clinical advisors. As a result, its criteria and categories appear to have stronger validity than those of the earlier versions of the DSM. But, again, many clinical theorists worry that at least some of the criteria and categories in DSM-5 are based on weak research and that others may reflect gender or racial bias (Frances, 2013; Freedman et al., 2013; Hyman, 2011; Yonkers & Clarke, 2011).

Call for Change

The effort to produce DSM-5 took more than a decade. After years of preliminary work, a DSM-5 task force and numerous work groups were formed in 2006; their goal was to develop a DSM that addressed the limitations of previous DSM editions. As noted earlier, the task force and work groups conducted scientific reviews and gathered input from a wide range of clinical advisors to help develop a DSM that would reflect current insights, research findings, and clinical concerns (APA, 2012).

Between 2010 and 2012, the task force released several drafts of DSM-5 online, and clinical researchers and practitioners were asked to offer their suggestions. Given the outreach of the Internet, the response from the clinical community was enormous—beyond anything the previous DSM task forces had experienced. And, not surprisingly, given the diversity of orientations in the clinical field today, the response was wide-ranging—including an onslaught of criticism from many quarters. The DSM-5 task force took the online feedback into consideration and completed the new edition of the classification system. In December 2012, the American Psychiatric Association (APA) Board of Trustees approved the final version of DSM-5. It also publicly announced which of the proposed categories and criteria from the various drafts had been retained, changed, or eliminated in the final version. Finally, DSM-5, the new diagnostic and classification system, was published in May 2013. The categories and criteria of DSM-5 are featured throughout this textbook (APA, 2013, 2012; Chapman, 2013; Fawcett, 2012; Jeste, 2012).

Some of the key changes in DSM-5 are the following:

- Adding a new category, "autism spectrum disorder," that combines certain past categories such as "autistic disorder" and "Asperger's syndrome" (see Chapter 17).

- Viewing "obsessive-compulsive disorder" as a problem that is different from the anxiety disorders and grouping it instead along with other compulsive-like disorders such as "hoarding disorder," "body dysmorphic disorder," "hair-pulling disorder," and "excoriation (skin-picking) disorder" (see Chapter 5).

- Viewing "posttraumatic stress disorder" as a problem that is distinct from the anxiety disorders (see Chapter 6).

- Adding a new category, "somatic symptom disorder" (see Chapter 7).

- Replacing the term "hypochondriasis" with the new term "illness anxiety disorder" (see Chapter 7).

- Adding a new category, "premenstrual dysphoric disorder" (see Chapter 8).

- Adding a new category, "disruptive mood dysregulation disorder" (see Chapters 8 and 17).

- Adding a new category, "binge eating disorder" (see Chapter 11).

- Adding a new category, "substance use disorder," that combines past categories "substance abuse" and "substance dependence" (see Chapter 12).

- Viewing "gambling disorder" as a problem that should be grouped as an addictive disorder alongside the "substance use disorders" (Chapters 12).

- Replacing the term "gender identity disorder" with the new term "gender dysphoria" (see Chapter 13).

- Replacing the term "mental retardation" with the new term "intellectual developmental disorder" ("intellectual disability") (Chapter 17).

- Adding a new category, "specific learning disorder," that combines past categories "reading disorder," "mathematics disorder," and "disorder of written expression" (see Chapter 17).

- Replacing the term "dementia" with the new term "neurocognitive disorder" (Chapter 18).

- Adding a new category, "mild neurocognitive disorder" (see Chapter 18).

Can Diagnosis and Labeling Cause Harm?

Even with trustworthy assessment data and reliable and valid classification categories, clinicians will sometimes arrive at a wrong conclusion (Faust & Ahern, 2012; Fernbach et al., 2011; Norman & Eva, 2010). Like all human beings, they are flawed information processors. Studies show that they are overly influenced by information gathered early in the assessment process (Dawes, Faust, & Meehl, 2002; Meehl, 1996, 1960). They sometimes pay too much attention to certain sources of information, such as a parent's report about a child, and too little to others, such as the child's point of view (McCoy, 1976). Finally, their judgments can be distorted by any number of personal biases—gender, age, race, and socioeconomic status, to name just a few (Vasquez, 2007). Given the limitations of assessment tools, assessors, and classification systems, it is small wonder that studies sometimes uncover shocking errors in diagnosis, especially in hospitals (Mitchell, 2010; Vickrey, Samuels, & Ropper, 2010).

In a classic study, for example, a clinical team was asked to reevaluate the records of 131 patients at a mental hospital in New York, conduct interviews with many of these persons, and arrive at a diagnosis for each one (Lipton & Simon, 1985). The researchers then compared the team's diagnoses with the original diagnoses for which the patients were hospitalized. Although 89 of the patients had originally received a diagnosis of schizophrenia, only 16 received it upon reevaluation. And whereas 15 patients originally had been given a diagnosis of a mood disorder, 50 received it now. It is obviously important for clinicians to be aware that such huge disagreements can occur.

Why are medical diagnoses usually valued, while the use of psychological diagnoses is often criticized?

Beyond the potential for misdiagnosis, the very act of classifying people can lead to unintended results. As you read in Chapter 3, for example, many family-social theorists believe that diagnostic labels can become self-fulfilling prophecies. When people are diagnosed as mentally disturbed, they may be viewed and reacted to correspondingly. If others expect them to take on a sick role, they may begin to consider themselves sick as well and act that way. Furthermore, our society attaches a stigma to abnormality (Bell et al., 2011; Rosenberg, 2011). People labeled mentally ill may find it difficult to get a job, especially a position of responsibility, or to be welcomed into social relationships. Once a label has been applied, it may stick for a long time.

Because of these problems, some clinicians would like to do away with diagnoses. Others disagree. They believe we must simply work to increase what is known about psychological disorders and improve diagnostic techniques. They hold that classification and diagnosis are critical to understanding and treating people in distress.

Elizabeth Eckert, Middletown, NY. From L. Gamwell and N. Tomes, *Madness in America*, 1995, Cornell University Press.

The power of labeling
When looking at this late-nineteenth-century photograph of a baseball team at the State Homeopathic Asylum for the Insane in Middletown, New York, most observers assume that the players are patients. As a result, they tend to "see" depression or confusion in the players' faces and posture. In fact, the players are members of the asylum staff, some of whom even sought their jobs for the express purpose of playing for the hospital team.

BETWEEN THE LINES

Famous Movie Clinicians

Dr. Banks (*Side Effects*, 2013) ‹‹

Dr. Patel (*The Silver Linings Playbook*, 2012) ‹‹

Dr. Logue (*The King's Speech*, 2010) ‹‹

Dr. Cawley (*Shutter Island*, 2010) ‹‹

Dr. Steele (*Changeling*, 2008) ‹‹

Dr. Rosen (*A Beautiful Mind*, 2001) ‹‹

Dr. Crowe (*The Sixth Sense*, 1999) ‹‹

Dr. McGuire (*Good Will Hunting*, 1997) ‹‹

Dr. Lecter (*The Silence of the Lambs*, 1991; *Hannibal*, 2001; and *Red Dragon*, 2002) ‹‹

Dr. Marvin (*What About Bob?*, 1991) ‹‹

Dr. Sayer (*Awakenings*, 1990) ‹‹

Dr. Sobel (*Analyze This*, 1999; and *Analyze That*, 2002) ‹‹

Dr. Berger (*Ordinary People*, 1980) ‹‹

Dr. Dysart (*Equus*, 1977) ‹‹

Nurse Ratched (*One Flew Over the Cuckoo's Nest*, 1975) ‹‹

Drs. Petersen and Murchison (*Spellbound*, 1945) ‹‹

•empirically supported treatment•
A movement in the clinical field that seeks to identify which therapies have received clear research support for each disorder, to develop corresponding treatment guidelines, and to spread such information to clinicians. Also known as *evidence-based treatment*.

Treatment: How Might the Client Be Helped?

Over the course of 10 months, Angela Savanti was treated for depression and related symptoms. She improved considerably during that time, as the following report describes:

> Angela's depression eased as she began to make progress in therapy. A few months before the termination of treatment, she and Jerry resumed dating. Angela discussed with Jerry her greater comfort in expressing her feelings and her hope that Jerry would also become more expressive with her. They discussed the reasons why Angela was ambivalent about getting married, and they began to talk again about the possibility of marriage. Jerry, however, was not making demands for a decision by a certain date, and Angela felt that she was not as frightened about marriage as she previously had been. . . .
>
> Psychotherapy provided Angela with the opportunity to learn to express her feelings to the persons she was interacting with, and this was quite helpful to her. Most important, she was able to generalize from some of the learning experiences in therapy and modify her behavior in her renewed relationship with Jerry. Angela still had much progress to make in terms of changing the characteristic ways she interacted with others, but she had already made a number of important steps in a potentially happier direction.
>
> *(Leon, 1991, 1984, pp. 118, 125)*

Clearly, treatment helped Angela, and by its conclusion she was a happier, more functional person than the woman who had first sought help 10 months earlier. But how did her therapist decide on the treatment program that proved to be so helpful?

Treatment Decisions

Angela's therapist began, like all therapists, with assessment information and diagnostic decisions. Knowing the specific details and background of Angela's problem (*idiographic data*) and combining this individual information with broad information about the nature and treatment of depression (*nomothetic data*), the clinician arrived at a treatment plan for her.

Yet therapists may be influenced by additional factors when they make treatment decisions. Their treatment plans typically reflect their theoretical orientations and how they have learned to conduct therapy (Sharf, 2012). As therapists apply a favored model in case after case, they become more and more familiar with its principles and treatment techniques and tend to use them in work with still other clients.

Current research may also play a role. Most clinicians say that they value research as a guide to practice (Beutler et al., 1995). However, not all of them actually read research articles, so they cannot be directly influenced by them (Rivett, 2011; Stewart & Chambless, 2007). In fact, according to surveys, therapists gather most of their information about the latest developments in the field from colleagues, professional newsletters, workshops, conferences, Web sites, books, and the like (Simon, 2011; Corrie & Callanan, 2001). Unfortunately, the accuracy and usefulness of these sources vary widely.

To help clinicians become more familiar with and apply research findings, there is an ever-growing movement in the United States, the United Kingdom, and elsewhere called **empirically supported,** or **evidence-based, treatment** (Carroll, 2012; Sharf, 2012; Pope & Wedding, 2011). Proponents of this movement have formed task forces that seek to identify which therapies have received clear research support for each disorder, to propose corresponding treatment guidelines, and to spread such information to clinicians. Critics of the movement worry that such efforts have thus far been simplistic, biased, and, at times, misleading (Nairn, 2012; Hagemoser, 2009; Weinberger & Rasco, 2007). However, the empirically supported treatment movement has been gaining momentum in recent years.

The Effectiveness of Treatment

Altogether, more than 400 forms of therapy are currently practiced in the clinical field (Corsini & Wedding, 2011). Naturally, the most important question to ask about each of them is whether it does what it is supposed to do. Does a particular treatment really help people overcome their psychological problems (see *PsychWatch* on the next page)? If so, the practitioner has performed a major service for the client. On the surface, the question may seem simple. In fact, it is one of the most difficult questions for clinical researchers to answer.

The first problem is how to *define* "success." If, as Angela's therapist suggests, she still has much progress to make at the conclusion of therapy, should her recovery be considered successful? The second problem is how to *measure* improvement (Lambert, 2010; Luborsky, 2004). Should researchers give equal weight to the reports of clients, friends, relatives, therapists, and teachers? Should they use rating scales, inventories, therapy insights, observations, or some other measure?

Perhaps the biggest problem in determining the effectiveness of treatment is the *variety* and *complexity* of the treatments currently in use. People differ in their problems, personal styles, and motivations for therapy. Therapists differ in skill, experience, orientation, and personality. And therapies differ in theory, format, and setting. Because an individual's progress is influenced by all these factors and more, the findings of a particular study will not always apply to other clients and therapists.

Proper research procedures address some of these problems. By using control groups, random assignment, matched research participants, and the like, clinicians can draw certain conclusions about various therapies. Even in studies that are well designed, however, the variety and complexity of treatment limit the conclusions that can be reached (Kazdin, 2011, 2006, 2004, 1994).

Despite these difficulties, the job of evaluating therapies must be done, and clinical researchers have plowed ahead with it. Investigators have, in fact, conducted thousands of *therapy outcome studies*, studies that measure the effects of various treatments. The studies typically ask one of three questions: (1) Is therapy *in general* effective? (2) Are *particular* therapies generally effective? (3) Are *particular* therapies effective for *particular* problems?

Is Therapy Generally Effective?
Studies suggest that therapy often is more helpful than no treatment or than placebos. A pioneering review examined 375 controlled studies, covering a total of almost 25,000 people seen in a wide assortment of therapies (Smith, Glass, & Miller, 1980; Smith & Glass, 1977). The reviewers combined the findings of these studies by using a special statistical technique called *meta-analysis.* According to this analysis, the average person who received treatment was better off than 75 percent of the untreated persons (see Figure 4-4). Other meta-analyses have found similar relationships between treatment and improvement (Sharf, 2012; Bickman, 2005).

"Can you describe this china shop?"

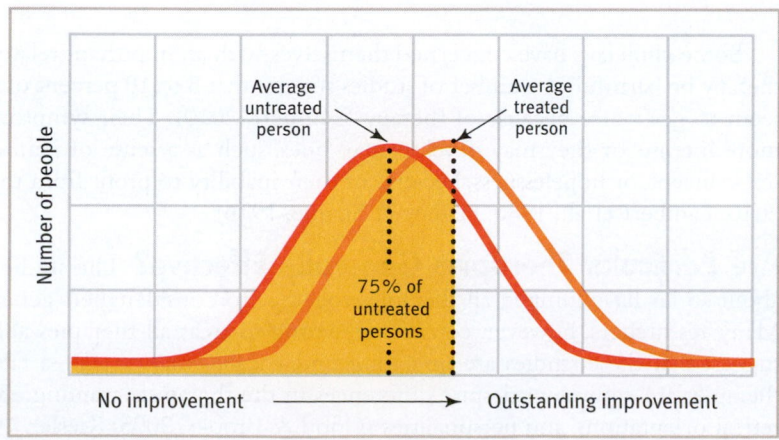

Figure 4-4
Does therapy help? Combining participants and results from hundreds of studies, investigators have determined that the average person who receives psychotherapy experiences greater improvement than do 75 percent of all untreated people with similar problems. (Adapted from Prochaska & Norcross, 2010; Lambert et al., 1993; Smith et al., 1980.)

Dark Sites

As you have seen, clinicians try to combat psychological disorders, either by preventive efforts or, if those fail, through assessment, diagnosis, and effective treatment. Unfortunately, today there are also other—more sinister—forces operating that run counter to the work of mental health professionals. Among the most common are so-called *dark sites* on the Internet—sites with the goal of promoting behaviors that the clinical community, and most of society, consider abnormal and destructive. *Pro-anorexia sites* and *suicide sites* are two examples.

Pro-anorexia sites

The Eating Disorders Association reports that there are more than 500 pro-anorexia Internet sites with names such as "Dying to Be Thin" and "Starving for Perfection" (Borzekowski et al., 2010). Users of these sites exchange tips on how they can starve themselves and disguise their weight loss from family, friends, and doctors (Christodoulou, 2012). The sites also offer support and feedback about starvation diets. One site of this kind sponsors a contest, "The Great Ana Competition," and awards a diploma to the girl who consumes the fewest calories in a two-week period. Another site endorses what it calls

the *Pro-Anorexia Ten Commandments*—assertions such as "Being thin is more important than being healthy" and "Thou shall not eat without feeling guilty" (Catan, 2007; Barrett, 2000).

Suicide sites

Suicide sites are another Internet phenomenon. Teens and young adults seem to be at particularly high risk for imitative suicidal behavior, and they are also more likely to visit suicide chat rooms. Suicide forums and chat rooms vary in their messages, but they pose clear risks to depressed or impressionable users. Some pro-suicide Web sites celebrate former users who have committed suicide; others help set up appointments for joint or partner suicides; and several offer specific instructions about suicide methods and locations and writing suicide notes (Davey, 2010; Becker & Schmidt, 2004).

During a two-month period in 2008, for example, 30 people committed suicide across Japan, all of them involving the use of detergent mixtures that produce a deadly hydrogen sulfide gas—a technique repeatedly described and encouraged on Internet suicide sites (CNN, 2008). A 31-year-old man took his life in a car using a mixture of detergent and bath salts, a 42-year-old woman killed herself in her bathroom using toilet cleaner and bath powder, and a 14-year-old girl mixed laundry detergent with cleanser to commit suicide in her apartment. Such detergent mixtures release powerful fumes that can also endanger innocent bystanders, so almost all of those who killed themselves in this way hung warning signs at the locations of their suicide saying "Stay Away" or "Poisonous Gas Being Emitted"—warnings apparently also suggested on the Internet suicide sites.

Many individuals worry that Internet suicide sites place vulnerable people at great risk, and they have called for the banning of these sites. Others argue, however, that despite their dangers, the sites represent basic freedoms that should not be violated—freedom of speech, for example, and perhaps even the freedom to do oneself harm.

Some clinicians have concerned themselves with an important related question: Can therapy be harmful? A number of studies suggest that 5 to 10 percent of patients actually seem to get worse because of therapy (Lambert, 2010). Their symptoms may become more intense, or they may develop new ones, such as a sense of failure, guilt, reduced self-concept, or hopelessness, because of their inability to profit from therapy (Lambert, 2010; Lambert et al., 1986; Hadley & Strupp, 1976).

Are Particular Therapies Generally Effective? The studies you have read about so far have lumped all therapies together to consider their general effectiveness. Many researchers, however, consider it wrong to treat all therapies alike. Some critics suggest that these studies are operating under a *uniformity myth*—a false belief that all therapies are equivalent despite differences in the therapists' training, experience, theoretical orientations, and personalities (Good & Brooks, 2005; Kiesler, 1995, 1966).

•**rapprochement movement**•An effort to identify a set of common strategies that run through the work of all effective therapists.

•**psychopharmacologist**•A psychiatrist who primarily prescribes medications.

Thus, an alternative approach examines the effectiveness of *particular* therapies. Most research of this kind shows each of the major forms of therapy to be superior to no treatment or to placebo treatment (Prochaska & Norcross, 2010). A number of other studies have compared particular therapies with one another and found that no one form of therapy generally stands out over all others (Luborsky et al., 2006, 2003, 2002, 1975).

If different kinds of therapy have similar successes, might they have something in common? A **rapprochement movement** has tried to identify a set of common strategies that may run through the work of all effective therapists, regardless of the clinicians' particular orientation (Sharf, 2012; Bohart & Tallman, 2010). Surveys of highly successful therapists suggest, for example, that most give feedback to clients, help clients focus on their own thoughts and behavior, pay attention to the way they and their clients are interacting, and try to promote self-mastery in their clients. In short, effective therapists of any type may practice more similarly than they preach.

How can people make wise decisions about therapists and treatment approaches when they are seeking treatment?

Are Particular Therapies Effective for Particular Problems?

People with different disorders may respond differently to the various forms of therapy (Beutler, 2011). In an oft-quoted statement, influential clinical theorist Gordon Paul said decades ago that the most appropriate question regarding the effectiveness of therapy may be "*What* specific treatment, by *whom,* is most effective for *this* individual with *that* specific problem, and under *which* set of circumstances?" (Paul, 1967, p. 111). Researchers have investigated how effective particular therapies are at treating particular disorders, and they often have found sizable differences among the various therapies. Behavioral therapies, for example, appear to be the most effective of all in treating phobias (Wilson, 2011), whereas drug therapy is the single most effective treatment for schizophrenia (Minzenberg, Yoon, & Carter, 2011).

As you read previously, studies also show that some clinical problems may respond better to *combined* approaches (Bandelow et al., 2012; Kim et al., 2012). Drug therapy is sometimes combined with certain forms of psychotherapy, for example, to treat depression. In fact, it is now common for clients to be seen by two therapists—one of them a **psychopharmacologist,** a psychiatrist who primarily prescribes medications, and the other a psychologist, social worker, or other therapist who conducts psychotherapy.

Obviously, knowledge of how particular therapies fare with particular disorders can help therapists and clients alike make better decisions about treatment (Beutler, 2011, 2002, 2000; Beutler et al., 2011) (see Figure 4-5). We will keep returning to this issue as we examine the various disorders throughout the book.

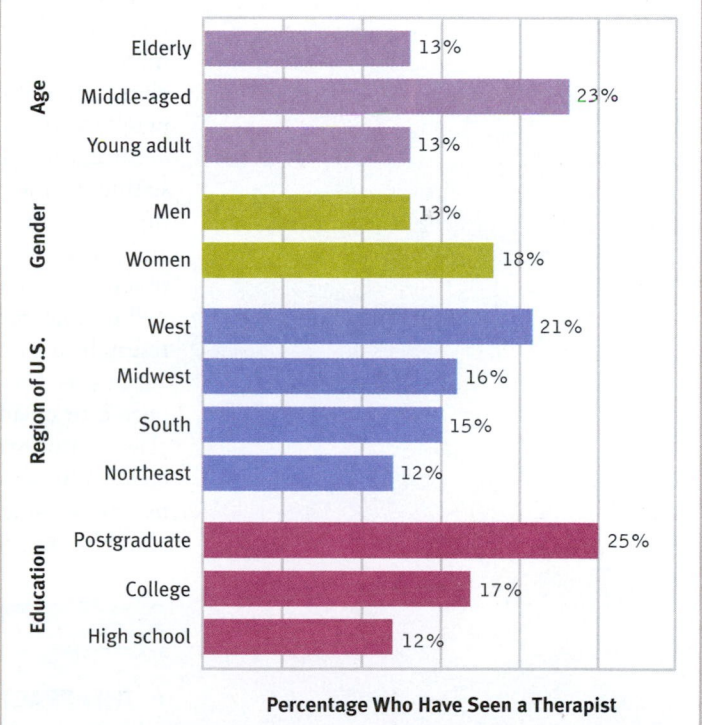

Percentage Who Have Seen a Therapist

Figure 4-5

Who seeks therapy? According to surveys conducted in the United States, people who are middle-aged, female, from Western states, and highly educated are the most likely to have been in therapy at some point in their lives. (Adapted from Howes, 2008; Fetto, 2002.)

PUTTING IT together

Assessment and Diagnosis at a Crossroads

In Chapter 3 you read that today's leading models of abnormal behavior often differ widely in their assumptions, conclusions, and treatments. It should not surprise you, then, that clinicians also differ considerably in their approaches to assessment and diagnosis. Yet when all is said and done, no assessment technique stands out as superior to the rest. Each of the hundreds of available tools has major limitations, and each produces at best an incomplete picture of how a person is functioning and why.

HERE LIES
FREDERICK
JONES

VERBAL — MATH
680   720

In short, the present state of assessment and diagnosis argues against relying exclusively on any one approach. As a result, more and more clinicians now use *batteries* of assessment tools in their work. Such batteries already are providing invaluable guidance in the assessment of Alzheimer's disease and certain other disorders that are particularly difficult to diagnose, as you shall see later.

Attitudes toward clinical assessment have shifted back and forth over the past several decades. Before the 1950s, assessment was a highly regarded part of clinical practice. As the number of clinical models grew during the 1960s and 1970s, however, followers of each model favored certain tools over others, and the practice of assessment became fragmented. Meanwhile, research began to reveal that a number of tools were inaccurate or inconsistent. In this atmosphere, many clinicians lost confidence in and abandoned systematic assessment and diagnosis.

Today, however, respect for assessment and diagnosis is on the rise once again. One reason for this renewal of interest is the development of more precise diagnostic criteria, as presented in the current and future editions of the DSM. Another is the drive by researchers for more rigorous tests to help them select appropriate participants for clinical studies. Still another factor is the clinical field's awareness that certain disorders can be properly identified only after careful assessment procedures. A final factor is the field's growing confidence that brain-scanning techniques may soon offer assessment information about a wide range of psychological disorders, not just neurological disturbances.

Along with heightened respect for assessment and diagnosis has come increased research. Indeed, today's researchers are carefully examining every major kind of assessment tool—from projective tests to personality inventories. This work is helping many clinicians perform their work with more accuracy and consistency—welcome news for people with psychological problems.

Ironically, just as today's clinicians and researchers are rediscovering systematic assessment, rising costs and economic factors seem to be discouraging the use of assessment tools. In particular, managed care insurance plans, which emphasize lower costs and shorter treatments, often refuse to provide coverage for extensive clinical testing or observations (Wedding, 2010; Martin, 2009; Wood et al., 2002). Which of these forces will ultimately have a greater influence on clinical assessment and diagnosis—promising research or economic pressure? Only time will tell.

Finally, the practice of assessment and diagnosis of psychological disorders is expected to be affected tremendously by the use of DSM-5. Will this new edition of the classification system prove to be an improvement? Will it be embraced by more clinicians? Will it unite or divide the clinical field? What impact will DSM-5 have on the use of assessment procedures? Once again, only time will tell. Clearly, the practice of clinical assessment and diagnosis is currently at a crossroads.

Summing Up

- **THE PRACTITIONER'S TASK** Clinical practitioners are interested primarily in gathering *idiographic* information about their clients. They seek an understanding of the specific nature and origins of a client's problems through *clinical assessment* and *diagnosis*. *p. 83*

- **CLINICAL ASSESSMENT** To be useful, assessment tools must be *standardized, reliable,* and *valid.* Most clinical assessment methods fall into three general categories: *clinical interviews, tests,* and *observations.* A clinical interview permits the practitioner to interact with a client and generally get a sense of who he or she is. It may be either *unstructured* or *structured.* Types of clinical tests include *projective, personality, response, psychophysiological, neurological, neuropsychological,* and *intelligence tests.* Types of observation include *naturalistic observation* and *analog observation.* Practitioners also employ *self-monitoring:* clients observe themselves and record designated behaviors, feelings, or cognitions as they occur. *pp. 83–98*

BETWEEN THE LINES

Believe It or Not

By a strange coincidence, Hermann Rorschach's young schoolmates gave him the nickname Klex, a variant of the German *Klecks,* which means "inkblot" (Schwartz, 1993). ‹‹

■ **DIAGNOSIS** After collecting assessment information, clinicians form a *clinical picture* and decide upon a *diagnosis*. The diagnosis is chosen from a *classification system*. The system used most widely in the United States is the *Diagnostic and Statistical Manual of Mental Disorders (DSM)*. *pp. 98–99*

■ **DSM-5** The most recent version of the DSM, known as *DSM-5,* lists approximately 400 disorders. DSM-5 contains numerous additions and changes to the diagnostic categories, criteria, and organization found in past editions of the DSM. The reliability and validity of DSM-5 are currently receiving clinical review and, in some circles, criticism. *pp. 99–104*

■ **DANGERS OF DIAGNOSIS AND LABELING** Even with trustworthy assessment data and reliable and valid classification categories, clinicians will not always arrive at the correct conclusion. They are human and so fall prey to various biases, misconceptions, and expectations. Another problem related to diagnosis is the prejudice that labels arouse, which may be damaging to the person who is diagnosed. *pp. 104–106*

■ **TREATMENT** The *treatment decisions* of therapists may be influenced by assessment information, the diagnosis, the clinician's theoretical orientation and familiarity with research, and the field's state of knowledge. Determining the *effectiveness of treatment* is difficult because therapists differ in their ways of defining and measuring success. The variety and complexity of today's treatments also present a problem. *Therapy outcome studies* have led to three general conclusions: (1) people in therapy are usually better off than people with similar problems who receive no treatment; (2) the various therapies do not appear to differ dramatically in their general effectiveness; and (3) certain therapies or combinations of therapies do appear to be more effective than others for certain disorders. Some therapists currently advocate *empirically supported treatment*—the active identification, promotion, and teaching of those interventions that have received clear research support. *pp. 106–109*

PsychPortal

Visit **PsychPortal**
www.yourpsychportal.com
to access the e-book, videocases and other case materials and activities, and study aids, including flashcards, crossword puzzles, quizzes, FAQs, and research exercises.

BETWEEN THE LINES

Bands with Psychological Labels

Widespread Panic ‹‹

Madness ‹‹

Obsession ‹‹

Bad Brains ‹‹

Placebo ‹‹

Fear Factory ‹‹

Mood Elevator ‹‹

Neurosis ‹‹

Disturbed ‹‹

10,000 Maniacs ‹‹

Grupo Mania ‹‹

The Insane Clown Posse ‹‹

Unsane ‹‹

ANXIETY, OBSESSIVE-COMPULSIVE, AND RELATED DISORDERS

Tomas, a 25-year old web designer, was afraid that he was "losing his mind." He had always been a worrier. He worried about his health, his girlfriend, his work, his social life, his future, his finances, and so on. Would his best friend get angry at him? Was his girlfriend tiring of him? Was he investing his money wisely? Were his clients pleased with his work?

But, lately, those worries had increased to an unbearable level. He was becoming consumed with the notion that something terrible was about to happen to him. Within an hour's time, he might have intense concerns about going broke, developing cancer, losing one of his parents, offending his friends, and more. He was certain that disaster awaited him at every turn. No amount of reassurance, from himself or from others, brought relief for very long.

He started therapy with Dr. Adena Morven, a clinical psychologist. Dr. Morven immediately noticed how disturbed Tomas appeared. He looked tense and frightened and could not sit comfortably in his chair; he kept tapping his feet and jumped when he heard traffic noise from outside the office building. He kept sighing throughout the visit, fidgeting and shifting his position, and he appeared breathless while telling Dr. Morven about his difficulties.

Tomas described his frequent inability to concentrate to the therapist. When designing client websites, he would lose his train of thought. Less than 5 minutes into a project, he'd forget much of his overall strategy. During conversations, he would begin a sentence and then forget the point he was about to make. TV watching had become impossible. He found it almost impossible to concentrate on anything for more than 5 minutes; his mind kept drifting away from the task at hand.

To say the least, he was worried about all of this. "I'm worried about being so worried," he told Dr. Morven, almost laughing at his own remark. At this point, Tomas expected the worst whenever he began a conversation, task, plan, or outing. If an event or interaction did in fact start to go awry, he would find himself overwhelmed with uncomfortable feelings—his heart would beat faster, his breathing would increase, and he'd sweat profusely. On some occasions, he thought he was actually having a heart attack—at the ripe old age of 25.

Typically, such physical reactions lasted but a matter of seconds. However, those few seconds felt like an eternity to Tomas. He acknowledged coming back down to earth after those feelings subsided—but, for him, "back down to earth" meant back to worrying and then worrying some more.

Dr. Morven empathized with Tomas about how upsetting this all must be. She asked him why he had decided to come into therapy now—as opposed to last year, last month, or last week. Tomas was able to pinpoint several things. First, all the worrying and anxiety seemed to be on the increase. Second, he was finding it hard to sleep. His nights were filled by tossing and turning—and, of course, more worrying. Third, he suspected that all of his worrying, physical symptoms, and lack of sleep were bad for his health. Wouldn't they eventually lead to a major medical problem of some kind? And finally, his constant anxiety had begun to interfere with his life. Although his girlfriend and other acquaintances did not seem to realize how much he was suffering, he was growing weary of covering it all up. He found himself turning down social invitations and work opportunities more and more. He had even quit his once-beloved weekly poker game. Not that staying home helped in any real way. He wondered how much longer he could go on this way.

•**fear**•The central nervous system's physiological and emotional response to a serious threat to one's well-being.

•**anxiety**•The central nervous system's physiological and emotional response to a vague sense of threat or danger.

•**generalized anxiety disorder**•A disorder marked by persistent and excessive feelings of anxiety and worry about numerous events and activities.

You don't need to be as troubled as Tomas to experience fear and anxiety. Think about a time when your breathing quickened, your muscles tensed, and your heart pounded with a sudden sense of dread. Was it when your car almost skidded off the road in the rain? When your professor announced a pop quiz? What about when the person you were in love with went out with someone else, or your boss suggested that your job performance ought to improve? Any time you face what seems to be a serious threat to your well-being, you may react with the state of immediate alarm known as **fear.** Sometimes you cannot pinpoint a specific cause for your alarm, but still you feel tense and edgy, as if you expect something unpleasant to happen. The vague sense of being in danger is usually called **anxiety,** and it has the same features—the same increase in breathing, muscular tension, perspiration, and so forth—as fear.

If fear is so unpleasant, why do many people seek out the feelings of fear brought about by amusement park rides, scary movies, bungee jumping, and the like?

Although everyday experiences of fear and anxiety are not pleasant, they often are useful. They prepare us for action—for "fight or flight"—when danger threatens. They may lead us to drive more cautiously in a storm, keep up with our reading assignments, treat our friends more sensitively, and work harder at our jobs. Unfortunately, some people suffer such disabling fear and anxiety that they cannot lead normal lives. Their discomfort is too severe or too frequent, lasts too long, or is triggered too easily. These people are said to have an *anxiety disorder* or a related kind of disorder.

Anxiety disorders are the most common mental disorders in the United States (Hollander & Simeon, 2011). In any given year around 18 percent of the adult population suffer from one or another of the anxiety disorders identified by DSM-5, while close to 29 percent of all people develop one of the disorders at some point in their lives (Daitch, 2011; Kessler et al., 2010, 2009, 2005). Only around one-fifth of these individuals seek treatment (Wang et al., 2005).

People with *generalized anxiety disorder* experience general and persistent feelings of worry and anxiety. People with *specific phobias* experience a persistent and irrational fear of a particular object, activity, or situation. Individuals with *agoraphobia* fear traveling to public places such as stores or movie theaters. Those with *social anxiety disorder* are intensely afraid of social or performance situations in which embarrassment may occur. And people with *panic disorder* have recurrent attacks of terror. Most individuals with one anxiety disorder suffer from a second one as well (Merikangas & Swanson, 2010) (see Figure 5-1). Tomas, for example, experiences the excessive worry found in generalized anxiety disorder and the repeated attacks of terror that mark panic disorder. In addition, many individuals with an anxiety disorder also experience depression (Fawcett et al., 2010; Goldberg et al., 2010).

Anxiety also plays a major role in a different group of problems called *obsessive-compulsive and related disorders.* People with these disorders feel overrun by recurrent thoughts that cause anxiety or by the need to perform certain repetitive actions to reduce anxiety. Because anxiety is so prominent in these disorders, this chapter will examine them along with the anxiety disorders.

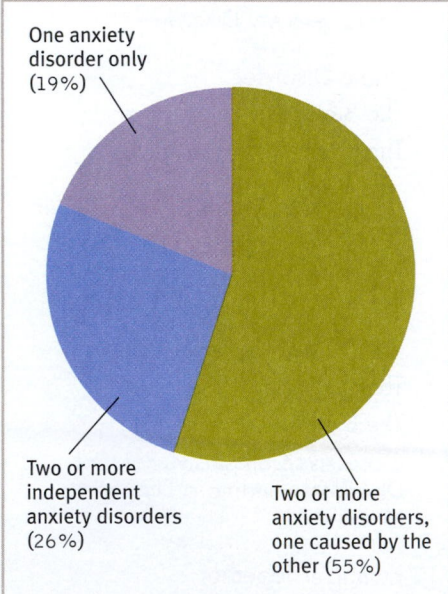

One anxiety disorder only (19%)

Two or more independent anxiety disorders (26%)

Two or more anxiety disorders, one caused by the other (55%)

Figure 5-1

Does anxiety beget anxiety? People with one anxiety disorder usually experience another as well, either simultaneously or at another point in their lives. (Adapted from Merikangas & Swanson, 2010; Ruscio et al., 2007; Rodriguez et al., 2004; Hunt & Andrews, 1995.)

Generalized Anxiety Disorder

People with **generalized anxiety disorder** experience excessive anxiety under most circumstances and worry about practically anything (Turk & Mennin, 2011). In fact, their problem is sometimes described as *free-floating anxiety.* Like the young web designer Tomas, they typically feel restless, keyed up, or on edge; tire easily; have difficulty concentrating; suffer from muscle tension; and have sleep problems (see Table 5-1). The symptoms last at least six months (APA, 2013, 2012). Nevertheless, most people with the disorder are able, although with some difficulty, to carry on social relationships and job activities.

Generalized anxiety disorder is common in Western society. Surveys suggest that as many as 4 percent of the U.S. population have the symptoms of this disorder in any given year, a rate that holds across Canada, Britain, and other Western countries (Kessler et al., 2010, 2005; Ritter, Blackmore, & Heimberg, 2010). Altogether, close to 6 percent of all people develop generalized anxiety disorder sometime during their lives. It may emerge at any age, but usually it first appears in childhood or adolescence. Women diagnosed with the disorder outnumber men 2 to 1. Around one-quarter of individuals with generalized anxiety disorder are currently in treatment (NIMH, 2011; Wang et al., 2005).

A variety of factors have been cited to explain the development of this disorder. Here you will read about the views and treatments offered by the sociocultural, psychodynamic, humanistic, cognitive, and biological models. The behavioral perspective will be examined when we turn to phobias later in the chapter because that model approaches generalized anxiety disorder and phobias in basically the same way.

The Sociocultural Perspective: Societal and Multicultural Factors

According to sociocultural theorists, generalized anxiety disorder is most likely to develop in people who are faced with ongoing societal conditions that are dangerous. Studies have found that people in highly threatening environments are indeed more likely to develop the general feelings of tension, anxiety, and fatigue and the sleep disturbances found in this disorder (Jacob, Prince, & Goldberg, 2010; Stein & Williams, 2010).

Take, for example, a classic study that was done on the psychological impact of living near the Three Mile Island nuclear power plant after the nuclear reactor accident of March 1979 (Baum et al., 2004; Wroble & Baum, 2002). In the months following the accident, local mothers of preschool children were found to display five times as many anxiety or depression disorders as mothers living elsewhere. Although the number of disorders decreased during the next year, the Three Mile Island mothers still displayed high levels of anxiety or depression a year later. Similarly, studies conducted more recently have found that in the months and years following Hurricane Katrina in 2005 and the Haitian earthquake in 2010, the rate of generalized and other anxiety disorders was twice as high among area residents who lived through the disasters as among unaffected persons living elsewhere (McShane, 2011; Galea et al., 2007).

One of the most powerful forms of societal stress is poverty. People without financial means are likely to live in rundown communities with high crime rates, have fewer educational and job opportunities, and run a greater risk for health problems (López & Guarnaccia, 2008, 2005, 2000). As sociocultural theorists would predict, such people also have a higher rate of generalized anxiety disorder (Jacob et al., 2010; Stein & Williams, 2010). In the United States, the rate is almost twice as high among people with low incomes as among those with higher incomes (Sareen et al., 2011; Kessler et al., 2010, 2005). As wages decrease, the rate of generalized anxiety disorder steadily increases (see Table 5-2).

Since race is closely tied to stress in the United States (from experiences of discrimination to low income and reduced job opportunities), it is not surprising that it too is sometimes tied to the prevalence of generalized anxiety disorder (Marques et al., 2011; Soto et al., 2011; HHS, 2009). In any given year African Americans are

table: 5-1

DSM-5 Checklist
Generalized Anxiety Disorder

1. Excessive or ongoing anxiety and worry, for at least six months, about two or more activities or events.

2. At least three of the following symptoms: restlessness, fatigue, poor concentration, irritability, muscle tension, sleep disturbance.

3. Significant distress or impairment.

Based on APA, 2013, 2012.

table: 5-2

Eye on Culture:
Prevalence of Anxiety Disorders and Obsessive-Compulsive Disorder (Compared to Rate in Total Population)

	Female	Low Income	African American	Hispanic American	Elderly
Generalized anxiety disorder	Higher	Higher	Higher	Same	Higher
Specific phobias	Higher	Higher	Higher	Higher	Lower
Agoraphobia	Higher	Higher	Same	Same	Higher
Social anxiety disorder	Higher	Higher	Higher	Lower	Lower
Panic disorder	Higher	Higher	Same	Same	Lower
Obsessive-compulsive disorder	Same	Higher	Same	Same	Lower

Source: Polo et al., 2011; Sareen et al., 2011; Bharani & Lantz, 2008; Hopko et al., 2008; Nazarian & Craske, 2008; Schultz et al., 2008.

AP Photo/The Monterey County Herald/Orville Myers

The role of society

Bishop Richard Garcia hugs the father of a 6-year-old child who was killed by a stray bullet fired by gang members outside his house. People who live in dangerous environments experience greater anxiety and have a higher rate of generalized anxiety disorder than those residing in other settings.

30 percent more likely than white Americans to suffer from this disorder. Moreover, although multicultural researchers have not consistently found a heightened rate of generalized anxiety disorder among Hispanics in the United States, they have noted that many Hispanics in both the United States and Latin American suffer from *nervios* ("nerves"), a culture-bound disorder that bears great similarity to generalized anxiety disorder (Lopez & Guarnaccia, 2005, 2000; APA, 2000). People with *nervios* experience enormous emotional distress, somatic symptoms such as headaches and stomachaches, so-called brain aches marked by poor concentration and nervousness, and symptoms of irritability, tearfulness, and trembling.

Although poverty and various societal and cultural pressures may help create a climate in which generalized anxiety disorder is more likely to develop, sociocultural variables are not the only factors at work. After all, most people in poor or dangerous environments do not develop this disorder. Even if sociocultural factors play a broad role, theorists still must explain why some people develop the disorder and others do not. The psychodynamic, humanistic-existential, cognitive, and biological schools of thought have all tried to explain why and have offered corresponding treatments.

The Psychodynamic Perspective

Sigmund Freud (1933, 1917) believed that all children experience some degree of anxiety as part of growing up and that all use ego defense mechanisms to help control such anxiety (see pages 53–55). Children experience *realistic anxiety* when they face actual danger; *neurotic anxiety* when they are repeatedly prevented, by parents or by circumstances, from expressing their id impulses; and *moral anxiety* when they are punished or threatened for expressing their id impulses. According to Freud, some children experience particularly high levels of such anxiety, or their defense mechanisms are particularly inadequate, and these individuals may develop generalized anxiety disorder.

Psychodynamic Explanations: When Childhood Anxiety Goes Unresolved According to Freud, when a child is overrun by neurotic or moral anxiety, the stage is set for generalized anxiety disorder. Early developmental experiences may produce an unusually high level of anxiety in such a child. Say that a boy is spanked

every time he cries for milk as an infant, messes his pants as a 2-year-old, and explores his genitals as a toddler. He may eventually come to believe that his various id impulses are very dangerous, and he may experience overwhelming anxiety whenever he has such impulses.

Alternatively, a child's ego defense mechanisms may be too weak to cope with even normal levels of anxiety. Overprotected children, shielded by their parents from all frustrations and threats, have little opportunity to develop effective defense mechanisms. When they face the pressures of adult life, their defense mechanisms may be too weak to cope with the resulting anxieties.

Today's psychodynamic theorists often disagree with specific aspects of Freud's explanation for generalized anxiety disorder. Most continue to believe, however, that the disorder can be traced to inadequacies in the early relationships between children and their parents (Sharf, 2012). Researchers have tested the psychodynamic explanations in various ways. In one strategy, they have tried to show that people with generalized anxiety disorder are particularly likely to use defense mechanisms. For example, one team of investigators examined the early therapy transcripts of patients with this diagnosis and found that the patients often reacted defensively. When asked by therapists to discuss upsetting experiences, they would quickly forget (*repress*) what they had just been talking about, change the direction of the discussion, or deny having negative feelings (Luborsky, 1973).

In another line of research, investigators have studied people who as children suffered extreme punishment for id impulses. As psychodynamic theorists would predict, these people have higher levels of anxiety later in life (Busch, Milrod, & Shear, 2010; Chiu, 1971). In addition, several studies have supported the psychodynamic position that extreme protectiveness by parents may often lead to high levels of anxiety in their children (Manfredi et al., 2011; Hudson & Rapee, 2004; Jenkins, 1968).

Although these studies are consistent with psychodynamic explanations, some scientists question whether they show what they claim to show. When people have difficulty talking about upsetting events early in therapy, for example, they are not necessarily repressing those events. They may be focusing purposely on the positive aspects of their lives, or they may be too embarrassed to share personal negative events until they develop trust in the therapist.

Psychodynamic Therapies

Psychodynamic therapists use the same general techniques to treat all psychological problems: *free association* and the therapist's interpretations of *transference, resistance,* and *dreams. Freudian psychodynamic therapists* use these methods to help clients with generalized anxiety disorder become less afraid of their id impulses and more successful in controlling them. Other psychodynamic therapists, particularly *object relations therapists,* use them to help anxious patients identify and settle the childhood relationship problems that continue to produce anxiety in adulthood (Lucas, 2006).

Controlled studies have typically found psychodynamic treatments to be of only modest help to persons with generalized anxiety disorder (Craske, 2010). An exception to this trend is *short-term psychodynamic therapy* (see Chapter 3), which has in some cases significantly reduced the levels of anxiety, worry, and social difficulty of patients with this disorder (Salzer et al., 2011; Crits-Christoph et al., 2005, 2004).

The Humanistic Perspective

Humanistic theorists propose that generalized anxiety disorder, like other psychological disorders, arises when people stop looking at themselves honestly and acceptingly. Repeated denials of their true thoughts, emotions, and behavior make these people extremely anxious and unable to fulfill their potential as human beings.

The humanistic view of why people develop this disorder is best illustrated by Carl Rogers' explanation. As you saw in Chapter 3, Rogers believed that children who fail to receive *unconditional positive regard* from others may become overly critical of themselves and develop harsh self-standards, what Rogers called *conditions of worth.* They try

"Dear Mom and Dad: Thanks for the happy childhood. You've destroyed any chance I had of becoming a writer."

•client-centered therapy•The humanistic therapy developed by Carl Rogers in which clinicians try to help clients by being accepting, empathizing accurately, and conveying genuineness.

•basic irrational assumptions•The inaccurate and inappropriate beliefs held by people with various psychological problems, according to Albert Ellis.

to meet these standards by repeatedly distorting and denying their true thoughts and experiences. Despite such efforts, however, threatening self-judgments keep breaking through and causing them intense anxiety. This onslaught of anxiety sets the stage for generalized anxiety disorder or some other form of psychological dysfunctioning.

Practitioners of Rogers's treatment approach, **client-centered therapy,** try to show unconditional positive regard for their clients and to empathize with them. The therapists hope that an atmosphere of genuine acceptance and caring will help clients feel secure enough to recognize their true needs, thoughts, and emotions. When clients eventually are honest and comfortable with themselves, their anxiety or other symptoms will subside. In the following excerpt, Rogers describes the progress made by a client with anxiety and related symptoms:

> Therapy was an experiencing of herself, in all its aspects, in a safe relationship . . . the experiencing of self as having a capacity for wholeness . . . a self that cared about others. This last followed . . . the realization that the therapist cared, that it really mattered to him how therapy turned out for her, that he really valued her. . . . She gradually became aware of the fact that . . . there was nothing fundamentally bad, but rather, at heart she was positive and sound.
>
> *(Rogers, 1954, pp. 261–264)*

Despite such optimistic case reports, controlled studies have failed to offer strong support for this approach. Although research does suggest that client-centered therapy is usually more helpful to anxious clients than no treatment, the approach is only sometimes superior to placebo therapy (Prochaska & Norcross, 2010, 2006, 2003). In addition, researchers have found, at best, only limited support for Rogers' explanation of generalized anxiety disorder and other forms of abnormal behavior. Nor have other humanistic theories and treatment received much research support.

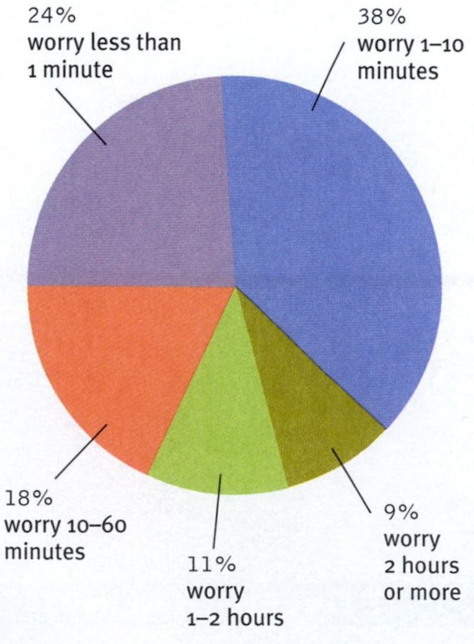

The Cognitive Perspective

Followers of the cognitive model suggest that psychological problems are often caused by dysfunctional ways of thinking (Ferreri, Leann, & Peretti, 2011) (see *PsychWatch* on the next page). Given that excessive worry—a cognitive symptom—is a key characteristic of generalized anxiety disorder (see Figure 5-2), it is not surprising that cognitive theorists have had much to say about the causes of and treatments for this particular disorder.

Maladaptive Assumptions Initially, cognitive theorists suggested that generalized anxiety disorder is primarily caused by *maladaptive assumptions,* a notion that continues to be influential. Albert Ellis, for example, proposed that many people are guided by irrational beliefs that lead them to act and react in inappropriate ways (Ellis, 2011, 2002, 1962). Ellis called these **basic irrational assumptions,** and he claimed that people with generalized anxiety disorder often hold the following ones:

"It is a dire necessity for an adult human being to be loved or approved of by virtually every significant other person in his community."

"It is awful and catastrophic when things are not the way one would very much like them to be."

"If something is or may be dangerous or fearsome, one should be terribly concerned about it and should keep dwelling on the possibility of its occurring."

"One should be thoroughly competent, adequate, and achieving in all possible respects if one is to consider oneself worthwhile."

(Ellis, 1962)

Figure 5-2

How long do your worries last? In one survey, 62 percent of college students said they spend less than 10 minutes at a time worrying about something. In contrast, 20 percent worry for more than an hour. (Adapted from Tallis et al., 1994.)

Pie chart labels: 24% worry less than 1 minute; 38% worry 1–10 minutes; 18% worry 10–60 minutes; 11% worry 1–2 hours; 9% worry 2 hours or more.

PsychWatch

Fears, Shmears: The Odds Are Usually on Our Side

People with anxiety disorders have many unreasonable fears, but millions of other people, too, worry about disaster every day. Most of the catastrophes they fear are not probable. Perhaps the ability to live by laws of *probability* rather than *possibility* is what separates the fearless from the fearful. What are the odds, then, that commonly feared events will happen? The range of probability is wide, but the odds are usually heavily in our favor.

A city resident will be a victim of a violent crime . . . 1 in 60

A suburbanite will be a victim of a violent crime . . . 1 in 1,000

A small-town resident will be a victim of a violent crime . . . 1 in 2,000

A child will suffer a high-chair injury this year . . . 1 in 6,000

Build with care The chance of a construction worker being injured at work during the year is 1 in 27.

The IRS will audit you this year . . . 1 in 100

You will be murdered this year . . . 1 in 12,000

You will be a victim of burglary this year . . . 1 in 25

You will be a victim of robbery this year . . . 1 in 83

You will be killed on your next bus ride . . . 1 in 500 million

You will be hit by a baseball at a major-league game . . . 1 in 300,000

You will drown in the tub this year . . . 1 in 685,000

Your house will have a fire this year . . . 1 in 200

Your carton will contain a broken egg . . . 1 in 10

You will develop a tooth cavity . . . 1 in 6

You will contract AIDS from a blood transfusion . . . 1 in 100,000

You will die in a tsunami . . . 1 in 500,000

You will be attacked by a shark . . . 1 in 4 million

You will receive a diagnosis of cancer this year . . . 1 in 8,000

A woman will develop breast cancer during her lifetime . . . 1 in 9

A piano player will eventually develop lower back pain . . . 1 in 3

You will be killed on your next automobile outing . . . 1 in 4 million

Condom use will eventually fail to prevent pregnancy . . . 1 in 10

An IUD will eventually fail to prevent pregnancy . . . 1 in 10

Coitus interruptus will eventually fail to prevent pregnancy . . . 1 in 5

You will die as a result of a collision between an asteroid and the earth . . . 1 in 500,000

You will die as a result of a lightning strike . . . 1 in 84,000

(ADAPTED FROM QUILLIAN & PAGER, 2012; BRITT, 2005)

When people who make these assumptions are faced with a stressful event, such as an exam or a first date, they are likely to interpret it as dangerous, to overreact, and to experience fear. As they apply the assumptions to more and more events, they may begin to develop generalized anxiety disorder.

Similarly, cognitive theorist Aaron Beck argued that people with generalized anxiety disorder constantly hold silent assumptions (for example, "A situation or a person is unsafe until proven to be safe" or "It is always best to assume the worst") that imply they are in imminent danger (Clark & Beck, 2012, 2010; Beck & Emery, 1985). Since the

Worry-free workers

This famous Bill Jones motivational poster, displayed in workplaces throughout the United States in the 1920s, reflects the view of today's new-wave cognitive theorists—that worrying is a dysfunctional process that can be brought under control.

---

table: 5-3

Worrying About Worrying: Items from the Meta-Worry Questionnaire

I am going crazy with worry.

My worrying will escalate and I'll cease to function.

I'm making myself ill with worry.

I'm abnormal for worrying.

My mind can't take the worrying.

I'm losing out in life because of worrying.

My body can't take the worrying.

Source: Wells, 2011, 2010, 2005.

---

time of Ellis' and Beck's initial proposals, researchers have repeatedly found that people with generalized anxiety disorder do indeed hold maladaptive assumptions, particularly about dangerousness (Ferreri et al., 2011; Clark & Beck, 2010).

New-Wave Cognitive Explanations In recent years, several new explanations for generalized anxiety disorder, sometimes called the *new-wave cognitive explanations,* have emerged (Fisher & Wells, 2011). Each of them builds on the work of Ellis and Beck and their emphasis on danger.

The *metacognitive theory,* developed by the researcher Adrian Wells (2011, 2010, 2005), suggests that people with generalized anxiety disorder implicitly hold both positive and negative beliefs about worrying. On the positive side, they believe that worrying is a useful way of appraising and coping with threats in life. And so they look for and examine all possible signs of danger—that is, they worry constantly.

At the same time, Wells argues, individuals with generalized anxiety disorder also hold negative beliefs about worrying, and these negative attitudes are the ones that open the door to the disorder. Because society teaches them that worrying is a bad thing, the individuals come to believe that their repeated worrying is in fact harmful (mentally and physically) and uncontrollable. Now they further worry about the fact that they always seem to be worrying (so-called *metaworries*) (see Table 5-3). The net effect of all this worrying: generalized anxiety disorder.

Why might many people believe, at least implicitly, that worrying is useful— even necessary—for problems to work out?

This explanation has received considerable research support. Studies indicate, for example, that individuals who generally hold both positive and negative beliefs about worrying are particularly prone to developing generalized anxiety disorder and that repeated metaworrying is a powerful predictor of developing the disorder (Ferreri et al., 2011; Wells, 2011, 2010, 2005).

According to another new explanation for generalized anxiety disorder, the *intolerance of uncertainty theory,* certain individuals cannot tolerate the knowledge that negative events *may* occur, even if the possibility of occurrence is very small. Inasmuch as life is filled with uncertain events, these individuals worry constantly that such events are about to occur. Such intolerance and worrying leave them highly vulnerable to the development of generalized anxiety disorder (Fisher & Wells, 2011; Dugas et al., 2010, 2004). Think of when you meet someone you're attracted to and how you then feel prior to texting or calling call him or her for the first time—or how you feel while you're waiting for that person to contact you for the first time. The worry that you experience in such instances—the sense of sometimes unbearable uncertainty over the possibility of an unacceptable negative outcome—is, according to this theory, how people with generalized anxiety disorder feel all the time.

Proponents of this theory believe people with generalized anxiety disorder keep worrying and worrying in efforts to find "correct" solutions for various situations in their lives and to restore certainty to the situations. However, because they can never really be sure that a given solution is a correct one, they are always left to grapple with intolerable levels of uncertainty, triggering new rounds of worrying and new efforts to find correct solutions. Like the metacognitive theory of worry, considerable research supports this theory. Studies have found, for example, that people with generalized anxiety disorder display greater levels of intolerance of uncertainty than people with normal degrees of anxiety (Daitch, 2011; Dugas et al., 2010, 2009, 2002).

Finally, a third new explanation for generalized anxiety disorder, the *avoidance theory,* developed by researcher Thomas Borkovec, suggests that people with this disorder have greater bodily arousal (higher heart rate, perspiration, respiration) than other people and that worrying actually serves to *reduce* this arousal, perhaps by distracting the individuals from their unpleasant physical feelings (Newman et al., 2011; Borkovec, Alcaine, & Behar, 2004). In short, the avoidance theory holds that people with generalized anxiety disorder worry repeatedly in order to reduce or avoid uncomfortable states of bodily arousal. When, for example, they find themselves in an uncomfortable job situation or social relationship, they implicitly choose to intellectualize (that is, worry about) losing their job or losing their friend rather than having to stew in a state of intense negative arousal. The worrying serves as a quick, though ultimately maladaptive, way of coping with unpleasant bodily states.

Borkovec's explanation has also been supported by numerous studies. Research reveals that people with generalized anxiety disorder experience particularly fast and intense bodily reactions, find such reactions overwhelming and unpleasant, worry more than other people upon becoming aroused, and successfully reduce their arousal whenever they worry (Aldao & Mennim, 2012; Fisher & Wells, 2011).

Cognitive Therapies

Two kinds of cognitive approaches are used in cases of generalized anxiety disorder (Hoyer et al., 2011). In one, based on the pioneering work of Ellis and Beck, therapists help clients change the maladaptive assumptions that characterize their disorder. In the other, new-wave cognitive therapists help clients to understand the special role that worrying may play in their disorder and to change their views about and reactions to worrying.

CHANGING MALADAPTIVE ASSUMPTIONS In Ellis' technique of **rational-emotive therapy,** therapists point out the irrational assumptions held by clients, suggest more appropriate assumptions, and assign homework that gives the individuals practice at challenging old assumptions and applying new ones (Ellis, 2011, 2008, 2005). Studies suggest that this approach and similar cognitive approaches bring at least modest relief to persons suffering from generalized anxiety (Clark & Beck, 2012, 2010). Ellis' approach is illustrated in the following discussion between him and an anxious client who fears failure and disapproval at work, especially over a testing procedure that she has developed for her company:

> *Client:* I'm so distraught these days that I can hardly concentrate on anything for more than a minute or two at a time. My mind just keeps wandering to that damn testing procedure I devised, and that they've put so much money into; and whether it's going to work well or be just a waste of all that time and money. . . .
>
> *Ellis:* Point one is that you must admit that you are telling yourself something to start your worrying going, and you must begin to look, and I mean really look, for the specific nonsense with which you keep reindoctrinating yourself. . . . The false statement is: "If, because my testing procedure doesn't work and I am functioning inefficiently on my job, my co-workers do not want me or approve of me, then I shall be a worthless person." . . .
>
> *Client:* But if I want to do what my firm also wants me to do, and I am useless to them, aren't I also useless to me?
>
> *Ellis:* No—not unless you think you are. You are frustrated, of course, if you want to set up a good testing procedure and you can't. But need you be desperately unhappy because you are frustrated? And need you deem yourself completely unworthwhile because you can't do one of the main things you want to do in life?
>
> (Ellis, 1962, pp. 160–165)

BREAKING DOWN WORRYING Alternatively, some of today's new-wave cognitive therapists specifically guide clients with generalized anxiety disorder to recognize and change their dysfunctional use of worrying (Newman et al., 2011; Ritter et al., 2010; Wells,

•**rational-emotive therapy**• A cognitive therapy developed by Albert Ellis that helps clients identify and change the irrational assumptions and thinking that help cause their psychological disorder.

Fearful delights

Many people enjoy the feeling of fear as long as it occurs under controlled circumstances, as when they are safely watching the tension grow in the hugely popular series of movies *Paranormal Activity 1, 2, 3, 4, and 5,* among the most profitable films ever made. In this scene from the first film, lead character Katie Featherston tries to escape the impact of a supernatural presence in her house.

2010). They begin by educating the clients about the role of worrying in their disorder and have them observe their bodily arousal and cognitive responses across various life situations. In turn, the clients come to appreciate the triggers of their worrying, their misconceptions about worrying, and their misguided efforts to control their lives by worrying. As their insights grow, clients are expected to see the world as less threatening (and so less arousing), try out more constructive ways of dealing with arousal, and worry less about the fact that they worry so much. Research has begun to indicate that a concentrated focus on worrying is indeed a helpful addition to the traditional cognitive treatment for generalized anxiety disorder (Wells, 2011, 2010; Ritter et al., 2010).

Treating individuals with generalized anxiety disorder by helping them to recognize their inclination to worry is similar to another cognitive approach that has gained popularity in recent years. The approach, *mindfulness-based cognitive therapy,* was developed by psychologist Steven Hayes and his colleagues as part of their broader treatment approach called *acceptance and commitment therapy* (Hayes & Lillis, 2012; Antony, 2011; Treanor, 2011). Here therapists help clients to become aware of their streams of thoughts, including their worries, as they are occurring and to *accept* such thoughts as mere events of the mind. By accepting their thoughts rather than trying to eliminate them, the clients are expected to be less upset and affected by them.

Mindfulness-based cognitive therapy has also been applied to a range of other psychological problems, such as depression, posttraumatic stress disorder, personality disorders, and substance use disorders, often with promising results (Hayes & Lillis, 2012; Orsillo & Roemer, 2011). As you'll see in the next chapter, this cognitive approach borrows heavily from a form of meditation called *mindfulness meditation,* which teaches individuals to pay attention to the thoughts and feelings that flow through their minds during meditation and to accept such thoughts in a nonjudgmental way.

The Biological Perspective

Biological theorists believe that generalized anxiety disorder is caused chiefly by biological factors. For years this claim was supported primarily by **family pedigree studies,** in which researchers determine how many and which relatives of a person with a disorder have the same disorder. If biological tendencies toward generalized anxiety disorder are inherited, people who are biologically related should have similar probabilities of developing this disorder. Studies have in fact found that biological relatives of persons with generalized anxiety disorder are more likely than nonrelatives to have the disorder also (Schienle et al., 2011; Domschke & Deckert, 2010). Approximately 15 percent of the relatives of people with the disorder display it themselves—

much more than the prevalence rate found in the general population. And the closer the relative (an identical twin, for example), the greater the likelihood that he or she will also have the disorder.

Of course, investigators cannot have full confidence in biological interpretations of such findings. Because relatives are likely to share aspects of the same environment, their shared disorders may reflect similarities in environment and upbringing rather than similarities in biological makeup. And, indeed, the closer the relatives, the more similar their environmental experiences are likely to be. Because identical twins are more physically alike than fraternal twins, they may even experience more similarities in their upbringing.

Biological Explanations: GABA Inactivity
In recent decades important discoveries by brain researchers have offered clearer evidence that generalized anxiety disorder is related to biological factors (Craig & Chamberlain, 2010; Martin & Nemeroff, 2010). One of the first such discoveries occurred in the 1950s, when researchers determined that **benzodiazepines,** the family of drugs that includes *alprazolam* (Xanax), *lorazepam* (Ativan), and *diazepam* (Valium), provide relief from anxiety. At first, no one understood why benzodiazepines reduce anxiety. Eventually, however, the development of radioactive techniques enabled researchers to pinpoint the exact sites in the brain that are affected by benzodiazepines (Mohler & Okada, 1977). Apparently certain neurons have receptors that receive the benzodiazepines, just as a lock receives a key.

Investigators soon discovered that these benzodiazepine receptors ordinarily receive **gamma-aminobutyric acid (GABA),** a common neurotransmitter in the brain. As you read in Chapter 3, neurotransmitters are chemicals that carry messages from one neuron to another. GABA carries *inhibitory* messages: when GABA is received at a receptor, it causes the neuron to stop firing.

On the basis of such findings, biological researchers eventually pieced together several scenarios of how fear reactions may occur. A leading one began with the notion that in normal fear reactions, key neurons throughout the brain fire more rapidly, triggering the firing of still more neurons and creating a general state of excitability throughout the brain and body. Perspiration, breathing, and muscle tension increase. This state is experienced as fear or anxiety. Continuous firing of neurons eventually triggers a feedback system—that is, brain and body activities that reduce the level of excitability. Some neurons throughout the brain release the neurotransmitter GABA, which then binds to GABA receptors on certain neurons and instructs those neurons to stop firing. The state of excitability ceases, and the experience of fear or anxiety subsides (Atack, 2010; Ator, 2005; Costa, 1985, 1983).

Some researchers have concluded that a malfunction in this feedback system can cause fear or anxiety to go unchecked (Atak, 2010; Bremner & Charney, 2010; Roy-Byrne, 2005). In fact, when investigators reduced GABA's ability to bind to GABA receptors, they found that animal subjects reacted with a rise in anxiety (Costa, 1985; Mohler et al., 1981). This finding suggested that people with generalized anxiety disorder might have ongoing problems in their anxiety feedback system. Perhaps they have too few GABA receptors, or perhaps their GABA receptors do not readily capture the neurotransmitter.

This explanation continues to have many supporters, but it is also problematic. First, according to recent biological discoveries, other neurotransmitters may also play important roles in anxiety and generalized anxiety disorder, either acting alone or in conjunction with GABA (Martin & Nemeroff, 2010; Burijon, 2007). Second, biological theorists are faced with the problem of establishing a causal relationship. The abnormal GABA responses of anxious persons may be the result, rather than the cause, of their anxiety disorders. Perhaps long-term anxiety eventually leads to poorer GABA reception, for example.

In fact, research conducted in recent years indicates that the root of generalized anxiety disorder is probably more complicated than a single neurotransmitter or group of neurotransmitters. Researchers have determined, for example, that emotional reactions of various kinds are tied to brain *circuits*—networks of brain structures that work together, triggering each other into action with the help of neurotransmitters

•family pedigree study•A research design in which investigators determine how many and which relatives of a person with a disorder have the same disorder.

•benzodiazepines•The most common group of antianxiety drugs, which includes Valium and Xanax.

•GABA•The neurotransmitter gamma-aminobutyric acid, whose low activity has been linked to generalized anxiety disorder.

Do monkeys experience anxiety?
Clinical researchers must be careful in interpreting the reactions of animal subjects. This infant monkey was considered "fearful" after being separated from its mother. But perhaps it was feeling depressed or experiencing a level of arousal that does not correspond to either fear or depression.

University of Wisconsin Primate Laboratory, Madison

Figure 5-3

The biology of anxiety The circuit in the brain that helps produce anxiety reactions includes areas such as the amygdala, prefrontal cortex, and anterior cingulate cortex.

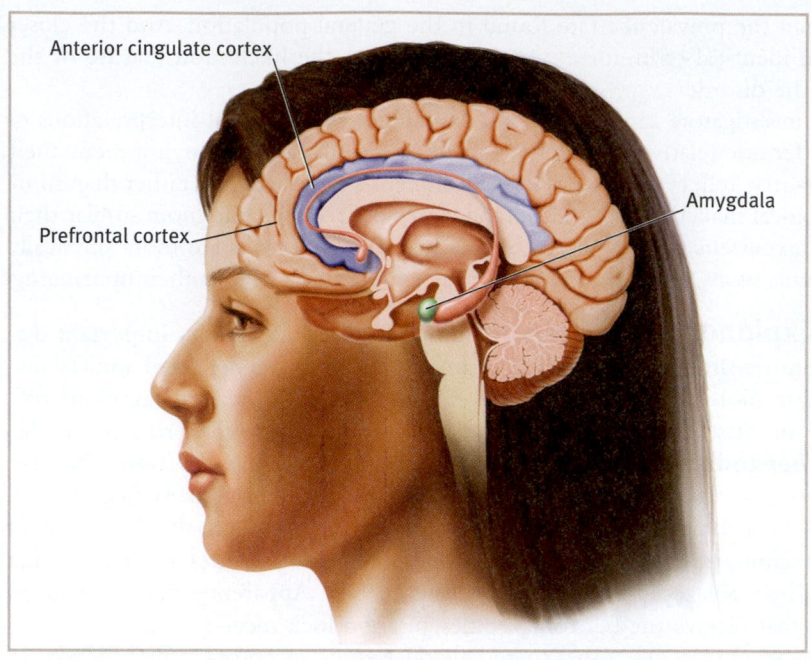

Anterior cingulate cortex

Prefrontal cortex

Amygdala

and producing a particular kind of emotional reaction. It turns out that the circuit that produces anxiety reactions includes the *prefrontal cortex, anterior cingulate cortex,* and *amygdala,* a small almond-shaped brain structure that usually starts the emotional ball rolling. Recent studies suggest that this circuit often functions improperly in people with generalized anxiety disorder (Schienle et al., 2011; McClure et al., 2007) (see Figure 5-3).

Biological Treatments

The leading biological treatment for generalized anxiety disorder is *drug therapy* (see Table 5-4). Other biological interventions are *relaxation training* and *biofeedback.*

ANTIANXIETY DRUG THERAPY In the late 1950s benzodiazepines were originally marketed as **sedative-hypnotic drugs**—drugs that calm people in low doses and help them fall asleep in higher doses. These new antianxiety drugs seemed less addictive than previous sedative-hypnotic medications, such as *barbiturates,* and they appeared to produce less tiredness. Thus, they were quickly embraced by both doctors and patients.

Only years later did investigators come to understand the reasons for the effectiveness of benzodiazepines. As you have read, researchers eventually learned that there are specific neuron sites in the brain that receive benzodiazepines and that these same receptor sites ordinarily

Why are antianxiety drugs so popular in today's world? Does their popularity say something about our society?

receive the neurotransmitter GABA. Apparently, when benzodiazepines bind to these neuron receptor sites, particularly those receptors known as *GABA-A receptors,* they increase the ability of GABA to bind to them as well, and so improve GABA's ability to stop neuron firing and reduce anxiety (Treit, Engin, & McEown, 2010; Dawson et al., 2005).

Studies indicate that benzodiazepines often provide relief for people with generalized anxiety disorder (Hadley et al., 2012; Van Ameriingen et al., 2010). However, clinicians have come to realize the potential dangers of these drugs. First, when the medications are stopped, many persons' anxieties return as strong as ever. Second, we now know that people who take benzodiazepines in large

table: 5-4

Some Benzodiazepine Drugs

Generic Name	Trade Name(s)
Alprazolam	Xanax, Xanax XR
Bromazepam	Lectopam, Lexotan, Bromaze
Chlordiazepoxide	Librium
Clonazepam	Klonopin
Clorazepate	Tranxene
Diazepam	Valium
Estazolam	ProSom
Flunitrazepam	Rohypnol
Flurazepam	Dalmadorm, Dalmane
Halazepam	Paxipam
Lorazepam	Ativan
Midazolam	Versed
Nitrazepam	Mogadon, Alodorm, Pacisyn, Dumolid
Oxazepam	Serax
Prazepam	Lysanxia, Centrax
Quazepam	Doral
Temazepam	Restoril
Triazolam	Halcion

doses for an extended time can become physically dependent on them. Third, the drugs can produce undesirable effects such as drowsiness, lack of coordination, memory loss, depression, and aggressive behavior. Finally, the drugs mix badly with certain other drugs or substances. If, for example, people on benzodiazepines drink even small amounts of alcohol, their breathing can slow down dangerously (Meyer & Quenzer, 2005).

In recent decades, still other kinds of drugs have become available for people with generalized anxiety disorder. In particular, it has been discovered that a number of *antidepressant* medications, drugs that are usually used to lift the moods of depressed persons, and *antipsychotic* medications, drugs commonly given to people who lose touch with reality, are also helpful to many people with generalized anxiety disorder. In fact, a number of today's clinicians are more inclined to prescribe antidepressants or antipsychotics to treat generalized anxiety disorder than the GABA-enhancing benzodiazepines (Baldwin et al., 2011; Comer et al., 2011).

RELAXATION TRAINING A nonchemical biological technique commonly used to treat generalized anxiety disorder is **relaxation training**. The notion behind this approach is that physical relaxation will lead to a state of psychological relaxation. In one version, therapists teach clients to identify individual muscle groups, tense them, release the tension, and ultimately relax the whole body. With continued practice, they can bring on a state of deep muscle relaxation at will, reducing their state of anxiety.

Research indicates that relaxation training is more effective than no treatment or placebo treatment in cases of generalized anxiety disorder. The improvement it produces, however, tends to be modest (Leahy, 2004), and other techniques that are known to relax people, such as *meditation,* often seem to be equally effective (Bourne et al., 2004). Relaxation training is of greatest help to people with generalized anxiety disorder when it is combined with cognitive therapy or with biofeedback (Lang, 2004).

BIOFEEDBACK In **biofeedback,** therapists use electrical signals from the body to train people to control physiological processes such as heart rate or muscle tension. Clients are connected to a monitor that gives them continuous information about their bodily activities. By attending to the signals from the monitor, they may gradually learn to control even seemingly involuntary physiological processes.

The most widely applied method of biofeedback for the treatment of anxiety uses a device called an **electromyograph (EMG),** which provides feedback about the level of muscular tension in the body. Electrodes are attached to the client's muscles—usually the forehead muscles—where they detect the minute electrical activity that accompanies muscle tension (see Figure 5-4). The device then converts electric potentials coming from the muscles into an image, such as lines on a screen, or into a tone whose pitch changes along with changes in muscle tension. Thus clients "see" or "hear" when their muscles are becoming more or less tense. Through repeated trial and error, the individuals become skilled at voluntarily reducing muscle tension and, theoretically, at reducing tension and anxiety in everyday stressful situations.

• **sedative-hypnotic drugs**•Drugs that calm people at lower doses and help them to fall asleep at higher doses.

• **relaxation training**•A treatment procedure that teaches clients to relax at will so they can calm themselves in stressful situations.

• **biofeedback**•A technique in which a client is given information about physiological reactions as they occur and learns to control the reactions voluntarily.

• **electromyograph (EMG)**•A device that provides feedback about the level of muscular tension in the body.

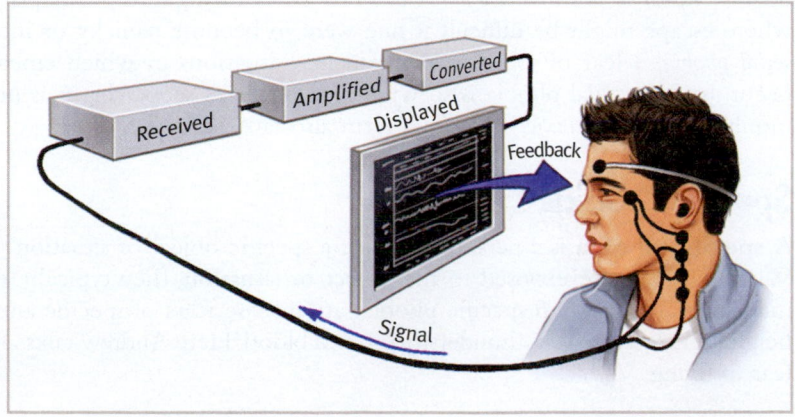

Figure 5-4

Biofeedback at work This biofeedback system records tension in the forehead muscles of an anxious person. The system receives, amplifies, converts, and displays information about the tension, allowing the client to "observe" it and to try to reduce his tension responses.

•phobia• A persistent and unreasonable fear of a particular object, activity, or situation.

•specific phobia• A severe and persistent fear of a specific object or situation (other than agoraphobia and social phobia).

•classical conditioning• A process of learning in which two events that repeatedly occur close together in time become tied together in a person's mind and so produce the same response.

Research finds that, in most cases, EMG biofeedback, like relaxation training, has only a modest effect on a person's anxiety level (Brambrink, 2004). As you will see in the next chapter, biofeedback has had its greatest impact when it plays *adjunct* roles in the treatment of certain medical problems, including headaches and back pain (Astin, 2004; Engel et al., 2004).

Phobias

Most of us are none too eager to confront a spider or to be caught in a thunderstorm, but few of us have such dread as Marianne or Trisha:

Marianne: *Seeing a spider makes me rigid with fear, hot, trembling and dizzy. I have occasionally vomited and once fainted in order to escape from the situation. These symptoms last three or four days after seeing a spider. Realistic pictures can cause the same effect, especially if I inadvertently place my hand on one.*

(Melville, 1978, p. 44)

Trisha: *At the end of March each year, I start getting agitated because summer is coming and that means thunderstorms. I have been afraid since my early twenties, but the last three years have been the worst. I have such a heartbeat that for hours after a storm my whole left side is painful. . . . I say I will stay in the room, but when it comes I am a jelly, reduced to nothing. I have a little cupboard and I go there, I press my eyes so hard I can't see for about an hour, and if I sit in the cupboard over an hour my husband has to straighten me up.*

(Melville, 1978, p. 104)

A **phobia** (from the Greek word for "fear") is a persistent and unreasonable fear of a particular object, activity, or situation. People with a phobia become fearful if they even think about the object or situation they dread, but they usually remain comfortable as long as they avoid it or thoughts about it.

We all have our areas of special fear, and it is normal for some things to upset us more than other things. How do such common fears differ from phobias? DSM-5 indicates that a phobia is more intense and persistent and the desire to avoid the object or situation is greater (APA, 2013, 2012). People with phobias often feel so much distress that their fears may interfere dramatically with their lives.

Most phobias technically fall under the category of *specific phobias,* DSM-5's label for an intense and persistent fear of a specific object or situation. In addition, there are two broader kinds of phobias: *agoraphobia,* a fear of venturing into public places or situations where escape might be difficult if one were to become panicky or incapacitated, and *social phobia,* a fear of social or performance situations in which embarrassment may occur. In fact, social phobia is so wide-ranging in its scope that it is now more commonly called *social anxiety disorder,* a term also favored by DSM-5.

Specific Phobias

A **specific phobia** is a persistent fear of a specific object or situation (see Table 5-5). When sufferers are exposed to the object or situation, they typically experience immediate fear. Common specific phobias are intense fears of specific animals or insects, heights, enclosed spaces, thunderstorms, and blood. Here Andrew talks about his phobic fear of flying:

table: 5-5

DSM-5 Checklist

Specific Phobia

1. Marked, persistent, and disproportionate fear of a specific object or situation, typically lasting six months or more.

2. Immediate anxiety is usually produced by exposure to the object.

3. Avoidance of the feared situation.

4. Significant distress or impairment.

Based on APA, 2013, 2012.

We got on board, and then there was the take-off. There it was again, that horrible feeling as we gathered speed. It was creeping over me again, that old feeling of panic. I kept seeing everyone as puppets, all strapped to their seats with no control over their destinies, me included. Every time the plane did a variation of speed or route, my heart would leap and I would hurriedly ask what was happening. When the plane started to lose height, I was terrified that we were about to crash.

(Melville, 1978, p. 59)

Each year close to 9 percent of all people in the United States have the symptoms of a specific phobia (Kessler et al., 2010, 2009, 2005). More than 12 percent of individuals develop such phobias at some point during their lives, and many people have more than one at a time. Women with the disorder outnumber men by at least 2 to 1. For reasons that are not clear, the prevalence of specific phobias also differs among racial and ethnic minority groups. In some studies, African Americans and Hispanic Americans report having at least 50 percent more specific phobias than do white Americans, even when economic factors, education, and age are held steady across the groups (Stein & Williams, 2010; Hopko et al., 2008; Breslau et al., 2006). It is worth noting, however, that these heightened rates are at work only among African and Hispanic Americans who were born in the United States, not those who emigrated to the United States at some point during their lives (Hopko et al., 2008).

The impact of a specific phobia on a person's life depends on what arouses the fear (Gamble, Harvey, & Rapee, 2010; Scher et al., 2006). People whose phobias center on dogs, insects, or water will keep encountering the objects they dread. Their efforts to avoid them must be elaborate and may greatly restrict their activities. Urban residents with snake phobias have a much easier time. The vast majority of people with a specific phobia do not seek treatment (NIMH, 2011). They try instead to avoid the objects they fear (Roth & Fonagy, 2005).

What Causes Specific Phobias? Each of the models offers explanations for specific phobias. Evidence tends to support the behavioral explanations. Behaviorists believe that people with such phobias first learn to fear certain objects, situations, or events through conditioning (Field & Purkis, 2012; Gamble et al., 2010; Wolfe, 2005). Once the fears are acquired, the individuals avoid the dreaded object or situation, permitting the fears to become all the more entrenched.

BEHAVIORAL EXPLANATIONS: HOW ARE FEARS LEARNED? Behaviorists propose **classical conditioning** as a common way of acquiring phobic reactions. Here, two events that occur close together in time become closely associated in a person's mind, and, as you saw in Chapter 3, the person then reacts similarly to both of them. If one event triggers a fear response, the other may also.

In the 1920s a clinician described the case of a young woman who apparently acquired a phobia of running water through classical conditioning (Bagby, 1922). When she was 7 years old she went on a picnic with her mother and aunt and ran off by herself into the woods after lunch. While she was climbing over some large rocks, her feet were caught between two of them. The harder she tried to free herself, the more trapped she became. No one heard her screams, and she grew more and more terrified. In the language of behaviorists, the entrapment was eliciting a fear response.

Crossing over

A fear of heights is one of the most common human phobias. Nevertheless, victims need not be stuck with this phobia. Here dentist Jason Bodnar crosses the finish line and wins the Annual Seven Mile Bridge Run in Florida for the fifth time, a clear victory over his phobia of crossing bridges.

Reuters/Andy Newman/Corbis

•**modeling**•A process of learning in which a person observes and then imitates others. Also, a therapy approach based on the same principle.

•**stimulus generalization**•A phenomenon in which responses to one stimulus are also produced by similar stimuli.

Phobia free

Most explanations of specific phobias focus on behavioral causes. However, this so-called knockout mouse at Rutgers University was genetically engineered without certain fear-related genes. Consequently, it experiences less fear than other mice and is less prone to acquire laboratory-induced phobias.

Entrapment → Fear response

As she struggled to free her feet, the girl heard a waterfall nearby. The sound of the running water became linked in her mind to her terrifying battle with the rocks, and she developed a fear of running water as well.

Running water → Fear response

Eventually the aunt found the screaming child, freed her from the rocks, and comforted her, but the psychological damage had been done. From that day forward, the girl was terrified of running water. For years family members had to hold her down to bathe her. When she traveled on a train, friends had to cover the windows so that she would not have to look at any streams. The young woman had apparently acquired a specific phobia through classical conditioning.

In conditioning terms, the entrapment was an *unconditioned stimulus* (*US*) that understandably elicited an *unconditioned response* (*UR*) of fear. The running water represented a *conditioned stimulus* (*CS*), a formerly neutral stimulus that became associated with entrapment in the child's mind and came also to elicit a fear reaction. The newly acquired fear was a *conditioned response* (*CR*).

US: Entrapment → UR: Fear

CS: Running water → CR: Fear

Another way of acquiring a fear reaction is through **modeling,** that is, through observation and imitation (Bandura & Rosenthal, 1966). A person may observe that others are afraid of certain objects or events and develop fears of the same things. Consider a young boy whose mother is afraid of illnesses, doctors, and hospitals. If she frequently expresses those fears, before long the boy himself may fear illnesses, doctors, and hospitals.

Why should one or a few upsetting experiences or observations develop into a long-term specific phobia? Shouldn't the trapped girl see later that running water will bring her no harm? Shouldn't the boy see later that illnesses are temporary and doctors and hospitals helpful? Behaviorists believe that after acquiring a fear response, people try to *avoid* what they fear. They do not get close to the dreaded objects often enough to learn that the objects are really quite harmless.

Behaviorists also propose that specific learned fears will blossom into a generalized anxiety disorder when a person acquires a large number of them. This development is presumed to come about through **stimulus generalization**: responses to one stimulus are also elicited by similar stimuli. The fear of running water acquired by the girl in the rocks could have generalized to such similar stimuli as milk being poured into a glass or even the sound of bubbly music. Perhaps a person experiences a series of upsetting events, each event produces one or more feared stimuli, and the person's reactions to each of these stimuli generalize to yet other stimuli. That person may then build up a large number of fears and eventually develop generalized anxiety disorder.

HOW HAVE BEHAVIORAL EXPLANATIONS FARED IN RESEARCH? Some laboratory studies have found that animals and humans can indeed be taught to fear objects through classical conditioning (Miller, 1948; Mowrer, 1947, 1939). In one famous report, psychologists John B. Watson and Rosalie Rayner (1920) described how they taught a baby boy called Little Albert to fear white rats. For weeks Albert was allowed to play with a white rat and appeared to enjoy doing so. One time when Albert reached for the rat, however, the experimenter struck a steel bar with a hammer, making a very loud noise that frightened Albert. The next several times that Albert reached for the rat, the experimenter again made the loud noise. Albert acquired a fear and avoidance response to the rat.

What concerns might today's human-participant research review boards raise about the study on Little Albert?

Research has also supported the behavioral position that fears can be acquired through modeling. Psychologists Albert Bandura and Theodore Rosenthal (1966), for example, had human research participants observe a person apparently being shocked by electricity whenever a buzzer sounded. The victim was actually the experimenter's accomplice—in research terminology, a *confederate*—who pretended to experience pain by twitching and yelling whenever the buzzer went on. After the unsuspecting participants had observed several such episodes, they themselves experienced a fear reaction whenever they heard the buzzer.

Although these studies support behaviorists' explanations of specific phobias, other research has called those explanations into question (Gamble et al., 2010; Ressler & Davis, 2003). Several laboratory studies with children and adults have failed to condition fear reactions. In addition, although most case studies trace specific phobias to incidents of classical conditioning or modeling, quite a few fail to do so. So, although it appears that such a phobia *can* be acquired by classical conditioning or modeling, researchers have not established that the disorder is *ordinarily* acquired in this way.

A BEHAVIORAL-EVOLUTIONARY EXPLANATION Some specific phobias are much more common than others. Phobic reactions to animals, heights, and darkness are more common than phobic reactions to meat, grass, and houses. Theorists often account for these differences by proposing that human beings, as a species, have a predisposition to develop certain fears (Scher et al., 2006; Lundqvist & Ohman, 2005; Seligman, 1971). This idea is referred to as **preparedness** because human beings, theoretically, are "prepared" to acquire some specific phobias and not others. The following case makes the point:

> A four-year-old girl was playing in the park. Thinking that she saw a snake, she ran to her parents' car and jumped inside, slamming the door behind her. Unfortunately, the girl's hand was caught by the closing car door, the results of which were severe pain and several visits to the doctor. Before this, she may have been afraid of snakes, but not phobic. After this experience, a phobia developed, not of cars or car doors, but of snakes. The snake phobia persisted into adulthood, at which time she sought treatment from me.
>
> (Marks, 1977, p. 192)

Where might such predispositions to fear come from? According to some theorists, the predispositions have been transmitted genetically through an evolutionary process. Among our ancestors, the ones who more readily acquired fears of animals, darkness, heights, and the like were more likely to survive long enough to reproduce and to pass on their fear inclinations to their offspring (Hofer, 2010; Ohman & Mineka, 2003).

How Are Specific Phobias Treated?
Surveys reveal that 19 percent of individuals with specific phobias are currently in treatment (Wang et al., 2005). Every theoretical model has its own approach to treating these phobias, but behavioral techniques are more widely used than the rest. The major behavioral approaches are *desensitization, flooding,* and *modeling.* Together, these approaches are called **exposure treatments** because in all of them individuals are exposed to the objects or situations they dread (Abramowitz, Deacon, & Whiteside, 2011).

People treated by **systematic desensitization,** a technique developed by Joseph Wolpe (1997, 1987, 1969), learn to relax while gradually facing the objects or situations they fear. Since relaxation and fear are incompatible, the new

•**preparedness**•A predisposition to develop certain fears.

•**exposure treatments**•Behavioral treatments in which persons are exposed to the objects or situations they dread.

•**systematic desensitization**•A behavioral treatment that uses relaxation training and a fear hierarchy to help clients with phobias react calmly to the objects or situations they dread.

Recovering lost revenues
These individuals scream out as they experience a sudden steep drop from the top of an amusement park ride. Several parks offer behavioral programs to help prospective customers overcome their fears of roller coasters and other horror rides. After "treatment," some clients are able to ride the rails with the best of them. For others, it's back to the relative calm of the Ferris wheel.

Flight without fear

No, these people are not sleeping, or worse. They are going through relaxation and meditation exercises prior to going on an airplane flight from Kansas City to Denver. They are students in an eight-week course called "Flight Without Fear" that applies the principles of behavioral desensitization to help individuals overcome their phobic fear of flying.

relaxation response is thought to substitute for the fear response. Desensitization therapists first offer *relaxation training* to clients, teaching them how to bring on a state of deep muscle relaxation at will. In addition, the therapists help clients create a *fear hierarchy*, a list of feared objects or situations, ordered from mildly to extremely upsetting.

Then clients learn how to pair relaxation with the objects or situations they fear. While the client is in a state of relaxation, the therapist has the client face the event at the bottom of his or her hierarchy. This may be an actual confrontation, a process called *in vivo desensitization*. A person who fears heights, for example, may stand on a chair or climb a stepladder. Or the confrontation may be imagined, a process called *covert desensitization*. In this case, the person imagines the frightening event while the therapist describes it. The client moves through the entire list, pairing his or her relaxation responses with each feared item. Because the first item is only mildly frightening, it is usually only a short while before the person is able to relax totally in its presence. Over the course of several sessions, clients move up the ladder of their fears until they reach and overcome the one that frightens them most of all.

Another behavioral treatment for specific phobias is **flooding.** Flooding therapists believe that people will stop fearing things when they are exposed to them repeatedly and made to see that they are actually quite harmless. Clients are forced to face their feared objects or situations without relaxation training and without a gradual buildup. The flooding procedure, like desensitization, can be either in vivo or covert.

When flooding therapists guide clients in imagining feared objects or situations, they often exaggerate the description so that the clients experience intense emotional arousal. In the case of a woman with a snake phobia, the therapist had her imagine the following scene, among others:

> *Close your eyes again. Picture the snake out in front of you, now make yourself pick it up. Reach down, pick it up, put it in your lap, feel it wiggling around in your lap, leave your hand on it, put your hand out and feel it wiggling around. Kind of explore its body with your fingers and hand. You don't like to do it, make yourself do it. Make yourself do it. Really grab onto the snake. Squeeze it a little bit, feel it. Feel it kind of start to wind around your hand. Let it. Leave your hand there, feel it touching your hand and winding around it, curling around your wrist.*

(Hogan, 1968, p. 423)

•**flooding**•A treatment for phobias in which clients are exposed repeatedly and intensively to a feared object and made to see that it is actually harmless.

•**agoraphobia**•An anxiety disorder in which a person is afraid to be in public places or situations from which escape might be difficult (or embarrassing) or help unavailable if panic-like symptoms were to occur.

In *modeling* it is the therapist who confronts the feared object or situation while the fearful person observes (Bandura, 2011, 1977, 1971; Bandura et al., 1977). The behavioral therapist acts as a model to demonstrate that the person's fear is groundless. After several sessions many clients are able to approach the objects or situations calmly. In one version of modeling, *participant modeling,* the client is actively encouraged to join in with the therapist.

Clinical researchers have repeatedly found that each of the exposure treatments helps people with specific phobias (Antony & Roemer, 2011; Gamble et al., 2010). The key to success in all of these therapies appears to be *actual* contact with the feared object or situation. In vivo desensitization is more effective than covert desensitization, in vivo flooding more effective than covert flooding, and participant modeling more helpful than strictly observational modeling. In addition, a growing number of therapists are using *virtual reality*—3D computer graphics that simulate real-world objects and situations—as a useful exposure tool (Antony, 2011).

Agoraphobia

People with **agoraphobia** are afraid of being in public places or situations where escape might be difficult or help unavailable, should they experience panic or become incapacitated (APA, 2013, 2012) (see Table 5-6). This is a pervasive and complex phobia. In any given year 2.2 percent of the adult population experience this problem, women twice as frequently as men (NIMH, 2012). The disorder also is twice as common among poor people as wealthy people (Sareen et al., 2011). At least one-fifth of individuals with agoraphobia are currently in treatment (NIMH, 2011).

People typically develop agoraphobia in their 20s or 30s, as Veronica did:

For several months prior to her application for treatment Veronica had been unable to leave her home. . . . "It is as if something dreadful would happen to me if I did not immediately go home." Even after she would return to the house, she would feel shaken inside and unable to speak to anyone or do anything for an hour or so. However, as long as she remained in her own home or garden, she was able to carry on her routine life without much problem. . . . Because of this agoraphobia, she had been unable to return to her position as a mathematics teacher in the local high school after the summer vacation.

. . . [Veronica] stated that she had always been a somewhat shy person who generally preferred keeping to herself, but that up until approximately a year ago she had always been able to go to her job, shop, or go to church without any particular feelings of dread or uneasiness. It was difficult for her to recall the first time . . . but it seemed to her that the first major experience was approximately a year before, when she and her mother had been Christmas shopping. They were standing in the middle of a crowded department store when she suddenly felt the impulse to flee. She left her mother without an explanation and drove home as fast as she could. . . . After the Christmas vacation she seemed to recover for a while and was at least able to return to her classroom duties without any ill effect. During the ensuing several months she had several similar experiences, usually when she was off duty; but by late spring these fears were just as likely to occur in the classroom. . . . In thinking further about the occurrence of her phobia, it seemed to Veronica that there was actually no particular stress which might account for her fear.

(Goldstein & Palmer, 1975, pp. 163–164)

It is typical of people with agoraphobia to avoid entering crowded streets or stores, driving in parking lots or on bridges, and traveling on public transportation or in airplanes. If they venture out of the house at all, it is usually only in the company of close relatives or friends. Some people with agoraphobia further insist that family members or friends stay with them at home, but even at home and in the company of others they may continue to feel anxious.

In many cases the intensity of the agoraphobia fluctuates, as it did for Veronica. In severe cases, people become virtual prisoners in their own homes. Their social life dwindles, and they cannot hold a job. Persons with agoraphobia may also become depressed, sometimes as a result of the severe limitations that their disorder places on their lives.

table: **5-6**

DSM-5 Checklist

Agoraphobia

1. Marked, disproportionate, and immediate fear about being in at least two of the following situations: public transportation (e.g., auto travel) • open spaces (e.g., parking lots) • shops, theaters, or cinemas • line or crowds • outside at home alone.

2. Fear of agoraphobic situations is related to concern that escape might be hard or help unavailable if one were to experience panic or become incapacitated.

3. Avoidance of agoraphobic situations.

4. Symptoms typically last six or more months

5. Significant distress or impairment.

Based on APA, 2013, 2012.

Explanations for Agoraphobia Although broader than specific phobias, agoraphobia is often explained in ways similar to specific phobias. Behaviorists, for example, often point to classical conditioning, modeling, and stimulus generalizations as key processes in the acquisition of this disorder. In addition, many people with agoraphobia actually experience extreme and sudden explosions of fear, called *panic attacks,* when they enter public places, a problem that can leave them particularly vulnerable to the development of agoraphobia. Such individuals may in fact receive two diagnoses— agoraphobia and *panic disorder,* an anxiety disorder that you'll be reading about later in this chapter—because their difficulties extend considerably beyond an excessive fear of venturing away from home into public places (APA, 2013, 2012).

Treatments for Agoraphobia For years clinicians made little impact on agoraphobia, the fear of leaving one's home and entering public places. However, approaches have now been developed that enable many such people to venture out with less anxiety. These new approaches do not always bring as much relief to sufferers as the highly successful treatments for specific phobias, but they do offer considerable relief to many people.

Once again behaviorists have led the way by developing a variety of exposure approaches for agoraphobia (Gloster et al., 2011; Emmelkamp, 1994). Therapists typically help clients to venture farther and farther from their homes and to gradually enter outside places, one step at a time. They may use systematic desensitization, support, and/or coaxing to get clients to confront the outside world.

Exposure therapy for people with agoraphobia often includes additional features, particularly the use of support groups and home-based self-help programs, to motivate clients to work hard at their treatment. In the *support group* approach, a small number of people with agoraphobia go out together for exposure sessions that last for several hours. The group members support and encourage one another, and eventually coax one another to move away from the safety of the group and perform exposure tasks on their own. In the *home-based self-help programs,* clinicians give clients and their families detailed instructions for carrying out exposure treatments themselves.

Between 60 and 80 percent of agoraphobic clients who receive exposure treatment find it easier to enter public places, and the improvement persists for years after the beginning of treatment (Gloster et al., 2011; Klein et al., 2011; Craske & Barlow, 2008, 1993). Unfortunately, these improvements are often partial rather than complete, and relapses may occur in as many as half of successfully treated clients, although these people readily recapture previous gains if they are treated again. Those whose agoraphobia is accompanied by a panic disorder seem to benefit less than others from exposure therapy alone. We shall take a closer look at this group when we investigate treatments for panic disorder.

Social Anxiety Disorder

Many people are uncomfortable when interacting with others or talking or performing in front of others. A number of entertainers and sports figures, from singer Barbra Streisand to baseball pitcher Zack Greinke, have described experiences of significant anxiety before performing. Social fears of this kind certainly are unpleasant, but usually the people who have them manage to function adequately.

People with **social anxiety disorder,** by contrast, have severe, persistent, and irrational anxiety about social or performance situations in which scrutiny by others and embarrassment may occur (APA, 2013, 2012) (see Table 5-7). The social anxiety may be narrow, such as a fear of talking in public or eating in front of others, or it may be broad, such as a general fear of functioning poorly in front of others. In both forms, people repeatedly judge themselves as performing less compe-

Why do so many professional performers seem prone to performance anxiety? Might their repeated exposure to audiences have a therapeutic effect?

table: 5-7

DSM-5 Checklist

Social Anxiety Disorder

1. Marked, disproportionate, and persistent fear or anxiety about one or more social situations in which individual is exposed to possible scrutiny by others, typically lasting six months or more.

2. Fear of being negatively evaluated by or offensive to others.

3. Anxiety is almost always produced by exposure to the social situation.

4. Avoidance of feared situations.

5. Significant distress or impairment.

Based on APA, 2013, 2012.

tently than they actually do. As you read earlier, it is because of its wide-ranging scope that this disorder is now typically called social anxiety disorder rather than *social phobia,* the label it had in past editions of the DSM.

Social anxiety disorder can interfere greatly with one's life (Ravindran & Stein, 2011). A person who cannot interact with others or speak in public may fail to carry out important responsibilities. One who cannot eat in public may reject meal invitations and other social offerings. Since many people with this disorder keep their fears secret, their social reluctance is often misinterpreted as snobbery, lack of interest, or hostility.

Surveys reveal that 7.1 percent of people in the United States and other Western countries (around 60 percent of them female) experience social anxiety disorder in any given year (see Table 5-8 on the next page). Around 12 percent develop this disorder at some point in their lives (Alfano & Beidel, 2011; Kessler et al., 2010). It tends to begin in late childhood or adolescence and may continue into adulthood. At least one-quarter of individuals with social anxiety disorder are currently in treatment (NIMH, 2011).

Research finds that poor people are 50 percent more likely than wealthier people to experience social anxiety disorder (Sareen et al., 2011). Moreover, in several studies African Americans and Asian Americans, but not Hispanic Americans, have scored higher than white Americans on surveys of social anxiety (Polo et al., 2011; Stein & Williams, 2010; Schultz et al., 2008, 2006). In addition, a culture-bound disorder called *taijn kyofusho* seems to be particularly common in Asian countries such as Japan and Korea. Although this disorder is traditionally defined as a fear of making other people feel uncomfortable, a number of clinicians now suspect that its sufferers primarily fear being evaluated negatively by other people, a key feature of social anxiety disorder.

What Causes Social Anxiety Disorder?

The leading explanation for social anxiety disorder has been proposed by cognitive theorists and researchers (Heimberg, Brozovich, & Rapee, 2010; Hofmann, 2007; Clark & Wells, 1995). They contend that people with this disorder hold a group of social beliefs and expectations that consistently work against them. These include:

▸ They hold unrealistically high social standards and so believe that they must perform perfectly in social situations.

▸ They view themselves as unattractive social beings.

▸ They view themselves as socially unskilled and inadequate.

▸ They believe they are always in danger of behaving incompetently in social situations.

▸ They believe that inept behaviors in social situations will inevitably lead to terrible consequences.

▸ They believe that they have no control over feelings of anxiety that emerge during social situations.

Cognitive theorists hold that, because of these beliefs, people with social anxiety disorder keep anticipating that social disasters will occur, and they repeatedly perform "avoidance" and "safety" behaviors to help prevent or reduce such disasters (Rosenberg, Ledley, & Heimberg, 2010). Avoidance behaviors include, for example, talking only to persons they already know well at gatherings or parties. Safety behaviors include wearing makeup to cover up blushing.

Beset by such beliefs and expectations, people with social anxiety disorder find that their anxiety levels increase as soon as they enter into a social situation. Moreover, because they are convinced that their social flaws are the cause of the anxiety, certain that they do not have the social skills to deal with the situation, and concerned that they cannot contain their negative arousal, they become filled with anxiety.

Later, after the social event has occurred, the individuals repeatedly review the details of the event. They overestimate how poorly things went and what

•**social anxiety disorder**•A severe and persistent fear of social or performance situations in which embarrassment may occur.

Word limits

In 2004, Austrian author Elfriede Jelinek, the Nobel prize winner in literature, had to accept this prestigious honor and present her Nobel lecture by video transmission because her social anxiety disorder prevented her from attending the festivities in Stockholm in person. She was the first literature winner in 40 years not to attend the prize ceremony.

AP Photo/Jonas Ekstromer

table: 5-8

Profile of Anxiety Disorders and Obsessive-Compulsive Disorder

	One-Year Prevalence	Female to Male Ratio	Typical Age at Onset	Prevalence Among Close Relatives	Percentage Currently Receiving Clinical Treatment
Generalized anxiety disorder	4.0%	2:1	0–20 years	Elevated	25.5%
Specific phobia	8.7%	2:1	Variable	Elevated	19.0%
Agoraphobia	2.2%	2:1	15–35 years	Elevated	20.9%
Social anxiety disorder	7.1%	3:2	10–20 years	Elevated	24.7%
Panic disorder	2.8%	5:2	15–35 years	Elevated	34.7%
Obsessive-compulsive disorder	1.0–2.0%	1:1	4–25 years	Elevated	41.3%

Source: NIMH, 2011; Kessler et al., 2010, 2005, 1999, 1994; Ritter et al., 2010; Ruscio et al., 2007; Wang et al., 2005; Regier et al., 1993.

negative results may take place. These persistent thoughts actually keep the event alive and further increase the individuals' fears about future social situations.

Researchers have indeed found that people with social anxiety disorder manifest the beliefs, expectations, interpretations, and feelings listed here (Rosenberg et al., 2010; Moscovitch, 2009). At the same time, cognitive theorists often differ on why some individuals have such cognitions and others do not. Various factors have been uncovered by researchers, including genetic predispositions, trait tendencies, biological abnormalities, traumatic childhood experiences, and overprotective parent-child interactions during childhood (Brozovich & Heimberg, 2011; Kuo et al., 2011).

Treatments for Social Anxiety Disorder

Only in the past 15 years have clinicians been able to treat social anxiety disorder successfully (Rosenberg et al., 2010). Their newfound success is due in part to the growing recognition that the disorder has two distinct features that may feed upon each other: (1) sufferers have overwhelming social fears, and (2) they often lack skill at starting conversations, communicating their needs, or meeting the needs of others (Beck, 2010). Armed with this insight, clinicians now treat social anxiety disorder by trying to reduce social fears, by providing training in social skills, or both.

HOW CAN SOCIAL FEARS BE REDUCED? Social fears are often reduced through medication (Ravindran & Stein, 2011). Somewhat surprisingly, it is *antidepressant medications* that seem to be the drugs of most help for this disorder, often more helpful than benzodiazepines or other kinds of antianxiety medications. At the same time, several types of psychotherapy have proved to be at least as effective as medication at reducing social fears, and people helped by such psychological treatments appear less likely to relapse than those treated with medications alone (Abramowitz et al., 2011). This finding suggests to some clinicians that the psychological approaches should always be included in the treatment of social fears.

One psychological approach is *exposure therapy,* the behavioral intervention so effective with phobias (Antony & Roemer, 2011). Exposure therapists encourage clients with social fears to expose themselves to the dreaded social situations and to remain until their fears subside. Usually the exposure is gradual, and it often includes homework assignments that are carried out in the social situations. In addition, group therapy offers an ideal setting for exposure treatments by allowing people to face social situations in an atmo-

See and do

The exposure technique of modeling is applied to both specific phobias and social anxiety disorder. Here, therapist Pete Cohen treats clients who manifest ophidiophobia (fear of snakes) by first handling a snake himself, then encouraging the clients to handle it. Similarly, therapists may model appropriate social behaviors for clients with social anxiety disorder, then encourage the clients to try out the same behaviors.

Kent News & Picture/Corbis Sygma

sphere of support and caring (McEvoy, 2007). In one group, for example, a man who was afraid that his hands would tremble in the presence of other people had to write on a blackboard in front of the group and serve tea to the other members (Emmelkamp, 1982).

Cognitive therapies have also been widely used to treat social fears, often in combination with behavioral techniques (Goldin et al., 2012; Kim, Parr, & Alfano, 2011). In the following discussion, cognitive therapist Albert Ellis uses rational-emotive therapy to help a man who fears he will be rejected if he speaks up at gatherings. The discussion took place after the man had done a homework assignment in which he was to identify his negative social expectations and force himself to say anything he had on his mind in social situations, no matter how stupid it might seem to him:

After two weeks of this assignment, the patient came into his next session of therapy and reported: "I did what you told me to do. . . . [Every] time, just as you said, I found myself retreating from people, I said to myself: 'Now, even though you can't see it, there must be some sentences. What are they?' And I finally found them. And there were many of them! And they all seemed to say the same thing."

"What thing?"

"That I, uh, was going to be rejected. . . . [If] I related to them I was going to be rejected. And wouldn't that be perfectly awful if I was to be rejected. And there was no reason for me, uh, to take that, uh, sort of thing, and be rejected in that awful manner." . . .

"And did you do the second part of the homework assignment?"

"The forcing myself to speak up and express myself?"

"Yes, that part."

"That was worse. That was really hard. Much harder than I thought it would be. But I did it."

"And?"

"Oh, not bad at all. I spoke up several times; more than I've ever done before. Some people were very surprised. Phyllis was very surprised, too. But I spoke up." . . .

"And how did you feel after expressing yourself like that?"

"Remarkable! I don't remember when I last felt this way. I felt, uh, just remarkable—good, that is. It was really something to feel! But it was so hard. I almost didn't make it. And a couple of other times during the week I had to force myself again. But I did. And I was glad!"

(Ellis, 1962, pp. 202–203)

Studies show that rational-emotive therapy and other cognitive approaches do indeed help reduce social fears (Boden et al., 2012; Kim et al., 2011). And these reductions typically persist for years. On the other hand, research also suggests that while cognitive therapy often reduces social fears, it does not consistently help people perform effectively in social settings. This is where social skills training has come to the forefront.

HOW CAN SOCIAL SKILLS BE IMPROVED? In **social skills training,** therapists combine several behavioral techniques in order to help people improve their social skills. They usually *model* appropriate social behaviors for clients and encourage the individuals to try them out. The clients then *role-play* with the therapists, *rehearsing* their new behaviors until they become more effective. Throughout the process, therapists provide frank *feedback* and *reinforce* (praise) the clients for effective performances.

Reinforcement from other people with similar social difficulties is often more powerful than reinforcement from a therapist alone. In *social skills training groups* and *assertiveness training groups,* members try out and rehearse new social behaviors with other group members. The group can also provide guidance on what is socially appropriate. According to research, social skills training, both individual and group formats, has helped many people perform better in social situations (Kim et al., 2011; Fisher et al., 2004).

•**social skills training**•A therapy approach that helps people learn or improve social skills and assertiveness through role playing and rehearsing of desirable behaviors.

•**panic attacks**•Periodic, short bouts of panic that occur suddenly, reach a peak within minutes, and gradually pass.

•**panic disorder**•An anxiety disorder marked by recurrent and unpredictable panic attacks.

•**norepinephrine**•A neurotransmitter whose abnormal activity is linked to panic disorder and depression.

•**locus ceruleus**•A small area of the brain that seems to be active in the regulation of emotions. Many of its neurons use norepinephrine.

•**amygdala**•A small, almond-shaped structure in the brain that processes emotional information.

Panic Disorder

Sometimes an anxiety reaction takes the form of a smothering, nightmarish panic in which people lose control of their behavior and, in fact, are practically unaware of what they are doing. Anyone can react with panic when a real threat looms up suddenly (see *PsychWatch* on page 139). Some people, however, experience **panic attacks**—periodic, short bouts of panic that occur suddenly, reach a peak within 10 minutes, and gradually pass (APA, 2013, 2012).

The attacks feature at least four of the following symptoms of panic: palpitations of the heart, tingling in the hands or feet, shortness of breath, sweating, hot and cold flashes, trembling, chest pains, choking sensations, faintness, dizziness, and a feeling of unreality (APA, 2013, 2012). Small wonder that during a panic attack many people fear they will die, go crazy, or lose control.

> I was inside a very busy shopping precinct and all of a sudden it happened: in a matter of seconds I was like a mad woman. It was like a nightmare, only I was awake; everything went black and sweat poured out of me—my body, my hands and even my hair got wet through. All the blood seemed to drain out of me; I went as white as a ghost. I felt as if I were going to collapse; it was as if I had no control over my limbs; my back and legs were very weak and I felt as though it were impossible to move. It was as if I had been taken over by some stronger force. I saw all the people looking at me—just faces, no bodies, all merged into one. My heart started pounding in my head and in my ears; I thought my heart was going to stop. I could see black and yellow lights. I could hear the voices of the people but from a long way off. I could not think of anything except the way I was feeling and that now I had to get out and run quickly or I would die. I must escape and get into the fresh air.
>
> *(Hawkrigg, 1975)*

More than one-quarter of all people have one or more panic attacks at some point in their lives (Kessler et al., 2010; 2006). Some people, however, have panic attacks repeatedly and unexpectedly and without apparent reason. They may be suffering from **panic disorder**. In addition to the panic attacks, people who are diagnosed with panic disorder experience dysfunctional changes in their thinking or behavior as a result of the attacks (see Table 5-9). They may, for example, worry persistently about having additional attacks, have concerns about what such attacks mean ("Am I losing my mind?"), or plan their lives around the possibility of future attacks (APA, 2013, 2012).

Around 2.8 percent of all people in the United States suffer from panic disorder in a given year; close to 5 percent develop it at some point in their lives (Kessler et al., 2010, 2009, 2005). The disorder tends to develop in late adolescence or early adulthood and is at least twice as common among women as among men (McGrath, 2012; APA, 2000). Poor people are 50 percent more likely than wealthier people to experience panic disorder (Sareen et al., 2011).

The prevalence of this disorder is the same across various cultural and racial groups in the United States, although the features of panic attacks may differ somewhat from group to group (Barrera et al., 2010). For example, Asian Americans appear more likely than white Americans to experience dizziness, unsteadiness, and choking, while African Americans seem less likely than white Americans to experience those particular symptoms. Similarly, panic disorder seems to occur in equal numbers in cultures across the world (Nazarian & Craske, 2008). Surveys indicate that at least one-third of individuals with panic disorder in the United States are currently in treatment (NIMH, 2011; Wang et al., 2005).

As you read earlier, panic disorder is often accompanied by agoraphobia, the broad phobia in which people are afraid to travel to public places where escape might be difficult should they experience panic symptoms or become incapacitated. In such cases,

table: 5-9

DSM-5 Checklist

Panic Disorder

1. Recurrent unexpected panic attacks.

2. A month or more of one of the following symptoms after at least one of the attacks.

   (a) Persistent concern or worry about having additional attacks.

   (b) Significant maladaptive change in behavior related to the attacks.

Based on APA, 2013, 2012.

the panic disorder typically sets the stage for the development of agoraphobia. That is, after experiencing multiple unpredictable panic attacks, the individuals become increasingly fearful of having new attacks in public places.

The Biological Perspective

In the 1960s, clinicians made the surprising discovery that panic disorder was helped more by certain *antidepressant drugs,* drugs that are usually used to reduce the symptoms of depression, than by most of the benzodiazepine drugs, the drugs useful in treating generalized anxiety disorder (Klein, 1964; Klein & Fink, 1962). This observation led to the first biological explanations and treatments for panic disorder.

What Biological Factors Contribute to Panic Disorder?

To understand the biology of panic disorder, researchers worked backward from their understanding of the antidepressant drugs that seemed to control it. They knew that these particular antidepressant drugs operate in the brain primarily by changing the activity of **norepinephrine,** yet another one of the neurotransmitters that carry messages between neurons. Given that the drugs were so helpful in eliminating panic attacks, researchers began to suspect that panic disorder might be caused in the first place by abnormal norepinephrine activity.

Several studies produced evidence that norepinephrine activity is indeed irregular in people who suffer from panic attacks. For example, the **locus ceruleus** is a brain area rich in neurons that use norepinephrine. When this area is electrically stimulated in monkeys, the monkeys have a panic-like reaction, suggesting that panic reactions may be related to increases in norepinephrine activity in the locus ceruleus (Redmond, 1981, 1979, 1977). Similarly, in another line of research, scientists were able to produce panic attacks in human beings by injecting them with chemicals known to increase the activity of norepinephrine (Bourin et al., 1995; Charney et al., 1990, 1987).

These findings strongly tied norepinephrine and the locus ceruleus to panic attacks. However, research conducted in recent years suggests that the root of panic attacks is probably more complicated than a single neurotransmitter or a single brain area. It turns out that panic reactions are produced in part by a brain circuit consisting of areas such as the **amygdala,** *ventromedial nucleus of the hypothalamus, central gray matter,* and *locus ceruleus* (Etkin, 2010; Ninan & Dunlop, 2005) (see Figure 5-5). When a person confronts a frightening object or situation, the amygdala is stimulated. In turn, the amygdala stimulates the other brain areas in the circuit, temporarily setting into motion an "alarm-and-escape" response (increased heart rate, respiration, blood pressure, and the like) that is very similar to a panic reaction (Gray & McNaughton, 1996). Most of today's researchers believe that this brain circuit—including the neurotransmitters at work throughout the circuit—probably functions improperly in people who experience panic disorder (Bremner & Charney, 2010; Burijon, 2007).

Note that the brain circuit responsible for panic reactions appears to be different from the one responsible for broad and worry-dominated *anxiety* reactions—the circuit that we came across on page 124. Although some of the brain areas and neurotransmitters in the two circuits obviously overlap—particularly the amygdala, which seems to be at the center of each circuit—the finding that the panic brain circuit and the anxiety brain circuit are different has further convinced researchers that panic disorder is biologically different from generalized anxiety disorder and, for that matter, from other kinds of anxiety disorders.

"Weekends I like to be able to panic without having all the distractions."

Figure 5-5

The biology of panic The circuit in the brain that produces panic reactions includes areas such as the amygdala, ventromedial nucleus of the hypothalamus, central gray matter, and locus ceruleus. This circuit appears to be different from the one limited to anxiety reactions, although the panic and anxiety circuits do share the amygdala.

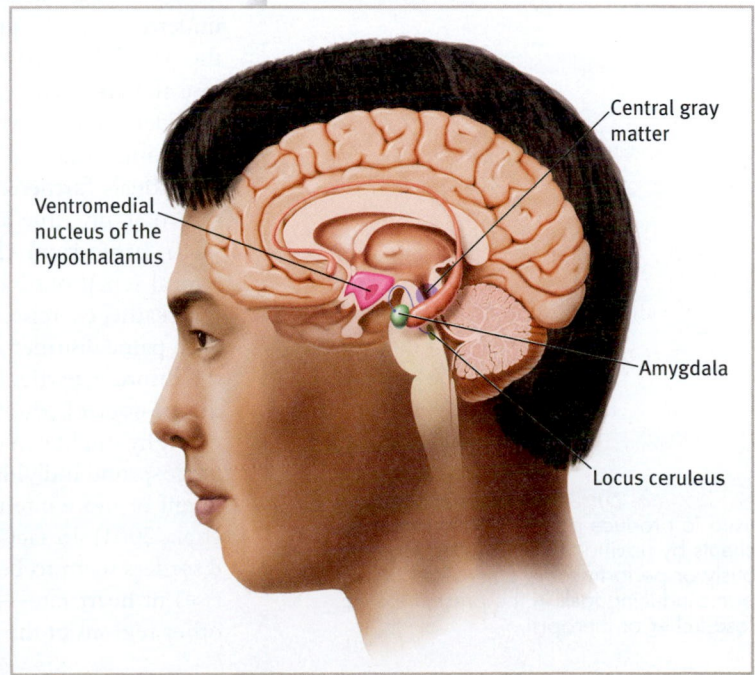

Why might some people have abnormalities in norepinephrine activity, locus ceruleus functioning, and other parts of the panic brain circuit? One possibility is that a predisposition to develop such abnormalities is inherited (Burijon, 2007; Torgersen, 1990, 1983). Once again, if a genetic factor is at work, close relatives should have higher rates of panic disorder than more distant relatives. Studies do find that among identical twins (twins who share all of their genes), if one twin has panic disorder, the other twin has the same disorder in as many as 31 percent of cases (Tsuang et al., 2004). Among fraternal twins (who share only some of their genes), if one twin has panic disorder, the other twin has the same disorder in only 11 percent of cases (Kendler et al., 1995, 1993).

Drug Therapies As you have just read, researchers discovered in 1962 that certain antidepressant drugs could prevent panic attacks or reduce their frequency. Since the time of this surprising finding, studies across the world have repeatedly confirmed the initial observation (Bandelow & Baldwin, 2010; Stein et al., 2010).

It appears that all antidepressant drugs that restore proper activity of norepinephrine in the locus ceruleus and other parts of the panic brain circuit are able to help prevent or reduce panic symptoms (Pollack, 2005; Redmond, 1985). Such drugs bring at least some improvement to 80 percent of patients who have panic disorder, and the improvement can last indefinitely, as long as the drugs are continued. In recent years *alprazolam* (Xanax) and other powerful benzodiazepine drugs have also proved effective in the treatment of panic disorder (Bandelow & Baldwin, 2010; Stein et al., 2010). Apparently, the benzodiazepines help individuals with this disorder by *indirectly* affecting the activity of norepinephrine throughout the brain. Clinicians also have found the same antidepressant drugs and powerful benzodiazepines to be helpful in cases of panic disorder accompanied by agoraphobia.

The Cognitive Perspective

Cognitive theorists have come to recognize that biological factors are only part of the cause of panic attacks. In their view, full panic reactions are experienced only by people who further *misinterpret* the physiological events that are occurring within their bodies. Cognitive treatments are aimed at correcting such misinterpretations.

The Cognitive Explanation: Misinterpreting Bodily Sensations
Cognitive theorists believe that panic-prone people may be very sensitive to certain bodily sensations; when they unexpectedly experience such sensations, they misinterpret them as signs of a medical catastrophe (Clark & Beck, 2012, 2010; Wenzel, 2011). Rather than understanding the probable cause of their sensations as "something I ate" or "a fight with the boss," the panic-prone grow increasingly upset about losing control, fear the worst, lose all perspective, and rapidly plunge into panic. For example, many people with panic disorder seem to "overbreathe," or hyperventilate, in stressful situations. The abnormal breathing makes them think that they are in danger of suffocation, so they panic. Such individuals further develop the belief that these and other "dangerous" sensations may return at any time and so set themselves up for future panic attacks.

In **biological challenge tests,** researchers produce hyperventilation or other biological sensations by administering drugs or by instructing clinical research participants to breathe, exercise, or simply think in certain ways. As you might expect, participants with panic disorder experience greater upset during these tests than participants without the disorder, particularly when they believe that their bodily sensations are dangerous or out of control (Bunaciu et al., 2012; Masdrakis & Papakostas, 2004).

Why might some people be prone to such misinterpretations? One possibility is that panic-prone individuals generally experience, through no fault of their own, more frequent or more intense bodily sensations than other people do (Nillni et al., 2012; Nardi et al., 2001). In fact, the kinds of sensations that are most often misinterpreted in panic disorders seem to be carbon dioxide increases in the blood, shifts in blood pressure, and rises in heart rate—bodily events that are controlled in part by the locus ceruleus and other regions of the panic brain circuit. Another possibility, supported by some research,

•**biological challenge test**• A procedure used to produce panic in participants or clients by having them exercise vigorously or perform some other potentially panic-inducing task in the presence of a researcher or therapist.

PsychWatch

Panic: Everyone Is Vulnerable

People with panic disorder are not the only ones to experience panic. In fact, many people panic when faced with a threat that unfolds very rapidly. The following news report describes the crowd reaction and human stampede that occurred at a trendy Chicago nightclub on February 17, 2003, after a security guard used pepper spray or mace to break up a fight between two women:

Police and fire officials yesterday began an investigation into how a fight in a Chicago nightclub caused a stampede in which 21 people were crushed to death. Witnesses claimed a fight between two women led to security guards using a pepper spray or mace to separate them early yesterday morning. As the fumes caused a panic, the fleeing clubbers found the rear doors of the E2 club were chained shut, forcing an estimated 1,500 people inside to surge down a narrow stairwell as they attempted to flee.

About 150 people, including two firefighters involved in the rescue operation, were injured, at least ten of whom were in critical condition last night. Eyewitnesses described how a "mound of people" built up on the stairs as they fled towards an exit, with many trampled and suffocated in the panic. Others passed out from the effect of the chemical fumes, it was claimed.

Cory Thomas, 33, who was waiting outside to collect two friends, said: "People were stacking on top of each other screaming and gagging. The door got blocked because there were too many people stacked up against it. I saw at least ten lifeless bodies." Others staggered from the building breathless and incoherent. "Everybody smashed; people crying, couldn't breathe," said one clubber, Reggie Clark. "Two ladies next to me died. A guy under me passed out." Tonita Matthews, a young woman inside the club who tried to help the injured, said: "People just died in my arms." As the bodies of the dead and injured lay in the street outside, another woman who escaped described a young man fighting to breathe in a tangle of bodies, who had asked her to tell his mother he loved her. . . .

The incident occurred at about 2 A.M. local time on a busier than usual night at E2, a dance club above the upmarket Epitome restaurant in a predominantly black district on Chicago's south side, which is famed for its nightclubs. The dance club is a popular late-night party spot, known for attracting rock and rap stars. . . .

Most of those who died were killed at the bottom of the main front door stairwell. Kristy Mitchell, 22, was one of those rescued after falling on the stairway and being trampled as the crowd continued to pour over her. She said: "People were stomping my legs. When they pulled me up, I was dizzy and I couldn't breathe." Another of those rescued, Lamont James, said: "We heard the DJ say there was a fight and that caused a panic. People started heading for the corridor leading to the exit. There were people on top of me, people underneath me, people pressed up against the wall. I heard people screaming 'I can't breathe'." Ms Matthews blacked out but later managed to scramble out of the front door, turning back to see casualties pressed up against the glass.

It was by far the worst fatal incident of its kind in the US. In 1979, 11 people were killed in Cincinnati in a crush to get into a concert by The Who, and in 1991 nine young people were crushed to death in a gym stairwell while awaiting a celebrity basketball game in New York. . . .

Amishoov Blackwell, 30, who was knocked backwards down the stairs by the screaming crowd as he emerged from the cloakroom, lay on top of a pile of dead bodies for 30 minutes before he was freed by firefighters. "It wasn't anything but two girls fighting," he said. "Why did they have to spray mace?"

(From the article "Revellers Crushed to Death in Club," by Jacqui Goddard, February 18, 2003, *The Scotsman*)

Tasos Katopodis/Getty Images

Panic's aftermath One year after the E2 nightclub stampede, friends and family members held a memorial at the site of the nightclub for the 21 people killed in the incident. Each victim was memorialized by a cross bearing his or her name and photograph.

"I'm sorry, I didn't hear what you said. I was listening to my body."

is that people prone to bodily misinterpretations have experienced more trauma-filled events over the course of their lives than other persons (Hawks et al., 2011).

Whatever the precise causes of such misinterpretations may be, research suggests that panic-prone individuals generally have a high degree of what is called **anxiety sensitivity;** that is, they focus on their bodily sensations much of the time, are unable to assess them logically, and interpret them as potentially harmful (Wilson & Hayward, 2005). Studies have found that people who scored high on anxiety sensitivity surveys are up to five times more likely than other people to develop panic disorder (Hawks et al., 2011; Maller & Reiss, 1992). Other studies have found that individuals with panic disorder typically earn higher anxiety sensitivity scores than other persons do (Reinecke et al., 2011; Dattilio, 2001).

Cognitive Therapy Cognitive therapists try to correct people's misinterpretations of their body sensations (Clark & Beck, 2012, 2010; Baker, 2011). The first step is to educate clients about the general nature of panic attacks, the actual causes of bodily sensations, and the tendency of clients to misinterpret their sensations. The next step is to teach clients to apply more accurate interpretations during stressful situations, thus short-circuiting the panic sequence at an early point (Teachman, 2011). Therapists may also teach clients to cope better with anxiety—for example, by applying relaxation and breathing techniques—and to distract themselves from their sensations, perhaps by striking up a conversation with someone.

In addition, cognitive therapists may use biological challenge procedures to induce panic sensations, so that clients can apply their new skills under watchful supervision (Baker, 2011; Meuret et al., 2005). Individuals whose attacks typically are triggered by a rapid heart rate, for example, may be told to jump up and down for several minutes or to run up a flight of stairs. They can then practice interpreting the resulting sensations appropriately, without dwelling on them.

According to research, cognitive treatments often help people with panic disorder (Teachman, 2011; Hofmann, Rief, & Spiegel, 2010; Elkins & Moore, 2001). In studies across the world, around 80 percent of participants given these treatments have become free of panic, compared to only 13 percent of control participants. Cognitive therapy has proved to be at least as helpful as antidepressant drugs or alprazolam in the treatment of panic disorder, sometimes even more so (Baker, 2011; McCabe & Antony, 2005). In view of the effectiveness of both cognitive and drug treatments, many clinicians have tried combining them. It is not yet clear, however, whether this strategy is more effective than cognitive therapy alone. For individuals who display both panic disorder and agoraphobia, research suggests that it is most helpful to combine behavioral exposure techniques with cognitive treatments and/or drug therapy (Arch & Craske, 2011; Gloster et al., 2011).

Obsessive-Compulsive Disorder

Obsessions are persistent thoughts, ideas, impulses, or images that seem to invade a person's consciousness. **Compulsions** are repetitive and rigid behaviors or mental acts that people feel they must perform in order to prevent or reduce anxiety. As Figure 5-6 indicates, minor obsessions and compulsions are familiar to almost everyone. You may find yourself filled with thoughts about an upcoming performance or exam or keep wondering whether you forgot to turn off the stove or lock the door. You may feel better when you avoid stepping on cracks, turn away from black cats, or arrange your closet in a particular manner.

Minor obsessions and compulsions can play a helpful role in life. Little rituals often calm us during times of stress. A person who repeatedly hums a tune or taps his or her

•**anxiety sensitivity**•A tendency to focus on one's bodily sensations, assess them illogically, and interpret them as harmful.

•**obsession**•A persistent thought, idea, impulse, or image that is experienced repeatedly, feels intrusive, and causes anxiety.

•**compulsion**•A repetitive and rigid behavior or mental act that a person feels driven to perform in order to prevent or reduce anxiety.

•**obsessive-compulsive disorder**•A disorder in which a person has recurrent and unwanted thoughts, a need to perform repetitive and rigid actions, or both.

fingers during a test may be releasing tension and thus improving performance. Many people find it comforting to repeat religious or cultural rituals, such as touching a mezuzah, sprinkling holy water, or fingering rosary beads.

According to DSM-5, a diagnosis of **obsessive-compulsive disorder** is called for when obsessions or compulsions feel excessive or unreasonable, cause great distress, take up much time, or interfere with daily functions (see Table 5-10). The disorder is classified as an anxiety disorder because the obsessions cause intense anxiety, while the compulsions are aimed at preventing or reducing anxiety. In addition, anxiety rises if individuals try to resist their obsessions or compulsions.

An individual with this disorder observed: "I can't get to sleep unless I am sure everything in the house is in its proper place so that when I get up in the morning, the house is organized. I work like mad to set everything straight before I go to bed, but, when I get up in the morning, I can think of a thousand things that I ought to do. . . . I can't stand to know something needs doing and I haven't done it" (McNeil, 1967, pp. 26–28). Research indicates that several additional disorders are closely related to obsessive-compulsive disorder in their features, causes, and treatment responsiveness, and so, as you will soon see, DSM-5 has grouped them together with obsessive-compulsive disorder.

Between 1 and 2 percent of the people in the United States and other countries throughout the world suffer from obsessive-compulsive disorder in any given year (Kessler et al., 2010; Björgvinsson & Hart, 2008; Wetherell et al., 2006). As many as 3 percent develop the disorder at some point during their lives. It is equally common in men and women and among people of different races and ethnic groups (Matsunaga & Seedat, 2011). The disorder usually begins by young adulthood and typically persists for many years, although its symptoms and their severity may fluctuate over time (Angst et al., 2004). It is estimated that more than 40 percent of people with obsessive-compulsive disorder seek treatment (Kessler et al., 1999, 1994).

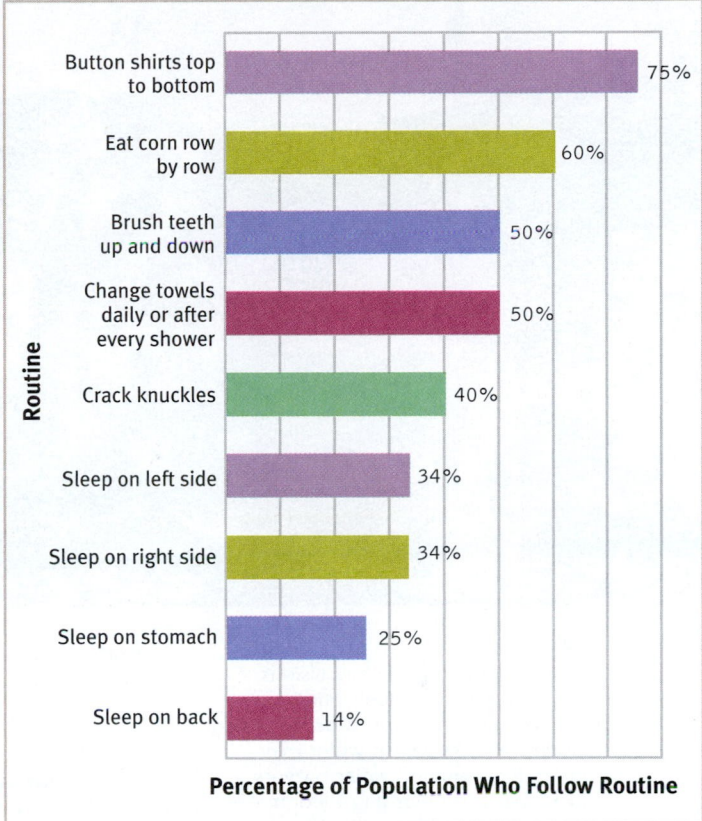

Percentage of Population Who Follow Routine

Figure 5-6
Normal routines Most people find it comforting to follow set routines when they carry out everyday activities, and, in fact, 40 percent become irritated if they must depart from their routines. (Adapted from Kanner, 2005, 1998, 1995.)

What Are the Features of Obsessions and Compulsions?

Obsessive thoughts feel both intrusive and foreign to the people who experience them. Attempts to ignore or resist these thoughts may arouse even more anxiety, and before long they come back more strongly than ever. People with obsessions typically are quite aware that their thoughts are excessive.

Obsessions often take the form of obsessive *wishes* (for example, repeated wishes that one's spouse would die), *impulses* (repeated urges to yell out obscenities at work or in church), *images* (fleeting visions of forbidden sexual scenes), *ideas* (notions that germs are lurking everywhere), or *doubts* (concerns that one has made or will make a wrong decision). In the following excerpt, a clinician describes a 20-year-old college junior who was plagued by obsessive doubts.

He now spent hours each night "rehashing" the day's events, especially interactions with friends and teachers, endlessly making "right" in his mind any and all regrets. He likened the process to playing a videotape of each event over and over again in his mind, asking himself if he had behaved properly and telling himself that he had done his best, or had said the right thing every step of the way. He would do this while sitting at his desk, supposedly studying; and it was not unusual for him to look at the clock after such a period of rumination and note that, to his surprise, two or three hours had elapsed.

(Spitzer et al., 1981, pp. 20–21)

table: 5-10

DSM-5 Checklist
Obsessive-Compulsive Disorder

1. Presence of recurrent obsessions, compulsions, or both.

2. The obsessions and/or compulsions are time-consuming or cause clinically significant distress or impairment.

Based on APA, 2013, 2012.

Cultural rituals

Rituals do not necessarily reflect compulsions. Indeed, cultural and religious rituals often give meaning and comfort to their practitioners. Here Buddhist monks splash water over themselves during their annual winter prayers at a temple in Tokyo. This cleansing ritual is performed to pray for good luck.

Certain basic themes run through the thoughts of most people troubled by obsessive thinking (Abramowitz, McKay, & Taylor, 2008). The most common theme appears to be dirt or contamination (Tolin & Meunier, 2008). Other common ones are violence and aggression, orderliness, religion, and sexuality. The prevalence of such themes may vary from culture to culture (Matsunaga & Seedat, 2011). Religious obsessions, for example, seem to be more common in cultures or countries with strict moral codes and religious values (Björgvinsson & Hart, 2008).

Compulsions are similar to obsessions in many ways. For example, although compulsive behaviors are technically under voluntary control, the people who feel they must do them have little sense of choice in the matter. Most of these individuals recognize that their behavior is unreasonable, but they believe at the same time something terrible will happen if they don't perform the compulsions. After performing a compulsive act, they usually feel less anxious for a short while. For some people the compulsive acts develop into detailed *rituals.* They must go through the ritual in exactly the same way every time, according to certain rules.

Like obsessions, compulsions take various forms. *Cleaning compulsions* are very common. People with these compulsions feel compelled to keep cleaning themselves, their clothing, or their homes. The cleaning may follow ritualistic rules and be repeated dozens or hundreds of times a day. People with *checking compulsions* check the same items over and over—door locks, gas taps, important papers—to make sure that all is as it should be (Coleman et al., 2011). Another common compulsion is the constant effort to seek *order* or *balance* (Coles & Pietrefesa, 2008). People with this compulsion keep placing certain items (clothing, books, foods) in perfect order in accordance with strict rules. *Touching, verbal,* and *counting* compulsions are also common.

Although some people with obsessive-compulsive disorder experience obsessions only or compulsions only, most of them experience both (Clark & Guyitt, 2008). In fact, compulsive acts are often a response to obsessive thoughts. One study found that in most cases, compulsions seemed to represent a *yielding* to obsessive doubts, ideas, or urges (Akhtar et al., 1975). A woman who keeps doubting that her house is secure may yield to that obsessive doubt by repeatedly checking locks and gas jets. Or a man who obsessively fears contamination may yield to that fear by performing cleaning rituals. The study also found that compulsions sometimes serve to help *control* obsessions. A teenager describes how she tried to control her obsessive fears of contamination by performing counting and verbal rituals:

> *Patient:* If I heard the word, like, something that had to do with germs or disease, it would be considered something bad, and so I had things that would go through my mind that were sort of like "cross that out and it'll make it okay" to hear that word.
>
> *Interviewer:* What sort of things?
>
> *Patient:* Like numbers or words that seemed to be sort of like a protector.
>
> *Interviewer:* What numbers and what words were they?
>
> *Patient:* It started out to be the number 3 and multiples of 3 and then words like "soap and water," something like that; and then the multiples of 3 got really high, and they'd end up to be 124 or something like that. It got real bad then.
>
> *(Spitzer et al., 1981, p. 137)*

BETWEEN THE LINES

Losing Battle

People who try to avoid all contamination and rid themselves and their world of all germs are fighting a losing battle. While talking, the average person sprays 300 microscopic saliva droplets per minute, or 2.5 per word. ‹‹

Many people with obsessive-compulsive disorder worry that they will act out their obsessions. A man with obsessive images of wounded loved ones may worry that he is but a step away from committing murder, or a woman with obsessive urges to yell out in church may worry that she will one day give in to them and embarrass herself. Most such concerns are unfounded. Although many obsessions lead to compulsive acts—particularly to cleaning and checking compulsions—they usually do not lead to violence or immoral conduct.

Obsessive-compulsive disorder was once among the least understood of the psychological disorders. In recent decades, however, researchers have begun to learn more about it. The most influential explanations and treatments come from the psychodynamic, behavioral, cognitive, and biological models.

The Psychodynamic Perspective

As you have seen, psychodynamic theorists believe that an anxiety disorder develops when children come to fear their own id impulses and use ego defense mechanisms to lessen the resulting anxiety. What distinguishes obsessive-compulsive disorder from other anxiety disorders, in their view, is that here the battle between anxiety-provoking id impulses and anxiety-reducing defense mechanisms is not buried in the unconscious but is played out in overt thoughts and actions. The id impulses usually take the form of obsessive thoughts, and the ego defenses appear as counterthoughts or compulsive actions. A woman who keeps imagining her mother lying broken and bleeding, for example, may counter those thoughts with repeated safety checks throughout the house.

According to psychodynamic theorists, three ego defense mechanisms are particularly common in obsessive-compulsive disorder: *isolation, undoing,* and *reaction formation.* People who resort to **isolation** simply disown their unwanted thoughts and experience them as foreign intrusions. People who engage in **undoing** perform acts that are meant to cancel out their undesirable impulses. Those who wash their hands repeatedly, for example, may be symbolically undoing their unacceptable id impulses. People who develop a **reaction formation** take on a lifestyle that directly opposes their unacceptable impulses. A person may live a life of compulsive kindness and devotion to others in order to counter unacceptable aggressive impulses.

Sigmund Freud traced obsessive-compulsive disorder to the *anal stage* of development (occurring at about 2 years of age). He proposed that during this stage some children experience intense rage and shame as a result of negative toilet-training experiences. Other psychodynamic theorists have argued instead that such early rage reactions are rooted in feelings of insecurity (Erikson, 1963; Sullivan, 1953; Horney, 1937). Either way, these children repeatedly feel the need to express their strong aggressive id impulses while at the same time knowing they should try to restrain and control the impulses. If this conflict between the id and ego continues, it may eventually blossom into obsessive-compulsive disorder. Overall, research has not clearly supported the psychodynamic explanation (Busch et al., 2010; Fitz, 1990).

When treating patients with obsessive-compulsive disorder, psychodynamic therapists try to help the individuals uncover and overcome their underlying conflicts and defenses, using the customary techniques of free association and therapist interpretation. Research has offered little evidence, however, that a traditional psychodynamic approach is of much help (Bram & Björgvinsson, 2004). Thus some psychodynamic therapists now prefer to treat these patients with short-term psychodynamic therapies, which, as you saw in Chapter 3, are more direct and action-oriented than the classical techniques.

The Behavioral Perspective

Behaviorists have concentrated on explaining and treating compulsions rather than obsessions. They propose that people happen upon their compulsions quite randomly. In a fearful situation, they happen just coincidentally to wash their hands, say, or dress a

"Is the Itsy Bitsy Spider obsessive-compulsive?"

Michael Shaw/CartoonBank.com

•**isolation**•An ego defense mechanism in which people unconsciously isolate and disown undesirable and unwanted thoughts, experiencing them as foreign intrusions.

•**undoing**•An ego defense mechanism whereby a person unconsciously cancels out an unacceptable desire or act by performing another act.

•**reaction formation**•An ego defense mechanism whereby a person suppresses an unacceptable desire by taking on a lifestyle that expresses the opposite desire.

Getting down and dirty

In one *exposure and response prevention* assignment, clients with cleaning compulsions might be instructed to do heavy-duty gardening and then resist washing their hands or taking a shower. They may never go so far as to participate in and enjoy mud wrestling, like these delightfully filthy individuals at the annual Mud Day event in Westland, Michigan, but you get the point.

•**exposure and response prevention**•
A behavioral treatment for obsessive-compulsive disorder that exposes a client to anxiety-arousing thoughts or situations and then prevents the client from performing his or her compulsive acts. Also called *exposure and ritual prevention*.

•**neutralizing**•A person's attempt to eliminate unwanted thoughts by thinking or behaving in ways that put matters right internally, making up for the unacceptable thoughts.

certain way. When the threat lifts, they link the improvement to that particular action. After repeated accidental associations, they believe that the action is bringing them good luck or actually changing the situation, and so they perform the same actions again and again in similar situations. The act becomes a key method of avoiding or reducing anxiety (Frost & Steketee, 2001).

The famous clinical scientist Stanley Rachman and his associates have shown that compulsions do appear to be rewarded by a reduction in anxiety. In one of their experiments, for example, 12 research participants with compulsive hand-washing rituals were placed in contact with objects that they considered contaminated (Hodgson & Rachman, 1972). As behaviorists would predict, the hand-washing rituals of these participants seemed to lower their anxiety.

If people keep performing compulsive behaviors in order to prevent bad outcomes and ensure positive outcomes, can't they be taught that such behaviors are not really serving this purpose? In a behavioral treatment called **exposure and response prevention** (or **exposure and ritual prevention**), first developed by psychiatrist Victor Meyer (1966), clients are repeatedly exposed to objects or situations that produce anxiety, obsessive fears, and compulsive behaviors, but they are told to *resist* performing the behaviors they feel so bound to perform. Because people find it very difficult to resist such behaviors, therapists may set an example first.

Many behavioral therapists now use exposure and response prevention in both individual and group therapy formats. Some of them also have people carry out *self-help* procedures at home (Abramowitz et al., 2011; Simpson et al., 2011; Foa et al., 2005). That is, they assign homework in exposure and response prevention, such as these assignments given to a woman with a cleaning compulsion:

> Have you ever tried an informal version of exposure and response prevention in order to stop behaving in certain ways?

- Do not mop the floor of your bathroom for a week. After this, clean it within three minutes, using an ordinary mop. Use this mop for other chores as well without cleaning it.

- Buy a fluffy mohair sweater and wear it for a week. When taking it off at night do not remove the bits of fluff. Do not clean your house for a week.

- You, your husband, and children all have to keep shoes on. Do not clean the house for a week.

- Drop a cookie on the contaminated floor, pick the cookie up and eat it.

- Leave the sheets and blankets on the floor and then put them on the beds. Do not change these for a week.

(Emmelkamp, 1982, pp. 299–300)

Eventually this woman was able to set up a reasonable routine for cleaning herself and her home.

Between 55 and 85 percent of clients with obsessive-compulsive disorder have been found to improve considerably with exposure and response prevention, improvements that often continue indefinitely (Abramowitz et al., 2011, 2008; McKay, Taylor, & Abramowitz, 2010). The effectiveness of this approach suggests that people with this disorder are like the superstitious man in the old joke who keeps snapping his fingers to keep elephants away. When someone points out, "But there aren't any elephants around here," the man replies, "See? It works!" One review concludes, "With hindsight, it is possible to see that the [obsessive-compulsive] individual has been snapping his fingers, and unless he stops (response prevention) and takes a look around at the same time (exposure), he isn't going to learn much of value about elephants" (Berk & Efran, 1983, p. 546).

At the same time, research has revealed key limitations in exposure and response prevention. Few clients who receive the treatment overcome all their symptoms, and as many as one-quarter fail to improve at all (Foa et al., 2005; Frost & Steketee, 2001). Also, the approach is of limited help to those who have obsessions but no compulsions (Hohagen et al., 1998).

The Cognitive Perspective

Cognitive theorists begin their explanation of obsessive-compulsive disorder by pointing out that everyone has repetitive, unwanted, and intrusive thoughts. Anyone might have thoughts of harming others or being contaminated by germs, for example, but most people dismiss or ignore them with ease. Those who develop this disorder, however, typically blame themselves for such thoughts and expect that somehow terrible things will happen (Clark & Beck, 2010; Shafran, 2005; Salkovskis, 1999, 1985). To avoid such negative outcomes, they try to **neutralize** the thoughts—thinking or behaving in ways meant to put matters right or to make amends (Salkovskis et al., 2003).

Neutralizing acts might include requesting special reassurance from others, deliberately thinking "good" thoughts, washing one's hands, or checking for possible sources of danger. When a neutralizing effort brings about a temporary reduction in discomfort, it is reinforced and will likely be repeated. Eventually the neutralizing thought or act is used so often that it becomes, by definition, an obsession or compulsion. At the same time, the individual becomes more and more convinced that his or her unpleasant intrusive thoughts are dangerous. As the person's fear of such thoughts increases, the thoughts begin to occur more frequently and they, too, become obsessions.

In support of this explanation, studies have found that people who have obsessive-compulsive disorder experience intrusive thoughts more often than other people, resort to more elaborate neutralizing strategies, and experience reductions in anxiety after using neutralizing techniques (Shafran, 2005; Salkovskis et al., 2003).

Although everyone sometimes has undesired thoughts, only some people develop obsessive-compulsive disorder. Why do these individuals find such normal thoughts so disturbing to begin with? Researchers have found that this population tends (1) to be more depressed than other people (Hong et al., 2004), (2) to have exceptionally high standards of conduct and morality (Rachman, 1993), (3) to have an inflated sense of responsibility in life and believe that their intrusive negative thoughts are equivalent to actions and capable of causing harm (Lawrence & Williams, 2011; Steketee et al., 2003), and (4) generally to believe that they should have perfect control over all of their thoughts and behaviors (Coles et al., 2005).

Cognitive therapists help clients focus on the cognitive processes involved in their obsessive-compulsive disorder. Initially, they educate the clients, pointing out how misinterpretations of unwanted thoughts, an excessive sense of responsibility, and neutralizing acts help produce and maintain their symptoms. The therapists then guide the clients to identify, challenge, and change their distorted cognitions. It appears that cognitive techniques of this kind often help reduce the number and impact of obsessions and compulsions (Clark & Beck, 2010; Rufer et al., 2005).

While the behavioral approach (exposure and response prevention) and the cognitive approach have each been of help to clients with obsessive-compulsive disorder, some research suggests that a combination of the two approaches is often more effective than either intervention alone (McKay et al., 2010; Sookman & Steketee, 2010). In such *cognitive-behavioral treatments*, clients are first taught to view their obsessive thoughts as inaccurate occurrences rather than as valid and dangerous cognitions for which they are responsible and upon which they must act. As they become better able to identify and recognize the thoughts for what they are, they also become less inclined to act on them, more willing to subject themselves to the rigors of exposure and response prevention, and more likely to make gains in that behavioral technique.

•**serotonin**• A neurotransmitter whose abnormal activity is linked to depression, obsessive-compulsive disorder, and eating disorders.

•**orbitofrontal cortex**• A region of the brain in which impulses involving excretion, sexuality, violence, and other primitive activities normally arise.

•**caudate nuclei**• Structures in the brain, within the region known as the basal ganglia, that help convert sensory information into thoughts and actions.

Personal knowledge

The HBO hit series *Girls* follows the struggles of Hannah Horvath and her friends as they navigate their twenties, "one mistake at a time." The show's creator and star, Lena Dunham, says that Hannah's difficulties often are inspired by her own real-life experiences, including her childhood battle with OCD and anxiety. As a young girl, Dunham was obsessed with the number 8. "I'd count eight times. . . . I'd look on both sides of me eight times, I'd make sure nobody was following me down the street, I touched different parts of my bed before I went to sleep, I'd imagine a murder, and I'd imagine that murder eight times."

The Biological Perspective

Family pedigree studies provided the earliest clues that obsessive-compulsive disorder may be linked in part to biological factors (Lambert & Kinsley, 2005). Studies of twins found that if one identical twin displays this disorder, the other twin also develops it in 53 percent of cases. In contrast, among fraternal twins (twins who share half rather than all of their genes), both twins display the disorder in only 23 percent of the cases. In short, the more similar the gene composition of two individuals, the more likely both are to experience obsessive-compulsive disorder, if indeed one of them displays the disorder.

In recent years two lines of research have uncovered more direct evidence that biological factors play a key role in obsessive-compulsive disorder, and promising biological treatments for the disorder have been developed as well. This research points to (1) abnormally low activity of the neurotransmitter *serotonin* and (2) abnormal functioning in key regions of the brain.

Abnormal Serotonin Activity

Serotonin, like GABA and norepinephrine, is a brain chemical that carries messages from neuron to neuron. The first clue to its role in obsessive-compulsive disorder was, once again, a surprising finding by clinical researchers—this time that two antidepressant drugs, *clomipramine* and *fluoxetine* (Anafranil and Prozac), reduce obsessive and compulsive symptoms (Stein & Fineberg, 2007). Since these particular drugs increase serotonin activity, some researchers concluded that the disorder might be caused by low serotonin activity. In fact, only those antidepressant drugs that increase serotonin activity help in cases of obsessive-compulsive disorder; antidepressants that mainly affect other neurotransmitters typically have no effect on it (Jenike, 1992).

Although serotonin is the neurotransmitter most often cited in explanations of obsessive-compulsive disorder, recent studies have suggested that other neurotransmitters, particularly *glutamate, GABA,* and *dopamine,* may also play important roles in the development of this disorder (Spooren et al., 2010; Lambert & Kinsley, 2005). Some researchers even argue that, with regard to obsessive-compulsive disorder, serotonin may act largely as a *neuromodulator,* a chemical whose primary function is to increase or decrease the activity of other key neurotransmitters.

Abnormal Brain Structure and Functioning

Another line of research has linked obsessive-compulsive disorder to abnormal functioning by specific regions of the brain, particularly the **orbitofrontal cortex** (just above each eye) and the **caudate nuclei** (structures located within the brain region known as the *basal ganglia*). These regions are part of a brain circuit that usually converts sensory information into thoughts and actions (Craig & Chamberlain, 2010; Stein & Fineberg, 2007). The circuit begins in the orbitofrontal cortex, where sexual, violent, and other primitive impulses normally arise. These impulses next move on to the caudate nuclei, which act as filters that send only the most powerful impulses on to the *thalamus,* the next stop on the circuit (see Figure 5-7). If impulses reach the thalamus, the person is driven to think further about them and perhaps to act. Many theorists now believe that either the orbitofrontal cortex or the caudate nuclei of some people are too active, leading to a constant eruption of troublesome thoughts and actions (Endrass et al., 2011; Lambert & Kinsley, 2005). Additional parts of this brain circuit have also been identified in recent years, including the *cingulate cortex* and, once again, the *amygdala* (Stein & Fineberg, 2007). It may turn out that these regions also play key roles in obsessive-compulsive disorder.

In support of this brain circuit explanation, medical scientists have observed for years that obsessive-compulsive symptoms do sometimes arise or subside after the orbitofrontal cortex, caudate nuclei, or other regions in the circuit are damaged by accident or illness (Coetzer, 2004). Similarly, brain scan studies have shown that the caudate nuclei and the orbitofrontal cortex of research participants with obsessive-compulsive disorder are more active than those of control participants (Chamberlain et al., 2005; Baxter et al., 2001, 1990). Some research further suggests that the serotonin and brain circuit abnormalities that characterize obsessive-compulsive disorder are at least partly the result of genetic inheritance (Nicolini et al., 2011).

The serotonin and brain circuit explanations may themselves be linked. It turns out that serotonin—along with the neurotransmitters glutamate, GABA, and dopamine—plays a key role in the operation of the orbitofrontal cortex, caudate nuclei, and other parts of the brain circuit; certainly abnormal activity by one or more of these neurotransmitters could be contributing to the improper functioning of the circuit.

Biological Therapies Ever since researchers first discovered that certain antidepressant drugs help to reduce obsessions and compulsions, these drugs have been used to treat obsessive-compulsive disorder (Fineberg & Craig, 2010; Simpson, 2010). We now know that the drugs not only increase brain serotonin activity but also help produce more normal activity in the orbitofrontal cortex and caudate nuclei (Stein & Fineberg, 2007; Baxter et al., 2000, 1992). Studies have found that clomipramine (Anafranil), fluoxetine (Prozac), fluvoxamine (Luvox), and similar antidepressant drugs bring improvement to between 50 and 80 percent of those with obsessive-compulsive disorder (Bareggi et al., 2004). The obsessions and compulsions do not usually disappear totally, but on average they are cut almost in half within eight weeks of treatment (DeVeaugh-Geiss et al., 1992). People who are treated with such drugs alone, however, tend to relapse if their medication is stopped. Thus, more and more individuals with obsessive-compulsive disorder are now being treated by a combination of behavioral, cognitive, and drug therapies. According to research, such combinations often yield higher levels of symptom reduction and bring relief to more clients than do each of the approaches alone—improvements that may continue for years (Abramowitz, 2010; Simpson, 2010).

Obviously, the treatment picture for obsessive-compulsive disorder has improved greatly over the past 15 years, and indeed, this disorder is now helped by several forms of treatment, often used in combination. In fact, some studies suggest that the behavioral, cognitive, and biological approaches may ultimately have the same effect on the brain. In these investigations, both participants who responded to cognitive-behavioral treatments and those who responded to antidepressant drugs showed marked reductions in activity in the caudate nuclei (Freyer et al., 2011; Stein & Fineberg, 2007; Baxter et al., 2000, 1992).

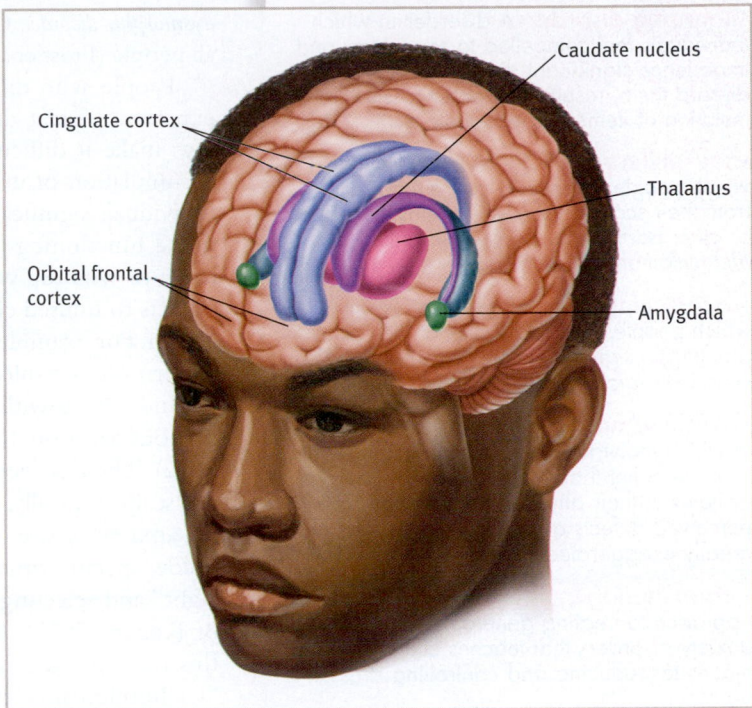

Figure 5-7
The biology of obsessive-compulsive disorder Brain structures that have been linked to obsessive-compulsive disorder include the orbitofrontal cortex, caudate nucleus, thalamus, amygdala, and cingulate cortex. The structures may be too active in people with the disorder.

Obsessive-Compulsive-Related Disorders: Finding a Diagnostic Home

Many people perform particular patterns of repetitive and excessive behavior that greatly disrupt their lives. Among the most common such patterns are excessive appearance-checking, hoarding, hair-pulling, skin-picking, exercising, video game-playing, and sex. Over the years, clinicians have tried to figure out how to best think about and classify these patterns. At various times, the disorders have been called "excessive behaviors," "repetitive behaviors," "habit disorders," "addictions," and "impulse-control disorders." In recent years, however, a growing number of clinical researchers have linked the patterns to obsessive-compulsive disorder, based on the driven nature of the behaviors and the obsessive-like concerns that typically trigger the behaviors. They have used the term "obsessive-compulsive spectrum disorders" to describe such patterns (Hollander et al., 2011).

Following the lead of these researchers, DSM-5 has created the group name **obsessive-compulsive-related disorders** and assigned four of these patterns to that group: *hoarding disorder, hair-pulling disorder, excoriation (skin-picking) disorder,* and *body*

•**obsessive-compulsive-related disorders**•A group of disorders in which obsessive-like concerns drive people to repeatedly and excessively perform specific patterns of behavior that greatly disrupt their lives.

•**hoarding disorder**•A disorder in which individuals feel compelled to save items and experience significant distress if they try to discard them, resulting in an excessive accumulation of items and possessions.

•**hair-pulling disorder**•A disorder in which people repeatedly pull out hair from their scalp, eyebrows, eyelashes, or other parts of the body. Also called *trichotillomania.*

•**excoriation disorder**•A disorder in which people repeatedly pick at their skin, resulting in significant sores or wounds. Also called *skin-picking disorder.*

•**body dysmorphic disorder**•A disorder in which individuals become preoccupied with the belief that they have certain defects or flaws in their physical appearance. The perceived defects or flaws are imagined or greatly exaggerated.

•**stress management program**•An approach to treating generalized and other anxiety disorders that teaches clients techniques for reducing and controlling stress.

dysmorphic disorder. Collectively, these four disorders are displayed by at least 5 percent of all people (Frost et al., 2012; Keuthen et al., 2012, 2010; Wolrich, 2011; Duke et al., 2009).

People who display **hoarding disorder** feel that they must save items, and they experience great distress if they try to discard them (APA, 2013, 2012). These feelings make it difficult for them to part with possessions, resulting in an extraordinary accumulation of items that clutters their lives and living areas. This pattern causes the individuals significant distress and may greatly impair their personal, social, or occupational functioning (Frost et al., 2012; Mataix-Cols & Pertusa, 2012). It is common for them to wind up with numerous useless and valueless items, from junk mail to broken objects to unused clothes. Parts of their homes may become inaccessible because of the clutter. For example, sofas, kitchen appliances, or beds may be unusable. In addition, the pattern often results in fire hazards, unhealthful sanitation conditions, or other dangers.

Individuals with **hair-pulling disorder,** also known as trichotillomania, repeatedly pull out hair from their scalp, eyebrows, eyelashes, or other parts of the body (APA, 2013, 2012). The disorder usually centers on just one or two of these body sites, most often the scalp. Typically, individuals with the disorder pull one hair at a time. It is common for anxiety or stress to trigger or accompany the hair-pulling behavior. Some sufferers follow specific rituals as they pull their hair, including pulling until the hair feels "just right" and selecting certain types of hairs for pulling (Keuthen et al., 2012; Mansueto & Rogers, 2012). Because of the distress, impairment, or embarrassment caused by this behavior, the individuals often try to reduce or stop the hair-pulling. The term "trichotillomania" is derived from the Greek for "frenzied hair-pulling."

Persons with **excoriation (skin-picking) disorder** keep picking at their skin, resulting in significant sores or wounds (APA, 2013). Like those with hair-pulling disorder, they often try to reduce or stop the behavior. Most sufferers pick with their fingers and center their picking on one area, most often the face (Grant et al., 2012; Odlaug & Grant, 2012). Other common areas of focus include the arms, legs, lips, scalp, chest, and extremities such as fingernails and cuticles. The behavior is typically triggered or accompanied by anxiety or stress.

People with **body dysmorphic disorder** become preoccupied with the belief that they have a particular defect or flaw in their physical appearance. Actually, the perceived defect or flaw is imagined or greatly exaggerated in the person's mind (APA, 2013, 2012). Such beliefs drive the persons to repeatedly check themselves in the mirror, groom themselves, pick at the perceived flaw, compare themselves to others, seek reassurance, or perform similar behaviors. Here too, individuals with the problem experience significant distress or impairment. Body dysmorphic disorder will be discussed more fully in Chapter 7, where we examine disorders featuring somatic symptoms.

Theorists typically account for obsessive-compulsive-related disorders by using the same kinds of explanations, both psychological and biological, that have been applied to obsessive-compulsive disorder (Witthöft & Hiller, 2010). Similarly, clinicians typically treat clients with these disorders by applying the kinds of treatment used with obsessive-compulsive disorder, particularly antidepressant drugs, exposure and response prevention, and cognitive therapy (Krebs et al., 2012; Phillips & Rogers, 2011).

Now that the body dysmorphic, hoarding, hair-pulling, and excoriation disorders are being grouped together in DSM-5 along with obsessive-compulsive disorder, it is hoped that they will be better researched, understood, and treated (Snowdon et al., 2012). DSM-5 has determined that other kinds of excessive patterns need further study before a decision can be made about their inclusion in this same group.

PUTTING IT... together

Diathesis-Stress in Action

Clinicians and researchers have developed many ideas about generalized anxiety disorder, phobias, panic disorder, and obsessive-compulsive disorder. At times, however, the sheer quantity of concepts and findings makes it difficult to grasp what is really known about the disorders.

Overall, it is fair to say that clinicians currently know more about the causes of phobias, panic disorder, and obsessive-compulsive disorder than about generalized anxiety disorder and social anxiety disorder. It is worth noting that the insights about panic disorder and obsessive-compulsive disorder—once among the field's most puzzling patterns—did not emerge until clinical theorists took a look at the disorders from more than one perspective and integrated those views. Today's cognitive explanation of panic disorder, for example, builds squarely on the biological idea that the disorder begins with abnormal brain activity and unusual physical sensations. Similarly, the cognitive explanation of obsessive-compulsive disorder takes its lead from the biological position that some people are predisposed to experience more unwanted and intrusive thoughts than others.

It may be that a fuller understanding of generalized anxiety disorder and social anxiety disorder await a similar integration of the various models. In fact, such integrations have already begun to unfold. Recall, for example, that one of the new wave cognitive explanations for generalized anxiety disorder links the cognitive process of worrying to heightened bodily arousal in individuals with the disorder.

Similarly, a growing number of theorists are adopting a *diathesis-stress* view of generalized anxiety disorder. They believe that certain individuals have a biological vulnerability toward developing the disorder—a vulnerability that is eventually brought to the surface by psychological and sociocultural factors. Indeed, genetic investigators have discovered that certain genes may determine whether a person reacts to life's stressors calmly or in a tense manner, and developmental researchers have found that even during the earliest stages of life some infants become particularly aroused when stimulated (Burijon, 2007; Kalin, 1993). Perhaps these easily aroused infants have inherited defects in GABA functioning or other biological limitations that predispose them to generalized anxiety disorder. If, over the course of their lives, the individuals also face intense societal pressures, learn to interpret the world as a dangerous place, or come to regard worrying as a useful tool, they may be candidates for developing generalized anxiety disorder.

In the treatment realm, integration of the models is already on display for each of the anxiety disorders and for obsessive-compulsive disorder. Therapists have discovered, for example, that treatment is at least sometimes more effective when medications are combined with cognitive techniques to treat panic disorder and when medications are combined with cognitive-behavioral techniques to treat obsessive-compulsive disorder. Similarly, cognitive techniques are often combined with relaxation training or biofeedback in the treatment of generalized anxiety disorder—a treatment package known as a **stress management program**. For the millions of people who suffer from these various anxiety disorders, such treatment combinations are a welcome development.

Bella C. Landauer Collection of Business and Advertising Art, The New York Historical Society

Sprinkle lightly

In the early twentieth century, drug companies did not have to prove the safety or value of their products. Brain Salt, a patent medicine for anxiety and related difficulties, promised to cure nervous disability, headaches, indigestion, heart palpitations, and sleep problems.

Summing Up

- **GENERALIZED ANXIETY DISORDER** People with *generalized anxiety disorder* experience excessive anxiety and worry about a wide range of events and activities. The various explanations and treatments for this anxiety disorder have received only limited research support, although recent cognitive and biological approaches seem to be promising.

   According to the *sociocultural* view, *societal dangers, economic stress,* or related *racial and cultural pressures* may create a climate in which cases of generalized anxiety disorder are more likely to develop.

In the original *psychodynamic* explanation, Freud said that generalized anxiety disorder may develop when anxiety is excessive and defense mechanisms break down and function poorly. Psychodynamic therapists use free association, interpretation, and related psychodynamic techniques to help people overcome this problem.

Carl Rogers, the leading *humanistic* theorist, believed that people with generalized anxiety disorder fail to receive *unconditional positive regard* from significant others during their childhood and so become overly critical of themselves. He treated such individuals with *client-centered therapy*.

Cognitive theorists believe that generalized anxiety disorder is caused by *maladaptive assumptions* and *beliefs* that lead people to view most life situations as dangerous. Many cognitive theorists further believe that implicit beliefs about the power and value of *worrying* are particularly important in the development and maintenance of this disorder. Cognitive therapists help their clients to change such thinking and to find more effective ways of coping during stressful situations.

Biological theorists hold that generalized anxiety disorder results from low activity of the neurotransmitter *GABA*. Common biological treatments are *antianxiety drugs*, particularly *benzodiazepines*, and serotonin-enhancing *antidepressant drugs*. *Relaxation training* and *biofeedback* are also applied in many cases. *pp. 114–126*

- **PHOBIAS** A phobia is a severe, persistent, and unreasonable fear of a particular object, activity, or situation. There are three main categories of phobias: *specific phobias, agoraphobia,* and *social anxiety disorder*.

Behaviorists believe that specific phobias and agoraphobia are often learned from the environment through *classical conditioning* or through *modeling,* and then are maintained by avoidance behaviors. Specific phobias and agoraphobia have been treated most successfully with behavioral *exposure techniques* by which people are led to confront the objects they fear. The exposure may be gradual and relaxed (*desensitization*), intense (*flooding*), or vicarious (*modeling*). For people who suffer from agoraphobia and panic disorder, exposure therapy alone is not as effective.

Cognitive theorists believe that social anxiety disorder is particularly likely to develop among people who hold and act on certain dysfunctional social beliefs and expectations. Therapists who treat this disorder typically distinguish two components: *social fears* and *poor social skills*. They try to reduce social fears by *drug therapy, exposure techniques, group therapy, various cognitive approaches,* or *a combination of these interventions*. They may try to improve social skills by *social skills training*. *pp. 126–135*

- **PANIC DISORDER** *Panic attacks* are periodic, discrete bouts of panic that occur suddenly. Sufferers of *panic disorder* experience panic attacks repeatedly and unexpectedly and without apparent reason. Panic disorder may be accompanied by *agoraphobia* in some cases, leading to two diagnoses.

Some biological theorists believe that abnormal *norepinephrine* activity in the brain's *locus ceruleus* may be the key to panic disorder. Others believe that related neurotransmitters or a panic brain circuit may also play key roles. Biological therapists use certain *antidepressant drugs* or powerful *benzodiazepines* to treat people with this disorder.

Cognitive theorists suggest that panic-prone people become preoccupied with some of their bodily sensations, misinterpret them as signs of medical catastrophe, panic, and in some cases develop panic disorder. Such persons have a high degree of *anxiety sensitivity* and also experience greater anxiety during *biological challenge tests*. Cognitive therapists teach patients to interpret their physical sensations more accurately and to cope better with anxiety. *pp. 136–140*

BETWEEN THE LINES

Famous Movie Phobias

Number 23 (*The Number 23*) ‹‹

Enclosed spaces (*The Da Vinci Code*) ‹‹

Bats (*Batman Begins*) ‹‹

Spiders (*Harry Potter* movies) ‹‹

Snakes (*Raiders of the Lost Ark*) ‹‹

Illness (*Hannah and Her Sisters*) ‹‹

The outside world (*Copycat*) ‹‹

Social situations (*Annie Hall*) ‹‹

Social situations (*The 40-Year-Old Virgin*) ‹‹

Social situations (*Coyote Ugly*) ‹‹

Air travel (*Rain Man*) ‹‹

Air travel (*Red Eye*) ‹‹

Heights (*Vertigo*) ‹‹

The color red (*Marnie*) ‹‹

Enclosed spaces (*Body Double*) ‹‹

Spiders (*Arachnophobia*) ‹‹

■ **OBSESSIVE-COMPULSIVE DISORDER** People with *obsessive-compulsive disorder* are beset by *obsessions*, perform *compulsions*, or display both. Compulsions are often a response to a person's obsessive thoughts.

According to the psychodynamic view, obsessive-compulsive disorder arises out of a battle between id impulses, which appear as obsessive thoughts, and ego defense mechanisms, which take the form of counterthoughts or compulsive actions. Behaviorists believe that compulsive behaviors develop through chance associations. The leading behavioral treatment combines prolonged *exposure* with *response prevention*. Cognitive theorists believe that obsessive-compulsive disorder grows from a normal human tendency to have *unwanted and unpleasant thoughts*. The efforts of some people to understand, eliminate, or avoid such thoughts actually lead to obsessions and compulsions. Cognitive therapy for this disorder includes psychoeducation and, at times, *habituation training*. While the behavioral and cognitive therapies are each helpful to clients with obsessive-compulsive disorder, research suggests that a combined *cognitive-behavioral approach* may be more effective than either therapy alone.

Biological researchers have tied obsessive-compulsive disorder to low *serotonin* activity and abnormal functioning in the *orbitofrontal cortex* and in the *caudate nuclei*. Antidepressant drugs that raise serotonin activity are a useful form of treatment.

In addition to obsessive-compulsive disorder, DSM-5 lists a group of *obsessive-compulsive-related disorders*, disorders in which obsessive-like concerns drive individuals to repeatedly and excessively perform specific patterns of behavior that greatly disrupt their lives. This group consists of *hoarding disorder, hair-pulling disorder, excoriation (skin-picking) disorder,* and *body dysmorphic disorder. pp. 140–148*

PsychPortal

Visit **PsychPortal**
www.yourpsychportal.com
to access the e-book, videocases and other case materials and activities, and study aids, including flashcards, crossword puzzles, quizzes, FAQs, and research exercises.

BETWEEN THE LINES

Famous People, Famous Fears

Adele	Seagulls ‹‹
Rihanna	Fish ‹‹
Justin Bieber	Elevators, enclosed places ‹‹
Aretha Franklin	Air travel ‹‹
Napoleon	Cats ‹‹
Kristen Stewart	Public speaking ‹‹
Johnny Depp	Clowns, spiders, ghosts ‹‹
Jennifer Aniston	Air travel ‹‹
Justin Timberlake	Snakes ‹‹
Keanu Reeves	Darkness ‹‹
Scarlett Johansson	Cockroaches ‹‹
Miley Cyrus	Spiders ‹‹
Nicole Kidman	Butterflies ‹‹
Madonna	Thunder ‹‹

STRESS DISORDERS

Specialist Latrell Robinson, a 25-year-old single African American man, was an activated National Guardsman [serving in the Iraq war]. He [had been] a full-time college student and competitive athlete raised by a single mother in public housing....

Initially trained in transportation, he was called to active duty and retrained as a military policeman to serve with his unit in Baghdad. He described enjoying the high intensity of his deployment and [became] recognized by others as an informal leader because of his aggressiveness and self-confidence. He [had] numerous [combat] exposures while performing convoy escort and security details [and he came] under small arms fire on several occasions, witnessing dead and injured civilians and Iraqi soldiers and on occasion feeling powerless when forced to detour or take evasive action. He began to develop increasing mistrust of the [Iraq] environment as the situation "on the street" seemed to deteriorate. He often felt that he and his fellow soldiers were placed in harm's way needlessly.

On a routine convoy mission [in 2003], serving as driver for the lead HUMVEE, his vehicle was struck by an Improvised Explosive Device showering him with shrapnel in his neck, arm, and leg. Another member of his vehicle was even more seriously injured.... He was evacuated to the Combat Support Hospital (CSH) where he was treated and returned to duty ... after several days despite requiring crutches and suffering chronic pain from retained shrapnel in his neck. He began to become angry at his command and doctors for keeping him in [Iraq] while he was unable to perform his duties effectively. He began to develop insomnia, hypervigilance, and a startle response. His initial dreams of the event became more intense and frequent and he suffered intrusive thoughts and flashbacks of the attack. He began to withdraw from his friends and suffered anhedonia, feeling detached from others, and he feared his future would be cut short. He was referred to a psychiatrist at the CSH....

After two months of unsuccessful rehabilitation for his battle injuries and worsening depressive and anxiety symptoms, he was evacuated to a ... military medical center [in the United States].... He was screened for psychiatric symptoms and was referred for outpatient evaluation and management. He met DSM-IV criteria for acute PTSD and was offered medication management, supportive therapy, and group therapy.... He was ambivalent about taking passes or convalescent leave to his home because of fears of being "different, irritated, or aggressive" around his family or girlfriend. After three months at the military service center, he was [deactivated from service and] referred to his local VA Hospital to receive follow-up care.

National Center for PTSD, 2008

During the horror of combat, soldiers often become highly anxious and depressed and physically ill. Moreover, for many, like Latrell, these reactions to extraordinary stress continue well beyond the combat experience itself.

But it is not just combat soldiers who are affected by stress. Nor does stress have to rise to the level of combat trauma to have a profound effect on psychological and physical functioning. Stress comes in all sizes and shapes, and we are all greatly affected by it.

We feel some degree of stress whenever we are faced with demands or opportunities that require us to change in some manner. The state of stress has two components: a *stressor*, the event that creates the demands, and a *stress response*, the person's reactions to the demands. The stressors of life may include annoying everyday hassles, such as rush-hour traffic; turning-point events, such as college graduation or marriage; long-term problems, such as poverty or poor health; or traumatic events, such as major accidents, assaults, tornadoes, or military combat (Almeida, Stawski, & Cichy, 2011). Our response to such stressors is influenced by the way we *judge* both the events and our capacity to react to them in an effective way (Smith & Kirby, 2011; Lazarus & Folkman, 1984). People who sense that they have the ability and the resources to cope are more likely to take stressors in stride and to respond well.

When we view a stressor as threatening, a natural reaction is arousal and a sense of fear—a response frequently on display in Chapter 5. As you saw in that chapter, fear is actually a package of responses that are *physical, emotional,* and *cognitive.* Physically, we perspire, our breathing quickens, our muscles tense, and our hearts beat faster. Turning pale, developing goose bumps, and feeling nauseated are other physical reactions. Emotional responses to extreme threats include horror, dread, and even panic, while in the cognitive realm fear can disturb our ability to concentrate and distort our view of the world. We may exaggerate the harm that actually threatens us or remember things incorrectly.

Stress reactions, and the sense of fear they produce, are often at play in psychological disorders. People who experience a large number of stressful events are particularly vulnerable to the onset of the anxiety disorders that you read about in Chapter 5. Similarly, increases in stress have been linked to the onset of depression, schizophrenia, sexual dysfunctioning, and other psychological problems.

Stress plays an even more central role in certain psychological and physical disorders. In such disorders, the features of stress become severe and debilitating, linger for a long period of time, and may make it impossible for the individual to live a normal life. The key *psychological* stress disorders are *acute stress disorder* and *posttraumatic stress disorder* (*PTSD*), problems that DSM-5 lists within a group called "trauma- and stressor-related disorders." These disorders are triggered by traumatic stressors and include symptoms such as heightened arousal, anxiety and mood disturbance, and memory difficulties. The *physical* stress disorders are typically called *psychophysiological disorders,* problems that DSM-5 technically lists under the heading *psychological factors affecting other medical conditions.* Here significant stressors set in motion an interaction of biological, psychological, and sociocultural factors to help produce or worsen a physical illness or ailment. The psychological and physical stress disorders are the focus of this chapter. Before examining them, however, you need to understand just how the brain and body react to stress.

Stress and Arousal: The Fight-or-Flight Response

The features of arousal and fear are set in motion by the brain area called the *hypothalamus.* When our brain interprets a situation as dangerous, neurotransmitters in the hypothalamus are released, triggering the firing of neurons throughout the brain and the

Different strokes for different folks
Some individuals are exhilarated by the opportunity to chase bulls through the streets of Pamplona, Spain, during the annual "running of the bulls" (left). Others are terrified by such a prospect and prefer instead to engage tamer animals, such as ostriches, during the "running of the ostriches" fiesta in Irurzun, Spain (right).

release of chemicals throughout the body. Actually, the hypothalamus activates two important systems—the *autonomic nervous system* and the *endocrine system* (Lundberg, 2011). The **autonomic nervous system (ANS)** is the extensive network of nerve fibers that connect the *central nervous system* (the brain and spinal cord) to all the other organs of the body. These fibers help control the *involuntary* activities of the organs—breathing, heartbeat, blood pressure, perspiration, and the like (see Figure 6-1). The **endocrine system** is the network of *glands* located throughout the body. (As you read in Chapter 3, glands release *hormones* into the bloodstream and on to the various body organs.) The autonomic nervous system and the endocrine system often overlap in their responsibilities. There are two pathways, or routes, by which these systems produce arousal and fear reactions—the *sympathetic nervous system* pathway and the *hypothalamic-pituitary-adrenal* pathway.

When we face a dangerous situation, the hypothalamus first excites the **sympathetic nervous system,** a group of autonomic nervous system fibers that work to quicken our heartbeat and produce the other changes that we experience as fear or anxiety. These nerves may stimulate the organs of the body directly—for example, they may directly stimulate the heart and increase heart rate. The nerves may also influence the organs indirectly, by stimulating the *adrenal glands* (glands located on top of the kidneys), particularly an area of these glands called the *adrenal medulla*. When the adrenal medulla is stimulated, the chemicals *epinephrine* (*adrenaline*) and *norepinephrine* (*noradrenaline*) are released. You have already seen that these chemicals are important neurotransmitters

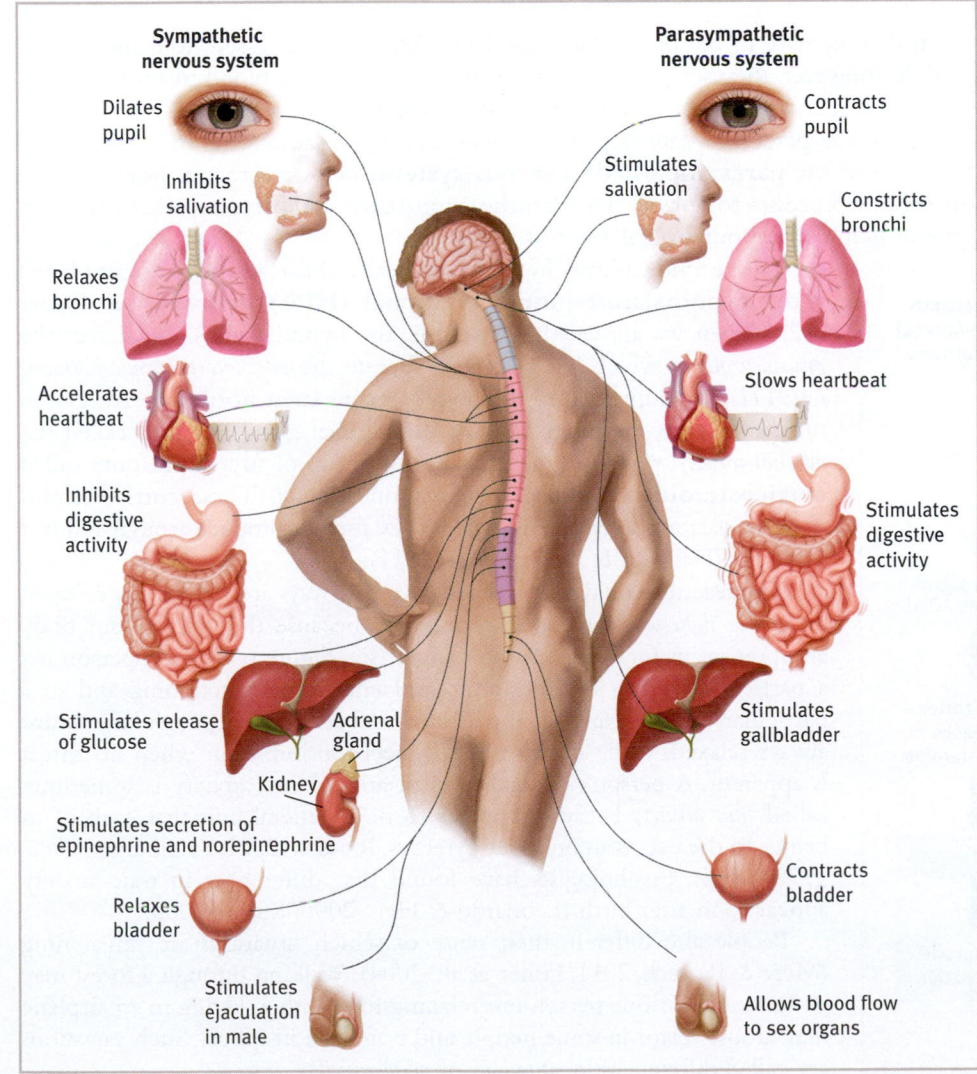

Figure 6-1

The autonomic nervous system (ANS)
When the sympathetic division of the ANS is activated, it stimulates some organs and inhibits others. The result is a state of general arousal. In contrast, activation of the parasympathetic division leads to an overall calming effect.

•**autonomic nervous system (ANS)**•The network of nerve fibers that connect the central nervous system to all the other organs of the body.

•**endocrine system**•The system of glands located throughout the body that help control important activities such as growth and sexual activity.

•**sympathetic nervous system**•The nerve fibers of the autonomic nervous system that quicken the heartbeat and produce other changes experienced as arousal and fear.

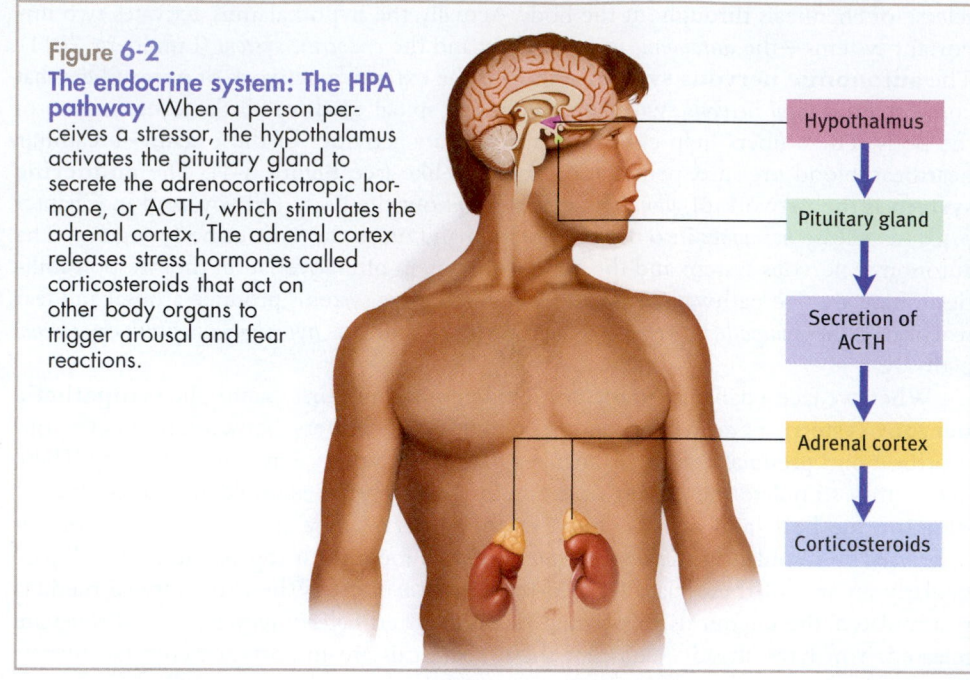

Figure 6-2

The endocrine system: The HPA pathway When a person perceives a stressor, the hypothalamus activates the pituitary gland to secrete the adrenocorticotropic hormone, or ACTH, which stimulates the adrenal cortex. The adrenal cortex releases stress hormones called corticosteroids that act on other body organs to trigger arousal and fear reactions.

Figure 6-3

Pathways of arousal and fear When we are confronted by a stressor, our bodies produce arousal and fear reactions through two pathways. In one, the hypothalamus sends a message to the sympathetic nervous system, which then activates key body organs, either directly or by causing the adrenal medulla to release epinephrine and norepinephrine into the bloodstream. In the other pathway, the hypothalamus sends a message to the pituitary gland, which then signals the adrenal cortex to release corticosteroids—the stress hormones—into the bloodstream.

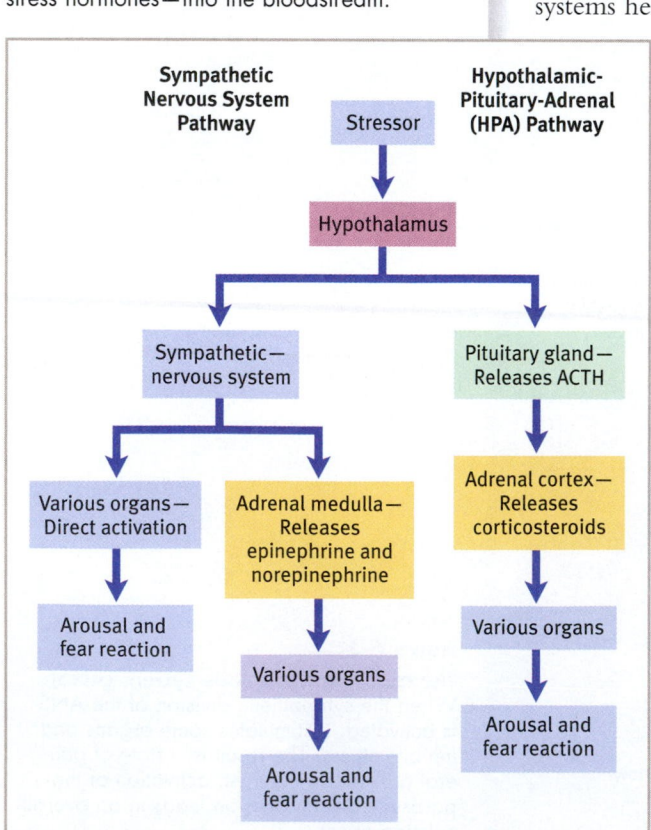

when they operate in the brain (see pages 136–138). When released from the adrenal medulla, however, they act as hormones and travel through the bloodstream to various organs and muscles, further producing arousal and fear.

When the perceived danger passes, a second group of autonomic nervous system fibers, called the **parasympathetic nervous system,** helps return our heartbeat and other body processes to normal. Together the sympathetic and parasympathetic nervous systems help control our arousal and fear reactions.

The second pathway by which arousal and fear reactions are produced is the **hypothalamic-pituitary-adrenal (HPA) pathway** (see Figure 6-2). When we are faced by stressors, the hypothalamus also signals the *pituitary gland,* which lies nearby, to secrete the *adrenocorticotropic hormone* (*ACTH*), sometimes called the body's "major stress hormone." ACTH, in turn, stimulates the outer layer of the adrenal glands, an area called the *adrenal cortex,* triggering the release of a group of stress hormones called **corticosteroids,** including the hormone *cortisol.* These corticosteroids travel to various body organs, where they further produce arousal and fear reactions (Dallman & Hellhammer, 2011).

The reactions on display in these two pathways are collectively referred to as the *fight-or-flight* response, precisely because they arouse our body and prepare us for a response to danger (see Figure 6-3). Each person has a particular pattern of autonomic and endocrine functioning and so a particular way of experiencing arousal and fear. Some people are almost always relaxed, while others typically feel tension, even when no threat is apparent. A person's general level of arousal and anxiety is sometimes called *trait anxiety* because it seems to be a general trait that each of us brings to the events in our lives (Merz & Roesch, 2011; Spielberger, 1985, 1972, 1966). Psychologists have found that differences in trait anxiety appear soon after birth (Leonardo & Hen, 2006; Kagan, 2003).

People also differ in their sense of which situations are threatening (Merz & Roesch, 2011; Fisher et al., 2004). Walking through a forest may be fearsome for one person but relaxing for another. Flying in an airplane may arouse terror in some people and boredom in others. Such variations are called differences in *situation,* or *state, anxiety.*

The Psychological Stress Disorders: Acute and Posttraumatic Stress Disorders

Of course when we actually confront stressful situations, we do not think to ourselves, "Oh, there goes my autonomic nervous system," or "My fight-or-flight seems to be kicking in." We just feel aroused psychologically and physically and experience a growing sense of fear. If the stressful situation is truly extraordinary and unusually dangerous, we may temporarily experience levels of arousal, anxiety, and depression that are beyond anything we have ever known.

For most people, such reactions subside soon after the danger passes. For others, however, the symptoms of anxiety and depression, as well as other kinds of symptoms, persist well after the upsetting situation is over. These people may be suffering from *acute stress disorder* or *posttraumatic stress disorder*, patterns that arise in reaction to a psychologically traumatic event. A traumatic event is one in which individuals are exposed to actual or threatened death, serious injury, or sexual violation (APA, 2013, 2012). Unlike the anxiety disorders that you read about in Chapter 5, which typically are triggered by situations that most people would not find threatening, the situations that cause acute stress disorder or posttraumatic stress disorder—combat, rape, an earthquake, an airplane crash—would be traumatic for anyone.

If the symptoms begin within four weeks of the traumatic event and last for less than a month, DSM-5 assigns a diagnosis of **acute stress disorder** (APA, 2013, 2012). If the symptoms continue longer than a month, a diagnosis of **posttraumatic stress disorder (PTSD)** is given. The symptoms of PTSD may begin either shortly after the traumatic event or months or years afterward (see Table 6-1).

Studies indicate that as many as 80 percent of all cases of acute stress disorder develop into posttraumatic stress disorder (Bryant et al., 2005). Think back to Latrell, the soldier in Iraq whose case opened this chapter. As you'll recall, Latrell became overrun by anxiety, insomnia, worry, anger, depression, irritability, intrusive thoughts, flashback memories, and social detachment within days of the attack on his convoy mission—thus qualifying him for a diagnosis of acute stress disorder. As his symptoms worsened and continued beyond one month—even long after his return to the United States—this diagnosis became PTSD. Aside from the differences in onset and duration, the symptoms of acute stress disorder and PTSD are almost identical:

Reexperiencing the traumatic event People may be battered by recurring thoughts, memories, dreams, or nightmares connected to the event (Ruzek et al., 2011; Geraerts, 2010). A few relive the event so vividly in their minds (flashbacks) that they think it is actually happening again.

Avoidance People will usually avoid activities that remind them of the traumatic event and will try to avoid related thoughts, feelings, or conversations (APA, 2013, 2012; Marx & Sloan, 2005).

Reduced responsiveness People feel detached from other people or lose interest in activities that once brought enjoyment. Some experience symptoms of *dissociation*, or psychological separation (APA, 2013, 2012; Ruzek et al., 2011): they feel dazed, have trouble remembering things, or have a sense of derealization (feeling that the environment is unreal or strange).

Increased arousal, negative emotions, and guilt People with these disorders may feel overly alert (hyperalertness), be easily startled, have trouble concentrating, and develop sleep problems (APA, 2013, 2012). They may display anxiety, anger, or depression and feel extreme guilt because they survived the traumatic event while others did not. Some also feel guilty about what they may have had to do to survive.

table: 6-1

DSM-5 Checklist

Posttraumatic Stress Disorder

1. Exposure to a traumatic event—actual or threatened death, serious injury, or sexual violation.

2. One or more of the following intrusive symptoms:
   • recurrent, involuntary, and distressing memories
   • recurrent distressing dreams • dissociative reactions, such as flashbacks • significant distress at exposure to cues of the event(s) • marked physiological reactions to reminders of the event(s).

3. Persistent avoidance of stimuli associated with the event(s).

4. Negative changes in cognitions and moods, such as the inability to remember important aspects of the event(s), exaggerated negative beliefs about oneself, or persistent negative emotions.

5. Marked changes in arousal and reactivity, such as hypervigilance, extreme startle response, or sleep disturbances.

6. Significant distress or impairment, with symptoms lasting more than one month.

Based on APA, 2013, 2012.

•**parasympathetic nervous system**• The nerve fibers of the autonomic nervous system that help return bodily processes to normal.

•**hypothalamic-pituitary-adrenal (HPA) pathway**•One route by which the brain and body produce arousal and fear.

•**corticosteroids**•A group of hormones, including cortisol, released by the adrenal glands at times of stress.

•**acute stress disorder**•A disorder in which fear and related symptoms are experienced soon after a traumatic event and last less than a month.

•**posttraumatic stress disorder (PTSD)**• A disorder in which fear and related symptoms continue to be experienced long after a traumatic event.

You can see these symptoms in the recollections of a Vietnam combat veteran years after he returned home:

I can't get the memories out of my mind! The images come flooding back in vivid detail, triggered by the most inconsequential things, like a door slamming or the smell of stir-fried pork. Last night I went to bed, was having a good sleep for a change. Then in the early morning a storm-front passed through and there was a bolt of crackling thunder. I awoke instantly, frozen in fear. I am right back in Vietnam, in the middle of the monsoon season at my guard post. I am sure I'll get hit in the next volley and convinced I will die. My hands are freezing, yet sweat pours from my entire body. I feel each hair on the back of my neck standing on end. I can't catch my breath and my heart is pounding. I smell a damp sulfur smell.

(Davis, 1992)

What Triggers a Psychological Stress Disorder?

An acute or posttraumatic stress disorder can occur at any age, even in childhood, and can affect one's personal, family, social, or occupational life (Smith et al., 2010). People with these stress disorders may also experience depression, another anxiety disorder, or substance abuse or become suicidal. Surveys indicate that at least 3.5 percent of people in the United States experience one of the stress disorders in any given year; 7 to 9 percent suffer from one of them during their lifetimes (Peterlin et al., 2011; Taylor, 2010; Kessler et al., 2009, 2005). Around two-thirds of these individuals seek treatment at some point in their lives, but few do so when they first develop the disorder (Wang et al., 2005).

? **What types of events in modern society might trigger acute stress disorder and posttraumatic stress disorder?**

Women are at least twice as likely as men to develop stress disorders: around 20 percent of women who are exposed to a serious trauma may develop one, compared to 8 percent of men (Koch & Haring, 2008; Russo & Tartaro, 2008). Moreover, people with low incomes are twice as likely as people with higher incomes to experience one of the stress disorders (Sareen et al., 2011).

Any traumatic event can trigger a stress disorder; however, some are particularly likely to do so. Among the most common are combat, disasters, and abuse and victimization.

Combat and Stress Disorders For years clinicians have recognized that many soldiers develop symptoms of severe anxiety and depression *during* combat. It was called "shell shock" during World War I and "combat fatigue" during World War II and the Korean War (Figley, 1978). Not until after the Vietnam War, however, did clinicians learn that a great many soldiers also experience serious psychological symptoms *after* combat (Ruzek et al., 2011).

By the late 1970s, it became apparent that many Vietnam combat veterans were still experiencing war-related psychological difficulties (Roy-Byrne et al., 2004). We now know that as many as 29 percent of all Vietnam veterans, male and female, suffered an acute or posttraumatic stress disorder, while another 22 percent experienced at least some stress symptoms (Krippner & Paulson, 2006;

A range of symptoms
Posttraumatic stress disorder is characterized by a range of symptoms from anxiety to depression, detachment, guilt, and anger. Here a veteran of the war in Iraq displays both rage and anxiety during therapy for PTSD.

Lynn Johnson/National Geographic Society/Corbis

Weiss et al., 1992). In fact, 10 percent of the veterans of that war still experience post-traumatic stress symptoms, including flashbacks, night terrors, nightmares, and persistent images and thoughts.

A similar pattern has been unfolding among the nearly 2 million veterans of the wars in Afghanistan and Iraq (Ramchand et al., 2011; Ruzek et al., 2011). Recently, the RAND Corporation, a nonprofit research organization, conducted a large-scale study of military service members who have served in those two wars since 2001 (RAND Corporation, 2010, 2008; Gever, 2008). It found that nearly 20 percent of the Americans deployed to the wars have so far reported symptoms of posttraumatic stress disorder. Given that not all of the individuals studied were in fact exposed to prolonged periods of combat-related stress, this is indeed a very large percentage. Half of the veterans interviewed in this study described traumas in which they had seen friends seriously wounded or killed, 45 percent reported seeing dead or gravely wounded civilians, and 10 percent said they themselves had been injured and hospitalized.

It is also worth noting that the wars in Afghanistan and Iraq have involved repeated deployments of many of the combat veterans and that the individuals who have served such multiple deployments are 50 percent more likely than those with one tour of service to have experienced severe combat stress, significantly raising their risk of developing posttraumatic stress disorder (Tyson, 2006).

Disasters and Stress Disorders Acute and posttraumatic stress disorders may also follow natural and accidental disasters such as earthquakes, floods, tornadoes, fires, airplane crashes, and serious car accidents (see Table 6-2). Researchers have found, for example, unusually high rates of posttraumatic stress disorder among the survivors of 2005's Hurricane Katrina and the BP Gulf Coast oil spill of 2010 (Voelker, 2010). In fact, because they occur more often, civilian traumas have been the trigger of stress disorders at least 10 times as often as combat traumas

Children too
A 10-year-old boy sits in a devastated area of Japan shortly after the 2011 earthquake and tsunami. Children too may develop posttraumatic stress disorder after large-scale natural disasters, leading clinicians to worry about the mental health of the many Japanese children who experienced the magnitude 9.0 earthquake.

table: **6-2**

Worst Natural Disasters of the Past 100 Years

Disaster	Year	Location	Number Killed
Flood	1931	Huang He River, China	3,700,000
Tsunami	2004	South Asia	280,000
Earthquake	1976	Tangshan, China	255,000
Heat wave	2003	Europe	35,000
Volcano	1985	Nevado del Ruiz, Colombia	23,000
Hurricane	1998	(Mitch) Central America	18,277
Landslide	1970	Yungay, Peru	17,500
Avalanche	1916	Italian Alps	10,000
Blizzard	1972	Iran	4,000
Tornado	1989	Shaturia, Bangladesh	1,300

Adapted from USGS, 2011; CBC, 2008; Ash, 2001.

•**rape**•Forced sexual intercourse or another sexual act committed against a nonconsenting person or intercourse with an underage person.

Julien Behal/PA Wire URN:10506509 (Press Association via AP Images)

Raising awareness and sensitivity
This woman joins a rally in front of Ireland's national parliament to protest "jokes" made by three policemen about raping women they had recently arrested. A recording of the police conversation was leaked to the public in 2011, causing a public uproar.

(Bremner, 2002). Studies have even found that as many as 40 percent of victims of serious traffic accidents—adult or child—may develop PTSD within a year of the accident (Hickling & Blanchard, 2007).

Victimization and Stress Disorders People who have been abused or victimized often experience lingering stress symptoms. Research suggests that more than one-third of all victims of physical or sexual assault develop posttraumatic stress disorder (Koss et al., 2011; Burijon, 2007). Similarly, as many as half of all people who are directly exposed to terrorism or torture may develop this disorder (Basoglu et al., 2001).

SEXUAL ASSAULT A common form of victimization in our society today is sexual assault. **Rape** is forced sexual intercourse or another sexual act committed against a nonconsenting person or intercourse with an underage person. In the United States, approximately 200,000 cases of rape or attempted rape are reported to police each year (Koss, White, & Kazdin, 2011; Wolitzky-Taylor et al., 2011; Ahrens et al., 2008). Most rapists are men and most victims are women. Around one in six women is raped at some time during her life. Surveys also suggest that most rape victims are young: 29 percent are under 11 years old, 32 percent are between the ages of 11 and 17, and 29 percent are between 18 and 29 years old. Approximately 70 percent of the victims are raped by acquaintances or relatives.

The rates of rape differ from race to race. Around 46 percent of rape victims in the United States are white American, 27 percent are African American, and 19 percent are Hispanic American (Ahrens et al., 2008; Tjaden & Thoennes, 2000). These rates are in marked contrast to the general population distribution of 63 percent white American, 12 percent African American, and 17 percent Hispanic American (Yen, 2012).

The psychological impact of rape on a victim is immediate and may last a long time (Koss et al., 2011, 2008; Koss, 2005, 1993). Rape victims typically experience enormous distress during the week after the assault. Stress continues to rise for the next 3 weeks, maintains a peak level for another month or so, and then starts to improve. In one study, 94 percent of rape victims fully qualified for a clinical diagnosis of acute stress disorder when they were observed around 12 days after the assault (Rothbaum et al., 1992). Although most rape victims improve psychologically within 3 or 4 months, the effects may persist for up to 18 months or longer. Victims typically continue to have higher-than-average levels of anxiety, suspiciousness, depression, self-esteem problems, self-blame, flashbacks, sleep problems, and sexual dysfunction (Street et al., 2011; Ahrens et al., 2008).

How might physicians, police, the courts, and other agents better meet the psychological needs of rape victims?

Female victims of rape and other crimes also are much more likely than other women to suffer serious long-term health problems (Koss et al., 2011; Koss & Heslet, 1992). Interviews with 390 women revealed that such victims had poorer physical well-being for at least five years after the crime and made twice as many visits to physicians.

As you will see in Chapter 17, ongoing victimization and abuse in the family—specifically child and spouse abuse—may also lead to psychological stress disorders. Because these forms of abuse may occur over the long term and violate family trust, many victims develop other symptoms and disorders as well (Koss et al., 2011).

TERRORISM People who are victims of terrorism or who live under the threat of terrorism often experience posttraumatic stress symptoms (Mitka, 2011; La Greca & Silverman, 2009). Unfortunately, this source of traumatic stress is on the rise in our society. Few will ever forget the events of September 11, 2001, when hijacked airplanes crashed into and brought down the World Trade Center in New York City and partially destroyed the Pentagon in Washington, DC, killing thousands of victims and rescue workers and forcing thousands more to desperately run, crawl, and even dig their way to safety. One of the many legacies of this infamous event is the lingering psychological effect, particularly severe stress reactions, that it has had on those people who were immediately affected, on their family members, and on tens of millions of others who were traumatized simply by watching images of the disaster on their television sets as the day unfolded (see *PsychWatch* below). Studies of subsequent acts of terrorism, such as the 2004 commuter train bombings in Madrid and the 2005 London subway and bus bombings, tell a similar story (Chacón & Vecina, 2007).

PsychWatch

September 11, 2001: The Psychological Aftermath

On September 11, 2001, the United States experienced the most catastrophic act of terrorism in history when four commercial airplanes were hijacked—two of them were crashed into the twin towers of the World Trade Center in New York City; one into the Pentagon in Arlington County, Virginia; and one into a field near Shanksville, Pennsylvania. Studies conducted since that fateful day have confirmed what psychologists knew all too well would happen—that in the aftermath of September 11, many individuals experienced immediate and long-term psychological effects, ranging from brief stress reactions, such as shock, fear, and anger, to en-

during psychological disorders, such as posttraumatic stress disorder (Mitka, 2011; Galea et al., 2007).

In a survey conducted a week after the terrorist attacks, 560 randomly selected adults across the United States were interviewed. Forty-four percent of them reported substantial stress symptoms; 90 percent reported at least some increase in stress (Schuster et al., 2001). Individuals closest to the disaster site experienced the greatest stress reactions, but millions of other people who had remained glued to their TV sets throughout the day experienced stress reactions and disorders as well.

Follow-up studies suggest that many such individuals continue to struggle with terrorism-related stress reactions (Mitka, 2011; Tramontin & Halpern, 2007; Adams & Boscarino, 2005). Indeed, even years after the attacks, 42 percent of all adults in the United States and 70 percent of all New York adults report high terrorism fears; 23 percent of all adults in the United States report feeling less safe in their homes; 15 percent of all U.S. adults report drinking more alcohol than they did prior to the attacks; and 9 percent of New York adults display PTSD, compared to the national annual prevalence of 3.5 percent.

No place for psychologists
California protesters rally in 2007 against participation by psychologists in military and CIA interrogations of suspected terrorists at Guantanamo Bay. In response to a public and professional uproar over this issue, the American Psychological Association voted in 2008 to ban its members from participating in all forms of interrogation at U.S. detention centers.

TORTURE Torture refers to the use of "brutal, degrading, and disorienting strategies in order to reduce victims to a state of utter helplessness" (Okawa & Hauss, 2007). Often, it is done on the orders of a government or another authority to force persons to yield information or make a confession (Gerrity, Keane, & Tuma, 2001). The question of the morality of torturing prisoners who are considered suspects in the "war on terror" has been the subject of much discussion over the past several years.

It is hard to know how many people are in fact tortured around the world because such numbers are typically hidden by governments (Basoglu et al., 2001). It has been estimated, however, that between 5 and 35 percent of the world's 15 million refugees have suffered at least one episode of torture and that more than 400,000 torture survivors from around the world now live in the United States (ORR, 2011, 2006; Basoglu et al., 2001; AI, 2000; Baker, 1992). Of course, these numbers do not take into account the many thousands of victims who have remained in their countries even after being tortured.

People from all walks of life are subjected to torture worldwide—from suspected terrorists to student activists and members of religious, ethnic, and cultural minority groups. The techniques used on them may include *physical torture* (beatings, waterboarding, electrocution), *psychological torture* (threats of death, mock executions, verbal abuse, degradation), *sexual torture* (rape, violence to the genitals, sexual humiliation), or *torture through deprivation* (sleep, sensory, social, nutritional, medical, or hygiene deprivation).

Torture victims often experience physical ailments as a result of their ordeal, from scarring and fractures to neurological problems and chronic pain. But many theorists believe that the lingering psychological effects of torture are even more problematic (Okawa & Hauss, 2007; Basoglu et al., 2001). It appears that between 30 and 50 percent of torture victims develop posttraumatic stress disorder (Punamäki et al., 2010; Basoglu et al., 2001). Even for those who do not develop a full-blown disorder, symptoms such as nightmares, flashbacks, repressed memories, depersonalization, poor concentration, anger outbursts, sadness, and suicidal thoughts are common (Okawa & Hauss, 2007).

Why Do People Develop a Psychological Stress Disorder?

Clearly, extraordinary trauma can cause a stress disorder. The stressful event alone, however, may not be the entire explanation. Certainly, anyone who experiences an unusual trauma will be affected by it, but only some people develop a stress disorder (see *PsychWatch* on the next page) (Elhai, Ford, & Naifeh, 2010). To understand the development of these disorders more fully, researchers have looked to the survivors' biological processes, personalities, childhood experiences, social support systems, and cultural backgrounds and to the severity of the traumas.

Biological and Genetic Factors Investigators have learned that traumatic events trigger physical changes in the brain and body that may lead to severe stress reactions and, in some cases, to stress disorders (Pace & Heim, 2011; Walderhaug et al., 2011). They have, for example, found abnormal activity of the hormone *cortisol* and the neurotransmitter/hormone *norepinephrine* in the urine, blood, and saliva of combat soldiers, rape victims, concentration camp survivors, and survivors of other severe stresses (Gerardi et al., 2010; Delahanty et al., 2005).

Evidence from brain studies also shows that once a stress disorder sets in, individuals experience further biochemical arousal and this continuing arousal may eventually damage key brain areas (Pace & Heim, 2011; Rosen et al., 2010). As we have seen in earlier chapters, researchers have determined that emotional reactions of various kinds are tied to brain circuits networks of brain structures that trigger each other into action with the help of neurotransmitters to produce various emotions. It appears that abnormal activity in one such circuit may contribute to posttraumatic stress reactions. This circuit includes the *hippocampus* and *amygdala,* which send and receive messages to and from each other (Bremner & Charney, 2010; Yehuda et al., 2010).

Normally, the hippocampus plays a major role both in memory and in the regulation of the body's stress hormones. Clearly, a dysfunctional hippocampus may help produce

•**torture**•The use of brutal, degrading, and disorienting strategies to reduce victims to a state of utter helplessness.

Adjustment Disorders: A Category of Compromise?

Some people react to a major stressor in their lives with extended and excessive feelings of anxiety, depressed mood, or antisocial behaviors. The symptoms do not quite add up to acute stress disorder or posttraumatic stress disorder, nor do they reflect an anxiety or mood disorder, but they do cause considerable distress or interfere with the person's job, schoolwork, or social life. Should we consider such reactions normal? No, says DSM-5. Somewhere between effective coping strategies and stress disorders lie the *adjustment disorders,* patterns that are included in DSM-5's group of trauma- and stressor-related disorders (APA, 2013, 2012).

DSM-5 lists several types of adjustment disorders, including *adjustment disorder with anxiety* and *adjustment disorder with depressed mood.* People receive such diagnoses if they develop their symptoms within three months of the onset of a stressor. If the stressor is long-term, such as a medical condition, the adjustment disorder may last indefinitely.

Almost any kind of stressor may trigger an adjustment disorder. Common ones

Candidates for dysfunction? A stock trader—exhausted, worried, and stunned—sits on the floor of the New York Stock Exchange after one of numerous bad financial days in 2008. Business difficulties are among the most common stressors known to trigger adjustment disorders.

are the breakup of a relationship, marital problems, business difficulties, and living in a crime-ridden neighborhood. The disorder may also be triggered by developmental events such as going away to school, getting married, or retiring from a job.

Up to 30 percent of all people in outpatient therapy receive this diagnosis; it accounts for far more treatment claims submitted to insurance companies than any other. However, some experts doubt that adjustment disorders are as common as this figure suggests. Rather, the diagnosis seems to be a favorite among clinicians—it can easily be applied to a range of problems yet is less stigmatizing than many other categories.

the intrusive memories and constant arousal found in posttraumatic stress disorder (Bremner et al., 2004). Similarly, as you read in Chapter 5, the amygdala helps control anxiety and many other emotional responses. It also works with the hippocampus to produce the emotional components of memory. Thus, a dysfunctional amygdala may help produce the repeated emotional symptoms and strong emotional memories experienced by persons with posttraumatic stress disorder (Protopopescu et al., 2005). In short, the arousal produced by extraordinary traumatic events may lead to stress disorders in some people, and the stress disorders may produce yet further brain abnormalities, locking in the disorders all the more firmly.

It may also be that posttraumatic stress disorder leads to the transmission of biochemical abnormalities to the children of persons with the disorder. One team of researchers examined the cortisol levels of women who had been pregnant during the September 11, 2001, terrorist attacks and had developed PTSD (Yehuda & Bierer, 2007). Not only did these women have higher-than-average cortisol levels, but the babies to whom they gave birth after the attacks also displayed higher cortisol levels, suggesting that the babies inherited a predisposition to develop the same disorder.

Many theorists believe that people whose biochemical reactions to stress are unusually strong are more likely than others to develop acute and posttraumatic stress disorders (Burijon, 2007). But why would certain people be prone to such strong biological reactions? One possibility is that the propensity is inherited (McCaffery, 2011). Clearly,

Building resiliency
Noting that a resilient, or "hardy," personality style may help protect people from developing stress disorders, many programs now claim to build resiliency. Here young South Korean schoolchildren fall on a mud flat at a five-day winter military camp designed to strengthen them mentally and physically.

this is suggested by the mother-offspring studies just discussed. Similarly, studies conducted on thousands of pairs of twins who have served in the military find that if one twin develops stress symptoms after combat, an identical twin is more likely than a fraternal twin to develop the same problem (Koenen et al., 2003; True & Lyons, 1993).

Personality Some studies suggest that people with certain personalities, attitudes, and coping styles are particularly likely to develop acute and posttraumatic stress disorders (Burijon, 2007; Chung et al., 2005). In the aftermath of Hurricane Hugo in 1989, for example, children who had been highly anxious before the storm were more likely than other children to develop severe stress reactions (Hardin et al., 2002). Research has also found that people who generally view life's negative events as beyond their control tend to develop more severe stress symptoms after sexual or other kinds of criminal assaults than people who feel greater control over their lives (Taylor, 2006; Bremner, 2002). Similarly, individuals who generally find it difficult to derive anything positive from unpleasant situations adjust more poorly after traumatic events than people who are generally resilient and who typically find value in negative events (Algoe & Fredrickson, 2011; Kunst, 2011).

Childhood Experiences Researchers have found that certain childhood experiences seem to leave some people at risk for later acute and posttraumatic stress disorders. People whose childhoods have been marked by poverty appear more likely to develop these disorders in the face of later trauma. So do people whose family members suffered from psychological disorders; who experienced assault, abuse, or catastrophe at an early age; or who were younger than 10 when their parents separated or divorced (Yehuda et al., 2010; Koch & Haring, 2008; Koopman et al., 2004).

Do the vivid images seen daily on the Web, on TV, and in video games make people more vulnerable to developing psychological stress disorders or less vulnerable?

Social Support It has been found that people whose social and family support systems are weak are also more likely to develop acute or posttraumatic stress disorder after a traumatic event (Uchino & Birmingham, 2011; Ozer, 2005). Rape victims who feel loved, cared for, valued, and accepted by their friends and relatives recover more successfully (Street et al., 2011). So do those treated with dignity and respect by the criminal justice system (Mouilso et al., 2011; Patterson, 2011). In contrast, clinical reports have suggested that poor social support contributes to the development of posttraumatic stress disorder in some combat veterans (Charuvastra & Cloitre, 2008).

Multicultural Factors There is a growing suspicion among clinical researchers that the rates of posttraumatic stress disorder may differ among ethnic groups in the United States. In particular, Hispanic Americans may have a greater vulnerability to the disorder than other cultural groups (Koch & Haring, 2008; Galea et al., 2006). Some cases in point: (1) Studies of combat veterans from the wars in Afghanistan, Iraq, and Vietnam have found higher rates of posttraumatic stress disorder among Hispanic American veterans than among white American and African American veterans (RAND Corporation, 2010, 2008; Kulka et al., 1990). (2) In surveys of police officers, Hispanic American officers typically report more severe duty-related stress symptoms than their non-Hispanic counterparts (Pole et al., 2001). (3) Data on hurricane victims reveal that after some hurricanes Hispanic American victims have had a significantly higher rate of PTSD than victims from other ethnic groups (Perilla et al.,

BETWEEN THE LINES

Gender and Posttraumatic Stress Disorder

Many researchers believe that women's higher rates of posttraumatic stress disorder are tied to the types of violent traumas they experience—namely, interpersonal assaults such as rape or sexual abuse (Street et al., 2011; Russo & Tartaro, 2008). ‹‹

2002). (4) surveys of New York City residents conducted in the months following the terrorist attacks of September 11, 2001, revealed that 14 percent of Hispanic American residents developed PTSD, compared to 9 percent of African American residents and 7 percent of white American residents (Galea et al., 2002).

Why might Hispanic Americans be more vulnerable to posttraumatic stress disorder than other racial or ethnic groups? Several explanations have been suggested. One holds that as part of their cultural belief system, many Hispanic Americans tend to view traumatic events as inevitable and unalterable, a coping response that may heighten their risk for posttraumatic stress disorder (Perilla et al., 2002). Another explanation suggests that their culture's emphasis on social relationships and social support may place Hispanic American victims at special risk when traumatic events deprive them—temporarily or permanently—of important relationships and support systems. Indeed, a study conducted almost three decades ago found that among Hispanic American Vietnam combat veterans with stress disorders, those with poor family and social relationships suffered the most severe symptoms (Escobar et al., 1983).

Severity of Trauma As you might expect, the severity and nature of traumatic events help determine whether one will develop acute and posttraumatic stress disorders. Some events can override even a nurturing childhood, positive attitudes, and social support (Tramontin & Halpern, 2007). One study examined 253 Vietnam War prisoners five years after their release. Some 23 percent qualified for a clinical diagnosis, though all had been evaluated as well adjusted before their imprisonment (Ursano et al., 1981).

Generally, the more severe the trauma and the more direct one's exposure to it, the greater the likelihood of developing a stress disorder (Burijon, 2007). Mutilation and severe physical injury in particular seem to increase the risk of stress reactions, as does witnessing the injury or death of other people (Koren et al., 2005; Ursano et al., 2003).

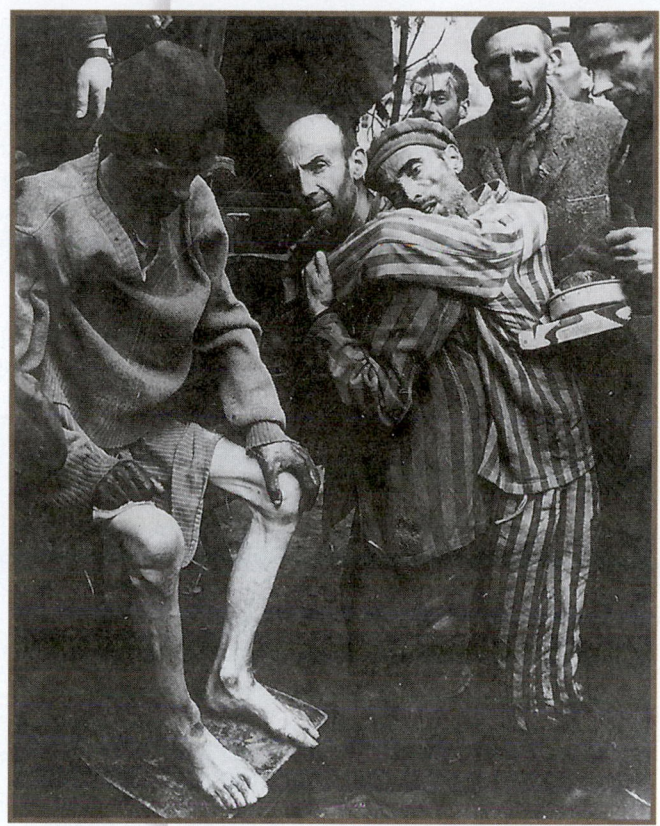

Victimization and posttraumatic stress disorder

Many survivors of Nazi concentration camps faced a long road back to psychological health. However, because knowledge of posttraumatic stress disorder was nonexistent until recent years, most survivors had to find their way back without professional help.

How Do Clinicians Treat the Psychological Stress Disorders?

Treatment can be very important for persons who have been overwhelmed by traumatic events (Taylor, 2010). Overall, about half of all cases of posttraumatic stress disorder improve within six months (Asnis et al., 2004). The remainder of cases may persist for years, and, indeed, more than one-third of people with PTSD fail to respond to treatment even after many years (Cigrang et al., 2011; Burijon, 2007).

Today's treatment procedures for troubled survivors typically vary from trauma to trauma. Was it combat, an act of terrorism, sexual molestation, or a major accident? Yet all the programs share basic goals: they try to help survivors put an end to their stress reactions, gain perspective on their painful experiences, and return to constructive living (Taylor, 2010). Programs for combat veterans who suffer from PTSD illustrate how these issues may be addressed.

Treatment for Combat Veterans Therapists have used a variety of techniques to reduce veterans' posttraumatic symptoms. Among the most common are *drug therapy, behavioral exposure techniques, insight therapy, family therapy,* and *group therapy.* Typically the approaches are combined, as no one of them successfully reduces all the symptoms (Vogt et al., 2011; Bryant, 2010).

Antianxiety drugs help control the tension that many veterans experience. In addition, antidepressant medications may reduce the occurrence of nightmares, panic attacks, flashbacks, and feelings of depression (Suavé & Stahl, 2011; Koch & Haring, 2008).

Behavioral exposure techniques, too, have helped reduce specific symptoms, and they have often led to improvements in overall adjustment (Peterson, Foa, & Riggs, 2011).

•**eye movement desensitization and reprocessing (EMDR)**•An exposure treatment in which clients move their eyes in a rhythmic manner from side to side while flooding their minds with images of objects and situations they ordinarily avoid.

In fact, some studies indicate that exposure treatment is the single most helpful intervention for persons with posttraumatic stress disorder (Powers et al., 2010; Williams, Cahill, & Foa, 2010). This finding suggests to many clinical theorists that exposure of one kind or another should always be part of the treatment picture. In one case, the exposure technique of *flooding,* along with relaxation training, helped rid a 31-year-old veteran of frightening flashbacks and nightmares (Fairbank & Keane, 1982). The therapist and the veteran first singled out combat scenes that the man had been reexperiencing frequently. The therapist then helped the veteran to imagine one of these scenes in great detail and urged him to hold on to the image until his anxiety stopped. After each of these flooding exercises, the therapist had the veteran switch to a positive image and led him through relaxation exercises.

A widely applied form of exposure therapy is **eye movement desensitization and reprocessing (EMDR),** in which clients move their eyes in a rhythmic manner from side to side while flooding their minds with images of the objects and situations they ordinarily try to avoid. Case studies and controlled studies suggest that this treatment can often be helpful to persons with posttraumatic stress disorder (Rothbaum et al., 2011; Luber, 2009). Many theorists argue that it is the exposure feature of EMDR, rather than the eye movement, that accounts for its success with the disorder (Lamprecht et al., 2004).

Although drug therapy and exposure techniques bring some relief, most clinicians believe that veterans with posttraumatic stress disorder cannot fully recover with these approaches alone: they must also come to grips in some way with their combat experiences and the impact those experiences continue to have (Rothbaum et al., 2011; Burijon, 2007) (see *MediaSpeak* on the next page). Thus clinicians often try to help veterans bring out deep-seated feelings, accept what they have done and experienced, become less judgmental of themselves, and learn to trust other people once again (Turner et al., 2005). In a similar vein, cognitive therapists typically guide such veterans to examine and change the dysfunctional attitudes and styles of interpretation that have emerged as a result of their traumatic experiences (Iverson et al., 2011; Karlin et al., 2010).

AP Photo/Ted S. Warren

"Virtual" exposure

In recent years, exposure therapy for combat veterans has been enhanced by the use of virtual reality software that enables clients to confront more vividly the objects and situations that continue to haunt them. Here a soldier's headset and video-game-type controller take him to a battle scene in Iraq.

Combat stress relief

To help prevent stress disorders among troops fighting in Afghanistan and Iraq, the U.S. military has developed stress and trauma release exercises for soldiers to perform, particularly soon after battles. Here active duty army and air force personnel learn one of the exercises.

Lynn Johnson/National Geographic Society/Corbis

Combat Trauma Takes the Stand

By Deborah Sontag And Lizette Alvarez, *New York Times*

When it came time to sentence James Allen Gregg for his conviction on murder charges, the judge in South Dakota took a moment to reflect on the defendant as an Iraq combat veteran who suffered from severe post-traumatic stress disorder. "This is a terrible case, as all here have observed," said Judge Charles B. Kornmann of United States District Court. "Obviously not all the casualties coming home from Iraq or Afghanistan come home in body bags.". . .

When combat veterans like Mr. Gregg stand accused of killings and other offenses on their return from Iraq and Afghanistan, prosecutors, judges and juries are increasingly prodded to assess the role of combat trauma in their crimes. . . . [M]ore and more, with the troops' mental health a rising concern, these defendants . . . are arguing that war be seen as the backdrop for these crimes, most of which are committed by individuals without criminal records. . . . "I think they should always receive some kind of consideration for the fact that their mind has been broken by war," said [a] Western regional defense counsel for the Marines. . . .

On the evening of July 3, 2004, Mr. Gregg, then 22, spent the night with friends in a roving pre-Independence Day celebration on the reservation where he grew up, part of a small non-Indian population. They drank at a Quonset hut bar . . . and finally at a mint farm where they built a bonfire, roasted marshmallows and made s'mores.

According to the prosecutor, Mr. Gregg got upset because a young woman accompanying him gravitated to another man. This, the prosecutor said, led to Mr. Gregg spinning the wheels of his truck and spraying gravel on a car belonging to James Fallis, 26, a former high school football lineman. . . . Some time later, a confrontation ensued. Mr. Gregg was severely beaten by Mr. Fallis and, primarily, by another man, suffering facial fractures. Later that night, with one eye swollen shut and a fat lip, he drove to Mr. Fallis's neighborhood.

Mr. Fallis emerged from a trailer, removed his jacket, asked Mr. Gregg if he had come back for more and opened the door to Mr. Gregg's pickup truck. Mr. Gregg then reached for the pistol that he carried with him after his return from Iraq. He pointed it at Mr. Fallis and warned him to back away. Mr. Fallis moved toward the trunk of his car, and Mr. Gregg testified that he believed Mr. Fallis was going to get a weapon. He started shooting to stop him, he said, and then Mr. Fallis veered toward his house. Mr. Gregg fired nine times, and struck [and killed] Mr. Fallis with five bullets.

Mr. Gregg drove quickly away, ending up in a pasture near his parents' house. According to Mr. Gregg's testimony, he then put a magazine of more bullets in his gun, chambered a round and pointed it at his chest. "Jim, why were you going to kill yourself?" his lawyer asked in court. . . . "Because it felt like Iraq had come back," Mr. Gregg said. "I felt hopeless. . . . I never wanted to shoot him. Never wanted to hurt him. Never. Everything happened just so fast. I mean, it was almost instinct that I had to protect myself."

Mental health experts for the defense said, as one psychiatrist testified, that "PTSD was the driving force behind Mr. Gregg's actions" when he shot his victim. Having suffered a severe beating, they said, he experienced an exaggerated "startle reaction"—a characteristic of PTSD—when Mr. Fallis reached for his car door, and responded instinctively. . . .

The jury found Mr. Gregg guilty of second-degree but not first-degree murder. . . . The Sentence: 21 Years. . . . If all efforts to free him fail, he is projected to be released on July 22, 2023, a few weeks shy of his 42nd birthday.

Veterans who have posttraumatic stress disorder may be further helped in a couple, family, or group therapy format (Maack et al., 2011; Vogt et al., 2011). The symptoms of PTSD are particularly apparent to family members, who may be directly affected by the client's anxieties, depressive mood, or angry outbursts (Monson et al., 2011). With the help and support of their family members, individuals may come to examine their impact on others, learn to communicate better, and improve their problem-solving skills.

•**rap group**•A group that meets to talk about and explore members' problems in an atmosphere of mutual support.

•**psychological debriefing**•A form of crisis intervention in which victims are helped to talk about their feelings and reactions to traumatic incidents. Also called *critical incident stress debriefing.*

•**psychophysiological disorders**•Stress-induced disorders in which biological, psychological, and sociocultural factors interact to cause or worsen a physical illness. Also known as *psychological factors affecting medical condition.*

A change of direction

A Chilean miner is helped by rescue workers after being pulled out of the gold and copper mine in which he and 32 other miners had been trapped for over two months in 2010. On the advice of international psychologists, Chilean officials decided to make counseling *available,* but not required, for the rescued miners. This advice was a departure from the widely used procedure of psychological debriefing, which has failed to receive consistent research support in recent years.

In group therapy, often provided in a form called **rap groups,** the veterans meet with others like themselves to share experiences and feelings (particularly guilt and rage), develop insights, and give mutual support (Foy et al., 2011; Vogt et al., 2011).

Today hundreds of small *Veterans Outreach Centers* across the country, as well as treatment programs in Veterans Administration hospitals and mental health clinics, provide group treatments (Ruzek & Batten, 2011; Welch, 2007). These agencies also offer individual therapy, counseling for spouses and children, family therapy, and aid in seeking jobs, education, and benefits. Clinical reports suggest that these programs offer a necessary, sometimes life-saving, treatment opportunity.

Psychological Debriefing People who are traumatized by disasters, victimization, or accidents profit from many of the same treatments that are used to help survivors of combat (D'Arienzo, 2010; Gist & Devilly, 2010). In addition, because their traumas occur in their own community, where mental health resources are close at hand, these individuals may, according to many clinicians, further benefit from immediate community interventions.

One of the leading such approaches is called **psychological debriefing**, or **critical incident stress debriefing,** an intervention applied widely over the past 25 years. The use of this intervention has, however, come under careful scrutiny in recent years, reminding the clinical field of the ongoing need for systematic research into its assumptions and applications.

Psychological debriefing is a form of crisis intervention that has victims of trauma talk extensively about their feelings and reactions within days of the critical incident (Gist & Devilly, 2010; Mitchell, 2003, 1983). Based on the assumption that such sessions prevent or reduce stress reactions, they are often applied to trauma victims who have not yet displayed any symptoms at all, as well as those who have. During the sessions, often conducted in a group format, counselors guide the individuals to describe the details of the recent trauma, to vent and relive the emotions provoked at the time of the event, and to express their current feelings. The clinicians then clarify to the victims that their reactions are perfectly normal responses to a terrible event, offer stress management tips, and, in some cases, refer the victims to professionals for long-term counseling.

Many thousands of counselors, both professionals and nonprofessionals, have been trained in psychological debriefing since its inception in the early 1980s, and the intense approach has been applied in the aftermath of countless traumatic events (Wei et al., 2010; McNally, 2004). Indeed, when a traumatic incident affects numerous individuals, debriefing-trained counselors may come from far and wide to conduct debriefing sessions with the victims. Large mobilizations of this kind have offered free emergency mental health services at disaster sites such as the 1999 shooting of 23 persons at Columbine High School in Colorado, the 2001 World Trade Center attack, the 2004 tsunami in South Asia, the floods caused by Hurricane Katrina in 2005, and the Haitian and Japanese earthquakes in 2010 and 2011.

In such community-wide mobilizations, the counselors may knock on doors or approach victims at shelters. Although victims from all socioeconomic groups may be engaged, those who live in poverty have been viewed traditionally as most in need and so have been targeted for psychological debriefing most often.

Does Psychological Debriefing Work? Over the years, personal testimonials for rapid mobilization programs have often been favorable (Watson & Shalev,

2005; Mitchell, 2003). However, as you read earlier, a growing number of studies conducted in the twenty-first century have called into question the effectiveness of this kind of intervention (Gist & Devilly, 2010).

Actually, an investigation conducted in the early 1990s was the first to raise concerns about disaster debriefing programs (Bisson & Deahl, 1994). Crisis counselors offered immediate debriefing sessions to 62 British soldiers whose job during the Gulf War was to handle and identify the bodies of individuals who had been killed. Despite such sessions, half of the soldiers displayed posttraumatic stress symptoms when interviewed nine months later.

In a properly controlled study conducted a few years later on hospitalized burn victims, researchers separated the victims into two groups (Bisson et al., 1997). One group received a single one-on-one debriefing session within days of their burn accidents, while the other (control) group of burn victims received no such intervention. Three months later, it was found that the debriefed and the control patients had similar rates of posttraumatic stress disorder. Moreover, researchers found that 13 months later, the rate of posttraumatic stress disorder was actually *higher* among the debriefed burn victims (26 percent) than among the control victims (9 percent).

More recent studies, focusing on yet other kinds of disasters, have yielded similar patterns of findings, raising important questions about the effectiveness of psychological debriefing (Szumilas et al., 2010; Wei et al., 2010). Some clinicians have come to believe that the early intervention programs may encourage victims to dwell too long on the traumatic events that they have experienced. And a number worry that early disaster counseling may unintentionally "suggest" problems to certain victims, thus helping to produce stress disorders (McNally, 2004; McClelland, 1998).

Many mental health professionals continue to believe in psychological debriefing programs. However, given the unsupportive and even contradictory research findings of recent years, the current clinical climate is moving away from outright acceptance. A number of clinical theorists now believe that certain *high-risk* individuals may profit from debriefing programs and that those people should receive debriefing techniques immediately after a traumatic event, but that other trauma victims should not receive such interventions (Delahanty, 2011). Of course, a key to this notion is the ability to effectively identify the risk factors that predict PTSD and the personality factors that predict responsiveness to psychological debriefing. Research into these issues is now under way (Delahanty, 2011).

The Physical Stress Disorders: Psychophysiological Disorders

As you have seen, stress can greatly affect our psychological functioning (see Figure 6-4). It can also have great impact on our physical functioning, contributing in some cases to the onset or worsening of medical problems. The idea that stress and related psychosocial factors may contribute to physical illnesses has ancient roots, yet it had few supporters before the twentieth century. Seventeenth-century French philosopher René Descartes went so far as to claim that the mind, or soul, is separate from the body—a position called *mind-body dualism*.

The belief that stress can contribute to physical illness began to take hold about 80 years ago, when clinicians first identified a group of physical illnesses that seemed to result from an *interaction* of biological, psychological, and sociocultural factors (Dunbar, 1948; Bott, 1928). Early editions of the DSM labeled these illnesses **psychophysiological,** or **psychosomatic, disorders,** but DSM-5 labels them as **psychological factors affecting other medical conditions** (see Table 6-3). The more familiar term "psychophysiological" will be used in this chapter.

It is important to recognize that psychophysiological disorders bring about *actual* physical damage (APA, 2013, 2012). They are different from "apparent" physical

table: **6-3**

DSM-5 Checklist

Psychological Factors Affecting Other Medical Conditions

1. The presence of a general medical condition.

2. Psychological factors adversely affect the general medical condition in one of the following ways:
   - Influence the course of the medical condition
   - Interfere with the treatment of the medical condition
   - Pose additional health risks
   - Influence underlying pathological physiology, triggering or worsening the medical condition

Based on APA, 2013, 2012.

Figure 6-4
What do people do to relieve stress?
According to surveys, most of us go on the Internet, watch television, read, or listen to music. Tweeting is on the rise (IWS, 2011; Pew Research Center, 2011, 2010; NPD Group, 2008; MHA, 2008).

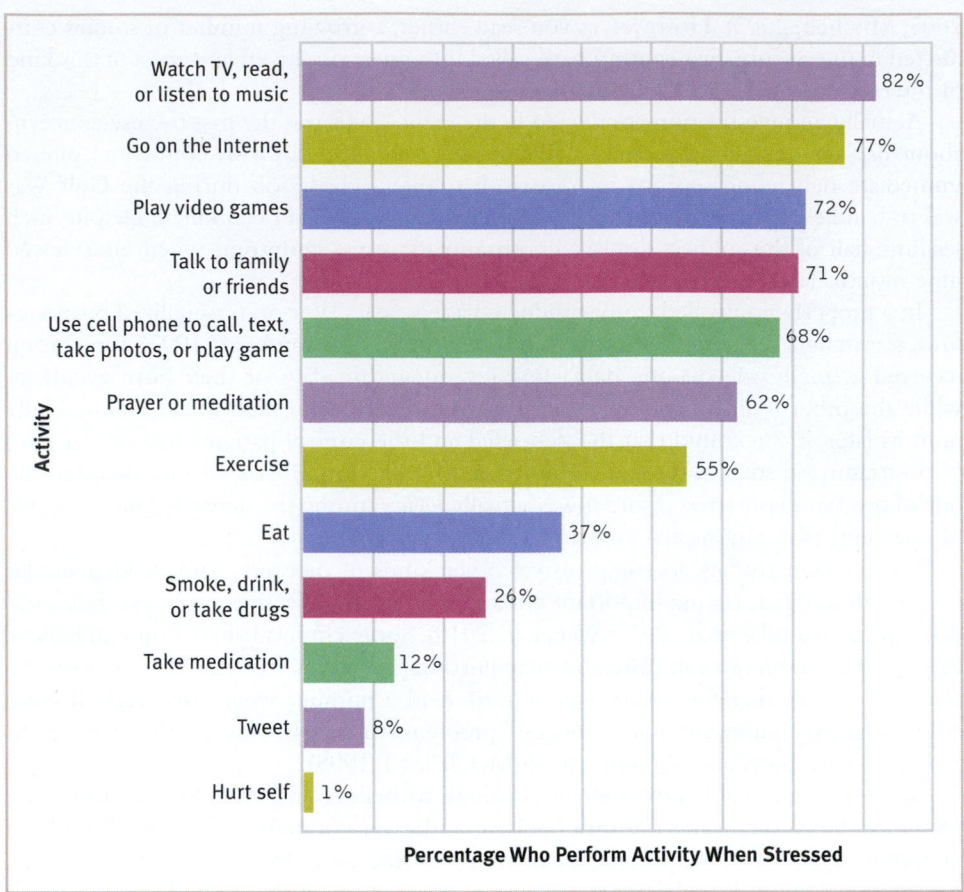

Watch TV, read, or listen to music — 82%
Go on the Internet — 77%
Play video games — 72%
Talk to family or friends — 71%
Use cell phone to call, text, take photos, or play game — 68%
Prayer or meditation — 62%
Exercise — 55%
Eat — 37%
Smoke, drink, or take drugs — 26%
Take medication — 12%
Tweet — 8%
Hurt self — 1%

Activity

Percentage Who Perform Activity When Stressed

Treating asthma
Children who suffer from asthma may use an aerochamber, or inhaler, to help them inhale helpful medications. With the aid of such devices, many asthmatic children are able to lead active and relatively normal lives.

illnesses—*factitious disorder, conversion disorder,* and *illness anxiety disorder*—disorders that are accounted for primarily by psychological factors. Those kinds of problems will be examined in the next chapter.

Traditional Psychophysiological Disorders

Before the 1970s, clinicians believed that only a limited number of illnesses were psychophysiological. The best known and most common of these disorders were ulcers, asthma, insomnia, chronic headaches, high blood pressure, and coronary heart disease. Recent research, however, has shown that many other physical illnesses—including bacterial and viral infections—may also be caused by an interaction of psychosocial and physical factors. Let's look first at the traditional psychophysiological disorders and then at the newer illnesses in this category.

Ulcers are lesions (holes) that form in the wall of the stomach or of the duodenum, resulting in burning sensations or pain in the stomach, occasional vomiting, and stomach bleeding. This disorder is experienced by over 25 million people in the United States at some point during their lives and is responsible for an estimated 6,500 deaths each year (CDC, 2010, 2005). Ulcers often are caused by an interaction of stress factors, such as environmental pressure or intense feelings of anger or anxiety, and physiological factors, such as the bacteria *H. pylori* (Fink, 2011; Carr, 2001).

Asthma causes the body's airways (the trachea and bronchi) to narrow periodically, making it hard for air to pass to and from the lungs. The resulting symptoms are shortness of breath, wheezing, coughing, and a terrifying choking sensation. Some 25 million people in the United States currently suffer from asthma, twice as many as 25 years ago (Akinbami, Moorman, & Liu, 2011). Most victims are children or young teenagers at the time of the first attack. Seventy percent of all cases appear to be caused by an interaction of stress factors, such as environmental pressures or anxiety, and physiological factors, such as allergies to specific substances, a slow-acting sympathetic nervous system, or a weakened respiratory system (CDC, 2011; Dhabhar, 2011).

Insomnia, difficulty falling asleep or maintaining sleep, plagues more than one-fourth of the population each year (CDC, 2011) (see *PsychWatch* on page 173). Although many of us have temporary bouts of insomnia that last a few nights or so, a large number of people—10 percent of the population—experience insomnia that lasts months or years (Riemann et al., 2011). Chronic insomniacs feel as though they are almost constantly awake. They often are very sleepy during the day and may have difficulty functioning. Their problem may be caused by a combination of psychosocial factors, such as high levels of anxiety or depression, and physiological problems, such as an overactive arousal system or certain medical ailments (Bastien, 2011; Belleville et al., 2011).

Chronic headaches are frequent intense aches of the head or neck that are not caused by another physical disorder. There are two major types. **Muscle contraction,** or **tension, headaches** are marked by pain at the back or front of the head or the back of the neck. These occur when the muscles surrounding the skull tighten, narrowing the blood vessels. Approximately 45 million Americans suffer from such headaches (CDC, 2010). **Migraine headaches** are extremely severe, often near-paralyzing headaches that are located on one side of the head and are sometimes accompanied by dizziness, nausea, or vomiting. Migraine headaches are thought by some medical theorists to develop in two phases: (1) blood vessels in the brain narrow, so that the flow of blood to parts of the brain is reduced, and (2) the same blood vessels later expand, so that blood flows through them rapidly, stimulating many neuron endings and causing pain. Migraines are suffered by about 23 million people in the United States.

Research suggests that chronic headaches are caused by an interaction of stress factors, such as environmental pressures or general feelings of helplessness, anger, anxiety, or depression, and physiological factors, such as abnormal activity of the neurotransmitter serotonin, vascular problems, or muscle weakness (Young & Skorga, 2011; Engel, 2009).

Hypertension is a state of chronic high blood pressure. That is, the blood pumped through the body's arteries by the heart produces too much pressure against the artery walls. Hypertension has few outward signs, but it interferes with the proper functioning of the entire cardiovascular system, greatly increasing the likelihood of stroke, heart disease, and kidney problems. It is estimated that 75 million people in the United States have hypertension, thousands die directly from it annually, and millions more perish because of illnesses caused by it (CDC, 2011; Ford & LaVan, 2011). Around 10 percent of all cases are caused by physiological abnormalities alone; the rest result from a combination of psychosocial and physiological factors and are called *essential hypertension.* Some of the leading psychosocial causes of essential hypertension are constant

•**ulcer**•A lesion that forms in the wall of the stomach or of the duodenum.

•**asthma**•A medical problem marked by narrowing of the trachea and bronchi, which results in shortness of breath, wheezing, coughing, and a choking sensation.

•**insomnia**•Difficulty falling or staying asleep.

•**muscle contraction headache**•A headache caused by a narrowing of muscles surrounding the skull. Also known as *tension headache.*

•**migraine headache**•A very severe headache that occurs on one side of the head, often preceded by a warning sensation and sometimes accompanied by dizziness, nausea, or vomiting.

•**hypertension**•Chronic high blood pressure.

Keeping workers healthy
Given that work stress is often tied to both physical and psychological stress disorders, many employers now take measures to help reduce such stress, even during the economic downturn. A nurse (left) prepares a worker for a physical stress test at a steel-processing company in Ohio. A time management instructor (right) uses props to illustrate how employees at a business in California can make better use of their time and, in turn, reduce their feelings of stress.

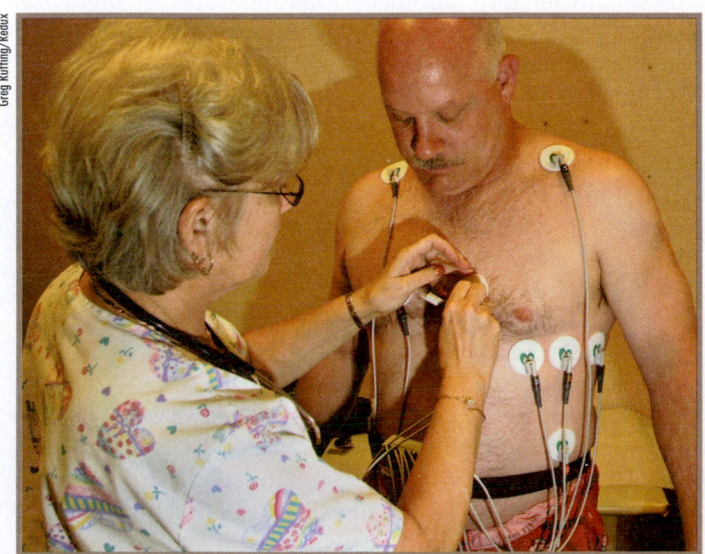

•coronary heart disease•Illness of the heart caused by a blockage in the coronary arteries.

stress, environmental danger, and general feelings of anger or depression. Physiological factors include obesity, smoking, poor kidney function, and an unusually high proportion of the gluey protein *collagen* in an individual's blood vessels (Brooks, McCabe, & Schneiderman, 2011; Landsbergis et al., 2011; Kluger, 2004).

Coronary heart disease is caused by a blocking of the *coronary arteries,* the blood vessels that surround the heart and are responsible for carrying oxygen to the heart muscle. The term actually refers to several problems, including blockage of the coronary arteries and *myocardial infarction* (a "heart attack"). Nearly 18 million people in the United States suffer from some form of coronary heart disease. It is the leading cause of death in men over the age of 35 and of women over 40 in the United States, accounting for close to 1 million deaths each year, around 40 percent of all deaths in the nation (AHA, 2011; Travis

What jobs in our society might be particularly stressful and traumatizing? Might certain lifestyles be more stressful than others?

& Meltzer, 2008). The majority of all cases of coronary heart disease are related to an interaction of psychosocial factors, such as job stress or high levels of anger or depression, and physiological factors, such as a high level of cholesterol, obesity, hypertension, smoking, or lack of exercise (Bekkouche et al., 2011; Kendall-Tackett, 2010).

Over the years, clinicians have identified a number of variables that may generally contribute to the development of psychophysiological disorders (see Figure 6-5). It should not surprise us that several of these variables are the same as those that contribute to the onset of the psychological stress disorders—acute and posttraumatic stress disorders. The variables may be grouped as biological, psychological, and sociocultural factors.

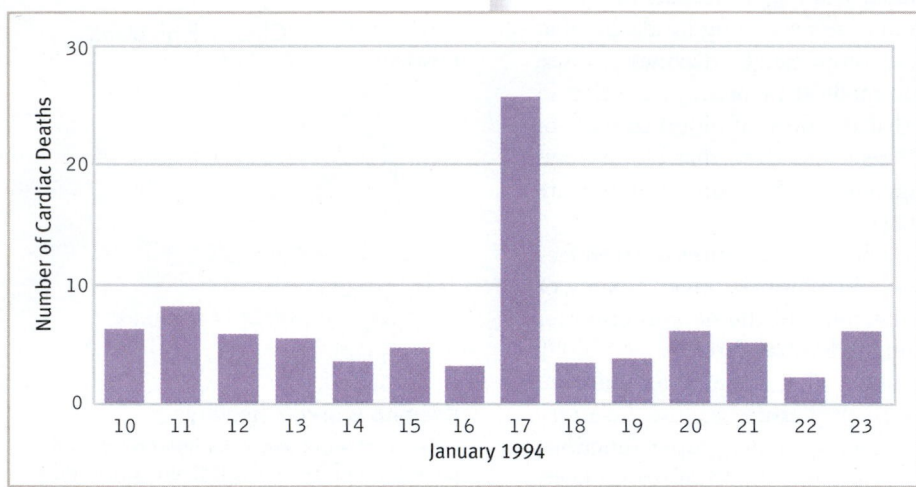

Figure 6-5

Coronary heart disease and stress On January 17, 1994, Los Angeles was struck by an enormous earthquake. Twenty-four city residents with cardiovascular disease died of heart attacks on that day, five times the usual total (Leor et al., 1996). This underlines the important role played by stress and other psychosocial variables in coronary heart disease.

Biological Factors You saw earlier that one way the brain activates body organs is through the operation of the *autonomic nervous system* (*ANS*), the network of nerve fibers that connect the central nervous system to the body's organs. Defects in this system are believed to contribute to the development of psychophysiological disorders (Lundberg, 2011; Hugdahl, 1995). If one's ANS is stimulated too easily, for example, it may overreact to situations that most people find only mildly stressful, eventually damaging certain organs and causing a psychophysiological disorder. Other more specific biological problems may also contribute to psychophysiological disorders. A person with a weak gastrointestinal system, for example, may be a prime candidate for an ulcer, whereas someone with a weak respiratory system may develop asthma readily.

In a related vein, people may display favored biological reactions that raise their chances of developing psychophysiological disorders. Some individuals perspire in response to stress, others develop stomachaches, and still others experience a rise in blood pressure (Lundberg, 2011; Fahrenberg et al., 1995). Research has indicated, for example, that some individuals are particularly likely to experience temporary rises in blood pressure when stressed (Gianaros & O'Connor, 2011; Gianaros et al., 2005). It may be that they are prone to develop hypertension.

Consistent with these notions, a team of cardiologists at Johns Hopkins Medical Institutes offered an interesting report several years ago on 19 patients who had symptoms of a severe heart attack (Wittstein et al., 2005). In fact, none of the patients had heart-tissue damage or clogged coronary arteries—that is, none had suffered a heart attack—but all had recently had a highly stressful experience and all displayed extraordinarily abnormal ANS and hormonal activity. Although such brain and bodily activity did not lead to an actual heart attack during that hospitalization, some of their cardiologists

Sleep, Perchance to Sleep

Sleep is affected by both physical and psychosocial factors. Sleep deprivation for 100 hours or more leads to hallucinations, paranoia, and bizarre behavior. When people remain awake for over 200 hours, they frequently experience periods of "microsleep," naps lasting two to three seconds. The body simply refuses to be entirely deprived of sleep for long.

To learn more about sleep, researchers bring people into the laboratory and record their activities as they sleep, using various types of recording devices. One important discovery has been that eyes move rapidly about 25 percent of the time a person is asleep, a phenomenon known as *rapid eye movement,* or *REM.* Despite small movements and muscle twitches during REM sleep, the body is immobilized, almost paralyzed. Eighty percent of participants who are awakened from REM sleep report that they were dreaming.

DSM-5 identifies a number of sleep-wake disorders (APA, 2013, 2012). Disorders called *dyssomnias* (insomnia disorder, hypersomnolence disorders, narcolepsy/hypocretin deficiency, sleep apnea, and circadian rhythm sleep-wake disorder) involve disturbances in the amount, quality, or timing of sleep. Disorders called *parasomnias* (nightmare disorder and disorders of arousal) involve abnormal events that occur during sleep.

The most common of these disorders is *insomnia disorder,* in which people repeatedly have great difficulty falling asleep or maintaining sleep. More than 25 percent of the entire population experiences this pattern each year (CDC, 2011). People with insomnia disorder feel as though they are almost constantly awake. Often they are very sleepy during the day and have difficulty functioning effectively. The problem may be caused by factors such as stress, anxiety, depression, medical ailments, pain, or medication effects (Bastien, 2011; Belleville et al., 2011; Reimann et al., 2011).

In contrast to insomnia disorder, *hypersomnolence disorder* is marked by a heightened need for sleep and excessive

sleepiness. Sufferers may need extra hours of sleep each night and perhaps during the daytime as well (APA, 2013, 2012).

Narcolepsy/hypocretin deficiency, a disorder marked by repeated sudden and irrepressible bouts of REM sleep during waking hours, afflicts more than 155,000 people in the United States (NINDS, 2010). Although it is a biological disorder, the bouts of sleep are often triggered by strong emotions. Sufferers may suddenly fall into REM sleep in the midst of an argument or during an exciting part of a football game (Goswami et al., 2010).

Sleep apnea is a respiratory problem in which persons are periodically deprived of oxygen to the brain during sleep, so that they frequently wake up. It may occur in more than 10 percent of the elderly population; it is less common in younger age groups (Wickwire et al., 2008; APA, 2000). Its victims, typically overweight persons who are heavy snorers, actually stop breathing for up to 30 seconds or more as they sleep. Hundreds of episodes may occur nightly, without the victim's awareness.

People with *circadian rhythm sleep-wake disorder* experience excessive sleepiness or insomnia as a result of a mismatch between their own sleep-wake pattern and the sleep-wake schedule of most other people in their environment. Often the disorder takes the form of falling asleep late and awakening late. This dyssomnia can result from night-shift work, frequent

changes in work shifts, or other factors (Ohayon et al., 2002).

Nightmare disorder is the most common of the parasomnias. Although most people experience nightmares from time to time, in this disorder nightmares become frequent and cause such great distress that the individual must receive treatment. Such nightmares often increase under stress.

Disorders of arousal takes various forms. In one kind, *sleep terrors,* sufferers awaken suddenly during the first third of their evening sleep, screaming in extreme fear and agitation. They are in a state of panic, are often incoherent, and have a heart rate to match. Sleep terrors most often appear in children and disappear during adolescence.

In another kind of disorder of arousal, *sleepwalking,* sufferers—usually children—repeatedly leave their beds and walk around, without being conscious of the episode or remembering it later. The episodes occur in the first third of the individuals' nightly sleep. Those who are awakened while sleepwalking are confused for several moments. If allowed to continue sleepwalking, they eventually return to bed. Sleepwalkers usually manage to avoid obstacles, climb stairs, and perform complex activities, in a seemingly emotionless state, but accidents do sometimes happen. Up to 5 percent of children experience this disorder, and as many as 40 percent have occasional sleepwalking episodes (Dogu & Pressman, 2011; Wickwire et al., 2008).

"You're not ill yet, Mr. Blendell, but you've got potential."

believed that repeated episodes could indeed contribute to coronary heart disease in the future.

Psychological Factors According to many theorists, certain needs, attitudes, emotions, or coping styles may cause people to overreact repeatedly to stressors, and so increase their chances of developing psychophysiological disorders (Williams et al., 2011). Researchers have found, for example, that men with a *repressive coping style* (a reluctance to express discomfort, anger, or hostility) tend to experience a particularly sharp rise in blood pressure and heart rate when they are stressed (Myers, 2010; Pauls & Stemmler, 2003).

Another personality style that may contribute to psychophysiological disorders is the **Type A personality style,** an idea introduced a half-century ago by two cardiologists, Meyer Friedman and Raymond Rosenman (1959). People with this style are said to be consistently angry, cynical, driven, impatient, competitive, and ambitious. They interact with the world in a way that, according to Friedman and Rosenman, produces continual stress and often leads to coronary heart disease. People with a **Type B personality style,** by contrast, are thought to be more relaxed, less aggressive, and less concerned about time and thus, in turn, are less likely to experience cardiovascular deterioration.

The link between the Type A personality style and coronary heart disease has been supported by many studies. In one well-known investigation of more than 3,000 people, Friedman and Rosenman (1974) separated healthy men in their forties and fifties into Type A and Type B categories and then followed their health over the next eight years. More than twice as many Type A men developed coronary heart disease. Later studies found that Type A functioning correlates similarly with heart disease in women (Haynes et al., 1980).

Recent studies indicate that the link between the Type A personality style and heart disease may not be as strong as the earlier studies suggested. These studies do suggest, however, that several of the characteristics that supposedly make up the Type A style, particularly *hostility* and *time urgency,* may indeed be strongly related to heart disease (Elovainio et al., 2011; Myrtek, 2007).

Sociocultural Factors: The Multicultural Perspective Adverse social conditions may set the stage for psychophysiological disorders. Such conditions produce ongoing stressors that trigger and interact with the biological and personality factors just discussed. One of society's most negative social conditions, for example, is poverty (see *MediaSpeak* on page 176). In study after study, it has been found that relatively wealthy people have fewer psychophysiological disorders, better health in general, and better health outcomes than poor people (Chandola & Marmot, 2011; Matsumoto & Juang, 2008). One obvious reason for this relationship is that poorer people typically experience higher rates of crime, unemployment, overcrowding, and other negative stressors than wealthier people. In addition, they typically receive inferior medical care.

The relationship between race and psychophysiological and other health problems is complicated. On the one hand, as one might expect from the economic trends just discussed, African Americans have more such problems than do white Americans. African Americans have, for example, higher rates of high blood pressure, diabetes, and asthma (CDCP, 2011; Mendes, 2010). They are also more likely than white Americans to die of heart disease and stroke. Certainly, economic factors may help explain this racial difference. Many African Americans live in poverty and, in turn, experience the high rates of crime and unemployment that often result in poor health conditions.

•**Type A personality style**•A personality pattern characterized by hostility, cynicism, drivenness, impatience, competitiveness, and ambition.

•**Type B personality style**•A personality pattern in which persons are more relaxed, less aggressive, and less concerned about time.

Research further suggests that the high rate of psychophysiological and other medical disorders among African Americans probably extends beyond economic factors. Consider, for example, the finding that 42 percent of African Americans have high blood pressure, compared to 29 percent of white Americans (CDCP, 2011). Although this difference may be explained, in part, by the dangerous environments in which so many African Americans live and the unsatisfying jobs at which so many must work (Gilbert et al., 2011; Jackson et al., 2010), other factors may also be operating. A physiological predisposition among African Americans may, for example, increase their risk of developing high blood pressure. Or it may be that repeated experiences of racial discrimination constitute special stressors that help raise the blood pressure of African Americans (Brandolo et al., 2011) (see Figure 6-6).

One recent investigation found that the more discrimination people experience over a one-year period, the greater their daily rise in blood pressure (Smart-Richman et al., 2010). In a related study, African American and white American women were instructed to talk about three hypothetical scenarios (Lepore et al., 2006). For one scenario, considered a *racial* stressor, the research participants had to describe being unjustly accused of shoplifting. For another scenario, considered a *nonracial* stressor, they discussed being caught in airport delays. And, for the third scenario, which involved little or no stressors of any kind, the participants had to describe giving a campus tour. The African American participants displayed significantly greater rises in blood pressure than the white American participants when discussing the racial stressor scenario. Based on this finding, the experimenters concluded that perceptions of racism produce greater physiological stress for African American women, setting the stage for high blood pressure, other psychophysiological disorders, and generally poorer health.

Looking at the health picture of African Americans, one might expect to find a similar trend among Hispanic Americans. After all, a high percentage of Hispanic Americans also live in poverty, are exposed to discrimination, experience high rates of crime and unemployment, and have inferior medical care. Indeed, census data reveal that more than half of all people who have no health care insurance are either Hispanic American or African American, and Hispanic American women have the worst access to health care in the United States (U.S. Census Bureau, 2010; Travis & Meltzer, 2008). However, despite such economic disadvantages, the health of Hispanic Americans is, on average, at least as good and often better than that of both white Americans and African Americans (CDCP, 2011; Mendes, 2010). As you can see in Table 6-4, for example, Hispanic Americans have lower rates of high blood pressure, high cholesterol, asthma, and cancer than white Americans or African Americans do.

The relatively positive health picture for Hispanic Americans in the face of clear economic disadvantage has been referred to in the clinical field as the "Hispanic Health

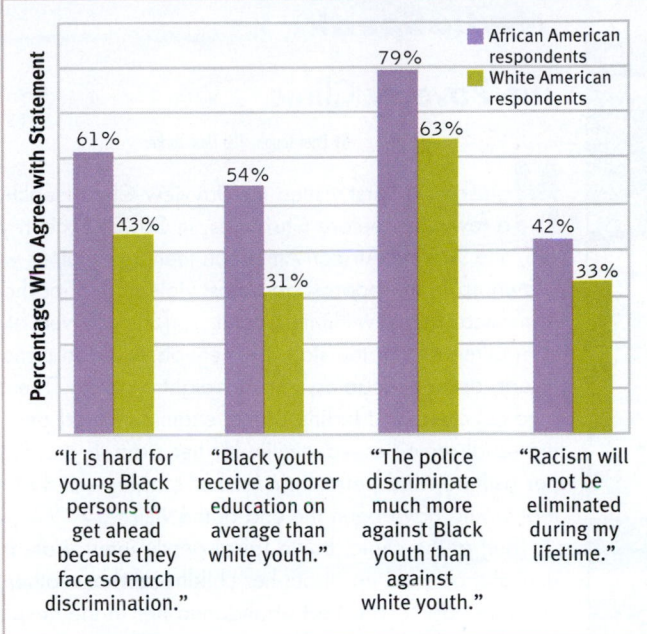

Figure 6-6

How much discrimination do racial minority teenagers face? It depends on who's being asked the question. In a recent survey of 1,590 teenagers and young adults, African American respondents were more likely than white American respondents to recognize that African American teens experience various forms of discrimination (Black Youth Project, 2011).

table: 6-4

Prevalence of Medical Disorders Among U.S. Racial Groups

	High Blood Pressure	High Cholesterol	Diabetes	Asthma	Cancer
African Americans	42%	24%	16%	13%	5%
White Americans	29%	30%	11%	11%	8%
Hispanic Americans	21%	20%	11%	9%	3%

Based on CDCP, 2011; Mendes, 2010.

MediaSpeak

The Poverty Clinic

By Paul Tough, *The New Yorker*

Monisha . . . first visited the Bayview Child Health Center a few days before Christmas, in 2008. Sixteen years old, she was an African-American teen-age mother who had grown up in the poorest and most violent neighborhood in San Francisco, Bayview-Hunters Point. . . . [She] arrived at the clinic with ailments that the staff routinely observed in patients: strep throat, asthma, scabies, and a weight problem. The clinic's medical director, Nadine Burke, examined [her] and prescribed the usual remedies—penicillin for her strep throat, ProAir for her asthma, and permethrin for her scabies—and at most clinics that would have been the end of the visit. . . .

[But] at the clinic, Burke [also] gently interrogated [Monisha] until she opened up about her childhood: her mother was a cocaine addict who had abandoned her in the hospital only a few days after she was born, prematurely, weighing just three and a half pounds. As a child, [Monisha] lived with her father and her older brother in a section of Hunters Point that is notorious for its gang violence; her father, too, began taking drugs, and at the age of ten she and her brother were removed from their home, separated, and placed in foster care. Since then, she had been in nine placements, staying with a family or in a group home until, inevitably, fights erupted over food or homework or TV and [Monisha] ran away—or her caregivers gave up. She longed to be with her father, despite his shortcomings, but there was always some reason that he couldn't take her back. . . .

As she listened . . . Burke found herself inching toward a diagnosis that, a year earlier, would have struck her as implausible. What if [the teenager's] anxiety wasn't merely an emotional side effect of her difficult life but the central issue affecting her health? According to the research Burke had been reading, the traumatic events that [Monisha] experienced in childhood had likely caused significant and long-lasting chemical changes in both her brain and her body, and these changes could well be making her sick, and also increasing her chances of serious medical problems in adulthood. And [this] case wasn't unusual; Burke was seeing the same patterns of trauma, stress, and symptoms every day in many of her patients.

Two years after [Monisha's] first visit, Burke has transformed her practice. Her methodology remains rooted in science, but it goes beyond the typical boundaries of medicine. Burke believes that regarding childhood trauma as a medical issue helps her to treat more effectively the symptoms of patients like [Monisha]. Moreover, she believes, this approach, when applied to a large population, might help alleviate the broader dysfunction that plagues poor neighborhoods. In the view of Burke and the researchers she has been following, many of the problems that we think of as social issues—and therefore the province of economists and sociologists—might better be addressed on the molecular level, among neurons and cytokines and interleukins. If these researchers are right, it could be time to reassess the relationship between poverty, child development, and health, and the Bayview clinic may turn out to be a place where a new kind of pediatric medicine is taking its tentative first steps. . . .

[Research on psychoneuroimmunology] provided Nadine Burke with a new way to evaluate what she was seeing in her clinic, and in Bayview-Hunters Point as a whole. "In many cases, what looks like a social situation is actually a neurochemical situation," Burke explained one afternoon at the clinic. "You can trace the pathology as it moves from the molecular level to the social level. You have a girl who grows up in a household where there's domestic violence, or some kind of horrible arguing between her parents. That triggers her fight-or-flight response, which affects the way the hormone receptors in her brain develop, and as she grows up her stress-regulation systems goes off track. Maybe she overreacts to confrontation, or maybe it's the opposite—that she doesn't recognize risky situations, and feels comfortable only around a lot of drama. So she ends up with a partner who's abusive. Then the pathology moves from the individual level to the household level, because that partner beats their kids, and then their son goes to a school where ten out of thirty kids are experiencing the same thing. Those kids create in the classroom a culture of hitting, of fighting—not just for the ten kids but for all thirty. Then those kids get a little older, and they're teen-agers, and they behave violently, and then they beat *their* kids. And it's just accepted. It becomes a cultural norm. It goes from the individual fight-or-flight adrenaline response to a social culture where it's, like, 'Oh, black people beat our kids. That's what we do.'"

Paradox." Generally, researchers are puzzled by this pattern, but a few explanations have been offered. It may be, for example, that the strong emphasis on social relationships, family support, and religiousness that often characterize the Hispanic American culture increase health resilience among its members (Dubowitz, Bates, & Acevedo-Garcia, 2010; Gallo et al., 2009). Or Hispanic Americans may have a physiological predisposition that heightens their likelihood of better health outcomes. Again, the field is simply not yet clear on the factors at work in this health pattern.

Alexandria Sanguinetti/Magnum Photos

The earlier the better Dr. Nadine Burke examines a young patient at her San Francisco medical clinic.

In the nineteen-sixties, federal policy-makers were influenced by scientific research that established direct connections between childhood disadvantage and diminished educational outcomes. . . . Fifty years later, another generation of scientific advocates has begun to make the case for a broader approach, one that aims at protecting children from both the mental and the physical consequences of early adversity.

Jack P. Shonkoff, a professor of pediatrics at Harvard Medical School, has emerged as a leader of this campaign. . . . [He says], "We now know that adversity early in life can not only disrupt brain circuits that lead to problems with literacy; it can also affect the development of the cardiovascular system and the immune system and metabolic regulatory systems, and lead to not only more problems learning in school but also greater risk for diabetes and hypertension and heart disease and cancer and depression and substance abuse. . . ."

Shonkoff and Burke are still struggling to figure out how to put this new theory into clinical practice. The science does pro-vide powerful evidence that intervening early can improve later outcomes in an individual's health—as well as in his education and his behavior. And researchers working with rats say they have found indications that the physiological effects of stress can be reversed well into adolescence, or even adulthood. But there's not yet a lot of good data to tell us which kinds of interventions are most effective. . . .

Now Burke [and several of her colleagues] are working to open a new center for child services in Bayview-Hunters Point that would include a medical clinic, family-support services, a child-abuse-response program, and an expanded staff of social workers and psychotherapists, as well as space for biofeedback and other stress-reduction therapies. . . . Burke says that the new center is on track to open next year.

Burke's goal is a treatment protocol, like the one doctors use when they're dealing with cancer or diabetes. "For cancer patients, someone comes in, they have stage-four breast cancer, they're BRCA-negative, they have these different types of comor-bid factors," she explained one day last fall. "As a doctor, you can look up that combination of indicators, and you know what to do. I would love to see a treatment protocol that says, you know, this child comes in, she's six years old. She has a history of intrauterine drug exposure and domestic violence." Burke ticked her way down an imaginary medical chart. "She is here today following removal from the home and foster-care place-ment after six years of physical and emotional abuse by dad and neglect by mom. And she's manifesting A, B, and C symp-toms. And you could say, 'O.K., let's start with twelve weeks of biofeedback, overlaid with a one-year course of insight-oriented therapy, and go from there.'" One patient might need to be removed from an abusive home; another might benefit from a course of antidepressants or a better diet. . . .

Burke is realistic about the challenges that [Monisha] and other patients face, and there are plenty of days, she says, when their problems feel overwhelming, even for her. Neverthe-less, she is convinced that her new methodology will give pa-tients a better chance at good health and a good future. . . .

New Psychophysiological Disorders

Clearly, biological, psychological, and sociocultural factors combine to produce psycho–physiological disorders. In fact, the interaction of such factors is now considered the *rule* of bodily functioning, not the exception, and, as the years have passed, more and more illnesses have been added to the list of traditional psychophysiological disorders and researchers have found many links between psychosocial stress and a wide range of physical illnesses. Let's look first at how these links were established and then at *psycho-neuroimmunology,* the area of study that ties stress and illness to the body's immune system.

Are Physical Illnesses Related to Stress?

Back in 1967 two research-ers, Thomas Holmes and Richard Rahe, developed the *Social Adjustment Rating Scale,* which assigns numerical values to the stresses that most people experience at some time in their lives (see Table 6-5). Answers given by a large sample of participants indicated that the most stressful event on the scale is the death of a spouse, which receives a score of 100 *life change units* (*LCUs*). Lower on the scale is retirement (45 LCUs), and still lower is a minor violation of the law (11 LCUs). This scale gave researchers a yardstick for measuring the total amount of stress a person faces over a period of time. If, for example, in the course of a year a woman started a new business (39 LCUs), sent her son off to college (29 LCUs), moved to a new house (20 LCUs), and experienced the death of a close friend (37 LCUs), her stress score for the year would be 125 LCUs, a considerable amount of stress for such a period of time.

With this scale in hand, Holmes and Rahe (1989, 1967) examined the relation-ship between life stress and the onset of illness. They found that the LCU scores of sick people during the year before they fell ill were much higher than those of healthy people. If persons' life changes totaled more than 300 LCUs over the course of a year, they were particularly likely to develop serious health problems.

Using the Social Adjustment Rating Scale or similar scales, studies have since linked stresses of various kinds to a wide range of physical conditions, from trench mouth and upper respiratory infection to cancer (Baum, Trevino, & Dougall, 2011; Rook, August, & Sorkin, 2011). Overall, the greater the amount of life stress, the greater the likelihood of illness (see Figure 6-7). Researchers even have found a relation-ship between traumatic stress and death. Widows and widowers, for example, display an increased risk of death during their period of bereavement (Möller et al., 2011; Rees & Lutkin, 1967; Young et al., 1963). A particularly striking instance of death after the loss of a loved one is seen in the following case:

> Charlie and Josephine had been inseparable companions for 13 years. In a senseless act of violence Charlie, in full view of Josephine, was shot and killed in a melee with police. Josephine first stood motionless, then slowly approached his prostrate form, sunk to her knees, and silently rested her head on the dead and bloody body. Concerned persons attempted to help her away, but she refused to move. Hoping she would soon surmount her overwhelming grief, they let her be. But she never rose again; in 15 minutes she was dead. Now the remarkable part of the story is that Charlie and Josephine were llamas in the zoo! They had escaped from their pen during a snow storm and Charlie, a mean animal to begin with, was shot when he proved unmanageable. I was able to establish from the zoo keeper that to all intents and purposes Josephine had been normally frisky and healthy right up to the moment of the tragic event.
>
> *(Engel, 1968)*

One shortcoming of Holmes and Rahe's Social Adjustment Rating Scale is that it does not take into consideration the particular life stress reactions of specific populations. For example, in their development of the scale, the researchers sampled white Americans predominantly. Few of the respondents were African Americans or Hispanic Americans. But since their ongoing life experiences often differ in key ways, might not members of minority groups and white Americans differ in their stress reactions to various kinds of life events? Research indicates that indeed they do (Bennett & Olugbala, 2010; Johnson, 2010). One study found, for example, that African Americans experience greater stress than white Americans in response to a major personal injury or illness, a major change

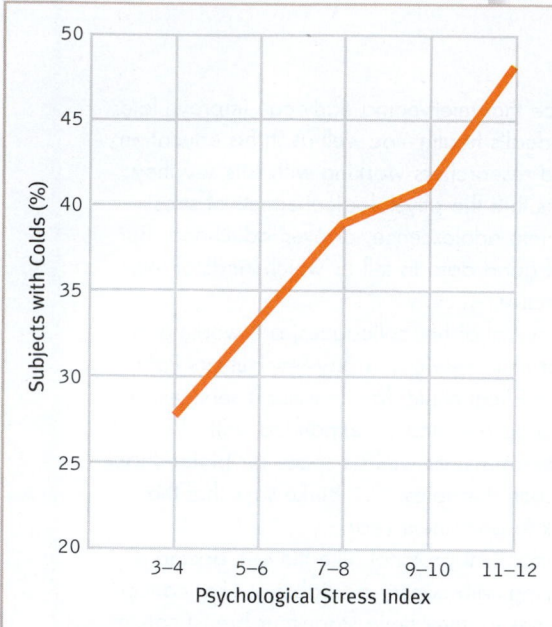

Figure 6-7

Stress and the common cold In a landmark study, healthy individuals were administered nasal drops containing common cold viruses and then quarantined (Cohen et al., 1991). It was found that those participants who had recently experienced higher levels of stress were much more likely to come down with a cold than participants who had experienced fewer recent stressors.

BETWEEN THE LINES

Stress and Coping: Eye on Culture

- 57 percent of American Indians and African Americans feel stressed by finances, compared to 47 percent of the entire American population. ‹‹

- 41 percent of Hispanic Americans feel stressed by employment issues, compared to 32 percent of the entire American population. ‹‹

(MHA, 2010, 2008)

table: 6-5

Most Stressful Life Events

Adults: Social Adjustment Rating Scale*	Students: Undergraduate Stress Questionnaire†
1. Death of spouse	1. Death (family member or friend)
2. Divorce	2. Had a lot of tests
3. Marital separation	3. It's finals week
4. Jail term	4. Applying to graduate school
5. Death of close family member	5. Victim of a crime
6. Personal injury or illness	6. Assignments in all classes due the same day
7. Marriage	7. Breaking up with boy-/girlfriend
8. Fired at work	8. Found out boy-/girlfriend cheated on you
9. Marital reconciliation	9. Lots of deadlines to meet
10. Retirement	10. Property stolen
11. Change in health of family member	11. You have a hard upcoming week
12. Pregnancy	12. Went into a test unprepared
13. Sex difficulties	13. Lost something (especially wallet)
14. Gain of new family member	14. Death of a pet
15. Business readjustment	15. Did worse than expected on test
16. Change in financial state	16. Had an interview
17. Death of close friend	17. Had projects, research papers due
18. Change to different line of work	18. Did badly on a test
19. Change in number of arguments with spouse	19. Parents getting divorce
20. Mortgage over $10,000	20. Dependent on other people
21. Foreclosure of mortgage or loan	21. Having roommate conflicts
22. Change in responsibilities at work	22. Car/bike broke down, flat tire, etc.
*Full scale has 43 items. Source: Holmes & Rahe, 1967.	†Full scale has 83 items. Source: Crandall et al., 1992.

in work responsibilities, or a major change in living conditions (Komaroff et al., 1989, 1986). Similarly, studies have shown that women and men differ in their reactions to a number of life changes (Wang et al., 2007; Miller & Rahe, 1997).

Finally, college students may face stressors that are different from those listed in the Social Adjustment Rating Scale. Instead of having marital difficulties, being fired, or applying for a job, a college student may have trouble with a roommate, fail a course, or apply to graduate school. When researchers use special scales to measure life events in this population, they find the expected relationships between stressful events and illness (Roddenberry & Renk, 2010; Crandall et al., 1992) (see Table 6-5 again).

Psychoneuroimmunology
How do stressful events result in a viral or bacterial infection? An area of study called **psychoneuroimmunology** seeks to answer this question by uncovering the links between psychosocial stress, the immune system, and health.

The **immune system** is the body's network of activities and cells that identify and destroy **antigens**—foreign invaders, such as bacteria, viruses, fungi, and parasites—and cancer cells. Among the most important cells in this system are billions of **lymphocytes,** white blood cells that circulate through the lymph system and the bloodstream.

•**psychoneuroimmunology**•The study of the connections between stress, the body's immune system, and illness.

•**immune system**•The body's network of activities and cells that identify and destroy antigens and cancer cells.

•**antigen**•A foreign invader of the body, such as a bacterium or virus.

•**lymphocytes**•White blood cells that circulate through the lymph system and bloodstream, helping the body identify and destroy antigens and cancer cells.

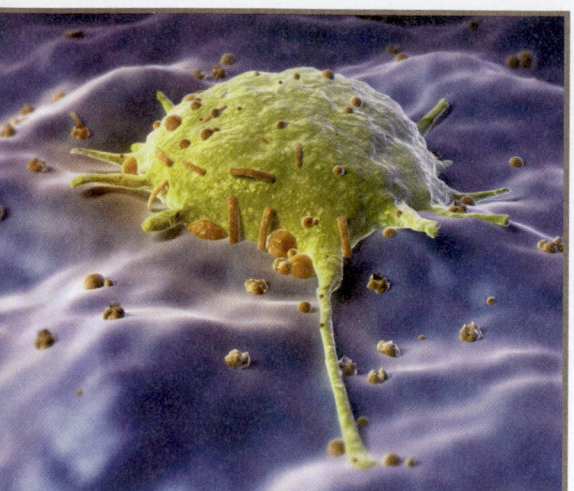

First line of defense

How do lymphocytes meet up with invading antigens? The lymphocytes are first alerted by *macrophages,* a group of big white blood cells in the immune system that recognize an antigen, engulf it, break it down, and hand off its dissected parts to the lymphocytes. Here a macrophage stretches its long "arms" (pseudopods) to detect and capture the suspected antigens.

When stimulated by antigens, lymphocytes spring into action to help the body overcome the invaders.

One group of lymphocytes, called *helper T-cells,* identifies antigens and then multiplies and triggers the production of other kinds of immune cells. Another group, *natural killer T-cells,* seeks out and destroys body cells that have already been infected by viruses, thus helping to stop the spread of a viral infection. A third group of lymphocytes, *B-cells,* produces *antibodies,* protein molecules that recognize and bind to antigens, mark them for destruction, and prevent them from causing infection.

Researchers now believe that stress can interfere with the activity of lymphocytes, slowing them down and thus increasing a person's susceptibility to viral and bacterial infections (Dhabhar, 2011). In a landmark study, investigator Roger Bartrop and his colleagues (1977) in New South Wales, Australia, compared the immune systems of 26 people whose spouses had died eight weeks earlier with those of 26 matched control group participants whose spouses had not died. Blood samples revealed that lymphocyte functioning was much lower in the bereaved people than in the controls. Still other studies have shown slow immune functioning in persons who are exposed to long-term stress. For example, researchers have found poorer immune functioning among people who face the challenge of providing ongoing care for a relative with Alzheimer's disease (Lovell & Wetherall, 2011; Kiecolt-Glaser et al., 2002, 1996).

These studies seem to be telling a remarkable story. During periods when healthy individuals happened to experience unusual levels of stress, they remained healthy on the surface, but their experiences apparently slowed their immune systems so that they became susceptible to illness. If stress affects our capacity to fight off illness, it is no wonder that researchers have repeatedly found a relationship between life stress and illnesses of various kinds. But why and when does stress interfere with the immune system? Several factors influence whether stress will result in a slowdown of the system, including *biochemical activity, behavioral changes, personality style,* and *degree of social support.*

BIOCHEMICAL ACTIVITY Excessive activity of the neurotransmitter *norepinephrine* apparently contributes to slowdowns of the immune system. Remember that stress leads to increased activity by the sympathetic nervous system, including an increase in the release of norepinephrine throughout the brain and body. Research indicates that if stress continues for an extended time, norepinephrine eventually travels to receptors

Everyone is vulnerable to stress

A male koala receives a swab test at the Sydney Wildlife World in Australia to detect an often-fatal disease called chlamydiosis. Chlamydiosis is caused by a virus that often breaks out in koalas when their immune systems are weakened during times of stress, such as when they are forced to find new habitats. Fewer than 100,000 koalas are now left in Australia, down from millions of them two centuries ago.

on certain lymphocytes and gives them an *inhibitory message* to stop their activity, thus slowing down immune functioning (Groer, Meagher, & Kendall-Tickett, 2010; Lekander, 2002).

In a similar manner, *corticosteroids*—cortisol and other so-called stress hormones—apparently contribute to poorer immune system functioning. Remember that when a person is under stress, the adrenal glands release corticosteroids. As in the case of norepinephrine, if stress continues for an extended time, the stress hormones eventually travel to receptor sites located on certain lymphocytes and give an inhibitory message, again causing a slowdown of the activity of the lymphocytes (Groer et al., 2010; Bauer, 2005; Bellinger et al., 1994).

Recent research has further indicated that another action of the corticosteroids is to trigger an increase in the production of *cytokines,* proteins that bind to receptors throughout the body. At moderate levels of stress, the cytokines, another key player in the immune system, help combat infection. But as stress continues and more corticosteroids are released, the growing production and spread of cytokines lead to *chronic inflammation* throughout the body, contributing at times to heart disease, stroke, and other illnesses (Brooks et al., 2011; Burg & Pickering, 2011).

BEHAVIORAL CHANGES Stress may set in motion a series of behavioral changes that indirectly affect the immune system. Some people under stress may, for example, become anxious or depressed, perhaps even develop an anxiety or mood disorder. As a result, they may sleep badly, eat poorly, exercise less, or smoke or drink more—behaviors known to slow down the immune system (Brooks et al., 2011; Kibler, Joshi, & Hughes, 2010).

PERSONALITY STYLE According to research, people who generally respond to life stress with optimism, constructive coping, and resilience—that is, people who welcome challenges and are willing to take control in their daily encounters—experience better immune system functioning and are better prepared to fight off illness (Kern & Friedman, 2011; Williams et al., 2011). Some studies have found, for example, that people with "hardy" or resilient personalities remain healthy after stressful events, while those whose personalities are less hardy seem more susceptible to illness (Bonanno & Mancini, 2010; Ouellette & DiPlacido, 2001). Researchers have even discovered that men with a general sense of hopelessness die at above-average rates from heart disease and other causes (Kangelaris

Student stress-busters: East and West
According to research, frequent testing is the second most stressful life event for high school and college students. To reduce such stress, college applicants from Beijing give each other head massages in preparation for China's college entrance exams (above). In the meantime, students at a dorm at Northwestern University in the United States try to blow off steam by performing "primal screams" during their final exam period (right).

•**behavioral medicine**•A field that combines psychological and physical interventions to treat or prevent medical problems.

et al., 2010; Everson et al., 1996). Similarly, a growing body of research suggests that people who are spiritual tend to be healthier than individuals without spiritual beliefs, and a few studies have linked spirituality to better immune system functioning (Jackson & Bergeman, 2011; Cadge & Fair, 2010).

In related work, researchers have found a relationship between certain personality characteristics and an individual's ability to cope effectively with cancer (Baum et al., 2011; Floyd et al., 2011). They have found, for example, that patients with certain forms of cancer who display a helpless coping style and who cannot easily express their feelings, particularly anger, tend to experience a poorer quality of life in the face of their disease than patients who do express their emotions. A few investigators have even suggested a relationship between personality and cancer *outcome,* but this claim has not been supported clearly by research (Kern & Friedman, 2011; Urcuyo et al., 2005).

SOCIAL SUPPORT Finally, people who have few social supports and feel lonely seem to display poorer immune functioning in the face of stress than people who do not feel lonely (Uchino & Birmingham, 2011; Cohen, 2002). In a pioneering study, medical students were given the *UCLA Loneliness Scale* and then divided into "high" and "low" loneliness groups (Kiecolt-Glaser et al., 1984). The high-loneliness group showed lower lymphocyte responses during a final exam period.

Other studies have found that social support and affiliation may actually help protect people from stress, poor immune system functioning, and subsequent illness or help speed up recovery from illness or surgery (Rook et al., 2011). Similarly, some studies have suggested that patients with certain forms of cancer who receive social support in their personal lives or supportive therapy often have better immune system functioning and, in turn, more successful recoveries than patients without such supports (Dagan et al., 2011; Kim et al., 2010; Spiegel & Fawzy, 2002).

Psychological Treatments for Physical Disorders

As clinicians have discovered that stress and related psychosocial factors may contribute to physical disorders, they have applied psychological treatments to more and more medical problems. The most common of these interventions are relaxation training, biofeedback, meditation, hypnosis, cognitive interventions, support groups, and therapies to increase awareness and expression of emotions. The field of treatment that combines psychological and physical approaches to treat or prevent medical problems is known as **behavioral medicine.**

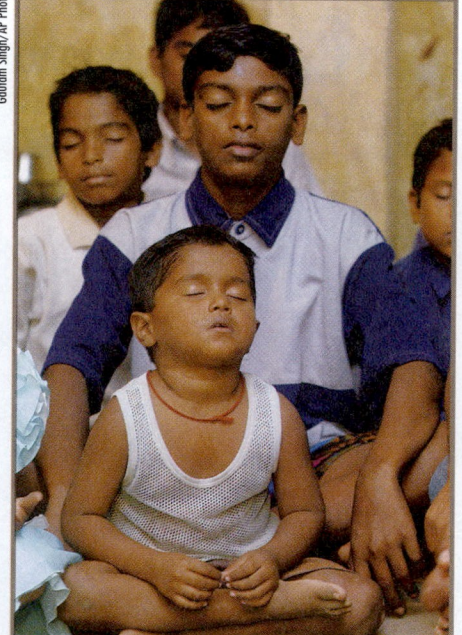

Relaxation Training
As you saw in Chapter 5, people can be taught to relax their muscles at will, a process that sometimes reduces feelings of anxiety. Given the positive effects of relaxation on anxiety and the nervous system, clinicians believe that *relaxation training* can help prevent or treat medical illnesses that are related to stress.

Relaxation training, often in combination with medication, has been widely used in the treatment of high blood pressure (Moffatt et al., 2010; Stetter & Kupper, 2002). It has also been of some help in treating headaches, insomnia, asthma, diabetes, pain after surgery, certain vascular diseases, and the undesirable effects of certain cancer treatments (Nezu et al., 2011; Devineni & Blanchard, 2005).

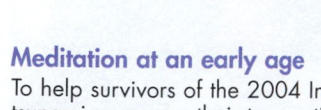

Meditation at an early age
To help survivors of the 2004 Indian Ocean tsunami overcome their traumatic ordeal, the Art and Living Foundation organized meditation sessions throughout Asia. In this session a 4-year-old Indian child, along with several older survivors, learns how to meditate, with the hope that this technique, among others, will help prevent the onset of physical and psychological disorders.

Biofeedback As you also saw in Chapter 5, patients given *biofeedback training* are connected to machinery that gives them continuous readings about their involuntary body activities. This information enables them gradually to gain control over those activities. Somewhat helpful in the treatment of anxiety disorders, the procedure has also been applied to a growing number of physical disorders.

In a classic study, *electromyograph* (*EMG*) feedback was used to treat 16 patients who were experiencing facial pain caused in part by tension in their jaw muscles (Dohrmann & Laskin, 1978). In an EMG procedure, electrodes are attached to a person's muscles so that the muscle contractions are detected and converted into a tone for the individual to hear (see pages 125–126). Changes in the pitch and volume of the tone indicate changes in muscle tension. After "listening" to EMG feedback repeatedly, the 16 patients in this study learned how to relax their jaw muscles at will and later reported a reduction in facial pain.

EMG feedback has also been used successfully in the treatment of headaches and muscular disabilities caused by strokes or accidents. Still other forms of biofeedback training have been of some help in the treatment of heartbeat irregularities, asthma, migraine headaches, high blood pressure, stuttering, and pain (Stokes & Lappin, 2010; Martin, 2002; Moss, 2002).

Meditation Although meditation has been practiced since ancient times, Western health care professionals have only recently become aware of its effectiveness in relieving physical distress. *Meditation* is a technique of turning one's concentration inward, achieving a slightly changed state of consciousness, and temporarily ignoring all stressors. In the most common approach, meditators go to a quiet place, assume a comfortable posture, utter or think a particular sound (called a *mantra*) to help focus their attention, and allow their minds to turn away from all outside thoughts and concerns. Many people who meditate regularly report feeling more peaceful, engaged, and creative. Meditation has been used to help manage pain and to treat high blood pressure, heart problems, asthma, skin disorders, diabetes, insomnia, and even viral infections (Gregoski et al., 2011; Stein, 2003; Andresen, 2000).

One form of meditation that has been applied in particular to patients suffering from severe pain is *mindfulness meditation* (Labbé, 2011; Kabat-Zinn, 2005). Here meditators pay attention to the feelings, thoughts, and sensations that are flowing through their minds during meditation, but they do so with detachment and objectivity and, most

Fighting HIV on all fronts
As part of his treatment at the Wellness Center in San Francisco, this man meditates and writes letters to his HIV virus.

BETWEEN THE LINES

Room with a View

According to one hospital's records of individuals who underwent gallbladder surgery, those in rooms with a good view from their window had shorter hospitalizations and needed fewer pain medications than those in rooms without a good view (Ulrich, 1984). ‹‹

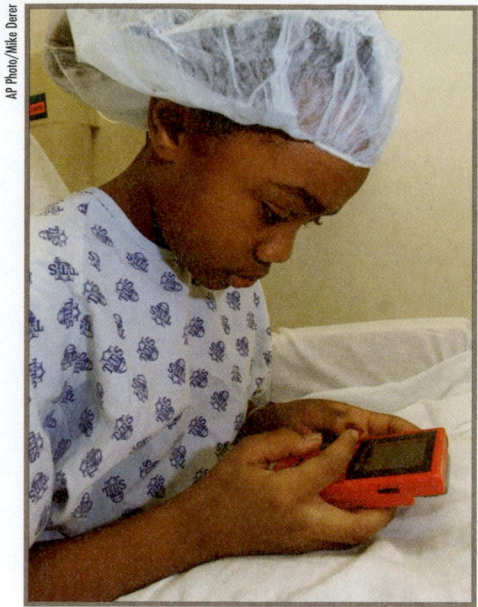

The power of distraction

Researchers at a medical center in New Jersey had this 10-year-old girl and other young presurgical patients play with handheld Game Boys while waiting for their anesthesia to take effect. It was found that such game-playing was more effective than antianxiety drugs or parent hand-holding at relaxing the young patients. Still other research suggests that patients who are more relaxed often have better surgical outcomes.

importantly, without judgment. By just being mindful but not judgmental of their feelings and thoughts, including feelings of pain, they are less inclined to label them, fixate on them, or react negatively to them.

Hypnosis As you saw in Chapter 1, individuals who undergo *hypnosis* are guided by a hypnotist into a sleeplike, suggestible state during which they can be directed to act in unusual ways, experience unusual sensations, remember seemingly forgotten events, or forget remembered events. With training some people are even able to induce their own hypnotic state (*self-hypnosis*). Hypnosis is now used as an aid to psychotherapy and to help treat many physical conditions.

Hypnosis seems to be particularly helpful in the control of pain (Gatchel, Howard, & Haggard, 2011; Jensen et al., 2011). One case study describes a patient who underwent dental surgery under hypnotic suggestion: After a hypnotic state was induced, the dentist suggested to the patient that he was in a pleasant and relaxed setting listening to a friend describe his own success at undergoing similar dental surgery under hypnosis. The dentist then proceeded to perform a successful 25-minute operation (Gheorghiu & Orleanu, 1982). Although only some people are able to undergo surgery while anesthetized by hypnosis alone, hypnosis combined with chemical forms of anesthesia is apparently helpful to many patients (Lang, 2010). Beyond its use in the control of pain, hypnosis has been used successfully to help treat such problems as skin diseases, asthma, insomnia, high blood pressure, warts, and other forms of infection (Gupta & Levenson, 2010; Modlin, 2002; Hornyak & Green, 2000).

Cognitive Interventions People with physical ailments have sometimes been taught new attitudes or cognitive responses toward their ailments as part of treatment (Nezu et al., 2011; Diefenbach et al., 2010). For example, an approach called *self-instruction training,* or *stress inoculation training,* has helped patients cope with severe pain (D'Arienzo, 2010; Meichenbaum, 1997, 1993, 1977, 1975). In this training therapists teach people to identify and eventually rid themselves of unpleasant thoughts that keep emerging during pain episodes (so-called *negative self-statements,* such as "Oh, no, I can't take this pain") and to replace them with *coping self-statements* instead (for example, "When pain comes, just pause; keep focusing on what you have to do").

Emotion Expression and Support Groups If anxiety, depression, anger, and the like contribute to a person's physical ills, interventions to reduce these negative emotions should help reduce the ills. Thus it is not surprising that some medically ill people have profited from support groups and from therapies that guide them to become more aware of and express their emotions and needs (Bell et al., 2010; Hsu et al., 2010; Antoni, 2005). Research suggests that the discussion, or even the writing down, of past and present emotions or upsets may help improve a person's health, just as it may help one's psychological functioning (Kelly & Barry, 2010; Smyth & Pennebaker, 2001). In one study, asthma and arthritis patients who wrote down their thoughts and feelings about stressful events for a handful of days showed lasting improvements in their conditions. Similarly, stress-related writing was found to be beneficial for patients with either HIV infections or cancer (Corter & Petrie, 2011; Petrie et al., 2004).

Combination Approaches Studies have found that the various psychological interventions for physical problems tend to be equal in effectiveness (Devineni & Blanchard, 2005). Relaxation and biofeedback training, for example, are equally helpful (and more helpful than placebos) in the treatment of high blood pressure, headaches, and asthma. Psychological interventions are, in fact, often of greatest help when they are combined with other psychological interventions and with medical treatments (Jensen et al., 2011; Hembree & Foa, 2010). In a classic study, ulcer patients who were given relaxation, self-instruction, and assertiveness training along with medication were found to be less anxious and more comfortable, to have fewer symptoms, and to have a better long-term outcome than patients who received medication only (Brooks & Richardson, 1980). Combination interventions have also been helpful in changing Type A patterns and in reducing the risk of coronary heart disease among people who display Type A kinds of behavior (Burke & Riley, 2010; Harlapur et al., 2010; Cohen et al., 1997).

Clearly, the treatment picture for physical illnesses has been changing dramatically. While medical treatments continue to dominate, today's medical practitioners are traveling a course far removed from that of their counterparts in centuries past.

PUTTING IT... together

Expanding the Boundaries of Abnormal Psychology

The concept of stress is familiar to everyone, yet only in recent decades have clinical scientists and practitioners had much success in understanding and treating it and recognizing its powerful impact on our functioning. Now that the impact of stress has been identified, however, research efforts in this area are moving forward at near-lightning speed. What researchers once saw as a vague connection between stress and psychological dysfunctioning or between stress and physical illness is now understood as a complex interaction of many variables. Such factors as life changes, individual psychological states, social support, biochemical activity, and slowing of the immune system are all recognized as contributors to psychological and physical stress disorders.

Insights into the treatment of the various stress disorders have been accumulating just as rapidly. In recent years clinicians have learned that a combination of approaches—from drug therapy to behavioral techniques to community interventions—may be of help to people with acute and posttraumatic stress disorders. Similarly, psychological approaches such as relaxation training and cognitive therapy are being applied to various physical ills, usually in combination with traditional medical treatments. Small wonder that many practitioners are convinced that such treatment combinations will eventually be the norm in treating the majority of physical ailments.

One of the most exciting aspects of these recent developments is the field's growing emphasis on the *interrelationship* of the social environment, the brain, and the rest of the body. Researchers have observed repeatedly that mental disorders are often best understood and treated when sociocultural, psychological, and biological factors are all taken into consideration. They now know that this interaction also helps explain medical problems. We are reminded that the brain is part of the body and that both are part of a social context. For better and for worse, the three are closely linked.

Another exciting aspect of this work on stress and its wide-ranging impact is the interest it has sparked in *illness prevention* and *health promotion* (Bowen & Boehmer, 2010; Weidner & Kendel, 2010). If stress is indeed key to the development of both psychological and physical disorders, perhaps such disorders can be prevented by eliminating or reducing stress—for example, by helping people to cope better generally or by better preparing their bodies for stress's impact (Carver, 2011). With this notion in mind, illness prevention and health promotion programs are now being developed around the world. Clinical theorists have, for example, designed school-curriculum programs to help promote *social competence* in children and to teach children more *optimistic ways of thinking.* Similarly, to help head off acute and posttraumatic stress disorders down the line, some military psychologists have developed the Comprehensive Soldier Fitness program, a program that seeks to build resilience in soldiers prior to their combat experiences (Cornum et al., 2011; Reivich et al., 2011).

Amidst these exciting and rapidly unfolding developments also lies a cautionary tale. When problems are studied heavily, it is common for the public, as well as some researchers and clinicians, to draw conclusions that may be too bold. In the psychological realm, for example, many individuals—perhaps too many—are now receiving diagnoses of posttraumatic stress disorder partly because the symptoms of the disorder are many, a variety of life events can be considered traumatic, and the disorder has received so much attention (Wakefield & Horwitz, 2010).

Similarly, given the growing body of work on psychophysiological disorders and psychoneuroimmunology, some people, including a number of clinicians, are all too

Dominic Lipinski/PA Wire URN:9802817 (Press Association via AP Images)

Can Facebook trigger asthma attacks?
Yes, according to a case reported by three physicians in the medical journal *Lancet.* The physicians described a depressed 18-year-old in Italy who was dumped by his girlfriend and then saw her picture on Facebook. That sighting triggered an asthma attack, which was repeated each time he logged on and accessed his ex's profile. Although the case report prompted warnings about the psychological dangers of social networking sites, the villain here seems to be stress—from whatever source.

quick to explain medical problems by pointing simplistically to psychosocial factors such as counterproductive attitudes, too little faith, or lack of social support. Explanations of this kind reflect a misapplication of the complex research that has been unfolding in the study of stress and health.

We shall see such potential problems again when we look at other forms of pathology that are currently receiving great focus, such as bipolar disorder among children, attention-deficit/hyperactivity disorder, repressed memories of childhood abuse, and dissociative identity disorder. The line between enlightenment and overenthusiasm is often thin.

Summing Up

- **EFFECTS OF STRESS** When we appraise a *stressor* as threatening, we often experience a *stress response* consisting of arousal and a sense of fear. The features of arousal and fear are set in motion by the *hypothalamus*, a brain area that activates the *autonomic nervous system* and the *endocrine system*. There are two pathways by which these systems produce arousal and fear—the *sympathetic nervous system* pathway and the *hypothalamic-pituitary-adrenal* pathway. *pp. 154–156*

- **PSYCHOLOGICAL STRESS DISORDERS** People with *acute stress disorder* or *posttraumatic stress disorder* react with arousal, anxiety and mood problems, and other stress symptoms after a traumatic event, including reexperiencing the traumatic event, avoiding related events, being markedly less responsive than normal, and feeling guilt. Traumatic events may include *combat experiences, disasters*, or episodes of *victimization*. The symptoms of *acute stress disorder* begin soon after the trauma and last less than a month. Those of *posttraumatic stress disorder* may begin at any time (even years) after the trauma and may last for months or years.

  In attempting to explain why some people develop a psychological stress disorder and others do not, researchers have focused on *biological factors, personality, childhood experiences, social support, multicultural factors*, and the *severity of the traumatic event*. Techniques used to treat the stress disorders include drug therapy, behavioral exposure, cognitive and other insight therapies, family therapy, and group therapy (including *rap groups* for combat veterans). Rapidly mobilized community interventions often follow the principles of *critical incident stress debriefing*. Such approaches initially appeared helpful after large-scale disasters; however, some recent studies have raised questions about their usefulness. *pp. 157–169*

- **PSYCHOPHYSIOLOGICAL DISORDERS** *Psychophysiological disorders* are stress-induced disorders in which psychosocial and physiological factors interact to cause or worsen a physical problem. Factors linked to these disorders are biological factors, such as defects in the autonomic nervous system or particular organs; psychological factors, such as particular needs, attitudes, or personality styles; and sociocultural factors, such as aversive social conditions and cultural pressures.

  For years clinical researchers singled out a limited number of physical illnesses as psychophysiological. These traditional psychophysiological disorders include *ulcers, asthma, insomnia, chronic headaches, hypertension*, and *coronary heart disease*. Recently many other psychophysiological disorders have been identified. Scientists have linked many physical illnesses to stress and have developed a new area of study called *psychoneuroimmunology*. *pp. 169–179*

- **PSYCHONEUROIMMUNOLOGY** The body's *immune system* consists of *lymphocytes* and other cells that fight off *antigens*—bacteria, viruses, and other foreign invaders—and cancer cells. Stress can slow *lymphocyte* activity, thereby interfering with the immune system's ability to protect against illness during times of stress. Factors that seem to affect immune functioning include *norepinephrine and corticosteroid activity, behavioral changes, personality style*, and *social support*. *pp. 179–182*

■ **PSYCHOLOGICAL TREATMENTS FOR PHYSICAL DISORDERS** *Behavioral medicine* combines psychological and physical interventions to treat or prevent medical problems. Psychological approaches such as *relaxation training, biofeedback training, meditation, hypnosis, cognitive techniques, support groups, and therapies that heighten the awareness and expression of emotions and needs* are increasingly being included in the treatment of various medical problems. *pp. 182–185*

■ **ILLNESS PREVENTION AND HEALTH PROMOTION** In recent years clinicians increasingly have designed programs that aim to eliminate or reduce stress by helping people generally to cope better or to prepare their bodies for stress's impact. The logic behind such programs is that the better people handle stress, the less likely they will be to develop the psychological and physical disorders that often result from stress. *pp. 185–186*

PsychPortal

Visit **PsychPortal**
www.yourpsychportal.com
to access the e-book, videocases and other case materials and activities, and study aids, including flashcards, crossword puzzles, quizzes, FAQs, and research exercises.

DISORDERS FOCUSING ON SOMATIC AND DISSOCIATIVE SYMPTOMS

Brian was spending Saturday sailing with his wife, Helen. The water was rough but well within what they considered safe limits. They were having a wonderful time and really didn't notice that the sky was getting darker, the wind blowing harder, and the sailboat becoming more difficult to control. After a few hours of sailing, they found themselves far from shore in the middle of a powerful and dangerous storm.

The storm intensified very quickly. Brian had trouble controlling the sailboat amidst the high winds and wild waves. He and Helen tried to put on the safety jackets they had neglected to wear earlier, but the boat turned over before they were finished. Brian, the better swimmer of the two, was able to swim back to the overturned sailboat, grab the side, and hold on for dear life, but Helen simply could not overcome the rough waves and reach the boat. As Brian watched in horror and disbelief, his wife disappeared from view.

After a time, the storm began to lose its strength. Brian managed to right the sailboat and sail back to shore. Finally he reached safety, but the personal consequences of this storm were just beginning. The next days were filled with pain and further horror: the Coast Guard finding Helen's body . . . texts, emails, and conversations with family members and friends . . . self-blame . . . grief . . . and more.

Compounding this horror, the accident had left Brian with a severe physical impairment—he could not walk properly. He first noticed this terrible impairment when he sailed the boat back to shore, right after the accident. As he tried to run from the sailboat to get help, he could hardly make his legs work. By the time he reached the nearby beach restaurant, all he could do was crawl. Two patrons had to lift him to a chair, and after he told his story and the authorities were alerted, he had to be taken to a hospital.

At first Brian and the hospital physician assumed that he must have been hurt during the accident. One by one, however, the hospital tests revealed nothing—no broken bones, no spinal damage, nothing. Nothing that could explain such severe impairment.

By the following morning, the weakness in his legs had become near paralysis. Because the physicians could not pin down the nature of his injuries, they decided to keep his activities to a minimum. He was not allowed to talk long with the police. To his deep regret, he was not even permitted to attend Helen's funeral.

The mystery deepened over the following days and weeks. As Brian's paralysis continued, he became more and more withdrawn, unable to see more than a few friends and family members and unable to take care of the many unpleasant tasks attached to Helen's death. He could not bring himself to return to work or get on with his life. Texting, emailing, and phone conversations slowly came to a halt. At most, he was able to go online and surf the Internet. Almost from the beginning, Brian's paralysis had left him self-absorbed and drained of emotion, unable to look back and unable to move forward.

In the previous two chapters you saw how stress and anxiety can negatively affect functioning. Indeed, anxiety is the key feature of disorders such as generalized anxiety disorder, phobias, and panic disorder. And stress can produce the lingering reactions seen in acute stress disorder, posttraumatic stress disorder, and psychophysiological disorders. Stress and anxiety also contribute to several other kinds of disorders, particularly disorders that focus on somatic and dissociative symptoms—the subject of this chapter.

Disorders focusing on somatic symptoms include *factitious disorder, conversion disorder, somatic symptom disorder, illness anxiety disorder,* and *body dysmorphic disorder.* The first four of these disorders are listed in DSM-5 within a group called "somatic symptom and related disorders." The last of the disorders, body dysmorphic disorder, is listed within the group called "obsessive-compulsive-related disorders," as you read in Chapter 5. In these disorders, the somatic symptoms are primarily caused by psychosocial factors or the symptoms trigger excessive anxiety and concern. They are different from *psychophysiological disorders,* the patterns you read about in the previous chapter. In psychophysiological disorders, psychosocial factors interact with genuine physical ailments to produce or worsen significant medical problems. In contrast, in cases of factitious disorder and conversion disorder, psychological symptoms masquerade as physical ones, and in cases of somatic symptom disorder, illness anxiety disorder, and body dysmorphic disorder, the clinical focus is on the disproportionate upset caused by somatic symptoms.

Disorders focusing on dissociative symptoms include *dissociative amnesia, dissociative identity disorder,* and *depersonalization-derealization disorder.* These patterns, collectively called *dissociative disorders,* are each characterized by significant memory loss or identity disruption. As you read in the previous chapter, dissociative reactions may also appear in cases of acute or posttraumatic stress disorder, but in the dissociative disorders, these reactions are the main or only symptoms, and the symptoms are particularly intense, extensive, and disruptive.

Disorders that focus on somatic symptoms and those that focus on dissociative symptoms have much in common. Both groups of disorders, for example, may occur in response to severe stress, and both have traditionally been viewed as forms of escape from that stress. In addition, as you will see, a number of individuals suffer from both a somatic-related and a dissociative disorder (Kukla et al., 2010). Indeed, theorists and clinicians often explain and treat the two groups of disorders in similar ways.

Disorders Focusing on Somatic Symptoms

Think back to Brian, the young man whose tragic boating accident left him unable to walk. As medical test after test failed to explain his paralysis, physicians became convinced that the cause of his problem lay elsewhere. When a physical ailment has no apparent medical cause, doctors may suspect that the pattern of physical complaints has more to do with psychological factors than physical ones.

As we noted above, DSM-5 lists a number of psychological disorders in which bodily symptoms or concerns are the primary features of the disorders. In *factitious disorder,* patients intentionally produce or feign physical symptoms. Individuals with *conversion disorder* experience medically unexplained physical symptoms that affect their voluntary motor or sensory functioning. People with *somatic symptom disorder* become disproportionately concerned, distressed, and disrupted by bodily symptoms. In *illness anxiety disorder,* health-anxious individuals become preoccupied with the notion that they are seriously ill despite the absence of bodily symptoms. And persons with *body dysmorphic disorder* become preoccupied that some aspect of their physical appearance is defective.

Factitious Disorder

Like Brian, people who become physically impaired or sick usually come to the attention of a physician. Sometimes, however, the physician cannot find a medical cause for the problem and may suspect that other factors are involved. Perhaps the patient is *malingering*—intentionally feigning illness to achieve some external gain, such as financial compensation or deferment from military service (McCullumsmith & Ford, 2011).

Alternatively, a patient may intentionally produce or feign physical symptoms from a wish to be a patient; that is, the motivation for assuming the sick role may be the role itself. Physicians would then decide that the patient is manifesting **factitious disorder** (see Table 7-1). Consider, for example, the symptoms of this lab technician:

A 29-year-old female laboratory technician was admitted to the medical service via the emergency room because of bloody urine. The patient said that she was being treated for lupus erythematosus by a physician in a different city. She also mentioned that she had had Von Willebrand's disease (a rare hereditary blood disorder) as a child. On the third day of her hospitalization, a medical student mentioned to the resident that she had seen this patient several weeks before at a different hospital in the area, where the patient had been admitted for the same problem. A search of the patient's belongings revealed a cache of anticoagulant medication. When confronted with this information she refused to discuss the matter and hurriedly signed out of the hospital against medical advice.

(Spitzer et al., 1981, p. 33)

•factitious disorder• A disorder in which an individual feigns or induces physical or psychological symptoms, typically for the purpose of assuming the role of a sick person.

Factitious disorder is known popularly as *Munchausen syndrome,* a label derived from the exploits of Baron Munchausen, an eighteenth-century cavalry officer who journeyed from tavern to tavern in Europe telling fantastical tales about his supposed military adventures (Ayoub, 2010). People with factitious disorder often go to extremes to create the appearance of illness (APA, 2013, 2012; Boone, 2011). Many give themselves medications secretly. Some, like the woman just described, inject drugs to cause bleeding. Still others use laxatives to produce chronic diarrhea. High fevers are especially easy to create. In a classic study of patients with prolonged mysterious fever, more than 9 percent were eventually diagnosed with factitious disorder (Feldman et al., 1994).

People with factitious disorder often research their supposed ailments and are impressively knowledgeable about medicine (Miner & Feldman, 1998). Many eagerly undergo painful testing or treatment, even surgery (McDermott et al., 2012). When confronted with evidence that their symptoms are factitious, they typically deny the charges and leave the hospital; they may enter another hospital the same day.

Clinical researchers have had a hard time determining the prevalence of factitious disorder since patients hide the true nature of their problem. Overall, the pattern appears to be more common in women than men. Severe cases, however, may be more frequent among men. The disorder usually begins during early adulthood.

Factitious disorder seems to be particularly common among people who (1) received extensive treatment for a medical problem as children, (2) carry a grudge against the medical profession, or (3) have worked as a nurse, laboratory technician, or medical aide. A number have poor social support, few enduring social relationships, and little family life (McDermott et al., 2012; Feldman et al., 1994).

The precise causes of factitious disorder are not understood, although clinical reports have pointed to factors such as depression, unsupportive parental relationships during childhood, and an extreme need for social support that is not otherwise available (McDermott et al., 2012; Ozden & Canat, 1999; Feldman et al., 1994). Nor have clinicians been able to develop dependably effective treatments for this disorder (McDermott et al., 2012; Feldman & Feldman, 1995).

Psychotherapists and medical practitioners often report feelings of annoyance or anger toward people with factitious disorder, feeling that these people are, at the very least, wasting their time. Yet people with the disorder feel they have no control over the problem, and they often experience great distress.

In a related pattern, *factitious disorder imposed on another,* known popularly as *Munchausen syndrome by proxy,* parents or caretakers make up or produce physical illnesses in their children, leading in some cases to repeated painful diagnostic tests, medication, and surgery (Bass & Jones, 2011; Ayoub, 2010). If the children are removed from their parents and placed in the care of others, their symptoms disappear (see *PsychWatch* on the next page).

Should society treat or punish those parents who produce Munchausen syndrome by proxy in their children?

table: 7-1

DSM-5 Checklist

Factitious Disorder Imposed on Self

1. Deceptive falsification of physical or psychological symptoms, or deceptive production of injury or disease, even in the absence of external rewards.

2. Presentation of oneself as ill, impaired, or injured.

Factitious Disorder Imposed on Another

1. Deceptive falsification of physical or psychological symptoms, or deceptive production of injury or disease, in another person, even in the absence of external rewards.

2. Presentation of another person (victim) as ill, impaired, or injured.

Based on APA, 2013, 2012.

PsychWatch

Munchausen Syndrome by Proxy

[Jennifer] had been hospitalized 200 times and undergone 40 operations. Physicians removed her gallbladder, her appendix and part of her intestines, and inserted tubes into her chest, stomach and intestines. [The 9-year-old from Florida] was befriended by the Florida Marlins and served as a poster child for health care reform, posing with Hillary Rodham Clinton at a White House rally. Then police notified her mother that she was under investigation for child abuse. Suddenly, Jennifer's condition improved dramatically. In the next nine months, she was hospitalized only once, for a viral infection. . . . Experts said Jennifer's numerous baffling infections were "consistent with someone smearing fecal matter" into her feeding line and urinary catheter.

(KATEL & BECK, 1996)

Cases like Jennifer's have horrified the public and called attention to *Munchausen syndrome by proxy*. This form of factious disorder is caused by a caregiver who uses various techniques to induce symptoms in a child—giving the child drugs, tampering with medications, contaminating a feeding tube, or even smothering the child, for example. The illness can take almost any form, but the most common symptoms are bleeding, seizures, asthma, comas, diarrhea, vomiting, "accidental" poisonings, infections, fevers, and sudden infant death syndrome.

Between 6 and 30 percent of the victims of Munchausen syndrome by proxy die as a result of their symptoms, and 8 percent of those who survive are permanently disfigured or physically impaired (Ayoub, 2006; Mitchell, 2001). Psychological, educational, and physical development are also affected (Schreier et al., 2010; Libow & Schreier, 1998).

Convalescent, 1867, by Frank Holl

The syndrome is very hard to diagnose and may be more common than clinicians once thought (Deimel et al., 2012; Day & Moseley, 2010; Feldman, 2004). The parent (usually the mother) seems to be so devoted and caring that others sympathize with and admire her. Yet the physical problems disappear when the child and parent are separated. In many cases siblings of the sick child have also been victimized (Ayoub, 2010, 2006).

What kind of parent carefully inflicts pain and illness on her own child? The typical Munchausen mother is emotionally needy: she craves the attention and praise she receives for her devoted care of her sick child (Ayoub, 2010; Noeker, 2004). She may have little social support outside the medical system. Often the mothers have a medical background of some

kind—perhaps having worked formerly in a doctor's office. A number have medically unexplained physical problems of their own (Bass & Jones, 2011). Typically they deny their actions, even in the face of clear evidence, and refuse to undergo therapy (Bluglass, 2001).

Law enforcement authorities approach Munchausen syndrome by proxy as a crime—a carefully planned form of child abuse (Schreier et al., 2010; Slovenko, 2006). They almost always require that the child be separated from the mother (Ayoub, 2010, 2006). At the same time, a parent who resorts to such actions is seriously disturbed and greatly in need of clinical help. Thus clinical researchers and practitioners must now work to develop clearer insights and more effective treatments for such parents and their young victims.

Conversion Disorder

Think back to Brian, the boating accident victim whose paralysis seemed to defy medical explanation. Eventually, Brian received a diagnosis of **conversion disorder** (see Table 7-2). People with this disorder display physical symptoms that affect voluntary motor or sensory functioning, but the symptoms are inconsistent with known medical diseases (APA, 2013, 2012). In short, the individuals experience neurological-like symptoms—for example, paralysis, blindness, or loss of feeling—that have no neurological basis.

Conversion disorder often is hard, even for physicians, to distinguish from a genuine medical problem (Parish & Yutzy, 2011). In fact, it is always possible that a diagnosis of conversion disorder is a mistake and that the patient's problem has an undetected neuro-

•**conversion disorder**•A disorder in which medically unexplained bodily symptoms affect voluntary motor and sensory functions.

•**somatic symptom disorder**•A disorder in which persons become excessively distressed, concerned, and anxious about bodily symptoms they are experiencing.

logical or other medical cause. Because conversion disorders are so similar to "genuine" medical ailments, physicians sometimes rely on oddities in the patient's medical picture to help distinguish the two (Boone, 2011). The symptoms of a conversion disorder may, for example, be at odds with the way the nervous system is known to work. In a conversion symptom called *glove anesthesia,* numbness begins sharply at the wrist and extends evenly right to the fingertips. As Figure 7-1 shows, real neurological damage is rarely as abrupt or evenly spread out.

The physical effects of a conversion disorder may also differ from those of the corresponding medical problem. For example, when paralysis from the waist down, or paraplegia, is caused by damage to the spinal cord, a person's leg muscles may *atrophy,* or waste away, unless physical therapy is applied. People whose paralysis is the result of a conversion disorder, in contrast, do not usually experience atrophy. Perhaps they exercise their muscles without being aware that they are doing so. Similarly, people with conversion blindness have fewer accidents than people who are organically blind, an indication that they have at least some vision even if they are unaware of it.

Unlike people with factitious disorder, those with conversion disorder do not consciously want or purposely produce their symptoms. Like Brian, they almost always believe that their problems are genuinely medical (Lahman et al., 2010). This pattern is called "conversion" disorder because clinical theorists used to believe that individuals with the disorder are converting psychological needs or conflicts into their neurological-like symptoms. Although some theorists still believe that conversion is at work in the disorder, others prefer alternative kinds of explanations, as you'll see later.

Conversion disorder usually begins between late childhood and young adulthood; it is diagnosed at least twice as often in women as in men. It typically appears suddenly, at times of extreme stress, and lasts a matter of weeks (Kukla et al., 2010). Some research suggests that people who develop the disorder tend to be generally suggestible; many are highly susceptible to hypnotic procedures, for example (Parish & Yutzy, 2011; Roelofs et al., 2002). It is thought to be a rare problem, occurring in at most 5 of every 1,000 persons.

Somatic Symptom Disorder

People with **somatic symptom disorder** become excessively distressed, concerned, and anxious about bodily symptoms that they are experiencing, and their lives are greatly disrupted by the symptoms (APA, 2013, 2012) (see Table 7-3 on the next page). The symptoms are longer-lasting but less dramatic than those found in conversion disorder. In some cases, the somatic symptoms have no known cause; in others, the cause can be identified. Either way, the person's concerns are disproportionate to the seriousness of the bodily problems.

Two patterns of somatic symptom disorder have received particular attention. In one, sometimes called a *somatization pattern,* the individual experiences a large and varied number of bodily symptoms. In the other, called a *predominant pain pattern,* the person's primary bodily problem is the experience of pain.

Somatization Pattern Sheila baffled medical specialists with the wide range of her symptoms:

> Sheila reported having abdominal pain since age 17, necessitating exploratory surgery that yielded no specific diagnosis. She had several pregnancies, each with severe nausea, vomiting, and abdominal pain; she ultimately had a hysterectomy for a "tipped uterus." Since age 40 she had experienced dizziness and "blackouts," which she eventually was told

table: **7-2**

DSM-5 Checklist

Conversion Disorder

1. Presence of one or more symptoms or deficits that affect voluntary or sensory function.

2. Symptoms are found to be inconsistent or incompatible with known neurological or medical disease.

3. Significant distress or impairment.

Based on APA, 2013, 2012.

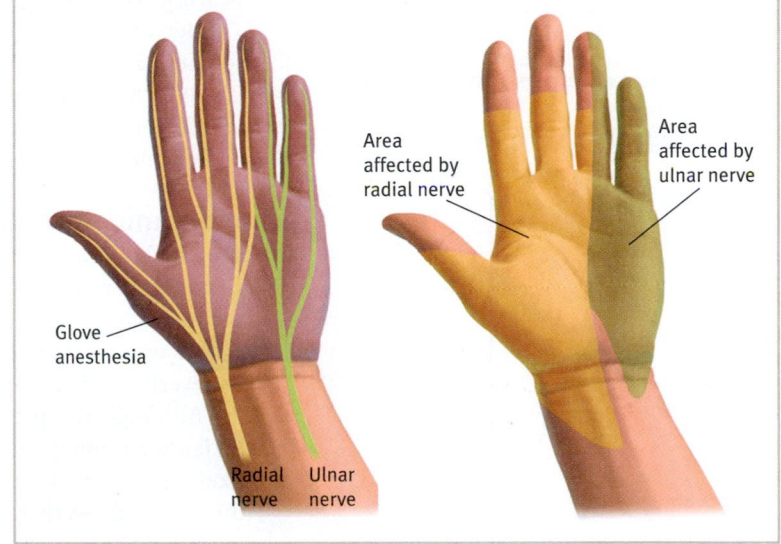

Figure 7-1

Glove anesthesia In this conversion symptom (left) the entire hand, extending from the fingertips to the wrist, becomes numb. Actual physical damage (right) to the ulnar nerve, in contrast, causes anesthesia in the ring finger and little finger and beyond the wrist partway up the arm; damage to the radial nerve causes loss of feeling only in parts of the ring, middle, and index fingers and the thumb and partway up the arm. (Adapted from Gray, 1959.)

table: 7-3

DSM-5 Checklist

Somatic Symptom Disorder

1. Presence of one or more somatic symptoms that are distressing and/or significantly disruptive to daily life.

2. Excessive thoughts, feelings, and behaviors regarding the somatic symptom(s) or related health concerns, including one of the following:

   - Disproportionate and persistent thoughts about the seriousness of the symptoms

   - Persistent and high anxiety about health or the symptoms

   - Excessive time and energy devoted to the symptoms or health concerns

3. Symptoms are persistent, although not necessarily continuous, typically lasting more than 6 months.

Based on APA, 2013, 2012.

---

might be multiple sclerosis or a brain tumor. She continued to be bedridden for extended periods of time, with weakness, blurred vision, and difficulty urinating. At age 43 she was worked up for a hiatal hernia because of complaints of bloating and intolerance of a variety of foods. She also had additional hospitalizations for neurological, hypertensive, and renal workups, all of which failed to reveal a definitive diagnosis.

(Spitzer et al., 1994, 1981, pp. 185, 260)

Like Sheila, people with a somatization pattern of somatic symptom disorder experience many long-lasting physical ailments—ailments that typically have little or no physical basis. This pattern, first described by Pierre Briquet in 1859, is also known as *Briquet's syndrome.* A sufferer's ailments often include pain symptoms (such as headaches or chest pain), gastrointestinal symptoms (such as nausea or diarrhea), sexual symptoms (such as erectile or menstrual difficulties), and neurological-type symptoms (such as double vision or paralysis).

People with a somatization pattern usually go from doctor to doctor in search of relief. They often describe their many symptoms in dramatic and exaggerated terms. Most also feel anxious and depressed (Dimsdale & Creed, 2010; Leiknes, Finset, & Moum, 2010). The pattern typically lasts for many years, fluctuating over time but rarely disappearing completely without therapy (Parish & Yutzy, 2011; Abbey, 2005).

Between 0.2 and 2.0 percent of all women in the United States may experience a somatization pattern in any given year, compared to less than 0.2 percent of men (North, 2005; APA, 2000). The pattern often runs in families; as many as 20 percent of the close female relatives of women with the pattern also develop it. It usually begins between adolescence and young adulthood.

Predominant Pain Pattern If the primary feature of somatic symptom disorder is pain, the individual is said to have a predominant pain pattern. Patients with conversion disorder or another somatic symptom disorder may also experience pain, but it is the key symptom in this pattern. The source of the pain may be known or unknown. Either way, the concerns and disruption produced by the pain are disproportionate to its severity and seriousness.

Although the precise prevalence has not been determined, this pattern appears to be fairly common (Nickel et al., 2010). It may begin at any age, and women seem more likely than men to experience it (APA, 2000). Often it develops after an accident or during an illness that has caused genuine pain, which then takes on a life of its own. For example, Laura, a 36-year-old woman, reported pains that went far beyond the usual symptoms of her tubercular disease, called sarcoidosis:

Before the operation I would have little joint pains, nothing that really bothered me that much. After the operation I was having severe pains in my chest and in my ribs, and those were the type of problems I'd been having after the operation, that I didn't have before.... I'd go to an emergency room at night, 11:00, 12:00, 1:00 or so. I'd take the medicine, and the next day it stopped hurting, and I'd go back again. In the meantime this is when I went to the other doctors, to complain about the same thing, to find out what was wrong; and they could never find out what was wrong with me either....

...At certain points when I go out or my husband and I go out, we have to leave early because I start hurting....A lot of times I just won't do things because my chest is hurting for one reason or another.... Two months ago when the doctor checked me and another doctor looked at the x-rays, he said he didn't see any signs of the sarcoid then and that they were doing a study now, on blood and various things, to see if it was connected to sarcoid....

(Green, 1985, pp. 60–63)

What Causes Conversion and Somatic Symptom Disorders?

For many years, conversion and somatic symptom disorders were referred to by clinical practitioners and scientists as *hysterical* disorders. This label was meant to convey the prevailing belief that excessive and uncontrolled emotions underlie the bodily symptoms found in these disorders.

Work by Ambroise-Auguste Liébault and Hippolyte Bernheim in the late nineteenth century helped foster the notion that such psychological factors were at the root of hysterical disorders. These researchers founded the Nancy School in Paris for the study and treatment of mental disorders. There they were able to produce hysterical symptoms in normal people—deafness, paralysis, blindness, and numbness—by hypnotic suggestion, and they could remove the symptoms by the same means (see Chapter 1).

Why do the terms "hysteria" and "hysterical" currently have such negative connotations in our society, as in "mass hysteria" and "hysterical personality"?

If hypnotic suggestion could both produce and reverse physical dysfunctioning, they concluded, hysterical disorders might themselves be caused by psychological processes.

Today's leading explanations for conversion and somatic symptom disorders come from the psychodynamic, behavioral, cognitive, and multicultural models. None has received much research support, however, and the disorders are still poorly understood (Kirmayer & Looper, 2007).

The Psychodynamic View As you read in Chapter 1, Sigmund Freud's theory of psychoanalysis began with his efforts to explain hysterical symptoms. Indeed, he was one of the few clinicians of his day to treat patients with these symptoms seriously, as people with genuine problems. After studying the technique of hypnosis in Paris, Freud became interested in the work of an older physician, Josef Breuer (1842–1925). Breuer had successfully used hypnosis to treat a female patient he called Anna O., who suffered from hysterical deafness, disorganized speech, and paralysis (Ellenberger, 1972). On the basis of this and similar cases, Freud (1894) came to believe that hysterical disorders represented a *conversion* of underlying emotional conflicts into physical symptoms and concerns.

Observing that most of his patients with hysterical disorders were women, Freud centered his explanation of such disorders on the needs of girls during their *phallic stage* (ages 3 through 5). At that time in life, he believed, all girls develop a pattern of desires called the *Electra complex:* each girl experiences sexual feelings for her father and at the same time recognizes that she must compete with her mother for his affection. However, aware of her mother's more powerful position and of cultural taboos, the child typically represses her sexual feelings and rejects these early desires for her father.

Freud believed that if a child's parents overreact to her sexual feelings—with strong punishments, for example—the Electra conflict will be unresolved and the child may reexperience sexual anxiety throughout her life. Whenever events trigger sexual feelings, she may experience an unconscious need to hide them from both herself and others. Freud concluded that some women hide their sexual feelings by unconsciously converting them into physical symptoms and concerns.

Most of today's psychodynamic theorists take issue with parts of Freud's explanation of conversion and somatic symptom disorders (Nickel et al., 2010), but they continue to believe that sufferers of the disorders have unconscious conflicts carried forth from childhood, which arouse anxiety, and that the individuals convert this anxiety into "more tolerable" physical symptoms (Brown et al., 2005).

Psychodynamic theorists propose that two mechanisms are at work in these disorders—primary gain and secondary gain. People achieve

Electra complex goes awry
Freud argued that a hysterical disorder may result when parents overreact to their daughter's early displays of affection for her father, by repeatedly punishing her, for example. The child may go on to exhibit sexual repression in adulthood and convert sexual feelings into physical ailments.

Susan Barr/Getty Images

Mind over matter

The opposite of conversion and somatic symptom disorders—although again demonstrating the power of psychological processes—are instances in which people "ignore" pain or other physical symptoms. Here a London performance artist manages to smile comfortably at onlookers while her skin is being pierced with sharp hooks that help suspend her from the ceiling above. Her action was part of a protest to end shark finning—the practice of cutting off a shark's fin and throwing its still living body back into the sea so that the fins can be used in the production of shark fin soup (a food delicacy) and other goods.

•**primary gain**•In psychodynamic theory, the gain achieved when somatic symptoms keep internal conflicts out of awareness.

•**secondary gain**•In psychodynamic theory, the gain achieved when somatic symptoms elicit kindness from others or provide an excuse to avoid unpleasant activities.

primary gain when their bodily symptoms keep their internal conflicts out of awareness. During an argument, for example, a man who has underlying fears about expressing anger may develop a conversion paralysis of the arm, thus preventing his feelings of rage from reaching consciousness. People achieve **secondary gain** when their bodily symptoms further enable them to avoid unpleasant activities or to receive sympathy from others. When, for example, a conversion paralysis allows a soldier to avoid combat duty or conversion blindness prevents the breakup of a relationship, secondary gain may be at work. Similarly, the conversion paralysis of Brian, the man who lost his wife in the boating accident, seemed to help him avoid many painful duties after the accident, such as attending her funeral and returning to work.

The Behavioral View Behavioral theorists propose that the physical symptoms of conversion and somatic symptom disorders bring *rewards* to sufferers (see Table 7-4). Perhaps the symptoms remove the individuals from an unpleasant relationship or bring attention from other people (Witthöft & Hiller, 2010). In response to such rewards, the sufferers learn to display the bodily symptoms more and more prominently. Behaviorists also hold that people who are familiar with an illness will more readily adopt its physical symptoms. In fact, studies find that many sufferers develop their bodily symptoms after they or their close relatives or friends have had similar medical problems (Marshall et al., 2007).

Clearly, the behavioral focus on rewards is similar to the psychodynamic idea of secondary gains. The key difference is that psychodynamic theorists view the gains as indeed secondary—that is, as gains that come only after underlying conflicts produce the disorders. Behaviorists view them as the primary cause of the development of the disorders.

Like the psychodynamic explanation, the behavioral view of conversion and somatic symptom disorders has received little research support. Even clinical case reports only occasionally support this position. In many cases the pain and upset that surround the disorders seem to outweigh any rewards the symptoms might bring.

The Cognitive View Some cognitive theorists propose that conversion and somatic symptom disorders are forms of *communication,* providing a means for people to express emotions that would otherwise be difficult to convey (Hallquist et al., 2010; Koh et al., 2005). Like their psychodynamic colleagues, these theorists hold that the emotions of people with the disorders are being converted into physical symptoms. They suggest, however, that the purpose of the conversion is not to defend against anxiety but to communicate extreme feelings—anger, fear, depression, guilt, jealousy—in a "physical language" that is familiar and comfortable for the individual.

According to this view, people who find it particularly hard to recognize or express their emotions are candidates for conversion and somatic symptom disorders. So are those who "know" the language of physical symptoms through firsthand experience with a genuine physical ailment. Because children are less able to express their emotions verbally, they are particularly likely to develop physical symptoms as a form of communication (Shaw et al., 2010). Like the other explanations, this cognitive view has not been widely tested or supported by research.

The Multicultural View Most Western clinicians believe that it is inappropriate to produce or focus excessively on somatic symptoms in response to personal distress (Shaw et al., 2010; So, 2008; Escobar, 2004). That is, in part, why conversion and somatic

table: 7-4

Disorders That Have Somatic Symptoms

Disorder	Voluntary Control of Symptoms?	Symptoms Linked to Psychosocial Factor?	An Apparent Goal?
Malingering	Yes	Maybe	Yes
Factitious disorder	Yes	Yes	No*
Conversion disorder	No	Yes	Maybe
Somatic symptom disorder	No	Yes	Maybe
Illness anxiety disorder	No	Yes	No
Body dysmorphic disorder	No	Yes	No
Psychophysiological disorder	No	Yes	No
Physical illness	No	Maybe	No

*Except for medical attention.

symptom disorders are included in DSM-5. Some theorists believe, however, that this position reflects a Western bias—a bias that sees somatic reactions as an *inferior* way of dealing with emotions (Moldavsky, 2004; Fábrega, 1990).

In fact, the transformation of personal distress into somatic complaints is the norm in many non-Western cultures (Draguns, 2006; Kleinman, 1987). In such cultures, the formation of such complaints is viewed as a socially and medically correct—and less stigmatizing—reaction to life's stressors. Studies have found very high rates of stress-caused bodily symptoms in non-Western medical settings throughout the world, including those in China, Japan, and Arab countries (Matsumoto & Juang, 2008). Individuals throughout Latin America seem to display the greatest number of somatic reactions (Escobar, 2004, 1995; Escobar et al., 1998, 1992). Even within the United States, Hispanic Americans display more somatic reactions in the face of stress than do other populations.

In Chapter 6 you saw that posttraumatic stress disorder may be more common among Hispanic Americans than among other ethnic groups in the United States (see pages 164–165). Interestingly, however, research clarifies that this trend exists only among Hispanic Americans who were born in the United States or have lived in the United States for a number of years (Escobar, 2004, 1998). Indeed, recent Latin immigrants display a *lower* rate of posttraumatic stress disorder than do other individuals throughout the country. It may be that recent immigrants, not yet influenced by the Western bias against somatic complaints, react to traumatic events with familiar somatic symptoms and that those symptoms help prevent the onset of a full-blown posttraumatic stress disorder.

The lesson to be learned from such multicultural findings is not that somatic reactions to stress are superior to psychological ones or vice versa, but rather, once again, that reactions to life's stressors are often influenced by one's culture. Overlooking this point can lead to knee-jerk mislabels or misdiagnoses.

A Possible Role for Biology
Although conversion and somatic symptom disorders are, by definition, thought to result largely from psychological and sociocultural factors, the impact of

Deliverance from danger
A man clings to one of his few remaining belongings and hopes for rescue as his Mexican village is flooded during Hurricane Frank in 2010. Conversion disorders may emerge during or shortly after life-threatening traumas such as this.

Max Nunez/epa/Corbis

"If this doesn't help you don't worry, it's a placebo."

biological processes should not be overlooked (Witthöft & Hiller, 2010; Ovsiew, 2006). To understand this point, consider first what researchers have learned about *placebos* and the *placebo effect*.

For centuries physicians have observed that patients suffering from many kinds of illnesses, from seasickness to angina, often find relief from **placebos,** substances that have no known medicinal value. Some studies have raised questions about the actual number of patients helped by placebos (Hróbjartsson & Gøtzsche, 2007, 2006, 2001), but it is generally agreed that such "pretend" treatments do bring help to many people.

Why do placebos have a medicinal effect? Theorists used to believe that they operated in purely psychological ways—that the power of suggestion worked almost magically upon the body. More recently, however, researchers have found that a belief or expectation can trigger certain chemicals throughout the body into action, and these chemicals then may produce a medicinal effect (Witthoft & Hiller, 2010; Price et al., 2008). The body chemicals most often mentioned are *hormones* and *lymphocytes,* chemicals that you observed at work in Chapter 6, and *endorphins,* natural opioid substances that you will read about in Chapter 12. Howard Brody, a leading theorist on the subject, compares the placebo effect to visiting a pharmacy:

> Our bodies are capable of producing many substances that can heal a wide variety of illnesses, and make us feel generally healthier and more energized. When the body simply secretes these substances on its own, we have what is often termed "spontaneous healing." Some of the time, our bodies seem slow to react, and a message from outside can serve as a wake-up call to our inner pharmacy. The placebo response can thus be seen as the reaction of our inner pharmacies to that wake-up call.
>
> *(Brody, 2000, p. 61)*

If placebos can "wake up" our inner pharmacies in this way, perhaps traumatic events and related concerns or needs are doing the same thing (although in a negative way) in cases of conversion or somatic symptom disorder. That is, such events and reactions may, in fact, be triggering our inner pharmacies and setting in motion the bodily symptoms and related concerns of these disorders.

How Are Conversion and Somatic Symptom Disorders Treated?

People with conversion and somatic symptom disorders usually seek psychotherapy only as a last resort. They believe that their problems are completely medical and at first reject all suggestions to the contrary (Lahmann et al., 2010). When a physician tells them that their symptoms or concerns have a psychological dimension, they often go to another physician. Eventually, however, many patients with these disorders do consent to psychotherapy, psychotropic drug therapy, or both.

Many therapists focus on the *causes* of these disorders (the trauma or anxiety tied to the physical symptoms) and apply insight, exposure, and drug therapies (Boone, 2011). Psychodynamic therapists, for example, try to help individuals with somatic symptoms become conscious of and resolve their underlying fears, thus eliminating the need to convert anxiety into physical symptoms (Nickel et al., 2010; Hawkins, 2004). Alternatively, behavioral therapists use exposure treatments. They expose clients to features of the horrific events that first triggered their physical symptoms, expecting that the individuals will become less anxious over the course of repeated exposures and, in turn, more able to face those upsetting events directly rather than through physical channels

•**placebo**•A sham treatment that a patient believes to be genuine.

•**illness anxiety disorder**•A disorder in which persons are chronically anxious about and preoccupied with the notion that they have or are developing a serious medical illness, despite the absence of substantial somatic symptoms. Previously known as *hypochondriasis*.

(Stuart et al., 2008). And biological therapists use antianxiety drugs or certain antidepressant drugs to help reduce the anxiety of clients with conversion and somatic symptom disorders (Boone, 2011; Parish & Yutzy, 2011).

Other therapists try to address the *physical symptoms* of these disorders rather than the causes, applying techniques such as suggestion, reinforcement, or confrontation (Parish & Yutzy, 2011). Those who employ *suggestion* offer emotional support to patients and tell them persuasively (or hypnotically) that their physical symptoms will soon disappear (Hallquist et al., 2010; Lahmann et al., 2010). Therapists who take a *reinforcement* approach arrange the removal of rewards for a client's "sickness" symptoms and an increase of rewards for healthy behaviors (North, 2005). And therapists who take a *confrontational* approach try to force patients out of the sick role by straightforwardly telling them that their bodily symptoms are without medical basis (Sjolie, 2002). Researchers have not fully evaluated the effects of these particular approaches on conversion and somatic symptom disorders (Boone, 2011).

Illness Anxiety Disorder

People with **illness anxiety disorder,** previously known as *hypochondriasis,* experience chronic anxiety about their health and are convinced that they have or are developing a serious medical illness, despite the absence of substantial somatic symptoms (see Table 7-5). They repeatedly check their bodies for signs of illness and misinterpret various bodily events as signs of serious medical problems. Typically the events are merely normal bodily changes, such as occasional coughing, sores, or sweating. The individuals persist in such misinterpretations no matter what friends, relatives, and physicians say. Some such people recognize that their concerns are excessive, but many do not.

Although illness anxiety disorder can begin at any age, it starts most often in early adulthood, among men and women in equal numbers. Between 1 and 5 percent of all people experience the disorder (Abramowitz & Braddock, 2011). Their symptoms tend to rise and fall over the years. Physicians report seeing many cases (Dimsdale et al., 2011). As many as 7 percent of all patients seen by primary care physicians may display the disorder.

Theorists typically explain illness anxiety disorder much as they explain various anxiety disorders (see Chapter 5). Behaviorists, for example, believe that the illness fears are acquired through classical conditioning or modeling (Marshall et al., 2007). Cognitive theorists suggest that people with the disorder are so sensitive to and threatened by bodily cues that they come to misinterpret them (Witthöft & Hiller, 2010 Williams, 2004).

The positive side of swearing
Famous English soccer player Wayne Rooney yells out in pain after being struck by a ball in the groin. Research indicates that swearing can help reduce pain, and not just pain on display in conversion and somatic symptom disorders, but even pain like Rooney's (Stephens et al., 2009).

table: **7-5**

DSM-5 Checklist

Illness Anxiety Disorder

1. Preoccupation with having or acquiring a serious illness.

2. Somatic symptoms are absent or only mild in intensity.

3. Anxiety and easily triggered alarm about one's health.

4. Performance of excessive health-related behaviors (e.g., checking one's body for signs of illness).

5. Preoccupation with health is chronic, although not necessarily continuous, lasting at least 6 months.

Based on APA, 2013, 2012.

BETWEEN THE LINES

Strictly a Coincidence?

On February 17, 1673, French actor-playwright Molière collapsed onstage and died while performing in *Le Malade Imaginaire* (*The Hypochondriac*). ‹‹

Mark Henley/Panos

Worldwide influence
A lingerie advertisement in a subway station in Shanghai, China, displays a woman in a push-up bra. As West meets East, Asian women have been bombarded by ads encouraging them to undergo Western-like cosmetic surgery, from facial changes (the most common procedures) to changes in other body parts. Perhaps not so coincidentally, Asian cases of body dysmorphic disorder are becoming more and more similar to Western cases.

People with illness anxiety disorder usually receive the kinds of treatments that are applied to obsessive-compulsive disorder (see pages 143–147). Studies reveal, for example, that clients with the disorder often improve considerably when treated with the same *antidepressant drugs* that are helpful in cases of obsessive-compulsive disorder (Bouman, 2008). Many clients also improve when treated with the behavioral approach of *exposure and response prevention* (Abramowitz & Braddock, 2011; Allen & Woolfolk, 2010). In this approach, the therapists repeatedly point out bodily variations to the clients while, at the same time, preventing them from seeking their usual medical attention. In addition, cognitive therapists guide the clients to identify, challenge, and change the illness-related beliefs that are helping to maintain their disorder.

Body Dysmorphic Disorder

People who experience **body dysmorphic disorder,** also known as **dysmorphophobia,** become deeply concerned about some imagined or minor defect in their appearance (see Table 7-6). As you read in Chapter 5, DSM-5 technically lists this disorder as an *obsessive-compulsive-related disorder* because the concerns of such individuals recur and dominate their thoughts and because the individuals often seem driven to repeatedly check or fix their imagined physical defects.

Most often, sufferers focus on wrinkles; spots on the skin; excessive facial hair; swelling of the face; or a misshapen nose, mouth, jaw, or eyebrow (Marques et al., 2011; McKay et al., 2008). Some worry about the appearance of their feet, hands, breasts, penis, or other body parts (see *PsychWatch* on page 202). Still others are concerned about bad odors coming from sweat, breath, genitals, or the rectum (Rocca et al., 2010; Phillips & Castle, 2002). Here we see such a case:

> A woman of 35 had for 16 years been worried that her sweat smelled terrible. The fear began just before her marriage when she was sharing a bed with a close friend who said that someone at work smelled badly, and the patient felt that the remark was directed at her. For fear that she smelled, for 5 years she had not gone out anywhere except when accompanied by her husband or mother. She had not spoken to her neighbors for 3 years because she thought she had overheard them speak about her to some friends. She avoided cinemas, dances, shops, cafes, and private homes.... Her husband was not allowed to invite any friends home; she constantly sought reassurance from him about her smell.... Her husband bought all her new clothes as she was afraid to try on clothes in front of shop assistants. She used vast quantities of deodorant and always bathed and changed her clothes before going out, up to 4 times daily.
>
> *(Marks, 1987, p. 371)*

It is common in our society to worry about appearance (see Figure 7-2). Many teenagers and young adults worry about acne, for instance. The concerns of people with body dysmorphic disorder, however, are extreme. Sufferers may severely limit contact with other people, be unable to look others in the eye, or go to great lengths to conceal their "defects"—say, always wearing sunglasses to cover their supposedly misshapen eyes (Didie et al., 2010; Phillips, 2005). As many as half of people with this disorder seek plastic surgery or dermatology treatment, and often they feel worse rather than better afterward (McKay et al., 2008). Research has found that as many as 30 percent of people with body dysmorphic disorder are housebound and as many as 22 percent may attempt suicide (Buhlmann et al., 2010; Phillips et al., 1993).

•**body dysmorphic disorder**•A disorder marked by excessive worry that some aspect of one's physical appearance is defective. The perceived defect is imagined or greatly exaggerated. Also known as *dysmorphophobia.*

Most cases of body dysmorphic disorder begin during adolescence (Phillips & Rogers, 2011). Often, however, people don't reveal their concerns for many years (McKay et al., 2008). Up to 5 percent of people in the United States—including many college students—suffer from the disorder (Buhlmann et al., 2010; Ovsiew, 2006; Miller, 2005). Clinical reports suggest that it may be equally common among women and men.

Why do some people carry their culture's aesthetic ideals to an extreme, whereas others stay within normal boundaries?

Theorists typically account for body dysmorphic disorder by using the same kinds of explanations, both psychological and biological, that have been applied to anxiety disorders and obsessive-compulsive disorder (Witthöft & Hiller, 2010). Similarly, clinicians typically treat clients with this disorder by applying the kinds of treatment used with obsessive-compulsive disorder, particularly antidepressant drugs, exposure and response prevention, and cognitive therapy (Krebs et al., 2012; Phillips & Rogers, 2011).

In one study, for example, 17 individuals with body dysmorphic disorder were treated with exposure and response prevention. Over the course of four weeks, the clients were repeatedly reminded of their perceived physical defects and, at the same time, prevented from doing anything to help reduce their discomfort (such as checking their

table: 7-6

DSM-5 Checklist

Body Dysmorphic Disorder

1. Preoccupation with having one or more defects or flaws in physical appearance that are not observable or appear slight to others.

2. Performance of repetitive behaviors (e.g., mirror checking) or mental acts (e.g., comparison of one's appearance to that of others) in response to concerns about appearance.

3. Significant distress or impairment.

Based on APA, 2013, 2012.

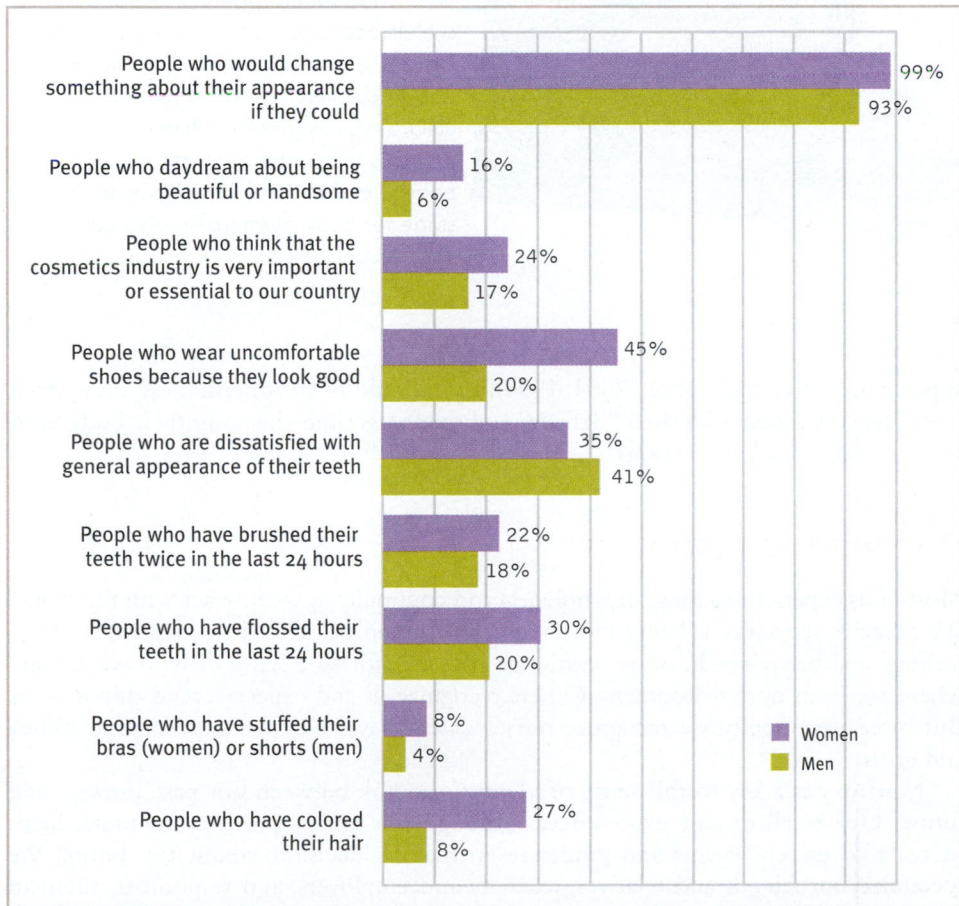

Figure 7-2

"Mirror, mirror, on the wall . . ."

People with body dysmorphic disorder are not the only ones who have concerns about their appearance. Surveys find that in our appearance-conscious society, large percentages of people regularly think about and try to change the way they look (Samorodnitzky-Naveh et al., 2007; Noonan, 2003; Kimball, 1993; Poretz & Sinrod, 1991; Weiss, 1991; Simmon, 1990).

Beauty Is in the Eye of the Beholder

People almost everywhere want to be attractive, and they tend to worry about how they appear in the eyes of others. At the same time, these concerns take different forms in different cultures.

Whereas people in Western society worry in particular about their body size and facial features, women of the Padaung tribe in Myanmar focus on the length of their neck and wear heavy stacks of brass rings to try to extend it. Many of them seek desperately to achieve what their culture has taught them is the perfect neck size. Said one, "It is most beautiful when the neck is really long. . . . I will never take off my rings. . . . I'll be buried in them" (Mydans, 1996).

Similarly, for centuries women of China, in response to the preferences of men in that country, worried greatly about the size and appearance of their feet and practiced *foot binding* to stop the growth of these extremities (Wang

Steve McCurry/Magnum Photos

Ping, 2000). In this procedure, which began in the year 900 and was widely practiced until it was outlawed in 1911, young girls were instructed to wrap a long bandage tightly around their feet each day, forcing the four toes under the sole of the foot. The procedure, which was carried out for about two years, caused the feet to become narrower and smaller. Typically the practice led to serious medical problems and poor mobility, but it did produce the small feet that were considered attractive.

Western society also falls victim to such cultural influences. Recent decades have witnessed staggering increases in such procedures as *rhinoplasty* (reshaping of the nose), *breast augmentation*, and *body piercing*—all reminders that cultural values greatly influence each person's ideas and concerns about beauty, and in some cases may set the stage for body dysmorphic disorder.

appearance) (Neziroglu et al., 2004, 1996). By the end of treatment, these individuals were less concerned with their "defects" and spent less time checking their body parts and avoiding social interactions.

Dissociative Disorders

Most of us experience a sense of wholeness and continuity as we interact with the world. We perceive ourselves as being more than a collection of isolated sensory experiences, feelings, and behaviors. In other words, we have an *identity,* a sense of who we are and where we fit in our environment. Others recognize us and expect certain things of us. But more importantly, we recognize ourselves and have our own expectations, values, and goals.

Memory is a key to this sense of identity, the link between our past, present, and future. Our recall of past experiences, although not always precisely accurate, helps us react to present events and guides us in making decisions about the future. We recognize our friends and relatives, teachers and employers, and respond to them in appropriate ways. Without a memory, we would always be starting over; with it, life moves forward.

People sometimes experience a major disruption of their memory or identity. They may, for example, have trouble remembering things, feel dazed, or have a sense of derealization. When such changes in memory or identity are significant and lack a clear physical cause, they are called **dissociative disorders.** In these disorders, one part of

•**memory**•The faculty for recalling past events and past learning.

•**dissociative disorders**•Disorders marked by major changes in memory that do not have clear physical causes.

the person's memory or identity typically seems to be *dissociated,* or separated, from the rest.

There are several kinds of dissociative disorders. People with *dissociative amnesia* are unable to recall important personal events and information. Individuals with *dissociative identity disorder,* also known as *multiple personality disorder,* have two or more separate identities that may not always be aware of each other's memories, thoughts, feelings, and behavior. And persons with *depersonalization-derealization disorder* feel as though they have become detached from their own mental processes or bodies or are observing themselves from the outside.

Several famous books and movies have portrayed dissociative disorders. Two classics are *The Three Faces of Eve* and *Sybil,* each about a woman who developed multiple personalities after experiencing traumatic childhood events. The topic is so fascinating that most television drama series seem to include at least one case of dissociation every season, creating the impression that the disorders are very common. Many clinicians, however, believe that they are rare.

At risk
The stunned look on the face of this Israeli soldier after a fierce battle in the Gaza Strip suggests confusion, shock, and exhaustion. Combat soldiers are particularly vulnerable to amnesia and other dissociative reactions. They may forget specific horrors, personal information, or even their identities.

Dissociative Amnesia

At the beginning of this chapter you met the unfortunate man named Brian. As you will recall, Brian developed a conversion disorder after a traumatic boating accident in which his wife was killed. To help examine dissociative amnesia, let us now revisit that case, changing the reactions and symptoms that Brian develops in the aftermath of the traumatic event.

Brian was spending Saturday sailing with his wife, Helen. The water was rough but well within what they considered safe limits. They were having a wonderful time and really didn't notice that the sky was getting darker, the wind blowing harder, and the sailboat becoming more difficult to control. After a few hours of sailing, they found themselves far from shore in the middle of a powerful and dangerous storm.

The storm intensified very quickly. Brian had trouble controlling the sailboat amidst the high winds and wild waves. He and Helen tried to put on the safety jackets they had neglected to wear earlier, but the boat turned over before they were finished. Brian, the better swimmer of the two, was able to swim back to the overturned sailboat, grab the side, and hold on for dear life, but Helen simply could not overcome the rough waves and reach the boat. As Brian watched in horror and disbelief, his wife disappeared from view.

After a time, the storm began to lose its strength. Brian managed to right the sailboat and sail back to shore. Finally he reached safety, but the personal consequences of this storm were just beginning. The next days were filled with pain and further horror: the Coast Guard finding Helen's body . . . discussions with authorities . . . breaking the news to Helen's parents . . . texts, emails, and conversations with family members and friends . . . self-blame . . . grief . . . and more. On Wednesday, four days after that fateful afternoon, Brian collected himself and attended Helen's funeral and burial. It was the longest and most difficult day of his life. Most of the time, he felt as though he were in a trance.

Soon after awakening on Thursday morning, Brian realized that something was terribly wrong with him. Try though he might, he couldn't remember the events of the past few days. He remembered the accident, Helen's death, and the call from the Coast Guard after they had found her body. But just about everything else was gone, right up through the funeral. At first he had even thought that it was now Sunday, and that his discussions

(continued on the next page)

Reuters/Amir Cohen

BETWEEN THE LINES

In Their Words

"Every man's memory is his private literature." ‹‹

Aldous Huxley

"There are lots of people who mistake their imagination for their memory." ‹‹

Josh Billings

table: 7-7

DSM-5 Checklist

Dissociative Amnesia

1. Inability to recall important auto-biographical information, usually of a traumatic or stressful nature, that is beyond ordinary forgetting.

2. Significant distress or impairment.

3. Symptoms are not attributable to a substance or medical condition.

Dissociative Identity Disorder

1. Disruption of identity, characterized by two or more distinct personality states or by an experience of possession.

2. Recurrent gaps in the recall of everyday events, important personal information, and/or traumatic events, beyond ordinary forgetting.

3. Significant distress or impairment.

4. Symptoms are not attributable to a substance or medical condition.

Based on APA, 2013, 2012.

•**dissociative amnesia**•A disorder marked by an inability to recall important personal events and information.

•**dissociative fugue**•A form of dissociative amnesia in which a person travels to a new location and may assume a new identity, simultaneously forgetting his or her past.

with family and friends and the funeral were all ahead of him. But the funeral guestbook, a phone conversation with his brother, and numerous texts and emails expressing condolences soon convinced him that he had lost the past four days of his life.

In this revised scenario, Brian is reacting to his traumatic experience with symptoms of **dissociative amnesia.** People with this disorder are unable to recall important information, usually of an upsetting nature, about their lives (APA, 2013, 2012). The loss of memory is much more extensive than normal forgetting and is not caused by physical factors (see Table 7-7). Often an episode of amnesia is directly triggered by a specific upsetting event (Kikuchi et al., 2010).

Dissociative amnesia may be *localized, selective, generalized,* or *continuous.* Any of these kinds of amnesia can be triggered by a traumatic experience such as Brian's, but each represents a particular pattern of forgetting. Brian was suffering from *localized amnesia,* the most common type of dissociative amnesia, in which a person loses all memory of events that took place within a limited period of time, almost always beginning with some very disturbing occurrence. Recall that Brian awakened on the day after the funeral and could not recall any of the events of the past difficult days, beginning after the boating tragedy. He remembered everything that happened up to and including the accident. He could also recall everything from the morning after the funeral onward, but the days in between remained a total blank. The forgotten period is called the *amnestic episode.* During an amnestic episode, people may appear confused; in some cases they wander about aimlessly. They are already experiencing memory difficulties but seem unaware of them. In the revised case, for example, Brian felt as though he were in a trance on the day of Helen's funeral.

Why do many people question the authenticity of individuals who seem to lose their memories at times of severe stress?

People with *selective amnesia,* the second most common form of dissociative amnesia, remember some, but not all, events that occurred during a period of time. If Brian had selective amnesia, he might remember certain conversations with friends but perhaps not the funeral itself.

In some cases the loss of memory extends back to times long before the upsetting period. Brian might awaken after the funeral and find that, in addition to forgetting events of the past few days, he could not remember events that occurred earlier in his life. In this case, he would be experiencing *generalized amnesia.* In extreme cases, Brian might not even remember who he was and might fail to recognize relatives and friends.

In the forms of dissociative amnesia just discussed, the period affected by the amnesia has an end. In *continuous amnesia,* however, forgetting continues into the present. Brian might forget new and ongoing experiences as well as what happened before and during the tragedy. Continuous forgetting of this kind is actually quite rare in cases of dissociative amnesia but not, as you will see in Chapter 18, in cases of organic amnesia.

All of these forms of dissociative amnesia are similar in that the amnesia interferes mostly with a person's memory of personal material. Memory for abstract or encyclopedic information usually remains. People with dissociative amnesia are as likely as anyone else to know the name of the president of the United States and how to read or drive a car. Recall, for example, that after the trauma of his wife's fatal accident, Brian fully retained his abilities to text and to use his computer.

Clinicians do not know how common dissociative amnesia is (Pope et al., 2007), but they do know that many cases seem to begin during serious threats to health and safety, as in wartime and natural disasters. Combat veterans often report memory gaps of hours or days, and some forget personal information, such as their names and addresses (Bremner, 2002). It appears that childhood abuse, particularly child sexual abuse, can also sometimes trigger dissociative amnesia; indeed, the 1990s witnessed many reports

"I think I accidentally repressed my good memories."

in which adults claimed to recall long-forgotten experiences of childhood abuse (see *PsychWatch* on the next page). In addition, dissociative amnesia may occur under more ordinary circumstances, such as the sudden loss of a loved one through rejection or death or guilt over certain actions (for example, an extramarital affair) (Koh et al., 2000).

The personal impact of dissociative amnesia depends on how much is forgotten. Obviously, an amnestic episode of two years is more of a problem than one of two hours. Similarly, an amnestic episode during which a person's life changes in major ways causes more difficulties than one that is quiet.

An extreme version of dissociative amnesia is called **dissociative fugue.** Here, persons not only forget their personal identities and details of their past lives but also flee to an entirely different location. Some individuals travel a short distance and make few social contacts in the new setting (APA, 2013, 2012). Their fugue may be brief—a matter of hours or days—and end suddenly. In other cases, however, the person may travel far from home, take a new name, and establish a new identity, new relationships, and even a new line of work. Such people may also display new personality characteristics; often they are more outgoing. This pattern is seen in the century-old case of the Reverend Ansel Bourne, whose last name was the inspiration for Jason Bourne, the memory-deprived secret agent in the modern-day Bourne books and movies.

On January 17, 1887, [the Reverend Ansel Bourne, of Greene, R.I.] drew 551 dollars from a bank in Providence with which to pay for a certain lot of land in Greene, paid certain bills, and got into a Pawtucket horsecar. This is the last incident which he remembers. He did not return home that day, and nothing was heard of him for two months. He was published in the papers as missing, and foul play being suspected, the police sought in vain his whereabouts. On the morning of March 14th, however, at Norristown, Pennsylvania, a man calling himself A. J. Brown who had rented a small shop six weeks previously, stocked it with stationery, confectionery, fruit and small articles, and carried on his quiet trade without seeming to any one unnatural or eccentric, woke up in a fright and called in the people of the house to tell him where he was. He said that his name was Ansel Bourne, that he was entirely ignorant of Norristown, that he knew nothing of shop keeping, and that the last thing he remembered—it seemed only yesterday—was drawing the money from the bank, etc. in Providence. . . . He was very weak, having lost apparently over twenty pounds of flesh during his escapade, and had such a horror of the idea of the candy-store that he refused to set foot in it again.

(James, 1890, pp. 391–393)

Approximately 0.2 percent of the population experience dissociative fugue. Like other kinds of dissociative amnesia, a fugue usually follows a severely stressful event (APA, 2013, 2012). Some adolescent runaways may be in a state of fugue (Loewenstein,

Repressed Childhood Memories or False Memory Syndrome?

Throughout the 1990s, reports of *repressed childhood memory of abuse* attracted much public attention. Adults with this type of *dissociative amnesia* seemed to recover buried memories of sexual and physical abuse from their childhood. A woman might claim, for example, that her father had sexually molested her repeatedly between the ages of 5 and 7. Or a young man might remember that a family friend had made sexual advances on several occasions when he was very young. Often the repressed memories surfaced during therapy for another problem.

Although the number of such claims has declined in recent years, experts remain split on this issue (Birrell, 2011; Haaken & Reavey, 2010). Some believe that recovered memories are just what they appear to be—horrible memories of abuse that have been buried for years in the person's mind. Other experts believe that the memories are actually illusions—false images created by a mind that is confused. Opponents of the repressed memory concept hold that the details of childhood sexual abuse are often remembered all too well, not completely wiped from memory (Loftus & Cahill, 2007). They also point out that memory in general is often flawed (Haaken & Reavey, 2010; Lindsay et al., 2004). Moreover, false memories of various kinds can be created in the laboratory by tapping into research participants' imaginations (Weinstein & Shanks, 2010; Brainerd et al., 2008).

If the alleged recovery of childhood memories is not what it appears to be, what is it? According to opponents of the concept, it may be a powerful case of suggestibility (Loftus & Cahill, 2007; Loftus, 2003, 2001). These theorists hold that the attention paid to the phenomenon by both clinicians and the public has led some therapists to make the diagnosis without sufficient evidence (Haaken & Reavey, 2010). The therapists may actively search for signs of early abuse in clients and even encourage clients to

Early recall These three siblings, all born on the same day in different years, have very different reactions to their cakes at a 1958 birthday party. But how do they each remember that party today? Research suggests that our memories of early childhood may be influenced by the reminiscences of family members, our dreams, television and movie plots, and our present self-image.

produce repressed memories (McNally & Garaerts, 2009). Certain therapists in fact use special memory recovery techniques, including hypnosis, regression therapy, journal writing, dream interpretation, and interpretation of bodily symptoms. Perhaps some clients respond to the techniques by unknowingly forming false memories of abuse. The apparent memories may then become increasingly familiar to them as a result of repeated therapy discussions of the alleged incidents.

Of course, repressed memories of childhood sexual abuse do not emerge only in clinical settings. Many individuals come forward on their own. Opponents of the repressed memory concept explain these cases by pointing to various books, articles, websites, and television shows that seem to validate repressed memories of childhood abuse (Haaken & Reavey,

2010; Loftus, 1993). Still other opponents of the repressed memory concept believe that, for biological or other reasons, some individuals are more prone than others to experience false memories—either of childhood abuse or of other kinds of events (McNally et al., 2005).

It is important to recognize that the experts who question the recovery of repressed childhood memories do not in any way deny the problem of child sexual abuse. In fact, proponents and opponents alike are greatly concerned that the public may take this debate to mean that clinicians have doubts about the scope of the problem of child sexual abuse. Whatever may be the final outcome of the repressed memory debate, the problem of childhood sexual abuse is all too real and all too common.

1991). And like other cases of dissociative amnesia, fugues usually affect personal memories rather than encyclopedic or abstract knowledge (Maldonado & Spiegel, 2007).

Fugues tend to end abruptly. In some cases, as with Reverend Bourne, the person "awakens" in a strange place, surrounded by unfamiliar faces, and wonders how he or she got there. In other cases, the lack of personal history may arouse suspicion. Perhaps a traffic accident or legal problem leads police to discover the false identity; at other times friends search for and find the missing person. When people are found before their state of fugue has ended, therapists may find it necessary to ask them many questions about the details of their lives, repeatedly remind them who they are, and even begin psychotherapy before they recover their memories. As these people recover their past, some forget the events of the fugue period.

The majority of people who experience dissociative fugue regain most or all of their memories and never have a recurrence. Since fugues are usually brief and totally reversible, individuals tend to experience few aftereffects. People who have been away for months or years, however, often do have trouble adjusting to the changes that have occurred during their flights. In addition, some people commit illegal or violent acts in their fugue state and later must face the consequences.

Lost and found

Cheryl Ann Barnes is helped off a plane by her grandmother and stepmother upon arrival in Florida in 1996. The 17-year-old high school honor student had disappeared from her Florida home and was found one month later in a New York City hospital listed as Jane Doe, apparently suffering from fugue.

Dissociative Identity Disorder (Multiple Personality Disorder)

Dissociative identity disorder is both dramatic and disabling, as we see in the case of Eric:

Dazed and bruised from a beating, Eric, 29, was discovered wandering around a Daytona Beach shopping mall on Feb. 9. . . . Transferred six weeks later to Daytona Beach's Human Resources Center, Eric began talking to doctors in two voices: the infantile rhythms of "young Eric," a dim and frightened child, and the measured tones of "older Eric," who told a tale of terror and child abuse. According to "older Eric," after his immigrant German parents died, a harsh stepfather and his mistress took Eric from his native South Carolina to a drug dealers' hideout in a Florida swamp. Eric said he was raped by several gang members and watched his stepfather murder two men.

One day in late March an alarmed counselor watched Eric's face twist into a violent snarl. Eric let loose an unearthly growl and spat out a stream of obscenities. "It sounded like something out of The Exorcist," says Malcolm Graham, the psychologist who directs the case at the center. "It was the most intense thing I've ever seen in a patient." That disclosure of a new personality, who insolently demanded to be called Mark, was the first indication that Graham had been dealing with a rare and serious emotional disorder: true multiple personality. . . .

Eric's other manifestations emerged over the next weeks: quiet, middle-aged Dwight; the hysterically blind and mute Jeffrey; Michael, an arrogant jock; the coquettish Tian, whom Eric considered a whore; and argumentative Phillip, the lawyer. "Phillip was always asking about Eric's rights," says Graham. "He was kind of obnoxious. Actually, Phillip was a pain."

To Graham's astonishment, Eric gradually unfurled 27 different personalities, including three females. . . . They ranged in age from a fetus to a sordid old man who kept trying to persuade Eric to fight as a mercenary in Haiti. In one therapy session, reports Graham, Eric shifted personality nine times in an hour. "I felt I was losing control of the sessions," says the psychologist, who has eleven years of clinical experience. "Some personalities would not talk to me, and some of them were very insightful into my behavior as well as Eric's."

(Time, October 25, 1982, p. 70)

Dissociative identity disorder: Hollywood style

Unfortunately, dissociative identity disorder is often trivialized or sensationalized in the arts and media, as this movie poster of the 1957 movie *The Three Faces of Eve* illustrates. Such treatments contribute to the public's skepticism about the disorder.

A person with **dissociative identity disorder,** or **multiple personality disorder,** develops two or more distinct personalities, often called **subpersonalities,** or **alternate personalities,** each with a unique set of memories, behaviors, thoughts, and emotions (see again Table 7-7 on page 204). At any given time, one of the subpersonalities takes center stage and dominates the person's functioning. Usually one subpersonality, called the *primary,* or *host,* personality, appears more often than the others.

The transition from one subpersonality to another, called *switching,* is usually sudden and may be dramatic. Eric, for example, twisted his face, growled, and yelled obscenities while changing personalities. Switching is usually triggered by a stressful event, although clinicians can also bring about the change with hypnotic suggestion.

Cases of dissociative identity disorder were first reported almost three centuries ago (Rieber, 2006, 2002). Many clinicians consider the disorder to be rare, but some reports suggest that it may be more common than was once thought. Most cases are first diagnosed in late adolescence or early adulthood, but, more often than not, the symptoms actually began in early childhood after episodes of abuse (often sexual abuse), perhaps even before the age of 5 (Steele, 2011; Ross & Ness, 2010; Maldonado & Spiegel, 2007). Women receive this diagnosis at least three times as often as men.

> **Why might women be much more likely than men to receive a diagnosis of dissociative identity disorder?**

How Do Subpersonalities Interact? How subpersonalities relate to or recall one another varies from case to case. Generally, however, there are three kinds of relationships. In *mutually amnesic relationships,* the subpersonalities have no awareness of one another (Ellenberger, 1970). Conversely, in *mutually cognizant patterns,* each subpersonality is well aware of the rest. They may hear one another's voices and even talk among themselves. Some are on good terms, while others do not get along at all.

In *one-way amnesic relationships,* the most common relationship pattern, some subpersonalities are aware of others, but the awareness is not mutual. Those who are aware, called *co-conscious subpersonalities,* are "quiet observers" who watch the actions and thoughts of the other subpersonalities but do not interact with them. Sometimes while another subpersonality is present, the co-conscious personality makes itself known through indirect means, such as auditory hallucinations (perhaps a voice giving commands) or "automatic writing" (the current personality may find itself writing down words over which it has no control).

Investigators used to believe that most cases of dissociative identity disorder involved two or three subpersonalities. Studies now suggest, however, that the average number of subpersonalities per patient is much higher—15 for women and 8 for men (APA, 2000). In fact, there have been cases in which 100 or more subpersonalities were observed. Often the subpersonalities emerge in groups of two or three at a time.

In the case of "Eve White," made famous in the book and movie *The Three Faces of Eve,* a woman had three subpersonalities—Eve White, Eve Black, and Jane (Thigpen & Cleckley, 1957). Eve White, the primary personality, was quiet and serious; Eve Black was carefree and mischievous; and Jane was mature and intelligent. According to the book, these three subpersonalities eventually merged into Evelyn, a stable personality who was really an integration of the other three.

The book was mistaken, however; this was not to be the end of Eve's dissociation. In an autobiography 20 years later, she revealed that altogether 22 subpersonalities had come forth during her life, including 9 subpersonalities after Evelyn. Usually they appeared in groups of three, and so the authors of *The Three Faces of Eve* apparently never knew about her previous or subsequent subpersonalities. She has now overcome her disorder, achieving a single, stable identity, and has been known as Chris Sizemore for over 35 years (Ramsland & Kuter, 2011; Sizemore, 1991).

How Do Subpersonalities Differ?

As in Chris Sizemore's case, subpersonalities often exhibit dramatically different characteristics. They may also have their own names and different *identifying features, abilities and preferences,* and even *physiological responses.*

IDENTIFYING FEATURES The subpersonalities may differ in features as basic as age, gender, race, and family history, as in the case of Sybil Dorsett, whose real-life disorder is described in the famous novel *Sybil* (Schreiber, 1973). According to the novel, Sybil displayed 17 subpersonalities, all with different identifying features. They included adults, a teenager, and even a baby. One subpersonality, Vicky, saw herself as attractive and blonde, while another, Peggy Lou, believed herself to be "a pixie with a pug nose." Yet another, Mary, was plump with dark hair, and Vanessa was a tall, thin redhead. (It is worth noting that the accuracy of the real-life case on which this novel was based has been challenged in recent years.)

ABILITIES AND PREFERENCES Although memories of abstract or encyclopedic information are not usually affected in dissociative amnesia or fugue, they are often disturbed in dissociative identity disorder. It is not uncommon for the different subpersonalities to have different abilities: one may be able to drive, speak a foreign language, or play a musical instrument, while the others cannot (Coons & Bowman, 2001). Their handwriting can also differ. In addition, the subpersonalities usually have different tastes in food, friends, music, and literature. Chris Sizemore ("Eve") later pointed out, "If I had learned to sew as one personality and then tried to sew as another, I couldn't do it. Driving a car was the same. Some of my personalities couldn't drive" (Sizemore & Pitillo, 1977, p. 4).

PHYSIOLOGICAL RESPONSES Researchers have discovered that subpersonalities may have physiological differences, such as differences in autonomic nervous system activity, blood pressure levels, and allergies (Spiegel, 2009; Putnam, Zahn, & Post, 1990). A famous study looked at the brain activities of different subpersonalities by measuring their *evoked potentials*—that is, brain-response patterns recorded on an electroencephalograph (Putnam, 1984). The brain pattern a person produces in response to a specific stimulus (such as a flashing light) is usually unique and consistent. However, when an evoked potential test was administered to four subpersonalities of each of 10 people with dissociative identity disorder, the results were dramatic. The brain-activity pattern of each subpersonality was unique, showing the kinds of variations usually found in totally different people.

The evoked potential study also used control participants who pretended to have different subpersonalities. These normal individuals were instructed to create and rehearse alternate personalities. The brain-reaction patterns of these participants, in contrast to those of real patients, did not vary as they shifted from subpersonality to subpersonality, suggesting that simple faking cannot produce the variations in brain reaction found in cases of multiple personality.

How Common Is Dissociative Identity Disorder?

As you have seen, dissociative identity disorder has traditionally been thought of as rare. Some researchers even argue that many or all cases are *iatrogenic*—that is, unintentionally produced by practitioners (Lynn & Deming, 2010; Piper & Merskey, 2005, 2004). They believe that therapists create this disorder by subtly suggesting the existence of other personalities during therapy or by explicitly asking a patient to produce different personalities while under hypnosis. In addition, they believe, a therapist who is looking for multiple personalities may reinforce these patterns by displaying greater interest when a patient displays symptoms of dissociation.

These arguments seem to be supported by the fact that many cases of dissociative identity disorder first come to attention while the person is already in treatment for a less serious problem. But such is not true of all cases; many people seek treatment because they have noticed time lapses throughout their lives or because relatives and friends have observed their subpersonalities (Putnam, 2006, 2000).

•**dissociative identity disorder**•A dissociative disorder in which a person develops two or more distinct personalities. Also known as *multiple personality disorder*.

•**subpersonalities**•The two or more distinct personalities found in individuals suffering with dissociative identity disorder. Also known as *alternate personalities*.

Cultural Ties

Some clinical theorists argue that dissociative identity disorder is culture-bound (tied to one culture) (Escobar, 2004). While the prevalence of this disorder has grown in North America, it is rare or nonexistent in Great Britain, Sweden, Russia, India, and Southeast Asia (Chaturvedi et al., 2010). Moreover, within the United States it is particularly rare among Hispanic Americans and Asian Americans. ‹‹

The number of people diagnosed with dissociative identity disorder has been increasing (Sar et al., 2007). Although the disorder is still uncommon, thousands of cases have now been diagnosed in the United States and Canada alone. Two factors may account for this increase. First, a growing number of today's clinicians believe that the disorder does exist and are willing to diagnose it (Merenda, 2008; Lalonde et al., 2002, 2001). Second, diagnostic procedures tend to be more accurate today than in past years. For much of the twentieth century, schizophrenia was one of the clinical field's most commonly applied diagnoses. It was applied, often incorrectly, to a wide range of unusual behavioral patterns, perhaps including dissociative identity disorder (Tschöke & Steinert, 2010). Under the stricter criteria of recent editions of the DSM, clinicians are now more accurate in diagnosing schizophrenia, allowing more cases of dissociative identity disorder to be recognized (Welburn et al., 2003). In addition, several diagnostic tests have been developed to help detect dissociative identity disorder (Ross & Ness, 2010; Cardena, 2008). Despite such changes, however, many clinicians continue to question the legitimacy of this category.

What verdict is appropriate for accused criminals who experience dissociative identity disorder and whose crimes are committed by one of their subpersonalities?

How Do Theorists Explain Dissociative Amnesia and Dissociative Identity Disorder?

A variety of theories have been proposed to explain dissociative amnesia and dissociative identity disorder. Older explanations, such as those offered by psychodynamic and behavioral theorists, have not received much investigation (Merenda, 2008). However, newer viewpoints, which combine cognitive, behavioral, and biological principles and highlight such factors as *state-dependent learning* and *self-hypnosis,* have captured the interest of clinical scientists.

The Psychodynamic View Psychodynamic theorists believe that these dissociative disorders are caused by repression, the most basic ego defense mechanism: people fight off anxiety by unconsciously preventing painful memories, thoughts, or impulses from reaching awareness. Everyone uses repression to a degree, but people with dissociative disorders are thought to repress their memories excessively (Henderson, 2010; Fayek, 2002).

In the psychodynamic view, dissociative amnesia is a *single episode* of massive repression. A person unconsciously blocks the memory of an extremely upsetting event to avoid the pain of facing it (Kikuchi et al., 2010). Repressing may be his or her only protection from overwhelming anxiety.

In contrast, dissociative identity disorder is thought to result from a *lifetime* of excessive repression (Howell, 2011; Wang & Jiang, 2007). Psychodynamic theorists believe that continuous use of repression is motivated by traumatic childhood events, particularly abusive parenting (Baker, 2010; Ross & Ness, 2010). The novel *Sybil,* for example, describes young Sybil's abuse at the hands of her disturbed mother, Hattie:

Courtesy of Chris Sizemore/Towers Productions/The Everett Collection

Early beginnings
The dissociative identity disorder of Chris Sizemore (*The Three Faces of Eve*) developed long before this photograph of her was taken at age 10. It emerged during her preschool years after she experienced several traumas (witnessing two deaths and a horrifying accident) within a three-month period.

A favorite ritual . . . was to separate Sybil's legs with a long wooden spoon, tie her feet to the spoon with dish towels, and then string her to the end of a light bulb cord, suspended from the ceiling. The child was left to swing in space while the mother proceeded to the water faucet to wait for the water to get cold. After muttering, "Well, it's not going to get any colder," she would fill the adult-sized enema bag to capacity and return with it to her daughter. As the child swung in space, the mother would insert the enema tip into the child's urethra and fill the bladder with cold water. "I did it," Hattie would scream triumphantly when her mission was accomplished. "I did it." The scream was followed by laughter, which went on and on.

(Schreiber, 1973, p. 160)

According to psychodynamic theorists, children who experience such traumas may come to fear the dangerous world they live in and take flight from it by pretending to be another person who is looking on safely from afar. Abused children may also come to fear the impulses that they believe are the reasons for their excessive punishments. Whenever they experience "bad" thoughts or impulses, they unconsciously try to disown and deny them by assigning them to other personalities.

Most of the support for the psychodynamic position is drawn from case histories, which report such brutal childhood experiences as beatings, cuttings, burnings with cigarettes, imprisonment in closets, rape, and extensive verbal abuse (Ross & Ness, 2010). Yet some individuals with dissociative identity disorder do not seem to have experiences of abuse in their background (Ross & Ness, 2010; Bliss, 1980). Moreover, child abuse appears to be far more common than dissociative identity disorder. Why might only a small fraction of abused children develop this disorder?

The Behavioral View

Behaviorists believe that dissociation grows from normal memory processes such as drifting of the mind or forgetting (see *PsychWatch* on page 213). Specifically, they hold that dissociation is a response learned through *operant conditioning* (Casey, 2001). People who experience a horrifying event may later find temporary relief when their minds drift to other subjects. For some, this momentary forgetting, leading to a drop in anxiety, increases the likelihood of future forgetting. In short, they are reinforced for the act of forgetting and learn—without being aware that they are learning—that such acts help them escape anxiety. Thus, like psychodynamic theorists, behaviorists see dissociation as escape behavior. But behaviorists believe that a reinforcement process rather than a hardworking unconscious is keeping the individuals unaware that they are using dissociation as a means of escape. Like psychodynamic theorists, behaviorists have relied largely on case histories to support their view of dissociative disorders. Moreover, the behavioral explanation fails to explain precisely how temporary and normal escapes from painful memories grow into a complex disorder or why more people do not develop dissociative disorders.

State-Dependent Learning

If people learn something when they are in a particular situation or state of mind, they are likely to remember it best when they are again in that same condition. If they are given a learning task while under the influence of alcohol, for example, their later recall of the information may be strongest under the influence of alcohol. Similarly, if they smoke cigarettes while learning, they may later have better recall when they are again smoking.

This link between state and recall is called **state-dependent learning**. It was initially observed in experimental animals who learned things while under the influence of certain drugs (Ardjmand et al., 2011; Overton, 1966, 1964). Research with human participants later showed that state-dependent learning can be associated with mood states as well: material learned during a happy mood is recalled best when the participant is again happy, and sad-state learning is recalled best during sad states (de l'Etoile, 2002; Bower, 1981) (see Figure 7-3 on the next page).

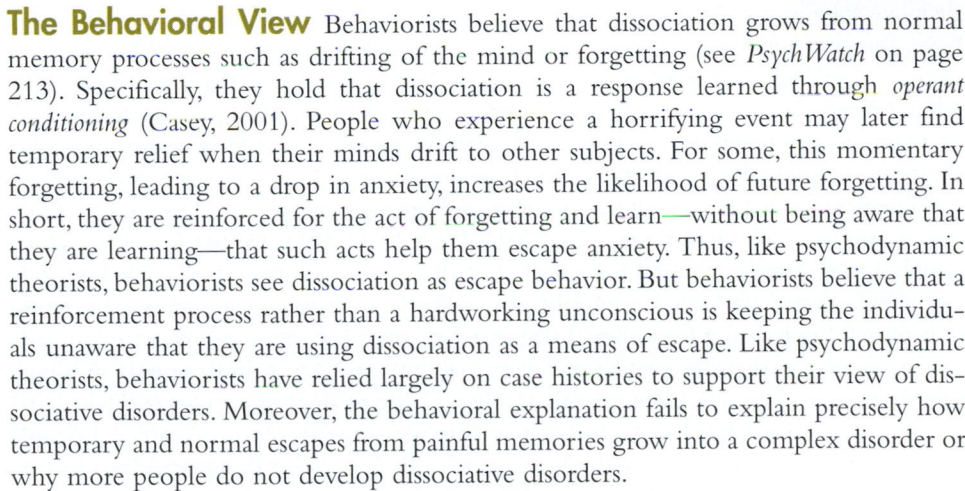

Might it be possible to use the principles of state-dependent learning to produce better results in school or at work?

Real or not real?

False claims of dissociation are sometimes used to excuse bad deeds or cover up illegal acts. In 2007, former teacher John Darwin walked into a police station and said that he had no memory of the events that had taken place in his life since his disappearance five years earlier while canoeing off Britain's coast. An investigation revealed, however, that his disappearance was a case of life insurance fraud. Shortly after Darwin had been declared dead, he and his wife had collected the insurance money, paid off their debts, and moved to Panama. Here a police officer holds up the photo Darwin had used on a fake passport.

•**state-dependent learning**•Learning that becomes associated with the conditions under which it occurred, so that it is best remembered under the same conditions.

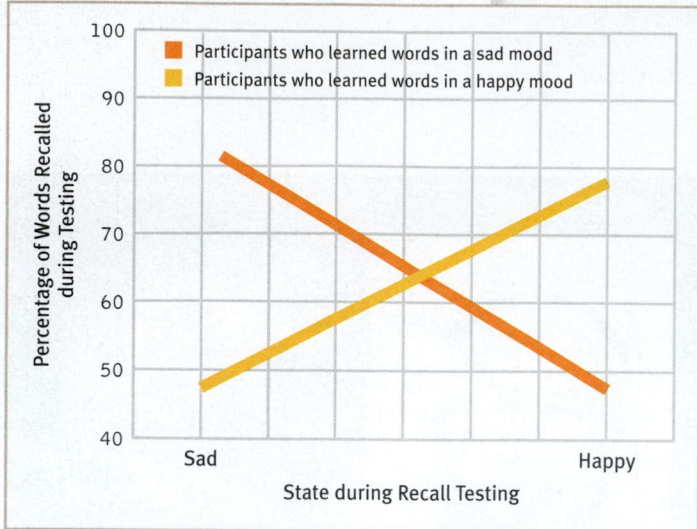

Figure 7-3

State-dependent learning In one study, participants who learned a list of words while in a hypnotically induced happy state remembered the words better if they were in a happy mood when tested later than if they were in a sad mood. Conversely, participants who learned the words when in a sad mood recalled them better if they were sad during testing than if they were happy (Bower, 1981).

Figure 7-4

Hypnotic susceptibility and age A person's hypnotic susceptibility increases until just before adolescence, then generally declines. (Adapted from Morgan & Hilgard, 1973.)

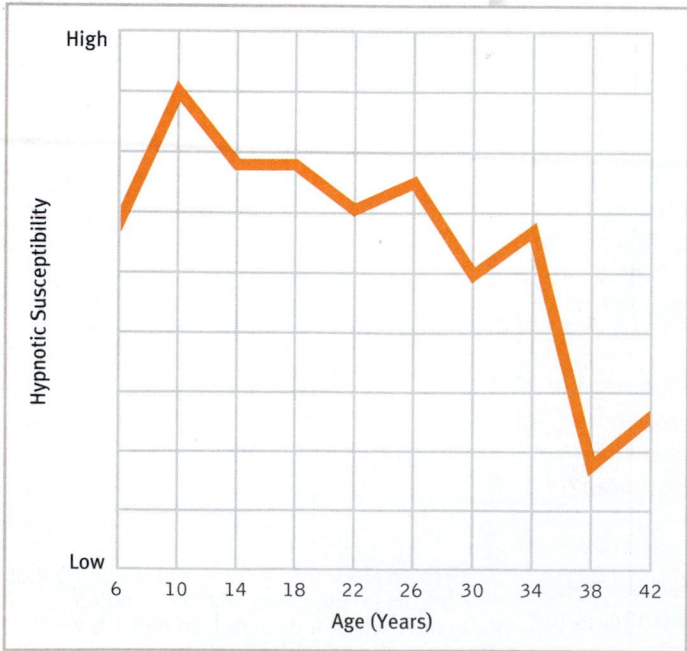

What causes state-dependent learning? One possibility is that *arousal* levels are an important part of learning and memory. That is, a particular level of arousal will have a set of remembered events, thoughts, and skills attached to it. When a situation produces that particular level of arousal, the person is more likely to recall the memories linked to it.

Although people may remember certain events better in some arousal states than in others, most can recall events under a variety of states. However, perhaps people who are prone to develop dissociative disorders have state-to-memory links that are unusually rigid and narrow (Barlow, 2011). Maybe each of their thoughts, memories, and skills is tied *exclusively* to a particular state of arousal, so that they recall a given event only when they experience an arousal state almost identical to the state in which the memory was first acquired. When such people are calm, for example, they may forget what occurred during stressful times, thus laying the groundwork for dissociative amnesia. Similarly, in dissociative identity disorder, different arousal levels may produce entirely different groups of memories, thoughts, and abilities—that is, different subpersonalities (Dorahy & Huntjens, 2007). This could explain why personality transitions in dissociative identity disorder tend to be sudden and stress-related.

Self-Hypnosis As you first saw in Chapter 1, people who are *hypnotized* enter a sleeplike state in which they become very suggestible. While in this state, they can behave, perceive, and think in ways that would ordinarily seem impossible. They may, for example, become temporarily blind, deaf, or insensitive to pain. Hypnosis can also help people remember events that occurred and were forgotten years ago, a capability used by many psychotherapists. Conversely, it can make people forget facts, events, and even their personal identities—an effect called *hypnotic amnesia*.

The parallels between hypnotic amnesia and the dissociative disorders we have been examining are striking (Terhune et al., 2011; Dell, 2010). Both are conditions in which people forget certain material for a period of time yet later remember it. And in both, the people forget without any insight into why they are forgetting or any awareness that something is being forgotten. These parallels have led some theorists to conclude that dissociative disorders may be a form of **self-hypnosis** in which people hypnotize themselves to forget unpleasant events (Dell, 2010; Gillig, 2009). Dissociative amnesia may occur, for example, in people who, consciously or unconsciously, hypnotize themselves into forgetting horrifying experiences that have recently occurred in their lives. If the self-induced amnesia covers all memories of a person's past and identity, that person may further experience a fugue.

Self-hypnosis might also be used to explain dissociative identity disorder. On the basis of several investigations, some theorists believe that this disorder often begins between the ages of 4 and 6, a time when children are generally very suggestible and excellent hypnotic subjects (Kohen & Olness, 2011; Kluft, 2001, 1987) (see Figure 7-4). These theorists argue that some children who experience abuse or other horrifying events manage to escape their threatening world by self-hypnosis, mentally separating themselves from their bodies and fulfilling their wish to become some other person or persons (Giesbrecht & Merckelbach, 2009). One patient with multiple personalities observed, "I was in a trance often [during my childhood]. There was a little place where I could sit, close my eyes and imagine, until I felt very relaxed just like hypnosis" (Bliss, 1980, p. 1392).

PsychWatch

Peculiarities of Memory

Usually memory problems must interfere greatly with a person's functioning before they are considered a sign of a disorder. Peculiarities of memory, on the other hand, fill our daily lives. Memory investigators have identified a number of these peculiarities—some familiar, some useful, some problematic, but none abnormal (Baars, 2010; Turkington & Harris, 2009, 2001; Mathews & Wang, 2007).

- **Absentmindedness** Often we fail to register information because our thoughts are focusing on other things. If we haven't absorbed the information in the first place, it is no surprise that later we can't recall it.

- **Déjà vu** Almost all of us have at some time had the strange sensation of recognizing a scene that we happen upon for the first time. We feel sure we have been there before.

- **Jamais vu** Sometimes we have the opposite experience: a situation or scene that is part of our daily life seems suddenly unfamiliar. "I knew it was my car, but I felt as if I'd never seen it before."

- **The tip-of-the-tongue phenomenon** To have something on the tip of the tongue is an acute "feeling of

"Did you ever start to do something and then forget what the heck it was?"

knowing": we are unable to recall some piece of information, but we know that we know it.

- **Eidetic images** Some people experience visual afterimages so vividly that they can describe a picture in detail after looking at it just once. The images may be memories of pictures, events, fantasies, or dreams.

- **Memory while under anesthesia** As many as 2 of every 1,000 anesthetized patients process enough of what is said in their presence during surgery to affect their recovery. In many such cases, the ability to understand language has continued under anesthesia, even though the patient cannot explicitly recall it.

- **Memory for music** Even as a small child, Mozart could memorize and reproduce a piece of music after having heard it only once. While no one yet has matched the genius of Mozart, many musicians can mentally hear whole pieces of music, so that they can rehearse anywhere, far from their instruments.

- **Visual memory** Most people recall visual information better than other kinds of information: they easily can bring to their mind the appearance of places, objects, faces, or the pages of a book. They almost never forget a face, yet they may well forget the name attached to it. Other people have stronger verbal memories: they remember sounds or words particularly well, and the memories that come to their minds are often puns or rhymes.

There are different schools of thought about the nature of hypnosis (Dell, 2010; Lynn, Rhue, & Kirsch, 2010; Spanos & Coe, 1992). Some theorists see hypnosis as a *special process,* an out-of-the-ordinary kind of functioning. Accordingly, these theorists contend that people with dissociative amnesia and dissociative identity disorder place themselves in internal trances during which their conscious functioning is significantly altered. Other theorists believe that hypnotic behaviors, and hypnotic amnesia in particular, are produced by *common social and cognitive processes,* such as high motivation, focused attention, role enactment, and self-fulfilling expectations. According to this point of view, hypnotized people are simply highly motivated individuals performing tasks that are asked of them, while believing all along that the hypnotic state is doing the work for them. Common-process theorists hold that people with dissociative amnesia and dissociative identity disorder provide themselves (or are provided by others) with powerful suggestions to forget and that social and cognitive mechanisms then put the suggestions into practice. Whether hypnosis consists of special or common processes, hypnosis research effectively demonstrates the power of our normal thought processes, and so renders the notion of dissociative disorders somewhat less remarkable.

•**self-hypnosis**•The process of hypnotizing oneself, sometimes for the purpose of forgetting unpleasant events.

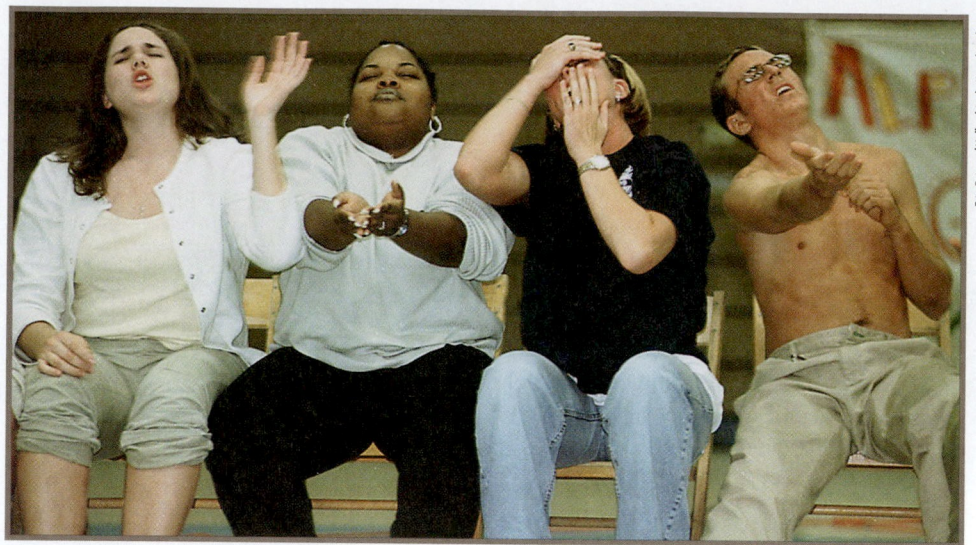

Erin Painter/Midland Daily News/AP Photo

Hypnotic recall

Northwood University students react while under hypnosis to the suggestion of being on a beach in Hawaii and needing suntan lotion. Many clinicians use hypnotic procedures to help clients recall past events, but research reveals that such procedures often create false memories.

How Are Dissociative Amnesia and Dissociative Identity Disorder Treated?

As you have seen, people with dissociative amnesia often recover on their own (see *MediaSpeak* on page 218). Only sometimes do their memory problems linger and require treatment. In contrast, people with dissociative identity disorder usually require treatment to regain their lost memories and develop an integrated personality. Treatments for dissociative amnesia tend to be more successful than those for dissociative identity disorder, probably because the former pattern is less complex.

How Do Therapists Help People with Dissociative Amnesia? The leading treatments for dissociative amnesia are *psychodynamic therapy, hypnotic therapy,* and *drug therapy,* although support for these interventions comes largely from case studies rather than controlled investigations (Maldonado & Spiegel, 2007, 2003). Psychodynamic therapists guide patients to search their unconscious in the hope of bringing forgotten experiences back to consciousness (Howell, 2011; Bartholomew, 2000). The focus of psychodynamic therapy seems particularly well suited to the needs of people with dissociative amnesia. After all, the patients need to recover lost memories, and the general approach of psychodynamic therapists is to try to uncover memories—as well as other psychological processes—that have been repressed. Thus many theorists, including some who do not ordinarily favor psychodynamic approaches, believe that psychodynamic therapy may be the most appropriate treatment for dissociative amnesia.

Another common treatment for dissociative amnesia is **hypnotic therapy,** or **hypnotherapy** (see Table 7-8). Therapists hypnotize patients and then guide them to recall forgotten events (Degun-Mather, 2002). Given the possibility that dissociative amnesia may be a form of self-hypnosis, hypnotherapy may be a particularly useful intervention. It has been applied both alone and in combination with other approaches (Colletti, Lynn, & Laurence, 2010).

Sometimes injections of barbiturates such as *sodium amobarbital* (Amytal) or *sodium pentobarbital* (Pentothal) have been used to help patients with dissociative amnesia regain lost memories. These drugs are often called "truth serums," but actually their effect is to calm people and free their inhibitions, thus helping them to recall anxiety-producing events (Ahern et al., 2000; Fraser, 1993). These drugs do not always work, however, and if used at all, they are likely to be combined with other treatment approaches.

How Do Therapists Help Individuals with Dissociative Identity Disorder? Unlike victims of dissociative amnesia, people with dissociative identity disorder do not typically recover without treatment (Howell, 2011; Maldonado & Spiegel,

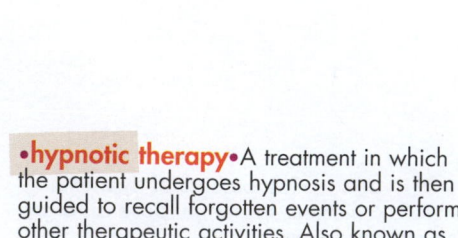

•**hypnotic therapy**•A treatment in which the patient undergoes hypnosis and is then guided to recall forgotten events or perform other therapeutic activities. Also known as *hypnotherapy.*

table: 7-8

Some Myths about Hypnosis

Myth	Reality
Hypnosis relies on having a good imagination.	Vivid imaginations are unrelated to hypnotizability.
Hypnosis is dangerous.	Hypnosis is no more distressing than a lecture.
It has something to do with a sleeplike state.	Hypnotized subjects are fully awake.
Hypnotized people lose control of themselves.	Hypnotized people are perfectly capable of saying no.
People remember more accurately under hypnosis.	Hypnosis can help create false memories.
Hypnotized people can be led to do immoral acts.	Hypnotized subjects fully adhere to their usual values.

Source: Nash, 2006, 2005, 2004, 2001.

2007, 2003). Treatment for this pattern is complex and difficult, much like the disorder itself. Therapists usually try to help the clients (1) recognize fully the nature of their disorder, (2) recover the gaps in their memory, and (3) integrate their subpersonalities into one functional personality (Baker, 2010; North & Yutzy, 2005).

RECOGNIZING THE DISORDER Once a diagnosis of dissociative identity disorder is made, therapists typically try to bond with the primary personality and with each of the subpersonalities (Howell, 2011). As bonds are formed, therapists try to educate patients and help them to recognize fully the nature of their disorder (Krakauer, 2001). Some therapists actually introduce the subpersonalities to one another, by hypnosis, for example, or by having patients look at videos of their other personalities (Howell, 2011; Ross & Gahan, 1988). A number of therapists have also found that group therapy helps to educate patients (Fine & Madden, 2000). In addition, family therapy may be used to help educate spouses and children about the disorder and to gather helpful information about the patient (Kluft, 2001, 2000).

RECOVERING MEMORIES To help patients recover the missing pieces of their past, therapists use many of the approaches applied in other dissociative disorders, including psychodynamic therapy, hypnotherapy, and drug treatment (Howell, 2011; Kluft, 2001, 1991, 1985). These techniques work slowly for patients with dissociative identity disorder, as some subpersonalities may keep denying experiences that the others recall. One of the

Columbia/The Kobal Collection

Close encounters of a false kind?
In the popular 1977 movie *Close Encounters of the Third Kind,* Earth is visited by space aliens—entertainment for most people, but some 3 million Americans believe that they have had encounters with space aliens. Many clinical theorists believe that such recollections are actually false memories; they note that the recollections are often "recovered" memories brought out by hypnosis or other unreliable memory-retrieval techniques (Warner, 2004).

BETWEEN THE LINES

At the Movies: Recent Films about Memory Disturbances

The Bourne series (2012, 2007, 2004, 2002) ‹‹

Black Swan (2010) ‹‹

The Hangover (2009) ‹‹

The Number 23 (2007) ‹‹

Eternal Sunshine of the Spotless Mind (2004) ‹‹

The Manchurian Candidate (2004, 1962) ‹‹

Memento (2000) ‹‹

subpersonalities may even assume a "protector" role to prevent the primary personality from suffering the pain of recollecting traumatic experiences.

INTEGRATING THE SUBPERSONALITIES The final goal of therapy is to merge the different subpersonalities into a single, integrated identity. Integration is a continuous process that occurs throughout treatment until patients "own" all of their behaviors, emotions, sensations, and knowledge. **Fusion** is the final merging of two or more subpersonalities. Many patients distrust this final treatment goal, and their subpersonalities may see integration as a form of death (Howell, 2011; Kluft, 2001, 1999, 1991). Therapists have used a range of approaches to help merge subpersonalities, including psychodynamic, supportive, cognitive, and drug therapies (Baker, 2010; Goldman, 1995).

Once the subpersonalities are integrated, further therapy is typically needed to maintain the complete personality and to teach social and coping skills that may help prevent later dissociations. In case reports, some therapists note high success rates (Howell, 2011; Rothschild, 2009), but others find that patients continue to resist full integration. A few therapists have in fact questioned the need for full integration.

Depersonalization-Derealization Disorder

As you read earlier, DSM-5 categorizes **depersonalization–derealization disorder** as a dissociative disorder, even though it is not characterized by the memory difficulties found in the other dissociative disorders. Its central symptom is persistent and recurrent episodes of *depersonalization* (the sense that one's own mental functioning or body are unreal or detached) and/or *derealization* (the sense that one's surroundings are unreal or detached).

> A 24-year-old graduate student sought treatment because he felt he was losing his mind. He had begun to doubt his own reality. He felt he was living in a dream in which he saw himself from without, and did not feel connected to his body or his thoughts. When he saw himself through his own eyes, he perceived his body parts as distorted—his hands and feet seemed quite large. As he walked across campus, he often felt the people he saw might be robots; he began to ruminate about his dizzy spells—did this mean that he had a brain tumor? . . . He often noted that he spent so much time thinking about his situation that he lost contact with all feelings except a pervasive discomfort about his own predicament.
>
> In his second session, he was preoccupied with his perception that his feet had grown too large for his shoes, and fretted over whether to break up with his girlfriend because he doubted the reality of his feelings for her, and had begun to perceive her in a distorted manner. He said he had hesitated before returning for his second appointment, because he wondered whether his therapist was really alive. He was very pessimistic that he could be helped, and had vague suicidal ideation. A thorough medical and neurological evaluation found no organic etiology.
>
> *(Kluft, 1988, p. 580)*

Like this graduate student, people experiencing depersonalization feel as though they have become separated from their body and are observing themselves from outside. Occasionally their mind seems to be floating a few feet above them—a sensation known as *doubling*. Their body parts feel foreign to them, the hands and feet smaller or bigger than usual. Many sufferers describe their emotional state as "mechanical," "dreamlike," or "dizzy." Throughout the whole experience, however, they are aware that their perceptions are distorted, and in that sense they remain in contact with reality. In some cases this sense of unreality also extends to other sensory experiences and behavior. People may, for example, experience distortions in their sense of touch or smell or their judgments of time or space, or they may feel that they have lost control over their speech or actions.

•**fusion**•The final merging of two or more subpersonalities in dissociative identity disorder.

•**depersonalization-derealization disorder**•A dissociative disorder marked by the presence of persistent and recurrent episodes of depersonalization, derealization, or both.

Daniel Morel/Reuters/Corbis

In contrast to depersonalization, derealization is characterized by feeling that the external world is unreal and strange. Objects may seem to change shape or size; other persons may seem removed, mechanical, or even dead. The graduate student, for example, began to perceive his girlfriend in a distorted manner, and he hesitated to return for a second session of therapy because he wondered whether his therapist was really alive.

Depersonalization and derealization experiences by themselves do not indicate a depersonalization-derealization disorder. Transient depersonalization or derealization reactions are fairly common (Michal, 2011). One-third of all people say that on occasion they have felt as though they were watching themselves in a movie. Similarly, one-third of individuals who confront a life-threatening danger experience feelings of depersonalization or derealization (van Duijl et al., 2010). People sometimes have feelings of depersonalization after practicing meditation, and individuals who travel to new places often report a temporary sense of depersonalization. Young children may also experience depersonalization from time to time as they are developing their capacity for self-awareness. In most such cases, the individuals are able to compensate for the distortion and continue to function with reasonable effectiveness until the temporary episode eventually ends.

If you have ever experienced feelings of depersonalization or derealization, how did you explain them at the time?

The symptoms of depersonalization-derealization disorder, in contrast, are persistent or recurrent, cause considerable distress, and may impair social relationships and job performance (Michal, 2011; Simeon et al., 2003). The disorder occurs most frequently in adolescents and young adults, hardly ever in people over 40 (Moyano, 2010). It usually comes on suddenly and may be triggered by extreme fatigue, physical pain, intense stress, or recovery from substance abuse. Survivors of traumatic experiences or people caught in life-threatening situations, such as hostages or kidnap victims, seem to be particularly vulnerable to this disorder (van Duijl et al., 2010). The disorder tends to be long-lasting; the symptoms may improve and even disappear for a time, only to return or intensify during times of severe stress. Like the graduate student in our case discussion, many sufferers fear that they are losing their minds and become preoccupied with worry about their symptoms. Few theories have been offered to explain this disorder.

A Life, Interrupted

By Rebecca Flint Marx and Vytenis Didziulis

The young woman was floating face down in the water, about a mile southwest of the southern tip of Manhattan. Wearing only red running shorts and a black sports bra, she was barely visible to the naked eye of the captain of the Staten Island Ferry. . . . Less than four minutes later, a skiff piloted by two of the ferry's deckhands pulled up alongside the woman. One man took hold of her ankles while the other grabbed her shoulders. As she was lifted from the water, she gasped. . . .

On Aug. 28, a Thursday, a 23-year-old schoolteacher from Hamilton Heights named Hannah Emily Upp went for a jog along Riverside Drive. That jog is the last thing that Ms. Upp says she remembers before the deckhands rescued her from the waters of New York Harbor on the morning of Tuesday, Sept. 16.

Rumors and speculation abounded about what befell Ms. Upp. She disappeared the day before the start of a new school year at Thurgood Marshall Academy, a Harlem school, where she taught Spanish. She left behind her wallet, her cellphone, her ID and a host of troubling questions.

It was as if the city had simply opened wide and swallowed her whole—until she was seen on a security camera at the Midtown Apple store checking her e-mail. Then she vanished again. And then reappeared, not only at the Apple store but also at a Starbucks and several New York Sports Clubs, where news reports said she went to shower. . . .

After her rescue, while she was recovering from hypothermia and dehydration . . . she was told that she was suffering from dissociative fugue, a rare form of amnesia that causes people to forget their identity, suddenly and without warning, and can last from a few hours to years.

"It's weird," Ms. Upp said a few weeks ago over a cup of tea in a Hell's Kitchen café, the first time in the five months since her rescue that she had talked publicly about her experience. "How do you feel guilty for something you didn't even know you did? It's not your fault, but it's still somehow you. So it's definitely made me reconsider everything. Who was I before? Who was I then—is that part of me? Who am I now?" . . .

The medical condition diagnosed in Ms. Upp is so uncommon that few psychiatrists ever see it. . . . [D]issociative fugue demonstrates the glasslike fragility of memory and identity.

Its most famous sufferer is the fictional Jason Bourne, the secret agent made flesh on film by Matt Damon. The Bourne character takes his name from Ansel Bourne, a Rhode Island preacher who suffered the earliest recorded case of the condition when he was en route to Providence in 1887. . . .

When Ms. Upp failed to return to her apartment after four days, her roommates contacted the police. After a week with no word, and fearing that she had been a victim of a kidnapping or another violent crime, her friends and family posted messages on blogs and started a Facebook page called "We're Not Giving Upp (on Hannah)," which was dedicated to tracking her down. . . .

Ms. Upp credits the police with helping her piece together what happened during the missing weeks. . . . According to police reports, Ms. Upp spent a lot of time in places like Riverside Drive, "where if you're in running gear, no one's going to look at you twice," she said. . . .

Ms. Upp's doctors have helped her make sense of other clues, like her stops at the Apple store, where she was seen . . . checking her e-mail. . . .

"I was on a computer, but there's no evidence in my Gmail account of any e-mails being sent or read," Ms. Upp said. She did log in, something her doctors attributed to a muscle memory: How many times in our lives have we typed in our name and password without even thinking? "So their theory," Ms. Upp said, "is that I thought, hey, this is a computer, this is what I do with a computer." But once she opened her e-mail,

PUTTING IT...together

Disorders Rediscovered

Disorders focusing on somatic and dissociative symptoms include some of the clinical field's earliest identified psychological disorders. Indeed, as you read in Chapter 1, they were key to the development of the psychogenic perspective. Despite this early impact, the clinical field stopped paying much attention to these disorders during the middle part of the twentieth century. The feeling among many clinical theorists was that the number of such cases was shrinking. And more than a few questioned the legitimacy of the diagnoses.

Hannah Emily Upp disappeared while jogging and was rescued nearly three weeks later off Staten Island, New York.

Nicole Bengiveno/New York Times/Redux

she couldn't figure out who Hannah was and why everyone was looking for her. "So I logged out and left." . . .

The one tangible clue to the extent of her travels was the large blister on her heel. In addition to the hypothermia, dehydration and a sunburn, the blister was the only physical record of her three weeks spent on the move, and it suggests why she eventually left the city's streets for its waterways: Her feet hurt.

"They think that just as I was wandering on land, I wandered in the water," Ms. Upp said. "I don't think I had a purpose. But I had that really big blister, so maybe I just didn't want my shoes on anymore." . . .

"From what I can piece together, I left Manhattan late at night," she said. "I've gone back over lunar records to figure out if there was a full moon then, which sounds right. At that point in the tidal records, the current would have been in my favor, so whether I was Olympic swimming or doggy paddling, I could have made it."

Made it, that is, to Robbins Reef [Staten Island], where she pulled herself ashore after swimming for several hours. She believes that she spent the next day sitting on the rocks around the lighthouse, a theory supported by the fresh sunburn she sported when she was rescued. She remained on the island until she returned to the water around 11 the following morning.

Then she was in an ambulance speeding toward the hospital. When her family and friends arrived, Ms. Upp said, "It was, wow, I'm happy to see you, but why are you so happy to see me?" . . .

Initially, Ms. Upp said she believed that once she returned to her apartment, she would leave her ordeal in the past. But in some ways, it was just beginning. [T]he larger question was whether she could resume her daily life without worrying about stumbling into another fugue. And would she forever be known as "that missing teacher"? . . .

Recovery has been slow. Simple social routines like seeing friends and taking a dance class have helped her re-establish her personal identity. . . . She wonders, too, about what caused the fugue state. So far, a possible catalyst has yet to emerge.

"That's the hardest thing," Ms. Upp acknowledged. "If I don't feel confident about the trigger, how do you start with prevention?"

She has learned, however, that fugues are usually isolated events.

"If you work through it, you can usually go on to live a normal life," she said." . . . And day by day, she works to put the "missing teacher" label behind her. . . .

Much of that thinking has changed in the past three decades. The field's keen interest in the impact of stress upon health and physical illness has, by association, reawakened interest in disorders that feature somatic symptoms. Similarly, as you will see in Chapter 18, the field has greatly intensified its efforts to understand and treat Alzheimer's disease in recent years, and that work has sparked a broad interest in the operation of memory, including an interest in dissociative disorders.

Over the past 30 years there has been considerable research seeking to help clinicians recognize, understand, and treat unexplained physical and memory disorders. Although this research has yet to produce clear insights or highly effective treatments, it has already suggested that the disorders may be more common than clinical theorists had come to believe. Moreover, there is growing evidence that the disorders may be rooted in

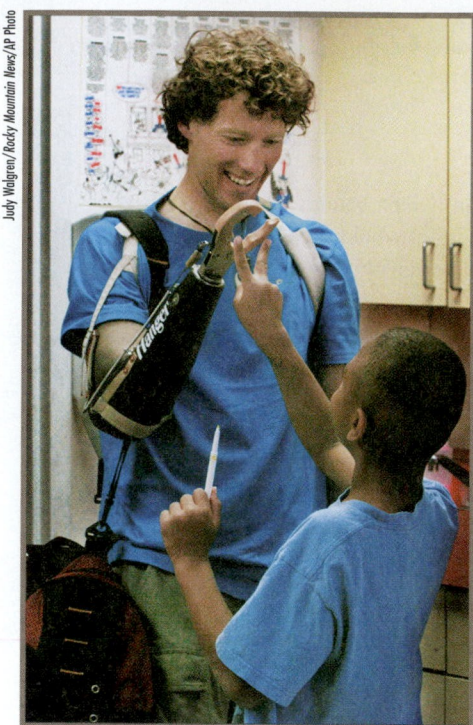

Phantom limb syndrome
While hiking in Utah, Aron Ralston's arm became pinned under a boulder and he had to amputate it himself, a horrific experience depicted by actor James Franco in the movie *127 Hours*. People who have lost their limbs often continue to feel pain and other sensations where their limbs used to be. A conversion or somatic symptom disorder? No. After amputation, brain areas that used to trigger sensations in the limbs remain intact and may sometimes produce sensations where the missing limbs used to be.

processes that are already well known from other areas of study, such as overattentiveness to bodily processes, cognitive misinterpretations, state-dependent learning, and self-hypnosis. Given this increased interest and research, we may witness significant growth in our understanding and treatment of these disorders in the coming years.

At the same time, many of today's clinicians worry that the clinical field's focus on somatic and dissociative symptoms is swinging back too far—that the high degree of interest in these kinds of symptoms may be creating a false impression of their prevalence or importance. Some clinicians note, for example, that physicians are often quick to assign the label "conversion disorder" or "somatic symptom disorder" to elusive medical problems such as chronic fatigue syndrome and lupus—clearly a disservice to patients with such severe problems and to the progress of medical science. Similarly, a number of clinicians worry that at least some of the many legal defenses based on dissociative identity disorder or other dissociative disorders are contrived or inaccurate. Of course, such possibilities serve to highlight even further the importance of continued investigations into all aspects of the disorders.

Summing Up

- **DISORDERS FOCUSING ON SOMATIC SYMPTOMS** Several DSM-5 disorders focus on somatic symptoms, including *factitious disorder, conversion disorder, somatic symptom disorder, illness anxiety disorder,* and *body dysmorphic disorder.* In these disorders, the somatic symptoms are primarily caused by psychosocial factors, or the symptoms trigger excessive anxiety or concern. pp. 189–190

- **FACTITIOUS DISORDER** Persons with *factitious disorder* feign or induce physical disorders, typically for the purpose of assuming the role of a sick person. The disorder is not well understood or treated. In a related pattern, *factious disorder imposed on another,* a parent fabricates or induces a physical illness in his or her child. pp. 190–192

- **CONVERSION AND SOMATIC SYMPTOM DISORDERS** *Conversion disorder* features bodily symptoms that affect voluntary motor and sensory functions, but the symptoms are inconsistent with known medical diseases. Diagnosticians are sometimes able to distinguish conversion disorder from a "true" medical problem by observing oddities in the patient's medical picture. In *somatic symptom disorder,* people become excessively distressed, concerned, and anxious about bodily symptoms that they are experiencing, and their lives are greatly and disproportionately disrupted by the symptoms. Current explanations for conversion and somatic symptom disorders include psychodynamic, behavioral, and cognitive explanations. Treatments for these disorders include insight, exposure, and drug therapies and may feature techniques such as suggestion, reinforcement, or confrontation. pp. 192–199

- **ILLNESS ANXIETY DISORDER AND BODY DYSMORPHIC DISORDER** People with *illness anxiety disorder* are chronically anxious about and preoccupied with the notion that they have or are developing a serious medical illness, despite the absence of substantial somatic symptoms. Those with *body dysmorphic disorder* worry excessively about some imagined or minor defect in their appearance. Theorists explain these disorders much as they do anxiety and obsessive-compulsive disorders. Treatment includes drug, behavioral, and cognitive approaches originally developed for obsessive-compulsive disorder. pp. 199–202

- **DISSOCIATIVE DISORDERS** People with *dissociative disorders* experience major changes in *memory* and *identity* that are not caused by clear physical factors—changes that often emerge after a traumatic event. Typically, one part of the memory or identity is *dissociated,* or *separated,* from the other parts. People with *dissociative amnesia* are unable to recall important personal information or past events in their lives. Those with *dissociative fugue,* an extreme form of dissociative amnesia, not only fail to remember personal information, but also flee to a different location and may establish a new identity. In another dissociative disorder, *dissociative identity disorder* (multiple personality disorder), persons display two or more distinct subpersonalities. pp. 202–203

■ **DISSOCIATIVE AMNESIA AND DISSOCIATIVE IDENTITY DISORDER** Dissociative amnesia and dissociative identity disorder are not well understood. Among the processes that have been cited to explain them are extreme *repression, operant conditioning, state-dependent learning,* and *self-hypnosis.* The latter two phenomena, in particular, have excited the interest of clinical scientists.

Dissociative amnesia may end on its own or may require treatment. Dissociative identity disorder typically requires treatment. Approaches commonly used to help people with dissociative amnesia recover their lost memories are *psychodynamic therapy, hypnotic therapy,* and *sodium amobarbital* or *sodium pentobarbital.* Therapists who treat people with dissociative identity disorder use the same approaches and also try to help the clients *recognize the nature and scope of their disorder, recover the gaps in their memory,* and *integrate their subpersonalities into one functional personality.* pp. 203–216

■ **DEPERSONALIZATION-DEREALIZATION DISORDER** People with yet another kind of dissociative disorder, *depersonalization-derealization disorder,* feel as though they are detached from their own mental processes or body and are observing themselves from the outside, or feel as though the individuals or objects around them are unreal or detached. Transient depersonalization and derealization experiences seem to be relatively common, while depersonalization-derealization disorder is not. pp. 216–217

KevinMazur/WireImage/Getty Images

Tanorexia?

A delighted fan photographs herself with Snooki Polizzi, star of the reality TV show *Jersey Shore.* One of the most talked-about features in the show is the constant pursuit of a dark tan by Snooki. Some clinicians consider "tanorexia"—a pop term for the addictive pursuit of a tan, both outdoors and in tanning beds—to be a mild form of body dysmorphic disorder.

PsychPortal

Visit **Psych**Portal

www.yourpsychportal.com

to access the e-book, videocases and other case materials and activities, and study aids, including flashcards, crossword puzzles, quizzes, FAQs, and research exercises.

DISORDERS OF MOOD

For ... a six-month period, her irritability bordered on the irrational. She screamed in anger or sobbed in despair at every dirty dish left on the coffee table or on the bedroom floor. Each day the need to plan the dinner menu provoked agonizing indecision. How could all the virtues or, more likely, vices of hamburgers be accurately compared to those of spaghetti? ... She had her whole family walking on eggs. She thought they would be better off if she were dead.

Beatrice could not cope with her job. As a branch manager of a large chain store, she had many decisions to make. Unable to make them herself, she would ask employees who were much less competent for advice, but then she could not decide whose advice to take. Each morning before going to work, she complained of nausea. ...

Beatrice's husband loved her, but he did not understand what was wrong. He thought that she would improve if he made her life easier by taking over more housework, cooking, and child care. His attempt to help only made Beatrice feel more guilty and worthless. She wanted to make a contribution to her family. She wanted to do the chores "like normal people" did but broke down crying at the smallest impediment to a perfect job. ... Months passed, and Beatrice's problem became more serious. Some days she was too upset to go to work. She stopped seeing her friends. She spent most of her time at home either yelling or crying. Finally, Beatrice's husband called the psychiatrist and insisted that something was seriously wrong.

Lickey & Gordon, 1991, p. 181

Most people's moods come and go. Their feelings of elation or sadness are understandable reactions to daily events and do not affect their lives greatly. However, the moods of people with mood disorders tend to last a long time. As in Beatrice's case, their moods color all of their interactions with the world and even interfere with normal functioning. Depression and mania are the key emotions in disorders of mood. **Depression** is a low, sad state in which life seems dark and its challenges overwhelming. **Mania,** the opposite of depression, is a state of breathless euphoria, or at least frenzied energy, in which people may have an exaggerated belief that the world is theirs for the taking.

Mood problems are at the center of two groups of disorders—depressive disorders and bipolar disorders (APA, 2013). People with **depressive disorders** suffer only from depression, a pattern called **unipolar depression.** They have no history of mania and return to a normal or nearly normal mood when their depression lifts. In contrast, those who display **bipolar disorders** experience periods of mania that alternate with periods of depression. You might logically expect a third pattern of mood disorder, *unipolar mania,* in which people suffer from mania only, but this pattern is uncommon.

Mood problems have always captured people's interest, in part because so many famous people have suffered from them. The Bible speaks of the severe depressions of Nebuchadnezzar, Saul, and Moses. Queen Victoria of England and Abraham Lincoln seem to have experienced recurring depressions. Mood difficulties also have plagued writers Ernest Hemingway and Sylvia Plath, comedians Jim Carrey

•**depression**•A low, sad state marked by significant levels of sadness, lack of energy, low self-worth, guilt, or related symptoms.

•**mania**•A state or episode of euphoria or frenzied activity in which people may have an exaggerated belief that the world is theirs for the taking.

•**depressive disorders**•The group of disorders marked by unipolar depression.

•**unipolar depression**•Depression without a history of mania.

•**bipolar disorder**•A disorder marked by alternating or intermixed periods of mania and depression.

and Rodney Dangerfield, and musical performers Eminem and Beyonce Knowles. Their mood problems have been shared by millions, and today the economic costs amount to many billions of dollars each year (Dilsaver, 2011). Of course, the human suffering that mood disorders cause is beyond calculation.

Unipolar Depression: The Depressive Disorders

Whenever we feel particularly unhappy, we are likely to describe ourselves as "depressed." In all likelihood, we are merely responding to sad events, fatigue, or unhappy thoughts. This loose use of the term confuses a perfectly normal mood swing with a clinical syndrome. All of us experience dejection from time to time, but only some experience a depressive disorder.

Normal dejection is seldom severe enough to influence daily functioning significantly or persist very long. Such downturns in mood can even be beneficial. Periods spent in contemplation can lead us to explore our inner selves, our values, and our way of life, and we often emerge with a sense of greater strength, clarity, and resolve.

Almost every day we experience ups and downs in mood. How can we distinguish the everyday blues from clinical depression?

Depressive disorders, on the other hand, have no redeeming characteristics. They bring severe and long-lasting psychological pain that may intensify as time goes by. Those who suffer from such disorders may lose their will to carry out the simplest of life's activities; some even lose their will to live.

How Common Is Unipolar Depression?

Around 8 percent of adults in the United States suffer from a severe unipolar pattern of depression in any given year, while as many as 5 percent suffer from mild forms (González et al., 2010; Kessler et al., 2010, 2005). Around 19 percent of all adults experience an episode of severe unipolar depression at some point in their lives. These prevalence rates are similar in Canada, England, France, and many other countries (see Table 8-1). Moreover, the rate of depression—mild or severe—is higher among poor people than wealthier people (Sareen et al., 2011).

People of any age may suffer from unipolar depression. In most countries, however, people in their forties are more likely than those in any other age group to experience this problem (Blanchflower & Oswald, 2007). The median age for its onset, now 26 in the United States, keeps dropping for each generation, and worldwide research projects suggest that the risk of experiencing unipolar depression has increased steadily since 1915 (Gonzalez et al., 2010; Weissman et al., 1992, 1991).

Women are at least twice as likely as men to experience episodes of severe unipolar depression (Astbury, 2010). As many as 26 percent of women may have an episode at some time in their lives, compared with 12 percent of men. As you will see in Chapter 17, among children the prevalence of unipolar depression is similar for girls and boys.

Approximately 85 percent of people with unipolar depression recover, some without treatment. Around 40 percent of them have at least one other episode of depression later in their lives (Monroe, 2010; Whisman & Schonbrun, 2010; Eaton et al., 2008).

What Are the Symptoms of Depression?

The picture of depression may vary from person to person. Earlier you saw how Beatrice's indecisiveness, uncontrollable sobbing, and feelings of despair, anger, and worthlessness brought her job and social life to a standstill. Other depressed people

table: 8-1

Across the World: What Percentage of Adults Suffer from Mood Disorders Each Year?

United States	9.6%
Ukraine	9.1%
France	8.5%
Colombia	6.8%
Lebanon	6.6%
Spain	4.9%
Mexico	4.8%
Italy	3.8%
Germany	3.6%
Japan	3.1%

Note: Mood disorders considered are major depressive disorder, dysthymic disorder, and bipolar disorder.
Source: Van Dusen, 2007; WHO, 2004.

have symptoms that are less severe. They manage to function, although their depression typically robs them of much effectiveness or pleasure, as you can see in the case of Derek:

Derek has probably suffered from depression all of his adult life but was unaware of it for many years. Derek called himself a night person, claiming that he could not think clearly until after noon even though he was often awake by 4:00 A.M. He tried to schedule his work as editorial writer for a small . . . newspaper so that it was compatible with his depressed mood at the beginning of the day. Therefore, he scheduled meetings for the mornings; talking with people got him moving. He saved writing and decision making for later in the day.

. . . Derek's private thoughts were rarely cheerful and self-confident. He felt that his marriage was a mere business partnership. He provided the money, and she provided a home and children. Derek and his wife rarely expressed affection for each other. Occasionally, he had images of his own violent death in a bicycle crash, in a plane crash, or in a murder by an unidentified assailant.

Derek felt that he was constantly on the edge of job failure. He was disappointed that his editorials had not attracted the attention of larger papers. He was certain that several of the younger people on the paper had better ideas and wrote more skillfully than he did. He scolded himself for a bad editorial that he had written ten years earlier. Although that particular piece had not been up to his usual standards, everyone else on the paper had forgotten it a week after it appeared. But ten years later, Derek was still ruminating over that one editorial. . . .

Derek brushed off his morning confusion as a lack of quick intelligence. He had no way to know that it was a symptom of depression. He never realized that his death images might be suicidal thinking. People do not talk about such things. For all Derek knew, everyone had similar thoughts.

(Lickey & Gordon, 1991, pp. 183–185)

As the cases of Beatrice and Derek indicate, depression has many symptoms other than sadness. The symptoms, which often exacerbate one another, span five areas of functioning: emotional, motivational, behavioral, cognitive, and physical.

Emotional Symptoms

Most people who are depressed feel sad and dejected. They describe themselves as feeling "miserable," "empty," and "humiliated." They tend to lose their sense of humor, report getting little pleasure from anything, and in some cases display *anhedonia,* an inability to experience any pleasure at all. A number also experience anxiety, anger, or agitation (Brown, 2010). This sea of misery may lead to crying spells. A successful writer and editor describes the agony she experienced each morning as her depression was unfolding:

? Research participants often prefer listening to sad songs over happy songs, even though they make them depressed. Why?

Nights I could handle. I fell asleep easily, and sleep allowed me to forget. But my mornings were unmanageable. To wake up each morning was to remember once again that the world by which I defined myself was no more. Soon after opening my eyes, the crying bouts would start and I'd sit alone for hours, weeping and mourning my losses.

(Williams, 2008, p. 9)

Motivational Symptoms Depressed people typically lose the desire to pursue their usual activities. Almost all report a lack of drive, initiative, and spontaneity. They may have to force themselves to go to work, talk with friends, eat meals, or have sex. This state has been described as a "paralysis of will" (Beck, 1967). Terrie Williams, author of *Black Pain,* a book about depression in African Americans, describes her social withdrawal during a depressive episode:

> *I woke up one morning with a knot of fear in my stomach so crippling that I couldn't face light, much less day, and so intense that I stayed in bed for three days with the shades drawn and the lights out.*
>
> *Three days. Three days not answering the phone. Three days not checking my e-mail. I was disconnected completely from the outside world, and I didn't care. Then on the morning of the fourth day there was a knock on my door. Since I hadn't ordered food I ignored it. The knocking kept up and I kept ignoring it. I heard the sound of keys rattling in my front door. Slowly the bedroom door opened and in the painful light from the doorway I saw the figures of two old friends. "Terrie, are you in there?"*
>
> *(Williams, 2008, p. xxiv)*

Suicide represents the ultimate escape from life's challenges. As you will see in Chapter 10, many depressed people become uninterested in life or wish to die; others wish they could kill themselves, and some actually do. It has been estimated that between 6 and 15 percent of people who suffer from severe depression commit suicide (Mulholland, 2010; Taube-Schiff & Lau, 2008).

Behavioral Symptoms Depressed people are usually less active and less productive. They spend more time alone and may stay in bed for long periods. One man recalls, "I'd awaken early, but I'd just lie there—what was the use of getting up to a miserable day?" (Kraines & Thetford, 1972, p. 21). Depressed people may also move and even speak more slowly (Joiner, 2002).

Cognitive Symptoms Depressed people hold extremely negative views of themselves. They consider themselves inadequate, undesirable, inferior, perhaps evil (Sowislo & Orth, 2012). They also blame themselves for nearly every unfortunate event, even things that have nothing to do with them, and they rarely credit themselves for positive achievements.

Another cognitive symptom of depression is pessimism. Sufferers are usually convinced that nothing will ever improve, and they feel helpless to change any aspect of their lives. Because they expect the worst, they are likely to procrastinate. Their sense of hopelessness and helplessness makes them especially vulnerable to suicidal thinking (Wilson & Deane, 2010).

People with depression frequently complain that their intellectual ability is poor. They feel confused, unable to remember things, easily distracted, and unable to solve even the smallest problems. In laboratory studies, depressed individuals do perform more poorly than nondepressed persons on some tasks of memory, attention, and reasoning (Hammar et al., 2011; Lyche et al., 2011). It may be, however, that these difficulties sometimes reflect motivational problems rather than cognitive ones.

Physical Symptoms People who are depressed frequently have such physical ailments as headaches, indigestion, constipation, dizzy spells, and general pain (Goldstein et al., 2011). In fact, many depressions are misdiagnosed as medical problems at first (Parker & Hyett, 2010). Disturbances in appetite and sleep are particularly common (Armitage & Arnett, 2011). Most depressed people eat less, sleep less, and feel more fatigued than they did prior to the disorder. Some, however, eat and sleep excessively. Terrie Williams describes the changes in the pattern of her sleep:

At first I didn't notice the change. Then things got worse. I always hated waking up, but slowly it was turning into something deeper; it was less like I didn't want to wake up, and more like I couldn't. I didn't feel tired, but I had no energy. I didn't feel sleepy, but I would have welcomed sleep with open arms. I had the sensation of a huge weight, invisible but gigantic, pressing down on me, almost crushing me into the bed and pinning me there.

(Williams, 2008, p. xxii)

Diagnosing Unipolar Depression

According to DSM-5, a *major depressive episode* is a period of two or more weeks marked by at least five symptoms of depression, including sad mood and/or loss of pleasure (see Table 8-2). In extreme cases, the episode may include psychotic symptoms, ones marked by a loss of contact with reality, such as *delusions*—bizarre ideas without foundation— or *hallucinations*—perceptions of things that are not actually present. A depressed man

table: 8-2

DSM-5 Checklist

Major Depressive Episode

1. The presence of five or more of the following symptoms during the same two-week period, including at least one of the first two symptoms: • daily depressed mood for most of the day • daily diminished interest or pleasure in almost all activities for most of the day • significant weight loss or weight gain, or daily decrease or increase in appetite • daily insomnia or hypersomnia • daily psychomotor agitation or retardation • daily fatigue or loss of energy • daily feelings of worthlessness or excessive guilt • daily reduced ability to think or concentrate, or indecisiveness • recurrent thoughts of death or suicide, a suicide attempt, or a specific plan for committing suicide.

2. Significant distress or impairment.

Major Depressive Disorder

1. The presence of a major depressive episode.

2. No history of a manic or hypomanic episode.

Dysthymic Disorder (One Form of *Persistent Depressive Disorder*)

1. Depressed mood for most of the day, for more days than not, for at least two years.

2. Presence, while depressed, of at least two of the following: • poor appetite or overeating • insomnia or hypersomnia • low energy or fatigue • low self-esteem • poor concentration or difficulty making decisions • feelings of hopelessness.

3. During the two-year period, symptoms not absent for more than two months at a time.

4. No history of a manic or hypomanic episode.

5. Significant distress or impairment.

Based on APA, 2013, 2012.

•**major depressive disorder**•A severe pattern of depression that is disabling and is not caused by such factors as drugs or a general medical condition.

•**dysthymic disorder**•A mood disorder that is similar to but longer-lasting and less disabling than a major depressive disorder.

•**premenstrual dysphoric disorder**•A disorder marked by repeated experiences of significant depression and related symptoms during the week before menstruation.

with psychotic symptoms may imagine that he cannot eat "because my intestines are deteriorating and will soon stop working," or he may believe that he sees his dead wife.

DSM-5 lists several types of depressive disorders. People who experience a major depressive episode without having any history of mania receive a diagnosis of **major depressive disorder** (APA, 2013, 2012) (see Table 8-2 again). The disorder may be additionally categorized as *recurrent* if it has been preceded by previous episodes, *seasonal* if it changes with the seasons (for example, if the depression recurs each winter), *catatonic* if it is marked by either immobility or excessive activity, *postpartum* if it occurs within four weeks of giving birth (see *PsychWatch* on the next page), or *melancholic* if the person is almost totally unaffected by pleasurable events. It sometimes turns out that an apparent case of major depressive disorder is, in fact, a depressive episode occurring within a larger pattern of bipolar disorder—a pattern in which the individual's manic episode has not yet appeared. When the person experiences a manic episode at a later time, the diagnosis is changed to bipolar disorder.

If a case of unipolar depression is chronic, it is technically called *persistent depressive disorder* (APA, 2013). Some people with this chronic pattern experience major depressive episodes. Others experience less severe and less disabling symptoms, a form of persistent depressive disorder called **dysthymic disorder** (see Table 8-2 again). When dysthymic disorder leads to major depressive disorder, the sequence is called *double depression* (Arnow & Post, 2010).

A third type of depressive disorder is **premenstrual dysphoric disorder,** a diagnosis given to certain women who repeatedly experience clinically significant depressive and related symptoms during the week before menstruation (see *PsychWatch* on page 230).

Yet another kind of depressive disorder, *disruptive mood dysregulation disorder,* is characterized by a combination of persistent depressive symptoms and recurrent outbursts of severe temper. This disorder emerges during mid-childhood or adolescence and so will be discussed in Chapter 17, *Disorders of Childhood and Adolescence.*

What Causes Unipolar Depression?

Episodes of unipolar depression often seem to be triggered by stressful events (Gutman & Nemeroff, 2011; Brown, 2010). In fact, researchers have found that depressed people experience a greater number of stressful life events during the month just before the onset of their disorder than do other people during the same period of time. Of course, stressful life events also precede other psychological disorders, but depressed people often report more such events than anybody else.

Why do you think stressful events or periods in life might trigger depressed feelings and other negative emotions?

Some clinicians consider it important to distinguish a *reactive (exogenous) depression,* which follows clear-cut stressful events, from an *endogenous depression,* which seems to be a response to internal factors. But can one ever know for certain whether a depression is reactive or not? Even if stressful events occurred before the onset of depression, that depression may not be reactive. The events could actually be a coincidence (Paykel, 2003). Thus, today's clinicians usually concentrate on recognizing both the situational and the internal aspects of any given case of unipolar depression.

The current explanations of unipolar depression point to biological, psychological, and sociocultural factors. Just as clinicians now recognize both internal and situational features in each case of depression, many believe that the various explanations should be viewed collectively for unipolar depression to be understood fully.

The Biological View

Medical researchers have been aware for years that certain diseases and drugs produce mood changes. Could unipolar depression itself have biological causes? Evidence from genetic, biochemical, anatomical, and immune system studies suggests that often it does.

BETWEEN THE LINES

Paternal Postpartum Depression

Considerable research has already indicated that a mother's postpartum depression can lead to disturbances in a child's social, behavioral, and cognitive development. Research suggests that a father's postpartum depression can have similar effects (Edoka et al., 2011; Ramchandani et al., 2005). ‹‹

Sadness at the Happiest of Times

Women usually expect the birth of a child to be a happy experience. But for 10 to 30 percent of new mothers, the weeks and months after childbirth bring clinical depression (Kendall-Tackett, 2010; Mauthner, 2010; Grace et al., 2003; O'Hara, 2003). Postpartum depression typically begins within four weeks after the birth of a child (APA, 2000), and it is far more severe than simple "baby blues." It is also different from other postpartum syndromes such as *postpartum psychosis,* a problem that will be examined in Chapter 14.

The "baby blues" are so common—as many as 80 percent of women experience them—that most researchers consider them normal. As new mothers try to cope with the wakeful nights, rattled emotions, and other stresses that accompany the arrival of a new baby, they may experience crying spells, fatigue, anxiety, insomnia, and sadness. These symptoms usually disappear within days or weeks (Kendall-Tackett, 2010; Horowitz et al., 2005, 1995).

In postpartum depression, however, depressive symptoms continue and may last up to a year. The symptoms include extreme sadness, despair, tearfulness, insomnia, anxiety, intrusive thoughts, compulsions, panic attacks, feelings of inability to cope, and suicidal thoughts. The mother–infant relationship and the psychological and physical health of the child may suffer as a result (Kendall-Tacket, 2010; Monti et al., 2004). Women who experience postpartum depression have a 25 to 50 percent chance of developing it again with a subsequent birth (Stevens et al., 2002).

Many clinicians believe that the hormonal changes accompanying childbirth trigger postpartum depression. All women experience a kind of hormone "withdrawal" after delivery, as estrogen and progesterone levels, which rise as much as 50 times above normal during pregnancy, now drop sharply to levels far below normal (Horowitz et al., 2005, 1995). Perhaps some women are particularly

Bryan Bedder/WireImage/Getty Images

Singing away depression
Actress and musician Gwyneth Paltrow performs at the Annual Country Music Awards in Nashville, Tennessee. Paltrow recently revealed that she suffered from postpartum depression after giving birth to her second child in 2006. Said Paltrow, "I felt like a zombie. . . . I couldn't connect. . . . I thought it meant I was a terrible mother and person. . . . I felt like a failure."

influenced by these dramatic hormone changes. Still other theorists suggest a genetic predisposition to postpartum depression (Comasco et al., 2011). A woman with a family history of mood disorders appears to be at high risk, even if she herself has not previously had a mood disorder (Phillips, 2011; APA, 2000).

At the same time, psychological and sociocultural factors may play important roles in the disorder (Mauthner, 2010). The birth of a baby brings enormous psychological and social change. A woman typically faces changes in her marital relationship, daily routines, and social roles. Sleep and relaxation are likely to decrease, and financial pressures may increase. Perhaps she feels the added stress of giving up a career—or of trying to maintain one. This pileup of stress may heighten the risk of depression (Phillips, 2011; Kendall-Tackett, 2010). Mothers whose infants are sick or temperamentally "difficult" may experience yet additional pressure.

Fortunately, treatment can make a big difference for most women with postpartum depression. Self-help support groups have proved extremely helpful for many women with the disorder (Evans et al., 2012). In addition, many respond well to the same approaches that are applied to other forms of depression—antidepressant medications, cognitive therapy, interpersonal psychotherapy, or a combination of these approaches (Miller & LaRusso, 2011; Phillips, 2011).

However, many women who would benefit from treatment do not seek help because they feel ashamed about being sad at a time that is supposed to be joyous and are concerned about being judged harshly (Mauthner, 2010). For them, and for the spouses and family members close to them, a large dose of education is in order. Even positive events, such as the birth of a child, can be stressful if they also bring major change to one's life. Recognizing and addressing such feelings are in everyone's best interest.

PsychWatch

Premenstrual Dysphoric Disorder: Déjà vu All Over Again

Back in the early 1990s, one of the biggest controversies in the development of DSM-IV centered on the category *premenstrual dysphoric disorder* (*PMDD*). The DSM-IV work group recommended that PMDD be formally listed as a new kind of depressive disorder. The category was to be applied when a woman was regularly impaired by at least 5 of 11 symptoms during the week before menstruation: depressed or hopeless feelings; tense or anxious feelings; marked mood changes; frequent irritability or anger and increased interpersonal conflicts; decreased interest in her usual activities; poor concentration; lack of energy; changes in appetite; insomnia or sleepiness; a sense of being overwhelmed or out of control; and physical symptoms such as swollen breasts, headaches, muscle pain, a "bloated" sensation, or weight gain.

This recommendation set off an uproar. Many clinicians (including some dissenting members of the work group), several national organizations, interest groups, and the media warned that this diagnostic category would "pathologize" severe cases of *premenstrual syndrome,* or *PMS,* the premenstrual discomforts that are common and normal, and might cause women's behavior in general to be attributed largely to

David Cheskin/PA Wire URN:10819660 (Press Association via AP Images)

"raging hormones" (a stereotype that society was finally rejecting). They argued that data were lacking to include the new category (Chase, 1993; DeAngelis, 1993).

The solution? A compromise. PMDD was not listed as a formal category in DSM-IV, but the pattern was listed in the DSM-IV appendix, with the suggestion that it be studied more thoroughly. Critics hoped that PMDD would die a quiet death there. However, two decades later

the category has gained new life. When, in 2011, the DSM-5 task force published a list of changes being considered for the new edition of the DSM, PMDD was included as one of the depressive disorders. The reaction? As you might expect, another uproar among many clinicians and interest groups. This time, however, the proponents prevailed, citing several studies conducted over the past 20 years. PMDD is now an official category in DSM-5.

•**norepinephrine**•A neurotransmitter whose abnormal activity is linked to depression and panic disorder.

•**serotonin**•A neurotransmitter whose abnormal activity is linked to depression, obsessive-compulsive disorder, and eating disorders.

Genetic Factors Four kinds of research—family pedigree, twin, adoption, and molecular biology gene studies—suggest that some people inherit a predisposition to unipolar depression (Elder & Mosack, 2011). *Family pedigree studies* select people with unipolar depression as *probands* (the proband is the person who is the focus of a genetic study), examine their relatives, and see whether depression also afflicts other members of the family. If a predisposition to unipolar depression is inherited, a proband's relatives should have a higher rate of depression than the population at large. Researchers have in fact found that as many as 20 percent of those relatives are depressed (see Table 8–3), compared with fewer than 10 percent of the general population (Kamali & McInnis, 2011; Berrettini, 2006).

If a predisposition to unipolar depression is inherited, you might also expect to find a particularly large number of cases among the close relatives of a proband. *Twin studies* have supported this expectation (Kamali & McInniss, 2011; Richard & Lyness, 2006). One study looked at nearly 200 pairs of twins. When a monozygotic (identical) twin had unipolar depression, there was a 46 percent chance that the other twin would have the same disorder. In contrast, when a dizygotic (fraternal) twin had unipolar depression, the other twin had only a 20 percent chance of developing the disorder (McGuffin et al., 1996).

Adoption studies have also implicated a genetic factor, at least in cases of severe unipolar depression. One study looked at the families of adopted persons who had been hospitalized for this disorder in Denmark. The biological parents of these adoptees turned out to have a higher incidence of severe depression (but not mild depression) than did the biological parents of a control group of nondepressed adoptees (Kamali & McInnis, 2011). Some theorists interpret these findings to mean that severe depression is more likely than mild depression to be caused by genetic factors.

Finally, today's scientists have at their disposal techniques from the field of molecular biology to help them directly identify genes and determine whether certain gene abnormalities are related to depression. Using such techniques, researchers have found evidence that unipolar depression may be tied to genes on chromosomes 1, 4, 9, 10, 11, 12, 13, 14, 17, 18, 20, 21, 22, and X (Kamali & McInnis, 2011). For example, a number of researchers have found that individuals who are depressed often have an abnormality of their *5-HTT* gene, a gene located on chromosome 17. This gene is responsible for the brain's production of *serotonin transporters,* or *5-HTTs,* proteins that help the neurotransmitter serotonin carry messages from one neuron to another (Brockmann et al., 2011; Selvaraj et al., 2011). As you will read in the next section, low activity of serotonin is closely tied to depression. People with an abnormality of the serotonin transporter gene are more likely than others to display low serotonin activity in their brains and may in turn be more prone to experience depression.

Biochemical Factors
Low activity of two neurotransmitter chemicals, **norepinephrine** and **serotonin,** has been strongly linked to unipolar depression. In the 1950s, several pieces of evidence began to point to this relationship. First, medical researchers discovered that *reserpine* and other medications for high blood pressure often caused depression (Ayd, 1956). As it turned out, some of these medications lowered norepinephrine activity and others lowered serotonin. A second piece of evidence was the discovery of the first truly effective antidepressant drugs. Although these drugs were discovered by accident, researchers soon learned that they relieve depression by increasing either norepinephrine or serotonin activity.

George P. A. Healy, 1887, The National Portrait Gallery, Smithsonian Institution

Lincoln's private war

In 1841 Abraham Lincoln wrote to a friend, "I am now the most miserable man living. If what I feel were equally distributed to the whole human family, there would be not one cheerful face on earth."

table: 8-3

Comparing Disorders of Mood

	One-year Prevalence (Percent)	Female to Male Ratio	Typical Age at Onset (Years)	Prevalence among First-Degree Relatives	Percentage Currently Receiving Treatment
Major depressive disorder	8.0%	2:1	24–29	Elevated	50.0%
Dysthymic disorder	1.5–5.0%	Between 3:2 and 2:1	10–25	Elevated	36.8%
Bipolar I disorder	1.6%	1:1	15–44	Elevated	33.8%
Bipolar II disorder	1.0%	1:1	15–44	Elevated	33.8%
Cyclothymic disorder	0.4%	1:1	15–25	Elevated	Unknown

Source: González et al., 2010; Taube-Schiff & Lau, 2008; Kessler et al., 2005, 1994; APA, 2000, 1994; Regier et al., 1993; Weissman et al., 1991.

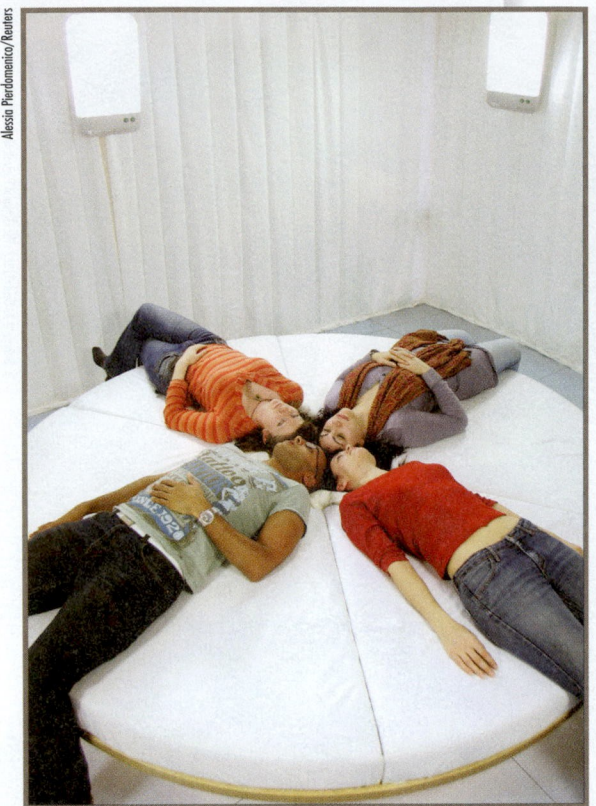

The Light Lounge

These visitors to the Science Museum in London make themselves comfortable in the Light Lounge, a white enclosure containing four light boxes where individuals can relax and experience "light therapy" to help beat the winter blues and prevent seasonal recurrences of depression, called *seasonal affective disorder*. Winter depression has been linked to a decrease in the amount of light people are exposed to and an accompanying shift in secretions of the hormone *melatonin*.

For years it was thought that low activity of *either* norepinephrine or serotonin was capable of producing depression, but investigators now believe that their relation to depression is more complicated (Goldstein et al., 2011). Research suggests that interactions between serotonin and norepinephrine activity, or between these and other kinds of neurotransmitters in the brain, rather than the operation of any one neurotransmitter alone, may account for unipolar depression. Some studies hint, for example, that depressed people have an overall imbalance in the activity of the neurotransmitters serotonin, norepinephrine, dopamine, and acetylcholine. In a variation of this theory, some researchers believe that serotonin is actually a *neuromodulator,* a chemical whose primary function is to increase or decrease the activity of other key neurotransmitters. If so, perhaps low serotonin activity serves to disrupt the activity of the other neurotransmitters, resulting in depression.

Biological researchers have also learned that the body's *endocrine system* may play a role in unipolar depression (Goldstein et al., 2011). As you have seen, endocrine glands throughout the body release *hormones,* chemicals that in turn spur body organs into action (see Chapter 6). People with unipolar depression have been found to have abnormally high levels of *cortisol,* one of the hormones released by the adrenal glands during times of stress (Gao & Bao, 2011; Veen et al., 2011). This relationship is not all that surprising, given that stressful events often seem to trigger depression. Another hormone that has been tied to depression is *melatonin,* sometimes called the "Dracula hormone" because it is released only in the dark.

Still other biological researchers are starting to believe that unipolar depression is tied more closely to what happens *within* neurons than to the chemicals that carry messages between neurons. They believe that activity by key neurotransmitters or hormones ultimately leads to deficiencies of certain proteins and other chemicals within neurons, particularly to deficiencies of *brain-derived neurotrophic factor (BDNF)*, a chemical that promotes the growth and survival of neurons (Goldstein et al., 2011; Higgins & George, 2007). Such deficiencies within neurons may impair the health of the neurons and lead, in turn, to depression.

The biochemical explanations of unipolar depression have produced much enthusiasm, but research in this area has certain limitations. Some of it has relied on *analogue studies,* which create depression-like symptoms in laboratory animals. Researchers cannot be certain that these symptoms do in fact reflect the human disorder. Similarly, until recent years, technology was limited, and studies of human depression had to measure brain biochemical activity indirectly. As a result, investigators could never be certain of the biochemical events that were occurring in the brain. Current studies using newer technology, such as PET and MRI scans, are helping to eliminate such uncertainties about such brain activity.

Brain Anatomy and Brain Circuits In Chapters 5 and 6, you read that many biological researchers now believe that the root of psychological disorders is more complicated than a single neurotransmitter or single brain area (see pages 123–124, 137–138, and 162–163). They have determined that emotional reactions of various kinds are tied to brain *circuits*—networks of brain structures that work together, triggering each other into action and producing a particular kind of emotional reaction. It appears that one brain circuit is tied largely to generalized anxiety disorder, another to panic disorder, and yet another to obsessive-compulsive disorder. Although research is far from complete, a brain circuit responsible for unipolar depression has also begun to emerge (Brockmann et al., 2011). An array of brain-imaging studies point to several brain areas that are likely members of this circuit, particularly the *prefrontal cortex,* the *hippocampus,* the *amygdala,* and *Brodmann Area 25,* an area located just under the brain part called the *cingulate cortex* (see Figure 8-1). Not surprisingly, this circuit is filled with serotonin transporters, or 5-HTTs, those proteins that help serotonin carry messages from one neuron to another (Selvaraj et al., 2011). Earlier you read that people with an abnormal 5-HTT gene are more prone to develop depression.

The *prefrontal cortex* is located within the frontal cortex of the brain. Because it receives information from a number of other brain areas, the prefrontal cortex is involved in many important functions, including mood, attention, and immune functioning. Several imaging studies have found lower activity and blood flow in the prefrontal cortex of depressed research participants than in the prefrontal cortex of nondepressed individuals (Lambert & Kinsley, 2005; Rajkowska, 2000). However, other studies, focusing on select areas of the prefrontal cortex, have found increases in activity during depression (Lemogne et al., 2010; Drevets, 2001, 2000). Correspondingly, research finds that the prefrontal cortex activity of depressed individuals increases after successful treatment by some antidepressant drugs, but decreases after successful treatment by other kinds of antidepressant drugs (Cook & Leuchter, 2001). Given these varied findings, researchers currently believe that the prefrontal cortex plays a critical role in depression but that the specific nature of this role has yet to be clearly defined (Lim et al., 2011; Goldstein et al., 2011).

The prefrontal cortex has strong neural connections with another part of the depression brain circuit, the *hippocampus.* Indeed, messages are both sent and received between the two brain areas. The hippocampus is one of the few brain areas to produce new neurons throughout adulthood, an activity known as *neurogenesis.* Several studies indicate that such hippocampal neurogenesis decreases dramatically when individuals become depressed (Kubera et al., 2011; Airan et al., 2007). Correspondingly, when depressed individuals are successfully treated by antidepressant drugs, neurogenesis in the hippocampus returns to normal (Malberg & Schechter, 2005). Moreover, some imaging studies have detected a reduction in the size of the hippocampus among depressed persons (Goldstein et al., 2011; Campbell et al., 2004). Recall from Chapter 6 that the hippocampus helps to control the brain's and body's reactions to stress and plays a role in the formation and recall of emotional memories. Thus, its role in depression is not surprising.

You may also recall from Chapters 5 and 6 that the *amygdala* is a brain area that repeatedly seems to be involved in the expression of negative emotions and memories. It has been found to be a key area in each of the brain circuits tied to generalized anxiety disorder, panic disorder, and posttraumatic stress disorder. Apparently, it also plays a role in depression. PET and fMRI scans indicate that activity and blood flow in the amygdala is 50 percent greater among depressed persons than nondepressed persons (Goldstein et al., 2011; Drevets, 2001). In fact, one study suggests that as a patient's depression increases in severity, the activity in his or her amygdala increases proportionately (Abercrombie et al., 1998). Moreover, among nondepressed research participants, activity in the amygdala increases as they are looking at pictures of sad faces; and among depressed participants, amygdala activity increases when they recall sad moments in their lives (Carlson, 2008; Liotti et al., 2002; Drevets, 2000).

The fourth part of the depression brain circuit, *Brodmann Area 25,* has received enormous attention over the past decade (Hamani et al., 2011; Mayberg et al., 2005, 2000, 1997). This area tends to be smaller in depressed people than nondepressed people. Moreover, like the amygdala, it is significantly more active among depressed people than among nondepressed people. In fact, brain scans reveal that when a person's depression subsides, the activity in his or her Area 25 decreases significantly. Because activation of Area 25 comes and goes with episodes of depression, some theorists believe that it may in fact be a "depression switch," a kind of junction box whose malfunction might be necessary and sufficient for depression to occur.

Immune System As you read in Chapter 6, the *immune system* is the body's network of activities and body cells that fight off bacteria, viruses, and other foreign invaders. When people are under intense stress for a while, their immune systems may become

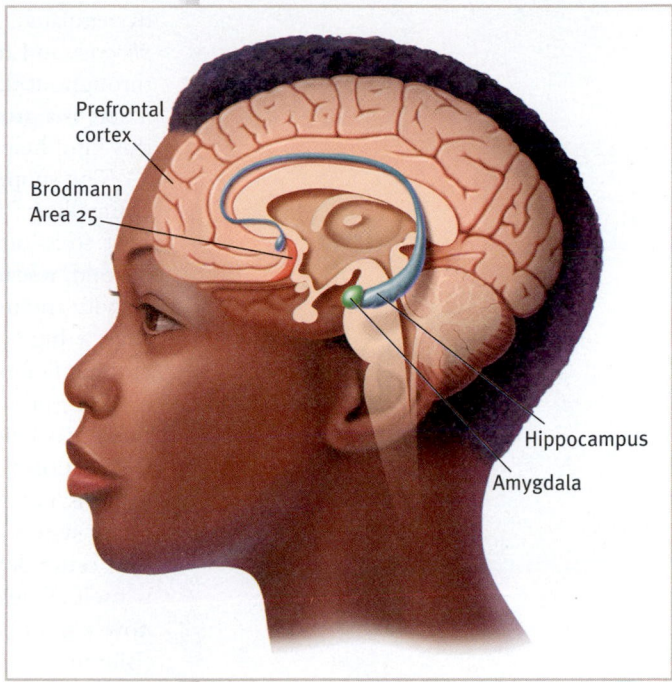

Figure 8-1

The biology of depression Researchers believe that the brain circuit involved in unipolar depression includes the prefrontal cortex, hippocampus, amygdala, and Brodmann Area 25.

Prefrontal cortex

Brodmann Area 25

Hippocampus

Amygdala

BETWEEN THE LINES

Medical Problems and Depression

50% Stroke victims who experience clinical depression ‹‹

30% Cancer patients who experience depression ‹‹

20% Heart attack victims who become depressed ‹‹

18% People with diabetes who are depressed ‹‹

(Jiang et al., 2011; Kerber et al., 2011; NIMH, 2004; Simpson, 1996)

dysregulated, leading to lower functioning of important white blood cells called *lymphocytes* and to increased production of *C-reactive protein* (*CRP*), a protein that spreads throughout the body and causes inflammation and various illnesses (see pages 179–181). There is a growing belief among some researchers that immune system dysregulation of this kind helps produce depression.

The support for an immune system explanation of depression is circumstantial but compelling (Yoon et al., 2012; Blume, Douglas, & Evans, 2011; Gardner & Boles, 2011). First, stress often triggers depression, just as it leads to poor immune system functioning. Second, researchers have found that people with depression display lower lymphocyte activity and increased CRP production and body inflammation. Third, depressed people have a higher incidence than other people of migraines, irritable bowel syndrome, chronic fatigue syndrome, rheumatoid arthritis, and other illnesses known to be caused by CRP production and body inflammation. And, finally, antidepressant drugs, medications that help reduce depression for many individuals, help combat CRP-related inflammation throughout the body.

It is not yet clear how to interpret the relationship between depression and immune system dysregulation. It could be that such dysregulation and chronic inflammation cause depression, just as they help produce other illnesses. Or, perhaps, depression is itself a stressor that leads to immune system problems. A number of researchers are now conducting studies that should help clarify this relationship in the coming years (Blume et al., 2011).

Psychological Views

The psychological models that have been most widely applied to unipolar depression are the psychodynamic, behavioral, and cognitive models. The psychodynamic explanation has not been strongly supported by research, and the behavioral view has received only modest support. In contrast, cognitive explanations have received considerable research support and have gained a large following.

The Psychodynamic View

Sigmund Freud (1917) and his student Karl Abraham (1916, 1911) developed the first psychodynamic explanation of depression. They began by noting the similarity between clinical depression and grief in people who lose loved ones: constant weeping, loss of appetite, difficulty sleeping, loss of pleasure in life, and general withdrawal.

According to Freud and Abraham, a series of unconscious processes is set in motion when a loved one dies. Unable to accept the loss, mourners at first regress to the *oral stage* of development, the period of total dependency when infants cannot distinguish themselves from their parents. By regressing to this stage, the mourners merge their own identity with that of the person they have lost, and so symbolically regain the lost person. In this process, called *introjection,* they direct all their feelings for the loved one, including sadness and anger, toward themselves.

For most mourners, introjection is temporary. For some, however, grief worsens over time. They feel empty, they continue to avoid social relationships, and their sense of loss increases. They become depressed. Freud and Abraham believed that two kinds of people are particularly likely to become clinically depressed in the face of loss: those whose parents failed to nurture them and meet their needs during the oral stage and those whose parents gratified those needs excessively. Infants whose needs are inadequately met remain overly dependent on others throughout their lives, feel unworthy of love, and have low self-esteem. Those

Why do you think so many comedians and other entertainers report that they have grappled with depression earlier in their lives?

Early loss
The young daughter of a policewoman killed during the September 11, 2001, terrorist attacks stands onstage holding her father's hand while the names of attack victims are read during ceremonies at Ground Zero marking the fifth anniversary of the event. Research has found that individuals who lose their parents as children have an increased likelihood of experiencing depression as adults.

Spencer Platt/Getty Images

whose needs are excessively gratified find the oral stage so pleasant that they resist moving on to subsequent stages. Either way, the individuals may devote their lives to others, desperately searching for love and approval. They are likely to feel a greater sense of loss when a loved one dies (Busch et al., 2004; Bemporad, 1992).

Of course, many people become depressed without losing a loved one. To explain why, Freud proposed the concept of **symbolic,** or **imagined, loss,** in which persons equate other kinds of events with loss of a loved one. A college student may, for example, experience failure in a calculus course as the loss of her parents, believing that they love her only when she excels academically.

Although many psychodynamic theorists have parted company with Freud and Abraham's theory of depression, it continues to influence current psychodynamic thinking (Zuckerman, 2011; Busch et al., 2004). For example, *object relations theorists,* the psychodynamic theorists who emphasize relationships, propose that depression results when people's relationships leave them feeling unsafe and insecure (Allen et al., 2004; Blatt, 2004). People whose parents pushed them toward either excessive dependence or excessive self-reliance are more likely to become depressed when they later lose important relationships.

The following therapist description of a depressed middle-aged woman illustrates the psychodynamic concepts of dependence, loss of a loved one, symbolic loss, and introjection:

> *Marie Carls ... had always felt very attached to her mother.... She always tried to placate her volcanic [emotions], to please her in every possible way....*
>
> *After marriage [to Julius], she continued her pattern of submission and compliance. Before her marriage she had difficulty in complying with a volcanic mother, and after her marriage she almost automatically assumed a submissive role....*
>
> *[W]hen she was thirty years old ... [Marie] and her husband invited Ignatius, who was single, to come and live with them. Ignatius and the patient soon discovered that they had an attraction for each other. They both tried to fight that feeling; but when Julius had to go to another city for a few days, the so-called infatuation became much more than that. There were a few physical contacts.... There was an intense spiritual affinity.... A few months later everybody had to leave the city.... Nothing was done to maintain contact. Two years later.... Marie heard that Ignatius had married. She felt terribly alone and despondent....*
>
> *Her suffering had become more acute as she [came to believe] that old age was approaching and she had lost all her chances. Ignatius remained as the memory of lost opportunities.... Her life of compliance and obedience had not permitted her to reach her goal.... When she became aware of these ideas, she felt even more depressed.... She felt that everything she had built in her life was false or based on a false premise.*
>
> *(Arieti & Bemporad, 1978, pp. 275–284)*

Studies have offered general support for the psychodynamic idea that depression may be triggered by a major loss. In a famous study of 123 infants who were placed in a nursery after being separated from their mothers, René Spitz (1946, 1945) found that 19 of the infants became very weepy and sad upon separation and withdrew from their surroundings—a pattern called **anaclitic depression.** Studies of infant monkeys who are separated from their mothers have noted a similar pattern of apparent depression (Harlow & Zimmermann, 1996; Harlow & Harlow, 1965).

Other research, involving both human participants and animal subjects, suggests that losses suffered early in life may set the stage for later depression (Gutman & Nemeroff, 2011; Pryce et al., 2005). When, for example, a depression scale was administered to 1,250 medical patients during visits to their family physicians, the patients whose fathers had died during their childhood scored higher on depression (Barnes & Prosen, 1985).

•**symbolic loss**•According to Freudian theory, the loss of a valued object (for example, a loss of employment) that is unconsciously interpreted as the loss of a loved one. Also called *imagined loss.*

•**anaclitic depression**•A pattern of depressed behavior found among very young children that is caused by separation from one's mother.

Across the species
Researcher Harry Harlow and his colleagues found that infant monkeys reacted with apparent despair to separation from their mothers. Even monkeys raised with surrogate mothers—wire cylinders wrapped with foam rubber and covered with terry cloth—formed an attachment to them and mourned their absence.

University of Wisconsin Primate Laboratory, Madison

Related research supports the psychodynamic idea that people whose childhood needs were improperly met are particularly likely to become depressed after experiencing loss (Goodman, 2002). In some studies, depressed patients have filled out a scale called the Parental Bonding Instrument, which indicates how much care and protection people feel they received as children. Many have identified their parents' child-rearing style as "affectionless control," consisting of a mixture of low care and high protection (Martin et al., 2004; Parker et al., 1995).

These studies offer some support for the psychodynamic view of unipolar depression, but this support has key limitations. First, although the findings indicate that losses and inadequate parenting *sometimes* relate to depression, they do not establish that such factors are *typically* responsible for the disorder. In the studies of young children and young monkeys, for example, only some of the research participants who were separated from their mothers showed depressive reactions. In fact, it is estimated that less than 10 percent of all people who experience major losses in life actually become depressed (Bonanno, 2004; Paykel & Cooper, 1992). Second, many findings are inconsistent. Though some studies find evidence of a relationship between childhood loss and later depression, others do not (Parker, 1992). Finally, certain features of the psychodynamic explanation are nearly impossible to test. Because symbolic loss is said to operate at an unconscious level, for example, it is difficult for researchers to determine if and when it is occurring.

The Behavioral View

Behaviorists believe that unipolar depression results from significant changes in the number of rewards and punishments people receive in their lives (Martell et al., 2010). Clinical researcher Peter Lewinsohn was one of the first clinical theorists to develop a behavioral explanation (Lewinsohn et al., 1990, 1984). He suggested that the positive rewards in life dwindle for some persons, leading them to perform fewer and fewer constructive behaviors. The rewards of campus life, for example, disappear when a young woman graduates from college and takes a job; and an aging baseball player loses the rewards of high salary and adulation when his skills deteriorate. Although many people manage to fill their lives with other forms of gratification, some become particularly disheartened. The positive features of their lives decrease even more, and the decline in rewards leads them to perform still fewer constructive behaviors. In this manner, the individuals spiral toward depression.

In a number of studies, behaviorists have found that the number of rewards people receive in life is indeed related to the presence or absence of depression. Not only do depressed participants typically report fewer positive rewards than nondepressed participants, but when their rewards begin to increase, their mood improved as well (Bylsma et al., 2011; Lewinsohn, Youngren, & Grosscup, 1979). Similarly, other investigations have found a strong relationship between positive life events and feelings of life satisfaction and happiness (Carvalho & Hopko, 2011; Martell et al., 2010).

Lewinsohn and other behaviorists have further proposed that *social* rewards are particularly important in the downward spiral of depression (Martell et al., 2010; Farmer & Chapman, 2008). This claim has been supported by research showing that depressed persons experience fewer social rewards than nondepressed persons and that as their mood improves, their social rewards increase. Although depressed people are sometimes the victims of social circumstances, it may also be that their dark mood and flat behaviors help produce a decline in social rewards (Joiner, 2002; Coyne, 2001).

Behaviorists have done an admirable job of compiling data to support this theory, but this research, too, has limitations. It has relied heavily on the self-reports of depressed individuals, and, as you saw in Chapter 4, measures of this kind can be biased and inaccurate; reports by depressed persons may be influenced heavily by a

When the applause stops According to behaviorists, the reduction in rewards brought about by retirement places high achievers at particular risk for depression. Former New York Giants running back Tiki Barber, seen here eluding a defender, recently described the severe depression he experienced after he retired from pro football in 2006, lost his job as a TV network correspondent, and ended his marriage, in quick succession. "I remember there were days where I would literally . . . sit on the couch and do nothing for 10 hours. . . . I started to shrivel. . . . I didn't have . . . that aura any more."

Stefan Zaklin/epa/Corbis

gloomy mood and negative outlook. Moreover, the behavioral studies have been largely correlational and do not establish that decreases in rewarding events are the initial cause of depression. As you have just read, for example, a depressed mood in itself may lead to negative behaviors and decreases in activities and hence to fewer rewards.

Cognitive Views Cognitive theorists believe that people with unipolar depression persistently view events in negative ways and that such perceptions lead to their disorder. The two most influential cognitive explanations are the *theory of negative thinking* and the *theory of learned helplessness*.

NEGATIVE THINKING Aaron Beck believes that negative thinking, rather than underlying conflicts or a reduction in positive rewards, lies at the heart of depression (Beck & Weishaar, 2011; Beck, 2002, 1991, 1967). Other cognitive theorists—Albert Ellis, for one—also point to maladaptive thinking as a key to depression, but Beck's theory is the one most often associated with the disorder. According to Beck, *maladaptive attitudes, a cognitive triad, errors in thinking,* and *automatic thoughts* combine to produce unipolar depression.

Beck believes that some people develop *maladaptive attitudes* as children, such as "My general worth is tied to every task I perform" or "If I fail, others will feel repelled by me." The attitudes result from their own experiences, their family relationships, and the judgments of the people around them (see Figure 8-2 on the next page). Many failures are inevitable in a full, active life, so such attitudes are inaccurate and set the stage for all kinds of negative thoughts and reactions. Beck suggests that later in these people's lives, upsetting situations may trigger an extended round of negative thinking. That thinking typically takes three forms, which he calls the **cognitive triad**: the individuals repeatedly interpret (1) their *experiences,* (2) *themselves,* and (3) their *futures* in negative ways that lead them to feel depressed. The cognitive triad is at work in the thinking of this depressed person:

One-third of people who felt unhappy as children continue to feel unhappy as adults. Why might this be so?

> *I can't bear it. I can't stand the humiliating fact that I'm the only woman in the world who can't take care of her family, take her place as a real wife and mother, and be respected in her community. When I speak to my young son Billy, I know I can't let him down, but I feel so ill-equipped to take care of him; that's what frightens me. I don't know what to do or where to turn; the whole thing is too overwhelming. . . . I must be a laughing stock. It's more than I can do to go out and meet people and have the fact pointed up to me so clearly.*
>
> *(Fieve, 1975)*

According to Beck, depressed people also make errors in their thinking. In one common error of logic, they draw arbitrary inferences—negative conclusions based on little evidence. A man walking through the park, for example, passes a woman who is looking at nearby flowers and concludes, "She's avoiding looking at me." Similarly, depressed people often minimize the significance of positive experiences or magnify that of negative ones. A college student receives an A on a difficult English exam, for example, but concludes that the grade reflects the professor's generosity rather than her own ability (minimization). Later in the week the same student must miss an English class and is convinced that she will be unable to keep up the rest of the semester (magnification).

Finally, depressed people experience **automatic thoughts,** a steady train of unpleasant thoughts that keep suggesting to them that they are inadequate and that their situation is hopeless. Beck labels these thoughts "automatic" because they seem to just

•**cognitive triad**•The three forms of negative thinking that Aaron Beck theorizes lead people to feel depressed. The triad consists of a negative view of one's experiences, oneself, and the future.

•**automatic thoughts**•Numerous unpleasant thoughts that help to cause or maintain depression, anxiety, or other forms of psychological dysfunction.

Figure 8-2

How depressed parents and their children interact Depressed parents are less likely than nondepressed parents to play with, hug, read to, or sing to their young children each day or to employ the same routine each day. They are also more likely to get frustrated with their children on a daily basis. Such problematic interactions may help explain the repeated research finding that children of depressed parents are more likely than other children to experience emotional, cognitive, or behavioral difficulties (Turney, 2011; Princeton Survey Research Associates, 1996).

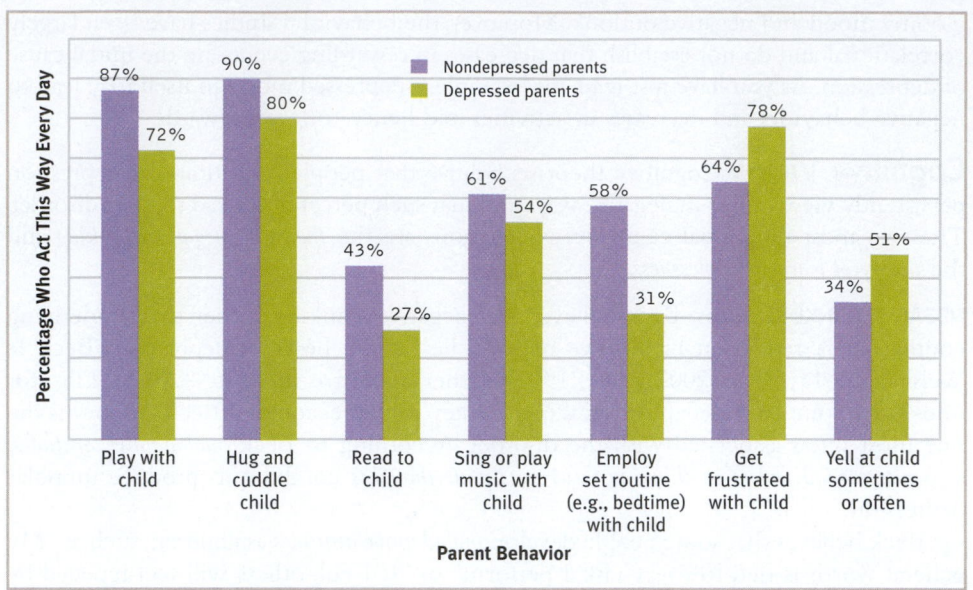

Tracking those thoughts
The brain waves of this college student are measured with an EEG to help detect what happens in her brain while her mind is wandering. Researchers have discovered that people who make ruminative responses during their unhappy moods are more likely to develop clinical depression, but little is known about why some people are particularly prone to ruminate.

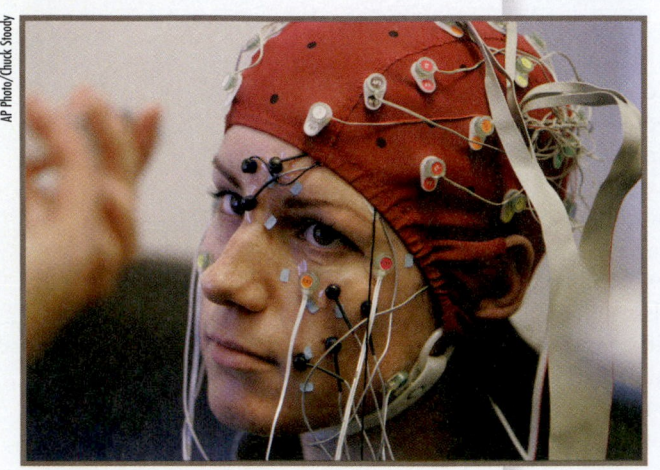

happen, as if by reflex. In the course of only a few hours, depressed people may be visited by hundreds of such thoughts: "I'm worthless. . . . I'll never amount to anything. . . . I let everyone down. . . . Everyone hates me. . . . My responsibilities are overwhelming. . . . I've failed as a parent. . . . I'm stupid. . . . Everything is difficult for me. . . . Things will never change." One therapist said of a depressed client, "By the end of the day, she is worn out, she has lived a thousand painful accidents, participated in a thousand deaths, mourned a thousand mistakes" (Mendels, 1970).

Many studies have produced evidence in support of Beck's explanation (Rehm, 2010). Several of them confirm that depressed people hold maladaptive attitudes and that the more of these maladaptive attitudes they hold, the more depressed they tend to be (Evans et al., 2005). Still other research has found the cognitive triad at work in depressed people (Benas & Gibb, 2011; Punkanen et al., 2011). In various studies, depressed individuals seem to recall unpleasant experiences more readily than positive ones, rate their performances on laboratory tasks lower than nondepressed people do, and select pessimistic statements in storytelling tests (for example, "I expect my plans will fail").

Beck's claims about errors in logic have also received research support. In one study, female participants—some depressed, some not—were asked to read and interpret paragraphs about women in difficult situations. Depressed participants made more errors in logic (such as arbitrary inference) in their interpretations than nondepressed women did (Hammen & Krantz, 1976).

Finally, research has supported Beck's claim that automatic thoughts are tied to depression. In several studies, nondepressed participants who are tricked into reading negative automatic-thought-like statements about themselves become increasingly depressed (Bates, Thompson, & Flanagan, 1999; Strickland, Hale, & Anderson, 1975). In a related line of research, it has been found that people who generally make *ruminative responses* during their depressed moods—that is, repeatedly dwell mentally on their mood without acting to change it—experience dejection longer and are more likely to develop clinical depression later in life than people who avoid such ruminations (Zetsche et al., 2012; McLaughlin & Nolen-Hoeksema, 2011).

This body of research shows that negative thinking is indeed linked to depression, but it fails to show that such patterns of thought are the cause and core of unipolar depression. It could be that a central mood problem leads to thinking difficulties that then take a further toll on mood, behavior, and physiology.

LEARNED HELPLESSNESS Feelings of helplessness fill this account of a young woman's depression:

> Mary was 25 years old and had just begun her senior year in college. . . . Asked to recount how her life had been going recently, Mary began to weep. Sobbing, she said that for the last year or so she felt she was losing control of her life and that recent stresses (starting school again, friction with her boyfriend) had left her feeling worthless and frightened. Because of a gradual deterioration in her vision, she was now forced to wear glasses all day. "The glasses make me look terrible," she said, and "I don't look people in the eye much any more." Also, to her dismay, Mary had gained 20 pounds in the past year. She viewed herself as overweight and unattractive. At times she was convinced that with enough money to buy contact lenses and enough time to exercise she could cast off her depression; at other times she believed nothing would help. . . . Mary saw her life deteriorating in other spheres, as well. She felt overwhelmed by schoolwork and, for the first time in her life, was on academic probation. . . . In addition to her dissatisfaction with her appearance and her fears about her academic future, Mary complained of a lack of friends. Her social network consisted solely of her boyfriend, with whom she was living. Although there were times she experienced this relationship as almost unbearably frustrating, she felt helpless to change it and was pessimistic about its permanence. . . .
>
> *(Spitzer et al., 1983, pp. 122–123)*

Mary feels that she is "losing control of her life." According to psychologist Martin Seligman (1975), such feelings of helplessness are at the center of her depression. Since the mid-1960s Seligman has developed the **learned helplessness** theory of depression. It holds that people become depressed when they think (1) that they no longer have control over the reinforcements (the rewards and punishments) in their lives and (2) that they themselves are responsible for this helpless state.

Seligman's theory first began to take shape when he was working with laboratory dogs. In one procedure, he strapped dogs into an apparatus called a hammock, in which they received shocks periodically no matter what they did. The next day each dog was placed in a *shuttle box,* a box divided in half by a barrier over which the animal could jump to reach the other side (see Figure 8-3). Seligman applied shocks to the dogs in the box, expecting that they, like other dogs in this situation, would soon learn to escape by jumping over the barrier. However, most of these dogs failed to learn anything in the shuttle box. After a flurry of activity, they simply "lay down and quietly whined" and accepted the shock.

Seligman decided that while receiving inescapable shocks in the hammock the day before, the dogs had learned that they had no control over unpleasant events (shocks) in their lives. That is, they had learned that they were helpless to do anything to change negative situations. Thus, when later they were placed in a new situation (the shuttle box) where they could in fact control their fate, they continued to believe that they were generally helpless. Seligman noted that the effects of learned helplessness greatly resemble the symptoms of human depression, and he proposed that people in fact become depressed after developing a general belief that they have no control over reinforcements in their lives.

In numerous human and animal studies, participants who undergo helplessness training have displayed reactions similar to depressive symptoms. When, for example, human participants are exposed to uncontrollable negative events, they later score higher than other individuals on a depressive mood survey (Miller & Seligman, 1975). Similarly, helplessness-trained animal subjects lose interest in sexual and social activities—a common symptom of human depression (Lindner, 1968). Finally, uncontrollable negative

•learned helplessness• The perception, based on past experiences, that one has no control over one's reinforcements.

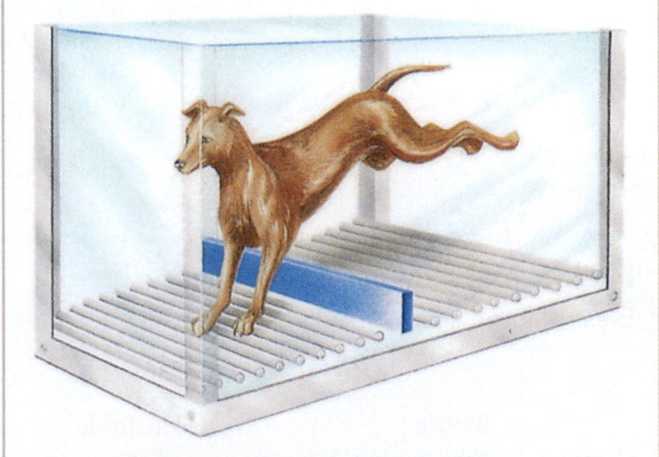

Figure 8-3
Jumping to safety Experimental animals learn to escape or avoid shocks that are administered on one side of a shuttle box by jumping to the other (safe) side.

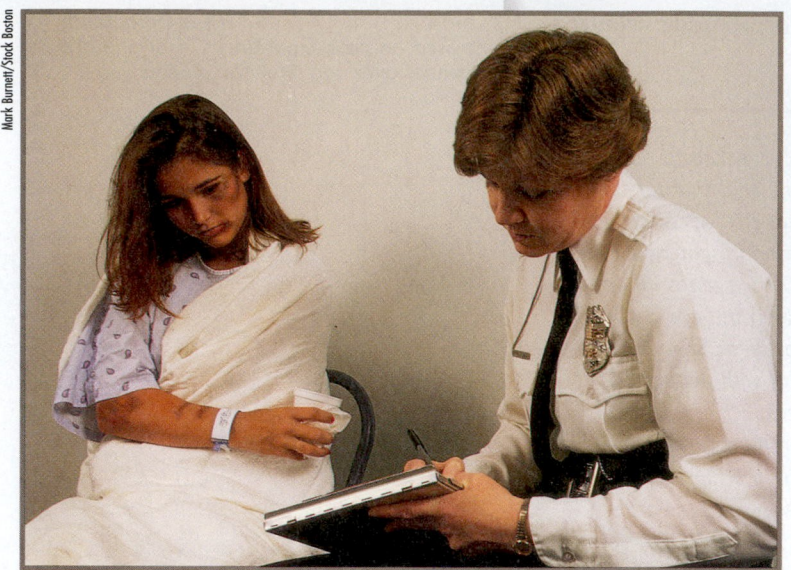

Mark Burnett/Stock Boston

Spouse abuse: victimization and learned helplessness

Spouse abuse occurs in at least 4 million American homes each year. Psychologists believe that many victims of spouse abuse develop feelings of helplessness over the course of their ordeal, thus explaining their "decision" to stay with their abusive husbands. Many such women come to believe that nothing they can do will stop the repeated episodes of violence, that they have no economic alternatives, and that the criminal justice system will be unable to protect them. In turn, they may develop feelings of depression, low self-esteem, and self-blame.

events result in lower norepinephrine and serotonin activity in rats (Wu et al., 1999). This, of course, is similar to the neurotransmitter activity found in the brains of people with unipolar depression.

The learned helplessness explanation of depression has been revised somewhat over the past two decades. According to a new version of the theory, the *attribution-helplessness theory,* when people view events as beyond their control, they ask themselves why this is so (Taube-Schiff & Lau, 2008; Abramson et al., 2002, 1989, 1978) (see Table 8-4). If they attribute their present lack of control to some *internal* cause that is both *global* and *stable* ("I am inadequate at everything and I always will be"), they may well feel helpless to prevent future negative outcomes and they may experience depression. If they make other kinds of attributions, this reaction is unlikely.

Consider a college student whose girlfriend breaks up with him. If he attributes this loss of control to an internal cause that is both global and stable—"It's my fault [internal], I ruin everything I touch [global], and I always will [stable]"—he then has reason to expect similar losses of control in the future and may generally experience a sense of helplessness. According to the learned helplessness view, he is a prime candidate for depression. If the student had instead attributed the breakup to causes that were more *specific* ("The way I've behaved the past couple of weeks blew this relationship"), *unstable* ("I don't know what got into me—I don't usually act like that"), or *external* ("She never did know what she wanted"), he might not expect to lose control again and would probably not experience helplessness and depression.

Hundreds of studies have supported the relationship between styles of attribution, helplessness, and depression (Roberts et al., 2010; Taube-Schiff & Lau, 2008). In one, depressed persons were asked to fill out an *Attributional Style Questionnaire* both before and after successful therapy. Before therapy, their depression was accompanied by the internal/global/stable pattern of attribution. At the end of therapy and again one year later, their depression was improved and their interpretive styles were less likely to be limited to internal, global, and stable attributions (Seligman et al., 1988).

Some theorists have refined the helplessness model yet again in recent years. They suggest that attributions are likely to cause depression only when they further produce a sense of *hopelessness* in an individual (Wain et al., 2011; Abramson et al., 2002, 1989). By taking this factor into consideration, clinicians are often able to predict depression with still greater precision (Robinson & Alloy, 2003).

Although the learned helplessness theory of unipolar depression has been very influential, it too has imperfections. First, laboratory helplessness does not parallel depression

table: 8-4

Internal and External Attributions

Event: "I failed my psych test today."

	INTERNAL		EXTERNAL	
	Stable	**Unstable**	**Stable**	**Unstable**
Global	"I have a problem with test anxiety."	"Getting into an argument with my roommate threw my whole day off."	"Written tests are an unfair way to assess knowledge."	"No one does well on tests that are given the day after vacation."
Specific	"I just have no grasp of psychology."	"I got upset and froze when I couldn't answer the first two questions."	"Everyone knows that this professor enjoys giving unfair tests."	"This professor didn't put much thought into the test because of the pressure of her book deadline."

in every respect. Uncontrollable shocks in the laboratory, for example, almost always produce anxiety along with the helplessness effects (Seligman, 1975); in contrast, human depression is often, but not always, accompanied by anxiety (Brown, 2010). Second, much of the learned helplessness research relies on animal subjects. It is impossible to know whether the animals' symptoms do in fact reflect the clinical depression found in humans. Third, the attributional feature of the theory raises difficult questions. What about the dogs and rats who learn helplessness? Can animals make attributions, even implicitly?

Sociocultural Views

Sociocultural theorists propose that unipolar depression is greatly influenced by the social context that surrounds people. Their belief is supported by the finding, discussed earlier, that this disorder is often triggered by outside stressors. Once again, there are two kinds of sociocultural views—the *family-social perspective,* which looks at the role played by interpersonal factors in the development of depression, and the *multicultural perspective,* which ties depression to factors such as gender, race, and economic status.

The Family-Social Perspective

Earlier you read that some behaviorists believe that a decline in social rewards is particularly important in the development of depression. Although presented as part of their behavioral explanation, this view is consistent with the family-social perspective.

The connection between declining social rewards and depression is a two-way street. On the one hand, researchers have found that depressed persons often display weak social skills and communicate poorly (Taube-Shiff & Lau, 2008; Joiner, 2002). They typically speak more slowly and quietly and in more of a monotone than nondepressed persons, pause longer between words and sentences, and take longer to respond to others. They also seek repeated reassurances from others. Such social deficits make other people uncomfortable and may cause them to avoid the depressed individuals. As a result, the social contacts and rewards of depressed persons decrease, and, as they participate in fewer and fewer social interactions, their social skills deteriorate still further. Not surprisingly, over time depressed people, particularly those who have experienced repeated episodes of depression, seem to lower their expectations of what they can get from social relationships and scale back their social ambitions (Coyne & Calarco, 1995).

Consistent with these findings, depression has been tied repeatedly to the unavailability of social support such as that found in a happy marriage (Whisman & Schonbrun, 2010; Kendler et al., 2005). People who are separated or divorced display at least three times the depression rate of married or widowed persons and double the rate of people who have never been married (Schultz, 2007; Weissman et al., 1991). In some cases, the spouse's depression may contribute to marital discord, a separation, or divorce, but often the interpersonal conflicts and low social support found in troubled relationships seem to lead to depression (Highet et al., 2005; Whisman, 2001).

Generally, there is a high correlation between level of marital conflict and degree of sadness: .37 for men and .42 for women (Whisman & Schonbrun, 2010; Whisman, 2001). Among those who are clinically depressed, the correlation rises to .66. In one study, researchers first assessed how satisfying the marital relationships of research participants were. They then discovered that over the next 12 months, participants who were in an unsatisfying relationship were three times more likely to experience a major depressive episode than those in a satisfying relationship (Whisman & Bruce, 1999). Such findings led the experimenters to estimate that one-third of cases of major depression could be prevented if marital stress were eliminated.

Finally, it appears that people whose lives are isolated and without intimacy are particularly likely to become depressed at times of stress (Hölzel et al., 2011; Nezlek et al.,

Why might problems in the social arena—for example, social loss, social ties, and social rewards—be particularly tied to depression?

2000). Some highly publicized studies conducted in England several decades ago showed that women who had three or more young children, lacked a close confidante, and had no outside employment were more likely than other women to become depressed after experiencing stressful events (Brown, 2002; Brown & Harris, 1978). Studies have also found that depressed people who lack social support remain depressed longer than those who have a supportive spouse or warm friendships.

The Multicultural Perspective Two kinds of relationships have captured the interest of multicultural theorists: (1) links between *gender and depression* and (2) ties between *cultural and ethnic background and depression*. In the case of gender, a strong relationship has been found, but a clear explanation for that relationship has yet to emerge. The clinical field is still sorting out whether and what ties exist between cultural factors and depression.

GENDER AND DEPRESSION As you have read, a strong link exists between gender and depression. Women in places as far apart as France, Sweden, Lebanon, New Zealand, and the United States are at least twice as likely as men to receive a diagnosis of unipolar depression (Astbury, 2010; McSweeney, 2004). Women also appear to be younger when depression strikes, to have more frequent and longer-lasting bouts, and to respond less successfully to treatment. Why the huge difference between the sexes? A variety of theories have been offered.

The *artifact theory* holds that women and men are equally prone to depression but that clinicians often fail to detect depression in men (Emmons, 2010; Brommelhoff et al., 2004). Perhaps men find it less socially acceptable to admit feeling depressed or to seek treatment. Perhaps depressed women display more emotional symptoms, such as sadness and crying, which are easily diagnosed, while depressed men mask their depression behind traditionally "masculine" symptoms such as anger. Although a popular explanation, this view has failed to receive consistent research support. It turns out that women are actually no more willing or able than men to identify their depressive symptoms and to seek treatment (McSweeney, 2004; Nolen-Hoeksema, 1990).

The *hormone explanation* holds that hormone changes trigger depression in many women (Parker & Brotchie, 2004; Dunn & Steiner, 2000). A woman's biological life from her early teens to middle age is marked by frequent changes in hormone levels. Gender differences in rates of depression also span these same years. Research suggests, however, that hormone changes alone are not responsible for the high levels of depression in women (Kessler et al., 2006; Whiffen & Demidenko, 2006). Important social and life events that occur at puberty, pregnancy, and menopause could likewise have an effect. Hormone explanations have also been criticized as sexist, since they imply that a woman's normal biology is flawed.

The *life stress theory* suggests that women in our society experience more stress than men (Astbury, 2010; Keyes & Goodman, 2006). On average they face more poverty, more menial jobs, less adequate housing, and more discrimination than men—all factors that have been linked to depression. And in many homes, women bear a disproportionate share of responsibility for child care and housework.

The *body dissatisfaction explanation* states that females in Western society are taught, almost from birth, to seek a low body weight and slender body shape—goals that are unreasonable, unhealthy, and often unattainable. As you will observe in Chapter 11, the cultural standard for males is much more lenient. As girls approach adolescence, peer pressure may produce greater and greater dissatisfaction with their weight and body, increasing the likelihood of depression. Consistent with this theory, gender differences in depression do indeed first appear during adolescence (Naninck et al., 2011; Nolen-Hoeksema & Girgus, 1995), and persons with eating disorders often experience high levels of depression (Touchette et al., 2011). However, it is not clear that eating and weight concerns actually cause depression; they may instead be the result of depression.

The *lack-of-control theory* picks up on the learned helplessness research and argues that women may be more prone to depression because they feel less control than men over their lives. Some studies have, in fact, suggested that women are more prone than men to develop learned helplessness in the laboratory (Le Unes, Nation, & Turley, 1980). In addition, it has been found that victimization of any kind, from burglary to rape, often produces a general sense of helplessness and increases the symptoms of depression. Women in our society are more likely than men to be victims, particularly of sexual assault and child abuse (Astbury, 2010; Nolen-Hoeksema, 2002).

A final explanation for the gender differences found in depression is the *rumination theory*. As you read earlier, *rumination* is the tendency to keep focusing on one's feelings when depressed and to consider repeatedly the causes and consequences of that depression ("Why am I so down? . . . I won't be able to finish my work if I keep going like this. . . ."). Research shows that people who ruminate whenever they feel sad are more likely to become depressed and stay depressed longer. It turns out that women are more likely than men to ruminate when their moods darken, perhaps making them more vulnerable to the onset of clinical depression (Nolen-Hoeksema & Corte, 2004; Nolen-Hoeksema, 2002, 2000).

Each of these explanations for the gender difference in unipolar depression offers food for thought. Each has gathered just enough supporting evidence to make it interesting and just enough evidence to the contrary to raise questions about its usefulness (Russo & Tartaro, 2008). Thus, at present, the gender difference in depression remains one of the most talked-about but least understood phenomena in the clinical field.

CULTURAL BACKGROUND AND DEPRESSION Depression is a worldwide phenomenon, and certain symptoms of this disorder seem to be constant across all countries. A landmark study of four countries—Canada, Switzerland, Iran, and Japan—found that the great majority of depressed people in those very different countries reported symptoms of sadness, joylessness, anxiety, tension, lack of energy, loss of interest, loss of ability to concentrate, ideas of insufficiency, and thoughts of suicide (Matsumoto & Juang, 2008). Beyond such core symptoms, however, research suggests that the precise picture of depression varies from country to country (Kleinman, 2004). Depressed people in non-Western countries—China and Nigeria, for example—are more likely to be troubled by physical symptoms such as fatigue, weakness, sleep disturbances, and weight loss. Depression in those countries is less often marked by cognitive symptoms such as self-blame, low self-esteem, and guilt. As countries become more Westernized, depression seems to take on the more cognitive character it has in the West (Matsumoto & Juang, 2008; Okello & Ekblad, 2006).

Within the United States, researchers have found few differences in the symptoms of depression among members of different ethnic or racial groups. Nor have they found significant differences in the *overall* rates of depression between such minority groups. On the other hand, recent research has revealed that there are often striking differences between ethnic/racial groups in the chronicity of depression. Chronicity refers to how likely it is that an individual will experience recurrent episodes of a disorder. Hispanic Americans and African Americans are 50 percent more likely than white Americans to have recurrent episodes of depression (González et al., 2010).

How might this difference in chronicity be explained? Data on the treatment of depression may provide a clue. As you will read in the next chapter, 54 percent of depressed white Americans receive treatment for their disorders (medication and/or psychotherapy), compared to 34 percent of depressed Hispanic Americans and 40 percent of depressed African Americans (González et al., 2010). It may be that minority groups in the United States are more vulnerable to repeated experiences of depression partly because many of their members have more limited treatment opportunities when they are depressed.

A close look at research findings also reveals that although the overall rates of depression are similar among minority groups, specific ethnic populations living under unusually oppressive circumstances sometimes do have strikingly high rates of depression (Matsumoto & Juang, 2008; Ayalon & Young, 2003). A study of one American

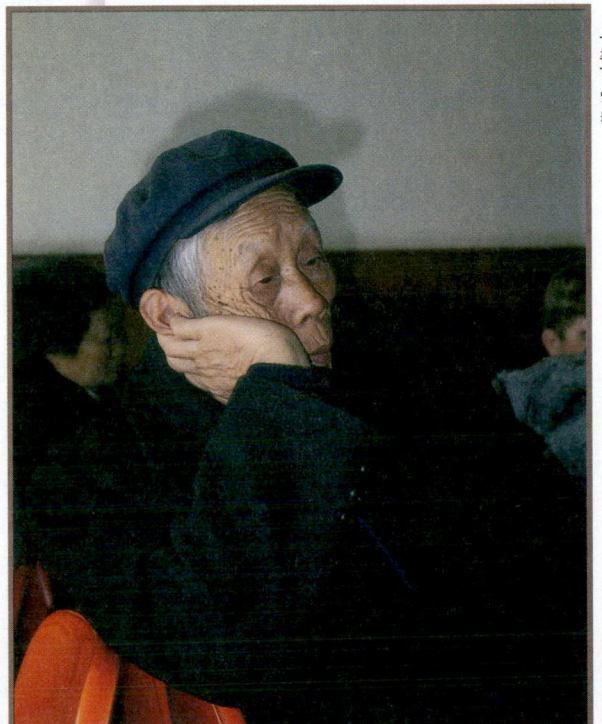

Mimi Forsyth/Monkmeyer

Non-Western depression
Depressed people in non-Western countries tend to have fewer cognitive symptoms, such as self-blame, and more physical symptoms, such as fatigue, weakness, and sleep disturbances.

Indian community in the United States, for example, showed that the lifetime risk of developing depression was 37 percent among women, 19 percent among men, and 28 percent overall, much higher than the risk in the general United States population (Kinzie et al., 1992). High prevalence rates of this kind may be linked to the terrible social and economic pressures faced by the people who live on American Indian reservations. Similarly, in one survey of Hispanic and African Americans residing in public housing, almost half of the respondents reported that they were suffering from depression (Bazargan et al., 2005). Within these minority populations, the likelihood of being depressed rose along with the individual's degree of poverty, family size, and number of health problems.

Finally, research has revealed that depression is distributed unevenly within some minority groups. This is not totally surprising, given that each minority group itself is comprised of persons of varied backgrounds and cultural values. For example, depression is more common among Hispanic and African Americans born in the United States than among Hispanic and African American immigrants (González et al., 2010; Matsumoto & Juang, 2008). Moreover, within the Hispanic American population, Puerto Ricans display a higher rate of depression than do Mexican Americans or Cuban Americans, whereas among African Americans, individuals whose families originally came to the United States from Africa and those whose families came by way of a Caribbean island experience similar rates of depression (González et al., 2010; Miranda et al., 2005).

How would you explain the relatively low rate of depression found among immigrants in the United States? Why do their depression rates eventually rise?

Bipolar Disorders

People with a *bipolar disorder* experience both the lows of depression and the highs of mania. Many describe their life as an emotional roller coaster, as they shift back and forth between extreme moods. A number of sufferers eventually become suicidal. Their roller coaster ride also has a dramatic impact on relatives and friends (Lee et al., 2011; Lowe & Cohen, 2010).

What Are the Symptoms of Mania?

Unlike people sunk in the gloom of depression, those in a state of mania typically experience dramatic and inappropriate rises in mood. The symptoms of mania span the same areas of functioning—*emotional, motivational, behavioral, cognitive,* and *physical*—as those of depression, but mania affects those areas in an opposite way.

A person in the throes of mania has active, powerful emotions in search of an outlet. The mood of euphoric joy and well-being is out of all proportion to the actual happenings in the person's life. One person with mania explained, "I feel no sense of restriction or censorship whatsoever. I am afraid of nothing and no one" (Fieve, 1975, p. 68). Not every person with mania is a picture of happiness, however. Some instead become very irritable and angry, especially when others get in the way of their exaggerated ambitions.

In the motivational realm, people with mania seem to want constant excitement, involvement, and companionship. They enthusiastically seek out new friends and old, new interests and old, and have little awareness that their social style is overwhelming, domineering, and excessive.

The behavior of people with mania is usually very active. They move quickly, as though there were not enough time to do everything they want to do. They may talk rapidly and loudly, their conversations filled with jokes and efforts to be clever or, conversely, with complaints and verbal outbursts. Flamboyance is not uncommon: dressing in flashy clothes, giving large sums of money to strangers, or even getting involved in dangerous activities.

In the cognitive realm, people with mania usually show poor judgment and planning, as if they feel too good or move too fast to consider possible pitfalls. Filled with optimism, they rarely listen when others try to slow them down, interrupt their buying sprees, or prevent them from investing money unwisely. They may also hold an inflated opinion of themselves, and sometimes their self-esteem approaches grandiosity. During severe episodes of mania, some have trouble remaining coherent or in touch with reality.

Finally, in the physical realm, people with mania feel remarkably energetic. They typically get little sleep yet feel and act wide awake (Armitage & Arnedt, 2011). Even if they miss a night or two of sleep, their energy level may remain high.

Diagnosing Bipolar Disorders

People are considered to be in a full *manic episode* when for at least one week they display an abnormally high or irritable mood, increased activity or energy, and at least three other symptoms of mania (see Table 8-5). The episode may even include psychotic features such as delusions or hallucinations. When the symptoms of mania are less severe (causing little impairment), the person is said to be experiencing a *hypomanic episode* (APA, 2013, 2012).

DSM-5 distinguishes two kinds of bipolar disorders—bipolar I and bipolar II. People with **bipolar I disorder** have full manic and major depressive episodes. Most of them experience an *alternation* of the episodes, for example, weeks of mania followed by a period of wellness, followed, in turn, by an episode of depression. Some, however, have *mixed* features, in which they display both manic and depressive symptoms within the

"Bi-Winning"
In spring 2011, successful actor Charlie Sheen went on an extended tirade against his CBS employers and other forces in society that had many friends and family members questioning his state of mind. Sheen made his own views on the subject clear by declaring, "I'm not bi-polar, I'm bi-winning," a phrase that he registered as a trademark phrase.

table: 8-5

DSM-5 Checklist

Manic Episode

1. A one-week (or longer) period of abnormally and persistently elevated, expansive, or irritable mood and abnormally and persistently increased activity or energy, for most of the day, nearly every day.

2. Presence of at least three of the following: • inflated self-esteem or grandiosity • decreased need for sleep • increased talkativeness, or pressure to keep talking • flight of ideas or the experience that thoughts are racing • distractibility • increase in goal-directed activity or psychomotor agitation • excessive involvement in activities that have a high potential for painful consequences.

3. Significant distress or impairment.

Bipolar I Disorder

1. Presence of manic episode. Or, if current episode is hypomanic or depressive, history of manic episode(s).

2. Significant distress or impairment.

Bipolar II Disorder

1. Presence or history of major depressive episode(s).

2. Presence or history of hypomanic episode(s).

3. No history of a manic episode.

4. Significant distress or impairment.

Based on APA, 2013, 2012.

•**bipolar I disorder**•A type of bipolar disorder marked by full manic and major depressive episodes.

"It's good, but it doesn't say 'bipolar.'"

same episode—for example, having racing thoughts amidst feelings of extreme sadness (Mazza et al., 2012; Mitchell et al., 2011). In **bipolar II disorder,** hypomanic—that is, mildly manic—-episodes alternate with major depressive episodes over the course of time. Some people with this pattern accomplish huge amounts of work during their mild manic periods (see *PsychWatch* on page 248).

Without treatment, the mood episodes tend to recur for people with either type of bipolar disorder (Ketter, 2010). If people experience four or more episodes within a one-year period, their disorder is further considered to be *rapid cycling*. Terri Cheney, author of the autobiography *Manic: A Memoir,* describes her rapid cycling in the following excerpt.

The precise term for my disorder is "ultradian rapid cycler," which means that without medication I am at the mercy of my own spectacular mood swings: "up" for days (charming, talkative, effusive, funny and productive, but never sleeping and ultimately hard to be around), then "down," and essentially immobile, for weeks at a time. . . .

. . . In love there's no hiding: You have to let someone know who you are, but I didn't have a clue who I was from one moment to the next. When dating me, you might go to bed with Madame Bovary and wake up with Hester Prynne. Worst of all, my manic, charming self was constantly putting me into situations that my down self couldn't handle.

For example: One morning I met a man in the supermarket produce aisle. I hadn't slept for three days, but you wouldn't have known it to look at me. My eyes glowed green, my strawberry blond hair put the strawberries to shame, and I literally sparkled (I'd worn a gold sequined shirt to the supermarket—manic taste is always bad). I was hungry, but not for produce. I was hungry for him, in his well-worn jeans, Yankees cap slightly askew.

I pulled my cart alongside his and started lasciviously squeezing a peach. . . . That's all I needed, an opening, and I was off. I told him my name, asked him his likes and dislikes in fruit, sports, presidential candidates and women. I talked so quickly I barely had time to hear his answers. I didn't buy any peaches, but I left with a dinner date on Saturday, two nights away, leaving plenty of time to rest, shave my legs and pick out the perfect outfit.

But by the time I got home, the darkness had already descended. I didn't feel like plowing through my closet or unpacking the groceries. I just left them on the counter to rot or not rot—what did it matter? I didn't even change my sequined shirt. I tumbled into bed as I was, and stayed there. My body felt as if I had been dipped in slow-drying concrete.

•bipolar II disorder• A type of bipolar disorder marked by mildly manic (hypomanic) episodes and major depressive episodes.

It was all I could do to draw a breath in and push it back out, over and over. I would have cried from the sheer monotony of it, but tears were too much effort.

On Saturday afternoon the phone rang. I was still in bed, and had to force myself to roll over, pick it up and mutter hello. "It's Jeff, from the peaches. Just calling to confirm your address." Jeff? Peaches? I vaguely remembered talking to someone who fit that description, but it seemed a lifetime ago. And that wasn't me doing the talking then, or at least not this me—I'd never wear sequins in the morning. But my conscience knew better. "Get up, get dressed!" it hissed in my ear. "It doesn't matter if she made the date, you've got to see it through."

When Jeff showed up at 7, I was dressed and ready, but more for a funeral than a date. I was swathed in black and hadn't put on any makeup, so my naturally fair skin looked ghostly and wan. But I opened the door, and even held up my cheek to be kissed. I took no pleasure in the feel of his lips on my skin. Pleasure was for the living.

I had nothing to say, not then or at dinner. So Jeff talked, a lot at first, then less and less until finally, during dessert, he asked, "You don't by any chance have a twin, do you?" And yet I was crushed when he didn't call.

A couple of weeks later, I awoke to a world gone Disney: daffodil sunshine, robin's egg sky. Birds were trilling outside my window, a song no doubt created especially for me. I couldn't stand it a minute longer. I flung back the covers and danced in my nightie—my gray flannel prison-issue nightie. I caught one glimpse of it in the mirror, shuddered, and flung it off, too.

I rifled through my closet for something decent to wear, but everything I put my hands on was wrong, wrong, wrong. For starters, it was all black. I hated black, even more than I hated gray. Redheads should be true to their colors, whatever the cost. I dug deeper, and there, shoved way in the back, was a pair of skin-tight jeans and something silky and sparkly and just what I needed: an exquisite gold sequined shirt.

I slipped it on and preened for a minute. Damn, I looked good. . . .

Jeff?

Jeff! I kicked the nightie out of my way and grabbed the bedside phone. Was 6:30 A.M. too early to call? No, not for good old Jeff! It rang and rang. I was about to give up when a thick, sleepy voice said "Hello?"

"It's me! Why haven't you called?"

It took a while to establish who "me" was, but eventually he remembered. "You sound different," he said. "Or no, maybe you sound more like yourself. I'm not sure. It's so early." Soon I had him laughing so hard he got the hiccups and had to get off the phone. But before he did, he asked me out for Friday, three nights away. No, I insisted, it had to be tonight, or even this afternoon. . . . We compromised on dinner that evening at 8. I spent the afternoon ridding my house of all evidence of depression. I soaped and scoured and dusted and vacuumed, using every attachment, even the ones that frightened me. . . .

When the house looked perfect, I turned on myself with the same fury. I buffed and polished and creamed and plucked. . . . As I was shadowing my eyes, . . . my hand started trembling and I couldn't finish applying my mascara. Suddenly I didn't look radiant. There were lines around my mouth and a hollowness to my eyes that aged me 10 years. My skin, despite the carefully applied foundation and blush, was so deathly pale I recoiled from my reflection.

I sat on the toilet and started to cry. I had met the enemy enough times to know it by sight. Not now, I prayed. Please not now. Globs of mascara ran down my cheeks, and I wiped them away, heedless of the streaks they left. It was 7:57. I had three minutes to wrestle my brain chemistry into submission. . . .

Maybe he would understand. Maybe I would find the courage. Maybe they would invent a cure. Maybe, but not tonight. As the doorbell rang and rang, I huddled in the bathroom, shivering. . . . When it was finally quiet, I rinsed off the rest of my mascara and tossed my cocktail dress into the hamper. Then I buttoned up my gray flannel nightie, and settled in for the long night to come.

I never heard from Jeff again.

(Cheney, 2008)

PsychWatch

Abnormality and Creativity: A Delicate Balance

Up to a point, states of depression, mania, anxiety, and even confusion can be useful. This may be particularly true in the arts. The ancient Greeks believed that various forms of "divine madness" inspired creative acts, from poetry to performance (Ludwig, 1995). Even today many people expect "creative geniuses" to be psychologically disturbed. A popular image of the artist includes a glass of liquor, a cigarette, and a tormented expression. Classic examples include writer William Faulkner, who suffered from alcoholism and received electroconvulsive therapy for depression; poet Sylvia Plath, who experienced depression most of her life and eventually committed suicide at age 31; and dancer Vaslav Nijinsky, who suffered from schizophrenia and spent many years in institutions. In fact, a number of studies indicate that artists and writers are somewhat more likely than others to suffer from mental disorders, particularly mood disorders (Galvez et al., 2011; Simonton, 2010; Sample, 2005).

Why might creative people be prone to psychological disorders? Some may be predisposed to such disorders long before they begin their artistic careers; the careers may simply bring attention to their emotional struggles (Simonton, 2010; Ludwig, 1995). Indeed, creative people often have a family history of psychological problems. A number also have experienced intense psychological trauma during childhood. English novelist and essayist Virginia Woolf, for example, endured sexual abuse as a child.

Another reason for the creativity link may be that creative endeavors create emotional turmoil that is overwhelming. Truman Capote said that writing his famous book *In Cold Blood* "killed" him psychologically. Before writing this account of the brutal murders of a family, he considered himself "a stable person. . . . Afterward something happened to me" (Ludwig, 1995).

Yet a third explanation for the link between creativity and psychological disorders is that the creative professions offer a welcome climate for those with psychological disturbances. In the worlds of poetry, painting, and acting, for example, emotional expression, unusual thinking, and/or personal turmoil are valued as sources of inspiration and success (Galvez et al., 2011; Sample, 2005; Ludwig, 1995).

Much remains to be learned about the relationship between emotional turmoil and creativity, but work in this area has already clarified two important points. First, psychological disturbance is hardly a requirement for creativity. Many "creative geniuses" are, in fact, psychologically stable and happy throughout their entire lives (Schlesinger & Ismail, 2004). Second, *mild* psychological disturbances relate to creative achievement much more strongly than severe disturbances do (Galvez et al., 2011; Simonton, 2010). For example, nineteenth-century composer Robert Schumann produced 27 works during one hypomanic year but next to nothing during years when he was severely depressed and suicidal (Jamison, 1995).

Some artists worry that their creativity would disappear if their psychological suffering were to stop. In fact, however, research suggests that successful treatment for severe psychological disorders more often than not improves the creative process (Jamison, 1995; Ludwig, 1995). Romantic notions aside, severe mental dysfunctioning has little redeeming value, in the arts or anywhere else.

Hulton-Deutsch Collection/Corbis

The price of creativity? The influential English novelist and essayist Virginia Woolf (1882–1941) suffered major episodes of depression and mania at the ages of 13, 22, 28, and 30, and less severe mood swings throughout the rest of her life. She took her own life by drowning at the age of 59 during a depressive episode, fearing that she was "going mad again."

Regardless of their particular pattern, individuals with a bipolar disorder tend to experience depression more than mania over the years (Julien et al., 2011). In most cases, their depressive episodes occur three times as often as manic ones, and the depressive episodes also last longer.

Surveys from around the world indicate that between 1 and 2.6 percent of all adults suffer from a bipolar disorder at any given time (Khare et al., 2011 Merikangas et al., 2011). As many as 4 percent experience one of the bipolar disorders over the course of their lives. Bipolar I disorder seems to be a bit more common than bipolar II disorder. The bipolar disorders are equally common in women and men. However, women may experience more depressive episodes and more rapid cycling than men (Curtis, 2005; Papadimitriou et al., 2005). The disorders are more common among people with low incomes than those with higher incomes (Sareen et al., 2011).

Onset of bipolar disorder usually occurs between the ages of 15 and 44 years. In most untreated cases, the manic and depressive episodes eventually subside, only to recur at a later time. Generally, when episodes recur, the intervening periods of normality grow shorter and shorter (Goodwin & Jamison, 1984). It also appears that over time people with bipolar disorders develop more medical ailments than the rest of the population (Weiner, Warren, & Fiedorowitz, 2011).

When a person experiences numerous periods of hypomanic symptoms and *mild* depressive symptoms, DSM-5 assigns a diagnosis of **cyclothymic disorder**. The symptoms of this milder form of bipolar disorder continue for two or more years, interrupted occasionally by normal moods that may last for only days or weeks. This disorder, like bipolar I and bipolar II disorders, usually begins in adolescence or early adulthood and is equally common among women and men. At least 0.4 percent of the population develops cyclothymic disorder. In some cases, the milder symptoms eventually blossom into a bipolar I or II disorder (Goto et al., 2011).

What Causes Bipolar Disorders?

Throughout the first half of the twentieth century, the search for the cause of bipolar disorders made little progress. Various explanations were proposed, but research did not support their validity. Psychodynamic theorists, for example, suggested that mania, like depression, emerges from the loss of a love object. Whereas some people introject the lost object and become depressed, others deny the loss and become manic. To avoid the terrifying conflicts generated by the loss, they escape into a dizzying round of activity (Lewin, 1950). Although case reports sometimes fit this explanation, only a few controlled studies have found a relationship between loss early or later in life and the onset of manic episodes (Post & Miklowitz, 2010; Tsuchiya et al., 2005).

More recently, biological research has produced some promising clues. The biological insights have come from research into *neurotransmitter activity, ion activity, brain structure,* and *genetic factors.*

Neurotransmitters Remember from Chapter 3 that neurotransmitters released from neurons' axon endings carry messages to the dendrites of neighboring neurons by binding to receptor sites there. As you read, different psychological disorders have been linked to the abnormal functioning of various neurotransmitters, including norepinephrine. Could *overactivity* of norepinephrine be related to mania? This was the expectation of clinicians back in the 1960s after investigators first found a relationship between low norepinephrine activity and unipolar depression (Schildkraut, 1965). One study did indeed find the norepinephrine activity of persons with mania to be higher than that of depressed or control research participants (Post et al., 1980, 1978). In another study patients with a bipolar disorder were given *reserpine,* the blood pressure drug known to reduce norepinephrine activity in the brain, and the manic symptoms of some subsided (Telner et al., 1986).

Because serotonin activity often parallels norepinephrine activity in unipolar depression, theorists at first expected that mania would also be related to high serotonin

•cyclothymic disorder•A disorder marked by numerous periods of hypomanic symptoms and mild depressive symptoms.

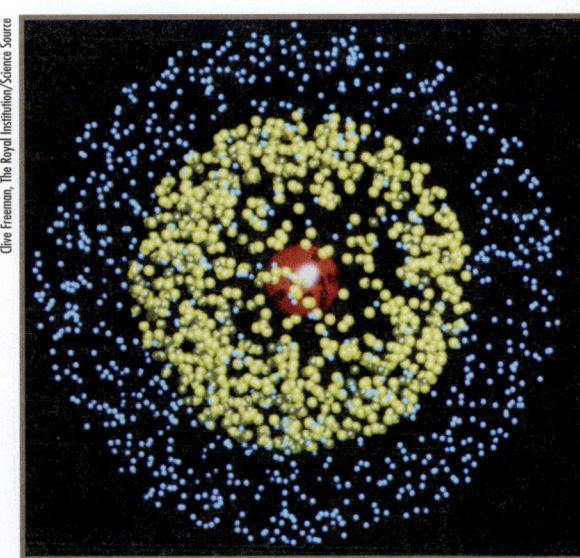

Clive Freeman, The Royal Institution/Science Source

Breakthrough

As you'll see in the next chapter, in the mid-1900s scientists discovered by accident that the moods of people with bipolar disorders often are stabilized by lithium, one of the earth's 98 basic chemical elements. Researchers have since worked backward, determining how lithium affects the cells of the brain and body and, in turn, identifying the possible biological causes of bipolar disorders. A computer graphic representation of the electronic structure of lithium is shown in this photo.

activity, but no such relationship has been found. Instead, research suggests that mania, like depression, may be linked to *low* serotonin activity (Shastry, 2005; Sobczak et al., 2002). Perhaps low activity of serotonin, acting again as a neuromodulator, opens the door to a mood disorder and *permits* the activity of norepinephrine (or perhaps other neurotransmitters) to define the particular form the disorder will take. That is, low serotonin activity accompanied by low norepinephrine activity may lead to depression; low serotonin activity accompanied by high norepinephrine activity may lead to mania. In recent years, researchers have found that bipolar disorder may also be tied to the abnormal activity of other neurotransmitters, such as GABA, the brain chemical you read about in Chapter 5 (Benes, 2011; Walderhaug et al., 2011).

Ion Activity While neurotransmitters play a significant role in the communication *between* neurons, ions seem to play a critical role in relaying messages *within* a neuron. That is, ions help transmit messages down the neuron's axon to the nerve endings. Positively charged *sodium ions* (*Na+*) sit on both sides of a neuron's cell membrane. When the neuron is at *rest*, more sodium ions sit outside the membrane. When the neuron receives an incoming message at its receptor sites, pores in the cell membrane open, allowing the sodium ions to flow to the inside of the membrane, thus increasing the positive charge inside the neuron. This starts a wave of electrical activity that travels down the length of the neuron and results in its "firing." After the neuron "fires," *potassium ions* (*K+*) flow from the inside of the neuron across the cell membrane to the outside, helping to return the neuron to its original resting state (see Figure 8-4).

Figure 8-4

Ions and the firing of neurons Neurons relay messages in the form of electrical impulses that travel down the axon toward the nerve endings. As an impulse travels along the axon, sodium ions (Na+), on the outside of the neuron's membrane, flow inside, causing the impulse to continue down the axon. Once sodium ions flow in, potassium ions (K+) flow out, returning the membrane's electrical balance to its resting state, ready for the arrival of a new impulse.

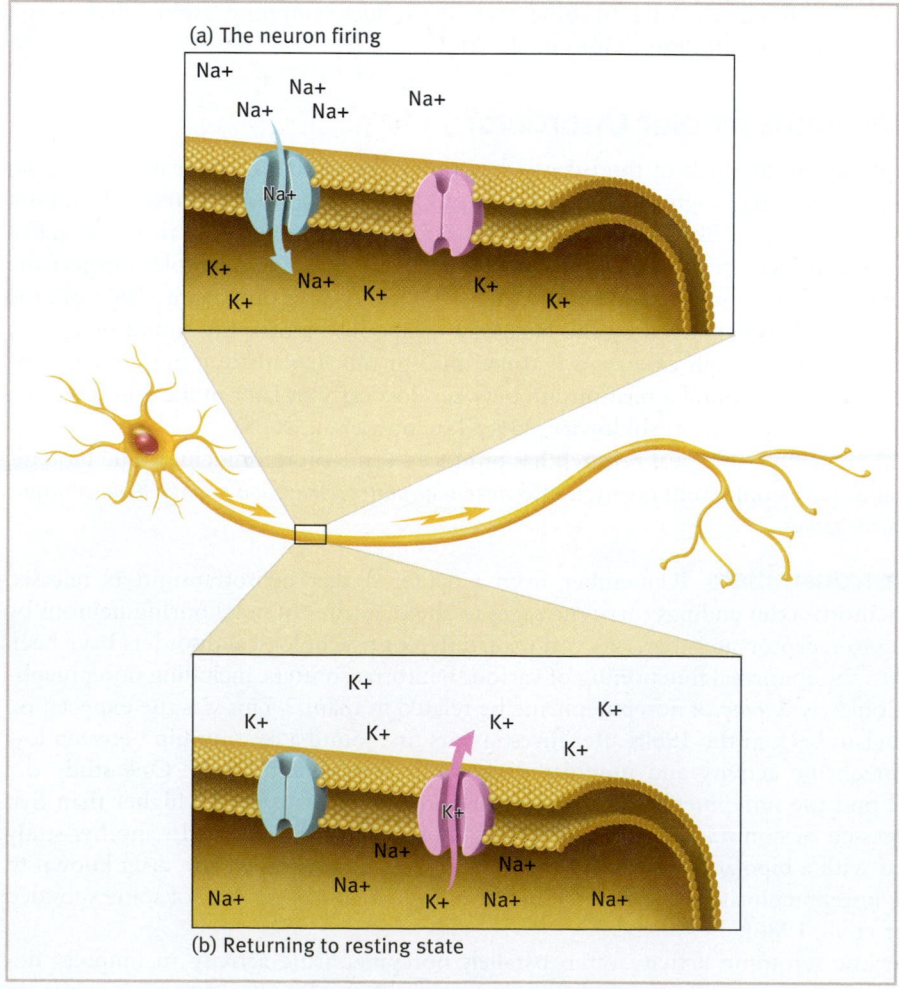

Sunset Boulevard/Corbis

War of a different kind
While starring as Princess Leia, the invincible heroine in the *Star Wars* movies from 1977 to 1983, actress Carrie Fisher received a diagnosis of bipolar disorder. The disorder is now under control with the help of medication, and Fisher says, "I don't want peace [in my life], I just don't want war" (Epstein, 2001, p. 36).

If messages are to be relayed effectively down the axon, the ions must be able to travel easily between the outside and the inside of the neural membrane. Some theorists believe that irregularities in the transport of these ions may cause neurons to fire too easily (resulting in mania) or to stubbornly resist firing (resulting in depression) (Manji & Zarate, 2011; Li & El-Mallakh, 2004). Not surprisingly, investigators have found membrane defects in the neurons of people suffering from bipolar disorder and have observed abnormal functioning in the proteins that help transport ions across a neuron's membrane (Sassi & Soares, 2002).

Brain Structure Brain imaging and postmortem studies have identified a number of abnormal brain structures in people with bipolar disorders (Chen et al., 2011; Savitz & Drevets, 2011). For example, the basal ganglia and cerebellum of these individuals tend to be smaller than those of other people, they have lower volumes of gray matter in the brain, and their dorsal raphe nucleus, striatum, amygdala, hippocampus, and prefrontal cortex have some structural abnormalities. It is not clear what role such structural abnormalities play in bipolar disorders. It may be that they help produce the neurotransmitter and ion abnormalities that you read about earlier. The dorsal raphe nucleus, for example, is one of the brain sites where serotonin is produced. Alternatively, the structural problems may simply be the result of the neurotransmitter or ion abnormalities or of the medications that many patients with bipolar disorders now take.

Genetic Factors Many theorists believe that people inherit a biological predisposition to develop bipolar disorders (Glahn & Burdick, 2011; Gershon & Nurnberger, 1995). Family pedigree studies support this idea. Identical twins of persons with a bipolar disorder have a 40 percent likelihood of developing the same disorder, and fraternal twins, siblings, and other close relatives of such persons have a 5 to 10 percent likelihood, compared to the 1 to 2.6 percent prevalence rate in the general population.

Researchers have also conducted *genetic linkage* studies to identify possible patterns in the inheritance of bipolar disorders. They select large families that have had high rates of a disorder over several generations, observe the pattern of distribution of the disorder among family members, and determine whether it closely follows the distribution pattern of a known genetically transmitted family trait (called a *genetic marker*), such as color blindness, red hair, or a particular medical syndrome.

> **BETWEEN THE LINES**
>
> **Criminal Conduct**
>
> People with bipolar disorder are more likely than other people to perform criminal behaviors, particularly during manic episodes (Swann et al., 2011). ‹‹

Teakwood Lane Productions/Cherry Pie Productions/Keshnet/Fox21/Showtime/The Kobal Collection

Powerful plot device

In *Homeland*, one of television's most popular series, actress Claire Danes plays Carrie Mathison, a CIA operative who is obsessed with Marine-turned-terrorist Nicholas Brody (played by actor Damien Lewis). One of the show's key features is Mathison's bipolar disorder, which both heightens and hinders her effectiveness in the pursuit of Brody and his terrorist associates. Danes and Lewis have received Emmy awards for their portrayals of these two troubled individuals.

After studying the records of Israeli, Belgian, and Italian families that had shown high rates of bipolar disorders across several generations, one team of researchers seemed to have linked bipolar disorders to genes on the X chromosome (Mendlewicz et al., 1987, 1980). Other research teams, however, later used techniques from *molecular biology* to examine genetic patterns in large families, and they linked bipolar disorders to genes on chromosomes 1, 4, 6, 10, 11, 12, 13, 15, 18, 21, and 22 (Wendland et al., 2011; Baron, 2002). Such wide-ranging findings suggest that a number of genetic abnormalities probably combine to help bring about bipolar disorders (Cruceanu et al., 2011).

PUTTING IT... together

Making Sense of All That Is Known

With mood problems so prevalent in all societies, it is no wonder that they have been the focus of so much research. Great quantities of data about disorders of mood have been gathered. Still, clinicians have yet to understand fully all that they know.

Several factors have been tied closely to unipolar depression, including biological abnormalities, a reduction in positive reinforcements, negative ways of thinking, a perception of helplessness, and life stress and other sociocultural influences. Indeed, more contributing factors have been associated with unipolar depression than with most other psychological disorders. Precisely how all of these factors relate to unipolar depression, however, is unclear. Several relationships are possible:

1. *One of the factors* may be the key cause of unipolar depression. That is, one theory may be more useful than any of the others for predicting and explaining how unipolar depression occurs. If so, cognitive or biological factors are leading candidates, for these kinds of factors have each been found, at times, to precede and predict depression.

2. *Different factors* may be capable of initiating unipolar depression in different persons (Goldstein et al., 2011). Some people may, for example, begin with low serotonin activity, which predisposes them to react helplessly in stressful situations, interpret events negatively, and enjoy fewer pleasures in life.

Others may first suffer a severe loss, which triggers helplessness reactions, low serotonin activity, and reductions in positive rewards. Regardless of the initial cause, these factors may merge into a "final common pathway" of unipolar depression.

3. An *interaction between two or more specific factors* may be necessary to produce unipolar depression. Perhaps people will become depressed only if they have low levels of serotonin activity, feel helpless, *and* repeatedly blame themselves for negative events.

4. The *various factors may play different roles* in unipolar depression. Some may cause the disorder, some may result from it, and some may keep it going. Peter Lewinsohn and his colleagues (1988) assessed more than 500 non-depressed persons on the various factors linked to depression. They then assessed the study's participants again eight months later to see who had in fact become depressed and which of the factors had predicted depression. Negative thinking, self-dissatisfaction, and life stress were found to precede and predict depression; poor social relationships and reductions in positive rewards did not. The researchers concluded that the former factors help cause unipolar depression, while the latter simply accompany or result from depression and perhaps help maintain it.

As with unipolar depression, clinicians and researchers have learned much about bipolar disorders during the past 35 years. But bipolar disorders appear to be best explained by a focus on *one* kind of variable—biological factors. The evidence suggests that biological abnormalities, perhaps inherited and perhaps triggered by life stress, cause bipolar disorders (Bender & Alloy, 2011). Whatever roles other factors may play, the primary one appears to lie in this realm.

Thus we see that one kind of mood disorder may result from multiple causes, while another may result largely from a single factor. Although today's theorists are increasingly looking for intersecting factors to explain various psychological disorders, this is not always the most enlightening course. It depends on the disorder. What is important is that the cause or causes of a disorder be recognized. Scientists can then invest their energies more efficiently and clinicians can better understand the persons with whom they work.

There is no question that investigations into the symptoms and causes of mood disorders have been fruitful and enlightening (see *MediaSpeak* on the next page). And it is more than reasonable to expect that important research findings and insights will continue to unfold in the years ahead. Now that clinical researchers have gathered so many important pieces of the puzzle, they must put the pieces together into a still more meaningful picture that will suggest even better ways to predict, prevent, and treat these disorders.

Ognen Teofilovski/Reuters

Loneliness and depression: not for humans only
A chimpanzee named Koko looks out from his cage at the Skopje Zoo in Macedonia, a poor country in southeastern Europe. Authorities believe that Koko, the only chimp in the zoo, suffers from depression after having lived alone and in terrible conditions for many years.

Summing Up

- **DISORDERS OF MOOD** People with disorders of mood have mood problems that tend to last for months or years, dominate their interactions with the world, and disrupt their normal functioning. *Depression* and *mania* are the key moods in these disorders. *pp. 223–224*

- **UNIPOLAR DEPRESSION: THE DEPRESSIVE DISORDERS** People with *unipolar depression,* the most common pattern of mood disorder, suffer exclusively from depression. The symptoms of depression span five areas of functioning: emotional, motivational, behavioral, cognitive, and physical. Depressed people are also at greater risk for suicidal thinking and behavior. Women are at least twice as likely as men to experience severe unipolar depression. *pp. 224–228*

MediaSpeak

The Crying Game: Male Versus Female Tears

By Jocelyn Noveck, The Associated Press

"Please, please, please, just give the dog back," Ellen DeGeneres wept on national TV. . . . It was a moment that quickly established itself in the pop-culture firmament, less for the plight of Iggy the adopted terrier than for the copious crying itself.

(To recap: DeGeneres had adopted Iggy from a rescue organization, then given it to her hairdresser's family when the dog didn't get along with her cats. That was against the rules, and the rescue group took the dog back.)

Setting aside the question of whether those sobs were 100 percent genuine, tears are a natural human response, and public figures are obviously not immune. But some who study this most basic expression of feeling will tell you that in this day and age, it can be easier for a crying man to be taken seriously than a crying woman.

In politics, it's a far cry from 1972, when Sen. Ed Muskie's presidential campaign was derailed by what were perceived to be tears in response to a newspaper attack on his wife. But decades later, an occasional Clintonesque tear is seen as a positive thing. Bill Clinton, that is.

"Bill could cry, and did, but Hillary can't," says Tom Lutz, a professor at the University of California, Riverside, who authored an exhaustive history of crying. The same tearful response that would be seen as sensitivity in Bill could be seen as a lack of control in his wife.

But there are additional rules for acceptable public crying. "We're talking about dropping a tear," Lutz notes, "no more than a tear or two." And it all depends on the perceived seriousness of the subject matter. Thus Jon Stewart or David Letterman could choke up with impunity just after Sept. 11. But a dog-adoption problem is another matter.

In a recently published study at Penn State, researchers sought to explore differing perceptions of crying in men and women, presenting their 284 subjects with a series of hypothetical vignettes. Reactions depended on the type of crying, and who was doing it. A moist eye was viewed much more posi-

Bill O'Leary/The Washington Post/Getty Images

Tears of leadership? Speaker of the House John Boehner sheds tears during an election night celebration. Boehner is notorious for such displays of emotion, a behavior that has endeared him to his political supporters. Apparently, when it comes to crying, the double standard between the sexes continues to grow.

tively than open crying, and males got the most positive responses.

"Women are not making it up when they say they're damned if they do, damned if they don't," said Stephanie Shields, the psychology professor who conducted the study. "If you don't express any emotion, you're seen as not human, like Mr. Spock on 'Star Trek,'" she said. "But too much crying, or the wrong kind, and you're labeled as overemotional, out of control and possibly irrational."

That comes as no surprise to Suzyn Waldman, a broadcaster of Yankee games on New York's WCBS Radio. Earlier this month, she choked up on live radio after the Yankees had just been eliminated from the playoffs. She was describing the scene as [the] coaches choked up themselves. . . . Her tearful report quickly became an Internet hit, and she was mocked far and wide, especially on radio. . . . "When men express anger they gain status, but when women express anger they lose status," Yale social psychologist Victoria Brescoll . . . said in an interview. . . .

For a little historical perspective, says Lutz, author of "Crying: The Natural and Cultural History of Tears," it's helpful to look back to the 19th century, when skillful politicians like Abraham Lincoln used tears as a natural part of their oratory.

The tide later shifted against male crying, but in the past 30 to 40 years male crying has gained in acceptability. "Every president since Ronald Reagan has used tears at some point," says Shields, the Penn State psychologist. . . . Military figures have cried at critical moments. Gen. Norman Schwarzkopf cried at a Christmas Eve ceremony in front of his troops, and when interviewed by Barbara Walters, Lutz notes. . . .

But in DeGeneres' case, along with the strong support from fans and many dog lovers, she also endured some criticism and mockery. . . .

■ **EXPLANATIONS OF UNIPOLAR DISORDER** Each of the leading models has offered explanations for unipolar depression. The biological, cognitive, and sociocultural views have received the greatest research support.

According to the *biological view,* low activity of two neurotransmitters, *norepinephrine* and *serotonin,* helps cause depression. *Hormonal factors* may also be at work. So too may deficiencies of key proteins and other chemicals *within* certain neurons. Brain imaging research has also tied depression to abnormalities in a circuit of brain areas, including the *prefrontal cortex, hippocampus, amygdala,* and *Brodmann Area 25.* All such biological problems may be linked to *genetic factors.*

According to the *psychodynamic view,* certain people who experience *real or imagined losses* may *regress* to an earlier stage of development, *introject* feelings for the lost object, and eventually become depressed.

The *behavioral view* says that when people experience a large reduction in their positive rewards in life, they may display fewer and fewer positive behaviors. This response leads to a still lower rate of positive rewards and eventually to depression.

The leading *cognitive explanations* of unipolar depression focus on *negative thinking* and *learned helplessness.* According to Beck's theory of negative thinking, *maladaptive attitudes,* the *cognitive triad, errors in thinking,* and *automatic thoughts* help produce unipolar depression. According to Seligman's learned helplessness theory, people become depressed when they believe that they have lost control over the reinforcements in their lives and when they attribute this loss to causes that are *internal, global,* and *stable.*

Sociocultural theories propose that unipolar depression is influenced by social and cultural factors. *Family-social* theorists point out that a low level of social support is often linked to unipolar depression. And *multicultural* theorists have noted that the character and prevalence of depression often vary by gender and sometimes by culture. *pp. 228–244*

■ **BIPOLAR DISORDERS** In *bipolar disorders,* episodes of mania alternate or intermix with episodes of depression. These disorders are much less common than unipolar depression. They may take the form of *bipolar I, bipolar II,* or *cyclothymic disorder. pp. 244–249*

■ **EXPLANATIONS OF BIPOLAR DISORDERS** Mania may be related to *high norepinephrine activity along with a low level of serotonin activity.* Some researchers have also linked bipolar disorders to *improper transport of ions* back and forth between the outside and the inside of a neuron's membrane, others have focused on deficiencies of key proteins and other chemicals within certain neurons, and still others have uncovered abnormalities in key brain structures. Genetic studies suggest that people may *inherit* a predisposition to these biological abnormalities. *pp. 249–252*

PsychPortal

Visit **PsychPortal**
www.yourpsychportal.com
to access the e-book, videocases and other case materials and activities, and study aids, including flashcards, crossword puzzles, quizzes, FAQs, and research exercises.

BETWEEN THE LINES

Football Injuries and Depression

According to a study of 2,500 retired National Football League players, those who suffer three concussions during their careers are three times more likely later to develop a depressive disorder than those who had no concussions. ‹‹

Players who experience one or two concussions are 1.5 times more likely than other players to develop a depressive disorder. ‹‹

Around 26 percent of all former professional football players have suffered three or more concussions. ‹‹

(Schwarz, 2010; McConnaughey, 2007)

TREATMENTS FOR MOOD DISORDERS

Mid-twenties life circumstances were poor and I really plummeted. . . . The thing that made me go for help . . . was probably my daughter. She was something that earthed me, grounded me, and I thought, this isn't right, this can't be right, she cannot grow up with me in this state. . . . I got counseling . . . She absolutely saved me.

J. K. Rowling, author of "Harry Potter" books (in Amini, 2008)

I will take Zoloft for the rest of my life. I'm quite content to do it.

Mike Wallace, television news journalist (in Biddle et al., 1996)

In my case, ECT [electroconvulsive therapy] was miraculous. My wife was dubious, but when she came into my room afterward, I sat up and said, "Look who's back among the living." It was like a magic wand.

Dick Cavett, talk show host (in Cavett, 1992)

[T]he hospital was my salvation, and it is something of a paradox that in this austere place with its locked and wired doors and desolate green hallways . . . I found the repose, the assuagement of the tempest in my brain, that I was unable to find in my quiet farmhouse. . . . For me the real healers were seclusion and time.

William Styron, novelist (in Styron, 1990, pp. 68–69)

Because I thought I ought to be able to handle my increasingly violent mood swings by myself, for the first ten years I did not seek any kind of treatment. Even after my condition became a medical emergency, I still intermittently resisted the medications. . . . Having finally cottoned onto the disastrous consequences of starting and stopping lithium, I took it faithfully and found that life was a much stabler and more predictable place than I had ever reckoned. My moods were still intense and my temperament rather quick to the boil, but I could make plans with far more certainty and the periods of absolute blackness were fewer and less extreme. . . . I am [now] too frightened that I will again become morbidly depressed or virulently manic—either of which would, in turn, rip apart every aspect of my life, relationships, and work that I find most meaningful—to seriously consider any change in my medical treatment.

Kay Redfield Jamison, clinical researcher (in Jamison, 1995, pp. 5, 153, 212)

Each of these people suffered from and overcame a severe disorder of mood. And, clearly, all believe that the treatment they received was the key to their improvement—the key that opened the door to a normal, stable, and productive life. Yet the treatments that seemed to help them differed greatly. Psychotherapy helped bring control, compassion, and meaning back to the life of J. K. Rowling. Electroconvulsive therapy, popularly known as shock treatment, lifted Dick Cavett from the black hole of severe unipolar depression. Hospitalization and its temporary retreat were the answer for William Styron, and antidepressant drugs were the key for Mike Wallace. Kay Jamison escaped the roller-coaster ride of bipolar disorders with the help of lithium, a common, inexpensive element found in mineral salts.

How could such diverse therapies be so helpful to people suffering from the same or similar disorders? As this chapter will show, disorders of mood—as painful

Figure 9-1

How do people feel about depression and treatment? According to a recent survey, more than 80 percent of Americans believe that depression is a serious condition that requires treatment. However, 19 percent consider depression to be a sign of personal weakness (Armstrong, 2010).

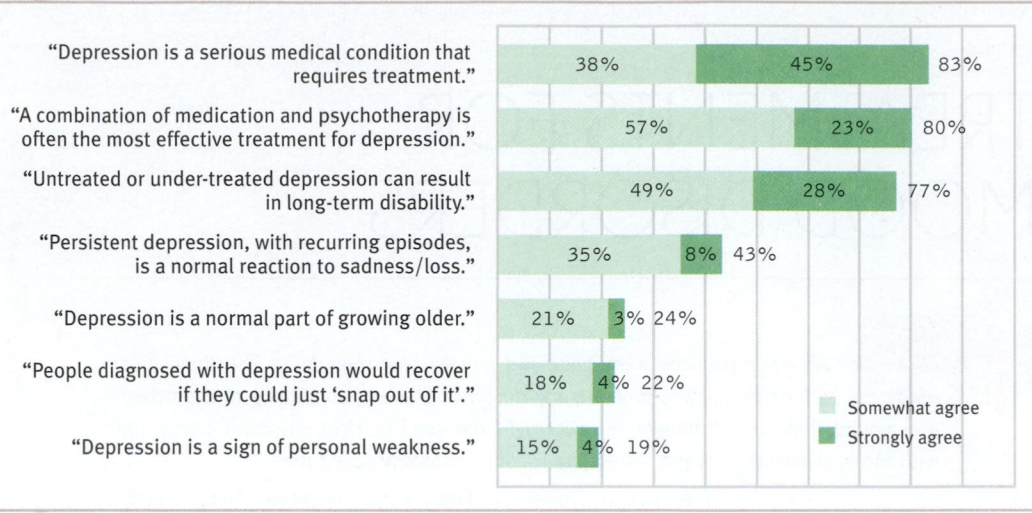

"Depression is a serious medical condition that requires treatment." — 38% / 45% / 83%

"A combination of medication and psychotherapy is often the most effective treatment for depression." — 57% / 23% / 80%

"Untreated or under-treated depression can result in long-term disability." — 49% / 28% / 77%

"Persistent depression, with recurring episodes, is a normal reaction to sadness/loss." — 35% / 8% / 43%

"Depression is a normal part of growing older." — 21% / 3% / 24%

"People diagnosed with depression would recover if they could just 'snap out of it'." — 18% / 4% / 22%

"Depression is a sign of personal weakness." — 15% / 4% / 19%

Somewhat agree
Strongly agree

A place for laughter

Many comedians have histories of depression. Drew Carey, for example, suffered from severe depression for much of his life. The popular host of the TV game show *The Price Is Right* reports that he has been able to overcome this mood disorder successfully by developing a positive outlook—through reading psychology books, listening to tapes on positive thinking, and, of course, generating and communicating humorous thoughts.

AP Photo/Kevork Djansezian

and disabling as they tend to be—respond more successfully to more kinds of treatment than do most other forms of psychological dysfunction. This range of treatment options has been a source of reassurance and hope for the millions of people who desire desperately to regain some measure of control over their moods (see Figure 9-1).

Treatments for Unipolar Depression

In the United States, around half of persons with unipolar depression—major depressive disorder or dysthymic disorder—receive treatment from a mental health professional each year (González et al., 2010). Access to such treatment differs among ethnic and racial groups. As you read in the previous chapter, only 34 percent of depressed Hispanic Americans and 40 percent of depressed African Americans receive treatment, compared to 54 percent of depressed white Americans (González et al., 2010).

In addition, many people in therapy experience depressed feelings as part of another disorder, such as an eating disorder, or in association with changes or general problems that they are encountering in life (see *MediaSpeak* on page 260). Thus much of the therapy being done today includes a focus on unipolar depression.

A variety of treatment approaches are currently in widespread use for unipolar depression. This chapter will first look at the psychological approaches, focusing on the psychodynamic, behavioral, and cognitive therapies. You will then read about the sociocultural approaches, including a highly regarded intervention called *interpersonal psychotherapy*. Next, the chapter will look at effective biological approaches, including electroconvulsive therapy, antidepressant drugs, and new brain stimulation interventions. In the process, you will see that unipolar patterns of depression are indeed among the most successfully treated of all psychological disorders.

Psychological Approaches

The psychological treatments used most often to combat unipolar depression come from the psychodynamic, behavioral, and cognitive schools of thought. Psychodynamic therapy, the oldest of all modern psychotherapies, continues to be used widely for depression even though research has not offered strong evidence of its effectiveness. Behavioral therapy, effective primarily for mild or moderate depression, is practiced less often today than it was in past decades. Cognitive therapy and cognitive-behavioral therapies have performed so well in research that they have a large and growing following among clinicians (Rehm, 2010).

Psychodynamic Therapy Believing that unipolar depression results from unconscious grief over real or imagined losses, compounded by excessive dependence on other people, psychodynamic therapists seek to help clients bring these underlying issues to consciousness and work them through. Using the arsenal of basic psychodynamic procedures, they encourage the depressed client to associate freely during therapy; suggest interpretations of the client's associations, dreams, and displays of resistance and transference; and

What kinds of transference issues might psychodynamic therapists expect to see in treatment with depressed clients?

help the person review past events and feelings (Busch et al., 2004). Free association, for example, helped one man recall the early experiences of loss that, according to his therapist, had set the stage for his depression:

> *Among his earliest memories, possibly the earliest of all, was the recollection of being wheeled in his baby cart under the elevated train structure and left there alone. Another memory that recurred vividly during the analysis was of an operation around the age of five. He was anesthetized and his mother left him with the doctor. He recalled how he had kicked and screamed, raging at her for leaving him.*
>
> *(Lorand, 1968, pp. 325–326)*

Psychodynamic therapists expect that in the course of treatment depressed clients will eventually gain awareness of the losses in their lives, become less dependent on others, cope with losses more effectively, and make corresponding changes in their functioning. The transition of a therapeutic insight into a real-life change is seen in the case of a middle-aged executive:

> *The patient's father was still living and in a nursing home, where the patient visited him regularly. On one occasion, he went to see his father full of high expectations, as he had concluded a very successful business transaction. As he began to describe his accomplishments to his father, however, the latter completely ignored his son's remarks and viciously berated him for wearing a pink shirt, which he considered unprofessional. Such a response from the father was not unusual, but this time, as a result of the work that had been accomplished in therapy, the patient could objectively analyze his initial sense of disappointment and deep feeling of failure for not pleasing the older man. Although this experience led to a transient state of depression, it also revealed to the patient his whole dependent lifestyle—his use of others to supply him with a feeling of worth. This experience added a dimension of immediate reality to the insights that had been achieved in therapy and gave the patient the motivation to change radically his childhood system of perceiving himself in relation to paternal transference figures.*
>
> *(Bemporad, 1992, p. 291)*

Despite successful case reports such as this, researchers have found that long-term psychodynamic therapy is only occasionally helpful in cases of unipolar depression (Prochaska & Norcross, 2007). Two features of the approach may help limit its

MediaSpeak

How Well Do Colleges Treat Depression?

By Daniel Mcginn and Ron Depasquale, *Newsweek*

On the long list of worries that Mom and Dad have when a child goes to college—grades, homesickness, partying— there's a new issue gaining prominence: the apparent rise in mental illness on campus. More than 1,100 college students commit suicide each year, according to estimates by mental-health groups. And even when students aren't in acute distress, they're suffering in surprisingly large numbers. In a 2003 survey by the American College Health Association, more than 40 percent of students reported feeling "so depressed it was difficult to function" at least once during the year. Thirty percent identified themselves as suffering from an anxiety disorder or depression. . . .

Given that kind of assessment, it's inevitable that mental-health issues are starting to filter into admissions conversations. One counselor at an East Coast private high school says that during the 2003–04 admissions cycle, officials from two colleges confided they were particularly focused on admitting a class that was "rock solid" emotionally, both to help prevent suicides and to reduce the toll on overbooked school therapists. . . .

Since the admissions process requires students to appear flawless, many families avoid disclosing a child's history of emotional problems, especially before they get an acceptance letter. However, parents are starting to ask tough questions about just which kind of mental-health services they can expect from schools. . . .

. . . While nearly every school has a counseling office, almost half lack a full-fledged staff psychiatrist, according to Robert Gallagher, a University of Pittsburgh professor who conducts an annual survey of college counseling offices. That means it may be difficult for a student to receive prescription drugs to treat depression or anxiety, and that students with serious problems may be referred off campus for treatment. "Not only are the [on-campus] services more accessible, but the people providing the services are more familiar with college pressures," says Gallagher. And while some schools offer unlimited therapy for students, others restrict them to eight or 10 appointments a year. That may be fine for the average student, who often sees a counselor just once or twice to discuss homesickness, a bad grade or a relationship breakup. For those with more serious problems, such limits may mean rushed care.

Nathan Lau/Design Pics/Corbis

Experts cite a mix of reasons that campus therapists' offices are so crowded. . . . [According to one explanation], the quest to get into a top college has grown so cutthroat for many that more students are emerging from it emotionally damaged. "Kids are burning out sooner and sooner," says Leigh Martin Lowe, director of college counseling at Roland Park Country School in Baltimore. "They're not being allowed to enjoy their teenage years, and many of them end up in college and they don't have the energy or stamina to really turn it on." . . .

For students with [emotional problems], college counselors and therapists say that fact should play some role in their college search. . . . There may also be benefits in choosing smaller schools. . . . According to the University of Pittsburgh study, at colleges with 2,500 or fewer students, health centers had one counselor for every 818 students. At colleges with more than 15,000 students, the counselor-to-student ratio jumped to 1 to 2,426.

The trickiest task faces parents whose children seem 100 percent healthy when they leave for college. Donna Satow . . . and her husband run the Jed Foundation, which helps colleges develop strategies for dealing with student depression. . . . Satow advises parents of every student to become informed about mental-health services at their child's school. . . . [I]n a world where families agonize over finding the cushiest dorm room and the perfect meal plan, it's a question that deserves to be asked.

effectiveness. First, depressed clients may be too passive and feel too weary to join fully into the subtle therapy discussions. And second, they may become discouraged and end treatment too early when this long-term approach is unable to provide the quick relief that they desperately seek. Generally, psychodynamic therapy seems to be of greatest help in cases of depression that clearly involve a history of childhood loss or trauma, a long-standing sense of emptiness, feelings of perfectionism, and extreme self-criticism

(Luyten & Blatt, 2011; Blatt, 1999, 1995). Short-term psychodynamic therapies have performed better than the traditional approaches (Lemma, Target, & Fonagy, 2011; Hollon & Ponniah, 2010).

Behavioral Therapy Behaviorists, whose theories of depression tie mood to the rewards in a person's life, have developed corresponding treatments for unipolar depression. Most such treatments are modeled after the intervention proposed by Peter Lewinsohn, the behavioral theorist whose theory of depression was described in Chapter 8 (see page 236). In a typical behavioral approach, therapists (1) reintroduce depressed clients to pleasurable events and activities, (2) appropriately reinforce their depressive and non-depressive behaviors, and (3) help them improve their social skills (Farmer & Chapman, 2008).

First, the therapist selects activities that the client considers pleasurable, such as going shopping or taking photos, and encourages the person to set up a weekly schedule for engaging in them. Studies have shown that adding positive activities to a person's life—sometimes called *behavioral activation*—can indeed lead to a better mood (Martell et al., 2010). The following case description exemplifies this process:

> *This patient was a forty-nine-year-old [woman]. . . . Her major interest in life was painting, and indeed she was an accomplished artist. She developed a depression characterized by apathy, self-derogation, and anxiety while she was incapacitated with a severe respiratory infection. She was unable to paint during her illness and lost interest and confidence in her art work when she became depressed. Her therapist thought that she could reinstitute her sources of "reinforcement" if she could be motivated to return to the easel. After providing a supportive relationship for a month, the therapist scheduled a home visit to look at her paintings and to watch and talk with her while she picked up her brush and put paint to canvas. By the time he arrived, she had already begun to paint and within a few weeks experienced a gradual lessening of her depression.*
>
> (Liberman & Raskin, 1971, p. 521)

While reintroducing pleasurable events into a client's life, the therapist makes sure that the person's various behaviors are rewarded correctly. Behaviorists argue that when people become depressed, their negative behaviors—crying, ruminating, complaining, or self-depreciation—keep others at a distance, reducing chances for rewarding experiences and interactions. To change this pattern, therapists guide clients to monitor their negative behaviors and to try new, more positive ones (Martell et al., 2010; Farmer & Chapman, 2008). In addition, the therapist may use a *contingency management* approach, systematically ignoring a client's depressive behaviors while praising or otherwise rewarding constructive statements and behavior, such as going to work. Sometimes family members and friends are recruited to help with this feature of treatment (Liberman & Raskin, 1971).

Finally, behavioral therapists may train clients in effective social skills (Segrin, 2000; Hersen et al., 1984). In group therapy programs, for example, members may work together to improve eye contact, facial expression, posture, and other behaviors that send social messages.

These behavioral techniques seem to be of only limited help when just one of them is applied. In one study, for example, depressed people who were instructed to increase their pleasant activities showed no more improvement than those in a control group who were told simply to keep track of their activities (Hammen & Glass, 1975). However, when two or more behavioral techniques are combined, behavioral treatment does appear to reduce depressive symptoms, particularly if the depression is mild

Stretching one's emotions
Although formal treatment is typically needed for severe depression, personal efforts such as going on vacation or spending time with friends can often make a significant difference for people who are struggling with mild depression. Research shows, for example, that regular exercise can help prevent or reduce feelings of depression as well as other psychological symptoms (Dunn et al., 2005).

Pete Saloutos/Corbis

	Monday	Tuesday	Wednesday	Thursday	Fr
9–10		Go to grocery store	Go to museum	Get ready to go out	
10–11		Go to grocery store	Go to museum	Drive to doctor's appointment	
11–12	Doctor's appointment	Call friend	Go to museum	Doctor's appointment	
12–1	Lunch	Lunch	Lunch at museum		
1–2	Drive home	Clean front room	Drive home		
2–3	Read novel	Clean front room	Washing		
3–4	Clean bedroom	Read novel	Washing		
4–5	Watch TV	Watch TV	Watch TV		
5–6	Fix dinner	Fix dinner	Fix dinner		
6–7	Eat with family	Eat with family	Eat with family		
7–8	Clean kitchen	Clean kitchen	Clean kitchen		
8–12	Watch TV, read novel, sleep	Call sister, watch TV, read novel, sleep	Work on rug, read novel, sleep		

Figure 9-2

Increasing activity In the early stages of cognitive therapy for depression, the client and therapist prepare an activity schedule such as this. Activities as simple as watching television and calling a friend are specified. (Adapted from Beck et al., 1979, p. 122.)

(Lazzari, Egan, & Rees, 2011; Martell et al., 2010; Jacobson et al., 2001, 1996). It is worth noting that Lewinsohn himself has combined behavioral techniques with cognitive strategies in recent years, in an approach similar to the cognitive-behavioral treatments discussed in the next section.

Cognitive Therapy In Chapter 8 you saw that Aaron Beck viewed unipolar depression as resulting from a pattern of negative thinking that may be triggered by current upsetting situations. *Maladaptive attitudes* lead people repeatedly to view themselves, their world, and their future in negative ways—the so-called *cognitive triad*. Such biased views combine with *illogical thinking* to produce *automatic thoughts,* unrelentingly negative thoughts that flood the mind and produce the symptoms of depression.

To help clients overcome this negative thinking, Beck has developed a treatment approach that he calls **cognitive therapy.** He uses this label because the approach is designed primarily to help clients recognize and change their negative cognitive processes and thus to improve their mood (Beck & Weishaar, 2011; Wright, Thase, & Beck, 2011). However, as you will see, the approach also includes a number of *behavioral* techniques (Figure 9-2), particularly as therapists try to get clients moving again and encourage them to try out new behaviors. Thus, many theorists consider this approach a *cognitive-behavioral therapy* rather than the purely cognitive intervention implied by its name. Beck's approach is similar to Albert Ellis' *rational-emotive therapy* (discussed in Chapters 3 and 5), but it is tailored to the specific cognitive errors found in depression. The approach follows four phases and usually requires fewer than 20 sessions (see Table 9-1).

Phase 1: Increasing activities and elevating mood Using behavioral techniques to set the stage for cognitive treatment, therapists first encourage individuals to become more active and confident. Clients spend time during each session preparing a detailed schedule of hourly activities for the coming week. As they become more active from week to week, their mood is expected to improve.

Phase 2: Challenging automatic thoughts Once people are more active and feeling some emotional relief, cognitive therapists begin to educate them about their negative automatic thoughts. The individuals are instructed to recognize and record automatic thoughts as they occur and to bring their lists to each session. Therapist and client

table: 9-1

Mood Disorders and Treatment

Disorder	Treatment	Average Duration of Treatment	Percent Improved by Treatment
Major Depressive Disorder	Cognitive/Cognitive-Behavioral Therapy	20 sessions	60%
	Interpersonal Psychotherapy	20 sessions	60
	Antidepressant Drugs	Indefinite	60
	ECT	9 sessions	60
	Vagus Nerve Stimulation	1 session (plus follow-up)	60
	Transcranial Magnetic Stimulation	25 sessions	60
Bipolar Disorder	Psychotropic Drugs: Mood Stabilizers, Anitpsychotics, and Antidepressants	Indefinite	60

then test the reality behind the thoughts, often concluding that they are groundless. Beck offers the following exchange as an example of this sort of review:

> **Therapist:** *Why do you think you won't be able to get into the university of your choice?*
> **Patient:** *Because my grades were really not so hot.*
> **Therapist:** *Well, what was your grade average?*
> **Patient:** *Well, pretty good up until the last semester in high school.*
> **Therapist:** *What was your grade average in general?*
> **Patient:** *A's and B's.*
> **Therapist:** *Well, how many of each?*
> **Patient:** *Well, I guess, almost all of my grades were A's but I got terrible grades my last semester.*
> **Therapist:** *What were your grades then?*
> **Patient:** *I got two A's and two B's.*
> **Therapist:** *Since your grade average would seem to me to come out to almost all A's, why do you think you won't be able to get into the university?*
> **Patient:** *Because of competition being so tough.*
> **Therapist:** *Have you found out what the average grades are for admission to the college?*
> **Patient:** *Well, somebody told me that a B+ average would suffice.*
> **Therapist:** *Isn't your average better than that?*
> **Patient:** *I guess so.*
>
> *(Beck et al., 1979, p. 153)*

Phase 3: Identifying negative thinking and biases As people begin to recognize the flaws in their automatic thoughts, cognitive therapists show them how illogical thinking processes are contributing to these thoughts. The depressed student, for example, was using dichotomous (all-or-nothing) thinking when she concluded that any grade lower than A was "terrible." The therapists also guide clients to recognize that almost all their interpretations of events have a negative bias and to change that style of interpretation.

Phase 4: Changing primary attitudes Therapists help clients change the maladaptive attitudes that set the stage for their depression in the first place. As part of the process, therapists often encourage clients to test their attitudes, as in the following therapy discussion:

> **Therapist:** *On what do you base this belief that you can't be happy without a man?*
> **Patient:** *I was really depressed for a year and a half when I didn't have a man.*
> **Therapist:** *Is there another reason why you were depressed?*
> **Patient:** *As we discussed, I was looking at everything in a distorted way. But I still don't know if I could be happy if no one was interested in me.*
> **Therapist:** *I don't know either. Is there a way we could find out?*
> **Patient:** *Well, as an experiment, I could not go out on dates for a while and see how I feel.*
> **Therapist:** *I think that's a good idea. Although it has its flaws, the experimental method is still the best way currently available to discover the facts. You're fortunate in being able to run this type of experiment. Now, for the first time in your adult life you aren't attached to a man. If you find you can be happy without a man, this will greatly strengthen you and also make your future relationships all the better.*
>
> *(Beck et al., 1979, pp. 253–254)*

BETWEEN THE LINES

Self-Help Goes Awry

In 1991 the Gloucester branch of Depressives Anonymous ejected several members because they were too cheerful. Said the group chairperson, "Those with sensitive tender feelings have been put off by more robust members who have not always been depressives" (Shaw, 2004). ‹‹

•**cognitive therapy**•A therapy developed by Aaron Beck that helps people identify and change the maladaptive assumptions and ways of thinking that help cause their psychological disorders.

"You're sad about the wrong things, Albert."

Over the past several decades, hundreds of studies have shown that Beck's therapy and similar cognitive and cognitive-behavioral approaches help with unipolar depression. Depressed adults who receive these therapies improve much more than those who receive placebos or no treatment at all (Manicavasgar et al., 2011; Hollon et al., 2006, 2005, 2002). Around 50 to 60 percent show a near-total elimination of their symptoms. In view of this strong research support, many depression therapists have adopted cognitive and cognitive-behavioral approaches, some offering them in group therapy formats (Petrocelli, 2002).

It is worth noting that a growing number of today's cognitive-behavioral therapists do not agree with Beck's proposition that individuals must fully discard their negative cognitions in order to overcome depression. These therapists, the new-wave cognitive-behavioral therapists about whom you read in Chapters 3 and 5, including those who practice *acceptance and commitment therapy* (ACT), guide depressed clients to recognize and accept their negative cognitions simply as streams of thinking that flow through their minds, rather than as valuable guides for behavior and decisions. As clients increasingly accept their negative thoughts for what they are, they can better work around the thoughts as they navigate their way through life (Wells et al., 2012; Hollon & DiGiuseppe, 2011; Hayes et al., 2006).

Sociocultural Approaches

As you read in Chapter 8, sociocultural theorists trace the causes of unipolar depression to the broader social structure in which people live and the roles they are required to play. Two groups of sociocultural treatments are now widely applied in cases of unipolar depression—*multicultural approaches* and *family-social approaches.*

Multicultural Treatments
In Chapter 3, you read that *culture-sensitive therapies* seek to address the unique issues faced by members of cultural minority groups (Comas-Diaz, 2011, 2006). Such approaches typically include special cultural training of the therapists; heightened awareness by therapists of their clients' cultural values and the culture-related stressors, prejudices, and stereotypes faced by the clients; and efforts by therapists to help clients achieve a comfortable (for them) bicultural balance and recognize the impact of their own culture and the dominant culture on their self-views and behaviors (Prochaska & Norcross, 2010).

In the treatment of unipolar depression, culture-sensitive approaches increasingly are being combined with traditional forms of psychotherapy to help maximize the likelihood of minority clients overcoming their disorders. A number of today's therapists, for example, offer cognitive-behavioral therapy for depressed minority clients while also focusing on the clients' economic pressures, minority identity, and related cultural issues (Stacciarini et al., 2007). A range of studies indicate that Hispanic American, African American, American Indian, and Asian American clients are more likely to overcome their depressive disorders when a culture-sensitive focus is added to the form of psychotherapy that they are otherwise receiving (Comas-Diaz, 2011; Ward, 2007). Unfortunately, this kind of combination therapy for depression, while on the increase, is still unavailable to most minority clients (Dwight-Johnson & Lagomasino, 2007).

It also appears that the medication needs of many depressed minority clients, especially those who are poor, are inadequately addressed. As you will see later in this chapter, for example, minority clients are less likely than white American clients to receive the most helpful antidepressant medications.

Do you think culture-sensitive therapies might be more useful for some kinds of disorders than for other kinds? Why or why not?

Family-Social Treatments Therapists who use family and social approaches to treat depression help clients change how they deal with the close relationships in their lives. The most effective family-social approaches are *interpersonal psychotherapy* and *couple therapy.*

INTERPERSONAL PSYCHOTHERAPY Developed by clinical researchers Gerald Klerman and Myrna Weissman, **interpersonal psychotherapy (IPT)** holds that any of four interpersonal problem areas may lead to depression and must be addressed: interpersonal loss, interpersonal role dispute, interpersonal role transition, and interpersonal deficits (Frank & Levenson, 2011; O'Hara, Schiller, & Stuart, 2010). Over the course of around 16 sessions, IPT therapists address these areas.

First, depressed persons may, as psychodynamic theorists suggest, be experiencing a grief reaction over an important *interpersonal loss,* the loss of a loved one. In such cases, IPT therapists encourage clients to explore their relationship with the lost person and express any feelings of anger they may discover. Eventually clients develop new ways of remembering the lost person and also seek new relationships.

Second, depressed people may find themselves in the midst of an *interpersonal role dispute.* Role disputes occur when two people have different expectations of their relationship and of the role each should play. IPT therapists help clients examine whatever role disputes they may be involved in and then develop ways of resolving them.

Depressed people may also be experiencing an *interpersonal role transition,* brought about by major life changes such as divorce or the birth of a child. They may feel overwhelmed by the role changes that accompany the life change. In such cases IPT therapists help them develop the social supports and skills the new roles require.

Finally, some depressed people display *interpersonal deficits,* such as extreme shyness or social awkwardness, that prevent them from having intimate relationships. IPT therapists may help such individuals recognize their deficits and teach them social skills and assertiveness in order to improve their social effectiveness. In the following discussion, the therapist encourages a depressed man to recognize the effect his behavior has on others:

> *Client:* (After a long pause with eyes downcast, a sad facial expression, and slumped posture) People always make fun of me. I guess I'm just the type of guy who really was meant to be a loner, damn it. (Deep sigh)
>
> *Therapist:* Could you do that again for me?
>
> *Client:* What?
>
> *Therapist:* The sigh, only a bit deeper.
>
> *Client:* Why? (Pause) Okay, but I don't see what . . . okay. (Client sighs again and smiles)
>
> *Therapist:* Well, that time you smiled, but mostly when you sigh and look so sad I get the feeling that I better leave you alone in your misery, that I should walk on eggshells and not get too chummy or I might hurt you even more.
>
> *Client:* (A bit of anger in his voice) Well, excuse me! I was only trying to tell you how I felt.
>
> *Therapist:* I know you felt miserable, but I also got the message that you wanted to keep me at a distance, that I had no way to reach you.
>
> *Client:* (Slowly) I feel like a loner, I feel that even you don't care about me—making fun of me.
>
> *Therapist:* I wonder if other folks need to pass this test, too?
>
> *(Beier & Young, 1984, p. 270)*

Studies suggest that IPT and related interpersonal treatments for depression have a success rate similar to that of cognitive and cognitive-behavioral therapies (Frank & Levenson, 2011; O'Hara et al., 2010). That is, symptoms almost totally disappear in 50

Tom Moran

Role transition

Major life changes such as marriage, the birth of a child, or divorce can present difficulties in role transition, one of the interpersonal problem areas addressed by IPT therapists in their work with depressed clients.

•interpersonal psychotherapy (IPT)• A treatment for unipolar depression that is based on the belief that clarifying and changing one's interpersonal problems will help lead to recovery.

Treating the relationship
In cases where depression is closely tied to marital difficulties, couple therapy is often as helpful or more helpful than individual therapy.

to 60 percent of clients who receive treatment. After IPT, clients not only experience a reduction of depressive symptoms but also function more effectively in their social and family interactions. Not surprisingly, IPT is considered especially useful for depressed people who are struggling with social conflicts or undergoing changes in their careers or social roles.

COUPLE THERAPY As you have read, depression can result from marital discord, and recovery from depression is often slower for people who do not receive support from their spouse (Whisman & Schonbrun, 2010). In fact, as many as half of all depressed clients may be in a dysfunctional relationship. Thus it is not surprising that many cases of depression have been treated by **couple therapy,** the approach in which a therapist works with two people who share a long-term relationship.

Therapists who offer *behavioral marital therapy* help spouses change harmful marital behavior by teaching them specific communication and problem-solving skills (see Chapter 3). When the depressed person's marriage is filled with conflict, this approach and similar ones may be as effective as individual cognitive therapy, interpersonal psychotherapy, or drug therapy in helping to reduce depression (Whisman & Shonbrun, 2010; Franchi, 2004). In addition, depressed clients who receive couple therapy are more likely than those in individual therapy to be more satisfied with their marriage after treatment.

Biological Approaches

Like several of the psychological and sociocultural therapies, biological treatments can bring great relief to people with unipolar depression. Usually biological treatment means *antidepressant drugs* or popular herbal supplements (see *PsychWatch* on the next page), but for severely depressed individuals who do not respond to other forms of treatment, it sometimes means *electroconvulsive therapy,* an approach that has been around for more than 70 years, or *brain stimulation,* a relatively new group of approaches.

Electroconvulsive Therapy One of the most controversial forms of treatment for depression is **electroconvulsive therapy,** or **ECT.** One patient describes his experience:

> *Strapped to a stretcher, you are wheeled into the ECT room. The electroshock machine is in clear view. It is a solemn occasion; there is little talk. The nurse, the attendant, and the anesthetist go about their preparation methodically. Your psychiatrist enters. He seems quite matter-of-fact, businesslike—perhaps a bit rushed. "Everything is going to be just fine. I have given hundreds of these treatments. No one has ever died." You flinch inside. Why did he say that? But there is no time to dwell on it. They are ready. The electrodes are in place. The long clear plastic tube running from the bottle above ends with a needle in your vein. An injection is given. Suddenly—terrifyingly—you can no longer breathe; and then . . . You awaken in your hospital bed. There is a soreness in your legs and a bruise on your arm you can't explain. You are confused to find it so difficult to recover memories. Finally, you stop struggling in the realization that you have no memory for what has transpired. You were scheduled to have ECT, but something must have happened. Perhaps it was postponed. But the nurse keeps coming over to you and asking, "How are you feeling?" You think to yourself: "It must have been given"; but you can't remember. Confused and uncomfortable, you begin to dread the return to the ECT room. You have forgotten, but something about it remains. You are frightened.*
>
> *(Taylor, 1975)*

•**couple therapy**•A therapy format in which the therapist works with two people who share a long-term relationship.

•**electroconvulsive therapy (ECT)**•A treatment for depression in which electrodes attached to a patient's head send an electrical current through the brain, causing a convulsion.

Clinicians and patients alike vary greatly in their opinions of ECT. Some consider it a safe biological procedure with minimal risks; others believe it to be an extreme measure that can cause troublesome memory loss and even neurological damage. Despite

Nature's Way

Today more than half of all Americans take "herbal" supplements and "natural" hormones to help combat ills ranging from depression to pain (Vosburgh, 2011; Magee, 2007). Such supplements—collectively called *dietary supplements* or *nutraceuticals*—are experiencing a remarkable growth in popularity, but they are hardly new. Chinese healers compiled the first of their 11,000 medicinal herb formulas as far back as 3000 B.C.

Dietary supplements are a multi-billion dollar industry in the United States, with sales increasing by about $1 billion each year (Thurston, 2008). This sales explosion can be traced to the 1994 passage of the Dietary Supplement Health and Education Act, which provides that dietary supplements are not bound by the same legal requirements as medicinal drugs. As you read in Chapter 3, to receive approval for a drug, its manufacturer must prove it safe and effective through a testing process that costs manufacturers hundreds of millions of dollars. Dietary supplements, in contrast, are assumed to be safe unless the U.S. Food and Drug Administration (FDA) can prove them harmful. In the wake of this law, 4,000 manufacturers have rushed dietary supplements into the marketplace, typically without research and often with a number of extraordinary claims about their healing powers.

Compounding these research problems is the reluctance of many patients to discuss their use of supplements with their therapists or physicians (Niv et al., 2010; Kessler, 2002). Yet nutraceuticals can be potent, and some interact dangerously with conventional medications (NIH, 2011;

Patrick Johns/Corbis

Flower power *Hypericum perforatum,* known as *Saint-John's-wort,* is a low, wild-growing shrub. It is currently among the hottest-selling products in health stores, with studies indicating that it can be quite helpful in cases of mild or moderate depression.

Magee, 2007). In addition, patients often take nutraceuticals incorrectly, partly because they learn about them primarily from friends or from the Internet, where misinformation on this subject abounds.

Here are some of today's most popular nutraceuticals:

Gingko biloba This herb, extracted from the leaves of the tree of the same name, is sold as a memory and concentration enhancer (Serby et al., 2010). Research has been divided regarding its usefulness in everyday life. It does seem to be modestly helpful to individuals suffering memory loss due to dementia, but it cannot help prevent dementia.

SAM-e In 1999, *s-adenosylmethionine,* or *SAM-e* (pronounced "Sammy"), entered the United States marketplace after more than 20 years of use in Italy and 13 other countries. A common molecule produced by all living cells, this compound is used in cases of depression.

Saint-John's-wort Research suggests that this common flower can be quite helpful in cases of moderate to mild depression (Solomon et al., 2011; McIntosh & Kleiman, 2007). Moreover, it is relatively inexpensive and produces few undesired effects. However, it does not appear to benefit people with severe depression.

Black cohosh This herb shows some promise as a treatment for the symptoms of premenstrual syndrome and menopause (Briese et al., 2007). A host of other herbs also have been touted for these conditions, including *evening primrose oil, wild yam,* and *chaste berry* (Chavez & Spitzer, 2002).

Melatonin This hormone, which is secreted naturally by the brain's pineal gland, has been touted to do everything from alleviating depression to improving sexual performance and even increasing the life span. The hormone has not received clear research support in most of these realms, but it does appear to be of help to people with sleep problems (Jan et al., 2011; Hollway & Aman, 2011; Braam et al., 2008).

---

the heat of this controversy, ECT is used frequently, largely because it is an effective and fast-acting intervention for unipolar depression (Pfeiffer et al., 2011; Loo, 2010).

THE TREATMENT PROCEDURE In an ECT procedure, two electrodes are attached to the patient's head, and 65 to 140 volts of electricity are passed through the brain for half a second or less. This results in a *brain seizure* that lasts from 25 seconds to a few minutes. After 6 to 12 such treatments, spaced over two to four weeks, most patients feel less depressed (Loo, 2010; Fink, 2007, 2001). In *bilateral ECT* one electrode is applied to each

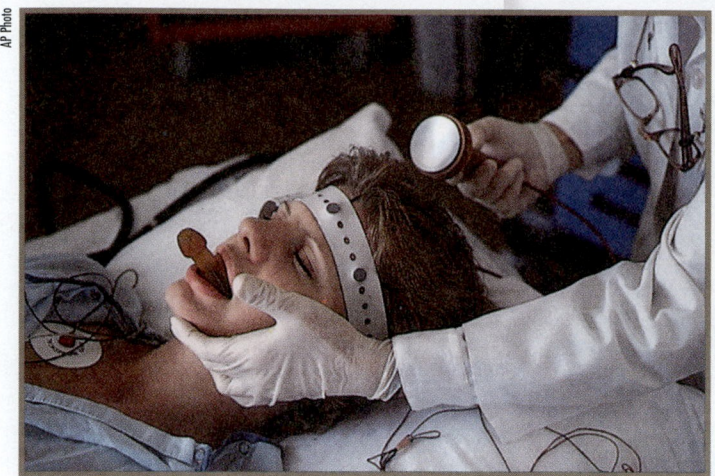

ECT today

The techniques for administering ECT have changed significantly since the treatment's early days. Today, patients are given drugs to help them sleep, muscle relaxants to prevent severe jerks of the body and broken bones, and oxygen to guard against brain damage.

side of the forehead, and a current passes through both sides of the brain. In *unilateral ECT,* the electrodes are placed so that the current passes through only one side.

THE ORIGINS OF ECT The discovery that electric shock can be therapeutic was made by accident. In the 1930s, clinical researchers mistakenly came to believe that brain seizures, or the *convulsions* (severe body spasms) that accompany them, could cure schizophrenia and other psychotic disorders. They observed that people with psychosis rarely suffered from *epilepsy* (*brain seizure disorder*) and that people with epilepsy rarely were psychotic, and so concluded that brain seizures or convulsions somehow prevented psychosis. We now know that the observed correlation between seizures and lack of psychotic symptoms does not necessarily imply that one event caused the other. Nevertheless, swayed by faulty logic, clinicians in the 1930s searched for ways to induce seizures as a treatment for patients with psychosis.

A Hungarian physician named Joseph von Meduna gave the drug *metrazol* to patients suffering from psychosis, and a Viennese physician named Manfred Sakel gave them large doses of insulin (*insulin coma therapy*). These procedures produced the desired brain seizures, but each was quite dangerous and sometimes even caused death. Finally, an Italian psychiatrist named Ugo Cerletti discovered that he could produce seizures more safely by applying electric currents to patients' heads, and he and his colleague Lucio Bini soon developed electroconvulsive therapy as a treatment for psychosis (Cerletti & Bini, 1938). As you might expect, much uncertainty and confusion accompanied their first clinical application of ECT. Did experimenters have the right to impose such an untested treatment against a patient's will?

> The schizophrenic arrived by train from Milan without a ticket or any means of identification. Physically healthy, he was bedraggled and alternately was mute or expressed himself in incomprehensible gibberish made up of odd neologisms. The patient was brought in but despite their vast animal experience there was great apprehension and fear that the patient might be damaged, and so the shock was cautiously set at 70 volts for one-tenth of a second. The low dosage predictably produced only a minor spasm, after which the patient burst into song. Cerletti suggested another shock at a higher voltage, and an excited and voluble discussion broke out among the spectators.... All of the staff objected to a further shock, protesting that the patient would probably die. Cerletti was familiar with committees and knew that postponement would inevitably mean prolonged and possibly permanent procrastination, and so he decided to proceed at 110 volts for one-half second. However, before he could do so, the patient who had heard but so far not participated in the discussion sat up and pontifically proclaimed in clear Italian without hint of jargon, "Non una seconda! Mortifera!" (Not again! It will kill me!). Professor Bini hesitated but gave the order to proceed. After recovery, Bini asked the patient "What has been happening to you?" and the man replied "I don't know; perhaps I've been asleep." He remained jargon-free and gave a complete account of himself, and was discharged completely recovered after 11 complete and 3 incomplete treatments over a course of 2 months.
>
> (Brandon, 1981, pp. 8–9)

BETWEEN THE LINES

Source of Inspiration

Like everyone else, Ugo Cerletti initially believed that the application of electric currents to people's heads would kill them. One day, however, he visited a slaughterhouse, where he observed that before slaughtering hogs with a knife, butchers clamped the animals' heads with metallic tongs and applied an electric current. The hogs fell unconscious and had convulsions, but they did not die from the current itself. Said Cerletti: "At this point I felt we could venture to experiment on man." ‹‹

ECT soon became popular and was tried out on a wide range of psychological problems, as new techniques so often are. Its effectiveness with severe depression in particular became apparent. Ironically, however, doubts were soon raised concerning its usefulness for psychosis, and many researchers have since judged it ineffective for psychotic disorders, except for cases that also include severe depressive symptoms (Freudenreich & Goff, 2011; Taube-Schiff & Lau, 2008).

CHANGES IN ECT PROCEDURES Although Cerletti gained international fame for his procedure, eventually he abandoned ECT and spent his later years seeking other treatments for mental disorders (Karon, 1985). The reason: he abhorred the broken bones and dislocations of the jaw or shoulders that sometimes resulted from ECT's severe convulsions, as well as the memory loss, confusion, and brain damage that the seizures could cause. Other clinicians have stayed with the procedure, however, and have changed it over the years to reduce its undesirable consequences. Today's practitioners give patients strong *muscle relaxants* to minimize convulsions, thus eliminating the danger of fractures or dislocations. They also use *anesthetics* (*barbiturates*) to put patients to sleep during the procedure, reducing their terror. With these precautions, ECT is medically more complex than it used to be, but also less dangerous and somewhat less disturbing (Pfeiffer et al., 2011; Gitlin, 2002).

Patients who receive ECT, particularly bilateral ECT, typically have difficulty remembering some events, most often events that took place immediately before and after their treatments (Merkl et al., 2011). In most cases, this memory loss clears up within a few months, but some patients experience gaps in more distant memory, and this form of amnesia can be permanent (Hanna et al., 2009; Wang, 2007; Squire, 1977). Understandably, these individuals may be left embittered by the procedure.

EFFECTIVENESS OF ECT ECT is clearly effective in treating unipolar depression. Studies find that between 60 and 80 percent of ECT patients improve (Perugi et al., 2011; Loo, 2010). The procedure seems to be particularly effective in severe cases of depression that include delusions (Rothschild, 2010). It has been difficult, however, to determine why ECT works so well (Cassidy et al., 2010). After all, this procedure delivers a broad insult to the brain that activates a number of brain areas, causes neurons all over the brain to fire, and leads to the release of all kinds of neurotransmitters, and it affects many other systems throughout the body as well.

Although ECT is effective and ECT techniques have improved, its use has generally declined since the 1950s. Two reasons for this decline are the memory loss caused by ECT and the frightening nature of the procedure. Another is the emergence of effective *antidepressant drugs*.

Antidepressant Drugs
Two kinds of drugs discovered in the 1950s reduce the symptoms of depression: *monoamine oxidase* (*MAO*) *inhibitors* and *tricyclics*. These drugs have now been joined by a third group, the so-called *second-generation antidepressants* (see Table 9-2 on the next page).

MAO INHIBITORS The effectiveness of **MAO inhibitors** as a treatment for unipolar depression was discovered accidentally. Physicians noted that *iproniazid*, a drug being tested on patients with tuberculosis, had an interesting effect: it seemed to make the patients happier (Sandler, 1990). It was found to have the same effect on depressed patients (Kline, 1958; Loomer, Saunders, & Kline, 1957). What this and several related drugs had in common biochemically was that they slowed the body's production of the enzyme *monoamine oxidase* (*MAO*). Thus they were called MAO inhibitors.

Normally, brain supplies of the enzyme MAO break down, or degrade, the neurotransmitter norepinephrine. MAO inhibitors block MAO from carrying out this activity and thereby stop the destruction of norepinephrine. The result is a rise in norepinephrine activity and, in turn, a reduction of depressive symptoms. Approximately half of depressed patients who take MAO inhibitors are helped by them (Ciraulo, Shader, & Greenblatt, 2011; Thase, Trivedi, & Rush, 1995). There is, however, a potential danger with regard to these drugs. People who take MAO inhibitors experience a dangerous rise in blood pressure if they eat foods containing the chemical *tyramine*, including such common foods as cheeses, bananas, and

•**MAO inhibitor**•An antidepressant drug that prevents the action of the enzyme monoamine oxidase.

"Katia, I knew that with the right combination of therapy and medication I could have a committed relationship with you."

table: 9-2

Drugs That Reduce Unipolar Depression

Class/Generic Name	Trade Name
Monoamine oxidase inhibitors	
Isocarboxazid	Marplan
Phenelzine	Nardil
Tranylcypromine	Parnate
Selegiline	Eldepryl
Tricyclics	
Imipramine	Tofranil
Amitriptyline	Elavil
Doxepin	Sinequan; Silenor
Trimipramine	Surmontil
Desipramine	Norpramin
Nortriptyline	Aventil; Pamelor
Protriptyline	Vivactil
Clomipramine	Anafranil
Second-Generation Antidepressants	
Vilazodone	Viibryd
Maprotiline	Ludiomil
Amoxapine	Asendin
Trazodone	Desyrel
Fluoxetine	Prozac
Sertraline	Zoloft
Paroxetine	Paxil
Venlafaxine	Effexor
Fluvoxamine	Luvox
Nefazodone	Serzone
Bupropion	Wellbutrin, Aplenzin
Mirtazapine	Remeron
Citalopram	Celexa
Escitalopram	Lexapro
Duloxetine	Cymbalta
Viloxazine	Vivalan
Desvenlafaxine	Pristiq

(Julien et al., 2011)

•**tricyclic**•An antidepressant drug such as imipramine that has three rings in its molecular structure.

•**selective serotonin reuptake inhibitors (SSRIs)**•A group of second-generation antidepressant drugs that increase serotonin activity specifically, without affecting other neurotransmitters.

certain wines. Thus people on these drugs must stick to a rigid diet. In recent years, a new MAO inhibitor has become available in the form of a *skin patch* that allows for slow, continuous absorption of the drug into the client's body (Julien et al., 2011). Because the doses absorbed across the skin are low, dangerous food interactions do not appear to be as common with this kind of MAO inhibitor.

TRICYCLICS The discovery of **tricyclics** in the 1950s was also accidental. Researchers who were looking for a new drug to combat schizophrenia ran some tests on a drug called *imipramine* (Kuhn, 1958). They discovered that imipramine was of no help in cases of schizophrenia, but it did relieve unipolar depression in many people. The new drug (trade name Tofranil) and related ones became known as tricyclic antidepressants because they all share a three-ring molecular structure.

In hundreds of studies, depressed patients taking tricyclics have improved much more than similar patients taking placebos, although the drugs must be taken for at least 10 days before such improvements take hold (Julien et al., 2011). About 60 to 65 percent of patients who take tricyclics are helped by them. The case of Derek, whom you met in Chapter 8, is typical:

One winter Derek signed up for an evening course called "The Use and Abuse of Psychoactive Drugs" because he wanted to be able to provide accurate background information in future news … articles on drug use among high school and college students. The course covered psychiatric as well as recreational drugs. When the professor listed the symptoms of … mood disorders on the blackboard, Derek had a flash of recognition. Perhaps he suffered from depression. …

Derek then consulted with a psychiatrist, who confirmed his suspicion and prescribed [an antidepressant drug]. A week later, Derek was sleeping until his alarm went off. Two weeks later, at 9:00 A.M. he was writing his column and making difficult decisions about editorials on sensitive topics. He started writing some feature stories on drugs just because he was interested in the subject. Writing was more fun than it had been in years. His images of his own violent death disappeared. His wife found him more responsive. He conversed with her enthusiastically and answered her questions without … long delays.

(Lickey & Gordon, 1991, p. 185)

If depressed people stop taking tricyclics immediately after obtaining relief, they run a high risk of relapsing within a year. If, however, they continue taking the drugs for five months or more after being free of depressive symptoms—a practice called "continuation therapy"—their chances of relapse decrease considerably (Kim et al., 2011; Ballas, Benton, & Evans, 2010). Certain studies further suggest that patients who take these antidepressant drugs for three or more years after initial improvement—a practice called "maintenance therapy"—may reduce the risk of relapse even more. As a result, clinicians often keep patients on the antidepressant drugs indefinitely.

Most researchers have concluded that tricyclics reduce depression by acting on neurotransmitter "reuptake" mechanisms (Ciraulo et al., 2011). Remember from Chapter 3 that messages are carried from the "sending" neuron across the synaptic space to a receiving neuron by a neurotransmitter, a chemical released from the axon ending of the sending neuron. However, there is a complication in this process. While the sending neuron releases the neurotransmitter, a pumplike mechanism in the neuron's ending immediately starts to reabsorb it in a process called *reuptake*. The purpose of this reuptake process is to control how long the neurotransmitter remains in the synaptic space and to prevent it from overstimulating the receiving neuron. Unfortu-

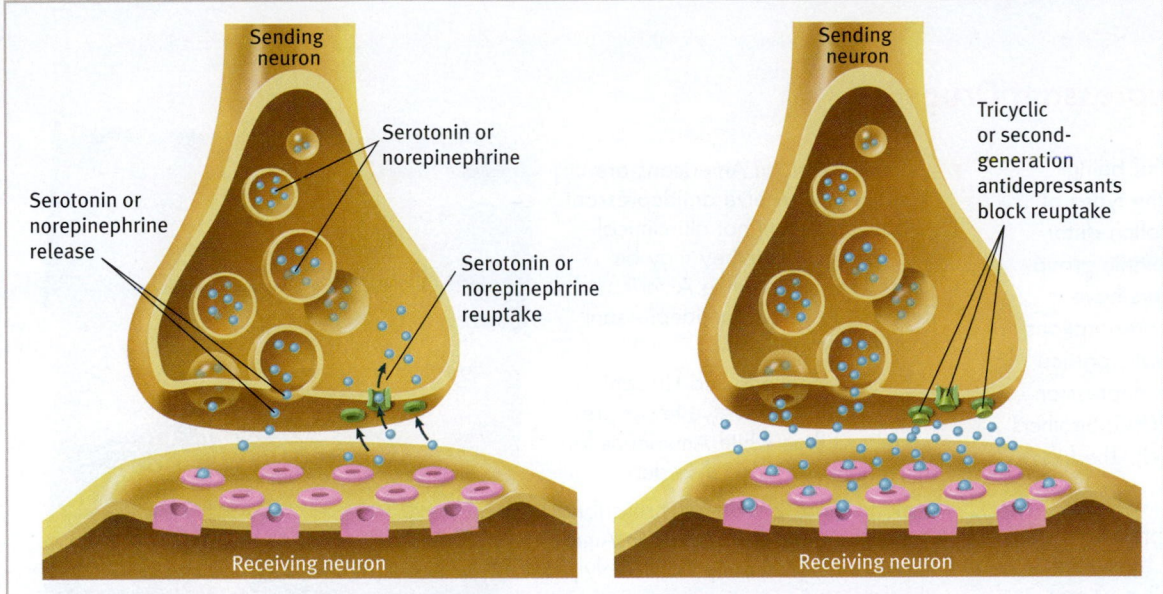

Figure 9-3
Reuptake and antidepressants (Left) Soon after a neuron releases neurotransmitters such as norepinephrine or serotonin into its synaptic space, it activates a pumplike reuptake mechanism to reabsorb excess neurotransmitters. In depression, however, this reuptake process is too active, removing too many neurotransmitters before they can bind to a receiving neuron. (Right) Tricyclic and most second-generation antidepressant drugs block this reuptake process, enabling norepinephrine or serotonin to remain in the synapse longer and bind to the receiving neuron.

nately, reuptake does not always progress properly. The reuptake mechanism may be too efficient in some people—cutting off norepinephrine or serotonin activity too soon, preventing messages from reaching the receiving neurons, and producing clinical depression. Tricyclics *block* this reuptake process, allowing neurotransmitters to remain in the synapse longer, and thus increasing their stimulation of the receiving neurons (see Figure 9-3).

If tricyclics act immediately to increase norepinephrine and serotonin activity, why do the symptoms of depression continue for 10 or more days after drug therapy begins? Growing evidence suggests that when tricyclics are ingested, they initially slow down the activity of the neurons that use norepinephrine and serotonin (Ciraulo et al., 2011; Lambert & Kinsley, 2005). Granted, the reuptake mechanisms of these cells are immediately corrected, thus allowing more efficient transmission of the neurotransmitters, but the neurons themselves respond to the change by releasing smaller amounts of the neurotransmitters. After a week or two, the neurons finally adapt to the tricyclic drugs and go back to releasing normal amounts of the neurotransmitters. Now the corrections in the reuptake mechanisms begin to have the desired effect: the neurotransmitters reach the receiving neurons in greater numbers, hence triggering more neural firing and producing a decrease in depression.

Soon after the discovery of tricyclics, this group of antidepressant drugs started being prescribed more often than MAO inhibitors. Tricyclics did not require dietary restrictions as MAO inhibitors did, and people taking them typically showed higher rates of improvement than those taking MAO inhibitors. On the other hand, some individuals respond better to MAO inhibitors than to either tricyclics or the new antidepressants described next, and such persons continue to be given MAO inhibitors (Julien et al., 2011; Thase, 2006).

If antidepressant drugs are effective, why do many people seek out herbal supplements, such as Saint-John's-wort or melatonin, for depression?

SECOND-GENERATION ANTIDEPRESSANTS A third group of effective antidepressant drugs, structurally different from the MAO inhibitors and tricyclics, has been developed during the past few decades. Most of these second-generation antidepressants are labeled **selective serotonin reuptake inhibitors (SSRIs)** because they increase serotonin activity specifically, without affecting norepinephrine or other neurotransmitters. The SSRIs include *fluoxetine* (trade name Prozac), *sertraline* (Zoloft), and *escitalopram* (Lexapro). Newly

PsychWatch

First Dibs on Antidepressant Drugs?

In our society, the likelihood of being treated for depression and the types of treatment received by clients often differ greatly from ethnic group to ethnic group. In revealing studies, researchers have examined the antidepressant prescriptions written for depressed individuals, particularly Medicaid recipients with depression (Kirby et al., 2010; Stagnitti, 2005; Strothers et al., 2005; Melfi et al., 2000). The following patterns have emerged:

▸ Almost 40 percent of depressed Medicaid recipients are seen by mental health providers irrespective of gender, race, or ethnic group.

▸ White Americans are twice as likely as Hispanic Americans and over five times as likely as African Americans to be prescribed antidepressant medications during the early stages of treatment.

▸ Although African Americans are less likely to receive antidepressant drugs, some (but not all) clinical trials suggest that they may be more likely than white Americans to respond to proper antidepressant medications.

▸ African Americans and Hispanic Americans also receive fewer prescriptions than white Americans for most nonpsychiatric disorders.

▸ Among those individuals prescribed antidepressant drugs, African Americans are significantly more likely than white Americans to receive older antidepressant drugs, while white Americans are more likely than African Americans to receive newly marketed second-generation antidepressant drugs. The older drugs tend to be less expensive for insurance providers.

Ariel Skelley/Blend Images/Getty Images

developed *selective norepinephrine reuptake inhibitors,* such as *atomoxetine* (Strattera), which increase norepinephrine activity only, and *serotonin-norepinephrine reuptake inhibitors,* such as *venlafaxine* (Effexor), which increase both serotonin and norepinephrine activity, are also now available (Ciraulo et al., 2011).

In effectiveness and speed of action the second-generation antidepressant drugs are about on a par with the tricyclics (Carr & Lucki, 2011), yet their sales have skyrocketed. Clinicians often prefer the new antidepressants because it is harder to overdose on them than on the other kinds of antidepressants. In addition, they do not pose the dietary problems of the MAO inhibitors or produce some of the unpleasant effects of the tricyclics, such as dry mouth and constipation. At the same time, the new antidepressants can produce undesirable side effects of their own. Some people experience weight gain or a reduction in their sex drive, for example (Uher et al., 2011; Taube-Schiff & Lau, 2008). Decisions about which kinds of antidepressants are prescribed for patients can also be influenced by other factors, such as insurance coverage or financial means (see *PsychWatch* above).

As popular as the antidepressants are, it is important to recognize that they do not work for everyone. In fact, as you have read, even the most successful of them *fails* to help at least 35 percent of clients with depression. In fact, some recent reviews have raised the possibility that the failure rate is higher still, especially for people with mild or modest levels of depression (Hegeri et al., 2012; Isacsson & Alder, 2012; Pigott et al., 2010). How are individuals who do not respond to antidepressant drugs treated currently? Researchers have noted that, all too often, their psychiatrists or family physicians simply prescribe alternative antidepressants or antidepressant mixtures—one after another—without directing the clients to psychotherapy or counseling of some kind. Melissa, a depressed woman for whom psychotropic drug treatment has failed to work over many years, reflects on this issue:

[S]he spoke, in a wistful manner, of how she wished her treatment could have been different. "I do wonder what might have happened if [at age 16] I could have just talked to someone, and they could have helped me learn about what I could do on my own to be a healthy person. I never had a role model for that. They could have helped me with my eating problems, and my diet and exercise, and helped me learn how to take care of myself. Instead, it was you have this problem with your neurotransmitters, and so here, take this pill Zoloft, and when that didn't work, it was take this pill Prozac, and when that didn't work, it was take this pill Effexor, and then when I started having trouble sleeping, it was take this sleeping pill," she says, her voice sounding more wistful than ever. "I am so tired of the pills."

(Whitaker, 2010)

BETWEEN THE LINES

Publication Bias

A review of 74 *FDA-registered* antidepressant drug studies revealed a troubling pattern (Turner et al., 2008). Only 38 of the studies yielded positive findings (the drug was effective), and all but one of these studies were published. The other 36 studies yielded findings that were negative or questionable, and 22 of them were *not* published. This publication bias may make the antidepressant drugs appear more effective than they actually are (Pigott et al., 2010). ‹‹

Brain Stimulation In recent years, three additional biological approaches have been developed—*vagus nerve stimulation, transcranial magnetic stimulation,* and *deep brain stimulation.*

VAGUS NERVE STIMULATION We each have two *vagus nerves,* one on each side of our body. The vagus nerve, the longest nerve in the human body, runs from the brain stem through the neck down the chest and on to the abdomen, serving as a primary channel of communication between the brain and major organs such as the heart, lungs, and intestines.

A number of years ago, a group of depression researchers surmised that they might be able to stimulate the brain by electrically stimulating the vagus nerve. They were hoping to mimic the positive effects of ECT without producing the undesired effects or trauma associated with ECT. Their efforts gave birth to a new treatment for depression—**vagus nerve stimulation.**

In this procedure, a surgeon implants a small device called a *pulse generator* under the skin of the chest. The surgeon then guides a wire, which extends from the pulse generator, up to the neck and attaches it to the left vagus nerve (see Figure 9-4). Electrical signals travel from the pulse generator through the wire to the vagus nerve. In turn, the stimulated vagus nerve delivers electrical signals to the brain. Typically in this procedure, the pulse generator, which runs on battery power, is programmed to stimulate the vagus nerve (and, in turn, the brain) every five minutes for a period of 30 seconds.

In 2005, the U.S. Food and Drug Administration (FDA) approved this treatment procedure for long-term, recurrent, and/or severe depression and for cases of depression

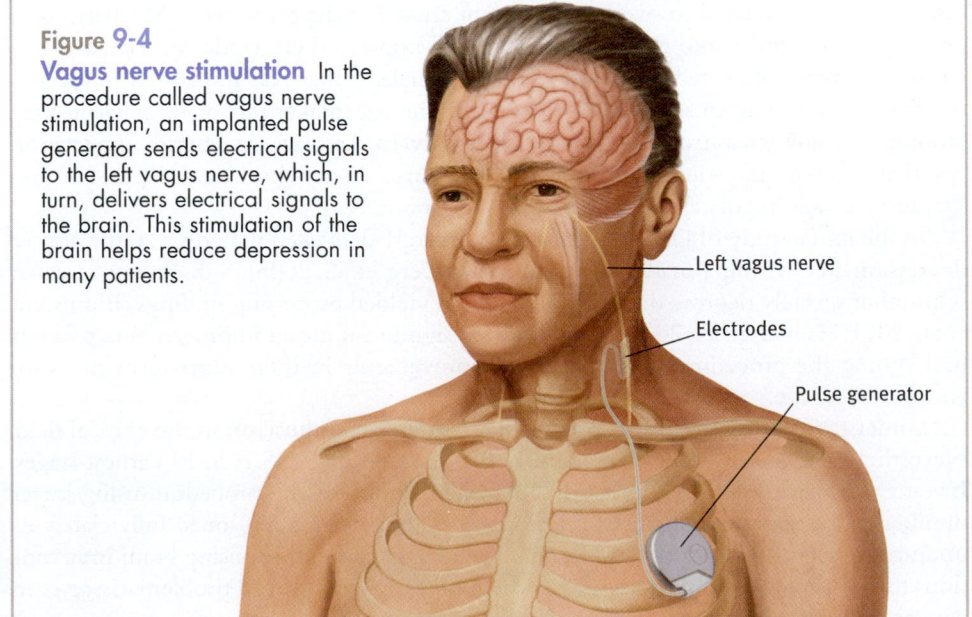

Figure 9-4

Vagus nerve stimulation In the procedure called vagus nerve stimulation, an implanted pulse generator sends electrical signals to the left vagus nerve, which, in turn, delivers electrical signals to the brain. This stimulation of the brain helps reduce depression in many patients.

Left vagus nerve

Electrodes

Pulse generator

•**vagus nerve stimulation**•A treatment procedure for depression in which an implanted pulse generator sends regular electrical signals to a person's vagus nerve; the nerve, in turn, stimulates the brain.

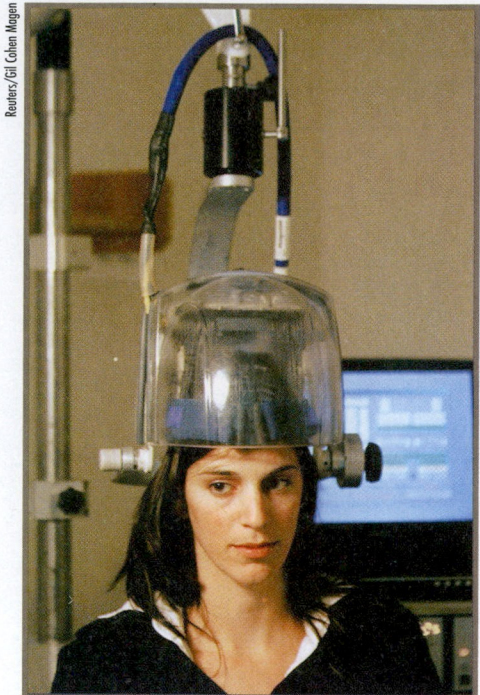

Stimulating the brain

In this version of transcranial magnetic stimulation, a woman sits under a helmet. The helmet contains an electromagnetic coil that sends currents into and stimulates her brain.

•**transcranial magnetic stimulation (TMS)**•A treatment procedure for depression in which an electromagnetic coil, which is placed on or above a person's head, sends a current into the individual's brain.

•**deep brain stimulation (DBS)**•A treatment procedure for depression in which a pacemaker powers electrodes that have been implanted in Brodmann Area 25, thus stimulating that brain area.

that have not improved even after the use of at least four other treatments. The reason for this approval? Ever since vagus nerve stimulation was first tried on depressed human beings in 1998, research has found that the procedure brings significant relief. Indeed, in studies of severely depressed people who have not responded to any other form of treatment, as many as 40 percent improve significantly when treated with vagus nerve stimulation (Howland et al., 2011; Graham, 2007; Nahas et al., 2005).

As with ECT, researchers do not yet know precisely why vagus nerve stimulation reduces depression. After all, like ECT, the procedure activates neurotransmitters and brain areas all over the brain. This includes, but is not limited to, serotonin and norepinephrine and the brain areas that have been implicated in depression (Kosel et al., 2011; George et al., 2000).

TRANSCRANIAL MAGNETIC STIMULATION Transcranial magnetic stimulation (TMS) is another technique that seeks to stimulate the brain without subjecting depressed individuals to the undesired effects or trauma of electroconvulsive therapy. In this procedure, first developed in 1985, the clinician places an electromagnetic coil on or above the patient's head. The coil sends a current into the prefrontal cortex. As you'll remember from the previous chapter, at least some parts of the prefrontal cortex of depressed people are underactive; TMS appears to increase neuron activity in those regions.

TMS has been tested by researchers on a range of disorders, including depression. A number of studies have found that the procedure reduces depression when it is administered daily for two to four weeks (Fox et al., 2011; Fitzgerald & Daskalakis, 2011; Rosenberg et al., 2011). Moreover, according to a few investigations, TMS may be just as helpful as electroconvulsive therapy when it is administered to severely depressed people who have been unresponsive to other forms of treatment (Rasmussen, 2011; Grunhaus et al., 2003). In 2008, TMS was approved by the FDA as a treatment for major depressive disorder.

DEEP BRAIN STIMULATION As you read in the previous chapter, researchers have recently linked depression to high activity in *Brodmann Area 25,* a brain area located just below the cingulate cortex, and some suspect that this area may be a kind of "depression switch." This finding led neurologist Helen Mayberg and her colleagues (2005) to administer an experimental treatment called **deep brain stimulation (DBS)** to six severely depressed patients who had previously been unresponsive to all other forms of treatment, including electroconvulsive therapy.

Mayberg's approach was modeled after deep brain stimulation approaches that had been applied successfully in cases of brain seizure disorder and Parkinson's disease, both disorders that are related to overly active brain areas. For depression, the Mayberg team drilled two tiny holes into the patient's skull and implanted electrodes in Area 25. The electrodes were connected to a battery, or "pacemaker," that was implanted in the patient's chest (for men) or stomach (for women). The pacemaker powered the electrodes, sending a steady stream of low-voltage electricity to Area 25. Mayberg's expectation was that this repeated stimulation would reduce Area 25 activity to a normal level and "recalibrate" and regulate the depression brain circuit.

In the initial study of DBS, four of the six severely depressed patients became almost depression-free within a matter of months (Mayberg et al., 2005). Subsequent research with other severely depressed individuals has also yielded promising findings (Blomstedt et al., 2011; Hamani et al., 2011). In addition to significant mood improvements, patients undergoing the procedure have reported improvements in their short-term memory and quality of life.

Understandably, all of this has produced considerable enthusiasm in the clinical field. Nevertheless, it is important to recognize that research on DBS is in its earliest stages. Investigators have yet to run properly controlled studies of the procedure using larger numbers of research participants, to determine its long-term safety, or to fully clarify its undesired effects. We must remember that in the past, certain promising brain interventions for psychological disorders, such as the lobotomy, later proved problematic or even dangerous upon closer inspection.

How Do the Treatments for Unipolar Depression Compare?

For most kinds of psychological disorders, no more than one or two treatments or combinations of treatments, if any, emerge as highly successful. Unipolar depression seems to be an exception. One of the most treatable of all abnormal patterns, it may respond to any of several approaches. During the past 20 years researchers have conducted a number of treatment outcome studies, which have revealed some important trends:

1. Cognitive, cognitive-behavioral, interpersonal, and biological therapies are all highly effective treatments for unipolar depression, from mild to severe (Hollon & Ponniah, 2010; Rehm, 2010). In most head-to-head comparisons, they seem to be equally effective at reducing depressive symptoms; however, there are indications that some populations of depressed patients respond better to one therapy than to another.

   In a pioneering six-year study of this issue, experimenters separated 239 moderately and severely depressed people into four treatment groups (Elkin, 1994; Elkin et al., 1989, 1985). One group was treated with 16 weeks of Beck's cognitive therapy, another with 16 weeks of interpersonal psychotherapy, and a third with the tricyclic drug *imipramine.* The fourth group received a placebo. A total of 28 therapists conducted these treatments.

   Using a depression assessment instrument called the *Hamilton Rating Scale for Depression,* the investigators found that each of the three therapies almost completely eliminated depressive symptoms in 50 to 60 percent of the participants who completed treatment. Only 29 percent of those who received the placebo showed such improvement. This trend also held, although somewhat less powerfully, when other assessment measures were used. These findings are consistent with those of most other comparative outcome studies.

   The study found that drug therapy reduced depressive symptoms more quickly than the cognitive and interpersonal therapies did, but these psychotherapies had matched the drugs in effectiveness by the final four weeks of treatment. In addition, more recent studies suggest that cognitive and cognitive-behavioral therapy may be more effective than drug therapy at preventing recurrences of depression except when drug therapy is continued for an extended period of time (Hollon & Ponniah, 2010). Despite the comparable or even superior showing of cognitive and cognitive-behavioral therapies, the past few decades have witnessed a significant increase in the number of physicians prescribing antidepressants. Indeed, the number of antidepressant prescriptions has grown from 2.5 million in 1980 to 4.7 million in 1990 to 164 million today (Gutierrez, 2010; Horwitz & Wakefield, 2007; Koerner, 2007).

2. Although the cognitive, cognitive-behavioral, and interpersonal therapies may lower the likelihood of relapse, they are hardly relapse-proof. Some studies suggest that as many as 30 percent of the depressed patients who respond to these approaches may, in fact, relapse within a few years after the completion of treatment. In an effort to head off relapse, some of today's cognitive, cognitive-behavioral, and interpersonal therapists continue to offer treatment, perhaps on a less frequent basis and sometimes in group or classroom formats, after the depression lifts—an approach similar to the "continuation" or "maintenance" approaches used with antidepressant drugs. Early indications are that treatment extensions of this kind do in fact reduce the rate of relapse among successfully treated patients (Bockting, Spinhoven, & Huibers, 2010; Hollon & Ponniah, 2010). In fact, some research suggests that people who have recovered from depression are less likely to relapse if they receive continuation

"Universal" health care
Dartmouth psychologist Mark Hegel displays a computer program, "The Virtual Space Station," that he has developed to guide astronauts through treatment for depression and other problems while they are in space.

Reverse order

Now that antidepressants have proved helpful for so many humans, many veterinarians are administering the drugs to animals in distress. Here a dose of Prozac is given to Phoenix, an unhappy and stressed-out cockatiel who has been plucking out his feathers.

or maintenance therapy in either drug or psychotherapy form, irrespective of which kind of therapy they originally received (Flynn & Himle, 2011).

3. When people with unipolar depression experience significant discord in their marriages, couple therapy tends to be as helpful as cognitive, cognitive-behavioral, interpersonal, or drug therapy (Whisman & Schonbrun, 2010).

4. In head-to-head comparisons, depressed people who receive strictly behavioral therapy have shown less improvement than those who receive cognitive, cognitive-behavioral, interpersonal, or biological therapy. Behavioral therapy has, however, proved more effective than placebo treatments or no attention at all (Hollon & Ponniah, 2010; Farmer & Chapman, 2008). Also, as you have seen, behavioral therapy is of less help to people who are severely depressed than to those with mild or moderate depression.

5. Most studies suggest that traditional psychodynamic therapies are less effective than these other therapies in treating all levels of unipolar depression (Hollon & Ponniah, 2010; Svartberg & Stiles, 1991). Many psychodynamic clinicians argue, however, that this system of therapy simply does not lend itself to empirical research, and its effectiveness should be judged more by therapists' reports of individual recovery and progress (Busch et al., 2004).

6. Studies have found that a combination of psychotherapy (usually cognitive, cognitive-behavioral, or interpersonal) and drug therapy is modestly more helpful to depressed people than either treatment alone (Ballas et al., 2010; Rehm, 2010).

7. As you will see in Chapter 17, these various trends do not always carry over to the treatment of depressed children and adolescents. For example, a broad six-year project called the *Treatment for Adolescents with Depression Study* (*TADS*) indicates that a combination of cognitive and drug therapy may be *much* more helpful to depressed teenagers than either treatment alone (NIMH, 2010; TADS, 2007).

8. Among biological treatments, ECT appears to be somewhat more effective than antidepressant drugs for reducing depression. ECT also acts more quickly. Half of patients treated by either intervention, however, relapse within a year unless the initial treatment is followed up by continuing drug treatment or by psychotherapy (Trevino et al., 2010; Fink, 2007, 2001). In addition, the new brain stimulation treatments seem helpful for some severely depressed individuals who have been repeatedly unresponsive to drug therapy, ECT, or psychotherapy.

When clinicians today choose a biological treatment for mild to severe unipolar depression, they most often prescribe one of the antidepressant drugs. In some cases, clients may actually request specific ones based on recommendations from friends or on ads they have seen (see *PsychWatch* on the next page). Clinicians are not likely to refer patients for ECT unless the depression is severe and has been unresponsive to drug therapy and psychotherapy (Gitlin, 2002). ECT appears to be helpful for 50 to 80 percent of the severely depressed patients who do not respond to other such interventions (Perugi et al., 2011; APA, 1993). If depressed persons seem to be at high risk for suicide, clinicians sometimes refer them for ECT treatment more readily (Kobeissi et al., 2011; Fink, 2007, 2001). Although ECT clearly has a beneficial effect on suicidal behavior in the short run, studies do not clearly indicate that it has a long-term effect on suicide rates (Prudic & Sackeim, 1999).

"Ask Your Doctor If This Medication Is Right for You"

"**M**aybe you are suffering from depression" . . . "Ask your doctor about Cymbalta" . . . "There is no need to suffer any longer." Anyone who watches television or surfs the Internet is familiar with phrases such as these. They are at the heart of *direct-to-consumer* (*DTC*) drug advertising—advertisements in which pharmaceutical companies appeal directly to consumers, coaxing them to ask their physicians to prescribe particular drugs for them. DTC drug ads on television are so commonplace that it is easy to forget they have been a major part of our viewing pleasure for only a short while (Koerner, 2007). It was not until 1997, when the FDA relaxed the rules of pharmaceutical advertising, that these ads really took off.

Antidepressants are among the leading drugs to receive DTC television advertising, along with oral antihistamines, cholesterol reducers, and anti-ulcer drugs (Koerner, 2007; Rosenthal et al., 2002). Altogether, pharmaceutical companies now spend around $3 billion a year on American television and online advertising (Iskowitz, 2011; Nielsen, 2010). In fact, 30 percent of adults say they have asked their doctors about specific medications that they saw advertised, and half of these individuals report that their doctors gave them a prescription for the advertised drug (Hausman, 2008; Kaiser Family Foundation, 2001).

How did we get here? Where did this tidal wave of advertising come from? And what's with those endless "side effects" that are recited so rapidly at the end of each and every commercial? It's a long story, but here are some of the key plot twists that helped set the stage for the emergence of DTC television drug advertising.

1938: Food, Drug, and Cosmetic Act

Congress passed the *Food, Drug, and Cosmetic Act*, which gave the FDA jurisdiction

"I think the dosage needs adjusting. I'm not nearly as happy as the people in the ads."

B. Smaller

Barbara Smaller/ The New Yorker Collection/www.cartoonbank.com

over the labels on prescriptions and over-the-counter drugs and over most related forms of drug advertising (Kessler & Pines, 1990).

1962: Kefauver-Harris Drug Amendments

In the spirit of consumer protection, Congress passed a law requiring that all pharmaceutical drugs be proved safe and effective. The law also transferred still more authority for prescription drug ads from the Federal Trade Commission (which regulates most other kinds of advertising) to the FDA (Wilkes et al., 2000). Perhaps most important, the law set up rules that companies were required to follow in their drug advertisements, including a detailed summary of the drug's contraindications, side effects, and effectiveness and a "fair balance" coverage of risks and benefits.

1962–1981: Drug Ads for Physicians

For the next two decades, pharmaceutical companies targeted their ads to the physicians who were writing the prescriptions. As more and more *psychotropic* drugs were developed, psychiatrists were included among those targeted.

1981: First Pitch

The pharmaceutical drug industry proposed shifting the advertising of drugs directly to consumers. The argument was based on the notion that such advertising would protect consumers by directly educating them about those drugs that were available.

1983: First DTC Drug Ad

The first direct-to-consumer drug ad appeared. In turn, the FDA imposed a voluntary moratorium on such ads until it could develop a formal policy (Pines, 1999).

1985: Lifting the Ban

The FDA lifted the moratorium and allowed DTC drug ads as long as the ads adhered to the physician-directed promotion standards. That is, each consumer-oriented ad also had to include a summary of the drug's side effects, contraindications, and effectiveness; avoid false advertising; and offer a fair balance in its information about effectiveness and risks (Curtiss, 2002; Ostrove, 2001). Because so much background information was required in each ad, most DTC ads were limited to magazines and ad brochures.

1997: FDA Makes Television-Friendly Changes

Recognizing that its previous guidelines could not readily be applied to brief TV ads, which may run for only 30 seconds, the FDA changed its guidelines for DTC television drug ads. It ruled that DTC television advertisements must simply mention a drug's important risks and must indicate where consumers can get further information about the drug—often a Web site or phone number. In addition, the ads must recommend that consumers speak with a doctor about the drug (Wilkes et al., 2000).

Going public

Actress Catherine Zeta-Jones received praise from mental health advocacy groups when she announced in 2011 that she was receiving treatment for bipolar disorder. Entering a treatment program after the extended stress of helping her husband Michael Douglas battle throat cancer, Jones said there was no need to suffer in silence and she hoped the publicity surrounding her treatment would help others.

Treatments for Bipolar Disorders

Until the latter part of the twentieth century, people with bipolar disorders were destined to spend their lives on an emotional roller coaster. Psychotherapists reported almost no success, and antidepressant drugs were of limited help. In fact, the drugs sometimes triggered a manic episode (Post, 2011, 2005). ECT, too, only occasionally relieved either the depressive or the manic episodes of bipolar disorders.

This gloomy picture changed dramatically in 1970 when the FDA approved the use of **lithium,** a silvery-white element found in various simple mineral salts throughout the natural world, as a treatment for bipolar disorder. Other **mood stabilizing,** or **antibipolar, drugs** have since been developed, and several of them are now used more widely than lithium, either because they produce fewer undesired effects or because they are even more effective than lithium.

Nevertheless, it was lithium that first brought hope to those suffering from bipolar disorder. Case descriptions of patients like Anna, who began taking lithium in the 1960s when it was still considered an experimental drug, helped capture the attention of both clinicians and the public.

•**lithium**•A metallic element that occurs in nature as a mineral salt and is an effective treatment for bipolar disorders.

•**mood stabilizing drugs**•Psychotropic drugs that help stabilize the moods of people suffering from bipolar mood disorder. Also known as *antibipolar drugs.*

Anna was a 21-year-old college student. Before she became ill, Anna was sedate and polite, perhaps even a bit prim. During the fall of her sophomore year at college, she had an episode of mild depression that began when she received a C on a history paper she had worked quite hard on. The same day she received a sanctimonious letter from her father reminding her of the financial hardships he was undergoing to send her to college. He warned her to stick to her books and not to play around with men. Anna became discouraged. She doubted that she deserved her parents' sacrifice. Anna's depression did not seem unusual to her roommate, to her other friends, or even to Anna herself. It seemed a natural reaction to her father's unreasonable letter and her fear that she could not live up to the standards he set. In retrospect, this mild depression was the first episode of her bipolar illness.

Several months later, Anna became restless, angry, and obnoxious. She talked continuously and rapidly, jumping from one idea to another. Her speech was filled with rhymes, puns, and sexual innuendos. During Christmas vacation, she made frequent and unwelcome sexual overtures to her brother's friend in the presence of her entire family. When Anna's mother asked her to behave more politely, Anna began to cry and then slapped her mother across the mouth. Anna did not sleep that night. She sobbed. Between sobs she screamed that no one understood her problems, and no one would even try. The next day, Anna's family took her to the hospital. . . . When she was discharged two weeks later, she was less angry and no longer assaultive. But she was not well and did not go back to school. Her thought and speech were still hypomanic. She had an exaggerated idea of her attractiveness and expected men to fall for her at the first smile. She was irritated when they ignored her attentions. Depressive symptoms were still mixed with the manic ones. She often cried when her bids for attention were not successful or when her parents criticized her dress or behavior.

Anna returned to school the following fall but suffered another depressive episode, followed by another attack of mania within seven months. She had to withdraw from school and enter the hospital. This time . . . the psychiatrists diagnosed her illness as bipolar disorder [and] began treatment with . . . lithium. . . . After seventeen days on lithium, Anna's behavior was quite normal. She was attractively and modestly dressed for her psychiatric interviews. Earlier, she had been sloppily seductive; hair in disarray, half-open blouse, smeared lipstick, bright pink rouge on her cheeks, and bright green make-up on her eyelids. With the help of lithium, she gained some ability to tolerate frustration. During the first week of her hospital stay, she had screamed at a nurse who would not permit her to read late into the night in violation of the ward's 11:00 P.M. "lights out" policy. On lithium, Anna was still annoyed by this "juvenile" rule, but she controlled her anger. She gained some insight into her illness, recognizing that her manic behavior was destructive to herself and others. She also recognized the depression that was often mixed with the mania. . . . She admitted, "Actually, when I'm high, I'm really feeling low. I need to exaggerate in order to feel more important."

Because Anna was on a research ward, the effectiveness of lithium had to be verified by removal of the drug. When she had been off lithium for four to five days, Anna began to show symptoms of both mania and depression. She threatened her psychiatrist, and as before, the threats were grandiose with sexual overtones. In a slinky voice, she warned, "I have ways to put the director of this hospital in my debt. He crawled for me before and he'll do it again. When I snap my fingers, he'll come down to this ward and squash you under his foot." Soon afterward, she threatened suicide. She later explained, "I felt so low last night that if someone had given me a knife or gun, POW." By the ninth day off lithium, Anna's speech was almost incomprehensible: "It's sad to be so putty, pretty, so much like water dripping from a faucet. . . ." Lithium therapy was reinstituted, and within about sixteen days, Anna again recovered and was discharged on lithium.

(Lickey & Gordon, 1991, pp. 236–239)

Lithium and Other Mood Stabilizers

The discovery that lithium effectively reduces bipolar symptoms was, like so many other medical discoveries, quite accidental. In 1949 an Australian psychiatrist, John Cade, hypothesized that manic behavior is caused by a toxic level of uric acid in the body. He set out to test this theory by injecting guinea pigs with uric acid, but first he combined it with lithium to increase its solubility.

To Cade's surprise, the guinea pigs became not manic but quite lethargic after their injections. Cade suspected that the lithium had produced this effect. When he later administered lithium to 10 human beings who had mania, he discovered that it calmed and normalized their mood. Many countries began using lithium for bipolar disorders soon after, but, as noted earlier, it was not until 1970 that the FDA approved it.

Determining the correct lithium dosage for a given patient is a delicate process requiring regular analyses of blood and urine samples and other laboratory tests. Too low a dose will have little or no effect on the bipolar mood swings, but too high a dose can

---

BETWEEN THE LINES

Race and Noncompliance

A study of bipolar outpatients found that half of the African American patients and half of the white American patients failed to take their antibipolar medications as prescribed (Fleck et al., 2005). Why? Patients of both races were equally likely to point to the medications' undesired effects. However, the African American patients were more likely than the white American patients to further cite a fear of becoming addicted to the drugs and a concern that the drugs symbolized severe illness. ‹‹

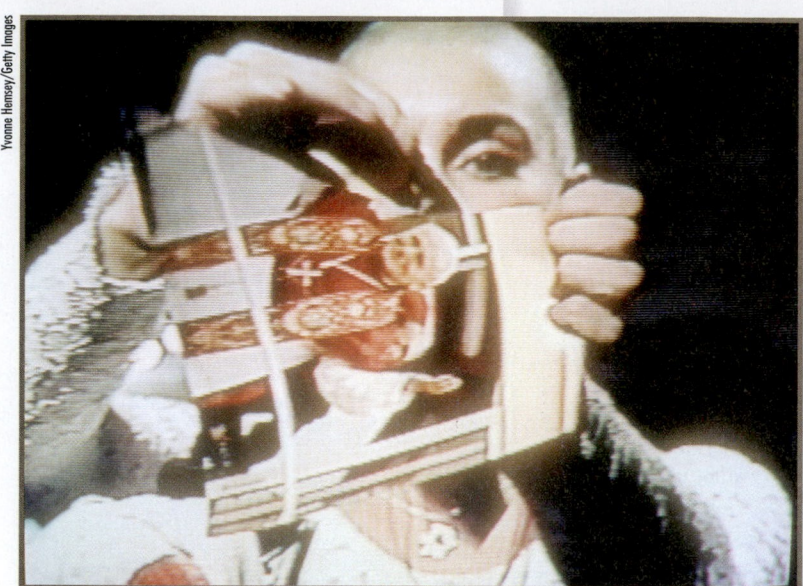

Bipolar struggle

Throughout the 1990s Grammy-winning Irish singer Sinead O'Connor was known for her shaved head, edgy songs, and notorious rebelliousness. In a 1992 appearance on the TV show *Saturday Night Live*, for example, she ripped up a picture of Pope John Paul II (left) to help bring attention to the problem of sex abuse in the Catholic church. In more recent times (right), she revealed that she received a diagnosis of bipolar disorder in 2003 and was treated successfully for it. She now performs spiritual kinds of music, on display in her 2007 CD album *Theology*, and songs about love, on display in her 2011 album *Home*, and is an advocate for a range of societal issues.

result in lithium intoxication (literally, poisoning), which can cause nausea, vomiting, sluggishness, tremors, dizziness, slurred speech, seizures, kidney dysfunction, and even death. With the correct dose, however, lithium often produces a noticeable change (Grof, 2010). Some patients respond better to the other mood stabilizing drugs, such as the antiseizure drugs *carbamazepine* (Tegretol) or *valproate* (Depakote), or to a combination of such drugs (Altamura et al., 2011; Bowden, 2011). And still others respond best to a combination of mood stabilizers and atypical antipsychotic drugs, medications that you will read about in Chapter 15 (Nivoli et al., 2011; Ketter & Wang, 2010).

Given the effectiveness of lithium and other mood stabilizers, around one-third of all persons with a bipolar disorder now seek treatment from a mental health professional in any given year. Another 15 percent are treated or monitored by family physicians (Wang et al., 2005).

Effectiveness of Lithium and Other Mood Stabilizers

All manner of research has attested to the effectiveness of lithium and other mood stabilizers in treating *manic* episodes (Grof, 2010, 2005). More than 60 percent of patients with mania improve on these medications. In addition, most such individuals experience fewer new episodes as long as they continue taking the medications (Gao et al., 2010). One study found that the risk of relapse is 28 times greater if patients stop taking a mood stabilizer (Suppes et al., 1991). These findings suggest that the mood stabilizers are also prophylactic drugs, ones that actually help prevent symptoms from developing. Thus, today's clinicians usually continue patients on some level of a mood stabilizing drug even after their manic episodes subside (Gao et al., 2010).

In the limited body of research that has been done on this subject, the mood stabilizers also seem to help those with bipolar disorder overcome their *depressive* episodes, though to a lesser degree than they help with their manic episodes (Post, 2011; Thase, 2010). In addition, continued doses of mood stabilizers may help reduce the risk of future depressive episodes and future suicide attempts, just as they seem to prevent the return of manic episodes (Gao et al., 2010; Carney & Goodwin, 2005). Given the drugs' less powerful impact on depressive episodes, many clinicians use a combination of mood stabilizers and antidepressant drugs to treat bipolar depression, although research suggests that antidepressants may trigger manic episodes in some cases (Nivoli et al., 2011; Post, 2011; Vazquez et al., 2011).

Mode of Operation of Mood Stabilizers

Researchers do not fully understand how mood stabilizing drugs operate (Aiken, 2010). They suspect that the drugs change synaptic activity in neurons, but in a way different from that of antidepressant drugs. The firing of a neuron actually consists of several phases that ensue at lightning speed. When the neurotransmitter binds to a receptor on the receiving neuron, a series of changes occur *within* the receiving neuron to set the stage for firing. The substances in the neuron that carry out those changes are often called **second messengers** because they relay the original message from the receptor site to the firing mechanism of the neuron. (The neurotransmitter itself is considered the *first messenger*.) Whereas antidepressant drugs affect a neuron's initial reception of neurotransmitters, mood stabilizers appear to affect a neuron's second messengers (Gawryluk & Young, 2011).

Different second-messenger systems are at work in different neurons. In one of the most important systems, chemicals called *phosphoinositides* are produced once neurotransmitters are received. Research suggests that lithium, and perhaps the other mood stabilizers as well, affect this particular messenger system (Gawryluk & Young, 2011). It may be that these drugs affect the activity of any neuron that uses this second-messenger system and in so doing correct the biological abnormalities that lead to bipolar disorders.

"He's bipolar."

In a similar vein, it has been found that lithium and other mood stabilizing drugs also increase the production of *neuroprotective proteins*—key proteins within certain neurons whose job is to prevent cell death. In so doing, the drugs may increase the health and functioning of those cells and, in turn, reduce bipolar symptoms (Aiken, 2010; Gray et al., 2003).

Alternatively, it may be that the mood stabilizers correct bipolar functioning by directly changing sodium and potassium ion activity in neurons (Swonger & Constantine, 1983). In Chapter 8 you read that bipolar disorders may be triggered by unstable alignments of ions along the membranes of certain neurons in the brain. If this instability is the key to bipolar problems, mood stabilizers would be expected to have some kind of effect on the ion activity. Several studies in fact suggest that lithium ions often substitute, although imperfectly, for sodium ions, and other research suggests that lithium changes the transport mechanisms that move ions back and forth across the neural membrane (Lambert & Kinsley, 2005; Soares et al., 1999; Baer et al., 1971).

Adjunctive Psychotherapy

Psychotherapy alone is rarely helpful for persons with bipolar disorders. At the same time, clinicians have learned that mood stabilizing drugs alone are not always sufficient either. Thirty percent or more of patients with these disorders may not respond to lithium or a related drug, may not receive the proper dose, or may relapse while taking it. In addition, a number of patients stop taking mood stabilizers on their own because they are bothered by the drugs' unwanted effects, feel too well to recognize the need for the drugs, miss the euphoria felt during manic episodes, or worry about becoming less productive when they take the drugs (Julien et al., 2011; Aiken, 2010).

In view of these problems, many clinicians now use individual, group, or family therapy as an *adjunct* to mood stabilizing drugs (Lee et al., 2011; Aiken, 2010; Culver & Pratchett, 2010). Most often, therapists use these formats to emphasize the importance of continuing to take medications; to improve social skills and relationships that may be affected by bipolar episodes; to educate patients and families about bipolar disorders; to help patients solve the family, school, and occupational problems caused by their disorder; and to help prevent patients from attempting suicide (Hollon & Ponniah, 2010). Few controlled studies have tested the effectiveness of such adjunctive therapy, but those that have been done, along with numerous clinical reports, suggest that it helps reduce hospitalization, improves social functioning, and increases patients' ability to obtain and hold a job (Culver & Pratchett, 2010). Psychotherapy plays a more central role in the treatment of cyclothymic disorder, the mild bipolar pattern that you read about in Chapter 8. In fact, patients with this problem typically receive psychotherapy, alone or in combination with mood stabilizers.

•**second messengers**•Chemical changes within a neuron just after the neuron receives a neurotransmitter message and just before it responds.

PUTTING IT....together

With Success Come New Questions

Mood disorders are among the most treatable of all psychological disorders. The choice of treatment for bipolar disorders is narrow and simple: drug therapy, perhaps accompanied by psychotherapy, is the single most successful approach. The picture for unipolar depression is more varied and complex, although no less promising. Cognitive, cognitive-behavioral, interpersonal, and antidepressant drug therapy are all helpful in cases of any severity; couple therapy is helpful in select cases; pure behavioral therapy helps in mild to moderate cases; and ECT is useful and effective in severe cases.

"Of course your daddy loves you. He's on Prozac— he loves everybody."

Why are several very different approaches highly effective in the treatment of unipolar depression? Two explanations have been proposed. First, if many factors contribute to unipolar depression, it is plausible that the removal of any one of them could improve all areas of functioning. In fact, studies have sometimes found that when one kind of therapy is effective, clients tend to function better in all spheres. When certain antidepressant drugs are effective, for instance, clients make the same improvements in their thinking and social functioning that cognitive and interpersonal therapy would bring about (Meyer et al., 2003; Weissman, 2000).

A second explanation suggests that there are various kinds of unipolar depression, each of which responds to a different kind of therapy. There is evidence that interpersonal psychotherapy is more helpful in depressions brought on by social problems than in depressions that seem to occur spontaneously (Frank & Levenson, 2011; Weissman & Markowitz, 2002). Similarly, antidepressant medications seem more helpful than other treatments in cases marked by appetite and sleep problems, sudden onset, and a family history of depression (McNeal & Cimbolic, 1986).

Whatever the ultimate explanation, the treatment picture is very promising both for people with unipolar depression and for those with bipolar disorders. The odds are that one or a combination of the therapies now in use will relieve their symptoms. Yet the sobering fact remains that as many as 40 percent of people with a mood disorder do not improve under treatment and must suffer their mania or depression until it has run its course (Gitlin, 2002).

Summing Up

- **TREATMENTS FOR MOOD DISORDERS** More than 60 percent of people with mood disorders can be helped by treatment. *pp. 257–258*

- **TREATMENTS FOR UNIPOLAR DEPRESSION** Various treatments have been used with unipolar depression. *Psychodynamic therapists* try to help depressed persons become aware of and work through their real or imagined losses and their excessive dependence on others. *Behavioral therapists* reintroduce clients to events and activities that they once found pleasurable, reinforce nondepressive behaviors, and teach interpersonal skills. *Cognitive therapists* help depressed persons identify and change their dysfunctional cognitions, and *cognitive-behavioral therapists* try to reduce depression by combining cognitive and behavioral techniques.

  Sociocultural theorists trace unipolar depression to interpersonal, social, and cultural factors. One family-social approach, *interpersonal psychotherapy,* is based on the premise that depression stems from social problems, and so therapists try to help clients develop insight into their interpersonal problems, change them and the conditions that are causing them, and learn skills to protect themselves in the future.

Another family-social approach, *couple therapy,* may be used when depressed people are in a dysfunctional relationship.

Most *biological treatments* consist of antidepressant drugs, but electroconvulsive therapy is still used to treat some severe cases of depression, and several *brain stimulation* techniques recently have been developed to treat severely depressed patients who are unresponsive to all other forms of treatment. *Electroconvulsive therapy (ECT)* remains a controversial procedure, although it is a fast-acting intervention that is particularly effective when depression is severe, unresponsive to other kinds of treatment, or characterized by delusions. *Antidepressant drugs* include three classes: MAO inhibitors, tricyclics, and second-generation antidepressants. *MAO inhibitors* block the degradation of norepinephrine, allowing the levels of this neurotransmitter to build up and relieve depressive symptoms. People taking MAO inhibitors must be careful to avoid eating foods with tyramine. *Tricyclics* improve depression by blocking neurotransmitter *reuptake* mechanisms, thereby increasing the activity of norepinephrine and serotonin. The *second-generation antidepressants* include *selective serotonin reuptake inhibitors,* or *SSRIs,* drugs that selectively increase the activity of serotonin. These drugs are as effective as tricyclics and have fewer undesired effects. And, finally, the *brain stimulation* techniques include *vagus nerve stimulation* (which has been approved by the FDA for use in cases of depression), *transcranial magnetic stimulation,* and *deep brain stimulation. pp. 258–274*

- **COMPARING TREATMENTS FOR UNIPOLAR DEPRESSION** The cognitive, interpersonal, and biological therapies appear to be the most successful for mild to severe depression. Couple therapy is helpful when the individual's depression is accompanied by significant marital discord. Behavioral therapy is helpful in mild to moderate cases. And ECT and brain stimulation treatments are effective in severe cases. Combinations of psychotherapy and drug therapy tend to be modestly more helpful than any one approach on its own. *pp. 275–277*

- **TREATMENTS FOR BIPOLAR DISORDERS** *Lithium* and other *mood stabilizing drugs,* such as *carbamazepine* or *valproate,* have proved to be effective in the treatment of bipolar disorders, particularly in the reduction and prevention of the disorders' manic episodes. In some cases these drugs are combined with antidepressant drugs or certain antipsychotic drugs. The various drug treatments are helpful in 60 percent of cases. The mood stabilizers may reduce bipolar symptoms by affecting the activity of *second-messenger* systems or key proteins or other chemicals in certain neurons throughout the brain. Alternatively, lithium and other mood stabilizers may directly change the activity of *sodium and other ions* in neurons, for example, by altering the transportation of the ions across neural membranes.

In recent years clinicians have learned that patients with bipolar disorders may fare better when mood stabilizers are supplemented by *adjunctive psychotherapy.* The issues most often addressed by psychotherapists are medication management, social skills and relationships, education of patients, and solving the family, school, and occupational problems caused by bipolar episodes. *pp. 278–281*

PsychPortal

Visit **PsychPortal**
www.yourpsychportal.com
to access the e-book, videocases and other case materials and activities, and study aids, including flashcards, crossword puzzles, quizzes, FAQs, and research exercises.

SUICIDE

The war in Iraq never ended for Jonathan Michael Boucher. Not when he flew home from Baghdad, not when he moved to Saratoga Springs for a fresh start and, especially, not when nighttime arrived.

Tortured by what he saw as an 18-year-old Army private during the 2003 invasion and occupation, Boucher was diagnosed with post-traumatic stress disorder (PTSD) and honorably discharged from the military less than two years later.

On May 15, three days before his 24th birthday, the young veteran committed suicide in his apartment's bathroom, stunning friends and family.... There was no note....

Johnny Boucher joined the Army right after graduating from East Lyme High School in Connecticut in 2002 because he was emotionally moved by the Sept. 11, 2001, terrorist attacks. "He felt it was his duty to do what he could for America," his father, Steven Boucher, 50, said.

Shortly after enlisting, the 6-foot-2-inch soldier deployed with the "Wolf Pack"—1st Battalion, 41st Field Artillery—and fought his way north in Iraq. He landed with his unit at Baghdad International Airport and was responsible for helping guard it. The battalion earned a Presidential Unit Citation for "exceptional bravery and heroism in the liberation of Baghdad."

But it was during those early months of the war that Johnny Boucher had the evils of combat etched into his mind. The soldier was devastated by seeing a young Iraqi boy holding his dead father, who had been shot in the head. Later, near the airport, the soldier saw four good friends in his artillery battery killed in a vehicle accident minutes after one of them relieved him from duty, his father said.

Boucher tried to rescue the soldiers. Their deaths and other things his son saw deeply impacted his soul after he returned because he was sensitive about family and very patriotic, Steven Boucher said....

But when the sun set, memories of combat and lost friends rose to the top, causing the former artilleryman severe nightmares. Sometimes he would curl up in a ball and weep, causing his parents to try to comfort him.... "At nighttime, he was just haunted," Steven Boucher said.... "Haunted, I think, by war." Bitterness about the war had crept in, and the troubled former soldier started drinking to calm himself....

Supported by a huge family he adored ..., Johnny Boucher recently got his own apartment on Franklin Street and appeared to be getting back on track. He seemed to be calm and enjoying life. But it was difficult to tell, and he was still fearful of sleep, his father said. They had plans for a hike, a birthday party and attending his brother Jeffrey's graduation. ... Then, without warning, Johnny Boucher was gone. He hanged himself next to a Bible, his Army uniform and a garden statue of an angel, said his mother, who discovered him after he failed to show up to work for two days....

Yusko, 2008

Salmon spawn and then die, after an exhausting upstream swim to their breeding ground. Lemmings rush to the sea and drown. But only humans knowingly take their own lives. The actions of salmon and lemmings are instinctual responses that may even help their species survive in the long run. Only in the human act of

table: 10-1

Most Common Causes of Death in the United States

Rank	Cause	Deaths Per Year
1	Heart disease	598,607
2	Cancer	568,668
3	Chronic respiratory diseases	137,082
4	Stroke	128,608
5	Accidents	117,176
6	Alzheimer's	78,889
7	Diabetes	68,504
8	Pneumonia and influenza	53,582
9	Kidney disease	48,714
10	**Suicide**	**36,547**

Source: National Center for Health Statistics, *National Vital Health Statistics Report* (2011).

suicide do beings act for the specific purpose of putting an end to their lives (Preti, 2011).

Suicide has been recorded throughout history. The Old Testament described King Saul's suicide: "There Saul took a sword and fell on it." The ancient Chinese, Greeks, and Romans also provided examples. In more recent times, twentieth-century suicides by such celebrated individuals as writer Ernest Hemingway, actress Marilyn Monroe, and rock star Kurt Cobain both shocked and fascinated the public.

> Before you finish reading this page, someone in the United States will try to kill himself. At least 60 Americans will have taken their own lives by this time tomorrow. . . . Many of those who attempted will try again, a number with lethal success.
>
> (Shneidman & Mandelkorn, 1983)

Today suicide is one of the leading causes of death in the world. It has been estimated that 1 million people die by it each year, more than 36,000 in the United States alone (NVSR, 2011; Rogers, Madura, & Hardy, 2011; Caine, 2010) (see Table 10-1). Around 25 million other people throughout the world—600,000 in the United States—make unsuccessful attempts to kill themselves; such attempts are called **parasuicides.** Actually, it is difficult to obtain accurate figures on suicide, and many investigators believe that estimates are often low. For one thing, suicide can be difficult to distinguish from unintentional drug overdoses, automobile crashes, drownings, and other accidents (Wertheimer, 2001; Lester, 2000). Many apparent "accidents" were probably intentional. For another, since suicide is frowned on in our society, relatives and friends often refuse to acknowledge that loved ones have taken their own lives.

Suicide is not officially classified as a mental disorder, although DSM-5's framers have proposed that a category called *suicidal behavior disorder* be studied for possible inclusion in future revisions of DSM-5. People would qualify for this diagnosis if they have tried to kill themselves within the last two years (APA, 2013, 2012). Regardless of whether suicidal acts themselves represent a distinct disorder, psychological dysfunctioning—a breakdown of coping skills, emotional turmoil, a distorted view of life—usually plays a role in such acts. For example, Jonathan Boucher, the young combat veteran about whom you read at the beginning of this chapter, had intense feelings of depression, developed a severe drinking problem, and displayed posttraumatic stress disorder.

What Is Suicide?

Not every self-inflicted death is a suicide. A man who crashes his car into a tree after falling asleep at the steering wheel is not trying to kill himself. Thus Edwin Shneidman (2005, 1993, 1963), a pioneer in this field, defined **suicide** as an intentioned death—a self-inflicted death in which one makes an intentional, direct, and conscious effort to end one's life.

Intentioned deaths may take various forms. Consider the following examples. All three of these people intended to die, but their motives, concerns, and actions differed greatly:

> **Dave** *was a successful man. By the age of 50 he had risen to the vice presidency of a small but profitable investment firm. He had a caring wife and two teenage sons who respected him. They lived in an upper-middle-class neighborhood, had a spacious house, and enjoyed a life of comfort.*
>
> *In August of his fiftieth year, everything changed. Dave was fired. Just like that. The economy had gone bad once again, the firm's profits were down, and the president wanted*

•**parasuicide**•A suicide attempt that does not result in death.

•**suicide**•A self-inflicted death in which the person acts intentionally, directly, and consciously.

to try new, fresher investment strategies and marketing approaches. Dave had been "old school." He didn't fully understand today's investors—didn't know how to reach out to them with Web-based advertising, engage them online in the investment process, or give his firm a high-tech look. Dave's boss wanted to try a younger person.

The experience of failure, loss, and emptiness was overwhelming for Dave. He looked for another position, but found only low-paying jobs for which he was overqualified. Each day as he looked for work Dave became more depressed, anxious, and desperate. He thought of trying to start his own investment company or to be a consultant of some kind, but, in the cold of night, he knew he was just fooling himself with such notions. He kept sinking, withdrew from others, and felt increasingly hopeless.

Six months after losing his job, Dave began to consider ending his life. The pain was too great, the humiliation unending. He hated the present and dreaded the future. Throughout February he went back and forth. On some days he was sure he wanted to die. On other days, an enjoyable evening or uplifting conversation might change his mind temporarily. On a Monday late in February he heard about a job possibility, and the anticipation of the next day's interview seemed to lift his spirits. But Tuesday's interview did not go well. He knew there'd be no job offer. He went home, took a recently purchased gun from his locked desk drawer, and shot himself.

Demaine never truly recovered from his mother's death. He was only 7 years old and unprepared for such a loss. His father sent him to live with his grandparents for a time, to a new school with new kids and a new way of life. In Demaine's mind, all these changes were for the worse. He missed the joy and laughter of the past. He missed his home, his father, and his friends. Most of all he missed his mother.

He did not really understand her death. His father said that she was in heaven now, at peace, happy. Demaine's unhappiness and loneliness continued day after day and he began to put things together in his own way. He believed he would be happy again if he could join his mother. He felt she was waiting for him, waiting for him to come to her. The thoughts seemed so right to him; they brought him comfort and hope. One evening, shortly after saying good night to his grandparents, Demaine climbed out of bed, went up the stairs to the roof of their apartment house, and jumped to his death. In his mind he was joining his mother in heaven.

Tya and Noah had met on a speed date. On a lark, Tya and a friend had registered at the speed date event, figuring, "What's the worst thing that can happen?" On the night of the big event, Tya talked to dozens of guys, none of whom appealed to her—except for Noah! He was quirky. He was witty. And he seemed as turned off by the whole speed date thing as she was. His was the only name that she put on her list. As it turned out, he also put her name down on his list, and a week later each of them received an email with contact information about the other. A flurry of email exchanges followed, and before long, they were going together. She marveled at her luck. She had beaten the odds. She had had a successful speed date experience.

It was Tya's first serious relationship; it became her whole life. Thus she was truly shocked and devastated when, on the one-year anniversary of their speed date, Noah told her that he no longer loved her and was leaving her for someone else.

As the weeks went by, Tya was filled with two competing feelings—depression and anger. Several times she texted or called Noah, begged him to reconsider, and pleaded for a chance to win him back. At the same time, she hated him for putting her through such misery.

Tya's friends became more and more worried about her. At first they sympathized with her pain, assuming it would soon lift. But as time went on, her depression and anger worsened, and Tya began to act strangely. Always a bit of a drinker, she started to drink heavily and to mix her drinks with various kinds of drugs.

One night Tya went into her bathroom, reached for a bottle of sleeping pills, and swallowed a handful of them. She wanted to make her pain go away, and she wanted Noah to know just how much pain he had caused her. She continued swallowing pill after pill,

(continued on the next page)

BETWEEN THE LINES

Sources of Information

Interviews indicate that elementary school children learn about suicide most often from television and discussions with other children and that they rarely discuss suicide with adults (Mishara, 1999). ‹‹

•**death seeker**•A person who clearly intends to end his or her life at the time of a suicide attempt.

•**death initiator**•A person who attempts suicide believing that the process of death is already under way and that he or she is simply hastening the process.

•**death ignorer**•A person who attempts suicide without recognizing the finality of death.

•**death darer**•A person who is ambivalent about the wish to die even as he or she attempts suicide.

•**subintentional death**•A death in which the victim plays an indirect, hidden, partial, or unconscious role.

•**retrospective analysis**•A psychological autopsy in which clinicians and researchers piece together information about a person's suicide from the person's past.

Death darers?

A sky surfer tries to ride the perfect cloud high above the hustle and bustle of the city below. Are thrill-seekers daredevils searching for new highs, as many of them claim, or are some actually death darers?

crying and swearing as she gulped them down. When she began to feel drowsy, she decided to call her close friend Dedra. She was not sure why she was calling, perhaps to say good-bye, to explain her actions, or to make sure that Noah was told; or perhaps to be talked out of it. Dedra pleaded and reasoned with her and tried to motivate her to live. Tya was trying to listen, but she became less and less coherent. Dedra hung up the phone and quickly called Tya's neighbor and the police. When reached by her neighbor, Tya was already in a coma. Seven hours later, while her friends and family waited for news in the hospital lounge, Tya died.

While Tya seemed to have mixed feelings about her death, Dave was clear in his wish to die. Whereas Demaine viewed death as a trip to heaven, Dave saw it as an end to his existence. Such differences can be important in efforts to understand and treat suicidal persons. Accordingly, Shneidman distinguished four kinds of people who intentionally end their lives: the *death seeker, death initiator, death ignorer,* and *death darer.*

Death seekers clearly intend to end their lives at the time they attempt suicide. This singleness of purpose may last only a short time. It can change to confusion the very next hour or day, and then return again in short order. Dave, the middle-aged investment counselor, was a death seeker. He had many misgivings about suicide and was ambivalent about it for weeks, but on Tuesday night he was a death seeker—clear in his desire to die and acting in a manner that virtually guaranteed a fatal outcome.

Death initiators also clearly intend to end their lives, but they act out of a belief that the process of death is already under way and that they are simply hastening the process. Some expect that they will die in a matter of days or weeks. Many suicides among the elderly and very sick fall into this category. Robust novelist Ernest Hemingway was profoundly concerned about his failing body as he approached his sixty-second birthday—a concern that some observers believe was at the center of his suicide.

Death ignorers do not believe that their self-inflicted death will mean the end of their existence. They believe they are trading their present lives for a better or happier existence. Many child suicides, like Demaine's, fall into this category, as do those of adult believers in a hereafter who commit suicide to reach another form of life. In 1997, for example, the world was shocked to learn that 39 members of an unusual cult named Heaven's Gate had committed suicide at an expensive house outside San Diego. It turned out that these members had acted out of the belief that their deaths would free their spirits and enable them to ascend to a "Higher Kingdom."

Death darers experience mixed feelings, or ambivalence, in their intent to die even at the moment of their attempt, and they show this ambivalence in the act itself. Although to some degree they wish to die, and they often do die, their risk-taking behavior does not guarantee death. The person who plays Russian roulette—that is, pulls the trigger of a revolver randomly loaded with one bullet—is a death darer. Tya might be considered a death darer. Although her unhappiness and anger were great, she was not sure that she wanted to die. Even while taking pills, she called her friend, reported her actions, and listened to her friend's pleas.

When individuals play *indirect, covert, partial,* or *unconscious* roles in their own deaths, Shneidman (2001, 1993, 1981) classified them in a suicide-like category called **subintentional death.** Traditionally, clinicians have cited drug, alcohol, or tobacco use, promiscuous sexual behavior, recurrent physical fighting, and medication mismanagement as behaviors that may contribute to subintentional deaths. Obviously, these kinds of behav-

? How should clinicians decide whether to hospitalize a person who is considering suicide or even one who has made an attempt?

Digital Vision

iors are dangerous in their own right. Moreover, researchers have found a correlation between the regular performance of such behaviors and later attempts at suicide (Juan et al., 2011).

In recent years, another behavioral pattern, *self-injury* or *self-mutilation,* has been added to this list—for example, cutting or burning oneself or banging one's head. Although this pattern is not officially classified as a mental disorder, the framers of DSM-5 have, here again, proposed that a category called *non-suicidal self-injury* be studied for possible inclusion in future revisions of DSM-5. People would qualify for this diagnosis if they intentionally injure themselves on five or more occasions over a one-year period—without the conscious intent of killing themselves (APA, 2013, 2012).

Self-injurious behavior is more common than previously recognized, particularly among teenagers and young adults, and it may be on the increase. Although the pattern is not well understood, it appears that the behavior becomes addictive in nature. The pain brought on by self-injury seems to offer some relief from emotional suffering, the behavior serves as a temporary distraction from problems, and the scars that result may provide a documentation of the individual's distress (Wilkinson & Goodyer, 2011). More generally, the pattern may help persons deal with chronic feelings of emptiness, boredom, and identity confusion. Although self-injury and the other risky behaviors mentioned earlier may indeed represent an indirect attempt at suicide, the true intent behind them is unclear, so, other than the *MediaSpeak* on the next page, these behaviors will not be included in the discussions of this chapter.

How Is Suicide Studied?

Suicide researchers face a major obstacle: the individuals they study are no longer alive. How can investigators draw accurate conclusions about the intentions, feelings, and circumstances of people who can no longer explain their actions? Two research methods attempt to deal with this problem, each with only partial success.

One strategy is **retrospective analysis,** a kind of psychological autopsy in which clinicians and researchers piece together data from the suicide victim's past (Schwartz, 2011; Wetzel & Murphy, 2005). Relatives, friends, therapists, or physicians may remember past statements, conversations, and behaviors that shed light on a suicide. Retrospective information may also be provided by the suicide notes that some victims leave behind (Wong et al., 2009).

However, such sources of information are not always available or reliable. Around half of all suicide victims have never been in psychotherapy (Stolberg et al., 2002), and less than one-third leave notes (Maris, 2001). Nor is retrospective information necessarily valid. A grieving, perhaps guilt-ridden relative or a distraught therapist may be incapable of objective recollections or simply reluctant to discuss an act that is so stigmatizing in our society (Kelleher & Campbell, 2011; Wurst et al., 2011).

Because of these limitations, many researchers also use a second strategy—*studying people who survive their suicide attempts.* It is estimated that there are 8 to 20 nonfatal suicide attempts for every fatal suicide (Maris, 2001). However, it may be that people who survive suicide attempts differ in important ways from those who do not. Many of them may not really have wanted to die, for example. Nevertheless, suicide researchers have found it useful to study survivors of suicide attempts, and this chapter shall consider those who attempt suicide and those who commit suicide as more or less alike.

Patterns and Statistics

Suicide happens within a larger social setting, and researchers have gathered many statistics regarding the social contexts in which such deaths take place. They have found, for example, that suicide rates vary from country to country (Kirkcaldy et al., 2010).

AP Photo/Ted S. Warren

Retrospective analysis
The very public *retrospective analysis* of the 1994 suicide of rock star Kurt Cobain, leader of the grunge band Nirvana, was given new impetus in 2002 with the publication of Journals—a collection of notebook pages in which Cobain had written about his thoughts and concerns, bouts with depression, and drug addiction during the final years of his life.

MediaSpeak

Self-Cutting: The Wound That Will Not Heal

By Scott Cooper, Citizen Correspondent, *Orato*

Self-injury is nothing new. From the hardcore 13th and 14th century Christian flagellators to Sid Vicious carving "Nancy" into his chest after a show to the stereotypical teenage girl taking out her adolescent angst on her skin with various instruments of mild disfigurement, self harm is here to stay. . . .

I am not a teenage girl. . . . Nor am I [Princess] Diana, under enormous pressure trying to live up to the insane demands of English royalty. Yet here I sit, newly 39 with brand new bandages and gauze to cover up the fresh cuts on my right arm.

I was on the phone with a friend the other night and decided to go because I said I was tired. I did not say, "I really need to talk because I feel like hurting myself." No. I had a ritual to do and nothing was going to get in the way. I gathered my necessary tools; paper towels for immediate covering, Band-Aids for eventual cover up, gauze in case bandages were not enough, tape to secure the gauze and a virgin razor.

Like my mother laying out a place setting for six at a formal Christmas dinner, I put each piece in its proper place. I placed them in a semi circle in front of me, located some music that would suit my needs and imbibed enough alcohol for the courage of the task. As I sat, smoking a cigarette, drinking a beer, and letting music rip through my headphones, I stopped trying to control my thoughts and let them escalate. . . .

Feelings of separation and loneliness bubbled beneath my volcanic surface. Anxiety and lack of self identity swirled in the whirlpool within. It's my fault, I did this, I'm to blame, I shouldn't be here, my body is a shroud that covers a terrible lie, something I said in '85 made my mother want to give up motherhood, I wish I'd succeeded with those pills in '88, I'm sorry I made you leave me, I didn't mean to traumatize your family, I still love you, tell your brother I'm sorry, don't, please, stop. . . .

Then, I went to work.

First a cross. . . . In closing, a couple of parallel lines along my wrist. . . .

My mind screamed from deep inside Dante's Inferno. . . . Blood dripped down my arm as a sign of life or something else secretly desired, I don't know. Paper towels spotted with dark red looking like a bad kitchen accident. In time, it was over and whatever psychological pain needed to be transferred to my body was complete.

I awoke the next day with alternate physical stings and pangs on my arm and my mind in conflict. Had I gone too far? . . . Whom do I tell, whom do I not tell and how long until these damn things heal? It is summer after all and wearing short sleeve shirts requires a new and detailed preparation for leaving the house.

This was not the first time, only the most recent. There have been deeper cuts, ER visits and stitches. Like each time before, there has been an urgency to engage in this ritual and, as always, an ambivalence of how far to go. While self-injury is often described as not including a suicidal impulse, more often than not, for me, that thought is never too far away. What if? Just a little bit deeper and a warm bath. Is this the time? Am I ready?

Cutting, like anorexia or bulimia, is intensely private and drenched in shame. Not the shame of the act per se but the shame that exists inside, always, as a catalyst for the act. Much like suicide, there are many people who have suffered any number of different horrors in their life who would never conceive of actually harming themselves. They can throw a plate against a wall, scream at someone who's hurt them, anything external to react to a situation. Others internalize. I wish I could yell. I wish I could break something. I need to. . . . "Why?" When I get in those moods, why cut? I do it to feel better, to relieve the tension in my mind via a physical act. I do it to feel worse because I'm trying to say something important about how this living hurts and I can't find the words. Because I deserve it. In some fantastical way, I want someone to see my wounds and immediately interpret what is wrong, to hold my hand and guide me through this life I can't navigate on my own. Above and beneath it all, like taking out the trash, I just do. . . .

In the end, despite my gender and age, I'm aware I'm not alone. And those who abuse themselves in any way are clearly not alone either. The saddest fact is, when that pull to self-harm comes on like a hurricane and the ability to escape it is futile, all the love, support and understanding of everyone stops at the door we simply cannot open.

And though I cannot open that door, to all my loved ones who will never read this, all I ask is, please, don't stop knocking.

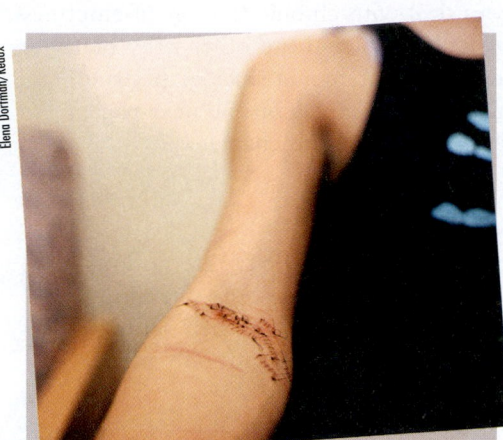

Elena Dorfman/Redux

Self-mutilation Given the growing problem of self-injury, many inpatient programs are now available for people who display this behavior. The self-inflicted knife wounds of this patient are evident as she receives treatment in one such program.

South Korea, Russia, Hungary, Germany, Austria, Finland, Denmark, China, and Japan have very high rates, more than 20 suicides annually per 100,000 persons; conversely, Egypt, Mexico, Greece, and Spain have relatively low rates, fewer than 5 per 100,000. The United States and Canada fall in between, each with a suicide rate of 11.5 per 100,000 persons; England has a rate of 9 per 100,000 (CDC, 2011, 2010; NVSR, 2011; U.S. Census Bureau, 2011; NVSR, 2010).

Religious affiliation and beliefs may help account for these national differences. For example, countries that are largely Catholic, Jewish, or Muslim tend to have low suicide rates. Perhaps in these countries, strict prohibitions against suicide or a strong religious tradition deter many people from committing suicide (Stack & Kposowa, 2008). Yet there are exceptions to this tentative rule. Austria, a largely Roman Catholic country, has one of the highest suicide rates in the world.

Research is beginning to suggest that religious doctrine may not help prevent suicide as much as the degree of an individual's *devoutness*. Regardless of their particular persuasion, very religious people seem less likely to commit suicide (Stack & Kposowa, 2008). Similarly, it seems that people who hold a greater reverence for life are less prone to consider or attempt self-destruction (Lee, 1985).

The suicide rates of men and women also differ. Three times as many women attempt suicide as men, yet men succeed at more than four times the rate of women (CDC, 2011; Claassen & Knox, 2011). Around the world 19 of every 100,000 men kill themselves each year; the suicide rate for women is 4 per 100,000 (Levi et al., 2003).

Although various explanations have been proposed for this gender difference (Fiori et al., 2011), a popular one points to the different methods used by men and women (Stack & Wasserman, 2009). Men tend to use more violent methods, such as shooting, stabbing, or hanging themselves, whereas women use less violent methods, such as drug overdose. Guns are used in nearly two-thirds of the male suicides in the United States, compared to 40 percent of the female suicides (Maris, 2001).

Suicide is also related to social environment and marital status (You, Van Orden, & Conner, 2011). In one study, around half of the individuals who had committed suicide were found to have no close friends (Maris, 2001). Fewer still had close relationships with parents and other family members. In a related vein, research has revealed that divorced persons have a higher suicide rate than married or cohabitating individuals (Roskar et al., 2011; Stolberg et al., 2002).

Finally, in the United States at least, suicide rates seem to vary according to race (see Figure 10-1). The overall suicide rate of white Americans is at least twice as high as that of African Americans, Hispanic Americans, and Asian Americans (CDC, 2011; Barnes, 2010). A major exception to this pattern is the very high suicide rate of American Indians, which overall is one and a half times the national average. Although the extreme poverty of many American Indians may partly explain this trend, studies show that factors such as alcohol use, modeling, and the availability of guns may also play a role (Lanier, 2010). In addition to differences across racial groups, researchers have found that suicide rates sometimes differ within groups. Among Hispanic Americans, for example, Puerto Ricans are significantly more likely to attempt suicide than any other Hispanic American group (Baca-Garcia et al., 2011).

Some of these statistics on suicide have been questioned. Analyses suggest, for example, that the actual rate of suicide may be 15 percent higher for African Americans and 6 percent higher for women than

Continuing trend
The rate of suicide among American Indians is much higher than the national average. Here a memorial is held for a young suicide victim at a middle school on the Fort Peck Indian Reservation in Poplar, Montana.

What factors besides religious affiliation and beliefs might help account for national variations in suicide rates?

Figure 10-1
Suicide, race, and gender In the United States, white Americans have a much higher suicide rate than all minority groups except American Indians (CDC, 2011, 2010; NVSS, 2011, 2010).

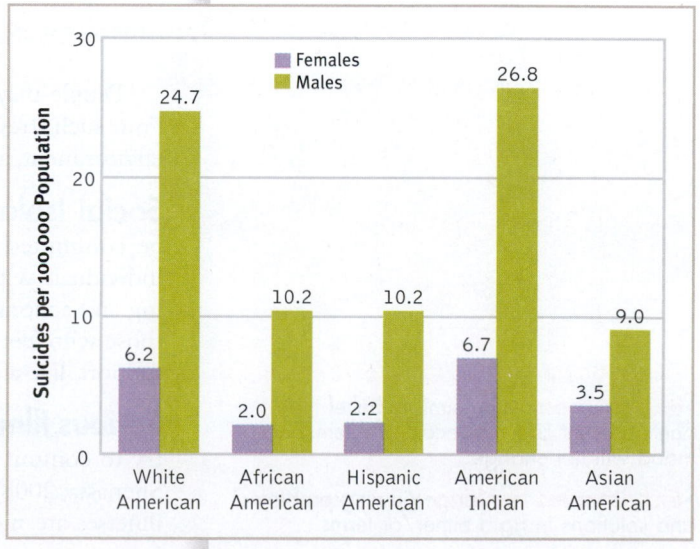

usually reported (Barnes, 2010; Phillips & Ruth, 1993). People in these groups are more likely than others to use methods of suicide that can be mistaken for causes of accidental death, such as poisoning, drug overdose, single-car crashes, and pedestrian accidents.

What Triggers a Suicide?

Suicidal acts may be connected to recent events or current conditions in a person's life. Although such factors may not be the basic motivation for the suicide, they can precipitate it. Common triggering factors include *stressful events, mood and thought changes, alcohol and other drug use, mental disorders,* and *modeling.*

Stressful Events and Situations

Researchers have counted more stressful events in the recent lives of suicide attempters than in the lives of nonattempters (Foster, 2011; Pompili et al., 2011). One stressor that has been consistently linked to suicide is combat stress. Research indicates that combat veterans across several wars are more than twice as likely to commit suicide as nonveterans (Jakupcak & Varra, 2011). At the beginning of this chapter, for example, you read about a young man who committed suicide upon returning to civilian life, after experiencing the enormous stressors of combat in Iraq.

The stressors that help lead to suicide do not need to be as horrific as those tied to combat. Common forms of *immediate stress* seen in cases of suicide are the loss of a loved one through death, divorce, or rejection (Roskar et al., 2011); loss of a job (Kuroki, 2010); and stress caused by hurricanes or other natural disasters, even among very young children. A suicide attempt may also be precipitated by a series of recent events that have a combined impact, rather than by a single event, as in the following case:

> Sally's suicide attempt took place in the context of a very difficult year for the family. Sally's mother and stepfather separated after 9 years of marriage. After the father moved out, he visited the family erratically. Four months after he moved out of the house, the mother's boyfriend moved into the house. The mother planned to divorce her husband and marry her boyfriend, who had become the major disciplinarian for the children, a fact that Sally intensely resented. Sally also complained of being "left out" in relation to the closeness she had with her mother. Another problem for Sally had been two school changes in the last 2 years which left Sally feeling friendless. In addition, she failed all her subjects in the last marking period.
>
> *(Pfeffer, 1986, pp. 129–130)*

People may also attempt suicide in response to long-term rather than recent stress. Four such stressors are particularly common—social isolation, serious illness, an abusive environment, and occupational stress.

Social Isolation As you saw in the cases of Dave, Demaine, and Tya, suicide may be committed by people from loving families or supportive social systems. However, individuals without such social supports are particularly vulnerable to suicidal thinking and actions. Researchers have found a heightened risk for suicidal behavior among those who feel little sense of "belongingness," believe that they have limited or no social support, live alone, and have ongoing conflicts with other people (You et al., 2011).

Serious Illness People whose illnesses cause them great pain or severe disability may try to commit suicide, believing that death is unavoidable and imminent (Schneider & Shenassa, 2008). They may also believe that the suffering and problems caused by their illnesses are more than they can endure. Studies suggest that as many as one-third of

•**hopelessness**•A pessimistic belief that one's present circumstances, problems, or mood will not change.

•**dichotomous thinking**•Viewing problems and solutions in rigid either/or terms.

individuals who die by suicide have been in poor physical health during the months prior to their suicidal acts (MacLean et al., 2011; Conwell et al., 1990). In fact, illness-linked suicides have become more common, and controversial, in recent years (Levy et al., 2011; Dickens et al., 2008). Although physicians can now keep seriously ill people alive much longer, they often fail to extend the quality and comfort of the patients' lives (Werth, 2001).

Abusive Environment Victims of an abusive or repressive environment from which they have little or no hope of escape sometimes commit suicide. For example, prisoners of war, inmates of concentration camps, abused spouses, abused children, and prison inmates have tried to end their lives (Fazel et al., 2011) (see Figure 10-2). Like those who have serious illnesses, these people may have felt that they could endure no more suffering and believed that there was no hope for improvement in their condition.

Occupational Stress Some jobs create feelings of tension or dissatisfaction that may trigger suicide attempts. Research has found particularly high suicide rates among psychiatrists and psychologists, physicians, nurses, dentists, lawyers, police officers, farmers, and unskilled laborers (Kleespies et al., 2011; Skegg et al., 2010). Such correlations do not necessarily mean that occupational pressures directly cause suicidal actions. Perhaps unskilled workers are responding to financial insecurity rather than job stress when they attempt suicide. Similarly, rather than reacting to the emotional strain of their work, suicidal psychiatrists and psychologists may have long-standing emotional problems that stimulated their career interest in the first place.

Mood and Thought Changes

Many suicide attempts are preceded by a change in mood (see *PsychWatch* on the next page). The change may not be severe enough to warrant a diagnosis of a mental disorder, but it does represent a significant shift from the person's past mood. The most common change is an increase in sadness. Also common are increases in feelings of anxiety, tension, frustration, anger, or shame (Reisch et al., 2010). In fact, Shneidman (2005, 2001) believed that the key to suicide is "psychache," a feeling of psychological pain that seems intolerable to the person. A study of 88 patients found that those who scored higher on a measure called the Psychological Pain Assessment Scale were indeed more likely than others to commit suicide (Pompili et al., 2008).

Suicide attempts may also be preceded by shifts in patterns of thinking. Individuals may become preoccupied with their problems, lose perspective, and see suicide as the only effective solution to their difficulties (Shneidman, 2005, 2001). They often develop a sense of **hopelessness**—a pessimistic belief that their present circumstances, problems, or mood will not change. In fact, one study found that individuals who generally expressed feelings of hopelessness were 11 times more likely to commit suicide over a 13-year follow-up period than people who did not feel hopeless (Kuo et al., 2004). Thus, some clinicians believe that a feeling of hopelessness is the single most likely indicator of suicidal intent, and they take special care to look for signs of hopelessness when they assess the risk of suicide (Sargalska et al., 2011).

Many people who attempt suicide fall victim to **dichotomous thinking,** viewing problems and solutions in rigid either/or terms (Shneidman, 2005, 2001, 1993). Indeed, Shneidman

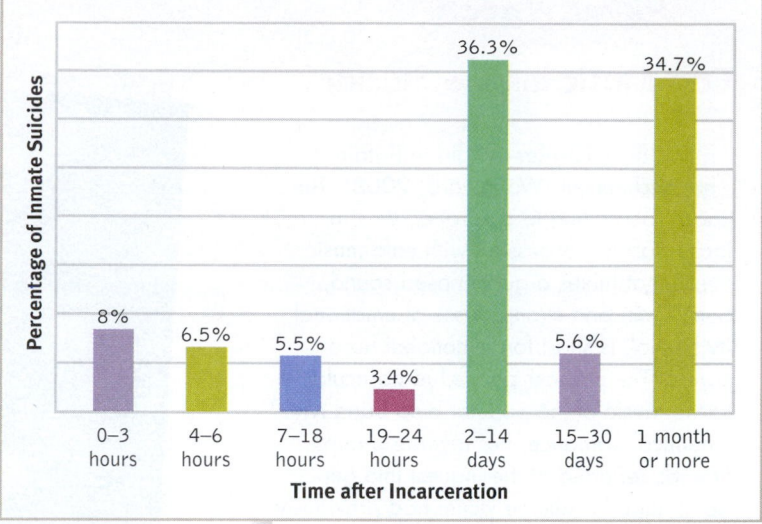

Figure 10-2
Suicide in prisons Approximately 107 of every 100,000 inmates in U.S. jails commit suicide each year, many times the national rate. Almost one-quarter of the suicides occur during the first day of incarceration. (Adapted from U.S. Department of Justice, 2010; Cerny & Noffsinger, 2006.)

Acting happy
Fans of actor Owen Wilson, known for his comic film portrayals, were shocked when they heard in 2007 that he had attempted suicide. Wilson (left) is seen here with actor Vince Vaughn in the movie *Wedding Crashers,* playing the happy-go-lucky character John Beckwith.

New Line/Avery Pix/The Kobal Collection/Richard Cartright

PsychWatch

Can Music Inspire Suicide?

In 2008, a 13-year-old girl in Britain hanged herself (Woodward, 2008). The cause, according to a coroner, was in large part her obsession with emo music, music that mixes a guitar-based sound, punk rock, and strong doses of emotionality ("emo" is short for "emotional hardcore"). The coroner pointed in particular to the music of the popular emo band My Chemical Romance, her favorite group. Friends reported at the inquest into her death that the suicide victim had previously discussed the "glamour of suicide" that attracted her to emo music and had posted a picture of an emo girl with bloody wrists online. The British press, in turn, described My Chemical Romance as a "suicide cult band," prompting the band to defend itself and emo music in general as "antisuicide" and filled with positive messages in its lyrics (Woodward, 2008).

This tragedy is hardly the first time that music has been blamed by the public for suicidal acts. In fact, over the years, music genres as varied as country, opera, heavy metal, and pop rock have been pointed to as negative influences, particularly on teenagers, that can lead to suicide attempts (Copley, 2008; Snipes & Maguire, 1995; Litman & Farberow, 1994; Stack et al., 1994; Wass et al, 1991). Little research has been conducted on this issue, and that which has been done fails to provide clear support for such claims. But the concerns go on. Indeed, such concerns helped lead to the current music rating system, which informs consumers (and their parents) about the kinds of language and themes that will appear on the CDs or music downloads.

Two famous cases in the 1980s first brought this concern into public awareness. One involved the music of Ozzy Osbourne, leader of the band Black Sabbath. In the early days of Black Sabbath, Osbourne and the band centered much of their music on psychological themes, and the band's music was even perceived by many as having a "satanic" bent.

Osbourne departed the band for a solo career between 1979 and the late 1990s. During this solo period, his music

Eye of the storm In a celebrated case, the British press have blamed the music of emo group My Chemical Romance for the recent suicide of a 13-year-old girl.

was blamed for three suicides. In 1984 a 19-year-old boy shot himself in the head while listening to Osbourne's song "Suicide Solution." A lawyer for the boy's family and lawyers for two other families whose children committed suicide claimed that the theme of the song encouraged suicide as an acceptable solution to one's problems. The lawyers also claimed that the song contained tones known as "hemisync" (a process that uses sound waves to influence an individual's mental state) and that these tones left the suicidal boys unable to resist what was being said in the song. Finally, the lawyers claimed that the song had *subliminal* lyrics—words sung much faster than the normal rate of speech and unrecognizable to first-time listeners. Supposedly, the subliminal lyrics in the song were "Why try, why try? Get the gun and try it! Shoot, Shoot, Shoot." Osbourne's lawyers rejected such claims, and the court agreed, dismissing all three cases by 1986.

A second famous case involved the music of the heavy metal band Judas Priest. In 1985 two boys died after shooting themselves in the head with a shotgun. The boys had been drunk and on drugs and shot themselves in a "suicide pact" after

listening to a Judas Priest album for hours. Lawyers for the boys' families claimed that Judas Priest's 1977 song "Better by You, Better Than Me" contained, when played backward, the subliminal message "Do it" as well as "Try suicide" and "Let's be dead." The band's lawyers countered that any song played backward might seem to have a hidden message. The trial judge agreed, and he dismissed the $6.2 million lawsuit in 1990. He ruled that even if the lyrics conveyed subliminal messages, such messages had been unintentional.

If the music in these cases did not itself lead to suicide, what did? A number of clinicians have argued that the individuals in these cases were probably suffering from several kinds of factors typically linked to suicide—depression, stress, drug abuse, and the like.

Of course, the dismissal of these suits did not put to rest the concerns of parents, and in fact such concerns grow still greater whenever parents read about a teenager—like the 13-year-old in Britain—who commits suicide while listening to death-themed music. While such events are not common in our society, they do, sadly, occur on occasion.

said that the "four–letter word" in suicide is "only," as in "suicide was the *only* thing I could do" (Maris, 2001). In the following statement a woman who survived her leap from a building describes her dichotomous thinking at the time. She saw death as the only alternative to her pain:

> *I was so desperate. I felt, my God, I couldn't face this thing. Everything was like a terrible whirlpool of confusion. And I thought to myself: There's only one thing to do. I just have to lose consciousness. That's the only way to get away from it. The only way to lose consciousness, I thought, was to jump off something good and high. . . .*
>
> *(Shneidman, 1987, p. 56)*

Alcohol and Other Drug Use

Studies indicate that as many as 70 percent of the people who attempt suicide drink alcohol just before the act (Crosby et al., 2009; McCloud et al., 2004). Autopsies reveal that about one-fourth of these people are legally intoxicated (Flavin et al., 1990). It may be that the use of alcohol lowers the individuals' fears of committing suicide, releases underlying aggressive feelings, or impairs their judgment and problem-solving ability. Research shows that the use of other kinds of drugs may have a similar tie to suicide, particularly in teenagers and young adults (Darke et al., 2005). A high level of heroin, for example, was found in the blood of Kurt Cobain at the time of his suicide in 1994 (Colburn, 1996).

Mental Disorders

Although people who attempt suicide may be troubled or anxious, they do not necessarily have a psychological disorder. Nevertheless, the majority of all suicide attempters do display such a disorder (Fountoulakis & Rihmer, 2011). Research suggests that as many as 70 percent of all suicide victims had been experiencing severe *depression,* 20 percent *chronic alcoholism,* and 10 percent *schizophrenia* (see Table 10-2). Correspondingly, as many as 25 percent of people with each of these disorders try to kill themselves. People who are both depressed and dependent on alcohol seem particularly prone to suicidal impulses (Nenadic-Sviglin et al., 2011). Certain anxiety disorders, including posttraumatic stress disorder and panic disorder, have also been linked to suicide, but in most cases of suicide these disorders occur in conjunction with major depressive disorder, a substance-related disorder, or schizophrenia (Bryan & Corso, 2011). It is also the case that many people with borderline personality disorder, a broad pattern that you will read about in Chapter 16, try to harm themselves or make suicidal gestures as part of their disorder (Paris, 2011). The issues with which these individuals are grappling are often quite different from those of other suicidal persons and so will be examined in Chapter 16.

As you saw in Chapter 8, people with major depressive disorder often experience suicidal thoughts. One program in Sweden was able to reduce the community suicide rate by teaching physicians how to recognize and treat depression at an early stage (Rihmer, Rutz, & Pihlgren, 1995). Similarly, a recent review in the United States found that treatments for depression consistently reduce the rate of suicidal thinking, attempts, or completions among patients

table: 10-2

Common Predictors of Suicide

1. Depressive disorder and certain other mental disorders
2. Alcoholism and other forms of substance abuse
3. Suicide ideation, talk, preparation; certain religious ideas
4. Prior suicide attempts
5. Lethal methods
6. Social withdrawal, isolation, living alone, loss of support
7. Hopelessness, feeling trapped, cognitive rigidity
8. Impulsivity and risk-taking behavior
9. Being an older white American male
10. Modeling, suicide in the family, genetics
11. Economic or work problems; certain occupations
12. Marital problems, family pathology
13. Dramatic changes in mood
14. Anxiety
15. Stress and stressful events
16. Anger, aggression, irritability
17. Psychosis
18. Physical illness
19. Sleep problems

Source: Adapted from Wong et al., 2011; Van Orden et al., 2008; Rudd et al., 2006; Papolos et al., 2005.

Fallen teammate

Prior to a 2010 game, the Denver Broncos football team observes a moment of silence for the team's wide receiver Kenny McKinley. McKinley shot himself to death a few days earlier, a suicide related to a combination of stressors, including a second-straight season-ending knee injury, financial problems, and feelings of depression.

(Sakinofsky, 2011). Even when depressed people are showing improvements in mood, however, they may remain high suicide risks. In fact, among those who are severely depressed, the risk of suicide may actually increase as their mood improves and they have more energy to act on their suicidal wishes. Recall, for example, Jonathan Boucher, the combat veteran whose case opened this chapter. Just prior to his suicide, he had seemed to be calm and enjoying life again, according to family members and friends.

Severe depression also may play a key role in suicide attempts by persons with serious physical illnesses (Werth, 2004). A study of 44 patients with terminal illnesses revealed that fewer than one-quarter of them had thoughts of suicide or wished for an early death and that those who did were all suffering from major depressive disorder (Brown et al., 1986).

A number of the people who drink alcohol or use drugs just before a suicide attempt actually have a long history of abusing such substances (Ries, 2010). The basis for the link between substance-related disorders and suicide is not clear. Perhaps the tragic lifestyle of many persons with these disorders or their sense of being hopelessly trapped by a substance leads to suicidal thinking. Alternatively, a third factor—psychological pain, for instance, or desperation—may cause both substance abuse and suicidal thinking (Sher et al., 2005). Such people may be caught in a downward spiral: they are driven toward substance use by psychological pain or loss, only to find themselves caught in a pattern of substance abuse that aggravates rather than solves their problems (Maris, 2001).

People with schizophrenia, as you will see in Chapter 14, may hear voices that are not actually present (hallucinations) or hold beliefs that are clearly false and perhaps bizarre (delusions). The popular notion is that when such persons kill themselves, they must be responding to an imagined voice commanding them to do so or to a delusion that suicide is a grand and noble gesture. Research indicates, however, that suicides by people with schizophrenia more often reflect feelings of demoralization or fears of further mental deterioration (Meltzer, 2011; Pompili & Lester, 2007). Many young and unemployed sufferers who have had relapses over several years come to believe that the disorder will forever disrupt their lives. Still others seem to be disheartened by their substandard living conditions. Suicide is the leading cause of premature death among people with schizophrenia.

Modeling: The Contagion of Suicide

It is not unusual for people, particularly teenagers, to try to commit suicide after observing or reading about someone else who has done so (Ali, Dwyer, & Rizzo, 2011; Feigelman & Gorman, 2008). Perhaps these people have been struggling with major problems and the other person's suicide seems to reveal a possible solution, or perhaps they have been thinking about suicide and the other person's suicide seems to give them permission or finally persuades them to act. Either way, one suicidal act apparently serves as a *model* for another. Suicides by family members and friends, those by celebrities, other highly publicized suicides, and ones by co-workers or colleagues are particularly common triggers.

Family Members and Friends Recent suicides by family members or friends increase the likelihood that individuals will attempt suicide (Ali et al., 2011). Of course, the death of a family member or friend, especially when self-inflicted, is a life-changing event, and suicidal thoughts or attempts may be tied largely to that trauma or sense of loss. Indeed, such losses typically have a lifelong impact on surviving relatives and friends, including a heightened risk of suicide that can continue for years (Roy, 2011). However, even when researchers factor out these issues, they find increases in the risk of suicide among the relatives and friends of people who recently committed suicide (Ali et al., 2011). This additional risk factor is often called the *social contagion effect*.

Celebrities Research suggests that suicides by entertainers, political figures, and other well-known persons are regularly followed by unusual increases in the number of suicides across the nation (Queinec et al., 2011). During the week after the suicide of Marilyn Monroe in 1963, for example, the national suicide rate rose 12 percent (Phillips, 1974).

Other Highly Publicized Cases Suicides with bizarre or unusual aspects often receive intense coverage by the news media. Such highly publicized accounts may lead to similar suicides (Blood et al., 2007; Gould et al., 2007). During the year after a widely publicized, politically motivated suicide by self-burning in England, for example, 82 other people set themselves on fire, with equally fatal results (Ashton & Donnan, 1981). Inquest reports revealed that most of those people had histories of emotional problems and that none of the suicides had the political motivation of the publicized suicide. The imitators seemed to be responding to their own problems in a manner triggered by the suicide they had observed or read about.

Even a media program that is clearly intended to educate and help viewers may have the paradoxical effect of spurring imitators. One study found a dramatic increase in the rate of suicide among West German teenagers after the airing of a television documentary showing the suicide of a teenager who jumped under a train (Schmidtke & Häfner, 1988). The number of railway suicides by male teenagers increased by 175 percent after the program was aired.

Some clinicians argue that more responsible reporting could reduce this frightening impact of highly publicized suicides (Mann & Currier, 2011; Blood et al., 2007). A careful approach to reporting was seen in the media's coverage of the suicide of Kurt Cobain. MTV's repeated theme on the evening of the suicide was "Don't do it!" In fact, thousands of young people called MTV and other radio and television stations in the hours after Cobain's death, upset, frightened, and in some cases suicidal. Some of the stations responded by posting the phone numbers of suicide prevention centers, presenting interviews with suicide experts, and offering counseling services and advice directly to callers. Perhaps because of such efforts, the usual rate of suicide both in Seattle, Cobain's hometown, and elsewhere held steady during the weeks that followed (Colburn, 1996).

Co-workers and Colleagues The word-of-mouth publicity that attends suicides in a school, workplace, or small community may trigger suicide attempts. The suicide of a recruit at a U.S. Navy training school, for example, was followed within two weeks by another and also by an attempted suicide at the school. To head off what threatened to become a suicide epidemic, the school began a program of staff education on suicide and group therapy sessions for recruits who had been close to the suicide victims (Grigg, 1988). Today, a number of schools, for individuals of all ages, put into action programs of this kind after a student commits suicide (Miller, 2011). Such postsuicide programs are often referred to by clinicians as *postvention*.

What Are the Underlying Causes of Suicide?

Most people faced with difficult situations never try to kill themselves. In an effort to understand why some people are more prone to suicide than others, theorists have proposed more fundamental explanations for self-destructive actions than the immediate

Suicidal thoughts

In a recent interview, J. K. Rowling, creator of the *Harry Potter* book series, revealed that she had "suicidal thoughts" while suffering from clinical depression in the mid-1990s. With this revelation, the author was hoping to counter the stigma associated with depression.

BETWEEN THE LINES

Military Risk

Suicide is the second leading cause of death in the Marine Corps. Combat is the leading cause. ‹‹

(Claassen & Knox, 2011)

AP Photo/Tennessee Department of Mental Health and Development Disabilities

BETWEEN THE LINES

Most Common Killings

More suicides (34,000) than homicides (18,000) are committed in the United States each year (CDC, 2011). ‹‹

triggers considered in the previous section. The leading theories come from the psychodynamic, sociocultural, and biological perspectives. As a group, however, these hypotheses have received limited research support and fail to address the full range of suicidal acts. Thus the clinical field currently lacks a satisfactory understanding of suicide.

The Psychodynamic View

Many psychodynamic theorists believe that suicide results from depression and from anger at others that is redirected toward oneself. This theory was first stated by Wilhelm Stekel at a meeting in Vienna in 1910, when he proclaimed that "no one kills himself who has not wanted to kill another or at least wished the death of another" (Shneidman, 1979). Some years later Sigmund Freud (1920) wrote, "No neurotic harbors thoughts of suicide which he has not turned back upon himself from murderous impulses against others." Agreeing with this notion, the influential psychiatrist Karl Menninger called suicide "murder in the 180th degree."

As you read in Chapter 8, Freud (1917) and Abraham (1916, 1911) proposed that when people experience the real or symbolic loss of a loved one, they come to "introject" the lost person; that is, they unconsciously incorporate the person into their own identity and feel toward themselves as they had felt toward the other. For a short while, negative feelings toward the lost loved one are experienced as self-hatred. Anger toward the loved one may turn into intense anger against oneself and finally into depression. Suicide is thought to be an extreme expression of this self-hatred and self-punishment (Campbell, 2010). The following description of a suicidal patient demonstrates how such forces may operate:

A 27-year-old conscientious and responsible woman took a knife to her wrists to punish herself for being tyrannical, unreliable, self-centered, and abusive. She was perplexed and frightened by this uncharacteristic self-destructive episode and was enormously relieved when her therapist pointed out that her invective described her recently deceased father much better than it did herself.

(Gill, 1982, p. 15)

Murder-suicide

Nowhere is the link between homicidal and suicidal behavior more evident than in cases of murder–suicide. In 2009, gifted National Football League quarterback Steve McNair was shot to death by a girlfriend who then proceeded to shoot herself as well. Ironically, in the public service video shown below, made by McNair shortly before his death, he urges young suicidal people to call a hot line and "live to see better days."

In support of Freud's view, researchers have often found a relationship between childhood losses—real or symbolic—and later suicidal behaviors (Fuller-Thomson & Dalton, 2011; Roy, 2011). A classic study of 200 family histories, for example, found that early parental loss was much more common among suicide attempters (48 percent) than among nonsuicidal individuals (24 percent) (Adam, Bouckoms, & Streiner, 1982). Common forms of loss were death of the father and divorce or separation of the parents. Similarly, a study of 343 depressed individuals found that those who had felt rejected or neglected as children by their parents were more likely than other individuals to attempt suicide as adults (Ehnvall et al., 2008).

Late in his career, Freud proposed that human beings have a basic "death instinct." He called this instinct *Thanatos* and said that it opposes the "life instinct." According to Freud, while most people learn to redirect their death instinct by aiming it toward others, suicidal people, caught in a web of self-anger, direct it squarely toward themselves.

Sociological findings are consistent with this explanation of suicide. National suicide rates have been found to drop in times of war (Maris, 2001), when, one could argue, people are encouraged to direct their self-destructive energy against "the enemy." In addition, in many parts of the world, societies with high rates of homicide tend to have low rates of suicide, and vice versa (Bills & Li, 2005). However, research has failed to establish that suicidal people are in fact dominated by intense feelings of anger. Although hostility is an important element in some suicides, several studies find that other emotional states are even more prevalent (Conner & Weisman, 2011; Castrogiovanni et al., 1998).

By the end of his career, Freud himself expressed dissatisfaction with his theory of suicide. Other psychodynamic theorists have also challenged his ideas over the years, yet themes of loss and self-directed aggression generally remain at the center of most psychodynamic explanations (King, 2003).

Durkheim's Sociocultural View

Toward the end of the nineteenth century, Emile Durkheim (1897), a sociologist, developed a broad theory of suicidal behavior. Today this theory continues to be influential and is often supported by research (Fernquist, 2007). According to Durkheim, the probability of suicide is determined by how attached a person is to such social groups as the family, religious institutions, and community. The more thoroughly a person belongs, the lower the risk of suicide. Conversely, people who have poor relationships with their society are at greater risk of killing themselves. He defined several categories of suicide, including *egoistic, altruistic,* and *anomic* suicide.

? Why might towns and countries in past times have been inclined to punish those who attempted suicide and their relatives?

Egoistic suicides are committed by people over whom society has little or no control. These people are not concerned with the norms or rules of society, nor are they integrated into the social fabric. According to Durkheim, this kind of suicide is more likely in people who are isolated, alienated, and nonreligious. The larger the number of such people living in a society, the higher that society's suicide rate.

Altruistic suicides, in contrast, are committed by people who are so well integrated into the social structure that they intentionally sacrifice their lives for its well-being. Soldiers who threw themselves on top of a live grenade to save others, Japanese kamikaze pilots who crashed their planes into enemy ships during World War II, and Buddhist monks and nuns who protested the Vietnam War by setting themselves on fire may have been committing altruistic suicide (Leenaars, 2004; Stack, 2004). According to Durkheim, societies that encourage people to sacrifice themselves for others and to preserve their own honor (as Far Eastern societies do) are likely to have higher suicide rates.

Anomic suicides, another category proposed by Durkheim, are those committed by people whose social environment fails to provide stable structures, such as family and religion, to support and give meaning to life. Such a societal condition, called *anomie* (literally, "without law"), leaves individuals without a sense of belonging. Unlike egoistic suicide, which is the act of a person who rejects the structures of a society, anomic suicide is the act of a person who has been let down by a disorganized, inadequate, often decaying society.

Durkheim argued that when societies go through periods of anomie, their suicide rates increase. Historical trends support this claim. Periods of economic depression may bring about some degree of anomie in a country, and national suicide rates tend to rise during such times (Noh, 2009; Maris, 2001). Periods of population change and increased immigration, too, tend to bring about a state of anomie, and again suicide rates rise (Kposowa et al., 2008).

A major change in an individual's immediate surroundings, rather than general societal problems, can also lead to anomic suicide. People who suddenly inherit a great deal of money, for example, may go through a period of anomie as their relationships with social, economic, and occupational structures are changed. Thus Durkheim predicted that societies with greater opportunities for change in individual wealth or status would have higher suicide rates, and this prediction, too, is supported by research (Cutright & Fernquist, 2001; Lester, 2000, 1985). Conversely, people who are removed from society

John Kaplan/Media Alliance

In the service of others
According to Durkheim, people who intentionally sacrifice their lives for others are committing altruistic suicide. Betsy Smith, a heart transplant recipient who was warned that she would probably die if she did not terminate her pregnancy, elected to have the baby and died giving birth.

Altruistic suicide?
A clay sculpture of a suicide bomber is displayed at a Baghdad art gallery. Some sociologists believe that the acts of such bombers fit Durkheim's definition of altruistic suicide, arguing that the bombers believe they are sacrificing their lives for the well-being of their society. Other theorists, however, point out that many such bombers seem indifferent to the innocent lives they are destroying and categorize the bombers instead as mass murderers motivated by hatred rather than feelings of altruism (Humphrey, 2006).

and sent to a prison environment may experience anomie. As you read earlier, research confirms that such individuals have a heightened suicide rate (Fazel et al., 2011).

Although today's sociocultural theorists do not always embrace Durkheim's particular ideas, most agree that social structure and cultural stress often play major roles in suicide. In fact, the sociocultural view pervades the study of suicide. Recall the earlier discussion of the many studies linking suicide to broad factors such as religious affiliation, marital status, gender, race, and societal stress. You will also see the impact of such factors when you read about the ties between suicide and age.

Despite the influence of sociocultural theories such as Durkheim's, these theories cannot by themselves explain why some people who experience particular societal pressures commit suicide while the majority do not. Durkheim himself concluded that the final explanation probably lies in the interaction between societal and individual factors.

The Biological View

For years biological researchers relied largely on family pedigree studies to support their position that biological factors contribute to suicidal behavior. They repeatedly have found higher rates of suicide among the parents and close relatives of suicidal people than among those of nonsuicidal people (Roy, 2011; Bronisch & Lieb, 2008; Brent & Mann, 2003). Such findings may suggest that genetic, and so biological, factors are at work.

Studies of twins also have supported this view of suicide. In a famous study, researchers who studied twins born in Denmark between 1870 and 1920 located 19 identical pairs and 58 fraternal pairs in which at least one twin had committed suicide (Juel-Nielsen & Videbech, 1970). In four of the identical pairs the other twin also committed suicide (21 percent), while none of the other twins among the fraternal pairs had done so.

As with all family pedigree and twin research, there are nonbiological interpretations for these findings as well. Psychodynamic clinicians might argue that children whose close relatives commit suicide are prone to depression and suicide because they have lost a loved one at a critical stage of development. Behavioral theorists might emphasize the modeling role played by parents or close relatives who attempt suicide.

Suicide sometimes runs in families. How might clinicians and researchers explain such family patterns?

In the past three decades, laboratory studies have offered more direct support for a biological view of suicide. One promising line of research focuses on *serotonin*. The activity level of this neurotransmitter has often been found to be low in people who commit suicide (Pompili et al., 2010; Mann & Currier, 2007). An early hint of this relationship came from a study by psychiatric researcher Marie Asberg and her colleagues (1976). They studied 68 depressed patients and found that 20 of the patients had particularly low levels of serotonin activity. It turned out that 40 percent of the low-serotonin research participants attempted suicide, compared with 15 percent of the higher-serotonin participants. The researchers interpreted this to mean that low serotonin activity may be "a predictor of suicidal acts." Later studies found that suicide attempters with low serotonin activity are 10 times more likely to make a repeat attempt and succeed than are suicide attempters with higher serotonin activity (Roy, 1992).

Subsequent studies that examined the autopsied brains of suicide victims pointed in the same direction (Pompili et al., 2010; Mann & Currier, 2007; Stanley et al., 2000, 1986, 1982). Some of these studies found, for example, that people who committed suicide tended to have fewer receptor sites on neurons that normally receive serotonin than did people who do not commit suicide. Similarly, recent PET scan studies have revealed that people who contemplate or attempt suicide display abnormal activity in areas of the brain that are comprised of many serotonin-using neurons—areas you read about in Chapters 5 and 8, such as the prefrontal cortex, orbitofrontal cortex, and cingulate cortex (Mann & Currier, 2007; Oquendo et al., 2003).

At first glance, these and related studies may appear to tell us only that depressed people often attempt suicide. After all, depression is itself related to low serotonin activity. On the other hand, there is evidence of low serotonin activity even among suicidal individuals who have no history of depression (Mann & Currier, 2007). That is, low serotonin activity also seems to play a role in suicide separate from depression.

How, then, might low serotonin activity increase the likelihood of suicidal behavior? One possibility is that it contributes to aggressive and impulsive behaviors (Preti, 2011). It has been found, for example, that serotonin activity is lower in aggressive men than in nonaggressive men and that serotonin activity is often low in those who commit such aggressive acts as arson and murder (Oquendo et al., 2006, 2004; Stanley et al., 2000). Moreover, PET scan studies of people who are aggressive and impulsive (but not necessarily depressed) reveal abnormal activity in the prefrontal cortex, orbitofrontal cortex, cingulate cortex, and other serotonin-rich areas of the brain (Mann & Currier, 2007; New et al., 2004, 2002). And, finally, studies have found that depressed patients with particularly low serotonin activity try to commit suicide more often, use more lethal methods, and score higher in hostility and impulsivity on personality inventories than do depressed patients with relatively higher serotonin activity (Moberg et al., 2011; Oquendo et al., 2003).

Collectively these findings suggest that low serotonin activity helps produce aggressive feelings and impulsive behavior. In people who are clinically depressed, low serotonin activity may produce aggressive tendencies that cause them to be particularly vulnerable to suicidal thoughts and acts. Even in the absence of a depressive disorder, however, people with low serotonin activity may develop such aggressive feelings that they, too, are dangerous to themselves or to others. Still other research indicates that low serotonin activity *combined* with key psychosocial factors (such as childhood traumas) may be the strongest suicide predictor of all (Moberg et al., 2011).

Is aggression the key?
Biological theorists believe that heightened feelings of aggression and impulsivity, produced by low serotonin activity, are key factors in suicide. In 2007, professional wrestling champion Chris Benoit—here receiving a body kick during a match—killed his wife and son and then hanged himself, a tragedy that seemed consistent with this theory. In addition, toxicology reports found steroids, drugs known to help cause aggression and impulsivity, in Benoit's body.

Is Suicide Linked to Age?

Generally speaking, the likelihood of committing suicide increases with age, although people of all ages may try to kill themselves (see Figure 10-3 on page 303). Currently, 1 of every 100,000 children in the United States kills himself or herself each year, compared to 7.3 of every 100,000 teenagers, 14.3 of every 100,000 young adults, 16.8 of every 100,000 middle-aged adults, and 16.3 of every 100,000 persons over age 75 (CDC, 2010; Cohen, 2008; NAHIC, 2006). It is worth noting that, these overall age trends not withstanding, the rate of middle-age suicides has been rising more than that of any other age group in recent years, a trend that is not fully understood.

Clinicians have paid particular attention to self-destructive behavior in three age groups: *children, adolescents,* and the *elderly.* Although the features and theories of suicide discussed throughout this chapter apply to all age groups, each group faces unique problems that may play key roles in the suicidal acts of its members.

Children

Tommy [age 7] and his younger brother were playing together, and an altercation arose that was settled by the mother, who then left the room. The mother recalled nothing to distinguish this incident from innumerable similar ones. Several minutes after she left, she considered Tommy strangely quiet and returned to find him crimson-faced and struggling for air, having knotted a jumping rope around his neck and jerked it tight.

(French & Berlin, 1979, p. 144)

(continued on the next page)

> *Dear Mom and Dad,*
>
> *I love you. Please tell my teacher that I cannot take it anymore. I quit. Please don't take me to school anymore. Please help me. I will run away so don't stop me. I will kill myself. So don't look for me because I will be dead. I love you. I will always love you. Remember me. Help me.*
>
> *Love Justin [age 10]*
>
> *(Pfeffer, 1986, p. 273)*

Although suicide is infrequent among children, it has been increasing over the past several decades (Dervic, Brent, & Oquendo, 2008). Indeed, more than 6 percent of all deaths among children between the ages of 10 and 14 years are caused by suicide (Arias et al., 2003). Boys outnumber girls by as much as 5 to 1. In addition, it has been estimated that 1 of every 100 children tries to harm himself or herself, and many thousands of children are hospitalized each year for deliberately self-destructive acts, such as stabbing, cutting, burning, or shooting themselves; overdosing; or jumping from high places (Fortune & Hawton, 2007; Cytryn & McKnew, 1996).

Researchers have found that suicide attempts by the very young are commonly preceded by such behavioral patterns as running away from home; accident-proneness; aggressive acting out; temper tantrums; self-criticism; social withdrawal and loneliness; extreme sensitivity to criticism by others; low tolerance of frustration; sleep problems; dark fantasies, daydreams, or hallucinations; marked personality change; and overwhelming interest in death and suicide (Wong et al., 2011; Dervic et al., 2008). Studies further have linked child suicides to the recent or anticipated loss of a loved one, family stress and a parent's unemployment, abuse by parents, and a clinical level of depression (Renaud et al., 2008; Van Orden et al., 2008).

Most people find it hard to believe that children fully comprehend the meaning of a suicidal act. They argue that because a child's thinking is so limited, children who attempt suicide fall into Shneidman's category of "death ignorers," like Demaine, who sought to join his mother in heaven. Many child suicides, however, appear to be based on a clear understanding of death and on a clear wish to die (Pfeffer, 2003). In addition, suicidal thinking among even normal children is apparently more common than most people once believed. Clinical interviews with schoolchildren have revealed that between 6 and 33 percent have thought about suicide (Riesch et al., 2008; Culp, Clyman, & Culp, 1995). Small wonder that many of today's elementary schools have tried to develop tools and procedures for better identifying and assessing suicide risk among their students (Miller, 2011; Whitney et al., 2011).

Student stress

The intense training and testing that characterize Japan's educational system produce high levels of stress in many students. This child, wearing a headband that reads "Struggle to Pass" in English, participates in summer *juku*, a camp where children receive special academic training, extra lessons, and exam practice 11 hours a day.

Adolescents

> *Dear Mom, Dad, and everyone else,*
>
> *I'm sorry for what I've done, but I loved you all and I always will, for eternity. Please, please, please don't blame it on yourselves. It was all my fault and not yours or anyone else's. If I didn't do this now, I would have done it later anyway. We all die some day, I just died sooner.*
>
> *Love,*
> *John*
>
> *(Berman, 1986)*

The suicide of John, age 17, was not an unusual occurrence. Suicidal actions become much more common after the age of 14 than at any earlier age. According to official records, overall 1,500 teenagers (age 15 to 19), or 7 of every 100,000, commit suicide in the United States each year (Van Orden et al., 2008). In addition, as many as 10 percent of teenagers may make suicide attempts and 1 in 6 may think about suicide each year (Pompili et al., 2011; Goldston et al., 2008). Because fatal illnesses are uncommon among the young, suicide has become the third leading cause of death in this age group, after accidents and homicides. Around 10 percent of all adolescent deaths are the result of suicide (Pompili et al, 2011; Shain, 2007).

About half of teenage suicides, like those of people in other age groups, have been tied to clinical depression (see *PsychWatch* on the next page), low self-esteem, and feelings of hopelessness, but many teenagers who try to kill themselves also appear to struggle with anger and impulsiveness or to have serious alcohol or drug problems (Renaud et al., 2008; Witte et al., 2008). In addition, some have deficiencies in their ability to sort out and solve problems (Brent, 2001).

Teenagers who consider or attempt suicide are often under great stress. They may experience long-term pressures such as poor (or missing) relationships with parents, family conflict, inadequate peer relationships, and social isolation (Capuzzi & Gross, 2008; Apter & Wasserman, 2007). Alternatively, their actions also may be triggered by more immediate stress, such as a parent's unemployment or medical illness, financial setbacks for the family, or a social loss such as a break-up with a boyfriend or girlfriend (Orbach & Iohan, 2007). Stress at school seems to be a particularly common problem for teenagers who attempt suicide. Some have trouble keeping up at school, while others may be high achievers who feel pressured to be perfect and to stay at the top of the class (Frazier & Cross, 2011). In many high schools, psychologists and teachers are now trained to look for these and other risk factors in students (Miller, 2011; Whitney et al., 2011).

Some theorists believe that the period of adolescence itself produces a stressful climate in which suicidal actions are more likely. Adolescence is a period of rapid growth that is often marked by conflicts, depressed feelings, tensions, and difficulties at home and school. Adolescents tend to react to events more sensitively, angrily, dramatically, and impulsively than individuals in other age groups; thus the likelihood of suicidal acts during times of stress is increased (Greening et al., 2008). Finally, the suggestibility of adolescents and their eagerness to imitate others, including others who attempt suicide, may set the stage for suicidal action (Apter & Wasserman, 2007). One study found that 93 percent of adolescent suicide attempters had known someone who had attempted suicide (Conrad, 1992).

Teen Suicides: Attempts Versus Completions

Far more teenagers attempt suicide than actually kill themselves—the ratio may be as high as 200 to 1. The unusually large number of unsuccessful suicides may mean that teenagers are less certain than older persons who make such attempts. While some do indeed wish to die, many may simply want to make others understand how desperate they are, get help, or teach others a lesson (Apter & Wasserman, 2007). Up to half of teenage attempters make new suicide attempts in the future, and as many as 14 percent eventually die by suicide (Wong et al., 2008; Borowsky et al., 2001).

Why is the rate of suicide attempts so high among teenagers (as well as among young adults)? Several explanations, most pointing to societal factors, have been proposed. First, as the number and proportion of teenagers and young adults in the general population have risen, the competition for jobs, college positions, and academic and athletic honors has intensified for them, leading

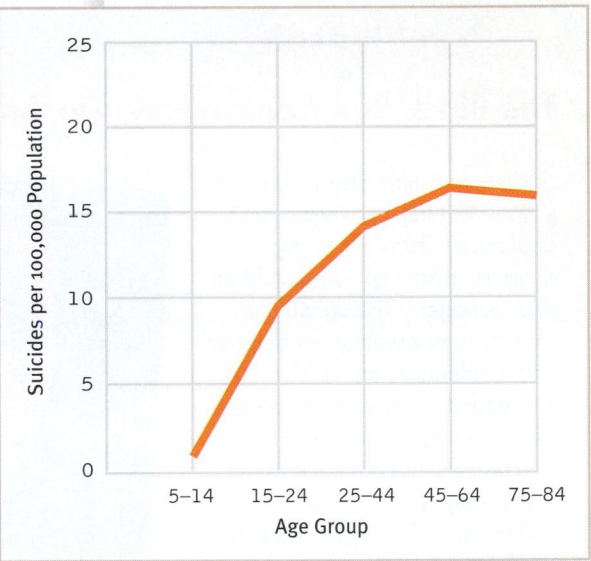

Figure 10-3

Suicide and age In the United States, suicide rates keep rising up to the age of 64 and then plateau among older age groups (CDC, 2011; U.S. Census Bureau, 2011; NVSS, 2010).

Telling his story

College student Bryce Mackie watches as his film, *Eternal High*, is played for a group of mental health professionals in Ohio. He made the film in high school chronicling his struggle with bipolar disorder and suicidal thoughts.

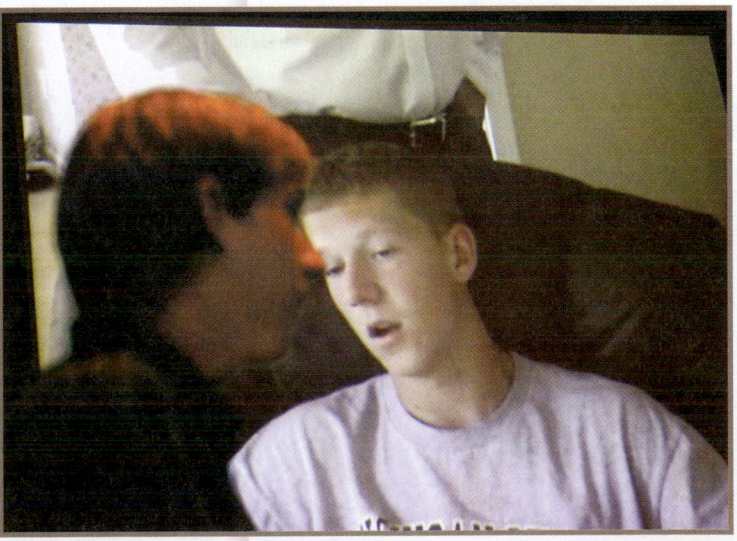

AP Photo/Ron Schwane

PsychWatch

The Black Box Controversy: Do Antidepressants Cause Suicide?

A major controversy in the clinical field is whether antidepressant drugs are highly dangerous for depressed children and teenagers. Throughout the 1990s, most psychiatrists believed that antidepressants—particularly the second-generation antidepressants—were safe and effective for children and adolescents, just as they seemed to be for adults, and they prescribed those medications readily (Hertzman, 2010; Kutcher & Gardner, 2008). However, after reviewing a large number of clinical reports and studying 3,300 patients on antidepressants, the United States Food and Drug Administration (FDA) concluded in 2004 that the drugs produce a real, though small, increase in the risk of suicidal behavior for certain children and adolescents, especially during the first few months of treatment, and it ordered that all antidepressant containers carry "black box" warnings stating that the drugs "increase the risk of suicidal thinking and behavior in children." In 2007 the FDA expanded this warning to include young adults.

Although many clinicians have been pleased by the FDA order, others worry that it may be ill-advised (Haliburn, 2010; Healy, Whitaker, & LaPierre, 2010). They argue that while the drugs may indeed

increase the risk of suicidal thoughts and attempts in as many as 2 to 3 percent of young patients, the risk of suicide is actually reduced in the vast majority of children and teenagers who take the drugs (Mulder, 2010). To support this argument, they point out that the overall rate of teenage suicides decreased by 30 percent in the decade leading up to 2004, as the number of antidepressant prescriptions provided to children and teenagers were soaring (Isaacsson et al., 2010).

The critics of the black box warnings also point to the initial effect that the warnings had on prescription patterns and teenage suicide rates in the United States and other countries. Some studies suggest that during the first two years following the institution of the black box warnings, the

number of antidepressant prescriptions fell 22 percent in the United States and the Netherlands while the rate of teenage suicides rose 14 percent in the United States, the largest suicide rate increases since 1979 (Fawcett, 2007). Although other studies challenge these numbers (Wheeler et al., 2008), it is certainly possible that black box warnings were indirectly depriving many young patients of a medication that they truly needed to help fight depression and head off suicide. Antidepressant prescriptions for depressed teenagers now seem to be rising again, and the effect of this trend reversal on teenage suicide rates certainly awaits careful scrutiny.

A major outgrowth and benefit of the black box controversy is that the FDA recently has expanded its interest in suicidal side effects to drugs other than antidepressants. It now requires pharmaceutical companies to test for suicidal side effects in certain newly developed drugs such as those for obesity and epilepsy, before such drugs receive FDA approval (Carey, 2008; Harris, 2008). In the past, lethal effects of this kind never came to light until well after drugs had been approved and used by millions of patients.

increasingly to shattered dreams and ambitions (Holinger & Offer, 1993, 1991, 1982). Other explanations point to weakening ties in the family (which may produce feelings of alienation and rejection in many of today's young people) and to the easy availability of alcohol and other drugs and the pressure to use them among teenagers and young adults (Brent, 2001; Cutler et al., 2001).

The mass media coverage of suicides by teenagers and young adults may also contribute to the high rate of suicide attempts among the young (Gould et al., 2007). The detailed descriptions of teenage suicide that the media and the arts often offer may serve as models for young people who are contemplating suicide (Cheng et al., 2007). In one of the most famous examples of this phenomenon, just days after the highly publicized suicides of four adolescents in a New Jersey town in 1987, dozens of teenagers across the United States took similar actions (at least 12 of them fatal)—two in the same garage just one week later. Similarly, one study found that the rate of adolescent suicide rose about 7 percent in New York City during the week following a television film on suicide, in contrast to a 0.5 percent increase in the adult suicide rate during the same week (Maris, 2001).

In Chapter 4 you read about pro-suicide sites on the Internet (see page 108). Although such sites are growing in number and influence, they do not appear to be a major factor in the rise of teenage suicide attempts—at least not yet. One study used a strategy called "hyperlink network analysis" to determine which websites are indeed visited by suicidal individuals (Kemp & Collings, 2011). The investigators found that pro-suicide sites were not readily accessible and in fact were visited relatively infrequently, whereas sites dedicated to suicide-related information, prevention, or treatment were very accessible and often visited.

Teen Suicides: Multicultural Issues Teenage suicide rates vary by ethnicity in the United States. Around 7.5 of every 100,000 white American teenagers commit suicide each year, compared to 5 of every 100,000 African American teens and 5 of every 100,000 Hispanic American teens (Goldston et al., 2008; NAHIC, 2006). Although these numbers certainly indicate that white American teens are more prone to suicide, the rates of the three groups are in fact becoming closer (Baca-Garcia et al., 2011). The white American rate was 150 percent greater than the African American and Hispanic American rates in 1980; today it is only 50 percent greater. This closing trend may reflect increasingly similar pressures on young African, Hispanic, and white Americans—competition for grades and college opportunities, for example, is now intense for all three groups (Barnes, 2010). The growing suicide rates for young African and Hispanic Americans may also be linked to rising unemployment among them, the many anxieties and economic pressures of inner-city life, and the rage felt by many of them over racial inequities and discrimination in our society (Baca-Garcia et al., 2011; Barnes, 2010; Goldston et al., 2008). Recent studies further indicate that 4.5 of every 100,000 Asian American teens now commit suicide each year.

The highest teenage suicide rate of all is displayed by American Indians. Currently, more than 15 of every 100,000 American Indian teenagers commit suicide each year, double the rate of white American teenagers and triple that of other minority teenagers. Clinical theorists attribute this extraordinarily high rate to factors such as the extreme poverty faced by most American Indian teens, their limited educational and employment opportunities, their particularly high rate of alcohol abuse, and the geographical isolation experienced by those who live on reservations (Alcantara & Gone, 2008; Goldston et al., 2008). In addition, it appears that certain American Indian reservations have extreme suicide rates—called *cluster suicides*—and that teenagers who live in such communities are unusually likely to be exposed to suicide, to have their lives disrupted, to observe suicidal models, and to be at risk for suicide contagion (Bender, 2006; Chekki, 2004).

The Elderly

Rose Ashby walks to the dry cleaner's to pick up her old but finest dinner dress. Although shaken at the cost of having it cleaned, Rose tells the sympathetic girl behind the counter, "Don't worry. It doesn't matter. I won't be needing the money any more."

Walking through the streets of St. Petersburg, Florida, she still wishes it had been Miami. The west coast of the fountain-of-youth peninsula is not as warm as the east. If only Chet had left more insurance money, Rose could have afforded Miami. In St. Petersburg, Rose failed to unearth de León's promised fount.

Last week, she told the doctor she felt lonely and depressed. He said she should perk up. She had everything to live for. What does he know? Has he lost a husband like Chet and his left breast to cancer all in one year? Has he suffered arthritis all his life? Were his ovaries so bad he had to undergo a hysterectomy? Did he have to suffer through menopause just to end up alone without family or friends? Does he have to live in a dungeon? Is his furniture worn, his carpet threadbare? What does he know? Might his every day be the last one for him?

(continued on the next page)

As Rose turns into the walk to her white cinderblock apartment building, fat Mrs. Green asks if she is coming to the community center that evening. Who needs it? The social worker did say Rose should come. Since Rose was in such good health, she could help those not so well as she.

Help them do what? Finger-paint like little children? Make baskets like insane people? Sew? Who can see to sew? Besides, who would appreciate it? Who would thank her? Who could she tell about her troubles? Who cares?

When she told the doctor she couldn't sleep, he gave her the prescription but said that all elderly people have trouble sleeping. What does he know? Does he have a middle-aged daughter who can only think about her latest divorce, or grandchildren who only acknowledge her birthday check by the endorsement on the back? Are all his friends dead and gone? Is all the money from her dead husband's insurance used up? What does he know? Who could sleep in this dungeon?

Back in her apartment, Rose washes and sets her hair. It's good she has to do it herself. Look at this hair. So thin, so sparse, so frowsy. What would a hairdresser think?

Then make-up. Base. Rouge. Lipstick. Bright red. Perfume? No! No cheap perfume for Rose today. Remember the bottles of Joy Chet would buy for her? He always wanted her to have the best. He would boast that she had everything, and that she never had to work a day in her life for it.

"She doesn't have to lift her little finger," Chet would say, puffing on his cigar. Where is the Joy now? Dead and gone. With Chet. Rose manages a wry laugh at the play on words.

Slipping into her dinner dress, she looks into the dresser mirror. "It's good you can't see this face now, Chet. How old and ugly it looks."

Taking some lavender notepaper from the drawer, she stands at the dresser to write. Why didn't anyone warn her that growing old was like this? It is so unfair. But they don't care. People don't care about anyone except themselves.

Leaving the note on the dresser, she suddenly feels excited. Breathing hard now, she rushes to the sink—who could call a sink in the counter in the living room a kitchen?—and gets a glass of water.

Trying to relax, Rose arranges the folds in her skirt as she settles down on the chaise. Carefully sipping the water as she takes all the capsules so as to not smear her lipstick, Rose quietly begins to sob. After a lifetime of tears, these will be her last. Her note on the dresser is short, written to no one and to everyone.

You don't know what it is like to have to grow old and die.

(Gernsbacher, 1985, pp. 227–228)

In Western society the elderly are more likely to commit suicide than people in most other age groups. More than 16 of every 100,000 persons over the age of 75 in the United States commit suicide. Elderly persons commit over 19 percent of all suicides in the United States, yet they account for only 12 percent of the total population.

Many factors contribute to this high suicide rate (Innamorati et al., 2011). As people grow older, all too often they become ill, lose close friends and relatives, lose control over their lives, and lose status in our society. Such experiences may result in feelings of hopelessness, loneliness, depression, "burdensomeness," or inevitability among aged persons and so increase the likelihood that they will attempt suicide (Cukrowicz et al., 2011; Jahn et al., 2011). One study found that two-thirds of elderly individuals (above 80 years old) who committed suicide had experienced a medical hospitalization within two years preceding the suicide (Erlangsen et al., 2005), and another found a heightened rate of vascular or respiratory illnesses among elderly people who attempted suicide (Levy et al., 2011). Still other research has revealed that the suicide rate of elderly people who have recently

Why do people often view the suicides of elderly or chronically sick persons as less tragic than that of young or healthy persons?

lost a spouse is particularly high (Ajdacic-Gross et al., 2008). The risk is greatest during the first weeks of bereavement, but it remains high in later months and years as well.

Elderly persons are typically more determined than younger persons in their decision to die and give fewer warnings, so their success rate is much higher (Dennis & Brown, 2011). Apparently one of every four elderly persons who attempts suicide succeeds (Demircin et al., 2011). Given the resolve of aged persons and their physical decline, some people argue that older persons who want to die are clear in their thinking and should be allowed to carry out their wishes (see *PsychWatch* on the next page). However, clinical depression appears to play an important role in as many as 60 percent of suicides by the elderly, suggesting that more elderly persons who are suicidal should be receiving treatment for their depressive disorders (Levy et al., 2011; Hirsch et al., 2009). In fact, research suggests that treating depression in older persons helps reduce their risk of suicide markedly (Lapierre et al., 2011).

The suicide rate among the elderly in the United States is lower in some minority groups (Alcantara & Gone, 2008; Leach & Leong, 2008; Utsey et al., 2008). Although American Indians have the highest overall suicide rate, for example, the rate among elderly American Indians is relatively low. The aged are held in high esteem by American Indians and are looked to for the wisdom and experience they have acquired over the years, and this may help account for their low suicide rate. Such high regard is in sharp contrast to the loss of status often experienced by elderly white Americans.

Similarly, the suicide rate is only one-third as high among elderly African Americans as among elderly white Americans (Barnes, 2010). One reason for this low suicide rate may be the pressures faced by African Americans: "only the strongest survive" (Seiden, 1981). Those who reach an advanced age have overcome great adversity and often feel proud of what they have accomplished. Because reaching old age is not in itself a form of success for white Americans, their attitude toward aging is more negative. Another possible explanation is that aged African Americans have successfully overcome the rage that prompts many suicides in younger African Americans.

Gruesome business
Vincent van Gogh's painting *Old Man with His Head in His Hands* conveys the psychological pain experienced by some elderly people.

The power of respect
Elderly persons are held in high esteem in many traditional societies because of the store of knowledge they have accumulated. Perhaps not so coincidentally, suicides among the elderly seem to be less common in these cultures than in those of many modern industrialized nations.

PsychWatch

The Right to Commit Suicide

In the fall of 1989, a Michigan doctor, Jack Kevorkian, built a "suicide device." A person using it could, at the touch of a button, change a saline solution being fed intravenously into the arm to one containing chemicals that would bring unconsciousness and a swift death. The following June, under the doctor's supervision, Mrs. J. Adkins took her life. She left a note explaining: "This is a decision taken in a normal state of mind and is fully considered. I have Alzheimer's disease and I do not want to let it progress any further. I do not want to put my family or myself through the agony of this terrible disease." Mrs. Adkins believed that she had a right to choose death. Michigan authorities promptly prohibited further use of Kevorkian's device, but the physician continued to assist in the suicides of medically ill persons throughout the 1990s.

(ADAPTED FROM BELKIN, 1990; MALCOLM, 1990)

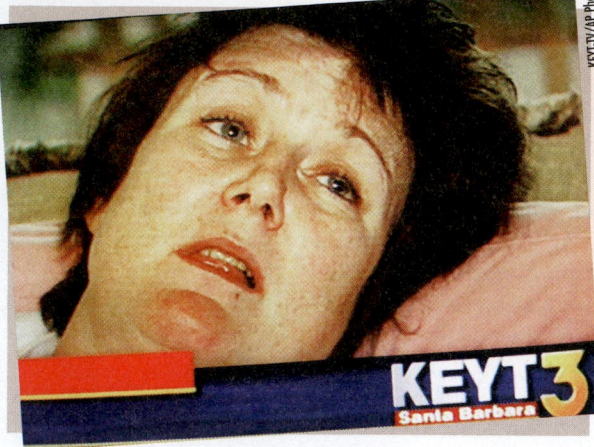

KEYT/AP Photo

A right to die? Multiple sclerosis patient Rebecca Badger conducts a TV interview from her bed in 1996, just two days before she committed suicide with the assistance of Dr. Jack Kevorkian. Badger stated that the constant pain and torment of immobility caused by her illness eventually made her long for death.

In 1999 Dr. Kevorkian was convicted of second-degree murder and sentenced to prison for an assisted suicide that he had conducted, filmed, and aired on the television news show *60 Minutes*. He was released from prison on parole in 2007 and died four years later. However, his many court battles have helped bring an important question to the public's attention: Do individuals have a right to commit suicide, or does society have the right to stop them (Dickens et al., 2008; Strate et al., 2005)?

The ancient Greeks valued physical and mental well-being in life and dignity in death. Therefore, individuals with a grave illness or mental anguish were permitted to commit suicide. Citizens could obtain official permission from the Senate to take their own lives, and judges were allowed to give them hemlock (Humphry & Wickett, 1986).

Western traditions, in contrast, discourage suicide, on the basis of belief in the "sanctity of life" (Dickens et al., 2008; Eser, 1981). People in Western cultures speak of "committing" suicide, as though it were a criminal act (Sharma, 2009), and allow the state to use force, including involuntary commitment to a mental hospital, to prevent it. But times and attitudes are changing. Today the ideas of a "right to suicide" and "rational suicide" are receiving more support from the public and from many psychotherapists and physicians (Canetto, 2011; Curlin et al., 2008).

Public support for a right to suicide seems strongest in connection with great pain and terminal illness (Breitbart et al., 2011; Werth, 2004, 2000, 1999, 1996). Surveys show that more than two-thirds of all Americans believe that terminally ill persons should be free to take their lives or to seek a physician's assistance to do so (Harris Poll, 2005). In line with this belief, the state of Oregon in 1997 passed the "Death with Dignity" Act, allowing a doctor to assist a suicide (by administering a lethal dose of drugs) if two physicians determine that the patient has less than six months to live and is not basing the decision to die on depression or another mental disorder. More than 500 people have used this law to end their lives since 1997, an average of 36 each year. Most of these individuals had cancer, and their median age was 74 (Hoffman, 2007). In 2006, after an extended legal battle between the federal government and Oregon, the U.S. Supreme Court upheld the law by a 6-to-3 vote. In recent years the states of Washington and Wisconsin have passed similar laws, and other states are currently considering such legislation. On the other hand, 34 states states have laws explicitly criminalizing assisted suicide.

Critics of the Oregon law and the right-to-suicide movement argue that the suicidal acts of patients with severe or fatal illnesses may often spring largely from psychological distress (Canetto, 2011). Indeed, a number of studies suggest that half or more of severely ill patients who are suicidal may be clinically depressed (Finlay & George, 2011; Werth, 2004). Thus, in some cases, it may be more beneficial to help individuals come to terms with a fatal illness than to offer them a license to end their lives. On the other hand, according to yet other research, decisions to seek physician-assisted suicide are often made in the absence of clinical depression (Canetto, 2011; Rosenfeld, 2004).

Some clinicians also worry that the right to suicide could be experienced more as a "duty to die" than as the ultimate freedom. Elderly people might feel selfish in expecting relatives to support and care for them when suicide is a socially approved alternative (Canetto, 2011; Brock, 2001; Sherlock, 1983). Moreover, as care for the terminally ill grows ever more costly, might suicide be subtly encouraged among the poor and disadvantaged? Could assisted suicide become a form of medical cost control (Brock, 2001)? In the Netherlands, where physician-assisted suicide and euthanasia were approved by law in 2001, euthanasia is clearly on the rise (Ferrell, 2011; Ruijs et al., 2011; Caldwell, 2010). In 2010, 2,700 people in that country chose to die by injection, up from 2,636 in 2009. Around 1.8 percent of all deaths in that country are now the result of physician-assisted suicide and voluntary euthanasia (Hendin, 2002).

How are these issues to be resolved? Understanding and preventing suicide remain challenges for the future, as do questions about whether and when we should stand back and do nothing. Whatever one's position on this issue, it is a matter of life and death.

Treatment and Suicide

Treatment of suicidal people falls into two major categories: *treatment after suicide has been attempted* and *suicide prevention*. Treatment may also be beneficial to relatives and friends of those who commit or attempt to commit suicide. Indeed, their feelings of loss, guilt, and anger after a suicide fatality or attempt can be intense (Feigelman & Feigelman, 2011). However, the discussion here is limited to the treatment afforded suicidal people themselves.

What Treatments Are Used After Suicide Attempts?

After a suicide attempt, most victims need medical care. Some are left with severe injuries, brain damage, or other medical problems. Once the physical damage is treated, psychotherapy or drug therapy may begin, on either an inpatient or outpatient basis.

Unfortunately, even after trying to kill themselves, many suicidal people fail to receive systematic follow-up care (Miret et al., 2009; Beautrais et al., 2000). In one study, for example, one-third of adolescent suicide attempters reported that they had not received any help after trying to end their lives (Larsson & Ivarsson, 1998). In some cases, health care professionals are at fault for this lack of follow-up. In others, the person who has attempted suicide refuses therapy. According to a recent review, the average number of therapy sessions attended by teenagers who receive follow-up care is 8; around 18 percent of such teens terminate treatment against their therapists' advice (Spirito et al., 2011).

The goals of therapy for persons who have attempted suicide are to keep the individuals alive, reduce their psychological pain, help them achieve a nonsuicidal state of mind, provide them with hope, and guide them to develop better ways of handling stress (Rudd & Brown, 2011). Various therapies have been employed, including drug, psychodynamic, cognitive-behavioral, group, and family therapies (Baldessarini & Tondo, 2011, 2007; Spirito et al., 2011). Treatment does appear to help. Studies have found that 30 percent of suicide attempters who do not receive treatment try again, compared with 16 percent of patients in treatment (Nordstrom et al., 1995; Allard et al., 1992).

Research indicates that cognitive-behavioral therapy may be particularly helpful for suicidal individuals (Brown et al., 2011, 2010; Ghahramanlou-Holloway et al., 2011, 2008). This approach focuses largely on the painful thoughts, sense of hopelessness, dichotomous thinking, poor coping skills, weak problem-solving abilities, and other cognitive and behavioral features that characterize suicidal persons. Using elements of Beck's cognitive therapy (see pages 262–264), the therapists may help their suicidal clients to assess, challenge, and change many of their negative attitudes and illogical thinking processes. Applying the principles of *mindfulness-based* cognitive therapy (see pages 64 and 264), the therapists may also guide the clients to become acutely aware of the painful thoughts and feelings that stream through their minds and to *accept* many such thoughts and feelings rather than try to eliminate them. Acceptance of this kind is expected to increase the clients' tolerance of psychological distress. And finally, employing therapy exercises, homework assignments, and other cognitive-behavioral tools, the therapists may try to teach clients better coping and problem-solving skills.

What Is Suicide Prevention?

During the past 50 years, emphasis around the world has shifted from suicide treatment to suicide prevention. In some respects this change is most appropriate: the last opportunity to keep many potential suicide victims alive comes before the first attempt.

The first **suicide prevention program** in the United States was founded in Los Angeles in 1955; the first in England, called the *Samaritans,* was started in 1953. There are now hundreds of suicide prevention centers in the United States and England. In addition, many of today's mental health centers, hospital emergency rooms, pastoral counseling centers, and poison control centers include suicide prevention programs among their services.

There are also hundreds of *suicide hot lines,* 24-hour-a-day telephone services, in the United States (Lester, 2011). Callers reach a counselor, typically a *paraprofessional, a*

•**suicide prevention program**•A program that tries to identify people who are at risk of killing themselves and to offer them crisis intervention.

Zhang Xiaoli/Color China Photo/AP Images

Working with suicide

Pedestrians and police work to rescue a young woman who had attempted to drown herself in a river in 2010. Police departments across the world typically provide special crisis intervention training so that officers can develop the skills to help suicidal individuals.

•**crisis intervention**•A treatment approach that tries to help people in a psychological crisis to view their situation more accurately, make better decisions, act more constructively, and overcome the crisis.

person trained in counseling but without a formal degree, who provides services under the supervision of a mental health professional.

Suicide prevention programs and hot lines respond to suicidal people as individuals *in crisis*—that is, under great stress, unable to cope, feeling threatened or hurt, and interpreting their situations as unchangeable. Thus the programs offer **crisis intervention:** they try to help suicidal people see their situations more accurately, make better decisions, act more constructively, and overcome their crises (Lester, 2011). Because crises can occur at any time, the centers advertise their hot lines and also welcome people who walk in without appointments.

Some prevention centers and hot lines reach out to particular suicidal populations. The *Trevor Lifeline,* for example, is a nationwide, around-the-clock hot line available for LGBTQ (lesbian, gay, bisexual, transgender, and questioning) teenagers who are thinking about suicide. This hot line is one of several services offered by the *Trevor Foundation,* a wide-reaching organization dedicated to providing support, guidance, and information and promoting acceptance of LGBTQ teens.

The public sometimes confuses suicide prevention centers and hot lines with online chat rooms and forums (message boards) to which some suicidal persons turn. However, such online sites operate quite differently, and, in fact, most of them do not seek out suicidal persons or try to prevent suicide. Typically, these chat rooms (where users communicate in real time) and forums (where users post messages without interacting directly) are not prepared to deal with suicidal persons, do not offer face-to-face support, do not involve professionals or paraprofessionals, and do not have ways of keeping out malevolent users (see *MediaSpeak* on the next page).

Today, suicide prevention takes place not only at prevention centers and hot lines but also in therapists' offices. Suicide experts encourage all therapists to look for and address signs of suicidal thinking in their clients, regardless of the broad reasons that the clients are seeking treatment (McGlothlin, 2008). With this in mind, a number of guidelines have been developed to help therapists effectively uncover, assess, prevent, and treat suicidal thinking and behavior in their daily work (Van Orden et al., 2008; Shneidman & Farberow, 1968).

Although specific techniques vary from therapist to therapist or from prevention center to prevention center, the approach developed originally by the Los Angeles Suicide Prevention Center continues to reflect the goals and techniques of many clinicians and organizations. During the initial contact at the center, the counselor has several tasks:

Establishing a positive relationship As callers must trust counselors in order to confide in them and follow their suggestions, counselors try to set a positive and comfortable tone for the discussion. They convey that they are listening, understanding, interested, nonjudgmental, and available.

Understanding and clarifying the problem Counselors first try to understand the full scope of the caller's crisis and then help the person see the crisis in clear and constructive terms. In particular, they try to help callers see the central issues and the transient nature of their crises and recognize the alternatives to suicide.

Assessing suicide potential Crisis workers at the Los Angeles Suicide Prevention Center fill out a questionnaire, often called a *lethality scale,* to estimate the caller's potential for suicide. It helps them determine the degree of stress the caller is under, relevant personality characteristics, how detailed the suicide plan is, the severity of symptoms, and the coping resources available to the caller.

Assessing and mobilizing the caller's resources Although they may view themselves as ineffectual, helpless, and alone, people who are suicidal usually have many strengths and resources, including relatives and friends. It is the counselor's job to recognize, point out, and activate those resources.

Formulating a plan Together the crisis worker and caller develop a plan of action. In essence, they are agreeing on a way out of the crisis, an alternative to suicidal action. Most plans include a series of follow-up counseling sessions over the next few days or weeks, either in person at the center or by phone. Each plan also requires the

MediaSpeak

Live Web Suicides: A Growing Phenomenon

By Brian Stelter, *New York Times*

For a 19-year-old community college student in Pembroke Pines, Fla., the message boards on BodyBuilding.com were a place to post messages, at least 2,300 of them, including more than one about his suicidal impulses. In a post last year, he wrote that online forums had "become like a family to me."

"I know its kinda sad," the student, Abraham Biggs, wrote in parentheses, adding that he posted about his "troubles and doubts" online because he did not want to talk to anyone about them in person.

Last Wednesday, when Mr. Biggs posted a suicide note and listed the drug cocktail he intended to consume, the Web site hardly acted like a family. On BodyBuilding.com, which includes discussions of numerous topics besides bodybuilding, and on a live video Web site, Justin.tv, Mr. Biggs was "egged on" by strangers who, investigators say, encouraged him to swallow the antidepressant pills that eventually killed him.

Mr. Biggs's case is the most recent example of a suicide that played out on the Internet. Live video of the death was shown online to scores of people, leading some viewers to cringe while others laughed. The case, which has prompted an outpouring of sympathy and second-guessing online, demonstrates the double-edged nature of online communities that millions of people flock to every day.

Online communities "are like the crowd outside the building with the guy on the ledge," Jeffrey Cole, a professor who studies technology's effects on society at the University of Southern California. "Sometimes there is someone who gets involved and tries to talk him down. Often the crowd chants, 'Jump, jump.' They can enable suicide or help prevent it." . . .

[A]ccording to a chronology posted by a fellow user, Mr. Biggs listed the pills he had obtained and posted a suicide note that he had copied from another Web site. He directed people to his page on Justin.tv, where anyone can plug in a webcam and stream live video onto the Internet. In a chat room adjacent to the live video, the "joking and trash talking" continued after Mr. Biggs consumed the pills and lay on his bed . . . .

Several . . . concerned users called the police when it appeared that Mr. Biggs had stopped breathing. As officers entered the room, according to a screen capture of the incident that circulated online, 181 people were watching the video. In the chat room, users typed the acronyms for "oh my God" and "laugh out loud" before the police covered the webcam. . . .

Mr. Biggs's family has said he suffered from bipolar disorder and was being treated for depression. . . . [I]n an interview with The Associated Press, [Mr. Biggs's] father said he was appalled by the lack of responsiveness on the part of the users and the operators.

"As a human being, you don't watch someone in trouble and sit back and just watch," he said. . . .

M. David Rudd, chairman of the psychology department at Texas Tech University, said the Internet did not fully live up to its potential to help with suicide prevention. "Most of what's available via the Internet only serves to make the problem worse," Mr. Rudd said, whether it is information about how to commit suicide or immature comments from chat room users.

Andrea Schoenrock/plainpicture

caller to take certain actions and make certain changes in his or her personal life. Counselors usually negotiate a *no-suicide contract* with the caller—a promise not to attempt suicide, or at least a promise to reestablish contact if the caller again considers suicide. Although such contracts are popular, their usefulness has been called into question in recent years (Rudd et al., 2006). In addition, if callers are in the midst of a suicide attempt, counselors will try to find out their whereabouts and get medical help to them immediately.

Although crisis intervention may be sufficient treatment for some suicidal people, longer-term therapy is needed for most (Lester et al., 2007; Stolberg et al., 2002). If a

Not just another bridge
This man, one of only 26 people to survive jumping off the Golden Gate Bridge, returns to the site of his suicide attempt—made at the age of 19. The bridge is believed to be the site of more jumping suicides than any other location in the world—with an estimated 1,400 suicides since the bridge opened in 1937.

crisis intervention center does not offer this kind of therapy, its counselors will refer the clients elsewhere.

As the suicide prevention movement spread during the 1960s, many clinicians came to believe that crisis intervention techniques should also be applied to problems other than suicide. Crisis intervention has emerged during the past several decades as a respected form of treatment for such wide-ranging problems as drug and alcohol abuse, rape victimization, and spouse abuse.

Yet another way to help prevent suicide may be to reduce the public's access to common means of suicide (Lester, 2011). In 1960, for example, around 12 of every 100,000 persons in Britain killed themselves by inhaling coal gas (which contains carbon monoxide). In the 1960s Britain replaced coal gas with natural gas (which contains no carbon monoxide) as an energy source, and by the mid-1970s the rate of coal gas suicide fell to zero (Maris, 2001). In fact, England's overall rate of suicide, at least for older people, dropped as well. On the other hand, the Netherlands' drop in gas-induced suicides was compensated for by an increase in other methods, particularly drug overdoses.

Similarly, ever since Canada passed a law in the 1990s restricting the availability of and access to certain firearms, a decrease in firearm suicides has been observed across the country (Leenaars, 2007). Some studies suggest that this decrease has not been displaced by increases in other kinds of suicides; other studies, however, have found an increase in the use of other suicide methods (Caron, Julien, & Huang, 2008). Thus, although many clinicians hope that measures such as gun control, safer medications, better bridge barriers, and car emission controls will lower suicide rates, there is no guarantee that they will.

Do Suicide Prevention Programs Work?

It is difficult for researchers to measure the effectiveness of suicide prevention programs (Lester, 2011). There are many kinds of programs, each with its own procedures and serving populations that vary in number, age, and the like. Communities with high suicide risk factors, such as a high elderly population or economic problems, may continue to have higher suicide rates than other communities regardless of the effectiveness of their local prevention centers.

Do suicide prevention centers reduce the number of suicides in a community? Clinical researchers do not know (Lester, 2011). Studies comparing local suicide rates before and after the establishment of community prevention centers have yielded different findings. Some find a decline in a community's suicide rates, others no change, and still others an increase (De Leo & Evans, 2004; Leenaars & Lester, 2004). Of course, even an increase may represent a positive impact, if it is lower than the larger society's overall increase in suicidal behavior.

Do suicidal people contact prevention centers? Apparently only a small percentage do. Moreover, the typical caller to an urban prevention center appears to be young, African American, and female, whereas the greatest number of suicides are committed by older white men (Maris, 2001; Lester, 2000, 1989, 1972). A key problem is that people who are suicidal do not necessarily admit or talk about their feelings in discussions with others, even with professionals (Stolberg et al., 2002).

Prevention programs do seem to reduce the number of suicides among those high-risk people who do call. One study identified 8,000 high-risk individuals who contacted the Los Angeles Suicide Prevention Center (Farberow & Litman, 1970). Approximately 2 percent of these callers later committed suicide, compared to the 6 percent suicide rate usually found in similar high-risk groups. Clearly, centers need to be more visible and available to people who are thinking of suicide. The growing number of advertisements

BETWEEN THE LINES

Still at Risk

Approximately 4 percent of all suicides are committed by people who are inpatients at mental hospitals or other psychiatric facilities. ‹‹

(Cassells et al., 2005)

AP Photo/PRNewsFoto/Montclair State University, Mike Peters

Raising public awareness
In order to better educate the public about suicide's far reach, many organizations now hold special remembrances. Here the organization Active Minds sponsors an exhibit of 1,100 backpacks at Montclair State University in New Jersey. The backpacks represent the number of college students who die by suicide each year.

and announcements on the web, television, radio, and billboards indicate a movement in this direction (Oliver et al., 2008).

Many theorists have called for more effective public education about suicide as the ultimate form of prevention, and a number of *suicide education programs* have emerged. Most of these programs take place in schools and concentrate on students and their teachers (Mann & Currier, 2011; Van Orden et al., 2008). There are also a growing number of sites online that provide education about suicide—targeting troubled persons, their family members, and friends. These various offerings often differ in content, curriculum, and style of presentation, but they all share the same goal and agree with the following statement by Shneidman:

? Why might some schools be reluctant to offer suicide education programs, especially if they have never experienced a suicide attempt by one of their students?

> The primary prevention of suicide lies in education. The route is through teaching one another and . . . the public that suicide can happen to anyone, that there are verbal and behavioral clues that can be looked for . . . , and that help is available. . . .
>
> In the last analysis, the prevention of suicide is everybody's business.
>
> *(Shneidman, 1985, p. 238)*

PUTTING IT... together

Psychological and Biological Insights Lag Behind

Once a mysterious and hidden problem, hardly acknowledged by the public and barely investigated by professionals, suicide today is the focus of much attention. During the past 40 years in particular, investigators have learned a great deal about this life-or-death problem.

In contrast to most other problems covered in this textbook, suicide has received much more examination from the sociocultural model than from any other. Sociocultural theorists have, for example, highlighted the importance of societal change and

BETWEEN THE LINES

Lethal Weapon
Altogether, 58% of all suicides in the United States are committed with firearms. ‹‹

(Claassen & Knox, 2011)

"Never was a story of more woe . . ."
Two of the most famous suicides in English literature are those of Shakespeare's star-crossed lovers Romeo and Juliet. They each ended their own life when confronted by the perceived death of the other.

stress, national and religious affiliation, marital status, gender, race, and the mass media. The insights and information gathered by psychological and biological researchers have been more limited.

Although sociocultural factors certainly shed light on the general background and triggers of suicide, they typically leave us unable to predict that a given person will attempt suicide. When all is said and done, clinicians do not yet fully understand why some people kill themselves while others in similar circumstances manage to find better ways of addressing their problems. Psychological and biological insights must catch up to the sociocultural insights if clinicians are truly to explain and understand suicide.

Treatments for suicide also pose some difficult problems. Clinicians have yet to develop clearly successful therapies for suicidal persons. Although suicide prevention programs certainly show the clinical field's commitment to helping people who are suicidal, it is not yet clear how much such programs actually reduce the overall risk or rate of suicide.

At the same time, the growth in the amount of research on suicide offers great promise. And perhaps most promising of all, clinicians are now enlisting the public in the fight against this problem. They are calling for broader public education about suicide—for programs aimed at both young and old. It is reasonable to expect that the current commitment will lead to a better understanding of suicide and to more successful interventions. Such goals are of importance to everyone. Although suicide itself is typically a lonely and desperate act, the impact of such acts is very broad indeed.

Summing Up

- **WHAT IS SUICIDE?** *Suicide* is a self-inflicted death in which one makes an intentional, direct, and conscious effort to end one's life. Four kinds of people who intentionally end their lives have been distinguished: the *death seeker,* the *death initiator,* the *death ignorer,* and the *death darer. pp. 286–289*

- **RESEARCH STRATEGIES** Two major strategies are used in the study of suicide: *retrospective analysis* (a psychological autopsy) and the *study of people who survive suicide attempts,* on the assumption that they are similar to those who commit fatal suicides. Each strategy has limitations. *p. 289*

- **PATTERNS AND STATISTICS** Suicide ranks among the top 10 causes of death in Western society. Rates vary from country to country. One reason seems to be cultural differences in *religious affiliation, beliefs,* or *degree of devoutness.* Suicide rates also vary according to *race, gender,* and *marital status. pp. 289–292*

- **FACTORS THAT TRIGGER SUICIDE** Many suicidal acts are triggered by the current events or conditions in a person's life. The acts may be triggered by *recent stressors,* such as loss of a loved one and job loss, or *long-term stressors,* such as serious illness, an abusive environment, and job stress. They may also be preceded by *changes in mood or thought,* particularly increases in one's sense of *hopelessness.* In addition, the *use of alcohol or other kinds of substances, mental disorders,* or *news of another's suicide* may precede suicide attempts. *pp. 292–297*

- **EXPLANATIONS** The leading explanations for suicide come from the psychodynamic, sociocultural, and biological models. Each has received only limited support. *Psychodynamic* theorists believe that suicide usually results from depression and self-directed anger. Emile Durkheim's *sociocultural* theory defines three categories of suicide based on the person's relationship with society: *egoistic, altruistic,* and *anomic* suicides. And *biological* theorists suggest that the activity of the neurotransmitter serotonin is particularly low in individuals who commit suicide. *pp. 297–301*

BETWEEN THE LINES

Deal Breaker

If clients state an intention to commit suicide, therapists may break the doctor-patient confidentiality agreement that usually governs treatment discussions. ‹‹

Paramount/The Kobal Collection

■ **SUICIDE IN DIFFERENT AGE GROUPS** The likelihood of suicide varies with age. It is uncommon among *children,* although it has been increasing in that group during the past several decades.

Suicide by *adolescents* is a more common occurrence than suicide by children, but it has been decreasing over the past decade. Adolescent suicide has been linked to clinical depression, anger, impulsiveness, major stress, and adolescent life itself. *Suicide attempts* by this age group are numerous. The high attempt rate among adolescents and young adults may be related to the growing number and proportion of young people in the general population, the weakening of family ties, the increased availability and use of drugs among the young, and the broad media coverage of suicide attempts by the young. The rate of suicide among American Indian teens is twice as high as that among white American teens and three times as high as the African, Hispanic, and Asian American teen suicide rates.

In Western society the *elderly* are more likely to commit suicide than people in any other age group. The loss of health, friends, control, and status may produce feelings of hopelessness, loneliness, depression, or inevitability in this age group. *pp. 301–308*

■ **TREATMENT AND SUICIDE** Treatment may *follow* a suicide attempt. In such cases, therapists seek to help the person achieve a nonsuicidal state of mind and develop better ways of handling stress and solving problems.

Over the past 50 years, emphasis has shifted to *suicide prevention.* Suicide prevention programs include 24-hour-a-day hot lines and walk-in centers staffed largely by *paraprofessionals.* During their initial contact with a suicidal person, counselors seek to establish a positive relationship, to understand and clarify the problem, to assess the potential for suicide, to assess and mobilize the caller's resources, and to formulate a plan for overcoming the crisis. Beyond such *crisis intervention,* most suicidal people also need *longer-term therapy.* In a still broader attempt at prevention, *suicide education programs* for the public are on the increase. *pp. 309–313*

PsychPortal

Visit **PsychPortal**
www.yourpsychportal.com
to access the e-book, videocases and other case materials and activities, and study aids, including flashcards, crossword puzzles, quizzes, FAQs, and research exercises.

BETWEEN THE LINES

Attitudes Toward Suicide

Hispanic Americans have certain beliefs that may make them less likely to attempt suicide. On average, they hold stronger moral objections to suicide than other groups do, have firmer beliefs about the need to cope and survive, and feel greater responsibility to their families (Oquendo et al., 2005). ‹‹

African Americans consider suicide "less acceptable" than do white Americans. This attitude has been linked to African Americans' higher degrees of orthodox religious belief and personal devotion and to their fear of giving others the power to end one's life (MacDonald, 1998; Neeleman et al., 1998). ‹‹

EATING DISORDERS

CHAPTER 11

Janet Caldwell was ... five feet, two inches tall and weighed 62 pounds.... Janet began dieting at the age of 12 when she weighed 115 pounds and was chided by her family and friends for being "pudgy." She continued to restrict her food intake over a two-year period, and as she grew thinner, her parents became increasingly more concerned about her eating behavior....

Janet ... felt that her weight problem began at the time of puberty. She said that her family and friends had supported her efforts to achieve a ten-pound weight loss when she first began dieting at age 12. Janet did not go on any special kind of diet. Instead, she restricted her food intake at meals, generally cut down on carbohydrates and protein intake, tended to eat a lot of salads, and completely stopped snacking between meals. At first, she was quite pleased with her progressive weight reduction, and she was able to ignore her feelings of hunger by remembering the weight loss goal she had set for herself. However, each time she lost the number of pounds she had set for her goal she decided to lose just a few more pounds. Therefore she continued to set new weight goals for herself. In this manner, her weight dropped from 115 pounds to 88 pounds during the first year of her weight loss regimen.

Janet felt that, in her second year of dieting, her weight loss had continued beyond her control.... She became convinced that there was something inside of her that would not let her gain weight.... Janet commented that although there had been occasions over the past few years when she had been fairly "down" or unhappy, she still felt driven to keep on dieting. As a result, she frequently went for walks, ran errands for her family, and spent a great deal of time cleaning her room and keeping it in a meticulously neat and unaltered arrangement.

When Janet's weight loss continued beyond the first year, her parents insisted that she see their family physician, and Mrs. Caldwell accompanied Janet to her appointment. Their family practitioner was quite alarmed at Janet's appearance and prescribed a high-calorie diet. Janet said that ... she often responded to her parents' entreaties that she eat by telling them that she indeed had eaten but they had not seen her do so. She often listed foods that she said she had consumed which in fact she had flushed down the toilet. She estimated that she only was eating about 300 calories a day.

Leon, 1984, pp. 179–184

It has not always done so, but Western society today equates thinness with health and beauty (see Figure 11-1). In fact, in the United States thinness has become a national obsession. Most of us are as preoccupied with how much we eat as with the taste and nutritional value of our food. Thus it is not surprising that during the past three decades we have also witnessed an increase in two eating disorders that have at their core a morbid fear of gaining weight. Sufferers of *anorexia nervosa,* like Janet Caldwell, are convinced that they need to be extremely thin, and they lose so much weight that they may starve themselves to death. People with *bulimia nervosa* go on frequent eating binges, during which they uncontrollably consume large quantities of food, and then force themselves to vomit or take other extreme steps to keep from gaining weight. A third eating disorder, *binge eating disorder,* in which people display frequent eating binges but not forced vomiting or other such behaviors, also appears to be on the rise. People with this disorder do not fear weight gain to the same degree as those with anorexia nervosa and

Figure 11-1

Undergraduates and body dissatisfaction
According to surveys, undergraduate women in the United States are less satisfied than undergraduate men with their bodies. Normal-weight women are much less satisfied with their bodies than underweight women (Frederick et al., 2007).

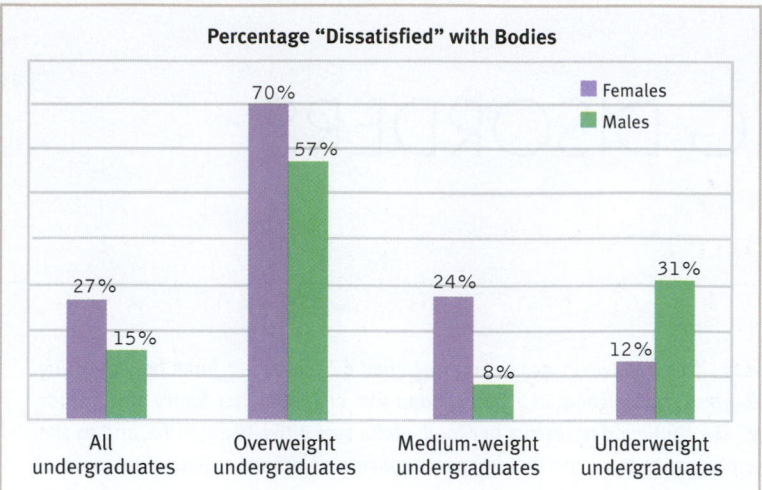

Percentage "Dissatisfied" with Bodies

- Females
- Males

	Females	Males
All undergraduates	27%	15%
Overweight undergraduates	70%	57%
Medium-weight undergraduates	24%	8%
Underweight undergraduates	12%	31%

table: 11-1

DSM-5 Checklist

Anorexia Nervosa

1. Restricted net intake of nourishment, leading to significantly low body weight.

2. Intense fear of gaining weight, even though significantly underweight, or persistent behavior that interferes with weight gain.

3. Disturbed body perception, undue influence of weight or shape on self-evaluation, or persistent denial of the seriousness of the current low weight.

Based on APA, 2013, 2012.

bulimia nervosa, but they do display many of the other features found in those disorders (Claudino & Morgan, 2012).

The news media have published many reports about the eating disorders. One reason for the surge in public interest is the frightening medical consequences that can result. The public first became aware of such consequences in 1983 when Karen Carpenter died from medical problems related to anorexia. Carpenter, the 32-year-old lead singer of the soft-rock brother-and-sister duo The Carpenters, had been enormously successful and was admired by many as a wholesome and healthy model to young women everywhere. Another reason for the current concern is the disproportionate prevalence of anorexia nervosa and bulimia nervosa among adolescent girls and young women.

Are girls and women in Western society destined to struggle with at least some issues of eating and appearance?

Anorexia Nervosa

Janet Caldwell, 14 years old and in the eighth grade, displays many symptoms of **anorexia nervosa** (APA, 2013, 2012). She purposely maintains a significantly low body weight, intensely fears becoming overweight, has a distorted view of her weight and shape, and is excessively influenced by her weight and shape in her self-evaluations (see Table 11-1).

Like Janet, at least half of the people with anorexia nervosa reduce their weight by restricting their intake of food, a pattern called *restricting-type anorexia nervosa*. First they tend to cut out sweets and fattening snacks; then, increasingly, they eliminate other foods. Eventually people with this kind of anorexia nervosa show almost no variability in diet. Others, however, lose weight by forcing themselves to vomit after meals or by abusing laxatives or diuretics, and they may even engage in eating binges, a pattern called *binge-eating/purging-type anorexia nervosa*, which you will read about in more detail in the section on bulimia nervosa.

Approximately 90 to 95 percent of all cases of anorexia nervosa occur in females. Although the disorder can appear at any age, the peak age of onset is between 14 and 18 years. Between 0.5 and 3.5 percent of all females in Western countries develop the disorder in their lifetime, and many more display at least some of its symptoms (Touchette et al., 2011; Crow, 2010). It seems to be on the increase in North America, Europe, and Japan.

Typically the disorder begins after a person who is slightly overweight or of normal weight has been on a diet (Stice & Presnell, 2010). The escalation toward anorexia nervosa may follow a stressful event such as separation of parents, a move away from home, or an experience of personal failure (Wilson et al., 2003). Although most victims recover, between 2 and 6 percent of them become so seriously ill that they die, usually from medical problems brought about by starvation or from suicide (Forcano et al., 2010).

The Clinical Picture

Becoming thin is the key goal for people with anorexia nervosa, but *fear* provides their motivation. People with this disorder are afraid of becoming obese, of giving in to their growing desire to eat, and more generally of losing control over the size and shape of their bodies. In addition, despite their focus on thinness and the severe restrictions they may place on their food intake, people with anorexia are *preoccupied with food*. They may spend considerable time thinking and even reading about food and planning their limited meals (Herzig, 2004). Many report that their dreams are filled with images of food and eating (Knudson, 2006).

This preoccupation with food may in fact be a result of food deprivation rather than its cause. In a famous "starvation study" conducted in the late 1940s, 36 normal-weight conscientious objectors were put on a semistarvation diet for six months (Keys et al., 1950). Like people with anorexia nervosa, the volunteers became preoccupied with food and eating. They spent hours each day planning their small meals, talked more about food than about any other topic, studied cookbooks and recipes, mixed food in odd combinations, and dawdled over their meals. Many also had vivid dreams about food.

Persons with anorexia nervosa also *think in distorted ways*. They usually have a low opinion of their body shape, for example, and consider themselves unattractive (Siep et al., 2011; Paxton & McLean, 2010). In addition, they are likely to overestimate their actual proportions. While most women in Western society overestimate their body size, the estimates of those with anorexia nervosa are particularly high. A 23-year-old patient said:

> I look in a full-length mirror at least four or five times daily and I really cannot see myself as too thin. Sometimes after several days of strict dieting, I feel that my shape is tolerable, but most of the time, odd as it may seem, I look in the mirror and believe that I am too fat.
>
> *(Bruch, 1973)*

This tendency to overestimate body size has been tested in the laboratory (Delinsky, 2011; Farrell, Lee, & Shafran, 2005). In a popular assessment technique, research participants look at a photograph of themselves through an adjustable lens. They are asked to adjust the lens until the image that they see matches their actual body size. The image can be made to vary from 20 percent thinner to 20 percent larger than actual appearance. In one study, more than half of the individuals with anorexia nervosa were found to overestimate their body size, stopping the lens when the image was larger than they actually were.

The distorted thinking of anorexia nervosa also takes the form of certain maladaptive attitudes and misperceptions (Fairburn et al., 2008). Sufferers tend to hold such beliefs as "I must be perfect in every way"; "I will become a better person if I deprive myself"; and "I can avoid guilt by not eating."

People with anorexia nervosa also display certain *psychological problems,* such as depression, anxiety, low self-esteem, and insomnia or other sleep disturbances (Halmi, 2010; Vögele & Gibson, 2010). A number grapple with substance abuse (Steiger & Israel, 2010). And many display obsessive-compulsive patterns (Friederich & Herzog, 2011; Lilenfeld, 2011). They may set rigid rules for food preparation or even cut food into specific shapes. Broader obsessive-compulsive patterns are common as well. Many,

Laboratory starvation

Thirty-six conscientious objectors who were put on a semistarvation diet for six months developed many of the symptoms seen in anorexia nervosa and bulimia nervosa (Keys et al., 1950).

Seeing is deceiving

In one research technique, people look at photographs of themselves through a special lens and adjust the lens until they see what they believe is their actual image. A research participant may change her actual image (left) from 20 percent thinner (middle) to 20 percent larger (right).

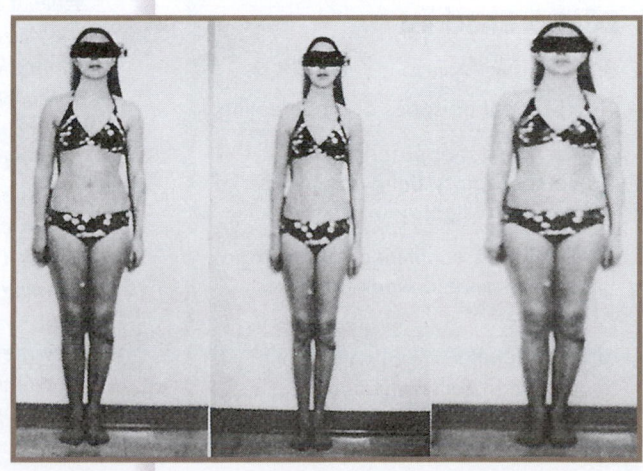

Turning point When soft-rock star Karen Carpenter (right) received an award from fellow musician Emmylou Harris at the 1977 Billboard Music Awards, few people paid much attention to her symptoms of anorexia nervosa. Carpenter's 1983 death helped change the public's view of this disorder.

table: **11-2**

DSM-5 Checklist

Bulimia Nervosa

1. Recurrent episodes of binge eating.

2. Recurrent inappropriate compensatory behavior in order to prevent weight gain.

3. Symptoms continuing, on average, at least once a week for three months.

4. Undue influence of weight or shape on self-evaluation.

Based on APA, 2013, 2012.

for example, exercise compulsively, giving this activity higher priority than most other activities in their lives (Fairburn et al., 2008). In some research, people with anorexia nervosa and others with obsessive–compulsive disorder score equally high for obsessiveness and compulsiveness. Finally, persons with anorexia nervosa tend to be perfectionistic, a characteristic that typically precedes the onset of the disorder (Lilenfeld, 2011).

Medical Problems

The starvation habits of anorexia nervosa cause medical problems (Birmingham, 2012; Mitchell & Crow, 2010). Women develop **amenorrhea,** the absence of menstrual cycles. Other problems include lowered body temperature, low blood pressure, body swelling, reduced bone mineral density, and slow heart rate. Metabolic and electrolyte imbalances also may occur and can lead to death by heart failure or circulatory collapse. The poor nutrition of people with anorexia nervosa may also cause skin to become rough, dry, and cracked; nails to become brittle; and hands and feet to be cold and blue. Some people lose hair from the scalp, and some grow lanugo (the fine, silky hair that covers some newborns) on their trunk, extremities, and face.

Bulimia Nervosa

People with **bulimia nervosa**—a disorder also known as **binge–purge syndrome**—engage in repeated episodes of uncontrollable overeating, or **binges.** A binge occurs over a limited period of time, often two hours, during which the person eats much more food than most people would eat during a similar time span (APA, 2013, 2012; Stewart & Williamson, 2008). In addition, people with this disorder repeatedly perform inappropriate *compensatory behaviors,* such as forcing themselves to vomit; misusing laxatives, diuretics, or enemas; fasting; or exercising excessively (see Table 11-2). A married woman, since recovered, describes a morning during her disorder:

Today I am going to be really good and that means eating certain predetermined portions of food and not taking one more bite than I think I am allowed. I am very careful to see that I don't take more than Doug does. I judge by his body. I can feel the tension building. I wish Doug would hurry up and leave so I can get going!

As soon as he shuts the door, I try to get involved with one of the myriad of responsibilities on the list. I hate them all! I just want to crawl into a hole. I don't want to do anything. I'd rather eat. I am alone, I am nervous, I am no good, I always do everything wrong anyway, I am not in control, I can't make it through the day, I just know it. It has been the same for so long.

I remember the starchy cereal I ate for breakfast. I am into the bathroom and onto the scale. It measures the same, BUT I DON'T WANT TO STAY THE SAME! I want to be thinner! I look in the mirror, I think my thighs are ugly and deformed looking. I see a lumpy, clumsy, pear-shaped wimp. There is always something wrong with what I see. I feel frustrated trapped in this body and I don't know what to do about it.

I float to the refrigerator knowing exactly what is there. I begin with last night's brownies. I always begin with the sweets. At first I try to make it look like nothing is missing, but my appetite is huge and I resolve to make another batch of brownies. I know there is half of a bag of cookies in the bathroom, thrown out the night before, and I polish them off immediately. I take some milk so my vomiting will be smoother. I like the full feeling I get after downing a big glass. I get out six pieces of bread and toast one side in the broiler, turn them over and load them with patties of butter and put them under the broiler again till they are bubbling. I take all six pieces on a plate to the television and go back for a bowl of cereal and a banana to have along with them. Before the last toast is finished, I am already preparing the next batch of six more pieces. Maybe another brownie or five, and a couple of large bowlfuls of ice cream, yogurt or cottage cheese. My stomach is stretched into a huge ball below my ribcage. I know I'll have to go into the bathroom soon, but I want to postpone it. I am in never-never land. I am waiting, feeling the pressure, pacing the floor in and out of the rooms. Time is passing. Time is passing. It is getting to be time.

I wander aimlessly through each of the rooms again tidying, making the whole house neat and put back together. I finally make the turn into the bathroom. I brace my feet, pull my hair back and stick my finger down my throat, stroking twice, and get up a huge pile of food. Three times, four and another pile of food. I can see everything come back. I am glad to see those brownies because they are SO fattening. The rhythm of the emptying is broken and my head is beginning to hurt. I stand up feeling dizzy, empty and weak. The whole episode has taken about an hour.

(Hall, 1980, pp. 5–6)

Like anorexia nervosa, bulimia nervosa usually occurs in females, again in 90 to 95 percent of the cases (Sanftner & Tantillo, 2011). It begins in adolescence or young adulthood (most often between 15 and 21 years of age) and often lasts for several years, with periodic letup. The weight of people with bulimia nervosa usually stays within a normal range, although it may fluctuate markedly within that range. Some people with this disorder, however, become seriously underweight and may eventually qualify for a diagnosis of anorexia nervosa instead (see Figure 11-2).

Many teenagers and young adults go on occasional eating binges or experiment with vomiting or laxatives after they hear about these behaviors from their friends or the media. Indeed, according to global studies, 25 to 50 percent of students report periodic binge eating or self-induced vomiting (Zerbe, 2008; McDermott & Jaffa, 2005). Only some of these individuals, however, qualify for a diagnosis of bulimia nervosa. Surveys in several Western countries suggest that as many as 5 percent of women develop the full syndrome (Touchette et al., 2011; Crow, 2010). Among college students the rate may be much higher (Zerbe, 2008).

Binges

People with bulimia nervosa may have between 1 and 30 binge episodes per week (Fairburn et al., 2008). In most cases, the binges are carried out in secret. The person eats massive amounts of food very rapidly, with minimal chewing—usually sweet, high-calorie foods with a soft texture, such as ice cream, cookies, doughnuts, and sandwiches.

•**amenorrhea**•The cessation of menstrual cycles.

•**bulimia nervosa**•A disorder marked by frequent eating binges that are followed by forced vomiting or other extreme compensatory behaviors to avoid gaining weight. Also known as *binge-purge syndrome*.

•**binge**•An episode of uncontrollable eating during which a person ingests a very large quantity of food.

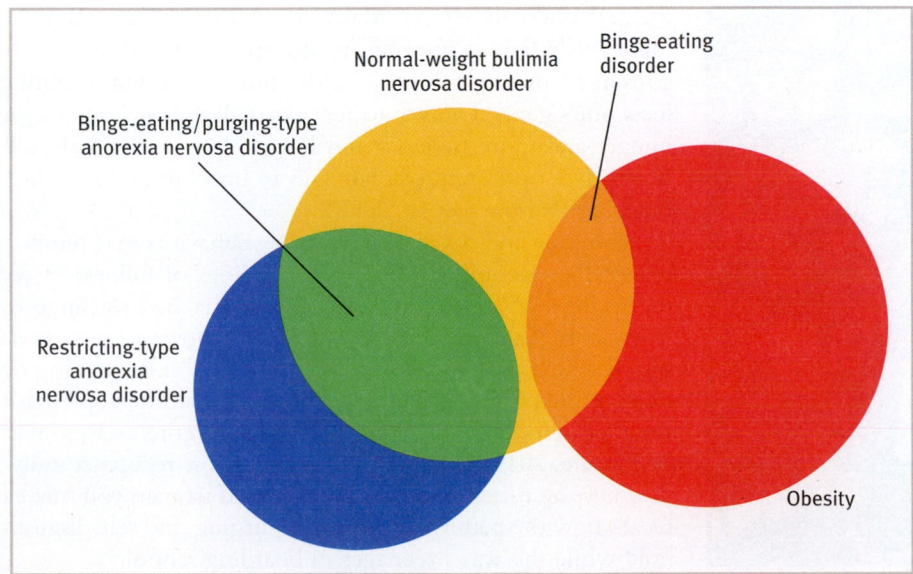

Figure 11-2
Overlapping patterns of anorexia nervosa, bulimia nervosa, and obesity
Some people with anorexia nervosa binge and purge their way to weight loss, and some obese persons binge-eat. However, most people with bulimia nervosa are not obese, and most overweight people do not binge-eat.

BETWEEN THE LINES

The Diet Business

Americans spend an estimated $40 billion each year on weight-reduction foods, products, and services (Tucker, 2010). ‹‹

Eating for sport

Many people go on occasional eating binges. In fact, sometimes binges are officially endorsed, as you see in this photo from the annual Nathan's Famous International Hot Dog Eating Contest at Brooklyn's Coney Island, New York. However, individuals are considered to have an eating disorder only when the binges recur, the pattern endures, and the issues of weight or shape dominate self-evaluation.

The food is hardly tasted or thought about. Binge-eaters commonly consume as many as 10,000 calories during an episode.

Binges are usually preceded by feelings of great tension. The person feels irritable, "unreal," and powerless to control an overwhelming need to eat "forbidden" foods. During the binge, the person feels unable to stop eating (APA, 2013, 2012). Although the binge itself may be experienced as pleasurable in the sense that it relieves the unbearable tension, it is followed by feelings of extreme self-blame, shame, guilt, and depression, as well as fears of gaining weight and being discovered (Sanftner & Tantillo, 2011; Goss & Allan, 2009). Such feelings are described by this public relations executive:

Here I had everything society tells us should make us happy: success, money, access, but not one thing in my life gave me pleasure. In the middle of all of this action and all of these people, I felt like I was in solitary confinement. And I began to cope with these feelings of emptiness and dread by numbing the pain with food—the only thing I looked forward to after a sixteen-hour day. On the way home, I would pick up snack foods, ice cream, party mix, cheese . . . mix them with leftovers from restaurant dinners, and eat until I was beyond full. But my hunger increased week by week, until every half hour I would get out of bed and go to the refrigerator for a snack. I was gaining weight; the more weight I gained the more disgust I felt; the more self-disgust I felt the more I wanted to hide from the pain by eating and sleeping. Like every drug, the food gave me less relief each day, but I clung to it. It was the only thing in my life that could soothe me—the only crutch I had to help me limp around my intolerable feelings. But what started as a source of comfort became another prison.

The saddest thing about all this is that I was able to go so long without anyone really noticing or at least feeling like they could say something. Every shred of energy I could muster after a night of sleep interrupted by binge eating went into servicing my clients and doing my superwoman act: competent, together, single woman making it on willpower alone; I was the poster girl for ambition and achievement, the Strong Black Woman. Strangely, sadly, the façade held up. As far as my colleagues and clients were concerned, the work got done and got done well.

(Williams, 2008, p. xxiii)

Compensatory Behaviors

After a binge, people with bulimia nervosa try to compensate for and undo its effects. Many resort to vomiting. But vomiting actually fails to prevent the absorption of half of the calories consumed during a binge. Furthermore, repeated vomiting affects one's general ability to feel satiated; thus it leads to greater hunger and more frequent and intense binges. Similarly, the use of laxatives or diuretics largely fails to undo the caloric effects of bingeing (Fairburn et al., 2008).

Vomiting and other compensatory behaviors may temporarily relieve the uncomfortable physical feelings of fullness or reduce the feelings of anxiety and self-disgust attached to binge eating (Stewart & Williamson, 2008). Over time, however, a cycle develops in which purging allows more bingeing, and bingeing necessitates more purging. The cycle eventually causes people with this disorder to feel powerless and disgusted with themselves (Sanftner & Tantillo, 2011; Hayaki et al., 2002). Most recognize fully that they have an eating disorder. The married woman you met earlier recalls how the pattern of bingeing, purging, and self-disgust took hold while she was a teenager in boarding school:

Every bite that went into my mouth was a naughty and selfish indulgence, and I became more and more disgusted with myself. . . .

The first time I stuck my fingers down my throat was during the last week of school. I saw a girl come out of the bathroom with her face all red and her eyes puffy. She had always talked about her weight and how she should be dieting even though her body was really shapely. I knew instantly what she had just done and I had to try it. . . .

I began with breakfasts which were served buffet-style on the main floor of the dorm. I learned which foods I could eat that would come back up easily. When I woke in the morning, I had to make the decision whether to stuff myself for half an hour and throw up before class, or whether to try and make it through the whole day without overeating. . . . I always thought people noticed when I took huge portions at mealtimes, but I figured they assumed that because I was an athlete, I burned it off. . . . Once a binge was under way, I did not stop until my stomach looked pregnant and I felt like I could not swallow one more time.

That year was the first of my nine years of obsessive eating and throwing up. . . . I didn't want to tell anyone what I was doing, and I didn't want to stop. . . . [Though] being in love or other distractions occasionally lessened the cravings, I always returned to the food.

(Hall, 1980, pp. 9–12)

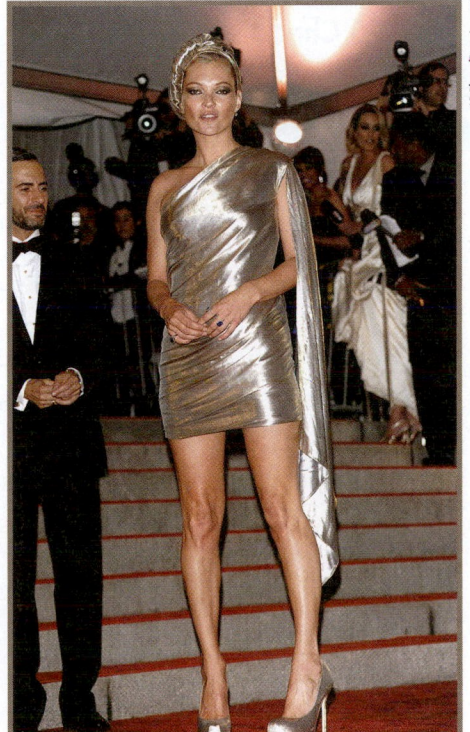

Wrong message
Supermodel Kate Moss arrives at a New York City fashion gala. Asked during a 2009 Web site interview whether she had any life mottos, Moss set off a firestorm by replying, "Nothing tastes as good as skinny feels." Noting that this phrase often appears on pro-anorexia Web sites, many critics accused the model of giving legitimacy to the pro-Ana movement. Moss countered that her answer had been misrepresented and clarified that she does not support self-starvation as a life-style choice.

As with anorexia nervosa, a bulimic pattern typically begins during or after a period of intense dieting, often one that has been successful and earned praise from family members and friends (Stice & Pressnell, 2010; Couturier & Lock, 2006). Studies of both animals and humans have found that normal research participants placed on very strict diets also develop a tendency to binge (Pankevich et al., 2010; Eifert et al., 2007). Some of the participants in the conscientious objector "starvation study," for example, later binged when they were allowed to return to regular eating, and a number of them continued to be hungry even after large meals (Keys et al., 1950).

Bulimia Nervosa Versus Anorexia Nervosa

Bulimia nervosa is similar to anorexia nervosa in many ways. Both disorders typically begin after a period of dieting by people who are fearful of becoming obese; driven to become thin; preoccupied with food, weight, and appearance; and struggling with depression, anxiety, obsessiveness, and the need to be perfect (Friederich & Herzog, 2011; Halmi, 2010). Individuals with either of the disorders have a heightened risk of attempts at suicide (Keel & McCormick, 2010; Pompili et al., 2007). Substance abuse may accompany either disorder, perhaps beginning with the excessive use of diet pills (Steiger & Israel, 2010). People with either disorder believe that they weigh too much and look too heavy regardless of their actual weight or appearance (Delinsky, 2011; Siep et al., 2011). And both disorders are marked by disturbed attitudes toward eating.

Yet the two disorders also differ in important ways. Although people with either disorder worry about the opinions of others, those with bulimia nervosa tend to be more concerned about pleasing others, being attractive to others, and having intimate relationships (Zerbe, 2010, 2008; Eddy et al., 2004). They also tend to be more sexually experienced and active than people with anorexia nervosa. Particularly troublesome, they are more likely to have long histories of mood swings, become easily frustrated or bored, and have trouble coping effectively or controlling their impulses and strong emotions (Lilenfeld, 2011; Halmi, 2010). More than one-third of them display the characteristics of a personality disorder, particularly borderline personality disorder, which you will be looking at more closely in Chapter 16 (Rowe et al., 2011, 2010).

Another difference is the nature of the medical complications that accompany the two disorders (Birmingham, 2011; Mitchell & Crow, 2010). Only half of women with bulimia nervosa are amenorrheic or have very irregular menstrual periods, compared to almost all of those with anorexia nervosa. On the other hand, repeated vomiting bathes teeth and gums in hydrochloric acid, leading some women with bulimia nervosa to experience serious dental problems, such as breakdown of enamel and even loss of teeth. Moreover, frequent vomiting or chronic diarrhea (from the use of laxatives) can cause dangerous potassium deficiencies, which may lead to weakness, intestinal disorders, kidney disease, or heart damage (see *MediaSpeak* on the next page).

Binge Eating Disorder

Like those who display bulimia nervosa, individuals with **binge eating disorder** engage in repeated eating binges during which they feel no control over their eating (APA, 2013, 2012). However, these individuals do *not* perform inappropriate compensatory behavior (see Table 11-3). As a result of their frequent binges, around two-thirds of people with binge eating disorder become overweight or even obese (Claudino & Morgan, 2012).

Binge eating disorder was first recognized more than 50 years ago as a pattern common among many overweight people (Stunkard, 1959). It is important to recognize, however, that most overweight persons do not engage in repeated binges; their weight results from frequent overeating and/or a combination of biological, psychological, and sociocultural factors (Claudino & Morgan 2012).

Between 2 and 7 percent of the population display binge eating disorder (Dove & Byne, 2011; Hudson et al., 2007). The binges that characterize this pattern are similar to those seen in bulimia nervosa, particularly the amount of food eaten and the sense of loss of control experienced during the binge. Moreover, like people with bulimia nervosa or anorexia nervosa, those with binge eating disorder typically are preoccupied with food, weight, and appearance; base their evaluation of themselves largely on their weight and shape; misperceive their body size and experience extreme body dissatisfaction; struggle with feelings of depression, anxiety, and perfectionism; may display substance abuse; and typically first develop the disorder in adolescence (Durso et al., 2012; Grilo et al., 2012; Zeeck et al., 2011). On the other hand, although these individuals aspire to limit their eating, they are not as driven to thinness as those with anorexia nervosa and bulimia nervosa. Also, unlike the other eating disorders, binge eating disorder does not necessarily begin with efforts at extreme dieting. Nor are there large gender differences in the prevalence of binge eating disorder (Grucza et al., 2007).

What Causes Eating Disorders?

Most of today's theorists and researchers use a **multidimensional risk perspective** to explain eating disorders. That is, they identify several key factors that place individuals at risk for these disorders (Jacobi & Fittig, 2010). The more of these factors that are present, the greater the likelihood that a person will develop an eating disorder. The factors cited most often include psychological, biological, and sociocultural ones. As you will see, most of the factors that have been cited and investigated center on anorexia nervosa and bulimia nervosa. Binge eating disorder, identified as a clinical syndrome more recently, is only now receiving broad investigation. Which of these factors are also at work in this "newer" disorder will probably become clearer in the coming years.

Psychodynamic Factors: Ego Deficiencies

Hilde Bruch, a pioneer in the study and treatment of eating disorders, developed a largely psychodynamic theory of the disorders. She argued that disturbed mother–child interactions lead to serious *ego deficiencies* in the child (including a poor sense of independence and control) and to severe *perceptual disturbances* that jointly help produce disordered eating (Bruch, 2001, 1991, 1962).

table: **11-3**

DSM-5 Checklist

Binge Eating Disorder

1. Recurrent episodes of binge eating.

2. Binge eating episodes are associated with 3 or more of the following: • Unusually rapid eating • Eating large amounts without physical hunger • Eating until uncomfortably full • Eating alone because of embarrassment • Feelings of self-disgust, depression, or severe guilt after episodes.

3. Significant distress regarding binge eating.

4. Binge eating occurs, on average, at least once a week for 3 months.

5. No pattern of inappropriate compensatory behavior

MediaSpeak

A Mother's Loss, a Daughter's Story

By Robin Pogrebin, *New York Times*

Andrew Avrin sits on a beige couch . . . while, off-camera, an unseen interviewer prompts him to talk about his sister, Melissa, who died last year at the age of 19 after a long battle with bulimia.

"There was no food in the house," he says, looking off to the side as his eyes fill. "If I went out with friends, I could not bring leftovers home because they would be gone by the next morning."

Once, he explains, in the middle of a bitterly cold night, he looked out the window and saw Melissa on the curb, going through the garbage. "I went outside and I yelled her name," he recounts in the interview, his voice breaking. "Just the way she looked back at me—it was so empty, vacant. It was a deer in the headlights, but that doesn't even explain it."

It is a hard scene for anyone to watch, but even more so for the film's producer—Judy Avrin, Melissa's mother, who decided to make a documentary about her daughter's life and, ultimately, her death. . . .

The film, called "Someday Melissa" . . . has become for Ms. Avrin salve, distraction and cause—a way to get the word out to other families grappling with eating disorders that they are not alone. . . .

Melissa died on May 6, 2009. Cause of death: heart attack due to complications from an eating disorder. Just a few days before, Melissa learned she had been admitted to Emerson College. The official letter of acceptance arrived a week after she died and sits unopened. . . .

Born Dec. 21, 1989, Melissa seemed in her early years to be a happy little girl. . . . Melissa did well in school—producing A's and short stories. . . . But at age 13, things started to change. Melissa's mood darkened; she didn't want to go to school or do extracurricular activities. She developed stomach problems and constipation. . . . In the early stages, the Avrins did not really see what was going on, in part because Melissa wasn't visibly under-

Courtesy of Judy Avrin

Losing battle Melissa Avrin is seen here with her mother, Judy, during better times. Judy Avrin's documentary, "Someday Melissa" (see also www .somedaymelissa.com), chronicles her daughter's struggles against bulimia nervosa.

weight, in part because they didn't want to. But clues started to show up that were too stark to ignore—logs of cookie dough that disappeared from the freezer along with whole boxes of cookies from the cabinet. Empty pizza boxes. "I found containers with chewed and spit-out food and I'd never heard of that before," Ms. Avrin tells Dr. Sanders during their filmed interview. . . .

Eventually, Melissa was sent away for professional help against her will. . . . It wasn't until Melissa's third round of in-patient treatment—when she and other young women testified about their eating disorders in front of their families—that her father began to fully understand. "I really said, 'Wow this is almost like heroin addiction,'" he says in his film interview. "They need to purge because it makes them feel high and it's something they need to do. I never appreciated that." . . .

Published April 21, 2010. © The New York Times Company. Reprinted with permission.

According to Bruch, parents may respond to their children either effectively or ineffectively. *Effective parents* accurately attend to their children's biological and emotional needs, giving them food when they are crying from hunger and comfort when they are crying out of fear. *Ineffective parents,* by contrast, fail to attend to their children's needs, deciding that their children are hungry, cold, or tired without correctly interpreting the children's actual condition. They may feed the children at times of anxiety rather than hunger or comfort them at times of tiredness rather than anxiety. Children who receive such parenting may grow up confused and unaware of their own internal needs, not knowing for themselves when they are hungry or full and unable to identify their own emotions.

Because they cannot rely on internal signals, these children turn instead to external guides, such as their parents. They seem to be "model children," but they fail to develop genuine self-reliance and "experience themselves as not being in control of their behavior, needs, and impulses, as not owning their own bodies" (Bruch, 1973, p. 55). Adolescence increases their basic desire to establish independence, yet they feel unable

•binge eating disorder• A disorder marked by frequent binges but not extreme compensatory behaviors.

•multidimensional risk perspective• A theory that identifies several kinds of risk factors that are thought to combine to help cause a disorder. The more factors present, the greater the risk of developing the disorder.

to do so. To overcome their sense of helplessness, they seek excessive control over their body size and shape and over their eating habits. Helen, an 18-year-old, describes her experience:

> There is a peculiar contradiction—everybody thinks you're doing so well and everybody thinks you're great, but your real problem is that you think that you are not good enough. You are afraid of not living up to what you think you are expected to do. You have one great fear, namely that of being ordinary, or average, or common—just not good enough. This peculiar dieting begins with such anxiety. You want to prove that you have control, that you can do it. The peculiar part of it is that it makes you feel good about yourself, makes you feel "I can accomplish something." It makes you feel "I can do something nobody else can do."
>
> *(Bruch, 1978, p. 128)*

Clinical reports and research have provided some support for Bruch's theory (Schultz & Laessle, 2012; Zerbe, 2010; Eifert et al., 2007). Clinicians have observed that the parents of teenagers with eating disorders do tend to define their children's needs rather than allow the children to define their own needs (Ihle et al., 2005; Steiner et al., 1991). When Bruch interviewed the mothers of 51 children with anorexia nervosa, many proudly recalled that they had always "anticipated" their young child's needs, never permitting the child to "feel hungry" (Bruch, 1973).

Research has also supported Bruch's belief that people with eating disorders perceive internal cues, including emotional cues, inaccurately (Siep et al., 2011; Fairburn et al., 2008). When research participants with an eating disorder are anxious or upset, for example, many of them mistakenly think they are also hungry (see Figure 11-3), and they respond as they might respond to hunger—by eating. In fact, people with eating disorders are often described by clinicians as *alexithymic*, meaning they have great difficulty putting descriptive labels on their feelings (Zerbe, 2010, 2008). And finally, studies support Bruch's argument that people with eating disorders rely excessively on the opinions, wishes, and views of others. They are more likely than other people to worry about how others view them, to seek approval, to be conforming, and to feel a lack of control over their lives (Amianto et al., 2011; Travis & Meltzer, 2008).

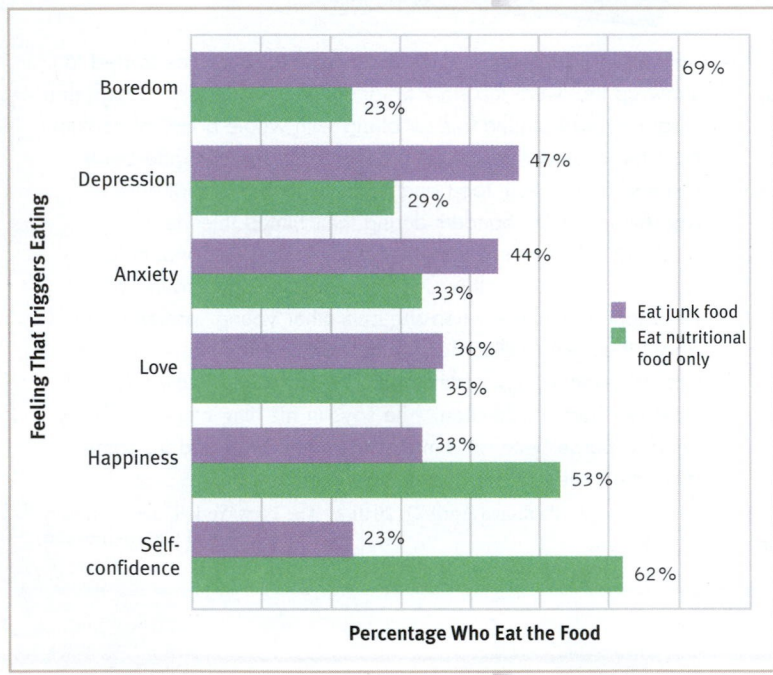

Figure 11-3

When do people seek junk food? Apparently, when they feel bad (Haberman, 2007; Hudd et al., 2000). People who eat junk food when they are feeling bad outnumber those who eat nutritional food under similar circumstances. In contrast, more people seek nutritional food when they are feeling good (Rowan, 2005; Lyman, 1982).

Cognitive Factors

If you look closely at Bruch's explanation of eating disorders, you'll see that it contains several *cognitive* features. She held, for example, that as a result of ineffective parenting, victims of eating disorders improperly label their internal sensations and needs, generally feel little control over their lives, and, in turn, desire excessive control over their body size, shape, and eating habits. According to cognitive theorists, these deficiencies contribute to a broad cognitive distortion that lies at the center of disordered eating, namely, people with anorexia nervosa and bulimia nervosa judge themselves—often exclusively—based on their shape and weight and their ability to control them (Murphy et al.,

How might you explain the finding that eating disorders tend to be less common in cultures that restrict a woman's freedom to make decisions about her life?

2010; Fairburn et al., 2008). This "core pathology," say cognitive theorists, gives rise to all other features of the disorders, including the individuals' repeated efforts to lose weight and their preoccupation with thoughts about shape, weight, and eating.

As you saw earlier in the chapter, research indicates that people with eating disorders do indeed display such cognitive deficiencies (Siep et al., 2011; Eifert et al., 2007). Although studies have not clarified that such deficiencies are the *cause* of eating disorders, many cognitive-behavioral therapists proceed from this assumption and center their treatment for the disorders on correcting the clients' cognitive distortions and their accompanying behaviors. As you'll soon see, cognitive-behavioral therapies of this kind are among the most widely used of all treatments for eating disorders (Fairburn et al., 2008).

Depression

Many people with eating disorders, particularly those with bulimia nervosa, experience symptoms of depression (Vögele & Gibson, 2010). This finding has led some theorists to suggest that depressive disorders set the stage for eating disorders.

Their claim is supported by four kinds of evidence. First, many more people with an eating disorder qualify for a clinical diagnosis of major depressive disorder than do people in the general population. Second, the close relatives of people with eating disorders seem to have a higher rate of depressive disorders than do close relatives of people without such disorders. Third, as you will soon see, many people with eating disorders, particularly bulimia nervosa, have low activity of the neurotransmitter serotonin, similar to the serotonin abnormalities found in people with depression. And finally, people with eating disorders are often helped by some of the same antidepressant drugs that reduce depression. Of course, although such findings suggest that depression may help cause eating disorders, other explanations are possible. For example, the pressure and pain of having an eating disorder may *cause* depression.

Biological Factors

Biological theorists suspect that certain genes may leave some persons particularly susceptible to eating disorders (Helder & Collier, 2011; Racine et al., 2011). Consistent with this idea, relatives of people with eating disorders are up to six times more likely than other individuals to develop the disorders themselves (Thornton et al., 2011; Strober et al., 2001, 2000). Moreover, if one identical twin has anorexia nervosa, the other twin also develops the disorder in as many as 70 percent of cases; in contrast, the rate for fraternal twins, who are genetically less similar, is 20 percent. Similarly, in the case of bulimia nervosa, identical twins display a concordance rate of 23 percent, compared to a rate of 9 percent among fraternal twins (Thornton et al., 2011; Kendler et al., 1995, 1991).

One factor that has interested investigators is the possible role of *serotonin*. Several research teams have found a link between eating disorders and the genes responsible for the production of this neurotransmitter, and still others have measured low serotonin activity in many people with eating disorders (Bailer & Kaye, 2011; Kaye, 2011). Given serotonin's role in depression and obsessive-compulsive disorder—problems that often accompany eating disorders—it is possible that low serotonin activity has more to do with those other disorders than with the eating disorders per se. On the other hand, perhaps low serotonin activity contributes directly to eating disorders—for example, by causing the body to crave and binge on high-carbohydrate foods (Kaye et al., 2012, 2011, 2005, 2002, 2000).

Other biological researchers explain eating disorders by pointing to the **hypothalamus**, a part of the brain that regulates many bodily functions (Fetissov & Mequid, 2010; Higgins & George, 2007). Researchers have located two separate areas in the hypothalamus that help control eating. One, the **lateral hypothalamus (LH)**, consisting of the side areas of the hypothalamus, produces hunger when it is activated. When the

•hypothalamus• A part of the brain that helps regulate various bodily functions, including eating and hunger.

•lateral hypothalamus (LH)• A brain region that produces hunger when activated.

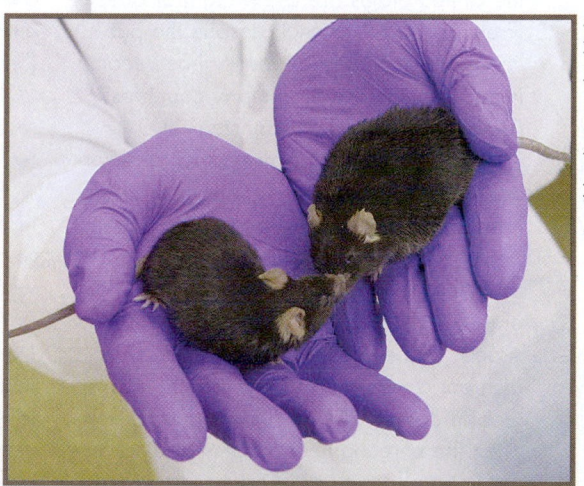

Penni Gladstone/San Francisco Chronicle/Corbis

Laboratory obesity
Biological theorists believe that certain genes leave some individuals particularly susceptible to eating disorders. To help support this view, researchers have created mutant ("knockout") mice—mice without certain genes. The mouse on the left is missing a gene that helps produce obesity, and it is thin. In contrast, the mouse on the right, which retains that gene, is indeed obese.

LH of a laboratory animal is stimulated electrically, the animal eats, even if it has been fed recently. In contrast, another area, the **ventromedial hypothalamus (VMH),** consisting of the bottom and middle of the hypothalamus, reduces hunger when it is activated. When the VMH is electrically stimulated, laboratory animals stop eating (see *PsychWatch* below).

These areas of the hypothalamus and related brain structures are apparently activated by chemicals from the brain and body, depending on whether the person is eating or fasting (Petrovich, 2011; Zerbe, 2008). Two such brain chemicals are the natural appetite suppressants *cholecystokinin* (*CCK*) and *glucagon-like peptide-1* (*GLP-1*) (Higgins & George, 2007; Turton et al., 1996). When one team of researchers collected and injected GLP-1 into the brains of rats, the chemical traveled to receptors in the hypothalamus and caused the rats to reduce their food intake almost entirely even though they had not eaten for 24 hours. Conversely, when "full" rats were injected with a substance that

PsychWatch

Obesity: To Lose or Not to Lose

Body-mass index (*BMI*) is a formula used to indicate whether a person's weight is appropriate for his or her height. It is calculated as the person's weight (in kilograms) divided by the square of his or her height (in meters). According to the World Health Organization, people whose BMI is above 25 are overweight; those with a BMI above 30 are considered obese. By such standards, one-third of adults in the United States are overweight or obese (Freking, 2007). In fact, despite the public's focus on thinness, obesity has become increasingly common in many countries (Dove & Byrne, 2011; Johnston, 2004).

Being overweight is not a mental disorder, nor in most cases is it the result of abnormal psychological processes (Mitchell et al., 2008). Nevertheless, it causes great anguish, and not just because of its physical effects. The media, people on the streets, and even many health professionals treat obesity as shameful (Rich, 2011; Goode & Vail, 2008). Obese people are often the unrecognized victims of discrimination in efforts to gain admission to college, obtain jobs, and receive promotions (Grilo, 2006).

Mounting evidence indicates that overweight persons are not to be sneered at as lacking in self-control and that obesity results from multiple factors (Dove & Byrne, 2011). First, genetic and biological factors seem to play large roles (Levin, 2010). Researchers have found that children of

obese biological parents are more likely to be obese than children whose biological parents are not obese, whether or not they are raised by obese parents (Higgins & George, 2007). Other researchers have identified several genes that seem to be linked to obesity (Helder & Collier, 2011; Stice et al., 2011). And still others have identified chemicals in the body, including the hormone *leptin* and the protein *glucagon-like peptide-1* (*GLP-1*), that apparently act as natural appetite suppressants (Stice et al., 2011; Figlewicz & Sipols, 2010). Suspicion is growing that the brain receptors for these chemicals may be defective in overweight persons.

Environment also plays a causal role in obesity (Petrovich, 2011; Levin, 2010). Studies have shown that people eat more when they are in the company of others, particularly if the other people are eating (Johnston & Tyler, 2008; Logue, 1991). In addition, research finds that people in low socioeconomic environments are more likely to be obese than those of high socioeconomic backgrounds (Martin et al., 2008; Benedict et al., 2007).

Health Risk?

Do mildly to moderately obese people have a greater risk of coronary disease, cancer, or other disease? Investigations into this question have produced conflicting results (Lagger et al., 2010; Mitchell et al., 2008). One long-term study found

that while moderately overweight participants had a 30 percent higher risk of early death, underweight participants had a low likelihood of dying at an early age as long as their thinness could not be attributed to smoking or illness (Manson et al., 2004, 1995). However, another study found that the mortality rate of underweight individuals was as high as that of overweight individuals regardless of smoking behavior or illness (Berrigan et al., 2006, 2003; Troiano et al., 1996). These conflicting findings suggest that the jury is still out on this issue.

Does Dieting Work?

There are scores of diets and diet pills. There is almost no evidence, however, that any diet yet devised can ensure long-term weight loss (de Zwaan, 2010; Mann et al., 2007). In fact, long-term studies reveal a *rebound effect,* a net gain in weight in obese people who have lost weight on very low-calorie diets. Research also suggests that the feelings of failure that accompany diet rebounds may lead to dysfunctional eating patterns, including binge eating (Eifert et al., 2007). Small wonder that the past decade has witnessed a significant rise in *bariatric surgery* for obese people, particularly those who are very obese (Berthoud, Shin, & Zheng, 2011). This kind of surgery changes the anatomy of the digestive system, limiting the amount of food that can be eaten and digested. It

blocked the reception of GLP-1 in the hypothalamus, they more than doubled their food intake.

Some researchers believe that the hypothalamus, related brain areas, and chemicals such as CCK and GLP-1, working together, comprise a "weight thermostat" of sorts in the body, which is responsible for keeping an individual at a particular weight level called the **weight set point.** Genetic inheritance and early eating practices seem to determine each person's weight set point (Sullivan et al., 2011; Levin, 2010). When a person's weight falls below his or her particular set point, the LH and certain other brain areas are activated and seek to restore the lost weight by producing hunger and lowering the body's *metabolic rate,* the rate at which the body expends energy. When a person's weight rises above his or her set point, the VMH and certain other brain areas are activated, and they seek to remove the excess weight by reducing hunger and increasing the body's metabolic rate.

•**ventromedial hypothalamus (VMH)**•
A brain region that depresses hunger when activated.

•**weight set point**•The weight level that a person is predisposed to maintain, controlled in part by the hypothalamus.

Trae Patton/NBC/NBCU Photo Bank via AP Images

HANNAH
STARTING WEIGHT
248
CURRENT WEIGHT
128
DIFFERENCE
-120

"The Biggest Loser" phenomenon Contestant Hannah Curlee proudly observes the results of her weigh-in on the 2011 season finale of the popular reality show "The Biggest Loser." In this TV series, which is also produced in dozens of other countries around the world, overweight contestants compete to lose the most weight for cash prizes. Although Curlee lost almost half her body weight, she was not the winner of the 2011 contest.

has proved very beneficial to many obese individuals (Levin, 2010).

What Is the Proper Goal?

Some researchers argue that, short of surgery, attempts to reduce obesity should focus less on weight loss and more on improving general health and attitudes. If poor eating habits can be corrected, if a poor self-concept and distorted body image can be improved, if proper exercise can be instituted, and if overweight people can be educated about the myths and truths regarding obesity, perhaps everyone will be better off. For very overweight in-dividuals in particular, the most promising path to long-term weight loss may be to set realistic, attainable goals, behaviors, and exercise levels rather than unrealistic ideals (de Zwaan, 2010; Travis & Meltzer, 2008; Brownell & O'Neil, 1993). In addition, it is critical that the public overcome its prejudice against people who are overweight.

Obesity Among Children and Adolescents

A matter of growing concern centers on recent increases in the rates of overweight children and adolescents, particularly in the United States (Lanigan, 2011; Johnston & Tyler, 2008). Indeed, since 1974, the obesity rate has quadrupled for children and doubled for adolescents in the United States. Compared to most European countries, the United States has by far the highest percentage of obese young people. Two key reasons for this difference are *diet* and *exercise.* American children and adolescents apparently drink more sugary soft drinks and eat more unhealthy food than young people in other countries (Malik et al., 2006). One study found, for example, that one-third of American teenagers eat at least one fast-food meal each day (Bowman et al., 2003). Moreover, on average, teenagers in the United States walk and bike less than their counterparts from other industrialized countries, and they are more likely to drive cars to get around (Matsumoto & Juang, 2008). Whatever the precise causes, the trend is alarming.

BETWEEN THE LINES

Smoking, Eating, and Weight

Smokers weigh less than nonsmokers. «

75 percent of people who quit smoking gain weight. «

Nicotine, a stimulant substance, suppresses appetites and increases metabolic rate, perhaps because of its impact on the lateral hypothalamus. «

(Higgins & George, 2007)

Models and mannequins

Mannequins were once made extra-thin to show the lines of the clothing for sale to best advantage. Today the shape of the ideal woman is indistinguishable from that of a mannequin (right), and a growing number of young women try to achieve this ideal.

According to the weight set point theory, when people diet and fall to a weight below their weight set point, their brain starts trying to restore the lost weight. Hypothalamic and related brain activity produce a preoccupation with food and a desire to binge. It also triggers bodily changes that make it harder to lose weight and easier to gain weight, however little is eaten (Monteleone, 2011; Higgins & George, 2007). Once the brain and body begin conspiring to raise weight in this way, dieters actually enter into a battle against themselves. Some people apparently manage to shut down the inner "thermostat" and control their eating almost completely. These people move toward restricting-type anorexia nervosa. For others, the battle spirals toward a binge-purge or binge-only pattern. Although the weight set point explanation has received considerable debate in the clinical field, it remains widely accepted by theorists and practitioners.

Societal Pressures

Eating disorders are more common in Western countries than in other parts of the world (see *PsychWatch* on page 333). Thus, many theorists believe that Western standards of female attractiveness are partly responsible for the emergence of the disorders (Levine & Maine, 2010; Russo & Tartaro, 2008). Western standards of female beauty have changed throughout history, with a noticeable shift toward preference for a thin female frame in recent decades (Gilbert et al., 2005). One study that tracked the height, weight, and age of contestants in the Miss America Pageant from 1959 through 1978 found an average decline of 0.28 pound per year among the contestants and 0.37 pound per year among winners (Garner et al., 1980). The researchers also examined data on all *Playboy* magazine centerfold models over the same time period and found that the average weight, bust, and hip measurements of these women had decreased steadily. More recent studies of Miss America contestants and *Playboy* centerfolds indicate that these trends have continued (Rubinstein & Caballero, 2000).

Because thinness is especially valued in the subcultures of fashion models, actors, dancers, and certain athletes, members of these groups are likely to be particularly concerned about their weight. Studies have indeed found that people in these professions are more prone than others to anorexia nervosa and bulimia nervosa (Sundgot-Borgen & Bratland-Sanda, 2011; Thompson & Sherman, 2010). In fact, many famous young women from these fields have publicly acknowledged grossly disordered eating patterns over the years. Surveys of athletes at colleges around the United States reveal that more than 9 percent of female college athletes suffer from an eating disorder and another 50 percent display eating behaviors that put them at risk for such disorders (Kerr et al., 2007; Johnson, 1995). A full 20 percent of surveyed gymnasts appear to have an eating disorder (see Figure 11-4).

Why do you think that fashion models, often called supermodels, have risen to celebrity status in recent decades?

Attitudes toward thinness may also help explain economic differences in the rates of eating disorders. In the past, women in the upper socioeconomic classes expressed more concern about thinness and dieting than women of the lower socioeconomic classes (Margo, 1985; Stunkard, 1975). Correspondingly, anorexia nervosa and bulimia nervosa were more common among women higher on the socioeconomic scale (Foreyt et al., 1996; Rosen et al., 1991). In recent years, however, dieting and preoccupation with thinness have increased to some degree in all socioeconomic classes, as has the prevalence of these eating disorders (Ernsberger, 2009; Striegel-Moore et al., 2005).

Western society not only glorifies thinness but also creates a climate of prejudice against overweight people (Levine & Maine, 2010; Goode & Vail, 2008). Whereas slurs based on ethnicity, race, and gender are considered unacceptable, cruel jokes about obesity are standard fare on the Web and television and in movies, books, and magazines. Research indicates that the prejudice against obese people is deep-rooted (Grilo et al., 2005). Prospective parents who were shown pictures of a chubby child and a medium-weight or thin child rated the former as less friendly, energetic, intelligent, and desirable than the latter. In another study, preschool children who were given a choice between a chubby and a thin rag doll chose the thin one, although they could not say why. It is small wonder that as many as half of elementary school girls have tried to lose weight and 61 percent of middle school girls are currently dieting (Hill, 2006; Stewart, 2004).

Given these trends, it is not totally surprising that a recent survey of 248 adolescent girls directly tied eating disorders and body dissatisfaction to social networking, Internet activity, and television browsing (Latzer, Katz, & Spivak, 2011). The survey found that the respondents who spent more time on Facebook were more likely to display eating disorders, experience negative body image, eat in dysfunctional ways, and want to diet. Similar tendencies were shown by those who spent more time on fashion and music Web sites and those who viewed more gossip- and leisure-related television programs (for example, *Gossip Girl*).

Family Environment

Families may play an important role in the development and maintenance of eating disorders (Konstantellou, Campbell, & Eisler, 2012; Treasure, Williams, & Schmidt, 2010). Research suggests that as many as half of the families of people with anorexia nervosa or bulimia nervosa have a long history of emphasizing thinness, physical appearance, and dieting. In fact, the mothers in these families are more likely to diet themselves and to be generally perfectionistic than are the mothers in other families (Zerbe, 2008; Woodside et al., 2002). Tina, a 16-year-old, describes her view of the roots of her eating disorder:

> When I was a kid, say 6 or 7, my Mom and I would go to the drugstore all the time. She was heavy and bought all kinds of books and magazines on how to lose weight. Whenever we talked, like after I got home from school, it was almost always about dieting and how to lose weight. . . . I [went] on diets with my Mom, to keep her company.
>
> I just got better at it than she did. My eating disorder is my Mom's therapy. . . . It's also the way we have time together—working on the diets and exercise and all of that. We've stopped talking about diets since I got anorexia, and now I don't know what we can talk about.
>
> *(Zerbe, 2008, pp. 20–21)*

Abnormal interactions and forms of communication within a family may also set the stage for an eating disorder (Konstantellou et al., 2011). Family systems theorists argue that the families of people who develop eating disorders are often dysfunctional to begin with and that the eating disorder of one member is a reflection of the larger problem. Influential family theorist Salvador Minuchin, for example, believes that what he calls an **enmeshed family pattern** often leads to eating disorders (Olson, 2011; Minuchin et al., 2006).

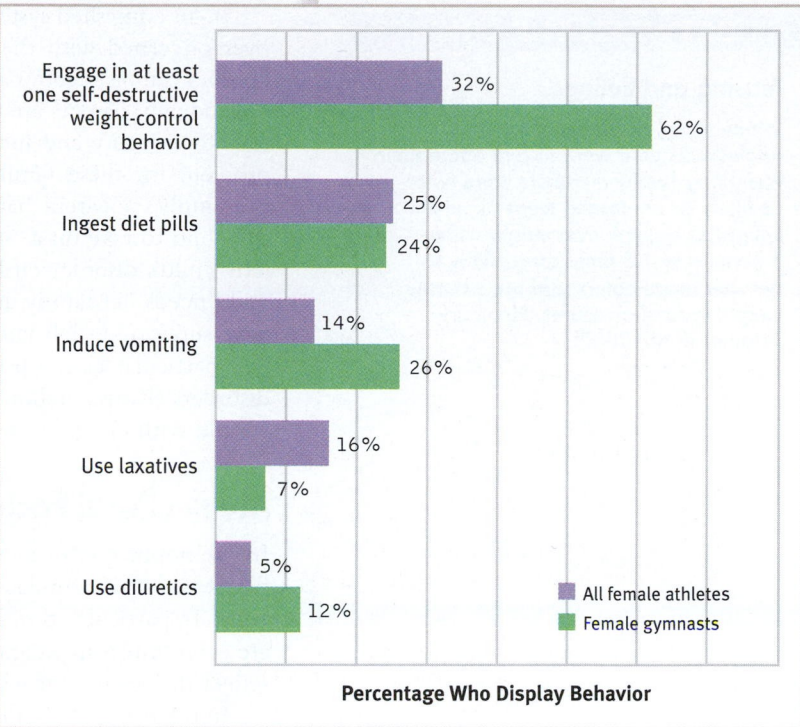

Figure 11-4

Dangerous shortcuts According to surveys, in sports ranging from field hockey to gymnastics, many female athletes engage in one or more self-destructive behaviors to control their weight (Kerr et al., 2007; Taylor & Ste. Marie, 2001). One study found that close to two-thirds of female college gymnasts engage in at least one such behavior. (Adapted from Rosen & Hough, 1988; Rosen et al., 1986.)

• **enmeshed family pattern** • A family system in which members are overinvolved with each other's affairs and overconcerned about each other's welfare.

BETWEEN THE LINES

Teasing and Eating

In one study, researchers found that adolescents who were teased about their weight by family members were twice as likely as nonteased teens of similar weight to become overweight within 5 years and 1.5 times more likely to become binge-eaters and use extreme weight control measures (Neumark-Sztainer et al., 2007). ‹‹

In an enmeshed system, family members are overinvolved in each other's affairs and overconcerned with the details of each other's lives. On the positive side, enmeshed families can be affectionate and loyal. On the negative side, they can be clingy and foster dependency. Parents are too involved in the lives of their children, allowing little room for individuality and independence. Minuchin argues that adolescence poses a special problem for these families. The teenager's normal push for independence threatens the family's apparent harmony and closeness. In response, the family may subtly force the child to take on a "sick" role—to develop an eating disorder or some other illness. The child's disorder enables the family to maintain its appearance of harmony. A sick child needs her family, and family members can rally to protect her. Some case studies have supported such family systems explanations, but systematic research fails to show that particular family patterns consistently set the stage for the development of eating disorders (Konstantellou et al., 2011; Wilson et al., 2003, 1996). In fact, the families of people with either anorexia nervosa or bulimia nervosa vary widely.

Multicultural Factors: Racial and Ethnic Differences

In the popular 1995 movie *Clueless,* Cher and Dionne, wealthy teenage friends of different races, have similar tastes, beliefs, and values about everything from boys to schoolwork. In particular, they have the same kinds of eating habits and beauty ideals, and they are even similar in weight and physical form. But does the story of these young women reflect the realities of white American and African American females in our society?

In the early 1990s, the answer to this question appeared to be a resounding no. Most studies conducted up to the time of the movie's release indicated that the eating behaviors, values, and goals of young African American women were considerably healthier than those of young white American women (Lovejoy, 2001; Cash & Henry, 1995; Parker et al., 1995). A widely publicized 1995 study at the University of Arizona, for example, found that the eating behaviors and attitudes of young African American women were more positive than those of young white American women. It found, specifically, that nearly 90 percent of the white American respondents were dissatisfied with their weight and body shape, compared to around 70 percent of the African American teens.

The study also suggested that white American and African American adolescent girls had different ideals of beauty. The white American teens, asked to define the "perfect girl," described a girl of 5′7″ weighing between 100 and 110 pounds—proportions that mirror those of so-called supermodels. Attaining a perfect weight, many said, was the key to being happy and popular. In contrast, the African American respondents

Scott Gries/Getty Images

Salt-N-Pepa: behind the scenes
When the pioneering female rap group Salt-N-Pepa suddenly disbanded in 2002, it was viewed by most as a "typical" band breakup. In fact, however, one of the performers, Cheryl "Salt" James (shown here), had been suffering from bulimia nervosa. She quit performing in order to recover from the disorder and to escape the pressures of her fame, including, in her words, "the pressure to be beautiful and management telling me 'You're gaining weight.'" With James now recovered, the group has reunited and is touring again.

Eating Disorders Across the World

Up until the past decade, anorexia nervosa and bulimia nervosa were generally considered culture-bound abnormalities. Although prevalent in the United States and other Western countries, they were uncommon in non-Western cultures. A study conducted during the mid-1990s, for example, compared students in the African nation of Ghana and those in the United States on issues such as eating disorders, weight, body perception, and attitudes toward thinness (Cogan et al., 1996). The Ghanaians were more likely to rate larger body sizes as ideal, while the Americans were more likely to diet and to display eating disorders. Similarly, in countries, such as Saudi Arabia, where attention was not drawn to the female figure and the female body was almost entirely covered, eating disorders were rarely mentioned in the clinical literature (Matsumoto & Juang, 2008; Al-Subaie & Alhamad, 2000).

However, studies conducted over the past decade reveal that disordered eating behaviors and attitudes are on the rise in non-Western countries, a trend that seems to correspond to those countries' increased exposure to Western culture (Caqueo-Urízar et al., 2011). Researchers have found, for example, that eating disorders are increasing in Pakistan, particularly among women

Chris Moore/Catwalking/Getty Images

who have been more exposed to Western culture (Suhail & Nisa, 2002).

The spread of eating disorders to non-Western lands has been particularly apparent in a series of studies conducted on the Fiji Islands in the South Pacific (Becker et al., 2010, 2007, 2003, 2002, 1999). In 1995 satellite television began beaming Western shows and fashions to remote parts of the islands for the first time. Just a few years later, researchers found that Fijian teenage girls who watched television at least three nights per week were more likely than others to feel "too big or fat." In addition, almost two-thirds of them had dieted in the previous month, and 15 percent had vomited to control weight within the previous year (compared to 3 percent before television).

Embracing diversity? The fashion industry prides itself on the range of nationalities now represented in its ranks. However, the Western ideal of extreme thinness remains the standard for all models, regardless of their cultural background. Many psychologists worry that the success of supermodels such as Ethiopia's Liya Kebede (shown here) and Sudan's Alek Wek may contribute to thinner body ideals, greater body dissatisfaction, and more eating disorders in their African countries.

emphasized personality traits over physical characteristics. They defined the "perfect" African American girl as smart, fun, easy to talk to, not conceited, and funny; she did not necessarily need to be "pretty," as long as she was well groomed. The body dimensions the African American teens described were more attainable for the typical girl; they favored fuller hips, for example. Moreover, the African American respondents were less likely than the white American respondents to diet for extended periods.

Unfortunately, research conducted over the past decade suggests that body image concerns, dysfunctional eating patterns, and anorexia nervosa and bulimia nervosa are on the rise among young African American women as well as among women of other minority groups (Gilbert, 2011; Levine & Smolak, 2010). For example, a survey conducted by *Essence,* the largest-circulation African American magazine, and studies by several teams of researchers have found that the risk of today's African American women developing these eating disorders is approaching that of white American women. Similarly, their attitudes regarding body image, weight, and eating are closing in on those of white American women (Annunziato et al., 2007). In the *Essence* survey, 65 percent of African American respondents reported dieting behavior, 39 percent said that food controlled their lives, 19 percent avoided eating when hungry, 17 percent used laxatives, and 4 percent vomited to lose weight.

Dangerous profession
The fashion world was shocked when 21-year-old Brazilian model Ana Carolina Reston died in 2006 of complications from anorexia nervosa. Told during a 2004 casting call that she was "too fat," Reston began restricting her diet to only apples and tomatoes, culminating in a generalized infection and eventually death. The 5'8" model weighed 88 pounds at the time of her death.

The shift in the eating behaviors and eating problems of African American women appears to be partly related to their *acculturation* (Gilbert, 2011). One study compared African American women at a predominately white American university with those at a predominately African American university. Those at the former school had significantly higher depression scores, and those scores were positively correlated with eating problems (Ford, 2000).

Still other studies indicate that Hispanic American female adolescents and young adults engage in disordered eating behaviors and express body dissatisfaction at rates about equal to those of white American women (Levine & Smolak, 2010; Germer, 2005). Moreover, those who consider themselves more oriented to the white American culture appear to have particularly high rates of anorexia nervosa and bulimia nervosa (Cachelin et al., 2006). These eating disorders also appear to be on the increase among young Asian American women and young women in several Asian countries (Stewart & Williamson, 2008). In one Taiwanese study, for example, 65 percent of the underweight girls aged 10 to 14 years said they wished they were thinner (Wong & Huang, 2000).

Despite these trends, the public apparently still believes that women from minority groups are relatively unlikely to develop anorexia nervosa and bulimia nervosa. In one study, 160 undergraduates read the diary of a 16-year-old girl, including passages that revealed disturbed patterns of eating (Gordon, Perez, & Joiner, 2002). The participants who were told that the diarist was white American were much more likely to recognize that she had an eating disorder than were those who were told she was African American or Hispanic American.

One would expect clinical professionals to be wiser in such assessments, and they are—for Hispanic Americans, but not for African Americans. Several years after conducting the study just mentioned, the research team ran the same design, except that they used mental health professionals and clinical psychology graduate students as participants (Gordon et al., 2006). These participants were more likely to believe that the diarist had an eating disorder if she were labeled white American or Hispanic American than if she were labeled African American.

Multicultural Factors: Gender Differences

Males account for only 5 to 10 percent of all cases of anorexia nervosa and bulimia nervosa. The reasons for this striking gender difference are not entirely clear, but Western society's double standard for attractiveness is, at the very least, one reason. Our society's emphasis on a thin appearance is clearly aimed at women much more than men, and some theorists believe that this difference has made women much more inclined to diet and more prone to eating disorders. Surveys of college men have, for example, found that the majority select "muscular, strong and broad shoulders" to describe the ideal male body and "thin, slim, slightly underweight" to describe the ideal female body (Toro et al., 2005; Kearney & Steichen-Ash, 1990).

A second reason for the different rates of anorexia nervosa and bulimia nervosa between men and women may be the different methods of weight loss favored by the two genders. According to some clinical observations, men are more likely to use exercise to lose weight, whereas women more often diet (Gadalla, 2009; Toro et al., 2005). And, as you have read, dieting often precedes the onset of these eating disorders.

Why do some men develop anorexia nervosa or bulimia nervosa? In a number of cases, the disorder is linked to the *requirements and pressures of a job or sport* (Morgan, 2012; Thompson & Sherman, 2011). According to one study, 37 percent of males with these eating disorders had jobs or played sports for which weight control was important, compared to 13 percent of women with such disorders (Braun, 1996). The highest rates of male eating disorders have been found among jockeys, wrestlers, distance runners, body

Why do you think that the prevalence of eating disorders among men has been on the increase in recent years?

builders, and swimmers. Jockeys commonly spend hours before a race in a sauna, shedding up to seven pounds of weight, and may restrict their food intake, abuse laxatives and diuretics, and force vomiting (Kerr et al., 2007). Herb McCauley, a top jockey who competed in more than 20,000 races and earned $70 million in winnings, suffered from an eating disorder for 20 years, until after his career ended. Using the laxative Ex-Lax and the diuretic Lasix to help him purge, he now says, "I took so many slabs of Ex-Lax that to this day I can't eat a Hershey bar" (Fountaino, 2000, p. 2). Similarly, male wrestlers in high school and college commonly restrict their food for up to three days before a match in order to "make weight." Some lose up to five pounds of water weight by practicing or running in several layers of warm or rubber clothing before weighing in for a match.

For other men who develop anorexia nervosa or bulimia nervosa, *body image* appears to be a key factor, just as it is in women. Many of them report that they want a "lean, toned, thin" shape similar to the ideal female body, rather than the muscular, broad-shouldered shape of the typical male ideal (Morgan, 2012; Hildebrandt & Alfano, 2009; Soban, 2006).

And, finally, yet other men seem to be caught up in a relatively new kind of eating disorder, called *reverse anorexia nervosa* or *muscle dysmorphobia*. This disorder is displayed by men who are very muscular but still see themselves as scrawny and small and therefore continue to strive for a perfect body through extreme measures such as excessive weight lifting or the abuse of steroids (Morgan, 2012; Stewart & Williamson, 2008). Individuals with muscle dysmorphobia typically experience shame about their bodies, and many have a history of depression, anxiety, and self-destructive compulsive behavior. About one-third of them also display related dysfunctional behaviors such as binge eating.

Not for women only
A growing number of today's men are developing eating disorders. Some of them aspire to a very lean body shape, such as that displayed by a new breed of ultra-thin male models (left), and develop anorexia nervosa or bulimia nervosa. Others aspire to the ultra-muscular look displayed by bodybuilders (above) and develop a new kind of eating disorder called *muscle dysmorphobia*. The men in this latter category inaccurately consider themselves to be scrawny and small and keep striving for a perfect body through excessive weight lifting and abuse of steroids.

How Are Eating Disorders Treated?

Today's treatments for eating disorders have two goals. The first is to correct the dangerous eating pattern as quickly as possible. The second is to address the broader psychological and situational factors that have led to and maintain the eating problem. Family and friends can also play an important role in helping to overcome the disorder.

Treatments for Anorexia Nervosa

The immediate aims of treatment for anorexia nervosa are to help individuals regain their lost weight, recover from malnourishment, and eat normally again. Therapists must then help them to make psychological and perhaps family changes to lock in those gains.

How Are Proper Weight and Normal Eating Restored? A variety of treatment methods are used to help patients with anorexia nervosa gain weight quickly and return to health within weeks. In the past, treatment almost always took place in a hospital (Olmsted et al., 2010), but now it is often offered in day hospitals or outpatient settings (Keel & McCormick, 2010).

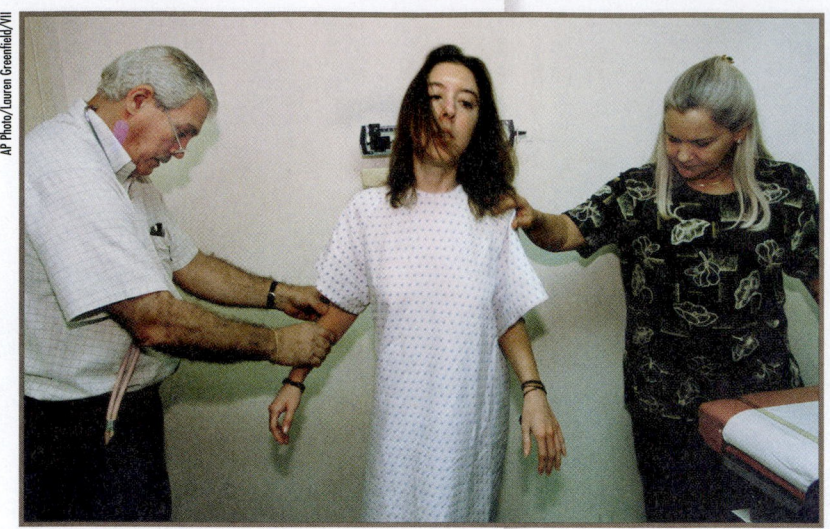

"Blind-weighed"

During inpatient treatment for anorexia nervosa, this 24-year-old woman, like many others in her program, cannot bear to see how much weight she may have gained. Thus she is "blind-weighed" by staff members: she mounts the scale backward so as not to view the weight gain. Clearly, gaining back her proper weight is a frightening and traumatic ordeal for her.

In life-threatening cases, clinicians may need to force *tube and intravenous feedings* on a patient who refuses to eat (Touyz & Carney, 2010; Tyre, 2005). Unfortunately, this use of force may breed distrust in the patient. In contrast, behavioral weight-restoration approaches have clinicians use *rewards* whenever patients eat properly or gain weight and offer no rewards when they eat improperly or fail to gain weight (Tacon & Caldera, 2001).

Perhaps the most popular weight-restoration technique of recent years has been a combination of *supportive nursing care,* nutritional counseling, and a relatively high-calorie diet (Hart & Abraham, 2011; Croll, 2010; Sorrentino et al., 2005). Here nurses *gradually* increase a patient's diet over the course of several weeks to more than 3,000 calories a day (Zerbe, 2010, 2008; Herzog et al., 2004). The nurses educate patients about the program, track their progress, provide encouragement, and help them recognize that their weight gain is under control and will not lead to obesity. Studies find that patients in nursing-care programs usually gain the necessary weight over 8 to 12 weeks.

How Are Lasting Changes Achieved? Clinical researchers have found that individuals with anorexia nervosa must overcome their underlying psychological problems in order to achieve lasting improvement. Therapists typically use a combination of education, psychotherapy, and family approaches to help achieve this broader goal (Wade & Watson, 2012; Zerbe, 2010, 2008). Psychotropic drugs have also been helpful in some cases, but research has found that such medications are typically of limited benefit over the long-term course of anorexia nervosa (David et al., 2012; McElroy et al., 2010).

COGNITIVE-BEHAVIORAL THERAPY In most treatment programs for anorexia nervosa, a combination of behavioral and cognitive interventions are included. Such techniques are designed to help clients appreciate and alter the behaviors and thought processes that help keep their restrictive eating going (Evans & Waller, 2011; Murphy et al., 2010). On the behavioral side, clients are typically required to monitor (perhaps by keeping a diary) their feelings, hunger levels, and food intake and the ties between these variables. On the cognitive side, they are taught to identify their "core pathology"—the deep-seated

Taking the first bite

Two terrified teenagers hold hands and try to support one another while struggling to take small bites of their desserts. The girls, in treatment for eating disorders at the Renfrew Center in Florida, are required to eat the desserts as part of their inpatient program.

A story of two billboards

In 1995, the Calvin Klein clothing brand posed young teenagers in sexually suggestive clothing ads (left). A public uproar forced the company to remove the ads from magazines and billboards across the United States, but, by then, a point had been made—that extreme thinness was in vogue for female fashion and, indeed, for females of all ages. In contrast, the Nolita clothing brand launched a major ad campaign *against* excessive thinness in 2007, displaying anti-anorexia billboards throughout Italy (right). Here two young women stare at one such billboard—that of an emaciated naked woman appearing beneath the words "No Anorexia." The billboard model, Isabelle Caro, died in 2010 of complications from anorexia nervosa.

belief that they should in fact be judged by their shape and weight and by their ability to control these physical characteristics. The clients may also be taught alternative ways of coping with stress and of solving problems.

The therapists who use these approaches are particularly careful to help patients with anorexia nervosa recognize their need for independence and teach them more appropriate ways to exercise control (Pike et al., 2010). The therapists may also teach them to identify better and trust their internal sensations and feelings (Wilson, 2010; Fairburn et al., 2008). In the following session, a therapist tries to help a 15-year-old client recognize and share her feelings:

Patient: I don't talk about my feelings; I never did.
Therapist: Do you think I'll respond like others?
Patient: What do you mean?
Therapist: I think you may be afraid that I won't pay close attention to what you feel inside, or that I'll tell you not to feel the way you do—that it's foolish to feel frightened, to feel fat, to doubt yourself, considering how well you do in school, how you're appreciated by teachers, how pretty you are.
Patient: (Looking somewhat tense and agitated) Well, I was always told to be polite and respect other people, just like a stupid, faceless doll. (Affecting a vacant, doll-like pose)
Therapist: Do I give you the impression that it would be disrespectful for you to share your feelings, whatever they may be?
Patient: Not really; I don't know.
Therapist: I can't, and won't, tell you that this is easy for you to do. . . . But I can promise you that you are free to speak your mind, and that I won't turn away.

(Strober & Yager, 1985, pp. 368–369)

BETWEEN THE LINES

In Their Words

"Girls should be encouraged to take an interest in their appearance when they are very young."
Ladies' Home Journal, 1940

Finally, cognitive-behavioral therapists help clients with anorexia nervosa change their attitudes about eating and weight (Evans & Waller, 2012; Pike et al., 2010) (see Table 11-4). The therapists may guide clients to identify, challenge, and change maladaptive assumptions, such as "I must always be perfect" or "My weight and shape determine my value" (Fairburn et al., 2008; Lask & Bryant-Waugh, 2000). They may also educate clients about the body distortions typical of anorexia nervosa and help them see that their own assessments of their size are incorrect. Even if a client never learns to judge her body shape accurately, she may at least reach a point where she says, "I know that a key feature of anorexia nervosa is a misperception of my own size, so I can expect to feel fat regardless of my actual size."

Although cognitive-behavioral techniques are often of great help to clients with anorexia nervosa, research suggests that the techniques typically must be supplemented by other approaches to bring about better results (Zerbe, 2010, 2008). Family therapy, for example, is often included in treatment.

CHANGING FAMILY INTERACTIONS Family therapy can be an invaluable part of treatment for anorexia nervosa, particularly for children and adolescents with the disorder. As in other family therapy situations, the therapist meets with the family as a whole, points out troublesome family patterns, and helps the members make appropriate changes. In particular, family therapists may try to help the person with anorexia nervosa separate her feelings and needs from those of other members of her family. Although the role of family in the development of anorexia nervosa is not yet clear, research strongly suggests that family therapy (or at least parent counseling) can be helpful in the treatment of this disorder (Hoste et al., 2012; Lock, 2011; Zucker et al., 2011; Treasure et al., 2010).

table: **11-4**

Sample Items from the Eating Disorder Inventory

For each item, decide if the item is true about you ALWAYS (A), USUALLY (U), OFTEN (O), SOMETIMES (S), RARELY (R), or NEVER (N). Circle the letter that corresponds to your rating.

A	U	O	S	R	N	I think that my stomach is too big.
A	U	O	S	R	N	I eat when I am upset.
A	U	O	S	R	N	I stuff myself with food.
A	U	O	S	R	N	I think about dieting.
A	U	O	S	R	N	I think that my thighs are too large.
A	U	O	S	R	N	I feel extremely guilty after overeating.
A	U	O	S	R	N	I am terrified of gaining weight.
A	U	O	S	R	N	I get confused about what emotion I am feeling.
A	U	O	S	R	N	I have gone on eating binges where I felt that I could not stop.
A	U	O	S	R	N	I get confused as to whether or not I am hungry.
A	U	O	S	R	N	I think my hips are too big.
A	U	O	S	R	N	If I gain a pound, I worry that I will keep gaining.
A	U	O	S	R	N	I have the thought of trying to vomit in order to lose weight.
A	U	O	S	R	N	I think my buttocks are too large.
A	U	O	S	R	N	I eat or drink in secrecy.
A	U	O	S	R	N	I would like to be in total control of my bodily urges.

Source: Clausen et al., 2011; Garner, 2005; Garner, Olmsted, & Polivy, 1991, 1984.

> **Mother:** *I think I know what [Susan] is going through: all the doubt and insecurity of growing up and establishing her own identity. (Turning to the patient, with tears) If you just place trust in yourself, with the support of those around you who care, everything will turn out for the better.*
>
> **Therapist:** *Are you making yourself available to her? Should she turn to you, rely on you for guidance and emotional support?*
>
> **Mother:** *Well, that's what parents are for.*
>
> **Therapist:** *(Turning to patient) What do you think?*
>
> **Susan:** *(To mother) I can't keep depending on you, Mom, or everyone else. That's what I've been doing, and it gave me anorexia. . . .*
>
> **Therapist:** *Do you think your mom would prefer that there be no secrets between her and the kids—an open door, so to speak?*
>
> **Older sister:** *Sometimes I do.*
>
> **Therapist:** *(To patient and younger sister) How about you two?*
>
> **Susan:** *Yeah. Sometimes it's like whatever I feel, she has to feel.*
>
> **Younger sister:** *Yeah.*
>
> *(Strober & Yager, 1985, pp. 381–382)*

What Is the Aftermath of Anorexia Nervosa?

The use of combined treatment approaches has greatly improved the outlook for people with anorexia nervosa, although the road to recovery can be difficult. The course and outcome of this disorder vary from person to person, but researchers have noted certain trends.

On the positive side, weight is often quickly restored once treatment for the disorder begins (McDermott & Jaffa, 2005), and treatment gains may continue for years (Haliburn, 2005). As many as 90 percent of patients continue to show improvement—either full or partial—when they are interviewed several years or more after their initial recovery (Brewerton & Costin, 2011; van Son et al., 2010; Zerbe, 2010, 2008).

Another positive note is that most females with anorexia nervosa menstruate again when they regain their weight, and other medical improvements follow (Mitchell & Crow, 2010; Zerbe, 2008). Also encouraging is that the death rate from anorexia nervosa seems to be falling (van Son et al., 2010). Earlier diagnosis and safer and faster weight-restoration techniques may account for this trend. Deaths that do occur are usually caused by suicide, starvation, infection, gastrointestinal problems, or electrolyte imbalance.

On the negative side, as many as 25 percent of persons with anorexia nervosa remain seriously troubled for years (Steinhausen, 2009; Steinhausen & Weber, 2009). Furthermore, recovery, when it does occur, is not always permanent. Anorexic behavior recurs in at least one-third of recovered patients, usually triggered by new stresses, such as marriage, pregnancy, or a major relocation (Eifert et al., 2007; Fennig et al., 2002). Even years later, many recovered individuals continue to express concerns about their weight and appearance. Some continue to restrict their diets to a degree, experience anxiety when they eat with other people, or hold some distorted ideas about food, eating, and weight (Fairburn et al., 2008).

About half of those who have suffered from anorexia nervosa continue to experience certain emotional problems—particularly depression, obsessiveness, and social anxiety—years after treatment. Such problems are particularly common in those who had not succeeded in reaching a fully normal weight by the end of treatment (Bodell & Mayer, 2011; Steinhausen, 2002).

Miss America speaks out Kirsten Haglund is crowned Miss America at the January 2008 pageant. During her one-year reign, Haglund openly acknowledged her past struggles with anorexia nervosa. In recent years, she has continued to travel and speak about body-image issues and eating disorders. She also has started a foundation to provide treatment services for women who have eating disorders.

Donald Kravitz/Getty Images

New efforts at prevention
A number of innovative educational programs have been developed to help promote healthy body images and prevent eating disorders. Here, a Winona State University freshman swings a maul over her shoulder and into bathroom scales as part of Eating Disorders Awareness Week. The scale smashing is an annual event.

The more weight persons had lost and the more time that had passed before they entered treatment, the poorer the recovery rate (Fairburn et al., 2008). Individuals who had psychological or sexual problems before the onset of the disorder tend to have a poorer recovery rate than those without such a history (Amianto et al., 2011; Finfgeld, 2002). Teenagers seem to have a better recovery rate than older patients (Richard, 2005; Steinhausen et al., 2000).

Treatments for Bulimia Nervosa

Treatment programs for bulimia nervosa are often offered in eating disorder clinics. Such programs share the immediate goal of helping clients to eliminate their binge-purge patterns and establish good eating habits and the more general goal of eliminating the underlying causes of bulimic patterns. The programs emphasize education as much as therapy (Zerbe, 2010, 2008; Fairburn et al., 2008). Cognitive-behavioral therapy is particularly helpful in cases of bulimia nervosa—perhaps even more helpful than in cases of anorexia nervosa (Campbell & Schmidt, 2011; Wilson, 2010). And antidepressant drug therapy, which is of limited help to people with anorexia nervosa, appears to be quite effective in many cases of bulimia nervosa (David et al., 2012; Zerbe, 2010, 2008).

Cognitive-Behavioral Therapy

When treating clients with bulimia nervosa, cognitive-behavioral therapists employ many of the same techniques that they apply in cases of anorexia nervosa. Here, however, they tailor the techniques to the unique features of bulimia (for example, bingeing and purging behavior) and to the specific beliefs at work in bulimia nervosa.

BEHAVIORAL TECHNIQUES The therapists often instruct clients with bulimia nervosa to keep diaries of their eating behavior, changes in sensations of hunger and fullness, and the ebb and flow of other feelings (Stewart & Williamson, 2008). This helps the clients to observe their eating patterns more objectively and recognize the emotions and situations that trigger their desire to binge.

One team of researchers studied the effectiveness of an online variation of the diary technique (Shapiro et al., 2010). They had 31 clients with bulimia nervosa, each an outpatient in a 12-week cognitive-behavioral therapy program, send nightly texts to their therapists, reporting on their bingeing and purging urges and episodes. In turn, the clients received feedback messages, including reinforcement and encouragement for the treatment goals they had been able to achieve that day. The clinical researchers reported that by the end of therapy, the clients showed significant decreases in binges, purges, other bulimic symptoms, and feelings of depression.

Cognitive-behavioral therapists may also use the behavioral technique of *exposure and response prevention* to help break the binge-purge cycle. As you read in Chapter 5, this approach consists of exposing people to situations that would ordinarily raise anxiety and then preventing them from performing their usual compulsive responses until they learn that the situations are actually harmless and their compulsive acts unnecessary. For bulimia nervosa, the therapists require clients to eat particular kinds and amounts of food and then prevent them from vomiting to show that eating can be a harmless and even constructive activity that needs no undoing (Wilson, 2010; Williamson et al., 2004). Typically the therapist sits with the client during the eating of forbidden foods and stays until the urge to purge has passed. Studies find that this treatment often helps reduce eating-related anxieties, bingeing, and vomiting.

COGNITIVE TECHNIQUES Beyond such behavioral techniques, a primary focus of cognitive-behavioral therapists is to help clients with bulimia nervosa recognize and change their maladaptive attitudes toward food, eating, weight, and shape (Campbell & Schmidt, 2011; Wilson, 2010). The therapists typically teach the individuals to identify and challenge the negative thoughts that regularly precede their urge to binge—"I have no self-control"; "I might as well give up"; "I look fat" (Fairburn, 1985). They may also guide clients to recognize, question, and eventually change their perfectionistic standards, sense

curvy thighs, bigger bums, rounder stomachs. What better way to test our firming range?

There's not much point in testing a new firming lotion on size-eight supermodel thighs, is there? That's why Dove's Firming range was tested on ordinary women with real lives to live – and real, curvy thighs to firm. After using Dove's nourishing and effective combination of moisturisers and seaweed extracts, we asked if they'd go in front of the camera. What better way to show how they felt about the unretouched, unairbrushed results?

new Dove Firming Range

Gel Cream · Body Wash · Lotion

The ad!

An advertising campaign that created a great stir in 2005 was the "Dove girls" ad. The manufacturer of Dove Firming products recruited six young women with no prior modeling experience, had them pose in their underwear, and displayed the ad across the United States. Many people praised Dove for "courageously" using less than perfectly shaped women in the ad (actually, their dress sizes ranged from 6 to 12). In a similar act of "courage," fashion magazine *Vogue Italia* featured three plus-sized models posing in their underwear on the cover of its July 2011 issue—the first time that ultra-thin women were not used for the cover.

of helplessness, and low self-concept (see *MediaSpeak* on the next page). Cognitive-behavioral approaches seem to help as many as 65 percent of patients stop bingeing and purging (Eifert et al., 2007).

Other Forms of Psychotherapy

Because of its effectiveness in the treatment of bulimia nervosa, cognitive-behavioral therapy is often tried first, before other therapies are considered. If clients do not respond to this approach, approaches with promising but less impressive track records may then be tried. A common alternative is *interpersonal psychotherapy,* the treatment that seeks to improve interpersonal functioning (Tanofsky-Kraff & Wilfley, 2010). *Psychodynamic therapy* has also been used in cases of bulimia nervosa, but only a few research studies have tested and supported its effectiveness (Cloak & Powers, 2010; Zerbe, 2010, 2008, 2001). The various forms of psychotherapy—cognitive-behavioral, interpersonal, and psychodynamic—are often supplemented by family therapy (Hoste et al., 2012; le Grange et al., 2011; Treasure et al., 2010).

Cognitive-behavioral, interpersonal, and psychodynamic therapy may each be offered in either individual or group therapy format. Group formats, including self-help groups, give clients with bulimia nervosa an opportunity to share their concerns and experiences with one another (Kalodner & Coughlin, 2004; Riess, 2002). Group members learn that their disorder is not unique or shameful, and they receive support from one another, along with honest feedback and insights. In the group they can also work directly on underlying fears of displeasing others or being criticized. Research suggests that group formats are at least somewhat helpful in as many as 75 percent of bulimia nervosa cases (Valbak, 2001).

Antidepressant Medications

During the past 15 years, antidepressant drugs—all forms of antidepressant drugs—have been used to help treat bulimia nervosa (Broft, Berner, & Walsh, 2010; McElroy et al, 2010). In contrast to anorexia nervosa, people with bulimia nervosa are often helped considerably by these drugs. According to research, the drugs help as many as 40 percent of patients, reducing their binges by an average of 67 percent and vomiting by 56 percent. Once again, drug therapy seems to work best in combination with other forms of therapy, particularly cognitive-behavioral therapy (Stewart & Williamson, 2008). Alternatively, some therapists wait to see whether cognitive-behavioral therapy or another form of psychotherapy is effective before trying antidepressants (Wilson, 2010, 2005).

MediaSpeak

The Sugar Plum Fairy

By Lisa Flam, AOL News

A dancer in the New York City Ballet's production of "The Nutcracker," criticized for looking "as if she'd eaten one sugar plum too many," said the review was embarrassing but she's moved past that single opinion and isn't looking for an apology.

The critique last month about the body of dancer Jenifer Ringer, who portrays the Sugar Plum Fairy, highlighted the pressure on ballerinas to be thin and set off an online uproar, with many commentators blasting New York Times writer Alastair Macaulay as cruel and hurtful.

Ringer, though, said the issue of whether dancers' bodies should be open to criticism "is a really complex question."

"As a dancer, I do put myself out there to be criticized, and my body is part of my art form," she said this morning on NBC's "Today" show. "At the same time, I'm not overweight. I do have, I guess a more womanly body type than the stereotypical ballerina."

Ringer, who has suffered from anorexia and compulsive overeating in the past, said the review made her feel bad.

"But I really had to tell myself it's one person's opinion out of the 2,000 people that were there that night," said Ringer, 37. "So where I am in my life right now, I was able to kind of move forward from it."

And, she said, she was pleasantly caught off guard by all the online support that came her way. "It's made me feel very loved and supported," she said. . . .

She spoke too of the pressures dancers face. "It is a field where our bodies are important," she said. "As dancers, we're taught to try to be perfect in every way."

Ringer said she wasn't prepared to deal with "just being in an adult performing world" when she became a professional dancer at age 16.

"My coping mechanism turned into eating disorders and body image issues," she said. "For me, I think it was an inability to cope."

Actress Natalie Portman, who lost 20 pounds to play a struggling ballerina in the . . . movie "Black Swan" came to Ringer's defense, saying in an interview last month, "In what other field is it acceptable to judge artists by how big they

Unfair critique Ballet dancer Jenifer Ringer performs with partner Jared Angle in *The Nutcracker*.

are? It was just amazing all of the pressure on dancers to starve themselves."

But Macaulay, noting the criticism his remark generated, wrote in a follow-up story that a dancer's body is relevant. "If you want to make your appearance irrelevant to criticism, do not choose ballet as a career," he wrote.

Ringer said she doesn't want an apology, noting that Macaulay's job is to give his opinion. . . .

Ringer noted that the New York City Ballet is made up of dancers of every body type: tall, petite, athletic, womanly and waif-like. "They can all dance like crazy. They're all gorgeous," she said.

"Seeing these beautiful woman with these different bodies all dancing to this gorgeous music—that's what should be celebrated," she said.

What Is the Aftermath of Bulimia Nervosa? Left untreated, bulimia nervosa can last for years, sometimes improving temporarily but then returning. Treatment, however, produces immediate, significant improvement in approximately 40 percent of clients: they stop or greatly reduce their bingeing and purging, eat properly, and maintain a normal weight (Richard, 2005). Another 40 percent show a moderate response—at least some decrease in binge eating and purging. As many as 20 percent show little immediate improvement. Follow-up studies, conducted years after treatment, suggest that as many as 75 percent of persons with bulimia nervosa have recovered—either fully or partially (Brewerton & Costin, 2011; Zeeck et al., 2011; Keel et al., 2010; van Son et al., 2010). Research also indicates that treatment helps many, but not all, people with bulimia nervosa attain lasting improvements in their overall psychological and social functioning (Keel et al., 2002, 2000; Stein et al., 2002).

Relapse can be a problem even among people who respond successfully to treatment (Olmsted et al., 2005). As with anorexia nervosa, relapses are usually triggered by a new life stress, such as an upcoming exam, job change, marriage, or divorce (Liu, 2007; Abraham & Llewellyn-Jones, 1984). One study found that close to one-third of persons who had recovered from bulimia nervosa relapsed within two years of treatment, usually within six months (Olmsted, Kaplan, & Rockert, 1994). Relapse is more likely among persons who had longer histories of bulimia nervosa before treatment,

Why might some people who recover from anorexia nervosa and bulimia nervosa remain vulnerable to relapse even after recovery?

had vomited more frequently during their disorder, continued to vomit at the end of treatment, had histories of substance abuse, made slower progress in the early stages of treatment, and continue to be lonely or to distrust others after treatment (Brewerton & Costin, 2011; Fairburn et al., 2004; Stewart, 2004).

Treatments for Binge Eating Disorder

Given the key role of binges in both bulimia nervosa and binge eating disorder (bingeing without purging), today's treatments for binge eating disorder are often similar to those for bulimia nervosa. In particular, cognitive-behavioral therapy, other forms of psychotherapy, and, in some cases, antidepressant medications are provided to help reduce or eliminate the binge eating patterns and to change disturbed thinking such as overconcern with weight and shape. Of course, most people with binge eating disorder also are overweight, a problem that requires additional kinds of intervention and is often resistant to long-term improvement (Claudino & Morgan, 2012; Zweig & Leahy, 2012; Wilson, 2011).

Now that binge eating disorder has been identified and is receiving considerable study, it is likely that specialized treatment programs, targeting the disorder's unique issues, will be emerging in the coming years. In the meantime, relatively little is known about the aftermath of this disorder (Claudino & Morgan, 2012). In one follow-up study of hospitalized patients with severe symptoms, the disorder was found to still be present in one-third of the individuals 12 years after hospitalization, and 36 percent of the individuals were still significantly overweight (Fichter et al., 2008).

PUTTING IT... together

A Standard for Integrating Perspectives

You have observed throughout this book that it is often useful to consider sociocultural, psychological, and biological factors jointly when trying to explain or treat various forms of abnormal functioning. Nowhere is the argument for combining these perspectives more powerful than in the case of eating disorders. According to the multidimensional risk perspective embraced by many theorists, varied factors act together to spark the development of eating disorders, particularly anorexia nervosa and bulimia nervosa. One case may result from societal pressures, autonomy issues, the physical and emotional changes of adolescence, and hypothalamic overactivity, while another case may result from family pressures, depression, and the effects of dieting. No wonder that the most helpful treatment programs for eating disorders combine sociocultural, psychological, and biological approaches. When the multidimensional risk perspective is applied to eating disorders, it demonstrates that scientists and practitioners who follow very different models can work together productively in an atmosphere of mutual respect.

New dolls for a new generation
During the 50-year reign of Barbie and her extremely thin waistline, manufacturers have periodically offered alternative dolls to the marketplace. For example, "Get Real Girls" dolls were introduced in 2001, emphasizing fitness and health, multicultural appearance, and sports and business roles for females. Observers hoped that the product would have a positive effect on the body satisfaction and self-image of young girls. However, production of the dolls apparently had to shut down within a few years—the result of low sales.

Research on eating disorders keeps revealing new surprises that force clinicians to adjust their theories and treatment programs. For example, researchers have learned that people with these disorders sometimes feel strangely positive about their symptoms (Williams & Reid, 2010; Serpell & Treasure, 2002). One recovered patient, for example, said, "I still miss my bulimia as I would an old friend who has died" (Cauwels, 1983, p. 173). Given such feelings, many therapists now help clients work through grief reactions over their lost symptoms, reactions that may occur as the individuals begin to overcome their eating disorders (Zerbe, 2008).

While clinicians and researchers seek more answers about eating disorders, clients themselves have begun to take an active role. A number of patient-run organizations now provide information, education, and support through Web sites, national telephone hot lines, schools, professional referrals, newsletters, workshops, and conferences (Musiat & Schmidt, 2010; Sinton & Taylor, 2010).

Summing Up

- **EATING DISORDERS** Rates of eating disorders have increased dramatically as thinness has become a national obsession. Two leading disorders in this category, *anorexia nervosa* and *bulimia nervosa,* share many similarities, as well as key differences. A third eating disorder, *binge eating disorder,* also seems to be on the rise. *pp. 317–318*

- **ANOREXIA NERVOSA** People with anorexia nervosa pursue extreme thinness and lose dangerous amounts of weight. They may follow a pattern of *restricting-type anorexia nervosa* or *binge-eating/purging-type anorexia nervosa.* The central features of anorexia nervosa are a drive for thinness, intense fear of weight gain, and disturbed body perception and other cognitive disturbances. Individuals with this disorder develop various medical problems, particularly *amenorhea.*

  Approximately 90 to 95 percent of all cases of anorexia nervosa occur among females. Typically the disorder begins after a person who is slightly overweight or of normal weight has been on a diet. *pp. 318–320*

- **BULIMIA NERVOSA** Individuals with bulimia nervosa go on frequent *eating binges* and then force themselves to vomit or perform other inappropriate *compensatory behaviors.* The binges often occur in response to increasing tension and are followed by feelings of guilt and self-blame.

  Compensatory behavior is at first reinforced by the temporary relief from uncomfortable feelings of fullness or the reduction of feelings of anxiety, self-disgust, and loss of control attached to bingeing. Over time, however, sufferers feel generally disgusted with themselves, depressed, and guilty.

  People with bulimia nervosa may experience mood swings or have difficulty controlling their impulses. Some display a personality disorder. Around half are amenorrheic, a number develop dental problems, and some develop a potassium deficiency. *pp. 320–324*

- **BINGE EATING DISORDER** People with binge eating disorder display frequent binge eating episodes but not inappropriate compensatory behaviors. Two-thirds of them become overweight, although most overweight people do not have this disorder. Between 2 and 7 percent of the population display binge eating disorder. Unlike anorexia nervosa and bulimia nervosa, this disorder is more evenly distributed among males and females and people of different races. *p. 324*

- **EXPLANATIONS** Most theorists now apply a *multidimensional risk perspective* to explain eating disorders and identify several key contributing factors. Principal among these are *ego deficiencies; cognitive factors; depression; biological factors* such as activity of the *hypothalamus, biochemical activity,* and the body's *weight set point; society's emphasis on thinness and bias against obesity; family environment; racial and ethnic differences;* and *gender differences. pp. 324–335*

■ **TREATMENTS** The first step in treating *anorexia nervosa* is to increase calorie intake and quickly restore the person's weight, using a strategy such as *supportive nursing care.* The second step is to deal with the underlying psychological and family problems, often using a combination of *education, cognitive-behavioral approaches,* and *family approaches.* As many as 90 percent of people who receive successful treatment for anorexia nervosa continue to show full or partial improvements years later. However, some of them relapse along the way, many continue to worry about their weight and appearance, and half continue to experience some emotional problems. Most menstruate again when they regain weight.

Treatments for *bulimia nervosa* focus first on stopping the binge-purge pattern and then on addressing the underlying causes of the disorder. Often several treatment strategies are combined, including *education, psychotherapy* (particularly *cognitive-behavioral therapy*), and *antidepressant medications.* As many as 75 percent of those who receive treatment eventually improve either fully or partially. While relapse can be a problem and may be precipitated by a new stress, treatment leads to lasting improvements in psychological and social functioning for many individuals. Similar treatments are provided to individuals with *binge eating disorder.* These individuals, however, may also require interventions to address their excessive weight. *pp. 335–343*

PsychPortal

Visit **PsychPortal**
www.yourpsychportal.com
to access the e-book, videocases and other case materials and activities, and study aids, including flashcards, crossword puzzles, quizzes, FAQs, and research exercises.

SUBSTANCE USE AND ADDICTIVE DISORDERS

"**I** am Duncan. I am an alcoholic." The audience settled deeper into their chairs at these familiar words. Another chronicle of death and rebirth would shortly begin [at] Alcoholics Anonymous. . . .

. . . "I must have been just past my 15th birthday when I had that first drink that everybody talks about. And like so many of them . . . it was like a miracle. With a little beer in my gut, the world was transformed. I wasn't a weakling anymore, I could lick almost anybody on the block. And girls? Well, you can imagine how a couple of beers made me feel like I could have any girl I wanted. . . .

"Though it's obvious to me now that my drinking even then, in high school, and after I got to college, was a problem, I didn't think so at the time. After all, everybody was drinking and getting drunk and acting stupid, and I didn't really think I was different. . . . I guess the fact that I hadn't really had any blackouts and that I could go for days without having to drink reassured me that things hadn't gotten out of control. And that's the way it went, until I found myself drinking even more—and more often—and suffering more from my drinking, along about my third year of college.

. . . "My roommate, a friend from high school, started bugging me about my drinking. It wasn't even that I'd have to sleep it off the whole next day and miss class, it was that he had begun to hear other friends talking about me, about the fool I'd made of myself at parties. He saw how shaky I was the morning after, and he saw how different I was when I'd been drinking a lot—almost out of my head was the way he put it. And he could count the bottles that I'd leave around the room, and he knew what the drinking and carousing was doing to my grades. . . . [P]artly because I really cared about my roommate and didn't want to lose him as a friend, I did cut down on my drinking by half or more. I only drank on weekends—and then only at night. . . . And that got me through the rest of college and, actually, through law school as well. . . .

"Shortly after getting my law degree, I married my first wife, and . . . for the first time since I started, my drinking was no problem at all. I would go for weeks at a time without touching a drop. . . .

"My marriage started to go bad after our second son, our third child, was born. I was very much career- and success-oriented, and I had little time to spend at home with my family. . . . My traveling had increased a lot, there were stimulating people on those trips, and, let's face it, there were some pretty exciting women available, too. So home got to be little else but a nagging, boring wife and children I wasn't very interested in. My drinking had gotten bad again, too, with being on the road so much, having to do a lot of entertaining at lunch when I wasn't away, and trying to soften the hassles at home. I guess I was putting down close to a gallon of very good scotch a week, with one thing or another.

"And as that went on, the drinking began to affect both my marriage and my career. With enough booze in me and under the pressures of guilt over my failure to carry out my responsibilities to my wife and children, I sometimes got kind of rough physically with them. I would break furniture, throw things around, then rush out and drive off in the car. I had a couple of wrecks, lost my license for two years because of one of them. Worst of all was when I tried to stop. By then I was totally hooked, so every time I tried to stop drinking, I'd experience withdrawal in all its horrors . . . with the vomiting and the 'shakes' and being unable to sit still or to lie down. And that would go on for days at a time. . . .

"Then, about four years ago, with my life in ruins, my wife given up on me and the kids with her, out of a job, and way down on my luck, [Alcoholics Anonymous] and I found each other. . . . I've been dry now for a little over two years, and with luck and support, I may stay sober. . . ."

Spitzer et al., 1983, pp. 87–89

Human beings enjoy a remarkable variety of foods and drinks. Every substance on earth probably has been tried by someone, somewhere, at some time. We also have discovered substances that have interesting effects—both medical and pleasurable—on our brains and the rest of our bodies. We may swallow an aspirin to quiet a headache, an antibiotic to fight an infection, or a tranquilizer to calm us down. We may drink coffee to get going in the morning or wine to relax with friends. We may smoke cigarettes to soothe our nerves. However, many of the substances we consume can harm us or disrupt our behavior or mood. The misuse of such substances has become one of society's biggest problems; it has been estimated that the cost of substance misuse is more than $600 billion each year in the United States alone (NIDA, 2011).

Not only are numerous substances available in our society: new ones are introduced almost every day. Some are harvested from nature, others derived from natural substances, and still others produced in the laboratory. Some, such as antianxiety drugs, require a physician's prescription for legal use. Others, such as alcohol and nicotine, are legally available to adults. Still others, such as heroin, are illegal under all circumstances. In 1962 only 4 million people in the United States had ever used marijuana, cocaine, heroin, or another illegal substance; today the number has climbed to more than 94 million (NSDUH, 2010). In fact, 22 million people have used illegal substances within the past month. Almost 24 percent of all high school seniors have used an illegal drug within the past month (Johnston et al., 2011).

A *drug* is defined as any substance other than food that affects our bodies or minds. It need not be a medicine or be illegal. The term "substance" is now frequently used in place of "drug," in part because many people fail to see that such substances as alcohol, tobacco, and caffeine are drugs, too. When a person ingests a substance—whether it be alcohol, cocaine, marijuana, or some form of medication—trillions of powerful molecules surge through the bloodstream and into the brain. Once there, the molecules set off a series of biochemical events that disturb the normal operation of the brain and body. Not surprisingly, then, substance misuse may lead to various kinds of abnormal functioning.

Substances may cause *temporary* changes in behavior, emotion, or thought. As Duncan found out, for example, an excessive amount of alcohol may lead to *intoxication* (literally, "poisoning"), a temporary state of poor judgment, mood changes, irritability, slurred speech, and poor coordination. Drugs such as LSD may produce a particular form of intoxication, sometimes called *hallucinosis,* which consists of perceptual distortions and hallucinations.

Some substances can also lead to *long-term* problems. People who regularly ingest them may develop **substance use disorders,** patterns of maladaptive behaviors and reactions brought about by repeated use of substances (APA, 2013, 2012). People with a substance use disorder may come to crave a particular substance and rely on it excessively, resulting in damage to their family and social relationships, poor functioning at work, and/or danger to themselves or others (see Table 12-1). In many cases, people with such a disorder also become physically dependent on the substance,

table: 12-1

DSM-5 Checklist

Substance Use Disorder

1. A maladaptive pattern of substance use leading to significant impairment or distress.

2. Presence of two or more of the following symptoms within a 12-month period:

   (a) Substance is often taken in larger amounts or over a longer period than intended.

   (b) Persistent desire or unsuccessful efforts to reduce or control substance use.

   (c) Excessive time spent trying to obtain, use, or recover from the effects of substance.

   (d) Failure to fulfill major role obligations at work, school, or home as a result of recurrent substance use.

   (e) Continued use of substance despite persistent social or interpersonal problems caused by it.

   (f) Cessation or reduction of important social, occupational, or recreational activities because of substance use.

   (g) Recurrent substance use in situations where use poses physical hazards.

   (h) Continued substance use despite awareness that it is causing or exacerbating a physical or psychological problem.

   (i) Tolerance effects.

   (j) Withdrawal reactions.

   (k) Craving or strong desire or urge to use substance.

Based on APA, 2013, 2012.

developing a *tolerance* for it and experiencing *withdrawal* reactions. When individuals develop **tolerance,** they need increasing doses of the substance to produce the desired effect. **Withdrawal** reactions consist of unpleasant and sometimes dangerous symptoms—cramps, anxiety attacks, sweating, nausea—that occur when the individuals suddenly stop taking or cut back on the substance. Duncan, who described his problems to fellow members at an Alcoholics Anonymous meeting, was caught in a form of substance use disorder called *alcohol use disorder.* When he was a college student and later a lawyer, alcohol damaged his family, social, academic, and work life. He also built up a tolerance for alcohol over time and experienced withdrawal symptoms such as vomiting and shaking when he tried to stop using it.

In any given year, 8.9 percent of all teens and adults in the United States, over 22 million people, display substance use disorders (NSDUH, 2010). The highest rate in the United States is found among American Indians (15.5 percent), while the lowest is among Asian Americans (3.5 percent). White Americans, Hispanic Americans, and African Americans display rates between 9 and 10 percent (NSDUH, 2010) (see Figure 12-1). Only 11 percent of all people with substance use disorders receive treatment from a mental health professional (NSDUH, 2010).

The substances people misuse fall into several categories: *depressants, stimulants, hallucinogens,* and *cannabis.* In this chapter you will read about some of the most problematic substances and the abnormal patterns they may produce. In addition, at the end of the chapter, you'll read about *gambling disorder,* a problem that DSM-5 lists as an additional addictive disorder. By listing this behavioral pattern alongside the substance use disorders, DSM-5 is suggesting that this problem has addictive-like symptoms and causes that share more than a passing similarity to those at work in substance use disorders.

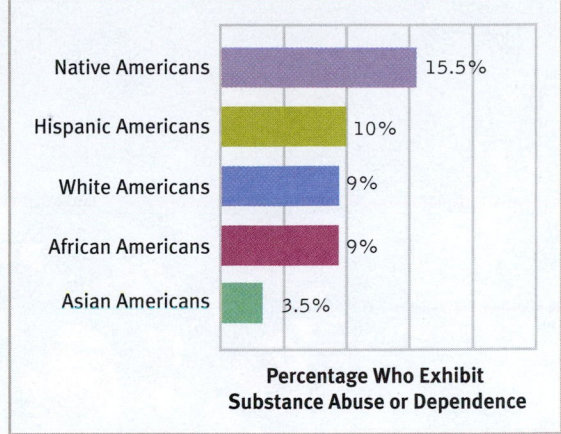

**Percentage Who Exhibit
Substance Abuse or Dependence**

Figure 12-1
How do races differ in substance use disorders? In the United States, American Indians are much more likely than members of other ethnic or cultural groups to display substance use disorders. Conversely, Asian Americans are less likely to display such disorders (NSDUH, 2010).

Depressants

Depressants slow the activity of the central nervous system. They reduce tension and inhibitions and may interfere with a person's judgment, motor activity, and concentration. The three most widely used groups of depressants are *alcohol, sedative-hypnotic drugs,* and *opioids.*

Alcohol

The World Health Organization estimates that 2 billion people worldwide consume **alcohol.** In the United States more than half of all residents at least from time to time drink beverages that contain alcohol (NSDUH, 2010). Purchases of beer, wine, and liquor amount to tens of billions of dollars each year in the United States alone.

When people consume five or more drinks on a single occasion, it is called a *binge-drinking* episode. Twenty-four percent of people in the United States over the age of 11, most of them male, binge-drink each month (NSDUH, 2010). Nearly 7 percent of persons over 11 years of age binge-drink at least five times each month (NSDUH, 2010). They are considered heavy drinkers. Among heavy drinkers, males outnumber females by more than two to one, around 8 percent to 4 percent.

All alcoholic beverages contain *ethyl alcohol,* a chemical that is quickly absorbed into the blood through the lining of the stomach and the intestine. The ethyl alcohol immediately begins to take effect as it is carried in the bloodstream to the central nervous system (the brain and spinal cord), where it acts to depress, or slow, functioning by binding to various neurons. One important group of neurons to which ethyl alcohol binds are those that normally receive the neurotransmitter GABA. As you saw in Chapter 5, GABA carries an *inhibitory* message—a message to stop firing—when it is received at certain neurons. When alcohol binds to receptors on those neurons, it apparently helps GABA to shut down the neurons, thus helping to relax the drinker (Kelm et al., 2011; Melón & Boehm, 2011; Nace, 2011, 2005).

At first ethyl alcohol depresses the areas of the brain that control judgment and inhibition; people become looser, more talkative, and often more friendly. As their inner

•**substance use disorder**•Pattern of maladaptive behaviors and reactions brought about by repeated use of a substance, sometimes also including tolerance for the substance and withdrawal reactions.

•**tolerance**•The adjustment that the brain and the body make to the regular use of certain drugs so that ever larger doses are needed to achieve the earlier effects.

•**withdrawal**•Unpleasant, sometimes dangerous reactions that may occur when people who use a drug regularly stop taking or reduce their dosage of the drug.

•**alcohol**•Any beverage containing ethyl alcohol, including beer, wine, and liquor.

AP Photo

Prohibition: Turkish style

Young adults gather in a public garden to protest Turkey's 2011 alcohol laws. The new laws, which build on previous restrictions, ban alcohol from sports advertising and events for young people and limit the sale of alcoholic beverages to licensed shops and restaurants.

control breaks down, they may feel relaxed, confident, and happy. When more alcohol is absorbed, it slows down additional areas in the central nervous system, leaving the drinkers less able to make sound judgments, their speech less careful and less coherent, and their memory weaker. Many people become highly emotional and perhaps loud and aggressive.

Motor difficulties increase as drinking continues, and reaction times slow. People may be unsteady when they stand or walk and clumsy in performing even simple activities. They may drop things, bump into doors and furniture, and misjudge distances. Their vision becomes blurred, particularly peripheral, or side, vision, and they have trouble hearing. As a result, people who have drunk too much alcohol may have great difficulty driving or solving simple problems.

The extent of the effect of ethyl alcohol is determined by its *concentration,* or proportion, in the blood. Thus a given amount of alcohol will have less effect on a large person than on a small one (see Table 12-2). Gender also affects the concentration of alcohol in the blood. Women have less of the stomach enzyme *alcohol dehydrogenase,* which breaks down alcohol in the stomach before it enters the blood. So women become more intoxicated than men on equal doses of alcohol, and women may be at greater risk for physical and psychological damage from alcohol than men who drink similar quantities of alcohol (Hart et al., 2010).

Levels of impairment are closely related to the concentration of ethyl alcohol in the blood. When the alcohol concentration reaches 0.06 percent of the blood volume, a person usually feels relaxed and comfortable. By the time it reaches 0.09 percent, however, the drinker crosses the line into intoxication. If the level goes as high as 0.55 percent, death will probably result. Most people lose consciousness before they can drink enough to reach this level; nevertheless, more than 1,000 people in the United States die each year from too high a blood alcohol level (Hart et al., 2010).

The effects of alcohol subside only when the alcohol concentration in the blood declines. Most of the alcohol is broken down, or *metabolized,* by the liver into carbon

Substance misuse and sports fans

A problem that has received growing attention in recent years is the excessive intake of alcohol by fans at sporting events. While two soccer players were jumping for a high ball at this 2002 playoff game in Athens, Greece, fans of the rival teams—many of them intoxicated—ripped out plastic seats, threw flares on the field, and hurled coins and rocks at the players.

Aris Messinis/AP Photo

dioxide and water, which can be exhaled and excreted. The average rate of this metabolism is 25 percent of an ounce per hour, but different people's livers work at different speeds; thus rates of "sobering up" vary. Despite popular belief, only time and metabolism can make a person sober. Drinking black coffee, splashing cold water on one's face, or "pulling oneself together" cannot hurry the process.

Alcohol Use Disorder Though legal, alcohol is actually one of the most dangerous of recreational drugs, and its reach extends across the life span. In fact, around 14 percent of elementary school students admit to some alcohol use, while 41 percent of high school seniors drink alcohol each month (most to the point of intoxication) and 3 percent report drinking every day (Johnston et al., 2011). Similarly, alcohol misuse is a major problem on college campuses (see *PsychWatch* on the next page).

Surveys indicate that over a one-year period, 7.4 percent of all adults in the United States display *alcohol use disorder,* known in popular terms as *alcoholism,* while over 13 percent of adults display it at some point in their lives (NSDUH, 2010). Men with this disorder outnumber women by at least 2 to 1. Many teenagers also experience the disorder (Johnston et al., 2011).

The prevalence of alcoholism in a given year is around the same (7 to 9 percent) for white Americans, African Americans, and Hispanic Americans (SAMHSA, 2008). The men in these groups, however, show strikingly different age patterns. For white American and Hispanic American men, the rate of alcoholism is highest—over 18

If alcohol is highly addictive and capable of causing so many psychological, physical, social, and personal problems, why does it remain legal in most countries?

table: **12-2**

Relationships Between Sex, Weight, Oral Alcohol Consumption, and Blood Alcohol Level

Absolute Alcohol (oz.)	Beverage Intake*	Female (100 lb.)	Male (100 lb.)	Female (150 lb.)	Male (150 lb.)	Female (200 lb.)	Male (200 lb.)
½	1 oz. spirits† / 1 glass wine / 1 can beer	0.045	0.037	0.03	0.025	0.022	0.019
1	2 oz. spirits / 2 glasses wine / 2 cans beer	0.090	0.075	0.06	0.050	0.045	0.037
2	4 oz. spirits / 4 glasses wine / 4 cans beer	0.180	0.150	0.12	0.100	0.090	0.070
3	6 oz. spirits / 6 glasses wine / 6 cans beer	0.270	0.220	0.18	0.150	0.130	0.110
4	8 oz. spirits / 8 glasses wine / 8 cans beer	0.360	0.300	0.24	0.200	0.180	0.150
5	10 oz. spirits / 10 glasses wine / 10 cans beer	0.450	0.370	0.30	0.250	0.220	0.180

*In 1 hour.
†100-proof spirits.
Source: Hart et al., 2010.

PsychWatch

College Binge Drinking: An Extracurricular Crisis

Drinking large amounts of alcohol in a short time, or *binge drinking,* is a serious problem on college campuses, as well as in many other settings (NSDUH, 2010). Studies show that 40 percent of college students binge-drink at least once each year, some of them six times or more per month (NCASA, 2007; Sharma, 2005). These are higher rates than those displayed by people of the same age who are not in college (Hart et al., 2010). In many circles, alcohol use is an accepted part of college life, but consider some of the following statistics:

▶ Alcohol-related arrests account for 83 percent of all campus arrests (NCASA, 2007).

▶ Alcohol may be a factor in nearly 40 percent of academic problems and 28 percent of all college dropouts (Anderson, 1994).

▶ Approximately 600,000 students each year are physically or emotionally traumatized or assaulted by a student drinker (NCASA, 2007; Hingson et al., 2002).

▶ Most undergraduates define binge drinking incorrectly and overestimate how many drinks constitute sensible drinking (Cooke et al., 2010).

▶ Binge drinking often has a lingering effect on mood, memory, brain functioning, and heart functioning (Heffernan et al., 2010; Howland et al., 2010; Zagroseck et al., 2010).

▶ Binge drinking is tied to 1,700 deaths, 500,000 injuries, and tens of thousands of cases of sexual assault, including date rape, every year (McCauley et al., 2010; NCASA,

Testing the limits Binge drinking, similar to this display at a college campus party, has led to a number of deaths in recent years.

2007; Wechsler & Wuethrich, 2002; Wechsler et al., 2000).

▶ The number of female binge drinkers among college students has increased 31 percent over the past decade.

These findings have led some educators to describe binge drinking as "the No. 1 public health hazard" for full-time college students, and many researchers and clinicians have turned their attention to it. Researchers at the Harvard School of Public Health, for example, have surveyed more than 50,000 students at 120 college campuses around the United States (Wechsler & Nelson, 2008; Wechsler et al., 2004, 1995, 1994). One of their surveys found that the students most likely to binge-drink were those who lived in a fraternity or sorority house, pursued a party-centered life-

style, and engaged in high-risk behaviors such as substance misuse or having multiple sex partners. Other surveys have also suggested that students who were binge drinkers in high school were more likely to binge-drink in college.

Efforts to change such patterns have begun. For example, some universities now provide substance-free dorms: 36 percent of the residents in such dorms continue to be occasional binge drinkers, according to one study, compared to 75 percent of those who live in a fraternity or sorority house (Wechsler et al., 2002). This and other current research efforts are promising. However, most people in the clinical field agree that much more work is needed to help us fully understand, prevent, and treat what has become a major societal problem.

percent—during young adulthood, compared to 8 percent among African American men in that age group. For African American men, the rate is highest during late middle age, 15 percent compared to 8 percent among white American and Hispanic American men in that age group.

American Indians, particularly men, tend to display a higher rate of alcohol use disorder than any of these groups (Dickerson, 2011). Overall 15 percent of them have this disorder, although their specific prevalence rates differ across the various American

Indian reservation communities (SAMHSA, 2008). Generally, Asians in the United States and elsewhere have a lower rate of alcoholism (3 percent) than do people from other cultures. As many as one-half of these individuals have a deficiency of alcohol dehydrogenase, the chemical responsible for breaking down alcohol, so they react quite negatively to even a modest intake of alcohol. Such reactions in turn help prevent extended use (Tsuang & Pi, 2011).

CLINICAL PICTURE Generally speaking, people with alcohol use disorder drink large amounts regularly and rely on it to enable them to do things that would otherwise make them anxious. Eventually the drinking interferes with their social behavior and ability to think and work. They may have frequent arguments with family members or friends, miss work repeatedly, and even lose their jobs. MRI scans of chronic heavy drinkers have revealed damage in various regions of their brains and, correspondingly, impairments in their short-term memory, speed of thinking, attention skills, and balance (Hernandez-Avila & Kranzler, 2011; Grilly, 2006).

Individually, people vary in their patterns of alcoholism. Some drink large amounts of alcohol every day and keep drinking until intoxicated. Others go on periodic binges of heavy drinking that can last weeks or months. They may remain intoxicated for days and later be unable to remember anything about the period. Still others may limit their excessive drinking to weekends, evenings, or both.

TOLERANCE AND WITHDRAWAL For many individuals, alcohol use disorder includes the symptoms of tolerance and withdrawal reactions. As their bodies build up a tolerance for alcohol, they need to drink ever greater amounts to feel its effects. In addition, they experience withdrawal symptoms when they stop drinking. Within hours their hands, tongue, and eyelids begin to shake; they feel weak and nauseated; they sweat and vomit; their heart beats rapidly; and their blood pressure rises. They may also become anxious, depressed, unable to sleep, or irritable (APA, 2013).

A small percentage of people with alcohol use disorder experience a particularly dramatic withdrawal reaction called **delirium tremens ("the DTs")**. It consists of terrifying visual hallucinations that begin within three days after they stop or reduce their drinking. Some people see small, frightening animals chasing or crawling on them or objects dancing about in front of their eyes. Mark Twain gave a classic picture of delirium tremens in Huckleberry Finn's description of his father:

> I don't know how long I was asleep, but ... there was an awful scream and I was up. There was Pap looking wild, and skipping around every which way and yelling about snakes. He said they was crawling up on his legs; and then he would give a jump and scream, and say one had bit him on the cheek—but I couldn't see no snakes. He started and run round ... hollering "Take him off! he's biting me on the neck!" I never see a man look so wild in the eyes. Pretty soon he ... fell down panting; then he rolled over ... kicking things every which way, and striking and grabbing at the air with his hands, and screaming ... there was devils a-hold of him. He wore out by and by. ... He says ...
>
> "Tramp-tramp-tramp: that's the dead; tramp-tramp-tramp; they're coming after me; but I won't go. Oh, they're here; don't touch me. ... They're cold; let go. ..."
>
> Then he went down on all fours and crawled off, begging them to let him alone. ...
>
> *(Twain, 1885)*

Like most other alcohol withdrawal symptoms, the DTs usually run their course in two to three days. However, people who experience severe withdrawal reactions such as this may also have seizures, lose consciousness, suffer a stroke, or even die. Today certain medical procedures can help prevent or reduce such extreme reactions (Doweiko, 2006).

•**delirium tremens (DTs)**•A dramatic withdrawal reaction experienced by some people who are alcohol-dependent. It consists of confusion, clouded consciousness, and terrifying visual hallucinations.

AP Photo/Matt York

Dealing with DUI

In an effort to better publicize, prevent, and punish intoxicated driving, Phoenix, Arizona, has recently created DUI chain gangs for all to see. Members of these chain gangs, men convicted of drunken driving, don bright pink shirts and perform tasks such as the burial of people who have died of alcohol abuse or dependence.

What Is the Personal and Social Impact of Alcoholism? Alcoholism destroys millions of families, social relationships, and careers (Hernandez–Avila & Kranzler, 2011; Murphy et al., 2005). Medical treatment, lost productivity, and losses due to deaths from alcoholism cost society many billions of dollars annually. The disorder also plays a role in more than one-third of all suicides, homicides, assaults, rapes, and accidental deaths, including 30 percent of all fatal automobile accidents in the United States (Gifford et al., 2010). Altogether, intoxicated drivers are responsible for 12,000 deaths each year. More than 30 million adults (12 percent) have driven while intoxicated at least once in the past year (NSDUH, 2010).

Alcoholism has serious effects on the 30 million children of persons with this disorder. Home life for these children is likely to include much conflict and perhaps sexual or other forms of abuse. In turn, the children themselves have higher rates of psychological problems (Hall & Webster, 2002). Many have low self-esteem, poor communication skills, poor sociability, and marital problems (Watt, 2002).

Long-term excessive drinking can also seriously damage one's physical health (Hernandez–Avila & Kranzler, 2011; Nace, 2011, 2005; Gifford et al., 2010). It so overworks the liver that people may develop an irreversible condition called *cirrhosis,* in which the liver becomes scarred and dysfunctional. Cirrhosis accounts for more than 29,000 deaths each year (CDC, 2010). Alcohol use disorder may also damage the heart and lower the immune system's ability to fight off cancer and bacterial infections and to resist the onset of AIDS after infection.

Long-term excessive drinking also causes major nutritional problems. Alcohol makes people feel full and lowers their desire for food, yet it has no nutritional value. As a result, chronic drinkers become malnourished, weak, and prone to disease. Their vitamin and mineral deficiencies may also cause problems. An alcohol-related deficiency of vitamin B (thiamine), for example, may lead to **Korsakoff's syndrome,** a disease marked by extreme confusion, memory loss, and other neurological symptoms (Hernandez–Avila & Kranzler, 2011; Nace, 2011, 2005). People with Korsakoff's syndrome cannot remember the past or learn new information and may make up for their memory losses by *confabulating*—reciting made-up events to fill in the gaps.

BETWEEN THE LINES

Alcohol and Auto Fatalities: A Special Relationship

Single-vehicle fatalities are more likely to involve alcohol than multiple-vehicle fatalities. ‹‹

There are proportionately more alcohol-related vehicle fatalities during the night than during the day and during the weekends than during the week. ‹‹

(Fatality Facts, 2004)

Finally, women who drink during pregnancy place their fetuses at risk (Gifford et al., 2010). Excessive alcohol use during pregnancy may cause a baby to be born with **fetal alcohol syndrome,** a pattern of abnormalities that can include intellectual developmental disorder, hyperactivity, head and face deformities, heart defects, and slow growth. It has been estimated that in the overall population around 1 of every 1,000 babies is born with this syndrome (Hart et al., 2010). The rate may increase to as many as 29 of every 1,000 babies of women who are problem drinkers. If all alcohol-related birth defects are counted (known as *fetal alcohol effect*), the rate becomes 80 to 200 such births per 1,000 heavy-drinking women. In addition, heavy drinking early in pregnancy often leads to a miscarriage. According to surveys, 10 percent of pregnant American women have drunk alcohol during the past month and 4.4 percent of pregnant women have had binge-drinking episodes (NSDUH, 2010).

Sedative-Hypnotic Drugs

Sedative-hypnotic drugs, also called **anxiolytic** (meaning "anxiety-reducing") **drugs,** produce feelings of relaxation and drowsiness. At low dosages, the drugs have a calming or sedative effect. At higher dosages, they are sleep inducers, or hypnotics. The sedative-hypnotic drugs include *barbiturates* and *benzodiazepines*.

Barbiturates

First discovered in Germany more than 100 years ago, **barbiturates** were widely prescribed in the first half of the twentieth century to fight anxiety and to help people sleep. Although still prescribed by some physicians, these drugs have been largely replaced by benzodiazepines, which are generally safer drugs. Barbiturates can cause many problems, not the least of which is misuse. Several thousand deaths a year are caused by accidental or suicidal overdoses.

Barbiturates are usually taken in pill or capsule form. In low doses they reduce a person's level of excitement in the same way that alcohol does, by attaching to receptors on the neurons that receive the inhibitory neurotransmitter GABA and by helping GABA operate at those neurons (Hart et al., 2010). People can get intoxicated from large doses of barbiturates, just as they do from alcohol. And, like alcohol, barbiturates are broken down in the liver. At too high a level, the drugs can halt breathing, lower blood pressure, and lead to coma and death.

Repeated use of barbiturates can quickly result in *sedative-hypnotic use disorder* (Dupont & Dupont, 2011, 2005). Users may spend much of the day intoxicated, irritable, and unable to do their work. Some organize their lives around the drug and need increasing amounts of it to calm down or fall asleep. A great danger of barbiturate tolerance is that the lethal dose of the drug remains the same even while the body is building up a tolerance for its sedating effects. Once the prescribed dose stops reducing anxiety or inducing sleep, the user is all too likely to increase it without medical supervision and eventually may ingest a dose that proves fatal. The individual may also experience withdrawal symptoms such as nausea, anxiety, and sleep problems. Barbiturate withdrawal is particularly dangerous because it can cause convulsions.

Benzodiazepines

Chapter 5 described **benzodiazepines,** the antianxiety drugs developed in the 1950s, as the most popular sedative-hypnotic drugs available. Xanax, Ativan, and Valium are just three of the dozens of these compounds in clinical use. Altogether, about 100 million prescriptions are written annually for this group of drugs (Bisaga, 2008). Like alcohol and barbiturates, they calm people by binding to receptors on the neurons that receive GABA and by increasing GABA's activity at those neurons (Dupont & Dupont, 2011, 2005). These drugs, however, relieve anxiety without making people as drowsy as other kinds of sedative-hypnotics. They are also less likely to slow a person's breathing, so they are less likely to cause death in the event of an overdose.

DURING THE HOLIDAYS **2–3 TIMES MORE PEOPLE DIE** IN ALCOHOL-RELATED **CRASHES** & **40%** OF TRAFFIC FATALITIES **INVOLVE A DRIVER WHO IS IMPAIRED BY ALCOHOL**

Source: National Highway Traffic Safety Administration, Traffic Safety Facts, December 2007.

AP Photo/PR Newswire

Holiday warning
Drinking and driving pose a significant danger throughout the year. However, alcohol-related automobile crashes and fatalities increase precipitously during Christmas and New Year, prompting the National Traffic Safety Administration to distribute informational ads such as this one during the holiday season.

•**Korsakoff's syndrome**•An alcohol-related disorder marked by extreme confusion, memory impairment, and other neurological symptoms.

•**fetal alcohol syndrome**•A cluster of problems in a child, including low birth weight, irregularities in the head and face, and intellectual deficits, caused by excessive alcohol intake by the mother during pregnancy.

•**sedative-hypnotic drug**•A drug used in low doses to reduce anxiety and in higher doses to help people sleep. Also called *anxiolytic drug*.

•**barbiturates**•Addictive sedative-hypnotic drugs that reduce anxiety and help produce sleep.

•**benzodiazepines**•The most common group of antianxiety drugs, which includes Valium and Xanax.

•**opioid**•Opium or any of the drugs derived from opium, including morphine, heroin, and codeine.

•**opium**•A highly addictive substance made from the sap of the opium poppy.

•**morphine**•A highly addictive substance derived from opium that is particularly effective in relieving pain.

•**heroin**•One of the most addictive substances derived from opium.

•**endorphins**•Neurotransmitters that help relieve pain and reduce emotional tension. They are sometimes referred to as the body's own opioids.

When benzodiazepines were first discovered, they seemed so safe and effective that physicians prescribed them generously, and their use spread. Eventually it became clear that in high enough doses the drugs can cause intoxication and lead to an addictive pattern of use (Bisaga, 2008). At some point in their lives, as many as 1 percent of the adults in North America display a sedative-hypnotic use disorder that centers on benzodiazepines and thus become subject to some of the same dangers that researchers have identified in barbiturate misuse (Berg, 2010; Sareen et al., 2004).

Opioids

Opioids include opium—taken from the sap of the opium poppy—and the drugs derived from it, such as heroin, morphine, and codeine. **Opium** itself has been in use for thousands of years. In the past it was used widely in the treatment of medical disorders because of its ability to reduce both physical and emotional pain. Eventually, however, physicians discovered that the drug was addictive.

In 1804 a new substance, **morphine,** was derived from opium. Named after Morpheus, the Greek god of sleep, this drug relieved pain even better than opium did and initially was considered safe. However, wide use of the drug eventually revealed that it, too, could lead to addiction. So many wounded soldiers in the United States received morphine injections during the Civil War that morphine addiction became known as "soldiers' disease."

Can you think of other substances or activities that, like opioids, can be helpful in controlled portions but dangerous when pursued excessively or uncontrollably?

In 1898 morphine was converted into yet another new pain reliever, **heroin.** For several years heroin was viewed as a wonder drug and was used as a cough medicine and for other medical purposes. Eventually, however, physicians learned that heroin is even more addictive than the other opioids. By 1917 the U.S. Congress had concluded that all drugs derived from opium were addictive (see Table 12-3), and it passed a law making opioids illegal except for medical purposes.

Still other drugs have been derived from opium, and *synthetic* (laboratory-blended) opioids such as *methadone* have also been developed (Dilts & Dilts, 2011, 2005). All these opioid drugs—natural and synthetic—are known collectively as *narcotics.* Each drug has a different strength, speed of action, and tolerance level. Morphine and *codeine* are

table: 12-3

Risks and Consequences of Drug Misuse

	Potential Intoxication	Addiction Potential	Risk of Organ Damage or Death	Risk of Severe Social or Economic Consequences	Risk of Severe or Long-Lasting Mental and Behavioral Change
Opioids	High	High	Low	High	Low to moderate
Sedative-hypnotics					
Barbiturates	Moderate	Moderate to high	Moderate to high	Moderate to high	Low
Benzodiazepines	Moderate	Moderate	Low	Low	Low
Stimulants (cocaine, amphetamines)	High	High	Moderate	Low to moderate	Moderate to high
Alcohol	High	Moderate	High	High	High
Cannabis	High	Low to moderate	Low	Low to moderate	Low
Mixed drugs	High	High	High	High	High

Source: Hart et al., 2010; APA, 2000.

medical narcotics usually prescribed to relieve pain. Heroin is illegal in the United States in all circumstances.

Narcotics are smoked, inhaled, snorted, injected by needle just beneath the skin ("skin popped"), or injected directly into the bloodstream ("mainlined"). Injection seems to be the most common method of narcotic use, although the other techniques have been used increasingly in recent years (NSDUH, 2008). An injection quickly brings on a *rush*—a spasm of warmth and ecstasy that is sometimes compared with orgasm. The brief spasm is followed by several hours of a pleasant feeling called a *high* or *nod*. During a high, the drug user feels relaxed, happy, and unconcerned about food, sex, or other bodily needs.

Opioids create these effects by depressing the central nervous system, particularly the centers that help control emotion. The drugs attach to brain receptor sites that ordinarily receive **endorphins**—neurotransmitters that help relieve pain and reduce emotional tension (Epstein, Phillips, & Preston, 2011; Hart et al., 2010). When neurons at these receptor sites receive opioids, they produce pleasurable and calming feelings just as they would do if they were receiving endorphins. In addition to reducing pain and tension, opioids cause nausea, narrowing of the pupils ("pinpoint pupils"), and constipation—bodily reactions that can also be brought about by releases of endorphins in the brain.

Opioid Use Disorder

Heroin use exemplifies the kinds of problems posed by opioids. After taking heroin repeatedly for just a few weeks, users may develop *opioid use disorder.* Their use of heroin interferes significantly with their social and occupational functioning, and their lives center around the drug. They may also build a tolerance for heroin and experience a withdrawal reaction when they stop taking it (Ahmed, 2011; Hart et al., 2010). At first the withdrawal symptoms are anxiety, restlessness, sweating, and rapid breathing; later they include severe twitching, aches, fever, vomiting, diarrhea, loss of appetite, high blood pressure, and weight loss of up to 15 pounds (due to loss of bodily fluids). These symptoms usually peak by the third day, gradually subside, and disappear by the eighth day. A person in heroin withdrawal can either wait out the symptoms or end withdrawal by taking the drug again.

Such individuals soon need heroin just to avoid going into withdrawal, and they must continually increase their doses in order to achieve even that relief. The temporary high becomes less intense and less important. The persons may spend much of their time planning their next dose, in many cases turning to criminal activities, such as theft and prostitution, to support the expensive "habit" (Allen, 2005).

Surveys suggest that close to 1 percent of adults in the United States display opioid use disorder at some time in their lives. The rate of such dependence dropped considerably during the 1980s, rose in the early 1990s, fell in the late 1990s, and now seems to be relatively high once again (NSDUH, 2010). The number of persons currently addicted to opioids of one kind or another is estimated to be at least 400,000. The actual number may be even higher, however, given the reluctance of many people to admit an illegal activity.

What Are the Dangers of Opioid Use?

Once again, heroin provides a good example of the dangers of opioid use. The most immediate danger of heroin use is an overdose, which closes down the respiratory center in the brain, almost paralyzing breathing and in many cases causing death. Death is particularly likely during sleep, when a person is unable to fight this effect by consciously working to breathe. People who resume heroin use after having avoided it for some time often make the fatal mistake of taking the same dose they

Purer blend
Heroin, derived from poppies such as this one in a poppy field in southern Afghanistan, is purer and stronger today than it was three decades ago (65 percent pure versus 5 percent pure).

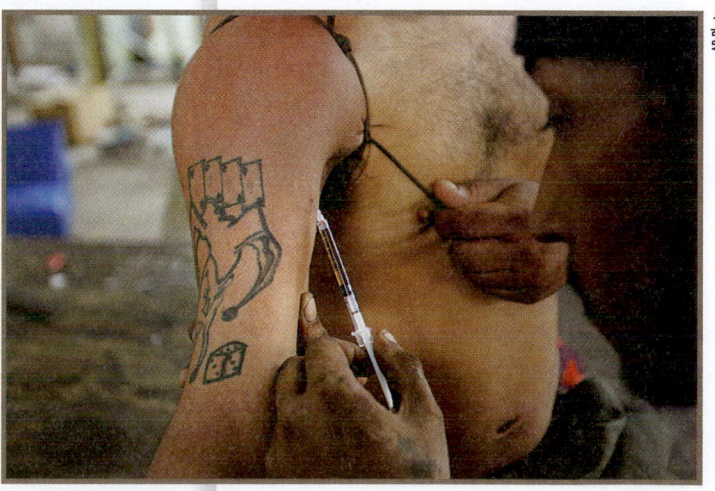

Injecting heroin
Opioids may be taken by mouth, inhaled, snorted, injected just beneath the surface of the skin, or injected intravenously. Here, one addict injects another with heroin inside one of the many so-called shooting galleries where addicts gather in downtown San Juan, Puerto Rico.

had built up to before. Because their bodies have been without heroin for some time, however, they can no longer tolerate this high level. Each year approximately 2 percent of persons addicted to heroin and other opioids die under the drug's influence, usually from an overdose (Theodorou & Haber, 2005; APA, 2000).

Heroin users run other risks as well. Often pushers mix heroin with a cheaper drug or even a deadly substance such as cyanide or battery acid. In addition, dirty needles and other unsterilized equipment spread infections such as AIDS, hepatitis C, and skin abscesses (Dilts & Dilts, 2011, 2005; Batki & Nathan, 2008). In some areas of the United States the HIV infection rate among active heroin users is reported to be as high as 60 percent (APA, 2000).

Stimulants

Stimulants are substances that increase the activity of the central nervous system, resulting in increased blood pressure and heart rate, greater alertness, and sped-up behavior and thinking. Among the most troublesome stimulants are *cocaine* and *amphetamines*, whose effects on people are very similar. When users report different effects, it is often because they have ingested different amounts of the drugs. Two other widely used and legal stimulants are *caffeine* and *nicotine* (see *PsychWatch* on page 360).

Cocaine

Cocaine—the central active ingredient of the coca plant, found in South America—is the most powerful natural stimulant now known (Acosta, Haller, & Schnoll, 2011, 2005). The drug was first separated from the plant in 1865. Native people of South America, however, have chewed the leaves of the plant since prehistoric times for the energy and alertness the drug offers. Processed cocaine (*hydrochloride powder*) is an odorless, white, fluffy powder. For recreational use, it is most often snorted so that it is absorbed through the mucous membrane of the nose. Some users prefer the more powerful effects of injecting cocaine intravenously or smoking it in a pipe or cigarette.

Sherlock Holmes took his bottle from the corner of the mantelpiece, and his hypodermic syringe from its neat morocco case. With his long white nervous fingers, he adjusted the delicate needle and rolled back his left shirtcuff. For some little time his eyes rested thoughtfully upon the sinewy forearm and wrist, all dotted and scarred with innumerable puncture-marks. Finally, he thrust the sharp point home, pressed down the tiny piston, and sank back into the velvet-lined armchair with a long sigh of satisfaction.

Three times a day for many months I had witnessed this performance, but custom had not reconciled my mind to it. . . .

"Which is it today," I asked, "morphine or cocaine?"

He raised his eyes languidly from the old black-letter volume which he had opened.

"It is cocaine," he said, "a seven-per-cent solution. Would you care to try it?"

"No, indeed," I answered brusquely. "My constitution has not got over the Afghan campaign yet. I cannot afford to throw any extra strain upon it."

He smiled at my vehemence. "Perhaps you are right, Watson," he said. "I suppose that its influence is physically a bad one. I find it, however, so transcendently stimulating and clarifying to the mind that its secondary action is a matter of small moment."

"But consider!" I said earnestly. "Count the cost! Your brain may, as you say, be roused and excited, but it is a pathological and morbid process which involves increased tissue-change and . . . a permanent weakness. You know, too, what a black reaction comes upon you. Surely, the game is hardly worth the candle."

(Doyle, 1938, pp. 91–92)

•**cocaine**•An addictive stimulant obtained from the coca plant. It is the most powerful natural stimulant known.

•**free-base**•A technique for ingesting cocaine in which the pure cocaine basic alkaloid is chemically separated from processed cocaine, vaporized by heat from a flame, and inhaled with a pipe.

•**crack**•A powerful, ready-to-smoke free-base cocaine.

For years people believed that cocaine posed few problems aside from intoxication and, on occasion, temporary psychosis. Like Sherlock Holmes, many felt that the benefits outweighed the costs. Only later did researchers come to appreciate its many dangers (Haile, 2012). Their insights came after society witnessed a dramatic increase in the drug's popularity and in problems related to its use. In the early 1960s an estimated 10,000 persons in the United States had tried cocaine. Today 28 million people have tried it, and 1.6 million—most of them teenagers or young adults—are using it currently (NSDUH, 2010). In fact, 3 percent of all high school seniors have used cocaine within the past month and almost 7 percent have used it within the past year (Johnston et al., 2011).

Cocaine brings on a euphoric rush of well-being and confidence. Given a high enough dose, this rush can be almost orgasmic, like the one produced by heroin. At first cocaine stimulates the higher centers of the central nervous system, making users feel excited, energetic, talkative, and even euphoric. As more is taken, it stimulates other centers of the central nervous system, producing a faster pulse, higher blood pressure, faster and deeper breathing, and further arousal and wakefulness.

Cocaine apparently produces these effects largely by increasing supplies of the neurotransmitter *dopamine* at key neurons throughout the brain (Haile, 2012; Haney, 2008; Kosten et al., 2008) (see Figure 12-2). Excessive amounts of dopamine travel to receiving neurons throughout the central nervous system and overstimulate them. In addition, cocaine appears to increase the activity of the neurotransmitters *norepinephrine* and *serotonin* in some areas of the brain (Haile, 2012; Hart et al., 2010).

High doses of the drug produce *cocaine intoxication*, whose symptoms are poor muscle coordination, grandiosity, bad judgment, anger, aggression, compulsive behavior, anxiety, and confusion. Some people experience hallucinations, delusions, or both, a condition called *cocaine-induced psychosis.*

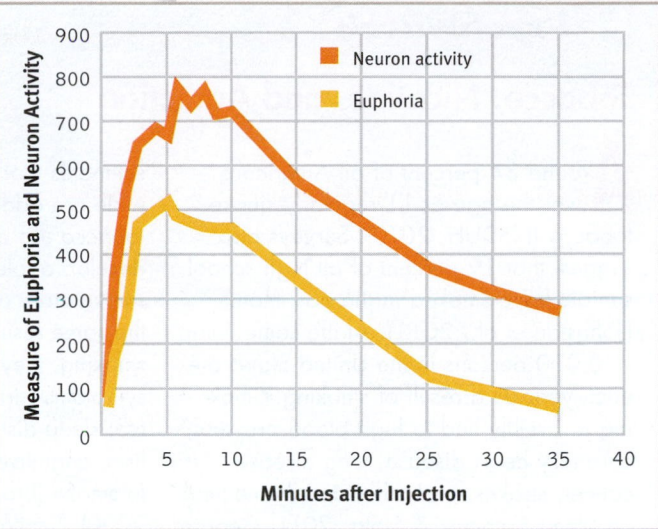

Figure 12-2
Biochemical euphoria The subjective experiences of euphoria after a cocaine injection closely parallel cocaine's action at dopamine-using neurons. The peak experience of euphoria seems to occur around the same time as the peak of neuron activity (Fowler, Volkow, & Wolf, 1995, p. 110; Cook, Jeffcoat, & Perez-Reyes, 1985).

A young man described how, after free-basing, he went to his closet to get his clothes, but his suit asked him, "What do you want?" Afraid, he walked toward the door, which told him, "Get back!" Retreating, he then heard the sofa say, "If you sit on me, I'll kick your ass." With a sense of impending doom, intense anxiety, and momentary panic, the young man ran to the hospital where he received help.

(Allen, 1985, pp. 19–20)

As the stimulant effects of cocaine subside, the user experiences a depression-like letdown, popularly called *crashing,* a pattern that may also include headaches, dizziness, and fainting (Acosta et al., 2011, 2005). For occasional users, the aftereffects usually disappear within 24 hours, but they may last longer for people who have taken a particularly high dose. These individuals may sink into a stupor, deep sleep, or, in some cases, coma.

Ingesting Cocaine In the past, cocaine use and impact were limited by the drug's high cost. Moreover, cocaine was usually snorted, a form of ingestion that has less powerful effects than either smoking or injection (Haile, 2012). Since 1984, however, the availability of newer, more powerful, and sometimes cheaper forms of cocaine has produced an enormous increase in the use of the drug. For example, many people now ingest cocaine by **free-basing,** a technique in which the pure cocaine basic alkaloid is chemically separated, or "freed," from processed cocaine, vaporized by heat from a flame, and inhaled through a pipe.

Millions more people use **crack,** a powerful form of free-base cocaine that has been boiled down into crystalline balls. It is smoked with a special pipe and makes a crackling

BETWEEN THE LINES

Cocaine Alert

Cocaine accounts for more drug treatment admissions than any other drug (Hart et al., 2010; SAMHSA, 2007). ‹‹

PsychWatch

Tobacco, Nicotine, and Addiction

Around 34 percent of all Americans over the age of 11 regularly smoke tobacco (NSDUH, 2010). Surveys also suggest that 19 percent of all high school seniors have smoked in the past month (Johnston et al., 2011). At the same time, 440,000 persons in the United States die each year as a result of smoking. Smoking is directly tied to high blood pressure, coronary heart disease, lung disease, cancer, strokes, and other deadly medical problems (Schmitz & Slotts, 2011; George & Weinberger, 2008; Hymowitz, 2005). Nonsmokers who inhale cigarette smoke from their environment have a higher risk of lung cancer and other diseases. And the 15.3 percent of all pregnant women who smoke are more likely than nonsmokers to deliver premature and underweight babies (Hart et al., 2010; NSDUH, 2010).

So why do people continue to smoke? Because *nicotine,* the active substance in tobacco and a stimulant of the central nervous system, is as addictive as heroin, perhaps even more so (Hart et al., 2010; Report of the Surgeon General, 1988). Indeed, the World Health Organization

estimates that 1.1 billion people worldwide are addicted to nicotine and display *tobacco use disorder.* Regular smokers develop a tolerance for nicotine and must smoke more and more in order to achieve the same results. When they try to stop smoking, they experience withdrawal symptoms—irritability, increased appetite, sleep disturbances, slower metabolism, cognitive difficulties, and cravings to smoke (Brandon et al., 2009; APA, 2000). Similarly, laboratory animals find nicotine addictive and readily learn to perform behaviors that lead to intravenous nicotine injections (Sorge & Clarke, 2011). As a stimulant, nicotine acts on the same neurotransmitters and reward center in the brain as amphetamines and cocaine (George & Weinberger, 2008).

The declining acceptability of smoking in our society has created a market for products and techniques to help people kick the habit. Most of these methods do not work very well. Self-help kits, commercial programs, and support groups are of limited help. Smokers who do quit permanently tend to be successful only after several failed attempts.

A fairly successful behavioral treatment for nicotine addiction is *aversion therapy.* In one version of this approach, known as *rapid smoking,* the smoker sits in a closed room and puffs quickly on a cigarette, as often as once every six seconds, until he or she begins to feel ill and cannot take another puff. The feelings of illness become associated with smoking, and the smoker develops an aversion to cigarettes (George & Weinberger, 2008).

Several biological treatments have also been developed. A common one is the use of *nicotine gum,* an over-the-counter product that contains a high level of nicotine that is released as the smoker chews. Theoretically, people who obtain nicotine by chewing will no longer feel a need to smoke. A similar approach is the *nicotine patch,* which is attached to the skin like a Band-Aid. Its nicotine is absorbed through the skin throughout the day, supposedly easing withdrawal and reducing the smoker's need for nicotine. Studies find that both nicotine gum and the nicotine patch help people to abstain from smoking (George & Weinberger, 2008). Still other popular biological products are *nicotine lozenges, nicotine nasal spray,* and certain antidepressant drugs.

Most smokers find such interventions on their own or through the advice of friends or physicians. A growing number, however, seek help from so-called "quitlines"— telephone-based programs that provide counseling or offer access to biological treatments (Lichtenstein et al., 2010).

The more one smokes, the harder it is to quit. On the positive side, however, former smokers' risk of disease and death decreases steadily the longer they continue to avoid smoking. This assurance may be a powerful motivator for many smokers, and, in fact, around 46 percent of regular smokers want to stop and are eventually able to stop permanently (NSDUH, 2010). In the meantime, more than 1,000 people die of smoking-related diseases each day.

Worth a thousand words The U.S. Department of Health and Human Services has ruled that graphic image warnings must appear soon on all cigarette packs. Its pictorial directive is similar to that initiated several years ago by the European Union. Each member country of the Union is required to display one of 42 illustrated warnings, including the one seen here, on cigarette packs sold within its boundaries.

CIGARETTES

Brand

Smoke contains benzene, nitrosamines, formaldehyde and hydrogen cyanide

European Community via Getty Images

sound as it is inhaled (hence the name). Crack is sold in small quantities at a fairly low cost, a practice that has resulted in crack epidemics among people who previously could not have afforded cocaine, primarily those in poor urban areas (Acosta et al., 2011, 2005). Around 1.4 percent of high school seniors report having used crack within the past year, the same rate as in 1993, yet down from a peak of 2.7 percent in 1999 (Johnston et al., 2011).

What Are the Dangers of Cocaine? Aside from cocaine's harmful effects on behavior, cognition, and emotion, the drug poses serious physical dangers (Paczynski & Gold, 2011). Its growing use in powerful forms has caused the annual number of cocaine-related emergency room incidents in the United States to multiply more than 100 times since 1982, from around 4,000 cases to 423,000 (DAWN, 2010). In addition, cocaine use has been linked to as many as 20 percent of all suicides by men under 61 years of age (Garlow, 2002).

Smoking crack
Crack, a powerful form of free-base cocaine, is produced by boiling cocaine down into crystalline balls and is smoked with a crack pipe.

The greatest danger of cocaine use is an overdose. Excessive doses have a strong effect on the respiratory center of the brain, at first stimulating it and then depressing it, to the point where breathing may stop. Cocaine can also create major, even fatal, heart irregularities or brain seizures that bring breathing or heart functioning to a sudden stop (Acosta et al., 2011, 2005). In addition, pregnant women who use cocaine run the risk of having a miscarriage and of having children with abnormalities in immune functioning, attention and learning, thyroid size, and dopamine and serotonin activity in the brain (Hart et al., 2010; Kosten et al., 2008).

Amphetamines

The **amphetamines** are stimulant drugs that are manufactured in the laboratory. Some common examples are amphetamine (Benzedrine), dextroamphetamine (Dexedrine), and methamphetamine (Methedrine). First produced in the 1930s to help treat asthma, amphetamines soon became popular among people trying to lose weight; athletes seeking an extra burst of energy; soldiers, truck drivers, and pilots trying to stay awake; and students studying for exams through the night (Haile, 2012). Physicians now know the drugs are far too dangerous to be used so casually, and they prescribe them much less freely.

Amphetamines are most often taken in pill or capsule form, although some people inject the drugs intravenously or smoke them for a quicker, more powerful effect. Like cocaine, amphetamines increase energy and alertness and reduce appetite when taken in small doses; produce a rush, intoxication, and psychosis in high doses; and cause an emotional letdown as they leave the body. Also like cocaine, amphetamines stimulate the central nervous system by increasing the release of the neurotransmitters dopamine, norepinephrine, and serotonin throughout the brain, although the actions of amphetamines differ somewhat from those of cocaine (Haile, 2012; Hart et al., 2010).

One kind of amphetamine, **methamphetamine** (nicknamed *crank*), has had a major surge in popularity in recent years and so warrants special focus. Almost 6 percent of all persons over the age of 11 in the United States have used this stimulant at least once. Around 0.2 percent use it currently (NSDUH, 2010). It is available in the form of crystals (also known by the street names *ice* and *crystal meth*), which are smoked by users.

Most of the nonmedical methamphetamine in the United States is made in small "stovetop laboratories," which typically operate for a few days in a remote area and then move on to a new—safer—location (Hart et al., 2010). Such laboratories have been around since the 1960s, but they have increased eightfold—in number, production, and confiscations by authorities—over the past decade. A major health concern is that the secret laboratories expel dangerous fumes and residue (Burgess, 2001).

•**amphetamine**•A stimulant drug that is manufactured in the laboratory.

•**methamphetamine**•A powerful amphetamine drug that has experienced a surge in popularity in recent years, posing major health and law enforcement problems.

DON'T LET DRUG DEALERS CHANGE
THE FACE OF YOUR NEIGHBOURHOOD.
Call Crimestoppers anonymously on 0800 555 111.

Methamphetamine dependence: spreading the word
This powerful ad shows the degenerative effects of methamphetamine addiction on a woman over a four-year period—from age 36 in the top photo to age 40 in the bottom one.

Since 1989, when the media first began reporting about the dangers of smoking methamphetamine crystals, the rise in usage has been dramatic. At this point, 15 million Americans have tried this stimulant at least once (NSDUH, 2010). Until recently, use of this drug has been much more prevalent in western parts of the United States, but its use has now spread east as well. Similarly, methamphetamine-linked emergency room visits are rising in hospitals throughout all parts of the country (DAWN, 2010).

Methamphetamine is about as likely to be used by women as men. Around 40 percent of current users are women (NSDUH, 2010). The drug is particularly popular today among biker gangs, rural Americans, and urban gay communities and has gained wide use as a "club drug," the term for those drugs that regularly find their way to all night dance parties, or "raves" (Hopfer, 2011; Hart et al., 2010).

Like other kinds of amphetamines, methamphetamine increases activity of the neurotransmitters dopamine, serotonin, and norepinephrine, producing increased arousal, attention, and related effects (Acosta et al., 2011, 2005; Dean & London, 2010). It can have serious negative effects on a user's physical, mental, and social life. Of particular concern is that it damages nerve endings, a problem called *neurotoxicity.* But users focus more on methamphetamine's immediate positive impact, including perceptions by many that it makes them feel hypersexual and uninhibited (Jefferson, 2005). Such perceived effects have contributed to several major societal problems. In the public health arena, for example, one-third of all men who tested positive for HIV in Los Angeles in 2004 reported having used this drug. In the area of law enforcement, one survey of police agencies had 58 percent of them reporting that methamphetamine is the leading drug they battle today.

Stimulant Use Disorder

Regular use of either cocaine or amphetamines may lead to *stimulant use disorder.* The stimulant comes to dominate the individual's life, and the person may remain under the drug's effects much of each day and function poorly in social relationships and at work. Regular stimulant use may also cause problems in short-term memory or attention (Lundqvist, 2010; Kubler et al., 2005). Tolerance and withdrawal reactions to the drug may also develop. Higher doses are needed to gain the desired effects, and stopping it results in deep depression, fatigue, sleep problems, irritability, and anxiety (Barr et al., 2011; Hill & Weiss, 2011). These withdrawal symptoms may last for weeks or even months after drug use has ended. In a given year, 0.5 percent of all people over the age of 11 display stimulant use disorder that is centered on cocaine, and 0.2 percent display stimulant use disorder centered on amphetamines (NSDUH, 2010).

Caffeine

Caffeine is the world's most widely used stimulant. Around 80 percent of the world's population consumes it daily. Most of this caffeine is taken in the form of coffee (from the coffee bean); the rest is consumed in tea (from the tea leaf), cola (from the kola nut), so-called *energy drinks,* chocolate (from the cocoa bean), and numerous prescription and over-the-counter medications, such as Excedrin.

Around 99 percent of ingested caffeine is absorbed by the body and reaches its peak concentration within an hour. It acts as a stimulant of the central nervous system, again producing a release of the neurotransmitters dopamine, serotonin, and norepinephrine in the brain (Julien et al., 2011; Cauli & Morelli, 2005). Thus it increases arousal and motor activity and reduces fatigue. It can also disrupt mood, fine motor movement, and reaction time and may interfere with sleep (Juliano, Anderson, & Griffiths, 2011; Hart et al., 2010; Judelson et al., 2005). Finally, at high doses, it increases the rate of breathing and gastric acid secretions in the stomach.

More than two to three cups of brewed coffee (250 milligrams of caffeine) can produce caffeine intoxication, which may include such symptoms as restlessness, nervousness, anxiety, stomach disturbances, twitching, and increased heart rate (Juliano et al., 2011; Paton & Beer, 2001). Grand mal seizures and fatal respiratory failure or circulatory failure can occur at doses greater than 10 grams of caffeine (about 100 cups of coffee).

Many people who suddenly stop or cut back on their usual intake of caffeine experience withdrawal symptoms—even some individuals whose regular consumption is low (two and a half cups of coffee daily or seven cans of cola). One study had adult participants consume their usual caffeine-filled drinks and foods for two days, then abstain from all caffeine-containing foods for two days while taking placebo pills that they thought contained caffeine, and then abstain from such foods for two days while taking actual caffeine pills (Silverman et al., 1992). More participants experienced headaches (52 percent), depression (11 percent), anxiety (8 percent), and fatigue (8 percent) during the two-day placebo period than during the caffeine periods. In addition, people reported using more unauthorized medications (13 percent) and performed experimental tasks more slowly during the placebo period than during the caffeine periods.

"It was the best of Starbucks. It was the worst of Starbucks."

Investigators often assess caffeine's impact by measuring coffee consumption, yet coffee also contains other chemicals that may be dangerous to one's health. Although some early studies hinted at links between caffeine and cancer (particularly pancreatic cancer), the evidence is not conclusive (Juliano et al., 2011; Hart et al., 2010). On the other hand, studies do suggest that there may be correlations between high doses of caffeine and heart rhythm irregularities (arrhythmias), high cholesterol levels, and risk of heart attacks (Hart et al., 2010). And it appears that high doses of caffeine during pregnancy increase the risk of miscarriage (Weng, Odouli, & Li, 2008). As public awareness of these possible health risks has increased, caffeine consumption has declined and the consumption of decaffeinated drinks has increased over the past few decades. There are, however, indications that caffeine consumption may currently be on the rise once again.

Hallucinogens, Cannabis, and Combinations of Substances

Other kinds of substances may also cause problems for their users and for society. *Hallucinogens* produce delusions, hallucinations, and other sensory changes. *Cannabis* produces sensory changes, but it also has depressant and stimulant effects, and so it is considered apart from hallucinogens in DSM-5. And many individuals take *combinations of substances.*

Hallucinogens

Hallucinogens are substances that cause powerful changes in sensory perception, from strengthening a person's normal perceptions to inducing illusions and hallucinations. They produce sensations so out of the ordinary that they are sometimes called "trips." The trips may be exciting or frightening, depending on how a person's mind interacts with the drugs. Also called *psychedelic drugs,* the hallucinogens include LSD, mescaline, psilocybin, and MDMA (Ecstasy) (see *PsychWatch* on page 365). Many of these substances come from plants or animals; others are laboratory-produced.

LSD (lysergic acid diethylamide), one of the most famous and most powerful hallucinogens, was derived by Swiss chemist Albert Hoffman in 1938 from a group

•**caffeine**•The world's most widely used stimulant, most often consumed in coffee.

•**hallucinogen**•A substance that causes powerful changes primarily in sensory perception, including strengthening perceptions and producing illusions and hallucinations. Also called *psychedelic drug.*

•**LSD (lysergic acid diethylamide)**• A hallucinogenic drug derived from ergot alkaloids.

Celebrities Who Have Died of Substance Overdose in the 21st Century

Whitney Houston, singer (cocaine and heart disease, 2012) ‹‹

Amy Winehouse, singer (alcohol poisoning, 2011) ‹‹

Michael Jackson, performer and songwriter (prescription polydrug, 2009) ‹‹

Heath Ledger, actor (prescription polydrug, 2008) ‹‹

Anna Nicole Smith, model (prescription polydrug, 2007) ‹‹

Ol' Dirty Bastard, rapper, Wu-Tang Clan (polydrug, 2004) ‹‹

Rick James, singer (cocaine, 2004) ‹‹

Dee Dee Ramone, musician, The Ramones (heroin, 2002) ‹‹

of naturally occurring drugs called *ergot alkaloids.* During the 1960s, a decade of social rebellion and experimentation, millions of persons turned to the drug as a way of expanding their experience. Within two hours of being swallowed, LSD brings on a state of *hallucinogen intoxication,* sometimes called *hallucinosis,* marked by a general strengthening of perceptions, particularly visual perceptions, along with psychological changes and physical symptoms. People may focus on small details—the pores of the skin, for example, or individual blades of grass. Colors may seem enhanced or take on a shade of purple. Illusions may be experienced in which objects seem distorted and may appear to move, breathe, or change shape. A person under the influence of LSD may also hallucinate—seeing people, objects, or forms that are not actually present.

> **Why do various club drugs (for example, Ecstasy and crystal meth), often used at "raves," seem to fall in and out of favor rather quickly?**

Hallucinosis may also cause one to hear sounds more clearly, feel tingling or numbness in the limbs, or confuse the sensations of hot and cold. Some people have been badly burned after touching flames that felt cool to them under the influence of LSD. The drug may also cause different senses to cross, an effect called *synesthesia.* Colors, for example, may be "heard" or "felt."

LSD can also induce strong emotions, from joy to anxiety or depression. The perception of time may slow dramatically. Long-forgotten thoughts and feelings may resurface. Physical symptoms can include sweating, palpitations, blurred vision, tremors, and poor coordination. All of these effects take place while the user is fully awake and alert, and they wear off in about six hours.

It seems that LSD produces these symptoms primarily by binding to some of the neurons that normally receive the neurotransmitter *serotonin,* changing the neurotransmitter's activity at those sites (Julien et al., 2011). These neurons ordinarily help the brain send visual information and control emotions (as you saw in Chapter 8); thus LSD's activity there produces various visual and emotional symptoms.

More than 14 percent of all persons in the United States have used LSD or another hallucinogen at some point in their lives. Around 0.5 percent, or 1.3 million persons, are currently using them (NSDUH, 2010). Although people do not usually develop tolerance to LSD or have withdrawal symptoms when they stop taking it, the drug

"It's only salvia"

When a picture of young pop star Miley Cyrus smoking from a bong surfaced on the Internet in 2010, Cyrus pointed out that she was simply using the legal psychoactive drug *salvia,* whose popularity is now growing in the United States. Salvia induces minutes-long hallucinations and feelings of disconnection from one's body. Advocates say the drug's short impact makes it safe, but its chronic use has been tied circumstantially to some violent acts.

Club Drugs: X Marks the (Wrong) Spot

You probably know of the drug *MDMA* (*3,4-methylenedioxymethamphetamine*) by its common street name, *Ecstasy*. It is also known as X, Adam, hug, beans, and love drug. This laboratory-produced drug is technically a *stimulant,* similar to amphetamines, but it also produces hallucinogenic effects and so is often considered a *hallucinogenic* drug (McDowell, 2011, 2005; Pechnick & Cunningham, 2011). MDMA was developed as far back as 1910, but only in the past 25 years has it gained life as a club drug. Today, in the United States alone, consumers collectively take hundreds of thousands of doses of MDMA weekly (Weaver & Schnoll, 2008; McDowell, 2005). Altogether, 12 million Americans over the age of 11 have now tried MDMA at least once in their lifetimes, 760,000 in the past year (NSDUH, 2010). Around 6.5 percent of all high school seniors have used it within the past year.

What is Ecstasy's allure? As a stimulant and hallucinogen, it helps to raise the mood of many partygoers and provides them with an energy boost that enables them to keep dancing and partying. Moreover, it produces strong feelings of attachment and connectedness in users. However, it also turns out to be a dangerous drug, particularly when taken repeatedly.

What Are the Dangers of Using Ecstasy?

As MDMA has gained wider and wider use, the drug has received increasing research scrutiny. As it turns out, the mood and energy lift produced by MDMA comes at a high price (Hart et al., 2010; Weaver & Schnoll, 2008; Wiegand et al., 2008). The problems that the drug may cause include the following:

- Immediate psychological problems such as confusion, depression, sleep difficulties, severe anxiety, and paranoid thinking. These symptoms may also continue for weeks after ingestion of MDMA.

- Significant impairment of memory and other cognitive skills.

Feeling the effects Shortly after taking MDMA, this couple manifests a shift in mood, energy, and behavior. Although this drug can feel pleasurable and energizing, often it produces undesired immediate effects, including confusion, depression, anxiety, sleep difficulties, and paranoid thinking.

- Physical symptoms such as muscle tension, nausea, blurred vision, faintness, and chills or sweating. MDMA also causes many people to clench and grind their teeth for hours at a time.

- Increases in heart rate and blood pressure, which place people with heart disease at special risk.

- Reduced sweat production. At a hot, crowded dance party, taking Ecstasy can even cause heat stroke, or *hyperthermia*. Users generally try to remedy this problem by drinking lots of water, but since the body cannot sweat under the drug's influence, the excess fluid intake can result in an equally perilous condition known as *hyponatremia*, or "water intoxication."

- Potential liver damage. This may happen when users take MDMA in combination with other drugs that are broken down by the same liver enzyme, such as the cheaper compound *DXM*, which is commonly mixed in with Ecstasy by dealers.

How Does MDMA Operate in the Brain?

MDMA works by causing the neurotransmitters *serotonin* and (to a lesser extent) *dopamine* to be released all at once throughout the brain, at first increasing and then depleting a person's overall supply of the neurotransmitters. MDMA also interferes with the body's ability to produce new supplies of serotonin. With repeated use, the brain eventually produces less and less serotonin (McDowell, 2011, 2005; Hart et al., 2010; Baggot & Mendelson, 2001).

Ecstasy's impact on these neurotransmitters accounts for its various psychological effects—and associated problems (Malberg & Bonson, 2001; Zakzanis et al., 2007). High levels of serotonin, such as those produced after one first ingests MDMA, produce feelings of well-being, sociability, and even euphoria. Conversely, abnormally low serotonin levels are associated with depression and anxiety. This is why "coming down" off a dose of Ecstasy often produces those psychological symptoms. Moreover, because repeated use of Ecstasy leads to long-term serotonin deficits, the depression and anxiety may be long-lasting. Finally, serotonin is linked to our ability to concentrate; thus the repeated use of Ecstasy may produce problems in memory and learning.

End of the Honeymoon?

The dangers of MDMA do not yet seem to outweigh its pleasures in the minds of many individuals. In fact, use of the drug is still expanding to many social settings beyond raves, dance clubs, and college scenes (Weaver & Schnoll, 2008). Clearly, despite the research indications listed here, the honeymoon for this drug is not yet over.

poses dangers for both one-time and long-term users. It is so powerful that any dose, no matter how small, is likely to produce enormous perceptual, emotional, and behavioral reactions. Sometimes the reactions are extremely unpleasant—an experience called a "bad trip." Reports of LSD users who injure themselves or others usually involve a reaction of this kind:

A 21-year-old woman was admitted to the hospital along with her lover. He had had a number of LSD experiences and had convinced her to take it to make her less constrained sexually. About half an hour after ingestion of approximately 200 microgm., she noticed that the bricks in the wall began to go in and out and that light affected her strangely. She became frightened when she realized that she was unable to distinguish her body from the chair she was sitting on or from her lover's body. Her fear became more marked after she thought that she would not get back into herself. At the time of admission she was hyperactive and laughed inappropriately. Her stream of talk was illogical and affect labile. Two days later, this reaction had ceased.

(Frosch, Robbins, & Stern, 1965)

Another danger is the long-term effect that LSD may have (Weaver & Schnoll, 2008). Some users eventually develop psychosis or a mood or anxiety disorder. And a number have *flashbacks*—a recurrence of the sensory and emotional changes after the LSD has left the body (Halpern et al., 2003). Flashbacks may occur days or even months after the last LSD experience.

Cannabis

Cannabis sativa, the hemp plant, grows in warm climates throughout the world. The drugs produced from varieties of hemp are, as a group, called **cannabis.** The most powerful of them is *hashish;* the weaker ones include the best-known form of cannabis, **marijuana,** a mixture derived from the buds, crushed leaves, and flowering tops of hemp plants. Each of these drugs is found in various strengths because the potency of a cannabis drug is greatly affected by the climate in which the plant is grown, the way it was prepared, and the manner and duration of its storage. Of the several hundred active chemicals in cannabis, **tetrahydrocannabinol (THC)** appears to be the one most responsible for its effects. The greater the THC content, the more powerful the cannabis; hashish contains a large portion, while marijuana's is small.

When smoked, cannabis produces a mixture of hallucinogenic, depressant, and stimulant effects. At low doses, the smoker typically has feelings of joy and relaxation and may become either quiet or talkative. Some smokers, however, become anxious, suspicious, or irritated, especially if they have been in a bad mood or are smoking in an upsetting environment. Many smokers report sharpened perceptions and fascination with the intensified sounds and sights around them. Time seems to slow down, and distances and sizes seem greater than they actually are. This overall "high" is technically called *cannabis intoxication.* Physical changes include reddening of the eyes, fast heartbeat, increases in blood pressure and appetite, dryness in the mouth, and dizziness. Some people become drowsy and may fall asleep.

In high doses, cannabis produces odd visual experiences, changes in body image, and hallucinations. Smokers may become confused or impulsive. Some worry that other people are trying to hurt them. Most of the effects of cannabis last two to six hours. The changes in mood, however, may continue longer.

Cannabis Use Disorder
Until the early 1970s, the use of marijuana, the weak form of cannabis, rarely led to a pattern of *cannabis use disorder.* Today, however, many people, including large numbers of high school students, are indeed developing this dis-

The source of marijuana
Marijuana is made from the leaves of the hemp plant, *Cannabis sativa.* The plant is an annual herb, reaches a height of between 3 and 15 feet, and is grown in a wide range of altitudes, climates, and soils.

order, getting high on marijuana regularly and finding their social and occupational or academic lives greatly affected (see Figure 12-3). Many regular users also develop a tolerance for marijuana and may experience flulike symptoms, restlessness, and irritability when they stop smoking (Chen et al., 2005). Around 1.7 percent of all persons in the United States have displayed cannabis use disorder in the past year, centered on marijuana in most cases; between 4 and 5 percent develop this disorder at some point in their lives (NSDUH, 2010).

Why have more and more marijuana users developed cannabis use disorder over the past three decades? Mainly because marijuana has changed. The marijuana widely available in the United States today is at least four times more powerful than that used in the early 1970s. The THC content of today's marijuana is, on average, 8 percent, compared to 2 percent in the late 1960s. Marijuana is now grown in places with a hot, dry climate, which increases the THC content.

Is Marijuana Dangerous?
As the strength and use of marijuana have increased, researchers have discovered that smoking it may pose certain dangers (Price, 2011). It occasionally causes panic reactions similar to the ones caused by hallucinogens, and some smokers may fear they are losing their minds (APA, 2000). Typically such reactions end in three to six hours, along with marijuana's other effects.

Because marijuana can interfere with the performance of complex sensorimotor tasks and with cognitive functioning, it has caused many automobile accidents (Ramaekers et al., 2006). Furthermore, people on a marijuana high often fail to remember information, especially anything that has been recently learned, no matter how hard they try to concentrate; thus heavy marijuana smokers are at a serious disadvantage at school or work (Budney et al., 2011; Jaffe & Klein, 2010; Lundqvist, 2010, 2005).

One study compared blood flow in the brain arteries of chronic marijuana users and nonusers (Herning et al., 2005). After one month of abstinence from smoking marijuana, chronic users continued to display higher blood flow than nonusers. Though still higher than normal, the blood flow of light marijuana users (fewer than 16 smokes per week) and of moderate users (fewer than 70 smokes per week) did improve somewhat over the course of the abstinence month. The blood flow of heavy users, however, showed no improvement. This lingering effect may help explain the memory and thinking problems of chronic heavy users of marijuana.

There are indications that regular marijuana smoking may also lead to long-term health problems (Budney et al., 2011; Whitten, 2010; Deplanque, 2005). It may, for example, contribute to lung disease. Studies show that marijuana smoking reduces the ability to expel air from the lungs (Tashkin, 2001) even more than tobacco smoking does (NIDA, 2002). In addition, marijuana smoke contains more tar and benzopyrene than tobacco smoke (Hart et al., 2010). Both of these substances have been linked to cancer. Another concern is the effect of regular marijuana smoking on human reproduction. Studies since the late 1970s have discovered lower sperm counts in men who are chronic smokers of marijuana, and abnormal ovulation has been found in female smokers (Schuel et al., 2002).

Efforts to educate the public about the growing dangers of repeated marijuana use appeared to have paid off throughout the 1980s. The percentage of high school seniors who smoked the substance on a daily basis decreased from 11 percent in 1978 to 2 percent in 1992 (Johnston et al., 1993). Today, however, 5 percent of high school seniors smoke marijuana daily, and as many as 50 percent of seniors do not believe that regular use poses a great risk (Johnston et al., 2011; NSDUH, 2010) (see Figure 12-4).

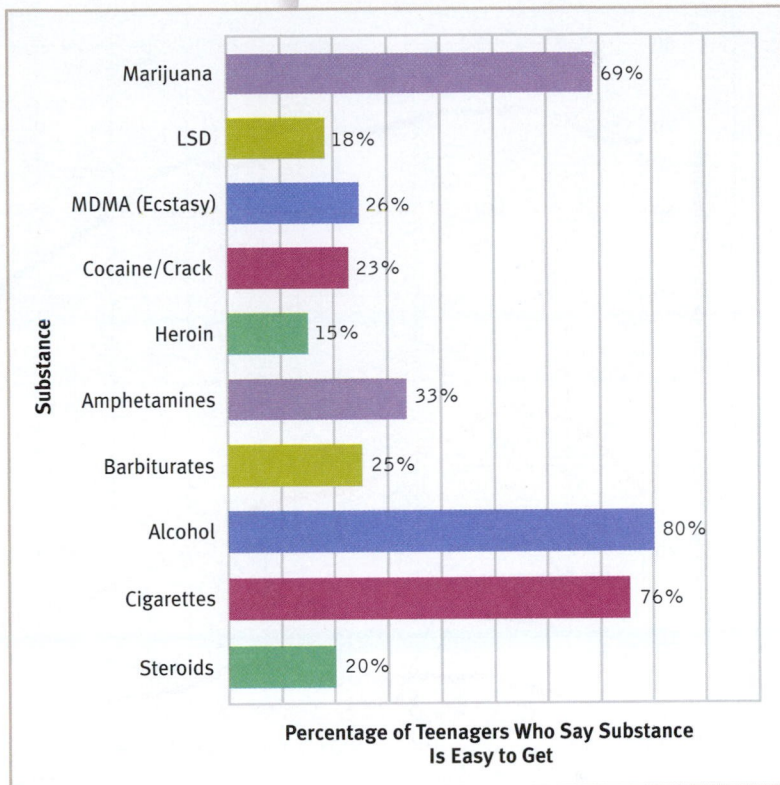

Figure 12-3

How easy is it for teenagers to acquire substances? Most surveyed tenth graders say it is easy to get cigarettes, alcohol, and marijuana, and more than one-fourth say it is easy to get Ecstasy, amphetamines, and barbiturates (Johnston et al., 2011).

•**cannabis drugs**•Drugs produced from the varieties of the hemp plant *Cannabis sativa*. They cause a mixture of hallucinogenic, depressant, and stimulant effects.

•**marijuana**•One of the cannabis drugs, derived from buds, leaves, and flowering tops of the hemp plant *Cannabis sativa*.

•**tetrahydrocannabinol (THC)**•The main active ingredient of cannabis substances.

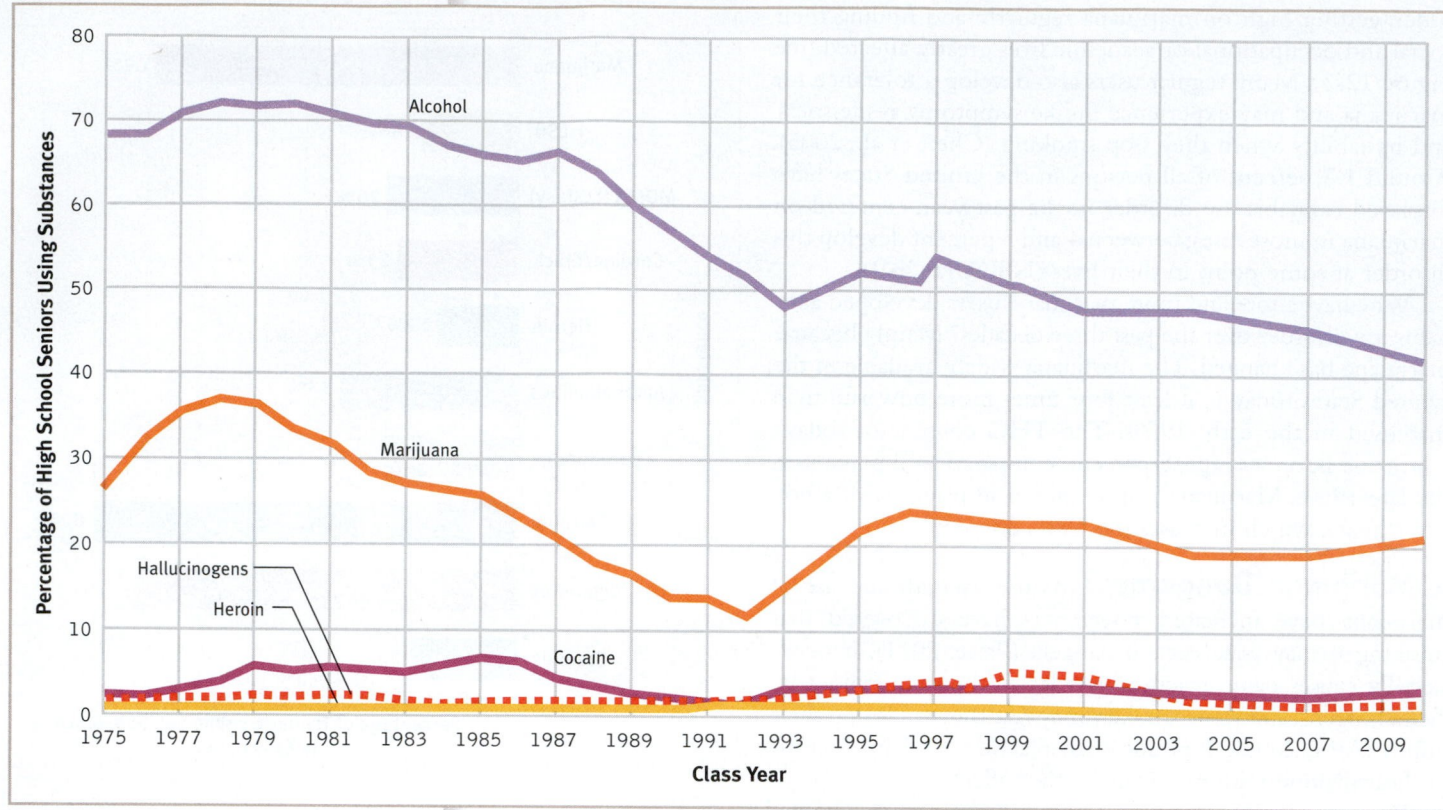

Figure 12-4

Teenagers and substance use The overall percentage of high school seniors who admitted to using substances illicitly at least once within the previous month rose in the 1970s, declined in the 1980s, rose again in the early 1990s, and has been declining slightly since 1997 (Johnston et al., 2011). In addition to the drugs shown in this figure, other drugs used by high school seniors within the past month include MDMA, or Ecstasy (1.4 percent); inhalants (1.4 percent); methamphetamine (0.5 percent); and steroids (1.1 percent).

Cannabis and Society: A Rocky Relationship For centuries cannabis played a respected role in medicine. It was recommended as a surgical anesthetic by Chinese physicians 2,000 years ago and was used in other lands to treat cholera, malaria, coughs, insomnia, and rheumatism. When cannabis entered the United States in the early twentieth century, mainly in the form of marijuana, it was likewise used for various medical purposes. Soon, however, more effective medicines replaced it, and the favorable view of cannabis began to change. Marijuana began to be used as a recreational drug, and its illegal distribution became a law enforcement problem. Authorities assumed it was highly dangerous and outlawed the "killer weed."

In the 1980s researchers developed precise techniques for measuring THC and for extracting pure THC from cannabis; they also developed laboratory forms of THC. These inventions opened the door to new medical applications for cannabis (Mack & Joy, 2001), such as its use in treating glaucoma, a severe eye disease. Cannabis was also found to help patients with chronic pain or asthma, to reduce the nausea and vomiting of cancer patients in chemotherapy, and to improve the appetites of AIDS patients and so combat weight loss in people with that disorder.

In light of these findings, several interest groups campaigned during the late 1980s for the *medical legalization* of marijuana, which operates on the brain and body more quickly than the THC capsules developed in the laboratory. Government agencies resisted this movement, saying prescriptions for pure THC served all needed medical functions. But the battle between advocates and opponents of the legalization of marijuana for medical purposes was just beginning, and, in fact, that battle has continued to the present day (Munsey, 2010).

In 2005, the United States Supreme Court ruled 6 to 3 that medically ill marijuana smokers and those who help them grow or obtain marijuana can be prosecuted, even if their physicians prescribe it and even if they live in states where medical marijuana use is legal. Although this ruling was initially considered a blow to the medical marijuana cause, proponents have fought on, and in 2009 the U.S. Attorney General directed federal prosecutors to not pursue cases against medical marijuana users or their caregivers who are complying with state laws. Moreover, in 2011 and 2012 several state governors and city mayors—from both political parties—petitioned the federal government to reclassify marijuana as a drug with accepted medical uses (Cooper, 2011). Some of them further proposed that the possession of marijuana—for any use—be decriminalized (Mak, 2012). And, in fact, in 2012 residents of the states of Colorado and Washington voted to legalize marijuana for use of any kind—although such state measures still can be blocked by the federal government.

In the meantime, the Canadian government has taken a different tack. Based on a series of studies and trial programs, Health Canada, the country's health care regulator, now legally permits the medical use of marijuana by individuals who are suffering from severe and debilitating illnesses, and it allows the sale of medical marijuana in select pharmacies, making Canada the second country in the world, after the Netherlands, to do so.

Combinations of Substances

Because people often take more than one drug at a time, a pattern called *polysubstance use,* researchers have studied the ways in which drugs interact with one another (De La Garza & Kalechstein, 2012). Two important discoveries have emerged from this work: the phenomena of *cross-tolerance* and *synergistic effects.*

Sometimes two or more drugs are so similar in their actions on the brain and the body that as people build a tolerance for one drug, they are simultaneously developing a tolerance for the other, even if they have never taken the latter. Correspondingly, users who display such **cross-tolerance** can reduce the symptoms of withdrawal from one drug by taking the other. Alcohol and antianxiety drugs are cross-tolerant, for example, so it is sometimes possible to reduce the alcohol withdrawal reaction of delirium tremens by administering benzodiazepines, along with vitamins and electrolytes (Hart et al., 2010).

When different drugs are in the body at the same time, they may multiply, or potentiate, each other's effects. The combined impact, called a **synergistic effect,** is often greater than the sum of the effects of each drug taken alone: a small dose of one drug mixed with a small dose of another can produce an enormous change in body chemistry.

One kind of synergistic effect occurs when two or more drugs have *similar actions* (McCance-Katz, 2010). For instance, alcohol, benzodiazepines, barbiturates, and opioids—all depressants—may severely depress the central nervous system when mixed (Hart et al., 2010). Combining them, even in small doses, can lead to extreme intoxication, coma, and even death. A young man may have just a few alcoholic drinks at a party, for example, and shortly afterward take a moderate dose of barbiturates to help him fall asleep. He believes he has acted with restraint and good judgment—yet he may never wake up.

A different kind of synergistic effect results when drugs have *opposite,* or *antagonistic, actions.* Stimulant drugs, for example, interfere with the liver's usual disposal of barbiturates and alcohol. Thus people who combine barbiturates or alcohol with cocaine or amphetamines may build up toxic, even lethal, levels of the depressant drugs in their systems. Students who take amphetamines to help them study late into the night and then take barbiturates to help them fall asleep are unknowingly placing themselves in serious danger.

Each year tens of thousands of people are admitted to hospitals with a multiple-drug emergency, and several thousand of them die (DAWN, 2010). Sometimes the cause is carelessness or ignorance. Often, however, people use multiple drugs precisely because

Medicinal use
A Canadian woman who suffers from multiple sclerosis holds her Health Canada cannabis permit while smoking a marijuana cigarette at an Ontario courthouse. She is expressing her support for Canada's legalization of marijuana for medicinal use.

Who has more impact on the drug behaviors of teenagers and young adults: rock performers who speak out against drugs or rock performers who praise drugs?

•**cross-tolerance**•Tolerance for a substance one has not taken before as a result of using another substance similar to it.

•**synergistic effect**•In pharmacology, an increase of effects that occurs when more than one substance is acting on the body at the same time.

Continuing problem
A number of popular performers have been victims of polysubstance misuse. The 2008 death of actor Heath Ledger, seen above as the Joker in the film *The Dark Knight,* was caused by a lethal combination of prescribed pain relievers, benzodiazepines, a sleep medication, and an antihistamine. The 2009 death of recording artist and entertainer Michael Jackson (left) was the result of a physician-assisted administration of both sedative and anesthetic drugs.

they enjoy the synergistic effects. In fact, as many as 90 percent of persons who use one illegal drug are also using another to some extent (Rosenthal & Levounis, 2011, 2005).

Fans still mourn the deaths of many celebrities who have been the victims of polysubstance use. Elvis Presley's delicate balancing act of stimulants and depressants eventually killed him. Janis Joplin's mixtures of wine and heroin were ultimately fatal. And John Belushi's and Chris Farley's liking for the combined effect of cocaine and opioids ("speedballs") also ended in tragedy.

What Causes Substance Use Disorders?

Clinical theorists have developed sociocultural, psychological, and biological explanations for why people develop substance use disorders. No single explanation, however, has gained broad support. Like so many other disorders, excessive and chronic drug use is increasingly viewed as the result of a combination of these factors (Brook, 2011).

Sociocultural Views

A number of sociocultural theorists propose that people are most likely to develop substance use disorders when they live under stressful socioeconomic conditions (Gardner et al., 2010). In fact, studies have found that regions with higher levels of unemployment have higher rates of alcoholism. Similarly, lower socioeconomic classes have rates of substance use disorder that are higher than those of the other classes (Marsiglia & Smith, 2010; Franklin & Markarian, 2005). In a related vein, 17 percent of unemployed adults currently use an illegal drug, compared to 8 percent of full-time employed workers and 11.5 percent of part-time employees (NSDUH, 2010).

Other sociocultural theorists propose that substance use disorders are more likely to appear in families and social environments where substance use is valued, or at least accepted. Researchers have, in fact, learned that problem drinking is more common

What factors might explain the finding that different ethnic, religious, and national groups have different rates of alcohol abuse?

among teenagers whose parents and peers drink, as well as among teenagers whose family environments are stressful and unsupportive (Andrews & Hops, 2011; Kliewer, 2010; Pandina et al., 2010). Moreover, lower rates of alcoholism are found among Jews and Protestants, groups in which drinking is typically acceptable only as long as it remains within clear limits, whereas alcoholism rates are higher among the Irish and Eastern Europeans, who do not, on average, draw as clear a line (Hart et al., 2010; Ledoux et al., 2002).

Psychodynamic Views

Psychodynamic theorists believe that people with substance use disorders have powerful *dependency* needs that can be traced to their early years (Dodes & Khantzian, 2011, 2005; Lightdale et al., 2011, 2008). They claim that when parents fail to satisfy a young child's need for nurturance, the child is likely to grow up depending excessively on others for help and comfort, trying to find the nurturance that was lacking during the early years. If this search for outside support includes experimentation with a drug, the person may well develop a dependent relationship with the substance.

Some psychodynamic theorists also believe that certain people respond to their early deprivations by developing a *substance abuse personality* that leaves them particularly prone to drug abuse. Personality inventories, patient interviews, and even animal studies have in fact indicated that individuals who abuse drugs tend to be more dependent, antisocial, impulsive, novelty-seeking, and depressive than other individuals (Hart et al., 2010; Wills & Ainette, 2010). However, these findings are correlational (at least, the findings from human studies), and do not clarify whether such traits lead to chronic drug use or whether repeated drug use causes individuals to be dependent, impulsive, and the like.

In an effort to establish clearer causation, one pioneering longitudinal study measured the personality traits of a large group of nonalcoholic young men and then kept track of each man's development (Jones, 1971, 1968). Years later, the traits of the men who developed alcohol problems in middle age were compared with the traits of those who did not. The men who developed alcohol problems had been more impulsive as teenagers and continued to be so in middle age, a finding suggesting that impulsive men are indeed more prone to develop alcohol problems. Similarly, in various laboratory investigations, "impulsive" rats—those that generally have trouble delaying their rewards—have been found to drink more alcohol when offered it than other rats (Bari et al., 2011; Poulos et al., 1995).

A major weakness of this line of argument is the wide range of personality traits that have been tied to substance use disorders. In fact, different studies point to different "key" traits (Wills & Ainette, 2010). Inasmuch as some people with these disorders appear to be dependent, others impulsive, and still others antisocial, researchers cannot presently conclude that any one personality trait or group of traits stands out in the development of the disorders (Chassin et al., 2001).

Cognitive-Behavioral Views

According to behaviorists, *operant conditioning* may play a key role in substance use disorders. They argue that the temporary reduction of tension or raising of spirits produced by a drug has a rewarding effect, thus increasing the likelihood that the user will seek this reaction again (Kassel et al., 2010; Witkiewitz & Wu, 2010). Similarly, the rewarding effects of a substance may eventually lead users to try higher dosages or more powerful methods of ingestion (see Table 12-4 on the next page). In addition, cognitive theorists argue that such rewards eventually produce an *expectancy* that substances will be rewarding, and this expectation helps motivate individuals to increase drug use at times of tension (Sussman, 2010).

Common substance, uncommon danger
A 13-year-old boy sniffs glue as he lies dazed near a garbage heap. In the United States, at least 6 percent of all people have tried to get high by inhaling the hydrocarbons found in common substances such as glue, gasoline, paint thinner, cleaners, and spray-can propellants (APA, 2013, 2012). Such behavior may lead to *inhalant use disorder* and poses a number of serious medical dangers.

BETWEEN THE LINES

Songs of Substance

Substance use is a popular theme in music. Hit songs include Amy Winehouse's "Rehab," the Velvet Underground's "Heroin," Evanescence's "Call Me When You're Sober," the Rolling Stones' "Sister Morphine," Snoop Dogg's "Gin and Juice," Eric Clapton's "Cocaine," Cyprus Hill's "I Wanna Get High," Eminem's "Drug Ballad," and Lil' Kim's "Drugs." «

Tragic Ending

For years, popular singer Amy Winehouse was caught in a web of substance abuse, including many binges involving alcohol and other drugs. Some of her most successful songs, such as "Rehab," "Addicted," and "Back to Black," were based on her personal struggles with drugs. Winehouse died suddenly in 2011 at age 27. The cause of her death was alcohol poisoning, brought about by binge drinking.

In support of these behavioral and cognitive views, studies have found that many people do in fact drink more alcohol or seek heroin when they feel tense (Kassel et al., 2010; McCarthy et al., 2010). In one study, as participants worked on a difficult anagram task, a confederate planted by the researchers unfairly criticized and belittled them (Marlatt, Kosturn, & Lang, 1975). The participants were then asked to participate in an "alcohol taste task," supposedly to compare and rate alcoholic beverages. The individuals who had been harassed drank more alcohol during the taste task than did the control participants who had not been criticized.

In a manner of speaking, the cognitive-behavioral theorists are arguing that many people take drugs to "medicate" themselves when they feel tense. If so, one would expect higher rates of substance use disorders among people who suffer from anxiety, depression, and other such problems. And, in fact, more than 22 percent of all adults who suffer from psychological disorders have displayed substance use disorders within the past year (Blanco et al., 2010; Nunes et al., 2010; NSDUH, 2010).

A number of behaviorists have proposed that *classical conditioning* may also play a role in these disorders. As you'll remember from Chapters 3 and 5, classical conditioning occurs when two stimuli that appear close together in time become connected in a person's mind, so that eventually, the person responds similarly to each stimulus. Cues or objects present in the environment at the time drugs are taken may act as classically conditioned stimuli and come to produce some of the same pleasure brought on by the drugs themselves (Cunningham et al., 2011; Grimm, 2011). Just the sight of a hypodermic needle, drug buddy, or regular supplier, for example, has been known to comfort people who are addicted to heroin or amphetamines and to relieve their withdrawal symptoms. In a similar manner, cues or objects that are present during withdrawal distress may *produce* withdrawal-like symptoms. One man who had formerly been dependent on heroin experienced nausea and other withdrawal symptoms when he returned to the neighborhood where he had gone through withdrawal in the past—a reaction that led him to start taking heroin again (O'Brien et al., 1975). Although classical conditioning certainly appears to be at work in particular cases of substance use disorder, it has not received widespread research support as the *key* factor in such disorders (Grimm, 2011).

table: 12-4

Methods of Taking Substances

Method	Route	Time to Reach Brain
Inhaling	Drug in vapor form is inhaled through mouth and lungs into circulatory system.	7 seconds
Snorting	Drug in powdered form is snorted into the nose. Some of the drug lands on the nasal mucous membranes, is absorbed by blood vessels, and enters the bloodstream.	4 minutes
Injection	Drug in liquid form directly enters the body through a needle. Injection may be intravenous or intramuscular (subcutaneous). intravenous intramuscular	20 seconds 4 minutes
Oral ingestion	Drug in solid or liquid form passes through esophagus and stomach and finally to the small intestines. It is absorbed by blood vessels in the intestines.	30 minutes
Other routes	Drugs can be absorbed through areas that contain mucous membranes. Drugs can be placed under the tongue, inserted anally and vaginally, and administered as eyedrops.	Variable

Source: Hart et al., 2010; Landry, 1994, p. 24.

Biological Views

In recent years researchers have come to suspect that drug misuse may have biological causes. Studies on genetic predisposition and specific biochemical processes have provided some support for these suspicions.

Genetic Predisposition
For years breeding experiments have been conducted to see whether certain animals are genetically predisposed to become addicted to drugs (Carroll & Meisch, 2011; Weiss, 2011). In several studies, for example, investigators have first identified animals that prefer alcohol to other beverages and then mated them to one another. Generally, the offspring of these animals have been found also to display an unusual preference for alcohol.

Similarly, some research with human twins has suggested that people may inherit a predisposition to misuse substances. One classic study found an alcoholism *concordance* rate of 54 percent in a group of identical twins; that is, if one identical twin displayed alcoholism, the other twin also displayed this disorder in 54 percent of the cases. In contrast, a group of fraternal twins had a concordance rate of only 28 percent (Kaij, 1960). Other studies have found similar twin patterns (Legrand et al., 2005; Tsuang et al., 2001). As you have read, however, such findings do not rule out other interpretations. For one thing, the parenting received by two identical twins may be more similar than that received by two fraternal twins.

A clearer indication that genetics may play a role in substance use disorders comes from studies of alcoholism rates in people adopted shortly after birth (Walters, 2002; Cadoret et al., 1995; Goldstein, 1994). These studies have compared adoptees whose biological parents abuse alcohol with adoptees whose biological parents do not. By adulthood, the individuals whose biological parents abuse alcohol typically show higher rates of alcoholism than those with nonalcoholic biological parents.

Genetic linkage strategies and *molecular biology* techniques provide more direct evidence in support of a genetic explanation (Gelernter & Kranzler, 2008). One line of investigation has found an abnormal form of the so-called *dopamine-2 (D2) receptor gene* in a majority of research participants with substance use disorders but in less than 20 percent of participants who do not display such disorders (Cosgrove, 2010; Blum et al., 1996, 1990). Other studies have tied still other genes to substance use disorders (Gelernter & Kransler, 2008; Kreek, 2008).

Biochemical Factors
Over the past few decades, researchers have pieced together several biological explanations of drug tolerance and withdrawal symptoms (Chung et al., 2012; Kosten, George, & Kleber, 2011, 2005; Schmidt et al., 2011). According to one of the leading explanations, when a particular drug is ingested, it increases the activity of certain neurotransmitters whose normal purpose is to calm, reduce pain, lift mood, or increase alertness. When a person keeps on taking the drug, the brain apparently makes an adjustment and reduces its own production of the neurotransmitters. Because the drug is increasing neurotransmitter activity or efficiency, release of the neurotransmitter by the brain is less necessary. As drug intake increases, the body's production of the neurotransmitters continues to decrease, leaving the person in need of more and more of the drug to achieve its effects. In this way, drug takers build tolerance for a drug, becoming more and more reliant on it rather than on their own biological processes to feel comfortable, happy, or alert. If they suddenly stop taking the drug, their natural supply of neurotransmitters will be low for a time, producing the symptoms of withdrawal. Withdrawal continues until the brain resumes its normal production of the neurotransmitters.

Which neurotransmitters are affected depends on the drug used. Repeated and excessive use of alcohol or benzodiazepines may lower the brain's production of the neurotransmitter GABA, regular use of opioids may reduce the brain's production of endorphins, and regular use of cocaine or amphetamines may lower the brain's production of dopamine (Kosten et al., 2011, 2005). In addition, researchers have identified

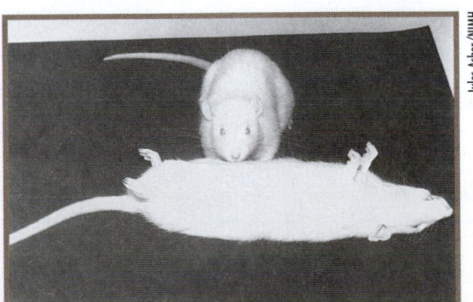

Jules Asher/NIMH

The GABA effect

After researchers blocked GABA receptors in the brain of the rat at the back of this photo, the rat showed no ill effects from ingesting alcohol. In contrast, the rat in front, whose unblocked GABA receptors remained open and available to alcohol, became obviously intoxicated when ingesting the same amount of alcohol. Clearly, GABA receptors play a key role in the effects of alcohol on the brain and body.

•reward center• A dopamine-rich pathway in the brain that produces feelings of pleasure when activated.

•reward-deficiency syndrome• A condition, suspected to be present in some individuals, in which the brain's reward center is not readily activated by the usual events in their lives.

•aversion therapy• A treatment in which clients are repeatedly presented with unpleasant stimuli while performing undesirable behaviors such as taking a drug.

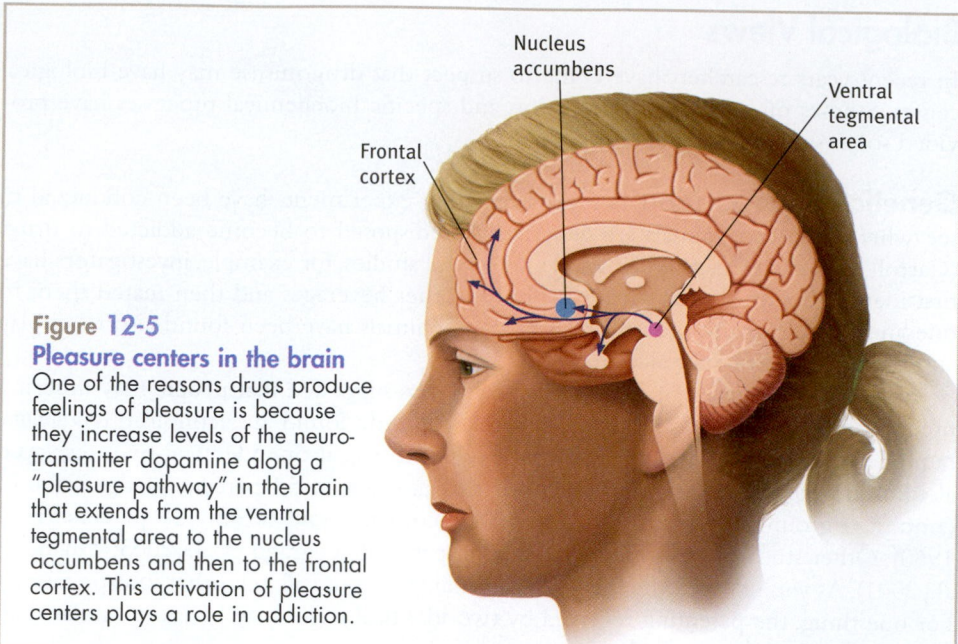

Figure 12-5
Pleasure centers in the brain
One of the reasons drugs produce feelings of pleasure is because they increase levels of the neurotransmitter dopamine along a "pleasure pathway" in the brain that extends from the ventral tegmental area to the nucleus accumbens and then to the frontal cortex. This activation of pleasure centers plays a role in addiction.

Victims of a reward deficiency syndrome?
The brain reward centers of people who develop substance use disorders may be inadequately activated by events in life—a problem called the *reward deficiency syndrome*. With the colors red and orange indicating greater brain activity, these PET scans show that prior to their use of drugs, the reward centers of cocaine, methamphetamine, and alcohol abusers (right) are generally less active than the reward centers of nonabusers (left) (Volkow et al., 2004, 2002).

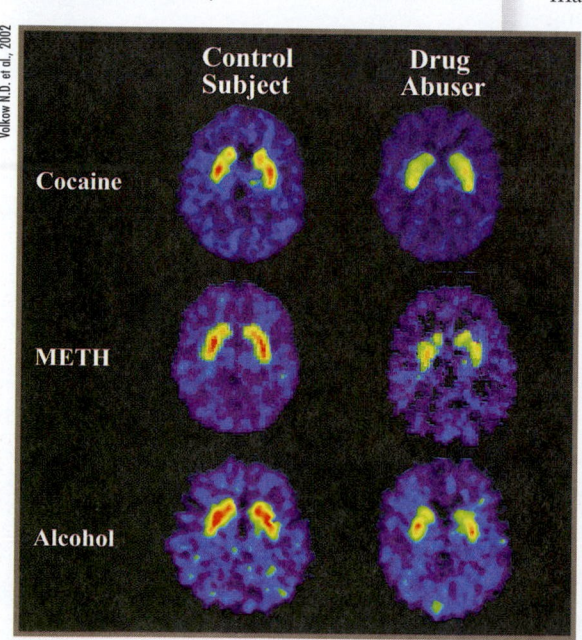

a neurotransmitter called *anandamide* that operates much like THC; excessive use of marijuana may reduce the production of this neurotransmitter (Budney et al., 2011; McDowell, 2011; Hitti, 2004).

This theory helps explain why people who regularly take substances experience tolerance and withdrawal reactions. But why are drugs so rewarding, and why do certain people turn to them in the first place? A number of brain-imaging studies suggest that many, perhaps all, drugs eventually activate a **reward center,** or "pleasure pathway," in the brain (de Wit & Phan, 2010). This reward center apparently extends from the brain area called the *ventral tegmental area* (in the midbrain) to an area known as the *nucleus accumbens* and on to the *frontal cortex* (see Figure 12-5). A key neurotransmitter in this pleasure pathway appears to be *dopamine* (Chung et al., 2012; Willuhn et al., 2010). When dopamine is activated along the pleasure pathway, a person experiences pleasure. Music may activate dopamine in the reward center. So may a hug or a word of praise. And so do drugs. Some researchers believe that other neurotransmitters may also play important roles in the reward center.

Certain drugs apparently stimulate the reward center directly. Remember that cocaine, amphetamines, and caffeine directly increase dopamine activity. Other drugs seem to stimulate it in roundabout ways. The biochemical reactions triggered by alcohol, opioids, and marijuana probably set in motion a series of chemical events that eventually lead to increased dopamine activity in the reward center.

A number of theorists further believe that when substances repeatedly stimulate this reward center, the center develops a hypersensitivity to the substances. Neurons in the center fire more readily when stimulated by the substances, contributing to future desires for them. This theory, called the *incentive-sensitization theory* of addiction, has received considerable support in animal studies (Loweth & Vezina, 2011; Vanderschuren & Pierce, 2010).

Still other theorists suspect that people who chronically use drugs may suffer from a **reward-deficiency syndrome:** Their reward center is not readily activated by the usual events in their lives, so they turn to drugs to stimulate this pleasure pathway, particularly in times of stress (Blum et al., 2000). Abnormal genes, such as the abnormal D2 receptor gene, have been cited as a possible cause of this syndrome (Müller, Likhodi, & Heinz, 2010; Finckh, 2001).

How Are Substance Use Disorders Treated?

Many approaches have been used to treat substance use disorders (see *MediaSpeak* on page 377), including psychodynamic, behavioral, cognitive-behavioral, and biological approaches, along with several sociocultural therapies (Brook, 2011; Margolis & Zweben, 2011). Although these treatments sometimes meet with great success, more often they are only moderately helpful (Myrick & Wright, 2008). Today the treatments are typically used on either an outpatient or inpatient basis or a combination of the two (see Figure 12-6).

The value of a treatment for substance use disorders can be difficult to determine. There are several reasons for this. First, different substance use disorders pose different problems. Second, many people with such disorders drop out of treatment very early (Radcliffe & Stevens, 2010). Third, some people recover without any intervention at all (Wilson, 2010), while many others recover and then relapse (Erb & Placenza, 2011). And, fourth, different criteria are used by different clinical researchers. How long, for example, must a person refrain from substance use in order to be called a treatment success? And is total abstention the only criterion, or is a reduction of drug use acceptable?

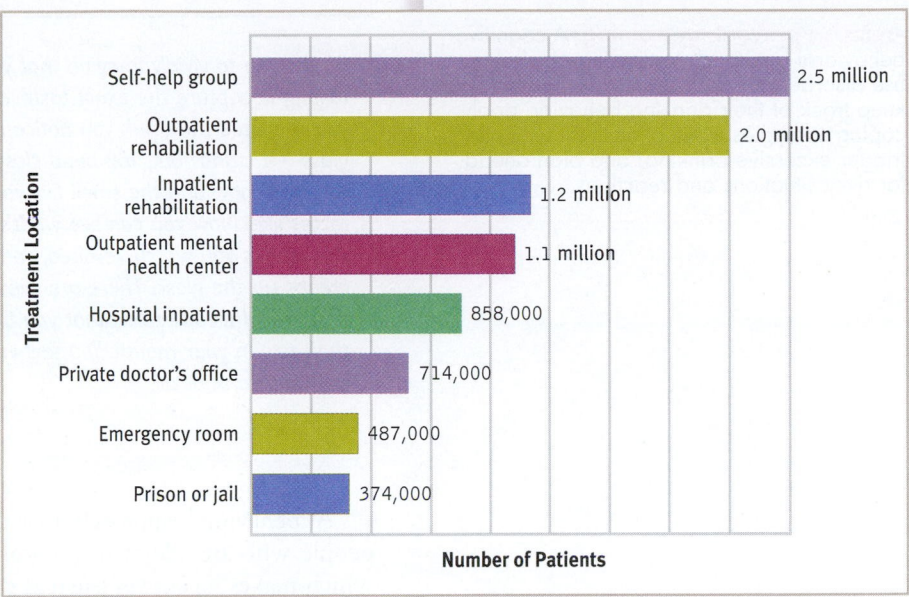

Number of Patients

Treatment Location	
Self-help group	2.5 million
Outpatient rehabiliation	2.0 million
Inpatient rehabilitation	1.2 million
Outpatient mental health center	1.1 million
Hospital inpatient	858,000
Private doctor's office	714,000
Emergency room	487,000
Prison or jail	374,000

Figure 12-6

Where do people receive treatment?
Most people receive treatment for substance use disorders in a self-help group, a rehabilitation program, or mental health center (NSDUH, 2010).

Psychodynamic Therapies

Psychodynamic therapists first guide clients to uncover and work through the underlying needs and conflicts that they believe have led to the substance use disorder. The therapists then try to help the individuals change their substance-related styles of living (Lightdale et al., 2011, 2008). Although often applied, this approach has not been found to be particularly effective (Cornish et al., 1995). It may be that substance use disorders, regardless of their causes, eventually become stubborn independent problems that must be the direct target of treatment if people are to become drug-free. Psychodynamic therapy tends to be of greater help when it is combined with other approaches in a multidimensional treatment program (Lightdale et al., 2011, 2008).

Sniffing for drugs

An increasingly common scene in schools, airports, storage facilities, and similar settings is that of trained dogs sniffing for marijuana, cocaine, opioids, and other substances. Here one such animal sniffs lockers at a school in Texas to see whether students have hidden any illegal substances among their books or other belongings.

Behavioral Therapies

A widely used behavioral treatment for substance use disorders is **aversion therapy,** an approach based on the principles of classical conditioning. Individuals are repeatedly presented with an unpleasant stimulus (for example, an electric shock) at the very moment that they are taking a drug. After repeated pairings, they are expected to react negatively to the substance itself and to lose their craving for it.

Aversion therapy has been applied to alcoholism more than to other substance use disorders. In one version of this therapy, drinking behavior is paired with drug-induced nausea and vomiting (Owen-Howard, 2001; Welsh & Liberto, 2001). The pairing of nausea with alcohol is expected to produce negative responses to alcohol itself. Another version of aversion therapy requires people with alcoholism to imagine extremely upsetting, repulsive, or frightening scenes while they are drinking. Here the pairing of the imagined scenes with alcohol is expected to produce negative responses to alcohol itself. Here is the kind of scene therapists may guide a client to imagine:

Paul Howell/Liaison/Getty Images

•relapse-prevention training• A cognitive-behavioral approach to treating alcohol use disorder in which clients are taught to keep track of their drinking behavior, apply coping strategies in situations that typically trigger excessive drinking, and plan ahead for risky situations and reactions.

I'd like you to vividly imagine that you are tasting the (beer, whiskey, etc.). See yourself tasting it, capture the exact taste, color and consistency. Use all of your senses. After you've tasted the drink you notice that there is something small and white floating in the glass—it stands out. You bend closer to examine it more carefully, your nose is right over the glass now and the smell fills your nostrils as you remember exactly what the drink tastes like. Now you can see what's in the glass. There are several maggots floating on the surface. As you watch, revolted, one manages to get a grip on the glass and, undulating, creeps up the glass. There are even more of the repulsive creatures in the glass than you first thought. You realise that you have swallowed some of them and you're very aware of the taste in your mouth. You feel very sick and wish you'd never reached for the glass and had the drink at all.

(Clarke & Saunders, 1988, pp. 143–144)

A behavioral approach that has been effective in the short-term treatment of people who are addicted to cocaine and several other drugs is *contingency management,* which makes incentives (such as cash, vouchers, prizes, or privileges) contingent on the submission of drug-free urine specimens (Dallery et al., 2012; Kaminer et al., 2011). In one pioneering study, 68 percent of cocaine abusers who completed a six-month contingency training program achieved at least eight weeks of continuous abstinence (Higgins et al., 2011, 1993).

Behavioral interventions for substance use disorders have usually had only limited success when they are the sole form of treatment (Carroll, 2008). A major problem is that the approaches can be effective only when individuals are motivated to continue with them despite their unpleasantness or demands (DiClemente et al., 2008). Generally, behavioral treatments work best in combination with either biological or cognitive approaches (Carroll & Kiluk, 2012; Rotgers, 2012).

Cognitive-Behavioral Therapies

Cognitive-behavioral treatments for substance use disorders help clients identify and change the behaviors and cognitions that keep contributing to their patterns of substance misuse (Yoon et al., 2012; Carroll, 2011). Practitioners of these approaches also help the clients develop more effective coping skills—skills that can be applied during times of stress, temptation, and substance craving.

Perhaps the most prominent cognitive-behavioral approach to substance misuse is **relapse-prevention training** (Daley et al., 2011; Marlatt, 2007, 1985). The overall goal of this approach is for clients to gain *control* over their substance-related behaviors. To achieve this, the individuals are taught to identify high-risk situations, appreciate the range of decisions that confront them in such situations, change their dysfunctional lifestyles, and learn from mistakes and lapses.

Several strategies typically are included in relapse-prevention training: (1) *Therapists have clients keep track of their drinking behavior.* Writing down the times, locations, emotions, bodily changes, and other circumstances of their drinking, the individuals become more aware of the situations that place them at risk for excessive drinking. (2) *Therapists teach clients coping strategies to use when such situations arise.* The individuals learn, for example, to recognize when their drinking limits are being approached, to control their rate of drinking (perhaps by spacing their drinks or by sipping them rather than gulping), and to practice relaxation techniques, assertiveness skills, and other coping behaviors in situations in which they would otherwise be drinking. (3) *Therapists teach clients to plan ahead of time.* The individuals may, for example, predetermine how many drinks are appropriate, what to drink, and under what circumstances.

This approach has been found to lower the frequency of intoxication and of binge drinking in some individuals, although such gains often occur only after repeated relapse prevention treatments (Borden et al., 2011; Margolis & Zweben, 2011). Individuals who

Jim West/Alamy

Spreading the word
Brett Ray, confined to a wheel chair since being hit by an intoxicated driver, participates in a demonstration organized by Mothers Against Drunk Driving (MADD). By raising public awareness, MADD has helped reduce the number of alcohol-related deaths by 47 percent over the past 3 decades.

MediaSpeak

Enrolling at Sober High

By Jeff Forester, TheFix.com (addiction website)

Jeff has been sober 22 months, he tells me. Without blinking or ducking, his clear blue eyes looking straight at me, he says that if it were not for Sobriety High, he'd be dead.

I believe him. Yet many recovery high schools now face cuts or closures which could have devastating consequences for the students who rely on them—and for wider society.

Sobriety High started in Minneapolis in 1989 with just two students. It has 100 more today, and sober high schools have sprung up in eight other states. While Minnesota, the land of ten thousand treatment centers, leads the pack with 11 of the 33, there are others in Dallas, Houston, and Los Angeles—though none in New York, Chicago, or San Francisco. According to a National Institute on Drug Abuse study, 78% of the students in sober high schools attend after receiving formal rehab. . . .

Enrollment is similar to any other school—students arrive with transcripts and all the typical paperwork. At Sobriety High, there is an interview with both the prospective student and the parents. The staff tries to determine where the teen is in their recovery and how committed they are. . . .

While it undoubtedly feels like a school, the wall banners feature phrases like "Turning It Over Is A Turning Point" rather than, say, a sign for the prom. The students are diverse, with hair of all different lengths and colors; some have the seemingly requisite addict tattoos while others are decked out in Goth garb and still others project a distinctly Midwestern Wonder Bread aura. Their journeys are also diverse, with the lucky ones landing here after treatment but many coming from the courts, detox or the streets. . . .

Recovery schools fill in the educational and emotional holes opened when kids use. The classes are small so that teachers can check in with each student regularly and the curriculum flexible so as to help them with what they missed while they were using or in treatment. Some programs help students—many with hair-raising records—find work. Some also work with chemically dependent parents and older siblings as well. Students typically have "group" each day, and while it is not an AA meeting, the DNA of AA is evident. . . .

All teenagers have low impulse control but the stakes are higher for chemically dependent kids trying to stay sober. Says Joe Schrank, founder of the Core Company and a board member of the National Youth Recovery Foundation (as well as a co-founder of The Fix), "When you put pot and booze on top of adolescent stupidity, kids are at risk." . . . [A teacher] adds, "We have to be the kids' prefrontal cortex and say, 'Stop and think before you act.'" . . .

Just try adding acne, constant temptation and regularly being heckled that you're a "pussy" to a standard newcomer's recovery and you'll see just how high the deck is stacked against teenage sobriety; the notion of placing them in an environment that caters to clean living thus makes sense. "In a regular high school, kids [would be] punished for making a good decision," says Schrank. By getting sober at a normal high school, . . . kids are setting themselves up as targets— essentially waving a red flag to the bullies. . . .

Ninety percent of students at Sobriety High have other mental health issues besides chemical dependency [and] need the extra support of counselors, psychologists, and ongoing mental health support, and this is costly. . . . "It takes more money per student, and the schools must be on a segregated site if they are to have a drug and alcohol free campus."

Minnesota's unresolved $5.2 billion deficit thus hangs over the campus like a meat axe. National funding cuts to education have been deep and painful. . . . [S]ober high school advocates . . . are quietly planning for more campus shut downs and staff reductions. . . .

For barely sober teens, . . . closing recovery schools will be disastrous. "Many of them will go back to the streets, or prison, or they will be dead," says . . . the Sobriety High social worker. . . .

Supporters . . . point out that closing recovery schools makes little fiscal sense. "Recovery school is a fraction of the cost of incarceration," says Joe Schrank. "If you like having these kids in high school, you'll love having them in prison."

"Look at Drug Courts," adds former Congressman Jim Ramstad. "The recidivism rate for those who complete the course is 24% while the rate for criminal court is 75%." . . .

No one can deny that there is need for more sober schools and more money to help the kids that want it. In 2008 and 2009, there were 4000 students being treated for chemical dependency in Minnesota, but only 400 school spaces available. And this is the state with a third of all the available recovery schools in the country. . . .

[Social worker Debbie Bolton] says plainly, "What we do is important. We save lives."

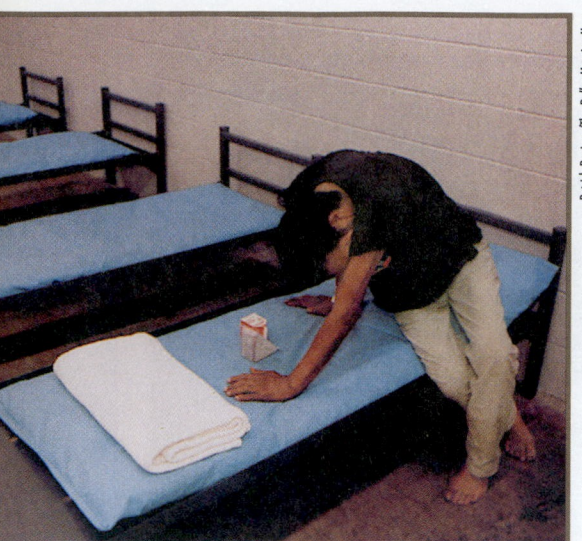

Forced detoxification
Abstinence is not always medically supervised, nor is it necessarily planned or voluntary. This sufferer of alcoholism begins to experience symptoms of withdrawal soon after being imprisoned for public intoxication.

are young and do not experience the tolerance and withdrawal features of chronic alcohol use seem to do best with this approach (Hart et al., 2010; Deas et al., 2008). The treatment has also been used in cases of marijuana and cocaine abuse as well as with other kinds of disorders such as sexual paraphilias (see Chapter 13).

Biological Treatments

Biological approaches may be used to help people withdraw from substances, abstain from them, or simply maintain their level of use without further increases. As with the other forms of treatment, biological approaches alone rarely bring long-term improvement, but they can be helpful when combined with other approaches.

Detoxification
Detoxification is systematic and medically supervised withdrawal from a drug. Some detoxification programs are offered on an outpatient basis. Others are located in hospitals and clinics and may also offer individual and group therapy, a "full-service" institutional approach that has become popular. One detoxification approach is to have clients withdraw gradually from the substance, taking smaller and smaller doses until they are off the drug completely. A second—often medically preferred—detoxification strategy is to give clients other drugs that reduce the symptoms of withdrawal (Day & Strang, 2011). Antianxiety drugs, for example, are sometimes used to reduce severe alcohol withdrawal reactions such as delirium tremens and seizures. Detoxification programs seem to help motivated people withdraw from drugs (Müller et al., 2010). However, relapse rates tend to be high for those who fail to receive a follow-up form of treatment—psychological, biological, or sociocultural—after successful detoxification (Day & Strang, 2011; Ford & Zarate, 2010).

Antagonist Drugs
After successfully stopping a drug, people must avoid falling back into a pattern of chronic use. As an aid to resisting temptation, some people with substance use disorders are given **antagonist drugs,** which block or change the effects of the addictive drug (Chung et al., 2012; O'Brien & Kampman, 2008). *Disulfiram* (Antabuse), for example, is often given to people who are trying to stay away from alcohol. By itself a low dose of this drug seems to have few negative effects, but a person who drinks alcohol while taking disulfiram will experience intense nausea, vomiting, blushing, faster heart rate, dizziness, and perhaps fainting. People taking disulfiram are less likely to drink alcohol because they know the terrible reaction that awaits them should they have even one drink. Disulfiram has proved helpful, but again only with people who are motivated to take it as prescribed (Diclemente et al., 2008). In addition to disulfiram, several other antagonist drugs are now being tested (De Sousa et al., 2008).

For substance use disorders centered on opioids, several *narcotic antagonists,* such as *naloxone,* are used (Harrison & Petrakis, 2011; Caldeiro et al., 2009). These antagonists attach to *endorphin* receptor sites throughout the brain and make it impossible for the opioids to have their usual effect. Without the rush or high, continued drug use becomes pointless. Although narcotic antagonists have been helpful—particularly in emergencies, to rescue people from an overdose of opioids—they can in fact be dangerous for persons with opioid addiction. The antagonists must be given very carefully because of their ability to throw such persons into severe withdrawal.

So-called *partial antagonists,* narcotic antagonists that produce less severe withdrawal symptoms, have also been developed (Dijkstra et al., 2010; Hart et al., 2010). Partial antagonists are now preferred over full antagonists by many clinicians to help people withdraw from opioid use—an approach often called *rapid detoxification* because the antagonists speed things along. The full antagonists remain the treatment of choice in emergency cases of overdose.

Recent studies indicate that narcotic antagonists may also be useful in the treatment of substance use disorders involving alcohol or cocaine (Harrison & Petrakis, 2011; Bishop, 2008). In some studies, for example, the narcotic antagonist *naltrexone* has helped reduce cravings for alcohol (O'Malley et al., 2000, 1996, 1992). Why should narcotic

•**detoxification**•Systematic and medically supervised withdrawal from a drug.

•**antagonist drugs**•Drugs that block or change the effects of an addictive drug.

•**methadone maintenance program**• An approach to treating heroin-centered substance use disorder in which clients are given legally and medically supervised doses of a substitute drug, methadone.

antagonists, which operate at the brain's endorphin receptors, help with alcoholism, which has been tied largely to activity at GABA sites? The answer may lie in the reward center of the brain. If various drugs eventually stimulate the same pleasure pathway, it seems reasonable that antagonists for one drug may, in a roundabout way, affect the impact of other drugs as well.

Drug Maintenance Therapy A drug-related lifestyle may be a greater problem than the drug's direct effects. Much of the damage caused by heroin addiction, for example, comes from overdoses, unsterilized needles, and an accompanying life of crime. Thus clinicians were very enthusiastic when **methadone maintenance programs** were developed in the 1960s to treat heroin addiction (Dole & Nyswander, 1967, 1965). In these programs, people with an addiction are given the laboratory opioid *methadone* as a substitute for heroin. Although they then become dependent on methadone, their new addiction is maintained under safe medical supervision. Unlike heroin, methadone can be taken by mouth, thus eliminating the dangers of needles, and needs to be taken only once a day.

> **?** Why has the legal, medically supervised use of heroin (in Great Britain) or heroin substitutes (in the United States) sometimes failed to combat drug problems?

At first, methadone programs seemed very effective, and many of them were set up throughout the United States, Canada, and England. These programs became less popular during the 1980s, however, because of the dangers of methadone itself. Many clinicians came to believe that substituting one addiction for another is not an acceptable "solution" for a substance use disorder, and many persons with an addiction complained that methadone addiction was creating an additional drug problem that simply complicated their original one (Winstock, Lintzeris, & Lea, 2011; McCance-Katz & Kosten, 2005). In fact, methadone is sometimes harder to withdraw from than heroin because the withdrawal symptoms can last longer (Day & Strang, 2011; Hart et al., 2010). Moreover, pregnant women maintained on methadone have the added concern of the drug's effect on their fetus.

Despite such concerns, maintenance treatment with methadone—or with other opioid substitute drugs—has again sparked interest among clinicians in recent years, partly because of new research support (Fareed et al., 2011; Saxon & Miotto, 2011; Meader, 2010) and partly because of the rapid spread of the HIV virus and the hepatitis C virus among intravenous drug abusers and their sex partners and children (Galanter & Kleber, 2008; Schottenfeld, 2008). Not only is methadone treatment safer than street opioid use, but many methadone programs now include AIDS education and other health instructions in their services (Sorensen & Copeland, 2000). Research suggests that methadone maintenance programs are most effective when they are combined with education, psychotherapy, family therapy, and employment counseling (Kouimtsidis & Drummond, 2010). Today thousands of clinics provide methadone treatment across the United States.

Sociocultural Therapies

As you have read, sociocultural theorists—both *family-social* and *multicultural* theorists—believe that psychological problems emerge in a social setting and are best treated in a social context. Three sociocultural approaches have been applied to substance use disorders: (1) *self-help programs*, (2) *culture- and gender-sensitive programs*, and (3) *community prevention programs*.

Self-Help and Residential Treatment Programs Many people with substance use disorders have organized among themselves to help one another recover without professional assistance. The drug self-help movement dates back to 1935, when two Ohio men suffering from alcoholism met and wound up discussing alternative treatment possibilities. The first discussion led to others and to the eventual formation of

Pros and cons of methadone treatment
Methadone is itself a narcotic that can be as dangerous as other opioids when not taken under safe medical supervision. Here a couple protest against a proposed methadone treatment facility in Maine. Their 19-year-old daughter, who was not an opioid addict, had died months earlier after taking methadone to get high.

AA: Reaching Out

As many as 9 percent of adults in the United States have been to an Alcoholics Anonymous meeting at some time in their lives. ‹‹

More than 3 percent have been to a meeting within the last year. ‹‹

(Moos & Timko, 2008)

a self-help group whose members discussed alcohol-related problems, traded ideas, and provided support. The organization became known as **Alcoholics Anonymous (AA)**.

Today AA has more than 2 million members in 116,000 groups across the United States and 180 other countries (AA World Services, 2011). It offers peer support along with moral and spiritual guidelines to help people overcome alcoholism. Different members apparently find different aspects of AA helpful. For some it is the peer support; for others it is the spiritual dimension. Meetings take place regularly, and members are available to help each other 24 hours a day.

By offering guidelines for living, the organization helps members abstain "one day at a time," urging them to accept as "fact" the idea that they are powerless over alcohol and that they must stop drinking entirely and permanently if they are to live normal lives (Nace, 2011, 2008). AA views alcoholism as a disease and takes the position that "Once an alcoholic, always an alcoholic" (Rosenthal, 2011; Rosenthal & Levounis, 2011, 2005; Pendery et al., 1982). Related self-help organizations, *Al-Anon* and *Alateen*, offer support for people who live with and care about persons with alcoholism. Self-help programs such as *Narcotics Anonymous* and *Cocaine Anonymous* have been developed for other substance use disorders (Jaffe & Kelly, 2011).

It is worth noting that the abstinence goal of AA directly opposes the controlled-drinking goal of relapse prevention training and several other interventions for substance misuse (see pages 376, 378). In fact, this issue—abstinence versus controlled drinking—has been debated for years (Rosenthal, 2011, 2005; Hart et al., 2010). Feelings about it have run so strongly that in the 1980s the people on one side challenged the motives and honesty of those on the other (Sobell & Sobell, 1984, 1973; Pendery et al., 1982).

Research indicates, however, that both controlled drinking and abstinence may be useful treatment goals, depending on the nature of the particular drinking problem. Studies suggest that abstinence may be a more appropriate goal for people who have a long-standing alcohol use disorder, whereas controlled drinking can be helpful to younger drinkers whose pattern does not include tolerance and withdrawal reactions. The latter persons may indeed need to be taught a nonabusive form of drinking (Hart et al., 2010; Witkiewitz & Marlatt, 2007, 2004). Studies also suggest that abstinence is appropriate for people who believe that it is the only answer for them (Rosenthal, 2011, 2005; Carbonari & DiClemente, 2000). These individuals are more likely to relapse after having just one drink.

Many self-help programs have expanded into **residential treatment centers,** or **therapeutic communities**—such as *Daytop Village* and *Phoenix House*—where people formerly addicted to drugs live, work, and socialize in a drug-free environment while undergoing individual, group, and family therapies and making a transition back to community life (O'Brien et al., 2011; Bonetta, 2010; Brook, 2008).

The evidence that keeps self-help and residential treatment programs going comes largely in the form of individual testimonials. Many tens of thousands of persons have revealed that they are members of these programs and credit them with turning their lives around. Studies of the programs have also had favorable findings, but their numbers have been limited (Moos & Timko, 2008).

Joshua Lutz/Redux

Fighting drug abuse while in prison
Inmates at a county jail in Texas exercise and meditate as part of a drug and alcohol rehabilitation program. The program also includes psychoeducation and other interventions to help inmates address their substance use disorders.

Culture- and Gender-Sensitive Programs Many persons with substance use disorders live in a poor and perhaps violent setting. A growing number of today's treatment programs try to be sensitive to the special sociocultural pressures and problems faced by drug abusers who are poor, homeless, or members of minority groups (el-Guebaly, 2011; Lawson et al., 2011; Ruiz, 2011). Therapists who are sensitive to their clients' life challenges can do more to address the stresses that often lead to relapse.

Similarly, therapists have become more aware that women often require treatment methods different from those designed for men (Greenfield et al., 2011; Brady & Back, 2008). Women and men often have different physical and psychological reactions to drugs, for example. In addition, treatment of women with substance use disorders may be complicated by the impact of sexual abuse, the possibility that they may be or may become pregnant while taking drugs, the stresses of raising children, and the fear of criminal prosecution for abusing drugs during pregnancy (Finnegan & Kandall, 2008). Thus many women with such disorders feel more comfortable seeking help at gender-sensitive clinics or residential programs; some such programs also allow children to live with their recovering mothers.

What different kinds of issues might be confronted by drug abusers from different minorities or genders?

Community Prevention Programs
Perhaps the most effective approach to substance use disorders is to prevent them (Botvin & Griffin, 2011; Hansen et al., 2010). The first drug-prevention efforts were conducted in schools. Today prevention programs are also offered in workplaces, activity centers, and other community settings and even through the media (NSDUH, 2010). Over 11 percent of adolescents report that they have participated in substance use prevention programs outside school within the past year. Around 77 percent have seen or heard a substance use prevention message. And almost 60 percent have talked to their parents in the past year about the dangers of alcohol and other drugs.

Some prevention programs argue for total abstinence from drugs, while others teach responsible use. Some seek to interrupt drug use; others try to delay the age at which people first experiment with drugs. Programs may also differ in whether they offer drug education, teach alternatives to drug use, try to change the psychological state of the potential user, seek to change relationships with peers, or combine these techniques.

Prevention programs may focus on the *individual* (for example, by providing education about unpleasant drug effects), the *family* (by teaching parenting skills), the *peer group* (by teaching resistance to peer pressure), the *school* (by setting up firm enforcement of drug policies), or the *community* at large. The most effective prevention efforts focus on several of these areas to provide a consistent message about drug misuse in all areas of individuals' lives (Hansen et al., 2010). Some prevention programs have even been developed for preschool children.

Two of today's leading community-based prevention programs are "TheTruth.com" and "Above the Influence." The Truth.com is an antismoking campaign, aimed at young people in particular, that provides "edgy" ads on the Web (e.g., YouTube), television, magazines, and newspapers. Above the Influence, conducted by the Office of National Drug Control Policy in the United States, is a similar advertising campaign that focuses on a range of substances abused by teenagers.

What impact might celebrity admissions of past drug use have on people's willingness to seek treatment for substance abuse?

Community-based prevention programs are not always effective, no matter how powerful and clever their ads may be. For example, after a five-year study, the Government Accountability Office concluded in 2006 that the highly regarded "My Anti-Drug" campaign of the late 1990s and early 2000s had been largely ineffective. Thus, it is encouraging that a recent nationwide survey of 3,000 students suggests that watching

•**Alcoholics Anonymous (AA)**•A self-help organization that provides support and guidance for persons with alcohol use disorder.

•**residential treatment center**•A place where people formerly addicted to drugs live, work, and socialize in a drug-free environment. Also called a *therapeutic community*.

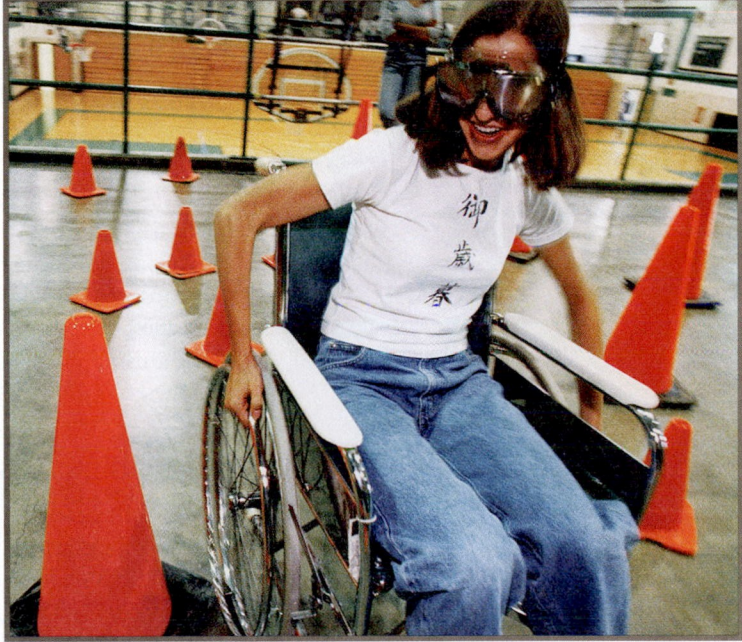

AP Photo/The Daily Times, Marc F. Henning

Simulation as prevention
A 16-year-old student weaves her way through an obstacle course while wearing a pair of alcohol-impaired goggles. The exercise is part of a DUI prevention program at her New Mexico high school, designed to give students hands-on experience regarding alcohol's effects on vision and balance.

Listen to my story
A prisoner stands shackled before students at an Ohio high school and discusses his drunk-driving conviction (his intoxicated driving resulted in a fatal automobile crash). Such high school visits by inmates are part of the school's "Make the Right Choice" prevention program.

Above the Influence ads may help reduce marijuana use by teenagers (Slater et al., 2011). The survey found that 8 percent of eighth graders familiar with the campaign have taken up marijuana use, in contrast to 12 percent of students who have never seen the ads.

Other Addictive Disorders

As you read at the beginning of this chapter, DSM-5 lists *gambling disorder* as an addictive disorder alongside the substance use disorders. This represents a significant broadening of the concept of addiction, which, in previous editions of the DSM, referred only to the misuse of substances. In essence, DSM-5 is suggesting that people may become addicted to behaviors and activities beyond substance use.

Gambling Disorder

It is estimated that as many as 2.3 percent of adults and 3 to 8 percent of teenagers and college students suffer from **gambling disorder** (Splevins et al., 2010; Griffiths, 2006). Clinicians are careful to distinguish between this disorder and social gambling (APA, 2013). Gambling disorder is defined less by the amount of time or money spent gambling than by the addictive nature of the behavior (Carragher & McWilliams, 2011). People with the disorder are preoccupied with gambling and typically cannot walk away from a bet. In many cases, repeated losses of money lead to more gambling in an effort to win the money back, and the gambling continues even in the face of financial, social, occupational, educational, and health problems (see Table 12-5). The gambling is usually more common when the individual feels distressed. Lying to cover up the extent of gambling is common. Finally, many individuals with gambling disorder need to gamble with increasing amounts of money to achieve the desired excitement, and they feel restless or irritable when they try to reduce or stop gambling—symptoms that are similar to the tolerance and withdrawal reactions often found in cases of substance use disorder (APA, 2013).

The explanations proposed for gambling disorder often parallel those offered for substance use disorders. Some studies suggest, for example, that people with gambling disorder may: (1) inherit a genetic predisposition to develop the disorder (Blanco, Myers, & Kendler, 2012); (2) experience heightened dopamine activity and operation of the brain's reward center (Balodis et al., 2012; Conversano et al., 2012); (3) have impulsive,

•**gambling disorder**•A disorder marked by persistent and recurrent gambling behavior, leading to a range of life problems.

•**Internet use gaming disorder**•A disorder marked by persistent, recurrent, and excessive Internet activity, particularly gaming. Recommended for further study by DSM-5. Also called *Internet addiction*.

novelty-seeking, and other personality styles that leave them prone to gambling disorder (Slutske et al., 2012); and (4) make repeated and cognitive mistakes such as inaccurate expectations and misinterpretations of their emotions and bodily states (Fortune & Goodie, 2012; Williams et al., 2012). However, the research on these theories has been limited thus far, leaving such explanations tentative at the present time.

Similarly, several of the leading treatments for substance use disorders have been adapted for use with gambling disorder. These treatments include cognitive-behavioral approaches like relapse-prevention training (Larimer et al., 2012; Grant et al., 2011) and biological approaches such as narcotic antagonists (Bosco et al., 2012). In addition, the self-help group program *Gamblers Anonymous,* a network modeled after *Alcoholics Anonymous,* is available to many thousands of people with gambling disorder (Marceaux & Melville, 2011). Individuals who attend such groups seem to have a heightened recovery rate.

Internet Use Gaming Disorder: Awaiting Official Status

As people increasingly turn to the Internet for activities that used to take place in the "real world"—communicating, networking, shopping, playing games, and participating in a community—a new psychological problem has emerged: an uncontrollable need to be online (Young, 2011). This pattern has been called *Internet use disorder, Internet addiction,* and *problematic Internet use,* among other names (Acier & Kern, 2011).

For people who display this pattern, the Internet has become a black hole. Sufferers —at least 1 percent of all people—spend all or most of their waking hours texting, tweeting, networking, gaming, Internet browsing, e-mailing, blogging, visiting virtual worlds, shopping online, or viewing online pornography (Kuss & Griffiths, 2012, Young & De Abreu, 2011). Specific symptoms of this pattern parallel those found in substance use disorders and gambling disorder, extending from loss of outside interests to possible withdrawal reactions when Internet use is not possible (APA, 2013, 2012).

Although clinicians, the media, and the public have shown enormous interest in this problem, DSM-5 has not listed it as a disorder. Rather, it has recommended that the pattern, which it calls **Internet gaming disorder,** receive further study for possible inclusion in future editions (APA, 2013, 2012). Moreover, DSM-5 has narrowed the disorder's criteria to emphasize excessive Internet *gaming* over the other kinds of Internet activities often associated with the pattern. Time—and research—will tell whether this pattern reaches the status of a formal clinical disorder.

PUTTING IT... together

New Wrinkles to a Familiar Story

In some respects the story of the misuse of drugs is the same today as in the past. Substance use is still rampant, often creating damaging psychological disorders. New drugs keep emerging, and the public goes through periods of believing, naively, that they are "safe." Only gradually do people learn that these drugs, too, pose dangers. And treatments for substance-related disorders continue to have only limited effect.

Yet there are important new wrinkles in this familiar story. Researchers have begun to develop a clearer understanding of how drugs act on the brain and body. In treatment, self-help groups and rehabilitation programs are flourishing. And preventive education to make people aware of the dangers of drug misuse is also expanding and seems to be having an effect. One reason for these improvements is that investigators and clinicians have stopped working in isolation and are instead looking for intersections between their own work and work from other models. The same kind of integrated efforts that have helped with other psychological disorders are bringing new promise and hope to the study and treatment of substance use disorders.

Perhaps the most important insight to be gained from these integrated efforts is that several of the models were already on the right track. Social pressures, personality

---

table: 12-5

DSM-5 Checklist

Gambling Disorder

Persistent and recurrent problematic gambling behavior, featuring 4 or more of the following symptoms in a 12-month period:

1. Need to gamble with increasing amounts of money to achieve desired excitement

2. Restlessness or irritability when trying to reduce or stop gambling

3. Repeated unsuccessful efforts to control, reduce, or stop gambling

4. Frequent preoccupation with gambling

5. Frequent gambling when feeling distressed

6. Frequent return to gambling to try to recoup losses

7. Lying in order to conceal extent of gambling

8. Jeopardizing or loss of a significant relationship, job, or educational/career opportunity because of gambling

9. Reliance on others for money to relieve gambling-induced financial problems.

Based on APA, 2013, 2012.

DSM-5 CONTROVERSY

Could Shopping Be an Addiction?

DSM-5 lists *gambling disorder* as an *addictive disorder* and is considering doing the same for *Internet gaming disorder* in a future DSM-5 revision. Critics worry that other excessive behaviors, such as shopping, exercising, having sex, and the like, may eventually be added to the list of diagnosable behavioral addictions. ‹‹

characteristics, rewards, and genetic predispositions all seem to play roles in substance use disorders, and in fact to operate together. For example, some people may inherit a malfunction of the biological reward center and so may need special doses of external stimulation—say, gambling, intense relationships, an abundance of certain foods, or drugs—to stimulate their reward center. Their pursuit of external rewards may take on the character of an addictive personality. Such individuals may be especially prone to experimenting with drugs, particularly when their social group makes the drugs available or when they are faced with intense social and personal stress.

Just as each model has identified important factors in the development of substance use disorders, each has made important contributions to treatment. As you have seen, the various forms of treatment seem to work best when they are combined with approaches from the other models, making integrated treatment the most productive approach.

Yet another new wrinkle to the addiction story is that the clinical field has now formally proclaimed that substances are not the only things to which people may develop an addiction. By grouping gambling disorder alongside substance use disorders and targeting Internet use gaming disorder for possible inclusion in the future, DSM-5 has opened the door for a broader view and perhaps broader treatments of addictive patterns—whether they are substance-induced or triggered by other kinds of experiences.

Summing Up

- **SUBSTANCE MISUSE** The misuse of *substances* (or *drugs*) may lead to temporary changes in behavior, emotion, or thought, including *intoxication*. Chronic and excessive use can lead to *substance use disorders*. Many people with such disorders also develop a *tolerance* for the substance in question and/or experience unpleasant *withdrawal symptoms* when they abstain from it. *pp. 348–349*

- **DEPRESSANTS** *Depressants* are substances that slow the activity of the central nervous system. Chronic and excessive use of these substances can lead to problems such as *alcohol use disorder, sedative-hypnotic use disorder,* or *opioid use disorder.*

  Alcoholic beverages contain *ethyl alcohol,* which is carried by the blood to the central nervous system, depressing its function. Intoxication occurs when the concentration of alcohol in the bloodstream reaches 0.09 percent. Among other actions, alcohol increases the activity of the neurotransmitter GABA at key sites in the brain. The *sedative-hypnotic drugs,* which produce feelings of relaxation and drowsiness, include *barbiturates* and *benzodiazepines.* These drugs also increase the activity of GABA. *Opioids* include *opium* and drugs derived from it, such as *morphine* and *heroin,* as well as laboratory-made opioids. They all reduce tension and pain and cause other reactions. Opioids operate by binding to neurons that ordinarily receive *endorphins. pp. 349–358*

- **STIMULANTS** *Stimulants* are substances that increase the activity of the central nervous system, including *cocaine, amphetamines, caffeine,* and *nicotine.* Abnormal use of cocaine or amphetamines can lead to *stimulant use disorder.* Stimulants produce their effects by increasing the activity of dopamine, norepinephrine, and serotonin in the brain. *pp. 358–363*

- **HALLUCINOGENS** *Hallucinogens,* such as *LSD,* are substances that cause powerful changes primarily in sensory perception. Perceptions are intensified and illusions and hallucinations can occur. LSD apparently causes such effects by disturbing the release of the neurotransmitter serotonin. *pp. 363–366*

- **CANNABIS** The main ingredient of *Cannabis sativa,* a hemp plant, is *tetrahydrocannabinol (THC). Marijuana,* the most popular form of cannabis, is more powerful today than it was in years past. It can cause intoxication, and regular use can lead to *cannabis use disorder. pp. 366–369*

- **COMBINATIONS OF SUBSTANCES** Many people take more than one drug at a time, and the drugs interact. The use of two or more drugs at the same time—*polysubstance use*—has become increasingly common. *pp. 369–370*

- **EXPLANATIONS FOR SUBSTANCE USE DISORDERS** Several explanations for substance use disorders have been put forward. Together they are beginning to shed light on the disorders. According to *sociocultural* theorists, the people most likely to develop these disorders are those living in socioeconomic conditions that generate stress or whose families value or tolerate drug use. In the *psychodynamic view*, people who develop substance use disorders have excessive *dependency* needs traceable to the early stages of life. Some psychodynamic theorists also believe that certain people have a *substance abuse personality* that makes them prone to drug use. The leading *behavioral* view proposes that drug use is reinforced initially because it reduces tensions and raises spirits. According to *cognitive* theorists, such reductions may also lead to an *expectancy* that drugs will be comforting and helpful.

  The *biological* explanations are supported by twin, adoptee, genetic linkage, and molecular biology studies, suggesting that people may inherit a predisposition to the disorders. Researchers have also learned that drug tolerance and withdrawal symptoms may be caused by cutbacks in the brain's production of particular neurotransmitters during excessive and chronic drug use. Finally, biological studies suggest that many, perhaps all, drugs may ultimately lead to increased *dopamine* activity in the brain's *reward center*. *pp. 370–374*

- **TREATMENTS FOR SUBSTANCE USE DISORDERS** Treatments for substance use disorders vary widely. Usually several approaches are combined. *Psychodynamic* therapies try to help clients become aware of and correct the underlying needs and conflicts that may have led to their use of drugs. A common *behavioral* technique is *aversion therapy*, in which an unpleasant stimulus is paired with the drug that the person is abusing. *Cognitive* and *behavioral* techniques have been combined in such forms as *relapse-prevention training*. *Biological* treatments include *detoxification, antagonist drugs,* and *drug maintenance therapy*. *Sociocultural* treatments approach substance use disorders in a social context by means of *self-help groups* (e.g., *Alcoholics Anonymous*), *culture-* and *gender-sensitive treatments,* and *community prevention programs*. *pp. 375–382*

- **OTHER ADDICTIVE DISORDERS** DSM-5 groups *gambling disorder* alongside the substance use disorders as an addictive disorder. The explanations for this disorder parallel those for substance use disorders, including genetic factors, dopamine activity, personality styles, and cognitive factors. Treatments for gambling disorder include cognitive-behavioral approaches, narcotic antagonists, and self-help groups. DSM-5 recommends that another addictive pattern, *Internet gaming disorder*, receive further study for possible inclusion in future DSM revisions. *pp. 382–383*

Cocaine and the heart
Pop icon Whitney Houston died in her bathtub on February 11, 2012. The coroner's report ruled that the cause of her death was accidental drowning caused in part by heart disease and her abuse of cocaine and perhaps other drugs. The suspicion is that her long-term use of cocaine helped produce her heart problems (Dolak & Murphy, 2012).

DISORDERS OF SEX AND GENDER

Robert, a 57-year-old man, came to sex therapy with his wife because of his inability to get erections. He had not had a problem with erections until six months earlier, when they attempted to have sex after an evening out, during which he had had several drinks. They attributed his failure to get an erection to his being "a little drunk," but he found himself worrying over the next few days that he was perhaps becoming impotent. When they next attempted intercourse, he found himself unable to get involved in what they were doing because he was so intent on watching himself to see if he would get an erection. Once again he did not, and they were both very upset. His failure to get an erection continued over the next few months. Robert's wife was very upset and ... frustrated, accusing him of having an affair, or of no longer finding her attractive. Robert wondered if he was getting too old, or if his medication for high blood pressure, which he had been taking for about a year, might be interfering with erection.... When they came for sex therapy, they had not attempted any sexual activity for over two months.

Sexual behavior is a major focus of both our private thoughts and public discussions. Sexual feelings are a crucial part of our development and daily functioning, sexual activity is tied to the satisfaction of our basic needs, and sexual performance is linked to our self-esteem. Most people are fascinated by the abnormal sexual behavior of others and worry about the normality of their own sexuality.

Experts recognize two general categories of sexual disorders: sexual dysfunctions and paraphilic disorders. People with *sexual dysfunctions* experience problems with their sexual responses. Robert, for example, had a dysfunction known as erectile disorder, a repeated failure to attain or maintain an erection during sexual activity. People with *paraphilic disorders* have repeated and intense sexual urges or fantasies in response to objects or situations that society deems inappropriate, and they may behave inappropriately as well. They may be aroused by the thought of sexual activity with a child, for example, or of exposing their genitals to strangers, and they may act on those urges. In addition to the sexual disorders, DSM-5 includes a diagnosis called *gender dysphoria,* a pattern in which people persistently feel that they have been born to the wrong sex and in fact identify with the other gender.

As you will see throughout this chapter, relatively little is known about racial and other cultural differences in sexuality. This is true for normal sexual patterns, sexual dysfunctions, and paraphilic disorders alike. Although different cultural groups have for years been labeled hypersexual, "hot blooded," exotic, passionate, submissive, and the like, such incorrect stereotypes have grown strictly from ignorance or prejudice, not from objective observations or research (McGoldrick et al., 2007). In fact, sex therapists and sex researchers have only recently begun to attend systematically to the importance of culture and race.

Sexual Dysfunctions

Sexual dysfunctions, disorders in which people cannot respond normally in key areas of sexual functioning, make it difficult or impossible to enjoy sexual intercourse. Studies suggest that as many as 31 percent of men and 43 percent of women in the United States suffer from such a dysfunction during their lives (Laumann et al., 2005, 1999). Sexual dysfunctions are typically very distressing, and they often lead to sexual frustration, guilt, loss of self-esteem, and interpersonal problems (McCarthy & McCarthy, 2012). Often these dysfunctions are interrelated; many patients with one dysfunction experience another as

Rates for sexual behavior are typically based on population surveys. What factors might affect the accuracy of such surveys?

well. Sexual dysfunctioning will be described here for heterosexual couples, the majority of couples seen in therapy. Homosexual couples have the same dysfunctions, however, and therapists use the same basic techniques to treat them (LoPiccolo, 2004, 1995).

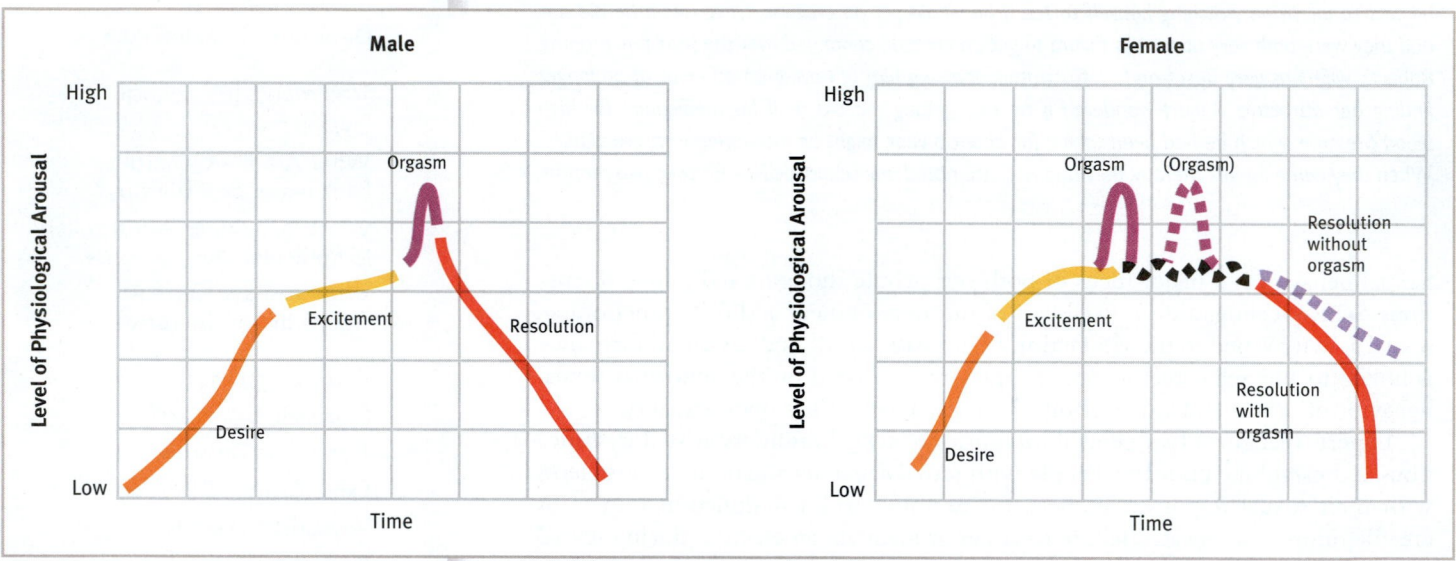

Figure 13-1

The normal sexual response cycle
Researchers have found a similar sequence of phases in both males and females. Sometimes, however, women do not experience orgasm; in that case, the resolution phase is less sudden. And sometimes women experience two or more orgasms in succession before the resolution phase. (Adapted from Kaplan, 1974; Masters & Johnson, 1970, 1966.)

The human sexual response can be described as a *cycle* with four phases: *desire, excitement, orgasm,* and *resolution* (Hayes, 2011) (see Figure 13-1). Sexual dysfunctions affect one or more of the first three phases. Resolution consists simply of the relaxation and reduction in arousal that follow orgasm. Some people struggle with a sexual dysfunction their whole lives (labeled *lifelong type*); in other cases, normal sexual functioning preceded the dysfunction (*acquired type*). In some cases the dysfunction is present during all sexual situations (*generalized type*); in others it is tied to particular situations (*situational type*) (APA, 2013, 2012).

Disorders of Desire

The **desire phase** of the sexual response cycle consists of an interest in or urge to have sex, sexual attraction to others, and, for many people, sexual fantasies. Two dysfunctions affect the desire phase—*male hypoactive sexual desire disorder* and *female sexual interest/arousal disorder.* The latter disorder actually cuts across both the desire and excitement phases of the sexual response cycle. It is considered a single disorder in DSM-5 because, according to research, desire and arousal overlap particularly highly for women, and many women express difficulty distinguishing feelings of desire from those of arousal (APA, 2013, 2012).

Men with **male hypoactive sexual desire disorder** persistently lack or have reduced interest in sex and, in turn, display little sexual activity (see Table 13-1 on the next page). Nevertheless, when these men do have sex, their physical responses may be normal and they may enjoy the experience. While our culture portrays men as wanting all the sex they can get, this disorder may be found in as many as 16 percent of men, and the number seeking therapy has increased during the past decade (McCarthy & Breetz, 2010; Laumann et al., 2005, 1999, 1994).

Women with **female sexual interest/arousal disorder** also lack normal interest in sex and rarely initiate sexual activity. In addition, many such women experience little excitement during sexual activity, are unaroused by erotic cues, and experience few genital or nongenital sensations during sexual activity (APA, 2013). Reduced sexual interest and arousal may be found in as many as 33 percent of women (Christensen et al., 2011; Laumann et al., 2005, 1999, 1994).

A number of people experience normal sexual interest but choose, as a matter of lifestyle, not to engage in sexual relations (see *PsychWatch* on page 391). These individuals are not diagnosed as having one of the sexual desire disorders.

A person's sex drive is determined by a combination of biological, psychological, and sociocultural factors, and any of them may reduce sexual desire (Carvalho & Nobre, 2011). Most cases of low sexual desire are caused primarily by sociocultural and psychological factors, but biological conditions can also lower sex drive significantly.

Biological Causes of Low Sexual Desire A number of hormones interact to help produce sexual desire and behavior (see Figure 13-2), and abnormalities in their activity can lower the sex drive (Heiman et al., 2011; Kruger et al., 2011). In both men and women, a high level of the hormone *prolactin*, a low level of the male sex hormone *testosterone*, and either a high or low level of the female sex hormone *estrogen* can lead to low sex drive (Davison & Davis, 2011; Korda, Goldstein, & Goldstein, 2010). Low sex drive has been linked to the high levels of estrogen contained in some birth control pills, for example. Conversely, it has also been tied to the low level of estrogen found in many postmenopausal women or women who have recently given birth.

•**sexual dysfunction**•A disorder marked by a persistent inability to function normally in some area of the sexual response cycle.

•**desire phase**•The phase of the sexual response cycle consisting of an urge to have sex, sexual fantasies, and sexual attraction.

•**male hypoactive sexual desire disorder**•A male dysfunction marked by a persistent reduction or lack of interest in sex and hence a low level of sexual activity.

•**female sexual interest/arousal disorder**•A female dysfunction marked by a persistent reduction or lack of interest in sex and low sexual activity, as well as, in some cases, limited excitement and few sexual sensations during sexual activity.

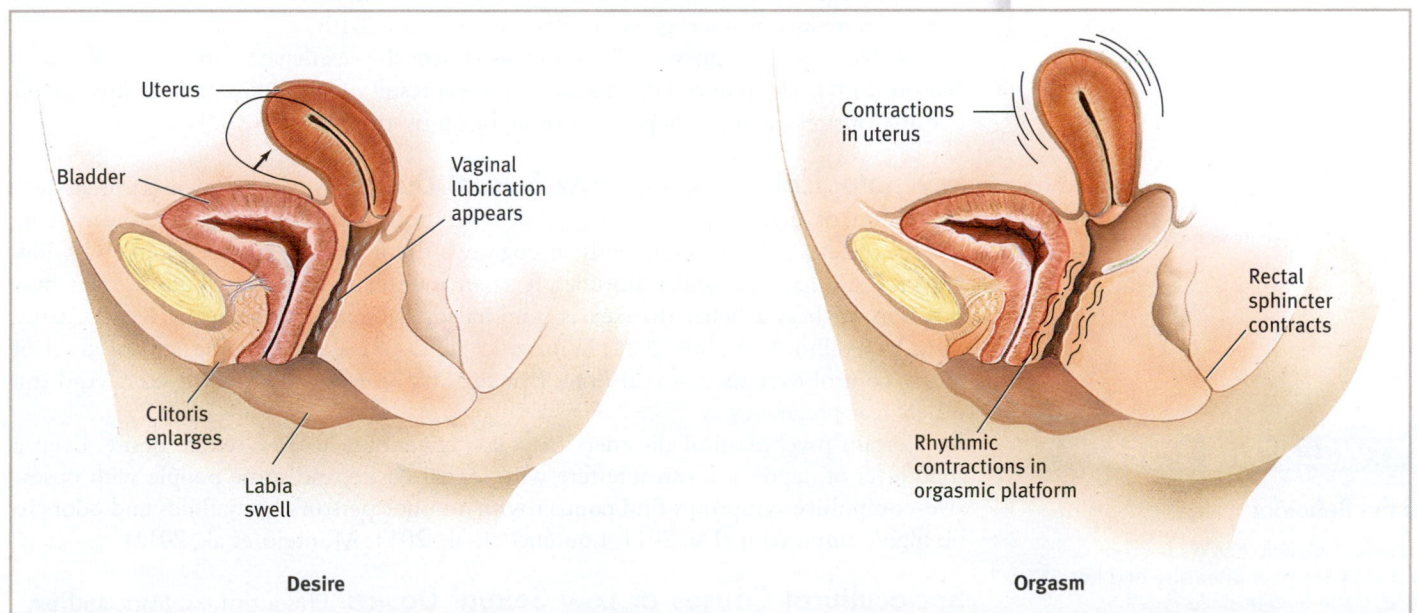

Figure 13-2
Normal female sexual anatomy
Changes in the female anatomy occur during the different phases of the sexual response cycle. (Adapted from Hyde, 1990, p. 200.)

table: 13-1

DSM-5 Checklist

Male Hypoactive Sexual Desire Disorder

1. Persistent or recurrent deficiency of sexual thoughts or fantasies and desire for sexual activity, lasting 6 months or more.

2. Significant distress or impairment.

Female Sexual Interest/Arousal Disorder

1. Lack of sexual interest and/or arousal, lasting for 6 months or more, and consisting of at least three of the following: • Absent/reduced frequency or intensity of sexual interest • Absent/reduced frequency or intensity of sexual thoughts or fantasies • Absent/reduced frequency of sexual initiation or receptiveness to a partner's sexual initiation • Absent/reduced frequency or intensity of sexual excitement or pleasure during almost all sexual encounters • Absent/reduced frequency or intensity of responsiveness to sexual cues • Absent/reduced frequency or intensity of genital or nongenital sensations during almost all sexual encounters.

2. Significant distress or impairment.

Based on APA, 2013, 2012.

Recent investigations also have suggested that low sexual desire may be linked to excessive activity of the neurotransmitters *serotonin* and *dopamine* (Chan et al., 2011). In one study, for example, female rats were administered *apomorphine,* a drug known to increase dopamine activity in certain areas of the brain (Snoeren et al., 2011). In turn, these rats avoided sexual contact with male rats.

Clinical practice and research have further indicated that sex drive can be lowered by certain pain medications, psychotropic drugs, and illegal drugs such as cocaine, marijuana, amphetamines, and heroin (Montejo et al., 2011; Shamloul & Bella, 2011). Low levels of alcohol may enhance the sex drive by lowering a person's inhibitions, yet high levels may reduce it (George et al., 2011; Hart et al., 2010).

Finally, long-term physical illness can also lower the sex drive (Anderson et al., 2011; Basson, 2007). The reduced drive may be a direct result of the illness or an indirect result because of stress, pain, or depression brought on by the illness.

Psychological Causes of Low Sexual Desire A general increase in anxiety, depression, or anger may reduce sexual desire in both men and women (Kashdan et al., 2011; Kim et al., 2011). Frequently, as cognitive theorists have noted, people with low sexual desire have particular attitudes, fears, or memories that contribute to their dysfunction, such as a belief that sex is immoral or dangerous (McCarthy & McCarthy, 2012; Carvalho & Nobre, 2011; Wincze et al., 2008). Other people are so afraid of losing control over their sexual urges that they try to resist them completely. And still others fear pregnancy.

Certain psychological disorders may also contribute to low sexual desire. Even a mild level of depression can interfere with sexual desire, and some people with obsessive-compulsive symptoms find contact with another person's body fluids and odors to be highly unpleasant (Lai, 2011; Lourenco et al., 2011; Montejo et al., 2011).

Sociocultural Causes of Low Sexual Desire The attitudes, fears, and psychological disorders that contribute to low sexual desire occur within a social context, and thus certain sociocultural factors have also been linked to disorders of sexual desire. Many sufferers are feeling situational pressures—divorce, a death in the family, job stress, infertility difficulties, having a baby (Meana, 2012; Basson, 2007). Others may be having problems in their relationships (Brotto et al., 2011). People who are in an unhappy

---

BETWEEN THE LINES

Eye of the Beholder

In the movie *Annie Hall,* Annie's psychotherapist asks her how often she and her boyfriend, Alvie Singer, sleep together. Simultaneously, across town, Alvie's therapist asks him the same question. Alvie answers, "Hardly ever, maybe three times a week," while Annie responds, "Constantly, I'd say three times a week." ‹‹

Lifetime Patterns of Sexual Behavior

Sexual dysfunctions are, by definition, different from the usual patterns of sexual functioning. But in the sexual realm, what is "the usual"? Studies conducted over the past two decades have provided a wealth of useful, sometimes eye-opening information about sexual patterns in the "normal" populations of North America (Chandra et al., 2011; Petersen & Hyde, 2011; Lindau et al., 2007; Laumann et al., 2005, 1999, 1994; Janus & Janus, 1993).

Teenagers

More than 90 percent of boys masturbate by the end of adolescence, compared to 50 percent of girls. For the vast majority of them, masturbation began by age 14. Males report masturbating an average of one to two times a week, females once a month.

Around 20 percent of teenagers have heterosexual intercourse by the age of 15, and 62 percent by age 19. Around 63 percent have oral sex by age 19. Thirty percent of teen girls and 24 percent of teen boys have no heterosexual sexual contact by age 19.

Most teens who are sexually experienced engage in only one sexual relationship at a time. Over the course of their teen years, however, most have at least two sex partners. Extended periods without sex are common, even for teenagers in a relationship. Half of sexually experienced adolescent girls have intercourse once a month or less. Sexually experienced teenage boys spend an average of six months of the year without intercourse.

Condom use by teenagers has increased somewhat during the past two decades, partly because of warnings about AIDS. However, at most half of teenagers report having used a condom the last time they had sex. Less than a third of teenagers use condoms consistently and appropriately.

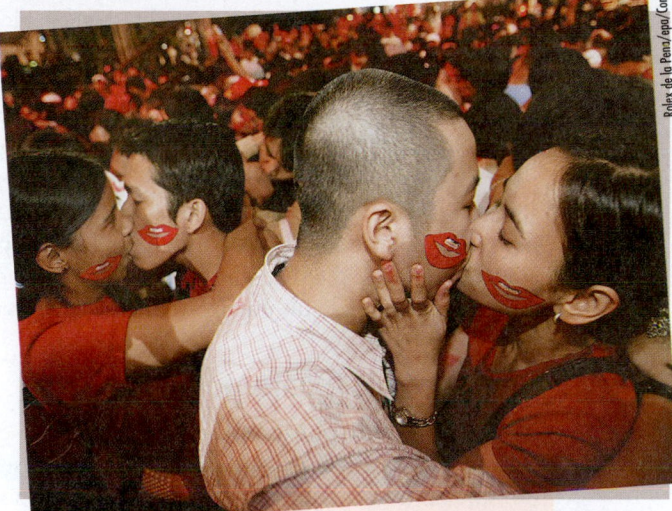

"Lovapalooza"
During early adulthood, more than 80 percent of individuals are sexually active. The feelings behind such activity are on display at the *Lovapalooza* kissing festival in Manila, Philippines, where more than 5,000 young couples lock lips for at least 10 seconds as part of the city's Valentine's Day celebration.

By age 19, 12 percent of teen girls and 4 percent of teen boys report having had at least one sexual experience with a partner of the same sex.

Early Adulthood (Ages 18–24)

Around 83 percent of unmarried young adults have intercourse in a given year. Of those who are sexually active, around a third have sexual contact two or three times a month and another third engage in it two or three times a week. Masturbation remains common in young adulthood: close to 60 percent of men masturbate, a third of them at least once a week, and 36 percent of women masturbate, a tenth of them at least once a week.

By age 24, 12 percent of women and 14 percent of men have had no heterosexual sexual contact. Also by age 24, 16 percent of women and 5.5 percent of men have had at least one sexual experience with a partner of the same sex.

Mid-Adulthood (Ages 25–59)

From the ages of 25 to 59, sexual relationships last longer and are more monogamous. Around 92 percent of people in this age range have sexual experiences in a given year. Half of the unmarried men have two or more partners in a given year, compared to a quarter of the unmarried women.

Among sexually active adults, close to 60 percent of men have intercourse up to three times a week and around 60 percent of women once or twice a week. Middle-aged adults are still masturbating. Half of all middle-aged men masturbate at least monthly. Half of all women between 25 and 50 masturbate at least monthly, but only a third of those between 51 and 64 do so.

Old Age (Ages 60 and Over)

More and more people stop having intercourse as the years go by—a total of 10 percent in their 40s, 15 percent in their 50s, 30 percent in their 60s, and 45 percent in their 70s. The decline in men's sexual activity usually comes gradually as they advance in age and their health fails. Sexual activity is more likely to drop off sharply for elderly women, commonly because of the death or illness of a partner. Elderly women also seem to lose interest in sex before elderly men do. Half of the women in their 60s report limited sexual interest, compared to fewer than 10 percent of the men.

Among elderly persons who remain sexually active, those in their 60s have intercourse an average of four times a month, those in their 70s two or three times a month. Around 70 percent of elderly men and 50 percent of elderly women continue to have sexual fantasies. Around half of men and a fourth of women continue to masturbate into their 90s.

•**excitement phase**•The phase of the sexual response cycle marked by changes in the pelvic region, general physical arousal, and increases in heart rate, muscle tension, blood pressure, and rate of breathing.

•**erectile disorder**•A dysfunction in which a man repeatedly fails to attain or maintain an erection during sexual activity.

•**nocturnal penile tumescence (NPT)**• Erection during sleep.

relationship, have lost affection for their partner, or feel powerless and dominated by their partner can lose interest in sex (Brenot, 2011). Even in basically happy relationships, if one partner is a very unskilled, unenthusiastic lover, the other can begin to lose interest in sex. And sometimes partners differ in their needs for closeness. The one who needs more personal space may develop low sexual desire as a way of keeping distance.

Cultural standards can also set the stage for low sexual desire. Some men adopt our culture's double standard and thus cannot feel sexual desire for a woman they love and respect (Maurice, 2007). More generally, because our society equates sexual attractiveness with youthfulness, many middle-aged and older men and women lose interest in sex as their self-image or their attraction to their partner diminishes with age (Leiblum, 2010).

The trauma of sexual molestation or assault is especially likely to produce the fears, attitudes, and memories found in disorders of sexual desire. Some victims of sexual abuse may feel repelled by sex, a condition that can persist for years, even decades (Brotto et al., 2011; Zwickl & Merriman, 2011). In some cases, individuals may experience vivid flashbacks of the assault during adult sexual activity.

Disorders of Excitement

The **excitement phase** of the sexual response cycle is marked by changes in the pelvic region, general physical arousal, and increases in heart rate, muscle tension, blood pressure, and rate of breathing. In men, blood pools in the pelvis and leads to erection of the penis; in women, this phase produces swelling of the clitoris and labia, as well as lubrication of the vagina. As you read earlier, female sexual interest/arousal disorder may include dysfunction during the excitement phase. In addition, a male disorder—*erectile disorder*—involves dysfunction during the excitement phase only.

Erectile Disorder Men with **erectile disorder** persistently fail to attain or maintain an erection during sexual activity (see Table 13-2). This problem occurs in as much as 10 percent of the general male population, including Robert, the man whose difficulties opened this chapter (Christensen et al., 2011; Laumann et al., 2005, 1999). Carlos Domera also has erectile disorder:

table: 13-2

DSM-5 Checklist

Erectile Disorder

1. Presence of one of the following symptoms during almost all occasions of sexual activity, lasting 6 months or more: • Marked difficulty obtaining an erection • Marked difficulty maintaining an erection until completion of sexual activity • Marked decrease in erectile rigidity that interferes with sexual activity.

2. Significant distress or impairment.

Based on APA, 2013, 2012.

Carlos Domera is a 30-year-old dress manufacturer who came to the United States from Argentina at age 22. He is married to . . . Phyllis, also age 30. They have no children. Mr. Domera's problem was that he had been unable to have sexual intercourse for over a year due to his inability to achieve or maintain an erection. He had avoided all sexual contact with his wife for the prior five months, except for two brief attempts at lovemaking which ended when he failed to maintain his erection.

The couple separated a month ago by mutual agreement due to the tension that surrounded their sexual problem and their inability to feel comfortable with each other. Both professed love and concern for the other, but had serious doubts regarding their ability to resolve the sexual problem. . . .

[Carlos] conformed to the stereotype of the "macho Latin lover," believing that he "should always have erections easily and be able to make love at any time." Since he couldn't "perform" sexually, he felt humiliated and inadequate, and he dealt with this by avoiding not only sex, but any expression of affection for his wife.

[Phyllis] felt "he is not trying; perhaps he doesn't love me, and I can't live with no sex, no affection, and his bad moods." She had requested the separation temporarily, and he readily agreed. However, they had recently been seeing each other twice a week. . . .

During the evaluation he reported that the onset of his erectile difficulties was concurrent with a tense period in his business. After several "failures" to complete intercourse, he concluded he was "useless as a husband" and therefore a "total failure." The anxiety of attempting lovemaking was too much for him to deal with.

He reluctantly admitted that he was occasionally able to masturbate alone to a full, firm erection and reach a satisfying orgasm. However, he felt ashamed and guilty about this, from both childhood masturbatory guilt and a feeling that he was "cheating" his wife. It was also noted that he had occasional firm erections upon awakening in the morning. Other than the antidepressant, the patient was taking no drugs, and he was not using much alcohol. There was no evidence of physical illness.

(Spitzer et al., 1983, pp. 105–106)

BETWEEN THE LINES

In Their Words

"Erection is chiefly caused by scuraum, eringoes, cresses, crymon, parsnips, artichokes, turnips, asparagus, candied ginger, acorns bruised to powder and drunk in muscadel, scallion, sea shell fish, etc." «

Aristotle, *The Masterpiece,*
fourth century B.C.

Unlike Carlos, most men with an erectile disorder are over the age of 50, largely because so many cases are associated with ailments or diseases of older adults (Cameron et al., 2005). The disorder is experienced by 7 percent of men who are under 30 years old and increases to 50 percent of men over 60 (Rosen, 2007). Moreover, according to surveys, half of all adult men experience erectile difficulty during intercourse at least some of the time. Most cases of erectile disorder result from an interaction of biological, psychological, and sociocultural processes (Rowland, 2012; Carvalho & Nobre, 2011; Rosen, 2007).

? Why has the clinical field been slow to investigate possible cultural and racial differences in sexual behaviors?

BIOLOGICAL CAUSES The same hormonal imbalances that can cause male hypoactive sexual desire disorder can also produce erectile disorder (Hyde, 2005). More commonly, however, vascular problems—problems with the body's blood vessels—are involved (Wincze et al., 2008; Rosen, 2007). An erection occurs when the chambers in the penis fill with blood, so any condition that reduces blood flow into the penis, such as heart disease or clogging of the arteries, may lead to the disorder (Meuleman, 2011). It can also be caused by damage to the nervous system as a result of diabetes, spinal cord injuries, multiple sclerosis, kidney failure, or treatment by dialysis (Anderson et al., 2011; Blackmore et al., 2011). In addition, as is the case with male hypoactive sexual desire disorder, the use of certain medications and various forms of substance abuse, from alcohol abuse to cigarette smoking, may interfere with erections (Herrick et al., 2011; Panjari, Bell, & Davis, 2011).

Medical procedures, including ultrasound recordings and blood tests, have been developed for diagnosing biological causes of erectile disorder. Measuring **nocturnal penile tumescence (NPT),** or erections during sleep, is particularly useful in assessing whether physical factors are responsible. Men typically have erections during *rapid eye movement (REM) sleep,* the phase of sleep in which dreaming takes place. A healthy man is likely to have two to five REM periods each night, and several penile erections as well (see Figure 13-3 on the next page). Abnormal or absent nightly erections usually (but not always) indicate some physical basis for erectile failure. As a rough screening device, a patient may be instructed to fasten a simple "snap gauge" band around his penis before going to sleep and then check it the next morning. A broken band indicates that erection has occurred during the night. An unbroken band indicates a lack of nighttime erections and suggests that the person's general erectile problem may have a physical basis. A newer version of this device further attaches the band to a computer, which provides precise measurements of erections throughout the night (Wincze et al., 2008). Such assessment devices are less likely to be used in clinical practice today than in past years. As you'll see later in the chapter, Viagra and other drugs for erectile disorder are typically given to patients without much formal evaluation of their problem (Rosen, 2007).

PSYCHOLOGICAL CAUSES Any of the psychological causes of male hypoactive sexual desire disorder can also interfere with arousal and lead to erectile disorder (Rowland, Georgoff, & Burnett, 2011). As many as 90 percent of all

Psychological or organic?
The *RigiScan* is a device that measures a male patient's erections during sleep. It consists of a computer and two bands that are worn around the penis. If the computer readout indicates that the bands have expanded throughout the night, it is concluded that the man has experienced normal erections during REM sleep and that his erectile failures during intercourse are probably caused by psychological factors.

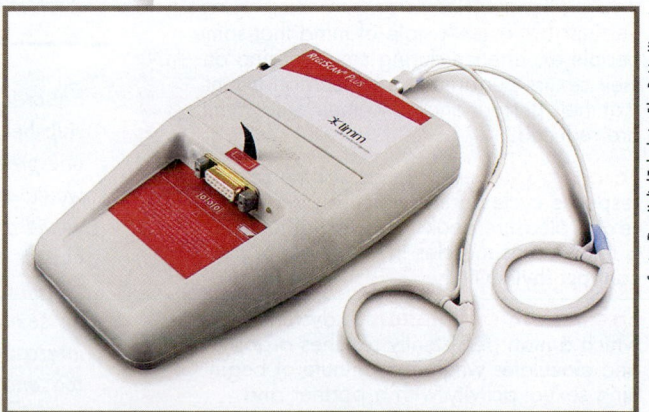

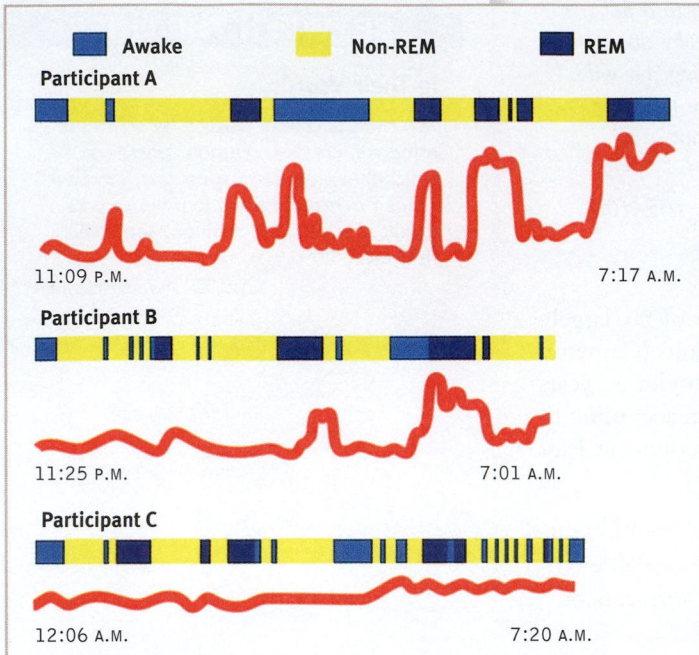

Figure 13-3

Measurements of erections during sleep
Research participant A, a man without erectile problems, has normal erections during REM sleep. Participant B has erectile problems that seem to be at least partly psychogenic—otherwise he would not have any erections during REM sleep. Participant C's erectile disorder is related to organic problems, an interpretation supported by his lack of erections during REM sleep. (Adapted from Bancroft, 1989.)

•**performance anxiety**•The fear of performing inadequately and a related tension experienced during sex.

•**spectator role**•A state of mind that some people experience during sex, focusing on their sexual performance to such an extent that their performance and their enjoyment are reduced.

•**orgasm phase**•The phase of the sexual response cycle during which an individual's sexual pleasure peaks and sexual tension is released as muscles in the pelvic region contract rhythmically.

•**premature ejaculation**•A dysfunction in which a man persistently reaches orgasm and ejaculates within one minute of beginning sexual activity with a partner and before he wishes to. Also called *early* or *rapid* ejaculation.

men with severe depression, for example, experience some degree of erectile dysfunction (Montejo et al., 2011; Stevenson & Elliott, 2007).

One well-supported psychological explanation for erectile disorder is the cognitive-behavioral theory developed by William Masters and Virginia Johnson (1970). The explanation emphasizes **performance anxiety** and the **spectator role.** Once a man begins to experience erectile problems, for whatever reason, he becomes fearful about failing to have an erection and worries during each sexual encounter (Carvalho & Nobre, 2011). Instead of relaxing and enjoying the sensations of sexual pleasure, he remains distanced from the activity, watching himself and focusing on the goal of reaching erection. Instead of being an aroused participant, he becomes a judge and spectator. Whatever the initial reason for the erectile dysfunction, the resulting spectator role becomes the reason for the ongoing problem. In this vicious cycle, the original cause of the erectile failure becomes less important than fear of failure.

SOCIOCULTURAL CAUSES Each of the sociocultural factors that contribute to male hypoactive sexual desire disorder has also been tied to erectile disorder. Men who have lost their jobs and are under financial stress, for example, are more likely to develop erectile difficulties than other men (Morokoff & Gilliland, 1993). Marital stress, too, has been tied to this dysfunction (Brenot, 2011; Wincze et al., 2008). Two relationship patterns in particular may contribute to it (Rosen, 2007; LoPiccolo, 2004, 1991). In one, a wife provides too little physical stimulation for her aging husband, who, because of normal aging changes, now requires more intense, direct, and lengthy physical stimulation of the penis for erection to occur. In the second relationship pattern, a couple believes that only intercourse can give the wife an orgasm. This idea increases the pressure on the man to have an erection and makes him more vulnerable to erectile dysfunction. If the wife reaches orgasm manually or orally during their sexual encounter, his pressure to perform is reduced.

Disorders of Orgasm

During the **orgasm phase** of the sexual response cycle, an individual's sexual pleasure peaks and sexual tension is released as the muscles in the pelvic region contract, or draw together, rhythmically (see Figure 13-4). The man's semen is ejaculated, and the outer third of the woman's vaginal wall contracts. Dysfunctions of this phase of the sexual response cycle are *premature ejaculation* and *delayed ejaculation* in men and *female orgasmic disorder* in women.

Premature (Early) Ejaculation
Eduardo is typical of many men in his experience of early ejaculation:

> Eduardo, a 20-year-old student, sought treatment after his girlfriend ended their relationship because his premature ejaculation left her sexually frustrated. Eduardo had had only one previous sexual relationship, during his senior year in high school. With two friends he would drive to a neighboring town and find a certain prostitute. After picking her up, they would drive to a deserted area and take turns having sex with her, while the others waited outside the car. Both the prostitute and his friends urged him to hurry up because they feared discovery by the police, and besides, in the winter it was cold. When Eduardo began his sexual relationship with his girlfriend, his entire sexual history consisted of this rapid intercourse, with virtually no foreplay. He found caressing his girlfriend's breasts and genitals and her touching of his penis to be so arousing that he sometimes ejaculated before complete entry of the penis, or after at most only a minute or so of intercourse.

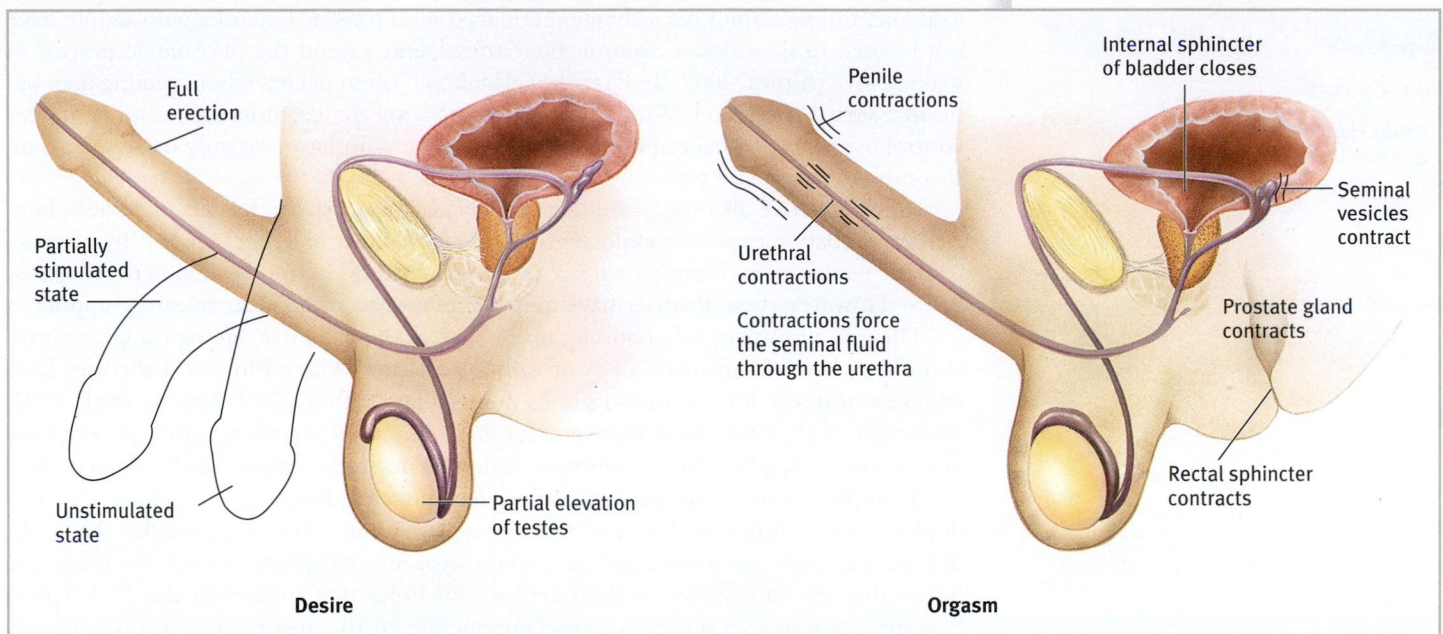

Desire

Full erection

Partially stimulated state

Unstimulated state

Partial elevation of testes

Orgasm

Penile contractions

Urethral contractions

Contractions force the seminal fluid through the urethra

Internal sphincter of bladder closes

Seminal vesicles contract

Prostate gland contracts

Rectal sphincter contracts

Figure 13-4

Normal male sexual anatomy Changes in the male anatomy occur during the different phases of the sexual response cycle. (Adapted from Hyde, 1990, p. 199.)

A man suffering from **early ejaculation** (also called *premature,* or *rapid,* ejaculation) persistently reaches orgasm and ejaculates within one minute of beginning sexual activity with a partner and before he wishes to (see Table 13-3). As many as 30 percent of men in the United States experience early ejaculation at some time (Jannini & Lenzi, 2005; Laumann et al., 2005, 1999, 1994). The typical duration of intercourse in our society has increased over the past several decades, in turn increasing the distress of men who experience early ejaculation. Although the dysfunction is certainly experienced by many young men, research suggests that men of any age may suffer from it (Rowland, 2012; Althof, 2007).

Psychological, particularly behavioral, explanations of early ejaculation have received more research support than other kinds of explanations. The dysfunction is common, for

table: 13-3

DSM-5 Checklist

Premature (Early) Ejaculation

1. During almost all occasions of sexual activity with a partner, ejaculation within one minute of beginning the activity and before the person wishes it.

2. Difficulty lasts 6 months or more.

3. Significant distress or impairment.

Delayed Ejaculation

1. Marked delay, infrequency, or absence of ejaculation during almost all occasions of sexual activity with a partner. Pattern lasts 6 months or more.

2. Significant distress or impairment.

Female Orgasmic Disorder

1. Presence of one of the following symptoms during almost all occasions of sexual activity, lasting 6 months or more: • Marked delay, infrequency, or absence of orgasm • Markedly reduced intensity of orgasmic sensation.

2. Significant distress or impairment.

Based on APA, 2013, 2012.

example, among young, sexually inexperienced men such as Eduardo, who simply have not learned to slow down, control their arousal, and extend the pleasurable process of making love (Althof, 2007). In fact, early ejaculation often occurs when a young man has his first sexual encounter. With continued sexual experience, most men acquire greater control over their sexual responses. Men of any age who have sex only occasionally are also prone to ejaculate early.

Clinicians have also suggested that early ejaculation may be related to anxiety, hurried masturbation experiences during adolescence (in fear of being "caught" by parents), or poor recognition of one's own sexual arousal (Althof, 2007; Westheimer & Lopater, 2005). However, these theories have only sometimes received clear research support.

There is a growing belief among many clinical theorists that biological factors may also play a key role in many cases of early ejaculation. Three biological theories have emerged from the limited investigations done so far (Althof, 2007; Mirone et al., 2001; Waldinger et al., 1998). One theory states that some men are born with a genetic predisposition to develop this dysfunction. Indeed, one study found that 91 percent of a small sample of men suffering from early ejaculation had first-degree relatives who also displayed the dysfunction. A second theory, based on animal studies, argues that the brains of men with early ejaculation contain certain serotonin receptors that are overactive and others that are underactive. A third explanation holds that men with this dysfunction experience greater sensitivity or nerve conduction in the area of their penis, a notion that has received inconsistent research support thus far.

Delayed Ejaculation A man with **delayed ejaculation** (previously called *male orgasmic disorder* or *inhibited male orgasm*) persistently is unable to ejaculate or has very delayed ejaculations during sexual activity with a partner (see Table 13-3 again). The disorder occurs in 8 percent of the male population (Hartmann & Waldinger, 2007; Laumann et al., 2005, 1999) and is typically a source of great frustration and upset, as in the case of John:

> John, a 38-year-old sales representative, had been married for 9 years. At the insistence of his 32-year-old wife, the couple sought counseling for their sexual problem—his inability to ejaculate during intercourse. During the early years of the marriage, his wife had experienced difficulty reaching orgasm until he learned to delay his ejaculation for a long period of time. To do this, he used mental distraction techniques and regularly smoked marijuana before making love. Initially, John felt very satisfied that he could make love for longer and longer periods of time without ejaculation and regarded his ability as a sign of masculinity.
>
> About 3 years prior to seeking counseling, after the birth of their only child, John found that he was losing his erection before he was able to ejaculate. His wife suggested different intercourse positions, but the harder he tried, the more difficulty he had in reaching orgasm. Because of his frustration, the couple began to avoid sex altogether. John experienced increasing performance anxiety with each successive failure, and an increasing sense of helplessness in the face of his problem.
>
> *(Rosen & Rosen, 1981, pp. 317–318)*

A low testosterone level, certain neurological diseases, and some head or spinal cord injuries can interfere with ejaculation (Stevenson & Elliott, 2007; McKenna, 2001). Substances that slow down the sympathetic nervous system (such as alcohol, some medications for high blood pressure, and certain psychotropic medications) can also affect ejaculation (Herrick et al., 2011). For example, certain serotonin-enhancing antidepressant drugs appear to interfere with ejaculation in at least 30 percent of men who take them (Montejo et al., 2011; Ashton, 2007).

A leading psychological cause of delayed ejaculation appears to be performance anxiety and the spectator role, the cognitive-behavioral factors also involved in erectile disorder (Carvalho & Nobre, 2011; Kashdan et al., 2011). Once a man begins to focus

•**delayed ejaculation**•A male dysfunction characterized by persistent inability to ejaculate or very delayed ejaculations during sexual activity with a partner.

•**female orgasmic disorder**•A dysfunction in which a woman persistently fails to reach orgasm, experiences orgasms of very low intensity, or has very delayed orgasms.

on reaching orgasm, he may stop being an aroused participant in his sexual activity and instead become an unaroused, self-critical, and fearful observer (Rowland, 2012; Hartmann & Waldinger, 2007; Wiederman, 2001). Another psychological cause of delayed ejaculation may be past masturbation habits. If, for example, a man has masturbated all his life by rubbing his penis against sheets, pillows, or other such objects, he may have difficulty reaching orgasm in the absence of the sensations tied to those objects (Wincze et al., 2008). Finally, delayed ejaculation may develop out of male hypoactive sexual desire disorder (Apfelbaum, 2000). A man who engages in sex largely because of pressure from his partner, without any real desire for it, simply may not get aroused enough to ejaculate.

? *Are there other areas in life that might also be explained by performance anxiety and the spectator role?*

Female Orgasmic Disorder Janel and Isaac, married for three years, came for sex therapy because of her lack of orgasm.

Janel had never had an orgasm in any way, but because of Isaac's concern, she had been faking orgasm during intercourse until recently. Finally she told him the truth, and they sought therapy together. Janel had been raised by a strictly religious family. She could not recall ever seeing her parents kiss or show physical affection for each other. She was severely punished on one occasion when her mother found her looking at her own genitals, at about age 7. Janel received no sex education from her parents, and when she began to menstruate, her mother told her only that this meant that she could become pregnant, so she mustn't ever kiss a boy or let a boy touch her. Her mother restricted her dating severely, with repeated warnings that "boys only want one thing." While her parents were rather critical and demanding of her (asking her why she got one B among otherwise straight A's on her report card, for example), they were loving parents and their approval was very important to her.

Women with **female orgasmic disorder** persistently fail to reach orgasm, experience orgasms of very low intensity, or have a very delayed orgasm (see Table 13-3 again). As many as 24 percent of women apparently have this problem to some degree—including more than a third of postmenopausal women (Heiman, 2007, 2002). Studies indicate that 10 percent or more of women have never had an orgasm, either alone or during intercourse, and at least another 9 percent rarely have orgasms (Bancroft et al., 2003). At the same time, half of all women experience orgasm in intercourse at least fairly regularly (LoPiccolo & Stock, 1987). Women who are more sexually assertive and more comfortable with masturbation tend to have orgasms more regularly (Carrobles et al., 2011; Hurlbert, 1991; Kelly et al., 1990). Female orgasmic disorder appears to be more common among single women than among women who are married or living with someone (Laumann et al., 2005, 1999, 1994).

? *Some theorists believe that the women's movement has helped to enlighten clinical views of sexual disorders. How might this be so?*

Most clinicians agree that orgasm during intercourse is not mandatory for normal sexual functioning (Meana, 2012; Wincze et al., 2008). Many women instead reach orgasm with their partners by direct stimulation of the clitoris (LoPiccolo, 2002, 1995). Although early psychoanalytic theory considered a lack of orgasm during intercourse to be pathological, evidence suggests that women who rely on stimulation of the clitoris for orgasm are entirely normal and healthy (Heiman, 2007).

Biological, psychological, and sociocultural factors may combine to produce female orgasmic disorder (Meana, 2012; Heiman, 2007). Because arousal plays a key role in

BETWEEN THE LINES

Nightly Visits

Orgasms can sometimes occur during sleep. Ancient Babylonians said that such nocturnal orgasms were caused by a "maid of the night" who visited men in their sleep and a "little night man" who visited women (Kahn & Fawcett, 1993). ‹‹

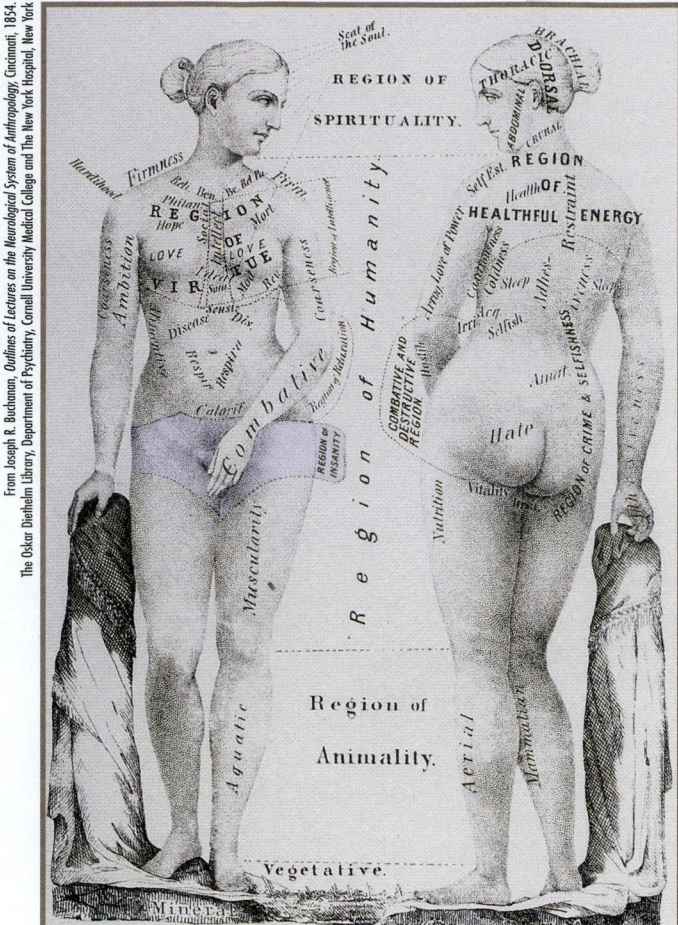

From Joseph R. Buchanan, *Outlines of Lectures on the Neurological System of Anthropology*. Cincinnati, 1854. The Oskar Diethelm Library, Department of Psychiatry, Cornell University Medical College and The New York Hospital, New York

"The region of insanity" Medical authorities described "excessive passion" in Victorian women as dangerous and as a possible cause of insanity (Gamwell & Tomes, 1995). This illustration from a nineteenth-century medical textbook even labels a woman's reproductive organs as her "region of insanity."

•**genito-pelvic pain/penetration disorder**• A sexual dysfunction characterized by significant physical discomfort during intercourse.

orgasms, arousal difficulties often are featured prominently in explanations of female orgasmic disorder.

BIOLOGICAL CAUSES A variety of physiological conditions can affect a woman's orgasm (Wincze et al., 2008; Heiman, 2007). Diabetes can damage the nervous system in ways that interfere with arousal, lubrication of the vagina, and orgasm. Lack of orgasm has sometimes been linked to multiple sclerosis and other neurological diseases, to the same drugs and medications that may interfere with ejaculation in men, and to changes, often postmenopausal, in skin sensitivity and structure of the clitoris, vaginal walls, or the labia—the folds of skin on each side of the vagina (Blackmore et al., 2011; Lombardi et al., 2011).

PSYCHOLOGICAL CAUSES The psychological causes of female sexual interest/arousal disorder, including depression, may also lead to female orgasmic disorder (Kashdan et al., 2011; Kim et al., 2011). In addition, as both psychodynamic and cognitive theorists might predict, memories of childhood traumas and relationships have sometimes been associated with orgasm problems. In one large study, memories of an unhappy childhood or loss of a parent during childhood were tied to lack of orgasm in adulthood (Raboch & Raboch, 1992). In other studies, childhood memories of a dependable father, a positive relationship with one's mother, affection between the parents, the mother's positive personality, and the mother's expression of positive emotions were all predictors of positive orgasm outcomes (Heiman, 2007; Heiman et al., 1986).

SOCIOCULTURAL CAUSES For years many clinicians have believed that female orgasmic problems may result from society's recurrent message to women that they should repress and deny their sexuality, a message that has often led to "less permissive" sexual attitudes and behavior among women than among men (see Figure 13-5). In fact, many women with both arousal and orgasmic difficulties report that they had an overly strict religious upbringing, were punished for childhood masturbation, received no preparation for the onset of menstruation, were restricted in their dating as teenagers, and were told that "nice girls don't" (LoPiccolo & Van Male, 2000).

A sexually restrictive history, however, is just as common among women who function well during sexual activity (LoPiccolo, 2002, 1997). In addition, cultural messages about female sexuality have been more positive in recent years, while the rate of arousal and orgasmic problems remains the same for women. Why, then, do some women and not others develop such problems? Researchers suggest that unusually stressful events, traumas, or relationships may help produce the fears, memories, and attitudes that often characterize these sexual problems (Meana, 2012; Westheimer & Lopater, 2005). For example, many women molested as children or raped as adults have female orgasmic disorder (Hall, 2007; Heiman, 2007).

Research has also related orgasmic behavior to certain qualities in a woman's intimate relationships (Brenot, 2011; Heiman et al., 1986). Studies have found, for example, that the likelihood of reaching orgasm may be tied to how much emotional involvement a woman had during her first experience of intercourse and how long that relationship lasted, the pleasure the woman obtained during the experience, her current attraction to her partner's body, and her marital happiness. Interestingly, the same studies have found that erotic fantasies during sex with their current partner are more common in orgasmic than in nonorgasmic women.

Disorders of Sexual Pain

Certain sexual dysfunctions are characterized by enormous physical discomfort during intercourse, a difficulty that does not fit neatly into a specific part of the sexual response cycle. Such dysfunctions, collectively called **genito-pelvic pain/penetration disorder,** are experienced by women much more often than men (APA, 2013, 2012).

Some women with genito-pelvic pain/penetration disorder experience involuntary contractions of the muscles around the outer third of the vagina that prevent entry of the penis (see Table 13-4). This problem, known in medical circles as *vaginismus,* can prevent a couple from ever having intercourse. The problem has received relatively little research, but estimates are that it occurs in fewer than 1 percent of all women (Christensen et al., 2011; Antony & Barlow, 2010, 2004). A number of women with this dysfunction enjoy sex greatly, have a strong sex drive, and reach orgasm with stimulation of the clitoris (Sánchez Bravo et al., 2010). They just fear the discomfort of penetration of the vagina.

Most clinicians agree with the cognitive-behavioral position that this form of genito-pelvic pain penetration disorder is usually a learned fear response, set off by a woman's expectation that intercourse will be painful and damaging (Huijding et al., 2011). A variety of factors apparently can set the stage for this fear, including anxiety and ignorance about intercourse, exaggerated stories about how painful and bloody the first occasion of intercourse is for women, trauma caused by an unskilled lover who forces his penis into the vagina before the woman is aroused and lubricated, and the trauma of childhood sexual abuse or adult rape (Zwickl & Merriman, 2011; Binik, 2010).

Alternatively, women may experience this form of genito-pelvic pain penetration disorder because of an infection of the vagina or urinary tract, a gynecological disease such as herpes simplex, or the physical effects of menopause. In such cases, the dysfunction can be overcome only if the women receive medical treatment for these conditions.

Other women with genito-pelvic pain/penetration disorder do not have involuntary contractions of their vaginal muscles, but they do experience severe vaginal or pelvic pain during sexual intercourse, a pattern known medically as *dyspareunia* (from Latin words meaning "painful mating"). Surveys suggest that as many as 14 percent of women suffer from this problem to some degree (Antony & Barlow, 2010, 2004; Laumann et al., 2004, 1999). Sufferers typically enjoy sex and get aroused but find their sex lives very limited by the pain that accompanies what used to be a positive event (Huijding et al., 2011).

This form of genito-pelvic pain/penetration disorder usually has a physical cause (Binik et al., 2007). Among the most common is an injury (for example, to the vagina or pelvic ligaments) during childbirth. Similarly, the scar left by an episiotomy (a cut often made to enlarge the vaginal entrance and ease delivery) can cause pain. Around 16 percent of women experience severe vaginal or pelvic pain during intercourse for up to a year after giving birth (Bertozzi et al., 2010). More generally, such pain has also been tied to collision of the penis with remaining parts of the hymen, infections of the vagina, wiry pubic hair that rubs against the labia during intercourse, pelvic diseases, tumors, cysts, and allergic reactions to the chemicals in vaginal douches and contraceptive creams, the rubber in condoms or diaphragms, or the protein in semen (Tripoli et al., 2011).

Although psychological factors (for instance, heightened anxiety or overattentiveness to one's body) or relationship problems may contribute to this problem (Granot et al., 2011), psychosocial factors alone are rarely responsible for it (Dewitte, Van Lankveld, & Crombez, 2011). In cases that are truly psychogenic, the woman may in fact be suffering from female sexual interest/arousal disorder. That is, penetration into an unaroused, unlubricated vagina is painful. It also is the case that around 3 percent of men suffer from pain in the genitals during intercourse, and many of these men also qualify for a diagnosis of genito-pelvic pain/penetration disorder.

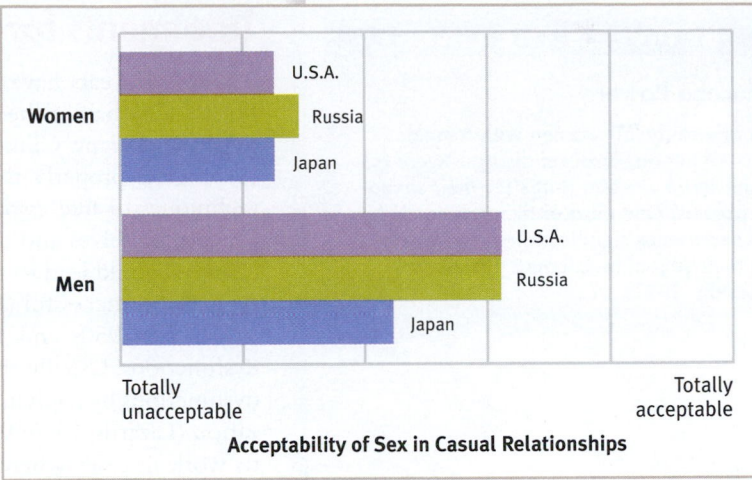

Acceptability of Sex in Casual Relationships

Figure 13-5
Is sex in a casual relationship acceptable? Men and women around the globe have different opinions on this issue. In one study, college women from the United States, Russia, and Japan rated casual sex as "unacceptable" on average, whereas the ratings by men in those countries ranged from "fairly acceptable" to "quite acceptable" (Sprecher & Hatfield, 1996).

table: 13-4

DSM-5 Checklist

Genito-Pelvic Pain/Penetration Disorder

1. Persistent or recurrent difficulties in one of the following areas for 6 months or more: •Marked difficulty having vaginal intercourse or penetration • Marked vaginal or pelvic pain during attempts at intercourse or penetration • Marked fear about vaginal or pelvic pain or vaginal penetration • Marked tensing or tightening of the pelvic floor muscles during attempts at vaginal penetration.

2. Significant distress or impairment.

Based on APA, 2013, 2012.

Treatments for Sexual Dysfunctions

The last 40 years have brought major changes in the treatment of sexual dysfunctions. For the first half of the twentieth century, the leading approach was long-term psychodynamic therapy. Clinicians assumed that sexual dysfunctioning was caused by failure to progress properly through the psychosexual stages of development, and they used techniques of free association and therapist interpretations to help clients gain insight about themselves and their problems. Although it was expected that broad personality changes would lead to improvement in sexual functioning, psychodynamic therapy was typically unsuccessful (Bergler, 1951).

In the 1950s and 1960s, behavioral therapists offered new treatments for sexual dysfunctions. Usually they tried to reduce the fears that they believed were causing the dysfunctions by applying such procedures as relaxation training and systematic desensitization (Lazarus, 1965; Wolpe, 1958). These approaches had some success, but they failed to work in cases where the key problems included misinformation, negative attitudes, and lack of effective sexual technique (LoPiccolo, 2002, 1995).

A revolution in the treatment of sexual dysfunctions occurred with the publication of William Masters and Virginia Johnson's landmark book *Human Sexual Inadequacy* in 1970. The *sex therapy* program they introduced has evolved into a complex approach, which now includes interventions from the various models, particularly cognitive-behavioral, couple, and family systems therapies (McCarthy & McCarthy, 2012; Meana, 2012; Leiblum, 2010, 2007). The goal of sex therapy is to help clients function better sexually and to achieve a higher level of sexual satisfaction and psychological well-being (Cuzin, 2011). In recent years, biological interventions, particularly drug therapies, have been added to the treatment arsenal (Korda et al., 2010; Leiblum, 2010, 2007).

What Are the General Features of Sex Therapy?

Modern sex therapy is short-term and instructive, typically lasting 15 to 20 sessions. It centers on specific sexual problems rather than on broad personality issues (Wincze et al., 2008). Carlos Domera, the Argentine man with erectile disorder whom you met earlier, responded successfully to the multiple techniques of modern sex therapy:

At the end of the evaluation session the psychiatrist reassured the couple that Mr. Domera had a "reversible psychological" sexual problem that was due to several factors, including his depression, but also more currently his anxiety and embarrassment, his high standards, and some cultural and relationship difficulties that made communication awkward and relaxation nearly impossible. The couple was advised that a brief trial of therapy, focused directly on the sexual problem, would very likely produce significant improvement within ten to fourteen sessions. They were assured that the problem was almost certainly not physical in origin, but rather psychogenic, and that therefore the prognosis was excellent.

Mr. Domera was shocked and skeptical, but the couple agreed to commence the therapy on a weekly basis, and they were given a typical first "assignment" to do at home: a caressing massage exercise to try together with specific instructions not to attempt genital stimulation or intercourse at all, even if an erection might occur.

Not surprisingly, during the second session Mr. Domera reported with a cautious smile that they had "cheated" and had had intercourse "against the rules." This was their first successful intercourse in more than a year. Their success and happiness were acknowledged by the therapist, but they were cautioned strongly that rapid initial improvement often occurs, only to be followed by increased performance anxiety in subsequent weeks and a return of the initial problem. They were humorously chastised and encouraged to try again to have sexual contact involving caressing and non-demand light genital stimulation, without an expectation of erection or orgasm, and to avoid intercourse.

During the second and fourth weeks [Carlos] did not achieve erections during the love play, and the therapy sessions dealt with helping him to accept himself with or without erections and to learn to enjoy sensual contact without intercourse. His wife helped him to believe genuinely that he could please her with manual or oral stimulation and that, although she enjoyed intercourse, she enjoyed these other stimulations as much, as long as he was relaxed.

[Carlos] struggled with his cultural image of what a "man" does, but he had to admit that his wife seemed pleased and that he, too, was enjoying the nonintercourse caressing techniques. He was encouraged to view his new lovemaking skills as a "success" and to recognize that in many ways he was becoming a better lover than many husbands, because he was listening to his wife and responding to her requests.

By the fifth week the patient was attempting intercourse successfully with relaxed confidence, and by the ninth session he was responding regularly with erections. If they both agreed, they would either have intercourse or choose another sexual technique to achieve orgasm. Treatment was terminated after ten sessions.

(Spitzer et al., 1983, pp. 106–107)

As Carlos Domera's treatment indicates, modern sex therapy includes a variety of principles and techniques. The following ones are applied in almost all cases, regardless of the dysfunction:

1. **Assessment and conceptualization of the problem.** Patients are initially given a medical examination and are interviewed concerning their "sex history." The therapist's focus during the interview is on gathering information about past life events and, in particular, current factors that are contributing to the dysfunction (Meana, 2012; Leiblum, 2010, 2007; Heiman, 2007). Sometimes proper assessment requires a team of specialists, perhaps including a psychologist, urologist, and neurologist.

2. **Mutual responsibility.** Therapists stress the principle of *mutual responsibility.* Both partners in the relationship share the sexual problem, regardless of who has the actual dysfunction, and treatment will be more successful when both are in therapy (McCarthy & McCarthy, 2012; Brenot, 2011; Hall, 2007).

3. **Education about sexuality.** Many patients who suffer from sexual dysfunctions know very little about the physiology and techniques of sexual activity (Rowland, 2012; Hinchliff & Gott, 2011; Heiman, 2007). Thus sex therapists may discuss these topics and offer educational materials, including instructional books, videos, and Internet sites.

4. **Emotion identification.** Sex therapists help patients identify and express upsetting emotions tied to past events that may keep interfering with sexual arousal and enjoyment (Kleinplatz, 2010).

5. **Attitude change.** Following a cardinal principle of cognitive therapy, sex therapists help patients examine and change any beliefs about sexuality that are preventing sexual arousal and pleasure (McCarthy & McCarthy, 2012; Hall, 2010; Wincze et al., 2008). Some of these mistaken beliefs are widely shared in our society and can result from past traumatic events, family attitudes, or cultural ideas.

6. **Elimination of performance anxiety and the spectator role.** Therapists often teach couples *sensate focus,* or *nondemand pleasuring,* a series of sensual tasks, sometimes called "petting" exercises, in which the partners focus on the sexual pleasure that can be achieved by exploring and caressing each other's body at home, without demands to have intercourse or reach orgasm—demands that may be interfering with arousal. Couples are told at first to refrain

Grooming is key
Humans are far from the only animals that follow a sexual response cycle or, for that matter, display sexual dysfunctions. Here a male Macaque monkey grooms a female monkey while they sit in a hot spring in the snow in central Japan. Research shows that such grooming triples the likelihood that the female will engage in sexual activity with the male.

AP Photo/Shuji Kajiyama

from intercourse at home and to restrict their sexual activity to kissing, hugging, and sensual massage of various parts of the body, but not of the breasts or genitals. Over time, they learn how to give and receive greater sexual pleasure and they build back up to the activity of sexual intercourse (Rowland, 2012).

7. **Increasing sexual and general communication skills.** Couples are taught to use their sensate-focus skills and apply new sexual techniques and positions at home. They may, for example, try sexual positions in which the person being caressed can guide the other's hands and control the speed, pressure, and location of sexual contact (Heiman, 2007). Couples are also taught to give instructions to each other in a nonthreatening, informative manner ("It feels better over here, with a little less pressure"), rather than a threatening uninformative manner ("The way you're touching me doesn't turn me on"). Moreover, couples are often given broader training in how best to communicate with each other (Brenot, 2011; Wincze et al., 2008).

8. **Changing destructive lifestyles and marital interactions.** A therapist may encourage a couple to change their lifestyle or take other steps to improve a situation that is having a destructive effect on their relationship—to distance themselves from interfering in-laws, for example, or to change a job that is too demanding. Similarly, if the couple's general relationship is marked by conflict, the therapist will try to help them improve it, often before work on the sexual problems per se begins (Brenot, 2011; Rosen, 2007).

9. **Addressing physical and medical factors.** When sexual dysfunctions are caused by a medical problem, such as disease, injury, medication, or substance abuse, therapists try to address that problem (Korda et al., 2010; Ashton, 2007). If antidepressant medications are causing erectile disorder, for example, the clinician may suggest lowering the dosage of the medication, changing the time of day when the drug is taken, or turning to a different antidepressant.

What Techniques Are Applied to Particular Dysfunctions?

In addition to the general components of sex therapy, specific techniques can help in each of the sexual dysfunctions.

Disorders of Desire Male hypoactive sexual desire disorder and female sexual interest/arousal disorder are among the most difficult dysfunctions to treat because of the many issues that may feed into them (Leiblum, 2010; Maurice, 2007). Thus therapists typically apply a combination of techniques. In a technique called *affectual awareness,* patients visualize sexual scenes in order to discover any feelings of anxiety, vulnerability, and other negative emotions they may have concerning sex (McCarthy & McCarthy, 2012; Kleinplatz, 2010). In another technique, patients receive cognitive *self-instruction training* to help them change their negative reactions to sex. That is, they learn to replace negative statements during sex with "coping statements," such as "I can allow myself to enjoy sex; it doesn't mean I'll lose control."

Therapists may also use behavioral approaches to help heighten a patient's sex drive. They may instruct clients to keep a "desire diary" in which they record sexual thoughts and feelings, to read books and view films with erotic content, and to fantasize about sex. Pleasurable shared activities such as dancing and walking together are also encouraged (LoPiccolo, 2002, 1997). If the reduced sexual desire has resulted from sexual assault or childhood molestation, additional techniques may be needed (Hall, 2010, 2007). A patient may, for example, be encouraged to remember, talk about, and think about the assault until the memories no longer arouse fear or tension. These and related psychological approaches apparently help many women and men with low sexual

"When I touch him he rolls into a ball."

desire eventually to have intercourse more than once a week (Meana, 2012; Rowland, 2012; Hurlbert, 1993). However, only a few controlled studies have been conducted.

Finally, biological interventions, such as *hormone* treatments, have been used, particularly for women whose problems arose after removal of their ovaries or later in life. These interventions have received some research support (Davison & Davis, 2011; Korda et al., 2010). In addition, several pharmaceutical drugs now are being developed specifically for the treatment of these disorders (Stahl, Sommer, & Allers, 2011).

Erectile Disorder Treatments for erectile disorder focus on reducing a man's performance anxiety, increasing his stimulation, or both, using a range of behavioral, cognitive, and relationship interventions (Rowland, 2012; Carroll, 2011; Segraves & Althof, 2002). In one technique, the couple may be instructed to try the *tease technique* during sensate-focus exercises: the partner keeps caressing the man, but if the man gets an erection, the partner stops caressing him until he loses it. This exercise reduces pressure on the man to perform and at the same time teaches the couple that erections occur naturally in response to stimulation, as long as the partners do not keep focusing on performance. In another technique, the couple may be instructed to use manual or oral sex to try to achieve the woman's orgasm, again reducing pressure on the man to perform (LoPiccolo, 2004, 2002, 1995).

"Everybody's a critic."

Biological approaches gained great momentum with the development in 1998 of *sildenafil* (trade name Viagra) (Rosen, 2007). This drug increases blood flow to the penis within one hour of ingestion; the increased blood flow enables the user to attain an erection during sexual activity (see *PsychWatch* on the next page). Sildenafil appears to be relatively safe except for men with certain coronary heart diseases and cardiovascular diseases, particularly those who are taking nitroglycerin and other heart medications (Stevenson & Elliott, 2007). Soon after Viagra emerged, two other erectile dysfunction drugs were also approved— *tadalafil* (Cialis) and *vardenafil* (Levitra)—and they are now actively competing with Viagra for a share of the lucrative marketplace. Collectively, the three drugs are the most common form of treatment for erectile disorder (Rosen, 2007). They effectively restore erections in 75 percent of men who use them.

Prior to the development of Viagra, Cialis, and Levitra, a range of other medical procedures were developed for erectile disorder. These procedures are now viewed as "second-line" treatments that are applied primarily when the medications are unsuccessful or too risky for individuals (Rosen, 2007; Frohman, 2002). Such procedures include gel suppositories, injections of drugs into the penis, and a *vacuum erection device* (*VED*), a hollow cylinder that is placed over the penis. Here a man uses a hand pump to pump air out of the cylinder, drawing blood into his penis and producing an erection.

Premature (Early) Ejaculation Early ejaculation has been treated successfully for years by behavioral procedures (Rowland, 2012; Althof, 2007; Masters & Johnson, 1970). In one such approach, the *stop-start,* or *pause, procedure,* the penis is manually stimulated until the man is highly aroused. The couple then pauses until his arousal subsides, after which the stimulation is resumed. This sequence is repeated several times before stimulation is carried through to ejaculation, so the man ultimately experiences much more total time of stimulation than he has ever experienced before (LoPiccolo, 2004, 1995). Eventually the couple progresses to putting the penis in the vagina, making sure to withdraw it and to pause whenever the man becomes too highly aroused. According to clinical reports, after two or three months many couples can enjoy prolonged intercourse without any need for pauses (Althof, 2007; LoPiccolo, 2004, 2002).

Some clinicians treat early ejaculation with SSRIs, the serotonin-enhancing antidepressant drugs. Because these drugs often reduce sexual arousal or orgasm, the reasoning goes, they may be helpful to men who experience early ejaculation. Many studies report positive results with this approach (Althof, 2007, 1995; Ashton, 2007). The effect

PsychWatch

Sexism, Viagra, and the Pill

Many of us believe that we live in an enlightened world, where sexism is declining and where health care and benefits are available to men and women in equal measure. Periodically, however, such illusions are shattered. The responses of government agencies and insurance companies to the discovery and marketing of Viagra in 1998 may be a case in point.

Consider, first, the nation of Japan. In early 1999, just six months after Viagra's introduction in the United States, the drug was approved for use among men in Japan (Martin, 2000). In contrast, low-dose contraceptives—"the pill"—were not approved for use among women in that country until June 1999—a full 40 years after their introduction elsewhere! Many observers believe that birth control pills would still be unavailable to women in Japan had Viagra not received its quick approval.

Has the United States been able to avoid such an apparent double standard in its health care system? Not really. Before Viagra was introduced, insurance companies were not required to reimburse women for the cost of prescription contraceptives. As a result, women had to pay 68 percent more out-of-pocket expenses for health care than did men,

largely because of uncovered reproductive health care costs (Hayden, 1998). Some legislators had sought to correct this problem by requiring contraceptive coverage in health insurance plans, but their efforts failed in state after state for more than a decade.

In contrast, when Viagra was introduced in 1998, many insurance companies readily agreed to cover the new drug, and many states included Viagra as part of Medicaid coverage. As the public outcry grew over the contrast between coverage of Viagra for men and lack of coverage of oral contraceptives for women, laws across the country finally began to change. In fact, by the end of 1998, nine states required prescription contraceptive coverage

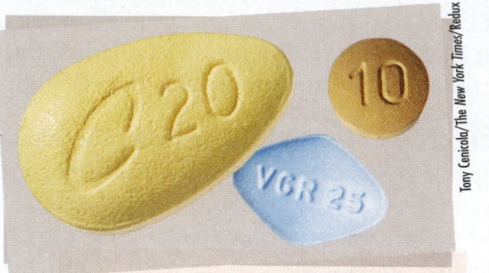

"The pills": Cialis, Viagra, and Levitra

(Hayden, 1998). Today 28 states require such coverage by private insurance companies (Guttmacher, 2011). The federal healthcare law of 2010 includes provisions that some interpret as a requirement for all insurance companies to cover contraceptives. However, this interpretation is being debated currently (Clabough, 2011).

In the meantime, wishful thinkers express hope that generous private donors will help foot the bill for oral contraceptives as some donors have done for Viagra. Immediately after Viagra's approval, one noted philanthropist donated $1 million to provide this drug to the needy. In explaining his action, he said, "I saw an article saying that at $10 apiece, a lot of impotent men wouldn't be able to afford it. So I said [to my wife], . . . 'let's help,' and by Tuesday we had it done" (Carlson, 1998).

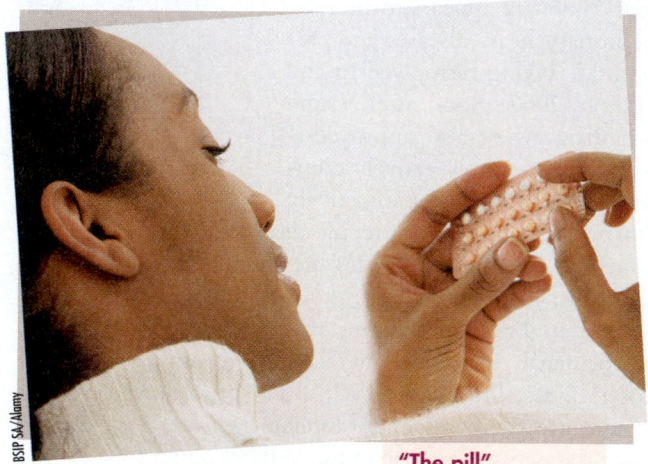

"The pill"

of this approach is consistent with the biological theory, mentioned earlier, that serotonin receptors in the brains of men with early ejaculation may function abnormally.

Delayed Ejaculation Therapies for delayed ejaculation include techniques to reduce performance anxiety and increase stimulation (Rowland, 2012; Hartmann & Waldinger, 2007; LoPiccolo, 2004). In one of many such techniques, a man may be instructed to masturbate to orgasm in the presence of his partner or to masturbate just short of orgasm before inserting his penis for intercourse (Marshall, 1997). This increases the likelihood that he will ejaculate during intercourse. He then is instructed to insert his penis at ever earlier stages of masturbation.

When delayed ejaculation is caused by physical factors such as neurological damage or injury, treatment may include a drug to increase arousal of the sympathetic nervous system (Stevenson & Elliott, 2007). However, few studies have systematically tested the effectiveness of such treatments (Hartmann & Waldinger, 2007).

Female Orgasmic Disorder Specific treatments for female orgasmic disorder include cognitive-behavioral techniques, self-exploration, enhancement of body awareness, and directed masturbation training (McCarthy & McCarthy, 2012; Meana, 2012; Heiman, 2007, 2002, 2000). These procedures are especially useful for women who have never had an orgasm under any circumstances. Biological treatments, including hormone therapy or the use of sildenafil (Viagra), have also been tried, but research has not consistently found such interventions to be helpful (Davison & Davis, 2011; Heiman, 2007).

In **directed masturbation training,** a woman is taught step by step how to masturbate effectively and eventually to reach orgasm during sexual interactions. The training includes use of diagrams and reading material, private self-stimulation, erotic material and fantasies, "orgasm triggers" such as holding her breath or thrusting her pelvis, sensate focus with her partner, and sexual positioning that produces stimulation of the clitoris during intercourse. This training program appears to be highly effective: over 90 percent of female clients learn to have an orgasm during masturbation, about 80 percent during caressing by their partners, and about 30 percent during intercourse (Heiman, 2007; LoPiccolo, 2002, 1997).

As you read earlier, a lack of orgasm during intercourse is not necessarily a sexual dysfunction, provided the woman enjoys intercourse and can reach orgasm through caressing, either by her partner or by herself. For this reason some therapists believe that the wisest course is simply to educate women whose only concern is lack of orgasm during intercourse, informing them that they are quite normal.

Genito-Pelvic Pain/Penetration Disorder

Genito-Pelvic Pain/Penetration Disorder Specific treatment for involuntary contractions of the muscles around the vagina typically involves two approaches (Rosenbaum, 2011). First, a woman may practice tightening and relaxing her vaginal muscles until she gains more voluntary control over them. Second, she may receive gradual behavioral exposure treatment to help her overcome her fear of penetration, beginning, for example, by inserting increasingly large dilators in her vagina at home and at her own pace and eventually ending with the insertion of her partner's penis. Most clients treated with such procedures eventually have pain-free intercourse (Engman et al., 2010; ter Kuile et al., 2009). Some medical interventions have also been applied. For example, several clinical investigators have injected the problematic vaginal muscles with Botox to help reduce spasms in those muscles (Ghazizadeh & Nikzad, 2004; Romito et al., 2004). However, studies of this approach have been unsystematic.

Different approaches are used to treat the other form of genito-pelvic pain/penetration disorder—severe vaginal or pelvic pain during intercourse. As you saw earlier, the most common cause of this problem is physical, such as pain-causing scars, lesions, or infection aftereffects. When the cause is known, pain management procedures (see pages 182–184) and sex therapy techniques may be tried, including helping a couple to learn intercourse positions that avoid putting pressure on the injured area (Dewitte et al., 2011). Medical interventions—from topical creams to surgery—may also be tried, but typically they must be combined with other sex therapy techniques to overcome the years of sexual anxiety and lack of arousal (Binik et al., 2007). Many experts believe that, in most cases, both forms of genito-pelvic pain/penetration disorder are best assessed and treated by a *team* of professionals, including a gynecologist, physical therapist, and sex therapist or other mental health professional (Rosenbaum, 2011, 2007).

What Are the Current Trends in Sex Therapy?

Sex therapists have now moved well beyond the approach first developed by Masters and Johnson. For example, today's sex therapists regularly treat partners who are living together but not married. They also treat sexual dysfunctions that arise from psychological disorders such as depression, mania, schizophrenia, and certain personality disorders (Leiblum, 2010, 2007; Bach et al., 2001). In addition, sex therapists no longer

---

BETWEEN THE LINES

Drugs That Sometimes Interfere with Sexual Functioning

Alcohol, opioids, sedative-hypnotics ‹‹

Cocaine, amphetamines ‹‹

Hallucinogens, marijuana ‹‹

Antidepressants, antipsychotics, diuretics, amyl nitrate, hypertension medications ‹‹

•**directed masturbation training**•A sex therapy approach that teaches women with female arousal or orgasmic problems how to masturbate effectively and eventually to reach orgasm during sexual interactions.

•paraphilias•Patterns in which individuals have recurrent and intense sexual urges, fantasies, or behaviors involving nonhuman objects, children, nonconsenting adults, or experiences of suffering or humiliation.

•paraphilic disorder•A disorder in which an individual's paraphilia causes great distress, interferes with social or occupational activities, or places the individual or others at risk of harm—either currently or in the past.

•fetishistic disorder•A paraphilic disorder consisting of recurrent and intense sexual urges, fantasies, or behaviors that involve the use of a nonliving object or nongenital part, often to the exclusion of all other stimuli.

screen out clients with severe marital discord, the elderly, the medically ill, the physically handicapped, gay clients, or individuals who have no long-term sex partner (Nichols & Shernoff, 2007; Stevenson & Elliott, 2007). Sex therapists are also paying more attention to excessive sexuality, sometimes called *hypersexuality* or *sexual addiction* (Lee, 2011; Kafka, 2007, 2000), although this condition is not listed as a disorder in DSM-5.

Many sex therapists have expressed concern about the sharp increase in the use of drugs and other medical interventions for sexual dysfunctions, particularly for the disorders characterized by low sexual desire and erectile disorder. Their concern is that therapists will increasingly choose the biological interventions rather than integrating biological, psychological, and sociocultural interventions. In fact, a narrow approach of any kind probably cannot fully address the complex factors that cause most sexual problems (Meana, 2012; Leiblum, 2010, 2007). It took sex therapists years to recognize the considerable advantages of an integrated approach to sexual dysfunctions. The development of new medical interventions should not lead to its abandonment.

Paraphilic Disorders

Paraphilias are patterns in which individuals repeatedly have intense sexual urges or fantasies or display sexual behaviors that involve objects or situations outside the usual sexual norms. The sexual focus may, for example, involve nonhuman objects, children, nonconsenting adults, or the experience of suffering or humiliation. Many people with a paraphilia can become aroused only when a paraphilic stimulus is present, fantasized about, or acted out. Others need the stimulus only during times of stress or under other special circumstances.

Some people with one kind of paraphilia display others as well. The large Internet and consumer market in paraphilic pornography leads clinicians to suspect that paraphilias are, in fact, quite common (Ahlers et al., 2011; Pipe, 2010). People whose paraphilias involve children or nonconsenting adults often come to the attention of clinicians as a result of legal issues generated by their inappropriate actions (Fabian, 2011).

According to DSM-5, a diagnosis of **paraphilic disorder** should be applied when paraphilias cause individuals significant distress or impairment *or* when the satisfaction of the paraphilias places the individuals or other people at risk of harm—either currently or in the past (APA, 2013, 2012) (see Table 13-5). People who initiate sexual contact with

Is the availability of sex chat groups and other sexual material on the Internet psychologically healthy or damaging?

table 13-5

DSM-5 Checklist

Paraphilic Disorder

1. Over a period of at least 6 months, the person experiences recurrent and intense sexually arousing fantasies, urges, or behaviors involving objects or situations outside the usual sexual norms (nonhuman objects; nongenital body parts; the suffering or humiliation of oneself or one's partner; or children or other nonconsenting persons).

2. Significant distress or impairment over the fantasies, urges, or behaviors. (In some paraphilic disorders—pedophilic disorder, exhibitionistic disorder, voyeuristic disorder, frotteuristic disorder, and sexual sadism disorder—the performance of the paraphilic behaviors indicates a disorder, even in the absence of distress or impairment.)

Based on APA, 2013, 2012.

children, for example, warrant a diagnosis of *pedophilic disorder* regardless of how troubled the individuals may or may not be over their behavior.

Although theorists have proposed various explanations for paraphilic disorders, there is little formal evidence to support such explanations (Becker et al., 2012; Raley, 2011). Moreover, none of the many treatments applied to these disorders have received much research or proved clearly effective (Becker et al., 2012; Roche & Quayle, 2007). Psychological and sociocultural treatments have been available the longest, but today's professionals are also using biological interventions.

Some practitioners administer drugs called *antiandrogens* that lower the production of testosterone, the male sex hormone, and reduce the sex drive (Korda & Sommer, 2010). Although antiandrogens may indeed reduce paraphilic patterns, several of them disrupt normal sexual feelings and behavior as well (Kirkpatrick & Clark, 2011; Thibaut et al., 2010). Thus the drugs tend to be applied primarily when the paraphilic disorders are of particular danger either to the individuals themselves or to other people. Clinicians are also increasingly administering SSRIs, the serotonin-enhancing antidepressant medications, to treat persons with paraphilic disorders, hoping that the drugs will reduce these compulsion-like sexual behaviors just as they help reduce other kinds of compulsions (Berner & Briken, 2010). In addition, of course, a common effect of the SSRIs is to lower sexual arousal.

Playful context

Dressing in clothes of the opposite sex does not necessarily convey a paraphilia. Here two members—both male—of Harvard University's Hasty Pudding Theatricals Club, known for staging musicals in which male undergraduates dress like women, plant a kiss on actress Anne Hathaway. Hathaway was receiving the club's 2010 Woman of the Year award.

Fetishistic Disorder

One relatively common paraphilic disorder is **fetishistic disorder**. Key features of this disorder are recurrent intense sexual urges, sexually arousing fantasies, or behaviors that involve the use of a nonliving object or nongenital body part, often to the exclusion of all other stimuli (APA, 2013, 2012). Usually the disorder, which is far more common in men than in women, begins in adolescence. Almost anything can be a fetish; women's underwear, shoes, and boots are particularly common. Some people with this disorder commit thievery in order to collect as many of the desired objects as possible. The objects may be touched, smelled, worn, or used in some other way while the person masturbates, or the individual may ask a partner to wear the object when they have sex (Marshall et al., 2008). Several of these features are seen in the following case:

A 32-year-old, single male . . . related that although he was somewhat sexually attracted by women, he was far more attracted by "their panties."

To the best of the patient's memory, sexual excitement began at about age 7, when he came upon a pornographic magazine and felt stimulated by pictures of partially nude women wearing "panties." His first ejaculation occurred at 13 via masturbation to fantasies of women wearing panties. He masturbated into his older sister's panties, which he had stolen without her knowledge. Subsequently he stole panties from her friends and from other women he met socially. He found pretexts to "wander" into the bedrooms of women during social occasions, and would quickly rummage through their possessions until he found a pair of panties to his satisfaction. He later used these to masturbate into, and then "saved them" in a "private cache." The pattern of masturbating into women's underwear had been his preferred method of achieving sexual excitement and orgasm from adolescence until the present consultation.

(Spitzer et al., 1994, p. 247)

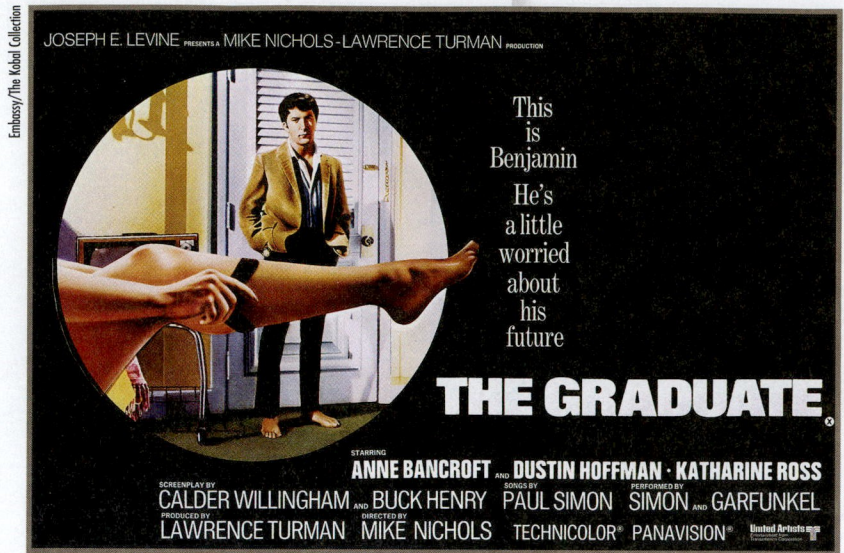

Embassy/The Kobal Collection

Mrs. Robinson's stockings
The 1967 film *The Graduate* helped define a generation by focusing on the personal confusion, apathy, and sexual adventures of a young man in search of meaning. Marketers promoted this film by using a fetishistic-like photo of Mrs. Robinson putting on her stockings under Benjamin's watchful eye, a scene forever identified with the movie.

•**masturbatory satiation**•A behavioral treatment in which a client masturbates for a long period of time while fantasizing in detail about a paraphilic object. The procedure is expected to produce a feeling of boredom that becomes linked to the object.

•**orgasmic reorientation**•A procedure for treating certain paraphilias by teaching clients to respond to new, more appropriate sources of sexual stimulation.

•**transvestic disorder**•A paraphilic disorder consisting of repeated and intense sexual urges, fantasies, or behaviors that involve dressing in clothes of the opposite sex. Also known as *transvestism* or *cross-dressing*.

•**exhibitionistic disorder**•A paraphilic disorder in which persons have repeated sexually arousing urges or fantasies about exposing their genitals to others, and may act upon those urges.

Researchers have not been able to pinpoint the causes of fetishistic disorder. Psychodynamic theorists view fetishes as defense mechanisms that help people avoid the anxiety produced by normal sexual contact. Psychodynamic treatment for this problem, however, has met with little success (Oncu et al., 2009; Zurolo & Napolitano, 2008).

Behaviorists propose that fetishes are acquired through classical conditioning (Dozier, Iwata, & Worsdell, 2011; Roche & Quayle, 2007). In a pioneering behavioral study, male participants were shown a series of slides of nude women along with slides of boots (Rachman, 1966). After many trials, the participants became aroused by the boot photos alone. If early sexual experiences similarly occur in the presence of particular objects, perhaps the stage is set for development of fetishes.

Behaviorists have sometimes treated fetishistic disorder with *aversion therapy* (Plaud, 2007; Krueger & Kaplan, 2002). In one study, an electric shock was administered to the arms or legs of participants with this disorder while they imagined their objects of desire (Marks & Gelder, 1967). After two weeks of therapy all men in the study showed at least some improvement. In another aversion technique, *covert sensitization,* people with fetishistic disorder are guided to *imagine* the pleasurable object and repeatedly to pair this image with an *imagined* aversive stimulus until the object of sexual pleasure is no longer desired.

Another behavioral treatment for fetishistic disorder is **masturbatory satiation** (Plaud, 2007; Wright & Hatcher, 2006). In this method, the client masturbates to orgasm while fantasizing about a sexually appropriate object, then switches to fantasizing in detail about fetishistic objects while masturbating again and continues the fetishistic fantasy for an hour. The procedure is meant to produce a feeling of boredom, which in turn becomes linked to the fetishistic object.

Yet another behavioral approach to fetishistic disorder, also used for other paraphilias, is **orgasmic reorientation,** which teaches individuals to respond to more appropriate sources of sexual stimulation (Wright & Hatcher, 2006). People are shown conventional stimuli while they are responding to unconventional objects. A person with a shoe fetish, for example, may be instructed to obtain an erection from pictures of shoes and then to begin masturbating to a picture of a nude woman. If he starts to lose the erection, he must return to the pictures of shoes until he is masturbating effectively, then change back to the picture of the nude woman. When orgasm approaches, he must direct all attention to the conventional stimulus.

Transvestic Disorder

Transvestic disorder, also known as **transvestism** or **cross-dressing,** features a recurrent and intense sexual arousal from dressing in clothes of the opposite sex—arousal expressed through fantasies, urges, or behaviors (APA, 2013, 2012). In the following passage, a 42-year-old married father describes his pattern:

I have been told that when I dress in drag, at times I look like Whistler's Mother [laughs], especially when I haven't shaved closely. I usually am good at detail, and I make sure when I dress as a woman that I have my nails done just so, and that my colors match. Honestly, it's hard to pin a date on when I began cross dressing. . . . If pressed, I would have to say it began when I was about 10 years of age, fooling around with and putting on my mom's clothes. . . . I was always careful to put everything back in its exact place, and in 18 years of doing this in her home, my mother never, I mean never, suspected, or questioned me about putting on her clothes. I belong to a transvestite support group . . . , a group for men who cross dress. Some of the group are homosexuals, but most are not. A true transvestite—and I am one, so I know—is not homosexual. We don't discriminate against them in the group at all; hey, we have enough trouble getting acceptance as normal people and not just a bunch of weirdos ourselves. They are a bunch of nice guys . . . , really. Most of them are like me.

Most of [the men in the group] have told their families about their dressing inclinations, but those that are married are a mixed lot; some wives know and some don't, they just suspect. I believe in honesty, and told my wife about this before we were married. We're separated now, but I don't think it's because of my cross dressing. . . . Some of my friends, when I was growing up, suggested psychotherapy, but I don't regard this as a problem. If it bothers someone else, then they have the problem. . . . I function perfectly well sexually with my wife, though it took her some time to be comfortable with me wearing feminine underwear; yes, sometimes I wear it while making love, it just makes it more exciting.

(Janus & Janus, 1993, p. 121)

Like this man, the typical person with transvestic disorder, almost always a heterosexual male, begins cross-dressing in childhood or adolescence (Marshall et al., 2008; Långström & Zucker, 2005). He is the picture of characteristic masculinity in everyday life and is usually alone when he cross-dresses. A small percentage of such men cross-dress to visit bars or social clubs. Some wear a single item of women's clothing, such as underwear or hosiery, under their masculine clothes. Others wear makeup and dress fully as women. Some married men with transvestic disorder involve their wives in their cross-dressing behavior. The disorder is often confused with *gender dysphoria,* but, as you will see, they are two separate patterns that overlap only in some individuals (Zucker et al., 2012).

The development of transvestic disorder sometimes seems to follow the behavioral principles of operant conditioning. In such cases, parents or other adults may openly encourage the individuals to cross-dress as children or even reward them for this behavior. In one case, a woman was delighted to discover that her young nephew enjoyed dressing in girls' clothes. She had always wanted a niece, and she proceeded to buy him dresses and jewelry and sometimes dressed him as a girl and took him out shopping.

A group approach
Crossroads is a self-help group for men with transvestic fetishism, a recurrent need to dress in women's clothing as a means to achieve sexual arousal.

Exhibitionistic Disorder

A person with **exhibitionistic disorder** experiences recurrent and intense sexual arousal from exposing his genitals to an unsuspecting individual—arousal reflected by fantasies, urges, or behaviors (APA, 2013, 2012). Most often, the person wants to provoke shock or surprise rather than initiate sexual activity with the victim. Sometimes an exhibitionist will expose himself in a particular neighborhood at particular hours. In a survey of 2,800 men, 4.3 percent of them reported that they perform exhibitionistic behavior (Långström & Seto, 2006). Yet between one-third and half of all women report having seen or had direct contact with an exhibitionist, or so-called flasher (Marshall et al., 2008). The urge to exhibit typically becomes stronger when the person has free time or is under significant stress.

Generally, exhibitionistic disorder begins before age 18 and is most common in males (APA, 2000). Some studies suggest that the individuals are typically immature in their dealings with the opposite sex and have difficulty in interpersonal relationships (Marshall et al., 2008; Murphy & Page, 2006). Around 30 percent of them are married and another 30 percent divorced or separated; their sexual relations with their wives are not usually satisfactory (Doctor & Neff, 2001). Many have doubts or fears about their masculinity, and some seem to have a strong bond to a possessive mother. As with other paraphilic disorders, treatment generally includes aversion therapy and masturbatory satiation, possibly combined with orgasmic reorientation, social skills training, or cognitive-behavioral therapy (Federoff & Marshall, 2010; Marshall et al., 2008).

Voyeuristic Disorder

A person with **voyeuristic disorder** experiences recurrent and intense sexual arousal from observing an unsuspecting individual who is naked, disrobing, or engaging in sexual activity. As with other paraphilic disorders, this arousal takes the form of fantasies, urges, or behaviors (APA, 2013, 2012). This disorder usually begins before the age of 15 and tends to persist (APA, 2013).

A person with voyeuristic disorder may masturbate during the act of observing or when thinking about it afterward but does not generally seek to have sex with the individual being spied on. The vulnerability of the people being observed and the probability that they would feel humiliated if they knew they were under observation are often part of the enjoyment. In addition, the risk of being discovered often adds to the excitement, as you can see in the following statement by a man with this disorder:

> Looking at a nude girlfriend wouldn't be as exciting as seeing her the sneaky way. It's not just the nude body but the sneaking out and seeing what you're not supposed to see. The risk of getting caught makes it exciting. I don't want to get caught, but every time I go out I'm putting myself on the line.
>
> *(Yalom, 1960, p. 316)*

Voyeurism, like exhibitionism, is often a source of sexual excitement in fantasy; it can also play a role in normal sexual interactions, but in such cases it is engaged in with the consent or understanding of the partner. The clinical disorder of voyeuristic disorder is marked by the repeated invasion of other people's privacy. Some people with the disorder are unable to have normal sexual relations; others, however, have a normal sex life apart from their disorder.

Many psychodynamic clinicians propose that people with voyeuristic disorder are seeking by their actions to gain power over others, possibly because they feel inadequate or are sexually or socially shy (Metzl, 2004). Behaviorists explain the disorder as a learned behavior that can be traced to a chance and secret observation of a sexually arousing scene (Lavin, 2008). If such observations are repeated on several occasions while the onlooker masturbates, a voyeuristic pattern may develop.

Frotteuristic Disorder

A person with **frotteuristic disorder** experiences repeated and intense sexual arousal from touching or rubbing against a nonconsenting person. Once again, the arousal may take the form of fantasies, urges, or behaviors. Frottage (from French *frotter*, "to rub") is usually committed in a crowded place, such as a subway or a busy sidewalk (Guterman, Martin, & Rudes, 2010). The person, almost always a male, may rub his genitals against

Lady Godiva and "Peeping Tom"
According to legend, Lady Godiva (shown in this 1890 illustration) rode naked through the streets of Coventry, England, in order to persuade her husband, the earl of Mercia, to stop taxing the city's poor. Although all townspeople were ordered to stay inside their homes with shutters drawn during her eleventh-century ride, a tailor named Tom "could not contain his sexual curiosity and drilled a hole in his shutter in order to watch Lady Godiva pass by" (Mann et al., 2008). Since then, the term "Peeping Tom" has been used to refer to people with voyeurism.

the victim's thighs or buttocks or fondle her genital area or breasts with his hands. Typically he fantasizes during the act that he is having a caring relationship with the victim. This paraphilia usually begins in the teenage years or earlier, often after the person observes others committing an act of frottage. After the person reaches the age of about 25, the acts gradually decrease and often disappear (APA, 2000).

Pedophilic Disorder

A person with **pedophilic disorder** experiences equal or greater sexual arousal from prepubescent or early pubescent children than from physically mature persons. This arousal is expressed through fantasies, urges, or behaviors (APA, 2013, 2012) (see *PsychWatch* on the next page). Individuals with the disorder may be attracted to prepubescent children (*classic* type), early pubescent children (*hebephilic* type), or both (*pedohebephilic* type). Some people with pedophilic disorder are satisfied by child pornography or seemingly innocent material such as children's underwear ads; others are driven to actually watch, touch, fondle, or engage in sexual intercourse with children (Quayle, 2011; Durkin & Hundersmarck, 2008). Some people with the disorder are attracted only to children; others are attracted to adults as well (Roche & Quayle, 2007). Both boys and girls can be pedophilic victims, but there is evidence suggesting that two-thirds of them are girls (Seto, 2008; Koss & Heslet, 1992).

People with pedophilic disorder usually develop their pattern of sexual need during adolescence. Some were themselves sexually abused as children, and many were neglected, excessively punished, or deprived of genuinely close relationships during their childhood. It is not unusual for them to be married and to have sexual difficulties or other frustrations in life that lead them to seek an area in which they can be masters. Often these individuals are immature: their social and sexual skills may be underdeveloped, and thoughts of normal sexual relationships fill them with anxiety (Seto, 2008; McAnulty, 2006).

Some people with pedophilic disorder also exhibit distorted thinking, such as, "It's all right to have sex with children as long as they agree" (Roche & Quayle, 2007; Abel et al., 2001, 1984). Similarly, it is not uncommon for pedophiles to blame the children for adult-child sexual contacts or to assert that the children benefited from the experience (Durkin & Hundersmarck, 2008; Lanning, 2001).

THERAPY: THE POSSIBILITY OF CHANGING BEHAVIOR

created by the mural crew, directed by california arts council artist in residence everett jensen with ted valli, john corbin, daniel chernia & kathleen keyes

•voyeuristic disorder• A paraphilic disorder in which a person has repeated and intense sexual desires to observe unsuspecting people in secret as they undress or to spy on couples having intercourse and may act upon these desires.

•frotteuristic disorder• A paraphilic disorder consisting of repeated and intense sexual urges, fantasies, or behaviors that involve touching and rubbing against a nonconsenting person.

•pedophilic disorder• A paraphilic disorder in which a person has repeated and intense sexual urges or fantasies about watching, touching, or engaging in sexual acts with children and may carry out these urges or fantasies.

Civil commitment for sex offenders
A mural painted by patients at the Atascadero state mental hospital in California is meant to depict the pain of inmates at the forensic facility. By law, certain sex offenders may be committed to the hospital (and later to a community treatment program) after they have completed a prison sentence if a court decides that they are not yet safe for release.

Serving the Public Good

As clinical practitioners and researchers conduct their work, should they consider the potential impact of their decisions on society? Many people, including a large number of clinicians, believe that the answer to this question is a resounding yes. In the 1990s two important clashes between the clinical field and the public interest—each centering on the disorder of *pedophilic disorder*—brought this issue to life.

In 1994, the then-newly published DSM-IV ruled that people should receive a diagnosis of pedophilic disorder only if their recurrent fantasies, urges, or behaviors involving sexual activity with children cause them significant distress or impairment in social, occupational, or other spheres of functioning. Critics worried that this criterion seemed to suggest that pedophilic behavior is acceptable, even normal, as long as it causes no distress or impairment. Even the U.S. Congress condemned the DSM-IV definition.

In response to these criticisms, the American Psychiatric Association clarified its position in 1997, stating, "An adult who engages in sexual activity with a child is performing a criminal and immoral act which never can be considered moral or socially acceptable behavior." In 2000 the Association went further still and changed the criteria for pedophilic disorder in a DSM revision; it decided that a diagnosis is appropriate if persons act on their sexual

Jens Meyer/AP Photo

Pedophilic disorders and public awareness
The growing public awareness of pedophilic disorders has led to an increase in the number of media and art presentations about the subject. Indeed, a recent production of the much-loved 1893 opera *Hansel and Gretel* was staged as an adults-only "study of pedophilia." Here, the witch gestures in front of a picture of one of the young victims.

urges, regardless of whether they experience distress or impairment (APA, 2000). Similarly, acting on one's recurrent sexual urges or fantasies warrants a diagnosis in cases of exhibitionistic, voyeuristic, frotteuristic, and sexual sadism disorders.

Another clash between the clinical field and public sensibilities occurred in 1998 when a review article in the prestigious journal *Psychological Bulletin* concluded

that the effects of child sexual abuse are not as long-lasting as usually believed. The study set off a firestorm, with critics arguing that the conclusion runs counter to evidence from a number of studies. Furthermore, many people worried that the article's conclusions could be used to legitimize pedophilia. After a groundswell of criticism, the American Psychological Association, publisher of the journal, acknowledged that it should have given more thought to how the study would be received and should have either presented the article with an introduction outlining the Association's stance against child abuse or paired it with articles offering different viewpoints. The Association also said that in the future it would more carefully weigh the potential consequences of research publications.

While many people with this disorder believe that their feelings are indeed wrong and abnormal, others consider adult sexual activity with children to be acceptable and normal. Some even have joined pedophile organizations that advocate abolishing the age of consent laws. The Internet has opened the channels of communication among such individuals. Indeed, there is now a wide range of Web sites, newsgroups, chat rooms, forums, and message boards centered on pedophilia and adult–child sex (Durkin & Hundersmarck, 2008).

Studies have found that most men with pedophilic disorder also display at least one additional psychological disorder (McAnulty, 2006). Some theorists have proposed that the pedophilic disorder may be related to biochemical or brain structure abnormalities, but clear biological factors have yet to emerge in research (Poeppl et al., 2011; Schiffer et al., 2007).

Most pedophilic offenders are imprisoned or forced into treatment if they are caught (Staller & Faller, 2010). After all, they are committing child sexual abuse when they take any steps toward sexual contact with a child. Moreover, there are now many residential registration and community notification laws across the United States that help law enforcement agencies and the public account for and control where convicted child sex offenders live and work (OJJDP, 2010).

Treatments for pedophilic disorder include those already mentioned for other paraphilic disorders, such as aversion therapy, masturbatory satiation, orgasmic reorientation, cognitive-behavioral therapy, and antiandrogen drugs (Plaud, 2007; Krueger & Kaplan, 2002). One widely applied cognitive-behavioral treatment for this disorder, *relapse-prevention training,* is modeled after the relapse-prevention training programs used in the treatment of substance use disorders (see pages 376, 378). In this approach, clients identify the kinds of situations that typically trigger their pedophilic fantasies and actions (such as depressed mood or distorted thinking). They then learn strategies for avoiding those situations or coping with them more effectively. Relapse-prevention training has sometimes, but not consistently, been of help in this and certain other paraphilic disorders (Federoff & Marshall, 2010; Marshall et al., 2008).

Sexual Masochism Disorder

A person with **sexual masochism disorder** is repeatedly and intensely sexually aroused by the act of being humiliated, beaten, bound, or otherwise made to suffer (APA, 2013, 2012). Again, this arousal may take such forms as fantasies, urges, or behaviors. Many people have fantasies of being forced into sexual acts against their will, but only those who are very distressed or impaired by the fantasies receive this diagnosis. Some people with the disorder act on the masochistic urges by themselves, perhaps tying, sticking pins into, or even cutting themselves. Others have their sexual partners restrain, tie up, blindfold, spank, paddle, whip, beat, electrically shock, "pin and pierce," or humiliate them (APA, 2013).

An industry of products and services has arisen to meet the desires of people with sexual masochism disorder. Here a 34-year-old woman describes her work as the operator of a sadomasochism facility:

> I get people here who have been all over looking for the right kind of pain they feel they deserve. Don't ask me why they want pain, I'm not a psychologist; but when they have found us, they usually don't go elsewhere. It may take some of the other girls an hour or even two hours to make these guys feel like they've had their treatment—I can achieve that in about 20 minutes. . . . Remember, these are businessmen, and they are not only buying my time, but they have to get back to work, so time is important.
>
> Among the things I do, that work really quickly and well, are: I put clothespins on their nipples, or pins in their [testicles]. Some of them need to see their own blood to be able to get off. . . .
>
> . . . All the time that a torture scene is going on, there is constant dialogue. . . . I scream at the guy, and tell him what a no-good rotten bastard he is, how this is even too good for him, that he knows he deserves worse, and I begin to list his sins. It works every time. Hey, I'm not nuts, I know what I'm doing. I act very tough and hard, but I'm really a very sensitive woman. But you have to watch out for a guy's health . . . you must not kill him, or have him get a heart attack. . . . I know of other places that have had guys die there. I've never lost a customer to death, though they may have wished for it during my "treatment." Remember, these are repeat customers. I have a clientele and a reputation that I value.
>
> *(Janus & Janus, 1993, p. 115)*

In one form of sexual masochism disorder, *hypoxyphilia,* people strangle or smother themselves (or ask their partner to strangle them) in order to enhance their sexual pleasure. There have, in fact, been a disturbing number of clinical reports of *autoerotic*

BETWEEN THE LINES

Cyber Danger
- In 2009, the state of New York enacted the *e-STOP* law, which prohibits many sexual offenders from using online social networking sites while on probation or parole. "
- Convicted sex offenders must also register all of their e-mail addresses and Internet identities under this law, and the information is shared with social networking sites. "
- Since the enactment of the law, Facebook and other social networking sites have purged thousands of user accounts. "

(Van Buskirk, 2009)

•**sexual masochism disorder**•A paraphilic disorder characterized by repeated and intense sexual urges, fantasies, or behaviors that involve being humiliated, beaten, bound, or otherwise made to suffer.

asphyxia, in which individuals, usually males and as young as 10 years old, may accidentally induce a fatal lack of oxygen by hanging, suffocating, or strangling themselves while masturbating (Hucker, 2011, 2008; Atanasijevic et al., 2010). There is some debate as to whether the practice should be characterized as sexual masochism disorder, but it is at least sometimes accompanied by other acts of bondage.

Most masochistic sexual fantasies begin in childhood. However, the person does not act out the urges until later, usually by early adulthood. The disorder typically continues for many years. Some people practice more and more dangerous acts over time or during times of particular stress (Krueger, 2010; APA, 2000).

In many cases sexual masochism disorder seems to have developed through the behavioral process of classical conditioning (Stekel, 2010; Akins, 2004). A classic case study tells of a teenage boy with a broken arm who was caressed and held close by an attractive nurse as the physician set his fracture, a procedure done in the past without anesthesia (Gebhard, 1965). The powerful combination of pain and sexual arousal the boy felt then may have been the cause of his later masochistic urges and acts.

Sexual Sadism Disorder

A person with **sexual sadism disorder,** usually male, is repeatedly and intensely sexually aroused by the physical or psychological suffering of another individual (APA, 2013, 2012). This arousal may be expressed through fantasies, urges, or behaviors, including acts such as dominating, restraining, blindfolding, cutting, strangling, mutilating, or even killing the victim. The label is derived from the name of the famous Marquis de Sade (1740–1814), who tortured others in order to satisfy his sexual desires.

People who fantasize about sexual sadism typically imagine that they have total control over a sexual victim who is terrified by the sadistic act. Many carry out sadistic acts with a consenting partner, often a person with sexual masochism disorder. Some, however, act out their urges on nonconsenting victims (Richards & Jackson, 2011; Marshall et al., 2008). A number of rapists and sexual murderers, for example, exhibit sexual sadism disorder (Chan, Heide, & Beauregard, 2011). In all cases, the real or fantasized victim's suffering is the key to arousal (Seto et al., 2012).

Fantasies of sexual sadism, like those of sexual masochism, may first appear in childhood or adolescence (Stone, 2010); the sadistic acts, when they occur, develop by early adulthood (APA, 2013, 2012). The pattern is long-term. Sadistic acts sometimes stay at

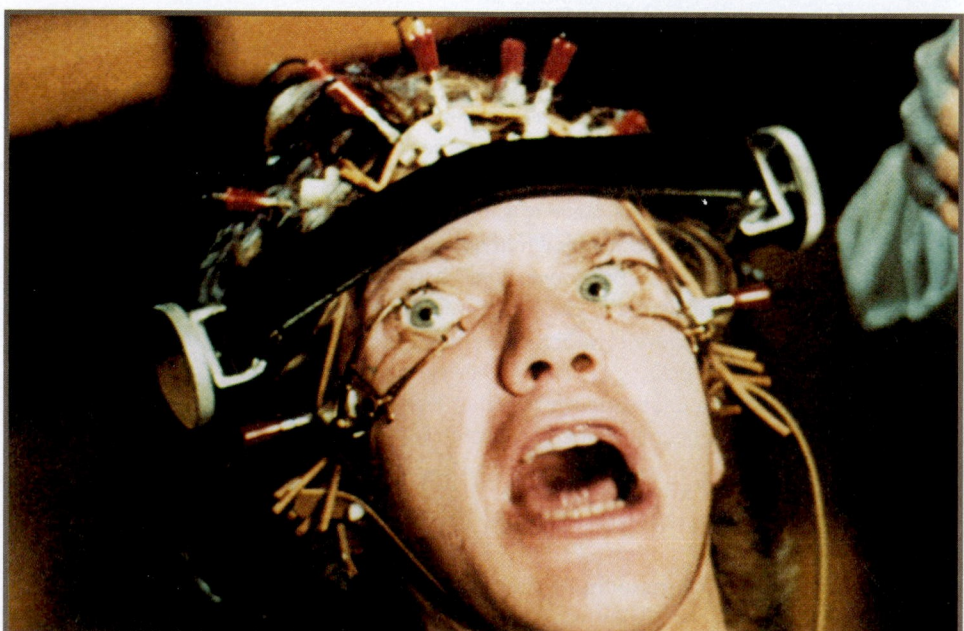

Courtesy of the Everett Collection

Cinematic introduction

In one of filmdom's most famous scenes, Alex, the sexually sadistic character in *A Clockwork Orange,* is forced to observe violent images while he experiences painful stomach spasms. Public attitudes toward aversion therapy were greatly influenced by this 1971 portrayal of the treatment approach.

the same level of cruelty, but often they become more and more severe over the years (Mokros et al., 2011; Santtila et al., 2006, 2002). Obviously, people with severe forms of the disorder may be highly dangerous to others.

Some behaviorists believe that classical conditioning is at work in sexual sadism disorder (Akins, 2004). While inflicting pain, perhaps unintentionally, on an animal or person, a teenager may feel intense emotions and sexual arousal. The association between inflicting pain and being aroused sexually sets the stage for a pattern of sexual sadism. Behaviorists also propose that the disorder may result from modeling, when adolescents observe others achieving sexual satisfaction by inflicting pain. The many Internet sex sites and sexual videos, magazines, and books in our society make such models readily available (Brophy, 2010; Seto, Maric, & Barbaree, 2001).

Both psychodynamic and cognitive theorists suggest that people with sexual sadism disorder inflict pain in order to achieve a sense of power or control, necessitated perhaps by underlying feelings of sexual inadequacy. The sense of power in turn increases their sexual arousal (Stekel, 2010; Rathbone, 2001). Alternatively, certain biological studies have found signs of possible brain and hormonal abnormalities in persons with sexual sadism (Harenski et al., 2012; Jacobs, 2011; Bradford et al., 2008). None of these explanations, however, has been thoroughly investigated.

The disorder has been treated by aversion therapy. The public's view of and distaste for this procedure have been influenced by Anthony Burgess' novel (later a movie) *A Clockwork Orange,* which describes simultaneous presentations of violent images and drug-induced stomach spasms to a sadistic young man until he is conditioned to feel nausea at the sight of such images. It is not clear that aversion therapy is helpful in cases of sexual sadism disorder. However, relapse-prevention training, used in some criminal cases, may be of value (Federoff & Marshall, 2010; Bradford et al., 2008).

A Word of Caution

The definitions of the various paraphilic disorders, like those of sexual dysfunctions, are strongly influenced by the norms of the particular society in which they occur (Bhugra et al., 2010). Some clinicians argue that except when people are hurt by them, at least some paraphilic behaviors should not be considered disorders at all (Wright, 2010). Especially in light of the stigma associated with sexual disorders and the self-revulsion that many people experience when they believe they have such a disorder, we need to be very careful about applying these labels to others or to ourselves. Keep in mind that for years clinicians considered homosexuality a paraphilic disorder, and their judgment was used to justify laws and even police actions against gay individuals (Dickinson et al., 2012; Kirby, 2000). Only when the gay rights movement helped change society's understanding of and attitudes toward homosexuality did clinicians stop considering it a disorder (Drescher, 2010). In the meantime, the clinical field had unintentionally contributed to the persecution, anxiety, and humiliation of millions of people because of personal sexual behavior that differed from the conventional norms.

? Sex is one of the topics most commonly searched on the Internet. Why might it be such a popular search topic?

Gender Dysphoria

As children and adults, most people feel like and identify themselves as males or females—a feeling and identity that is consistent with the gender to which they are born. But society has come to appreciate that many people do not experience such gender clarity. Instead, they have *transgender experiences*—a sense that their actual gender identity is different from the gender category to which they were born physically or a sense that it lies outside the usual male versus female categories (Carroll, 2007). Many people with

•**sexual sadism disorder**•A paraphilic disorder characterized by repeated and intense sexual urges, fantasies, or behaviors that involve inflicting suffering on others.

BETWEEN THE LINES

Tattoos and Sexuality

31% Percentage of people with tattoos who say that their tattoos make them feel sexier ‹‹

39% Percentage of people without tattoos who say that people with tattoos are less sexy ‹‹

(Harris Poll, 2008)

A delicate matter
A 5-year-old boy (left), who identifies and dresses as a girl and asks to be called "she," plays with a female friend. Sensitive to the gender identity rights movement and to the special needs of children with gender dysphoria, a growing number of parents, educators, and clinicians are now supportive of children like this boy.

such transgender experiences come to terms with their gender inconsistencies, but others experience extreme unhappiness with their given gender—and may seek treatment for their problem (Singh et al., 2010). DSM-5 categorizes these individuals as having **gender dysphoria,** a disorder in which people persistently feel that a vast mistake has been made, they have been born to the wrong sex, and gender changes would be desirable (see Table 13-6).

The DSM-5 categorization of gender dysphoria is controversial (Sennott, 2011; Dannecker, 2010). Many people believe that transgender experiences reflect alternative—not pathological—ways of experiencing one's gender identity. Moreover, they argue, even transgender experiences that bring unhappiness should not be considered a disorder. At the other end of the spectrum, many argue that gender dysphoria is in fact a medical problem that may produce personal unhappiness. They hold that gender dysphoria should not be categorized as a psychological disorder, just as kidney disease and cancer, medical conditions that may also produce unhappiness, are not categorized as psychological disorders. Although one of these views may eventually prove to be a more appropriate perspective, this chapter largely will follow DSM-5's position that gender dysphoria is more than a variant lifestyle and far from a clearly defined medical problem, and it will examine what clinical theorists believe they know about the pattern.

People with gender dysphoria typically would like to get rid of their primary and secondary sex characteristics—many of them find their own genitals repugnant—and acquire the characteristics of the other sex (APA, 2013, 2012). Men with this disorder outnumber women by around 2 to 1. The individuals experience anxiety or depression and may have thoughts of suicide (Hoshiai et al., 2010). Such reactions may be related to the confusion and pain brought on by the disorder itself, or they may be tied to the prejudice typically experienced by individuals who display this pattern (Iantaffi & Bockting, 2011; Bouman et al., 2010). Studies also suggest that some people with gender dysphoria further manifest a personality disorder (Singh et al., 2011). Today the term *gender dysphoria* has replaced the old term *transsexualism,* although the label "transsexual" is still commonly applied to those individuals who desire and seek *full* gender change.

Sometimes gender dysphoria emerges in children (APA, 2013, 2012; Dragowski et al., 2011; Nieder et al., 2011). Like adults with this disorder, the children feel uncomfortable about their assigned sex and yearn to be members of the opposite sex. This childhood pattern usually disappears by adolescence or adulthood, but in some cases it develops into adolescent and adult forms of gender dysphoria (Cohen-Kettenis, 2001).

table 13-6

DSM-5 Checklist

Gender Dysphoria in Adolescents and Adults

1. Marked inconsistency between one's assigned gender and one's experienced gender, lasting 6 months or more, and consisting of 2 of the following: • Marked inconsistency between one's experienced gender and primary or secondary sex characteristics • Strong desire to be rid of one's sex characteristics • Strong desire for the sex characteristics of the other gender • Strong desire to be a member of the other gender • Strong desire to be treated as a member of the other gender • Strong conviction that one has the typical feelings and reactions of the other gender.

2. Significant distress or impairment.

Based on APA, 2013, 2012

Growing acceptance
An important milestone in the gender identity rights movement was the 2006 election of actress and television personality Vladimir Luxuria to the Italian Parliament, the first transgender individual ever to attain such legislative status. Luxuria, sitting here at the tribune of the parliament, has not undergone sex change surgery and currently remains physically male. She lost her Parliament seat in the 2008 general election.

Thus adults with this disorder may have had a childhood form of gender dysphoria, but most children with the childhood form do not become adults with the disorder. Surveys of mothers indicate that about 1.5 percent of young boys wish to be a girl, and 3.5 percent of young girls wish to be a boy (Carroll, 2007; Zucker & Bradley, 1995), yet considerably less than 1 percent of adults manifest gender dysphoria (Zucker, 2010). This age shift in the prevalence of gender dysphoria is, in part, why leading experts on the disorder strongly recommend against any form of *physical* treatment for this pattern until individuals are at least 16 years of age (Cohen-Kettenis et al., 2011; HBIGDA, 2001).

Explanations of Gender Dysphoria

Many clinicians suspect that biological factors—perhaps genetic or prenatal—play a key role in gender dysphoria (Rametti et al., 2011; Nawata et al., 2010). Consistent with a genetic explanation, the disorder does sometimes run in families. Research indicates, for example, that people whose siblings have gender dysphoria are more likely to have the same disorder than are people without such siblings (Gómez-Gil et al., 2010). Indeed, one study of 23 pairs of identical twins found that when one of the twins displayed gender dysphoria, the other twin displayed it as well in 9 of the pairs (Heylens et al., 2012).

Biological investigators have recently detected differences between the brains of control participants and participants with gender dysphoria. One study found, for example, that those with the disorder had heightened blood flow in the *insula* and reduced blood flow in the *anterior cingulate cortex* (Nawata et al., 2010). These brain areas are known to play roles in human sexuality and consciousness.

Moreover, a biological study that was conducted more than 15 years ago continues to receive considerable attention (Zhou et al., 1997, 1995). Dutch investigators autopsied the brains of six people who had changed their sex from male to female. They found that a cluster of cells in the hypothalamus called the *bed nucleus of stria terminalis* (*BST*) was only half as large in these people as it was in a control group of "normal" men. Usually, a woman's BST is much smaller than a man's, so in effect the men with gender dysphoria were found to have a female-sized BST. Scientists do not know for certain what the BST does in humans, but they know that it helps regulate sexual behavior in male rats. Thus it may be that men who develop gender dysphoria have a key biological difference that leaves them very uncomfortable with their assigned sex characteristics.

•**gender dysphoria**•A disorder in which a person persistently feels extremely uncomfortable about his or her assigned sex and strongly wishes to be a member of the opposite sex. Also known as *transsexualism*.

Treatments for Gender Dysphoria

In order to more effectively assess and treat those with gender dysphoria, clinical theorists have tried to distinguish the most common patterns of the disorder encountered in clinical practice.

Client Patterns of Gender Dysphoria

Richard Carroll (2007), a leading theorist on gender dysphoria, has described the three patterns of gender dysphoria for which individuals most commonly seek treatment: (1) *female-to-male gender dysphoria,* (2) *male-to-female gender dysphoria: androphilic type,* and (3) *male-to-female gender dysphoria: autogynephilic type.*

FEMALE-TO-MALE GENDER DYSPHORIA People with a female-to-male gender dysphoria pattern are born female but appear or behave in a stereotypically masculine manner from early on—often as young as 3 years of age or younger. As children, they always play rough games or sports, prefer the company of boys, hate "girlish" clothes, and state their wish to be male. As adolescents, they become disgusted by the physical changes of puberty and are sexually attracted to females. However, lesbian relationships do not feel like a satisfactory solution to them because they want other women to be attracted to them as males, not as females.

MALE-TO-FEMALE GENDER DYSPHORIA: ANDROPHILIC TYPE People with an androphilic type of male-to-female gender dysphoria are born male but appear or behave in a stereotypically female manner from birth. As children, they are viewed as effeminate, pretty, and gentle; avoid rough games; and hate to dress in boys' clothing. As adolescents, they become sexually attracted to males, and they often come out as gay and develop gay relationships (the term "androphilic" means *attracted to males*). But by adulthood, it becomes clear to them that such gay relationships do not truly address their gender dysphoric feelings because they want to be with heterosexual men who are attracted to them as women.

MALE-TO-FEMALE GENDER DYSPHORIA: AUTOGYNEPHILIC TYPE People with an autogynephilic type of male-to-female gender dysphoria are not sexually attracted to males; rather, they are attracted to the fantasy of themselves being females (the term "autogynephilic" means *attracted to oneself as a female*). Like males with the paraphilic disorder *transvestic disorder* (see pages 408–409), persons with this form of gender dysphoria behave in a stereotypically masculine manner as children, start to enjoy dressing in female clothing during childhood, and, after puberty, become sexually aroused when they cross-dress. Also, like males with transvestic disorder, they are attracted to females during and beyond adolescence. However, unlike individuals with transvestic disorder, these persons have fantasies of becoming female that become stronger and stronger during adulthood. Eventually they are consumed with the need to be female.

In short, cross-dressing is characteristic of both men with transvestic disorder (the paraphilic disorder) and men with this type of male-to-female gender dysphoria (Zucker et al., 2012). But the former individuals cross-dress strictly to become sexually aroused, whereas the latter develop much deeper reasons for cross-dressing, reasons of gender identity.

Types of Treatment for Gender Dysphoria

Many adults with gender dysphoria receive psychotherapy (Affatati et al., 2004), but a large number of them further seek to address their concerns through biological interventions (see *MediaSpeak*). For example, many adults with this disorder change their sexual characteristics by means of *hormone treatments* (Traish & Gooren, 2010). Physicians prescribe the female sex hormone *estrogen* for male patients, causing breast development, loss of body and facial hair,

Lea T.

Transgender model Lea T. emerged in 2010 as the face of Givenchy, the famous French fashion brand. Born male, the Brazilian model has become a leading female figure in runway fashion shows and magazines, including *Vogue Paris, Cover* magazine, and *Love* magazine. In 2012 she underwent sexual reassignment surgery.

Splash News/Newscom

A Different Kind of Judgment

By Angela Woodall, *Oakland Tribune*

Few county judges command standing ovations before they say a word, nor do they compel hate mail from strangers halfway around the world.

Alameda County Superior Court Judge Victoria Kolakowski receives both. She is the first transgender person elected as a trial judge and one of the very few elected to any office.

"No, I am not going to be able to get you out of things," she said jokingly to an audience of transgender advocates . . . two weeks after her upset victory. . . . "I had a chance to serve. If my being visible helps a community that is often ignored and looked down upon, then I am happy. If not me, then who?"

But it took years of rejection and perseverance to get from Michael Kolakowski to 49-year-old Judge Victoria Kolakowski, even though as a child she hoped and prayed to wake up in a female body. "I guess the prayer was answered," she said. "But not for a long time afterward." . . .

Kolakowski, a New York native, is a carefully groomed, mildly spoken brunette of average build who usually appears wearing glasses, modest makeup, dark pantsuits and pumps. In other words, she looks a lot like a conservatively dressed judge.

Kolakowski said she has never "had problems" . . . aimed against transgender people, . . . but she came close the first time she appeared in public as "Vicky," short for Victoria, a name she came up with in high school. She was a college student on summer break when she sneaked away at night from her parents' home on Staten Island. She was heading for a bus stop when a man drove up to her. "Hey, he-she. Come here," he kept calling. He assumed that she must've been working the streets just because she was obviously a man dressed as a woman. She had to cross a freeway to get away from him. Looking back, she said she was lucky to have escaped being raped. Kolakowski rushed back home and didn't mention that night again until years later.

Back then, the Internet did not exist, and information about transsexuals was unavailable to minors, Kolakowski said. At Louisiana State University, she finally found some books in the college library about transsexuality and realized that she was not alone. But when she told her parents, they took her to the emergency room of the hospital. This started an on-again, off-again series of counseling and therapy that lasted for a decade.

Kolakowski eventually married, came out with her wife during law school and began her transition to becoming a woman on April 1, 1989. It was her last semester at LSU. She was 27. Three years later, she underwent surgery to complete her transition to a woman.

She was a 30-year-old lawyer with five degrees on her re-sume. So she had no problem attracting job offers—only to be rejected when she walked into the interview.

A new kind of role model Judge Victoria Kolakowski (left) waves during the 41st annual Gay Pride parade in San Francisco, June 26, 2011.

Rejection is one of the commonalities for transgender women and men, and the pain can run deep. Some of the transgender lawyers Kolakowski knew killed themselves.

Kolakowski attributes her resilience to her faith—she also holds a master's degree in divinity—and the support of "some very loving people." That includes her parents and her second wife. . . . They wed in 2006.

By then, Kolakowski had become an administrative law judge for the California Public Utilities Commission. . . . Her chance to run for the Superior Court bench came in 2008. [The mother of a murdered transgender teen] gave her the butterfly pin she wore at her daughter's murder trials and asked Kolakowski to wear it if elected to the bench. Kolakowski didn't win, but she tried again in 2010. "This time, things were different, and in June, I came in first," she said.

The spotlight turned in her direction because she became a symbol of success for the transgender community. But she also has become a target. The more successful you are, the more backlash you are likely to get, she said, "and that backlash can be violent.". . . [T]wo transgender women were killed in Houston last year, even though voters there elected a transgender municipal judge in November. . . . "We're dealing with people who don't know us and don't really understand who we are," she said.

Kolakowski is also mindful that she must be sensitive to the dignity of the office voters elected her to. Some people, she predicted, will accuse her of "acting inappropriately." But she said: "This is what it is. I was elected based on my qualifications. It just happens to be historic."

Pioneers James and Jan
Feeling like a woman trapped in a man's body, British writer James Morris (left) underwent sex-change surgery, described in his 1974 autobiography, *Conundrum*. Today Jan Morris (right) is a successful author and seems comfortable with her change of gender.

and change in body fat distribution. Similar treatments with the male sex hormone *testosterone* are given to women with gender dysphoria.

Hormone therapy and psychotherapy enable many persons with this disorder to lead a satisfactory existence in the gender role that they believe represents their true identity. For others, however, this is not enough, and they seek out one of the most controversial practices in medicine: **sex-change,** or **sexual reassignment, surgery** (Andreasen & Black, 2006). This surgery, which is preceded by one to two years of hormone therapy, involves, for men, partial removal of the penis and restructuring of its remaining parts into a clitoris and vagina. In addition, the men undergo face-changing plastic surgery. For women, surgery may include bilateral mastectomy and hysterectomy (Ott et al., 2010). The procedure for creating a functioning penis, called *phalloplasty,* is performed in some cases, but it is not perfected. Alternatively, doctors have developed a silicone prosthesis that can give patients the appearance of having male genitals. One review calculates that 1 of every 3,100 persons in the United States has had or will have sex-change surgery during their life time (Horton, 2008). For women, the incidence is 1 of every 4,200, and for men, it is 1 of every 2,500.

Clinicians have debated heatedly whether sexual reassignment surgery is an appropriate treatment for gender dysphoria (Gozlan, 2011). Some consider it a humane solution, perhaps the most satisfying one to people with the pattern. Others argue that sexual reassignment is a "drastic nonsolution" for a complex disorder. Either way, such surgery appears to be on the increase (Allison, 2010; Horton, 2008).

Research into the outcomes of sexual reassignment surgery has yielded mixed findings. On the one hand, in several studies, the majority of patients—both female and male—report satisfaction with the outcome of the surgery, improvements in self-satisfaction and interpersonal interactions, and improvements in sexual functioning (Johansson et al., 2010; Klein & Gorzalka, 2009; Carroll, 2007). On the other hand, several studies have yielded less favorable findings. A long-term follow-up study in Sweden, for example, found that although sexually reassigned participants did show a reduction in gender dysphoria, they also had a higher rate of psychological disorders and of suicide attempts than the general population (Dhejne et al., 2011). Individuals with serious pretreatment psychological disturbances (for example, a personality disorder) seem most likely to later regret the surgery (Carroll, 2007). All of this argues for careful screening prior to surgical interventions and, of course, for continued research to better understand both the patterns themselves and the long-term impact of the surgical procedure.

•**sex-change surgery**•A surgical procedure that changes a person's sex organs, features, and, in turn, sexual identity. Also known as *sexual reassignment surgery.*

PUTTING IT... together

A Private Topic Draws Public Attention

For all the public interest in sexual and gender disorders, clinical theorists and practitioners have only recently begun to understand their nature and how to treat them. As a result of research done over the past few decades, people with sexual dysfunctions are no longer doomed to a lifetime of sexual frustration. At the same time, however, insights into the causes and treatment of paraphilic disorders and gender dysphoria remain limited.

Studies of sexual dysfunctions have pointed to many psychological, sociocultural, and biological causes. Often, as you have seen with so many disorders, the various causes may *interact* to produce a particular dysfunction, as in erectile disorder and female orgasmic disorder. For some dysfunctions, however, one cause alone is dominant, and integrated explanations may be inaccurate and unproductive. Some sexual pain dysfunctions, for example, have a physical cause exclusively.

Recent work has also yielded important progress in the treatment of sexual dysfunctions, and people with such problems are now often helped greatly by therapy. Sex therapy today is usually a complex program tailored to the particular problems of an individual or couple. Techniques from the various models may be combined, although in some instances the particular problem calls primarily for one approach.

One of the most important insights to emerge from all of this work is that *education* about sexual dysfunctions can be as important as therapy. Sexual myths are still taken so seriously that they often lead to feelings of shame, self-hatred, isolation, and hopelessness—feelings that themselves contribute to sexual difficulty. Even a modest amount of education can help persons who are in treatment.

In fact, most people can benefit from a more accurate understanding of sexual functioning. Public education about sexual functioning—through the Internet, books, television and radio, school programs, group presentations, and the like—has become a major clinical focus. It is important that these efforts continue and even increase in the coming years.

BETWEEN THE LINES

Sexual Self-Satisfaction

- A Finnish study of almost 10,000 adults found that half of all male and female participants were satisfied with the appearance of their genitals. ‹‹
- Half of all women were satisfied with the appearance of their breasts. ‹‹
- Higher genital self-satisfaction was related to better sexual functioning for both genders. ‹‹

(Algars et al., 2011)

Summing Up

- **SEXUAL DYSFUNCTIONS** The *human sexual response cycle* consists of four phases: *desire, excitement, orgasm,* and *resolution. Sexual dysfunctions,* disorders in which people cannot respond normally in a key area of sexual functioning, make it difficult or impossible for a person to have or enjoy sexual activity. *pp. 387–388*

- **DISORDERS OF DESIRE** DSM-5 lists two disorders of the *desire phase* of the *sexual response cycle: male hypoactive sexual desire disorder* and *female sexual interest/arousal disorder.* Men with the former disorder persistently lack or have reduced interest in sex and, in turn, display little sexual activity. Women with the latter disorder also lack normal interest in sex, rarely initiate sexual activity, and may also experience little excitement during sexual activity or in the presence of erotic cues. Biological causes for these disorders include abnormal hormone levels, certain drugs, and some medical illnesses. Psychological and sociocultural causes include specific fears, situational pressures, relationship problems, and the trauma of having been sexually molested or assaulted. *pp. 388–392*

- **DISORDERS OF EXCITEMENT** Disorders of the *excitement phase* include *erectile disorder,* a repeated inability to attain or maintain an erection during sexual activity. Biological causes of erectile disorder include abnormal hormone levels, vascular problems, medical conditions, and certain medications. Psychological and sociocultural causes include the combination of *performance anxiety* and the *spectator role,* situational pressures such as job loss, and relationship problems. *pp. 392–394*

Paul Sakuma/AP Photo

Grand Theft Auto: the sexual controversy
One of today's most popular video game series is *Grand Theft Auto.* Fearing that the sexual material in one of the games, *Grand Theft Auto: San Andreas,* was too graphic and suggestive for children, parents and politicians pressured the producer to stop manufacturing the initial version of that game and to develop enhanced security measures to prevent children's access to the game's sexual features.

■ **DISORDERS OF ORGASM** *Premature (early) ejaculation* has been attributed most often to behavioral causes, such as inappropriate early learning and inexperience. In recent years, possible biological factors have been proposed as well. *Delayed ejaculation,* a repeated absence of or long delay in reaching orgasm, can have biological causes, such as low testosterone levels, neurological diseases, and certain drugs, and psychological causes, such as performance anxiety and the spectator role. The dysfunction may also develop from male hypoactive sexual desire disorder.

Female orgasmic disorder, which is often accompanied by arousal difficulties, has been tied to biological causes such as medical diseases and changes that occur after menopause, psychological causes such as memories of childhood traumas, and sociocultural causes such as relationship problems. Most clinicians agree that orgasm during intercourse is not critical to normal sexual functioning, provided a woman can reach orgasm with her partner during direct stimulation of the clitoris. *pp. 394–398*

■ **SEXUAL PAIN DISORDERS** *Genito-pelvic pain/penetration disorder* features significant pain during intercourse. In one form of this disorder, *vaginismus,* involuntary contractions of the muscles around the outer third of the vagina prevent entry of the penis. In another form, *dyspareunia,* the person experiences severe vaginal or pelvic pain during intercourse. This form of the disorder usually occurs in women and typically has a physical cause, such as injury resulting from childbirth. *p. 398–399*

■ **TREATMENTS FOR SEXUAL DYSFUNCTIONS** In the 1970s the work of William Masters and Virginia Johnson led to the development of *sex therapy.* Today sex therapy combines a variety of cognitive, behavioral, couple, and family systems therapies. It generally includes features such as careful assessment, education, acceptance of mutual responsibility, attitude changes, *sensate-focus* exercises, improvements in communication, and couple therapy. In addition, specific techniques have been developed for each of the sexual dysfunctions. The use of biological treatments for sexual dysfunctions is also increasing. *pp. 400–406*

■ **PARAPHILIC DISORDERS** *Paraphilias* are patterns characterized by recurrent and intense sexual urges, fantasies, or behaviors involving objects or situations outside the usual sexual norms—for example, nonhuman objects, children, nonconsenting adults, or experiences of suffering or humiliation. When an individual's paraphilia causes great distress, interferes with social or occupational functioning, or places the individual or others at risk of harm, a diagnosis of *paraphilic disorder* should be applied. Paraphilic disorders are found primarily in men. The paraphilic disorders include *fetishistic disorder, transvestic disorder, exhibitionistic disorder, voyeuristic disorder, frotteuristic disorder, pedophilic disorder, sexual masochism disorder,* and *sexual sadism disorder.*

Fetishistic disorder consists of recurrent and intense sexual fantasies, urges, or behaviors that involve the use of a nonliving object or nongenital part. *Transvestic disorder,* also known as *transvestism* or *cross-dressing,* is characterized by repeated and intense sexual fantasies, urges, or behaviors that involve dressing in clothes of the opposite sex. *Exhibitionistic disorder* features repeated and intense sexual fantasies, urges, or behaviors that involve exposing one's genitals to others. In *voyeuristic disorder,* a person has repeated and intense sexual fantasies, urges, or behaviors that involve secretly observing unsuspecting people who are naked, undressing, or engaging in sexual activity. In *frotteuristic disorder,* a person has repeated and intense sexual fantasies, urges, or behaviors that involve touching or rubbing against a non-consenting person. In *pedophilic disorder,* a person has repeated and intense sexual fantasies, urges, or behaviors that involve watching, touching, or engaging in sexual acts with children. *Sexual masochism disorder* is characterized by repeated and intense sexual fantasies, urges, or behaviors that involve being humiliated, beaten, bound, or otherwise made to suffer. *Sexual sadism disorder* is characterized by repeated and intense sexual fantasies, urges, or behaviors that involve inflicting suffering on others.

Although various explanations have been proposed for paraphilic disorders, research has revealed little about their causes. A range of treatments have been tried, including *aversion therapy, masturbatory satiation, orgasmic reorientation,* and *relapse-prevention training. pp. 406–415*

■ **GENDER DYSPHORIA** People with *gender dysphoria* persistently feel that they have been assigned to the wrong sex. Gender dysphoria in children usually disappears by adolescence or adulthood, but in some cases it develops into adolescent and adult forms of gender dysphoria. In recent years, a number of theorists have criticized the categorization of gender dysphoria as a clinical disorder. The causes of this disorder are not well understood. *Hormone treatments* and *psychotherapy* have been used to help some people adopt the gender role they believe to be right for them. *Sex-change operations* have also been performed, but the appropriateness of surgery as a form of "treatment" has been debated heatedly. *pp. 415–420*

PsychPortal

Visit **PsychPortal**
www.yourpsychportal.com
to access the e-book, videocases and other case materials and activities, and study aids, including flashcards, crossword puzzles, quizzes, FAQs, and research exercises.

BETWEEN THE LINES

Key Decision

On September 19, 2008, the Federal District Court for Washington, DC, ruled for the first time ever that discrimination against a transgender person constitutes illegal sex discrimination. Specifically, it held that the Library of Congress had discriminated against a woman (the plaintiff) by rescinding a job offer to her after she disclosed that she was changing from male to female. ‹‹

SCHIZOPHRENIA

Laura, **40 years old:** *Laura's desire was to become independent and leave home . . . as soon as possible. . . . She became a professional dancer at the age of 20 . . . and was booked for . . . theaters in many European countries. . . .*

It was during one of her tours in Germany that Laura met her husband. . . . They were married and went to live in a small . . . town in France where the husband's business was. . . . She spent a year in that town and was very unhappy. . . . [Finally] Laura and her husband decided to emigrate to the United States. . . .

They had no children, and Laura . . . showed interest in pets. She had a dog to whom she was very devoted. The dog became sick and partially paralyzed, and veterinarians felt that there was no hope of recovery. . . . Finally [her husband] broached the problem to his wife, asking her "Should the dog be destroyed or not?" From that time on Laura became restless, agitated, and depressed. . . .

. . . Later Laura started to complain about the neighbors. A woman who lived on the floor beneath them was knocking on the wall to irritate her. According to the husband, this woman had really knocked on the wall a few times; he had heard the noises. However, Laura became more and more concerned about it. She would wake up in the middle of the night under the impression that she was hearing noises from the apartment downstairs. She would become upset and angry at the neighbors. . . . Later she became more disturbed. She started to feel that the neighbors were now recording everything she said; maybe they had hidden wires in the apartment. She started to feel "funny" sensations. There were many strange things happening, which she did not know how to explain; people were looking at her in a funny way in the street. . . . She felt that people were planning to harm either her or her husband. . . . In the evening when she looked at television, it became obvious to her that the programs referred to her life. Often the people on the programs were just repeating what she had thought. They were stealing her ideas. She wanted to go to the police and report them.

(Arieti, 1974, pp. 165–168)

Richard, 23 years old: *In high school, Richard was an average student. After graduation from high school, he [entered] the army. . . . Richard remembered [the] period . . . after his discharge from the army . . . as one of the worst in his life. . . . Any, even remote, anticipation of disappointment was able to provoke attacks of anxiety in him. . . .*

Approximately two years after his return to civilian life, Richard left his job because he became overwhelmed by these feelings of lack of confidence in himself, and he refused to go look for another one. He stayed home most of the day. His mother would nag him that he was too lazy and unwilling to do anything. He became slower and slower in dressing and undressing and taking care of himself. When he went out of the house, he felt compelled "to give interpretations" to everything he looked at. He did not know what to do outside the house, where to go, where to turn. If he saw a red light at a crossing, he would interpret it as a message that he should not go in that direction. If he saw an arrow, he would follow the arrow interpreting it as a sign sent by God that he should go in that direction. Feeling lost and horrified, he would go home and stay there, afraid to go out because going out meant making decisions or choices that he felt unable to make. He reached the point where he stayed home most of the time. But even at

•schizophrenia•A psychotic disorder in which personal, social, and occupational functioning deteriorate as a result of strange perceptions, unusual emotions, and motor abnormalities.

•psychosis•A state in which a person loses contact with reality in key ways.

•positive symptoms•Symptoms of schizophrenia that seem to be excesses of or bizarre additions to normal thoughts, emotions, or behaviors.

•delusion•A strange false belief firmly held despite evidence to the contrary.

home, he was tortured by his symptoms. He could not act; any motion that he felt like making seemed to him an insurmountable obstacle, because he did not know whether he should make it or not. He was increasingly afraid of doing the wrong thing. Such fears prevented him from dressing, undressing, eating, and so forth. He felt paralyzed and lay motionless in bed. He gradually became worse, was completely motionless, and had to be hospitalized....

Being undecided, he felt blocked, and often would remain mute and motionless, like a statue, even for days.

(Arieti, 1974, pp. 153–155)

Eventually, Laura and Robert each received a diagnosis of **schizophrenia.** People who have this disorder, though they previously functioned well or at least acceptably, deteriorate into an isolated wilderness of unusual perceptions, odd thoughts, disturbed emotions, and motor abnormalities. In Chapter 15 you will see that schizophrenia is no longer the hopeless disorder of times past and that some sufferers, though certainly not all, now make remarkable recoveries. However, in this chapter let us first take a look at the symptoms of this disorder and at the theories that have been developed to explain them.

Like Laura and Robert, individuals with schizophrenia experience **psychosis,** a loss of contact with reality. Their ability to perceive and respond to the environment becomes so disturbed that they may not be able to function at home, with friends, in school, or at work (Figueira & Brissos, 2011). They may have hallucinations (false sensory perceptions) or delusions (false beliefs), or they may withdraw into a private world. As you saw in Chapter 12, taking LSD or abusing amphetamines or cocaine may produce psychosis (see *PsychWatch* on page 428). So may injuries or diseases of the brain. And so may mood disorders. Recall from Chapter 8 that some people with major depressive disorder or bipolar disorder develop symptoms of psychosis. Most commonly, however, psychosis appears in the form of schizophrenia. The term schizophrenia comes from the Greek words for "split mind."

Approximately 1 of every 100 people in the world suffers from schizophrenia during his or her lifetime (Lindenmayer & Khan, 2012). An estimated 24 million people worldwide are afflicted with this disorder, 2.5 million in the United States (NIMH, 2010). Its financial cost is enormous, and the emotional cost is even greater (Covell, Essock, & Frisman, 2011). In addition, sufferers have an increased risk of suicide and of physical—often fatal—illness (Messia & Dixon, 2012; an der Heiden & Häfner, 2011).

As you read in Chapter 10, it is estimated that as many as 25 percent of people with the disorder attempt suicide (Kasckow et al., 2011; Meltzer, 2011).

Although schizophrenia appears in all socioeconomic groups, it is found more frequently in the lower levels (Sareen et al., 2011) (see Figure 14-1). This has led some theorists to believe that the stress of poverty is itself a cause of the disorder. However, it could be that schizophrenia causes its victims to fall from a higher to a lower socioeconomic level or to remain poor because they are unable to function effectively (Jablensky, Kirkbride, & Jones, 2011). This is sometimes called the *downward drift* theory.

Equal numbers of men and women receive a diagnosis of schizophrenia. The average age of onset for men is 23 years, compared to 28 years for women (Lindenmayer & Khan, 2012). Almost 3 percent of all those who are divorced or separated suffer from schizophrenia sometime during their lives, compared to 1 percent of married people and 2 percent of people who remain single. Again, however, it is not clear whether marital problems are a cause or a result (Solter et al., 2004; Keith et al., 1991).

People today, like those of the past, show great interest in schizophrenia, flocking to plays and movies that explore or exploit our fascination with the disorder. Yet, as you will read, all too many people with schizophrenia are neglected in our country, their

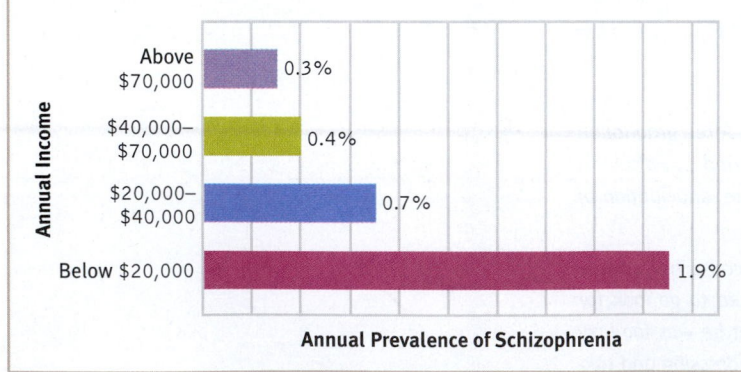

Figure 14-1
Socioeconomic class and schizophrenia
Poor people in the United States are more likely than wealthy people to experience schizophrenia. (Adapted from Sareen et al., 2011.)

needs almost entirely ignored. Although effective interventions have been developed, most sufferers live without adequate treatment and without nearly fulfilling their potential as human beings.

The Clinical Picture of Schizophrenia

For years schizophrenia was a "wastebasket category" for diagnosticians, particularly for those in the United States, where the label might be assigned to anyone who acted unpredictably or strangely. The disorder is defined more precisely today, but still its symptoms vary greatly, and so do its triggers, course, and responsiveness to treatment (APA, 2013; Seeman, 2011). In fact, a number of clinicians believe that schizophrenia is actually a group of distinct disorders that happen to have some features in common (Arango & Carpenter, 2011).

Regardless of whether schizophrenia is a single disorder or several disorders, the lives of people who experience its symptoms are filled with pain and turmoil. One particularly coherent and articulate patient described what it is like to live with this disorder:

What . . . does schizophrenia mean to me? It means fatigue and confusion, it means trying to separate every experience into the real and the unreal and sometimes not being aware of where the edges overlap. It means trying to think straight when there is a maze of experiences getting in the way, and when thoughts are continually being sucked out of your head so that you become embarrassed to speak at meetings. It means feeling sometimes that you are inside your head and visualizing yourself walking over your brain, or watching another girl wearing your clothes and carrying out actions as you think them. It means knowing that you are continually "watched," that you can never succeed in life because the laws are all against you and knowing that your ultimate destruction is never far away.

(Rollin, 1980, p. 162)

What Are the Symptoms of Schizophrenia?

Think back to Laura and Richard, the two individuals described at the beginning of the chapter. Both of them deteriorated from a normal level of functioning to become ineffective in dealing with the world. Each experienced some of the symptoms found in schizophrenia. The symptoms can be grouped into three categories: *positive symptoms* (excesses of thought, emotion, and behavior), *negative symptoms* (deficits of thought, emotion, and behavior), and *psychomotor symptoms* (unusual movements or gestures). Some people with schizophrenia are more dominated by positive symptoms and others by negative symptoms, although both kinds of symptoms are typically displayed to some degree. In addition, around half of people with schizophrenia display significant difficulties with memory and other kinds of cognitive functioning (Keefe & Eesley, 2012).

Positive Symptoms **Positive symptoms** are "pathological excesses," or bizarre additions, to a person's behavior. *Delusions, disorganized thinking and speech, heightened perceptions and hallucinations,* and *inappropriate affect* are the ones most often found in schizophrenia.

DELUSIONS Many people with schizophrenia develop **delusions,** ideas that they believe wholeheartedly but have no basis in fact. The deluded person may consider the ideas enlightening or may

Inner torment
Like this young woman, people with schizophrenia often appear to be trying to fight off the strange thoughts and perceptions that pervade their minds.

David Grossman/Photo Researchers

Mentally Ill Chemical Abusers

A state appeals court yesterday ordered Larry Hogue, who has for years frightened residents of Manhattan's Upper West Side with his bizarre behavior, to remain in a state mental hospital until a hearing next week. . . . Before he was arrested, Mr. Hogue had attacked passers-by and cars in the area around West 96th Street and Amsterdam Avenue. . . .

. . . Mr. Hogue has been arrested 30 times and served at least six terms in prison, ranging from five days to a year, according to law-enforcement records. He now faces charges of criminal mischief for scraping the paint off a car last August.

(*NEW YORK TIMES*, FEBRUARY 9, 1993)

Wild Man of West 96th Street The case of Larry Hogue, the so-called Wild Man of West 96th Street, helped bring the plight of MICAs to public attention. Here Hogue roams the streets in 1993 while displaying the combined effects of schizophrenia and substance abuse.

During the 1990s, Larry Hogue, nicknamed the "Wild Man of West 96th Street" by neighbors, became the best-known *mentally ill chemical abuser* (*MICA*) in the United States. MICAs, also known as *dual diagnosis* patients, are individuals who suffer from both a severe mental disorder (in Hogue's case schizophrenia) *and* a substance use disorder. Today the MICA problem in the United States appears to be bigger than ever (Kavanagh & Mueser, 2011; Kavanagh, 2008). Between 20 and 50 percent of all people with chronic mental disorders may be MICAs.

MICAs tend to be young and male. They often rate below average in social functioning and school achievement and above average in poverty, acting-out behavior, emergency room visits, and encounters with the criminal justice system (McKendrick et al., 2007; Sullivan et al., 2007). MICAs commonly report greater distress and have poorer treatment outcomes than people with mental disorders who do not abuse substances (Haddock & Spaulding, 2011; Potvin et al., 2008).

The relationship between substance abuse and mental dysfunctioning is complex. A mental disorder may precede substance abuse, and the drug may be taken as a form of self-medication or as a result of impaired judgment. Conversely, substance abuse may cause or exacerbate psychopathology. Cocaine and amphet-

amines, for example, exacerbate the symptoms of psychosis and can quickly intensify the symptoms of schizophrenia. Whichever begins first, substance abuse and mental disorders interact to create a complex and distinct problem that is greater than the sum of its parts (Kavanagh & Mueser, 2011; Wilson, 2010). The course and outcome of each disorder can be significantly influenced by the other.

Treatment of MICAs has been undermined by the tendency of patients to hide their drug abuse problems and for clinicians to underdiagnose them. Unrecognized substance abuse may lead to misdiagnosis and misunderstanding of the disorders. The treatment of MICAs is further complicated by the fact that many treatment facilities are designed and funded to treat *either* mental disorders *or* substance abuse; only some are equipped or willing to treat both. As a result, it is not uncommon for MICA patients to be rejected as inappropriate for treatment in both substance abuse and mental health programs. Many such individuals fall through the cracks in this way and find themselves in jail, like Larry Hogue, or in homeless shelters for

want of the treatment they sought in vain (Kooyman & Walsh, 2011).

The problem of falling through the cracks is perhaps most poignantly seen in the case of *homeless* MICAs (Kooyman & Walsh, 2011; Felix, 2008). Researchers estimate that 10 to 20 percent of the homeless population may be MICAs. MICAs typically remain homeless longer than other homeless people and are more likely to experience extremely harsh conditions, such as living on the winter streets rather than in a homeless shelter. They are also more likely to be jailed, to trade sexual favors for food or money, to share needles, to engage in unprotected sex, and to be victimized in other ways. Homeless MICAs need treatment programs committed to building trust and providing intensive case management and long-term practical assistance (Coldwell & Bender, 2007; Egelko et al., 2002). In short, therapists must tailor treatment programs to MICAs' unique combination of problems rather than expecting the MICAs to adapt to traditional forms of care.

feel confused by them. Some people hold a single delusion that dominates their lives and behavior, whereas others have many delusions. *Delusions of persecution* are the most common in schizophrenia (APA, 2013, 2012). People with such delusions believe they are being plotted or discriminated against, spied on, slandered, threatened, attacked, or deliberately victimized. Laura believed that her neighbors were trying to irritate her and that other people were trying to harm her and her husband.

? Philosopher Friedrich Nietzsche said, "Insanity in individuals is something rare—but in groups, parties, nations and epochs, it is the rule." What did he mean?

People with schizophrenia may also experience *delusions of reference:* they attach special and personal meaning to the actions of others or to various objects or events. Richard, for example, interpreted arrows on street signs as indicators of the direction he should take. People who experience *delusions of grandeur* believe themselves to be great inventors, religious saviors, or other specially empowered persons. And those with *delusions of control* believe their feelings, thoughts, and actions are being controlled by other people.

DISORGANIZED THINKING AND SPEECH People with schizophrenia may not be able to think logically and may speak in peculiar ways. These **formal thought disorders** can cause the sufferer great confusion and make communication extremely difficult. Often they take the form of positive symptoms (pathological excesses), as in *loose associations, neologisms, perseveration,* and *clang.*

People who have **loose associations,** or **derailment,** the most common formal thought disorder, rapidly shift from one topic to another, believing that their incoherent statements make sense. A single, perhaps unimportant word in one sentence becomes the focus of the next. One man with schizophrenia, asked about his itchy arms, responded:

> *The problem is insects. My brother used to collect insects. He's now a man 5 foot 10 inches. You know, 10 is my favorite number. I also like to dance, draw, and watch television.*

Some people with schizophrenia use *neologisms,* made-up words that typically have meaning only to the person using them. One individual stated, for example, "I am here from a foreign university . . . and you have to have a *'plausity'* of all acts of amendment to go through for the children's code . . . it is an *'amorition'* law . . . the children have to have this *'accentuative'* law so they don't go into the *'mortite'* law of the church" (Vetter, 1969, p. 189). Others may display the formal thought disorder of *perseveration,* in which they repeat their words and statements again and again. Finally, some use *clang,* or rhyme, to think or express themselves. When asked how he was feeling, one man replied, "Well, hell, it's well to tell." Another described the weather as "So hot, you know it runs on a cot." Research suggests that some disorganized speech or thinking may appear long before a full pattern of schizophrenia unfolds (Goldberg, David, & Gold, 2011; Covington et al., 2005).

HEIGHTENED PERCEPTIONS AND HALLUCINATIONS A deranged character in Edgar Allan Poe's "The Tell-Tale Heart" asks, "Have I not told you that what you mistake for madness is but the overacuteness of the senses?" Similarly, the perceptions and attention of some people with schizophrenia

•**formal thought disorder**•A disturbance in the production and organization of thought.

•**loose associations**•A common thinking disturbance in schizophrenia, characterized by rapid shifts from one topic of conversation to another. Also known as *derailment.*

Famous, but rare, delusion
In the MTV show *Teen Wolf,* a possessed man cries out in terror as his body changes into that of a wolf. *Lycanthropy,* the delusion of being an animal, is a rare psychological syndrome, but it has been the subject of many profitable books, movies, and TV shows over the years.

MGM/The Kobal Collection

seem to intensify. The persons may feel that their senses are being flooded by all the sights and sounds that surround them. This makes it almost impossible for them to attend to anything important:

> *Everything seems to grip my attention.... I am speaking to you just now, but I can hear noises going on next door and in the corridor. I find it difficult to shut these out, and it makes it more difficult for me to concentrate on what I am saying to you.*
>
> *(McGhie and Chapman, 1961)*

Laboratory studies repeatedly have found problems of perception and attention among people with schizophrenia (Goldberg et al., 2011; Park et al., 2011). In one study, participants were instructed to listen for a particular syllable recorded against an ongoing background of speech (Harris et al., 1985). As long as the background speech was kept simple, participants with and without schizophrenia were equally successful at picking out the syllable in question; but when the background speech was made more distracting, the individuals with schizophrenia became less able to identify the syllable. In many studies, people with this disorder have also demonstrated deficiencies in *smooth pursuit eye movement,* weaknesses that may be related again to attention problems. When asked to keep their head still and track a moving object back and forth with their eyes, research participants with schizophrenia tend to perform more poorly than those without schizophrenia (Egan & Cannon, 2011; Mitropoulou et al., 2011).

The various perception and attention problems found in schizophrenia may develop years before the onset of the actual disorder (Goldberg et al., 2011; Cornblatt & Keilp, 1994). It is also possible that such problems further contribute to the memory impairments that are experienced by many individuals with the disorder.

Another kind of perceptual problem in schizophrenia consists of **hallucinations,** perceptions that occur in the absence of external stimuli. People who have *auditory* hallucinations, by far the most common kind in schizophrenia, hear sounds and voices that seem to come from outside their heads. The voices may talk directly to the hallucinator, perhaps giving commands or warning of dangers, or they may be experienced as overheard:

> *The voices ... were mostly heard in my head, though I often heard them in the air, or in different parts of the room. Every voice was different, and each beautiful, and generally, speaking or singing in a different tone and measure, and resembling those of relations or friends. There appeared to be many in my head, I should say upwards of fourteen. I divide them, as they styled themselves, or one another, into voices of contrition and voices of joy and honour.*
>
> *("Perceval's Narrative," in Bateson, 1974)*

Research suggests that people with auditory hallucinations actually produce the nerve signals of sound in their brains, "hear" them, and then believe that external sources are responsible (Jardri et al., 2011; Plaze et al., 2011). One line of research measured blood flow in *Broca's area,* the region of the brain that helps people produce speech (Meyer-Lindenberg & Bullmore, 2011; Waters et al., 2007; McGuire et al., 1996). The investigators found more blood flow in Broca's area while patients were experiencing auditory hallucinations. A related study instructed six men with schizophrenia to press a button whenever they experienced an auditory hallucination (Silbersweig et al., 1995).

Jeff Morgan 03/Alamy

Poor tracking

A clinical researcher demonstrates a device that reveals how well a person's eyes track a moving laser dot. People with schizophrenia tend to perform poorly on this and other eye-pursuit tasks.

PET scans revealed increased activity near the surfaces of their brains, in the tissues of the auditory cortex, the brain's hearing center, when they pressed the button.

Hallucinations can also involve any of the other senses (Stevenson, Langdon, & McGuire, 2011). *Tactile* hallucinations may take the form of tingling, burning, or electric-shock sensations. *Somatic* hallucinations feel as if something is happening inside the body, such as a snake crawling inside one's stomach. *Visual* hallucinations may produce vague perceptions of colors or clouds or distinct visions of people or objects. People with *gustatory* hallucinations regularly find that their food or drink tastes strange, and people with *olfactory* hallucinations smell odors that no one else does, such as the smell of poison or smoke.

Hallucinations and delusional ideas often occur together. A woman who hears voices issuing commands, for example, may have the delusion that the commands are being placed in her head by someone else. A man with delusions of persecution may hallucinate the smell of poison in his bedroom or the taste of poison in his coffee. Might one symptom cause the other? Whatever the cause and whichever comes first, the hallucination and delusion eventually feed into each other.

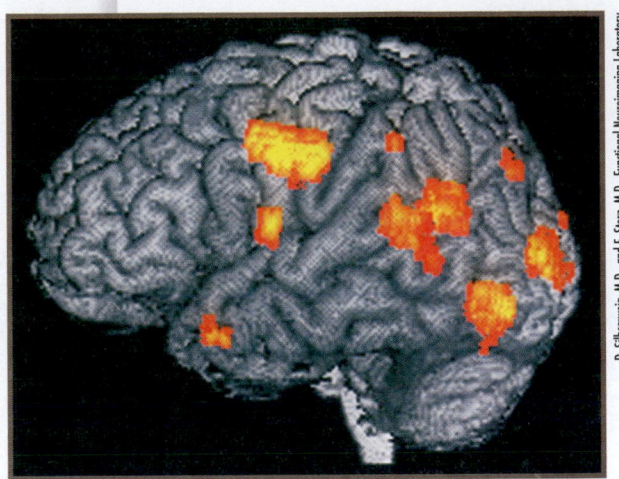

I thought the voices I heard were being transmitted through the walls of my apartment and through the washer and dryer and that these machines were talking and telling me things. I felt that the government agencies had planted transmitters and receivers in my apartment so that I could hear what they were saying and they could hear what I was saying.

(Anonymous, 1996, p. 183)

The human brain during hallucinations
This PET scan, taken at the moment a patient was experiencing auditory hallucinations, shows heightened activity (yellow-orange) in Broca's area, a brain region that helps people produce speech, and the auditory cortex, the brain area that helps people hear sounds (Silbersweig et al., 1995). Conversely, the front of the brain, which is responsible for determining the source of sounds, was quiet during the hallucinations. Thus persons who are hallucinating seem to hear sounds produced by their own brains, but the brains cannot recognize that the sounds are actually coming from within.

INAPPROPRIATE AFFECT Many people with schizophrenia display **inappropriate affect,** emotions that are unsuited to the situation (Gard et al., 2011). They may smile when making a somber statement or upon being told terrible news, or they may become upset in situations that should make them happy. They may also undergo inappropriate shifts in mood. During a tender conversation with his wife, for example, a man with schizophrenia suddenly started yelling obscenities at her and complaining about her inadequacies.

In at least some cases, these emotions may be merely a response to other features of the disorder. Consider a woman with schizophrenia who smiles when told of her husband's serious illness. She may not actually be happy about the news; in fact, she may not be understanding or even hearing it. She could, for example, be responding instead to another of the many stimuli flooding her senses, perhaps a joke coming from an auditory hallucination.

Negative Symptoms
Negative symptoms are those that seem to be "pathological deficits," characteristics that are lacking in an individual. *Poverty of speech, blunted and flat affect, loss of volition,* and *social withdrawal* are commonly found in schizophrenia (Messinger et al., 2011). Such deficits greatly affect one's life and activities.

POVERTY OF SPEECH People with schizophrenia often display **alogia,** or **poverty of speech,** a reduction in speech or speech content. Some people with this negative kind of formal thought disorder think and say very little. Others say quite a bit but still manage to convey little meaning (Birkett et al., 2011). These problems are revealed in the following diary entry written in 1919 by Vaslav Nijinsky, one of the twentieth century's great ballet dancers, as his pattern of schizophrenia was unfolding:

•**hallucination**•The experiencing of sights, sounds, or other perceptions in the absence of external stimuli.

•**inappropriate affect**•Display of emotions that are unsuited to the situation; a symptom of schizophrenia.

•**negative symptoms**•Symptoms of schizophrenia that seem to be deficits in normal thought, emotions, or behaviors.

•**alogia**•A decrease in speech or speech content; a symptom of schizophrenia. Also known as *poverty of speech.*

•flat affect• A marked lack of expressed emotions; a symptom of schizophrenia.

•avolition• A symptom of schizophrenia marked by apathy and an inability to start or complete a course of action.

•catatonia• A pattern of extreme psychomotor symptoms found in some forms of schizophrenia, which may include catatonic stupor, rigidity, or posturing.

I do not wish people to think that I am a great writer or that I am a great artist nor even that I am a great man. I am a simple man who has suffered a lot. I believe I suffered more than Christ. I love life and want to live, to cry but cannot—I feel such a pain in my soul—a pain which frightens me. My soul is ill. My soul, not my mind. The doctors do not understand my illness. I know what I need to get well. My illness is too great to be cured quickly. I am incurable. Everyone who reads these lines will suffer—they will understand my feelings. I know what I need. I am strong, not weak. My body is not ill—it is my soul that is ill. I suffer, I suffer. Everyone will feel and understand. I am a man, not a beast. I love everyone, I have faults, I am a man—not God. I want to be God and therefore I try to improve myself. I want to dance, to draw, to play the piano, to write verses, I want to love everybody. That is the object of my life.

(Nijinsky, 1936)

RESTRICTED AFFECT Many people with schizophrenia have a *blunted affect*—they show less anger, sadness, joy, and other feelings than most people (Gard et al., 2011). And some show almost no emotions at all, a condition known as **flat affect**. Their faces are still, their eye contact is poor, and their voices are monotonous. In some cases, people with these problems may have *anhedonia,* a general lack of pleasure or enjoyment (Cohen et al., 2011). In other cases, however, the restricted affect may reflect an inability to express emotions as others do. One study had participants view very emotional film clips. The participants with schizophrenia showed less facial expression than the others; however, they reported feeling just as much positive and negative emotion and in fact displayed greater skin arousal (Kring & Neale, 1996).

LOSS OF VOLITION Many people with schizophrenia experience **avolition,** or apathy, feeling drained of energy and of interest in normal goals and unable to start or follow through on a course of action (Arango & Carpenter, 2011). This problem is particularly common in people who have had schizophrenia for many years, as if they have been worn down by it. Similarly, individuals with the disorder may display *ambivalence,* or conflicting feelings, about most things. The avolition and ambivalence of Richard, the young man you read about earlier, made eating, dressing, and undressing impossible ordeals for him.

SOCIAL WITHDRAWAL People with schizophrenia may withdraw from their social environment and attend only to their own ideas and fantasies. Because their ideas are illogical and confused, the withdrawal has the effect of distancing them still further from reality. The social withdrawal seems also to lead to a breakdown of social skills, including the ability to recognize other people's needs and emotions accurately (Pinkham et al., 2012; Ziv et al., 2011; Kurtz & Mueser, 2008).

Psychomotor Symptoms People with schizophrenia sometimes experience *psychomotor symptoms,* for example, awkward movements or repeated grimaces and odd gestures. These unusual gestures often seem to have a private purpose—perhaps ritualistic or magical.

The psychomotor symptoms of schizophrenia may take certain extreme forms, collectively called **catatonia** (Weder et al., 2008). People in a *catatonic stupor* stop responding to their environment, remaining motionless and silent for long stretches of time. Recall how Richard would lie motionless and mute in bed for days. People who display *catatonic rigidity* maintain a rigid, upright posture for hours and resist efforts to be moved. Still others exhibit *catatonic posturing,* assuming awkward, bizarre positions for long periods of time. They may, for example, spend hours holding their arms out at a 90-degree angle or balancing in a squatting position. Finally, people who display *catatonic excitement,* a different form of catatonia, move excitedly, sometimes with wild waving of arms and legs.

A catatonic pose
These patients, photographed in the early 1900s, display features of catatonia, including catatonic posturing, in which they assume bizarre positions for long periods of time.

The Oskar Diethelm Library, History of Psychiatry Section, Department of Psychiatry, Cornell University Medical College and The New York Hospital, New York, NY

What Is the Course of Schizophrenia?

Schizophrenia usually first appears between the person's late teens and mid-30s (Lindenmayer & Khan, 2012). Although its course varies widely from case to case, many sufferers seem to go through three phases—prodromal, active, and residual (Perkins & Lieberman, 2012). During the *prodromal phase,* symptoms are not yet obvious, but the individuals are beginning to deteriorate (Addington & Lewis, 2011; French, 2010). They may withdraw socially, speak in vague or odd ways, develop strange ideas, or express little emotion. During the *active phase,* symptoms become apparent. Sometimes this phase is triggered by stress or trauma in the person's life (Bebbington & Kuipers, 2011; Callcott et al., 2011). For Laura, the middle-aged woman described earlier, the immediate trigger was the loss of her cherished dog. Finally, many people with schizophrenia eventually enter a *residual phase,* in which they return to a prodromal-like level of functioning. The striking symptoms of the active phase lessen, but some negative symptoms, such as blunted emotions, may remain. Although one-quarter or more of patients recover completely from schizophrenia, the majority continue to have at least some residual problems for the rest of their lives (an der Heiden & Hafner, 2011; Fischer & Carpenter, 2008).

Each of these phases may last for days or for years. A fuller recovery from schizophrenia is more likely in persons who functioned quite well before the disorder (had good *premorbid functioning*); whose initial disorder is triggered by stress, comes on abruptly, or develops during middle age; and who receive early treatment, preferably during the prodromal phase (Addington & Lewis, 2011; Conus et al., 2007). Relapses are apparently more likely during times of life stress (Bebbington & Kuipers, 2011, 2008).

Diagnosing Schizophrenia

DSM-5 calls for a diagnosis of schizophrenia only after symptoms of the disorder continue for six months or more. At least one of those months must be an active phase, marked by significant delusions, hallucinations, or disorganized speech. In addition, people suspected of having this disorder must show a deterioration in their work, social relations, and ability to care for themselves (see Table 14-1).

Many researchers believe that in order to help predict the course of schizophrenia, there should be a distinction between so-called Type I and Type II schizophrenia. People with *Type I schizophrenia* are thought to be dominated by positive symptoms, such as delusions, hallucinations, and certain formal thought disorders (Crow, 2008, 1995,

table: **14-1**

DSM-5 Checklist

Schizophrenia

1. During a one-month period, at least two of the following symptoms are present for a significant portion of time. One or more of the symptoms must be a, b, or c.
   (a) Delusions.
   (b) Hallucinations.
   (c) Disorganized speech.
   (d) Grossly abnormal psychomotor behavior, including catatonia.
   (e) Negative symptoms.

2. Functioning in school, work, interpersonal relations, or self-care is markedly below the level achieved prior to the onset of symptoms.

3. Continuous signs of the disturbance for at least six months, at least one month of which includes symptoms in full and active form.

Based on APA, 2013, 2012.

1985, 1980). Those with *Type II schizophrenia* display more negative symptoms, such as restricted affect, poverty of speech, and loss of volition. Type I patients generally seem to have a better adjustment prior to the disorder, later onset of symptoms, and greater likelihood of improvement (Blanchard et al., 2011). In addition, as you will soon see, the positive symptoms of Type I schizophrenia may be linked more closely to *biochemical* abnormalities in the brain, while the negative symptoms of Type II schizophrenia may be tied largely to *structural* abnormalities in the brain.

How Do Theorists Explain Schizophrenia?

As with many other kinds of disorders, biological, psychological, and sociocultural theorists have each proposed explanations for schizophrenia. So far, the biological explanations have received by far the most research support. This is not to say that psychological and sociocultural factors play no role in the disorder. Rather, a *diathesis-stress relationship* may be at work: people with a biological predisposition will develop schizophrenia only if certain kinds of events or stressors are also present. Similarly, a diathesis-stress relationship often seems to be operating in the development of other kinds of psychotic disorders (see *PsychWatch* on page 436).

Biological Views

What is arguably the most enlightening research on schizophrenia during the past several decades has come from genetic and biological investigations. These studies have revealed the key roles of inheritance and brain activity in the development of this disorder and have opened the door to important changes in its treatment.

Genetic Factors Following the principles of the diathesis-stress perspective, genetic researchers believe that some people inherit a biological predisposition to schizophrenia and develop the disorder later when they face extreme stress, usually during late adolescence or early adulthood (Riley & Kendler, 2011). The genetic view has been supported by studies of (1) relatives of people with schizophrenia, (2) twins with this disorder, (3) people with schizophrenia who are adopted, and (4) genetic linkage and molecular biology.

ARE RELATIVES VULNERABLE? Family pedigree studies have found repeatedly that schizophrenia is more common among relatives of people with the disorder (Tamminga et al., 2008). And the more closely related the relatives are to the person with schizophrenia, the greater their likelihood of developing the disorder (see Figure 14-2).

As you saw earlier, 1 percent of the general population develops schizophrenia. The prevalence rises to 3 percent among second-degree relatives with this disorder—that is, half-siblings, uncles, aunts, nephews, nieces, and grandchildren (Gottesman & Reilly, 2003)—and it reaches an average of 10 percent among first-degree relatives (parents, siblings, and children). Of course, this trend by itself does not establish a genetic basis for the disorder. Neuroscientist Solomon Snyder (1980) has pointed out, "Attendance at Harvard University also runs in families but would hardly be considered a genetic trait." Close family members are exposed to many of the same environmental influences as the person with schizophrenia, and it may be these influences that lead to the disorder.

Figure 14-2

Family links People who are biologically related to individuals with schizophrenia have a heightened risk of developing the disorder during their lifetimes. The closer the biological relationship (that is, the more similar the genetic makeup), the greater the risk of developing the disorder (Coon & Mitterer, 2007; Gottesman, 1991, p. 96).

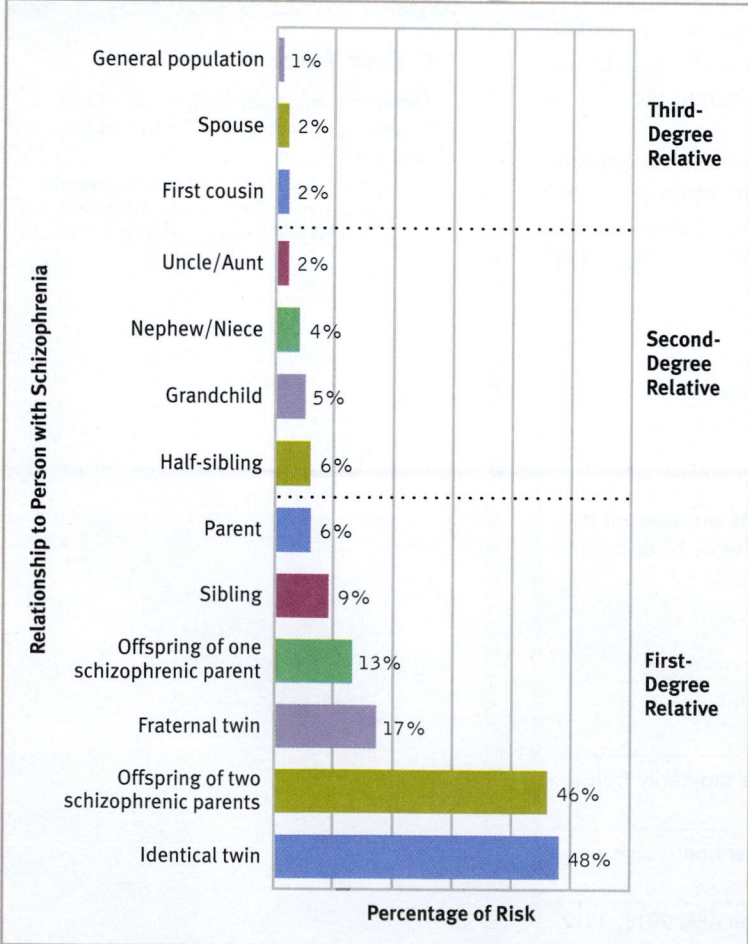

IS AN IDENTICAL TWIN MORE VULNERABLE THAN A FRATERNAL TWIN? Twins, who are among the closest of relatives, have received particular study by schizophrenia researchers. If both members of a pair of twins have a particular trait, they are said to be *concordant* for that trait. If genetic factors are at work in schizophrenia, identical twins (who share all their genes) should have a higher concordance rate for this disorder than fraternal twins (who share only some genes). This expectation has been supported consistently by research (Higgins & George, 2007; Gottesman, 1991). Studies have found that if one identical twin develops schizophrenia, there is a 48 percent chance that the other twin will do so as well. If the twins are fraternal, on the other hand, the second twin has approximately a 17 percent chance of developing the disorder.

Once again, however, factors other than genetics may explain these concordance rates. For example, if one twin is exposed to a particular danger during the prenatal period, such as an injury or virus, the other twin is likely to be exposed to it as well (Davis & Phelps, 1995). This is especially true for identical twins, whose prenatal environment is particularly similar. Thus a predisposition to schizophrenia could be the result of a prenatal problem, and twins, particularly identical twins, would still be expected to have a higher concordance rate.

ARE THE BIOLOGICAL RELATIVES OF AN ADOPTEE VULNERABLE? Adoption studies look at adults with schizophrenia who were adopted as infants and compare them with both their biological and their adoptive relatives. Because they were reared apart from their biological relatives, similar symptoms in those relatives would indicate genetic influences. Conversely, similarities to their adoptive relatives would suggest environmental influences. Repeatedly, researchers have found that the biological relatives of adoptees with schizophrenia are more likely than their adoptive relatives to experience schizophrenia or a schizophrenia–like disorder (see Table 14-2) (Andreasen & Black, 2006; Kety, 1988, 1968).

What factors, besides genetic ones, might account for the elevated rate of schizophrenia among relatives of people with this disorder?

table: **14-2**

An Array of Psychotic Disorders

Disorder	Key Features	Duration	Lifetime Prevalence
Schizophrenia	Various psychotic symptoms such as delusions, hallucinations, disorganized speech, restricted or inappropriate affect, and catatonia	6 months or more	1.0%
Brief psychotic disorder	Various psychotic symptoms such as delusions, hallucinations, disorganized speech, and catatonia	Less than 1 month	Unknown
Schizophreniform disorder	Various psychotic symptoms such as delusions, hallucinations, disorganized speech, restricted or inappropriate affect, and catatonia	1 to 6 months	0.2%
Schizoaffective disorder	Marked symptoms of both schizophrenia and a major depressive episode or a manic episode	6 months or more	Unknown
Delusional disorder	Persistent delusions that are not bizarre and not due to schizophrenia; persecutory, jealous, grandiose, and somatic delusions are common	1 month or more	0.1%
Psychotic disorder due to another medical condition	Hallucinations, delusions, or disorganized speech caused by a medical illness or brain damage	No minimum length	Unknown
Substance-induced psychotic disorder	Hallucinations, delusions, or disorganized speech caused directly by a substance, such as an abused drug	No minimum length	Unknown

Postpartum Psychosis: The Case of Andrea Yates

On the morning of June 20, 2001, the nation's television viewers watched in horror as officials escorted 36-year-old Andrea Yates to a police car. Just minutes before, she had called police and explained that she had drowned her five children in the bathtub because "they weren't developing correctly" and because she "realized [she had not been] a good mother to them." Homicide sergeant Eric Mehl described how she looked him in the eye, nodded, answered with a polite "Yes, sir" to many of his questions, and twice recounted the order in which the children had died: first 3-year-old Paul, then 2-year-old Luke, followed by 5-year-old John and 6-month-old Mary. She then described how she had had to drag 7-year-old Noah to the bathroom and how he had come up twice as he fought for air. Later she told doctors she wanted her hair shaved so she could see the number 666—the mark of the Antichrist—on her scalp (Roche, 2002).

In Chapter 8 you observed that as many as 80 percent of mothers experience "baby blues" soon after giving birth, while between 10 and 30 percent display the clinical syndrome of *postpartum depression*. Yet another postpartum disorder that has become all too familiar to the public in recent times, by way of cases such as that of Andrea Yates, is *postpartum psychosis* (Doucet et al., 2011; Worley, 2010).

Postpartum psychosis affects about 1 to 2 of every 1,000 mothers who have recently given birth (Posmontier, 2010). The symptoms apparently are triggered by the enormous shift in hormone levels that occur after delivery (Blackmore et al., 2008; Nonacs, 2007, 2002). Within days or at most a few months of childbirth, the woman develops signs of losing touch with reality, such as delusions (for example, she may become convinced that her baby is the devil); hallucinations (perhaps hearing voices); extreme anxiety, confusion, and disorientation; disturbed sleep; and illogical or chaotic thoughts (for example, thoughts about killing herself or her child).

Women with a history of bipolar disorder, schizophrenia, or depression are particularly vulnerable to the disorder (Read & Purse, 2007; Sit et al., 2006). In addition, women who have previously experienced postpartum depression or postpartum psychosis have an increased likelihood of developing this disorder after subsequent births (Nonacs, 2007; Ruta & Cohen, 1998). Andrea Yates, for example, had developed signs of postpartum depression (and perhaps postpartum psychosis) and attempted suicide after the birth of her fourth child. At that time, however, she appeared to respond well to a combination of medications, including antipsychotic drugs, and so she and her husband later decided to conceive a fifth child. Although they were warned that she was at risk for serious postpartum symptoms once again, they believed that the same combination of medications would help if the symptoms were to recur (King, 2002).

After the birth of her fifth child, the symptoms did in fact recur, along with features of psychosis. Yates again attempted suicide. Although she was hospitalized twice and treated with various medications, her condition failed to improve. Six months after giving birth to Mary, her fifth child, she drowned all five of her children.

Most clinicians who are knowledgeable about this rare disorder agree that Yates was indeed a victim of postpartum psychosis. Although only a fraction of women

Family tragedy In this undated photograph, Andrea Yates poses with her husband and four of the five children she later drowned.

with the disorder actually harm their children (estimates run as high as 4 percent), the Yates case reminds us that such an outcome is indeed possible (Posmontier, 2010; Read & Purse, 2007). The case also reminds us that early detection and treatment are critical (Doucet et al., 2011).

On March 13, 2002, a Texas jury found Andrea Yates guilty of murdering her children and she was sentenced to life in prison. She had pleaded *not guilty by reason of insanity* during her trial, but the jury concluded within hours that despite her profound disorder, she did know right from wrong. The verdict itself stirred debate throughout the United States, but clinicians and the public alike were united in the belief that, at the very least, the mental health system had tragically failed this woman and her five children.

A Texas appeals court later reversed Yates' conviction, citing the inaccurate testimony of a prosecution witness, and on July 26, 2006, after a new trial, Yates was found *not guilty by reason of insanity* and was sent to a high-security mental health facility for treatment. In 2007, she was transferred to a low-security state mental hospital, where she continues to receive treatment today.

WHAT DO GENETIC LINKAGE AND MOLECULAR BIOLOGY STUDIES SUGGEST? As with bipolar disorders (see Chapter 8), researchers have run studies of *genetic linkage* and *molecular biology* to pinpoint the possible genetic factors in schizophrenia (Sanders et al., 2012; O'Donovan & Owen, 2011). In one approach, they select large families in which schizophrenia is very common, take blood and DNA samples from all members of the families, and then compare gene fragments from members with and without schizophrenia. Applying this procedure to families from around the world, various studies have identified possible gene defects on chromosomes 1, 2, 6, 8, 10, 13, 15, 18, 20, and 22 and on the X chromosome, each of which may help predispose individuals to develop schizophrenia (Chen et al., 2012; Riley & Kendler, 2011).

These varied findings may indicate that some of the suspected gene sites are cases of mistaken identity and do not actually contribute to schizophrenia. Alternatively, it may be that different kinds of schizophrenia are linked to different genes. It is most likely, however, that schizophrenia, like a number of other disorders, is a *polygenic disorder,* caused by a combination of gene defects (Ikeda et al., 2011; Riley & Kendler, 2011).

How might genetic factors lead to the development of schizophrenia? Research has pointed to two kinds of biological abnormalities that could conceivably be inherited—*biochemical abnormalities* and *abnormal brain structure.*

Biochemical Abnormalities

As you have read, the brain is made up of neurons whose electrical impulses (or "messages") are transmitted from one to another by neurotransmitters. After an impulse arrives at a receiving neuron, it travels down the axon of that neuron until it reaches the nerve ending. The nerve ending then releases neurotransmitters that travel across the synaptic space and bind to receptors on yet another neuron, thus relaying the message to the next "station." This neuron activity is known as "firing."

Over the past four decades, researchers have developed a **dopamine hypothesis** to explain their findings on schizophrenia: certain neurons that use the neurotransmitter dopamine (particularly neurons in the striatum region of the brain) fire too often and transmit too many messages, thus producing the symptoms of the disorder (Abi-Dargham & Grace, 2011; Lyon et al., 2010). This hypothesis has undergone challenges and adjustments in recent years, but it is still the foundation for current biochemical explanations of schizophrenia. The chain of events leading to this hypothesis began with the accidental discovery of **antipsychotic drugs,** medications that help remove the symptoms of schizophrenia. As you will see in Chapter 15, the first group of antipsychotic medications, the **phenothiazines,** were discovered in the 1950s by researchers who were looking for better *antihistamine* drugs to combat allergies. Although phenothiazines failed as antihistamines, their effectiveness in reducing schizophrenic symptoms became obvious, and clinicians began to prescribe them widely (Geddes, Stroup, & Lieberman, 2011).

Researchers soon learned that these early antipsychotic drugs often produce troublesome muscular tremors, symptoms that are identical to the central symptom of *Parkinson's disease,* a disabling neurological illness (Haddad & Mattay, 2011). This undesired reaction to antipsychotic drugs offered the first important clue to the biology of schizophrenia. Scientists already knew that people who suffer from Parkinson's disease have abnormally low levels of the neurotransmitter dopamine in some areas of the brain and that lack of dopamine is the reason for their uncontrollable shaking. If antipsychotic drugs produce Parkinsonian symptoms in persons with schizophrenia while removing their psychotic symptoms, perhaps the drugs reduce dopamine activity. And, scientists reasoned further, if lowering dopamine activity helps remove the symptoms of schizophrenia, perhaps schizophrenia is related to excessive dopamine activity in the first place.

HOW STRONG IS THE DOPAMINE-SCHIZOPHRENIA LINK? Since the 1960s, research has supported and helped clarify the dopamine hypothesis. It has been found, for example, that some people with Parkinson's disease develop schizophrenia-like symptoms if they take too much *L-dopa,* a medication that raises dopamine levels in patients with that disease (Grilly, 2002). The L-dopa apparently raises the dopamine activity so much that it produces psychosis.

•**dopamine hypothesis**•The theory that schizophrenia results from excessive activity of the neurotransmitter dopamine.

•**antipsychotic drugs**•Drugs that help correct grossly confused or distorted thinking.

•**phenothiazines**•A group of antihistamine drugs that became the first group of effective antipsychotic medications.

Making a comeback

For years, rats were preferred over mice as animal lab subjects. However, in 1989, scientists developed a technique to make "knockout mice"—mice with specific genes eliminated—and mice became the preferred animals in studies on the causes of schizophrenia and other disorders. Until 2010, that is. With the recent discovery of techniques to make "knockout rats," rats may be on the verge of regaining their elite laboratory status.

•**atypical antipsychotic drugs**•A relatively new group of antipsychotic drugs whose biological action is different from that of the traditional antipsychotic drugs.

Support for the dopamine hypothesis has also come from research on *amphetamines,* drugs that, as you saw in Chapter 12, stimulate the central nervous system. Investigators first noticed during the 1970s that people who take high doses of amphetamines may develop *amphetamine psychosis*—a syndrome very similar to schizophrenia (Srisurapanont et al., 2011; Janowsky et al., 1973). They also found that antipsychotic drugs can reduce the symptoms of amphetamine psychosis, just as they reduce the symptoms of schizophrenia. Eventually researchers learned that amphetamines increase dopamine activity in the brain, thus producing schizophrenia-like symptoms.

Investigators have located areas of the brain that are rich in dopamine receptors and have found that phenothiazines and other antipsychotic drugs bind to many of these receptors (Abi-Dargham & Grace, 2011; Burt et al., 1977; Creese et al., 1977). Apparently the drugs are dopamine *antagonists*—drugs that bind to dopamine receptors, *prevent* dopamine from binding there, and so prevent the neurons from firing. Researchers have identified five kinds of dopamine receptors in the brain—called the D-1, D-2, D-3, D-4, and D-5 receptors—and have found that phenothiazines bind most strongly to the *D-2 receptors* (Remington et al., 2011; Seeman, 2011).

WHAT IS DOPAMINE'S PRECISE ROLE? These and related findings suggest that in schizophrenia, messages traveling from dopamine-sending neurons to dopamine receptors on other neurons, particularly to the D-2 receptors, may be transmitted too easily or too often. This theory is appealing because certain dopamine neurons are known to play a key role in guiding attention. People whose attention is severely disturbed by excessive dopamine activity might well be expected to suffer from the problems of attention, perception, and thought found in schizophrenia.

Why might dopamine be overactive in people with schizophrenia? It may be that people with this disorder have a larger-than-usual number of dopamine receptors, particularly D-2 receptors, or their dopamine receptors may operate abnormally (Tamminga et al., 2008). Remember that when dopamine carries a message to a receiving neuron, it must bind to a receptor on the neuron. A greater number of receptors or abnormal operation by the receptors could result in more dopamine binding and thus more neuron firing. Autopsies have in fact found an unusually large number of dopamine receptors in people with schizophrenia (Owen et al., 1987, 1978; Lee & Seeman, 1980), and imaging studies have revealed particularly high occupancy levels of dopamine at D-2 receptors in patients with schizophrenia (Abi-Dargham & Grace, 2011).

Though enlightening, the dopamine hypothesis has certain problems. The greatest challenge to it has come with the recent discovery of a new group of antipsychotic drugs, referred to as **atypical antipsychotic drugs,** which are often more effective than the traditional ones. The new drugs bind not only to D-2 dopamine receptors, like the traditional, or conventional, antipsychotic drugs, but also to many D-1 receptors and to receptors for other neurotransmitters such as *serotonin* (Waddington, O'Tuathaigh, & Remington, 2011; Goldman-Rakic et al., 2004). Thus, it may be that schizophrenia is related to abnormal activity or interactions of both dopamine and serotonin and perhaps other neurotransmitters (for example, *glutamate* and *GABA*) as well, rather than to abnormal dopamine activity alone (Krystal & Moghaddam, 2011; Lin et al., 2011; Winterer & McCarley, 2011).

In yet another challenge to the dopamine hypothesis, some theorists claim that excessive dopamine activity contributes primarily to the positive symptoms of schizophrenia such as delusions and hallucinations. In support of that notion, it turns out that positive symptoms respond well to the conventional antipsychotic drugs, which bind so strongly to D-2 receptors, whereas some of the negative symptoms (such as restricted affect and loss of volition) respond best to the atypical antipsychotic drugs, which bind less strongly to D-2 receptors (Julien et al., 2011). Still other studies suggest that negative symptoms may be related primarily to abnormal brain structure, rather than to dopamine overactivity.

Not-so-identical twins

The man on the left is normal, while his identical twin, on the right, has schizophrenia. Magnetic resonance imaging (MRI), shown in the background, clarifies that the brain of the twin with schizophrenia is smaller overall than his brother's and has larger ventricles, indicated by the dark butterfly-shaped spaces.

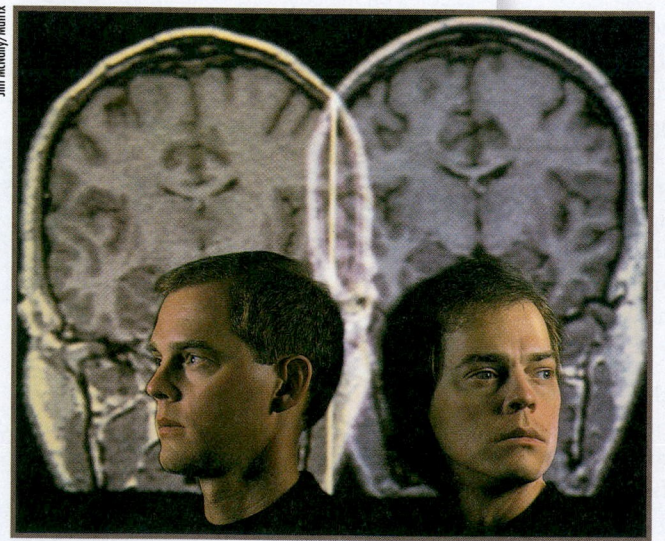

Jim McNally/Matrix

Abnormal Brain Structure During the past decade, researchers also have linked schizophrenia, particularly cases dominated by negative symptoms, to abnormalities in brain structure (Eyler, 2008; Weyandt, 2006). Using brain scans, they have found, for example, that many people with schizophrenia have *enlarged ventricles*—the brain cavities that contain cerebrospinal fluid (Hartberg et al., 2011; Cahn et al., 2002; Lieberman et al., 2001). In addition to displaying more negative symptoms and fewer positive ones, patients who have enlarged ventricles tend to experience a poorer social adjustment prior to the disorder, greater cognitive disturbances, and poorer responses to conventional antipsychotic drugs (Bornstein et al., 1992).

It may be that enlarged ventricles are actually a sign that nearby parts of the brain have not developed properly or have been damaged, and perhaps these problems are the ones that help produce schizophrenia. In fact, studies suggest that some patients with schizophrenia also have smaller temporal lobes and frontal lobes than other people, smaller amounts of cortical gray matter, and, perhaps most important, abnormal blood flow—either reduced or heightened—in certain areas of the brain (Lawrie & Pantelis, 2011; Walther et al., 2011). Still other studies have linked schizophrenia to abnormalities of the hippocampus, amygdala, and thalamus, among other brain structures (Goldberg et al., 2011; Harrison et al., 2011; Spoletini et al., 2011) (see Figure 14-3).

Viral Problems What might cause the biochemical and structural abnormalities found in many cases of schizophrenia? Various studies have pointed to genetic factors, poor nutrition, fetal development, birth complications, immune reactions, and toxins (Brown, 2012; Clarke et al., 2012; Borrajo et al., 2011). In addition, some investigators suggest that the brain abnormalities may result from exposure to *viruses* before birth. Perhaps the viruses enter the fetus' brain and interrupt proper brain development, or perhaps the viruses remain quiet until puberty or young adulthood, when, activated by changes in hormones or by another viral infection, they help to bring about schizophrenic symptoms (Fox, 2010; Torrey, 2001, 1991).

Some of the evidence for the viral theory comes from animal model investigations, and other evidence is circumstantial, such as the finding that an unusually large number of people with schizophrenia are born during the winter (Patterson, 2012; Fox, 2010). The winter birth rate among people with schizophrenia is 5 to 8 percent higher than among other persons (Harper & Brown, 2012; Tamminga et al., 2008). This finding could be because of an increase in fetal or infant exposure to viruses at that time of year. The viral theory has also received support from investigations of *fingerprints*. Normally, identical twins have almost identical numbers of fingerprint ridges. People with schizophrenia, however, often have significantly more or fewer ridges than their nonschizophrenic identical twins (van Os et al., 1997; Torrey et al., 1994). Fingerprints form in the fetus during the second trimester of pregnancy, just when the fetus is most vulnerable to certain viruses. Thus the fingerprint irregularities of some people with schizophrenia could reflect a viral infection contracted during the prenatal period, an infection that also predisposed the individuals to schizophrenia.

More direct evidence for the viral theory of schizophrenia comes from studies showing that mothers of individuals with schizophrenia were more likely to have been exposed to the influenza virus during pregnancy than were mothers of people without schizophrenia (Brown & Patterson, 2011; McGrath & Murray, 2011; Fox, 2010). Other studies have found antibodies to certain viruses, including viruses usually found in animals, in the blood of 40 percent of research participants with schizophrenia (Leweke et al., 2004; Torrey et al., 1994). The presence of such antibodies suggests that these people had at some time been exposed to those particular viruses.

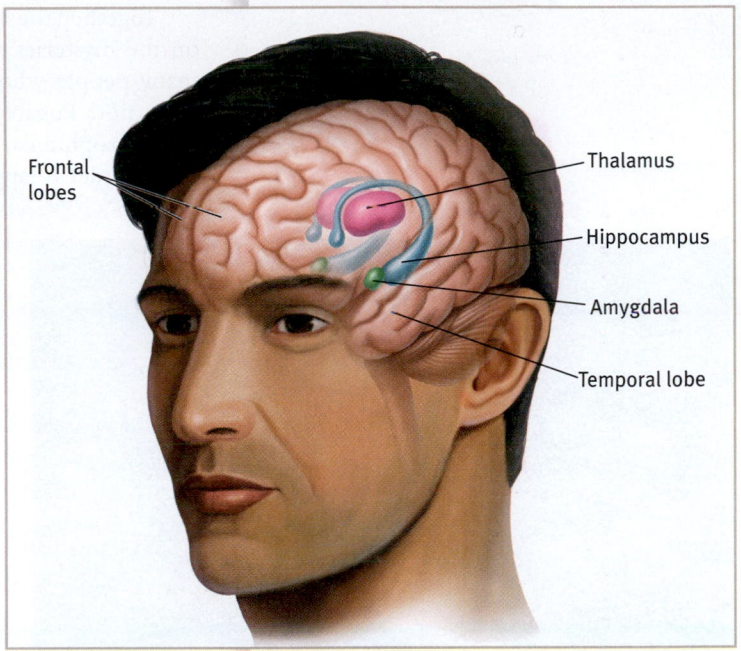

Labels: Frontal lobes, Thalamus, Hippocampus, Amygdala, Temporal lobe

Figure 14-3
Biology of schizophrenia Some studies show that people with schizophrenia have relatively small temporal and frontal lobes, as well as abnormalities in structures such as the hippocampus, amygdala, and thalamus.

Together, the biochemical, brain structure, and viral findings are shedding much light on the mysteries of schizophrenia. At the same time, it is important to recognize that many people who display these biological abnormalities never develop schizophrenia. Why not? Possibly, as you read earlier, because biological factors merely set the stage for schizophrenia, while key psychological and sociocultural factors must be present for the disorder to appear.

Psychological Views

When schizophrenia investigators began to identify genetic and biological factors during the 1950s and 1960s, many clinicians abandoned the psychological theories of the disorder. During the past few decades, however, the tables have been turned and psychological factors are once again being considered as important pieces of the schizophrenia puzzle. The leading psychological theories come from the psychodynamic, behavioral, and cognitive perspectives.

The Psychodynamic Explanation
Freud (1924, 1915, 1914) believed that schizophrenia develops from two psychological processes: (1) *regression* to a pre-ego stage and (2) efforts to *reestablish* ego control. He proposed that when their world has been extremely harsh or withholding—for example, when their parents have been cold or unnurturing or when they have experienced severe traumas—some individuals regress to the earliest point in their development, to the pre-ego state of *primary narcissism,* in which they recognize and meet only their own needs. This sets the stage for schizophrenia. Their near-total regression leads to self-centered symptoms such as neologisms, loose associations, and delusions of grandeur. Once people regress to such an infantile state, Freud continued, they then try to reestablish ego control and contact with reality. Their efforts give rise to yet other psychotic symptoms. Auditory hallucinations, for example, may be an individual's attempt to substitute for a lost sense of reality.

In support of Freud's theory, studies often reveal that people with schizophrenia experienced severe stress or traumas early in their lives (Bebbington & Kuipers, 2011). Beyond this finding, however, Freud's explanation for the disorder has received little research support.

Years later, noted psychodynamic clinician Frieda Fromm-Reichmann (1948) elaborated on Freud's notion that cold or unnurturing parents may set schizophrenia in motion. She described the mothers of people who develop this disorder as cold, domineering, and uninterested in their children's needs. According to Fromm-Reichmann, these mothers may appear to be self-sacrificing but are actually using their children to meet their own needs. At once overprotective and rejecting, they confuse their children and set the stage for schizophrenic functioning. She called them **schizophrenogenic** (schizophrenia-causing) **mothers.**

Fromm-Reichmann's theory, like Freud's, has received little research support (Willick, 2001). The majority of people with schizophrenia do not appear to have mothers who fit the schizophrenogenic description. Most of today's psychodynamic theorists have, in fact, rejected the views of Freud and Fromm-Reichmann. Typically, they believe that biological abnormalities leave certain persons particularly prone to extreme regression or other unconscious acts that may contribute to schizophrenia (Berzoff, Flanagan, & Hertz, 2008; Willick, Milrod, & Karush, 1998). For example, *self theorists,* who believe that schizophrenia reflects a struggling fragmented self, suggest that biological deficiencies explain the failure of people with this disorder to develop an integrated self (Lysaker & Hermans, 2007).

Why have parents and family life so often been blamed for schizophrenia, and why do such explanations continue to be influential?

Movie diagnosis
Since the film *Black Swan* debuted in 2010, clinicians have argued over the correct diagnosis for the principal character, a disturbed ballerina played by actress Natalie Portman. Most have settled on *schizophrenia,* pointing to the character's hallucinations, delusions, and extreme anxiety; the stress-precipitated onset of her psychotic symptoms; and the duration of her deteriorating condition (Villarreal, 2010).

•**schizophrenogenic mother**•A type of mother—supposedly cold, domineering, and uninterested in the needs of others—who was once thought to cause schizophrenia in her child.

The Behavioral View Behaviorists usually cite *operant conditioning* and principles of reinforcement as the cause of schizophrenia. They propose that most people become quite proficient at reading and responding to social cues—that is, other people's smiles, frowns, and comments. People who respond to such cues in a socially acceptable way are better able to satisfy their own emotional needs and achieve their goals (Bach, 2007). Some people, however, are not reinforced for their attention to social cues, either because of unusual circumstances or because important figures in their lives are socially inadequate. As a result, they stop attending to such cues and focus instead on irrelevant cues—the brightness of light in a room, a bird flying above, or the sound of a word rather than its meaning. As they attend more and more to irrelevant cues, their responses become increasingly bizarre. Because the bizarre responses are rewarded with attention or other types of reinforcement, they are likely to be repeated again and again.

Support for the behavioral position has been circumstantial. As you'll see in Chapter 15, researchers have found that patients with schizophrenia are capable of learning at least some appropriate verbal and social behaviors if hospital personnel consistently ignore their bizarre responses and reinforce normal responses with cigarettes, food, attention, or other rewards (Kopelowicz, Liberman, & Zarate, 2007). If bizarre verbal and social responses can be eliminated by appropriate reinforcements, perhaps they were acquired through improper learning in the first place. Of course, an effective treatment does not necessarily indicate the cause of a disorder. Today the behavioral view is usually considered at best a partial explanation for schizophrenia. Although it may help explain why a given person displays more psychotic behavior in some situations than in others, it is too limited, in the opinion of many, to account for schizophrenia's origins and its many symptoms.

The Cognitive View A leading cognitive explanation of schizophrenia agrees with the biological view that during hallucinations and related perceptual difficulties the brains of people with schizophrenia are actually producing strange and unreal sensations—sensations triggered by biological factors. According to the cognitive explanation, however, further features of the disorder emerge when the individuals attempt to understand their unusual experiences (Tarrier, 2008; Waters et al., 2007). When first confronted by voices or other troubling sensations, these people turn to friends and relatives. Naturally, the friends and relatives deny the reality of the sensations, and eventually the sufferers conclude that the others are trying to hide the truth. They begin to reject all feedback, and some develop beliefs (delusions) that they are being persecuted (Perez-Alvarez et al., 2008; Bach, 2007). In short, according to this theory, people with schizophrenia take a "rational path to madness" (Zimbardo, 1976).

Researchers have established that people with schizophrenia do indeed experience sensory and perceptual problems. As you saw earlier, many of them have hallucinations, for example, and most have trouble keeping their attention focused. But researchers have yet to provide clear, direct support for the cognitive notion that misinterpretations of such sensory problems actually produce a syndrome of schizophrenia.

Sociocultural Views

Sociocultural theorists, recognizing that people with mental disorders are subject to a wide range of social and cultural forces, claim that *multicultural factors, social labeling,* and *family dysfunctioning* all contribute to schizophrenia. At the same time, research has yet to clarify what the precise causal relationships might be.

Multicultural Factors Rates of schizophrenia appear to differ between racial and ethnic groups (Singh & Kunar, 2010), particularly between African Americans and white Americans. As many as 2.1 percent of African Americans receive a diagnosis of schizophrenia, compared with 1.4 percent of white Americans (Lawson, 2008; Folsom

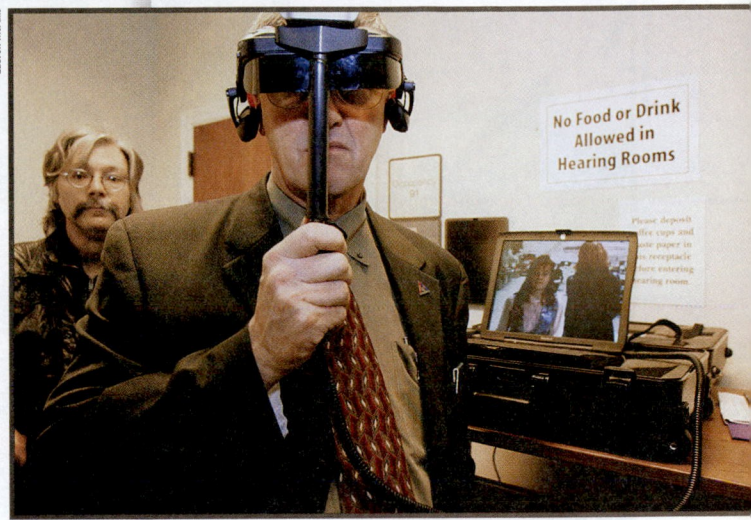

Virtual lobbying
This Washington state lawmaker wears the *Hallucinator Simulator,* a virtual-reality headset that produces disorienting sounds and visions similar to those experienced by people with psychosis. Mental health advocates convinced many of the state's legislators to wear the simulator prior to voting on a mental health funding bill, hoping that the experience would bring to life the needs of people with severe mental disorders.

Silvia Izquierdo/AP Photo

Coming together
Different countries and cultures each have their own way of viewing and interacting with schizophrenic people and other disturbed individuals. Here patients and members of the community come together and dance during the annual Carnival parade in front of the Psychiatric Institute in Rio de Janeiro, Brazil.

et al., 2006). Similarly, studies find that African American patients are more likely than white American patients to be assessed as having symptoms of hallucinations, paranoia, and suspiciousness (Mark et al., 2003; Trierweiler et al., 2000). And still other studies suggest that African Americans with schizophrenia are overrepresented in state hospitals (Lawson, 2008; Barnes, 2004). For example, in Tennessee's state hospitals 48 percent of those with a diagnosis of schizophrenia are African American, although only 16 percent of the state population is African American (Lawson, 2008; Barnes, 2004).

It is not clear why African Americans have a higher likelihood than white Americans of receiving this diagnosis. One possibility is that African Americans are more prone to develop the disorder. Another is that clinicians from majority groups are unintentionally biased in their diagnoses of African Americans or misread cultural differences as symptoms of schizophrenia (Lawson, 2008; Barnes, 2004).

Yet another explanation for the difference between African Americans and white Americans may lie in the economic sphere. On average, African Americans are more likely than white Americans to be poor, and, indeed, when economic differences are controlled for, the prevalence rates of schizophrenia become closer for the two racial groups. Consistent with the economic explanation is the finding that Hispanic Americans, who are, on average, also economically disadvantaged, appear to have a much higher likelihood of receiving a diagnosis of schizophrenia than white Americans, although their diagnostic rate is not as high as that of African Americans (Blow et al., 2004).

? *How might bias by diagnosticians contribute to race-linked and culture-linked differences in the diagnosis of schizophrenia?*

It also appears that schizophrenia differs from country to country in key ways. Although the overall prevalence of this disorder is stable—around 1 percent—in countries across the world, the *course* and *outcome* of the disorder may vary considerably. According to a 10-country study conducted by the World Health Organization (WHO), the 25 million schizophrenic patients who live in *developing* countries have better recovery rates than schizophrenic patients in Western and other *developed* countries (Vahia & Vahia, 2008; Jablensky, 2000). The WHO study followed the progress of 467 patients from developing countries (Colombia, India, and Nigeria) over a two-year period and compared it to that of 603 patients from developed countries (Czech Republic, Denmark, Ireland, Japan, Russia, the United Kingdom, and the United States). As you can see in Figure 14-4, during the course of a two-year observation period, the schizophrenic patients from the developing countries were more likely than those in the developed countries to recover from their disorder and less likely to experience continuous or episodic symptoms, display impaired social functioning, require heavy antipsychotic drugs, or require hospitalization.

Some clinical theorists believe that these differences partly reflect genetic differences from population to population. However, others argue that the psychosocial environments of developing countries tend to be more supportive and therapeutic than those of developed countries, leading to more favorable outcomes for people with schizophrenia (Vahia & Vahia, 2008; Jablensky, 2000). Developing countries, for example, seem to provide more family and social support to people with schizophrenia, make available more

Figure 14-4

Do the course and outcome of schizophrenia differ from country to country?
Yes, according to a World Health Organization study. In developing countries, patients with schizophrenia seem to recover more quickly, more often, and more completely than patients in developed countries. (Adapted from Jablensky, 2000.)

Patterns of Schizophrenia / Percentage of Patients Who Display Pattern

- Complete remission: Developing countries 63%, Developed countries 37%
- Continuous or episodic symptoms: Developing countries 36%, Developed countries 61%
- Receive heavy antipsychotic medications: Developing countries 16%, Developed countries 61%
- Undergo hospitalization: Developing countries 44%, Developed countries 92%
- Impaired social functioning: Developing countries 16%, Developed countries 42%

■ Developing countries
■ Developed countries

relatives and friends to help care for such individuals, and act less judgmental, critical, and hostile toward persons with schizophrenia. The Nigerian culture, for example, is generally more tolerant of the presence of voices than are Western cultures (Matsumoto & Juang, 2008).

Social Labeling

Many sociocultural theorists believe that the features of schizophrenia are influenced by the diagnosis itself (Modrow, 1992). In their opinion, society assigns the label "schizophrenic" to people who fail to conform to certain norms of behavior. Once the label is assigned, justified or not, it becomes a self-fulfilling prophecy that promotes the development of many schizophrenic symptoms. Certainly sufferers of schizophrenia have attested to the power that labeling has had on their lives:

Like any worthwhile endeavor, becoming a schizophrenic requires a long period of rigorous training. My training for this unique calling began in earnest when I was six years old. At that time my somewhat befuddled mother took me to the University of Washington to be examined by psychiatrists in order to find out what was wrong with me. These psychiatrists told my mother: "We don't know exactly what is wrong with your son, but whatever it is, it is very serious. We recommend that you have him committed immediately or else he will be completely psychotic within less than a year." My mother did not have me committed since she realized that such a course of action would be extremely damaging to me. But after that ominous prophecy my parents began to view and treat me as if I were either insane or at least in the process of becoming that way. Once, when my mother caught me playing with some vile muck I had mixed up—I was seven at the time—she gravely told me, "They have people put away in mental institutions for doing things like that." Fear was written all over my mother's face as she told me this. . . . The slightest odd behavior on my part was enough to send my parents into paroxysms of apprehension. My parents' apprehensions in turn made me fear that I was going insane. . . . My fate had been sealed not by my genes, but by the attitudes, beliefs, and expectations of my parents. . . . I find it extremely difficult to condemn my parents for behaving as if I were going insane when the psychiatric authorities told them that this was an absolute certainty.

(Modrow, 1992, pp. 1–2)

Like this man, people who are labeled schizophrenic may be viewed and treated as "crazy." Perhaps the expectations of other people subtly encourage the individuals to display psychotic behaviors. In turn, they come to accept their assigned role and learn to play it convincingly.

We have already seen the very real dangers of diagnostic labeling. In the famous Rosenhan (1973) study, discussed in Chapter 3, eight normal people presented themselves at various mental hospitals, complaining that they had been hearing voices utter the words "empty," "hollow," and "thud." They were quickly diagnosed as schizophrenic, and all eight were hospitalized. Although the pseudopatients then dropped all symptoms and behaved normally, they had great difficulty getting rid of the label and gaining release from the hospital.

Rosenhan's study is one of the most controversial in the field. What kinds of ethical, legal, and therapeutic concerns does it raise?

The pseudopatients reported that staff members were authoritarian in their behavior toward patients, spent limited time interacting with them, and responded curtly and uncaringly to questions. In fact, they generally treated patients as though they were invisible. "A nurse unbuttoned her uniform to adjust her brassiere in the presence of an entire ward of viewing men. One did not have the sense that she was being seductive. Rather, she didn't notice us." In addition, the pseudopatients described feeling powerless, bored, tired, and uninterested. The deceptive design and possible implications of this study have aroused the emotions of clinicians and researchers, pro and con. The investigation does demonstrate, however, that the label "schizophrenic" can itself have a negative effect not just on how people are viewed but also on how they themselves feel and behave.

Family Dysfunctioning

Theorists have suggested for years that certain patterns of family interactions can promote—or at least sustain—schizophrenic symptoms. One leading theory has focused on *double-bind communications*.

DO DOUBLE-BIND COMMUNICATIONS CAUSE SCHIZOPHRENIA? One of the best-known family theories of schizophrenia is the **double-bind hypothesis** (Visser, 2003; Bateson et al., 1956). It says that some parents repeatedly communicate pairs of mutually contradictory messages that place children in so-called double-bind situations: the children cannot avoid displeasing their parents because nothing they do is right. In theory, the symptoms of schizophrenia represent the child's attempt to deal with the double binds.

Double-bind messages typically consist of a verbal communication (the *primary communication*) and an accompanying—and contradictory—nonverbal communication (the *metacommunication*). If one person says to another, "I'm glad to see you," yet frowns and avoids eye contact, the two messages are incongruent. According to this theory, a child who is repeatedly exposed to double-bind communications will adopt a special life strategy for coping with them. One strategy, for example, is always to ignore primary communications and respond only to metacommunications: be suspicious of what anyone is saying, wonder about its true meaning, and focus on clues only in gestures or tones. People who increasingly respond to messages in this way may progress toward paranoid schizophrenia.

The double-bind hypothesis is closely related to the psychodynamic notion of a schizophrenogenic mother. When Fromm-Reichmann described schizophrenogenic mothers as overprotective and rejecting at the same time, she was in fact describing someone who is likely to send double-bind messages. Like the schizophrenogenic mother theory, the double-bind hypothesis has been popular in the clinical field over the years, but systematic investigations have not supported it (Chaika, 1990). In one study, clinicians analyzed letters written by parents to their children in the hospital (Ringuette & Kennedy, 1966). One group of parents had children with schizophrenia; the other had children with other disorders. On average, the letters of both groups of parents contained similar degrees of double-bind communication.

THE ROLE OF FAMILY STRESS Although the double-bind explanation and certain other family theories of schizophrenia have not received much research support, studies do suggest that schizophrenia, like a number of other mental disorders, is often linked to *family stress* (Bebbington & Kuipers, 2011; Roisko et al., 2011; Schiffman et al., 2002, 2001). Parents of people with this disorder often (1) display more conflict, (2) have greater difficulty communicating with one another, and (3) are more critical of and overinvolved with their children than other parents.

Family theorists have long recognized that some families are high in **expressed emotion**—that is, members frequently express criticism, disapproval, and hostility toward each other and intrude on one another's privacy. Individuals who are trying to recover from schizophrenia are almost four times more likely to relapse if they live with such a family than if they live with one low in expressed emotion (Bebbington & Kuipers, 2011; Ritsner & Gibel, 2007). Do such findings mean that family dysfunctioning helps cause and maintain schizophrenia? Not necessarily. It is also the case that individuals with schizophrenia greatly disrupt family life. In so doing, they themselves may help produce the family problems that clinicians and researchers continue to observe (McFarlane, 2011; Barrowclough & Lobban, 2008).

"Bad news—we're all out of our minds. You're going to have to be the lone healthy person in this family."

R. D. Laing's View One final sociocultural explanation of schizophrenia continues to have legions of supporters in the public at large despite the fact that it is controversial and largely untested by research. Famous clinical theorist R. D. Laing (1967, 1964, 1959) combined sociocultural principles with existential philosophy, arguing that schizophrenia is actually a *constructive* process in which people try to cure themselves of the confusion and unhappiness caused by their social environment. Laing believed that, left alone to complete this process, people with schizophrenia would indeed achieve a healthy outcome.

According to Laing's existential principles, human beings must be in touch with their *true* selves in order to give meaning to their lives. Unfortunately, said Laing, this is difficult to do in present-day society. Other people's expectations, demands, and standards require us to develop a *false* self rather than a true one. Moreover, Laing believed, some people—those who develop schizophrenia—have especially difficult obstacles to deal with. They experience a lifetime of confusing communications and demands from their families and community. Out of desperation they eventually undertake an inner search for strength and purpose. They withdraw from others and attend increasingly to their own inner cues in order to recover their wholeness as human beings. Laing argued that these people would emerge stronger and less confused if they were allowed to continue this inner search. Instead, as he saw it, society and its clinicians tell these individuals that they are sick, manipulate them into the role of patient, and subject them to treatments that actually produce further psychotic symptoms. In attempting to cure these people, he said, society dooms them to suspension in an inner world.

Most of today's theorists reject Laing's controversial notion that schizophrenia is constructive. For the most part, research simply has not addressed the issue. Laing's ideas do not lend themselves to empirical research, and the existentialists who embrace his view typically have little confidence in traditional research approaches (Burston, 2000). It is also worth noting that many persons with schizophrenia have themselves rejected the theory.

"Is there anybody out there?"
Schizophrenia is often depicted in positive terms in the arts. Pink Floyd's hugely popular album and movie *The Wall*, for example, follows the lead of R. D. Laing and portrays the disorder as a constructive inward search undertaken by some persons to cure themselves of confusion and unhappiness caused by society. Here former Pink Floyd band member Roger Waters tries to break down the societal wall during a recent concert.

> *"Schizophrenia's a reasonable reaction to an unreasonable society." It's great on paper. Poetic, noble, etc. But if you happen to be a schizophrenic, it's got some not-so-cheery implications. . . . One of R.D.'s worst sins is how blithely and misleadingly he glides over the suffering involved. . . . Pulling off a revolution and ushering in a new era in which truth and beauty reign triumphant seems unlikely when you're having trouble brushing your teeth or even walking.*
>
> *(Vonnegut, 1974, p. 91)*

PUTTING IT together

Psychological and Sociocultural Models Lag Behind

Schizophrenia—a bizarre and frightening disorder—was studied intensively throughout the twentieth century. Only since the discovery of antipsychotic drugs, however, have clinicians acquired any practical insight into its course and causes. Theories abounded before that time, but they typically failed to find empirical support and, in fact, contributed to inaccurate stereotyping of people with schizophrenia and their parents.

As with most other psychological disorders, clinical theorists now believe that schizophrenia is probably caused by a combination of factors (Riley & Kendler, 2011). At the same time, researchers have been far more successful in identifying the biological

Delusions of grandeur

In 1892, an artist who was a patient at a mental hospital claimed credit for this painting, *Self-Portrait as Christ*. Although few people with schizophrenia have his artistic skill, a number display similar delusions of grandeur.

influences than the psychological and sociocultural ones. While biological investigations have closed in on specific genes, abnormalities in brain biochemistry and structure, and even viral infections, most of the psychological and sociocultural research has been able to cite only general factors, such as the roles of family conflict and diagnostic labeling. Clearly, researchers must identify psychological and sociocultural factors with greater precision if we are to gain a full understanding of the disorder. The exciting progress now being made in the biological study of schizophrenia is indeed impressive, but it must not blind us to the significant gaps, uncertainties, and confusions that continue to obscure our view.

Summing Up

- **THE CLINICAL PICTURE OF SCHIZOPHRENIA** *Schizophrenia* is a disorder in which personal, social, and occupational functioning deteriorate as a result of disturbed thought processes, distorted perceptions, unusual emotions, and motor abnormalities. Approximately 1 percent of the world's population suffers from this disorder. *p. 427*

- **SYMPTOMS OF SCHIZOPHRENIA** The symptoms of schizophrenia fall into three groupings. *Positive symptoms* include *delusions*, certain *formal thought disorders*, *hallucinations* and other *disturbances in perception and attention*, and *inappropriate affect*. *Negative symptoms* include *poverty of speech, restricted affect, loss of volition*, and *social withdrawal*. The disorder may also include *psychomotor symptoms*, collectively called *catatonia* in their extreme form. Schizophrenia usually emerges during late adolescence or early adulthood and tends to progress through three phases: *prodromal, active,* and *residual*. *pp. 427–433*

- **DIAGNOSING SCHIZOPHRENIA** DSM-5 calls for a disgnosis of schizophrenia after symptoms of the disorder continue for *six months* or more. This diagnosis also requires that individuals display active symptoms for at least one of those months and show a deterioration from previous levels of functioning. *Type I schizophrenia* is often distinguished from *Type II schizophrenia*. Patients with the former type seem to be dominated by positive symptoms, and those with the latter type seem to display more negative ones. *pp. 433–434*

- **BIOLOGICAL EXPLANATIONS** The biological explanations of schizophrenia point to genetic, biochemical, structural, and viral causes. The *genetic* view is supported by studies of relatives, twins, adoptees, and genetic linkage and by molecular biology. The leading *biochemical* explanation holds that the brains of people with schizophrenia, particularly those with largely positive symptoms, may contain an unusually large number of *dopamine* receptors, especially *D-2 receptors,* leading to excessive dopamine activity. Brain-imaging techniques have also detected *abnormal brain structures* in many people with schizophrenia, particularly those with a number of negative symptoms, including *enlarged ventricles* and *abnormal blood flow* in certain parts of the brain. Finally, some researchers believe that schizophrenia is related to a *virus* that settles in the fetus and perhaps lies quiet until adolescence or young adulthood. *pp. 434–440*

- **PSYCHOLOGICAL EXPLANATIONS** The leading psychological explanations for schizophrenia come from the psychodynamic, behavioral, and cognitive models. In influential *psychodynamic* explanations, Freud held that schizophrenia involves *regression* to a state of primary narcissism and efforts to *restore* ego control, and Fromm-Reichmann proposed that *schizophrenogenic mothers* help produce this disorder. Contemporary psychodynamic theorists, however, ascribe the disorder to a combination of biological and psychodynamic factors. *Behaviorists* suggest that people with schizophrenia fail to learn to attend to appropriate social cues. And *cognitive*

BETWEEN THE LINES

The Wrong Split

Despite popular misconceptions, people with schizophrenia do not display a "split" or multiple personality. That pattern is indicative of dissociative identity disorder. ‹‹

theorists contend that when people with schizophrenia try to understand their strange biological sensations, they develop delusional thinking. None of these theories have received compelling research support. *pp. 440–441*

- ■ **SOCIOCULTURAL EXPLANATIONS** One sociocultural explanation holds that *multicultural* differences may influence the prevalence and character of schizophrenia, as well as recovery from this disorder, both within the United States and across the world. Another sociocultural explanation argues that society expects persons who are *labeled* as having schizophrenia to behave in certain ways and that these expectations actually lead to further symptoms. Still other sociocultural theorists point to *family dysfunctioning* as a cause of schizophrenia, including such features as *double-bind communications*. Such specific family features have not been implicated by research, although general *family stress and conflict* have repeatedly been linked to schizophrenia. Finally, R. D. Laing has presented schizophrenia as a *constructive* process by which people try to cure themselves of the confusion and unhappiness caused by their society and family. *pp. 441–445*

PsychPortal

Visit **PsychPortal**
www.yourpsychportal.com
to access the e-book, videocases and other case materials and activities, and study aids, including flashcards, crossword puzzles, quizzes, FAQs, and research exercises.

TREATMENTS FOR SCHIZOPHRENIA AND OTHER SEVERE MENTAL DISORDERS

*D*uring [Cathy's] second year in college . . . her emotional troubles worsened. . . .

Her thoughts about sex gradually bloomed into a fantasy about Steve Martin, the comedian. Unable to sleep through the night, she would awaken at four a.m. and go for walks, and at times, it seemed that Steve Martin was there on campus, stalking her. "I thought he was in love with me and was running through the bushes just out of sight," she says. "He was looking for me."

. . . The breaking point came one evening when she threw a glass object against the wall in her dorm room. "I didn't clean it up, but instead was walking around in it. I was, you know, taking the glass out of my feet. I was completely out of my mind." . . . She was . . . informed that she suffered from a chemical imbalance in the brain, and put on Haldol and lithium.

For the next sixteen years, Cathy cycled in and out of hospitals. She "hated the meds"—Haldol stiffened her muscles and caused her to drool, while the lithium made her depressed—and often she would abruptly stop taking them. . . . The problem was that off the drugs, she would "start to decompensate and become disorganized."

In early 1994, she was hospitalized for the fifteenth time. She was seen as chronically mentally ill, occasionally heard voices now, . . . and was on a cocktail of drugs: Haldol, Ativan, Tegretol, Halcion, and Cogentin, the last drug an antidote to Haldol's nasty side effects. But after she was released that spring, a psychiatrist told her to try Risperdal, a new antipsychotic that had just been approved by the FDA. "Three weeks later, my mind was much clearer," she says. "The voices were going away. I got off the other meds and took only this one drug. I got better. I could start to plan. I wasn't talking to the devil anymore. Jesus and God weren't battling it out in my head." Her father put it this way: "Cathy is back." . . .

. . . She went back to school and earned a degree in radio, film, and television. . . . In 1998, she began dating the man she lives with today. . . . In 2005, she took a parttime job. . . . Still, she remains on SSDI (Social Security Disability Insurance)—"I am a kept woman," she jokes—and although there are many reasons for that, she believes that Risperdal, the very drug that has helped her so much, nevertheless has proven to be a barrier to full-time work. Although she is usually energetic by the early afternoon, Risperdal makes her so sleepy that she has trouble getting up in the morning. The other problem is that she has always had trouble getting along with other people, and Risperdal exacerbates that problem, she says. . . . "The drugs may take care of aggression and anxiety and some paranoia, those sorts of symptoms, but they don't help with the empathy that helps you get along with people."

Risperdal has also taken a physical toll. . . . She has . . . developed some of the metabolic problems, such as high cholesterol, that the atypical antipsychotics regularly cause. "I can go toe-to-toe with an old lady with a recital of my physical problems," she says. "My feet, my bladder, my heart, my sinuses, the weight gain—I have it all." . . . But she can't do well without Risperdal. . . .

Such has been her life's course on medications. Sixteen terrible years, followed by fourteen pretty good years on Risperdal. She believes that this drug is essential to her mental health today, and indeed, she could be seen as a local poster child for promoting the wonders of that drug. Still, if you look at the long-term course of her illness . . . you have to ask: Is hers a story of a life made better by our drug-based . . . care for mental disorders, or a story of a life made worse? . . .

Cathy believes that this is a question that psychiatrists never contemplate.

"They don't have any sense about how these drugs affect you over the long term. They just try to stabilize you for the moment, and look to manage you from week to week, month to month. That's all they ever think about."

(Whitaker, 2010)

In many ways, Cathy's clumsy journey is typical of hundreds of thousands of people with schizophrenia and other severe mental disorders. To be sure, there are other patients whose efforts to overcome such disorders go more smoothly. And, at the other end of the spectrum, there are many whose struggles against severe mental dysfunctioning never comes close to Cathy's level of success. But in between, there are the Cathys.

This is today's treatment picture for schizophrenia and other severe mental disorders. It is a picture marked by miraculous triumph for some, modest success for others, and heartbreaking failure for still others. It is a picture typically characterized by medications, medication-linked health problems, compromised lifestyles, and a mixture of hope and frustration. All that said, today's treatment outlook for schizophrenia and other severe mental disorders is vastly superior to that of past years. In fact, for much of human history, persons with such disorders were considered beyond help. Few returned to any semblance of normal or functional living. Indeed, few returned home from the institutions to which they were sent.

Schizophrenia is still extremely difficult to treat, but clinicians are much more successful today than they were in the past. And, indeed, much of the credit goes to *antipsychotic drugs*—imperfect, troubling, and even dangerous though they may be. These medications help many people with schizophrenia and other psychotic disorders to think clearly and profit from psychotherapies that previously would have had little effect on them (Miller et al., 2012).

As you will see, each of the models offers treatments for schizophrenia, and all have been influential at one time or another. However, a mere description of the different approaches cannot convey the pain suffered by the victims of this disorder as the various methods of treatment evolved over the years. Indeed, people with schizophrenia have been subjected to more mistreatment and indifference than perhaps any other group of patients. Even today, at least half of them do not receive adequate care (Burns & Drake, 2011; Gill, 2010). To better convey the plight of people with schizophrenia, this chapter will depart from the usual format and discuss the treatments from a historical perspective.

As you saw in Chapter 14, throughout much of the twentieth century the label "schizophrenia" was assigned to most people with psychosis. However, clinical theorists now realize that many people with psychotic symptoms are instead manifesting a severe form of bipolar disorder or major depressive disorder and that such individuals were in past times inaccurately given a diagnosis of schizophrenia (Lake, 2012). Thus, our discussions of past treatments for schizophrenia, particularly the failures of institutional care, are as applicable to those other severe mental disorders as they are to schizophrenia. Moreover, our discussions about current approaches to schizophrenia, such as the community mental health movement, often apply to other severe mental disorders as well.

Institutional Care in the Past

For more than half of the twentieth century, most people diagnosed with schizophrenia were *institutionalized* in a public mental hospital. Because patients with this disorder failed to respond to traditional therapies, the primary goals of these establishments were to restrain them and give them food, shelter, and clothing. Patients rarely saw therapists and generally were neglected. Many were abused. Oddly enough, this state of affairs unfolded in an atmosphere of good intentions.

•**state hospitals**•Public mental hospitals in the United States, run by the individual states.

As you read in Chapter 1, the move toward institutionalization in hospitals began in 1793 when French physician Philippe Pinel "unchained the insane" at La Bicêtre asylum and began the practice of "moral treatment." For the first time in centuries, patients with severe disturbances were viewed as human beings who should be cared for with sympathy and kindness. As Pinel's ideas spread throughout Europe and the United States, they led to the creation of large mental hospitals rather than asylums to care for those with severe mental disorders (Goshen, 1967).

These new mental hospitals, typically located in isolated areas where land and labor were cheap, were meant to protect patients from the stresses of daily life and offer them a healthful psychological environment in which they could work closely with therapists (Grob, 1966). States throughout the United States were even required by law to establish public mental institutions, **state hospitals,** for patients who could not afford private ones.

Eventually, however, the state hospital system encountered serious problems. Between 1845 and 1955 nearly 300 state hospitals opened in the United States, and the number of hospitalized patients on any given day rose from 2,000 in 1845 to nearly 600,000 in 1955. During this expansion, wards became overcrowded, admissions kept rising, and state funding was unable to keep up. Too many aspects of treatment became the responsibility of nurses and attendants, whose knowledge and experience at that time were limited.

The priorities of the public mental hospitals, and the quality of care they provided, changed over those 110 years. In the face of overcrowding and understaffing, the emphasis shifted from giving humanitarian care to keeping order. In a throwback to the asylum period, difficult patients were restrained, isolated, and punished; individual attention disappeared. Patients were transferred to *back wards,* or chronic wards, if they failed to improve quickly (Bloom, 1984). Most of the patients on these wards suffered from schizophrenia (Hafner & an der Heiden, 1988). The back wards were in fact human warehouses filled with hopelessness. Staff members relied on straitjackets and handcuffs to deal with difficult patients. More "advanced" forms of treatment included medical approaches such as *lobotomy* (see *PsychWatch* on page 453).

? **Why have people with schizophrenia so often been victims of horrific treatments such as overcrowded wards, lobotomy, and, later, deinstitutionalization?**

A graphic reminder

During the rise of the state hospital system, tens of thousands of patients with severe mental disorders were abandoned by their families and spent the rest of their lives in the back wards of the public mental institutions. We are reminded of their tragic situation by the numerous brass urns filled with unclaimed ashes currently stored in a building at Oregon State Hospital.

Institutional life

In a scene reminiscent of public mental hospitals in the United States during the first half of the twentieth century, these patients spend their days crowded together on a hospital ward in central Shanghai. Because of a shortage of therapists, only a small fraction of Chinese people with psychological disorders receive proper professional care today.

Many patients not only failed to improve under these conditions but also developed additional symptoms, apparently as a result of institutionalization itself. The most common pattern of decline was called the *social breakdown syndrome:* extreme withdrawal, anger, physical aggressiveness, and loss of interest in personal appearance and functioning (Oshima et al., 2005). Often more troublesome than patients' original symptoms, this new syndrome made it impossible for them to return to society even if they somehow recovered from the symptoms that had first brought them to the hospital.

Institutional Care Takes a Turn for the Better

In the 1950s, clinicians developed two institutional approaches that finally brought some hope to patients who had lived in institutions for years: *milieu therapy,* based on humanistic principles, and the *token economy program,* based on behavioral principles. These approaches particularly helped improve the personal care and self-image of patients, problem areas that had been worsened by institutionalization. The approaches were soon adapted by many institutions and are now standard features of institutional care.

Milieu Therapy

In the opinion of humanistic theorists, institutionalized patients deteriorate because they are deprived of opportunities to exercise independence, responsibility, and positive self-regard and to engage in meaningful activities. Thus the premise of **milieu therapy** is that institutions cannot be of help to patients unless they can somehow create a social climate, or milieu, that promotes productive activity, self-respect, and individual responsibility.

The pioneer of this approach was Maxwell Jones, a London psychiatrist who in 1953 converted a ward of patients with various psychological disorders into a therapeutic community. The patients were referred to as "residents" and were regarded as capable of running their own lives and making their own decisions. They participated in community government, working with staff members to establish rules and determine sanctions. In fact, patients and staff members alike were valued as important therapeutic agents. The atmosphere was one of mutual respect, support, and openness. Patients could also take on special projects, jobs, and recreational activities. In short, their daily schedule was designed to resemble life outside the hospital.

Milieu-style programs have since been set up in institutions throughout the Western world. The programs vary from setting to setting, but at a minimum staff members try to encourage interactions (especially group interactions) between patients and staff, to keep patients active, and to raise patients' expectations of what they can accomplish.

Research over the years has shown that patients with schizophrenia and other severe mental disorders in milieu hospital programs often improve and that they leave the hospital at higher rates than patients in programs offering primarily custodial care (Paul, 2000; Paul & Lentz, 1977). Many of these persons remain impaired, however, and must live in sheltered settings after their release. Despite its limitations, milieu therapy continues to be practiced in many institutions, often combined with other hospital approaches (Gunter, 2005). Moreover, you will see later in this chapter that many of today's halfway houses and other community programs for individuals with severe mental disorders are run in accordance with the same principles of resident self-government and work schedules that have proved effective in hospital milieu programs.

The Token Economy

In the 1950s behaviorists had little status in mental institutions and were permitted to work only with patients whose problems seemed hopeless. Among the "hopeless" were patients diagnosed with schizophrenia. Through years of experimentation, behaviorists discovered that the systematic application of *operant conditioning* techniques on hospital wards could help change the behaviors of these individuals (Ayllon, 1963; Ayllon

•**milieu therapy**•A humanistic approach to institutional treatment based on the belief that institutions can help patients recover by creating a climate that promotes self-respect, responsible behavior, and meaningful activity.

•**token economy program**•A behavioral program in which a person's desirable behaviors are reinforced systematically throughout the day by the awarding of tokens that can be exchanged for goods or privileges.

PsychWatch

Lobotomy: How Could It Happen?

In 1949 a *New York Times* article reported on a medical procedure that appeared to offer hope to sufferers of severe mental disorders:

Hypochondriacs no longer thought they were going to die, would-be suicides found life acceptable, sufferers from persecution complex forgot the machinations of imaginary conspirators. Prefrontal lobotomy, as the operation is called, was made possible by the localization of fears, hates, and instincts [in the prefrontal cortex of the brain]. It is fitting, then, that the Nobel Prize in medicine should be shared by Hess and Moniz. Surgeons now think no more of operations on the brain than they do of removing an appendix.

We now know that the lobotomy was hardly a miracle treatment. Far from "curing" people with mental disorders, the procedure left thousands upon thousands extremely withdrawn, subdued, and even stuporous. The first lobotomy was performed by Portuguese neuropsychiatrist Egas Moniz in 1935 (Whitaker, 2010; Tierney, 2000). His particular procedure, called a *prefrontal leukotomy,* consisted of drilling two holes in either side of the skull and inserting an instrument resembling an icepick into the brain tissue to cut or destroy nerve fibers. Moniz believed that severe abnormal thinking could be changed by cutting the nerve pathways that carried such thoughts from one part of the brain to another. In the 1940s Walter Freeman and his surgical partner, James Watts, developed a second kind of psychosurgery called the *transorbital lobotomy,* in which the surgeon inserted

a needle into the brain through the eye socket and rotated it in order to destroy the brain tissue.

Altogether, an estimated 50,000 people in the United States alone received lobotomies (Johnson, 2005). Why was the procedure so enthusiastically accepted by the medical community in the 1940s and 1950s? Neuroscientist Elliot Valenstein (1986) points first to the extreme over-crowding in mental hospitals at the time. This crowding was making it difficult to maintain decent standards in the hospitals. Valenstein also points to the personalities of the inventors of the procedure as important factors. Although these individuals were gifted and dedicated physicians, Valenstein also believes that their professional ambi-

Lessons in psychosurgery Neuropsychiatrist Walter Freeman performs a lobotomy in 1949 before a group of interested onlookers by inserting a needle through a patient's eye socket into the brain.

Bettmann Archives

tions led them to move too quickly and boldly in applying the procedure. Indeed, in 1949 Moniz was awarded the Nobel Prize for his work.

The prestige of Moniz and Freeman were so great and the field of neurology was so small that their procedures drew little criticism. Physicians may also have been misled by the seemingly positive findings of early studies of the lobotomy, which, as it turned out, were not based on sound methodology.

By the 1950s, better studies revealed that in addition to having a fatality rate of 1.5 to 6 percent, lobotomies could cause serious problems such as brain seizures, huge weight gain, loss of motor coordination, partial paralysis, incontinence, endocrine malfunctions, and very poor intellectual and emotional responsiveness. Finally, the discovery of effective antipsychotic drugs put an end to this inhumane treatment for mental disorders (Krack et al., 2010).

Today's psychosurgical procedures are greatly refined and hardly resemble the lobotomies of 60 years back. Moreover, the procedures are considered experimental and are used only as a last resort in the most severe cases of disorders such as OCD and depression (Krack et al., 2010; McNeely et al., 2008). Even so, many professionals believe that any kind of surgery that destroys brain tissue is inappropriate and perhaps unethical and that it keeps alive one of the clinical field's most shameful and ill-advised efforts at cure.

& Michael, 1959). Programs that apply these techniques are called **token economy programs.**

In token economies patients are rewarded when they behave acceptably and are not rewarded when they behave unacceptably. The immediate rewards for acceptable behavior are often tokens that can later be exchanged for food, cigarettes, hospital privileges, and other desirable items, thus creating a "token economy." Acceptable behaviors likely to be targeted include caring for oneself and for one's possessions (making the bed, getting dressed), going to a work program, speaking normally, following ward rules, and showing self-control.

How Effective Are Token Economy Programs?
Researchers have found that token economies do help reduce psychotic and related behaviors (Swartz et al., 2012; Dickerson et al., 2005). In one early program, Gordon Paul and Robert Lentz (1977) set up a hospital token economy for 28 patients diagnosed with chronic schizophrenia, most of whom improved greatly. After four and a half years, 98 percent of the patients had been released, mostly to sheltered-care facilities, compared with 71 percent of patients treated in a milieu program and 45 percent of patients who received custodial care only.

What Are the Limitations of Token Economies?
Some clinicians have voiced reservations about the claims made for token economy programs. One problem is that many token economy studies, unlike Paul and Lentz's, are uncontrolled. When administrators set up a token economy, they usually bring all ward patients into the program rather than dividing the ward into a token economy group and a control group. As a result, patients' improvements can be compared only with their own past behaviors—a comparison that may be misleading. Changes in the physical setting, for example, or a general increase in staff attention could be causing patients' improvement, rather than the token economy.

Many clinicians have also raised ethical and legal concerns. If token economy programs are to be effective, administrators need to control the important rewards in a patient's life, perhaps including such basic ones as food and a comfortable bed. But aren't there some things in life to which all human beings are entitled? Court decisions have now ruled that patients do indeed have certain basic rights that clinicians cannot violate, regardless of the positive goals of a treatment program. They have a right to food, storage space, and furniture, as well as freedom of movement.

Still other clinicians have questioned the quality of the improvements made under token economy programs. Are behaviorists changing a patient's psychotic thoughts and perceptions or simply improving the patient's ability to imitate normal behavior? This issue is illustrated by the case of a middle-aged man named John, who had the delusion that he was the U.S. government (Comer, 1973). Whenever he spoke, he spoke as the government. "We are happy to see you. . . . We need people like you in our service. . . . We are carrying out our activities in John's body." When John's hospital ward was converted into a token economy, the staff members targeted his delusional statements and required him to identify himself properly to earn tokens. If he called himself John, he received tokens; if he insisted on describing himself as the government, he received nothing. After a few months on the token economy program, John stopped referring to himself as the government. When asked his name, he would say, "John." Although staff members were understandably pleased with his improvement, John himself had a different view of the situation. In a private discussion he said:

> We're tired of it. Every damn time we want a cigarette, we have to go through their bullshit. "What's your name? . . . Who wants the cigarette? . . . Where is the government?" Today, we were desperate for a smoke and went to Simpson, the damn nurse, and she made us do her bidding. "Tell me your name if you want a cigarette. What's your name?" Of course, we said, "John." We needed the cigarettes. If we told her the truth, no cigarettes. But we don't have time for this nonsense. We've got business to do, international business, laws to change, people to recruit. And these people keep playing their games.
>
> *(Comer, 1973)*

Critics of the behavioral approach would argue that John was still delusional and therefore as psychotic as before. Behaviorists, however, would argue that at the very least,

John's judgment about the consequences of his behavior had improved. Learning to keep his delusion to himself might even be a step toward changing his private thinking.

Last, it has often been difficult for patients to make a satisfactory transition from hospital token economy programs to community living. In an environment where rewards are contingent on proper conduct, proper conduct becomes contingent on continued rewards. Some patients who find that the real world doesn't reward them so concretely abandon their newly acquired behaviors.

Nevertheless, token economies have had a most important effect on the treatment of people with schizophrenia and other severe mental disorders. They were among the first hospital treatments that actually changed psychotic symptoms and got chronic patients moving again. These programs are no longer as popular as they once were, but they are still used in many mental hospitals, usually along with medication, and in many community residences as well (Kopelowicz, Liberman, & Zarate, 2008). The approach has also been applied to other clinical problems, including intellectual developmental disorder, delinquency, and hyperactivity, as well as in other fields, such as education and business (Spiegler & Guevremont, 2003).

Antipsychotic Drugs

Milieu therapy and token economy programs helped improve the gloomy outlook for patients diagnosed with schizophrenia, but it was the discovery of **antipsychotic drugs** in the 1950s that truly revolutionized treatment for this disorder. These drugs eliminate many of its symptoms and today are almost always a part of treatment (Barnes & Marder, 2011; Farmer, 2010).

The discovery of antipsychotic medications dates back to the 1940s, when researchers developed the first *antihistamine drugs* to combat allergies. The French surgeon Henri Laborit soon discovered that one group of antihistamines, *phenothiazines,* could also be used to help calm patients about to undergo surgery. After experimenting with several

•**antipsychotic drugs**•Drugs that help correct grossly confused or distorted thinking.

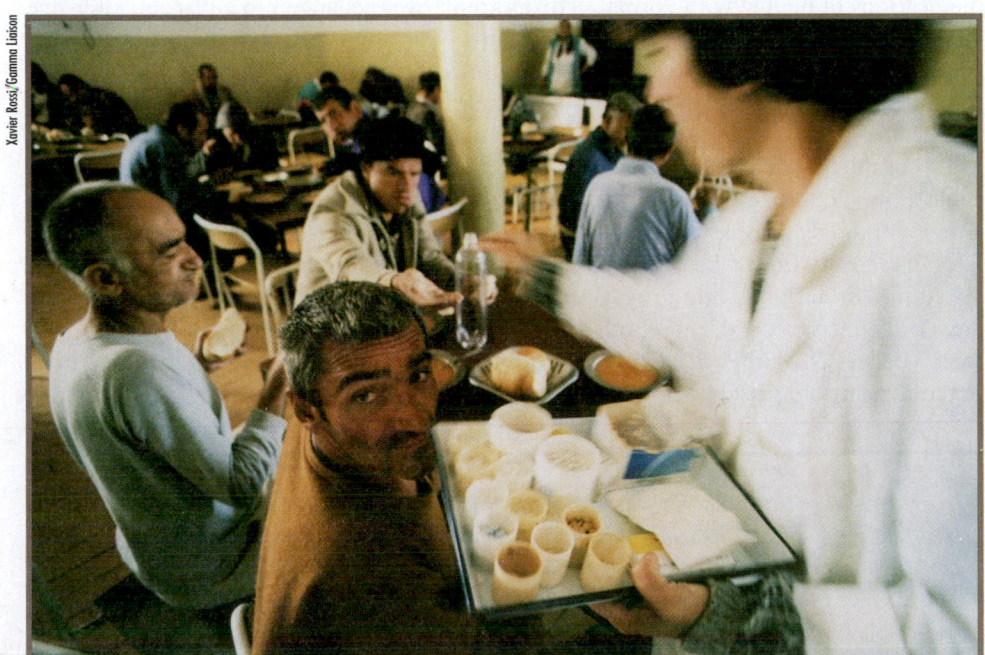

Xavier Rossi/Gamma Liaison

The drug revolution
Since the 1950s medications have become the center of treatment for patients with schizophrenia and other severe mental disorders. The medications have resulted in shorter hospitalizations that last weeks rather than years.

•**neuroleptic drugs**•Conventional antipsychotic drugs, so called because they often produce undesired effects similar to the symptoms of neurological disorders.

•**extrapyramidal effects**•Unwanted movements, such as severe shaking, bizarre-looking grimaces, twisting of the body, and extreme restlessness, sometimes produced by conventional antipsychotic drugs.

•**tardive dyskinesia**•Extrapyramidal effects that appear in some patients after they have taken conventional antipsychotic drugs for an extended time.

phenothiazine antihistamines and becoming most impressed with one called *chlorpromazine,* Laborit reported, "It provokes not any loss of consciousness, not any change in the patient's mentality but a slight tendency to sleep and above all 'disinterest' for all that goes on around him."

Laborit suspected that chlorpromazine might also have a calming effect on persons with severe psychological disorders. Psychiatrists Jean Delay and Pierre Deniker (1952) therefore tested the drug on six patients with psychotic symptoms and did indeed observe a sharp reduction in their symptoms. In 1954, chlorpromazine was approved for sale in the United States as an antipsychotic drug under the trade name Thorazine.

Since the discovery of the phenothiazines, other kinds of antipsychotic drugs have been developed. The ones developed throughout the 1960s, 1970s, and 1980s are now referred to as *"conventional" antipsychotic drugs* in order to distinguish them from the *"atypical" antipsychotics* (also called *"second generation" antipsychotic drugs*) that have been developed in recent years. The conventional drugs are also known as **neuroleptic drugs** because they often produce undesired movement effects similar to the symptoms of neurological diseases. Among the best known conventional drugs are *thioridazine* (Mellaril), *fluphenazine* (Prolixin), *trifluoperazine* (Stelazine), and *haloperidol* (Haldol). As you saw in Chapter 14, antipsychotic drugs reduce psychotic symptoms at least in part by blocking excessive activity of the neurotransmitter *dopamine,* particularly at the brain's dopamine D-2 receptors (Remington et al., 2011; Seeman, 2011).

How Effective Are Antipsychotic Drugs?

Research has shown that antipsychotic drugs reduce symptoms in at least 65 percent of patients diagnosed with schizophrenia (Ellenbroek, 2011; Geddes et al., 2011; Julien et al., 2011). Moreover, in direct comparisons the drugs appear to be a more effective treatment for schizophrenia than any of the other approaches used alone, such as psychotherapy, milieu therapy, or electroconvulsive therapy.

In most cases, the drugs produce the maximum level of improvement within the first six months of treatment; however, symptoms may return if patients stop taking the drugs too soon (Barnes & Marder, 2011; Kutscher, 2008). In one study, when the antipsychotic medications of people with chronic schizophrenia were changed to a placebo after five years, 75 percent of the patients relapsed within a year, compared to 33 percent of similar patients who continued to receive medication (Sampath et al., 1992).

As you read in Chapter 14, antipsychotic drugs, particularly the conventional ones, reduce the positive symptoms of schizophrenia, such as hallucinations and delusions, more completely, or at least more quickly, than the negative symptoms, such as restricted affect, poverty of speech, and loss of volition (Stroup et al., 2012; Blanchard et al., 2011). Correspondingly, people who display largely positive symptoms generally have better rates of recovery from schizophrenia than those with predominantly negative symptoms.

Although antipsychotic drugs are now widely accepted, patients often dislike the powerful effects of the drugs—both intended and unintended—and some refuse to take them (Barnes & Marder, 2011). But like Edward Snow, a writer who overcame schizophrenia, many are greatly helped by the medications.

BETWEEN THE LINES

Perinatal Impact

Some babies born to mothers who take antipsychotic drugs during their third trimester of pregnancy display abnormal muscle movements and withdrawal symptoms, such as increased or decreased muscle tone, tremors, breathing difficulty, or sleeping difficulty. The symptoms often subside on their own within hours or days; some of the newborns, however, require longer hospital stays. ‹‹

(FDA, 2011)

In my case it was necessary to come to terms with a specified drug program. I am a legalized addict. My dose: 100 milligrams of Thorazine and 60 milligrams of Stelazine daily. I don't feel this dope at all, but I have been told it is strong enough to flatten a normal person. It keeps me—as the doctors agree—sane and in good spirits. Without the brain candy, as I call it, I would go—zoom—right back into the bin. I've made the institution scene enough already to be familiar with what it's like and to know I don't want to go back.

(Snow, 1976)

The Unwanted Effects of Conventional Antipsychotic Drugs

In addition to reducing psychotic symptoms, the conventional antipsychotic drugs sometimes produce disturbing movement problems (Stroup et al., 2012; Geddes et al., 2011; Julien et al., 2011). These effects are called **extrapyramidal effects** because they appear to be caused by the drugs' impact on the extrapyramidal areas of the brain, areas that help control motor activity. These undesired effects include *Parkinsonian and related symptoms, neuroleptic malignant syndrome,* and *tardive dyskinesia.*

Parkinsonian and Related Symptoms
The most common extrapyramidal effects are *Parkinsonian symptoms,* reactions that closely resemble the features of the neurological disorder Parkinson's disease. At least half of patients on conventional antipsychotic drugs experience muscle tremors and muscle rigidity at some point in their treatment; they may shake, move slowly, shuffle their feet, and show little facial expression (Geddes et al., 2011; Haddad & Mattay, 2011). Some also display related symptoms such as movements of the face, neck, tongue, and back; and a number experience great restlessness and discomfort in the limbs, which causes individuals to move their arms and legs continually in search of relief.

The Parkinsonian and related symptoms seem to be the result of medication-induced reductions of dopamine activity in the *basal ganglia* and the *substantia nigra,* parts of the brain that coordinate movement and posture (Julien et al., 2011). In most cases, the symptoms can be reversed if an anti-Parkinsonian drug is taken along with the antipsychotic drug. Alternatively, clinicians may have to reduce the dose of the antipsychotic drug or stop it altogether.

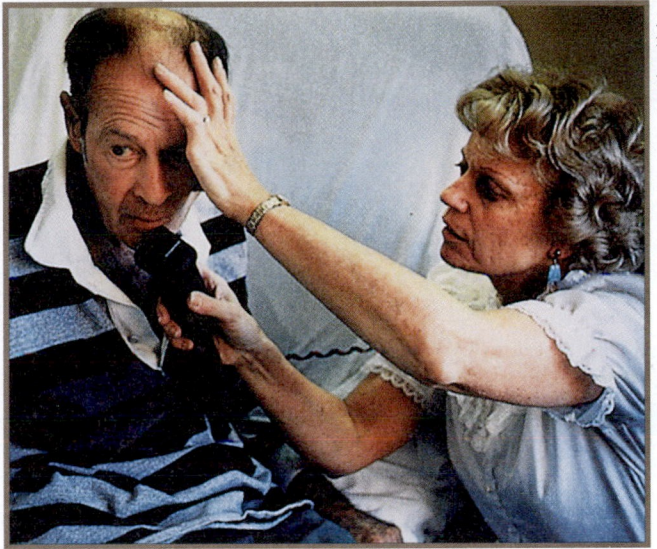

Unwanted effects
This man has a severe case of Parkinson's disease, a disorder caused by low dopamine activity, and his muscle tremors prevent him from shaving himself. The conventional antipsychotic drugs often produce similar Parkinsonian symptoms.

Neuroleptic Malignant Syndrome
In as many as 1 percent of patients, particularly elderly ones, conventional antipsychotic drugs produce *neuroleptic malignant syndrome,* a severe, potentially fatal reaction consisting of muscle rigidity, fever, altered consciousness, and improper functioning of the autonomic nervous system (Haddad & Mattay, 2011). As soon as the syndrome is recognized, drug use is discontinued and each neuroleptic symptom is treated medically. In addition, individuals may be given dopamine-enhancing drugs.

Tardive Dyskinesia
Whereas most undesired drug effects appear within days or weeks, a reaction called **tardive dyskinesia** (meaning "late-appearing movement disorder") does not usually unfold until after a person has taken conventional antipsychotic drugs for more than a year. Sometimes it does not even appear until after the medications are stopped (Julien et al., 2011). This syndrome may include involuntary writhing or ticlike movements of the tongue, mouth, face, or whole body; involuntary chewing, sucking, and lip smacking; and jerky movements of the arms, legs, or entire body. It is sometimes accompanied by memory difficulties (Haddad & Mattay, 2011).

Most cases of tardive dyskinesia are mild and involve a single symptom, such as tongue flicking; however, some are severe and include such features as continual rocking back and forth, irregular breathing, and grotesque twisting of the face and body. It is believed that more than 10 percent of the people who take conventional antipsychotic drugs for an extended time develop tardive dyskinesia to some degree, and the longer the drugs are taken, the greater the risk becomes (Geddes et al., 2011; Julien et al., 2011). Patients over 50 years of age seem to be at greater risk.

Tardive dyskinesia can be difficult, sometimes impossible, to eliminate (Combs et al., 2008). If it is discovered early and the conventional drugs are stopped immediately, it eventually disappears in most cases (APA, 2000). Early detection, however, is elusive because some of the symptoms are similar to psychotic symptoms. Clinicians may easily overlook them, continue to administer the drugs, and unintentionally create a more

•agranulocytosis• A life-threatening reduction in white blood cells. This condition is sometimes produced by the atypical antipsychotic drug *clozapine*.

serious case of tardive dyskinesia. Researchers do not fully understand why conventional antipsychotic drugs cause tardive dyskinesia; however, they suspect that, once again, the problem is related to the drugs' effect on dopamine receptors in the basal ganglia and substantia nigra (Julien et al., 2011).

How Should Conventional Antipsychotic Drugs Be Prescribed? Today clinicians are more knowledgeable and more cautious about prescribing conventional antipsychotic drugs than they were in the past. Previously, when patients did not improve with such a drug, their clinicians would keep increasing the dose; today a clinician will typically stop the drug (Leucht, Correll, & Kane, 2011). Similarly, today's clinicians try to prescribe the lowest effective dose for each patient and to gradually reduce or even stop medication weeks or months after the patient begins functioning normally (Barnes & Marder, 2011).

Why did psychiatrists of the past keep administering high dosages of antipsychotic drugs to adversely affected patients?

Newer Antipsychotic Drugs

Chapter 14 noted that "atypical" antipsychotic drugs have been developed in recent years (see Table 15-1). The most widely used of these new drugs include *clozapine* (trade name Clozaril), *risperidone* (Risperdal), *olanzapine* (Zyprexa), *quetiapine* (Seroquel), *ziprasidone* (Geodon), and *aripiprazole* (Abilify). As you have read, the drugs are called *atypical* because their biological operation differs from that of the conventional antipsychotic medications: the atypicals are received at fewer dopamine D-2 receptors and more D-1, D-4, and serotonin receptors than the others (Julien et al., 2011; Nord & Farde, 2011).

In fact, atypical antipsychotic drugs appear to be more effective than the conventional drugs (Geddes et al., 2011; Julien et al., 2011). Clozapine is often the most effective atypical drug, but the other atypicals also bring significant change in many cases. Recall, for example, Cathy, the woman whom we met at the beginning of this chapter, and how well she responded to risperidone after years of doing poorly on conventional antipsychotic drugs. Unlike the conventional drugs, the new drugs reduce not only the positive symptoms of schizophrenia, but also the negative ones (Waddington et al., 2011). Another major benefit of the atypical antipsychotic drugs is that they cause fewer extrapyramidal symptoms and seem less likely to produce tardive dyskinesia (Geddes et al., 2011; Edlinger et al., 2009) (see Figure 15-1).

Given such advantages, more than half of all medicated patients with schizophrenia now take the atypical drugs; indeed, the drugs are considered the first line of treatment for the disorder (Barnes & Marder, 2011; Combs et al., 2008) (see *PsychWatch* on the next page). Moreover, many patients with bipolar or other severe mental disorders also seem to be helped by several of the atypical antipsychotic drugs. Studies indicate, for example, that olanzapine, prescribed alone or in combination with mood-stabilizing drugs, is very effective in cases of acute mania (Julien et al., 2011).

Yet the atypical antipsychotic drugs have serious problems as well (Barnes & Marder, 2011; Haddad & Mattay, 2011; Waddington et al., 2011). For example, people who use one of the atypical drugs, clozapine, have around a 1 percent risk of developing **agranulocytosis**, a life-threatening drop in white blood cells (other atypical antipsychotic drugs do not produce this undesired effect). Patients who take clozapine must therefore have frequent blood tests so that this effect can be spotted early and the drug stopped. In addition, some of the atypical antipsychotic drugs may cause weight gain, particularly among women; dizziness; and significant elevations in blood sugar, as we also saw in the case of Cathy.

table: 15-1

Antipsychotic Drugs

Class/Generic Name	Trade Name
Conventional antipsychotics	
Chlorpromazine	Thorazine
Triflupromazine	Vesprin
Thioridazine	Mellaril
Mesoridazine	Serentil
Trifluoperazine	Stelazine
Fluphenazine	Prolixin, Permitil
Perphenazine	Trilafon
Acetophenazine	Tindal
Chlorprothixene	Taractan
Thiothixene	Navane
Haloperidol	Haldol
Loxapine	Loxitane
Molindone hydrochloride	Moban, Lidone
Pimozide	Orap
Atypical antipsychotics	
Risperidone	Risperdal
Clozapine	Clozaril
Olanzapine	Zyprexa
Quetiapine	Seroquel
Ziprasidone	Geodon
Aripiprazole	Abilify
Iloperidone	Ranapt
Lurasidone	Latuda
Paliperidone	Invega

PsychWatch

First Dibs on Atypical Antipsychotic Drugs?

As you saw in Chapter 9, depressed African Americans and Hispanic Americans in the United States are less likely than depressed white Americans to be prescribed second-generation antidepressant drugs (see page 272). Unfortunately, a similar pattern appears to be at work in cases of schizophrenia when people are prescribed *atypical antipsychotic medications*, the second-generation antipsychotic medications that are often more effective and have fewer undesired effects than conventional antipsychotic medications. Several prescription patterns have emerged

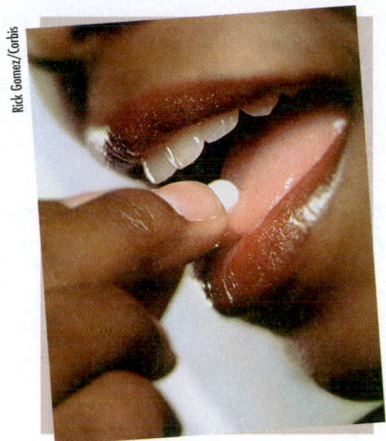

in the research literature (Herbeck et al., 2004; Ni & Cohen, 2004; Mark et al., 2003, 2002; Covell et al., 2002). They include the following:

> African Americans and Hispanic Americans with schizophrenia and other psychotic disorders are significantly less likely than white Americans to be prescribed atypical antipsychotic drugs.

> African Americans and Hispanic Americans with schizophrenia are much more likely than white Americans to be prescribed conventional antipsychotic drugs.

> In turn, African American and Hispanic American patients are less likely to be helped by their antipsychotic medications and more likely to experience tardive dyskinesia and extrapyramidal effects in response to their medications for schizophrenia.

> One reason for this racial disparity may be economic. On average, African American and Hispanic American patients are less likely than white Americans to have private health insurance or any health insurance at all. Schizophrenic patients

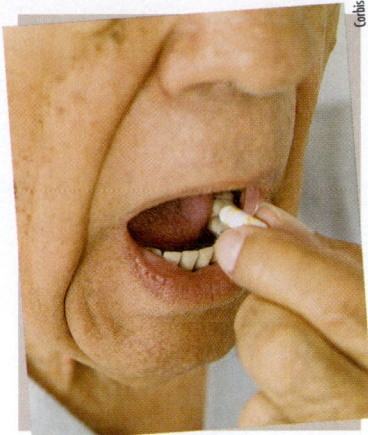

without private insurance are more likely to be prescribed conventional antipsychotic medications, which are much cheaper than atypical antipsychotics.

> Another reason for this racial disparity points to the kind of practitioner seen by patients. In general, African American and Hispanic American patients with severe mental disorders are more likely to have a family physician rather than a psychiatrist prescribe their psychotropic drugs. It turns out that many family physicians are more inclined to prescribe conventional antipsychotic drugs than atypical antipsychotic drugs.

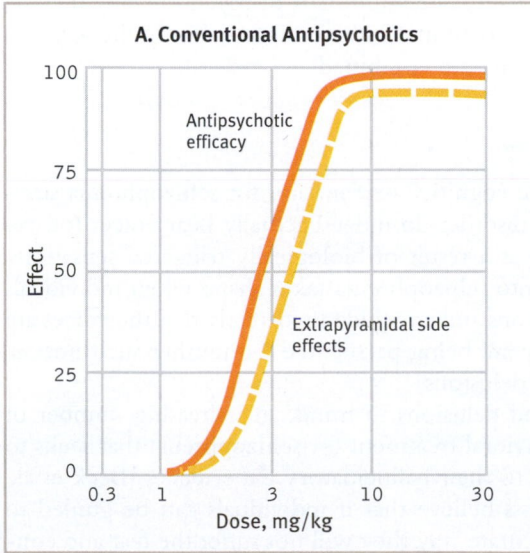

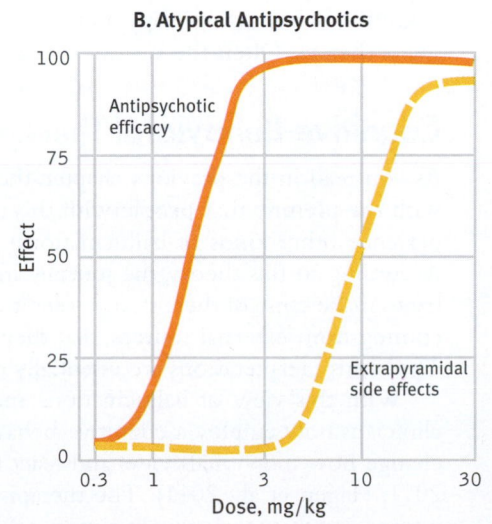

Figure 15-1
Conventional versus atypical antipsychotic drugs: the side effect advantage Conventional antipsychotic drugs are much more likely than atypical antipsychotic drugs to produce undesired extrapyramidal symptoms. (A) The dose-response curve for conventional drugs shows that, beginning with low doses of the drugs, extrapyramidal side effects emerge and keep intensifying right along with increases in the drug doses. (B) In contrast, the dose-response curve for atypical antipsychotic drugs indicates that extrapyramidal side effects typically do not even appear until a patient is taking relatively high doses of the drugs. (Adapted from Casey, 1995, p. 107.)

Psychotherapy

Before the discovery of antipsychotic drugs, psychotherapy was not really an option for people with schizophrenia. Most were too far removed from reality to profit from it. Only a handful of therapists, apparently blessed with extraordinary patience and skill, specialized in the psychotherapeutic treatment of this disorder and reported a measure of success (Will, 1967, 1961; Sullivan, 1962, 1953; Fromm-Reichmann, 1950, 1948, 1943). These therapists believed that the first task of such therapy was to win the trust of patients with schizophrenia and build a close relationship with them.

Well-known clinical theorist and therapist Frieda Fromm-Reichmann, for example, would initially tell her patients that they could continue to exclude her from their private world and hold onto their disorder as long as they wished. She reported that eventually, after much testing and acting out, the patients would accept, trust, and grow attached to her and begin to talk to her about their problems. Case studies seemed to attest to the effectiveness of such approaches and to the importance of trust and emotional bonding in treatment. Here a recovered woman tells her therapist how she had felt during their early interactions:

> At the start, I didn't listen to what you said most of the time but I watched like a hawk for your expression and the sound of your voice. After the interview, I would add all this up to see if it seemed to show love. The words were nothing compared to the feelings you showed. I sense that you felt confident I could be helped and that there was hope for the future....
>
> The problem with schizophrenics is that they can't trust anyone. They can't put their eggs in one basket. The doctor will usually have to fight to get in no matter how much the patient objects....
>
> Loving is impossible at first because it turns you into a helpless little baby. The patient can't feel safe to do this until he is absolutely sure the doctor understands what is needed and will provide it.
>
> *(Hayward & Taylor, 1965)*

Today psychotherapy is successful in many more cases of schizophrenia (Miller et al., 2012; Lencer et al., 2011). By helping to relieve thought and perceptual disturbances, antipsychotic drugs allow people with schizophrenia to learn about their disorder, participate actively in therapy, think more clearly about themselves and their relationships, make changes in their behavior, and cope with stressors in their lives (Swartz et al., 2012; Mueser & VandenBos, 2011). The most helpful forms of psychotherapy include cognitive-behavioral therapy and two sociocultural interventions—family therapy and social therapy. Often the various approaches are combined.

Cognitive-Behavioral Therapy

As you read in the previous chapter, the cognitive explanation for schizophrenia starts with the premise that people with this disorder do indeed actually hear voices (or experience other kinds of hallucinations) as a result of biologically triggered sensations. According to this theory, the journey into schizophrenia takes shape when individuals try to make sense of these strange sensations and conclude incorrectly that the voices are coming from external sources, that they are being persecuted, or another such notion. These misinterpretations are essentially delusions.

With this view of hallucinations and delusions in mind, an increasing number of clinicians now employ a cognitive-behavioral treatment for schizophrenia that seeks to change how individuals view and react to their hallucinatory experiences (Beck et al., 2011; Hagen et al., 2011). The therapists believe that if individuals can be guided to interpret such experiences in a more accurate way, they will not suffer the fear and con-

Joao Relvas/epa/Corbis

Spontaneous improvement?
For reasons unknown, the symptoms of some people with schizophrenia lessen during old age, even without treatment (Meeks & Jeste, 2008; Fisher et al., 2001). An example of this is the remarkable late-life improvement of John Nash, the subject of the book and movie *A Beautiful Mind.* Nash, seen here giving a presentation in 2010, received the 1994 Nobel Prize in Economic Science after struggling with schizophrenia for 35 years.

fusion produced by their delusional misinterpretations (Dudley & Turkington, 2011). Thus, the therapists use a combination of behavioral and cognitive techniques:

1. They provide clients with education and evidence about the biological causes of hallucinations.

2. They help clients learn more about the "comings and goings" of their own hallucinations and delusions. The individuals learn, for example, to monitor which kinds of events and situations trigger the voices in their heads.

3. The therapists challenge their clients' inaccurate ideas about the power of their hallucinations, such as their notions that the voices are all-powerful, uncontrollable, and must be obeyed. The therapists also have the clients conduct behavioral experiments to put such notions to the test. What happens, for example, if the clients occasionally resist following the orders from their hallucinatory voices?

4. The therapists teach clients to reattribute and more accurately interpret their hallucinations. Clients may, for example, increasingly adopt and apply alternative conclusions such as, "It's not a real voice, it's my illness."

5. The therapists teach clients techniques for coping with their unpleasant sensations (hallucinations). The clients may, for example, learn ways to reduce the physical arousal that accompanies hallucinations—applying special breathing and relaxation techniques, positive self-statements, and the like. Similarly, they may learn to refocus or distract themselves whenever the hallucinations occur. In one reported case, a therapist repeatedly walked behind his schizophrenic client and made harsh and critical statements, seeking to simulate the clients' auditory hallucinations and then guiding him to focus his attention past the voices and on to the task at hand (Veiga-Martinez et al., 2008).

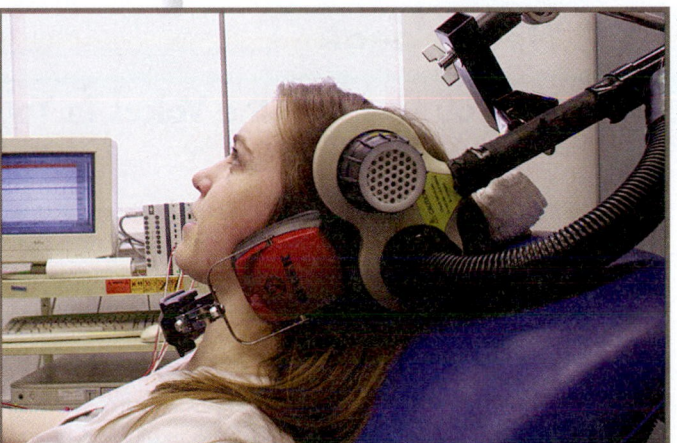

These behavioral and cognitive techniques often help schizophrenic individuals gain a greater sense of control over their hallucinations and reduce their delusional ideas. But they do not eliminate the hallucinations. They simply render the hallucinations less powerful and less destructive. Can anything be done further to lessen the hallucinations' unpleasant impact on the individual? Yes, say *new-wave cognitive-behavioral therapists,* including practitioners of *Acceptance and Commitment Therapy.*

As you read in Chapters 3 and 5, new-wave cognitive-behavioral therapists believe that the most useful goal of treatment is often to help clients *accept* their streams of problematic thoughts rather than to judge them, act on them, or try fruitlessly to change them (Hayes & Lillis, 2012; Hayes et al., 2004; Hayes, 2002). The therapists, for example, help highly anxious individuals to become simply *mindful* of the worries that engulf their thinking and to *accept* such negative thoughts as but harmless events of the mind (see pages 121–122). Similarly, in cases of schizophrenia, new-wave cognitive-behavioral therapists try to help clients become detached and comfortable observers of their hallucinations—merely mindful of the unusual sensations and accepting of them—while the individuals otherwise move forward with the tasks and events of their lives (Bach, 2007).

What are the differences between cognitive-behavioral therapies and self-help programs for people who regularly experience auditory hallucinations?

Reducing auditory sensations
While cognitive-behavioral therapists try to help people with schizophrenia more accurately interpret their hallucinations, biological researchers keep trying to rid sufferers of the sensations that produce the hallucinations. Researcher Ralph Hoffman and his colleagues, for example, have used a *transcranial magnetic stimulation* procedure to reduce neural excitability in the auditory brain centers of patients with schizophrenia. The procedure, shown here, has reduced the hallucinations of many patients (Hoffman, 2010; Hoffman et al., 2007, 2000).

Studies indicate that these various cognitive-behavioral treatments are often very helpful to clients with schizophrenia (Swartz et al., 2012; Gumley, 2011; Haddock & Spaulding, 2011). Many clients who receive such treatments report feeling less distressed by their hallucinations and display fewer delusions. Indeed, the individuals are often able to shed the diagnosis of schizophrenia. Rehospitalizations decrease by 50 percent among clients treated with cognitive-behavioral therapy.

The cognitive-behavioral view that hallucinations should be accepted (rather than misinterpreted or overreacted to) is compatible with a notion already held by some people who hallucinate. There are in fact a number of self-help groups comprised of people with auditory hallucinations whose guiding principles are that hallucinations themselves are harmless and valid experiences and that sufferers often do best if they simply can accept and learn to live with these experiences (see *MediaSpeak* below).

Family Therapy

Over 50 percent of persons who are recovering from schizophrenia and other severe mental disorders live with their families: parents, siblings, spouses, or children (Tsai et al., 2011; Barrowclough & Lobban, 2008). Such situations create special pressures; even if family stress was not a factor in the onset of the disorder, a patient's recovery may be influenced greatly by the behavior and reactions of his or her relatives at home (Macleod et al., 2011).

MediaSpeak

Can You Live with the Voices in Your Head?

By Daniel B. Smith, *New York Times*

Angelo, a London-born scientist in his early 30s with sandy brown hair, round wire-frame glasses and a slight, unobtrusive stammer, vividly recalls the day he began to hear voices. It was Jan. 7, 2001, and he had recently passed his Ph.D. oral exams in chemistry at an American university. . . . Angelo was walking home from the laboratory when, all of a sudden, he heard two voices in his head. "It was like hearing thoughts in my mind that were not mine," he explained recently. "They identified themselves as Andrew and Oliver, two angels." . . . What the angels said, to Angelo's horror, was that in the coming days, he would die of a brain hemorrhage. Terrified, Angelo hurried home and locked himself into his apartment. For three long days he waited out his fate, at which time his supervisor drove him to a local hospital, where Angelo was admitted to the psychiatric ward. It was his first time under psychiatric care. He had never heard voices before. His diagnosis was schizophrenia with depressive overtones.

Angelo remembers his time at the hospital as the deepening of a nightmare. . . . Angelo did not react well to the antipsychotic he'd been prescribed. . . . His voices remained strong and disturbing. . . . Several days into his stay, Angelo's parents flew to the United States from London and took him back home.

More than six years later, Angelo still lives at his parents' house. He currently takes a cocktail of antidepressants and antipsychotics, with tolerable side effects. . . . The pills help Angelo to manage his voices, but they have not been able to eradicate them. . . . Despite these setbacks, Angelo has maintained his optimism. He is eager to discover new ways to combat his voices. Not long ago, he found one. In November, his psychologist informed him of a local support group for people who hear voices, from which he thought Angelo might benefit. Angelo began to attend the group late last year.

I first met Angelo at a meeting of the group in mid-January. (I was given permission to sit in on the condition that I not divulge the participants' last names.) . . . The gathering was small but eclectic. In addition to the group's facilitators—Jo Kutchinsky, an occupational therapist, and Liana Kaiser, a social-work student—five men and women assembled in a circle. . . . Besides Angelo, there was Stewart, . . . Jenny, . . . Michelle, . . . and David. . . .

. . . When Kutchinsky opened the meeting by asking each member to discuss the previous week's experience hearing voices, . . . most of the members spoke of their voices in the way that comedians speak of mothers-in-law: burdensome and irritating, but an inescapable part of life that you might as well learn to deal with. When David's name was called, he lifted his head and discussed his struggle to accept his voices as part of his consciousness. "I've learned over time that my voices can't be rejected," he said. "No matter what I do, they won't go away. I have to find a way to live with them." Jenny discussed how keeping busy quieted her voices; she seemed to have taken a remarkable number of adult-education courses. Michelle expressed her belief that her voices were nothing more exotic than powerfully negative thoughts. "Negative thoughts are universal," she said. "Everyone has them. Everyone. What matters is how you cope with them: that's what counts."

. . .[A]fterward I pulled [Angelo] aside and asked him what he thought. "It's interesting to hear people's stories," he said. "Before I started coming, I hadn't realized just how long some people have suffered. I've heard voices for six years. Some people have heard them for 15 or 20." . . . It was comforting, he said, to speak at last with people who understood.

The meeting that I attended in London is one of dozens like it affiliated with a small but influential grass-roots organization

Generally speaking, persons with schizophrenia who feel positively toward their relatives do better in treatment (Camacho et al., 2005). As you saw in Chapter 14, recovered patients living with relatives who display high levels of *expressed emotion*—that is, relatives who are very critical, emotionally overinvolved, and hostile—often have a much higher relapse rate than those living with more positive and supportive relatives (Bebbington & Kuipers, 2011; Janicak et al., 2001). Moreover, for their part, family members may be greatly upset by the social withdrawal and unusual behaviors of a relative with schizophrenia (McFarlane, 2011).

To address such issues, clinicians now commonly include family therapy in their treatment of schizophrenia, providing family members with guidance, training, practical advice, psychoeducation about the disorder, and emotional support and empathy (Burbach, Fadden, & Smith, 2010). In family therapy, relatives develop more realistic expectations and become more tolerant, less guilt-ridden, and more willing to try new patterns of communication. Family therapy also helps the person with schizophrenia cope with the pressures of family life, make better use of family members, and avoid troublesome interactions.

"And only you can hear this whistle?"

known as Hearing Voices Network. . . . H.V.N. groups must accept all interpretations of auditory hallucinations as equally valid. If an individual comes to a group claiming that he is hearing the voice of the queen of England, and he finds this belief useful, no attempt is made to divest him of it, but rather to figure out what it means to him. . . .

. . . H.V.N.'s brief . . . can be boiled down to two core positions. The first is that many more people hear voices, and hear many more kinds of voices, than is usually assumed. The second is that auditory hallucination—or "voice-hearing," H.V.N.'s more neutral preference—should be thought of not as a pathological phenomenon in need of eradication but as a meaningful, interpretable experience. . . . .

The concept of "coping" is central to H.V.N., based on its belief that people feel better not when their voices are extinguished but when the person hearing voices learns to listen to his hallucinations without anguish. Jacqui Dillon, the national

chairwoman of H.V.N. . . . has heard voices for more than 30 years. . . . But she no longer heeds their commands or allows them to bother her. . . .

It was just before noon on a mild Friday in January when the . . . hearing-voices group reconvened after a 15-minute coffee break. . . . The participants were asked . . . to discuss [how they cope with the voices in their heads]. . . . The coping strategies that followed were . . . commonsensical lifestyle suggestions geared toward improving one's frame of mind, or sanding down the edges of the experience's effects. Liana chose "Exercise"; Jenny chose "Religious Activities"; David chose "Pamper Yourself." . . . The most novel strategy, and the only one that seemed to cause the group's members to perk up, came under the heading of "Mobile Phones." If you have the temptation to yell at your voices in public, one suggestion went, you should do so with a phone to your ear. That way you can feel free to let loose, and no one who sees you will think you're crazy. Chris in particular seemed to cozy to the suggestion. "I sometimes talk to my voices in public," he said matter-of-factly. "It's very upsetting. I have to bite my knuckles to suppress the urge."

Participants in H.V.N.'s self-help groups take comfort from strategies like these. . . . As for Angelo, his concern is not to choose one option over another—but only to recover. "I have found the group interesting," Angelo wrote via e-mail three weeks after we met. "It has made me realize that many voice-hearers have had the problem for many years, and that many . . . are able to hold down a job despite the voices. I hope to do this myself. Perhaps the right combination of drugs will make this possible."

Research has found that family therapy—particularly when it is combined with drug therapy—helps reduce tensions within the family and so helps relapse rates go down (Swartz et al., 2012; Haddock & Spaulding, 2011; Barrowclough & Loban, 2008). The principles of this approach are evident in the following description:

Mark was a 32-year-old single man living with his parents. He had a long and stormy history of schizophrenia with many episodes of psychosis, interspersed with occasional brief periods of good functioning. Mark's father was a bright but neurotically tormented man gripped by obsessions and inhibitions. Mark's mother appeared weary, detached, and embittered. Both parents felt hopeless about Mark's chances of recovery and resentful that needing to care for him would always plague their lives. They acted as if they were being intentionally punished. It gradually emerged that the father, in fact, was riddled with guilt and self-doubt; he suspected that his wife had been cold and rejecting toward Mark as an infant and that he had failed to intervene, due to his unwillingness to confront his wife and the demands of graduate school that distanced him from home life. He entertained the fantasy that Mark's illness was a punishment for this. Every time Mark did begin to show improvement—both in reduced symptoms and in increased functioning—his parents responded as if it were just a cruel torment designed to raise their hopes and then to plunge them into deeper despair when Mark's condition deteriorated. This pattern was especially apparent when Mark got a job. As a result, at such times, the parents actually became more critical and hostile toward Mark. He would become increasingly defensive and insecure, finally developing paranoid delusions, and usually would be hospitalized in a panicky and agitated state.

All of this became apparent during the psychoeducational sessions. When the pattern was pointed out to the family, they were able to recognize their self-fulfilling prophecy and were motivated to deal with it. As a result, the therapist decided to see the family together. Concrete instances of the pattern and its consequences were explored, and alternative responses by the parents were developed. The therapist encouraged both the parents and Mark to discuss their anxieties and doubts about Mark's progress, rather than to stir up one another's expectations of failure. The therapist had regular individual sessions with Mark as well as the family sessions. As a result, Mark has successfully held a job for an unprecedented 12 months.

(Heinrichs & Carpenter, 1983, pp. 284–285)

A place to call home

This man, recovering from schizophrenia and bipolar disorder, joyfully assumes a yoga pose in the living room of his new Chicago apartment. He found the residence with the help of a program called Direct Connect, which has helped many such individuals move into their own apartments.

AP Photo/M. Spencer Green

The families of persons with schizophrenia and other severe mental disorders may also turn to *family support groups* and *family psychoeducational programs* for encouragement and advice (McFarlane, 2011; Glentworth & Reed, 2010). In such programs, family members meet with others in the same situation to share their thoughts and emotions, provide mutual support, and learn about schizophrenia. Although research has yet to determine the usefulness of these groups, the approach has become popular.

Social Therapy

Many clinicians believe that the treatment of people with schizophrenia should include techniques that address social and personal difficulties in the clients' lives. These clinicians offer practical advice; work with clients on problem solving, decision making, and social skills; make sure that the clients are taking their medications properly; and may even help them find work, financial assistance, appropriate health care, and proper housing (Ridgway, 2008; Sherrer & O'Hare, 2008).

Research finds that this practical, active, and broad approach, called *social therapy* or *personal therapy,* does indeed help keep people out of the hospital (Haddock & Spaulding, 2011; Hogarty, 2002). One study compared the progress of four groups of patients with chronic schizophrenia after their discharge from a state hospital (Hogarty et al., 2006, 1986, 1974). One group received both antipsychotic medications and social therapy in the community, while the other groups received medication only, social therapy only, or no treatment of any kind. The researchers' first finding was that chronic patients need to continue taking medication after being released in order to avoid rehospitalization. Over a two-year period, 80 percent of those who did not continue medication needed to be hospitalized again, compared to 48 percent of those who received medication. They also found that among the patients on medication, those who also received social therapy adjusted to the community and avoided rehospitalization most successfully. Clearly, social therapy played an important role in their recovery.

The Community Approach

The broadest approach for the treatment of schizophrenia and other severe mental disorders is the *community approach*. In 1963, partly in response to the terrible conditions in public mental institutions and partly because of the emergence of antipsychotic drugs, the U.S. government ordered that patients be released and treated in the community. Congress passed the *Community Mental Health Act,* which stipulated that patients with psychological disorders were to receive a range of mental health services—outpatient therapy, inpatient treatment, emergency care, preventive care, and aftercare—in their communities rather than being transported to institutions far from home. The act was aimed at a variety of psychological disorders, but patients diagnosed with schizophrenia and other severe disorders, especially those who had been institutionalized for years, were affected most. Other countries around the world put similar sociocultural treatment programs into action shortly thereafter (Wiley-Exley, 2007).

? How might the "revolving door" syndrome itself worsen the symptoms and outlook of people with schizophrenia?

Thus began several decades of **deinstitutionalization,** an exodus of hundreds of thousands of patients with schizophrenia and other long-term mental disorders from state institutions into the community. On a given day in 1955 close to 600,000 patients were living in state institutions; today fewer than 40,000 patients reside in those settings

•**deinstitutionalization**•The discharge of large numbers of patients from long-term institutional care so that they might be treated in community programs.

Art that heals

Art and other creative activities can be therapeutic for people with schizophrenia and other severe mental disorders. Here, artist William Scott paints a San Francisco cityscape at the Creative Growth Art Center in California. Diagnosed with schizophrenia and autism, Scott has had his paintings and sculptures sold around the world.

AP Photo/Paul Sakuma

(Althouse, 2010). Clinicians have learned that patients recovering from schizophrenia and other severe disorders can profit greatly from community programs. As you will see, however, the actual quality of community care for these people has often been inadequate throughout the United States. The result is a "revolving door" syndrome for many patients. They are released to the community, readmitted to an institution within months, released a second time, admitted yet again, and so on, over and over (Burns & Drake, 2011; Torrey, 2001).

What Are the Features of Effective Community Care?

People recovering from schizophrenia and other severe disorders need medication, psychotherapy, help in handling daily pressures and responsibilities, guidance in making decisions, training in social skills, residential supervision, and vocational counseling—a combination of services sometimes called *assertive community treatment* (Burns & Drake, 2011; Meaden & Hacker, 2011). Those whose communities help them meet these needs make greater progress than those living in other communities (Swartz et al., 2012). Some of the key features of effective community care programs are (1) coordination of patient services, (2) short-term hospitalization, (3) partial hospitalization, (4) supervised residencies, and (5) occupational training.

Coordinated Services

When the Community Mental Health Act was first passed, it was expected that community care would be provided by a **community mental health center,** a treatment facility that would supply medication, psychotherapy, and inpatient emergency care to people with severe disturbances, as well as coordinate the services offered by other community agencies. When community mental health centers are available and do provide these services, patients with schizophrenia and other severe disorders often make significant progress (Burns & Drake, 2011; Rapp & Goscha, 2008). Coordination of services is particularly important for so-called *mentally ill chemical abusers* (*MICAs*), patients with psychotic disorders as well as substance use disorders.

Short-Term Hospitalization

When people develop severe psychotic symptoms, today's clinicians first try to treat them on an outpatient basis, usually with a combination of antipsychotic medication and psychotherapy (Addington & Addington, 2008). If this approach fails, *short-term hospitalization*—in a mental hospital or a general hospital's psychiatric unit—that lasts a few weeks (rather than months or years) may be tried (Craig & Power, 2010). Soon after the patients improve, they are released for **aftercare,** a general term for follow-up care and treatment in the community. Short-term hospitalization usually leads to greater improvement and a lower rehospitalization rate than extended institutionalization (Soliman et al., 2008). Countries throughout the world now favor this policy.

Partial Hospitalization

People's needs may fall between full hospitalization and outpatient therapy, and so some communities offer **day centers** or **day hospitals,** all-day programs in which patients return to their homes for the night. Such programs actually originated in Moscow in 1933, when a shortage of hospital beds necessitated the premature release of many patients. Today's day centers provide patients with daily supervised activities, therapy, and programs to improve social skills. People recovering from severe disorders in day centers often do better than those who spend extended periods in a hospital or in traditional outpatient therapy (Mayahara & Ito, 2002; Yoshimasu et al., 2002).

A long way to go

A man with schizophrenia lies on the floor of the emergency room at Hospital Delafontaine near Paris, France. The plight of this patient is a reminder that, despite the development of various effective interventions, the overall treatment picture for many individuals with severe mental disorders leaves much to be desired.

Alexandra Boulat/VII/Corbis

Another kind of institution that has become a popular setting for the treatment of people with schizophrenia and other severe disorders is the *semihospital,* or *residential crisis center.* Semihospitals are houses or other structures in the community that provide 24-hour nursing care for people with severe mental disorders (Soliman et al., 2008). Many individuals who would otherwise be cared for in state hospitals are now being transferred to these semihospitals.

Supervised Residences Many people do not require hospitalization but, at the same time, are unable to live alone or with their families. **Halfway houses,** also known as *crisis houses* or *group homes,* often serve individuals well (Lindenmayer & Khan, 2012; Levy et al., 2005). Such residences may shelter between one and two dozen people. The live-in staff usually are *paraprofessionals*—lay people who receive training and ongoing supervision from outside mental health professionals. The houses are usually run with a *milieu therapy* philosophy that emphasizes mutual support, resident responsibility, and self-government. Research indicates that halfway houses help many people recovering from schizophrenia and other severe disorders adjust to community life and avoid rehospitalization (Hansson et al., 2002; McGuire, 2000). Here is how one woman described living in a halfway house after 10 hospitalizations in 12 years:

> The halfway house changed my life. First of all, I discovered that some of the staff members had once been clients in the program! That one single fact offered me hope. For the first time, I saw proof that a program could help someone, that it was possible to regain control over one's life and become independent. The house was democratically run; all residents had one vote and the staff members, outnumbered 5 to 22, could not make rules or even discharge a client from the program without majority sentiment. There was a house bill of rights that was strictly observed by all. We helped one another and gave support. When residents were in a crisis, no staff member hustled them off or increased their medication to calm them down. Residents could cry, be comforted and hugged until a solution could be found, or until they accepted that it was okay to feel bad. Even anger was an acceptable feeling that did not have to be feared, but could be expressed and turned into constructive energy. If you disliked some aspect of the program or the behavior of a staff member, you could change things rather than passively accept what was happening. Choices were real, and failure and success were accepted equally.... Bit by bit, my distrust faltered and the fears lessened. I slept better and made friends.... Other residents and staff members who had hallucinated for years and now were able to control their hallucinations shared with me some of the techniques that had worked for them. Things like diet ... and interpersonal relationships became a few of my tools.
>
> *(Lovejoy, 1982, pp. 605–609)*

Occupational Training and Support Paid employment provides income, independence, self-respect, and the stimulation of working with others. It also brings companionship and order to one's daily life. For these reasons, occupational training and placement are important services for people with schizophrenia and other severe mental disorders (Bell, Choi, & Lysaker, 2011; Bio & Gattaz, 2011; Davis et al., 2010).

Many people recovering from such disorders receive occupational training in a **sheltered workshop**—a supervised workplace for employees who are not ready for competitive or complicated jobs. The workshop replicates a typical work environment: products such as toys or simple appliances are manufactured and sold, workers are paid according to performance, and all are expected to be at work regularly and on time. For some, the sheltered workshop becomes a permanent workplace. For others, it is an important step toward better-paying and more demanding employment or a return to a previous job (Becker, 2008; Chalamat et al., 2005). In the United States, however,

•**community mental health center**•A treatment facility that provides medication, psychotherapy, and emergency care for psychological problems and coordinates treatment in the community.

•**aftercare**•A program of posthospitalization care and treatment in the community.

•**day center**•A program that offers hospital-like treatment during the day only. Also known as a *day hospital.*

•**halfway house**•A residence for people with schizophrenia or other severe problems, often staffed by paraprofessionals. Also known as a *group home* or *crisis house.*

•**sheltered workshop**•A supervised workplace for people who are not yet ready for competitive jobs.

BETWEEN THE LINES

Treatment Delay

The average length of time between the first appearance of psychotic symptoms and the initiation of treatment is 2 years. ‹‹

(Brunet & Birchwood, 2010)

•**case manager**•A community therapist who offers a full range of services for people with schizophrenia or other severe disorders, including therapy, advice, medication, guidance, and protection of patients' rights.

Changing the unacceptable
A resident of a group home holds a sign during a rally in New York to protest the shortage of appropriate community residences for people with severe mental disorders. This shortage is one of the reasons that many such people have become homeless and/or imprisoned.

occupational training is not consistently available to people with severe mental disorders (Honberg, 2005).

An alternative work opportunity for individuals with severe psychological disorders is *supported employment*. Here vocational agencies and counselors help people find competitive jobs in the community and provide psychological support while the individuals are maintaining employment (Bell et al., 2011; Solar, 2011). Like sheltered workshops, supported employment opportunities are often in short supply.

How Has Community Treatment Failed?

There is no doubt that effective community programs can help people with schizophrenia and other severe mental disorders recover. However, fewer than half of all the people who need them receive appropriate community mental health services (Burns & Drake, 2011; Lehman et al., 2004; McGuire, 2000). In fact, in any given year, 40 to 60 percent of all people with schizophrenia and other severe mental disorders receive no treatment at all (Wang et al., 2002; Torrey, 2001). Two factors are primarily responsible: *poor coordination* of services and *shortage* of services.

Poor Coordination of Services The various mental health agencies in a community often fail to communicate with one another. There may be an opening at a nearby halfway house, for example, and the therapist at the community mental health center may not know about it. In addition, even within a community agency a patient may not have continuing contacts with the same staff members and may fail to receive consistent services. Still another problem is poor communication between state hospitals and community mental health centers, particularly at times of discharge (Torrey, 2001).

It is not surprising, then, that a growing number of community therapists have become **case managers** for people with schizophrenia and other severe mental disorders (Burns, 2010). Like the social therapists described earlier, they offer therapy and advice, teach problem-solving and social skills, ensure that medications are being taken properly, and keep an eye on possible health care needs. In addition, they try to coordinate available community services, guide clients through the community system, and, perhaps most importantly, help protect clients' legal rights. Many professionals now believe that effective case management is the key to success for a community program.

Shortage of Services The number of community programs—community mental health centers, halfway houses, sheltered workshops—available to people with severe mental disorders falls woefully short (Burns & Drake, 2011; Julien et al., 2011). In addition, the community mental health centers that do exist generally fail to provide adequate services for people with severe disorders. They tend to devote their efforts and money to people with less disabling problems, such as anxiety disorders or problems in social adjustment. Only a fraction of the patients treated by community mental health centers suffer from schizophrenia or other disorders marked by psychosis (Torrey, 2001).

There are various reasons for this shortage of services. Perhaps the primary one is economic (Covell et al., 2011). On the one hand, more public funds are available for people with psychological disorders now than in the past. In 1963 a total of $1 billion was spent in this area, whereas today approximately $171 billion in public funding is devoted each year to people with mental disorders (Gill, 2010; Nordal, 2010; Redick et al., 1992). This represents a significant increase even when inflation and so-called real dollars are factored in. On the other hand, rather little of the additional money is going to community treatment programs for people with severe disorders. Much of it goes instead to prescription drugs, monthly income payments such as *social security disability income,* services for persons with mental disorders in nursing homes and general hospitals, and community services for people who are less disturbed (Covell et al., 2011). Today the financial burden of providing community treatment for persons with long-term severe disorders often falls on local governments and nonprofit organizations rather than the federal or state government, and local resources cannot always meet this challenge.

What Are the Consequences of Inadequate Community Treatment?

What happens to persons with schizophrenia and other severe disorders whose communities do not provide the services they need and whose families cannot afford private treatment (see Figure 15-2)? As you have read, a large number receive no treatment at all; many others spend a short time in a state hospital or semihospital and are then discharged prematurely, often without adequate follow-up treatment (Burns & Drake, 2011; Gill, 2010).

Many of the people with schizophrenia and other severe disorders return to their families and receive medication and perhaps emotional and financial support, but little else in the way of treatment (Barrowclough & Lobban, 2008). Around 8 percent enter an alternative institution such as a nursing home or rest home, where they receive only custodial care and medication (Torrey, 2001). As many as 18 percent are placed in privately run residences where supervision often is provided by untrained individuals— foster homes (small or large), boardinghouses, care homes, and similar facilities (Lindenmayer & Khan, 2012). These residences vary greatly in quality. Some of them are legitimate "bed and care" facilities, providing three meals a day, medication reminders, and at least a small degree of staff supervision. However, many fail to offer even these minimal services.

Another 34 percent of people with schizophrenia and other severe disorders live in totally unsupervised settings. Some of these individuals are equal to the challenge of living alone, support themselves effectively, and maintain nicely furnished apartments. But many cannot really function independently and wind up in rundown single-room-occupancy hotels (SROs) or rooming houses, often located in inner-city neighborhoods (Torrey, 2001). They may live in conditions that are substandard and unsafe. Many of them survive on government disability payments, and a number spend their days wandering through neighborhood streets.

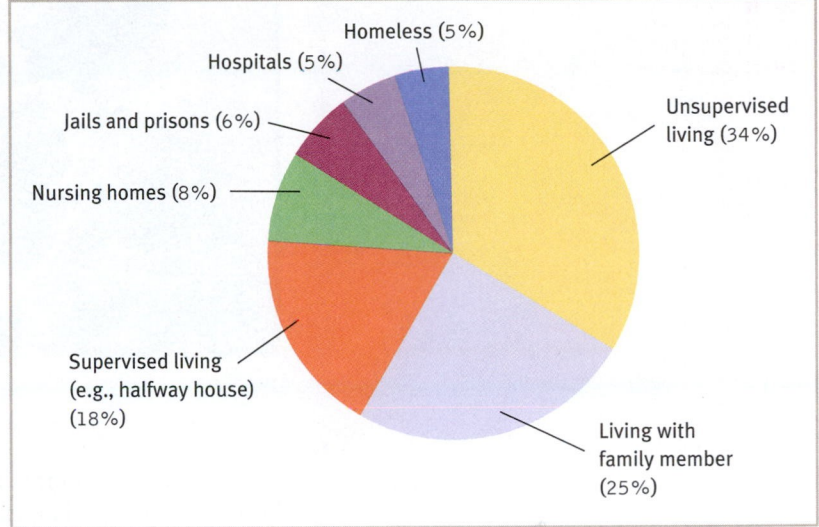

Figure 15-2

Where do people with schizophrenia live? More than one-third live in unsupervised residences, 6 percent in jails, and 5 percent on the streets or in homeless shelters (Kooyman & Walsh, 2011; Torrey, 2001).

David Duprey/AP Photo

Helping to meet the need
Because formal community services fall short for so many people with schizophrenia, the contributions of volunteers become especially important. Here a young man with schizophrenia tries a mountain bike while his volunteer friend of 12 years looks on. The volunteer was enlisted by Compeer Inc., an organization in Rochester, New York, dedicated to befriending community residents who have psychological disorders.

Counseling the homeless

As a result of the severe shortage of community services and related treatment offerings, many people with schizophrenia and other severe mental disorders have become homeless. Here a worker at the Phool Mandi homeless shelter in Delhi, India, comforts and counsels one such individual while they sit together on a stairway at the shelter.

Finally, a great number of people with schizophrenia and other severe disorders have become homeless (Kooyman & Walsh, 2011). There are between 400,000 and 800,000 homeless people in the United States, and approximately one-third have a severe mental disorder, commonly schizophrenia. Many such persons have been released from hospitals. Others are young adults who were never hospitalized in the first place. Another 135,000 or more people with severe mental disorders end up in prisons because their disorders have led them to break the law (Morrissey & Cuddeback, 2008; Peters et al., 2008) (see *MediaSpeak* on the next page). Certainly deinstitutionalization and the community mental health movement have failed these individuals, and many report actually feeling relieved if they are able to return to hospital life.

Why do so many people continue to perceive individuals with schizophrenia as dangerous and violent, despite evidence to the contrary?

The Promise of Community Treatment

Despite these very serious problems, proper community care has shown great potential for assisting in the recovery from schizophrenia and other severe disorders, and clinicians and many government officials continue to press to make it more available. In addition, a number of *national interest groups* have formed in countries around the world that push for better community treatment (Frese, 2008). In the United States, for example, the *National Alliance on Mental Illness* began in 1979 with 300 members and has expanded to around 240,000 members in more than 1,200 chapters (NAMI, 2011). Made up largely of families and people affected by severe mental disorders (particularly schizophrenia, bipolar disorders, and major depressive disorder), this group has become not only a source of information, support, and guidance for its members but also a powerful lobbying force in state and national legislatures; additionally, it has pressured community mental health centers to treat more persons with schizophrenia and other severe disorders.

Today community care is a major feature of treatment for people recovering from severe mental disorders in countries around the world. Both in the United States and abroad, well-coordinated community treatment is seen as an important part of the solution to the problem of severe mental dysfunctioning (Burns & Drake, 2011; DeLuca et al., 2008).

BETWEEN THE LINES

Easy Targets

Adults with schizophrenia are at far greater risk of dying by homicide than other people. ""

In the United States more than one-third of adults with schizophrenia are victims of violent crime. ""

In the United States, adults with schizophrenia are 14 times more likely to be victims of violent crime than to be arrested for committing such a crime. ""

(Kooyman & Walsh, 2011; Cuvelier, 2002; Hiroeh et al., 2001)

MediaSpeak

"Alternative" Mental Health Care

By Merrill Balassone, *Washington Post*

An 18-year-old schizophrenic pounds on the thick security glass of his single-man cell.

A woman lets out a long guttural scream to nobody in particular to turn off the lights.

A 24-year-old man drags his mattress under his bunk, fearful of the voices telling him to hurt himself.

This is not the inside of a psychiatric hospital. It's the B-Mental Health Unit [at a prison in California's] Stanislaus County. . . . Sheriff's deputy David Frost, who oversees the unit, says most of the inmates aren't difficult, just needy. "They do want help," Frost said.

Stanislaus County is not unique. Experts say U.S. prisons and jails have become the country's largest mental health institutions, its new asylums. Nearly four times more Californians with serious mental illnesses are housed in jails and prisons than in hospitals. . . . Nationally, 16 to 20 percent of prisoners are mentally ill, said Harry K. Wexler, a psychologist specializing in crime and substance abuse.

"I think it's a national tragedy," Wexler said. "Prisons are the institutions of last resort. The mentally ill are generally socially undesirable, less employable, more likely to be homeless and get on that slippery slope of repeated involvement in the criminal justice system."

Those who staff prisons and jails are understandably ill-equipped to be psychiatric caretakers. . . . Frost agrees. . . . "I'm not a mental health technician," he says, although he does hold a psychology degree. "I'm a sworn law enforcement officer." He walked the halls on a recent day, asking inmates if they were taking their medications and how they were feeling, and answering questions about upcoming court dates. . . .

Mentally ill offenders have higher recidivism rates than other inmates (they're called "frequent fliers" in the criminal justice world) because they receive little psychiatric care after their release, researchers say. They cost more to jail because of the cost of medications and psychiatric examinations, and they can cause security problems by their aggressive and destructive behavior in lockup.

Wexler said these inmates also are more likely to commit suicide. Because they're less capable of conforming to the rigid rules of a jailhouse, they can end up in isolation as punishment, Wexler said.

At 4:30 A.M. in the . . . jail—and again 12 hours later—it's "pill pass time," when the medical staff hands out about a dozen types of medications. . . . "You're making jailers our mental health treatment personnel," said Phil Trompetter, a Modesto police and forensic psychologist. "They're not trained to do that. . . . This population is not getting what they need." . . .

Because of the lack of hospital space, police are often forced to take the mentally ill who commit minor misdemeanors—from petty thefts to urinating in public—to jail instead. . . . "We have too many untreated mentally ill people who are getting criminalized because of the absence of resources," Trompetter said.

One nationally recognized solution is called a mental health treatment court, which gives offenders the choice between going to jail or following a treatment plan—including taking prescribed medications. [Such programs have had] success in decreasing the recidivism rate among mentally ill offenders and helping smooth their transition back into society.

But at the same time, [because of budget cuts, mental health treatment courts have been] forced to stop taking new offenders. . . . "We deal every day with this crisis of the mentally ill—in jail or out on the street," Frost said. "We do need the funding for these types of programs."

Debbie Noda/Modesto Bee/ZUMA Press/Corbis

Trying to help Sheriff's deputy David Frost talks with an inmate in the B-Mental Health Unit of the Public Safety Center, a prison in Stanislaus County, California.

PUTTING IT... together

An Important Lesson

After years of frustration and failure, clinicians now have an arsenal of weapons to use against schizophrenia and other disorders marked by psychosis—medication, institutional programs, psychotherapy, and community programs. It has become clear that antipsychotic medications open the door for recovery from these disorders, but in most cases other kinds of treatment are also needed to help the recovery process along. The various approaches must be combined in a way that meets each individual's specific needs.

Working with schizophrenia and other severe disorders has taught therapists an important lesson: no matter how compelling the evidence for biological causation may be, a strictly biological approach to the treatment of psychological disorders is a mistake more often than not. Largely on the basis of biological discoveries and pharmacological advances, hundreds of thousands of patients with schizophrenia and other severe mental disorders were released to their communities in the 1960s. Little attention was paid to the psychological and sociocultural needs of these individuals, and many of them have been trapped in their pathology ever since. Clinicians must remember this lesson, especially in today's climate, when managed care and government priorities often promote medication as the sole treatment for psychological problems.

When the pioneering clinical researcher Emil Kraepelin described schizophrenia at the end of the nineteenth century, he estimated that only 13 percent of its victims ever improved. Today, even with shortages in community care, many more such individuals show improvement (Abdel-Baki et al., 2011). Certainly the clinical field has advanced considerably since Kraepelin's day, yet it still has far to go. Studies suggest that the recovery rates could be considerably higher. It is unacceptable that so many people with this and other severe mental disorders receive few or none of the effective community interventions that have been developed, worse still that tens of thousands have become homeless. It is now up to clinicians, along with public officials, to address the needs of all people with schizophrenia and other severe disorders.

Healthy competition

As part of the community mental health philosophy, individuals with schizophrenia and other severe mental disorders are also encouraged to participate in normal activities, athletic endeavors, and artistic undertakings. Here mental health patients compete in the men's 100-meter event during an annual sports festival held in Havana, Cuba, for psychiatric patients.

BETWEEN THE LINES

Mistaken Impression

Most of the "violent" acts committed by people with schizophrenia are relatively minor, such as shoving or slapping. ‹‹
(Swanson, 2010)

Summing Up

- **OVERVIEW OF TREATMENT** For years all efforts to treat schizophrenia brought only frustration. The disorder is still difficult to treat, but today's therapies are more successful than those of the past. *pp. 449–450*

- **PAST INSTITUTIONAL CARE** For more than half of the twentieth century, the main treatment for schizophrenia and other severe mental disorders was *institutionalization* and *custodial care*. Because patients failed to respond to traditional therapies, they were usually placed in overcrowded public institutions (*state hospitals* in the United States), typically in *back wards* where the primary goal was to maintain and restrain them. Between 1845 and 1955 the number of state hospitals and mental patients rose steadily, while the quality of care declined. *pp. 450–452*

- **IMPROVED INSTITUTIONAL CARE** In the 1950s two in-hospital approaches were developed, *milieu therapy* and *token economy programs*. They often brought improvement and particularly helped patients to care for themselves and feel better about themselves. *pp. 452–455*

■ **ANTIPSYCHOTIC DRUGS** The discovery of *antipsychotic drugs* in the 1950s revolutionized the treatment of schizophrenia and other disorders marked by psychosis. Today they are almost always a part of treatment. Theorists believe that the first generation of antipsychotic drugs operate by reducing excessive dopamine activity in the brain. These "conventional" antipsychotic drugs reduce the positive symptoms of schizophrenia more completely, or more quickly, than the negative symptoms.

The *conventional* antipsychotic drugs can also produce dramatic unwanted effects, particularly movement abnormalities called extrapyramidal effects, which include *Parkinsonian and related symptoms, neuroleptic malignant syndrome,* and *tardive dyskinesia. Tardive dyskinesia* apparently occurs in more than 10 percent of the people who take conventional antipsychotic drugs for an extended time and can be difficult or impossible to eliminate, even when the drugs are stopped. Recently *atypical* antipsychotic drugs (such as clozapine, risperidone, and olanzapine) have been developed, which seem to be more effective than the conventional drugs and to cause fewer or no *extrapyramidal effects. pp. 455–459*

■ **PSYCHOTHERAPY** Today *psychotherapy* is often employed successfully in combination with antipsychotic drugs. Helpful forms include *cognitive-behavioral therapy, family therapy,* and *social therapy. Family support groups* and *family psychoeducational programs* are also growing in number. *pp. 460–465*

■ **THE COMMUNITY APPROACH** A *community approach* to the treatment of schizophrenia and other severe mental disorders began in the 1960s, when a policy of *deinstitutionalization* in the United States brought about a mass exodus of hundreds of thousands of patients from state institutions into the community. Among the key elements of effective community care programs are coordination of patient services by a *community mental health center, short-term hospitalization* (followed by *aftercare*), *day centers, halfway houses, occupational training and support,* and *case management.*

Unfortunately, the quality and funding of community care for people with schizophrenia and other severe disorders have been inadequate throughout the United States, often resulting in a "revolving door" syndrome. One consequence is that many people with such disorders are now homeless or in jail. Still others live in *nursing homes* or *rest homes* where they do not receive effective treatment, and many live in *boardinghouses* or *single-room-occupancy hotels. pp. 465–470*

■ **THE PROMISE OF COMMUNITY TREATMENT** The potential of proper community care to help people recovering from schizophrenia and other severe disorders continues to capture the interest of clinicians and policy makers. One major development has been the formation of *national interest groups* that are successfully promoting community treatment for people with these disorders. *p. 470*

PsychPortal

Visit **PsychPortal**
www.yourpsychportal.com
to access the e-book, videocases and other case materials and activities, and study aids, including flashcards, crossword puzzles, quizzes, FAQs, and research exercises.

BETWEEN THE LINES

Schizophrenia and Jail

There are more people with schizophrenia and other severe mental disorders in jails and prisons than there are in all hospitals and other treatment facilities. ‹‹

Persons with severe mental disorders account for 10 to 16 percent of the jail populations in the United States. ‹‹

Inmates in jails and prisons have rates of schizophrenia that are four times higher than that of the general public. ‹‹

The Los Angeles County Jail, where several thousand of the inmates require daily mental health services, is now de facto the largest mental institution in the United States. ‹‹

(Balassone, 2011; Morrissey & Cuddeback, 2008; Peters et al., 2008; Torrey, 2001)

PERSONALITY DISORDERS

While interviewing for the job of editor of a start-up news website, Frederick said, "This may sound self-serving, but I am extraordinarily gifted. I am certain that I will do great things in this position. I and the Osterman Post will soon set the standard for journalism and blogging in the country. Within a year, we'll be looking at The Huffington Post in the rearview mirror." The committee was impressed. Certainly, Frederick's credentials were strong, but even more important, his self-confidence and boldness had wowed them.

A year later, many of the same individuals were describing Frederick differently—arrogant, self-serving, cold, ego-maniacal, draining. He had performed well as editor (though not as spectacularly as he seemed to think), but that performance could not outweigh his impossible personality. Colleagues below and above him had grown weary of his manipulations, his emotional outbursts, his refusal ever to take the blame, his nonstop boasting, and his grandiose plans. Once again Frederick had outworn his welcome.

To be sure, Frederick had great charm, and he knew how to make others feel important, when it served his purpose. Thus he always had his share of friends and admirers. But in reality they were just passing through, until Frederick would tire of them or feel betrayed by their lack of enthusiasm for one of his self-serving interpretations or grand plans. Or until they simply could take Frederick no longer.

Bright and successful though he was, Frederick always felt entitled to more than he was receiving—to higher grades at school, greater compensation at work, more attention from girlfriends. If criticized even slightly, he reacted with fury, and was certain that the critic was jealous of his superior intelligence, skill, or looks. At first glance, Frederick seemed to have a lot going for him socially. Typically, he could be found in the midst of a deep, meaningful romantic relationship—in which he might be tender, attentive, and seemingly devoted to his partner. But Frederick would always tire of his partner within a few weeks or months and would turn cold or even mean. Often he started affairs with other women while still involved with the current partner. The breakups—usually unpleasant and sometimes ugly—rarely brought sadness or remorse to him, and he would almost never think about his former partner again. He always had himself.

Each of us has a *personality*—a set of uniquely expressed characteristics that influence our behaviors, emotions, thoughts, and interactions. Our particular characteristics, often called *personality traits,* lead us to react in fairly predictable ways as we move through life (see *PsychWatch* on page 478). Yet our personalities are also flexible. We learn from experience. As we interact with our surroundings, we try out various responses to see which feel better and which are more effective. This is a flexibility that people who suffer from a personality disorder usually do not have.

People with a **personality disorder** display an enduring, rigid pattern of inner experience and outward behavior that impairs their sense of self, emotional experiences, goals, capacity for empathy, and/or capacity for intimacy (APA, 2013, 2012). Put another way, they have personality traits that are much more extreme and dysfunctional than those of most other people in their culture, leading to significant problems and psychological pain for themselves or others.

Frederick seems to display a personality disorder. For most of his life, his extreme narcissism, grandiosity, and insensitivity have led to poor functioning in

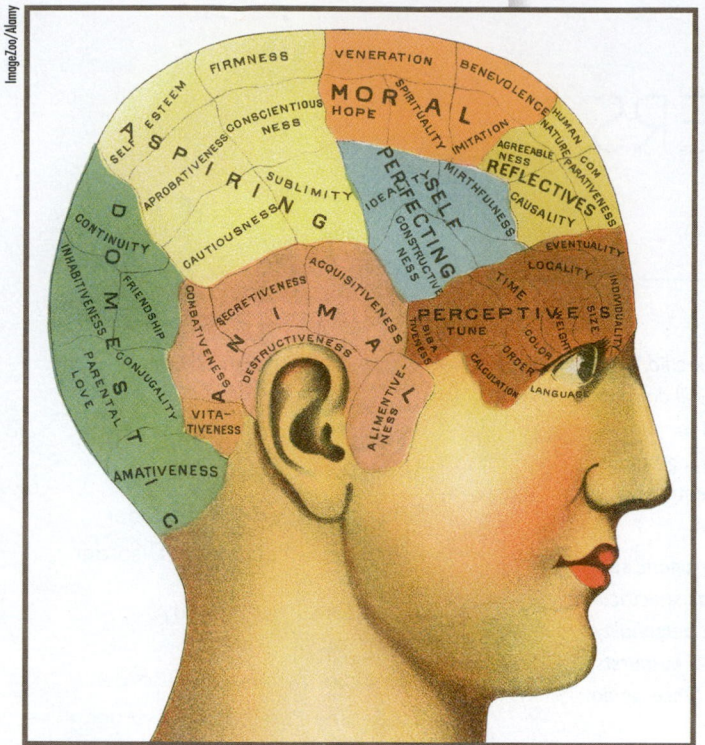

Early notions of personality

In the popular nineteenth-century theory of phrenology, Franz Joseph Gall (1758–1828) held that the brain consists of distinct portions, each responsible for some aspect of personality. Phrenologists tried to assess personality by feeling bumps and indentations on a person's head.

both the personal and social realms. They have caused him to repeatedly feel angry and unappreciated, deprived him of close personal relationships, and brought considerable pain to others. Witness the upset and turmoil experienced by Frederick's co-workers and girlfriends.

The symptoms of personality disorders last for years and typically become recognizable in adolescence or early adulthood, although some start during childhood (Westen et al., 2011). These disorders are among the most difficult psychological disorders to treat. Many sufferers are not even aware of their personality problems and fail to trace their difficulties to their maladaptive style of thinking and behaving. It has been estimated that as many as 9 to 13 percent of all adults have a personality disorder (Paris, 2010; O'Connor, 2008).

It is common for a person with a personality disorder to also suffer from another disorder, a relationship called *comorbidity*. As you will see later in this chapter, for example, many people with avoidant personality disorder, who fearfully shy away from all relationships, also display social anxiety disorder. Perhaps avoidant personality disorder predisposes people to develop social anxiety disorder. Or perhaps social anxiety disorder sets the stage for the personality disorder. Then again, some biological factor may create a predisposition to both the personality disorder and the anxiety disorder. Whatever the reason for the relationship, research indicates that the presence of a personality disorder complicates a person's chances for a successful recovery from other psychological problems (Abbass et al., 2011; Bock et al., 2010).

DSM-5, like its predecessor, DSM-IV-TR, identifies 10 personality disorders (APA, 2013). Often these disorders are separated into three groups, or *clusters*. One cluster, marked by odd or eccentric behavior, consists of the *paranoid, schizoid,* and *schizotypal* personality disorders. A second cluster features dramatic behavior and consists of the *antisocial, borderline, histrionic,* and *narcissistic* personality disorders. The final cluster features a high degree of anxiety and includes the *avoidant, dependent,* and *obsessive-compulsive* personality disorders.

These 10 personality disorders are each characterized by a group of problematic personality symptoms. For example, as you will soon see, *paranoid personality disorder* is diagnosed when individuals hold unjustified suspicions that others are harming them, have persistent unfound doubts about the loyalty of friends, read threatening meanings into benign events, persistently bear grudges, and have recurrent unjustified suspicions about the faithfulness of their life partners.

The DSM's listing of 10 distinct personality disorders is called a *categorical* approach. Like a light switch that is either on or off, this kind of approach assumes that (1) problematic personality traits are either present or absent in people, (2) a personality disorder is either displayed or not displayed by an individual, and (3) a person who suffers from a personality disorder is not markedly troubled by personality traits outside of that disorder.

It turns out, however, that these assumptions are frequently contradicted in clinical practice. In fact, the symptoms of the personality disorders listed in DSM-5 overlap so much that clinicians often find it difficult to distinguish one disorder from another (see Figure 16-1), resulting in frequent disagreements about which diagnosis is correct for a person with a personality disorder. Moreover, diagnosticians sometimes determine that particular individuals have more than one personality disorder (O'Connor, 2008). This lack of agreement has raised serious questions about the *validity* (accuracy) and *reliability* (consistency) of the 10 DSM-5 categories.

Given this state of affairs, many theorists have challenged the use of a categorical approach to personality disorders. They believe that personality disorders differ more in *degree* than in type of dysfunction and should instead be classified by the severity of personality traits rather than by the presence or absence of specific traits—a procedure called a *dimensional* approach (Skodol, 2010). In a dimensional approach each trait is seen as varying along a continuum extending from nonproblematic to extremely problematic.

People with a personality disorder are those who display extreme degrees of problematic traits—degrees not commonly found in the general population.

Given the inadequacies of a categorical approach and the growing enthusiasm for a dimensional one, the framers of DSM-5 initially proposed significant changes in how personality disorders should be classified. They proposed a largely dimensional system that would allow many additional kinds of personality problems to be classified as personality disorders and would require clinicians to assess the severity of each problematic trait exhibited by a person who receives a diagnosis of personality disorder. However, this proposal itself produced enormous concern and criticism in the clinical field, leading the

•**personality disorder**•An enduring, rigid pattern of inner experience and outward behavior that repeatedly impairs an individual's sense of self, emotional experiences, goals, capacity for empathy, and/or capacity for intimacy.

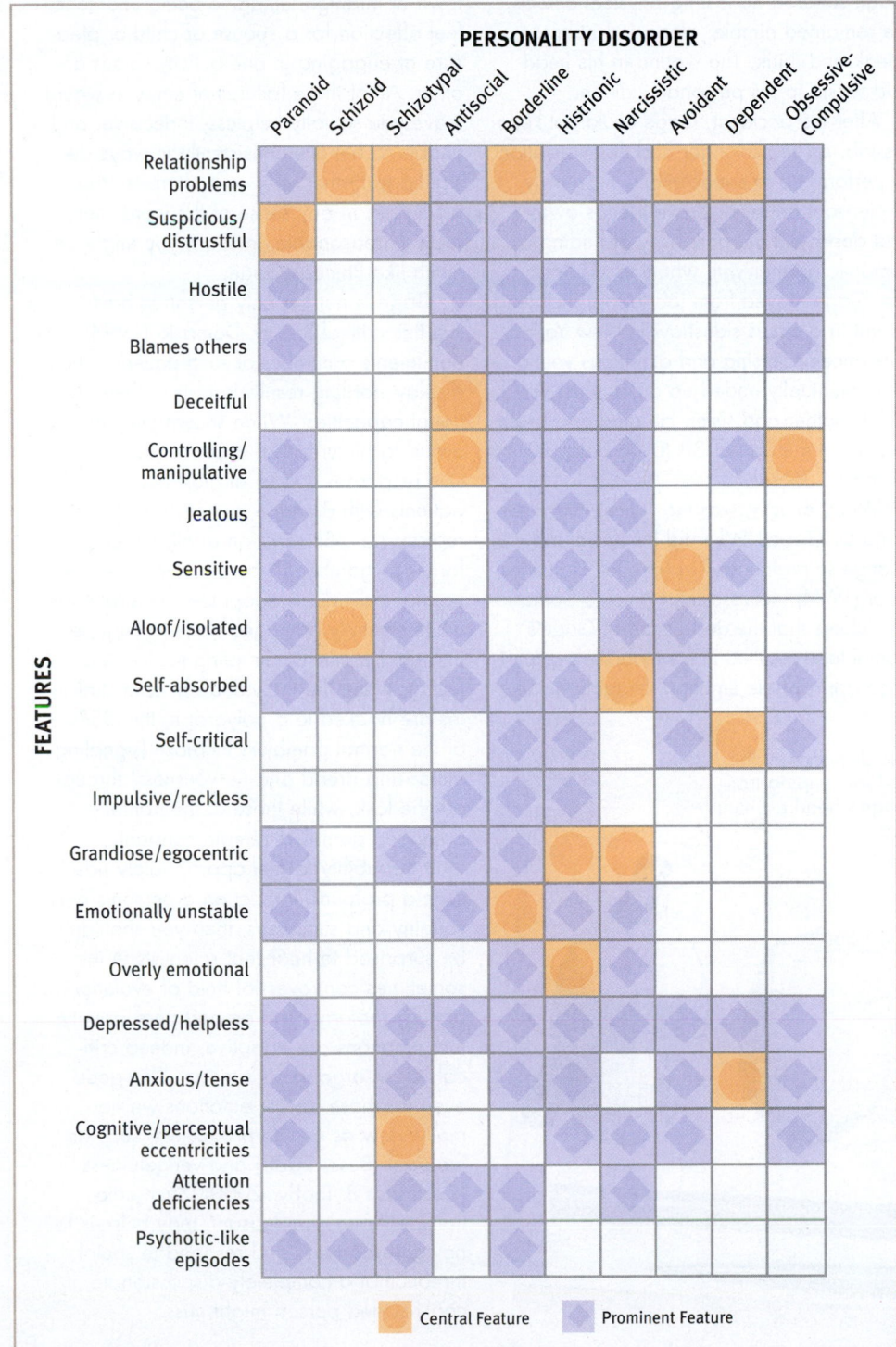

Figure 16-1

Prominent and central features of DSM-5's personality disorders The symptoms of the various personality disorders often overlap greatly, leading to frequent misdiagnosis or to multiple diagnoses for a given client.

Personality and the Brain: The Case of Phineas Gage

Most of us are aware that damage to particular regions in the brain can cause motor dysfunction, memory or language problems, or even the loss of particular senses such as vision or hearing. However, clinical scientists have come to appreciate that damage to the brain from strokes, injury, or tumors can also bring about major changes in personality. The tragic story of Phineas Gage provided science with history's most memorable evidence of this fact.

In 1848, 25-year-old Gage was laying tracks for a railroad, a hazardous but common occupation in those years. The smart, careful, and friendly Gage was admired and liked by the men he supervised, and the company that wrote the paychecks called him "the most efficient and capable" employee they had. But that was all to change in a few seconds' time, when a rock-blasting mishap hurled a three-foot-long tamping iron under Gage's left cheek and straight through the top of his skull, piercing a one-and-a-half-inch hole through his brain's frontal lobes (Della Sala, 2011).

Miraculously, Gage's body survived. But you could say that Gage himself, at least as others had known him, did not. From an even-tempered, responsible, and likable young man, Gage turned into a disrespectful, profane, impulsive, stubborn, and indecisive individual who had trouble planning for the future and sometimes had fits of temper. Beyond losing his sight in one eye, Gage suffered no lasting physical defects. He remained nimble, alert, and able to speak and think. The wound in his head laid waste to his personality alone.

After the accident, Gage could not keep his job, as he no longer had the motivation to perform up to expectations. His newly unpleasant behavior drove friends away and destroyed the possibility of finding a romantic partner with whom to share his life. Gage moved from job to job, including a stint in a circus sideshow in New York. This once-promising and ambitious young man eventually ended up a penniless ward of his mother and sister. He died of a brain seizure at the age of 38 (Della Sala, 2011; Damasio, 1994).

What, exactly, was the critical injury suffered by Gage? *Why* did his personality change so profoundly? In his book *Descartes' Error* (1994), neuroscientist Antonio Damasio speculates that the destruction of Gage's frontal lobe resulted in his inability to experience appropriate emotion. Imagine being unable to experience shame at saying rude things to your host at a dinner, anger at being duped by a con man who invests your money in a speculative venture, or fear at walking through a dangerous area of town at midnight. Imagine being unable to feel affection for a spouse or child or pleasure at engaging in one activity versus another. All of these failures of emotion would leave you socially helpless, indecisive, and unable to behave consistently in ways designed to further your own interests. You would be, in any sense of the word, perfectly unreasonable. In short, you might be much like Phineas Gage.

Gage is not the only person to have lost this critical faculty. Damasio (1994) documents a number of such patients who display startling results in tests of their emotional capacities. When shown emotion-arousing pictures that raise the galvanic skin responses (GSRs) of most people, patients with damage to their frontal lobes register no GSR reaction at all. When performing "gambling" tasks in certain studies, normal individuals adopt low-risk strategies, while frontally damaged patients engage in high-risk and bankrupting tactics. Most telling, when the individuals in such studies are hooked to a polygraph, the GSRs of the normal gamblers increase (signaling increasing dread and nervousness) throughout the task, while those of the frontally damaged gamblers remain constant.

If the ability to *feel* appropriately has such a profound impact on a person's personality and successes, then you shouldn't be surprised to hear that scientists in the sometimes controversial field of *evolutionary psychology* have argued persuasively that emotions are adaptive, indeed critical, to an organism's survival. This goes even for those darker emotions we normally view as counterproductive, such as jealousy (Buss, 2000) and vengefulness (Cosmides & Tooby, 2000). Such emotions, although unpleasant, may help us to navigate dangers and respond to social threats that a completely dispassionate, cool-headed person might miss.

Irreparable harm An 1850s artist offered these drawings of the injury suffered by Phineas Gage when a three-foot tamping iron penetrated his brain. Although the holes in Gage's head eventually healed, his previous personality did not survive.

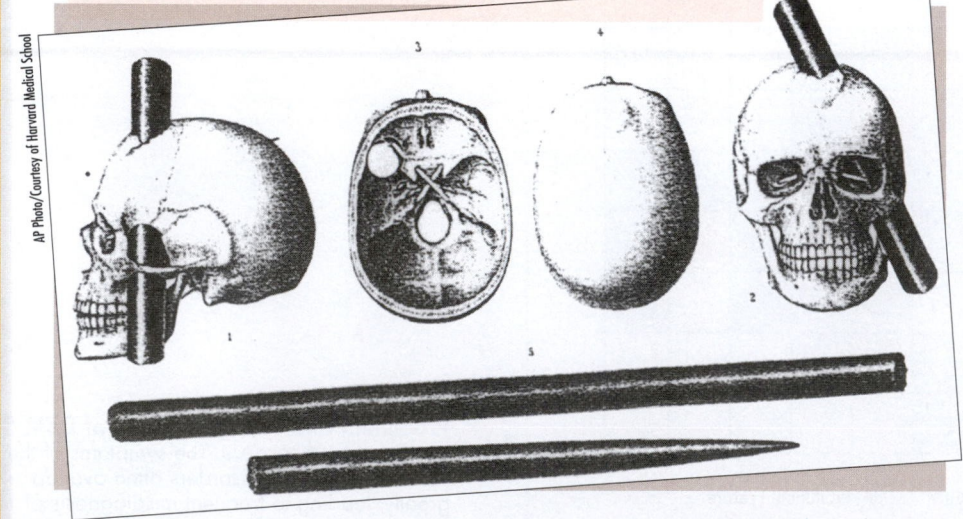

AP Photo/Courtesy of Harvard Medical School

framers of DSM-5 to change their mind and to retain a classic 10-disorder categorical approach in the new DSM. At the same time, they assigned their newly proposed dimensional approach for further study and possible inclusion in a future revision of DSM-5.

Most of the discussions in this chapter will be organized around the 10-disorder categorical approach currently used in DSM-5. Later in the chapter, however, we also will examine alternative—dimensional—approaches that are being considered for future use in the classification of personality disorders.

As you read about the various personality disorders, you should be clear that diagnoses of such disorders can easily be overdone. We may catch glimpses of ourselves or of people we know in the descriptions of these disorders, and we may be tempted to conclude that we or they have a personality disorder. In the vast majority of instances, such interpretations are incorrect. We all display personality traits. Only occasionally are they so maladaptive, distressful, and inflexible that they can be considered disorders.

> **Why do you think personality disorders are particularly subject to so many efforts at amateur psychology?**

"Odd" Personality Disorders

The cluster of *"odd" personality disorders* consists of the *paranoid, schizoid,* and *schizotypal* personality disorders. People with these disorders typically display odd or eccentric behaviors that are similar to but not as extensive as those seen in schizophrenia, including extreme suspiciousness, social withdrawal, and peculiar ways of thinking and perceiving things. Such behaviors often leave the person isolated. Some clinicians believe that these personality disorders are actually related to schizophrenia, and they call them *schizophrenia-spectrum disorders.* In support of this idea, people with these personality disorders often qualify for an additional diagnosis of schizophrenia or have close relatives with schizophrenia (Chemerinski & Siever, 2011; Bollini & Walker, 2007).

Clinicians have learned much about the symptoms of the odd personality disorders but have not been so successful in determining their causes or how to treat them. In fact, as you'll soon see, people with these disorders rarely seek treatment.

Paranoid Personality Disorder

As you read earlier, people with **paranoid personality disorder** deeply distrust other people and are suspicious of their motives (APA, 2013). Because they believe that everyone intends them harm, they shun close relationships. Their trust in their own ideas and abilities can be excessive, though, as you can see in the case of Amaya:

She believed, without cause, that her neighbors were harassing her by allowing their young children to make loud noise outside her apartment door. Rather than asking the neighbors to be more considerate, she stopped speaking to them and began a campaign of unceasingly antagonistic behavior: giving them "dirty looks," pushing past them aggressively in the hallway, slamming doors, and behaving rudely toward their visitors. After over a year had passed, when the neighbors finally confronted her about her obnoxious behavior, she accused them of purposely harassing her. "Everyone knows that these doors are paper thin," she said, "and that I can hear everything that goes on in the hallway. You are doing it deliberately." Nothing that the neighbors said could convince her otherwise. Despite their attempts to be more considerate about the noise outside her apartment, she continued to behave in a rude and aggressive manner toward them.

Neighbors and visitors commented that [Amaya] appeared tense and angry. Her face looked like a hard mask. She was rarely seen smiling. She walked around the neighborhood wearing dark sunglasses, even on cloudy days. She was often seen yelling at her children, behavior that had earned her the nickname "the screamer" among the parents

(continued on the next page)

BETWEEN THE LINES

In Their Words

"Personality disorders . . . are the only things left in psychiatry where people think you are bad." ‹‹
Gary M. Flaxenberg, psychiatrist, 1998

•**paranoid personality disorder**•A personality disorder marked by a pattern of distrust and suspiciousness of others.

at her children's school. She had forced her children to change schools several times within the same district because she was dissatisfied with the education they were receiving. An unstated reason, perhaps, was that she had alienated so many other parents. [Amaya] worked at home during the day at a job that required her to have little contact with other people. She had few social contacts, and in conversation was often perceived to be sarcastic and hypercritical.

(Bernstein & Useda, 2007, p. 42)

Ever on guard and cautious and seeing threats everywhere, people like Amaya continually expect to be the targets of some trickery (see Figure 16-2). They find "hidden" meanings, which are usually belittling or threatening, in everything. In a study that required individuals to role-play, participants with paranoia were more likely than control participants to read hostile intentions into the actions of others (Turkat et al., 1990). In addition, they more often chose anger as the appropriate role-play response.

Quick to challenge the loyalty or trustworthiness of acquaintances, people with paranoid personality disorder remain cold and distant. A woman might avoid confiding in anyone, for example, for fear of being hurt, or a husband might, without any justification, persist in questioning his wife's faithfulness. Although inaccurate and inappropriate, their suspicions are not usually *delusional;* the ideas are not so bizarre or so firmly held as to clearly remove the individuals from reality (Millon, 2011).

People with this disorder are critical of weakness and fault in others, particularly at work. They are unable to recognize their own mistakes, however, and are extremely sensitive to criticism. They often blame others for the things that go wrong in their lives, and they repeatedly bear grudges (Rotter, 2011). Between 0.5 and 3 percent of adults are believed to experience this disorder, apparently more men than women (Paris, 2010; O'Connor, 2008; Mattia & Zimmerman, 2001).

How Do Theorists Explain Paranoid Personality Disorder?

The proposed explanations of paranoid personality disorder, like those of most other personality disorders, have received little systematic research (Bernstein & Useda, 2007). Psychodynamic theories, the oldest of the explanations for this disorder, trace the pattern to early interactions with demanding parents, particularly distant, rigid fathers and overcontrolling, rejecting mothers (Caligor & Clarkin, 2010; Williams, 2010). (You will see that psychodynamic explanations for almost all the personality disorders begin the same way—with repeated mistreatment during childhood and lack of love.) According to one psychodynamic view, some individuals come to view their environment as hostile as a result of their parents' persistently unreasonable demands. They must always be on the alert because they cannot trust others, and they are likely to develop feelings of extreme anger. They also project these feelings onto others and, as a result, feel increasingly persecuted (Koenigsberg et al., 2001). Similarly, some cognitive theorists suggest that people with paranoid personality disorder generally hold broad maladaptive assumptions, such as "People are evil" and "People will attack you if given the chance" (Beck & Weishaar, 2011; Weishaar & Beck, 2006; Beck et al., 2004).

Biological theorists propose that paranoid personality disorder has genetic causes (Bernstein & Useda, 2007). One study that looked at self-reports of suspiciousness in 3,810 Australian twin pairs found that if one twin was excessively suspicious, the other had an increased likelihood of also being suspicious (Kendler et al., 1987). Once again, however, it is important to note that such similarities between twins might also be the result of common environmental experiences.

Treatments for Paranoid Personality Disorder
People with paranoid personality disorder do not typically see themselves as needing help, and few come to treatment willingly (Millon, 2011). Furthermore, many who are

Figure 16-2

Whom do you distrust? Although distrust and suspiciousness are the hallmarks of paranoid personality disorder, even persons without this disorder are surprisingly untrusting. In a broad survey, the majority of respondents said they distrust lawyers, congressional members, journalists, and television newscasters (Harris Poll, 2006).

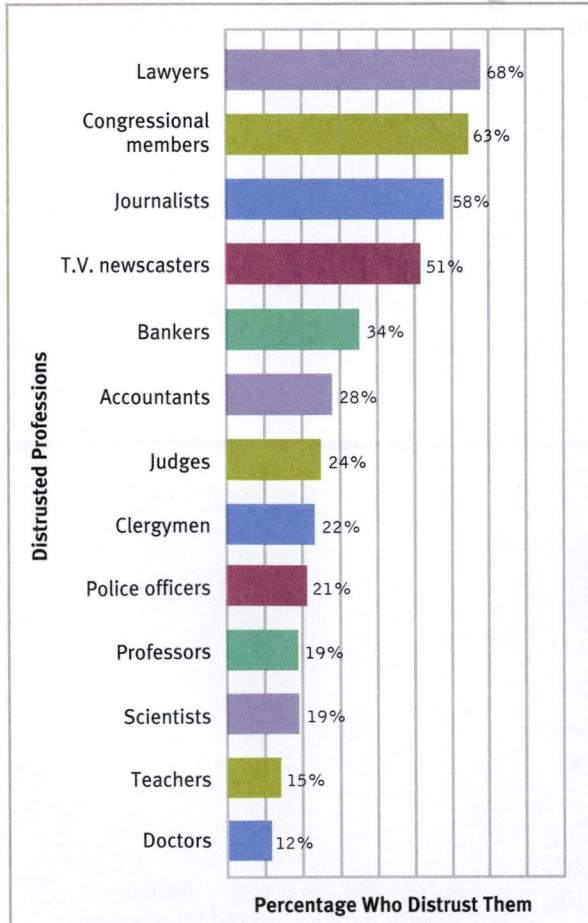

Distrusted Professions / Percentage Who Distrust Them

- Lawyers 68%
- Congressional members 63%
- Journalists 58%
- T.V. newscasters 51%
- Bankers 34%
- Accountants 28%
- Judges 24%
- Clergymen 22%
- Police officers 21%
- Professors 19%
- Scientists 19%
- Teachers 15%
- Doctors 12%

in treatment view the role of patient as inferior and distrust and rebel against their therapists (Bender, 2005). Thus it is not surprising that therapy for this disorder, as for most other personality disorders, has limited effect and moves very slowly (Piper & Joyce, 2001).

Object relations therapists—the psychodynamic therapists who give center stage to relationships—try to see past the patient's anger and work on what they view as his or her deep wish for a satisfying relationship (Caligor & Clarkin, 2010; Salvatore et al., 2005). Self-therapists—the psychodynamic clinicians who focus on the need for a healthy and unified self—try to help clients reestablish self-cohesion (a unified personality), which they believe has been lost in the person's continuing negative focus on others (Vermote et al., 2010; Silverstein, 2007). Cognitive and behavioral techniques have also been applied in cases of paranoid personality disorder, often combined into an integrated cognitive-behavioral approach. On the behavioral side, therapists help the individuals to master anxiety-reduction techniques and to improve their skills at solving interpersonal problems. On the cognitive side, therapists guide the clients to develop more realistic interpretations of other people's words and actions and to become more aware of other people's points of view (Farmer & Nelson-Gray, 2005; Leahy, Beck, & Beck, 2005). Drug therapy seems to be of limited help (Silk & Jibson, 2010; Agronin, 2006).

Schizoid Personality Disorder

People with **schizoid personality disorder** persistently avoid and are removed from social relationships and demonstrate little in the way of emotion (APA, 2013). Like people with paranoid personality disorder, these individuals do not have close ties with other people. The reason they avoid social contact, however, has nothing to do with paranoid feelings of distrust or suspicion; it is because they genuinely prefer to be alone. Take Eli:

"Zero Degrees of Empathy"
With the term "skinhead" tattooed on the back of his head, this man awaits trial in Germany for committing neo-Nazi crimes against foreigners and liberals. Clinicians sometimes confront extreme racism, homophobia, and even apparent evil in their practices, particularly among clients with paranoid, antisocial, and certain other personality disorders. Famous developmental psychologist Simon Baron-Cohen argues in his book *Zero Degrees of Empathy* that the common element in all such behaviors is a total lack of empathy—a condition he attributes to a combination of genetic and environmental factors.

Eli, a student at the local technical institute, had been engaged in several different Internet certificate programs over the past few years, and was about to engage in yet another, when his mother, confused as to why he would not apply for a traditional degree at a "real" college, insisted he seek therapy. A loner by nature, Eli preferred not to socialize in any traditional sense, having little to no desire to get to know much about the people in his immediate social context. The way Eli saw it, . . . "at least at my school you just go to class and go home."

Routinely, he slept through much of his day and then spent his evenings, nights, and weekends at the school's computer lab, "chatting" with others over the Internet while not in class. Notably, people that he chatted with often sought to meet Eli, but he always declined these invitations, stating that he didn't really have any desire to learn more about them than what they shared over the computer in the chat rooms. He described a family life that was similar to that of his social surroundings; he was mostly oblivious of his younger brother and sister, two outgoing teens, despite the fact that they seemed to hold him in the highest regard, and he had recently alienated himself entirely from his father, who had left the family several years earlier. . . .

A marked deficit in social interest was notable in Eli, as were frequent behavioral eccentricities. . . . At best, he had acquired a peripheral . . . role in social and family relationships. . . . Rather than venturing outward, he had increasingly removed himself from others and from sources of potential growth and gratification. Life was uneventful, with extended periods of solitude interspersed.

(Millon, 2011)

People like Eli, often described as "loners," make no effort to start or keep friendships, take little interest in having sexual relationships, and even seem indifferent to their families. They seek out jobs that require little or no contact with others. When necessary,

•schizoid personality disorder• A personality disorder characterized by persistent avoidance of social relationships and little expression of emotion.

A darker knight
In this scene from the hugely popular 2008 movie *The Dark Knight,* Bruce Wayne confronts Batman, Wayne's alter ego and only real friend. True to the vision of comic book artist and writer Frank Miller, this film and its sequel, *The Dark Knight Rises,* present the crime-fighter as a singularly driven loner incapable of forming or sustaining relationships. Indeed, some clinical observers have argued that in key ways the current *Dark Knight* version of Batman displays the features of schizoid personality disorder.

•**schizotypal personality disorder**•
A personality disorder characterized by extreme discomfort in close relationships, odd forms of thinking and perceiving, and behavioral eccentricities.

they can form work relations to a degree, but they prefer to keep to themselves. Many live by themselves as well. Not surprisingly, their social skills tend to be weak. If they marry, their lack of interest in intimacy may create marital or family problems.

People with schizoid personality disorder focus mainly on themselves and are generally unaffected by praise or criticism. They rarely show any feelings, expressing neither joy nor anger. They seem to have no need for attention or acceptance; are typically viewed as cold, humorless, or dull; and generally succeed in being ignored. This disorder is estimated to be present in fewer than 1 percent of the population (Paris, 2010; Mittal et al., 2007). It is slightly more likely to occur in men than in women, and men may also be more impaired by it (APA, 2000).

How Do Theorists Explain Schizoid Personality Disorder? Many psychodynamic theorists, particularly object relations theorists, propose that schizoid personality disorder has its roots in an unsatisfied need for human contact (Caligor & Clarkin, 2010; Kernberg & Caligor, 2005). The parents of people with this disorder, like those of people with paranoid personality disorder, are believed to have been unaccepting or even abusive of their children. Whereas individuals with paranoid symptoms react to such parenting chiefly with distrust, those with schizoid personality disorder are left unable to give or receive love. They cope by avoiding all relationships.

Cognitive theorists propose, not surprisingly, that people with schizoid personality disorder suffer from deficiencies in their thinking. Their thoughts tend to be vague, empty, and without much meaning, and they have trouble scanning the environment to arrive at accurate perceptions (Kramer & Meystre, 2010). Unable to pick up emotional cues from others, they simply cannot respond to emotions. As this theory might predict, children with schizoid personality disorder develop language and motor skills very slowly, whatever their level of intelligence (Wolff, 2000, 1991).

Treatments for Schizoid Personality Disorder Their social withdrawal prevents most people with schizoid personality disorder from entering therapy unless some other disorder, such as alcoholism, makes treatment necessary (Mittal et al., 2007). These clients are likely to remain emotionally distant from the therapist, seem not to care about their treatment, and make limited progress at best (Millon, 2011).

Cognitive-behavioral therapists have sometimes been able to help people with this disorder experience more positive emotions and more satisfying social interactions (Beck & Weishaar, 2011; Weishaar & Beck, 2006; Beck et al., 2004). On the cognitive end, their techniques include presenting clients with lists of emotions to think about or having them write down and remember pleasurable experiences. On the behavioral end, therapists have sometimes had success teaching social skills to such clients, using role-playing, exposure techniques, and homework assignments as tools. Group therapy is apparently useful when it offers a safe setting for social contact, although people with this disorder may resist pressure to take part (Piper & Joyce, 2001). As with paranoid personality disorder, drug therapy seems to offer limited help (Silk & Jibson, 2010; Koenigsberg et al., 2002).

Schizotypal Personality Disorder

People with **schizotypal personality disorder** display a range of interpersonal problems marked by extreme discomfort in close relationships, very odd patterns of thinking and perceiving, and behavioral eccentricities (APA, 2013). Anxious around others, they seek isolation and have few close friends. Some feel intensely lonely. The disorder is more severe than the paranoid and schizoid personality disorders, as we see in the case of 41-year-old Kevin:

Kevin was a night security guard at a warehouse, where he had worked since his high school graduation more than 20 years ago. His parents, both successful professionals, had been worried for many years, as Kevin seemed entirely disconnected from himself and his surroundings and had never taken initiative to make any changes, even toward a shift supervisory position. They therefore made the referral for therapy, and Kevin simply acquiesced. He explained that he liked his work, as it was a place where he could be by himself in a quiet atmosphere, away from anyone else. He described where he worked as "an empty warehouse; they don't use it no more but they don't want no one in there. It's nice; 'homey.'"

Throughout the . . . interview, Kevin remained aloof, never once looking at the counselor, usually answering questions with either one-word responses or short phrases, and usually waiting to respond until a second question was asked or the first question was repeated. He described, in . . . . short, bizarre answers, a life devoid of almost any human interconnectedness, almost his only tangible contact being his brother, whom he saw only during major holidays. Living alone, he could only remember one significant relationship, and that was with a girl in high school. Very simply, he stated, "We graduated, and then I didn't see her anymore." He expressed no apparent loneliness, however, and appeared entirely emotionless regarding any aspect of his life. . . .

Kevin . . . often seemed to experience a separation between his mind and his physical body. There was a strange sense of nonbeing or nonexistence, as if his floating conscious awareness carried with it a depersonalized or identityless human form. Behaviorally, his tendency was to be drab, sluggish, and inexpressive. He . . . appeared bland, indifferent, unmotivated, and insensitive to the external world. . . . Most people considered him to be [a] strange person . . . who faded into the background, self-absorbed . . . and lost to the outside world. . . . Bizarre "telepathic" powers enabled him to communicate with mythical or distant others. . . . Kevin also occasionally decompensated when faced with too much, rather than too little, stimulation. . . . He would simply fade out, becoming blank, losing conscious awareness, and turning off the pressures of the outer world.

(Millon, 2011)

BETWEEN THE LINES

In Their Words

"Everyone is a moon, and has a dark side which he never shows to anybody." ‹‹

Mark Twain

As with Kevin, the thoughts and behaviors of people with schizotypal personality disorder can be noticeably disturbed. These symptoms may include *ideas of reference*—beliefs that unrelated events pertain to them in some important way—and *bodily illusions,* such as sensing an external "force" or presence. A number of people with this disorder see themselves as having special extrasensory abilities, and some believe that they have magical control over others. Examples of schizotypal eccentricities include repeatedly arranging cans to align their labels, organizing closets extensively, or wearing an odd assortment of clothing. The emotions of these individuals may be inappropriate, flat, or humorless.

People with schizotypal personality disorder often have great difficulty keeping their attention focused. Correspondingly, their conversation is typically digressive and vague, even sprinkled with loose associations (Millon, 2011; O'Connor, 2008). Like Kevin, they tend to drift aimlessly and lead an idle, unproductive life. They are likely to choose undemanding jobs in which they can work below their capacity and are not required to interact with other people. It has been estimated that 2 to 4 percent of all people—slightly more males than females—may have a schizotypal personality disorder (Paris, 2010; Bollini & Walker, 2007; Mattia & Zimmerman, 2001).

How Do Theorists Explain Schizotypal Personality Disorder? Because

the symptoms of schizotypal personality disorder so often resemble those of schizophrenia, researchers have hypothesized that similar factors are at work in both disorders (Chemerinski & Siever, 2011). They have in fact found that schizotypal symptoms, like schizophrenic patterns, are often linked to family conflicts and to psychological

BETWEEN THE LINES

A Common Belief

People who think that they have extrasensory abilities are not necessarily suffering from schizotypal personality disorder. In fact, 73 percent of Americans believe in some form of the paranormal or occult—ESP, astrology, ghosts, communicating with the dead, or psychics (Gallup Poll, 2005). ‹‹

When personality disorders explode

In this video, Seung-Hui Cho, a student at Virginia Tech, described the slights he experienced throughout his life and displayed his desire for revenge. After mailing the video to NBC News, he proceeded, on April 16, 2007, to kill 32 people, including himself, and to wound 25 others in a campus shooting rampage. Most clinical observers agree that he displayed a combination of features from the antisocial, borderline, paranoid, schizoid, schizotypal, and narcissistic personality disorders, including boundless fury and hatred, extreme social withdrawal, persistent distrust, strange thinking, intimidating behavior and arrogance, disregard for others, and violation of social boundaries.

BETWEEN THE LINES

Portrait in Vanity

King Frederick V, ruler of Denmark from 1746 to 1766, had his portrait painted at least 70 times by the same artist, Carl Pilo (Shaw, 2004). ‹‹

disorders in parents (Millon & Grossman, 2007; Carlson & Fish, 2005). They have also learned that defects in attention and short-term memory may contribute to schizotypal personality disorder, just as they apparently do to schizophrenia (Goldstein et al., 2011). For example, research participants with either disorder perform poorly on *backward masking*, a laboratory test of attention that requires individuals to identify a visual stimulus immediately after a previous stimulus has flashed on and off the screen. People with these disorders have a hard time shutting out the first stimulus in order to focus on the second. Finally, researchers have begun to link schizotypal personality disorder to some of the same biological factors found in schizophrenia, such as high activity of the neurotransmitter dopamine, enlarged brain ventricles, smaller temporal lobes, and loss of gray matter (Hazlett et al., 2011; Bollini & Walker, 2007). As you read in Chapter 14, there are indications that these biological factors may have a genetic base.

Although these findings do suggest a close relationship between schizotypal personality disorder and schizophrenia, the personality disorder also has been linked to disorders of mood (Lentz, Robinson, & Bolton, 2010). Over half of people with the personality disorder also suffer from major depressive disorder at some point in their lives (APA, 2000). Moreover, relatives of people with depression have a higher than usual rate of schizotypal personality disorder, and vice versa. Thus, at the very least, this personality disorder is not tied exclusively to schizophrenia.

Treatments for Schizotypal Personality Disorder Therapy is as difficult in cases of schizotypal personality disorder as it is in cases of paranoid and schizoid personality disorders. Most therapists agree on the need to help these clients "reconnect" with the world and recognize the limits of their thinking and their powers. The therapists may thus try to set clear limits—for example, by requiring punctuality—and work on helping the clients recognize where their views end and those of the therapist begin. Other therapy goals are to increase positive social contacts, ease loneliness, reduce overstimulation, and help the individuals become more aware of their personal feelings (Sperry, 2003; Piper & Joyce, 2001).

Cognitive-behavioral therapists further combine cognitive and behavioral techniques to help people with schizotypal personality disorder function more effectively. Using cognitive interventions, they try to teach clients to evaluate their unusual thoughts or perceptions objectively and to ignore the inappropriate ones (Beck & Weishaar, 2011; Weishaar & Beck, 2006; Beck et al., 2004). Therapists may keep track of clients' odd or magical predictions, for example, and later point out their inaccuracy. When clients are speaking and begin to digress, the therapists might ask them to sum up what they are trying to say. In addition, specific behavioral methods, such as speech lessons, social skills training, and tips on appropriate dress and manners, have sometimes helped clients learn to blend in better with and be more comfortable around others (Farmer & Nelson-Gray, 2005).

Antipsychotic drugs have been given to people with schizotypal personality disorder, again because of the disorder's similarity to schizophrenia. In low doses the drugs appear to have helped some people, usually by reducing certain of their thought problems (Silk & Jibson, 2010; Koenigsberg et al., 2003, 2002).

"Dramatic" Personality Disorders

The cluster of *"dramatic" personality disorders* includes the *antisocial, borderline, histrionic,* and *narcissistic* personality disorders. The behaviors of people with these problems are so dramatic, emotional, or erratic that it is almost impossible for them to have relationships that are truly giving and satisfying.

These personality disorders are more commonly diagnosed than the others. However, only the antisocial and borderline personality disorders have received much study, partly because they create so many problems for other people. The causes of the disorders, like those of the odd personality disorders, are not well understood. Treatments range from ineffective to moderately effective.

Antisocial Personality Disorder

Sometimes described as "psychopaths" or "sociopaths," people with **antisocial personality disorder** persistently disregard and violate others' rights (APA, 2013). Aside from substance use disorders, this is the disorder most closely linked to adult criminal behavior. DSM-5 stipulates that a person must be at least 18 years of age to receive this diagnosis; however, most people with antisocial personality disorder displayed some patterns of misbehavior before they were 15, including truancy, running away, cruelty to animals or people, and destroying property.

Robert Hare (1993), a leading researcher of antisocial personality disorder, recalls an early professional encounter with a prison inmate named Ray:

In the early 1960s, I found myself employed as the sole psychologist at the British Columbia Penitentiary.... I wasn't in my office for more than an hour when my first "client" arrived. He was a tall, slim, dark-haired man in his thirties. The air around him seemed to buzz, and the eye contact he made with me was so direct and intense that I wondered if I had ever really looked anybody in the eye before. That stare was unrelenting—he didn't indulge in the brief glances away that most people use to soften the force of their gaze.

Without waiting for an introduction, the inmate—I'll call him Ray—opened the conversation: "Hey, Doc, how's it going? Look, I've got a problem. I need your help. I'd really like to talk to you about this."

Eager to begin work as a genuine psychotherapist, I asked him to tell me about it. In response, he pulled out a knife and waved it in front of my nose, all the while smiling and maintaining that intense eye contact.

Once he determined that I wasn't going to push the button, he explained that he intended to use the knife not on me but on another inmate who had been making overtures to his "protégé," a prison term for the more passive member of a homosexual pairing. Just why he was telling me this was not immediately clear, but I soon suspected that he was checking me out, trying to determine what sort of a prison employee I was....

From that first meeting on, Ray managed to make my eight-month stint at the prison miserable. His constant demands on my time and his attempts to manipulate me into doing things for him were unending. On one occasion, he convinced me that he would make a good cook ... and I supported his request for a transfer from the machine shop (where he had apparently made the knife). What I didn't consider was that the kitchen was a source of sugar, potatoes, fruit, and other ingredients that could be turned into alcohol. Several months after I had recommended the transfer, there was a mighty eruption below the floorboards directly under the warden's table. When the commotion died down, we found an elaborate system for distilling alcohol below the floor. Something had gone wrong and one of the pots had exploded. There was nothing unusual about the presence of a still in a maximum-security prison, but the audacity of placing one under the warden's seat shook up a lot of people. When it was discovered that Ray was the brains behind the bootleg operation, he spent some time in solitary confinement.

Once out of "the hole," Ray appeared in my office as if nothing had happened and asked for a transfer from the kitchen to the auto shop—he really felt he had a knack, he saw the need to prepare himself for the outside world, if he only had the time to practice he could have his own body shop on the outside.... I was still feeling the sting of having arranged the first transfer, but eventually he wore me down.

Soon afterward I decided to leave the prison to pursue a Ph.D. in psychology, and about a month before I left Ray almost persuaded me to ask my father, a roofing contractor, to offer him a job as part of an application for parole.

(continued on the next page)

•antisocial personality disorder• A personality disorder marked by a general pattern of disregard for and violation of other people's rights.

BETWEEN THE LINES

Previous Identity

Antisocial personality disorder was referred to as "moral insanity" during the nineteenth century. ‹‹

Notorious disregard

In 2009, financier Bernard Madoff was sentenced to 150 years in prison after defrauding thousands of investors, including many charities, of billions of dollars. Given his overwhelming disregard for others and other such qualities, some clinicians suggest that Madoff displays antisocial personality disorder.

Ray had an incredible ability to con not just me but everybody. He could talk, and lie, with a smoothness and a directness that sometimes momentarily disarmed even the most experienced and cynical of the prison staff. When I met him he had a long criminal record behind him (and, as it turned out, ahead of him); about half his adult life had been spent in prison, and many of his crimes had been violent. . . . He lied endlessly, lazily, about everything, and it disturbed him not a whit whenever I pointed out something in his file that contradicted one of his lies. He would simply change the subject and spin off in a different direction. Finally convinced that he might not make the perfect job candidate in my father's firm, I turned down Ray's request—and was shaken by his nastiness at my refusal.

Before I left the prison for the university, I took advantage of the prison policy of letting staff have their cars repaired in the institution's auto shop—where Ray still worked, thanks (he would have said no thanks) to me. The car received a beautiful paint job and the motor and drivetrain were reconditioned.

With all our possessions on top of the car and our baby in a plywood bed in the backseat, my wife and I headed for Ontario. The first problems appeared soon after we left Vancouver, when the motor seemed a bit rough. Later, when we encountered some moderate inclines, the radiator boiled over. A garage mechanic discovered ball bearings in the carburetor's float chamber; he also pointed out where one of the hoses to the radiator had clearly been tampered with. These problems were repaired easily enough, but the next one, which arose while we were going down a long hill, was more serious. The brake pedal became very spongy and then simply dropped to the floor—no brakes, and it was a long hill. Fortunately, we made it to a service station, where we found that the brake line had been cut so that a slow leak would occur. Perhaps it was a coincidence that Ray was working in the auto shop when the car was being tuned up, but I had no doubt that the prison "telegraph" had informed him of the owner of the car.

(Hare, 1993)

Like Ray, people with antisocial personality disorder lie repeatedly (APA, 2013). Many cannot work consistently at a job; they are absent frequently and are likely to quit their jobs altogether. Usually they are also careless with money and frequently fail to pay their debts. They are often impulsive, taking action without thinking of the consequences (Millon, 2011). Correspondingly, they may be irritable, aggressive, and quick to start fights. Many travel from place to place.

Recklessness is another common trait: people with antisocial personality disorder have little regard for their own safety or for that of others, even their children. They are self-centered as well, and are likely to have trouble maintaining close relationships. Usually they develop a knack for gaining personal profit at the expense of other people. Because the pain or damage they cause seldom concerns them, clinicians commonly say that they lack a moral conscience (Kantor, 2006) (see Table 16-1). They think of their victims as weak and deserving of being conned, robbed, or even physically harmed (see *PsychWatch* on the next page).

Surveys indicate that as many as 2 to 3.5 percent of people in the United States meet the criteria for antisocial personality disorder (Paris, 2010; O'Connor, 2008; Mattia & Zimmerman, 2001). The disorder is as much as four times more common among men than women.

Because people with this disorder are often arrested, researchers frequently look for people with antisocial patterns in prison populations (Black et al., 2010; Blair et al., 2005). In fact, it is estimated that around 30 percent of people in prison meet the diagnostic criteria for this disorder (O'Connor, 2008). Among men in urban jails, the antisocial personality pattern has been linked strongly to past arrests for crimes of violence

? How do various institutions in our society—business, government, science, religion—view lying? How might such views affect lying by individuals?

table: 16-1

Number of Annual Hate Crimes in the United States

Group Attacked	Number of Reported Incidents
Racial/ethnic groups	5,166
Religious groups	1,575
Sexual-orientation groups	1,482
Groups with disability	99

U.S. Department of Justice, Federal Bureau of Investigation, 2010

Mass Murders: Where Does Such Violence Come From?

On December 14, 2012, a young man entered the Sandy Hook Elementary School in Newtown, Connecticut, and killed 26 people, 20 of them young children, in a shooting rampage. In the months prior to this massacre, gunmen killed 7 people at a college in California, 12 moviegoers at a *Batman* movie in Colorado, 6 churchgoers at a Sikh temple in Wisconsin, and 5 workers at a sign company in Minnesota. Listening to some of the psychologists and psychiatrists interviewed immediately after these events, you might conclude that the mental health field has a clear understanding of why individuals commit mass murders and has effective treatments for persons capable of such acts. In fact, that is not the case. The clinical field has offered various theories about mass murderers, but enlightening research and effective interventions have been elusive (Ferguson et al., 2011; Bowers et al., 2010).

What do we know about mass killings? We know they involve, by definition, the murder of 4 or more people in the same location and at around the same time. FBI records also indicate that, on average, mass

killings occur in the United States every two weeks, 75 percent of them feature a lone killer, 67 percent involve the use of guns, and most are committed by males (Hoyer & Heath, 2012).

We also know that despite appearances, the number of mass killings is not on the rise *overall* (O'Neill, 2012). What is increasing, however, are certain kinds of mass killings. So-called pseudocommando mass murders, for example, are on the rise. A pseudocommando mass murderer "kills in public during the daytime, plans his offense well in advance, and comes prepared with a powerful arsenal of weapons. He has no escape planned and expects to be killed during the incident" (Knoll, 2010). Similarly, "autogenetic" (self-generated) massacres, in which individuals kill people indiscriminately to fulfill a personal agenda, seem be on the rise (Bowers et al., 2010; Mullen, 2004).

Theorists have suggested a number of factors to help explain pseudocommando, autogenetic, and other mass killings, including the availability of guns, bullying behavior, substance abuse, the proliferation of violent media and video games,

dysfunctional homes, contagion effects, and *mental illness*. In fact, regardless of one's position on gun control, media violence, or the like, almost everyone, including most clinicians, believes that mass killers typically suffer from a mental disorder (Archer, 2012). Which mental disorder? On this, there is little agreement. Each of the following has been suggested:

- Antisocial, borderline, paranoid, or schizotypal personality disorder
- Schizophrenia or severe bipolar disorder
- Intermittent explosive disorder—an impulse-control disorder featuring repeated, unprovoked verbal and/or behavioral outbursts (Coccaro, 2012)
- Severe disorder of mood, stress, or anxiety

Although these and yet other disorders have been proposed, none has received clear support in the limited research conducted on mass killings. On the other hand, several variables have emerged as a common denominator across the various studies: severe feelings of anger and resentment, feelings of being persecuted or grossly mistreated, and desires for revenge (Knoll, 2010). That is, regardless of which psychological disorder a mass killer may display, he usually is driven by this set of feelings. For a growing number of clinical researchers, this repeated finding suggests that research should focus less on diagnosis and much more on identifying and understanding these particular feelings.

Clearly, clinical research must expand its focus on this area of enormous social concern. Granted it is a difficult problem to investigate, partly because so few mass killers survive their crimes, but the clinical field has managed to gather useful insights about other elusive areas. And, indeed, in the aftermath of the horrific massacre of so many innocent children in the Newtown shooting rampage, a wave of heightened determination and commitment seems to have seized the clinical community (Archer, 2012).

AP Photo/Newtown Bee, Shannon Hicks

Unthinkable A police officer leads a line of frightened children to safety after the killing rampage at the Sandy Hook Elementary School in Connecticut.

(De Matteo et al., 2005). For many people with this disorder, criminal behavior declines after the age of 40; some, however, continue their criminal activities throughout their lives (Hurt & Oltmanns, 2002).

Studies and clinical observations also indicate higher rates of alcoholism and other substance use disorders among people with antisocial personality disorder than in the rest of the population (Brooner et al., 2010; Reese et al., 2010). Perhaps intoxication and substance misuse help trigger the development of antisocial personality disorder by loosening a person's inhibitions. Perhaps this personality disorder somehow makes a person more prone to abuse substances. Or perhaps antisocial personality disorder and substance use disorders both have the same cause, such as a deep-seated need to take risks. Interestingly, drug users with the personality disorder often cite the recreational aspects of drug use as their reason for starting and continuing it.

Finally, children with conduct disorder and an accompanying attention-deficit/hyperactivity disorder may have a heightened risk of developing antisocial personality disorder (Black et al., 2010; Lahey et al., 2005). These two childhood disorders, which you will read about in Chapter 17, often bear similarities to antisocial personality disorder. Like adults with antisocial personality disorder, children with a conduct disorder persistently lie and violate rules and other people's rights, and children with attention-deficit/hyperactivity disorder lack foresight and judgment and fail to learn from experience. Intriguing as these observations may be, however, the precise connection between the childhood disorders and antisocial personality disorder has been difficult to pinpoint.

Dark passenger

One of television's most famous sociopaths is Dexter Morgan, lead character in the drama series *Dexter*. A blood spatter analyst for the Miami Police Department by day and serial killer by night, Dexter experiences few genuine emotions. He avoids detection by being pleasant and generous and maintaining generally superficial relationships—skills taught to him by his stepfather so that he would not be discovered.

How Do Theorists Explain Antisocial Personality Disorder?

Explanations of antisocial personality disorder come from the psychodynamic, behavioral, cognitive, and biological models. As with many other personality disorders, psychodynamic theorists propose that this one, too, begins with an absence of parental love during infancy, leading to a lack of basic trust (Meloy & Yakeley, 2010; Sperry, 2003). In this view, some children—the ones who develop antisocial personality disorder—respond to the early inadequacies by becoming emotionally distant, and they bond with others through the use of power and destructiveness. In support of the psychodynamic explanation, researchers have found that people with this disorder are more likely than others to have had significant stress in their childhoods, particularly in such forms as family poverty, family violence, and parental conflict or divorce (Martens, 2005; Paris, 2001).

Many behavioral theorists have suggested that antisocial symptoms may be learned through *modeling,* or imitation (Gaynor & Baird, 2007). As evidence, they point to the higher rate of antisocial personality disorder found among the parents of people with this disorder (Paris, 2001). Other behaviorists have suggested that some parents unintentionally teach antisocial behavior by regularly rewarding a child's aggressive behavior (Kazdin, 2005). When the child misbehaves or becomes violent in reaction to the parents' requests or orders, for example, the parents may give in to restore peace. Without meaning to, they may be teaching the child to be stubborn and perhaps even violent.

The cognitive view says that people with antisocial personality disorder hold attitudes that trivialize the importance of other people's needs (Elwood et al., 2004). Such a philosophy of life, some theorists suggest, may be far more common in our society than people recognize (see Figure 16-3). Cognitive theorists further propose that people with this disorder have genuine difficulty recognizing a point of view other than their own.

Finally, studies suggest that biological factors may play an important role in antisocial personality disorder. Researchers have found that antisocial people, particularly

? Can you point to attitudes and events in today's world that may trivialize people's needs? What impact might they have on individual functioning?

those who are highly impulsive and aggressive, display lower serotonin activity than other individuals (Patrick, 2007). As you'll recall (see page 301), both impulsivity and aggression also have been linked to low serotonin activity in other kinds of studies, so the presence of this biological factor in people with antisocial personality disorder is not surprising.

Other studies further indicate that individuals with this disorder display deficient functioning in their frontal lobes, and particularly the prefrontal cortex (Morgan & Lilienfeld, 2000). Among other duties, this brain region helps individuals to plan and execute realistic strategies and to experience personal characteristics such as sympathy, judgment, and empathy. These are, of course, all qualities found wanting in people with antisocial personality disorder.

In yet another line of research, investigators have found that individuals with this disorder often experience less anxiety than other people, and so lack a key ingredient for learning (Blair et al., 2005). This would help explain why they have so much trouble learning from negative life experiences or tuning in to the emotional cues of others. Why should individuals with antisocial personality disorder experience less anxiety than other people? The answer may lie once again in the biological realm. Research participants with the disorder often respond to warnings or expectations of stress with low brain and bodily arousal, such as slow autonomic arousal and slow EEG waves (Perdeci et al., 2010; Gaynor & Baird, 2007). Perhaps because of the low arousal, the individuals easily tune out threatening or emotional situations, and so are unaffected by them.

It could also be argued that because of their physical underarousal, people with antisocial personality disorder would be more likely than other people to take risks and seek thrills. That is, they may be drawn to antisocial activity precisely because it meets an underlying biological need for more excitement and arousal. In support of this idea, as you read earlier, antisocial personality disorder often goes hand in hand with sensation-seeking behavior (Patrick, 2007).

Treatments for Antisocial Personality Disorder

Treatments for people with antisocial personality disorder are typically ineffective (Millon, 2011; Meloy & Yakeley, 2010). A major obstacle to treatment is the individuals' lack of conscience or desire to change (Kantor, 2006). Most of those in therapy have been forced to participate by an employer, their school, or the law, or they come to the attention of therapists when they also develop another psychological disorder (Agronin, 2006).

Some cognitive therapists try to guide clients with antisocial personality disorder to think about moral issues and about the needs of other people (Beck & Weishaar, 2011; Weishaar & Beck, 2006; Beck et al., 2004). In a similar vein, a number of hospitals and prisons have tried to create a therapeutic community for people with this disorder, a structured environment that teaches responsibility toward others (Harris & Rice, 2006). Some patients seem to profit from such approaches, but it appears that most do not. In recent years, clinicians have also used psychotropic medications, particularly atypical antipsychotic drugs, to treat people with antisocial personality disorder. Some report that these drugs help reduce certain features of the disorder, but systematic studies of this claim are still needed (Silk & Jibson, 2010; Markovitz, 2004).

Borderline Personality Disorder

People with **borderline personality disorder** display great instability, including major shifts in mood, an unstable self-image, and impulsivity (APA, 2013). These characteristics combine to make their relationships very unstable as well (Paris, 2010, 2005). Some of Ellen Farber's difficulties are typical:

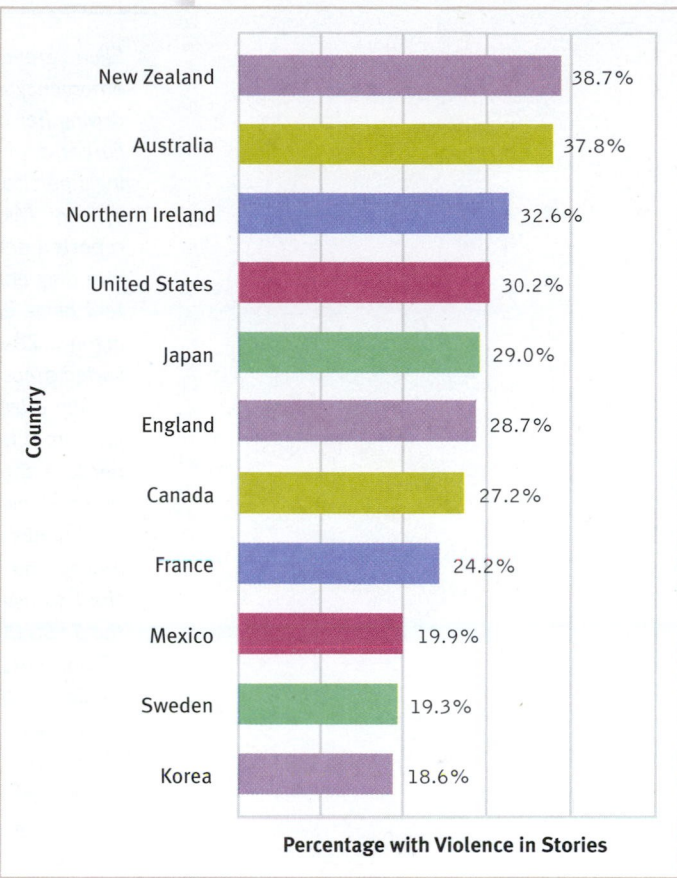

Figure 16-3

Are some cultures more antisocial than others? In a cross-cultural study, teenagers were asked to write stories describing how imaginary characters would respond to various conflicts. About one-third of the respondents from New Zealand, Australia, Northern Ireland, and the United States described violent responses, compared to less than one-fifth of the subjects from Korea, Sweden, and Mexico. (Adapted from Archer & McDaniel, 1995.)

•**borderline personality disorder**•A personality disorder characterized by repeated instability in interpersonal relationships, self-image, and mood and by impulsive behavior.

Ellen Farber, a 35-year-old, single insurance company executive, came to a psychiatric emergency room of a university hospital with complaints of depression and the thought of driving her car off a cliff. An articulate, moderately overweight, sophisticated woman, Ms. Farber appeared to be in considerable distress. She reported a 6-month period of increasingly persistent dysphoria and lack of energy and pleasure. Feeling as if she were "made of lead," Ms. Farber had recently been spending 15–20 hours a day in her bed. She also reported daily episodes of binge eating, when she would consume "anything I can find," including entire chocolate cakes or boxes of cookies. She reported problems with intermittent binge eating since adolescence, but these had recently increased in frequency, resulting in a 20-pound weight gain over the last few months. In the past her weight had often varied greatly as she had gone on and off a variety of diets. . . .

She attributed her increasing symptoms to financial difficulties. Ms. Farber had been fired from her job two weeks before coming to the emergency room. She claimed it was because she "owed a small amount of money." When asked to be more specific, she reported owing $150,000 to her former employers and another $100,000 to various local banks. Further questions revealed that she had always had difficulty managing her money and had been forced to declare bankruptcy at age 27. From age 30 to age 33, she had used her employer's credit cards to finance weekly "buying binges," accumulating the $150,000 debt. She . . . reported that spending money alleviated her chronic feelings of loneliness, isolation, and sadness. Experiencing only temporary relief, every few days she would impulsively buy expensive jewelry, watches, or multiple pairs of the same shoes. . . .

In addition to lifelong feelings of emptiness, Ms. Farber described chronic uncertainty about what she wanted to do in life and with whom she wanted to be friends. She had many brief, intense relationships with both men and women, but her quick temper led to frequent arguments and even physical fights. Although she had always thought of her childhood as happy and carefree, when she became depressed, she began to recall [being abused verbally and physically by her mother].

(Spitzer et al., 1994, pp. 395–397)

Personality disorders—at the movies

In this scene from the 1999 film *Girl, Interrupted,* based on a best-selling memoir, Susanna Kaysen (left, played by actress Winona Ryder) is befriended by Lisa Rowe (played by Angelina Jolie) at a mental hospital. Kaysen, who had recently made a suicide attempt, received a diagnosis of borderline personality disorder at the hospital, while Rowe's diagnosis was antisocial personality disorder. However, Rowe's rages, dramatic mood shifts, impulsivity, and other symptoms were actually more characteristic of a borderline picture than were Kaysen's.

Suzanne Tenner/Columbia Tristar/The Kobal Collection

Like Ellen Farber, people with borderline personality disorder swing in and out of very depressive, anxious, and irritable states that last anywhere from a few hours to a few days or more (see Table 16-3). Their emotions seem to be always in conflict with the world around them. They are prone to bouts of anger, which sometimes result in physical aggression and violence. Just as often, however, they direct their impulsive anger inward and inflict bodily harm on themselves. Many seem troubled by deep feelings of emptiness.

Borderline personality disorder is a complex disorder, and it is fast becoming one of the more common conditions seen in clinical practice. Many of the patients who come to mental health emergency rooms are individuals with this disorder who have intentionally hurt themselves. Their impulsive, self-destructive activities may range from alcohol and substance abuse to delinquency, unsafe sex, and reckless driving (Coffey et al., 2011; Sherry & Whilde, 2008). Many engage in so-called self-injurious or self-mutilation behaviors (see *MediaSpeak* on page 492), such as cutting or burning themselves or banging their heads (Chiesa, Sharp, & Fonagy, 2011). As you saw in Chapter 10, such behaviors typically cause immense physical suffering, but those with borderline personality disorder often feel as if the physical discomfort offers relief from their emotional suffering. It may serve as a distraction from their emotional or interpersonal upsets, "snapping" them out of an "emotional overload" (Stanley & Brodsky, 2005). Scars and bruises may also provide the individuals with a kind of documentation or concrete evidence of their emotional distress (Paris, 2010, 2005; Plante, 2006). Finally, many people with borderline personality disorder try to hurt themselves as a way of dealing with their chronic feelings of emptiness, boredom, and identity confusion. Many theorists believe that borderline patterns are more severe among individuals who injure themselves (Whipple & Fowler, 2011).

Suicidal threats and actions are also common. Studies suggest that around 75 percent of people with borderline personality disorder attempt suicide at least once in their lives; as many as 10 percent actually commit suicide (Gunderson, 2011; Leichsenring et al., 2011). It is common for people with this disorder to enter clinical treatment by way of the emergency room after a suicide attempt.

People with borderline personality disorder frequently form intense, conflict-ridden relationships in which their feelings are not necessarily shared by the other person. They may come to idealize another person's qualities and abilities after just a brief first encounter. They also may violate the boundaries of relationships (Skodol et al., 2002). Thinking in dichotomous (black-and-white) terms, they quickly experience feelings of rejection and become furious when their expectations are not met; yet they remain very attached to the relationships (Berenson et al., 2011). In fact, people with this disorder have recurrent fears of impending abandonment and frequently engage in frantic efforts to avoid real or imagined separations from important people in their lives (Gunderson, 2011; Sherry & Whilde, 2008). Sometimes they cut themselves or carry out other self-destructive acts to prevent partners from leaving.

Sufferers of borderline personality disorder typically experience dramatic shifts in their identity. An unstable sense of self may produce rapid shifts in goals, aspirations, friends, and even sexual orientation (Westen et al., 2011; Skodol, 2005). The individuals may also experience an occasional sense of dissociation, or detachment, from their own thoughts or bodies. Indeed, at times they may experience no sense of themselves at all, leading to the feelings of emptiness described earlier (Meares et al., 2011; Linehan, Cochran, & Kehrer, 2001).

Between 1 and 2.5 percent of the general population are thought to suffer from borderline personality disorder (Paris, 2010; Sherry & Whilde, 2008; Arntz, 2005). Close to 75 percent of the patients who receive the diagnosis are women (Gunderson, 2011). The course of the disorder varies from person to person. In the most common pattern, the individual's instability and risk of suicide peak during young adulthood and then gradually wane with advancing age (Hurt & Oltmanns, 2002). Males with borderline personality disorder may display more aggressive, disruptive, and antisocial behaviors than females (Bradley et al., 2005). Given the chaotic and unstable relationships characteristic of borderline personality disorder, it is not surprising that this disorder tends to interfere with job performance more than most other personality disorders do. Only about 25 percent of people with this disorder are employed full time (Gunderson, 2011).

How Do Theorists Explain Borderline Personality Disorder?
Because a fear of abandonment tortures so many people with borderline personality disorder, psychodynamic theorists have looked once again to early parental relationships to explain the disorder (Gabbard, 2010). Object relations theorists, for example, propose that an early lack of acceptance by parents may lead to a loss of self-esteem, increased dependence, and an inability to cope with separation (Caligor & Clarkin, 2010; Sherry & Whilde, 2008).

table: 16-2

Comparison of Personality Disorders

	Cluster	Similar Disorders	Responsiveness to Treatment
Paranoid	Odd	Schizophrenia; delusional disorder	Modest
Schizoid	Odd	Schizophrenia; delusional disorder	Modest
Schizotypal	Odd	Schizophrenia; delusional disorder	Modest
Antisocial	Dramatic	Conduct disorder	Poor
Borderline	Dramatic	Mood disorders	Moderate
Histrionic	Dramatic	Somatic symptom disorder; mood disorders	Modest
Narcissistic	Dramatic	Cyclothymic disorder (mild bipolar disorder)	Poor
Avoidant	Anxious	Social anxiety disorder	Moderate
Dependent	Anxious	Separation anxiety disorder; dysthymic disorder (mild depressive disorder)	Moderate
Obsessive-compulsive	Anxious	Obsessive-compulsive disorder	Moderate

MediaSpeak

Videos of Self-Injury Find an Audience

By Roni Caryn Rabin, *New York Times*

YouTube videos are spreading word of a self-destructive behavior already disturbingly common among many teenagers and young adults—"cutting" and other forms of self-injury that stop short of suicide, a new study reports.

As many as one in five young men and women are believed to have engaged at least once in what psychologists call nonsuicidal self-injury. Now the behavior is being depicted in hundreds of YouTube clips—most of which don't carry any warnings about the content—that show explicit videos and photographs of people injuring themselves, usually by cutting. They also depict burning, hitting and biting oneself, picking at one's skin, disturbing wounds and embedding objects under the skin. Most of the injuries are inflicted on the wrists and arms and, less commonly, on the legs, torso or other parts of the body.

Some of the videos weave text, music and photography together, which may glamorize self-harming behaviors even more, the paper's authors warn.

And the videos are popular. Many viewers rated the videos positively, selecting them as favorites more than 12,000 times, according to the new study, . . . whose authors reviewed the 100 most-viewed videos on self-harm.

Stephen P. Lewis, assistant professor of psychology at the University of Guelph in Ontario and the paper's lead author, calls the YouTube depictions of self-harm "an alarming new trend," especially considering how popular Internet use is among the population that engages most in self-injury already: teenagers and young adults.

"The risk is that these videos normalize self-injury, and foster a virtual community for some people in which self-injury is accepted, and the message of getting help is not necessarily

conveyed," Dr. Lewis said. "There's another risk, which is the phenomenon of 'triggering,' when someone who has a history of self-injury then watches a video or sees a picture, his or her urge to self-injure might actually increase in the moment."

Only about one in four of the 100 most-viewed videos sent a clear message against self-injury, the paper's analysis showed, and about the same proportion had an encouraging message that suggested the behavior could be overcome. About half the videos had a sad, melancholic tone, while about half described the behavior in a straightforward and factual manner.

About a quarter of the videos conveyed a mixed message about self-injury, while 42 percent were deemed neutral and 7 percent were clearly favorable toward self-injury.

Only 42 percent of the videos warned viewers about the content.

Research has found that the early childhoods of people with the disorder are often consistent with this view. In many cases, the parents of such individuals neglected or rejected them, verbally abused them, or otherwise behaved inappropriately (Huang, Yang, & Wu, 2010; Bradley et al., 2005). Similarly, their childhoods were often marked by multiple parent substitutes, divorce, death, or traumas such as physical or sexual abuse. Indeed, research suggests that early sexual abuse is a common contributor to the development of borderline personality disorder (Huang et al., 2010; Bradley et al., 2005); children who experience such abuse are four times more likely to develop the disorder than those who do not (Zelkowitz et al., 2001). At the same time, it is important to recognize that the vast majority of persons with histories of physical, sexual, or psychological abuse do not go on to develop this disorder (Skodol, 2005).

Borderline personality disorder also has been linked to certain biological abnormalities, such as an overly reactive *amygdala,* the brain structure so closely tied to fear and other negative emotions, and an underactive *prefrontal cortex,* the brain region linked to planning, self-control, and decision-making (Gunderson, 2011; Hall et al., 2010). Moreover, borderline individuals who are particularly impulsive—those who attempt suicide or are very aggressive toward others—apparently have lower brain serotonin activity

(Herpertz, 2011). Several studies have further tied this lower activity to an abnormality of the individuals' *5-HTT gene* (the *serotonin transporter gene*) (Ni et al., 2006). As you may recall, this gene also has been linked to major depressive disorder, suicide, aggression, and impulsivity (see page 231). In accord with these various biological findings, close relatives of those with borderline personality disorder are five times more likely than the general population to have the same personality disorder (Gunderson, 2011; Torgersen, 2000, 1984; Kendler et al., 1991).

A number of theorists currently use a *biosocial theory* to explain borderline personality disorder (Arens et al., 2011; Rizvi et al., 2011; Linehan, 1993). According to this view, the disorder results from a combination of internal forces (for example, difficulty identifying and controlling one's emotions, social skill deficits, abnormal neurotransmitter reactions) and external forces (for example, an environment in which a child's emotions are punished, ignored, trivialized, or disregarded). Parents may, for example, misinterpret their child's intense emotions as exaggerations or attempts at manipulation rather than as serious expressions of unsettled internal states. According to the biosocial theory, if children have intrinsic difficulties identifying and controlling their emotions and if their parents further teach them to ignore their intense feelings, the children may never learn how properly to recognize and control their emotional arousal, how to tolerate emotional distress, or when to trust their emotional responses (Gratz & Tull, 2011). In turn, such children will be at risk for the development of borderline personality disorder.

Note that the biosocial theory is similar to one of the leading explanations for eating disorders. As you saw in Chapter 11, theorist Hilde Bruch proposed that children whose parents do not respond accurately to the children's internal cues may never learn to identify cues of hunger, thus increasing their risk of developing an eating disorder (see pages 324–326). Small wonder that a large number of people with borderline personality disorder also display an eating disorder (Rowe et al., 2010; Zanarini et al., 2010). Recall, for example, Ellen Farber's dysfunctional eating pattern.

Finally, some sociocultural theorists suggest that cases of borderline personality disorder are particularly likely to emerge in cultures that change rapidly. As a culture loses its stability, they argue, it inevitably leaves many of its members with problems of identity, a sense of emptiness, high anxiety, and fears of abandonment (Paris, 2010, 1991). Family units may come apart, leaving people with little sense of belonging. Changes of this kind in society today may explain growing reports of the disorder (Millon, 2011).

Treatments for Borderline Personality Disorder It appears that psychotherapy can eventually lead to some degree of improvement for people with borderline personality disorder (Leichsenring et al., 2011). It is, however, extraordinarily difficult for a therapist to strike a balance between empathizing with the borderline client's dependency and anger and challenging his or her way of thinking (Gabbard, 2010; Sherry & Whilde, 2008). Given the emotionally draining demands of clients with borderline personality disorder, some therapists refuse to treat such individuals. The wildly fluctuating interpersonal attitudes of clients with the disorder can also make it difficult for therapists to establish collaborative working relationships with them (Bender & Oldham, 2005). Moreover, such clients may violate the boundaries of the client–therapist relationship (for example, calling the therapist's emergency contact number to discuss matters of a less urgent nature) (Gutheil, 2005).

Traditional psychoanalysis has not been effective with these individuals (Doering et al., 2010; Bender & Oldham, 2005). The clients often experience the psychoanalytic therapist's reserved style and encouragement of free association as suggesting disinterest and abandonment. The clients may also have difficulties tolerating interpretations made by psychoanalytic therapists, experiencing them as attacks.

Contemporary psychodynamic approaches, such as *relational psychoanalytic therapy* (see page 58), in which therapists take a more supportive and egalitarian posture, have been more effective than traditional psychoanalytic approaches (Muran et al., 2010; Yeomans & Diamond, 2010). In such contemporary approaches, therapists work to provide an empathic setting within which borderline clients can explore their unconscious conflicts and pay particular attention to their central relationship disturbance, poor sense of self, and pervasive loneliness and emptiness (Gabbard, 2010, 2001; Piper & Joyce, 2001). Research has found that contemporary psychodynamic approaches sometimes help reduce suicide attempts, self-harm behaviors, and the number of hospitalizations and bring at least some improvement to individuals with the disorder (Clarkin et al., 2010, 2001; Messer & Abbass, 2010).

Over the past two decades, an integrative treatment for borderline personality disorder, called *dialectical behavior therapy* (*DBT*), has received growing research support and is now considered the treatment of choice in many clinical circles (Kliem et al., 2010; Linehan et al., 2006, 2002, 2001). DBT, developed by psychologist Marsha Linehan, grows largely from the cognitive-behavioral treatment model (see *MediaSpeak* below). As such, it includes a number of the same cognitive and behavioral techniques that are

MediaSpeak

The Patient as Therapist

By Benedict Carey, *New York Times*

Are you one of us?

The patient wanted to know, and her therapist—Marsha M. Linehan of the University of Washington, creator of a treatment used worldwide for severely suicidal people—had a ready answer. It was the one she always used to cut the question short, whether a patient asked it hopefully, accusingly or knowingly, having glimpsed the macramé of faded burns, cuts and welts on Dr. Linehan's arms:

"You mean, have I suffered?"

"No, Marsha," the patient replied, in an encounter last spring. "I mean one of us. Like us. Because if you were, it would give all of us so much hope."

"That did it," said Dr. Linehan, 68, who told her story in public for the first time last week before an audience . . . at the Institute of Living, the Hartford clinic where she was first treated for extreme social withdrawal at age 17. "So many people have begged me to come forward, and I just thought—well, I have to do this. I owe it to them. I cannot die a coward." . . .

Dr. Linehan . . . was driven by a mission to rescue people who are chronically suicidal, often as a result of borderline personality disorder, an enigmatic condition characterized in part by self-destructive urges. "I honestly didn't realize at the time that I was dealing with myself," she said. "But I suppose it's true that I developed a therapy that provides the things I needed for so many years and never got."

"I Was in Hell"

She learned the central tragedy of severe mental illness the hard way, banging her head against the wall of a locked room.

Marsha Linehan arrived at the Institute of Living on March 9, 1961, at age 17, and quickly became the sole occupant of the seclusion room on the unit known as Thompson Two, for the most severely ill patients. The staff saw no alternative: The girl attacked herself habitually, burning her wrists with cigarettes,

slashing her arms, her legs, her midsection, using any sharp object she could get her hands on.

The seclusion room . . . had no such weapon. Yet her urge to die only deepened. So she did the only thing that made any sense to her at the time: banged her head against the wall and, later, the floor. Hard. . . .

[D]octors gave her a diagnosis of schizophrenia; dosed her with Thorazine, Librium and other powerful drugs, as well as hours of Freudian analysis; and strapped her down for electroshock treatments, 14 shocks the first time through and 16 the second, according to her medical records. Nothing changed, and soon enough the patient was back in seclusion on the locked ward. . . .

"I was in hell," she said. "And I made a vow: when I get out, I'm going to come back and get others out of here."

Radical Acceptance

. . . It was 1967, several years after she left the institute as a desperate 20-year-old whom doctors gave little chance of surviving outside the hospital. . . . "One night I was kneeling in [church], looking up at the cross, and the whole place became gold—and suddenly I felt something coming toward me," she said. "It was this shimmering experience, and I just ran back to my room and said, 'I love myself.' . . . I felt transformed."

The high lasted about a year, before the feelings of devastation returned in the wake of a romance that ended. But something was different. She could now weather her emotional storms without cutting or harming herself.

What had changed?

It took years of study in psychology—she earned a Ph.D. at Loyola in 1971—before she found an answer. On the surface, it seemed obvious: She had accepted herself as she was. . . . That basic idea—radical acceptance, she now calls it—became increasingly important as she began working with patients, first at a suicide clinic in Buffalo and later as a researcher. . . .

applied to other disorders: homework assignments, psychoeducation, the teaching of social and other skills, therapist modeling, clear goal setting, reinforcements for appropriate behaviors, ongoing assessment of the client's behaviors and treatment progress, and collaborative examinations by client and therapist of the client's ways of thinking (Rizvi et al., 2011; Sherry & Whilde, 2008).

DBT further borrows heavily from humanistic and contemporary psychodynamic approaches, placing the client-therapist relationship itself at the center of treatment interactions, making sure that appropriate treatment boundaries are adhered to, and, at the same time, providing acceptance and validation of the client. Indeed, DBT therapists regularly empathize with their borderline clients and with the emotional turmoil they are experiencing, locate kernels of truth in the clients' complaints or demands, and examine alternative ways for them to address valid needs.

Damon Winter/*New York Times*/Redux Pictures

Learning from within Psychologist Marsha Linehan drew from her own psychological struggles to develop dialectical behavior therapy.

No therapist could promise a quick transformation or even sudden "insight," much less a shimmering religious vision. But now Dr. Linehan was closing in on two seemingly opposed principles that could form the basis of a treatment: acceptance of life as it is, not as it is supposed to be; and the need to change, despite that reality and because of it. . . .

Getting Through the Day

"I decided to get supersuicidal people, the very worst cases, because I figured these are the most miserable people in the world—they think they're evil, that they're bad, bad, bad—and I understood that they weren't," she said. "I understood their suffering because I'd been there, in hell, with no idea how to get out."

In particular she chose to treat people with a diagnosis that she would have given her young self: borderline personality disorder. . . .

Yet even as she climbed the academic ladder, moving from the Catholic University of America to the University of Washington in 1977, she understood from her own experience that acceptance and change were hardly enough. . . . She relied on therapists herself, off and on over the years, for support and guidance (she does not remember taking medication after leaving the institute).

Dr. Linehan's own emerging approach to treatment—now called dialectical behavior therapy, or D.B.T.—would also have to include day-to-day skills. A commitment means very little, after all, if people do not have the tools to carry it out. She borrowed some of these from other behavioral therapies and added elements, like opposite action, in which patients act opposite to the way they feel when an emotion is inappropriate; and mindfulness meditation, a Zen technique in which people focus on their breath and observe their emotions come and go without acting on them. . . .

In studies in the 1980s and '90s, researchers at the University of Washington and elsewhere tracked the progress of hundreds of borderline patients at high risk of suicide who attended weekly dialectical therapy sessions. Compared with similar patients who got other experts' treatments, those who learned Dr. Linehan's approach made far fewer suicide attempts, landed in the hospital less often and were much more likely to stay in treatment. D.B.T. is now widely used for a variety of stubborn clients, including juvenile offenders, people with eating disorders and those with drug addictions. . . .

Most remarkably, perhaps, Dr. Linehan has reached a place where she can stand up and tell her story, come what will. "I'm a very happy person now." . . . "I still have ups and downs, of course, but I think no more than anyone else."

DBT is often supplemented by the clients' participation in social skill-building groups. In such groups, the individuals practice new ways of relating to other persons in a safe environment and at the same time receive validation and support from other group members.

DBT has received more research support than any other treatment for borderline personality disorder (Roepke et al., 2011; Linehan et al., 2006, 2002, 2001). Many clients who receive this treatment come to display an increased ability to tolerate stress; develop new, more appropriate, social skills; respond more effectively to life situations; and develop a more stable identity. Such individuals also display significantly fewer suicidal behaviors and require fewer hospitalizations than those who receive other forms of treatment (Klein & Miller, 2011). Finally, DBT clients are more likely to remain in treatment and to report less anger, greater social gratification, improved work performance, and reductions in substance abuse (Rizvi et al., 2011).

Finally, antidepressant, antibipolar, antianxiety, and antipsychotic drugs have helped calm the emotional and aggressive storms of some people with borderline personality disorder (Silk & Jibson, 2010; Agronin, 2006). However, given the numerous suicide attempts by individuals with this disorder, the use of drugs on an outpatient basis is controversial (Gunderson, 2011). Additionally, clients with the disorder have been known to adjust or discontinue their medication dosages without consulting their clinicians. Many professionals believe that psychotropic drug treatment for borderline personality disorder should be used largely as an adjunct to psychotherapy approaches, and indeed many clients seem to benefit from a combination of psychotherapy and drug therapy (Soloff, 2005).

Histrionic Personality Disorder

People with **histrionic personality disorder,** once called **hysterical personality disorder,** are extremely emotional—they are typically described as "emotionally charged"—and continually seek to be the center of attention (APA, 2013). Their exaggerated moods can complicate life considerably, as we see in the case of Hilde:

Hilde is a 42-year-old homemaker who [had] . . . a combination of complaints, including headaches, mild depression, and marital difficulties. . . . Hilde, still quite attractive, obviously spent a great deal of time on her personal appearance. She was cooperative in the initial interview with the psychiatrist, though at times rambled so much that he had to bring her back to the subject at hand. As she talked, it became apparent that she had not really reflected in any depth on the issues that she discussed and was only pumping out information, much as a computer would. She showed a significant amount of [emotion] during the interview, but it was often exaggerated in response to the content she was discussing at the time. She delighted in giving extensive historical descriptions of her past life. . . .

In fact, many of the descriptions she gave appeared to be more for the purpose of impressing the therapist than in order to come to grips with her problems. When confronted with any irrelevancies in her stories, she first adopted a cute and charming manner, and if this proved ineffective in persuading the psychiatrist to change topics, she then became petulant and irritated.

When she described her present difficulties, she was always inclined to ascribe the responsibility to some person or situation other than herself. She stated that her husband was indifferent to her. . . . This situation, along with a "lot of stress in my life" were given as the reason for [her] headaches and depression. When pressed for more details, she found it hard to describe interactions with her husband in any meaningful detail.

A parallel interview with her husband revealed that he felt he "had simply become tired of dealing with her." He admitted that his original attraction to Hilde was for her social status, her "liveliness," and her physical attractiveness. Over the years, it became clear that her liveliness was not the exuberance and love of life of an integrated personality, but simply a chronic flamboyance and intensity that was often misplaced. Her physical attractiveness was naturally declining, and she was spending inordinate amounts of time and money attempting to keep it up. . . . [He] had . . . grown tired of her childish and superficial manner. . . .

Hilde was raised as a prized child of a moderately wealthy family. Her father owned a successful [business]. Her mother was active socially, joining virtually every socially prominent activity that occurred in the city. She did not have much time for Hilde, yet delighted in showing her off to guests. Hilde was born with many gifts. . . . [Her] beauty was obviously prized, and she was taught many ways to maximize her attractiveness.

Her beauty and the response it received from friends in her parents' social circle also provided her with more than simple attention. Her mother delighted in having her stay up and greet guests at their parties, something she never consistently allowed Hilde's sisters to do. Also, Hilde soon discovered that if she misbehaved, a charmingly presented "I'm sorry" to her father usually voided any necessity for punishment.

As Hilde moved into adolescence, she developed a wide circle of friends, though it is interesting that she never maintained any one relationship for long. . . . Males came to her as bees come to a flower. . . .

Throughout high school, she was active as a cheerleader and as an organizer of class dances and parties. . . . Hilde remembers her junior high and high school years as "the happiest time of my life," an assessment that is probably accurate.

Hilde's college years were not unlike her high school years. . . . She dated many people. . . . When she did allow [sex], it was more to try it out than as a result of any strong desires on her part. . . .

After college, she took a job in a woman's clothing store whose clientele were primarily the rich and fashionable. One of her customers subtly introduced Hilde to her son, Steve, a young attorney with one of the most prestigious firms in the region. . . . They went out almost every night, usually attending the many parties to which they were both invited. Each was enraptured by the other, and they were married five months after they met. . . .

Over the years, [however], the bloom has worn off the romance that propelled them into marriage.

(Meyer, 2005)

People with histrionic personality disorder are always "on stage," using theatrical gestures and mannerisms and grandiose language to describe ordinary everyday events. Like chameleons, they keep changing themselves to attract and impress an audience, and in their pursuit they change not only their surface characteristics—according to the latest fads—but also their opinions and beliefs. In fact, their speech is actually scanty in detail and substance, and they seem to lack a sense of who they really are.

Approval and praise are the life's blood of these individuals; they must have others present to witness their exaggerated emotional states. Vain, self-centered, demanding, and unable to delay gratification for long, they overreact to any minor event that gets in the way of their quest for attention. Some make suicide attempts, often to manipulate others (Lambert, 2003; APA, 2000).

People with this disorder may draw attention to themselves by exaggerating their physical illnesses or fatigues. They may also behave very provocatively and try to achieve their goals through sexual seduction. Most obsess over how they look and how others will perceive them, often wearing bright, eye-catching clothes. They exaggerate the depth of their relationships, considering themselves to be the intimate friends of people who see them as no more than casual acquaintances. Often they become involved with romantic partners who may be exciting but who do not treat them well.

This disorder was once believed to be more common in women than in men, and clinicians long described the "hysterical wife" (Anderson et al., 2001). Research, however, has revealed gender bias in past diagnoses (Fowler et al., 2007). When evaluating

•**histrionic personality disorder**•A personality disorder characterized by a pattern of excessive emotionality and attention seeking. Once called *hysterical personality disorder.*

Transient hysterical symptoms

These avid Harry Potter fans expressed themselves with exaggerated emotionality and lack of restraint at the midnight launch of one of the books in the series. Similar reactions, along with fainting, tremors, and even convulsions, have been common at concerts by musical idols dating back to the 1940s. Small wonder that expressive fans of this kind are regularly described as "hysterical" or "histrionic" by the press—the same labels applied to the personality disorder that is marked by such behaviors and symptoms.

case studies of people with a mixture of histrionic and antisocial traits, clinicians in several studies gave a diagnosis of histrionic personality disorder to women more than men (Blagov et al., 2007; Ford & Widiger, 1989). The latest statistics suggest that as many as 2 to 3 percent of adults have this personality disorder, with males and females equally affected (Paris, 2010; O'Connor, 2008; Mattia & Zimmerman, 2001).

How Do Theorists Explain Histrionic Personality Disorder?

The psychodynamic perspective was originally developed to help explain cases of hysteria (see Chapter 7), so it is no surprise that these theorists continue to have a strong interest in histrionic personality disorder today. Most psychodynamic theorists believe that as children, people with this disorder experienced unhealthy relationships in which cold and controlling parents left them feeling unloved and afraid of abandonment (Horowitz & Lerner, 2010; Bender et al., 2001). To defend against deep-seated fears of loss, the individuals learned to behave dramatically, inventing crises that would require other people to act protectively.

Cognitive explanations look instead at the lack of substance and extreme suggestibility found in people with histrionic personality disorder. These theories see the individuals as becoming less and less interested in knowing about the world at large because they are so self-focused and emotional. With no detailed memories of what they never learned, they must rely on hunches or on other people to provide them with direction in life (Blagov et al., 2007). Some cognitive theorists also propose that people with this disorder hold a general assumption that they are helpless to care for themselves, and so they constantly seek out others who will meet their needs (Weishaar & Beck, 2006; Beck et al., 2004).

Finally, sociocultural, particularly multicultural, theorists believe that histrionic personality disorder is produced in part by cultural norms and expectations. Until recently, our society encouraged girls to hold on to childhood and dependency as they grew up. The vain, dramatic, and selfish behavior of the histrionic personality may actually be an exaggeration of femininity as our culture once defined it (Fowler et al., 2007). Similarly, some clinical observers claim that histrionic personality disorder is diagnosed less often in Asian and other cultures that discourage overt sexualization and more often in Hispanic American and Latin American cultures that are more tolerant of overt sexualization (Patrick, 2007; Trull & Widiger, 2003). Researchers have not, however, investigated this claim systematically.

Treatments for Histrionic Personality Disorder People with histrionic personality disorder are more likely than those with most other personality disorders to seek out treatment on their own (Tyrer et al., 2003). Working with them can be very difficult, however, because of the demands, tantrums, and seductiveness they are likely to deploy. Another problem is that these individuals may pretend to have important insights or to experience change during treatment merely to please the therapist. To head off such problems, therapists must remain objective and maintain strict professional boundaries (Blagov et al., 2007; Sperry, 2003).

Cognitive therapists have tried to help people with this disorder to change their belief that they are helpless and also to develop better, more deliberate ways of thinking and solving problems (Beck & Weishaar, 2011; Weishaar & Beck, 2006; Beck et al., 2004). Psychodynamic therapy and various group therapy formats have also been applied (Horowitz & Lerner, 2010). In all these approaches, therapists ultimately aim to help the clients recognize their excessive dependency, find inner satisfaction, and become more self-reliant. Clinical case reports suggest that each of the approaches can be useful. Drug therapy appears less successful except as a means of relieving the depressive symptoms experienced by some patients (Bock et al., 2010; Grossman, 2004; Koenigsberg et al., 2002).

Narcissistic Personality Disorder

People with **narcissistic personality disorder** are generally grandiose, need much admiration, and feel no empathy with others (APA, 2013). Convinced of their own great success, power, or beauty, they expect constant attention and admiration from those around them. Frederick, the man whom we met at the beginning of this chapter, was one such person. So is Steven, a 30-year-old artist, married, with one child:

> *Steven came to the attention of a therapist when his wife insisted that they seek marital counseling. According to her, Steve was "selfish, ungiving and preoccupied with his work." Everything at home had to "revolve about him, his comfort, moods and desires, no one else's." She claimed that he contributed nothing to the marriage, except a rather meager income. He shirked all "normal" responsibilities and kept "throwing chores in her lap," and she was "getting fed up with being the chief cook and bottlewasher, tired of being his mother and sleep-in maid."*
>
> *On the positive side, Steven's wife felt that he was basically a "gentle and good-natured guy with talent and intelligence." But this wasn't enough. She wanted a husband, someone with whom she could share things. In contrast, he wanted, according to her, "a mother, not a wife"; he didn't want "to grow up, he didn't know how to give affection, only to take it when he felt like it, nothing more, nothing less."*
>
> *Steve presented a picture of an affable, self-satisfied and somewhat disdainful young man. He was employed as a commercial artist, but looked forward to his evenings and weekends when he could turn his attention to serious painting. He claimed that he had to devote all of his spare time and energies to "fulfill himself," to achieve expression in his creative work....*
>
> *His relationships with his present co-workers and social acquaintances were pleasant and satisfying, but he did admit that most people viewed him as a "bit self-centered, cold and snobbish." He recognized that he did not know how to share his thoughts and feelings with others, that he was much more interested in himself than in them and that perhaps he always had "preferred the pleasure" of his own company to that of others.*
>
> *(Millon, 1969, pp. 261–262)*

The Greek myth has it that Narcissus died enraptured by the beauty of his own reflection in a pool, pining away with longing to possess his own image. His name

•**narcissistic personality disorder**• A personality disorder marked by a broad pattern of grandiosity, need for admiration, and lack of empathy.

has come to be synonymous with extreme self-involvement, and indeed people with narcissistic personality disorder have a grandiose sense of self-importance. They exaggerate their achievements and talents, expecting others to recognize them as superior, and often appear arrogant. They are very choosy about their friends and associates, believing that their problems are unique and can be appreciated only by other "special," high-status people. Because of their charm, they often make favorable first impressions, yet they can rarely maintain long-term relationships (Campbell & Miller, 2011; Shapiro & Bernadett-Shapiro, 2006).

Why do people often admire arrogant deceivers—art forgers, jewel thieves, or certain kinds of "con" artists, for example?

Like Steven, people with narcissistic personality disorder are seldom interested in the feelings of others. Indeed, they may not be able to empathize with such feelings (Ritter et al., 2011). Many take advantage of other people to achieve their own ends, perhaps partly out of envy; at the same time they believe others envy them (Millon, 2011; O'Connor, 2008). Though grandiose, some of these individuals react to criticism or frustration with bouts of rage, humiliation, or embitterment (Campbell & Miller, 2011; Rotter, 2011). Others may react with cold indifference. And still others become extremely pessimistic and filled with depression. Periods of zest may alternate with periods of disappointment (Ronningstam, 2011).

Around 1 percent of adults display narcissistic personality disorder, up to 75 percent of them men (Dhawan et al., 2010). Narcissistic-type behaviors and thoughts are common and normal among teenagers and do not usually lead to adult narcissism (APA, 2000).

How Do Theorists Explain Narcissistic Personality Disorder?

Psychodynamic theorists more than others have theorized about narcissistic personality disorder, and, again, they propose that the problem begins with cold, rejecting parents. They argue that some people with this background spend their lives defending against feeling unsatisfied, rejected, unworthy, and wary of the world (Ronningstam, 2011; Bornstein, 2005). They do so by repeatedly telling themselves that they are actually perfect and desirable, and also by seeking admiration from others. Object relations theorists—the psychodynamic theorists who emphasize relationships—interpret the grandiose self-image as a way for these people to convince themselves that they are totally self-sufficient and without need of warm relationships with their parents or anyone else (Kernberg, 2010; Kernberg & Caligor, 2005). In support of the psychodynamic theories, research has found that children who are abused or who lose parents through adoption, divorce, or death are at particular risk for the later development of narcissistic personality disorder (Kernberg, 2010, 1992, 1989). Studies also reveal that people with this disorder do indeed believe that other persons are basically unavailable to them (Bender et al., 2001).

A number of cognitive-behavioral theorists propose that narcissistic personality disorder may develop when people are treated *too positively* rather than too negatively in early life. They hold that certain individuals acquire a superior and grandiose attitude when their "admiring or doting parents" teach them to "overvalue their self worth," repeatedly rewarding them for minor accomplishments or for no accomplishment at all (Millon, 2011; Sperry, 2003).

What specific features of Western society may be contributing to today's apparent rise in narcissistic behavior?

Finally, many sociocultural theorists see a link between narcissistic personality disorder and "eras of narcissism" in society (Campbell & Miller, 2011). They suggest that family values and social ideals in certain societies periodically break down, producing

"I'm attracted to you, but then I'm attracted to me, too."

Richard Cline/cartoonbank.com

generations of youth who are self-centered and materialistic and have short attention spans. Western cultures in particular, which encourage self-expression, individualism, and competitiveness, are considered likely to produce such generations of narcissism. In fact, one worldwide study conducted on the Internet found that respondents from the United States had the highest narcissism scores, followed, in descending order, by individuals from Europe, Canada, Asia, and the Middle East (Foster, Campbell, & Twenge, 2003).

Treatments for Narcissistic Personality Disorder Narcissistic personality disorder is one of the most difficult personality patterns to treat because the clients are unable to acknowledge weaknesses, to appreciate the effect of their behavior on others, or to incorporate feedback from others (Campbell & Miller, 2011; Levy et al., 2007). The clients who consult therapists usually do so because of a related disorder, most commonly depression (Piper & Joyce, 2001). Once in treatment, the individuals may try to manipulate the therapist into supporting their sense of superiority. Some also seem to project their grandiose attitudes onto their therapists and develop a love-hate stance toward them (Shapiro, 2004).

Psychodynamic therapists seek to help people with this disorder recognize and work through their basic insecurities and defenses (Kernberg, 2010; Messer & Abbass, 2010). Cognitive therapists, focusing on the self-centered thinking of such clients, try to redirect the clients' focus onto the opinions of others, teach them to interpret criticism more rationally, increase their ability to empathize, and change their all-or-nothing notions (Beck & Weishaar, 2011; Weishaar & Beck, 2006; Beck et al., 2004). None of the approaches have had clear success, however (Dhawan et al., 2010).

"Anxious" Personality Disorders

The cluster of *"anxious" personality disorders* includes the *avoidant, dependent,* and *obsessive-compulsive personality disorders.* People with these patterns typically display anxious and fearful behavior. Although many of the symptoms of these personality disorders are similar to those of the anxiety and depressive disorders, researchers have not found direct links between this cluster and those disorders (O'Donohue et al., 2007). As with most of the other personality disorders, research support for the various explanations is very limited. At the same time, treatments for these disorders appear to be modestly to moderately helpful—considerably better than for other personality disorders.

Avoidant Personality Disorder

People with **avoidant personality disorder** are very uncomfortable and inhibited in social situations, overwhelmed by feelings of inadequacy, and extremely sensitive to negative evaluation (APA, 2013). They are so fearful of being rejected that they give no one an opportunity to reject them—or to accept them either:

Perhaps what made Malcolm pursue counseling was the painful awareness of his inability to socialize at a party hosted by a professor. A first-semester computer science graduate student, Malcolm watched other new students in his program fraternize at this gathering while he suffered in silence. He wanted desperately to join [in], but, as he described it, "I was totally at a loss as to how to go about talking to anyone." The best feeling in the world, he stated, was getting out of there. The following Monday, he came to the university counseling center, realizing he would have to be able to function in this group, but not before his first teaching experience that morning, which he described as "the most terrifying feeling I have ever encountered." As an undergrad, he spent most of his time alone in the computer lab working on new programs, which was what he most enjoyed as "no one was

(continued on the next page)

What Is the Difference Between an Egoist and an Egotist?

An *egoist* is a person concerned primarily with his or her own interests. An *egotist* has an inflated sense of self-worth. A boastful egotist is not necessarily a self-absorbed egoist. ‹‹

•**avoidant personality disorder**•A personality disorder characterized by consistent discomfort and restraint in social situations, overwhelming feelings of inadequacy, and extreme sensitivity to negative evaluation.

Peter Turnley/Corbis

BETWEEN THE LINES

Feelings of Shyness

Around 48 percent of people in the United States consider themselves to be shy to some degree (Carducci, 2000). ‹‹

looking over my shoulder or judging me." In contrast to this, with his teaching assistantship duties, . . . he felt he constantly ran the risk of being made to look like a fool in front of a large audience.

When asked about personal relationships he had previously enjoyed, Malcolm admitted that any interaction was a source of frustration and worry. From the moment he left home for undergraduate school, he lived alone, attended functions alone, and found it nearly impossible to make conversation with anyone. . . . The expectancy that people would be rejecting . . . precipitated profound gloom. . . . Despite a longing to relate and be accepted, Malcolm . . . maintained a safe distance from all emotional involvement. [He] became remote from others and from needed sources of support. He . . . had learned to be watchful, on guard against ridicule, and ever alert . . . to the most minute traces of annoyance expressed by others.

(Millon, 2011)

People like Malcolm actively avoid occasions for social contact. At the center of this withdrawal lies not so much poor social skills as a dread of criticism, disapproval, or rejection. They are timid and hesitant in social situations, afraid of saying something foolish or of embarrassing themselves by blushing or acting nervous. Even in intimate relationships they express themselves very carefully, afraid of being shamed or ridiculed.

People with this disorder believe themselves to be unappealing or inferior to others. They exaggerate the potential difficulties of new situations, so they seldom take risks or try out new activities (Rodebaugh et al., 2010). They usually have few or no close friends, though they actually yearn for intimate relationships, and frequently feel depressed and lonely. As a substitute, some develop an inner world of fantasy and imagination (Millon, 2011).

Avoidant personality disorder is similar to *social anxiety disorder* (see Chapter 5), and many people with one of these disorders also experience the other (Cox et al., 2011). The similarities include a fear of humiliation and low confidence. Some theorists believe that there is a key difference between the two disorders—namely, that people with social anxiety disorder primarily fear social *circumstances,* while people with the personality disorder tend to fear close social *relationships* (Kantor, 2010). Other theorists, however,

A lonely life

This woman paints a sad and lonely figure as she sits by the Paris grave of the late Jim Morrison, lead singer of the rock group The Doors. Legions of Morrison fans have visited the grave for a variety of reasons since his 1971 death. Clinicians believe, however, that in some cases the overly devoted fans of long-gone celebrities—particularly fans who build their lives around the celebrities—manifest avoidant personality disorder. Uncomfortable and inhibited in real social situations, some people with this personality disorder develop an inner world of fantasy and imagined relationships.

believe that the two disorders reflect the same core of psychopathology and should in fact be combined (Herbert, 2007).

As many as 1 to 2 percent of adults have avoidant personality disorder, men as frequently as women (Paris, 2010; O'Connor, 2008; Mattia & Zimmerman, 2001). Many children and teenagers are also painfully shy and avoid other people, but this is usually just a normal part of their development.

How Do Theorists Explain Avoidant Personality Disorder?

Theorists often assume that avoidant personality disorder has the same causes as anxiety disorders—such as early traumas, conditioned fears, upsetting beliefs, or biochemical abnormalities. However, with the exception of social anxiety disorder, research has not yet tied the personality disorder directly to the anxiety disorders (Herbert, 2007). In the meantime, psychodynamic, cognitive, and behavioral explanations of avoidant personality disorder are the most popular among clinicians.

Psychodynamic theorists focus mainly on the general sense of shame felt by people with avoidant personality disorder (Svartberg & McCullough, 2010). Some trace the shame to childhood experiences such as early bowel and bladder accidents. If parents repeatedly punish or ridicule a child for having such accidents, the child may develop a negative self-image. This may lead to the individual's feeling unlovable throughout life and distrusting the love of others.

Similarly, cognitive theorists believe that harsh criticism and rejection in early childhood may lead certain people to assume that others in their environment will always judge them negatively. These individuals come to expect rejection, misinterpret the reactions of others to fit that expectation, discount positive feedback, and generally fear social involvements—setting the stage for avoidant personality disorder (Kantor, 2010; Weishaar & Beck, 2006; Beck et al., 2004). In several studies, participants with this disorder were asked to recall their childhood, and their descriptions supported both the psychodynamic and the cognitive theories (Carr & Francis, 2010; Herbert, 2007). They remembered, for example, feeling criticized, rejected, and isolated; receiving little encouragement from their parents; and experiencing few displays of parental love or pride.

Finally, behavioral theorists suggest that people with avoidant personality disorder typically fail to develop normal social skills, a failure that helps maintain the disorder. In support of this position, several studies have indeed found social skills deficits among individuals with avoidant personality disorder (Kantor, 2010; Herbert, 2007). Most behaviorists agree, however, that the deficits first develop as a result of the individuals avoiding so many social situations.

Treatments for Avoidant Personality Disorder

People with avoidant personality disorder come to therapy in the hope of finding acceptance and affection. Keeping them in treatment can be a challenge, however, for many of them soon begin to avoid the sessions. Often they distrust the therapist's sincerity and start to fear his or her rejection. Thus, as with several of the other personality disorders, a key task of the therapist is to gain the individual's trust (Millon, 2011).

Beyond building trust, therapists tend to treat people with avoidant personality disorder much as they treat people with social anxiety disorder and other anxiety disorders (Svartberg, Stiles, & Seltzer, 2004; Markovitz, 2001). Such approaches have had at least modest success (Kantor, 2010; Porcerelli et al., 2007). Psychodynamic therapists try to help clients recognize and resolve the unconscious conflicts that may be operating (Messer & Abbass, 2010; Sperry, 2003). Cognitive therapists help them change their distressing beliefs and thoughts, carry on in the face of painful emotions, and improve their self-image (Beck & Weishaar, 2011; Weishaar & Beck, 2006; Beck et al., 2004). Behavioral therapists provide social skills training as well as exposure treatments that require people gradually to increase their social contacts (Herbert, 2007; Farmer & Nelson-Gray, 2005). Group therapy formats, especially groups that follow cognitive and behavioral principles, have the added advantage of providing clients with practice in social interactions (Herbert et al., 2005; Piper & Joyce, 2001). Antianxiety and

Rosanne Olson/Getty Images

Just a stage
Many children are painfully shy, withdrawn, easily embarrassed, and uncomfortable with people other than their parents, siblings, or close friends. Early temperament is often linked to adult personality traits, but research has not yet clarified whether extreme shyness, a common and normal part of childhood, can, in certain cases, predict the development of avoidant or dependent personality disorder in adulthood.

antidepressant drugs are sometimes useful in reducing the social anxiety of people with the disorder, although the symptoms may return when medication is stopped (Herbert, 2007; Fava et al., 2002).

Dependent Personality Disorder

People with **dependent personality disorder** have a pervasive, excessive need to be taken care of (APA, 2013). As a result, they are clinging and obedient, fearing separation from their parent, spouse, or other person with whom they are in a close relationship. They rely on others so much that they cannot make the smallest decision for themselves. Matthew is a case in point.

> *Matthew is a 34-year-old single man who lives with his mother and works as an accountant. He is seeking treatment because he is very unhappy after having just broken up with his girlfriend. His mother had disapproved of his marriage plans, ostensibly because the woman was of a different religion. Matthew felt trapped and forced to choose between his mother and his girlfriend, and because "blood is thicker than water," he had decided not to go against his mother's wishes. Nonetheless, he is angry at himself and at her and believes that she will never let him marry and is possessively hanging on to him. His mother "wears the pants" in the family and is a very domineering woman who is used to getting her way. Matthew is afraid of disagreeing with his mother for fear that she will not be supportive of him and he will then have to fend for himself. He criticizes himself for being weak, but also admires his mother and respects her judgment—"Maybe Carol wasn't right for me after all." He alternates between resentment and a "Mother knows best" attitude. He feels that his own judgment is poor.*
>
> *Matthew works at a job several grades below what his education and talent would permit. On several occasions he has turned down promotions because he didn't want the responsibility of having to supervise other people or make independent decisions. He has worked for the same boss for 10 years, gets on well with him, and is, in turn, highly regarded as a dependable and unobtrusive worker. He has two very close friends whom he has had since early childhood. He has lunch with one of them every single workday and feels lost if his friend is sick and misses a day.*
>
> *Matthew is the youngest of four children and the only boy. He was "babied and spoiled" by his mother and elder sisters. He had considerable separation anxiety as a child—he had difficulty falling asleep unless his mother stayed in the room, mild school refusal, and unbearable homesickness when he occasionally tried "sleepovers." As a child he was teased by other boys because of his lack of assertiveness and was often called a baby. He has lived at home his whole life except for 1 year of college, from which he returned because of homesickness.*
>
> *(Spitzer et al., 1994, pp. 179–180)*

It is normal and healthy to depend on others, but those with dependent personality disorder constantly need assistance with even the simplest matters and demonstrate extreme feelings of inadequacy and helplessness. Afraid that they cannot care for themselves, they cling desperately to friends or relatives.

As you just observed, people with avoidant personality disorder have difficulty *initiating* relationships. In contrast, people with dependent personality disorder have difficulty with *separation*. The individuals feel completely helpless and devastated when a close relationship ends, and they quickly seek out another relationship to fill the void. Many cling persistently to relationships with partners who physically or psychologically abuse them (Loas et al., 2011).

Lacking confidence in their own ability and judgment, people with this disorder seldom disagree with others and allow even important decisions to be made for them

•dependent personality disorder•
A personality disorder characterized by a pattern of clinging and obedience, fear of separation, and an ongoing need to be taken care of.

(Millon, 2011; Bornstein, 2007). They may depend on a parent or spouse to decide where to live, what job to have, and which neighbors to befriend. Because they so fear rejection, they are overly sensitive to disapproval and keep trying to meet other people's wishes and expectations, even if it means volunteering for unpleasant or demeaning tasks.

Many people with dependent personality disorder feel distressed, lonely, and sad; often they dislike themselves. Thus they are at risk for depressive, anxiety, and eating disorders (Bornstein, 2007). Their fear of separation and their feelings of helplessness may leave them particularly prone to suicidal thoughts, especially when they believe that a relationship is about to end (Kiev, 1989).

Studies suggest that over 2 percent of the population may experience dependent personality disorder (Paris, 2010; Mattia & Zimmerman, 2001). For years clinicians have believed that more women than men display this pattern, but some research suggests that the disorder is just as common in men (APA, 2000).

How Do Theorists Explain Dependent Personality Disorder? Psychodynamic explanations for this personality disorder are very similar to those for depression (Svartberg & McCullough, 2010). Freudian theorists argue, for example, that unresolved conflicts during the oral stage of development can give rise to a lifelong need for nurturance, thus heightening the likelihood of a dependent personality disorder (Bornstein, 2007, 2005). Similarly, object relations theorists say that early parental loss or rejection may prevent normal experiences of *attachment* and *separation,* leaving some children with fears of abandonment that persist throughout their lives (Caligor & Clarkin, 2010). Still other psychodynamic theorists suggest that, to the contrary, many parents of people with this disorder were overinvolved and overprotective, thus increasing their children's dependency, insecurity, and separation anxiety (Sperry, 2003).

Behaviorists propose that parents of people with dependent personality disorder unintentionally rewarded their children's clinging and "loyal" behavior, while at the same time punishing acts of independence, perhaps through the withdrawal of love. Alternatively, some parents' own dependent behaviors may have served as models for their children (Bornstein, 2007).

Finally, cognitive theorists identify two maladaptive attitudes as helping to produce and maintain this disorder: (1) "I am inadequate and helpless to deal with the world," and (2) "I must find a person to provide protection so I can cope" (Weishaar & Beck, 2006;

Cell phone dependence?
Many clinicians believe that the proliferation of cell phones has created a widespread psychological dependence on them. Although not a disorder, studies reveal that some users react with intense anxiety, physical discomfort, feelings of separation, and a loss of self-esteem when forced to shut down their phones for more than a few minutes (Chaparro, 2004).

Beck et al., 2004). Dichotomous (black–and–white) thinking may also play a key role: "If I am to be dependent, I must be completely helpless," or "If I am to be independent, I must be alone." Such thinking prevents sufferers from making efforts to be autonomous.

Treatments for Dependent Personality Disorder In therapy, people with this personality disorder usually place all responsibility for their treatment and well-being on the clinician (Gutheil, 2005). Thus a key task of therapy is to help patients accept responsibility for themselves. Because the domineering behaviors of a spouse or parent may help foster a patient's symptoms, some clinicians propose couple or family therapy as well, or even separate therapy for the partner or parent (Lebow & Uliaszek, 2010; Nichols, 2004).

Treatment for dependent personality disorder can be at least modestly helpful. Psychodynamic therapy for this pattern focuses on many of the same issues as therapy for depressed people, including the *transference* of dependency needs onto the therapist (Svartberg & McCullough, 2010; Gabbard, 2009, 2001). Cognitive-behavioral therapy combines behavioral and cognitive interventions to help the clients take control of their lives. On the behavioral end, the therapists often provide assertiveness training to help the individuals better express their own wishes in relationships (Farmer & Nelson-Gray, 2005). On the cognitive end, the therapists also try to help the clients challenge and change their assumptions of incompetence and helplessness (Beck & Weishaar, 2011; Weishaar & Beck, 2006; Beck et al., 2004). Antidepressant drug therapy has been helpful for persons whose personality disorder is accompanied by depression (Fava et al., 2002).

Finally, as with avoidant personality disorder, a group therapy format can be helpful because it provides opportunities for the client to receive support from a number of peers rather than from a single dominant person (Perry, 2005; Sperry, 2003). In addition, group members may serve as models for one another as they practice better ways to express feelings and solve problems.

Obsessive-Compulsive Personality Disorder

People with **obsessive-compulsive personality disorder** are so preoccupied with order, perfection, and control that they lose all flexibility, openness, and efficiency (APA, 2013). Their concern for doing everything "right" impairs their productivity, as in the case of Joseph:

Joseph was advised to seek assistance from a therapist following several months of relatively sleepless nights and a growing immobility and indecisiveness at his job. When first seen, he reported feelings of extreme self-doubt and guilt and prolonged periods of tension and diffuse anxiety. It was established early in therapy that he always had experienced these symptoms; they were now merely more pronounced than before.

The precipitant for this sudden increase in discomfort was a forthcoming change in his academic post. New administrative officers had assumed authority at the college, and he was asked to resign his deanship to return to regular departmental instruction. In the early sessions, Joseph spoke largely of his fear of facing classroom students again, wondered if he could organize his material well, and doubted that he could keep classes disciplined and interested in his lectures. It was his preoccupation with these matters that he believed was preventing him from concentrating and completing his present responsibilities.

At no time did Joseph express anger toward the new college officials for the demotion he was asked to accept; he repeatedly voiced his "complete confidence" in the "rationality of their decision." Yet, when face-to-face with them, he observed that he stuttered and was extremely tremulous.

Joseph was the second of two sons, younger than his brother by three years. His father was a successful engineer, and his mother a high school teacher. Both were "efficient,

•obsessive-compulsive personality disorder• A personality disorder marked by such an intense focus on orderliness, perfectionism, and control that the individual loses flexibility, openness, and efficiency.

orderly, and strict" parents. Life at home was "extremely well planned," with "daily and weekly schedules of responsibility posted" and "vacations arranged a year or two in advance." Nothing apparently was left to chance.... Joseph adopted the "good boy" image. Unable to challenge his brother either physically, intellectually, or socially, he became a "paragon of virtue." By being punctilious, scrupulous, methodical, and orderly, he could avoid antagonizing his perfectionistic parents, and would, at times, obtain preferred treatment from them. He obeyed their advice, took their guidance as gospel, and hesitated making any decision before gaining their approval. Although he recalled "fighting" with his brother before he was 6 or 7, he "restrained my anger from that time on and never upset my parents again."

(Millon, 2011, 1969, pp. 278–279)

In Joseph's concern with rules and order and doing things right, he has trouble seeing the larger picture. When faced with a task, he and others who have obsessive-compulsive personality disorder may become so focused on organization and details that they fail to grasp the point of the activity. As a result, their work is often behind schedule (some seem unable to finish any job), and they may neglect leisure activities and friendships.

People with this personality disorder set unreasonably high standards for themselves and others. Their behaviors extend well beyond the realm of conscientiousness (Samuel & Widiger, 2011). They can never be satisfied with their performance, but they typically refuse to seek help or to work with a team, convinced that others are too careless or incompetent to do the job right. Because they are so afraid of making mistakes, they may be reluctant to make decisions.

These individuals also tend to be rigid and stubborn, particularly in their morals, ethics, and values. They live by a strict personal code and use it as a yardstick for measuring others. They may have trouble expressing much affection, and their relationships are sometimes stiff and superficial. In addition, they are often stingy with their time or money. Some cannot even throw away objects that are worn out or useless (APA, 2000).

As many as 1 to 2 percent of the population are believed to display obsessive-compulsive personality disorder, with white, educated, married, and employed individuals receiving the diagnosis most often (Paris, 2010; Bartz et al., 2007; Mattia & Zimmerman, 2001). Men are twice as likely as women to display the disorder.

Many clinicians believe that obsessive-compulsive personality disorder and *obsessive-compulsive disorder* are closely related. Certainly, the two disorders share a number of features. Moreover, many people who suffer from one of the disorders meet the diagnostic criteria for the other disorder (Lochner et al., 2011). However, it is worth noting that people with the personality disorder are more likely to suffer from either major depressive disorder, generalized disorder, or a substance use disorder than from obsessive-compulsive disorder (Pinto et al., 2008). In fact, researchers have not found a specific link between obsessive-compulsive personality disorder and obsessive-compulsive disorder (Nydegger & Paludi, 2006; Albert et al., 2004).

How Do Theorists Explain Obsessive-Compulsive Personality Disorder?
Most explanations of obsessive-compulsive personality disorder borrow heavily from those of obsessive-compulsive disorder, despite the doubts concerning a link between the two disorders. As with so many of the personality disorders, psychodynamic explanations dominate and research evidence is limited.

Freudian theorists suggest that people with obsessive-compulsive personality disorder are *anal regressive.* That is, because of overly harsh toilet training during the anal stage, they become filled with anger, and they remain *fixated* at this stage. To keep their anger under control, they persistently resist both their anger and their instincts to have bowel movements. In turn, they become extremely orderly and

Toilet rage
According to Freud, toilet training often produces rage in a child. If parents are too harsh in their approach, the child may become fixated at the anal stage and prone to obsessive-compulsive functioning later in life.

restrained; many become passionate collectors. Other psychodynamic theorists suggest that any early struggles with parents over control and independence may ignite the aggressive impulses at the root of this personality disorder (Millon, 2011; Bartz et al., 2007).

Cognitive theorists have little to say about the origins of obsessive-compulsive personality disorder, but they do propose that illogical thinking processes help keep it going (Weishaar & Beck, 2006; Beck et al., 2004). They point, for example, to dichotomous thinking, which may produce rigidity and perfectionism. Similarly, they note that people with this disorder tend to misread or exaggerate the potential outcomes of mistakes or errors.

Treatments for Obsessive-Compulsive Personality Disorder

People with obsessive-compulsive personality disorder do not usually believe there is anything wrong with them. They therefore are not likely to seek treatment unless they are also suffering from another disorder, most frequently an anxiety disorder or depression, or unless someone close to them insists that they get treatment (Bartz et al., 2007). The individuals often respond well to psychodynamic or cognitive therapy (Messer & Abbass, 2010; Svartberg & McCullough, 2010; Weishaar & Beck, 2006). Psychodynamic therapists typically try to help them recognize, experience, and accept their underlying feelings and insecurities, and perhaps take risks and accept their personal limitations. Cognitive therapists focus on helping the clients to change their dichotomous—"all-or-nothing"—thinking, perfectionism, indecisiveness, procrastination, and chronic worrying. Finally, a number of clinicians report that people with obsessive-compulsive personality disorder, like those with obsessive-compulsive disorder, respond well to SSRIs, the serotonin-enhancing antidepressant drugs; however, researchers have yet to study this issue directly (Pinto et al., 2008).

Multicultural Factors: Research Neglect

Given the enormous interest in personality disorders, it is striking how little multicultural research has been conducted on the disorders (McGilloway et al., 2010). When all is said and done, clinical theorists have suspicions, but no compelling evidence that cultural differences exist in this realm or that such differences are important to the field's understanding and treatment of personality disorders (Bender et al., 2007).

The lack of multicultural research is of special concern with regard to borderline personality disorder, the pattern characterized by extreme mood fluctuations, outbursts of intense anger, self-injurious behavior, fear of abandonment, feelings of emptiness, problematic relationships, and identity confusion, because many theorists are convinced that gender and other cultural differences may be particularly important in both the development and diagnosis of this disorder.

Around 75 percent of all people who receive a diagnosis of borderline personality disorder are female. Although it may be that women are biologically more prone to the disorder or that diagnostic bias is at work, this gender difference may instead be a reflection of the extraordinary traumas to which many women are subjected as children. Recall, for example, that the childhoods of people with borderline personality disorder tend to be filled with emotional trauma, victimization, violence, and abuse, at times sexual abuse. It may be, a number of theorists argue, that experiences of this kind are *prerequisites* to the development of borderline personality disorder, that women in our society are particularly subjected to such experiences, and that, in fact, the disorder should more properly be viewed and treated as a special form of posttraumatic stress disorder (Sherry & Whilde, 2008; Hodges, 2003). In the absence of systematic research, however, alternative explanations like this remain untested and corresponding treatments undeveloped.

In a related vein, given the childhood experiences that typically precede borderline personality disorder, some multicultural theorists believe that the disorder may actually be a reaction to persistent feelings of marginality, powerlessness, and social failure

(Sherry & Whilde, 2008; Miller, 1999, 1994). That is, the disorder may be attributable more to social inequalities (including sexism, racism, or homophobia) than to psychological factors.

Given such possibilities, it is most welcome that at least a few multicultural studies of borderline personality disorder have been conducted over the past decade. In one, researchers assessed the prevalence of the personality disorder in racially diverse clinical populations from across the United States (Chavira et al., 2003). The study found that disproportionately more Hispanic American clients qualified for a diagnosis of borderline personality disorder than did white or African American clients. Could it be that Hispanic Americans generally are more likely than other cultural groups to display this disorder, and—if so—why?

Finally, some multicultural theorists have argued that the features of borderline personality disorder may be perfectly acceptable traits and behaviors in certain cultures. In Puerto Rican culture, for example, men are *expected* to display very strong emotions like anger, aggression, and sexual attraction (Sherry & Whilde, 2008; Casimir & Morrison, 1993). Could such culture-based characteristics help account for the higher rates of borderline personality disorder found among Hispanic American clients? And could these culturally based characteristics also help explain the fact that Hispanic men and women demonstrate similar rates of this disorder, in contrast to the usual 3-to-1 female-to-male ratio found in other cultural groups (Chavira et al., 2003)? Questions of this kind underline once again the need for more multicultural research into personality disorders.

Are There Better Ways to Classify Personality Disorders?

Most of today's clinicians believe that personality disorders represent important and troubling patterns. Yet, as you read at the beginning of this chapter, DSM-5's personality disorders are particularly hard to diagnose and easy to misdiagnose, difficulties that indicate serious problems with the validity and reliability of these categories. Consider, in particular, the following problems:

1. Some of the criteria used to diagnose the DSM-5 personality disorders cannot be observed directly. To separate paranoid from schizoid personality disorder, for example, clinicians must ask not only whether people avoid forming close relationships, but also *why*. In other words, the diagnoses often rely heavily on the impressions of the individual clinician.

2. Clinicians differ widely in their judgments about when a normal personality style crosses the line and deserves to be called a disorder. Some even believe that it is wrong ever to think of personality styles as mental disorders, however troublesome they may be.

3. The personality disorders often are very similar to one another. Thus it is common for people with personality problems to meet the diagnostic criteria for several DSM-5 personality disorders (Loas et al., 2011).

4. People with quite different personalities may qualify for the same DSM-5 personality disorder diagnosis.

In light of these problems, the leading criticism of DSM-5's approach to personality disorders is, as you read earlier, that the classification system defines such disorders by using *categories*—rather than *dimensions*—of personality (Widiger & Mullins-Sweatt, 2010; Widiger, 2007). A growing number of theorists believe that personality disorders differ more in *degree* than in type of dysfunction. Therefore, they propose that the disorders should be classified by the severity of key personality traits (or dimensions) rather than by the presence or absence of specific traits (Skodol, 2010). In such an approach,

---

BETWEEN THE LINES

Personality Disorder Demographics

19% Percentage of people with severe personality disorders who are racial or ethnic minority group members ‹‹

59% Individuals with severe personality disorders who are male ‹‹

6% Individuals with severe personality disorders who are unemployed ‹‹

23% Individuals with severe personality disorders who have never married ‹‹

10% Poor people with borderline personality disorder ‹‹

3% Wealthy people with borderline personality disorder ‹‹

(Sareen et al., 2011; Cloninger & Svrakic, 2005)

BETWEEN THE LINES

In Their Words

"We continue to shape our personality all our life. ‹‹

Albert Camus

Dysfunctional toons

As the technology found in film animation has become more complex over time, so have the personality problems of animated characters. (Left) Troubled characters of the past were usually defined by a single undesirable personality trait, as demonstrated by Snow White's friend Grumpy, second from left. (Right) Today's characters have "clusters" of problematic traits. For example, some critics suggest that the *South Park* kids (especially Cartman, second from left) display enduring grumpiness; disrespect for authority, irreverence, and self-absorption; disregard for the feelings of others; general lack of conscience; and a tendency to get into trouble.

each key trait (for example, disagreeableness, dishonesty, or self-absorption) would be seen as varying along a continuum in which there is no clear boundary between normal and abnormal. People with a personality disorder would be those who display extreme degrees of several of these key traits—degrees not commonly found in the general population (see *PsychWatch*).

What key personality dimensions should clinicians use to help identify people with personality problems? Some theorists believe that they should rely on the dimensions identified in the "Big Five" theory of personality, dimensions that have received enormous attention by personality psychologists over the years.

The "Big Five" Theory of Personality and Personality Disorders

A large body of research conducted with diverse populations consistently suggests that the basic structure of personality may consist of five "supertraits," or factors—*neuroticism, extroversion, openness to experiences, agreeableness,* and *conscientiousness* (Zuckerman, 2011). Each of these factors, which are frequently referred to as the "Big Five," consists of a number of subfactors. Anxiety and hostility, for example, are subfactors of the neuroticism factor, while optimism and friendliness are subfactors of the extroversion factor. Theoretically, everyone's personality can be summarized by a combination of these supertraits. One person may display high levels of neuroticism and agreeableness, medium extroversion, and low conscientiousness and openness to experiences. In contrast, another person may display high levels of agreeableness and conscientiousness, medium neuroticism and extroversion, and low openness to experiences. And so on.

Many proponents of the Big Five model have argued further that it would be best to describe all people with personality disorders as being high, low, or in between on the five supertraits and to drop the use of personality disorder categories altogether (Glover et al., 2011; Lawton et al., 2011). Thus a particular individual who currently qualifies for a diagnosis of avoidant personality disorder might instead be described as displaying a high degree of neuroticism, medium degrees of agreeableness and conscientiousness, and very low degrees of extroversion and openness to new experiences. Similarly, an individual currently diagnosed with narcissistic personality disorder might be described in the Big Five approach as displaying very high degrees of neuroticism and extroversion, medium degrees of conscientiousness and openness to new experiences, and a very low degree of agreeableness.

Lying: "Oh What a Tangled Web . . ."

A college student fakes her own kidnapping, triggering a massive manhunt to locate her.

A 59-year-old great-grandmother falsely claims to the national news media that she is pregnant with twins.

A woman disappears shortly before her wedding, setting off a three-day nationwide search, then calls home from across the country with the false claim that she had been kidnapped and sexually assaulted.

After emerging from a very troubled adolescence as a transgendered, abused, homeless drug addict and male prostitute, a young male writer achieves enormous literary success and a cult-like following. However, the writer turns out to be a 40-year-old woman who had made up this entire persona.

A 71-year-old woman reveals as false a best-selling memoir that describes her early years as a Jewish child wandering through Europe during the Holocaust in search of her deported parents.

These are some famous examples of lying that have surfaced almost daily on the Internet and in the media. Psychologists have offered various theories about why people lie, but research has produced limited insight into this subject (Grover, 2010). Currently, lying—even *extreme* or *compulsive lying*—is not, by itself, considered a psychological disorder, although it is sometimes characteristic of people with antisocial, borderline, or narcissistic personality disorders.

Let's take a brief look at what the field of psychology knows about lying. First, researchers have determined that most people lie some of the time. Almost everyone has been in a situation when lying seems preferable to telling the truth, where, for example, a lie enables them to save face or avoid getting into trouble. People are more likely to tell such "defensive" lies in some situations than in others. E-mail lying is, for example, more likely than hand-written lying or phone call lying, and all

three are more likely than face-to-face lying (Naquin et al., 2010; Whitty & Carville, 2008).

Few liars of this kind can be classified as "pathological" liars. Pathological liars do not lie to protect themselves or others; rather, their lies have no situational gain. Pathological lies tend to be compulsive or fantastic in nature and can often be refuted easily by others (Scott, 2010; Dike et al., 2006, 2005).

Sociocultural theorists suggest that lying is more acceptable in some cultures than in others. One study of college students, for example, found that white American students rated lies as more acceptable than Ecuadorian students (Mealy et al., 2007). In fact, in some cultures, the clever deceit of others may be highly regarded.

Biological researchers also have some things to say about lying. By observing brain activity on fMRIs, particularly activity in the prefrontal cortex, several researchers have been able to detect when study participants are lying (Ganis et al, 2011; Wu et al., 2011; Mameli et al, 2010). But beware: just as polygraphs can be fooled (see page 94), it turns out that participants can lower the accuracy of fMRIs by applying certain countermeasures (Ganis et al., 2011).

There are, of course, more people-oriented ways to try to detect when persons are lying (Vrij, 2008; Bond, 2004). Across the world, around 53 percent of people say that they can consistently detect lies in their interactions with others (Bond, 2004), although relatively few are willing to bet money on their detection skills (Holm & Kawago, 2010). Some cultures are more confident than others about their lie-detector abilities. Americans believe, for example, that they can detect lies less than half the time, and Norwegians and Swedes rate themselves even lower. At the other end of the spectrum, Turks and Armenians believe they can spot liars 70 percent of the time (Bond, 2004; Mann, 2004; Warner, 2004).

How can we tell when someone is lying to us? A variety of informal clues to detect lies have been cited by researchers (Boltz et al., 2010; Porter & ten Brinke, 2008; Bond, 2004). An observer may, for example, be able to spot deception from behavioral cues such as the deceiver's slowness to respond, frequent pauses, inappropriate message duration, or unusual physical gestures (e.g., arm raising and staring). When persons ask someone to "Look me in the eye when you say that," they are often trying to pick up on subtle cues to determine whether the speaker is uttering a falsehood or telling the truth. Once again, however, we should beware that such "telltale" signs are far from foolproof (Arciuli et al., 2010; Vrij, 2008; Geary & DePaulo, 2007).

"I would've told you all this yesterday, but I just made it up today."

"Personality Disorder Trait Specified": Another Dimensional Approach

The "Big-Five" approach to personality disorders is currently receiving considerable study and may wind up being used in the next edition of the World Health Organization's International Classification of Diseases (ICD), the classification system for medical and psychiatric diagnoses used in many countries outside the United States (Aldhous, 2012). In the meantime, as you read earlier, the DSM-5 framers have designed their own dimensional approach for possible use in a future revision of the DSM.

This approach begins with the notion that individuals whose traits significantly impair their functioning should receive a diagnosis called **personality disorder trait specified (PDTS)** (APA, 2013, 2012). When assigning this diagnosis, clinicians would further identify and list the problematic traits and rate the severity of impairment caused by them. According to the proposal, five groups of problematic traits would be eligible for a diagnosis of PDTS: *negative affectivity, detachment, antagonism, disinhibition,* and *psychoticism.*

> **Negative Affectivity** People who display negative affectivity experience negative emotions frequently and intensely. In particular, they exhibit one or more of the following traits: *emotional lability* (unstable emotions), *anxiousness, separation insecurity, perseveration* (repetition of certain behaviors despite repeated failures), *submissiveness, hostility, depressivity, suspiciousness,* and *strong emotional reactions* (overreactions to emotionally-arousing situations).

> **Detachment** People who manifest detachment tend to withdraw from other people and social interactions. They may exhibit any of the following traits: *restricted emotional reactivity* (little reaction to emotionally-arousing situations), *depressivity, suspiciousness, withdrawal, anhedonia* (inability to feel pleasure or take interest in things), and *intimacy avoidance.* You'll note that two of the traits in this group —"depressivity" and "suspiciousness"— are also found in the negative affectivity group.

> **Antagonism** Individuals who display antagonism behave in ways that put them at odds with other people. They may exhibit any of the following traits (including "hostility," which is also found in the negative affectivity group): *manipulativeness, deceitfulness, grandiosity, attention seeking, callousness,* and *hostility.*

> **Disinhibition** Persons who manifest disinhibition behave impulsively, without reflecting on potential future consequences. They may exhibit any of the following traits: *irresponsibility, impulsivity, distractibility, risk taking,* and *imperfection and disorganization.*

> **Psychoticism** People who display psychoticism have unusual and bizarre experiences. They may exhibit any of the following traits: *unusual beliefs and experiences, eccentricity,* and *cognitive and perceptual dysregulation* (odd thought processes or sensory experiences).

If a person is impaired significantly by any of the five trait groups, or even by just one of the 25 traits that comprise those groups, he or she would qualify for a diagnosis of *personality disorder trait specified.* In such cases, the diagnostician would indicate which traits are impaired.

Consider, for example, Matthew, the unhappy 34-year-old accountant described on page 504. As you'll recall, Matthew meets the criteria for a diagnosis of dependent personality disorder under DSM-5's current categorical approach, based largely on his lifetime of extreme dependence on his mother, friends, and coworkers. However, according to the dimensional approach being studied by DSM-5, Matthew would not receive this diagnosis. Instead, a diagnostician would take note that Matthew is greatly impaired by several of the traits that characterize the negative affectivity trait group. He is, for example, greatly impaired by "separation insecurity." This trait has prevented him from completing college, living on his own, marrying his girlfriend, ever disagreeing with his mother, advancing at work, and broadening his social life. In addition, Matthew seems to be impaired significantly by the traits of "anxiousness," "submissiveness," and

•**personality disorder trait specified (PDTS)**•A personality disorder currently undergoing study for possible inclusion in a future revision of DSM-5. Individuals would receive this diagnosis if they display significant impairment in their functioning as a result of one or more very problematic traits.

"depressivity." Given this picture, his therapist might assign him a diagnosis of *personality disorder trait specified, with problematic traits of separation insecurity, anxiousness, submissiveness, and depressivity.*

According to this dimensional approach, when clinicians assign a diagnosis of personality disorder trait specified, they also must rate the degree of dysfunctioning caused by each of the person's traits, using, as one possibility, a four-point scale ranging from "minimally descriptive" (Rating = 0) to "extremely descriptive" (Rating = 3).

Consider Matthew once again. He would probably warrant a rating of "0" on most of the 25 traits listed in the DSM-5 proposal, a rating of "2" on the trait of anxiousness and depressivity, and a rating of "3" on the traits of separation insecurity and submissiveness. Altogether, he would receive the following cumbersome, but informative, diagnosis:

Diagnosis: *Personality Disorder Trait Specified*
Separation insecurity: Rating 3
Submissiveness: Rating 3
Anxiousness: Rating 2
Depressivity: Rating 2
Other traits: Rating 0

"You'll have to excuse me—I'm myself today."

This dimensional approach to personality disorders may indeed prove superior to DSM-5's current categorical approach. Thus far, however, it has caused its own stir in the clinical community. Many clinicians believe that the proposed changes would give too much latitude to diagnosticians—allowing them to apply diagnoses of personality disorder to an enormous range of personality patterns. Still others worry that the requirements of the newly proposed system are too cumbersome or complicated. Only time and research will determine whether the alternative system is indeed a useful approach to the classification and diagnosis of personality disorders.

PUTTING IT... together

Disorders of Personality—Rediscovered, Then Reconsidered

During the first half of the twentieth century, clinicians believed deeply in the unique, enduring patterns we call personality, and they tried to define important personality traits. They then discovered how readily people can be shaped by the situations in which they find themselves, and a backlash developed. The concept of personality seemed to lose legitimacy, and for a while it became almost an obscene word in some circles. The clinical category of personality disorders experienced a similar rejection. When psychodynamic and humanistic theorists dominated the clinical field, *neurotic character disorders,* a set of diagnoses similar to today's personality disorders, were considered useful clinical categories (Millon et al., 2011, 2000). But their popularity declined as other models grew in influence.

? Why do some observers suggest that personality disorders are little more than descriptions of undesirable personal styles?

During the past two decades, serious interest in personality and personality disorders has rebounded. In case after case, clinicians have concluded that rigid personality traits do seem to pose special problems, and they have developed new objective tests and interview guides to assess these disorders, setting in motion a wave of systematic research (Millon, 2011). So far, only the antisocial and borderline personality disorders have received much study. However, with DSM-5 now considering a new—dimensional—classification approach for possible use in the future, additional research is likely to follow. In turn, clinicians may soon be better able to answer some pressing questions: How common are the various personality disorders?

Variations in personality
Like humans, animals of the same species vary widely in temperament. Brown bears, for example, are known for their aggressiveness—a trait that they express with loud growls, roars, woofs, champs, smacks, and outright attacks on other bears, animals, and, on occasion, humans. Yet many brown bears are shy, others relatively fearful, and some even playful, though few are as playful and carefree as this 800-pound brown bear seems to be.

How useful are personality disorder categories? How effective is a dimensional approach to diagnosing these disorders? And what treatments are most effective?

One of the most important questions is, "Why do people develop troubled patterns of personality?" As you have read, psychological, as opposed to biological and sociocultural, theories have offered the most suggestions so far, but these proposed explanations are not very precise, and they do not have strong research support. Given the current enthusiasm for biological explanations, genetic and biological factors are beginning to receive considerable study, a shift in the waters that should soon enable researchers to determine possible interactions between biological and psychological causes. And one would hope that sociocultural factors will be studied as well. As you have seen, sociocultural theorists have only occasionally offered explanations for personality disorders, and multicultural factors have received little research. However, sociocultural factors may well play an important role in these disorders and certainly should be examined more carefully.

DSM-5's proposal of a dimensional classification approach eventually may lead to major changes in the diagnosis of personality disorders. Similarly, the future is likely to bring significant changes to the explanations and treatments for these disorders. Now that clinicians have rediscovered personality disorders, they must determine the most appropriate ways to think about, explain, and treat them.

Summing Up

- **PERSONALITY DISORDERS AND DSM-5** People with a *personality disorder* display an enduring, rigid pattern of inner experience and outward behavior. Their personality traits are much more extreme and dysfunctional than those of most other people in their culture, resulting in significant problems for them or those around them. It has been estimated that as many as 9 to 13 percent of adults have such a disorder. DSM-5 uses a *categorical approach* that lists 10 distinct personality disorders. In addition, the framers of DSM-5 have proposed a *dimensional approach* to the classification of personality disorders, an approach that they assigned for further study and possible inclusion in a future revision of the DSM. *pp. 475–479*

- **"ODD" PERSONALITY DISORDERS** Three of the personality disorders in DSM-5 are marked by the kinds of odd or eccentric behavior often seen in schizophrenia. People with *paranoid personality disorder* display a broad pattern of distrust and suspiciousness. Those with *schizoid personality disorder* persistently avoid social relationships, have little or no social interests, and show little emotional expression. Individuals with *schizotypal personality disorder* display a range of interpersonal problems marked by extreme discomfort in close relationships, very odd forms of thinking and behavior, and behavioral eccentricities. People with these three kinds of disorders usually are resistant to treatment, and treatment gains tend to be modest at best. *pp. 479–484*

- **"DRAMATIC" PERSONALITY DISORDERS** Four of the personality disorders in DSM-5 are marked by highly dramatic, emotional, or erratic symptoms. People with *antisocial personality disorder* display a pattern of disregard for and violation of the rights of others. No known treatment is notably effective. People with *borderline personality disorder* display a pattern of instability in interpersonal relationships, self-image, and mood, along with extreme impulsivity. Treatment apparently can be helpful and lead to some improvement. People with *histrionic personality disorder* (once called *hysterical personality disorder*) display a pattern of extreme emotionality and attention seeking. Clinical case reports suggest that treatment is helpful on occasion. Finally, people with *narcissistic personality disorder* display a pattern of grandiosity, need for admiration, and lack of empathy. It is one of the most difficult disorders to treat. *pp. 484–501*

■ **"ANXIOUS" PERSONALITY DISORDERS** Three of the personality disorders in DSM-5 are marked by anxious and fearful behavior. People with *avoidant personality disorder* are consistently uncomfortable and inhibited in social situations, overwhelmed by feelings of inadequacy, and extremely sensitive to negative evaluation. People with *dependent personality disorder* have a persistent need to be taken care of, are submissive and clinging, and fear separation. Individuals with *obsessive-compulsive personality disorder* are so preoccupied with order, perfection, and control that they lose their flexibility, openness, and efficiency. A variety of treatment strategies have been used for people with these disorders and apparently have been modestly to moderately helpful. *pp. 501–508*

■ **MULTICULTURAL FACTORS** Despite the field's growing focus on personality disorders, relatively little research has been done on gender and other *multicultural* influences. Nevertheless, many clinicians believe that multicultural factors play key roles in the diagnosis and treatment of personality disorders, and researchers have recently begun to study this possibility. *pp. 508–509*

■ **ARE THERE BETTER WAYS TO CLASSIFY PERSONALITY DISORDERS?** The personality disorders listed in DSM-5 are commonly misdiagnosed, an indication of serious problems in the validity and reliability of the categories. Given the significant problems posed by the current *categorical approach,* a number of today's theorists believe that personality disorders should instead be described and classified by a *dimensional approach.* One such approach, the *"Big Five"* model, may be included in the next edition of the World Health Organization's International Classification of Diseases. Another dimensional approach, the *"personality disorder trait specified"* model, is under study for possible inclusion in a future revision of DSM-5. *pp. 509–513*

PsychPortal

Visit **PsychPortal**
www.yourpsychportal.com
to access the e-book, videocases and other case materials and activities, and study aids, including flashcards, crossword puzzles, quizzes, FAQs, and research exercises.

DISORDERS OF CHILDHOOD AND ADOLESCENCE

B illy, a 7-year-old . . . child, was brought to a mental health clinic by his mother because "he is unhappy and always complaining about feeling sick." . . . His mother describes Billy as a child who has never been very happy and never wanted to play with other children. From the time he started nursery school, he has complained about stomachaches, headaches, and various other physical problems. . . .

Billy did well in first grade, but in second grade he is now having difficulty completing his work. He takes a lot of time to do his assignments and frequently feels he has to do them over again so that they will be "perfect." Because of Billy's frequent somatic complaints, it is hard to get him off to school in the morning. If he is allowed to stay home, he worries that he is falling behind in his schoolwork. When he does go to school, he often is unable to do the work, which makes him feel hopeless about his situation. . . .

His worries have expanded beyond school, and frequently he is clinging and demanding of his parents. He is fearful that if his parents come home late or leave and go somewhere without him that something may happen to them. . . .

Although Billy's mother acknowledges that he has never been really happy, in the last 6 months, she feels, he has become much more depressed. He frequently lies around the house, saying that he is too tired to do anything. He has no interest or enjoyment in playing. His appetite has diminished. He has trouble falling asleep at night and often wakes up in the middle of the night or early in the morning. Three weeks ago, he talked, for the first time, about wanting to die. . . .

(Spitzer et al., 1994)

In the past year, Eddie [age 9] had been suspended twice for hyperactive and impulsive behavior. Most recently, he had climbed onto the overhead lights of the classroom and caused an uproar when he could not get himself down. His teachers complain that other children cannot concentrate when Eddie is in the room because he walks around constantly. Even when he is seated, his rapid foot and hand movements are disruptive to the other children. Eddie has almost no friends and does not play games with his classmates due to his impulsivity and overly active behavior. After school, he likes to play with his dog or ride his bike alone.

Eddie's mother reports that he has been excessively active since he was a toddler. At the age of three, Eddie would awaken at 4:30 AM each day and go downstairs without any supervision. Sometimes he would "demolish" the kitchen or living room, and at other times he would leave the house by himself. Once when he was four years old, he was found walking alone on a busy street in the early morning. Luckily, a passerby rescued him before he got into traffic.

After being rejected by a preschool because of his hyperactivity and impulsivity, Eddie attended a kindergarten and had a very difficult year. For first and second grade, he attended a special behavioral program. For third grade, he was allowed to attend a regular education class, with pull-out services for help with his behavior.

(Spitzer et al., 1994)

Billy and Eddie are both displaying psychological disorders. Their disorders are disrupting the boys' family ties, school performances, and social relationships, but each disorder does so in a particular way and for particular reasons. Billy, who may qualify for a diagnosis of *major depressive disorder,* struggles constantly with sadness, worry, and perfectionism, along with stomachaches and other physical ailments. Eddie's main problems, on the other hand, are that he cannot concentrate and is overly active and impulsive—difficulties that comprise attention-deficit/hyperactivity disorder (ADHD).

Abnormal functioning can occur at any time in life. Some patterns of abnormality, however, are more likely to emerge during particular periods—during childhood, for example, or, at the other end of the spectrum, during old age. In this chapter you will read about disorders that have their onset during childhood or early adolescence. In the next chapter you'll observe problems that are more common among the elderly.

Childhood and Adolescence

People often think of childhood as a carefree and happy time—yet it can also be frightening and upsetting (see Figure 17-1). In fact, children of all cultures typically experience at least some emotional and behavioral problems as they encounter new people and situations. Surveys reveal that *worry* is a common experience: close to half of all children in the United States have multiple fears, particularly concerning school, health, and personal safety (Beidel & Turner, 2005; Szabo & Lovibond, 2004). Bed-wetting, nightmares, temper tantrums, and restlessness are other problems experienced by many children. Adolescence can also be a difficult period. Physical and sexual changes, social and academic pressures, school violence, personal doubts, and temptations cause many teenagers to feel nervous, confused, and depressed.

A particular concern among children and adolescents is that of being bullied. Surveys throughout the world have revealed repeatedly that bullying ranks as a major problem in the minds of most young respondents, often a bigger problem than racism, AIDS, and peer pressure to try sex or alcohol (Jimerson et al., 2010; Cukan, 2001). More generally, over one-quarter of students report being bullied frequently, and more

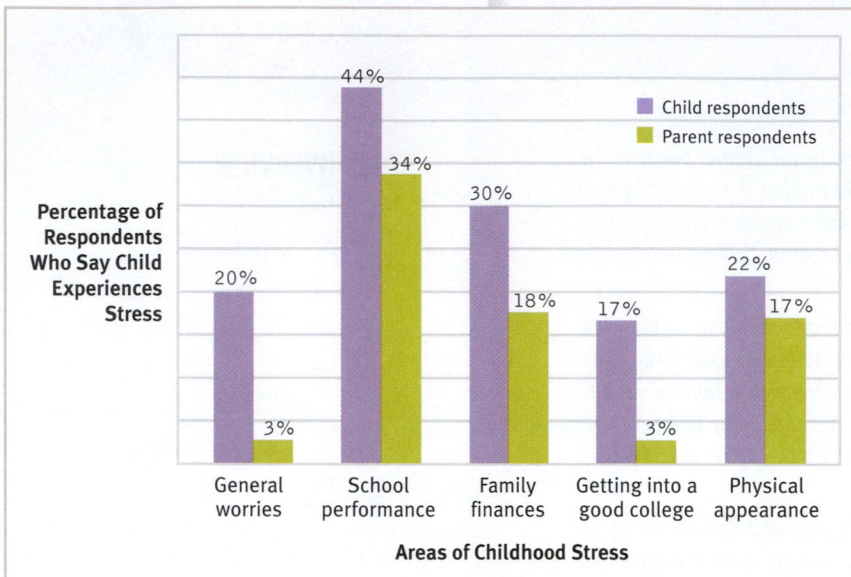

Figure 17-1

Are parents aware of their children's stress? Not always, according to a large survey of parents and their children aged 8 to 17. For example, although 44 percent of the child respondents report that they worry about school, only 34 percent of the parent respondents believe that their children have that concern. (Munsey, 2010).

"Is this the story you want to tell on your college application?"

than 70 percent report having been a victim at least once, with victims typically react-ing with feelings of humiliation, anxiety, or dislike for school (Jimerson et al., 2010; Smith, 2011, 2010; Jacobs, 2008). Just as troubling, the technological advances of today's world have broadened the ways in which children and adolescents can be bullied, and *cyberbullying*—bullying and humiliating by e-mail, text messages, and Facebook—is now on the rise (Schwartz, 2010; Smith & Slonje, 2010).

Beyond these common concerns and psy-chological difficulties, at least one-fifth of all children and adolescents in North America also experience a diagnosable psychological disorder (Winter & Bienvenu, 2011; Steele, Roberts, & Elkin, 2008). Boys with disorders outnumber girls, even though most of the adult psychological disorders are more common among women.

> **All victims of bullying are upset by it, but some individuals seem to be more traumatized by the experience than others. Why might this be so?**

Some disorders of children—childhood anxiety disorders, childhood depression, and disruptive disorders—have adult counterparts, although they are also distinct in certain ways. Other childhood disorders—elimination disorders, for example—usually disap-pear or radically change form by adulthood. There are also disorders that begin at birth or in childhood and persist in stable forms into adult life. These include autism spectrum disorder and intellectual developmental disorder (previously called mental retardation), the former marked by a lack of responsiveness to the environment, the latter by an extensive disturbance in intellect.

Childhood Anxiety Disorders

Anxiety is, to a degree, a normal part of childhood. Since children have had fewer experiences than adults, their world is often new and scary. They may be frightened by common events, such as the beginning of school, or by special upsets, such as mov-ing to a new house or becoming seriously ill. In addition, each generation of children is confronted by new sources of anxiety. Today's children, for example, are repeatedly warned, both at home and at school, about the dangers of Internet surfing and net-working, child abduction, drugs, and terrorism. They are bombarded by violent images on the Web, on television, or in movies. Even fairy tales and nursery rhymes contain frightening images that upset many children.

Children may also be affected greatly by parental problems or inadequacies. If, for example, parents typically react to events with high levels of anxiety or overprotect their children, the children may be more likely to respond to the world with anxiety (Becker et al., 2010; Levavi et al., 2010). Similarly, if parents repeatedly reject, disappoint, or avoid their children, the world may seem an unpleasant and anxious place for them. And if parents are divorced, become seriously ill, or must be separated from their children for a long period, childhood anxiety may result. Beyond such environmental problems, there is genetic evidence that some children are prone to an anxious temperament (Baldwin & Dadds, 2008).

For some children, such anxieties become long-lasting and debilitating, interfering with their daily lives and their ability to function appropriately (Pliszka, 2011). These children may be suffering from an anxiety disorder. Surveys indicate that between 8 and 29 percent of all children and adolescents display an anxiety disorder (Winter & Bienvenu, 2011; Mash & Wolfe, 2010; Costello et al., 2005). Some of the childhood anxiety disorders are similar to their adult counterparts. When specific phobias are expe-rienced by children, for example, they usually look and operate just like the phobias of adulthood (Pilecki & McKay, 2011). Indeed, a number of untreated childhood phobias grow into adult ones.

More often, however, the anxiety disorders of childhood take on a somewhat differ-ent character from that of adult anxiety disorders. Consider *generalized anxiety disorder,* marked by constant worrying, and *social anxiety disorder,* marked by fears of embarrassing

BETWEEN THE LINES

In Their Words

"It is an illusion that youth is happy, an illusion of those who have lost it." ‹‹

W. Somerset Maugham,
Of Human Bondage, 1915

BETWEEN THE LINES

Children in Need

Almost half of students identified with significant emotional disturbances drop out of high school. ‹‹

Currently there is 1 school counselor for every 476 students. The recommended ratio is 1 per 250 students. ‹‹

(ASCA, 2010; Planty et al., 2008; Gruttadaro, 2005)

oneself in front of others (Weems & Varela, 2011). In order to have such disorders, individuals must be able to anticipate future negative events (losing one's job, having a car accident, fainting in front of others), to take on the perspective of other people, and/or to recognize that the thoughts and beliefs of others differ from their own. These cognitive skills are simply beyond the capacity of very young children, and so the symptoms of generalized anxiety disorder and social anxiety disorder do not appear in earnest until children are 7 years old or older. In short, odd as it may sound, some patterns of anxiety cannot fully unfold until children are afforded the "benefits" of cognitive, physical, and emotional growth (Davis & Ollendick, 2011).

What, then, do the anxiety disorders of young children look like? Typically they are dominated by behavioral and somatic symptoms rather than cognitive ones—symptoms such as clinging, sleep difficulties, and stomach pains (Morris & Ale, 2011; Schulte & Petermann, 2011). They tend to center on specific, sometimes imaginary, objects and events, such as monsters, ghosts, or thunderstorms, rather than broad concerns about the future or one's place in the world (Davis & Ollendick, 2011). And they are more often than not triggered by current events and situations (Felix et al., 2011).

Separation Anxiety Disorder

Separation anxiety disorder, one of the most common childhood anxiety disorders, follows this profile (APA, 2013, 2012). This disorder is common (but not unique) to childhood, begins as early as the preschool years, and is displayed by 4 to 10 percent of all children (Mash & Wolfe, 2010; Van Dyke et al., 2009). Sufferers feel extreme anxiety, often panic, whenever they are separated from home or a parent (Eisen et al., 2011). Carrie, a 9-year-old girl, was referred to a local mental health center by her school counselor when she seemed to become extremely anxious at school for no apparent reason.

Oh, that first day!
The first day of kindergarten is overwhelming for this child and perhaps also for his mother. Such anxiety reactions to the beginning of school and to being temporarily separated from one's parents are common among young children.

She initially reported feeling sick to her stomach and later became quite concerned over being unable to get her breath. She stated that she was too nervous to stay at school and that she wanted her mother to come get her and take her home.... The counselor indicated that a similar incident occurred the next day with Carrie ending up going home again. She had not returned to school since....

At the time of the intake evaluation the mother indicated that she felt Carrie was just too nervous to go to school. She stated that she had encouraged her daughter to go to school on numerous occasions but that she seemed afraid to go and appeared to feel bad, so she had not forced her.... When asked if Carrie went places by herself, the mother stated that Carrie didn't like to do that and that the two of them typically did most everything together. The mother went on to note that Carrie really seemed to want to have her (the mother) around all the time and tended to become upset whenever the two of them were separated.

(Schwartz & Johnson, 1985, p. 188)

•**separation anxiety disorder**•A disorder marked by excessive anxiety, even panic, whenever the individual is separated from home, a parent, or another attachment figure.

•**play therapy**•An approach to treating childhood disorders that helps children express their conflicts and feelings indirectly by drawing, playing with toys, and making up stories.

Children like Carrie have great trouble traveling away from their family, and they often refuse to visit friends' houses, go on errands, or attend camp or school (see Table 17-1). Many cannot even stay alone in a room and cling to their parent around the house. Some also have temper tantrums, cry, or plead to keep their parents from leaving them. The children may fear that they will get lost when separated from their parents or that the parents will meet with an accident or illness. As long as the children are near their parents and not threatened by separation, they may function quite normally. At the first hint of separation, however, the dramatic pattern of symptoms may be set in motion.

As in Carrie's case, a separation anxiety disorder may further take the form of a *school phobia,* or *school refusal,* a common problem in which children fear going to school and often stay home for a long period. Many cases of school phobia, however, have causes other than separation fears, such as social or academic fears, depression, and fears of specific objects or persons at school.

Treatments for Childhood Anxiety Disorders

Despite the high prevalence of childhood and adolescent anxiety disorders, around two-thirds of anxious children go untreated (Winter & Bienvenu, 2011; Chavira et al., 2004). Among the children who do receive treatment, psychodynamic, cognitive-behavioral, family, and group therapies, separately or in combination, have been applied most often. Each approach has had some degree of success; however, cognitive-behavioral therapy has fared the best across a number of studies (Edmunds, O'Neil, & Kendall, 2011; Kendall, Furr, & Podell, 2010; Moore et al., 2010). Such treatments parallel the adult anxiety approaches that you read about in Chapter 5, but they are tailored to the child's cognitive abilities, unique life situation, and limited control over his or her life. In addition, clinicians may offer psychoeducation, provide parent training, and arrange school interventions to treat anxious children (Lewin, 2011).

Clinicians have also used drug therapy in a number of cases of childhood anxiety disorders, often in combination with psychotherapy (Bloch & McGuire, 2011; Watson, 2011). Not only do they prescribe antianxiety drugs, but antidepressant and antipsychotic drugs as well (Comer et al., 2011, 2010; Patel & Greydanus, 2010). Drug therapy for childhood anxiety appears to be helpful, but it has begun only recently to receive much research attention.

Because children typically have difficulty recognizing and understanding their feelings and motives, many therapists, particularly psychodynamic therapists, use **play therapy** as part of treatment (Landreth, 2012; Snow et al., 2009). In this approach, the children play with toys, draw, and make up stories; in doing so they reveal the conflicts in their lives and their related feelings. The therapists then introduce more play and fantasy to help the children work through their conflicts and change their emotions and behavior. In addition, because children are often excellent hypnotic subjects, some therapists use *hypnotherapy* to help them overcome intense fears.

AP Photo/Ahn Young-joon

table: 17-1

DSM-5 Checklist

Separation Anxiety Disorder

1. Developmentally inappropriate and excessive fear or anxiety concerning separation from those to whom the individual is attached. Symptoms include recurrent separation-related fears, worries, refusal to leave home, nightmares, and/or physical symptoms.

2. The symptoms are persistent, lasting at least 4 weeks in children and adolescents and typically 6 months or more in adults.

3. Significant distress or impairment.

Based on APA, 2013, 2012.

Surrounded by danger

These South Korean children wear medical masks and hold umbrellas amid fears that raindrops may contain radioactive materials from the damaged nuclear reactors in nearby Japan. In the aftermath of Japan's 2011 earthquake, tsunami, and nuclear plant meltdowns, children in Eastern Asia were bombarded by warnings of impending disaster and doom, causing a significant increase in the rate of childhood anxiety and mood disorders.

Childhood Mood Problems

Like Billy, the boy you read about at the beginning of this chapter, around 2 percent of children and 8 percent of adolescents currently experience major depressive disorder (Mash & Wolfe, 2010). Indeed, as many as 20 percent of adolescents experience at least one depressive episode during their teen years. In addition, many clinicians believe that children may experience bipolar disorder.

Major Depressive Disorder

As with anxiety disorders, very young children lack some of the cognitive skills that help produce clinical depression, thus accounting for the low rate of depression among the very young (Hankin et al., 2008). For example, in order to experience the sense of hopelessness typically found in depressed adults, children must demonstrate an ability to hold expectations about the future, a skill rarely in full bloom before the age of 7.

Nevertheless, if life situations or biological predispositions are significant enough, even very young children sometimes experience severe downward turns of mood (Swearer et al., 2011; Cummings & Fristad, 2008). Depression in the young may be triggered by negative life events (particularly losses), major changes, rejection, or ongoing abuse. Childhood depression is commonly characterized by such symptoms as headaches, stomach pain, irritability, and a disinterest in toys and games (Schulte & Petermann, 2011; Hankin et al., 2008).

Clinical depression is much more common among teenagers than among young children. Adolescence is, under the best of circumstances, a difficult and confusing time, marked by angst, hormonal and bodily changes, mood changes, complex relationships, and new explorations (see *MediaSpeak* on the next page). For some teens these "normal" upsets of adolescence cross the line into clinical depression. As you read in Chapter 10, suicidal thoughts and attempts are particularly common among adolescents—one in six teens think about suicide each year—and depression is the leading cause of such thoughts and attempts (Spirito & Esposito-Smythers, 2008).

Interestingly, while there is no difference between the rates of depression in boys and girls before the age of 13, girls are twice as likely as boys to be depressed by the age of 16 (Merikangas et al., 2010). Why this gender shift? Several factors have been suggested, including hormonal changes, the fact that females increasingly experience more stressors than males, and the tendency of girls to become more emotionally invested than boys in social and intimate relationships as they mature (Hankin et al., 2008). One explanation also focuses on teenage girls' growing dissatisfaction with their bodies. Whereas boys tend to like the increase in muscle mass and other body changes that accompany puberty, girls often detest the increases in body fat and weight gain that they experience during puberty and beyond. Raised in a society that values and demands extreme thinness as the aesthetic female ideal, many adolescent girls feel imprisoned by their own bodies, experience low self-esteem, and become depressed (Stice et al., 2000). Many also develop eating disorders, as you saw in Chapter 11.

For years, it was generally believed that childhood and teenage depression would respond well to the same treatments that have been of help to depressed adults—cognitive-behavioral therapy, interpersonal approaches, and antidepressant drugs—and, in fact, many studies have indicated the effectiveness of such approaches (Vela et al., 2011; Clarke & Debar, 2010; Jacobson & Mufson, 2010). Some recent studies and events, however, have raised questions about these approaches for teenagers.

In one development, the National Institute of Mental Health recently sponsored a massive six-year study called the *Treatments for Adolescents with Depression Study (TADS)*, which compared the effectiveness of cognitive-behavioral therapy alone, antidepressant therapy alone, cognitive-behavioral and antidepressant

Grief camp

A number of "grief camps" have been developed around the country for children and teenagers who have lost a loved one. At one such program, this young girl, whose uncle was killed while fighting in Iraq, puts a clipping representing what she feels about his death in a bag.

AP Photo/Al Grillo

MediaSpeak

Alone in a Parallel Life

By Bernadine Healy, M.D., *U.S. News & World Report*

The world wide web began as a platform for information, communication, and entertainment. It's now emerging as a powerful social medium, in which people build communities of newfound friends with whom they form personal and emotional bonds. One has to be concerned about this seemingly innocuous exercise in networking, however, if these bonds with people known only to the imagination—typically anonymous, sometimes misrepresented, and never accountable—interfere with or replace real intimacies, particularly in those who are in a formative stage of social development. Researchers at the Annenberg School Center for the Digital Future at the University of Southern California, which has been tracking Internet behavior for six years, were taken by surprise when their latest survey found that more than 40 percent of users feel that their online friends are every bit as important to them as their real-life ones.

Beyond communities of presumably real people is the Internet game world, in which emotional contacts are made in three-dimensional virtual reality with fantasy people in fantasy places. . . .

Little is known about what might be [the] safety concerns related to games in which young people create avatars [virtual representations of themselves] and interact freely in vivid imaginary worlds, largely unsupervised. Sometimes the play involves any number of supercharged violent or objectionable actions against other imaginary humans—taken without remorse or empathy or personal consequence. To be sure, there is disagreement on the impact of such experiences. Some psychologists argue that they might encourage the behavior in the real world; others that it has no effect and may even be a way to drain off aggressive feelings. Or, as in one study, a 15-year-old girl, whose avatar was a cyberprostitute, believed that her online behavior wasn't bad since it wasn't real. In essence, this girl is saying, just chill.

The unknown. Should we chill? As Harvard cyber-researcher and psychiatrist Steven Locke acknowledges, we've only scratched the surface when it comes to understanding how imaginary experiences that are so vividly realistic might

affect brain development in children. We know that real ones do. We also have to consider a broader but more subtle risk: that for some kids, a dependence on virtual human interactions, be they with real or with fantasy people, might influence their evolving social intelligence, affecting whom they trust and how they set expectations, how they deal with both affirmation and rejection, and how they give and receive emotional support. Remember, the virtual world can be just what you want it to be and can become an escape from reality.

In this regard, psychologists are concerned about one form of virtual escape—Internet addiction disorder [IAD], which can be a big relationship buster. Those with IAD become so immersed online that they neglect studies, work, friends, and family and when deprived of Internet access grow anxious or depressed. IAD has been reported worldwide in at least 2 percent of Internet users, and the young are most susceptible. Concerned, China last month mandated antiaddiction software to limit young people's Internet access to three hours per day.

But it's cybersmart parents who are best suited to influence their children's time online and also the places they go. Maybe the first question at the next PTA meeting should be, "Where was your 13-year-old's avatar last night?"

therapy combined, and placebo therapy for teenage depression (TADS, 2010, 2007, 2004; Curry & Becker, 2008). Three major surprises emerged from this highly regarded study. First, neither antidepressants alone nor cognitive-behavioral therapy alone was as effective for teenage depression as was a combination of antidepressants and cognitive-behavioral therapy. Second, antidepressants alone tended to be more helpful to depressed teens than cognitive-behavioral therapy alone. And third, cognitive-behavioral therapy alone was barely more helpful than placebo therapy. Many researchers believe that certain peculiarities in the participant population of the TADS study may have been responsible for the poor showing of cognitive-behavioral therapy. However, other clinical

Separation and depression
This 3-year-old boy hugs his father as the soldier departs for deployment to Iraq. Given research evidence that extended family separations often produce depression in children, clinical theorists have been particularly worried about the thousands of children from military families who have been left behind during the wars in Afghanistan and Iraq.

theorists believe that the TADS study is indeed a definitive research undertaking and that many depressed teens may in fact respond less well to cognitive-behavioral therapy than adults do.

A second development in recent years has been the discovery that antidepressant drugs may be highly dangerous for some depressed children and teenagers. Throughout the 1990s, most psychiatrists believed that second-generation antidepressants were safe and effective for children and adolescents, and they prescribed them readily (Vela et al., 2011). However, as you read in Chapter 10, the United States Food and Drug Administration (FDA) concluded in 2004, based on a number of clinical reports, that the drugs may produce a real, though small, increase in the risk of suicidal behavior for certain children and adolescents, especially during the first few months of treatment. In turn, it ordered that all antidepressant containers carry "black box" warnings stating that the drugs "increase the risk of suicidal thinking and behavior in children."

Arguments about the wisdom of this FDA order have since followed. Although most clinicians agree that the drugs may indeed increase the risk of suicidal thoughts and attempts in as many as 2 to 4 percent of young patients, many observers have noted that the overall risk of suicide may actually be reduced for the vast majority of children who take the drugs (Vela et al., 2011; Kutcher & Gardner, 2008). They point out, for example, that suicides among children and teenagers decreased by 30 percent in the decade leading up to 2004, as the number of antidepressant prescriptions provided to children and teenagers were soaring.

While the findings of the TADS study and questions about antidepressant drug safety continue to be sorted out, these two recent developments serve to highlight once again the importance of research, particularly in the treatment realm. We are reminded that treatments that work for individuals of a certain age, gender, race, or ethnic background may be ineffective or even dangerous for other groups of individuals.

Bipolar Disorder and Disruptive Mood Dysregulation Disorder

For decades, conventional clinical wisdom held that bipolar disorder is exclusively an *adult* mood disorder, whose earliest age of onset is the late teens. However, since the mid-1990s, clinical theorists have done an about-face, and a rapidly growing number of them now believe that many children display bipolar disorder (Chang et al., 2010; Diler et al., 2010; Grier et al., 2010). A review of national diagnostic trends from 1994 through 2003 found that the number of children—often very young children—and adolescents diagnosed and treated for bipolar disorder in United States increased 40-fold, from 25 such diagnoses per 100,000 individuals in 1994 to 1,000 per 100,000 individuals in 2003 (Moreno et al., 2007) . Correspondingly, as you can see in Figure 17-2, the number of

Figure 17-2

Rapid rise: Children and bipolar disorder
The number of private office visits for children and teenagers with a diagnosis of bipolar disorder rose from 20,000 in 1994 to 800,000 in 2003 (Whitaker, 2010; Moreno, 2007).

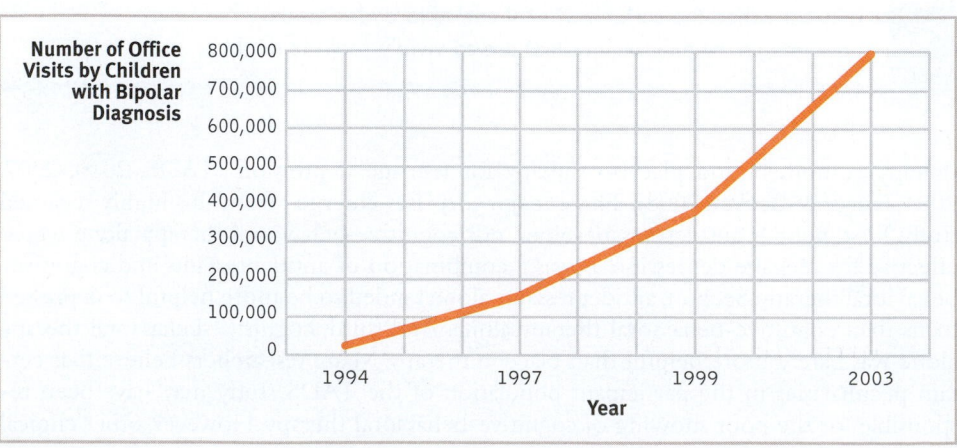

private office visits for children with bipolar disorders increased from 20,000 in 1994 to 800,000 in 2003. Furthermore, most clinical observers agree that the number of children and adolescents diagnosed with bipolar disorder has continued to rise sharply since 2003 (Mash & Wolfe, 2010).

Most theorists believe that these numbers reflect not an increase in the prevalence of bipolar disorders among children but, rather, a new diagnostic trend. The question is whether this trend is accurate. In a national survey of adults with bipolar disorders, 33 percent of the respondents recalled that their symptoms actually began before they reached 15 years of age, and another 27 percent said their symptoms first appeared between the ages of 15 and 19 (Hirschfeld et al., 2003). Such responses indicate that bipolar disorders among children and teenagers have indeed been around for years but were overlooked by diagnosticians and therapists (Chang et al., 2010).

Some clinical theorists, however, distrust the accuracy of such retrospective reports and believe that the diagnosis of bipolar disorder is currently being overapplied to children and adolescents (Mash & Wolfe, 2010; Moreno et al., 2007). Indeed, they suggest that the label has become a clinical "catchall" that is being applied to almost every explosive, aggressive child. In fact, symptoms of rage and aggression, along with depression, dominate the clinical picture of most children who receive a bipolar diagnosis (Diler et al., 2010; Miklowitz & Cichetti, 2010). The children may not even manifest the symptoms of mania or the mood swings that characterize cases of adult bipolar disorder. Moreover, two-thirds of the children and adolescents who receive a bipolar diagnosis are boys, while adult men and women have bipolar disorder in equal numbers.

The DSM-5 task force concluded that the childhood bipolar label has in fact been overapplied over the past two decades. To help rectify this problem, DSM-5 now includes a new category, **disruptive mood dysregulation disorder,** which is targeted for children with severe patterns of rage (see Table 17-2). It is expected that such children will receive this diagnosis increasingly in the coming years and that the number of childhood bipolar disorder diagnoses will decrease correspondingly.

This issue is particularly important because the rise in diagnoses of bipolar disorder has been accompanied by an increase in the number of children who receive adult medications (Chang et al., 2010; Grier et al., 2010). Around one-half of children in treatment for bipolar disorder receive an antipsychotic drug; one-third receive an antibipolar, or mood stabilizing, drug; and many others receive antidepressant or stimulant drugs. Yet relatively few of these drugs have been tested on and approved specifically for use with children.

•disruptive mood dysregulation disorder• A childhood disorder marked by severe recurrent temper outbursts along with a persistent irritable or angry mood.

•oppositional defiant disorder• A childhood disorder in which children are repeatedly argumentative and defiant, angry and irritable, and, in some cases, vindictive.

•conduct disorder• A childhood disorder in which the child repeatedly violates the basic rights of others and displays aggression, characterized by symptoms such as physical cruelty to people or animals, the deliberate destruction of other people's property, and the commission of various crimes.

table: **17-2**

DSM-5 Checklist

Disruptive Mood Dysregulation Disorder

1. Severe and recurrent temper outbursts (verbal or behavioral) that are grossly out of proportion to the situation.

2. Outbursts occur three or more times per week, for at least one year.

3. Persistent irritable or angry mood is displayed between outbursts.

4. Symptoms are present in at least two settings (home, school, with peers).

5. Individual is between 6 and 18 years of age.

Based on APA, 2013, 2012.

Oppositional Defiant Disorder and Conduct Disorder

Most children break rules or misbehave on occasion. If they consistently display extreme hostility and defiance, however, they may qualify for a diagnosis of oppositional defiant disorder or conduct disorder. Those with **oppositional defiant disorder** are argumentative and defiant, angry and irritable, and, in some cases, vindictive (APA, 2013, 2012). They may, for example, argue repeatedly with adults, ignore adult rules and requests, deliberately annoy other people, and feel great anger and resentment. As many as 10 percent of children qualify for a diagnosis of oppositional defiant disorder (Mash & Wolfe, 2010; Merikangas et al., 2010). The disorder is more common in boys than in girls before puberty but equal in both sexes after puberty.

Children with **conduct disorder,** a more severe problem, repeatedly violate the basic rights of others (APA, 2013, 2012). They are often aggressive and may be physically cruel to people or animals, deliberately destroy other people's property, skip school, or

BETWEEN THE LINES

Early Births and Psychological Disorders

A recent study conducted in Britain and Ireland found that 23 percent of children born very prematurely (6 months or less) displayed a psychological disorder at the age of 11, compared to 9 percent of full-term children. ''

(Johnson et al., 2010)

Unthinkable

A surveillance camera shows the 1993 abduction of 2-year-old James Bulger from a shopping mall in England. The child holds the hand of one of his abductors—two 10-year-old boys who were later convicted of his torture and murder. The legal case stirred the emotions of people around the world and clarified once again that some children are indeed capable of extreme antisocial behavior.

Photo by BWP Media via Getty Images

run away from home (see Table 17-3). Many steal from, threaten, or harm their victims, committing such crimes as firesetting, shoplifting, forgery, breaking into buildings or cars, mugging, and armed robbery. As they get older, their acts of physical violence may include rape or, in rare cases, homicide. The symptoms of conduct disorder are apparent in this summary of a clinical interview with a 15-year-old boy named Derek:

> Questioning revealed that Derek was getting into . . . serious trouble of late, having been arrested for shoplifting 4 weeks before. Derek was caught with one other youth when he and a dozen friends swarmed a convenience store and took everything they could before leaving in cars. This event followed similar others at [an electronics] store and a . . . clothing store. Derek blamed his friends for getting caught because they apparently left him behind as he straggled out of the store. He was charged only with shoplifting, however, after police found him holding just three candy bars and a bag of potato chips. Derek expressed no remorse for the theft or any care for the store clerk who was injured when one of the teens pushed her into a glass case. When informed of the clerk's injury, for example, Derek replied, "I didn't do it, so what do I care?"
>
> The psychologist decided to question Derek further about other legal violations in the past. He discovered a rather extended history of trouble. Ten months earlier, Derek had been arrested for vandalism—breaking windows and damaging cars—on school property. He was placed on probation for 6 months because this was his first offense. In addition, Derek boasted of other exploits for which he was not caught, including several shoplifting attempts, . . . joyriding, and missing school. . . . Derek had missed 23 days (50 percent) of school since the beginning of the academic year. . . . In addition, Derek described break-in attempts of his neighbors' apartments. . . . Only rarely during the interview did Derek stray from his bravado.
>
> *(Kearney, 1999, pp. 104–105)*

Conduct disorder usually begins between 7 and 15 years of age (APA, 2000). As many as 10 percent of children, three-quarters of them boys, qualify for this diagnosis (Mash & Wolfe, 2010; Nock et al., 2006; Hibbs & Jensen, 2005). Children with a relatively mild conduct disorder often improve over time, but severe cases may continue into adulthood and develop into antisocial personality disorder or other psychological problems (Mash & Wolfe, 2010). Usually, the earlier the onset of the conduct disorder, the poorer the eventual outcome. Research indicates that more than 80 percent of individuals who develop conduct disorder first display a pattern of oppositional defiant disorder (Lahey, 2008). More than one-third of children with conduct disorder also display attention-deficit/hyperactivity disorder (ADHD), a disorder that you will read about shortly (Jiron, 2010; Waschbusch, 2002). And a number of children with the disorder also experience depression and anxiety.

Some clinical theorists believe that there are actually several kinds of conduct disorder, including (1) the *overt-destructive* pattern, in which individuals display openly aggressive and confrontational behaviors; (2) the *overt-nondestructive* pattern, dominated by openly offensive but nonconfrontational behaviors such as lying; (3) the *covert-destructive* pattern, characterized by secretive destructive behaviors such as violating other people's property, breaking and entering, and setting fires; and (4) the *covert-nondestructive* pattern, in which individuals secretly commit nonaggressive behaviors, such as being truant from school (McMahon & Frick, 2007, 2005). It may be that the different patterns have different causes. In a similar vein,

DSM-5 instructs diagnosticians to distinguish those individuals whose conduct disorder is marked by particularly callous and unemotional behaviors (APA, 2013). They may be qualitatively different from others with the disorder.

Other researchers distinguish yet another pattern of aggression found in certain cases of conduct disorder, *relational aggression,* in which the individuals are socially isolated and primarily display social misdeeds such as slandering others, spreading rumors, and manipulating friendships (Keenan et al., 2010) (see *MediaSpeak* on page 529). Relational aggression is more common among girls than boys.

Many children with conduct disorder are suspended from school, placed in foster homes, or incarcerated (Weyandt et al., 2011). When children between the ages of 8 and 18 break the law, the legal system often labels them *juvenile delinquents* (Jiron, 2010; Lahey, 2008). More than half of the juveniles who are arrested each year are *recidivists,* meaning they have records of previous arrests. Boys are much more involved in juvenile crime than girls, although rates for girls are on the increase. Girls are most likely to be arrested for drug use, sexual offenses, and running away, boys for drug use and crimes against property. Arrests of teenagers for serious crimes have at least tripled during the past 25 years (U.S. Department of Justice, 2010, 2008).

table: **17-3**
DSM-5 Checklist
Conduct Disorder
1. Repetitive and persistent pattern of behavior in which the basic rights of others or major age-appropriate societal norms or rules are violated.
2. At least three of the following features are present in the past 12 months (and at least one in the past 6 months): • Frequent bullying or threatening of others • Frequent provoking of physical fights • Using dangerous weapons • Physical cruelty to people • Physical cruelty to animals • Stealing while confronting a victim • Forcing someone into sexual activity • Fire-setting • Deliberately destroying others' property. • Breaking into a house, building, or car • Frequent lying • Stealing items of nontrivial value without confronting a victim • Frequent staying out beyond curfews, beginning before the age of 13 • Running away from home overnight at least twice • Frequent truancy from school, beginning before the age of 13.
3. Significant impairment.
Based on APA, 2013, 2012.

What Are the Causes of Conduct Disorder?

Many cases of conduct disorder have been linked to genetic and biological factors, particularly cases marked by destructive behaviors (Cohen, 2010; Jiron, 2010). In addition, a number of cases have been tied to drug abuse, poverty, traumatic events, and exposure to violent peers or community violence (Weyandt et al., 2011; Webster-Stratton & Reid, 2010). Most often, however, conduct disorder has been tied to troubled parent-child relationships, inadequate parenting, family conflict, marital conflict, and family hostility (Mash & Wolfe, 2010; Biederman et al., 2001). Children whose parents reject, leave, coerce, or abuse them or fail to provide appropriate and consistent supervision are apparently more likely to develop conduct problems. Similarly, children seem more prone to this disorder when their parents themselves are antisocial, display excessive anger, or have substance use, mood, or schizophrenic disorders (Julien et al., 2011).

How Do Clinicians Treat Conduct Disorder?

Because aggressive behaviors become more locked in with age, treatments for conduct disorder are generally most effective with children younger than 13 (Webster-Stratton & Reid, 2010). A number of interventions, from sociocultural to child-focused, have been developed in recent years to treat children with the disorder. As you will see, several of these have had modest (and at times moderate) success, but clearly no one of them alone is the answer for this difficult problem. Today's clinicians are increasingly combining several approaches into a wide-ranging treatment program.

Sociocultural Treatments Given the importance of family factors in conduct disorder, therapists often use family interventions. One such approach, used with preschoolers, is called *parent-child interaction therapy* (Zisser & Eyberg, 2010; Querido & Eyberg, 2005). Here therapists teach parents to work with their child positively, to set appropriate limits, to act consistently, to be fair in their discipline decisions, and to establish more appropriate expectations regarding the child. The therapists also try to teach the child better social skills. Ideally, these efforts strengthen the relationship between the parents and child, improve the parents' attitudes, lead to greater parent control, and

BETWEEN THE LINES

Narrowing the Gender Gap

Today, one of every three teens arrested for violent crimes is female. ‹‹
(Department of Justice, 2008; Scelfo, 2005)

Antisocial behavior and the law

Many children and adolescents with conduct disorder wind up incarcerated in *juvenile detention,* or *juvenile training, centers* when their antisocial behaviors place them in conflict with the law. Here inmates at a juvenile detention center in Alabama spend Christmas waiting in line to go outside for physical training.

Figure 17-3

Teenage crime Although teenagers make up only 14 percent of the total population, they commit around 30 percent of all violent crimes and 34 percent of all murders. They are also the victims of 33 percent of all violent crimes. (Adapted from National Crime Victimization Survey, 2006, 1997, 1996, 1993; Levesque, 2002.)

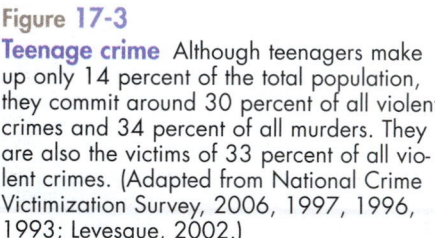

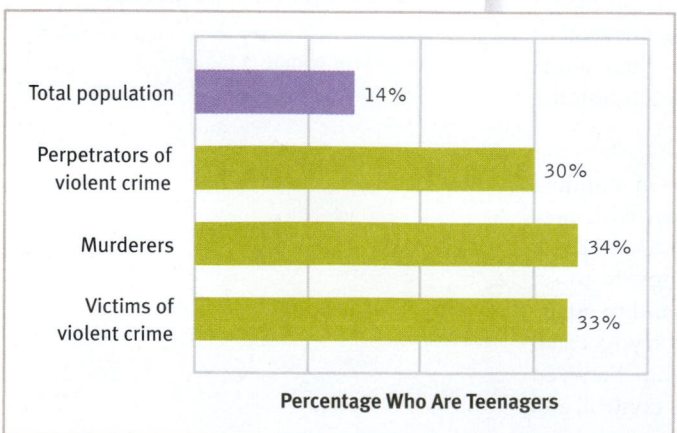

Percentage Who Are Teenagers

Total population	14%
Perpetrators of violent crime	30%
Murderers	34%
Victims of violent crime	33%

help bring about improvements in the child's behavior. A related family intervention for very young children, *video modeling,* works toward the same goals with the help of video tools (Webster-Stratton & Reid, 2010; Webster-Stratton, 2005).

When children reach school age, therapists often use a family intervention called *parent management training.* In this approach (1) parents are again taught more effective ways to deal with their children and (2) parents and children meet together in behavior-oriented family therapy (Forgatch & Patterson, 2010; Kazdin, 2010, 2002). Typically, the family and therapist target particular behaviors for change; then, with the help of written manuals, therapy rehearsals and practice, and homework, the parents are taught how to better identify problem behaviors, stop rewarding unwanted behaviors, and reward proper behaviors with consistency. Like the preschool family interventions, parent management training has often achieved a measure of success (Forgatch & Patterson, 2010; McMahon & Kotler, 2008).

Other sociocultural approaches, such as residential treatment in the community and programs at school, have also helped some children improve (Lebuffe, Robison, & Chamberlin-Elliot, 2010; Boxer & Frick, 2008). In one such approach, *treatment foster care,* delinquent boys and girls with conduct disorder are assigned to a foster home in the community by the juvenile justice system. While there, the children, foster parents, and biological parents all receive training and treatment interventions, including family therapy with both sets of parents, individual treatment for the child, and meetings with school, parole, and probation officers. In addition, the children and their parents continue to receive treatment and support after they leave foster care. This program is apparently most beneficial when all the intervention components are applied simultaneously.

In contrast to these sociocultural interventions, institutionalization in so-called *juvenile training centers* has not met with much success (Stahlberg et al., 2010; Heilbrun et al., 2005). In fact, such institutions frequently serve to strengthen delinquent behavior rather than resocialize young offenders (see Figure 17-3).

How might juvenile training centers themselves contribute to the high recidivism rate among teenage criminal offenders?

Targeted for Bullying

By Jesse McKinley, *New York Times*

When Seth Walsh was in the sixth grade, he turned to his mother one day and told her he had something to say.

"I was folding clothes, and he said, 'Mom, I'm gay,'" said Wendy Walsh, a hairstylist and single mother of four. "I said, 'O.K., sweetheart, I love you no matter what.'"

But last month, Seth went into the backyard of his home in the desert town of Tehachapi, Calif., and hanged himself, apparently unable to bear a relentless barrage of taunting, bullying and other abuse at the hands of his peers. After a little more than a week on life support, he died last Tuesday. He was 13.

The case of Tyler Clementi, the Rutgers University freshman who jumped off the George Washington Bridge after a sexual encounter with another man was broadcast online, has shocked many. But his death is just one of several suicides in recent weeks by young gay teenagers who had been harassed by classmates, both in person and online.

The list includes Billy Lucas, a 15-year-old from Greensburg, Ind., who hanged himself on Sept. 9 after what classmates reportedly called a constant stream of invective against him at school.

Less than two weeks later, Asher Brown, a 13-year-old from the Houston suburbs, shot himself after coming out. He, too, had reported being taunted at his middle school, according to The Houston Chronicle. His family has blamed school officials as failing to take action after they complained, something the school district has denied.

The deaths have set off an impassioned—and sometimes angry—response from gay activists and caught the attention of federal officials, including Secretary of Education Arne Duncan, who on Friday called the suicides "unnecessary tragedies" brought on by "the trauma of being bullied."

"This is a moment where every one of us—parents, teachers, students, elected officials and all people of conscience—needs to stand up and speak out against intolerance in all its forms," Mr. Duncan said. . . .

According to a recent survey, . . . nearly 9 of 10 gay, lesbian, transgender or bisexual middle and high school students suffered physical or verbal harassment in 2009, ranging from taunts to outright beatings. . . .

In a pair of blog postings last week, Dan Savage, a sex columnist based in Seattle, assigns the blame to negligent teachers and school administrators, bullying classmates and "hate groups that warp some young minds and torment others." . . .

"There are accomplices out there," he wrote Saturday. . . .

In late September, Mr. Savage began a project on YouTube called "It Gets Better," featuring gay adults talking about their experiences with harassment as adolescents. . . .

Valerie Macon/AFP/Getty Images

Important message Actor Chris Colfer won a Golden Globe Award in 2011 for his portrayal of bullied gay teen Kurt Hummel in the popular television series *Glee*. In his acceptance speech, Colfer, who is himself openly gay, said, "To all those amazing kids . . . who are constantly told . . . by bullies at school that they can't be who they are. . . . Well, screw that, kids."

In Tehachapi, in Kern County south of here, more than 500 mourners attended a memorial on Friday for Seth Walsh. One of those, Jamie Elaine Phillips, a classmate and friend, said Seth had long known he was gay and had been teased for years. "But this year it got much worse," Jamie said. "People would say, 'You should kill yourself,' 'You should go away,' 'You're gay, who cares about you?'"

Richard L. Swanson, superintendent of the local school district, said his staff had conducted quarterly assemblies on behavior, taught tolerance in the classroom and had "definite discipline procedures that respond to bullying."

"But these things didn't prevent Seth's tragedy," he said in an e-mail. "Maybe they couldn't have." . . .

For her part, Ms. Walsh said she had complained about Seth's being picked on but did not want to cast blame, though she hoped his death would teach people "not to discriminate, not be prejudiced."

"I truly hope," she said, "that people understand that."

Prevention: Scared Straight
Rather than waiting for children or adolescents to develop antisocial patterns, many clinicians call for better *prevention* programs. In one such program, "at-risk" children visit nearby prisons where inmates describe how drugs, gang life, and other antisocial behaviors led to their imprisonment.

Child-Focused Treatments Treatments that focus primarily on the child with conduct disorder, particularly cognitive-behavioral interventions, have achieved some success in recent years (Kazdin, 2010, 2007, 2003, 2002). In an approach called *problem-solving skills training,* therapists combine modeling, practice, role-playing, and systematic rewards to help teach children constructive thinking and positive social behaviors. During therapy sessions, the therapists may play games and solve tasks with the children and later help the children apply the lessons and skills derived from the games and tasks to real-life situations.

In another child-focused approach, the *Anger Coping and Coping Power Program,* children with conduct problems participate in group sessions that teach them to manage their anger more effectively, view situations in perspective, solve problems, become aware of their emotions, build social skills, set goals, and handle peer pressure. Studies indicate that child-focused approaches such as these do indeed help reduce aggressive behaviors and prevent substance use in adolescence (Lochman et al., 2011, 2010).

Recently, drug therapy has also been used on children with conduct disorder. Studies suggest that *stimulant drugs* may be helpful in reducing their aggressive behaviors at home and at school (Connor et al., 2002).

Prevention It may be that the greatest hope for dealing with the problem of conduct disorder lies in *prevention* programs that begin in the earliest stages of childhood (Boxer & Frick, 2008). These programs try to change unfavorable social conditions before a conduct disorder is able to develop. The programs may offer training opportunities for young people, recreational facilities, and health care and may try to ease the stresses of poverty and improve parents' child-rearing skills. All such approaches work best when they educate and involve the family.

Attention-Deficit/Hyperactivity Disorder

Children who display **attention-deficit/hyperactivity disorder (ADHD)** have great difficulty attending to tasks, or behave overactively and impulsively, or both (APA, 2013, 2012) (see Table 17-4). The disorder often appears before the child starts school, as with Eddie, one of the boys we met at the beginning of this chapter. Steven is another child whose symptoms began very early in life:

Steven's mother cannot remember a time when her son was not into something or in trouble. As a baby he was incredibly active, so active in fact that he nearly rocked his crib apart. All the bolts and screws became loose and had to be tightened periodically. Steven was also always into forbidden places, going through the medicine cabinet or under the kitchen sink. He once swallowed some washing detergent and had to be taken to the emergency room. As a matter of fact, Steven had many more accidents and was more clumsy than his older brother and younger sister. . . . He always seemed to be moving fast. His mother recalls that Steven progressed from the crawling stage to a running stage with very little walking in between.

Trouble really started to develop for Steven when he entered kindergarten. Since his entry into school, his life has been miserable and so has the teacher's. Steven does not seem capable of attending to assigned tasks and following instructions. He would rather be talking to a neighbor or wandering around the room without the teacher's permission. When he is seated and the teacher is keeping an eye on him to make sure that he works, Steven's body still seems to be in motion. He is either tapping his pencil, fidgeting,

•**attention-deficit/hyperactivity disorder (ADHD)**•A disorder marked by inability to focus attention, or overactive and impulsive behavior, or both.

or staring out the window and daydreaming. Steven hates kindergarten and has few long-term friends; indeed, school rules and demands appear to be impossible challenges for him. The effects of this mismatch are now showing in Steven's schoolwork and attitude. He has fallen behind academically and has real difficulty mastering new concepts; he no longer follows directions from the teacher and has started to talk back.

(Gelfand, Jenson, & Drew, 1982, p. 256)

The symptoms of ADHD often feed into one another (Stevens & Ward-Estes, 2006). Children who have trouble focusing attention may keep turning from task to task until they end up trying to run in several directions at once. Similarly, constantly moving

table: **17-4**

DSM-5 Checklist

Attention-Deficit/Hyperactivity Disorder

1. Either of the following groups:

   A. At least six of the following symptoms of *inattention,* persisting for at least six months to a degree that is maladaptive and inconsistent with development level:

      a. Frequent failure to give close attention to details, or making careless mistakes.

      b. Frequent difficulty in sustaining attention.

      c. Frequent failure to listen when spoken to directly.

      d. Frequent failure to follow through on instructions and failure to finish work.

      e. Difficulty organizing tasks and activities.

      f. Avoidance of, dislike of, and reluctance to engage in tasks that require sustained mental effort.

      g. Frequent loss of items necessary for tasks or activities.

      h. Easy distraction by irrelevant stimuli.

      i. Forgetfulness in daily activities.

   B. At least six of the following symptoms of *hyperactivity* and *impulsivity,* persisting for at least six months to a degree that is maladaptive and inconsistent with developmental level:

      a. Fidgeting with or tapping of hands or feet, or squirming in seat.

      b. Frequent wandering from seat in classroom or similar situation.

      c. Frequent running about or climbing excessively in situations in which it is inappropriate.

      d. Frequent difficulty playing or engaging in leisure activities quietly.

      e. Frequent "on the go" activity or acting as if "driven by a motor."

      f. Frequent excessive talking.

      g. Frequent blurting out of answers before questions have been completed.

      h. Frequent difficulty awaiting turn.

      i. Frequent interrupting of or intruding on others.

2. The presence of some symptoms before the age of 12.

3. The symptoms occur in at least two settings.

4. Significant impairment.

Based on APA, 2013, 2012.

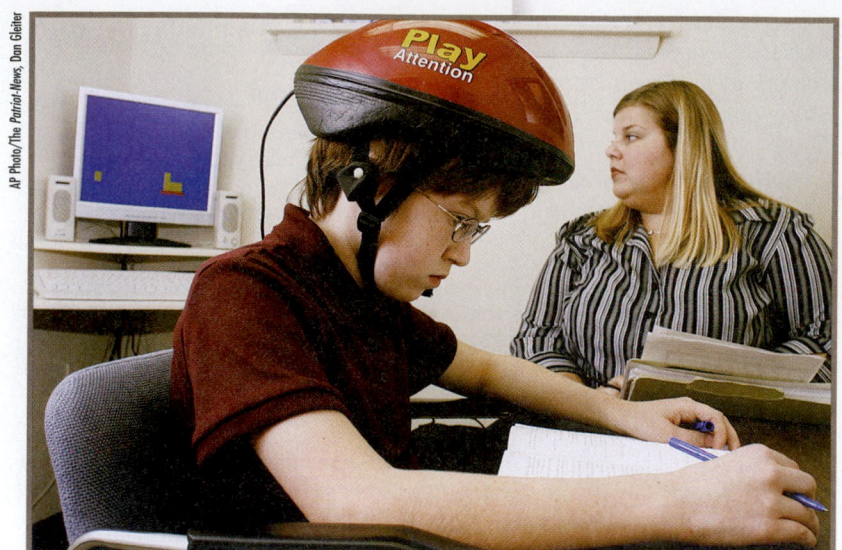

AP Photo/The Patriot-News, Dan Gleiter

"Playing" attention

A range of techniques have been used to help understand and treat children with ADHD, including a computer program called *Play Attention*. Here, under the watchful eye of a behavior specialist, a child wears a bike helmet that measures brain waves while she performs tasks that require attention.

children may find it hard to attend to tasks or show good judgment. In many cases one of these symptoms stands out much more than the other. About half of the children with ADHD also have learning or communication problems, many perform poorly in school, a number have difficulty interacting with other children, and about 80 percent misbehave, often quite seriously (Goldstein, 2011; Mash & Wolfe, 2010). It is also common for these children to have anxiety or mood problems (Günther et al., 2011; Julien et al., 2011).

Around 4 to 9 percent of schoolchildren display ADHD, as many as 70 percent of them boys (Merikangas et al., 2011; Mash & Wolfe, 2010). Those whose parents have had ADHD are more likely than others to develop it (APA, 2000). The disorder usually persists throughout childhood. Many children show a marked lessening of symptoms as they move into mid-adolescence, but between 35 and 60 percent of affected children continue to have ADHD as adults (Julien et al., 2011; Barkley & Benton, 2010; Ramsay, 2010). The symptoms of restlessness and overactivity are not usually as pronounced in adult cases.

ADHD is a difficult disorder to assess properly (Hale et al., 2010). Ideally, the child's behavior should be observed in several environmental settings (school, home, with friends) because the symptoms of hyperactivity and inattentiveness must be present across multiple settings in order to be diagnosed (APA, 2013). Because children with this disorder often give poor descriptions of their symptoms, it is important to obtain reports of the child's symptoms from his or her parents and teachers. And, finally, although diagnostic interviews, ratings scales, and psychological tests can be helpful in the assessment of ADHD (DuPaul & Kern, 2011), studies suggest that many children receive their diagnosis from pediatricians or family physicians rather than mental health professionals and that at most one-third of such diagnoses are based on psychological or educational testing (Millichap, 2010; Hoagwood et al., 2000).

What Are the Causes of ADHD?

Today's clinicians generally consider ADHD to have several interacting causes. Biological factors have been identified in many cases, particularly abnormal activity of the neurotransmitter *dopamine* and abnormalities in the *frontal-striatal* regions of the brain (Julien et al., 2011; Hale et al., 2010). The disorder has also been linked to high levels of stress and to family dysfunctioning (DuPaul & Kern, 2011; Rapport et al., 2008). In addition, sociocultural theorists have noted that ADHD symptoms and a diagnosis of ADHD may themselves create interpersonal problems and produce additional symptoms in the child. That is, children who are hyperactive tend to be viewed negatively by their peers and by their parents, and they often view themselves negatively as well (Chandler, 2010; Rapport et al., 2008).

How Is ADHD Treated?

Almost 80 percent of all children and adolescents with ADHD receive treatment (Winter & Bienvenu, 2011). There is, however, disagreement in the field about which kind of treatment is most effective. The most commonly applied approaches are drug therapy, behavioral therapy, or a combination of the two (Goldstein, 2011).

Drug Therapy Like Tom, millions of children and adults with ADHD are currently treated with **methylphenidate,** a stimulant drug that actually has been available for decades, or with certain other stimulants.

•**methylphenidate**•A stimulant drug, known better by the trade name *Ritalin*, commonly used to treat ADHD.

> *When Tom was born, he acted like a "crack baby," his mother, Ann, says. "He responded violently to even the slightest touch, and he never slept." Shortly after Tom turned two, the . . . day care center asked Ann to withdraw him. They deemed his behavior "just too aberrant," she remembers. Tom's doctors ran a battery of tests to screen for brain damage, but they found no physical explanation for his lack of self-control. In fact, his IQ was high—even though he performed poorly in school. Eventually, Tom was diagnosed with attention-deficit/hyperactivity disorder (ADHD). . . . The psychiatrist told Ann that in terms of severity, Tom was 15 on a scale of one to 10. As therapy, this doctor prescribed methylphenidate, a drug better known by its brand name, Ritalin.*
>
> *(Leutwyler, 1996, p. 13)*

Although a variety of manufacturers now produce methylphenidate, the drug continues to be known to the public by its most famous trade name, **Ritalin.** As researchers have confirmed Ritalin's quieting effect on children with ADHD and its ability to help them focus, solve complex tasks, perform better at school, and control aggression, use of the drug has increased enormously—according to some estimates, at least a threefold increase since 1990 alone (Mash & Wolfe, 2010; Scheffler et al., 2007). This increase in use also extends to preschoolers.

It is estimated that 2.2 million children in the United States, 3 percent of all school children, regularly take Ritalin or other stimulant drugs for ADHD (Mash & Wolfe, 2010). Collectively, the stimulant drugs are now the most common treatment for the disorder (Carlson et al., 2010). Many clinicians, however, worry about the possible long-term effects of the drugs, and others question whether the favorable findings of the drug studies (most of which have been done on white American children) are applicable to children from minority groups (Biederman et al., 2005, 2004).

Extensive investigations indicate that ADHD is overdiagnosed in the United States, so many children who are receiving stimulants may, in fact, have been inaccurately diagnosed (Rapport et al., 2008; DEA, 2000). In addition, a number of clinicians and parents have questioned the safety of stimulants. During the late 1980s, several lawsuits were filed against physicians, schools, and even the American Psychiatric Association, claiming misuse of Ritalin (Safer, 1994). Most of the suits were dismissed, yet the media blitz that surrounded them affected public perceptions. At the same time, Ritalin has become a popular recreational drug among teenagers; some snort it to get high, others use it to stay alert, and a number become dependent on it, further raising public concerns about the drug.

Why has there been a sizable increase in the diagnosis and treatment of ADHD over the past few decades?

On the positive side, stimulant drugs are apparently very helpful to children and adults who do suffer from ADHD (Carlson et al., 2010). As you will see, behavioral programs are also effective in many cases, but not in all. Moreover, the behavioral programs tend to be most effective when they are combined with stimulant drugs. When children with ADHD are taken off the drugs, many fare badly.

Most studies to date have indicated that stimulants are safe for the majority of people with ADHD (Rapport et al., 2008; Biederman et al., 2005). Their undesired effects are usually no worse than insomnia, stomachaches, headaches, or loss of appetite. However, some research and case reports suggest that, in a small number of cases, stimulants may increase the risk of having a heart attack (particularly in adults with high blood pressure) and produce psychotic symptoms or facial tics (Carey, 2006). They also apparently can affect the growth of some children, thus requiring "drug holidays" to prevent such an effect.

Jose Azel/Aurora

Behavioral intervention
Educational and treatment programs for children with ADHD use behavioral principles that clearly spell out target behaviors and program rewards and systematically reinforce appropriate behaviors by the children.

Behavior Therapy and Combination Therapies Behavioral therapy has been applied in many cases of ADHD. Here parents and teachers learn how to reward attentiveness or self-control in the children, often placing them on a token economy program (DuPaul et al., 2011). Such operant conditioning treatments have been helpful for a number of children, especially when combined with stimulant drug therapy (Dendy, 2011; Carlson et al., 2010; Barkley, 2006, 2004, 2002). Combining behavioral and drug therapies is also desirable because, according to research, children who receive both treatments require lower levels of medication, meaning, of course, that they are less subject to the medication's undesired effects (Hoza et al., 2008).

Multicultural Factors and ADHD

Throughout this book, you have seen that race often affects how persons are diagnosed and treated for various psychological disorders. Thus, you should not be totally surprised that race also seems to come into play with regard to ADHD.

A number of studies indicate that African American and Hispanic American children with significant attention and activity problems are less likely than white American children with similar symptoms to be assessed for ADHD, receive an ADHD diagnosis, or undergo treatment for this disorder (Bussing et al., 2005, 2003, 1998). Moreover, among those who do receive an ADHD diagnosis and treatment, children from racial minorities are less likely than white American children to be treated with stimulant drugs or a combination of stimulants and behavioral therapy—the interventions that seem to be of most help to those with ADHD (Pham et al., 2010; dos Reis et al., 2006; Stevens et al., 2005). And, finally, among children who do receive stimulant drug treatment for ADHD, children from racial minorities are less likely than white American children to receive the promising (but more expensive) *long-acting* stimulant drugs that have been developed in recent years (Cooper, 2004).

In part, these racial differences in diagnosis and treatment are tied to economic factors. Studies consistently reveal that poorer children are less likely than wealthier ones to be identified as having ADHD and are less likely to receive effective treatment, and racial minority families have, on average, lower incomes and weaker insurance coverage than white American families. Consistent with this point, one study found that privately insured African American children with ADHD do in fact receive higher, more effective doses of stimulant drugs than do Medicaid-insured African American children with ADHD (Lipkin et al., 2005).

Some clinical theorists further believe that social bias and stereotyping may contribute to the racial differences in diagnosis and treatment that have been observed. The theorists argue that our society often views the symptoms of ADHD as medical problems when exhibited by white American children but as indicators of poor parenting, lower IQ, substance use, or violence when displayed by African American and Hispanic American children (Duval-Harvey & Rogers, 2010; Kendall & Hatton, 2002). This notion has been supported by the finding that, all symptoms being equal, teachers are more likely to conclude that overactive white American children have ADHD but that overactive African American or Hispanic American children have other kinds of difficulties (Raymond, 1997; Samuel et al., 1997). Moreover, white American parents of ADHD children are more likely than African American and Hispanic American parents to believe that their children have ADHD or to seek ADHD evaluations and treatments for their children (Hillemeier et al., 2007; Stevens et al., 2005; Kendall & Hatton, 2002).

Whatever the reason—economic disadvantage, social bias, racial stereotyping, or other factors—it appears that children from racial minority groups are less likely to receive a proper ADHD diagnosis and treatment. While many of today's clinical theorists correctly alert us to the possibility that ADHD may be generally overdiagnosed and overtreated, it is important to also recognize that children from certain segments of society may, in fact, be underdiagnosed and undertreated.

Elimination Disorders

Children with elimination disorders repeatedly urinate or pass feces in their clothes, in bed, or on the floor. They already have reached an age at which they are expected to control these bodily functions, and their symptoms are not caused by physical illness.

Enuresis

Enuresis is repeated involuntary (or in some cases intentional) bed-wetting or wetting of one's clothes. It typically occurs at night during sleep but may also occur during the day. Children must be at least 5 years of age to receive this diagnosis. The problem may be triggered by stressful events, such as a hospitalization, entrance into school, or family problems. In some cases it is the result of physical or psychological abuse (see *PsychWatch* on page 537).

At the time of her initial assessment, Amber was in second grade. She was referred to the clinic by her father, Mr. Dillon, who was quite upset about his daughter's problems. During the telephone screening interview, he reported that Amber was wetting her bed more at night and often needed to urinate during school. She was also experiencing minor academic problems....

During [her] assessment session ... Amber said that she was getting into a lot of trouble at home and that her parents were mad at her. When asked why they were mad, Amber said she wasn't doing well in school and that she felt "nervous."... She said her grades had been getting worse over the course of the school year and that she was having trouble concentrating on her assigned work. She had apparently been a very good student the year before, especially in reading, but was now struggling with different subjects....

[Amber acknowledged that] she wet her bed at night about once or twice a week. In addition, she often had to use the bathroom at school, going about three or four times a

(continued on the next page)

•**enuresis**•A childhood disorder marked by repeated bed-wetting or wetting of one's clothes.

day. This was apparently a source of annoyance for her team teacher. . . . On one occasion, Amber said that she didn't make it to the bathroom in time and slightly wet her pants. Fortunately, this was not noticeable, but Amber was quite embarrassed about the incident. In fact, she now placed a wad of toilet tissue in her underwear to diminish the results of any possible mishaps in the future. . . .

[In a separate assessment interview, the psychologist asked Amber's parents] if any significant changes were going on at home. The question seemed to strike a nerve, as both parents paused and looked at each other nervously before answering. Finally, Mr. Dillon said that he and his wife had been having marital problems within the past year and that they were fighting more than usual. In fact, the possibility of divorce had been raised and both were now considering separation.

(Kearney, 1999, pp. 60–62)

The Bedwetter
Outrageous comedienne Sarah Silverman holds up a copy of her best-selling 2010 book *The Bedwetter*. In this memoir, she writes extensively about her childhood experiences with enuresis and other emotional difficulties—always with a blend of self-revelation, pain, and humor.

•**encopresis**•A childhood disorder characterized by repeated defecating in inappropriate places, such as one's clothing.

The prevalence of enuresis decreases with age. Between 13 and 33 percent of 5-year-old children have some bedwetting experiences and as many as 10 percent meet the criteria for enuresis; in contrast, 3 percent of 10-year-olds and 1 percent of 15-year-olds suffer from the disorder (Mash & Wolfe, 2010; Mellon & Houts, 2006). Those with enuresis typically have a close relative (parent, sibling) who has had or will have the same disorder.

Research has not favored one explanation for enuresis over the others (Christophersen & Friman, 2010; Friman, 2008; Fletcher, 2000). Psychodynamic theorists explain it as a symptom of broader anxiety and underlying conflicts. Family theorists point to disturbed family interactions. Behaviorists view the problem as the result of improper, unrealistic, or coercive toilet training. And biological theorists suspect that children with this disorder often have a small bladder capacity or weak bladder muscles.

Most cases of enuresis correct themselves even without treatment. However, therapy, particularly behavioral therapy, can speed up the process (Christophersen & Friman, 2010; Houts, 2010). In a widely used classical conditioning approach, the *bell-and-battery technique,* a bell and a battery are wired to a pad consisting of two metallic foil sheets, and the entire apparatus is placed under the child at bedtime (Houts, 2010; Mowrer & Mowrer, 1938). A single drop of urine sets off the bell, awakening the child as soon as he or she starts to wet. Thus the bell (unconditioned stimulus) paired with the sensation of a full bladder (conditioned stimulus) produces the response of waking. Eventually, a full bladder alone awakens the child.

Another effective behavioral treatment method is *dry-bed training,* in which children receive training in cleanliness and retention control, are awakened periodically during the night, practice going to the bathroom, and are appropriately rewarded (Christophersen & Friman, 2010; Friman, 2008). Like the bell-and-battery technique, this behavioral approach is often effective, according to research.

Encopresis

Encopresis, repeatedly defecating into one's clothing, is less common than enuresis, and it is also less well researched. This problem seldom occurs at night during sleep. It is usually involuntary, starts after the age of 4, and affects about 1.5 to 3 percent of all children (see Table 17-5 on page 538). The disorder is much more common in boys than in girls (Mash & Wolfe, 2010).

Encopresis causes intense social problems, shame, and embarrassment (Christophersen & Friman, 2010; Cox et al., 2002). Children who suffer from it usually try to hide their condition and to avoid situations, such as camp or school, in which they might embarrass themselves. Cases may stem from stress, biological factors such as constipation,

Child Abuse

What I remember most about my mother was that she was always beating me. She'd beat me with her high-heeled shoes, with my father's belt, with a potato masher. When I was eight, she black and blued my legs so badly, I told her I'd go to the police. She said, "Go, they'll just put you into the darkest prison." So I stayed. When my breasts started growing at 13, she beat me across the chest until I fainted. Then she'd hug me and ask forgiveness. . . . Most kids have nightmares about being taken away from their parents. I would sit on our front porch crooning softly of going far, far away to find another mother.

(*TIME,* SEPTEMBER 5, 1983, P. 20)

"Memories so strong that I can smell and taste them now" That is how actor and filmmaker Tyler Perry (left) describes his recollections of the physical and sexual abuse he suffered as a child. Similarly, mega-celebrity and producer Oprah Winfrey (right) has revealed her childhood experiences of sexual abuse to her many fans. The two have collaborated to bring attention to child abuse.

A problem that affects all too many children and has an enormous impact on their psychological development is *child abuse,* the nonaccidental use of excessive physical or psychological force by an adult on a child, often with the intention of hurting or destroying the child. At least 5 percent of children in the United States are physically abused each year (Mash & Wolfe, 2010). Surveys suggest that 1 of every 10 children is the victim of severe violence, such as being kicked, bitten, hit, beaten, or threatened with a knife or a gun. In fact, some observers believe that physical abuse and neglect are the leading causes of death among young children.

Overall, girls and boys are physically abused at approximately the same rate (Humphrey, 2006). Although such abuse occurs in all socioeconomic groups, it is apparently more common among the poor (Mammen et al., 2002).

Abusers are usually the child's parents (Faust et al., 2008; Humphrey, 2006). Clinical investigators have learned that abusive parents often have poor impulse control, low self-esteem, and weak parenting skills (Tolan et al., 2006; Mammen et al., 2002). Many have been abused themselves as children and have had poor role models (McCaghy et al., 2006). In some cases, they are experiencing the stress of marital discord or family unemployment (Faust et al., 2008).

Studies suggest that the victims of child abuse may suffer both immediate and long-term psychological effects. Research has revealed, for example, that they may experience psychological symptoms such as anxiety, depression, or bed-wetting, and tend to display more performance and behavior problems in school. Long-term negative effects include lack of social acceptance, a higher number of medical and psychological disorders during adulthood, more abuse of alcohol and other substances, more arrests during adolescence and adulthood, a greater risk of becoming criminally violent, a higher unemployment rate, and a higher suicide rate (Faust et al., 2008; Harkness & Lumley, 2008; Safren et al., 2002; Widom, 2001). Finally, as many as one-third of abuse victims grow up to be abusive, neglectful, or inadequate parents themselves (Heyman & Slep, 2002).

Two forms of child abuse have received special attention: psychological and sexual abuse. *Psychological abuse* may include severe rejection, excessive discipline, scapegoating and ridicule, isolation, and refusal to provide help for a child with psychological problems. It probably accompanies all forms of physical abuse and neglect and often occurs by itself. *Child sexual abuse,* the use of a child for gratification of adult sexual desires, may occur outside of or within the home (Faust et al., 2008; McCaghy et al., 2006). Surveys suggest that at least 13 percent of women were forced into sexual contact with an adult male during their childhood, many of them with their father or stepfather (Mash & Wolfe, 2010). At least 4 percent of men were also sexually abused during childhood. Child sexual abuse appears to be equally common across all socioeconomic classes, races, and ethnic groups (McCaghy et al., 2006).

A variety of therapies have been used in cases of child abuse, including groups sponsored by *Parents Anonymous,* which help parents to develop insight into their behavior, provide training on alternatives to abuse, and teach coping and parenting skills (Tolan et al., 2006; Wolfe et al., 1988). In addition, prevention programs, often in the form of home visitations and parent training, have proved promising (Wekerle et al., 2007).

Research suggests that the psychological needs of the child victims should be addressed as early as possible (Gray et al., 2000; Roesler & McKenzie, 1994). Clinicians and educators have launched valuable *early detection programs* that (1) educate all children about child abuse, (2) teach them skills for avoiding or escaping from abusive situations, (3) encourage children to tell another adult if they are abused, and (4) assure them that abuse is never their own fault (Goodman-Brown et al., 2003; Godenzi & DePuy, 2001; Finkelhor et al., 1995).

table: 17-5

Comparison of Childhood Disorders

Disorder	Usual Age of Identification	Prevalence Among All Children	Gender with Greater Prevalence	Elevated Family History	Recovery by Adulthood
Separation anxiety disorder	Before 12 years	4–10%	Females	Yes	Usually
Conduct disorder	7–15 years	1–10%	Males	Yes	Often
ADHD	Before 12 years	4–9%	Males	Yes	Often
Enuresis	5–8 years	5%	Males	Yes	Usually
Encopresis	After 4 years	1.5–3%	Males	Unclear	Usually
Specific learning disorders	6–9 years	5%	Males	Yes	Often
Autism spectrum disorder	0–3 years	0.2–1.1%	Males	Yes	Sometimes
Intellectual developmental disorder	Before 10 years	1–3%	Males	Unclear	Sometimes

improper toilet training, or a combination of these factors. In fact, most children with encopresis have a history of repeated constipation, a history that may contribute to improper intestinal functioning. Because physical problems are so often linked to this disorder, a medical examination is typically conducted first.

The most common and successful treatments for encopresis are behavioral and medical approaches or a combination of the two (Christophersen & Friman, 2010; Friman, 2008). Among other features of treatment, practitioners may use biofeedback training (see pages 125–126 and 183) to help the children better detect when their bowels are full, try to eliminate the children's constipation, and stimulate regular bowel functioning with high-fiber diets, mineral oil, laxatives, and lubricants. Family therapy has also proved helpful.

"I wish I'd started therapy at your age."

Long-Term Disorders That Begin in Childhood

As you read at the beginning of this chapter, many childhood disorders change or subside as the person ages. Two kinds of disorders that emerge during childhood, however, are likely to continue unchanged throughout life: *autism spectrum disorder* and *intellectual developmental disorder*. Researchers have investigated both of these disorders extensively. In addition, although it was not always so, clinicians have developed a range of treatment approaches that can make a major difference in the lives of people with these problems.

Autism Spectrum Disorder

Autism spectrum disorder, a pattern first identified by psychiatrist Leo Kanner in 1943, is marked by extreme unresponsiveness to other people, severe communication deficits, and highly rigid and repetitive behaviors, interests, and activities (APA, 2013, 2012) (see Table 17-6). These symptoms appear early in life, typically before 3 years of age. Just a decade ago, the disorder seemed to affect around 1 out of every 2,000 children. However, in recent years there has been a steady increase in the number of children diagnosed with autism spectrum disorder, and it now appears that at least 1 in 600 and perhaps as many as 1 in 88 children display this pattern (CDC, 2012; Mash & Wolfe, 2010). Mark is one such child:

> In retrospect [Susan, Mark's mother] can recall some things that appeared odd to her. For example, she remembers that . . . Mark never seemed to anticipate being picked up when she approached. In addition, despite Mark's attachment to a pacifier (he would complain if it were mislaid), he showed little interest in toys. In fact, Mark seemed to lack interest in anything. He rarely pointed to things and seemed oblivious to sounds. . . . Mark spent much of his time repetitively tapping on tables, seeming to be lost in his own world.
>
> After his second birthday, Mark's behavior began to trouble his parents. . . . Mark, they said, would "look through" people or past them, but rarely at them. He could say a few words but didn't seem to understand speech. In fact, he did not even respond to his own name. Mark's time was occupied examining familiar objects, which he would hold in front of his eyes while he twisted and turned them. Particularly troublesome were Mark's odd movements—he would jump, flap his arms, twist his hands and fingers, and perform all sorts of facial grimaces, particularly when he was excited—and what Robert [Mark's father] described as Mark's rigidity. Mark would line things up in rows and scream if they were disturbed. He insisted on keeping objects in their place and would become upset whenever Susan attempted to rearrange the living room furniture. . . .
>
> Slowly, beginning at age five, Mark began to improve. . . . The pronoun in the sentence was inappropriate and the sentence took the form of a question he had been asked previously, but the meaning was clear.
>
> *(Wing, 1976)*

Around 80 percent of all cases of autism spectrum disorder occur in boys. As many as 90 percent of children with the disorder remain significantly disabled into adulthood. They have enormous difficulty maintaining employment, performing household tasks, and leading independent lives (Hollander et al., 2011). Even the highest-functioning adults with autism typically have problems displaying closeness and empathy and have restricted interests and activities.

The individual's *lack of responsiveness and social reciprocity*—extreme aloofness, lack of interest in other people, low empathy, and inability to share attention with others—has long been considered a central feature of autism (Boyd et al., 2011; Constantino, 2011) (see *PsychWatch* on next page). Like Mark, children with this disorder typically do not

•**autism spectrum disorder**•A developmental disorder marked by extreme unresponsiveness to others, severe communication deficits, and highly repetitive and rigid behaviors, interests, and activities.

table: **17-6**

DSM-5 Checklist

Autism Spectrum Disorder

1. Persistent deficits in social communication and social interaction, featuring all of the following:
   • Deficits in social-emotional reciprocity • Deficits in nonverbal communicative behaviors used for social interactions • Deficits in developing and maintaining relationships.

2. Restricted and repetitive patterns of behaviors, interests, or activities, featuring two of the following:
   • Stereotyped or repetitive speech, motor movements, or use of objects • Excessive adherence to routines, ritualized patterns of behavior, or excessive resistance to change • Highly restricted, fixated, and abnormal interests • Hyper-reactive or hypo-reactive responses to sensory input or unusual interest in sensory aspects of environment.

3. Onset by early childhood.

4. Significant impairment.

Based on APA, 2013, 2012.

DSM-5 CONTROVERSY

Loss of Services?

In past editions of the DSM, people qualified for a diagnosis of *Asperger's disorder* if they displayed the severe social deficits and restricted and repetitive behaviors found in *autistic disorder* but otherwise had normal language, adaptive, and cognitive skills. With the elimination of Asperger's disorder from DSM-5, critics worry that some such individuals will fail to receive a diagnosis of *autism spectrum disorder,* the new category that subsumes Asperger's disorder. In turn, these individuals might not qualify for the special educational services previously made available for children with Asperger's disorder. ‹‹

reach for their parents during infancy. Instead they may arch their backs when they are held and appear not to recognize or care about those around them. In a similar vein, unlike other individuals of the same age, autistic children typically fail to include others in their play or to represent social experiences when they are playing; they often fail to see themselves as others see them and have no desire to imitate or be like others (Bodfish, 2011; Boyd et al., 2011).

Communication problems take various forms in autism spectrum disorder. The individuals' nonverbal behaviors are often at odds with their efforts at verbal communication. They may, for example, fail to use a proper tone when talking. It is also common for autistic persons to show few or no facial expressions or body gestures. In addition, a number are unable to maintain proper eye contact during interactions. Recall, for example, how Mark "looked through" people rather than at them.

Many autistic individuals have great difficulty understanding speech or using language for conversational purposes. In fact, approximately half fail to speak or develop language skills (Paul & Gilbert, 2011; Gillis & Romanczyk, 2007). Those who do talk may show rigidity and repetition in their speech. One of the most common speech peculiarities is *echolalia,* the exact echoing of phrases spoken by others. The individuals repeat the words with the same accent or inflection, but with no sign of understanding or intent of communicating. Some even repeat a sentence days after they have heard it (*delayed echolalia*). Another speech oddity is *pronominal reversal,* or confusion of pronouns—for example, the use of "you" instead of "I." When Mark was hungry, he would say, "Do you want dinner?"

Autistic individuals also display a wide range of *highly rigid and repetitive behaviors, interests, and activities* that extend beyond speech patterns. Typically they become very

PsychWatch

What Happened to Asperger's Disorder?

Around the time that Leo Kanner first identified autism in the early 1940s, a Viennese physician named Hans Asperger observed a similar syndrome that came to be known—for more than half a century—as *Asperger's disorder,* or *Asperger's syndrome.* Children with this disorder seemed to display certain autistic-like symptoms—social deficits, expressiveness difficulties, idiosyncratic interests, and restricted and repetitive behaviors—but at the same time they had normal (or near normal) intellectual, adaptive, and language skills (Miller & Ozonoff, 2011; Siegel & Ficcaglia, 2006). Individuals with Asperger's disorder wanted to fit in and interact with others, but their impaired social functioning made it hard for them to do so.

For decades, clinicians believed that Asperger's disorder was closely related to autism. The disorder was included in past editions of the DSM and was widely diagnosed. But then, with the publication of DSM-5 in 2013, the category disappeared from sight. Where did it go? Well,

Joshua Gunter/The Plain Dealer/AP Photo

Disappearing Diagnosis
Despite their impairments, a number of the individuals who received the past diagnosis of Asperger's disorder reached impressive heights. A butterfly perches on the nose of one such person, a 14-year-old boy who won a national award for activities such as playing the piano at nursing homes and raising chickens, peacocks, strawberries, and more on his family's farm in Ohio.

the DSM-5 task force decided that it was, in fact, not a distinct disorder. It concluded that many of the cases previously diagnosed as Asperger's disorder were really cases of high-functioning autism, while other cases were patterns that did not really involve autistic-like functioning. According to DSM-5, the former individuals

should now receive a diagnosis of *autism spectrum disorder,* whereas the latter individuals should be assigned to other categories, such as a new one called *social communication disorder*—a nonautistic disorder characterized by persistent difficulties in communication, social relationships, and social responsiveness.

upset at minor changes in objects, persons, or routines and resist any efforts to change their own repetitive behaviors. Mark, for example, lined things up and screamed if they were disturbed. Similarly, children with the disorder may react with tantrums if a parent wears an unfamiliar pair of glasses, a chair is moved to a different part of the room, or a word in a song is changed. Kanner (1943) labeled such reactions a *perseveration of sameness.* Many sufferers also become strongly attached to particular objects—plastic lids, rubber bands, buttons, water. They may collect these objects, carry them, or play with them constantly. Some are fascinated by movement and may watch spinning objects, such as fans, for hours.

Similarly, the *motor movements* of people with this disorder may be unusual, rigid, and repetitive. Mark would jump, flap his arms, twist his hands and fingers, rock, walk on his toes, spin, and make faces. These acts are called *self-stimulatory behaviors.* Some autistic individuals also perform *self-injurious behaviors,* such as repeatedly lunging into or banging their head against a wall, pulling their hair, or biting themselves (Aman & Farmer, 2011; Farmer & Aman, 2011).

Blocking out the world
An 8-year-old child with autism spectrum disorder peers vacantly through a hole in the netting of a baseball batting cage, seemingly unaware of other chldren and activities at the playground.

The symptoms of autism spectrum disorder suggest a very disturbed and contradictory pattern of reactions to stimuli (see *PsychWatch* on page 543). Sometimes the individuals seem overstimulated by sights and sounds and appear to be trying to block them out (called *hyper-reactivity*), while at other times they seem understimulated and appear to be performing self-stimulatory actions (called *hypo-reactivity*). They may, for example, fail to react to loud noises yet turn around when they hear soda being poured. Similarly, they may fail to recognize that they have reached the edge of a dangerous high place yet immediately spot a small object that is out of position in their room.

What Are the Causes of Autism Spectrum Disorder?

A variety of explanations have been offered for autism spectrum disorder. This is one disorder for which sociocultural explanations have probably been overemphasized. In fact, such explanations initially led investigators in the wrong direction. More recent work in the psychological and biological spheres has persuaded clinical theorists that cognitive limitations and brain abnormalities are the primary causes of this disorder.

SOCIOCULTURAL CAUSES At first, theorists thought that family dysfunction and social stress were the primary causes of autism spectrum disorder. When he first identified this disorder, for example, Kanner argued that particular personality characteristics of the parents created an unfavorable climate for development and contributed to the disorder (Kanner, 1954, 1943). He saw these parents as very intelligent yet cold—"refrigerator parents." These claims had enormous influence on the public and on the self-image of the parents themselves, but research has totally failed to support a picture of rigid, cold, rejecting, or disturbed parents (Vierck & Silverman, 2011; Jones & Jordan, 2008).

Similarly, some clinical theorists have proposed that a high degree of social and environmental stress is a factor in the disorder. Once again, however, research has not supported this notion. Investigators who have compared autistic children to nonautistic children have found no differences in the rate of parental death, divorce, separation, financial problems, or environmental stimulation (Landrigan, 2011; Cox et al., 1975).

PSYCHOLOGICAL CAUSES According to certain theorists, people with autism spectrum disorder have a central perceptual or cognitive disturbance that makes normal communication and interactions impossible. One influential explanation holds that individuals with the disorder fail to develop a **theory of mind**—an awareness that other people base their behaviors on their own beliefs, intentions, and other mental states, not on information that they have no way of knowing (Pisula, 2010; Frith, 2000).

•**theory of mind**•Awareness that other people base their behaviors on their own beliefs, intentions, and other mental states, not on information they have no way of knowing.

•**cerebellum**•An area of the brain that coordinates movement in the body and perhaps helps control a person's ability to shift attention rapidly.

By 3 to 5 years of age, most normal children can take the perspective of another person into account and use it to anticipate what the person will do. In a way, they learn to read others' minds. Let us say, for example, that we watch Jessica place a marble in a container and then we observe Frank move the marble to a nearby room while Jessica is taking a nap. We know that later Jessica will search first in the container for the marble because she is not aware that Frank moved it. We know that because we take Jessica's perspective into account. A normal child would also anticipate Jessica's search correctly. An autistic child would not. He or she would expect Jessica to look in the nearby room because that is where the marble actually is. Jessica's own mental processes would be unimportant to the person.

Studies show that people with autism spectrum disorder do indeed have this kind of "mind-blindness," although they are not the only kinds of individuals with this limitation (Pisula, 2010; Jones & Jordan, 2008). They thus have great difficulty taking part in make-believe play, using language in ways that include the perspectives of others, developing relationships, or participating in human interactions. Why do autistic persons have this and other cognitive limitations? Some theorists believe that they suffered early biological problems that prevented proper cognitive development.

BIOLOGICAL CAUSES For years researchers have tried to determine what biological abnormalities might cause theory-of-mind deficits and the other features of autism spectrum disorder. They have not yet developed a complete biological explanation, but they have uncovered some promising leads. First, examinations of the relatives of autistic people keep suggesting a *genetic factor* in this disorder (Sakurai et al., 2011). The prevalence of autism among their siblings, for example, is as high as 8 per 100 (Teicher et al., 2008; Gillis & Romanczyk, 2007), a rate much higher than the general population's. Moreover, the prevalence of autism among the identical twins of autistic people is 60 percent.

Some studies have also linked autism spectrum disorder to *prenatal difficulties* or *birth complications* (Reichenberg et al., 2011). For example, the chances of developing the disorder are higher when the mother had rubella (German measles) during pregnancy, was exposed to toxic chemicals before or during pregnancy, or had complications during labor or delivery.

Finally, researchers have identified specific *biological abnormalities* that may contribute to autism spectrum disorder. One line of research has pointed to the **cerebellum,** for example (Allen, 2011; Teicher et al., 2008; Pierce & Courchesne, 2002, 2001). Brain scans and autopsies reveal abnormal development in this brain area occurring early in the life of autistic people. Scientists have long known that the cerebellum coordinates movement in the body, but they now suspect that it also helps control a person's ability to shift attention rapidly. It may be that people whose cerebellum develops abnormally will have great difficulty adjusting their level of attention, following verbal and facial cues, and making sense of social information—all key features of autism.

In a similar vein, neuroimaging studies indicate that many autistic children have increased brain volume and white matter and structural abnormalities in the brain's limbic system, brain stem nuclei, and amygdala (Bachevalier, 2011; Bauman, 2011). Many individuals with the disorder also experience reduced activity in the brain's temporal and frontal lobes when they perform language and motor tasks (Escalante et al., 2003).

Given such findings, many researchers believe that autism spectrum disorder may in fact have multiple biological causes (Hollander et al., 2011). Perhaps each of the relevant biological factors (genetic, prenatal, birth, and postnatal) can eventually lead to a common problem in the brain—a "final common pathway," such as neurotransmitter abnormalities, that produces the cognitive problems and other features of the disorder.

Autistic acts

When upset, some children with autism spectrum disorder, particularly those who cannot express themselves verbally, display physical outbursts. This 6-year-old child throws a tantrum and exhibits self-stimulatory hand shaking while under the care of a doctor at Bretonneau Hospital in Tours, France.

Bernard Bisson/Corbis Sygma

A Special Kind of Talent

Most people are familiar with the savant syndrome, thanks to Dustin Hoffman's portrayal of a man with autism in the movie *Rain Man*. The savant skills that Hoffman portrayed—counting 246 toothpicks in the instant after they fall to the floor, memorizing the phone book through the Gs, and doing numerical calculations at lightning speed—were based on the astounding talents of certain real-life people who are otherwise limited by autism spectrum disorder or intellectual developmental disorder (formerly known as mental retardation).

A *savant* (French for "learned" or "clever") is a person with a major mental disorder or intellectual handicap who has some spectacular ability. Often these abilities are remarkable only in light of the handicap, but sometimes they are remarkable by any standard (Yewchuk, 1999).

A common savant skill is calendar calculating, the ability to calculate what day of the week a date will fall on, such as New Year's Day in 2050 (Kennedy & Squire, 2007; Heavey et al., 1999). A common musical skill such individuals may possess is the ability to play a piece of classical music flawlessly from memory after hearing it only once. Other individuals can paint exact replicas of scenes they saw years ago (Hou et al., 2000).

Some theorists believe that savant skills do indeed represent special forms of cognitive functioning; others propose that the skills are merely a positive side to certain cognitive deficits (Scheuffgen et al., 2000; Miller, 1999). Special memorization skills, for example, may be facilitated by the very narrow and intense focus often found in cases of autism spectrum disorder.

Special insights One of the world's highest achieving autistic individuals is Dr. Temple Grandin, a professor at Colorado State University. Applying her personal perspective and unique visualization skills, she has developed insight into the minds and sensitivities of cattle and has designed more humane animal-handling equipment and facilities. Indeed, she argues that autistic savants and animals share cognitive similarities.

Finally, because it has received so much attention over the past 15 years, it is worth examining a biological explanation for autism spectrum disorder that has *not* been borne out—the *MMR vaccine* theory. In 1998 a team of investigators published a study suggesting that a *postnatal event*—the vaccine for measles, mumps, and rubella (*MMR vaccine*)—might produce autistic symptoms in some children (Wakefield et al., 1998). Specifically, the researchers held that for certain children, this vaccine, which is usually given between the ages of 12 and 15 months, produces an increase in the measles virus throughout the body which in turn causes the onset of a powerful stomach disease and, ultimately, autism spectrum disorder.

However, virtually all research conducted since 1998 has argued against this theory (Ahearn, 2010; Uchiyama et al., 2007; Chen et al., 2004). First, epidemiological studies repeatedly have found that children throughout the world who receive the MMR vaccine have the same prevalence of autism as

Why do many people still believe that the MMR vaccine causes autism spectrum disorder, despite so much evidence to the contrary?

those who do not receive the vaccine. Second, according to research, children with autism do not have more measles viruses in their bodies than children without autism. Third, autistic children do not have the special stomach disease proposed by this theory. Finally, careful reexaminations of the original study have indicated that it was methodologically flawed and, perhaps, manipulated and that it, in fact, failed to demonstrate any relationship between the MMR vaccine and the development of autism spectrum disorder (*Lancet,* 2010). Unfortunately, despite this clear refutation, many concerned parents now choose to withhold the MMR vaccine from their young children, leaving them highly vulnerable to diseases that can be very dangerous.

How Do Clinicians and Educators Treat Autism Spectrum Disorder?

Treatment can help people with autism spectrum disorder adapt better to their environment, although no treatment yet known totally reverses the autistic pattern. Treatments of particular help are *cognitive-behavioral therapy, communication training, parent training,* and *community integration.* In addition, psychotropic drugs and certain vitamins have sometimes helped when combined with other approaches (Ristow et al., 2011; Hellings et al., 2010; Shaw & Dawkins, 2010).

COGNITIVE-BEHAVIORAL THERAPY Behavioral approaches have been used in cases of autism for more than 35 years to teach new, appropriate behaviors, including speech, social skills, classroom skills, and self-help skills, while reducing negative, dysfunctional ones. Most often, the therapists use modeling and operant conditioning. In modeling, they demonstrate a desired behavior and guide autistic individuals to imitate it. In operant conditioning, they reinforce desired behaviors, first by shaping them—breaking them down so they can be learned step by step—and then rewarding each step clearly and consistently. With careful planning and execution, these procedures often produce new, more functional behaviors.

A pioneering, long-term study compared the progress of two groups of children with autism spectrum disorder (Lovaas, 2003, 1987; McEachin et al., 1993). Nineteen received intensive behavioral treatments, and 19 served as a control group. The treatment began when the children were 3 years old and continued until they were 7. By the age of 7, the behavioral group was doing better in school and scoring higher on intelligence tests than the control group. Many were able to go to school in regular classrooms. The gains continued into the research participants' teenage years. Given the favorable findings of this and similar studies, many clinicians now consider early behavioral programs to be the preferred treatment for autism spectrum disorder (Peters-Scheffer et al., 2011; Soorya et al., 2011).

One behavioral program that has achieved considerable success is the *Learning Experiences . . . An Alternative Program (LEAP)* for preschoolers with autism (Kohler et al., 2005). In this program, 4 autistic children are integrated with 10 normal children in a classroom. The normal children learn how to use modeling and operant conditioning in order to help teach social, communication, play, and other skills to the autistic children. The program has been found to improve significantly the cognitive functioning of autistic children, as well as their social and peer interactions, play behaviors, and other behaviors. Moreover, the normal children in the classroom experience no negative effects as a result of serving as intervention agents.

As such programs suggest, therapies for people with autism spectrum disorder, particularly behavioral ones, tend to provide the most benefit when they are started early in the children's lives (Carter et al., 2011; Magiati et al., 2011). Very young autistic children often begin with services at home, but ideally, by the age of 3 they attend special programs outside the home. A federal law lists autism spectrum

Early intervention

This child with autism spectrum disorder waves as he follows the instructions on a motion exercise DVD. Formally diagnosed at 18 months, he was able to begin intensive behavioral therapy before the age of 2. Early assessment and treatment appear to improve the prognosis of individuals with this disorder.

AP Photo/Rich Pedroncelli

disorder as 1 of 10 disorders for which school districts must provide a free education from birth to age 22, in the least restrictive or most appropriate setting possible. Typically, services are provided by education, health, or social service agencies until the children reach 3 years of age; then the department of education for each state determines what services will be offered.

Given the recent increases in the prevalence of autism spectrum disorder, many school districts are now trying to provide education and training for autistic children in special classes that operate at the district's own facilities (Wilczynski et al., 2011). However, most school districts remain ill-equipped to meet the profound needs of students with this disorder. The most fortunate autistic students are sent by their school districts to attend special schools, where education and therapy are combined. At such schools, specially trained teachers help the children improve their skills, behaviors, and interactions with the world. Higher-functioning autistic students may eventually spend at least part of their school day returning to normal classrooms in their own school district (Hartford & Marcus, 2011; Smith et al., 2002).

COMMUNICATION TRAINING Even when given intensive behavioral treatment, half of the people with autism spectrum disorder remain speechless. As a result, they are often taught other forms of communication, including *sign language* and *simultaneous communication,* a method combining sign language and speech. They may also learn to use **augmentative communication systems,** such as "communication boards" or computers that use pictures, symbols, or written words to represent objects or needs (Prelock et al., 2011; Ramdoss et al., 2011). A child may point to a picture of a fork to give the message "I am hungry," for example, or point to a radio for "I want music."

Some programs now use *child-initiated interactions* to help improve the communication skills of autistic children (Koegel et al., 2010, 2005). In such programs, teachers try to identify *intrinsic* reinforcers rather than trivial ones like food or candy. The children are first encouraged to choose items that they are interested in, and they then learn to initiate questions ("What's that?" "Where is it?" "Whose is it?") in order to obtain the items. Studies find that child-directed interventions of this kind often increase self-initiated communications, language development, and social participation (Koegel et al., 2010, 2005).

PARENT TRAINING Today's treatment programs for autism spectrum disorder involve parents in a variety of ways. Behavioral programs, for example, often train parents so that they can apply behavioral techniques at home (Hollander et al., 2011; Schreibman & Koegel, 2005). Instruction manuals for parents and home visits by teachers and other professionals are typically included in such programs. Research consistently has demonstrated that the behavioral gains produced by trained parents are often equal to or greater than those generated by teachers.

In addition to parent-training programs, individual therapy and support groups are becoming more available to help the parents of autistic children deal with their own emotions and needs (Hastings, 2008). A number of parent associations and lobbies also offer emotional support and practical help.

COMMUNITY INTEGRATION Many of today's school-based and home-based programs for autism spectrum disorder teach self-help, self-management, and living, social, and work skills as early as possible to help the individuals function better in their communities. In addition, greater numbers of carefully run *group homes* and *sheltered workshops* are now available for teenagers and young adults with this disorder. These and related programs help the individuals become a part of their community; they also reduce the concerns of aging parents whose children will always need supervision.

Learning to communicate

Behaviorists have had success teaching many children with autism spectrum disorder to communicate. Here a speech language specialist combines behavioral techniques with the use of a communication board to teach a 3-year-old autistic child how to express herself better and understand others.

•**augmentative communication system**•A method for enhancing the communication skills of individuals with autism spectrum disorder, intellectual developmental disorder, or cerebral palsy by teaching them to point to pictures, symbols, letters, or words on a communication board or computer.

table: 17-7

DSM-5 Checklist

Intellectual Developmental Disorder (Intellectual Disability)

1. Deficits in general mental abilities such as reasoning, problem-solving, planning, abstract thinking, judgment, academic learning, and learning from experience.

2. Impairment in adaptive functioning in at least one aspect of daily life activities, such as communication, social participation, functioning at school or work, or personal independence at home or in the community. The limitations necessitate ongoing support at school, work, or independent life.

3. Onset during the developmental period (before the age of 18).

Based on APA, 2013, 2012.

Intellectual Developmental Disorder (Intellectual Disability)

Ed Murphy, aged 26, can tell us what it's like to be considered "mentally retarded":

What is retardation? It's hard to say. I guess it's having problems thinking. Some people think that you can tell if a person is retarded by looking at them. If you think that way you don't give people the benefit of the doubt. You judge a person by how they look or how they talk or what the tests show, but you can never really tell what is inside the person.

(Bogdan & Taylor, 1976, p. 51)

For much of his life Ed was labeled mentally retarded and was educated and cared for in special institutions. During his adult years, clinicians discovered that Ed's intellectual ability was in fact higher than had been assumed. In the meantime, however, he had lived the childhood and adolescence of a person labeled mentally retarded, and his statement reveals the kinds of difficulties often faced by people with this disorder.

In DSM-5, the term "mental retardation" has been replaced by *intellectual developmental disorder*. Actually, the manual lists two terms—intellectual development disorder and *intellectual disability*. In this section, we will use the former term, because it is expected to be the diagnostic label used internationally in the coming years. This term is applied to a varied population, including children in institutional wards who rock back and forth, young people who work in special job programs, and men and women who raise and support their families by working at undemanding jobs. As many as 3 of every 100 persons meet the criteria for this diagnosis (Harris, 2010). Around three-fifths of them are male, and the vast majority display a *mild* level of the disorder.

People receive a diagnosis of **intellectual developmental disorder (IDD)** when they display general *intellectual functioning* that is well below average, in combination with poor *adaptive behavior* (APA, 2013, 2012). That is, in addition to having a low IQ (a score of 70 or below), a person with IDD has great difficulty in areas such as communication, home living, self-direction, work, or safety (APA, 2013). The symptoms also must appear before the age of 18 (see Table 17-7).

Don Ryan/AP Photo

Getting a head start
Studies suggest that IQ scores and school performances of children from poor neighborhoods can be improved by enriching their daily environments at a young age. The teachers in this classroom try to stimulate further and enrich the lives of preschool children in a Head Start program in Oregon.

PsychWatch

Reading and 'Riting and 'Rithmetic

Between 15 and 20 percent of children, boys more often than girls, develop slowly and function poorly compared to their peers in a single area such as learning, communication, or coordination (Goldstein et al., 2011; Swanson, 2011). The children do not suffer from intellectual developmental disorder, and in fact they are often very bright, yet their problems may interfere with school performance, daily living, and in some cases social interactions. Similar difficulties may be seen in the children's close biological relatives (Watson et al., 2008). According to DSM-5, many of these children are suffering from a specific learning disorder, communication disorder, or developmental coordination disorder (APA, 2013, 2012).

Children with *specific learning disorder* have significant difficulties in the acquisition of reading, writing, arithmetic, or mathematical reasoning skills. Across the United States, children with such problems comprise the largest subgroup of individuals placed in special education classes (Watson et al., 2008). Some of these children read slowly or inaccurately or have difficulty understanding the meaning of what they are reading, difficulties also known as *dyslexia* (Peterson & Pennington, 2010). Others spell or write very poorly (Berninger, 2010). And still others have great trouble remembering number facts, performing calculations, or reasoning mathematically.

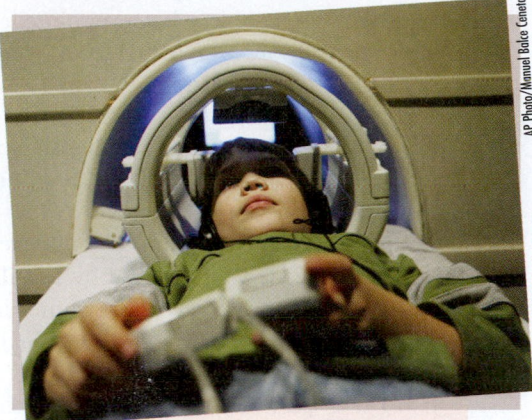

Dyslexia and the brain This child with dyslexia undergoes an MRI to help researchers determine which areas of the brain function abnormally when individuals with this problem are reading.

The *communication disorders* include language disorder and speech sound disorder (Gillam & Petersen, 2011). Children with *language disorder* have persistent difficulties acquiring, using, or comprehending spoken or written language. They may, for example, have trouble using language to express themselves, struggle at learning new words, confine their speech to short simple sentences, or show a general lag in language development. Children with *speech sound disorder* have persistent difficulties in speech production or speech fluency. Some, for example, fail to make correct speech sounds at an appropriate age, resulting in speech that sounds like baby talk. Others suffer from stuttering; they display a disturbance in the fluency and timing of their speech, characterized by repeating, prolonging, or interjecting sounds, pausing before finishing a word, or experiencing excessive tension in the muscles they use for speech.

Finally, children with *developmental coordination disorder* perform coordinated motor activities at a level well below that of others their age (APA, 2013, 2012). Younger children with this disorder are clumsy and slow to master skills such as tying shoelaces, buttoning shirts, and zipping pants. Older children with the disorder may have great difficulty assembling puzzles, building models, playing ball, and printing or writing.

Studies have linked these various disorders to genetic defects, birth injuries, lead poisoning, inappropriate diet, sensory or perceptual dysfunction, and poor teaching (Yeates et al., 2010; Golden, 2008; Teicher et al., 2008). Research implicating each of these factors has been limited, however, and the precise causes of the disorders remain unclear.

Some of the disorders respond to special treatment approaches (Feifer, 2010; Miller, 2010). Reading therapy, for example, is very helpful in mild cases of dyslexia, and speech therapy brings about complete recovery in many cases of speech sound disorder. Furthermore, the various disorders often disappear before adulthood, even without any treatment.

Assessing Intelligence Educators and clinicians administer intelligence tests to measure intellectual functioning (see Chapter 3). These tests consist of a variety of questions and tasks that rely on different aspects of intelligence, such as knowledge, reasoning, and judgment. Having difficulty in just one or two of these subtests or areas of functioning does not necessarily reflect low intelligence (see *PsychWatch*). It is an individual's overall test score, or **intelligence quotient (IQ),** that is thought to indicate general intellectual ability.

Many theorists have questioned whether IQ tests are indeed valid. Do they actually measure what they are supposed to measure? The correlation between IQ and school performance is rather high—around .50—indicating that many children with lower IQs do, as one might expect, perform poorly in school, while many of those with higher IQs perform better (Sternberg et al., 2001). At the same time, the correlation also suggests

•**intellectual developmental disorder (IDD)**•A disorder marked by intellectual functioning and adaptive behavior that are well below average. Also called intellectual disability. Also called *intellectual disability*. Previously called *mental retardation*.

•**intelligence quotient (IQ)**•A score derived from intelligence tests that theoretically represents a person's overall intellectual capacity.

that the relationship is far from perfect. That is, a particular child's school performance is often higher or lower than his or her IQ might predict. Moreover, the accuracy of IQ tests at measuring extremely low intelligence has not been evaluated adequately, so it is difficult to properly assess people with severe intellectual developmental disorder (AAIDD, 2010).

Are there other kinds of intelligence that IQ tests might fail to assess? What might that suggest about the validity and usefulness of these tests?

Intelligence tests also appear to be socioculturally biased, as you read in Chapter 3. Children reared in households at the middle and upper socioeconomic levels tend to have an advantage on the tests because they are regularly exposed to the kinds of language and thinking that the tests evaluate. The tests rarely measure the "street sense" needed for survival by people who live in poor, crime-ridden areas—a kind of know-how that certainly requires intellectual skills. Similarly, members of cultural minorities and people for whom English is a second language often appear to be at a disadvantage in taking these tests.

If IQ tests do not always measure intelligence accurately and objectively, then the diagnosis of intellectual developmental disorder also may be biased. That is, some people may receive the diagnosis partly because of test inadequacies, cultural differences, discomfort with the testing situation, or the bias of a tester.

Assessing Adaptive Functioning Diagnosticians cannot rely solely on a cutoff IQ score of 70 to determine whether a person suffers from intellectual developmental disorder. Some people with a low IQ are quite capable of managing their lives and functioning independently, while others are not. The cases of Brian and Jeffrey show the range of adaptive abilities.

Brian comes from a lower-income family. He always has functioned adequately at home and in his community. He dresses and feeds himself and even takes care of himself each day until his mother returns home from work. He also plays well with his friends. At school, however, Brian refuses to participate or do his homework. He seems ineffective, at times lost, in the classroom. Referred to a school psychologist by his teacher, he received an IQ score of 60.

Jeffrey comes from an upper-middle-class home. He was always slow to develop, and sat up, stood, and talked late. During his infancy and toddler years, he was put in a special stimulation program and given special help and attention at home. Still Jeffrey has trouble dressing himself today and cannot be left alone in the backyard lest he hurt himself or wander off into the street. Schoolwork is very difficult for him. The teacher must work slowly and provide individual instruction for him. Tested at age 6, Jeffrey received an IQ score of 60.

Brian seems well adapted to his environment outside of school. However, Jeffrey's limitations are pervasive. In addition to his low IQ score, Jeffrey has difficulty meeting challenges at home and elsewhere. Thus a diagnosis of intellectual developmental disorder may be more appropriate for Jeffrey than for Brian.

Several scales have been developed to assess adaptive behavior. Here again, however, some people function better in their lives than the scales predict, while others fall short. Thus to properly diagnose intellectual developmental disorder, clinicians should probably observe the adaptive functioning of each individual in his or her everyday environment, taking both the person's background and the community's standards into account. Even then, however, such judgments may be subjective, as clinicians may not be familiar with the standards of a particular culture or community.

•**mild IDD**• A level of intellectual developmental disorder (IQ between 50 and 70) at which people can benefit from education and can support themselves as adults.

Animal connection
At the National Aquarium in Havana, Cuba, regular sessions of stroking and touching dolphins, sea tortoises, and sea lions have helped many children with autism spectrum disorder and others with intellectual developmental disorder to become more spontaneous, independent, and sociable.

What Are the Features of Intellectual Developmental Disorder?

The most consistent feature of intellectual developmental disorder is that the person learns very slowly (AAIDD, 2010; Sturmey, 2008). Other areas of difficulty are attention, short-term memory, planning, and language. Those who are institutionalized with this disorder are particularly likely to have these limitations. It may be that the unstimulating environment and minimal interactions with staff in many institutions contribute to such difficulties. Traditionally, four levels of intellectual developmental disorder have been distinguished: *mild* (IQ 50–70), *moderate* (IQ 35–49), *severe* (IQ 20–34), and *profound* (IQ below 20).

Mild IDD Some 80 to 85 percent of all people with intellectual developmental disorder fall into the category of **mild IDD** (IQ 50–70). This is sometimes called the "educable" level because the individuals can benefit from schooling and can support themselves as adults. Mild IDD is not usually recognized until children enter school and are assessed there. The individuals demonstrate rather typical language, social, and play skills, but they need assistance when under stress—a limitation that becomes increasingly apparent as academic and social demands increase. Interestingly, the intellectual performance of individuals with mild IDD often seems to improve with age; some even seem to leave the label behind when they leave school, and they go on to function well in the community (Sturmey, 2008). Their jobs tend to be unskilled or semiskilled.

Research has linked mild IDD mainly to sociocultural and psychological causes, particularly poor and unstimulating environments during a child's early years, inadequate parent-child interactions, and insufficient learning experiences (Sturmey, 2008; Stromme & Magnus, 2000). These relationships have been observed in studies comparing deprived and enriched environments (see Figure 17-4). In fact, some community programs have sent workers into the homes of young children with low IQ scores to help enrich the environment there, and their interventions have often improved the children's functioning. When continued, programs of this kind also help improve the

Figure 17-4
Intellectual developmental disorder and socioeconomic class The prevalence of mild IDD is much higher in the lower socioeconomic classes than in the upper classes. In contrast, other levels of intellectual developmental disorder are evenly distributed among the various classes.

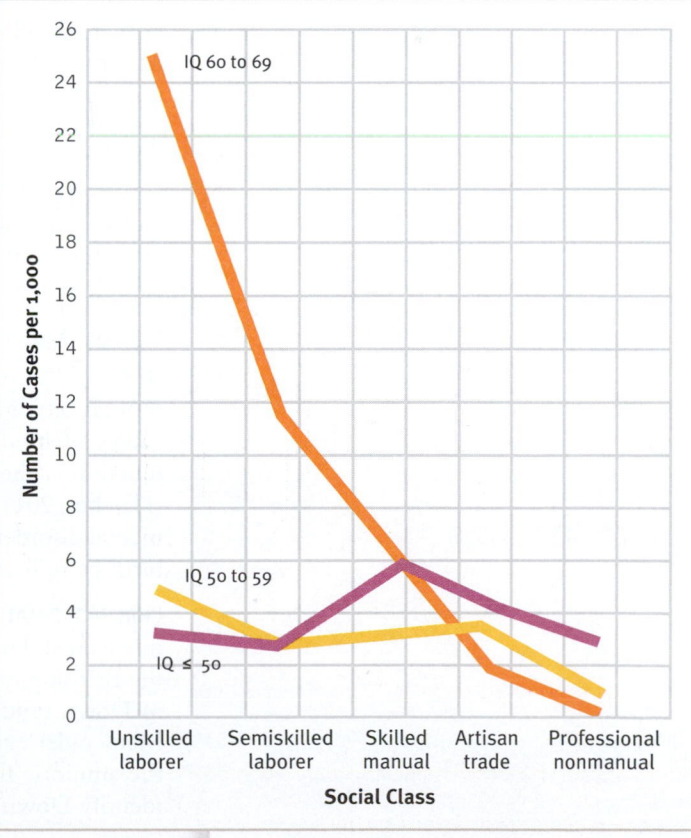

•**moderate IDD**•A level of intellectual developmental disorder (IQ between 35 and 49) at which people can learn to care for themselves and can benefit from vocational training.

•**severe IDD**•A level of intellectual developmental disorder (IQ between 20 and 34) at which individuals require careful supervision and can learn to perform basic work in structured and sheltered settings.

•**profound IDD**•A level of intellectual developmental disorder (IQ below 20) at which people need a very structured environment with close supervision.

•**Down syndrome**•A form of intellectual developmental disorder caused by an abnormality in the twenty-first chromosome.

individual's later performance in school and adulthood (Pungello et al., 2010; Ramey & Ramey, 2007, 2004, 1992).

Although sociocultural and psychological factors seem to be the leading causes of mild IDD, at least some biological factors also may be operating. Studies suggest, for example, that a mother's moderate drinking, drug use, or malnutrition during pregnancy may lower her child's intellectual potential (Hart et al., 2010). Similarly, malnourishment during a child's early years may hurt his or her intellectual development, although this effect can usually be reversed at least partly if a child's diet is improved before too much time goes by.

Moderate, Severe, and Profound IDD Approximately 10 percent of persons with intellectual developmental disorder function at a level of **moderate IDD** (IQ 35–49). They typically receive their diagnosis earlier in life than do individuals with mild IDD, as they demonstrate clear deficits in language development and play during their preschool years. By middle school they further display significant delays in their acquisition of reading and number skills and adaptive skills. By adulthood, however, many individuals with moderate IDD manage to acquire a fair degree of communication skill, learn to care for themselves, benefit from vocational training, and can work in unskilled or semiskilled jobs, usually under supervision. Most such persons also function well in the community if they have supervision (AAIDD, 2010).

Approximately 3 to 4 percent of people with intellectual developmental disorder display **severe IDD** (IQ 20–34). They typically demonstrate basic motor and communication deficits during infancy. Many also show signs of neurological dysfunction and have an increased risk for brain seizure disorder. In school, they may be able to string together only two or three words when speaking. The individuals usually require careful supervision, profit somewhat from vocational training, and can perform only basic work tasks in structured and sheltered settings. Their understanding of communication is usually better than their speech. Most are able to function well in the community if they live in group homes, in community nursing homes, or with their families (AAIDD, 2010).

Around 1 to 2 percent of all people with intellectual developmental disorder function at a level of **profound IDD** (IQ below 20). This level is very noticeable at birth or early infancy. With training, people with profound IDD may learn or improve basic skills such as walking, some talking, and feeding themselves. They need a very structured environment, with close supervision and considerable help, including a one-to-one relationship with a caregiver, in order to develop to the fullest (AAIDD, 2010).

Severe and profound levels of intellectual developmental disorder often appear as part of larger syndromes that include severe physical handicaps. The physical problems are often even more limiting than the individual's low intellectual functioning and in some cases can be fatal.

What Are the Biological Causes of Intellectual Developmental Disorder? As you read earlier, the primary causes of mild IDD are environmental, although biological factors may also be operating in many cases. In contrast, the main causes of moderate, severe, and profound IDD are biological, although people who function at these levels also are affected greatly by their family and social environment (Fletcher, 2011; Sturmey, 2008). The leading biological factors of intellectual developmental disorder are chromosomal abnormalities, metabolic disorders, prenatal problems, birth complications, and childhood diseases and injuries.

CHROMOSOMAL CAUSES The most common of the chromosomal disorders leading to intellectual developmental disorder is **Down syndrome,** named after Langdon Down, the British physician who first identified it. Fewer than 1 of every 1,000 live births result in Down syndrome, but this rate increases greatly when the mother's age is over 35. Many older expectant mothers are now encouraged to undergo *amniocentesis* (testing of the amniotic fluid that surrounds the fetus) during the fourth month of pregnancy to identify Down syndrome and other chromosomal abnormalities.

Individuals with Down syndrome may have a small head, flat face, slanted eyes, high cheekbones, and, in some cases, protruding tongue. The latter may affect their ability to pronounce words clearly. They are often very affectionate with family members but in general display the same range of personality characteristics as people in the general population.

Several types of chromosomal abnormalities may cause Down syndrome (Hazlett et al., 2011). The most common type (94 percent of cases) is *trisomy 21,* in which the individual has three free-floating twenty-first chromosomes instead of two. Most people with Down syndrome range in IQ from 35 to 55. The individuals appear to age early, and many even show signs of neurocognitive decline as they approach 40 (Bebko & Weiss, 2006; Lawlor et al., 2001). It may be that Down syndrome and early neurocognitive decline often occur together because the genes that produce them are located close to each other on chromosome 21 (Lamar et al., 2011; Selkoe, 1991).

Fragile X syndrome is the second most common chromosomal cause of intellectual developmental disorder. Children born with a fragile X chromosome (that is, an X chromosome with a genetic abnormality that leaves it prone to breakage and loss) generally display mild to moderate degrees of intellectual dysfunctioning, language impairments, and, in some cases, behavioral problems (Hagerman, 2011). Typically, these individuals are shy and anxious.

Brian Davies/The Appeal-Democrat

Reaching higher
Today people with Down syndrome are viewed as individuals who can learn and accomplish many things in their lives. Derek Finstad, a 16-year-old with this disorder, celebrates with his football teammates after the team's 56–0 season-opening victory.

METABOLIC CAUSES In metabolic disorders, the body's breakdown or production of chemicals is disturbed. The metabolic disorders that affect intelligence and development are typically caused by the pairing of two defective *recessive* genes, one from each parent. Although one such gene would have no influence if it were paired with a normal gene, its pairing with another defective gene leads to major problems for the child.

The most common metabolic disorder to cause intellectual developmental disorder is *phenylketonuria (PKU)*, which strikes 1 of every 14,000 children. Babies with PKU appear normal at birth but cannot break down the amino acid *phenylalanine*. The chemical builds up and is converted into substances that poison the system, causing severe intellectual dysfunction and several other symptoms (Waisbren, 2011). Today infants can be screened for PKU, and if started on a special diet before 3 months of age, they may develop normal intelligence.

Children with *Tay-Sachs disease,* another metabolic disorder resulting from a pairing of recessive genes, progressively lose their mental functioning, vision, and motor ability over the course of two to four years, and eventually die. One of every 30 persons of Eastern European Jewish ancestry carries the recessive gene responsible for this disorder, so that 1 of every 900 Jewish couples is at risk for having a child with Tay-Sachs disease.

PRENATAL AND BIRTH-RELATED CAUSES As a fetus develops, major physical problems in the pregnant mother can threaten the child's prospects for a normal life (AAIDD, 2010; Bebko & Weiss, 2006). When a pregnant woman has too little iodine in her diet, for example, her child may be born with *cretinism,* also called *severe congenital hypothyroidism,* marked by an abnormal thyroid gland, slow development, intellectual developmental disorder, and a dwarflike appearance. This condition is rare today because the salt in most diets now contains extra iodine. Also, any infant born with this problem may quickly be given thyroid extract to bring about a normal development.

Other prenatal problems may also cause intellectual developmental disorder. As you saw in Chapter 12, children whose mothers drink too much alcohol during pregnancy may be born with **fetal alcohol syndrome,** a group of very serious problems that includes mild to severe IDD (Kodituwakku & Kodituwakku, 2011; Blackburn et al., 2010). In fact, a generally safe level of alcohol consumption during pregnancy

•**fetal alcohol syndrome**•A group of problems in a child, including lower intellectual functioning, low birth weight, and irregularities in the hands and face, that result from excessive alcohol intake by the mother during pregnancy.

has not been established by research. In addition, certain maternal infections during pregnancy—*rubella* (German measles) and *syphilis,* for example—may cause childhood problems that include intellectual developmental disorder.

Birth complications also can lead to problems in intellectual functioning. A prolonged period without oxygen (*anoxia*) during or after delivery can cause brain damage and intellectual developmental disorder in a baby. Similarly, although premature birth does not necessarily lead to long-term problems for children, researchers have found that some babies with a premature birth weight of less than 3.5 pounds display low intelligence (AAIDD, 2010; Taylor, 2010).

CHILDHOOD PROBLEMS After birth, particularly up to age 6, certain injuries and accidents can affect intellectual functioning and in some cases lead to intellectual developmental disorder. Poisonings, serious head injuries caused by accident or abuse, excessive exposure to X-rays, and excessive use of certain drugs pose special dangers (AAIDD, 2010; Evans, 2006). For example, a serious case of *lead poisoning,* from eating lead-based paints or inhaling high levels of automobile fumes, can cause IDD in children. Mercury, radiation, nitrite, and pesticide poisoning may do the same. In addition, certain infections, such as *meningitis* and *encephalitis,* can lead to IDD if they are not diagnosed and treated in time (AAIDD, 2010; Durkin et al., 2000).

Interventions for People with Intellectual Developmental Disorder

The quality of life attained by people with intellectual developmental disorder depends largely on sociocultural factors: where they live and with whom, how they are educated, and the growth opportunities available at home and in the community. Thus intervention programs for these individuals try to provide comfortable and stimulating residences, a proper education, and social and economic opportunities. At the same time, the programs seek to improve the self-image and self-esteem of individuals with IDD. Once these needs are met, formal psychological or biological treatments are also of help in some cases.

WHAT IS THE PROPER RESIDENCE? Until recent decades, parents of children with intellectual developmental disorder would send them to live in public institutions—**state schools**—as early as possible (Harris, 2010). These overcrowded institutions provided basic care, but residents were neglected, often abused, and isolated from society.

Life lessons

The normalization movement calls for people with intellectual developmental disorder to be taught whatever skills are needed for normal and independent living. Here a psychologist (left) gives cooking lessons to young adults with IDD as part of a national program called You and I. The program also provides lessons in dating, self-esteem, social skills, and sex education.

AP Photo/Shiho Fukada

During the 1960s and 1970s, the public became more aware of these sorry conditions and, as part of the broader *deinstitutionalization* movement (see Chapter 15), demanded that many people with intellectual developmental disorder be released from the state schools (Harris, 2010). In many cases, the releases occurred without adequate preparation or supervision. Like deinstitutionalized people suffering from schizophrenia, the individuals were virtually dumped into the community. Often they failed to adjust and had to be institutionalized once again.

Since that time, reforms have led to the creation of *small institutions* and other *community residences* (group homes, halfway houses, local branches of larger institutions, and independent residences) that teach self-sufficiency, devote more staff time to patient care, and offer educational and medical services. Many of these settings follow the principles of **normalization** first started in Denmark and Sweden—they attempt to provide living conditions similar to those enjoyed by the rest of society, flexible routines, and normal developmental experiences, including opportunities for self-determination, sexual fulfillment, and economic freedom (Hemmings, 2010; Hodapp & Dykens, 2003).

Today the vast majority of children with intellectual developmental disorder live at home rather than in an institution. During adulthood and as their parents age, however, some individuals with IDD require levels of assistance and opportunities that their families are unable to provide. A community residence becomes an appropriate alternative for these persons. Most people with IDD, including almost all with mild IDD, now spend their adult lives either in the family home or in a community residence (Sturmey, 2008).

WHICH EDUCATIONAL PROGRAMS WORK BEST? Because early intervention seems to offer such great promise, educational programs for individuals with intellectual developmental disorder may begin during the earliest years. The appropriate education depends on the individual's level of functioning (Bebko & Weiss, 2006; Patton et al., 2000). Educators hotly debate whether special classes or mainstreaming is most effective once the children enter school (Hardman, Drew, & Egan, 2002). In **special education,** children with IDD are grouped together in a separate, specially designed educational program. In contrast, **mainstreaming,** or **inclusion,** places them in regular classes with students from the general school population. Neither approach seems consistently superior (Bebko & Weiss, 2006). It may well be that mainstreaming is better for some areas of learning and for some children, and special classes are better for others.

Teacher preparedness is another factor that may play into decisions about mainstreaming and special education classes. Many teachers report feeling inadequately prepared to provide training and support for children with intellectual development disorder, especially children who have additional problems (Scheuermann et al., 2003). Brief training courses for teachers appear to address such concerns (Campbell et al., 2003).

Teachers who work with individuals with IDD often use operant conditioning principles to improve the self-help, communication, social, and academic skills of the individuals (Sturmey, 2008; Ardoin et al., 2004). They break learning tasks down into small steps, giving positive reinforcement as each increment is accomplished. In addition, many institutions, schools, and private homes have set up *token economy programs*—the operant conditioning programs that have also been used to treat institutionalized patients suffering from schizophrenia.

WHEN IS THERAPY NEEDED? Like anyone else, people with intellectual developmental disorder sometimes experience emotional and behavioral problems. Around 30 percent or more of them have a psychological disorder other than IDD (Baker et al., 2010; Bouras & Holt, 2010). Furthermore, some suffer from low self-esteem, interpersonal problems, and difficulties adjusting to community life. These problems are helped to some degree

What might be the benefits of "mainstreaming" compared to special education classes and vice versa?

BETWEEN THE LINES

Residential Shift

91,592 Number of children and adolescents with intellectual developmental disorder who lived in large state institutions in 1964

1,641 Children and adolescents with intellectual developmental disorder currently living in large state institutions

(Breedlove et al., 2005)

•**state school**•A state-supported institution for people with intellectual developmental disorder.

•**normalization**•The principle that institutions and community residences should expose people with intellectual developmental disorder to living conditions and opportunities similar to those found in the rest of society.

•**special education**•An approach to educating children with intellectual developmental disorder in which they are grouped together and given a separate, specially designed education.

•**mainstreaming**•The placement of children with intellectual developmental disorder in regular school classes. Also known as *inclusion*.

Joe Klamar/AP Photo

Working for money, independence, and self-respect

This 28-year-old waiter serves beverages in a café in Slovakia. He is one of five waiters with intellectual developmental disorder who work at the café.

by either individual or group therapy (Fletcher, 2011). In addition, large numbers of people with IDD are given psychotropic medications (Sturmey, 2008). Many clinicians argue, however, that too often the medications are used simply for the purpose of making the individuals easier to manage.

HOW CAN OPPORTUNITIES FOR PERSONAL, SOCIAL, AND OCCUPATIONAL GROWTH BE INCREASED? People need to feel effective and competent in order to move forward in life. Those with intellectual developmental disorder are most likely to achieve these feelings if their communities allow them to grow and to make many of their own choices. Denmark and Sweden, where the normalization movement began, have again been leaders in this area, developing youth clubs that encourage those with IDD to take risks and function independently. The Special Olympics program has also encouraged those with IDD to be active in setting goals, to participate in their environment, and to interact socially with others (Glidden et al., 2011; Marks et al., 2010).

Socializing, sex, and marriage are difficult issues for people with intellectual developmental disorder and their families, but with proper training and practice, the individuals usually can learn to use contraceptives and carry out responsible family planning (Lumley & Scotti, 2001). National advocacy organizations and a number of clinicians currently offer guidance in these matters, and some have developed *dating skills programs* (Segal, 2008).

Some states restrict marriage for people with intellectual developmental disorder. These laws are rarely enforced, however, and in fact many people with mild IDD marry. Contrary to popular myths, the marriages can be very successful. Moreover, although some individuals may be incapable of raising children, many are quite able to do so, either on their own or with special help and community services (AAIDD, 2010; Sturmey, 2008).

Finally, adults with intellectual developmental disorder—whatever the severity—need the personal and financial rewards that come with holding a job (AAIDD, 2010; Kiernan, 2000). Many work in **sheltered workshops,** protected and supervised workplaces that train them at a pace and level tailored to their abilities. After training in the workshops, many with mild or moderate IDD move on to hold regular jobs.

Stephanie Maze/Stephanie Maze Photography

Normal needs

The interpersonal and sexual needs of people with intellectual developmental disorder are normal, and many, such as this engaged couple, demonstrate considerable ability to express intimacy.

Although training programs for people with intellectual developmental disorder have improved greatly in quality over the past 35 years, there are too few of them. Consequently, most of these individuals fail to receive a complete range of educational and occupational training services. Additional programs are required so that more people with IDD may achieve their full potential, as workers and as human beings.

PUTTING IT... together

Clinicians Discover Childhood and Adolescence

Early in the twentieth century, mental health professionals virtually ignored children. At best, they viewed them as small adults and treated their psychological disorders as they would adult problems (Peterson & Roberts, 1991). Today the problems and needs of young people have caught the attention of researchers and clinicians. Although all of the leading models have been used to help explain and treat these problems, the sociocultural perspective—especially the family perspective—is considered to play a special role.

Because children and adolescents have limited control over their lives, they are particularly affected by the attitudes and reactions of family members. Clinicians must therefore deal with those attitudes and reactions as they try to address the problems of the young. Treatments for conduct disorder, ADHD, intellectual developmental disorder, and other problems of childhood and adolescence typically fall short unless clinicians educate and work with the family as well.

At the same time, clinicians who work with children and adolescents have learned that a narrow focus on any one model can lead to problems. For years autism spectrum disorder was explained exclusively by family factors, misleading theorists and therapists alike and adding to the pain of parents already devastated by their child's disorder. Similarly, in the past, the sociocultural model often led professionals wrongly to accept anxiety among young children and depression among teenagers as inevitable, given the many new experiences confronted by the former and the latter group's preoccupation with peer approval.

The increased clinical focus on the young has also been accompanied by increased attention to their human and legal rights. More and more, clinicians have called on government agencies to protect the rights and safety of this often powerless group. In doing so, they hope to fuel the fights for greater educational resources and against child abuse and neglect, sexual abuse, malnourishment, and fetal alcohol syndrome.

As the problems and, at times, mistreatment of young people receive greater attention, the special needs of these individuals are becoming more visible. Thus the study and treatment of psychological disorders among children and adolescents are likely to continue at a rapid pace. Now that clinicians and public officials have "discovered" this population (see *MediaSpeak* on the next page), they are not likely to underestimate their needs and importance again.

•sheltered workshop• A protected and supervised workplace that offers job opportunities and training at a pace and level tailored to people with various psychological disabilities.

"We've been thinking a lot about what we want to do with your life."

Summing Up

■ **DISORDERS OF CHILDHOOD AND ADOLESCENCE** Emotional and behavioral problems are common in childhood and adolescence, but in addition, at least one-fifth of all children and adolescents in the United States experience a diagnosable psychological disorder. A particular concern among children is that of being *bullied*.

(continued on page 558)

The Etiology and Treatment of Childhood

Jordan W. Smoller

This tongue-in-cheek clinical review of the "disorder" called childhood originally appeared in the book Oral Sadism and the Vegetarian Personality edited by Glenn C. Ellenbogen.

Childhood is a syndrome that has only recently begun to receive serious attention from clinicians. The syndrome itself, however, is not at all recent. As early as the eighth century, the Persian historian Kidnom made reference to "short, noisy creatures," who may well have been what we now call "children." The treatment of children, however, was unknown until this century, when so-called child psychologists and child psychiatrists became common. Despite this history of clinical neglect, it has been estimated that well over half of all Americans alive today have experienced childhood directly (Seuss, 1983). In fact, the actual numbers are probably much higher, since these data are based on self-reports which may be subject to social desirability biases and retrospective distortion. Clinicians are still in disagreement about the significant clinical features of childhood, but the proposed DSM . . . will almost certainly include the following core features:

1. Congenital onset
2. [Diminutiveness]
3. Emotional lability and immaturity
4. Knowledge deficits
5. Legume anorexia

Congenital Onset

In one of the few existing literature reviews on childhood, Temple-Black (1982) has noted that childhood is almost always present at birth, although it may go undetected for years or even remain subclinical indefinitely. This observation has led some investigators to speculate on a biological contribution to childhood. As one psychologist has put it, "we may soon be in a position to distinguish organic childhood from functional childhood" (Rogers, 1979).

[Diminutiveness]

This is certainly the most familiar clinical marker of childhood. It is widely known that children are physically short relative to the population at large. Indeed, common clinical wisdom suggests that the treatment of the so-called small child (or "tot") is particularly difficult. These children are known to exhibit infantile behavior and display a startling lack of insight (Tom & Jerry, 1967).

Emotional Lability and Immaturity

This aspect of childhood is often the only basis for a clinician's diagnosis. As a result, many otherwise normal adults are misdiagnosed as children and must suffer the unnecessary social stigma of being labeled a "child" by professionals and friends alike.

Knowledge Deficits

While many children have IQs within or even above the norm, almost all will manifest knowledge deficits. Anyone who has known a real child has experienced the frustration of trying to discuss any topic that requires some general knowledge.

Legume Anorexia

This last identifying feature is perhaps the most unexpected. Folk wisdom is supported by empirical observation—children will rarely eat their vegetables (see Popeye, 1957, for review).

Causes of Childhood

Now that we know what it is, what can we say about the causes of childhood? Recent years have seen a flurry of theory and speculation from a number of perspectives. Some of the most prominent are reviewed below.

Sociological Model

Emile Durkind was perhaps the first to speculate about sociological causes of childhood. He points out two key observations about children: (1) the vast majority of children are unemployed, and (2) children represent one of the least educated segments of our society. In fact, it has been estimated that less than 20 percent of children have had more than a fourth-grade education. . . . One promising rehabilitation program (Spanky & Alfalfa, 1978) has trained victims of severe childhood to sell lemonade.

Ned Frisk Photography/Corbis

Biological Model

The observation that childhood is usually present from birth has led some to speculate on a biological contribution. An early investigation by Flintstone and Jetson (1939) indicated that childhood runs in families. Their survey of over 8,000 American families revealed that over half contained more than one child. Further investigation revealed that even most nonchild family members had experienced childhood at some point. . . .

Psychological Models

A considerable number of psychologically based theories of the development of childhood exist. They are too numerous to review here. Among the more familiar models are Seligman's "learned childishness" model. According to this model, individuals who are treated like children eventually give up and become children. As a counterpoint to such theories, some experts have claimed that childhood does not really exist. Szasz (1980) has called "childhood" an expedient label. In seeking conformity, we handicap those whom we find unruly or too short to deal with by labeling them "children."

Treatment of Childhood

Efforts to treat childhood are as old as the syndrome itself. Only in modern times, however, have humane and systematic treatment protocols been applied. The overwhelming number of children has made government intervention inevitable. The nineteenth century saw the institution of what remains the largest single program for the treatment of childhood—so-called public schools. Under this colossal program, individuals are placed into treatment groups on the basis of the severity of their condition. For example, those most severely afflicted may be placed in a "kindergarten" program. Patients at this level are typically short, unruly, emotionally immature, and intellectually deficient.

Unfortunately, the "school" system has been largely ineffective. Not only is the program a massive tax burden, but it has failed even to slow down the rising incidence of childhood.

Faced with this failure and the growing epidemic of childhood, mental health professionals are devoting increasing attention to the treatment of childhood. . . . The following case (taken from Gumbie & Pokey, 1957) is typical.

Billy J., age 8, was brought to treatment by his parents. Billy's affliction was painfully obvious. He stood only 4'3" high and weighed a scant 70 pounds, despite the fact that he ate voraciously. Billy presented a variety of troubling symptoms. His voice was noticeably high for a man. He displayed legume anorexia and, according to his parents, often refused to bathe. His intellectual functioning was also below normal—he had little general knowledge and could barely write a structured sentence. Social skills were also deficient. He often spoke inappropriately and exhibited "whining behavior." His sexual experience was nonexistent. Indeed, Billy considered women "icky." . . .

After years of this kind of frustration, startling new evidence has come to light which suggests that the prognosis in cases of childhood may not be all gloom. . . . Moe, Larrie, and Kirly (1974) began a large-scale longitudinal study. These investigators studied two groups. The first group comprised 34 children currently engaged in a long-term conventional treatment program. The second was a group of 42 children receiving no treatment. . . .

The results . . . of a careful 10-year follow-up were startling. . . . Shemp (1984) found subjects improved. Indeed, in most cases, the subjects appeared to be symptom-free. Moe et al. report a spontaneous remission rate of 95 percent, a finding that is certain to revolutionize the clinical approach to childhood.

These recent results suggest that the prognosis for victims of childhood may not be so bad as we have feared. We must not, however, become too complacent. Despite its apparently high spontaneous remission rate, childhood remains one of the most serious and rapidly growing disorders facing mental health professionals today. And beyond the psychological pain it brings, childhood has recently been linked to a number of physical disorders. Twenty years ago, Howdi, Doodi, and Beauzeau (1965) demonstrated a sixfold increased risk of chickenpox, measles, and mumps among children as compared with normal controls. Later, Barbie and Kenn (1971) linked childhood to an elevated risk of accidents—compared with normal adults, victims of childhood were much more likely to scrape their knees, lose their teeth, and fall off their bikes.

Clearly, much more research is needed before we can give any real hope to the millions of victims wracked by this insidious disorder.

Glenn C. Ellenbogen (Ed.), *Oral Sadism and the Vegetarian Personality* (New York: Brunner/Mazel, 1986).

According to surveys, over one-quarter of students are bullied frequently and more than 70 percent have been victims of bullying at least once. *Cyberbullying* is on the rise. *pp. 518–519*

Anxiety disorders are particularly common among children and adolescents. This group of problems includes adult-like disorders, such as social anxiety disorder and generalized anxiety disorder, and the childhood form of *separation anxiety disorder*, which is characterized by excessive anxiety, often panic, whenever a child is separated from a parent. Those with separation anxiety disorder have great trouble traveling away from their family, and they often refuse to visit friends' houses, go on errands, or attend camp or school. Many cannot even stay alone in a room and cling to their parent around the house. Some also have temper tantrums, cry, or plead to keep their parents from leaving them. *pp. 519–521*

Depression is found in 2 percent of children and 8 percent of adolescents. Depression in the young may be triggered by negative life events (particularly losses), major changes, rejection, or ongoing abuse. Childhood depression is often characterized by such symptoms as headaches, stomach pain, irritability, and a disinterest in toys and games. Although there is no difference between the rates of depression in boys and girls before the age of 13, girls are twice as likely as boys to be depressed by the age of 16. The past two decades have also witnessed an enormous increase in the number of children and adolescents who receive diagnoses of *bipolar disorder*. Such diagnoses are expected to decrease now that DSM-5 has added a new childhood category, *disruptive mood dysregulation disorder*. *pp. 522–525*

Children with *oppositional defiant disorder* and *conduct disorder* exceed the normal breaking of rules and act very aggressively. Children with oppositional defiant disorder argue repeatedly with adults, ignore adult rules and requests, and feel intense anger and resentment. Those with conduct disorder, a more severe pattern, repeatedly violate the basic rights of others. Children with this disorder often are violent and cruel and may deliberately destroy property, steal, and run away. Several types of conduct disorders have been identified. Clinicians have treated conduct disorders with approaches such as *parent-child interaction therapy, video modeling, parent management training, treatment foster care, problem-solving skills training*, and the *anger coping and coping power program*. Some individuals with this disorder have been institutionalized in *juvenile training centers*. A number of *prevention* programs have also been developed. *pp. 525–530*

Children who display *attention-deficit/hyperactivity disorder* (ADHD) attend poorly to tasks, behave overactively and impulsively, or both. *Ritalin* and other *stimulant drugs* and *behavioral programs* are often effective treatments. Children with an *elimination disorder—enuresis* or *encopresis*—repeatedly urinate or pass feces in inappropriate places. Behavioral approaches, such as the *bell-and-battery technique,* are effective treatments for enuresis. *pp. 530–538*

■ **LONG-TERM DISORDERS THAT BEGIN IN CHILDHOOD** *Autism spectrum disorder* and *intellectual developmental disorder* are problems that emerge early and typically continue throughout a person's life.

People with autism spectrum disorder are *extremely unresponsive to others, have severe communication deficits, and display very rigid and repetitive behaviors, interests, and activities.* The leading explanations of this disorder point to cognitive deficits, such as failure to develop a *theory of mind*, and biological abnormalities, such as abnormal development of the *cerebellum*, as causal factors. Although no treatment totally reverses the autistic pattern, significant help is available in the form of *cognitive-behavioral treatments, communication training, training and treatment for parents*, and *community integration. pp. 539–545*

People with intellectual developmental disorder are significantly below average in *intelligence* and *adaptive ability*. As many as 3 of every 100 people qualify for this diagnosis. *Mild IDD*, by far the most common level of intellectual developmental disorder, has been linked primarily to environmental factors such as unstimulating environments during a child's early years, inadequate parent-child interactions, and insufficient learning experiences. *Moderate, severe,* and *profound IDD* are caused primarily by biological factors, although individuals who function at these levels also are affected enormously by their family and social environment. The leading biological causes of intellectual developmental disorder are *chromosomal abnormalities, metabolic disorders, prenatal problems, birth complications, and childhood diseases and injuries.*

Today intervention programs for people with intellectual developmental disorder emphasize the importance of a comfortable and stimulating residence, either the family home or a small institution or group home that follows the principles of *normalization.* Other important interventions include *proper education, therapy for psychological problems,* and *programs offering training in socializing, sex, marriage, parenting, and occupational skills.* One of the most intense debates in the field of education centers on whether individuals with intellectual developmental disorder profit more from *special classes* or from *mainstreaming.* Research has not consistently favored one approach over the other. *pp. 546–555*

PsychPortal

Visit **PsychPortal**
www.yourpsychportal.com
to access the e-book, videocases and other case materials and activities, and study aids, including flashcards, crossword puzzles, quizzes, FAQs, and research exercises.

BETWEEN THE LINES

In Their Words

"The boy will come to nothing." ‹‹
   Jakob Freud, 1864 (*referring to his 8-year-old son Sigmund, after he had urinated in his parents' bedroom*)

DISORDERS OF AGING AND COGNITION

Harry appeared to be in perfect health at age 58. . . . He worked in the municipal water treatment plant of a small city, and it was at work that the first overt signs of Harry's mental illness appeared. While responding to a minor emergency, he became confused about the correct order in which to pull the levers that controlled the flow of fluids. As a result, several thousand gallons of raw sewage were discharged into a river. Harry had been an efficient and diligent worker, so after puzzled questioning, his error was attributed to the flu and overlooked.

Several weeks later, Harry came home with a baking dish his wife had asked him to buy, having forgotten that he had brought home the identical dish two nights before. Later that week, on two successive nights, he went to pick up his daughter at her job in a restaurant, apparently forgetting that she had changed shifts and was now working days. A month after that, he quite uncharacteristically argued with . . . the phone company; he was trying to pay a bill that he had already paid three days before. . . .

Months passed and Harry's wife was beside herself. She could see that his problem was worsening. Not only had she been unable to get effective help, but Harry himself was becoming resentful and sometimes suspicious of her attempts. He now insisted there was nothing wrong with him, and she would catch him narrowly watching her every movement. . . . Sometimes he became angry—sudden little storms without apparent cause. . . . More difficult for his wife was Harry's repetitiveness in conversation: He often repeated stories from the past and sometimes repeated isolated phrases and sentences from more recent exchanges. There was no context and little continuity to his choice of subjects. . . .

Two years after Harry had first allowed the sewage to escape, he was clearly a changed man. Most of the time he seemed preoccupied; he usually had a vacant smile on his face, and what little he said was so vague that it lacked meaning. . . . Gradually his wife took over getting him up, toileted, and dressed each morning. . . .

Harry's condition continued to worsen slowly. When his wife's school was in session, his daughter would stay with him some days, and neighbors were able to offer some help. But occasionally he would still manage to wander away. On those occasions he greeted everyone he met—old friends and strangers alike—with "Hi, it's so nice." That was the extent of his conversation, although he might repeat "nice, nice, nice" over and over again. . . . When Harry left a coffee pot on a unit of the electric stove until it melted, his wife, desperate for help, took him to see another doctor. Again Harry was found to be in good health. [However] the doctor ordered a [brain scan and eventually concluded] that Harry had "Pick-Alzheimer disease." . . .

Because Harry was a veteran . . . [he qualified for] hospitalization in a . . . veterans' hospital about 400 miles away from his home. . . .

At the hospital the nursing staff sat Harry up in a chair each day and, aided by volunteers, made sure he ate enough. Still, he lost weight and became weaker. He would weep when his wife came to see him, but he did not talk, and he gave no other sign that he recognized her. After a year, even the weeping stopped. Harry's wife could no longer bear to visit. Harry lived on until just after his sixty-fifth birthday, when he choked on a piece of bread, developed pneumonia as a consequence, and soon died.

(Heston, 1992, pp. 87–90)

Harry suffered from a form of *Alzheimer's disease.* This term is familiar to almost everyone in our society. It seems as if each decade is marked by a disease that everyone dreads—a diagnosis no one wants to hear because it feels like a death sentence. Cancer used to be such a diagnosis, then AIDS. But medical science has made remarkable strides with those diseases, and patients who now develop them have reason for hope and expectations of improvement. Alzheimer's disease, on the other hand, remains incurable and almost untreatable, although, as you will see later, researchers are currently making enormous progress toward understanding it and reversing, or at least slowing, its march.

What makes Alzheimer's disease particularly frightening is that it means not only eventual physical death but also, as in Harry's case, a slow psychological death—a progressive deterioration of one's memory and related cognitive faculties. Significant cognitive deterioration, previously called *dementia,* is now categorized as *neurocognitive disorder.* There are many types of neurocognitive disorders listed in DSM-5 (APA, 2013). Alzheimer's disease is the most common one.

Although neurocognitive disorders are currently the most publicized and feared psychological problems among the elderly, they are hardly the only ones. A variety of psychological disorders are tied closely to later life. As with childhood disorders, some of the disorders of old age are caused primarily by pressures that are particularly likely to appear at that time of life, others by unique traumatic experiences, and still others—like neurocognitive disorders—by biological abnormalities.

Old Age and Stress

Old age is usually defined in our society as the years past age 65. By this account, around 36 million people in the United States are "old," representing more than 12 percent of the total population; this is an 11-fold increase since 1900 (Cummings & Coffey, 2011) (see Figure 18-1). Moreover, it has been estimated that the U.S. population will consist of 70 million elderly people by the year 2030—over 20 percent of the population. Not only is the overall population of the elderly on the rise, but, furthermore, the number of people over 85 will double in the next 10 years. Indeed, people over 85 represent the fastest-growing segment of the population in the United States and in most countries around the world (Cherry et al., 2007). Older women outnumber older men by 3 to 2 (Etaugh, 2008).

Like childhood, old age brings special pressures, unique upsets, and major biological changes (Tucker-Drob, 2011). People become more prone to illness and injury as they age. About 40 percent of adults over 65 have three or more chronic illnesses, and 25 percent have four or more (Durso et al., 2010). And at least half of elderly people experience some measure of insomnia or other sleep problems (Jaussent et al., 2011). In addition, elderly people are likely to experience the stress of loss—the loss of spouses, friends, and adult children and the loss of former activities and roles (Shankar et al., 2011; Etaugh, 2008). Many lose their sense of purpose after they retire. Even favored pets and possessions are sometimes lost.

The stresses of elderly people need not necessarily result in psychological problems (Butler, 2010) (see *PsychWatch* on the next page). In fact, some older persons, particularly those who seek social contacts and those who maintain a sense of control over their lives, use the changes that come with aging as opportunities for learning and growth (Infurna et al., 2011; Windsor & Anstey, 2011). For example, the number of elderly—

What kinds of attitudes and activities might help individuals enter old age with peace of mind and positive anticipation?

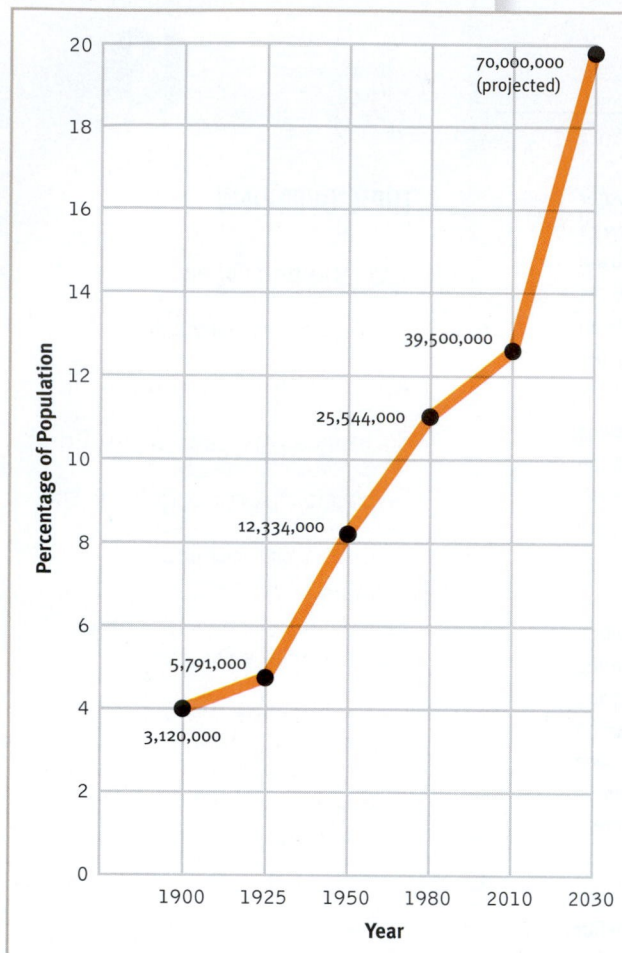

Figure 18-1

On the rise The population of people aged 65 and older in the United States has increased 11-fold since the beginning of the twentieth century. The percentage of elderly people in the population increased from 4 percent in 1900 to 13 percent in 2010 and is expected to be more than 20 percent in 2030 (Census Bureau, 2011; Cummings & Coffey, 2011; Edelstein et al., 2008).

PsychWatch

PsychWatch

The Oldest Old

Clinicians suggest that aging need not inevitably lead to psychological problems. Nor apparently does it always lead to physical problems.

There are currently around 65,000 centenarians in the United States—people whose age is 100 years or older. When researchers have studied these people—often called the "oldest old"—they have been surprised to learn that the individuals are on average more healthy, clear-headed, and agile than those in their 80s and early 90s (Zhou et al., 2011; Martin et al., 2010; Perls, 2010). Although some certainly experience cognitive declines, more than half remain perfectly alert. Many of the oldest old are, in fact, still employed, sexually active, and able to enjoy the outdoors and the arts. What is the greatest fear of these individuals? The fear of significant cognitive decline. According to one study, many people in their 90s and above fear the prospect of mental deterioration more than they fear death (Boeve et al., 2003).

Some scientists believe that individuals who live this long carry "longevity" genes

Welcome to the club A 100-year-old woman and a 99-year-old man chat during a party for centenarians in Woodbridge, Connecticut.

that make them resistant to disabling or terminal infections (Perls, 2010; Corliss & Lemonick, 2004). Others point to engaged lifestyles and "robust" personalities that help the individuals meet life's challenges with optimism and a sense of challenge (Martin et al., 2010, 2009; Poon et al., 2010). The individuals themselves often credit a good frame of mind or regular be-

haviors that they have maintained for many years—for example, eating healthful food, pursuing regular exercise, and not smoking. Said one 96-year-old retired math and science teacher, "You can't sit. . . . You have to keep moving" (Duenwald, 2003).

---

often physically limited—people who use the Internet to connect with people of similar ages and interests doubled between 2000 and 2004, doubled again between 2004 and 2007, and has doubled yet again since then (Oinas-Kukkonen & Mantila, 2010). For other elderly people, however, the stresses of old age do lead to psychological difficulties (Aldwin, Spiro, & Park, 2006). Studies indicate that as many as half of elderly people would benefit from mental health services, yet fewer than 20 percent actually receive them. **Geropsychology,** the field of psychology dedicated to the mental health of elderly people, has developed almost entirely within the last 30 years, and at present only a small percentage of all clinicians work primarily with elderly persons (Fiske et al., 2011; Knight & McCallum, 2011).

The psychological problems of elderly persons may be divided into two groups. One group consists of disorders that may be common among people in all age groups but are often connected to the process of aging when they occur in an elderly person. These include *depressive, anxiety,* and *substance use disorders.* The other group consists of disorders of cognition, such as *delirium, mild neurocognitive disorders,* and *major neurocognitive disorders,* that result from brain abnormalities. As in Harry's case, these brain abnormalities are most often tied to aging, but they also can sometimes occur in younger individuals. Elderly persons with one of these psychological problems often display other such problems. For example, many who suffer from neurocognitive disorders also experience depression and anxiety (Abdel-Rahman, 2012).

•**geropsychology**•The field of psychology concerned with the mental health of elderly people.

Depression in Later Life

Depression is one of the most common mental health problems of older adults. The features of depression are the same for elderly people as for younger people, including feelings of profound sadness and emptiness; low self-esteem, guilt, and pessimism; and loss of appetite and sleep disturbances. Depression is particularly common among those who have recently experienced a trauma, such as the loss of a spouse or close friend or the development of a serious physical illness (Coffey & Coffey, 2011; Edelstein et al., 2008).

[Oscar] was an 83-year-old married man with an episode of major depressive disorder.... He said that about one and one-half years prior to beginning treatment, his brother had died. In the following months, two friends whom he had known since childhood died. Following these losses, he became increasingly anxious [and] grew more and more pessimistic. Reluctantly, he acknowledged, "I even thought about ending my life." Review of his symptoms indicated that while ... anxiety was a prominent part of his clinical picture, so was depression....

During ... treatment, [Oscar] discussed his relationship with his brother. He discussed how distraught he was to watch his brother's physical deterioration from an extended illness. He described the scene at his brother's deathbed and the moment "when he took his final breath." He experienced guilt over the failure to carry out his brother's funeral services in a manner he felt his brother would have wanted. While initially characterizing his relationship with his brother as loving and amiable, he later acknowledged that he disapproved of many ways in which his brother acted. Later in therapy, he also reviewed different facets of his past relationships with his two deceased friends. He expressed sadness that the long years had ended.... [Oscar's] life had been organized around visits to his brother's home and outings with his friends.... [While] his wife had encouraged him to visit with other friends and family, it became harder and harder to do so as he became more depressed.

(Hinrichsen, 1999, p. 433)

Overall, as many as 20 percent of people experience depression at some point during old age (Mathys & Belgeri, 2010; Knight et al., 2006). The rate is highest in

Making a difference
To help prevent feelings of unimportance and low self-esteem, some older individuals now offer their expertise to young people who are trying to master new skills, undertake business projects, and the like. This elderly man, who volunteers regularly at an elementary school, is teaching math to a first grader.

Owen Franken/Corbis

Racing to mental health
Gerontologists propose that elderly people need to pursue pleasurable and personally meaningful activities. With this in mind, the elderly men on the left compete in a race in the Senior Olympics. In contrast, the elderly gentleman on the right, also interested in racing, watches a competition at the Saratoga Springs horse racing track with the daily post parade statistics program resting on his head. Which of these two activities might be more likely to contribute to successful psychological functioning during old age?

older women. This rate among the elderly is about the same as that among younger adults—even lower, according to some studies (Dubovsky & Dubovsky, 2011). However, it climbs much higher (as high as 32 percent) among aged persons who live in nursing homes, as opposed to those in the community (Mathys & Belgeri, 2010; Seitz, Purandare, & Conn, 2010).

Several studies suggest that depression raises an elderly person's chances of developing significant medical problems (Coffey & Coffey, 2011; Edelstein et al., 2008). For example, older depressed people with high blood pressure are almost three times as likely to suffer a stroke as older nondepressed people with the same condition. Similarly, elderly people who are depressed recover more slowly and less completely from heart attacks, hip fractures, pneumonia, and other infections and illnesses. Small wonder that among the elderly, increases in clinical depression are tied to increases in the mortality rate (Holwerda et al., 2007).

Is it more likely that positive thinking leads to good health or that good health produces positive thinking?

As you read in Chapter 10, elderly persons are also more likely to commit suicide than young people, and often their suicides are related to depression (Oyama et al., 2010). The overall rate of suicide in the United States is 11.5 per 100,000 persons; among the elderly it is 16 per 100,000 (CDC, 2011, 2010).

Like younger adults, older individuals who are depressed may be helped by cognitive-behavioral therapy, interpersonal therapy, antidepressant medications, or a combination of these approaches (Dubovsky & Dubovsky, 2011; McKenzie & Teri, 2011). Both individual and group therapy formats have been used. More than half of elderly patients with depression improve with these various treatments. At the same time, it is sometimes difficult to use antidepressant drugs effectively and safely with older persons because the body breaks the drugs down differently in later life (Ciraulo et al., 2011; Dubovsky & Dubovsky, 2011). Moreover, among elderly people, antidepressant drugs have a higher risk of causing some cognitive impairment. Electroconvulsive therapy, applied with certain modifications, also has been used for elderly people who are severely depressed and unhelped by other approaches (Coffey & Kellner, 2011).

Anxiety Disorders in Later Life

Anxiety is also common among elderly people (Lenze et al., 2011; Gum et al., 2009). At any given time, around 6 percent of elderly men and 11 percent of elderly women in the United States experience at least one of the anxiety disorders. Surveys indicate that generalized anxiety disorder is particularly common, experienced by up to 7 percent of all elderly persons (Holwerda et al., 2007). The prevalence of anxiety also increases throughout old age. For example, individuals over 85 years of age report higher rates of anxiety than those between 65 and 84 years. In fact, all of these numbers may be low, as anxiety in the elderly tends to be underreported (Jeste, Blazer, & First, 2005). Both the elderly individual and the clinician may interpret physical symptoms of anxiety, such as heart palpitations and perspiring, as symptoms of a medical condition.

There are many things about aging that may heighten the anxiety levels of certain individuals (Lenze et al., 2011). Declining health, for example, has often been pointed to, and in fact, older persons who experience significant medical illnesses or injuries report more anxiety than those who are healthy or injury-free. Researchers have not, however, been able to determine why certain individuals who experience such problems in old age become anxious while others who face similar circumstances remain relatively calm.

Older adults with anxiety disorders have been treated with psychotherapy of various kinds, particularly cognitive-behavioral therapy (McKenzie & Teri, 2011; Sorocco & Lauderdale, 2011). Many also receive benzodiazepines or other antianxiety medications. And a number are treated with serotonin-enhancing antidepressant drugs, particularly those with obsessive-compulsive disorder or panic disorder, just as younger sufferers are. Again, however, all such drugs must be used cautiously with older people (Dubovsky & Dubovsky, 2011).

Environmental comfort
Some long-term care facilities have redesigned their buildings so that the settings themselves have soothing effects on elderly residents. At this facility in Baltimore, an elderly woman feels one of the fiber-optic light curtains that decorate the rooms. The rooms are also made more peaceful by the use of soft changing colors and sounds of the ocean, woods, and streams.

Substance Misuse in Later Life

Although alcohol use disorder and other substance use disorders are significant problems for many older persons, the prevalence of such patterns actually appears to decline after age 65, perhaps because of declining health or reduced income (Blazer & Wu, 2011; Berks & McCormick, 2008). The majority of older adults do not misuse alcohol or other substances despite the fact that aging can sometimes be a time of considerable stress and that in our society alcohol and drugs are widely turned to in times of stress. At the same time, accurate data about the rate of substance abuse among older adults are difficult to gather because many elderly persons do not suspect or admit that they have such a problem (Jeste et al., 2005).

Surveys find that 4 to 7 percent of older people, particularly men, have alcohol use disorder in a given year (Knight et al., 2006). Men under 30 are four times as likely as men over 60 to display a behavioral problem associated with excessive alcohol use, such as repeated falling, spells of dizziness or blacking out, secretive drinking, or social withdrawal. Older patients who are institutionalized, however, do display high rates of problem drinking. For example, alcohol problems among older persons admitted to general and mental hospitals range from 15 percent to 49 percent, and estimates of alcohol-related problems among patients in nursing homes range from 26 percent to 60 percent (Klein & Jess, 2002; Gallagher-Thompson & Thompson, 1995).

Researchers often distinguish between older problem drinkers who have had alcohol use disorder for many years, perhaps since their 20s, and those who do not start the pattern until their 50s or 60s (sometimes called "late-onset alcoholism") (Volfson & Oslin, 2011). The latter group typically begins abusive drinking as a reaction to the negative events and pressures of growing older, such as the death of a spouse, living alone, or unwanted retirement (Ames et al., 2010; Onen et al., 2005). Alcohol use disorder in elderly people is treated much as in younger adults (see Chapter 12), with such approaches as detoxification, Antabuse, Alcoholics Anonymous (AA), and cognitive-behavioral therapy (Ames et al., 2010; Knight et al., 2006).

A leading kind of substance problem in the elderly is the *misuse of prescription drugs* (Cummings & Coffey, 2011; Volfson & Oslin, 2011). Most often it is unintentional. Elderly people buy 30 percent of all prescription drugs and 40 percent of all over-the-counter drugs. In fact, older people receive twice as many prescriptions as younger persons (Dubovsky & Dubovsky, 2011). Most take at least five prescription drugs and two over-the-counter drugs (Hajjar & Hanlon, 2010; Edelstein et al., 2008). Thus their risk of confusing medications or skipping doses is high. To help address this problem, physicians and pharmacists often try to simplify medications, educate older patients about their prescriptions, clarify directions, and teach them to watch for undesired effects (Rubin, 2005). On the other hand, physicians themselves are sometimes to blame in cases of prescription drug misuse, perhaps overprescribing medications for elderly patients or unwisely mixing certain medicines (Sleeper, 2010; Wilder-Smith, 2005).

? What changes in medical practice, patient education, or family interactions might address the problem of prescription drug misuse by the elderly?

Yet another drug-related problem, apparently on the increase, is the misuse of powerful medications at nursing homes (see *MediaSpeak* on the next page). Research suggests that antipsychotic drugs are currently being given to almost 30 percent of the total nursing home population in the United States, despite the fact that many such individuals do not display psychotic functioning (Lagnado, 2007). Apparently, these powerful and (for some elderly patients) dangerous drugs are often given to sedate and manage the patients (Ames et al., 2010).

Psychotic Disorders in Later Life

Elderly people have a higher rate of psychotic symptoms than younger persons (Devanand, 2011; Broadway & Mintzer, 2007). Among aged people, these symptoms are usually due to underlying medical conditions such as delirium and dementia, the disorders of cognition that you will read about in the next section. However, some elderly persons suffer from *schizophrenia* or *delusional disorder.*

Actually, schizophrenia is less common in older persons than in younger ones. In fact, many persons with schizophrenia find that their symptoms lessen in later life (Meeks & Jeste, 2008; Fisher et al., 2001). Improvement can occur in people who have displayed schizophrenia for 30 or more years, particularly in such areas as social skills and work capacity, as we are reminded by the remarkable late-life improvement of the Nobel Prize recipient John Nash, the subject of the book and movie *A Beautiful Mind.*

It is uncommon for *new* cases of schizophrenia to emerge in late life (Devanand, 2011). Thus some of the elderly people with schizophrenia have been receiving antipsychotic drugs and psychotherapeutic interventions for years and are continuing to do so in old age (Cummings & Coffey, 2011; Meeks & Jeste, 2008). Once again, however, antipsychotic drugs may pose more dangers (cognitive impairment, stroke, seizures) for elderly people than younger people, given the metabolism changes in older people (Debovsky & Dubovsky, 2011). In contrast, other elderly people with schizophrenia have been untreated for years and continue to be untreated as elderly persons, winding up in nursing homes, in run-down apartments, homeless, or in jail. Among the cases of schizophrenia that do emerge for the first time during old age, women outnumber men by at least 2 to 1 (Ames et al., 2010).

Another kind of psychotic disorder found among the elderly is *delusional disorder,* in which individuals develop beliefs that are false but not bizarre (Cummings & Coffey,

MediaSpeak

Doctor, Do No Harm

By Laurie Tarkan, *New York Times*

Ramona Lamascola thought she was losing her 88-year-old mother to dementia. Instead, she was losing her to overmedication.

Last fall her mother, Theresa Lamascola, of the Bronx, suffering from anxiety and confusion, was put on the antipsychotic drug Risperdal. When she had trouble walking, her daughter took her to another doctor—the younger Ms. Lamascola's own physician—who found that she had unrecognized hypothyroidism, a disorder that can contribute to dementia.

Theresa Lamascola was moved to a nursing home to get these problems under control. But things only got worse. "My mother was screaming and out of it, drooling on herself and twitching," said Ms. Lamascola, a pediatric nurse. The psychiatrist in the nursing home stopped the Risperdal, which can cause twitching and vocal tics, and prescribed a sedative and two other antipsychotics. "I knew the drugs were doing this to her," her daughter said. "I told him to stop the medications and stay away from Mom." Not until yet another doctor took Mrs. Lamascola off the drugs did she begin to improve.

The use of antipsychotic drugs to tamp down the agitation, combative behavior and outbursts of dementia patients has soared, especially in the elderly. Sales of newer antipsychotics like Risperdal, Seroquel and Zyprexa totaled $13.1 billion in 2007, up from $4 billion in 2000. . . . Part of this increase can be traced to prescriptions in nursing homes. Researchers estimate that about a third of all nursing home patients have been given antipsychotic drugs.

The increases continue despite a drumbeat of bad publicity. A 2006 study of Alzheimer's patients found that for most patients, antipsychotics provided no significant improvement over placebos in treating aggression and delusions. . . . [The] Food and Drug Administration . . . has not approved marketing of these drugs for older people with dementia, but they are commonly prescribed to these patients "off label." . . .

[M]any doctors say misuse of the drugs is widespread. "These antipsychotics can be overused and abused," said Dr. Johnny Matson, a professor of psychology at Louisiana State University. "And there's a lot of abuse going on in a lot of these places.". . .

Nursing homes are short staffed, and insurers do not generally pay for the attentive medical care and hands-on psychosocial therapy that advocates recommend. It is much easier to use sedatives and antipsychotics, despite their side effects. . . .

Used correctly, the drugs do have a role in treating some seriously demented patients, who may be incapacitated by

paranoia or are self-destructive or violent. Taking the edge off the behavior can keep them safe and living at home, rather than in a nursing home.

If patients are prescribed an antipsychotic, it should be a very low dose for the shortest period necessary, said Dr. Dillip V. Jeste, a professor of psychiatry and neuroscience at the University of California, San Diego. It may take a few weeks or months to control behavior. In many cases, the patient can then be weaned off of the drugs or kept at a very low dose. . . .

Some doctors point out that simply paying attention to a nursing home patient can ease dementia symptoms. They note that in randomized trials of antipsychotic drugs for dementia, 30 to 60 percent of patients in the placebo groups improved.

"That's mind boggling," Dr. Jeste said. "These severely demented patients are not responding to the power of suggestion. They're responding to the attention they get when they participate in a clinical trial.

"They receive both T.L.C. and good general medical and humane care, which they did not receive until now. That's a sad commentary on the way we treat dementia patients.". . .

[Fortunately, the physician Ramona Lamascola consulted did stop] her mother's antipsychotics and sedatives and prescribed Aricept. "It's not clear whether it was getting her . . . medical issues finally under control or getting rid of the offending medications," [the physician] said. "But she had a miraculous turnaround."

Theresa Lamascola still has dementia, but . . . as her daughter put it, "I got my mother back."

2011; Devanand, 2011). This disorder is rare in most age groups—around 3 of every 10,000 persons—but its prevalence appears to increase in the elderly population (Chae & Kang, 2006). Older persons with a delusional disorder may develop deeply held suspicions of persecution; they believe that other persons—often family members, doctors, or friends—are conspiring against, cheating, spying on, or maligning them. They may become irritable, angry, or depressed or pursue legal action because of such ideas. It is not clear why this disorder increases among elderly people, but some clinicians suggest that the rise is related to the deficiencies in hearing, social isolation, greater stress, or heightened poverty experienced by many elderly persons.

Disorders of Cognition

Most of us worry from time to time that we are losing our memory and other mental abilities. You rush out the door without your keys, you meet a familiar person and cannot remember her name, or you forget that you have seen a particular film. Actually such mishaps are a common and quite normal feature of stress or of aging. As people move through middle age, these memory difficulties and lapses of attention increase, and they may occur regularly by the age of 60 or 70. Sometimes, however, people experience memory and other cognitive changes that are far more extensive and problematic.

In Chapter 7 you saw that problems in memory and related cognitive processes can occur without biological causes, in the form of *dissociative disorders.* More often, however, cognitive problems do have organic roots, particularly when they appear late in life. The leading such disorders among the elderly are *delirium, major neurocognitive disorder,* and *mild neurocognitive disorder.*

Delirium

Delirium is a major disturbance in attention and orientation to the environment (see Table 18-1). As the person's focus becomes less clear, he or she has great difficulty concentrating and thinking in an organized way, which leads to misinterpretations, illusions, and, on occasion, hallucinations (Eeles & Bhat, 2010). Sufferers may believe that it is morning in the middle of the night or that they are home when actually they are in a hospital room.

This state of massive confusion typically develops over a short period of time, usually hours or days (APA, 2013, 2012). Delirium may occur in any age group, including children, but is most common in elderly persons. Fewer than 0.5 percent of the non-elderly population experience delirium, compared to 1 percent of people over 55 years of age and 14 percent of those over 85 years of age (Tune & DeWitt, 2011). When elderly people enter a hospital to be treated for a general medical condition, 1 in 10 of them shows the symptoms of delirium. At least another 10 percent develop delirium during their stay in the hospital (Ames et al., 2010; Inouye, 2006; Inouye et al., 2003). Delirium is experienced by 60 percent of nursing home residents older than 75 years of age, compared to 35 percent of similar people living independently with the assistance of home health services (Tune & DeWitt, 2011).

Fever, certain diseases and infections, poor nutrition, head injuries, strokes, and stress (including the trauma of surgery) may all cause delirium (Eeles & Bhat, 2010; Wetterling, 2005). So may intoxication by certain substances, such as prescription drugs. Partly because older people face so many of these problems, they are more likely than younger ones to experience delirium. If a clinician accurately identifies delirium, it can often be easy to correct—by treating the underlying infection, for example, or changing the patient's drug prescription. However, the syndrome typically fails to be recognized for what it is (Ames et al., 2010). One study on a medical ward, for example, found that admission doctors detected only 1 of 15 consecutive cases of delirium (Cameron et al., 1987). Incorrect diagnoses of this kind may contribute to a high death rate for older people with delirium (Trzepacz & Meagher, 2008).

•**delirium**•A rapidly developing, acute disturbance in attention and orientation that makes it very difficult to concentrate and think in a clear and organized manner.

table: 18-1

DSM-5 Checklist

Delirium

1. Disturbance in attention and orientation to the environment.

2. The disturbance develops over a short period of time and represents an acute change.

3. Accompanied by a change in an additional cognitive domain.

Based on APA, 2013, 2012.

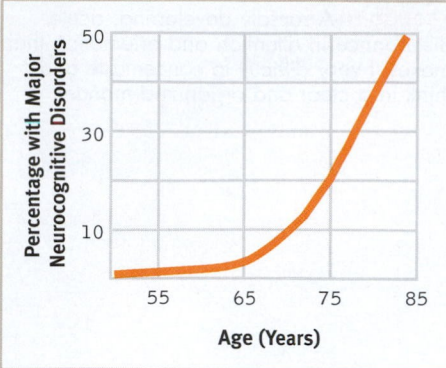

Figure 18-2

Substantial cognitive decline and age
The occurrence of substantial cognitive decline is closely related to age. Fewer than 1 percent of all 60-year-olds have major neurocognitive disorders, compared to as many as 50 percent of those who are 85. (Adapted from Julien et al., 2011; Ames et al., 2010; Nussbaum & Ellis, 2003.)

table: **18-2**

DSM-5 Checklist

Major Neurocognitive Disorder

1. Substantial decline in one or more of the following areas of cognitive function:
   - Memory and learning
   - Attention • Perceptual motor
   - Planning and decision-making
   - Language ability • Social cognition.

2. Cognitive deficits interfere with independence.

Mild Neurocognitive Disorder

1. Modest decline in one or more areas of cognitive functioning.

2. Cognitive deficits do not interfere with independence.

Based on APA, 2013, 2012.

Alzheimer's Disease and Other Neurocognitive Disorders

People with a **neurocognitive disorder** experience a significant decline in at least one (often more than one) area of cognitive functioning, such as memory and learning, attention, perceptual motor, planning and decision making, language ability, or social cognition (APA, 2013, 2012). In certain types of neurocognitive disorders, the individuals may also undergo personality changes—they may behave inappropriately, for example—and their symptoms may worsen steadily.

If the person's cognitive decline is substantial and interferes significantly with his or her ability to be independent, a diagnosis of **major neurocognitive disorder** is in order. If, however, the decline is modest and does not interfere with independent functioning, the appropriate diagnosis is **mild neurocognitive disorder** (see Table 18-2).

There are currently 24 to 36 million people with neurocognitive disorders around the world, with 4.6 million new cases emerging each year (Hollingworth et al., 2011; Ames et al., 2010). Indeed, at any given time, around 3 to 9 percent of the world's adult population are suffering from such disorders (Berr et al., 2005). Their occurrence is closely related to age (see Figure 18-2). Among people 65 years of age, the prevalence is around 1 to 2 percent, increasing to as much as 50 percent among those over the age of 85 (Ames et al., 2010; Apostolova & Cummings, 2008).

As you read earlier, **Alzheimer's disease** is the most common type of neurocognitive disorder, accounting for around two-thirds of all cases (Burke, 2011; Farlow, 2010). Around 5 million people in the United States currently have this disease, a number expected to triple by the year 2050 unless a cure is found (Wesson et al., 2011). Alzheimer's disease sometimes appears in middle age (*early onset*), but in the vast majority of cases it occurs after the age of 65 (*late onset*), and its prevalence increases markedly among people in their late 70s and early 80s. Around 17 percent of individuals with this disease also experience major depressive disorder (Abdel-Rahman, 2012; Mathys & Belgeri, 2010).

Alzheimer's disease is a gradually progressive disease in which memory impairment is the most prominent cognitive dysfunction (APA, 2013, 2012). Technically, sufferers receive a DSM-5 diagnosis of *mild neurocognitive disorder due to Alzheimer's disease* during the early and mild stages of the syndrome and *major neurocognitive disorder due to Alzheimer's disease* during the later, more severe stages (see Table 18-3 on page 572).

Alzheimer's disease is named after Alois Alzheimer, the German physician who formally identified it in 1907. Alzheimer first became aware of the syndrome in 1901 when a new patient, Auguste D., was placed under his care:

On November 25, 1901, a … woman with no personal or family history of mental illness was admitted to a psychiatric hospital in Frankfurt, Germany, by her husband, who could no longer ignore or hide quirks and lapses that had overtaken her in recent months. First, there were unexplainable bursts of anger, and then a strange series of memory problems. She became increasingly unable to locate things in her own home and began to make surprising mistakes in the kitchen. By the time she arrived at Städtische Irrenanstalt, the Frankfurt Hospital for the Mentally Ill and Epileptics, her condition was as severe as it was curious. The attending doctor, senior physician Alois Alzheimer, began the new file with these notes….

She sits on the bed with a helpless expression.

"What is your name?"

Auguste.

"Last name?"

Auguste.

"What is your husband's name?"

Auguste, I think.

"How long have you been here?"

(She seems to be trying to remember.)

Three weeks.

It was her second day in the hospital. Dr. Alzheimer, a thirty-seven-year-old neuropathologist and clinician, . . . observed in his new patient a remarkable cluster of symptoms: severe disorientation, reduced comprehension, aphasia (language impairment), paranoia, hallucinations, and a short-term memory so incapacitated that when he spoke her full-name, Frau Auguste D_____, and asked her to write it down, the patient got only as far as "Frau" before needing the doctor to repeat the rest.

He spoke her name again. She wrote "Augu" and again stopped.

When Alzheimer prompted her a third time, she was able to write her entire first name and the initial "D" before finally giving up, telling the doctor, "I have lost myself."

Her condition did not improve. It became apparent that there was nothing that anyone at this or any other hospital could do for Frau D. except to insure her safety and try to keep her as clean and comfortable as possible for the rest of her days. Over the next four and a half years, she became increasingly disoriented, delusional, and incoherent. She was often hostile.

"Her gestures showed a complete helplessness," Alzheimer later noted in a published report. "She was disoriented as to time and place. From time to time she would state that she did not understand anything, that she felt confused and totally lost. . . . Often she would scream for hours and hours in a horrible voice."

By November 1904, three and a half years into her illness, Auguste D. was bedridden, incontinent, and largely immobile. . . . Notes from October 1905 indicate that she had become permanently curled up in a fetal position with her knees drawn up to her chest, muttering but unable to speak, and requiring assistance to be fed.

(Shenk, 2001, pp. 12–14)

Although some people with Alzheimer's disease may survive for as many as 20 years, the time between onset and death is typically 8 to 10 years (Julien et al., 2011; Soukup, 2006). It usually begins with mild memory problems, lapses of attention, and difficulties in language and communication (Farlow, 2010). As symptoms worsen, the person has trouble completing complicated tasks or remembering important appointments. Eventually sufferers also have difficulty with simple tasks, distant memories are forgotten, and changes in personality often become very noticeable. For example, a man may become uncharacteristically aggressive.

People with Alzheimer's disease may at first deny that they have a problem, but they soon become anxious or depressed about their state of mind; many also become agitated. A woman from Virginia describes her memory loss as the disease progresses:

Very often I wander around looking for something which I know is very pertinent, but then after a while I forget about what it is I was looking for. . . . Once the idea is lost, everything is lost and I have nothing to do but wander around trying to figure out what it was that was so important earlier.

(Shenk, 2001, p. 43)

As the neurocognitive symptoms intensify, people with Alzheimer's disease show less and less awareness of their limitations. They may withdraw from others during the late stages of the disorder, become more confused about time and place, wander, and show very poor judgment. Eventually they become fully dependent on other people. They may lose almost all knowledge of the past and fail to recognize the faces of even close relatives. They also become increasingly uncomfortable at night and

•**neurocognitive disorder**•Disorder marked by a significant decline in at least one area of cognitive functioning.

•**major neurocognitive disorder**•Neurocognitive disorder in which the decline in cognitive functioning is substantial and interferes with the ability to be independent.

•**mild neurocognitive disorder**•Neurocognitive disorder in which the decline in cognitive functioning is modest and does not interfere with the ability to be independent.

•**Alzheimer's disease**•The most common type of neurocognitive disorder, usually occurring after the age of 65, marked most prominently by memory impairment.

Slipping away
Because of their short-term memory problems, people with advanced cases of Alzheimer's disease, one form of neurocognitive disorder, are often unable to draw or paint or do other simple tasks. In addition, their long-term memory deficits may prevent them from recognizing even close relatives or friends.

Richard Falco/Black Star

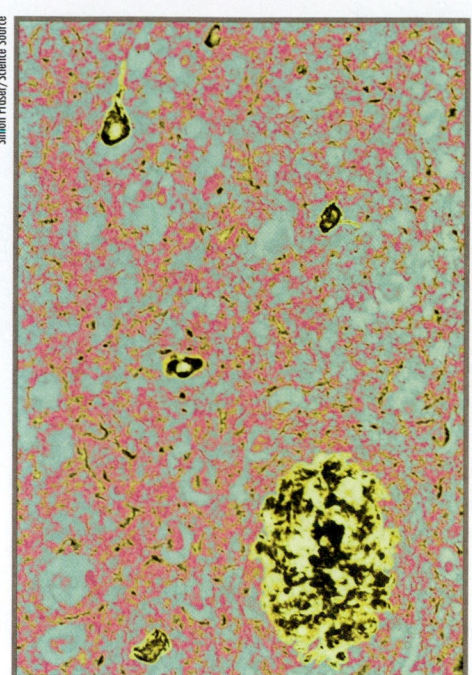

Simon Fraser/Science Source

Biological culprits
Tissue from the brain of an individual with Alzheimer's disease shows excessive amounts of plaque (large yellow-black sphere at lower right of photo) and neurofibrillary tangles (several smaller yellow blobs throughout photo).

take frequent naps during the day (Ames et al., 2010; Edelstein et al., 2008). During the late phases of the disorder, the individuals require constant care.

Alzheimer's victims usually remain in fairly good health until the later stages of the disease. As their mental functioning declines, however, they become less active and spend much of their time just sitting or lying in bed. As a result, they are prone to develop illnesses such as pneumonia, which can result in death (Ames et al., 2010). Alzheimer's disease is responsible for close to 75,000 deaths each year in the United States, which makes it the seventh leading cause of death in the country, the third leading cause among the elderly (CDC, 2010).

In most cases, Alzheimer's disease can be diagnosed with certainty only after death, when structural changes in the person's brain, such as excessive *senile plaques and neurofibrillary tangles,* can be fully examined. **Senile plaques** are sphere-shaped deposits of a small molecule known as the *beta-amyloid protein* that form in the spaces *between* cells in the hippocampus, cerebral cortex, and certain other brain regions, as well as in some nearby blood vessels. The formation of plaques is a normal part of aging, but it is exceptionally high in people with Alzheimer's disease (Fandrich et al., 2011; Selkoe, 2011, 2000, 1992). **Neurofibrillary tangles,** twisted protein fibers found *within* the cells of the hippocampus and certain other brain areas, also occur in all people as they age, but again people with Alzheimer's disease form an extraordinary number of them.

Scientists do not fully understand what role excessive numbers of plaques and tangles play in Alzheimer's disease, but they suspect they are very important. Today's leading explanations for this disease center on these plaques and tangles and on the various factors that may contribute to their formation.

What are the Genetic Causes of Alzheimer's Disease? To understand the genetic theories of Alzheimer's disease, we must first appreciate the nature and role of *proteins.* Proteins are fundamental components of all living cells, including, of course, brain cells. They are large molecules made up of chains of carbon, hydrogen, oxygen, nitrogen, and sulfur. There are many different kinds of proteins, each with a different function. Collectively, they are essential for the proper functioning of an organism.

The plaques and tangles that are so plentiful in the brains of Alzheimer's patients seem to occur when two important proteins start acting in a frenzied manner. Abnormal activity by the beta-amyloid protein is, as we noted above, key to the repeated formation of plaques (Fandrich et al., 2011). Similarly, abnormal activity by another protein, *tau,* is key to the excessive formation of tangles (Obulesu et al., 2011). A leading theory holds that the many plaques formed by beta amyloid proteins cause tau proteins in the brain to start breaking down, resulting in tangles and the death of many neurons (Hughes, 2011; Obulescu et al., 2011).

What causes this chain of events? Genetic factors are a major culprit. However, the genetic factors that are responsible differ for the early-onset and late-onset types of Alzheimer's disease.

EARLY-ONSET ALZHEIMER'S DISEASE As we noted earlier, Alzheimer's disease occurs before the age of 65 in relatively few cases. Such cases typically run in families. Researchers have learned that this form of Alzheimer's disease can be caused by abnormalities in the

table: 18-3

DSM-5 Checklist

Neurocognitive Disorder Due to Alzheimer's Disease

1. Individual meets criteria for major or mild neurocognitive disorder.

2. Gradual onset and progression of cognitive impairment, with memory and learning impairment as an early and prominent feature.

3. Symptoms are not due to other types of neurocognitive disorders or medical problems.

Based on APA, 2013, 2012.

genes responsible for the production of two proteins—the *beta-amyloid precursor protein* (*beta-APP*) and the *presenilin* protein. Apparently, some families transmit *mutations,* or abnormal forms, of one or both of these genes—mutations that lead ultimately to abnormal beta amyloid protein buildups and to plaque formations (Wesson et al., 2011).

LATE-ONSET ALZHEIMER'S DISEASE The vast majority of Alzheimer cases develop after the age of 65. Such cases typically do not run in families and are often called *sporadic* Alzheimer's disease. This late-onset form of the disease appears to result from a combination of genetic, environmental, and lifestyle factors. However, the genetic factor at play in late-onset Alzheimer's disease is different from the ones involved in early-onset Alzheimer's disease.

A gene called the *apolipoprotein E (ApoE) gene*, located on chromosome 19, is normally responsible for the production of a protein that helps carry various fats into the bloodstream. This gene comes in various forms. About 30 percent of the population inherit the form called *ApoE-4,* and these people appear to be particularly vulnerable to the development of Alzheimer's disease (Hollingsworth et al., 2011). Apparently, the ApoE-4 gene form promotes the excessive formation of beta-amyloid proteins, helping to spur the formation of plaques, and, in turn, the breakdown of the tau protein, the formation of numerous tangles, the death of many neurons, and, finally, Alzheimer's disease.

Although the ApoE-4 gene form appears to be a major contributor to the development of Alzheimer's disease, it is important to recognize that not everyone with this form of the gene develops the disease. Apparently, other factors—perhaps environmental, lifestyle, or stress-related—also have a significant impact in cases of late-onset Alzheimer's disease (Nation et al., 2011; Tran et al., 2011).

How Does Brain Structure Relate to Alzheimer's Disease?

Genetic factors may predispose individuals to Alzheimer's disease, but we still need to know what abnormalities in brain structure eventually result from such factors—that is, what brain structure abnormalities help promote Alzheimer's disease. Researchers have identified a number of possibilities. To understand these, we need first to appreciate some basic information about the operation and biology of memory.

The human brain has two memory systems that work together to help us learn and recall. **Short-term memory,** or **working memory,** gathers new information. **Long-term memory** is the accumulation of information that we have stored over the years, information that first made its way through the short-term memory system. The information held in short-term memory must be transformed, or *consolidated,* into long-term memory if we are to hold on to it. Remembering information that has been stored in long-term memory is called *retrieval* and is described as going into one's long-term memory to bring it out for use again in short-term, or working, memory.

Certain *brain structures* seem to be especially important in memory. Among the most important structures in short-term memory are the *prefrontal lobes,* located just behind the forehead. When animals or humans acquire new information, their prefrontal lobes become more active (Jiang et al., 2000). Apparently this activity enables them to hold information temporarily and to continue working with the information as long as it is needed. Among the brain areas most important to long-term memory are the *temporal lobes* (including the *hippocampus* and *amygdala,* key structures under the temporal lobes) and the *diencephalon* (including the *mammillary bodies, thalamus,* and *hypothalamus*), which seem to help transform short-term into long-term memory. Research indicates that cases of Alzheimer's disease involve damage to or improper functioning of one or more of these brain areas (van der Flier et al., 2005; Caine et al., 2001) (see Figure 18-3 on the next page).

•**senile plaques**•Sphere-shaped deposits of beta-amyloid protein that form in the spaces between certain brain cells and in certain blood vessels as people age. People with Alzheimer's disease have an excessive number of such plaques.

•**neurofibrillary tangles**•Twisted protein fibers that form within certain brain cells as people age. People with Alzheimer's disease have an excessive number of such tangles.

•**short-term memory**•The memory system that collects new information. Also known as *working memory.*

•**long-term memory**•The memory system that contains all the information that we have stored over the years.

Sacrificing for research
Nuns at the *School Sisters of Notre Dame* in Connecticut sit in the chapel for morning vespers. In a famous and ongoing longitudinal study spanning 30 years, hundreds of sisters from this convent have undergone cognitive and personality testing and eventual postmortem examinations to help shed light on the development, predictors, and progression of Alzheimer's disease and other neurocognitive disorders. The study has clarified that cognitive and other kinds of functioning in early, middle, and late life may help predict the eventual onset of such cognitive disorders.

Steve Liss/Time Life Pictures/Getty Images

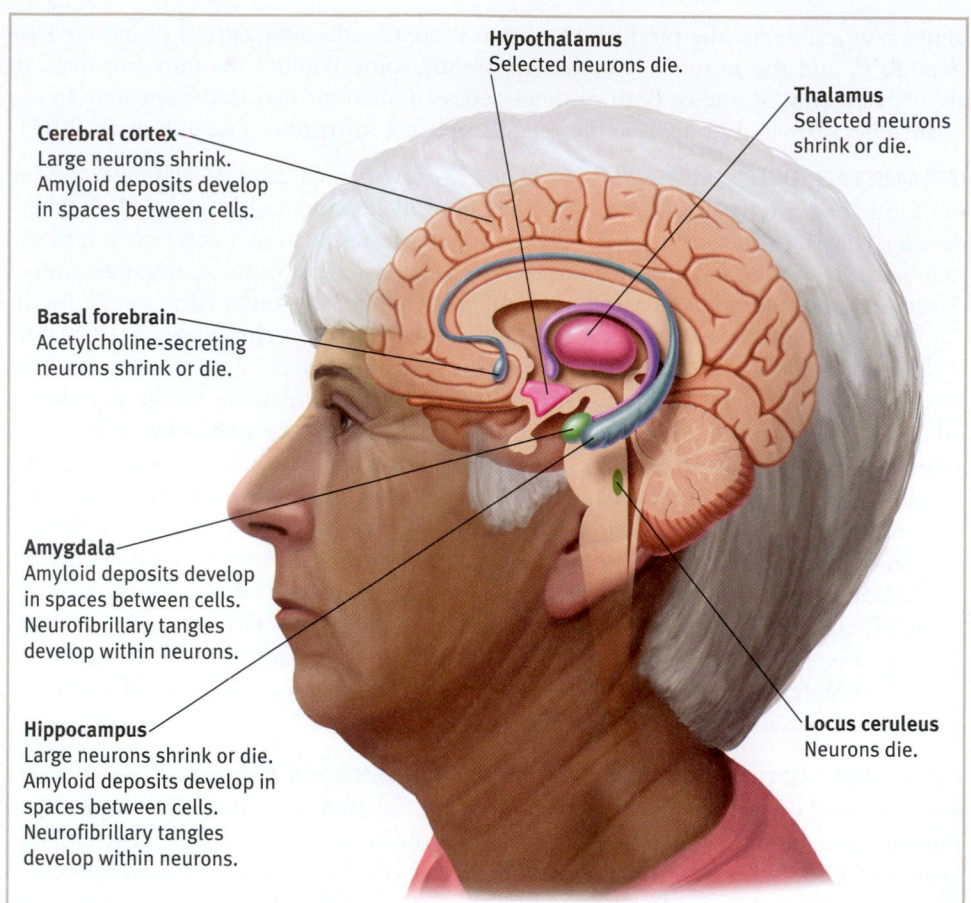

Figure 18-3

The aging brain In old age, the brain undergoes changes that affect cognitive functions such as memory, learning, and reasoning to some degree. These same changes occur to an excessive degree in people with Alzheimer's disease. (Adapted from Selkoe, 2011, 1992.)

Hypothalamus
Selected neurons die.

Thalamus
Selected neurons shrink or die.

Cerebral cortex
Large neurons shrink. Amyloid deposits develop in spaces between cells.

Basal forebrain
Acetylcholine-secreting neurons shrink or die.

Amygdala
Amyloid deposits develop in spaces between cells. Neurofibrillary tangles develop within neurons.

Hippocampus
Large neurons shrink or die. Amyloid deposits develop in spaces between cells. Neurofibrillary tangles develop within neurons.

Locus ceruleus
Neurons die.

What Biochemical Changes in the Brain Relate to Alzheimer's Disease?

Memory researchers have also identified *biochemical changes* that occur in cells as memories form. In order for new information to be acquired and stored, certain proteins must be produced in key brain cells. Several chemicals—for example, *acetylcholine, glutamate, RNA* (*ribonucleic acid*), and *calcium*—are responsible for the production of the memory-linked proteins. If the activity of any of these chemicals is disturbed, the proper production of proteins may be prevented and the formation of memories interrupted (Wu et al., 2008; Steward & Worley, 2002). For example, by blocking the activity of glutamate, animal researchers have prevented short-term memory. Similarly, by blocking the cellular production of RNA or of calcium, they have interrupted the formation of long-term memories (Berridge, 2011).

Some research suggests that abnormal activity by these various chemicals may contribute to the symptoms of Alzheimer's disease. Studies have found, for example, that *acetylcholine* and *glutamate* are in low supply, or at least function differently, in the brains of Alzheimer's victims (Chin et al., 2007; Akaike, 2006). Still other studies suggest that such victims display an imbalance in the breakdown of *calcium*.

Other Explanations of Alzheimer's Disease

Several lines of research suggest that certain substances found in nature may act as toxins, damage the brain, and contribute to the development of Alzheimer's disease. For example, researchers have detected high levels of *zinc* in the brains of some Alzheimer's victims (Schrag et al., 2011; Shcherbatykh & Carpenter, 2007). This finding has gained particular attention because in some animal studies zinc has been observed to trigger a clumping of the beta–amyloid protein, similar to the plaques found in the brains of Alzheimer's patients.

Another line of research suggests that the environmental toxin *lead* may contribute to the development of Alzheimer's disease (Ritter, 2008). Lead was phased out of gasoline products between 1976 and 1991, leading to an 80 percent drop of lead levels in people's blood. However, many of today's elderly population were exposed to high levels of lead in the 1960s and 1970s, regularly inhaling air pollution from vehicle exhausts—an exposure that might have damaged or destroyed many of their neurons. Several studies suggest that this previous absorption of lead and other pollutants may be having a negative effect on the current cognitive functioning of such individuals (Ritter, 2008; Hu et al., 2005).

One study, for example, examined elderly people and scanned their shinbones for lead (Schwartz & Stewart, 2007). Interpreting shinbone levels of lead as indicators of the individuals' lifetime exposures to this toxin, the researchers found that the higher a person's lifetime lead exposure, the more poorly he or she performed on memory and language tests. An important question here is: Why would cognitive dysfunction first appear decades after exposure to the toxin? Medical researcher Philip Landrigan (2007) suggests, "If a substance destroys brain cells in early life, the brain may cope by drawing on its reserve capacity until [eventually] it loses more cells with aging. . . . Only then would symptoms like forgetfulness or tremors begin."

Finally, two other explanations for Alzheimer's disease have been offered. One is the *autoimmune theory.* On the basis of certain irregularities found in the immune systems of people with Alzheimer's disease, several researchers have speculated that changes in aging brain cells may trigger an *autoimmune response* (that is, a mistaken attack by the immune system against itself) that helps lead to this disease (Zipp & Aktas, 2006). The other explanation is a *viral theory.* Because Alzheimer's disease resembles *Creutzfeldt-Jakob disease,* another type of neurocognitive disorder that is known to be caused by a slow-acting virus, some researchers propose that a similar virus may cause Alzheimer's disease (Doty, 2008; Prusiner, 1991). However, no such virus has been detected in the brains of Alzheimer's victims.

Assessing and Predicting Alzheimer's Disease As you read earlier, most cases of Alzheimer's disease can be diagnosed with absolute certainty only after death, when an autopsy is performed. However, brain scans, which reveal abnormalities in the living brain, now are used commonly as assessment tools and often provide clinicians with considerable confidence in their diagnoses of Alzheimer's disease (Yamasaki et al., 2012; Berkof et al., 2011; Berti et al., 2011). In addition, several research teams currently

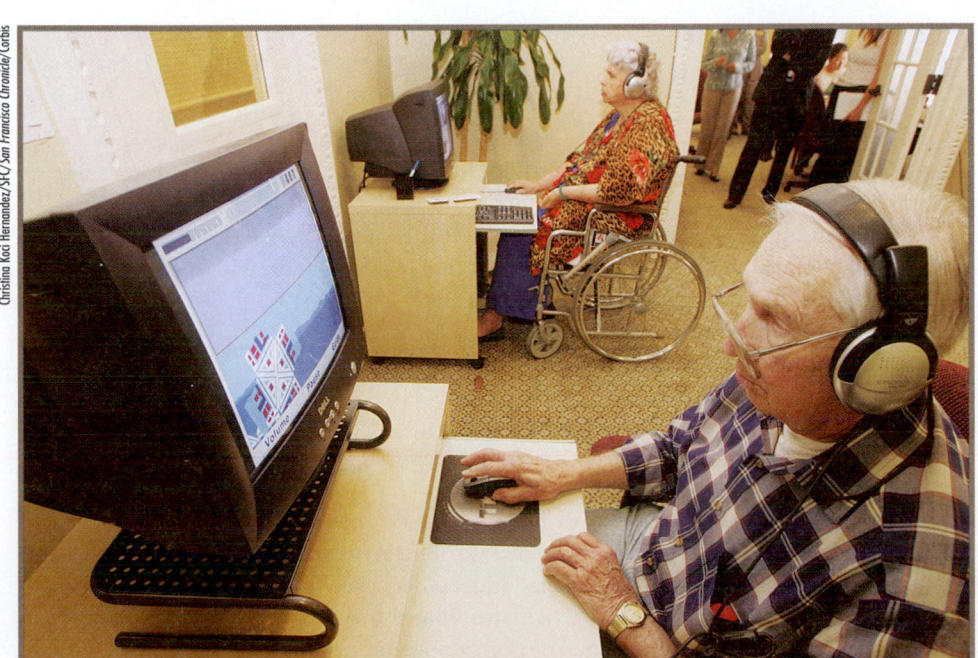

Cognitive fitness center

A number of senior living community programs now include cognitive fitness centers where elderly persons sit at computers and work on memory and cognitive software programs. Clinicians hope that "cognitive calisthenics" of this kind will help prevent or reverse certain symptoms of aging.

Damaging the Brain

A leading cause of neurocognitive disorders is damage to the brain—including damage brought about by drugs or head injuries. Among other effects, a damaged brain may produce significant amnesia.

Retrograde amnesia is an inability to remember events from the past. *Anterograde amnesia* is an ongoing inability to form new memories. In anterograde amnesia, it is as though information from short-term memory can no longer cross over into long-term memory. In severe cases, new acquaintances are forgotten almost immediately, and problems solved one day must be tackled again the next. Individuals may not remember anything that has happened since their brain damage first occurred. Nevertheless, sufferers may continue to possess all of their earlier verbal abilities and many problem-solving skills, and their IQ is not changed.

Korsakoff's Syndrome

Fred, a 69-year-old man, was admitted to a mental hospital in a state of confusion, the result of *Korsakoff's syndrome,* a disorder that causes its victims to keep forgetting newly learned information (anterograde amnesia):

Fred . . . had a history of many years of heavy drinking, although he denied drinking during the past several years. When seen in the admitting ward, the patient was neatly dressed, but there was some deterioration of his personal habits. Although pleasant and sociable with the interviewer and ward personnel, he was definitely confused. He wandered about the ward, investigating objects and trying on other people's clothing. He talked freely, though his speech tended to be rambling and at times incoherent. Most of his spontaneous conversation centered on himself, and there were a number of hypochondriacal complaints. Fred was disoriented for time and place, although he was able to give his name. He could not give his correct address, said his age was 91, and was unable to name the day, the month, or the year. He did not know where he was, although he said he was sent here by his landlord because he had been drinking. . . . [Fred] showed the characteristic symptom picture of Korsakoff's syndrome, with disorientation, confusion, and a strong tendency toward confabulation. When asked where he was, he said he was in a brewery. He gave the name of the brewery, but when asked the same question a few minutes later, he named another brewery. Similarly, he said that he knew the examiner, called him by an incorrect name, and a little later changed the name again. When leaving the examining room, he used still another name when he said politely, "Goodbye, Mr. Wolf!"

(KISKER, 1977, P. 308)

As you'll recall from Chapter 12, approximately 5 percent of people with chronic alcoholism develop Korsakoff's syndrome. A combination of excessive drinking and improper diet produce a deficiency of *vitamin B* (*thiamine*), which leads to damage in key memory regions of the brain (Hirstein, 2011; Fattal-Valevski, 2011). Sufferers of this disorder primarily lose memories of factual knowledge but still maintain their intellectual and language skills. Thus, like Fred, many of them *confabulate* repeatedly—they use their general intellect to make up elaborate stories and lies in an effort to replace the memories they keep losing.

Head Injuries and Brain Surgery

Both head injuries and brain surgery can cause significant memory problems (King & Kirwilliam, 2011; Zeckey et al., 2011; Bigler, 2009). Either may destroy memory-related brain structures. Television shows and movies often portray bumps on the head as a quick and easy way to lose one's memory. In fact, *mild* head injuries, such as a concussion that does not result in coma or a period of unconsciousness, seem unlikely to cause much memory loss.

---

are trying to develop tools that can identify persons likely to develop Alzheimer's disease and other types of neurocognitive disorders.

One promising line of work, for example, comes from the laboratory of neuroscientist Lisa Mosconi and her colleagues (Apostolova et al., 2010; Mosconi et al., 2010, 2008; de Leon et al., 2007). Using a special kind of PET scan, this research team examined activity in certain parts of the *hippocampus* in dozens of elderly research participants and then conducted follow-up studies of those individuals for up to 24 years. (Recall that the hippocampus plays a major role in memory.) Eventually, 43 percent of the study's participants developed either a mild or major neurocognitive disorder due to Alzheimer's disease. The researchers found that those who developed such cognitive impairments had indeed displayed lower hippocampus activity on their initial PET scans than the participants who remained healthy. Overall, the PET scans, administered years before the onset of symptoms, predicted mild neurocognitive

Would people be better off knowing that they will eventually develop a disease that has no known cure?

AP Photo/Steve Ruark

Part of the game? National Football League great John Mackey shows off his Super Bowl V and Hall of Fame rings. Mackey died at age 69 in 2011 of frontotemporal neurocognitive disorder, a condition marked by extreme confusion and the need for full-time assistance. Many cases of neurocognitive disorder, like Mackey's, are apparently the result of repeated sports injuries to the head, a link implicitly acknowledged by the NFL with their implementation of the "88 plan" (named after Mackey's jersey number), which helps pay the cost of nursing home care and day care for football veterans with such problems.

In contrast, almost half of all *severe* head injuries do cause some permanent learning and memory problems, both anterograde and retrograde. In everyday life, the leading causes of severe brain injuries are car accidents and falls.

Given these dangers, the public has become very concerned by the recent release of information that tens of thousands of U.S. soldiers who fought in Afghanistan and Iraq have suffered head injuries from exposure to blasts during combat. Estimates on the low end are that at least 20,000, and perhaps as many as 320,000, combat veterans have sustained such injuries (RAND, 2008; Marchione, 2007). While it may be that most such brain injuries are mild, clinical practitioners and researchers caution that they do not yet know how severe or long lasting these injuries will turn out to be.

Brain surgery may create more specific memory problems. The most famous case of memory loss as a result of brain surgery was that of a man called H.M. by researchers (Milner, 2010). In 1953, surgeons decided to treat H.M.'s *brain seizure disorder,* or *epilepsy,* by removing parts of both of his temporal lobes, along with the amygdala and hippocampus. At that time, the involvement of these brain areas in the formation of memories was not known. (Today temporal lobe surgery is usually limited to either the right or left side of the brain.) From that day forward, H.M. experienced severe anterograde amnesia. For the remaining half-century of his life, he was unable to recognize or recall anyone he met after his operation.

impairment with an accuracy rate of 71 percent and major neurocognitive impairment with an accuracy rate of 83 percent.

As you will see shortly, the most effective interventions for Alzheimer's disease and other types of neurocognitive disorders are those that help *prevent* these problems, or at least ones that are applied early. Clearly, then, it is essential to have tools that identify the disorders as early as possible, preferably years before the onset of symptoms. That is what makes the research advances in assessment and diagnosis so exciting.

Other Types of Neurocognitive Disorders There are a number of neurocognitive disorders in addition to Alzheimer's disease (Ringman & Vinters, 2011) (see *PsychWatch*). *Vascular neurocognitive disorder,* for example, follows a cerebrovascular accident, or *stroke,* during which blood flow to specific areas of the brain was cut off, thus damaging the areas (Ames et al., 2010). In many cases, the patient may not even be aware of the stroke (Moorhouse & Rockwood, 2010). Like Alzheimer's disease, this disorder is progressive, but its symptoms begin suddenly rather than gradually. Moreover, cognitive functioning may continue to be normal in areas of the brain that have not

Victims of Parkinson's disease
Two of today's most famous victims of Parkinson's disease, boxing legend Muhammad Ali (left) and actor Michael J. Fox (right), chat playfully prior to testifying before a Senate funding subcommittee about the devastating effects the disease has had on their lives and those of other persons.

Stephane Audras/REA/Redux

been affected by the stroke, in contrast to the broad cognitive deficiencies usually displayed by Alzheimer's patients. Some people have both Alzheimer's disease and vascular neurocognitive disorder.

Frontotemporal neurocognitive disorder, also known as *Pick's disease,* is a rare disorder that affects the frontal and temporal lobes. It offers a clinical picture similar to Alzheimer's disease, but the two diseases can be distinguished at autopsy.

Neurocognitive disorder due to prion disease, also called *Creutzfeldt-Jakob disease,* has symptoms that include spasms of the body. As we observed earlier, this disorder is caused by a slow-acting virus that may live in the body for years before the disease develops. Once launched, however, the disease has a rapid course.

Neurocognitive disorder due to Huntington's disease is an inherited progressive disease in which memory problems worsen over time, along with personality changes and mood difficulties. Huntington's victims have movement problems, too, such as severe twitching and spasms. Children of people with Huntington's disease have a 50 percent chance of developing it.

Parkinson's disease, the slowly progressive neurological disorder marked by tremors, rigidity, and unsteadiness, can result in n*eurocognitive disorder due to Parkinson's disease,* particularly in older people or individuals whose cases are advanced.

And, finally, yet other neurocognitive disorders may be caused by *HIV infections, traumatic brain injury, substance abuse,* or various *medical conditions* such as meningitis or advanced syphilis.

What Treatments Are Currently Available for Alzheimer's Disease and Other Neurocognitive Disorders?

Treatments for the cognitive features of Alzheimer's disease and most other types of neurocognitive disorders have been at best modestly helpful. A number of approaches have been applied, including drug therapy, cognitive techniques, behavioral interventions, support for caregivers, and sociocultural approaches.

DRUG TREATMENT The drugs currently prescribed for Alzheimer's patients are designed to affect acetylcholine and glutamate, the neurotransmitters that play important roles in memory. Such drugs include *tacrine* (trade name Cognex), *donepezil* (Aricept), *rivastigmine* (Exelon), *galantamine* (Reminyl), and *memantine* (Namenda). Some Alzheimer's patients who take these drugs improve slightly in short-term memory and reasoning ability, as well as in their use of language and their ability to cope under pressure (Patel & Grossberg, 2011). Although the benefits of the drugs are limited and the risk of harmful effects (particularly for tacrine) is sometimes high, these drugs have been approved by the Food and Drug Administration. Clinicians believe that they may be of greatest use to persons in the early, mild stage of Alzheimer's disease. Another approach, taking *vitamin E,* either alone or in combination with one of these drugs, also seems to help slow down further cognitive decline among people in the mild stage of Alzheimer's disease (Sano, 2003). In addition, numerous other possible drug treatments are being investigated currently (Assal, 2011).

The drugs just discussed are each administered *after* a person has developed Alzheimer's disease. In contrast, studies suggest that certain substances now available on the marketplace for other kinds of problems may help prevent or delay the onset of Alzheimer's disease. For example, some studies have found that women who took *estrogen,* the female sex hormone, for years after menopause cut their risk of developing Alzheimer's disease in half (Kawas et al., 1997). And other studies have suggested that the long-term use of *nonsteroid anti-inflammatory drugs* such as *ibuprofen* and *naprosyn* (drugs found in Advil, Motrin, Nuprin, and other pain relievers) may help reduce the risk of Alzheimer's disease, although recent findings on this possibility have been mixed (Julien et al., 2011).

COGNITIVE TECHNIQUES Cognitive treatments have been applied in cases of Alzheimer's disease, with some temporary success (Farlow, 2010; Knight et al., 2006). In Japan, for example, a number of persons with the disease meet regularly in classes, performing simple calculations and reading essays and novels aloud. Proponents of this approach claim that it serves as a mental exercise that helps rehabilitate those parts of the brain linked to memory, reasoning, and judgment. Similarly, some research suggests that cognitive activities, including computer-based cognitive stimulation programs, may help prevent or delay the onset of Alzheimer's disease (Schmiedek et al., 2010; Meyers, 2008). One study of 700 individuals in their eighties found that those research participants who had pursued cognitive activities over a five-year period (for example, writing letters, following the news, reading books, or attending concerts or plays) were less likely to develop Alzheimer's disease than mentally inactive participants (Wilson et al., 2007).

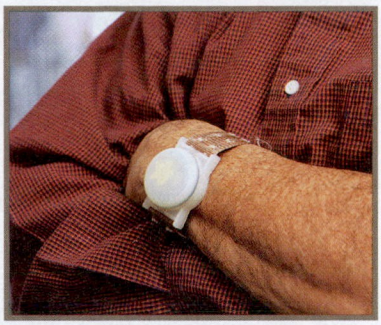

AP Photo/Mel Evans

Staying in touch
This Alzheimer's sufferer wears a tracking bracelet that enables his family members to locate him quickly if he wanders from home. This wrist device is a much less controversial solution for the problem of wandering than microchip implants or other invasive tracking techniques that have been proposed.

BEHAVIORAL INTERVENTIONS Behavioral interventions have also been applied with some success to Alzheimer's patients. First, it has become increasingly clear across many studies that physical exercise helps improve cognitive functioning—for people of all ages and states of health (Szabo et al., 2011; Van Stralen et al., 2011). Moreover, there is evidence that regular physical exercise may help reduce the risk of developing Alzheimer's disease and other types of neurocognitive disorders (Nation et al., 2011). Correspondingly, physical exercise is often a part of treatment programs for people with the disorders.

Behavioral interventions of a different kind have been applied to help improve specific symptoms displayed by Alzheimer's patients. The approaches typically focus on changing everyday patient behaviors that are stressful for the family, such as wandering at night, loss of bladder control, demands for attention, and inadequate personal care (Lancioni et al., 2011; Lindsey, 2011; Knight et al., 2006). The behavioral therapists use a combination of role-playing exercises, modeling, and practice to teach family members how and when to apply reinforcement in order to shape more positive behaviors.

Havakuk Levison/Reuters/Corbis

Much more than a pet
Bella, a smooth collie, is stroked by her owner, a man with Alzheimer's disease. Bella is one of many dogs trained to assist people with neurocognitive disorders in various tasks, including bringing them home if they get lost. The owner can command Bella to take him home, or his family can also summon the dog home with a special device.

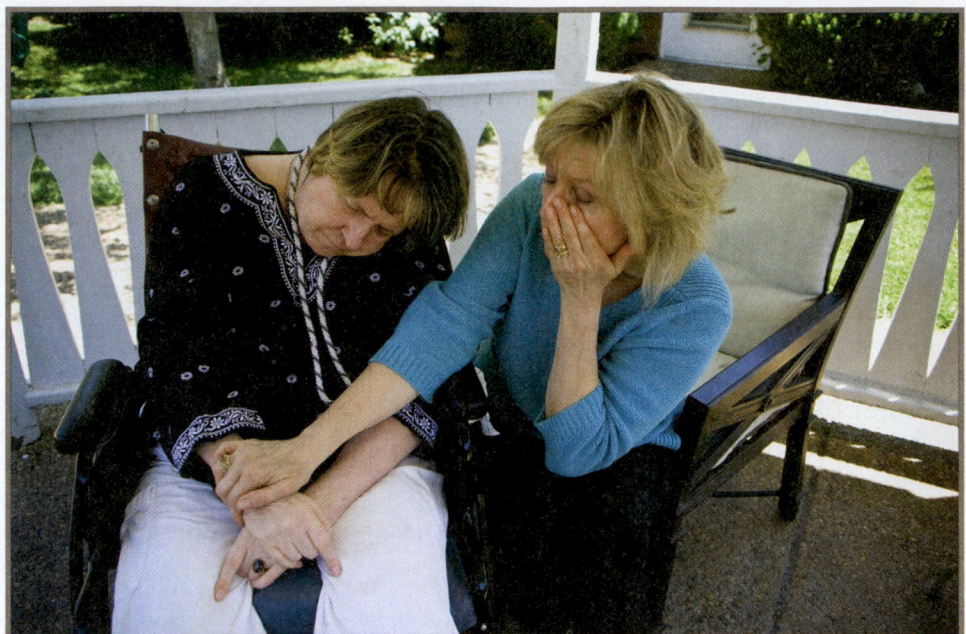

Jodi Cobb/National Geographic Society/Corbis

Toll on caregivers

A woman comforts her twin sister, who suffers from Alzheimer's disease. The psychological and physical burdens of caring for close relatives with neurocognitive disorders typically take a heavy toll on caregivers. Many develop, for example, feelings of depression, poorer immune system functioning, and declines in their physical and mental health.

SUPPORT FOR CAREGIVERS Caregiving can take a heavy toll on the close relatives of people with Alzheimer's disease and other types of neurocognitive disorders (McKenzie & Teri, 2011; Pinquart & Sörensen, 2011). Almost 90 percent of all people with Alzheimer's disease are cared for by their relatives (Alzheimer's Association, 2011, 2007). It is hard to take care of someone who is becoming increasingly lost, helpless, and medically ill (see Figure 18-4). And it is very painful to witness mental and physical decline in someone you love.

I have really struggled with the honesty issue. What do you say to someone who sits on her bed and says that she has never stayed out overnight without letting her parents know where she is? What do you say to someone who thinks she is a teacher and if she doesn't get home and into her classroom there will be a whole class of children left unattended? What do you say to someone who thinks she has no money to pay bills and will lose everything she owns if she doesn't get home to a job that you know she has been retired from for years? I couldn't find any reason for telling her over and over that she has a horrible terrible degenerating disease that was making her feel the way she does.

I found that she became less anxious if I just listened to what she was saying and feeling. Sometimes saying nothing was better than anything I could say. Telling her that I would take care of some of these things put her a bit more at ease. It may feel better for me to verbalize the facts, but what she needs is comfort and security—not the truth. The truth won't change anything.

(Shenk, 2001, p. 147)

BETWEEN THE LINES

Leading Causes of Death Among the Elderly

#1 Circulatory diseases (heart attacks and stroke) ‹‹

#2 Lung cancer ‹‹

#3 Alzheimer's disease ‹‹

#4 Renal failure ‹‹

#5 Chronic lung diseases ‹‹

One of the most frequent reasons for the institutionalization of Alzheimer's victims is that overwhelmed caregivers can no longer cope with the difficulties of keeping them at home (Di Rosa et al., 2011; Apostolova & Cummings, 2008). Many caregivers experience anger and depression, and their own physical and mental health often declines (Pinquart & Sorensen, 2011; Kantrowitz & Springen, 2007). Clinicians now recognize that one of the most important aspects of treating Alzheimer's disease and other types of neurocognitive disorders is to focus on the emotional needs of the caregivers, including their needs for regular time out, education about the disease, and psychotherapy

(McKenzie & Teri, 2011). Some clinicians also provide caregiver support groups (Ames et al., 2010).

SOCIOCULTURAL APPROACHES Sociocultural approaches have begun to play an important role in treatment (Ames et al., 2010; Brooks, 2005; Kalb, 2000) (see *MediaSpeak* on page 584). A number of *day-care facilities* for patients with neurocognitive disorders have been developed, providing treatment programs and activities for outpatients during the day and returning them to their homes and families at night. In addition, many *assisted-living facilities* have been built, in which individuals suffering from neurocognitive impairment live in cheerful apartments, receive needed supervision, and take part in various activities that bring more joy and stimulation to their lives. These apartments are typically designed to meet the special needs of the residents—providing more light, for example, or enclosing gardens with circular paths so the individuals can go for strolls alone without getting lost. Studies suggest that such facilities often help slow the cognitive decline of residents and enhance their enjoyment of life. In addition, a growing number of practical devices, such as tracking beacons worn on the wrists of Alzheimer's patients, have been developed to help locate patients who may wander off (Neergaard, 2007).

Given the progress now unfolding in the understanding and treatment of Alzheimer's disease and other types of neurocognitive disorders, researchers are looking forward to enormous advances in the coming years. The brain changes responsible for these disorders are tremendously complex, but most investigators believe that exciting breakthroughs are just over the horizon. Ironically, just when significant progress is being made and genuine reason for hope has emerged, the public seems to be losing patience. In a recent survey of more than 3,000 adults across the United States, only 48 percent of the respondents believed that at least "some" progress has been made toward curing Alzheimer's disease (Shriver, 2011). In contrast, 74 percent and 81 percent of them believed that at least some progress has been made toward curing cancer and heart disease, respectively.

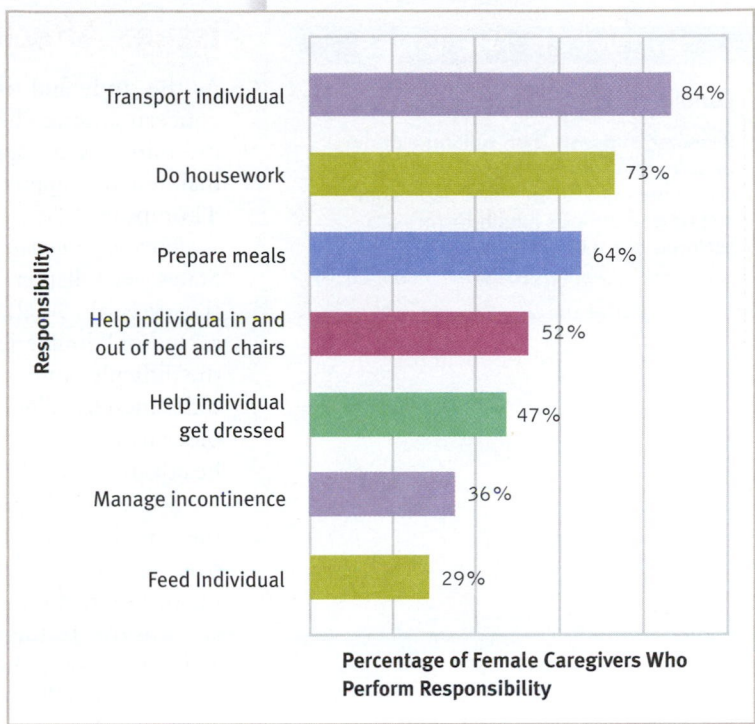

Percentage of Female Caregivers Who Perform Responsibility

Figure 18-4

What responsibilities must female caregivers of Alzheimer's sufferers perform? More than two of every three caregivers of Alzheimer's sufferers are women. Most of them provide transportation, do housework, and prepare meals, among other responsibilities. Some must also feed the Alzheimer's individual and manage episodes of incontinence (Shriver, 2011).

Day treatment
Two women go their separate ways in a New Jersey day-care facility for patients with Alzheimer's disease. The individuals return to their families each night.

Issues Affecting the Mental Health of the Elderly

As the study and treatment of elderly people have progressed, three issues have raised concern among clinicians: the problems faced by elderly members of racial and ethnic minority groups, the inadequacies of long-term care, and the need for a health-maintenance approach to medical care in an aging world (Gallagher-Thompson & Thompson, 1995).

First, *discrimination because of race and ethnicity* has long been a problem in the United States (see Chapter 3), and many people suffer as a result, particularly those who are old (Utsey et al., 2002). To be both old and a member of a minority group is considered a kind of "double jeopardy" by many observers. For older women in minority groups, the difficulties are sometimes termed "triple jeopardy," as many more older women than older men live alone, are widowed, and are poor. Clinicians must take into account their older patients' race, ethnicity, and gender as they try to diagnose and treat their mental health problems (Kwag et al., 2011; Knight et al., 2006) (see Figure 18-5).

Some elderly people in minority groups face language barriers that interfere with their medical and mental health care. Others may hold cultural beliefs that prevent them from seeking services. Moreover, many members of minority groups do not trust the majority establishment or do not know about medical and mental health services that are sensitive to their culture and their particular needs (Ayalon & Huyck, 2001). As a result, it is common for elderly members of racial and ethnic minority groups to rely largely on family members or friends for remedies and health care.

Today, 10 to 20 percent of elderly people live with their children or other relatives, usually because of increasing health problems (Etaugh, 2008). In the United States, this living arrangement is more common for elderly people from ethnic minority groups than for elderly white Americans. Elderly Asian Americans are most likely to live with their children, African Americans and Hispanic Americans are less likely to do so, and white Americans are least likely (Etaugh, 2008; Armstrong, 2001).

Second, many older people require care *long-term care,* a general term that may refer variously to the services offered outside the family in a partially supervised apartment, a senior housing complex for mildly impaired elderly persons, or a nursing home where skilled medical and nursing care are available around the clock (Samos et al., 2010). The quality of care in such residences varies widely.

At any given time in the United States, only about 5 percent of the elderly population actually live in nursing homes, but as many as 30 percent eventually wind up being placed in such facilities (Edelstein et al., 2008). Thus many older adults live in fear of being "put away." They fear having to move, losing independence, and living in a medical environment. Many also worry about the cost of long-term care facili-

Figure 18-5

Ethnicity and old age The elderly population is becoming racially and ethnically more diverse. In the United States today, almost 81 percent of all people over the age of 65 are white Americans. By 2050, only around 59 percent of the elderly will be in this group. (Adapted from Census Bureau, 2011; Pirkl, 2009; Hobbs, 1997).

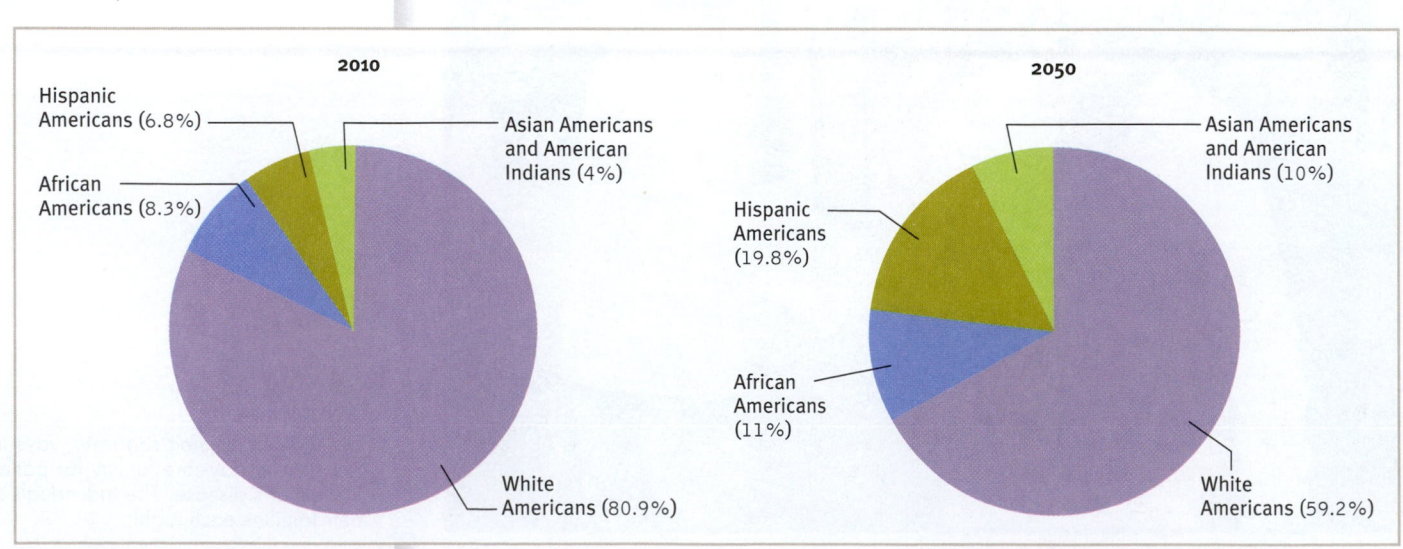

Social connections
Recognizing that elderly people continue to need social companionship and stimulation, many retirement homes now offer student visitation programs. The engaged looks on the faces of these residents during their interactions with students are a far cry from the lost and lonely faces often found in less stimulating nursing and retirement homes.

ties (Papastavrou et al., 2007). Around-the-clock nursing care is expensive, and nursing home costs continue to rise. The health insurance plans available today do not adequately cover the costs of long-term or permanent placement (Durso et al., 2010; Newcomer et al., 2001). Worry over these issues can greatly harm the mental health of older adults, perhaps leading to depression and anxiety as well as family conflict.

Finally, clinical scientists suggest that the current generation of young adults should take a *health-maintenance,* or *wellness promotion, approach* to their own aging process (Evans, 2010; Markle-Reid, Keller, & Browne, 2010; Pacala, 2010). In other words, they should do things that promote physical and mental health—avoid smoking, eat well-balanced and healthful meals, exercise regularly, engage in positive social relationships, and take advantage of psychoeducational, stress management, and other mental health

Every little bit helps
In line with research findings that all kinds of physical exercise help improve cognitive functioning, these elderly persons participate in an "arm chair" exercise program at the Dominican Association, a community center in Bradford, West Yorkshire, in the United Kingdom.

MediaSpeak

Focusing on Emotions

By Pam Belluck, *New York Times*

Margaret Nance was, to put it mildly, a difficult case. Agitated, combative, often reluctant to eat, she would hit staff members and fellow residents at nursing homes, several of which kicked her out. But when Beatitudes nursing home agreed to an urgent plea to accept her, all that changed.

Disregarding typical nursing-home rules, Beatitudes allowed Ms. Nance, 96 and afflicted with Alzheimer's, to sleep, be bathed and dine whenever she wanted, even at 2 A.M. She could eat anything, too, no matter how unhealthy, including unlimited chocolate.

And she was given a baby doll, a move that seemed so jarring that a supervisor initially objected until she saw how calm Ms. Nance became when she rocked, caressed and fed her "baby," often agreeing to eat herself after the doll "ate" several spoonfuls.

Dementia patients at Beatitudes are allowed practically anything that brings comfort, even an alcoholic "nip at night," said Tena Alonzo, director of research. "Whatever your vice is, we're your folks," she said. . . .

It is an unusual posture for a nursing home, but Beatitudes is actually following some of the latest science. Research suggests that creating positive emotional experiences for Alzheimer's patients diminishes distress and behavior problems. . . .

Other [studies] recommend making cosmetic changes to rooms and buildings to affect behavior or mood. A study in The Journal of the American Medical Association found that brightening lights in dementia facilities decreased depression, cognitive deterioration and loss of functional abilities. . . .

Stephane Audras/REA/Redux

Finding the right activity This patient picks tomatoes from a garden at Les Aurelias Home for Alzheimer's Victims in France. Consistent with the principles of emotion-focused treatment, the staff recognized the horticultural interests of this Alzheimer's patient and created a therapeutic garden where she could be active and experience pleasure and satisfaction.

Several German nursing homes have fake bus stops outside to keep patients from wandering; they wait for nonexistent buses until they forget where they wanted to go, or agree to come inside. . . .

New research suggests emotion persists after cognition deteriorates. In a University of Iowa study, people with . . . Alzheimer's-like amnesia viewed film clips evoking tears and

programs (Nation et al., 2011; Szabo et al, 2011). There is a growing belief that older adults will adapt more readily to changes and negative events if their physical and psychological health is good.

PUTTING IT... together

Clinicians Discover the Elderly

Early in the twentieth century, mental health professionals focused little on the elderly. But like the problems of children, those of aging persons have now caught the attention of researchers and clinicians. Current work is changing how we understand and treat the psychological problems of the elderly. No longer do clinicians simply accept depression or anxiety in elderly people as inevitable. No longer do they overlook the dangers of prescription drug misuse by the elderly. And no longer do they underestimate the dangers of delirium or the prevalence of neurocognitive disorders. Similarly,

sadness . . . or laughter and happiness. . . . Six minutes later, participants had trouble recalling the clips. But 30 minutes later, emotion evaluations showed they still felt sad or happy, often more than participants with normal memories. . . .

Justin Feinstein, the lead author, . . . said the results . . . suggest behavioral problems could stem from sadness or anxiety that patients cannot explain. . . . Similarly, happy emotions, even from socializing with patients, "could linger well beyond the memories that actually caused them."

One program for dementia patients cared for by relatives at home creates specific activities related to something they once enjoyed: arranging flowers, filling photo albums, snapping beans.

"A gentleman who loved fishing could still set up a tackle box, so we gave him a plastic tackle box" to set up every day, said the program's developer, Laura N. Gitlin, a sociologist . . . at Johns Hopkins University.

After four months, patients seemed happier and more active, and showed fewer behavior problems, especially repetitive questioning and shadowing, following caregivers around. . . .

Beatitudes, which takes about 30 moderate to severe dementia sufferers, introduced its program 12 years ago, focusing on individualized care. . . . Beatitudes eliminated anything potentially considered restraining, from deep-seated wheelchairs that hinder standing up to bedrails (some beds are lowered and protected by mats). It drastically reduced antipsychotics and medications considered primarily for "staff convenience," focusing on relieving pain, Ms. Alonzo said.

It encouraged keeping residents out of diapers if possible, taking them to the toilet to preserve feelings of independence. Some staff members resisted, Ms. Alonzo said, but now "like it because it saves time" and difficult diaper changes. . . .

For behavior management, Beatitudes plumbs residents' biographies, soothing one woman, Ruth Ann Clapper, by dabbing on White Shoulders perfume, which her biographical survey indicated she had worn before becoming ill. Food became available constantly, a canny move, Ms. Dougherty said, because people with dementia might be "too distracted" to eat during group mealtimes, and later "be acting out when what they actually need is food." Realizing that nutritious, low-salt, low-fat, doctor-recommended foods might actually discourage people from eating, Ms. Alonzo began carrying chocolate in her pocket. . .

Comforting food improves behavior and mood because it "sends messages they can still understand: 'it feels good, therefore I must be in a place where I'm loved,'" Ms. Dougherty said. . . .

Beatitudes also changed activity programming. Instead of group events like bingo, in which few residents could actually participate, staff members, including housekeepers, conduct one-on-one activities: block-building, coloring, simply conversing. . . .

These days, hundreds of Arizona physicians, medical students, and staff members at other nursing homes have received Beatitudes' training, and several Illinois nursing homes are adopting it. . . .

geropsychologists have become more aware of the importance of addressing the health care and financial needs of the elderly as keys to their psychological well-being.

As the elderly population lives longer and grows ever larger, the needs of people in this age group are becoming more visible. Thus the study and treatment of their psychological problems will probably continue at a rapid pace. Clinicians and public officials are not likely to underestimate their needs and importance again (Hinrichsen, 2010).

Particularly urgent is neurocognitive impairment and its devastating impact on the elderly and their families. As you have read throughout the chapter, Alzheimer's disease and other kinds of neurocognitive disorders can be tragic and debilitating problems that shatter the lives of both patients and caregivers. Indeed, they may rob patients of the essence of their identities. The complexity of the brain makes neurocognitive disorders difficult to understand, diagnose, and treat. However, researchers are now making important discoveries on a regular basis. To date, this research has been largely biological, but these disorders have such a powerful impact on patients and their families that psychological and sociocultural investigations are also starting to grow by leaps and bounds.

*"Am I the smart one and you're the pretty one
or is it the other way around?"*

In addition, society's interest in and focus on Alzheimer's disease and other types of neurocognitive disorders have reminded everyone about the importance of memory and related cognitive faculties. Memory is so central to our lives and to our self-concept that research in this area is of potential value to every person's well-being. Thus, it is important that such work continue to grow in the years to come.

Summing Up

- **DISORDERS OF LATER LIFE** The problems of elderly people are often linked to the losses and other stresses and changes that accompany advancing age. As many as 50 percent of the elderly would benefit from mental health services, yet fewer than 20 percent receive them. *Depression* is a common mental health problem among this age group. Older people may also suffer from *anxiety disorders*. Between 4 and 6 percent exhibit *alcohol use disorder* in any given year, and many others *misuse prescription drugs*. In addition, some elderly persons display psychotic disorders such as *schizophrenia* or *delusional disorder*. pp. 562–569

- **DISORDERS OF COGNITION** Older people are more likely than people of other age groups to experience *delirium*, a fast-developing disturbance marked by great difficulty focusing attention, staying oriented, concentrating, and following an orderly sequence of thought.

  Neurocognitive disorders, characterized by a significant decline in cognitive function, become increasingly common in older age groups. There are many types of neurocognitive disorders, the most common being *Alzheimer's disease*. Alzheimer's disease has been linked to an unusually high number of *senile plaques* and *neurofibrillary tangles* in the brain. According to a leading explanation of late-onset Alzheimer's disease, the most common kind of Alzheimer's disease, people who inherit *ApoE-4*, a particular form of the *apolipoprotein E (ApoE) gene*, are particularly vulnerable to the development of the disease. Apparently, the ApoE-4 gene form promotes the excessive formation of *beta-amyloid proteins*, helping to spur the formation of plaques and, in turn, the breakdown of the *tau protein*, the formation of numerous tangles, the death of many neurons, and, finally, Alzheimer's disease.

BETWEEN THE LINES

Varied Life Spans

79 years	Average human life span ‹‹
200 years	Life span of some marine clams ‹‹
150 years	Life span of some giant tortoises ‹‹
90 years	Life span of killer whales ‹‹
50 years	Life span of bats ‹‹
13 years	Life span of canaries ‹‹
2 years	Life span of mice ‹‹
24 days	Life span of worms ‹‹
17 days	Life span of male houseflies ‹‹

(Durso et al., 2010; CDC, 2011; Ash, 1999)

A number of other causes have also been proposed for this disease, including high levels of *zinc, lead,* or *other toxins; immune system problems;* and a *virus* of some kind.

Researchers are making significant strides at better assessing Alzheimer's disease and other types of neurocognitive disorders and even at identifying persons who will eventually develop these problems. Drug, cognitive, and behavioral therapies have been applied to Alzheimer's disease, with limited success. Addressing the needs of caregivers is now also recognized as a key part of treatment. In addition, sociocultural approaches such as day-care facilities are on the rise. The coming years are expected to see major treatment breakthroughs. *pp. 569–581*

- **KEY ISSUES** In studying and treating the problems of old age, clinicians have become concerned about three issues: *the problems of elderly members of racial and ethnic minority groups, inadequacies of long-term care,* and *the need for health maintenance by young adults. pp. 582–584*

PsychPortal

Visit **PsychPortal**
www.yourpsychportal.com
to access the e-book, videocases and other case materials and activities, and study aids, including flashcards, crossword puzzles, quizzes, FAQs, and research exercises.

BETWEEN THE LINES

Maximum Age

The maximum attainable age by human beings is thought to be 120 years (Durso et al., 2010). ‹‹

LAW, SOCIETY, AND THE MENTAL HEALTH PROFESSION

Dear Jodie:

There is a definite possibility that I will be killed in my attempt to get Reagan. It is for this very reason that I am writing you this letter now. As you well know by now, I love you very much. The past seven months I have left you dozens of poems, letters and messages in the faint hope you would develop an interest in me. . . . Jodie, I would abandon this idea of getting Reagan in a second if I could only win your heart and live out the rest of my life with you, whether it be in total obscurity or whatever. I will admit to you that the reason I'm going ahead with this attempt now is because I just cannot wait any longer to impress you. I've got to do something now to make you understand in no uncertain terms that I am doing all of this for your sake. By sacrificing my freedom and possibly my life I hope to change your mind about me. This letter is being written an hour before I leave for the Hilton Hotel. Jodie, I'm asking you please to look into your heart and at least give me the chance with this historical deed to gain your respect and love. I love you forever.

John Hinckley

John W. Hinckley Jr. wrote this letter to actress Jodie Foster in March 1981. Soon after writing it, he stood waiting, pistol ready, outside the Washington Hilton Hotel. Moments later, President Ronald Reagan came out of the hotel, and the popping of pistol fire was heard. As Secret Service men pushed Reagan into the limousine, a policeman and the president's press secretary fell to the pavement. The president had been shot, and by nightfall most of America had seen the face and heard the name of the disturbed young man from Colorado.

As you have seen throughout this book, the psychological dysfunctioning of an individual does not occur in isolation. It is influenced—sometimes caused—by societal and social factors, and it affects the lives of relatives, friends, and acquaintances. The case of John Hinckley demonstrates in powerful terms that individual dysfunction may, in some cases, also affect the well-being and rights of people the person does not know.

By the same token, clinical scientists and practitioners do not conduct their work in isolation. As they study and treat people with psychological problems, they are affecting and being affected by other institutions of society. We have seen, for example, how the government regulates the use of psychotropic medications, how clinicians helped carry out the government's policy of deinstitutionalization, and how clinicians have called the psychological ordeal of Iraq and Afghanistan combat veterans and, before them, Vietnam veterans, to the attention of society.

In short, like their clients, clinical professionals operate within a complex social system, and in fact, it is the system that defines and often regulates their professional responsibilities. Just as we must understand the social context in which abnormal behavior occurs in order to understand the behavior, so must we understand the context in which this behavior is studied and treated. This chapter will focus on the relationship between the mental health field and three major forces in society—the *legislative/judicial system,* the *business/economic* arena, and the world of *technology.*

Law and Mental Health

Two social institutions have a particularly strong impact on the mental health profession—the legislative and judicial systems. These institutions—collectively, the *legal field*—have long been responsible for protecting both the public good and the rights of individuals. Sometimes the relationship between the legal field and the mental health field has been friendly, and they have worked together to protect the rights and meet the needs of troubled individuals and of society at large. At other times they have clashed, and one field has imposed its will on the other.

This relationship has two distinct aspects. On the one hand, mental health professionals often play a role in the criminal justice system, as when they are called upon to help the courts assess the mental stability of people accused of crimes. They responded to this call in the Hinckley case, as you will see, and in thousands of other cases. This aspect of the relationship is sometimes termed *psychology in law;* that is, clinical practitioners and researchers operate within the legal system. On the other hand, there is another aspect to the relationship, called *law in psychology*. The legislative and judicial systems act upon the clinical field, regulating certain aspects of mental health care. The courts may, for example, force some individuals to enter treatment, even against their will. In addition, the law protects the rights of patients.

The intersections between the mental health field and the legal and judicial systems are collectively referred to as **forensic psychology** (Pinals & Mossman, 2012; Brendel & Glezer, 2010; Roesch, Zapf, & Hart, 2010). Forensic psychologists or psychiatrists (or related mental health professionals) may perform such varied activities as testifying in trials, researching the reliability of eyewitness testimony, or helping police profile the personality of a serial killer on the loose.

Psychology in Law: How Do Clinicians Influence the Criminal Justice System?

To arrive at just and appropriate punishments, the courts need to know whether defendants are *responsible* for the crimes they commit and *capable* of defending themselves in court. If not, it would be inappropriate to find individuals guilty or punish them in the usual manner. The courts have decided that in some instances people who suffer from severe *mental instability* may not be responsible for their actions or may not be able to defend themselves in court, and so should not be punished in the usual way. Although the courts make the final judgment as to mental instability, their decisions are guided to a large degree by the opinions of mental health professionals.

When people accused of crimes are judged to be mentally unstable, they are usually sent to a mental institution for treatment, a process called **criminal commitment**. Actually there are several forms of criminal commitment. In one, individuals are judged mentally unstable *at the time of their crimes* and so innocent of wrongdoing. They may plead **not guilty by reason of insanity (NGRI)** and bring mental health professionals into court to support their claim. When people are found not guilty on this basis, they are committed for treatment until they improve enough to be released.

In a second form of criminal commitment, individuals are judged mentally unstable *at the time of their trial* and so are considered unable to understand the trial procedures and defend themselves in court. They are committed for treatment until they are competent to stand trial. Once again, the testimony of mental health professionals helps determine the defendant's psychological functioning.

These judgments of mental instability have stirred many arguments. Some people consider the judgments to be loopholes in the legal system that allow criminals to escape proper punishment for wrongdoing. Others argue that a legal system simply cannot be just unless it allows for extenuating circumstances, such as mental instability. The practice of criminal commitment differs from country to country. In this chapter you will see primarily how it operates in the United States. Although the specific principles and

•**forensic psychology**•The branch of psychology concerned with intersections between psychological practice and research and the judicial system. Also related to the field of *forensic psychiatry*.

•**criminal commitment**•A legal process by which people accused of a crime are instead judged mentally unstable and sent to a mental health facility for treatment.

•**not guilty by reason of insanity (NGRI)**• A verdict stating that defendants are not guilty of committing a crime because they were insane at the time of the crime.

•**M'Naghten test**•A widely used legal test for insanity that holds people to be insane at the time they committed a crime if, because of a mental disorder, they did not know the nature of the act or did not know right from wrong. Also known as *M'Naghten rule*.

•**irresistible impulse test**•A legal test for insanity that holds people to be insane at the time they committed a crime if they were driven to do so by an uncontrollable "fit of passion."

•**Durham test**•A legal test for insanity that holds people to be insane at the time they committed a crime if their act was the result of a mental disorder or defect.

procedures of each country may differ, most countries grapple with the same issues, concerns, and decisions that you will be reading about here.

Criminal Commitment and Insanity During Commission of a Crime

Consider once again the case of John Hinckley. Was he insane at the time he shot the president? If insane, should he be held responsible for his actions? On June 21, 1982, 15 months after he shot four men in the nation's capital, a jury pronounced Hinckley not guilty by reason of insanity. Hinckley thus joined Richard Lawrence, a house painter who shot at Andrew Jackson in 1835, and John Schrank, a saloonkeeper who shot former president Teddy Roosevelt in 1912, as a would-be assassin who was found not guilty by reason of insanity.

Although most Americans were shocked by the Hinckley verdict, those familiar with the insanity defense were not so surprised. In this case, as in other federal court cases at that time, the prosecution had the burden of proving that the defendant was sane beyond a reasonable doubt. Many state courts placed a similar responsibility on the prosecution. To present a clear-cut demonstration of sanity can be difficult, especially when the defendant has exhibited bizarre behavior in other areas of life. In fact, a few years later, Congress passed a law making it the defense's burden in federal cases to prove that defendants are insane, rather than the prosecution's burden to prove them sane. Around 70 percent of state legislatures have since followed suit.

Which burden of proof is more appropriate—that defense attorneys must prove defendants "insane" or that prosecutors must prove defendants "not insane"?

It is important to recognize that "insanity" is a *legal* term (Simon & Gold, 2010). That is, the definition of "insanity" used in criminal cases was written by legislators, not by clinicians. Defendants may have mental disorders but not necessarily qualify for a legal definition of insanity. Modern Western definitions of insanity can be traced to the murder case of Daniel M'Naghten in England in 1843. M'Naghten shot and killed Edward Drummond, the secretary to British Prime Minister Robert Peel, while trying to shoot Peel. Because of M'Naghten's apparent delusions of persecution, the jury found him to be not guilty by reason of insanity. The public was outraged by this decision, and their angry outcry forced the British law lords to define the insanity defense more clearly. This legal definition, known as the **M'Naghten test,** or **M'Naghten rule,** stated that experiencing a mental disorder at the time of a crime does not by itself mean that the person was insane; the defendant also had to be *unable to know right from wrong.* The state and federal courts in the United States adopted this test as well.

In the late nineteenth century some state and federal courts in the United States, dissatisfied with the M'Naghten rule, adopted a different test—the **irresistible impulse test.** This test, which had first been used in Ohio in 1834, emphasized the inability to control one's actions. A person who committed a crime during an uncontrollable "fit of passion" was considered insane and not guilty under this test.

For years state and federal courts chose between the M'Naghten test and the irresistible impulse test to determine the sanity of criminal defendants. For a while a third test, called the **Durham test,** also became popular, but it was soon replaced in most courts. This test, based on a decision handed down by the Supreme Court in 1954 in the case of *Durham v. United States,* stated simply that people are not criminally responsible if their "unlawful act was the product of mental disease or mental defect." This test was meant to offer more flexibility in court decisions, but it proved too flexible. Insanity defenses could point to such problems as alcoholism or other forms of substance abuse and conceivably even headaches or ulcers, which were listed as psychophysiological disorders in DSM-I.

AP/Wide World Photos

Would-be assassin
Few courtroom decisions have spurred as much debate or legislative action as the jury's verdict that John Hinckley, having been captured in the act of shooting President Ronald Reagan, was not guilty by reason of insanity.

•American Law Institute test• A legal test for insanity that holds people to be insane at the time they committed a crime if, because of a mental disorder, they did not know right from wrong or could not resist an uncontrollable impulse to act.

In 1955 the American Law Institute (ALI) formulated a test that combined aspects of the M'Naghten, irresistible impulse, and Durham tests. The **American Law Institute test** held that people are not criminally responsible if at the time of a crime they had a mental disorder or defect that prevented them from knowing right from wrong *or* from being able to control themselves and to follow the law. For a time the new test became the most widely accepted legal test of insanity. After the Hinckley verdict, however, there was a public uproar over the "liberal" ALI guidelines, and people called for tougher standards.

Partly in response to this uproar, the American Psychiatric Association recommended in 1983 that people should be found not guilty by reason of insanity *only* if they did not know right from wrong at the time of the crime; an inability to control themselves and to follow the law should no longer be sufficient grounds for a judgment of insanity. In short, the association was calling for a return to the M'Naghten test. This test now is used in all cases tried in federal courts and in about half of the state courts. The more liberal ALI standard is still used in the remaining state courts, except in Idaho, Kansas, Montana, and Utah, which have, more or less, done away with the insanity plea altogether. Research has not found, however, that the stricter M'Naghten definition actually reduces the likelihood of verdicts of not guilty by reason of insanity (Ogloff et al., 1992).

People suffering from severe mental disorders in which confusion is a major feature may not be able to tell right from wrong or to control their behavior. It is therefore not surprising that approximately two-thirds of defendants who are acquitted of a crime by reason of insanity qualify for a diagnosis of schizophrenia (Novak et al., 2007; Steadman et al., 1993). The vast majority of these acquitted defendants have a history of past hospitalization, arrest, or both. About half who successfully plead insanity are white, and 86 percent are male. Their mean age is 32 years. The crimes for which defendants are found not guilty by reason of insanity vary greatly. However, approximately 65 percent are violent crimes of some sort (APA, 2003; Steadman et al., 1993). Close to 15 percent of those acquitted are accused specifically of murder (see Figure 19-1 and *PsychWatch* on the next page).

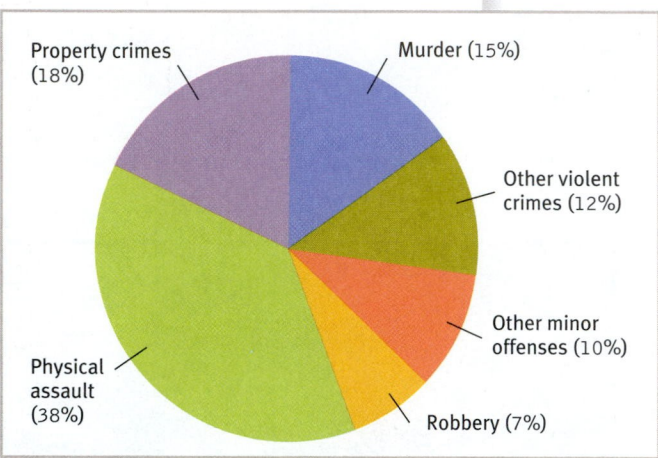

Figure 19-1
Crimes for which persons are found not guilty by reason of insanity (NGRI)
A review of NGRI verdicts in eight states revealed that most people who were acquitted on this basis had been charged with a crime of violence. (Based on APA, 2003; Steadman et al., 1993; Callahan et al., 1991.)

Pie chart labels: Property crimes (18%); Murder (15%); Other violent crimes (12%); Other minor offenses (10%); Robbery (7%); Physical assault (38%)

WHAT CONCERNS ARE RAISED BY THE INSANITY DEFENSE? Despite the changes in the insanity tests, criticism of the insanity defense continues (Slovenko, 2011, 2004, 2002; Sales & Shuman, 2005). One concern is the fundamental difference between the law and the science of human behavior (Pouncey & Lukens, 2010; Dennison, 2007). The law assumes that individuals have free will and are generally responsible for their actions. Several models of human behavior, in contrast, assume that physical or psychological forces act to determine the individual's behavior. Inevitably, then, legal definitions of insanity and responsibility will differ from those suggested by clinical research.

A second criticism points to the uncertainty of scientific knowledge about abnormal behavior. During a typical insanity defense trial, the testimony of defense clinicians conflicts with that of clinicians hired by the prosecution, and so the jury must weigh the claims of "experts" who disagree in their assessments (Sadoff, 2011; Schopp et al., 2010). Some people see this lack of professional agreement as evidence that clinical knowledge in some areas may be too incomplete to be allowed to influence important legal decisions. Others counter that the field has made great strides—for example, developing several psychological scales to help clinicians discriminate more consistently between the sane and insane as defined by the M'Naghten standard (Pinals & Mossman, 2012; Rogers, 2008).

Even with helpful scales in hand, however, clinicians making judgments of legal insanity face a problem that is difficult to overcome: they must evaluate a defendant's state of mind during an event that occurred weeks, months, or years earlier. Because mental states can and do change over time and across situations, clinicians can never be entirely certain that their assessments of mental instability at the time of the crime are accurate.

Famous Insanity Defense Cases

1977 In Michigan, Francine Hughes poured gasoline around the bed where her husband, Mickey, lay in a drunken stupor. Then she lit a match and set him on fire. At her trial she explained that he had beaten her repeatedly for 14 years and had threatened to kill her if she tried to leave him. The jury found her not guilty by reason of temporary insanity, making her into a symbol for many abused women across the nation.

1978 David "Son of Sam" Berkowitz, a serial killer in New York City, explained that a barking dog had sent him demonic messages to kill. Although two psychiatrists assessed him as psychotic, he was found guilty of his crimes. Long after his trial, he said that he had actually made up the delusions.

1979 Kenneth Bianchi, one of the pair known as the Hillside Strangler, entered a plea of not guilty by reason of insanity but was found guilty along with his cousin of sexually assaulting and murdering women in the Los Angeles area in late 1977 and early 1978. He claimed that he had multiple personality disorder.

1980 In December, Mark David Chapman murdered John Lennon. Chapman later explained that he had killed the rock music legend because he believed Lennon to be a "sell-out." Pleading not guilty by reason of insanity, he also described hearing the voice of God, considered himself his generation's "catcher in the rye" (from the J. D. Salinger novel), and compared himself to Moses. Chapman was convicted of murder.

1981 In an attempt to prove his love for actress Jodie Foster, John Hinckley Jr. tried to assassinate President Ronald Reagan. Hinckley was found not guilty by reason of insanity and was committed to St. Elizabeth's Hospital for the criminally insane in Washington, DC, where he remains today.

1992 Jeffrey Dahmer, a 31-year-old mass murderer in Milwaukee, was tried for the killings of 15 young men. Dahmer apparently drugged some of his victims, performed crude lobotomies on them, and dismembered their bodies and stored their parts to be eaten. Despite a plea of not guilty by reason of insanity, the jury found him guilty as charged. He was beaten to death by another inmate in 1995.

1994 On June 23, 1993, 24-year-old Lorena Bobbitt cut off her husband's penis with a 12-inch kitchen knife while he slept. During her trial, defense attorneys argued that after years of abuse by John Bobbitt, his wife suffered a brief psychotic episode and was seized by an "irresistible impulse" to cut off his penis after he came home drunk and raped her. In 1994, the jury found her not guilty by reason of temporary insanity. She was committed to a state mental hospital and released a few months later.

2003 For three weeks in October 2002, John Allen Muhammad and Lee Boyd Malvo went on a sniping spree in the Washington, DC, area, shooting 10 people dead and wounding 3 others. Attorneys for Malvo, a teenager, argued that he had acted under the influence of the middle-aged Muhammad and that he should be found not guilty of the crimes by reason of insanity. The jury, however, found Malvo guilty of capital murder and sentenced him to life in prison.

2006 On June 20, 2001, Andrea Yates, a 36-year-old woman, drowned each of her five children in the bathtub. Yates had a history of *postpartum depression* and *postpartum psychosis:* she believed that she was the devil, that she had failed to be a good mother, and that her children were not developing correctly. Given such problems and history, she pleaded not guilty by reason of insanity during her trial. In 2002, however, a Texas jury found her guilty and sentenced her to life in prison. This verdict was later overturned, and in 2006, after a new trial, Yates was found not guilty by reason of insanity and sent to a mental health facility for treatment.

Pool photo by Getty Images

Two verdicts Andrea Yates is led into a district court in Texas. In a 2002 trial Yates was found guilty of murder and sentenced to life in prison. In a 2006 retrial, however, she was judged not guilty by reason of insanity and sent to a mental institution for treatment.

Executing the mentally ill

One of the most controversial executions in the United States was that of Charles Singleton, a man who killed a store clerk in Arkansas, was sentenced to death in 1979, and then developed schizophrenia at some point after the trial. Inasmuch as the United States does not allow executions if persons cannot understand why they are being executed, state officials wanted Singleton to take medications to clear up his psychosis. After years of legal appeals, the U.S. Supreme Court ruled in 2003 that Singleton was, by then, taking medications voluntarily, and Singleton was executed by lethal injection in 2004.

•**guilty but mentally ill**•A verdict stating that defendants are guilty of committing a crime but are also suffering from a mental illness that should be treated during their imprisonment.

Perhaps the most often heard criticism of the insanity defense is that it allows dangerous criminals to escape punishment. Granted, some people who successfully plead insanity are released from treatment facilities just months after their acquittal. Yet the number of such cases is quite small (MHA, 2007, 2004; Steadman et al., 1993). According to surveys, the public dramatically overestimates the percentage of defendants who plead insanity, guessing it to be 30 to 40 percent, when in fact it is less than 1 percent. Moreover, only a minority of these persons fake or exaggerate their psychological symptoms (Resnick & Harris, 2002), and only 26 percent of defendants who plead insanity are actually found not guilty on this basis (APA, 2003; Callahan et al., 1991). In the end, less than 1 of every 400 defendants in the United States is found not guilty by reason of insanity. It is also worth noting that in 80 percent of those cases in which defendants are acquitted by reason of insanity, the prosecution has agreed to the appropriateness of the plea.

During most of U.S. history, a successful insanity plea amounted to the equivalent of a long-term prison sentence. In fact, treatment in a mental hospital often resulted in a longer period of confinement than a verdict of guilty would have brought (Nwokike, 2005; Perlin, 2000). Because hospitalization resulted in little, if any, improvement, clinicians were reluctant to predict that the offenders would not repeat their crimes. Moreover, tragic cases would occasionally call into question clinicians' ability to make such judgments and to predict dangerousness (Hooper et al., 2005). In Idaho, for example, a young man raped two women and was found not guilty by reason of insanity. He was released after less than a year of treatment, shot a nurse, and this time was convicted of assault with intent to kill. The uproar over this 1981 case led the Idaho state legislature to abolish the insanity plea.

Today, however, offenders are being released from mental hospitals earlier and earlier. This trend is the result of the increasing effectiveness of drug therapy and other treatments in institutions, the growing reaction against extended institutionalization, and a

? After patients have been criminally committed to institutions, why might clinicians be hesitant to later declare them unlikely to commit the same crime again?

greater emphasis on patients' rights (Slovenko, 2011, 2009, 2004; Salekin & Rogers, 2001). In 1992, in the case of *Foucha v. Louisiana,* the U.S. Supreme Court clarified that the *only* acceptable basis for determining the release of hospitalized offenders is whether or not they are still "insane"; they cannot be kept indefinitely in mental hospitals solely because they are dangerous. Some states are able to maintain control over offenders even after their release from hospitals (Swartz et al., 2002). The states may insist on community treatment, monitor the patients closely, and rehospitalize them if necessary.

WHAT OTHER VERDICTS ARE AVAILABLE? Over the past few decades, 14 states have added another verdict option—**guilty but mentally ill.** Defendants who receive this verdict are found to have had a mental illness at the time of their crime, but the illness was not fully related to or responsible for the crime. The guilty-but-mentally-ill option enables jurors to convict a person they view as dangerous while also suggesting that the individual receive needed treatment. Defendants found to be guilty but mentally ill are given a prison term with the added recommendation that they also undergo treatment if necessary.

After initial enthusiasm for this verdict option, legal and clinical theorists have increasingly found it unsatisfactory. According to research, it has not reduced the number of not-guilty-by-reason-of-insanity verdicts. Moreover, it often confuses jurors in both real and mock trials. And, perhaps most important, critics point out that appropriate mental health care is supposed to be available to all prisoners anyway, regardless of the verdict. They argue that the guilty-but-mentally-ill option differs from a guilty verdict in name only (Slovenko, 2011, 2009, 2004, 2002).

Some states allow still another kind of defense, *guilty with diminished capacity*. Here a defendant's mental dysfunctioning is viewed as an extenuating circumstance that the court should take into consideration in determining the precise crime of which he or she is guilty (Benitez & Chamberlain, 2008; Leong, 2000). The defense lawyer argues that because of mental dysfunctioning, the defendant could not have *intended* to commit a particular crime. The person can then be found guilty of a lesser crime—of manslaughter (unlawful killing without intent), say, instead of murder in the first degree (planned murder). The famous case of Dan White, who shot and killed Mayor George Moscone and City Supervisor Harvey Milk of San Francisco in 1978, illustrates the use of this verdict.

On the morning of November 27, 1978, Dan White loaded his .38 caliber revolver. White had recently resigned his position as a San Francisco supervisor because of family and financial pressures. Now, after a change of heart, he wanted his job back. When he asked Mayor George Moscone to reappoint him, however, the mayor refused. Supervisor Harvey Milk was among those who had urged Moscone to keep White out, for Milk was America's first openly gay politician, and Dan White had been an outspoken opponent of measures supporting gay rights.

White avoided the metal detector at City Hall's main entrance [and] went straight to the mayor's office. . . . White pulled out his gun and . . . from only inches away, fired twice into Moscone's head.

White then reloaded his gun, ran down the hall, and spotted Harvey Milk. . . . Once again White from point-blank range fired two more bullets into his victim's head. Shortly afterward he turned himself in to the police. Several months later the jury rendered its verdict: Dan White was not guilty of murder, only voluntary manslaughter. . . .

Defense attorney Douglas Schmidt argued that a patriotic, civic-minded man like Dan White—high school athlete, decorated war veteran, former fireman, policeman, and city supervisor—could not possibly have committed such an act unless something had snapped inside him. The brutal nature of the two final shots to each man's head only proved that White had lost his wits. White was not fully responsible for his actions because he suffered from "diminished capacity." Although White killed Mayor George Moscone and Supervisor Harvey Milk, he had not planned his actions. On the day of the shootings, White was mentally incapable of planning to kill, or even of wanting to do such a thing.

Well known in forensic psychiatry circles, Martin Blinder, professor of law and psychiatry at the University of California's Hastings Law School in San Francisco, brought a good measure of academic prestige to White's defense. White had been, Blinder explained to the jury, "gorging himself on junk food: Twinkies, Coca-Cola. . . . The more he consumed, the worse he'd feel and he'd respond to his ever-growing depression by consuming ever more junk food." Schmidt later asked Blinder if he could elaborate on this. "Perhaps if it were not for the ingestion of this junk food," Blinder responded, "I would suspect that these homicides would not have taken place." From that moment on, Blinder became known as the author of the Twinkie defense. . . .

Dan White was convicted only of voluntary manslaughter, and was sentenced to seven years, eight months. (He was released on parole January 6, 1984.) Psychiatric testimony convinced the jury that White did not wish to kill George Moscone or Harvey Milk.

The angry crowd that responded to the verdict by marching, shouting, trashing City Hall, and burning police cars was in good part homosexual. Gay supervisor Harvey Milk had worked well for their cause, and his loss was a serious setback for human rights in San Francisco. Yet it was not only members of the gay community who were appalled at the outcome. Most San Franciscans shared their feelings of outrage.

(Coleman, 1984, pp. 65–70)

Justice served?
Mass protests took place in San Francisco after Dan White was convicted of voluntary manslaughter rather than premeditated murder in the killings of Mayor George Moscone and Supervisor Harvey Milk, one of the nation's leading gay activists. For many, the 1979 verdict highlighted the serious pitfalls of the "diminished capacity" defense.

Because of possible miscarriages of justice, many legal experts have argued against the "diminished capacity" defense. And, indeed, a number of states have eliminated it, including California shortly after the Dan White verdict (Slovenko, 2011, 2009, 2002, 1992; Gado, 2008).

WHAT ARE SEX-OFFENDER STATUTES? Since 1937, when Michigan passed the first "sexual psychopath" law, a number of states have placed sex offenders in a special legal category (Ewing, 2011; Miller, 2010; Zonana et al., 2004). These states believe that some of the individuals who are repeatedly found guilty of sex crimes have a mental disorder, and so the states categorize them as *mentally disordered sex offenders.*

People classified in this way are convicted of a criminal offense and are thus judged to be responsible for their actions. Nevertheless, mentally disordered sex offenders are sent to a mental health facility instead of a prison. In part, such laws reflect a belief held by many legislators that such sex offenders are psychologically disturbed. On a practical level, the laws help protect sex offenders from the physical abuse that they often receive in prison society.

Over the past two decades, however, most states have been changing or abolishing their mentally disordered sex offender laws, and at this point only a handful still have them (Ewing, 2011; Miller, 2010). There are several reasons for this trend. First, states typically have found the laws difficult to apply. Some of the laws, for example, require that the offender be found "sexually dangerous beyond a reasonable doubt"—a judgment that is often beyond the reach of the clinical field's expertise. Similarly, the state laws may require that in order to be classified as mentally disordered sex offenders, individuals must be good candidates for treatment, another judgment that is difficult for clinicians to make, especially for this population (Marshall et al., 2011; Bradford et al., 2010). Third, evidence exists that racial bias often affects the use of the mentally disordered sex offender classification. From a defendant's perspective, this classification is considered an attractive alternative to imprisonment—an alternative available to white Americans much more often than to members of racial minority groups. White Americans are twice as likely to be granted mentally disordered sex offender status as African Americans or Hispanic Americans who have been convicted of similar crimes.

But perhaps the primary reason that mentally disordered sex offender laws have lost favor is that state legislatures and courts are now less concerned than they used to be about the rights and needs of sex offenders, given the growing number of sex crimes

•**mental incompetence**•A state of mental instability that leaves defendants unable to understand the legal charges and proceedings they are facing and unable to prepare an adequate defense with their attorney.

taking place across the country (Laws & Ward, 2011), particularly ones in which children are victims. In fact, in response to public outrage over the high number of sex crimes, 21 states and the federal government have instead passed *sexually violent predator* laws (or *sexually dangerous persons* laws). These new laws call for certain sex offenders who have been convicted of sex crimes and have served their sentence in prison to be removed from prison before their release and committed involuntarily to a mental hospital for treatment if a court judges them likely to engage in further "predatory acts of sexual violence" as a result of "mental abnormality" or "personality disorder" (Ewing, 2011; Miller, 2010). That is, in contrast to the mentally disordered sex offender laws, which call for sex offenders to receive treatment *instead* of imprisonment, the sexually violent predator laws require certain sex offenders to receive imprisonment and then, *in addition,* be committed for a period of involuntary treatment. The constitutionality of the sexually violent predator laws was upheld by the Supreme Court in the 1997 case of *Kansas v. Hendricks* by a 5-to-4 margin. In California, one of the states with such a law, around 1 to 2 percent of convicted sex offenders have been committed to mental health treatment programs after serving their prison sentences (Miller, 2010; Sreenivasan et al., 2003).

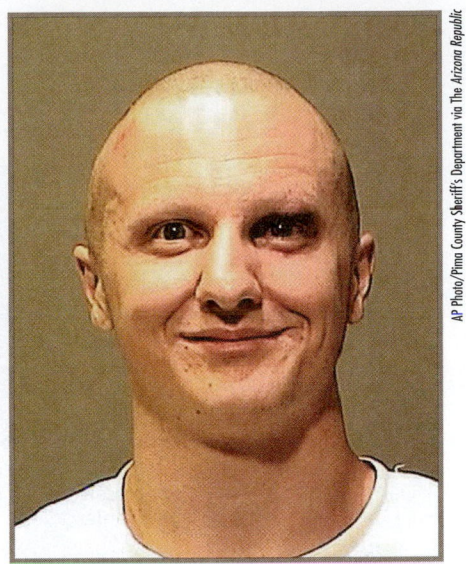

Incompetent to stand trial
Jared Loughner, shown here in a police photo taken on the day of his shooting rampage in 2011 in Tucson, Arizona. For 18 months following his crime, Loughner was ruled incompetent to stand trial.

Criminal Commitment and Incompetence to Stand Trial

Regardless of their state of mind at the time of a crime, defendants may be judged to be **mentally incompetent** to stand trial. The competence requirement is meant to ensure that defendants understand the charges they are facing and can work with their lawyers to prepare and conduct an adequate defense (Schopp et al., 2010; Zapf & Roesch, 2009). This minimum standard of competence was specified by the Supreme Court in the case of *Dusky v. United States* (1960).

The issue of competence is most often raised by the defendant's attorney, although prosecutors, arresting police officers, and even the judge may raise it as well. They prefer to err on the side of caution because some convictions have been reversed on appeal when a defendant's competence was not established at the beginning. When the issue of competence is raised, the judge orders a psychological evaluation, usually on an inpatient basis (see Table 19-1). As many as 60,000 competency evaluations are conducted in the United States each year (Roesch et al., 2010, 1999; Zapf & Roesch, 2009, 2006). Approximately 20 percent of defendants who receive such an evaluation are in fact found to be incompetent to stand trial. If the court decides that the defendant is incompetent, the individual is typically assigned to a mental health facility until competent to stand trial.

A recent, famous case of incompetence to stand trial is that of Jared Lee Loughner. On January 8, 2011, Loughner went to a political gathering at a shopping center in Tucson, Arizona, and opened fire on 20 persons. Six people were killed and 14 injured, including U.S. Representative Gabrielle Giffords. Giffords, the apparent target of the attack, survived, although she was shot in the head. After Loughner underwent five weeks of psychiatric assessment, a judge ruled that he was incompetent to stand trial. Indeed, it was not until 18 months later, after extended treatment with antipsychotic drugs, that Loughner was ruled competent to stand trial. In November 2012, he pleaded guilty to murder and was sentenced to life imprisonment.

Sometimes, rulings of incompetence can continue even longer. In another famous case, a man named Russell Weston entered the United States Capitol building in 1998 apparently seeking out then–House Majority Whip Tom DeLay, among others. Weston proceeded to shoot two police officers to death. In 1999, the defendant, who had stopped taking

table 19-1

Multicultural Issues: Race and Forensic Psychology

- Psychologically disturbed people from racial minority groups are more likely than disturbed white Americans to be sent to prison, as opposed to mental health facilities.

- Among defendants evaluated for competence to stand trial, those from racial minority groups are more likely than white American defendants to be referred for *inpatient* evaluations.

- Among defendants evaluated for competence to stand trial, those from racial minority groups are more likely than white Americans to have the evaluation occur in a *strict-security inpatient* setting, rather than in the noncorrectional mental health system.

- When nonwhite and white defendants are evaluated for competence to stand trial, the defendants from racial minority groups are more likely to be found incompetent to stand trial.

- In New York State, 42 percent of all individuals ordered into *involuntary outpatient commitment* are African American, 34 percent are white American, and 21 percent are Hispanic American. In contrast, these three groups comprise, respectively, 17 percent, 61 percent, and 16 percent of New York's general population.

Source: Haroules, 2007; Pinals et al., 2004; Grekin et al., 1994; Arvanites, 1989.

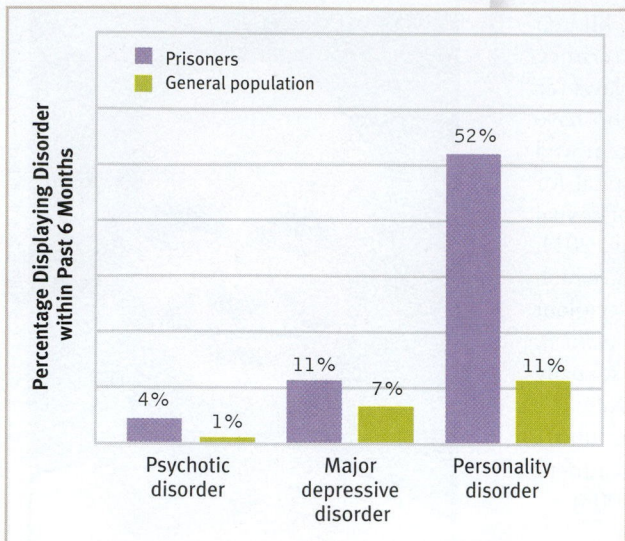

Figure 19-2

Prison and mental health According to studies conducted in several Western countries, psychological disorders are much more prevalent in prison populations than in the general population. For example, schizophrenia is 4 times more common and personality disorders 5 times more common among prisoners than among nonprisoners. In fact, antisocial personality disorder is 10 times more common. (Based on Butler et al., 2006; Fazel & Danesh, 2002.)

•**civil commitment**•A legal process by which an individual can be forced to undergo mental health treatment.

medications for his severe psychosis, was found incompetent to stand trial and sent to a psychiatric institution. In 2001, a judge ruled that he should be forced to take medications again, but even with such drugs Weston continued to have severe symptoms and to this day remains incompetent to stand trial for the 1998 shootings.

Many more cases of criminal commitment result from decisions of mental incompetence than from verdicts of not guilty by reason of insanity (Roesch et al., 2010; Zapf & Roesch, 2006). However, the majority of criminals currently institutionalized for psychological treatment in the United States are not from either of these two groups. Rather, they are convicted inmates whose psychological problems have led prison officials to decide they need treatment—either in mental health units within the prison or in mental hospitals (Metzner & Dvoskin, 2010; Senior et al., 2007) (see Figure 19-2).

It is possible that an innocent defendant, ruled incompetent to stand trial, could spend years in a mental health facility with no opportunity to disprove the criminal accusations. Some defendants have, in fact, served longer "sentences" in mental health facilities awaiting a ruling of competence than they would have served in prison had they been convicted. Such a possibility was reduced when the Supreme Court ruled, in the case of *Jackson v. Indiana* (1972), that an incompetent defendant cannot be indefinitely committed. After a reasonable amount of time, he or she should either be found competent and tried, set free, or transferred to a mental health facility under *civil* commitment procedures.

Until the early 1970s, most states required that mentally incompetent defendants be committed to maximum-security institutions for the "criminally insane." Under current law, however, the courts have greater flexibility. In fact, when the charges are relatively minor, such defendants are often treated on an outpatient basis, an arrangement often called *jail diversion* because the disturbed individual is "diverted" from jail to the community for mental health care (Morrissey & Cuddeback, 2008).

Law in Psychology: How Do the Legislative and Judicial Systems Influence Mental Health Care?

Just as clinical science and practice have influenced the legal system, so the legal system has had a major impact on clinical practice. First, courts and legislatures have developed the process of **civil commitment,** which allows certain people to be forced into mental health treatment. Although many people who show signs of mental disturbance seek treatment voluntarily, a large number are not aware of their problems or are simply not interested in undergoing therapy. For such individuals, civil commitment guidelines may be put into action.

Second, the legal system, on behalf of the state, has taken on the responsibility for protecting patients' rights during treatment. This protection extends not only to patients who have been involuntarily committed but also to those who seek treatment voluntarily, even on an outpatient basis.

Civil Commitment
Every year in the United States large numbers of people with mental disorders are involuntarily committed to treatment. Typically they are committed to *mental institutions,* but 44 states also have some form of *outpatient* civil commitment laws that allow patients to be forced into community treatment programs (Dawson, 2010). Civil commitments have long caused controversy and debate. In some ways the law provides greater protection for people suspected of being criminals than for people suspected of being psychotic (Strachan, 2008; Burton, 1990).

WHY COMMIT? Generally our legal system permits involuntary commitment of individuals when they are considered to be *in need of treatment* and *dangerous to themselves or others.* People may be dangerous to themselves if they are suicidal or if they act recklessly (for example, drinking a drain cleaner to prove that they are immune to its chemicals).

They may be dangerous to others if they seek to harm them (see *PsychWatch* below) or if they unintentionally place others at risk. The state's authority to commit disturbed individuals rests on its duties to protect the interests of the individual and of society: the principles of *parens patriae* and *police power*. Under *parens patriae* ("parent of the country"), the state can make decisions that protect patients from self-harm, including a decision of involuntary hospitalization. Conversely, *police power* allows the state to take steps to protect society from a person who is dangerous.

> **How do you think a physical attack by a client might affect a clinician's subsequent professional behavior?**

WHAT ARE THE PROCEDURES FOR CIVIL COMMITMENT? Civil commitment laws vary from state to state. Some basic procedures, however, are common to most of these laws. Often family members begin commitment proceedings. In response to a son's psychotic behavior and repeated assaults on other people, for example, his parents may try to persuade him to seek admission to a mental institution. If the son refuses, the parents may go to court and seek an involuntary commitment order. If the son is a minor, the process is simple. The Supreme Court, in the case of *Parham v. J. R.* (1979), has ruled that a hearing is

---

PsychWatch

Violence Against Therapists

On a winter night in 2008, a 39-year-old man named David Tarloff went to the New York City office of psychiatrist Kent Shinbach with robbery on his mind. Tarloff had a long history of severe mental disorders, and apparently Dr. Shinbach had played a role in one of his diagnoses and institutionalizations back in 1991. Upon his arrival, however, Tarloff first came upon psychologist Dr. Kathryn Faughey, whose office was near Dr. Shinbach's. In the course of events, Tarloff slashed Dr. Faughey to death with a meat cleaver and seriously wounded Dr. Shinbach, who tried to come to the psychologist's aid.

As you have read, the vast majority of people with severe mental disorders are not violent and in fact are much more likely to be victims of violence than perpetrators. Nevertheless, periodic cases, like the tragic murder of Dr. Faughey, do occur, reminding psychotherapists that there is indeed some degree of danger attached to their profession—a profession in which clients are invited to expose and address their innermost feelings and concerns. Such danger is particularly a possibility in cases in which clients have displayed a history of violence.

AP Photo/Andy Kropa

Justice postponed
David Tarloff is walked out of a police precinct a few days after killing psychologist Kathryn Faughey in February 2008. Declared incompetent to stand trial for several years, Tarloff did not go on trial until March 2013.

According to surveys, more than 80 percent of therapists have on at least one occasion feared that a client might physically attack them (Pope et al., 2006; Pope & Tabachnick, 1993). It is estimated that as many as 13 percent of therapists have been attacked in some form by a patient at least once in private therapy, and an even larger percentage have been assaulted in mental hospitals (Barron, 2008; Tryon, 1987; Bernstein, 1981). Similarly, a number of therapists have been stalked or harassed by patients (Hudson-Allez, 2006).

Patients have used a variety of weapons in their attacks, including such common objects as shoes, lamps, fire extinguishers, and canes. Some have used guns or knives and have severely wounded or even killed a therapist, as we saw in the case of Dr. Faughey.

As you can imagine, many therapists who have been attacked continue to feel anxious and insecure in their work for a long time afterward. Some try to be more selective in accepting patients and to look for cues that signal impending violence. It is possible that such concerns represent a significant distraction from the task at hand when they are in session with clients.

AP/AFP/Getty Images

Dangerous to oneself

The public often thinks that the term "dangerous to oneself" refers exclusively to those who are suicidal. There are, however, other ways that people may pose a danger to themselves, be in need of treatment, and be subject to civil commitment. This sequence of photos shows a man being attacked by a lion at the zoo after he crossed a barbed wire fence to "preach" to two of the animals.

not necessary in such cases, as long as a qualified mental health professional considers commitment necessary. If the son is an adult, however, the process is more involved. The court usually will order a mental examination and allow the person to contest the commitment in court, often represented by a lawyer.

Although the Supreme Court has offered few guidelines concerning specific procedures of civil commitment, one important decision, in the case of *Addington v. Texas* (1979), outlined the *minimum standard of proof* needed for commitment. Here the Court ruled that before an individual can be committed, there must be "clear and convincing" proof that he or she is mentally ill and has met the state's criteria for involuntary commitment. The ruling does not suggest what criteria should be used. That matter is still left to each state. But, whatever the state's criteria, clinicians must offer clear and convincing proof that the individual meets those criteria. When is proof clear and convincing, according to the Court? When it provides 75 percent certainty that the criteria of commitment have been met. This is far less than the near-total certainty ("beyond a reasonable doubt") required to convict people of committing a crime.

EMERGENCY COMMITMENT Many situations require immediate action; no one can wait for commitment proceedings when a life is at stake. Consider, for example, an emergency room patient who is suicidal or hearing voices demanding hostile actions against others. He or she may need immediate treatment and round-the-clock supervision. If treatment could not be given in such situations without the patient's full consent, the consequences could be tragic.

Therefore, many states give clinicians the right to certify that certain patients need temporary commitment and medication. In past years, these states required certification by two *physicians* (not necessarily psychiatrists in some of the states). Today states may allow certification by other mental health professionals as well. The clinicians must declare that the state of mind of the patients makes them dangerous to themselves or others. By tradition, the certifications are often referred to as *two-physician certificates,* or *2 PCs.* The length of such emergency commitments varies from state to state, but three days is often the limit (Strachan, 2008). Should clinicians come to believe that a longer stay is necessary, formal commitment proceedings may be initiated during the period of emergency commitment.

WHO IS DANGEROUS? In the past, people with mental disorders were actually less likely than others to commit violent or dangerous acts. This low rate of violence was apparently related to the fact that so many such individuals lived in institutions. As a result of deinstitutionalization, however, hundreds of thousands of people with severe disturbances now live in the community, and many of them receive little, if any, treatment. Some of these individuals are indeed dangerous to themselves or others.

Although approximately 90 percent of people with mental disorders are in no way violent or dangerous, studies now suggest at least a small relationship between severe mental disorders and violent behavior (Palijan et al., 2010; Norko & Baranoski, 2008). After reviewing a number of studies, John Monahan (2010, 2001, 1993, 1992), a law and psychology professor, concluded that the rate of violent behavior among persons with severe mental disorders is at least somewhat higher than that of people without such disorders:

- Approximately 15 percent of patients in mental hospitals have assaulted another person prior to admission.

- Around 25 percent of patients in mental hospitals assault another person during hospitalization.

- Approximately 12 percent of all people with schizophrenia, major depression, or bipolar disorder have assaulted other people, compared with 2 percent of persons without a severe mental disorder.

- Approximately 4 percent of people who report having been violent during the past year suffer from schizophrenia, whereas 1 percent of nonviolent persons suffer from schizophrenia.

Monahan cautions that the findings do not suggest that people with mental disorders are generally dangerous. Nor do they justify the "caricature of the mentally disordered" that is often portrayed by the media or the "lock 'em up" laws proposed by some politicians. But they do indicate that a severe mental disorder may be more of a risk factor for violence than mental health experts used to believe.

A judgment of *dangerousness* is often required for involuntary civil commitment. But can mental health professionals accurately predict who will commit violent acts? Research suggests that psychiatrists and psychologists are wrong more often than right when they make *long-term* predictions of violence (Mills, Kroner, & Morgan, 2011; Palijan et al., 2010). Most often they overestimate the likelihood that a patient will eventually be violent. On the other hand, studies suggest that *short-term* predictions—that is, predictions of imminent violence—can be more accurate (Otto & Douglas, 2010; Litwack et al, 2006). Researchers are now working, with some success, to develop new assessment techniques that use statistical approaches and are more objective in their predictions of dangerousness than the subjective judgments of clinicians (Pinals & Mossman, 2012; Mills et al., 2011).

Failure to predict

A school surveillance camera shows Dylan Klebold and Eric Harris in the midst of their killing rampage at Columbine High School in Littleton, Colorado, in 1999. Although the teenagers had built a violent Web site, threatened other students, experienced problems with the law, and, in the case of one of the boys, received treatment for psychological problems, professionals were not able to predict or prevent their violent behavior.

Nowhere else to go
A man with a severe mental disorder talks to a mental health team inside a maximum security prison in Idaho. He was sent to the prison for treatment because there is no place else in the state for him to receive care. He is considered too disturbed for treatment as an outpatient and too dangerous for lower-level security hospitals.

WHAT ARE THE PROBLEMS WITH CIVIL COMMITMENT? Civil commitment has been criticized on several grounds (Petrila, 2010; Winick, 2008; Morse, 1982). First is the difficulty of assessing a person's dangerousness (Falzer, 2011). If judgments of dangerousness are often inaccurate, how can one justify using them to deprive people of liberty? Second, the legal definitions of "mental illness" and "dangerousness" are vague. The terms may be defined so broadly that they could be applied to almost anyone an evaluator views as undesirable. Indeed, many civil libertarians worry about the use of involuntary commitment to control people, as occurred in the former Soviet Union and now seems to be taking place in China, where mental hospitals house people with unpopular political views. A third problem is the sometimes questionable therapeutic value of civil commitment (Petrila, 2010; Winick, 2008). Research suggests that many people committed involuntarily do not typically respond well to therapy.

On the basis of these and other arguments, some clinicians suggest that involuntary commitment should be abolished (McSherry et al., 2010; Szasz, 2007, 1977, 1963). Others, however, advocate finding a more systematic way to evaluate dangerousness when decisions are to be made about commitment (Falzer, 2011). They suggest instituting a process of *risk assessment* that would arrive at statements such as, "The patient is believed to have X likelihood of being violent to the following people or under the following conditions over Y period of time." Proponents argue that this would be a more useful and appropriate way of deciding where and how people with psychological disorders should be treated (Mills et al., 2011; Heilbrun & Erickson, 2007).

TRENDS IN CIVIL COMMITMENT The flexibility of the involuntary commitment laws probably reached a peak in 1962. That year, in the case of *Robinson v. California,* the Supreme Court ruled that imprisoning people who suffered from drug addictions might violate the Constitution's ban on cruel and unusual punishment, and it recommended involuntary civil commitment to a mental hospital as a more reasonable action. This ruling encouraged the civil commitment of many kinds of "social deviants." In the years immediately following, civil commitment procedures granted far fewer rights to "defendants" than the criminal courts did (Holstein, 1993). In addition, involuntarily committed patients found it particularly difficult to obtain release.

During the late 1960s and early 1970s, reporters, novelists, civil libertarians, and others spoke out against the ease with which so many people were being unjustifiably committed to mental hospitals. As the public became more aware of these issues, state legislatures started to pass stricter standards for involuntary commitment (Pekkanen, 2007, 2002; Perlin, 2000). Some states, for example, spelled out specific types of behavior that had to be observed before an assessment of dangerousness could be made. Rates of involuntary commitment then declined and release rates rose.

Fewer people are institutionalized through civil commitment procedures today than in the past. The lower commitment rate has not led to more violence-related arrests of people who would have been committed under more flexible criteria (Hiday, 2006; Hiday & Wales, 2003; Teplin et al., 1994). Nevertheless, some clinicians and states are concerned that commitment criteria are now too strict, and they are moving toward broadening the criteria once again (Large et al., 2008; Bloom, 2004). It is not yet clear whether this broadening will lead to a return to the vague commitment procedures of the past.

How are people who have been institutionalized viewed and treated by other people in society today?

Protecting Patients' Rights Over the past two decades, court decisions and state and federal laws have significantly expanded the rights of patients with mental disorders, in particular the *right to treatment* and the *right to refuse treatment* (Petrila, 2010; Weller, 2010).

HOW IS THE RIGHT TO TREATMENT PROTECTED? When people are committed to mental institutions and do not receive treatment, the institutions become, in effect, prisons for the unconvicted. To many patients in the late 1960s and the 1970s, large state mental institutions were just that. Thus some patients and their attorneys began to demand that the state honor their **right to treatment**. In the landmark case of *Wyatt v. Stickney*, a suit on behalf of institutionalized patients in Alabama in 1972, a federal court ruled that the state was constitutionally obligated to provide "adequate treatment" to all people who had been committed involuntarily. Because conditions in the state's hospitals were so terrible, the judge laid out goals that state officials had to meet, including more therapists, better living conditions, more privacy, more social interactions and physical exercise, and a more proper use of physical restraint and medication. Other states have since adopted many of these standards.

John Stanmeyer/VII/Corbis

Another important decision was handed down in 1975 by the Supreme Court in the case of *O'Connor v. Donaldson*. After being held in a Florida mental institution for more than 14 years, Kenneth Donaldson sued for release. Donaldson repeatedly had sought release and had been overruled by the institution's psychiatrists. He argued that he and his fellow patients were receiving poor treatment, were being largely ignored by the staff, and were allowed little personal freedom. The Supreme Court ruled in his favor, fined the hospital's superintendent, and said that such institutions must review patients' cases periodically. The justices also ruled that the state cannot continue to institutionalize people against their will if they are not dangerous and are capable of surviving on their own or with the willing help of responsible family members or friends. In a later case of importance, *Youngberg v. Romeo* (1982), the Supreme Court further ruled that people committed involuntarily have a right to "reasonably nonrestrictive confinement conditions" as well as "reasonable care and safety."

To help protect the rights of patients, Congress passed the Protection and Advocacy for Mentally Ill Individuals Act in 1986. This law set up *protection and advocacy systems* in all states and U.S. territories and gave public advocates who worked for patients the power to investigate possible abuse and neglect and to correct those problems legally.

In recent years public advocates have argued that the right to treatment also should be extended to the tens of thousands of people with severe mental disorders who are repeatedly released from hospitals into ill-equipped communities. Many such people have no place to go and are unable to care for themselves, often winding up homeless or in prisons (Althouse, 2010). A number of advocates are now suing federal and state agencies throughout the country, demanding that they fulfill the promises of the community mental health movement (see Chapter 15).

HOW IS THE RIGHT TO REFUSE TREATMENT PROTECTED? During the past two decades the courts have also decided that patients, particularly those in institutions, have the **right to refuse treatment** (Rolon & Jones, 2008; Perlin, 2004, 2000). The courts have been reluctant to make a single general ruling on this right because there are so many different kinds of treatment, and a general ruling based on one of them might have unintended effects. Therefore, rulings usually target one specific treatment at a time.

Most of the right-to-refuse-treatment rulings center on *biological treatments* (Rolon & Jones, 2008). These treatments are easier to impose on patients without their cooperation than psychotherapy, and they often seem more hazardous. For example, state rulings have consistently granted patients the right to refuse *psychosurgery,* the most irreversible form of physical treatment—and therefore often the most dangerous.

Hospital neglect
While some countries increasingly have attended to the rights of patients in recent decades, including their rights to treatment and to humane treatment conditions, other countries, especially poor ones, have lagged behind. This scene inside a government-run center for mental patients in Jakarta, Indonesia, underscores this point.

•**right to treatment**•The legal right of patients, particularly those who are involuntarily committed, to receive adequate treatment.

•**right to refuse treatment**•The legal right of patients to refuse certain forms of treatment.

Jeff Topping/Getty Images

"The Taser solution"
Police use of stun guns, or Tasers, to subdue people with mental disorders is not uncommon. Tasers, weapons that affect neuromuscular control and temporarily incapacitate people, are viewed by mental health advocates as a violation of the rights of mental patients—a quick but inhumane intervention when dealing with extremely confused or frightened people.

Some states have also acknowledged a patient's right to refuse *electroconvulsive therapy (ECT)*, the treatment used in many cases of severe depression (see Chapter 9). However, the right-to-refuse issue is more complex with regard to ECT than to psychosurgery. ECT is very effective for many people with severe depression; yet it can cause great upset and can also be misused. Today many states grant patients—particularly voluntary patients—the right to refuse ECT. Usually a patient must be informed fully about the nature of the treatment and must give written consent to it. A number of states continue to permit ECT to be forced on committed patients (Baldwin & Oxlad, 2000), whereas others require the consent of a close relative or other third party in such cases.

In the past, patients did not have the right to refuse *psychotropic medications.* As you have read, however, many psychotropic drugs are very powerful, and some produce effects that are unwanted and dangerous. As these harmful effects have become more apparent, some states have granted patients the right to refuse medication. Typically, these states require physicians to explain the purpose of the medication to patients and obtain their written consent. If a patient's refusal is considered incompetent, dangerous, or irrational, the state may allow it to be overturned by an independent psychiatrist, medical committee, or local court (Rolon & Jones, 2008). However, the refusing patient is supported in this process by a lawyer or other patient advocate.

WHAT OTHER RIGHTS DO PATIENTS HAVE? Court decisions have protected still other patient rights over the past several decades. Patients who perform work in mental institutions, particularly private institutions, are now guaranteed at least a *minimum wage.* In addition, a district court ruled in 1974 that patients released from state mental hospitals have a right to *aftercare* and to an *appropriate community residence,* such as a group home, a right later confirmed by the Supreme Court in the 1999 case of *Olmstead v. L.C. et al.* And in the 1975 case of *Dixon v. Weinberger,* another district court ruled that people with psychological disorders should receive treatment in the *least restrictive facility* available. If an inpatient program at a community mental health center is available, for example, then that is the facility to which they should be assigned, not a mental hospital.

THE "RIGHTS" DEBATE Certainly, people with psychological disorders have civil rights that must be protected at all times. However, many clinicians express concern that the patients' rights rulings and laws may unintentionally deprive these patients of opportunities for recovery. Consider the right to refuse medication. If medications can help a patient with a severe mental disorder to recover, doesn't the patient have the right to that recovery? If confusion causes the patient to refuse medication, can clinicians in good conscience delay medication while legal channels are cleared? Psychologist Marilyn Whiteside raised similar concerns in her description of a 25-year-old patient with intellectual developmental disorder:

> *He was 25 and severely retarded. And after his favorite attendant left, he became self-abusive. He beat his fists against the side of his head until a football helmet had to be ordered for his protection. Then he clawed at his face and gouged out one of his eyes.*
>
> *The institution psychologists began a behavior program that had mildly aversive consequences: they squirted warm water in his face each time he engaged in self-abuse. When that didn't work, they requested permission to use an electric prod. The Human Rights Committee vetoed this "excessive and inhumane form of correction" because, after all, the young man was retarded, not criminal.*
>
> *Since nothing effective could be done that abridged the rights and negated the dignity of the developmentally disabled patient, he was verbally reprimanded for his behavior—and allowed to push his thumb through his remaining eye. He is now blind, of course, but he has his rights and presumably his dignity.*
>
> *(Whiteside, 1983, p. 13)*

Despite such legitimate concerns, keep in mind that the clinical field has not always done an effective job of protecting patients' rights. Over the years, many patients have been overmedicated and received improper treatments. Furthermore, one must ask whether the field's present state of knowledge justifies clinicians' overriding of patients' rights. Can clinicians confidently say that a given treatment will help a patient? Can they predict when a treatment will have harmful effects? Since clinicians themselves often disagree, it seems appropriate for patients, their advocates, and outside evaluators to play key roles in decision making.

In What Other Ways Do the Clinical and Legal Fields Interact?

Mental health and legal professionals may influence each other's work in other ways as well. During the past 25 years, their paths have crossed in four key areas: *malpractice suits, professional boundaries, jury selection,* and *psychological research of legal topics.*

Law in Psychology: Malpractice Suits

The number of **malpractice suits** against therapists has risen so sharply in recent years that clinicians have coined terms for the fear of being sued—"litigaphobia" and "litigastress." Claims have been made against clinicians in response to a patient's attempted suicide, sexual activity with a patient, failure to obtain informed consent for a treatment, negligent drug therapy, omission of drug therapy that would speed improvement, improper termination of treatment, and wrongful commitment (Appelbaum, 2011; Simon & Shuman, 2011; Shapiro & Smith, 2011).

Improper termination of treatment was at issue in one highly publicized case in 1985. A man being treated for alcohol-related depression was released from a state hospital in Alabama. Two and a half months later, he shot and killed a new acquaintance in a motel lounge. He was convicted of murder and sentenced to life in prison. The victim's father, claiming negligence, filed a civil suit against a psychologist, physician, and social worker at the state hospital, and after two years of legal action a jury awarded him a total of almost $7 million. The state supreme court later overturned the verdict, saying that a state hospital is entitled to a certain degree of immunity in such cases.

Two investigators who studied the effects of this case found that the hospital had released 11 percent of its patients during the six months before the lawsuit was filed, 10 percent during the two years it was being litigated, but only 7 percent during the

•**malpractice suit**•A lawsuit charging a therapist with improper conduct in the course of treatment.

six months after the verdict (Brodsky & Poythress, 1990). Although judgments about a patient's improvement are supposed to be made on their own merits, they were apparently being affected by a heightened fear of litigation at this hospital.

Similarly, a more recent study of 98 psychiatrists in northern England found that most of them were practicing "defensive medicine" at least some of the time—selecting certain treatments, tests, and procedures to protect themselves from criticism, rather than because such approaches were clearly best for their clients (Beezhold, 2002). Seventy-one of the psychiatrists reported that during the month preceding the study, they had indeed taken some defensive action in their work, including admitting patients to hospitals overcautiously (21 percent) and placing hospitalized patients on higher levels of staff observation (29 percent). Clearly, malpractice suits, or the fear of them, can have significant effects on clinical decisions and practice, for better or for worse (Appelbaum, 2011; Feldman et al., 2005).

Law in Psychology: Professional Boundaries Over the past two decades, the legislative and judicial systems have helped to change the *boundaries* that distinguish one clinical profession from another. In particular, they have given more authority to psychologists and blurred the lines that once separated psychiatry from psychology. A growing number of states, for example, are ruling that psychologists can admit patients to the state's hospitals, a power previously held only by psychiatrists (Halloway, 2004).

In 1991, with the blessings of Congress, the Department of Defense (DOD) started to reconsider the biggest difference of all between the practices of psychiatrists and psychologists—the authority to prescribe drugs, a role previously denied to psychologists. The DOD set up a trial training program for Army psychologists. Given the apparent success of this trial program, the American Psychological Association later recommended that all psychologists be allowed to attend a special educational program in prescription services and receive certification to prescribe medications if they pass (McGrath & Moore, 2010). New Mexico and Louisiana and the U.S. territory of Guam now do in fact grant prescription privileges to psychologists who receive special pharmacological training.

> **Most psychiatrists oppose the idea of prescription rights for psychologists. Why do some psychologists also oppose this idea?**

As the action by the American Psychological Association in the prescription matter suggests, the legislative and judicial systems do not simply take it upon themselves to interfere in the affairs of clinical professionals. In fact, professional associations of psychologists, psychiatrists, and social workers lobby in state legislatures across the country for laws and decisions that may increase the authority of their members. In each instance, clinicians seek the involvement of other institutions as well, a further demonstration of the way the mental health system interacts with other sectors of our society.

Psychology in Law: Jury Selection During the past 30 years, more and more lawyers have turned to clinicians for psychological advice in conducting trials (Crocker & Kovera, 2011; Hope, 2010; Lieberman & Olson, 2008). A new breed of clinical specialists, known as "jury specialists," has evolved. They advise lawyers about which jury candidates are likely to favor their side and which strategies are likely to win jurors' support during trials. The jury specialists make their suggestions on the basis of surveys, interviews, analyses of jurors' backgrounds and attitudes, and laboratory simulations of upcoming trials. However, it is not clear that a clinician's advice is more valid than a lawyer's instincts or that the judgments of either are particularly accurate.

Psychology in Law: Psychological Research of Legal Topics Psychologists have sometimes conducted studies and developed expertise on topics of great importance to the criminal justice system. In turn, these studies influence how the system carries out its work. Psychological investigations of two topics, *eyewitness testimony* and *patterns of criminality,* have gained particular attention.

EYEWITNESS TESTIMONY In criminal cases testimony by eyewitnesses is extremely influential. It often determines whether a defendant will be found guilty or not guilty. But how accurate is eyewitness testimony? This question has become urgent, as a troubling number of prisoners (many on death row) have had their convictions overturned after DNA evidence revealed that they could not have committed the crimes of which they had been convicted. It turns out that more than 75 percent of such wrongful convictions were based in large part on mistaken eyewitness testimony (Garrett, 2011; Hope, 2010).

While some witnesses may have reason to lie (for example, prosecutors may reduce an eyewitness's own punishment in exchange for testimony), most eyewitnesses undoubtedly try to tell the truth about what or who they saw. Yet research indicates that eyewitness testimony can be highly unreliable, partly because most crimes are unexpected and fleeting and therefore not the sort of events remembered well (Kapardis, 2010; Roesch et al., 2010). During the crime, for example, lighting may be poor or other distractions may be present. Witnesses may have had other things on their minds, such as concern for their own safety or that of bystanders. Such concerns may greatly impair later memory.

Moreover, in laboratory studies researchers have found it easy to fool research participants who are trying to recall the details of an observed event simply by introducing misinformation (Laney & Loftus, 2010). After a suggestive description by the researcher, stop signs can be transformed into yield signs, white cars into blue ones, and Mickey Mouse into Minnie Mouse (Pickel, 2004; Loftus, 2003). In addition, laboratory studies indicate that persons who are highly suggestible have the poorest recall of observed events (Liebman et al., 2002).

As for identifying actual perpetrators, research has found that accuracy is greatly influenced by the method used in identification (Garrett, 2011; Roesch et al., 2010; Semmier & Brewer, 2010). The traditional police lineup, for example, is not always a highly reliable technique, and witnesses' errors committed during lineups tend to stick (Wells, 2008). Researchers have also learned that witnesses' confidence is not necessarily related to accuracy (Allwood, 2010; Ghetti et al., 2004). Witnesses who are "absolutely certain" may be no more correct in their recollections than those who are only "fairly sure." Yet the degree of a witness's confidence often influences whether jurors believe his or her testimony. In fact, judges often instruct jurors that they can use witness confidence as an indicator of accuracy (Greene & Ellis, 2007).

Psychological investigations into eyewitnesses' memory have not yet undone the judicial system's reliance on or respect for those witnesses' testimony. Nor should it. The distance between laboratory studies and real-life events is often great, and the implications of such research must be applied carefully (Roesch et al., 2010). Still, eyewitness research has begun to make an impact. Studies of hypnosis and of its ability to create false memories, for example, have led most states to prohibit eyewitnesses from testifying about events or details if their recall of the events was initially helped by hypnosis (Knight, Meyer, & Goldstein, 2007).

PATTERNS OF CRIMINALITY A growing number of television shows, movies, and books suggest that clinicians often play a major role in criminal investigations by providing police with *psychological profiles* of perpetrators—"He's probably white, in his 30s, has a history of animal torture, has few friends, and is subject to emotional outbursts." The study of criminal behavior patterns and of profiling has increased in recent years; however, it is not nearly as revealing or influential as the media and the arts would have us believe (Salfati, 2011; Crighton, 2010; Turvey, 2008).

On the positive side, researchers have gathered information about the psychological features of various criminals, and they have indeed found that perpetrators of particular kinds of crimes—serial murder or serial sexual assault, for example—frequently share a

Chuck Burton/AP Photo

Eyewitness error

Psychological research indicates that eyewitness testimony is often invalid. Here a woman talks to the man whom she had identified as her rapist back in 1984. DNA testing eventually proved that a different person had, in fact, raped her, and the incorrectly identified man was released. In the meantime, however, he had served 11 years of a life sentence in prison.

BETWEEN THE LINES

Recent TV Series Featuring Psychological Profilers

NCIS ‹‹

NUMB3RS ‹‹

Dexter ‹‹

The Mentalist ‹‹

Without a Trace ‹‹

Criminal Minds and *Criminal Minds: Suspect Behavior* ‹‹

Law and Order: Criminal Intent ‹‹

Law and Order: Special Victims Unit ‹‹

Waking the Dead (British television series) ‹‹

Wire in the Blood (British television series) ‹‹

number of traits and background features (see *PsychWatch* below). But while such traits are *often* present, they are not *always* present, and so applying profile information to a particular crime can be wrong and misleading. Increasingly police are consulting psychological profilers, and this practice appears to be helpful as long as the limitations of profiling are recognized (Salfati, 2011; Crighton, 2010; Palermo et al., 2005).

A reminder of the limitations of profiling information comes from the case of the snipers who terrorized the Washington, DC, area for three weeks in October 2002,

PsychWatch

Serial Murderers: Madness or Badness?

In late 2001, a number of anthrax-tainted letters were mailed to people throughout eastern parts of the United States, leading to 5 deaths and to severe illness in 13 other people. Finally, in 2008 the FBI targeted a biodefense researcher named Bruce Ivins as the killer. With a murder indictment imminent, Ivins committed suicide on July 29, 2008. It appeared that the FBI had finally found the perpetrator of these terrible deeds.

Although Ivins' suicide left behind unanswered questions, the FBI has concluded that this troubled man was indeed the anthrax killer. As such, he appears to have been one of a growing list of serial killers who have fascinated and horrified Americans over the years: Theodore Kaczynski ("Unabomber"), Ted Bundy, David Berkowitz ("Son of Sam"), Albert DeSalvo, John Wayne Gacy, Jeffrey Dahmer, John Allen Muhammad, John Lee Malvo, Dennis Rader ("BTK killer"), and more.

The FBI estimates that there are between 35 and 100 serial killers at large in the United States at any given time (Hickey, 2002). Each such killer follows his or her own pattern (Kocsis, 2008; Homant & Kennedy, 2006), but many of them appear to have certain characteristics in common.

Most—but certainly not all—are white males between 25 and 34 years old, of average to high intelligence, generally clean-cut, smooth-talking, attractive, and skillful manipulators (Gray, 2010; Kocsis, 2008; Fox & Levin, 2005).

A number of serial killers seem to display severe personality disorders (Waller, 2010; Whitman & Akutagawa, 2004). Lack of conscience and an utter disregard for people and the rules of society—key features of antisocial personality disorder—are typical. Narcissistic thinking is quite common as well. The feeling of being special may even give the killer an unrealistic belief that he will not get caught (Kocsis, 2008; Wright et al., 2006). Often it is this sense of invincibility that leads to his capture.

Sexual dysfunction and fantasy also seem to play a part (Waller, 2010; Wright et al., 2006; Arndt et al., 2004). Studies have found that vivid fantasies, often sexual and sadistic, may help drive the killer's behavior (Kocsis, 2008; Homant & Kennedy, 2006). Some clinicians also believe that the killers may be trying to overcome general feelings of powerlessness by controlling, hurting, or eliminating those who are momentarily weaker (Fox & Levin, 2005, 1999). A number of the killers were abused as children—physically, sexually, and emotionally (Wright et al., 2006; Hickey, 2002).

Despite such profiles and suspicions, clinical theorists do not yet understand why serial killers behave as they do. But most agree with Park Dietz, a highly regarded forensic expert, when he asserts, "It's hard to imagine any circumstance under which they should be released to the public again" (Douglas, 1996, p. 349).

Photo by Alex Wong/Getty Images

Serial murder by mail In 2001, a hazardous-material worker sprays his colleagues as they depart the Senate Office Building after searching the building for traces of anthrax, an acute infectious disease caused by a spore-forming bacterium.

shooting 10 people dead and seriously wounding 3 others. Most of the profiling done by FBI psychologists had suggested that the sniper was acting alone; it turned out that the attacks were conducted by a pair: a middle-aged man, John Allen Muhammad, and a teenage boy, Lee Boyd Malvo. Although profiles had suggested a young thrill-seeker, Muhammad was 41. Profilers had believed the attacker to be white, but neither Muhammad nor Malvo was white. The prediction of a *male* attacker was correct, but then again female serial killers are relatively rare.

AP Photo/Ron Edmonds

Misleading profile
Massive numbers of police search for clues outside a Home Depot in Virginia in 2002, hoping to identify and capture the serial sniper who killed 10 people and terrorized residents throughout Washington, DC, Maryland, and Virginia. As it turned out, psychological profiling in this case offered limited help and, in fact, misled the police in certain respects.

What Ethical Principles Guide Mental Health Professionals?

Discussions of the legal and mental health systems may sometimes give the impression that clinicians as a group are uncaring and are considerate of patients' rights and needs only when they are forced to be. This, of course, is not true. Most clinicians care greatly about their clients and strive to help them while at the same time respecting their rights and dignity (Pope & Vasquez, 2011). In fact, clinicians do not rely exclusively on the legislative and court systems to ensure proper and effective clinical practice. They also regulate themselves by continually developing and revising ethical guidelines for members of the clinical field. Many legal decisions do nothing more than place the power of the law behind these already existing professional guidelines.

Each profession within the mental health field has its own **code of ethics** (Nagy, 2011; Brown, 2010; Koocher & Keith-Spiegel, 2008). The code of the American Psychological Association (2010, 2002, 1992) is typical. This code, highly respected by other mental health professionals and public officials, includes specific guidelines:

1. **Psychologists are permitted to offer advice** in self-help books, on DVDs, on television and radio programs, in newspaper and magazines, through mailed material, and in other places, provided they do so responsibly and professionally and base their advice on appropriate psychological literature and practices. Psychologists are bound by these same ethical requirements when they offer advice and ideas online, whether on individual Web pages, blogs, bulletin boards, or chat rooms (Koocher & Keith-Spiegel, 2008). Internet-based professional advice has proved difficult to regulate, however, because the number of such offerings keeps getting larger and larger and so many advice-givers (at least one-third of them) do not appear to have any professional training or credentials.

2. **Psychologists may not conduct fraudulent research, plagiarize the work of others, or publish false data.** During the past 30 years cases of scientific fraud or misconduct have been discovered in all of the sciences, including psychology. These acts have led to misunderstandings of important issues, taken scientific research in the wrong direction, and damaged public trust. Unfortunately, the impressions created by false findings may continue to influence the thinking of both the public and other scientists for years.

3. **Psychologists must acknowledge their limitations** with regard to patients who are disabled or whose gender, ethnicity, language, socioeconomic status, or sexual orientation differs from that of the therapist (Elwyn et al., 2010). This guideline often requires psychotherapists to obtain additional training or supervision, consult with more knowledgeable colleagues, or refer clients to more appropriate professionals.

•**code of ethics**•A body of principles and rules for ethical behavior, designed to guide decisions and actions by members of a profession.

The ethics of giving professional advice
Like enormously popular psychologist Phil McGraw ("Dr. Phil"), many of today's clinicians offer advice in books, at workshops, on television and radio, on DVDs, and online. Their presentations are bound by the field's ethics code to act responsibly and to base their advice on appropriate psychological theories and findings.

• **confidentiality** • The principle that certain professionals will not divulge the information they obtain from a client.

• **duty to protect** • The principle that therapists must break confidentiality in order to protect a person who may be the intended victim of a client.

• **employee assistance program** • A mental health program offered by a business to its employees.

• **stress-reduction and problem-solving seminar** • A workshop or series of group sessions offered by a business in which mental health professionals teach employees how to cope with and solve problems and reduce stress.

4. **Psychologists who make evaluations and testify in legal cases must base their assessments on sufficient information and substantiate their findings appropriately** (Carlin, 2010; Gutheil, 2010). If an adequate examination of the individual in question is not possible, psychologists must make clear the limited nature of their testimony.

5. **Psychologists may not take advantage of clients and students, sexually or otherwise.** This guideline relates to the widespread social problem of sexual harassment, as well as the problem of therapists who take sexual advantage of clients in therapy. The code specifically forbids a sexual relationship with a present or former therapy client for at least two years after the end of treatment—and even then such a relationship is permitted only in "the most unusual circumstances." Furthermore, psychologists may not accept as clients people with whom they have previously had a sexual relationship.

Research has clarified that clients may suffer great emotional damage from sexual involvement with their therapists (Pope & Vasquez, 2011; Pope & Wedding, 2011; Koocher & Keith-Spiegel, 2008). How many therapists actually have a sexual relationship with a client? On the basis of various surveys, reviewers have estimated that some form of sexual misconduct with patients may be engaged in by around 5 to 6 percent of today's therapists, down from 10 percent more than a decade ago (Pope & Wedding, 2011; Koocher & Keith-Spiegel, 2008).

Although the vast majority of therapists do not engage in sexual behavior of any kind with clients, their ability to control private feelings is apparently another matter. In surveys, close to 90 percent of therapists reported having been sexually attracted to a client, at least on occasion (Pope & Vasquez, 2011; Pope et al., 2006). Although few of these therapists acted on their feelings, most of them felt guilty, anxious, or concerned about the attraction. Given such issues, it is not surprising that sexual ethics training is given high priority in many of today's clinical training programs (Lamb et al., 2003).

6. **Psychologists must adhere to the principle of confidentiality.** All of the state and federal courts have upheld laws protecting therapist **confidentiality**. For peace of mind and to ensure effective therapy, clients must be able to trust that their private exchanges with a therapist will not be repeated to others (Nagy, 2011; Brendel & Glezer, 2010). There are times, however, when the principle of confidentiality must be compromised (Pope & Vasquez, 2011; Koocher & Keith-Spiegel, 2008). A therapist in training, for example, must discuss cases on a regular basis with a supervisor. Clients, in turn, must be informed that such discussions are occurring.

A second exception arises in cases of outpatients who are clearly dangerous. The 1976 case of *Tarasoff v. Regents of the University of California,* one of the most important cases to affect client-therapist relationships, concerned an outpatient at a University of California hospital. He had confided to his therapist that he wanted to harm his former girlfriend, Tanya Tarasoff. Several days after ending therapy, the former patient fulfilled his promise. He stabbed Tanya Tarasoff to death.

Should confidentiality have been broken in this case? The therapist, in fact, felt that it should. Campus police were notified, but the patient was released after some questioning. In their suit against the hospital and therapist, the victim's parents argued that the therapist should have also warned them and their daughter that the patient intended to harm Ms. Tarasoff. The California Supreme Court agreed: "The protective privilege ends where the public peril begins."

The current code of ethics for psychologists thus declares that therapists have a **duty to protect**—a responsibility to break confidentiality, even without the client's consent, when it is necessary "to protect the client or others from harm." Since the *Tarasoff* ruling, California's courts further have held that therapists must also protect people who are close to a client's intended victim and thus in danger. A child, for example, is likely to be at risk when a client plans to assault the child's mother. In addition, the California courts have ruled that therapists must act to protect people even when information about the dangerousness of a client is received from the client's family, rather than from the client (Thomas, 2005). Many, but not all, states have adopted the California court rulings or similar ones, and a number have passed "duty to protect" bills that clarify the rules of confidentiality for therapists and protect them from certain civil suits (Sonne, 2012; Benjamin et al., 2009; Koocher & Keith-Spiegel, 2008).

Mental Health, Business, and Economics

The legislative and judicial systems are not the only social institutions with which mental health professionals interact. The *business* and *economic* fields are two other sectors that influence and are influenced by clinical practice and study.

Bringing Mental Health Services to the Workplace

Untreated psychological disorders are, collectively, among the 10 leading categories of work-related disorders and injuries (Brough & Biggs, 2010; Kessler & Stang, 2006; Kemp, 1994). In fact, almost one-third of all employees are estimated to experience psychological problems that are serious enough to affect their work (Larsen et al., 2010). Psychological problems contribute to 60 percent of all absenteeism from work, up to 90 percent of industrial accidents, and to 65 percent of work terminations. Alcohol abuse and other substance use disorders are particularly damaging. The business world has often turned to clinical professionals to help prevent and correct such problems (Pomaki et al., 2012; Gold, 2010; Wang, 2007). Two common means of providing mental health care in the workplace are *employee assistance programs* and *problem-solving seminars*.

Employee assistance programs, mental health services made available by a place of business, are run either by mental health professionals who work directly for a company or by outside mental health agencies (Pomaki et al., 2012; Merrick et al., 2011; Armour, 2006). Companies publicize such programs at the work site, educate workers about psychological dysfunctioning, and teach supervisors how to identify workers who are having psychological problems. Businesses believe that employee assistance programs save them money in the long run by preventing psychological problems from interfering with work performance and by reducing employee insurance claims, although these beliefs have not undergone extensive testing (Wang, 2007).

Stress-reduction and problem-solving seminars are workshops or group sessions in which mental health professionals teach employees techniques for coping, solving problems, and handling and reducing stress (Ashcraft, 2012; Russell, 2007; Daw, 2001). Programs of this kind are just as likely to be aimed at high-level executives as at assembly-line workers. Often employees are required to attend such workshops, which may run for several days, and are given time off from their jobs to do so.

The Economics of Mental Health

You have already seen how economic decisions by the government may influence the clinical field's treatment of people with severe mental disorders. For example, the desire of the state and federal governments to reduce costs was an important consideration in the country's deinstitutionalization movement, which contributed to the premature release of hospital patients into the community. Economic decisions by government agencies may affect other kinds of clients and treatment programs as well.

As you read in Chapter 15, government funding for services to people with psychological disorders has risen sharply over the past five decades, from $1 billion in 1963 to

AP Photo/Jacquelyn Martin

Failure to protect
The father of one of the 32 students and teachers slain in the 2007 massacre at Virginia Tech listens to a review panel investigating the shootings. The panel blamed mental health professionals and school administrators for failing to notice clear warning signs of psychological deterioration displayed by killer Seung-Hui Cho for two years prior to the shooting and for failing to force him into proper treatment.

BETWEEN THE LINES

Mental Health Parity

Until recently, 35 states had passed laws requiring insurance companies to provide clients with equal coverage (*parity*) for medical and mental disorders. However, several of these states excluded certain mental disorders from the insurance parity laws. In 2008, Congress passed a health parity bill that eliminated most such exclusions, but that bill did not go into effect until mid-2011 (APA, 2011; Clay, 2011). ‹‹

•**managed care program**•An insurance program in which the insurance company decides the cost, method, provider, and length of treatment.

•**peer review system**•A system by which clinicians paid by an insurance company may periodically review a patient's progress and recommend the continuation or termination of insurance benefits.

around $171 billion in 2011, to an estimated $239 billion in 2014 (Gill, 2010; Nordal, 2010; Redick et al., 1992). Around 30 percent of that money is spent on prescription drugs, but much of the rest is targeted for income support, housing subsidies, and other such expenses rather than direct mental health services (Daly, 2010; Nordal, 2010). The result is that government funding for mental health services is, in fact, insufficient. People with severe mental disorders are hit hardest by the funding shortage. The number of people on waiting lists for community-based services grew from 200,000 in 2002 to 393,000 in 2008, and that number has continued to rise in recent years (Daly, 2010).

Government funding currently covers around two-thirds of all mental health services, leaving a mental health expense of tens of billions of dollars for individual patients and their private insurance companies (Nordal, 2010; Mark et al., 2008, 2005). This large economic role of private insurance companies has had a significant effect on the way clinicians go about their work. As you'll remember from Chapter 1, to reduce their expenses, most of these companies have developed **managed care programs,** in which the insurance company decides such questions as which therapists clients may choose, the cost of sessions, and the number of sessions for which a client may be reimbursed (Domino, 2012; Glasser, 2010). These and other insurance plans may also control expenses through the use of **peer review systems,** in which clinicians who work for the insurance company periodically review a client's treatment program and recommend that insurance benefits be either continued or stopped. Typically, insurers require reports or session notes from the therapist, often including intimate personal information about the patient.

As you read in Chapter 1, many therapists and clients dislike managed care programs and peer reviews (Merrick & Reif, 2010; Scheid, 2010). They believe that the reports required of therapists breach confidentiality, even when efforts are made to protect anonymity, and that the importance of therapy in a given case is sometimes difficult to convey in a brief report. They also argue that the priorities of managed care programs inevitably shorten therapy, even if longer-term treatment would be advisable in particular cases. The priorities may also favor treatments that offer short-term results (for example, drug therapy) over more costly approaches that might achieve a more promising long-term improvement. As in the medical field, disturbing stories are often heard about patients who are prematurely cut off from mental health services by their managed care programs. In short, many clinicians fear that the current system amounts to regulation of therapy by insurance companies rather than by therapists.

? What are the costs to clients and practitioners when insurance companies make decisions about the methods, frequency, and duration of treatment?

Technology and Mental Health

Technology is always changing, and, like most other fields, the mental health field is in the position of trying to keep pace with that change. This is not a new state of affairs. Technological change occurred 25, 50, 100 years ago and beyond. What is new, however, is the breathtaking *rate* of technological change that characterizes today's world. The rate of change has increased exponentially in the past decade alone. On the one hand, we often take for granted the digital and hyperconnected world in which we now live. On the other hand, it has had a profound impact on how we conduct our lives, how we feel, and how we think. As such, today's ever-changing technology has begun to have significant effects—both positive and negative—on the mental health field, and it will undoubtedly affect the field even more in the coming years.

Consider for a moment the nature and breadth of technological change in today's world. Around 2.1 billion people across the world

"I can't wait to see what you're like online."

Paul Noth/The New Yorker Collection/www.cartoonbank.com

currently use the Internet—272 million in the United States alone (MMG, 2011). The Internet has now become the primary medium through which people access and disseminate all kinds of information. More than half of all people say that the Internet is their preferred and most useful source of news, scientific enlightenment, and other kinds of information (GSS, 2008).

Closely aligned with the Internet, *cell phone* use has proliferated. There are currently 5.3 billion cell phone owners worldwide—that's 77 percent of the world population (MobiThinking, 2011). Close to 85 percent of all Americans own a cell phone (Smith, 2010; Wilson & Kimball, 2010), and 96 percent of 18- to 29-year-olds own one. Almost 70 percent of all cell phone owners in the United States use them for texting, among other services—itself a relatively new form of technology (MobiThinking, 2011) (see Figure 19-3). Small wonder that cell phone use throughout the country tops 6 billion minutes each day (Henry, 2011).

Video games have emerged as yet another force in our digital society. Over 70 percent of Americans play computer, console, or video games (ESA, 2011). They are a passion across all ages, with the average age of game players being 37. One-third of all gamers say that playing video games is their favorite entertainment activity. Often gaming is a social experience: 65 percent of gamers play with other individuals in person, and many interact online with numerous other players in virtual game environments called MMOGs (Massively Multiplayer Online Games). Teenage game players have been of special interest to psychologists. Surveys reveal that virtually all teenagers play video games (ESA, 2011; Lenhart et al., 2008), and almost one-third of them play games that are considered appropriate for adults only.

Finally, there is the spectacular growth of social networking in recent years, set in motion when Facebook expanded its audience in 2006 from college and high school students to users of all ages. The number of registered users on Facebook increased from 10.5 million in 2006 to almost 600 million in 2010, and it is expected to climb to 2.3 billion by 2017 (Trefis, 2011). Teenagers and young adults comprise almost half of all Facebook users (Trefis, 2011). Altogether, nearly three-quarters of all online teens and young adults use social networking sites (Lenhart et al., 2010).

Social networking is also expanding in ways beyond Facebook. Witness, for example, the growth of *Twitter,* an online social networking and micro-blogging service that enables users to send and receive brief text-based messages to and from large numbers of friends, colleagues, and other people. Twitter, which was launched in 2006, has already become a major part of cell phone use and of broader online behavior. Around 200 million tweets (messages sent through Twitter) are sent out by users and 350 billion tweets are received by followers each day (Olivarez-Giles, 2011). In contrast, only 2 million tweets were sent each day in 2009.

Given these changes and trends in technology and their impact on the daily lives of most people, it is not surprising that the focus, tools, and research directions of the mental health field have themselves expanded over the past decade—a shift that is expected to increase precipitously as we move further into the twenty-first century. Let's consider just a small sample of the ways that the mental health field has been affected by and dealt with technological advances. You have already come across many of them throughout the textbook.

New Triggers and Vehicles for Psychopathology

Our digital world provides new triggers and vehicles for the expression of abnormal behavior. Many individuals who grapple with gambling disorder, for example, have found the ready availability of Internet gambling to be all too inviting. Similarly, the Internet, texting, and social networks have become convenient tools for those who wish to stalk or bully others, express sexual exhibitionism, pursue pedophilic desires, or satisfy other

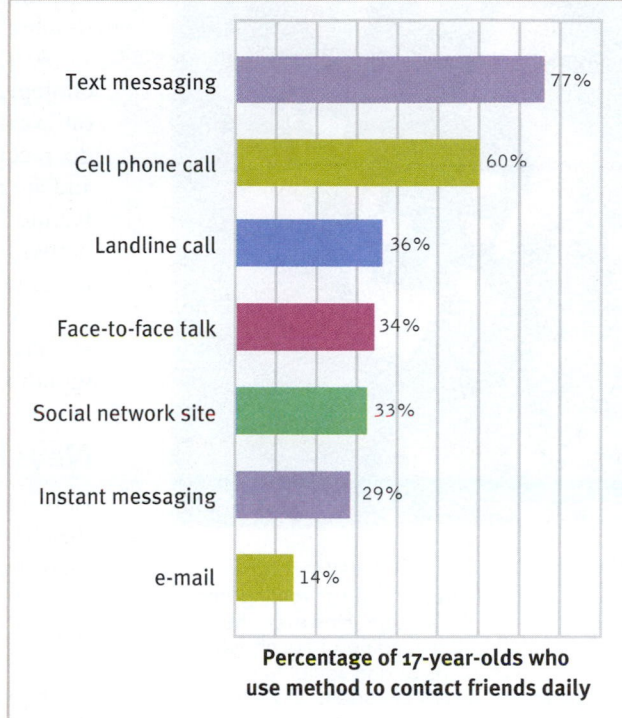

Percentage of 17-year-olds who use method to contact friends daily

- Text messaging — 77%
- Cell phone call — 60%
- Landline call — 36%
- Face-to-face talk — 34%
- Social network site — 33%
- Instant messaging — 29%
- e-mail — 14%

Figure 19-3

How do today's teenagers connect each day with their friends? A large survey of American teenagers reveals that 77 percent of high school seniors use text messaging each day to connect with their friends, 34 percent talk face-to-face with them, and 14 percent e-mail them (Pew Internet, 2010).

The impact of social networks
Facebook has turned social networking into a fixture of the digital age. However, the clinical field's understanding of Facebook's effect on psychological and social functioning awaits the results of current and future research.

paraphilias (see pages 518–519, 409–415) (Taylor & Quayle, 2010). Likewise, some clinicians believe that violent video games may contribute to the development of antisocial behavior, and perhaps even to the onset of conduct disorders (Zhuo, 2010). And, in the opinion of many clinicians, constant texting, tweeting, and Internet browsing may help shorten people's attention spans and establish a foundation for attention problems (Richtel, 2010).

A number of clinicians also worry that social networking can contribute to psychological dysfunctioning in certain cases. On the positive side, research indicates that, on average, social network users maintain more close relationships than other people do, receive more social support, are more trusting and open to differing points of view, and are more likely to participate in groups and lead active lives (Hampton et al., 2011; Rainie et al., 2011). On the negative side, however, there is research suggesting that social networking sites may provide a new venue for peer pressure that increases social anxiety in some adolescents (Charles, 2011; Hampton et al., 2011). The sites may, for example, cause some individuals to develop fears that others in their network will exclude them socially. Similarly, there is clinical concern that sites such as Facebook may facilitate the withdrawal of shy or socially anxious people from valuable face-to-face relationships.

New Forms of Psychopathology

Beyond providing new triggers and vehicles for abnormal behavior, research indicates that today's technology also is helping to produce new psychological disorders. One such disorder, sometimes called *Internet addiction,* is marked by excessive and dysfunctional levels of texting, tweeting, networking, Internet browsing, e-mailing, blogging, online shopping, or online pornographic use. At least 1 percent of all people are thought to display this pattern, leading some clinical theorists to argue that it should be a category in the DSM (Young & de Abreu, 2011). Indeed, as you read in Chapter 5, the framers of DSM-5 have designated *Internet gaming disorder* as a disorder that should receive further study for possible inclusion in future revisions of the DSM.

Similarly, the Internet has brought a new exhibitionistic feature to certain kinds of abnormal behavior. For example, as you read in Chapter 16 (see page 492), a growing number of individuals now use YouTube to post videos of their self-cutting behaviors, acts that traditionally have been conducted in private.

Cybertherapy

As you have seen throughout the textbook, cybertherapy is growing as a treatment option by leaps and bounds (Carrard et al., 2011; Pope & Vasquez, 2011; Gunter, 2010). It takes such forms as long-distance therapy between clients and therapists using Skype (see page 69), therapy offered by computer programs (page 69), treatment enhanced by the use of video gamelike avatars and other virtual reality experiences (pages 69, 131, 166), and Internet-based support groups (page 69). Similarly, countless Web sites offer a wealth of mental health information, enabling people to better inform themselves, their friends, and their family members about psychological dysfunctioning and treatment options. In addition, of the 300,000 new apps created over the past three years (MobiThinking, 2011), a number are devoted to relaxing people, cheering them up, or otherwise improving their psychological states (Leis-Newman, 2011; Krüger et al., 2010). And, finally, many computer exercise programs—cognitive and physical—have been developed with the goal of improving both mental health (particularly, cognitive functioning and mood) and physical health (see pages 575, 579, and 583–584).

Unfortunately, the cybertherapy movement is not without its problems, as you read in Chapters 3, 4, 10, and 11. Along with the wealth of mental health information now available online comes an enormous amount of misinformation about psychological problems and their treatments, offered by persons and sites that are far from knowledgeable. Similarly, the issue of quality control is a major problem for Internet-based therapy, support groups, and the like. Moreover, there are now numerous antitreatment Web sites that try to guide people away from seeking help for their psychological problems (Davey, 2010). You read in Chapters 4, 10, and 11, for example, about the growing phenomenon of pro-anorexia and pro-suicide websites and the dangerous influences they exert on vulnerable people. Research has yet to clarify exactly how influential such sites are. However, a quick browse through the Internet reveals how destructive their messages can be.

Clearly, the impact of technological change on the mental health field today is wide-ranging and both positive and negative. Its impact presents formidable challenges for clinicians and researchers alike. Few of the phenomena and applications discussed in this section are well understood, and fewer still have been subjected to comprehensive research. Yet, as we mentioned earlier, the relationship between technology and mental health is expected to grow precipitously in the coming years. It behooves everyone in the field to understand and be ready for this growth and its implications.

The Person Within the Profession

The actions of clinical researchers and practitioners not only influence and are influenced by other forces in society but also are closely tied to their personal needs and goals. You have seen that the human strengths, imperfections, wisdom, and clumsiness of clinical professionals may affect their theoretical orientations, their interactions with clients, and the kinds of clients with whom they choose to work. You have also seen how personal leanings may sometimes override professional standards and scruples and, in extreme cases, lead clinical scientists to commit research fraud and clinical practitioners to engage in sexual misconduct with clients.

Surveys of the mental health of therapists have found that as many as 84 percent report having been in therapy at least once (Klitzman, 2008; Pope et al., 2006; Pope & Tabachnick, 1994). Their reasons are largely the same as those of other clients, with emotional problems, depression, and anxiety topping the list. And, like other people, therapists often are reluctant to acknowledge their psychological problems (see *MediaSpeak* on the next page).

It is not clear why so many therapists seem to experience psychological problems. Perhaps it is because their jobs are highly stressful; research suggests that therapists often experience some degree of job burnout (Clay, 2011; Rosenberg & Pace, 2006). Or perhaps therapists are simply more aware of their own negative feelings or are more likely to pursue treatment for their problems. Alternatively, individuals with personal concerns may be more inclined to choose clinical work as a profession. Whatever the reason, clinicians bring to their work a set of psychological issues that may, along with other important factors, affect how they listen and respond to clients (Friedman, 2008).

The science and profession of abnormal psychology seek to understand, predict, and change abnormal functioning. But we must not lose sight of the fact that mental health

"Look, you're not the only one with problems."

"Mad Pride" Fights a Stigma

By Gabrielle Glaser, *New York Times*

In the YouTube video, Liz Spikol is smiling and animated, the light glinting off her large hoop earrings. Deadpan, she holds up a diaper. It is not, she explains, a hygienic item for a giantess, but rather a prop to illustrate how much control people lose when they undergo electroconvulsive therapy, or ECT, as she did 12 years ago.

In other videos and blog postings, Ms. Spikol, a 39-year-old writer in Philadelphia who has bipolar disorder, describes a period of psychosis so severe she jumped out of her mother's car and ran away like a scared dog.

In lectures across the country, Elyn Saks, a law professor and associate dean at the University of Southern California, recounts the florid visions she has experienced during her life-long battle with schizophrenia—dancing ashtrays, houses that spoke to her—and hospitalizations where she was strapped down with leather restraints and force-fed medications.

Like many Americans who have severe forms of mental illness such as schizophrenia and bipolar disorder, Ms. Saks and Ms. Spikol are speaking candidly and publicly about their demons. Their frank talk is part of a conversation about mental illness (or as some prefer to put it, "extreme mental states") that stretches from college campuses to community health centers, from YouTube to online forums.

"Until now, the acceptance of mental illness has pretty much stopped at depression," said Charles Barber, a lecturer in psychiatry at the Yale School of Medicine. "But a newer generation, fueled by the Internet and other sophisticated delivery systems, is saying, 'We deserve to be heard, too.'"

Just as gay-rights activists reclaimed the word queer as a badge of honor rather than a slur, these advocates proudly call themselves mad; they say their conditions do not preclude them from productive lives. Mad pride events, organized by loosely connected groups in at least seven countries including Australia, South Africa and the United States, draw thousands of participants. . . . Recent mad pride activities include a Mad Pride Cabaret in Vancouver, British Columbia; a Mad Pride March in Accra, Ghana; and a Bonkersfest in London that drew 3,000 participants. . . . In recent years, groups have started anti-stigma campaigns, and even the federal government embraces the message, with an ad campaign aimed at young adults to encourage them to support friends with mental illness. . . .

Ms. Spikol writes about her experiences with bipolar disorder in The Philadelphia Weekly, and posts videos on her blog, the Trouble With Spikol. . . . Thousands have watched her joke about her weight gain and loss of libido, and her giggle-punctuated portrayal of ECT. But another video shows her face pale and her eyes red-rimmed as she reflects on the dark

Shea Roggio/The New York Times/Redux

"Mad pride" Writer and blogger Liz Spikol sits in front of a laptop that displays her Web site. With both wit and self-revelation, Spikol, who suffers from bipolar disorder, speaks out on her trials and tribulations—seeking to increase awareness and remove the stigma of mental disorders.

period in which she couldn't care for herself, or even shower. "I knew I was crazy but also sane enough to know that I couldn't make myself sane," she says in the video. . . .

Ms. Saks, the U.S.C. professor, who recently published a memoir, "The Center Cannot Hold: My Journey Through Madness," has come to accept her illness. She manages her symptoms with a regimen that includes psychoanalysis and medication. But stigma, she said, is never far away. She said she waited until she had tenure at U.S.C. before going public with her experience. . . . Ms. Saks said she hopes to help others in her position, find tolerance, especially those with fewer resources. "I have the kind of life that anybody, mentally ill or not, would want: a good place to live, nice friends, loved ones," she said. "For an unlucky person," Ms. Saks said, "I'm very lucky."

researchers and clinicians are human beings, living within a society of human beings, working to serve human beings. The mixture of discovery, misdirection, promise, and frustration that you have encountered throughout this book is thus to be expected. When you think about it, could the study and treatment of human behavior really proceed in any other way?

PUTTING IT... together

Operating Within a Larger System

At one time clinical researchers and professionals conducted their work largely in isolation. Today, however, their activities have numerous ties to the legislative, judicial, and economic systems, and to technological forces as well. One reason for this growing interconnectedness is that the clinical field has achieved a high level of respect and acceptance in our society. Clinicians now serve millions of people in many ways. They have much to say about almost every aspect of society, from education to ecology, and are widely looked to as sources of expertise. When a field achieves such prominence, it inevitably affects how other institutions are run. It also attracts public scrutiny, and various institutions begin to keep an eye on its activities.

Today, when people with psychological problems seek help from a therapist, they are entering a complex system consisting of many interconnected parts. Just as their personal problems have grown within a social structure, so will their treatment be affected by the various parts of a larger system—the therapist's values and needs, legal and economic forces, societal attitudes, technological changes, and yet other forces. These many forces influence clinical research as well.

The effects of this larger system on an individual's psychological needs can be positive or negative, like a family's impact on each of its members. When the system protects a client's rights and confidentiality, for example, it is serving the client well. When economic, legal, or other societal forces limit treatment options, cut off treatment prematurely, or stigmatize a person, the system is adding to the person's problems.

Because of the enormous growth and impact of the mental health profession in our society, it is important that we understand its strengths and weaknesses. As you have seen throughout this book, the field has gathered much knowledge, especially during the past several decades. What mental health professionals do not know and cannot do, however, still outweigh what they do know and can do. Everyone who turns to the clinical field—directly or indirectly—must recognize that it is young and imperfect. Society is vastly curious about behavior and often in need of information and help. What we as a society must remember, however, is that the field is still *putting it all together.*

Summing Up

- **LAW AND MENTAL HEALTH** The mental health profession interacts with the *legislative and judicial systems* in two key ways. First, clinicians help assess the mental stability of people accused of crimes. Second, the legislative and judicial systems help regulate mental health care. *p. 590*

- **CRIMINAL COMMITMENT** The punishment of persons convicted of crimes depends on the assumption that individuals are *responsible for their acts* and are *capable of defending themselves in court.* Evaluations by clinicians may help judges and juries decide the culpability of defendants and sometimes result in criminal commitment.

  If defendants are judged to have been *mentally unstable at the time they committed a crime,* they may be found *not guilty by reason of insanity* and placed in a treatment facility rather than a prison. "Insanity" is a legal term, one defined by legislators, not by clinicians. In federal courts and about half the state courts, insanity is judged in accordance with the *M'Naghten test,* which holds that defendants were insane at the time of a criminal act if they did not know the nature or quality of the act or did not know right from wrong at the time they committed it. Other states use the broader *American Law Institute test.*

The insanity defense has been criticized on several grounds, and some states have added an additional option, *guilty but mentally ill.* Defendants who receive this verdict are sentenced to prison with the proviso that they will also receive psychological treatment. Still another verdict option is *guilty with diminished capacity.* A related category consists of convicted *sex offenders,* who are considered in some states to have a mental disorder and are therefore assigned to treatment in a mental health facility.

Regardless of their state of mind at the time of the crime, defendants may be found *mentally incompetent to stand trial,* that is, incapable of fully understanding the charges or legal proceedings that confront them. If so, they are typically sent to a mental hospital until they are competent to stand trial. *pp. 590–598*

■ **CIVIL COMMITMENT** The legal system also influences the clinical profession. First, courts may be called upon to commit noncriminals to mental hospitals for treatment, a process called *civil commitment.* Society allows involuntary commitment of people considered to be *in need of treatment* and *dangerous to themselves or others.* Laws governing civil commitment procedures vary from state to state, but a *minimum standard of proof*—clear and convincing evidence of the necessity of commitment—has been defined by the Supreme Court. *pp. 598–602*

■ **PROTECTING PATIENTS' RIGHTS** The courts and legislatures significantly affect the mental health profession by specifying legal rights to which patients are entitled. The rights that have received the most attention are the *right to treatment* and the *right to refuse treatment. pp. 603–605*

■ **OTHER CLINICAL-LEGAL INTERACTIONS** Mental health and legal professionals also cross paths in four other areas. First, *malpractice suits* against therapists have increased in recent years. Second, the legislative and judicial systems help define *professional boundaries.* Third, lawyers may solicit the advice of mental health professionals regarding the *selection of jurors* and case strategies. Fourth, psychologists may *investigate legal phenomena* such as *eyewitness testimony* and *patterns of criminality. pp. 605–609*

■ **ETHICAL PRINCIPLES** Each clinical profession has a *code of ethics.* The psychologists' code includes prohibitions against *engaging in fraudulent research* and against *taking advantage of clients and students, sexually or otherwise.* It also establishes guidelines for respecting patient *confidentiality.* The case of *Tarasoff v. Regents of the University of California* helped to determine the circumstances in which therapists have a *duty to protect* the client or others from harm and must break confidentiality. *pp. 609–611*

■ **MENTAL HEALTH, BUSINESS, AND ECONOMICS** Clinical practice and study also intersect with the business and economic worlds. Clinicians often help to address psychological problems in the workplace, for example, through *employee assistance programs* and *stress-reduction and problem-solving seminars.*

Reductions in government funding of clinical services have left much of the expense for these services to be paid by insurance companies. Private insurance companies are setting up *managed care programs* whose structure and reimbursement procedures influence and often reduce the duration and focus of therapy. Their procedures, which include *peer review systems,* may also compromise patient confidentiality and the quality of therapy services. *pp. 611–612*

■ **TECHNOLOGY AND MENTAL HEALTH** The remarkable technological advances of recent times have affected the mental health field, just as they have affected all other fields and professions. In particular, these advances have contributed to new vehicles and triggers for psychopathology, new forms of psychopathology, and various kinds of cybertherapy *pp. 612–615*

■ **THE PERSON WITHIN THE PROFESSION** Mental health activities are affected by the personal needs, values, and goals of the human beings who provide the clinical services. These factors inevitably affect the choice, direction, and even quality of their work. *pp. 615–617*

PsychPortal

Visit **PsychPortal**
www.yourpsychportal.com
to access the e-book, videocases and other case materials and activities, and study aids, including flashcards, crossword puzzles, quizzes, FAQs, and research exercises.

BETWEEN THE LINES

In Their Words

"I think John Hinckley will be a threat the rest of his life. He is a time bomb." ‹‹
(U.S. Attorney, 1982)

"Without doubt, [John Hinckley] is the least dangerous person on the planet." ‹‹
Attorney for John Hinckley, applying for increased privileges for his client, 2003

glossary

ABAB design A single-subject experimental design in which behavior is measured during a baseline period, after a treatment has been applied, after baseline conditions have been reintroduced, and after the treatment has been reintroduced. Also called a *reversal design*.

Abnormal psychology The scientific study of abnormal behavior in order to describe, predict, explain, and change abnormal patterns of functioning.

Acceptance and commitment therapy A cognitive-behavioral therapy that teaches clients to accept and be mindful of (i.e., just notice) their dysfunctional thoughts or worries.

Acetylcholine A neurotransmitter that has been linked to depression and dementia.

Acute stress disorder A disorder in which fear and related symptoms are experienced soon after a traumatic event and last less than a month.

Addiction Persistent, compulsive dependence on a substance or behavior.

Adjustment disorders Disorders characterized by clinical symptoms such as depressed mood or anxiety in response to significant stressors.

Affect An experience of emotion or mood.

Aftercare A program of post-hospitalization care and treatment in the community.

Agoraphobia An anxiety disorder in which a person is afraid to be in public places or situations from which escape might be difficult (or embarrassing) or help unavailable if panic-like symptoms were to occur.

Alcohol Any beverage containing ethyl alcohol, including beer, wine, and liquor.

Alcohol dehydrogenase An enzyme that breaks down alcohol in the stomach before it enters the blood.

Alcohol use disorder A pattern of behavior in which a person repeatedly abuses or depends on alcohol. Also known as *alcoholism*.

Alcoholics Anonymous (AA) A self-help organization that provides support and guidance for persons with alcoholism.

Alcoholism A pattern of behavior in which a person repeatedly abuses or depends on alcohol. Also known as *alcohol use disorder*.

Alogia A decrease in speech or speech content; a symptom of schizophrenia. Also known as *poverty of speech*.

Alprazolam A benzodiazepine drug shown to be effective in the treatment of anxiety disorders. Marketed as *Xanax*.

Altruistic suicide Suicide committed by people who intentionally sacrifice their lives for the well-being of society.

Alzheimer's disease The most common type of neurocognitive disorder, usually occurring after the age of 65, marked most prominently by memory impairment.

Amenorrhea The cessation of menstrual cycles.

American Law Institute test A legal test for insanity that holds people to be insane at the time of committing a crime if, because of a mental disorder, they did not know right from wrong or could not resist an uncontrollable impulse to act.

Amnesia Loss of memory.

Amniocentesis A prenatal procedure used to test the amniotic fluid that surrounds the fetus for the possibility of birth defects.

Amphetamines Stimulant drugs that are manufactured in the laboratory.

Amphetamine psychosis A syndrome characterized by psychotic symptoms brought on by high doses of amphetamines. Similar to *cocaine psychosis*.

Amygdala A structure in the brain that plays a key role in emotion and memory.

Analog observation A method for observing behavior in which people are observed in artificial settings such as clinicians' offices or laboratories.

Analogue experiment A research method in which the experimenter produces abnormal-like behavior in laboratory participants and then conducts experiments on the participants.

Anal stage In psychoanalytic theory, the second 18 months of life, during which the child's focus of pleasure shifts to the anus.

Anesthesia A lessening or loss of sensation of touch or for pain.

Anomic suicide Suicide committed by individuals whose social environment fails to provide stability, thus leaving them without a sense of belonging.

Anorexia nervosa A disorder marked by the pursuit of extreme thinness and by an extreme loss of weight.

Anoxia A complication of birth in which the baby is deprived of oxygen.

Antabuse (disulfiram) A drug that causes intense nausea, vomiting, increased heart rate, and dizziness when taken with alcohol. It is often taken by people who are trying to refrain from drinking alcohol.

Antagonist drugs Drugs that block or change the effects of an addictive drug.

Antianxiety drugs Psychotropic drugs that help reduce tension and anxiety. Also called *minor tranquilizers* or *anxiolytics*.

Antibipolar drugs Psychotropic drugs that help stabilize the moods of people suffering from a bipolar mood disorder. Also known as *mood stabilizing drugs*.

Antibodies Bodily chemicals that seek out and destroy foreign invaders such as bacteria or viruses.

Antidepressant drugs Psychotropic drugs that improve the mood of people with depression.

Antigen A foreign invader of the body, such as a bacterium or virus.

Antipsychotic drugs Drugs that help correct grossly confused or distorted thinking.

Antisocial personality disorder A personality disorder marked by a general pattern of disregard for and violation of other people's rights.

Anxiety The central nervous system's physiological and emotional response to a vague sense of threat or danger.

Anxiety disorder A disorder in which anxiety is a central symptom.

Anxiety sensitivity A tendency to focus on one's bodily sensations, assess them illogically, and interpret them as harmful.

Anxiolytics Drugs that reduce anxiety.

Arbitrary inference An error in logic in which a person draws negative conclusions on the basis of little or even contrary evidence.

Aripiprazole An atypical antipsychotic drug whose brand name is Abilify.

Asperger's disorder One of the patterns found in autism spectrum disorder, in which individuals display profound social impairment yet maintain a relatively high level of cognitive functioning and language skills.

Assertiveness training A cognitive-behavioral approach to increasing assertive behavior that is socially desirable.

Assessment The process of collecting and interpreting relevant information about a client or research participant.

Asthma A medical problem marked by narrowing of the trachea and bronchi, which results in shortness of breath, wheezing, coughing, and a choking sensation.

Asylum A type of institution that first became popular in the sixteenth century to provide care for persons with mental disorders. Most became virtual prisons.

Attention-deficit/hyperactivity disorder (ADHD) A disorder marked by inability to focus attention, overactive and impulsive behavior, or both.

Attribution An explanation of things we see going on around us that points to particular causes.

Atypical antipsychotic drugs A relatively new group of antipsychotic drugs whose biological action is different from that of the conventional antipsychotic drugs.

Auditory hallucination A hallucination in which a person hears sounds or voices that are not actually present.

Augmentative communication system A method for enhancing the communication skills of individuals with autism spectrum disorder, intellectual developmental disorder, or cerebral palsy by teaching them to point to pictures, symbols, letters, or words on a communication board or computer.

Aura A warning sensation that may precede a migraine headache.

Autism spectrum disorder A developmental disorder marked by extreme unresponsiveness to others, severe communication deficits, and highly repetitive and rigid behaviors, interests, and activities.

Autoerotic asphyxia A fatal lack of oxygen that persons may unintentionally produce while hanging, suffocating, or strangling themselves during masturbation.

Automatic thoughts Numerous unpleasant thoughts that help to cause or maintain depression, anxiety, or other forms of psychological dysfunction.

Autonomic nervous system (ANS) The network of nerve fibers that connect the central nervous system to all the other organs of the body.

Aversion therapy A treatment in which clients are repeatedly presented with unpleasant stimuli while performing undesirable behaviors such as taking a drug.

Avoidant personality disorder A personality disorder characterized by consistent discomfort and restraint in social situations, overwhelming feelings of inadequacy, and extreme sensitivity to negative evaluation.

Avolition A symptom of schizophrenia marked by apathy and an inability to start or complete a course of action.

Axon A long fiber extending from the body of a neuron.

Barbiturates One group of sedative-hypnotic drugs that reduce anxiety and help produce sleep.

Baroreceptors Sensitive nerves in the blood vessels that are responsible for signaling the brain that blood pressure is becoming too high.

Baseline data An individual's initial response level on a test or scale.

Basic irrational assumptions The inaccurate and inappropriate beliefs held by people with various psychological problems, according to Albert Ellis.

Battery A series of tests, each of which measures a specific skill area.

B-cell A lymphocyte that produces antibodies.

Behavioral medicine A field that combines psychological and physical interventions to treat or prevent medical problems.

Behavioral model A theoretical perspective that emphasizes behavior and the ways in which it is learned.

Behavioral therapy A therapeutic approach that seeks to identify problem-causing behaviors and change them. Also known as *behavior modification*.

Behaviors The responses an organism makes to its environment.

Bender Visual-Motor Gestalt Test A neuropsychological test in which a subject is asked to copy a set of nine simple designs and later reproduce the designs from memory.

Benzodiazepines The most common group of antianxiety drugs, which includes Valium and Xanax.

Bereavement The process of working through the grief that one feels when a loved one dies.

Beta-amyloid protein A small molecule that forms sphere-shaped deposits called senile plaques, linked to aging and to Alzheimer's disease.

"Big Five" theory of personality A leading theory that holds that personality can be effectively organized and described by five broad dimensions of personality—openness, conscientiousness, extraversion, agreeableness, and neuroticism.

Binge An episode of uncontrollable eating during which a person ingests a very large quantity of food.

Binge drinking A pattern of alcohol consumption in which five or more drinks are consumed on a single occasion.

Binge-eating disorder A disorder marked by frequent binges but not extreme compensatory behaviors.

Binge-eating/purging-type anorexia nervosa A type of anorexia nervosa in which people have eating binges but still lose excessive weight by forcing themselves to vomit after meals or by abusing laxatives or diuretics.

Biofeedback A technique in which a client is given information about physiological reactions as they occur and learns to control the reactions voluntarily.

Biological challenge test A procedure used to produce panic in participants or clients by having them exercise vigorously or perform some other potentially panic-inducing task in the presence of a researcher or therapist.

Biological model The theoretical perspective that points to biological processes as the key to human behavior.

Biological therapy The use of physical and chemical procedures to help people overcome psychological problems.

Biopsychosocial theories Explanations that attribute the cause of abnormality to an interaction of genetic, biological, developmental, emotional, behavioral, cognitive, social, and societal influences.

Bipolar disorder A disorder marked by alternating or intermixed periods of mania and depression.

Bipolar I disorder A type of bipolar disorder marked by full manic and major depressive episodes.

Bipolar II disorder A type of bipolar disorder marked by mild manic and major depressive episodes.

Birth complications Problematic biological conditions during birth that can affect the physical and psychological well-being of the child.

Blind design An experiment in which participants do not know whether they are in the experimental or the control condition.

Blunted affect A symptom of schizophrenia in which a person shows less emotion than most people.

Body dysmorphic disorder A disorder marked by excessive worry that some aspect of one's physical appearance is defective. Also known as *dysmorphophobia*.

Borderline personality disorder A personality disorder characterized by repeated instability in interpersonal relationships, self-image, and mood and by impulsive behavior.

Brain circuits Networks of brain structures that work together, triggering each other into action with the help of neurotransmitters.

Brain region A distinct area of the brain formed by a large group of neurons.

Brain wave The fluctuations of electrical potential that are produced by neurons in the brain.

Breathing-related sleep disorder A sleep disorder in which sleep is frequently disrupted by a breathing problem, causing excessive sleepiness or insomnia.

Brief psychotic disorder Psychotic symptoms that appear suddenly after a very stressful event or a period of emotional turmoil and last anywhere from a few hours to a month.

Brodmann Area 25 Brain structure whose abnormal activity has been linked to depression.

Bulimia nervosa A disorder marked by frequent eating binges that are followed by forced vomiting or other extreme compensatory behaviors. Also known as *binge-purge syndrome*.

Caffeine The world's most widely used stimulant, most often consumed in coffee.

Cannabis Substance produced from the varieties of the hemp plant, *Cannabis sativa*. It causes a mixture of hallucinogenic, depressant, and stimulant effects.

Case manager A community therapist who offers a full range of services for people with schizophrenia or other severe disorders, including therapy, advice, medication, guidance, and protection of patients' rights.

Case study A detailed account of a person's life and psychological problems.

Catatonia A pattern of extreme psychomotor symptoms, found in some forms of schizophrenia, which may include catatonic stupor, rigidity, or posturing.

Catatonic excitement A form of catatonia in which a person moves excitedly, sometimes with wild waving of the arms and legs.

Catatonic stupor A symptom associated with schizophrenia in which a person becomes almost totally unresponsive to the environment, remaining motionless and silent for long stretches of time.

Catharsis The reliving of past repressed feelings in order to settle internal conflicts and overcome problems.

Caudate nuclei Structures in the brain, within the region known as the basal ganglia, that help convert sensory information into thoughts and actions.

Central nervous system The brain and spinal cord.

Cerebellum An area of the brain that coordinates movement in the body and perhaps helps control a person's rapid attention to things.

Checking compulsion A compulsion in which people feel compelled to check the same things over and over.

Child abuse The nonaccidental use of excessive physical or psychological force by an adult on a child, often aimed at hurting or destroying the child.

Chlorpromazine A phenothiazine drug commonly used for treating schizophrenia. Marketed as *Thorazine*.

Chromosomes The structures located within a cell that contain genes.

Chronic headaches Frequent intense aches in the head or neck that are not caused by another medical disorder.

Circadian rhythms Internal "clocks" consisting of repeated biological fluctuations.

Circadian rhythm sleep disorder A sleep disorder caused by a mismatch between the sleep-wake cycle in a person's environment and the person's own circadian sleep-wake cycle.

Cirrhosis An irreversible condition, often caused by excessive drinking, in which the liver becomes scarred and begins to change in anatomy and functioning.

Civil commitment A legal process by which an individual can be forced to undergo mental health treatment.

Clang A rhyme used by some persons with schizophrenia as a guide to forming thoughts and statements.

Classical conditioning A process of learning in which two events that repeatedly occur close together in time become tied together in a person's mind and so produce the same response.

Classification system A list of disorders, along with descriptions of symptoms and guidelines for making appropriate diagnoses.

Cleaning compulsion A common compulsion in which people feel compelled to keep cleaning themselves, their clothing, and their homes.

Client-centered therapy The humanistic therapy developed by Carl Rogers in which clinicians try to help clients by being accepting, empathizing accurately, and conveying genuineness.

Clinical interview A face-to-face encounter in which clinicians ask questions of clients, weigh their responses and reactions, and learn about them and their psychological problems.

Clinical psychologist A mental health professional who has earned a doctorate in clinical psychology.

Clinical psychology The study, assessment, treatment, and prevention of abnormal behavior.

Clitoris The female sex organ located in front of the urinary and vaginal openings. It becomes enlarged during sexual arousal.

Clozapine A commonly prescribed atypical antipsychotic drug.

Cocaine An addictive stimulant obtained from the coca plant. It is the most powerful natural stimulant known.

Code of ethics A body of principles and rules for ethical behavior, designed to guide decisions and actions by members of a profession.

Cognition The capacity to think, remember, and anticipate.

Cognitive behavior Thoughts and beliefs, many of which remain private.

Cognitive-behavioral therapies Therapy approaches that seek to help clients change both counterproductive behaviors and dysfunctional ways of thinking.

Cognitive model A theoretical perspective that emphasizes the process and content of thinking as causes of psychological problems.

Cognitive therapy A therapy developed by Aaron Beck that helps people identify and change the maladaptive assumptions and ways of thinking that help cause their psychological disorders.

Cognitive triad The three forms of negative thinking that theorist Aaron Beck theorizes lead people to feel depressed. The triad consists of a negative view of one's experiences, oneself, and the future.

Coitus Sexual intercourse.

Communication disorders Disorders characterized by marked impairment in language and/or speech.

Community mental health center A treatment facility that provides medication, psychotherapy, and emergency care to patients and coordinates treatment in the community.

Community mental health treatment A treatment approach that emphasizes community care.

Comorbidity The occurrence of two or more disorders in the same person.

Compulsion A repetitive and rigid behavior or mental act that persons feel they must perform in order to prevent or reduce anxiety.

Compulsive ritual A detailed, often elaborate, set of actions that a person often feels compelled to perform, always in an identical manner.

Computerized axial tomography (CAT scan) A composite image of the brain created by compiling X-ray images taken from many angles.

Concordance A statistical measure of the frequency with which family members (often both members of a pair of twins) have the same particular characteristic.

Concurrent validity The degree to which the measures gathered from one assessment tool agree with the measures gathered from other assessment techniques.

Conditioned response (CR) A response previously associated with an unconditioned stimulus that comes to be produced by a conditioned stimulus.

Conditioned stimulus (CS) A previously neutral stimulus that comes to be associated with a nonneutral stimulus, and can then produce responses similar to those produced by the nonneutral stimulus.

Conditioning A simple form of learning.

Conditions of worth According to client-centered theorists, the internal standards by which a person judges his or her own lovability and acceptability, determined by the standards to which the person was held as a child.

Conduct disorder A childhood disorder in which the child repeatedly violates the basic rights of others and displays aggression, characterized by symptoms such as physical cruelty to people or animals, the deliberate destruction of other people's property, and the commission of various crimes.

Confabulation A made-up description of one's experience to fill in a gap in one's memory.

Confederate An experimenter's accomplice, who helps create a particular impression in a study while pretending to be just another subject.

Confidentiality The principle that certain professionals will not divulge the information they obtain from a client.

Confound In an experiment, a variable other than the independent variable that is also acting on the dependent variable.

Continuous amnesia An inability to recall newly occurring events as well as certain past events.

Control group In an experiment, a group of participants who are not exposed to the independent variable.

Conversion disorder A disorder in which bodily symptoms affect voluntary motor and sensory functions, but the symptoms are inconsistent with known medical diseases.

Convulsion A brain seizure.

Coronary arteries Blood vessels that surround the heart and are responsible for carrying oxygen to the heart muscle.

Coronary heart disease Illness of the heart caused by a blockage in the coronary arteries.

Correlation The degree to which events or characteristics vary along with each other.

Correlation coefficient (r) A statistical term that indicates the direction and the magnitude of a correlation, ranging from–1.00 to +1.00.

Correlational method A research procedure used to determine how much events or characteristics vary along with each other.

Corticosteroids A group of hormones, including cortisol, released by the adrenal glands at times of stress.

Cortisol A hormone released by the adrenal glands when a person is under stress.

Counseling psychology A mental health specialty similar to clinical psychology that requires completion of its own graduate training program.

Countertransference A phenomenon of psychotherapy in which therapists' own feelings, history, and values subtly influence the way they interpret a patient's problems.

Couple therapy A therapy format in which the therapist works with two people who share a long-term relationship.

Covert desensitization Desensitization that focuses on imagining confrontations with the frightening objects or situations while in a state of relaxation.

Covert sensitization A behavioral treatment for eliminating unwanted behavior by pairing the behavior with unpleasant mental images.

Crack A powerful, ready-to-smoke freebase cocaine.

C-reactive protein (CRP) A protein that spreads throughout the body and causes inflammation and various illnesses and disorders.

Cretinism A disorder marked by intellectual deficiencies and physical abnormalities; caused by low levels of iodine in the mother's diet during pregnancy.

Creutzfeldt-Jakob disease A form of neurocognitive disorder caused by a slow-acting virus that may live in the body for years before the disease unfolds.

Criminal commitment A legal process by which persons accused of a crime are instead judged mentally unstable and sent to a mental health facility for treatment.

Crisis intervention A treatment approach that tries to help people in a psychological crisis view their situation more accurately, make better decisions, act more constructively, and overcome the crisis.

Critical incident stress debriefing Training in how to help victims of disasters or other horrifying events talk about their feelings and reactions to the traumatic incidents.

Cross-tolerance Tolerance that a person develops for a substance as a result of regularly using another substance similar to it.

Culture A people's common history, values, institutions, habits, skills, technology, and arts.

Culture-sensitive therapies Approaches that seek to address the unique issues faced by members of minority groups.

Cyberbullying The use of e-mail, texting, chat rooms, cell phones, or other digital devices to harass, threaten, or intimidate persons.

Cyclothymic disorder A disorder marked by numerous periods of hypomanic symptoms and mild depressive symptoms.

Day center A program that offers hospital-like treatment during the day only. Also known as a *day hospital*.

Death darer A person who is ambivalent about the wish to die even as he or she attempts suicide.

Death ignorer A person who attempts suicide without recognizing the finality of death.

Death initiator A person who attempts suicide believing that the process of death is already under way and that he or she is simply quickening the process.

Death seeker A person who clearly intends to end his or her life at the time of a suicide attempt.

Deep brain stimulation (DBS) A treatment procedure for depression in which a pacemaker powers electrodes that have been implanted in Brodmann Area 25, thus stimulating that brain area.

Deinstitutionalization The discharge, begun during the 1960s, of large numbers of patients from long-term institutional care so that they might be treated in community programs.

Déjà vu The haunting sense of having previously seen or experienced a new scene or situation.

Delayed ejaculation A male dysfunction characterized by persistent inability to ejaculate or very delayed ejaculations during sexual activity with a partner.

Delirium A rapidly developing, acute disturbance in attention and orientation that make it very difficult to concentrate and think in a clear and organized manner.

Delirium tremens (DTs) A dramatic withdrawal reaction experienced by some people with alcoholism. It consists of confusion, clouded consciousness, and terrifying visual hallucinations.

Delusion A strange false belief firmly held despite evidence to the contrary.

Delusion of control The belief that one's impulses, feelings, thoughts, or actions are being controlled by other people.

Delusion of grandeur The belief that one is a great inventor, historical figure, or other specially empowered person.

Delusion of persecution The belief that one is being plotted or discriminated against, spied on, slandered, threatened, attacked, or deliberately victimized.

Delusion of reference A belief that attaches special and personal meaning to the actions of others or to various objects or events.

Delusional disorder A disorder consisting of persistent delusions that are not part of a schizophrenic disorder.

Demonology The belief that abnormal behavior results from supernatural causes such as evil spirits.

Dendrite An extension located at one end of a neuron that receives impulses from other neurons.

Denial An ego defense mechanism in which a person fails to acknowledge unacceptable thoughts, feelings, or actions.

Dependent personality disorder A personality disorder characterized by a pattern of clinging and obedience, fear of separation, and a persistent, excessive need to be taken care of.

Dependent variable The variable in an experiment that is expected to change as the independent variable is manipulated.

Depersonalization-derealization disorder A dissociative disorder marked by the presence of persistent and recurrent episodes of depersonalization, derealization, or both.

Depressant A substance that slows the activity of the central nervous system and in sufficient dosages causes a reduction of tension and inhibitions.

Depression A low, sad state marked by significant levels of sadness, lack of energy, low self-worth, guilt, or related symptoms.

Depressive disorders The group of disorders marked by unipolar depression.

Derailment A common thinking disturbance in schizophrenia, involving rapid shifts from one topic of conversation to another. Also called *loose associations*.

Desensitization *See* Systematic desensitization.

Desire phase The phase of the sexual response cycle consisting of an urge to have sex, sexual fantasies, and sexual attraction.

Detoxification Systematic and medically supervised withdrawal from a drug.

Developmental coordination disorder Disorder characterized by marked impairment in the development and performance of coordinated motor activities.

Deviance Variance from common patterns of behavior.

Diagnosis A determination that a person's problems reflect a particular disorder.

Diagnostic and Statistical Manual of Mental Disorders (DSM) The classification system for mental disorders developed by the American Psychiatric Association.

Dialectical behavior therapy A therapy approach developed by psychologist Marsha Linehan to treat people with borderline personality disorder and other psychological disorders, consisting of cognitive-behavioral techniques in combination with various emotion regulation, mindfulness, humanistic, and other techniques.

Diathesis-stress view The view that a person must first have a predisposition to a disorder and then be subjected to immediate psychosocial stress in order to develop the disorder.

Diazepam A benzodiazepine drug, marketed as *Valium*.

Dichotomous thinking Viewing problems and solutions in rigid "either/ or" terms.

Diencephalon A brain area (consisting of the mammillary bodies, thalamus, and hypothalamus) that plays a key role in transforming short-term to long-term memory, among other functions.

Directed masturbation training A sex therapy approach that teaches women with female arousal or orgasmic disorders how to masturbate effectively and eventually reach orgasm during sexual interactions.

Disaster Response Network (DRN) A network of thousands of volunteer mental health professionals who mobilize to provide free emergency psychological services at disaster sites throughout North America.

Displacement An ego defense mechanism that channels unacceptable id impulses toward another, safer substitute.

Disruptive mood dysregulation disorder A disorder of childhood or adolescence marked by severe recurrent temper outbursts along with a persistent irritable or angry mood.

Dissociative amnesia A dissociative disorder marked by an inability to recall important personal events and information.

Dissociative disorders A group of disorders in which some parts of one's memory or identity seem to be dissociated, or separated, from other parts of one's memory or identity.

Dissociative identity disorder A disorder in which a person develops two or more distinct personalities. Also called *multiple personality disorder*.

Disulfiram (Antabuse) An antagonist drug used in treating alcohol abuse or dependence.

Dopamine The neurotransmitter whose high activity has been shown to be related to schizophrenia.

Dopamine hypothesis The theory that schizophrenia results from excessive activity of the neurotransmitter dopamine.

Double-bind hypothesis A theory that some parents repeatedly communicate pairs of messages that are mutually contradictory, helping to produce schizophrenia in their children.

Double-blind design Experimental procedure in which neither the participant nor the experimenter knows whether the participant has received the experimental treatment or a placebo.

Double depression A sequence in which dysthymic disorder leads to a major depressive disorder.

Down syndrome A form of intellectual developmental disorder caused by an abnormality in the twenty-first chromosome.

Dream A series of ideas and images that form during sleep.

Drug Any substance other than food that affects the body or mind.

Drug maintenance therapy An approach to treating substance dependence in which clients are given legally and medically supervised doses of the drug on which they are dependent or a substitute drug.

Drug therapy The use of psychotropic drugs to reduce the symptoms of psychological disorders.

DSM-5 (Diagnostic and Statistical Manual of Mental Disorders, Fifth Edition) The newest edition of the DSM, published in 2013.

Durham test A legal test for insanity that holds people to be insane at the time they committed a crime if their act was the result of a mental disorder or defect.

Duty to protect The principle that therapists must break confidentiality in order to protect a person who may be the intended victim of a client.

Dyslexia A type of specific learning disorder in which persons show a marked impairment in the ability to recognize words and to comprehend what they read.

Dyssomnias Sleep disorders in which the amount, quality, or timing of sleep is disturbed.

Dysthymic disorder A mood disorder that is similar to but longer-lasting and less disabling than major depressive disorder. Technically, one form of *persistent depressive disorder*.

Early ejaculation A dysfunction in which a man persistently reaches orgasm and ejaculates within one minute of beginning sexual activity with a partner and before he wishes to. Also called *premature ejaculation* and *rapid ejaculation*.

Eccentric Person who deviates from conventional norms in odd, irregular, or even bizarre ways, but is not displaying a psychological disorder.

Echolalia A symptom of autism or schizophrenia in which a person responds to statements by repeating the other person's words.

Ecstasy (MDMA) A drug chemically related to amphetamines and hallucinogens, used illicitly for its euphoric and hallucinogenic effects.

Ego According to Freud, the psychological force that employs reason and operates in accordance with the reality principle.

Ego defense mechanisms According to psychoanalytic theory, strategies developed by the ego to control unacceptable id impulses and to avoid or reduce the anxiety they arouse.

Ego theory The psychodynamic theory that emphasizes the ego and considers it an independent force.

Egoistic suicide Suicide committed by people over whom society has little or no control, people who are not concerned with the norms or rules of society.

Eidetic imagery A strong visual image of an object or scene that persists in some persons long after the object or scene is removed.

Ejaculation Contractions of the muscles at the base of the penis that cause sperm to be ejected.

Electra complex According to Freud, the pattern of desires all girls experience during the phallic stage, in which they develop a sexual attraction to their father.

Electroconvulsive therapy (ECT) A treatment for depression in which electrodes attached to a patient's head send an electrical current through the brain, causing a seizure.

Electroencephalograph (EEG) A device that records electrical impulses in the brain.

Electromyograph (EMG) A device that provides feedback about the level of muscular tension in the body.

Emergency commitment Temporary commitment to a mental hospital of a patient who is behaving in a bizarre or violent way.

Empirically supported treatment A movement in the clinical field that seeks to identify which therapies have received clear research support for each disorder, to develop corresponding treatment guidelines, and to spread such information to clinicians. Also known as *evidence-based treatment*.

Employee assistance program A mental health program offered by a business to its employees.

Encopresis A childhood disorder characterized by repeated defecation in inappropriate places, such as one's clothing.

Endocrine system The system of glands located throughout the body that help control important activities such as growth and sexual activity.

Endogenous depression A depression that appears to develop without external reasons and is assumed to be caused by internal factors.

Endorphins Neurotransmitters that help relieve pain and reduce emotional tension. They are sometimes referred to as the body's own opioids.

Enmeshed family pattern A family system in which members are overinvolved with each other's affairs and overconcerned about each other's welfare.

Enuresis A childhood disorder marked by repeated bed-wetting or wetting of one's clothes.

Epidemiological study A study that measures the incidence and prevalence of a disorder in a given population.

Erectile disorder A dysfunction in which a man persistently fails to attain or maintain an erection during sexual activity.

Ergot alkaloid A naturally occurring compound from which LSD is derived.

Essential hypertension High blood pressure caused by a combination of psychosocial and physiological factors.

Estrogen The primary female sex hormone.

Ethyl alcohol The chemical compound in all alcoholic beverages that is rapidly absorbed into the blood and immediately begins to affect the person's functioning.

Evoked potentials The brain response patterns recorded on an electroencephalograph while a person performs a task such as observing a flashing light.

Excitement phase The phase of the sexual response cycle marked by changes in the pelvic region, general physical arousal, and increases in heart rate, muscle tension, blood pressure, and rate of breathing.

Excoriation disorder A disorder in which persons keep picking at their skin, resulting in significant sores or wounds. Also called *skin-picking disorder*.

Exhibitionistic disorder A paraphilic disorder in which persons have repeated sexually arousing urges or fantasies about exposing their genitals to others and may act upon those urges.

Existential anxiety According to existential theorists, a universal fear of the limits and responsibilities of one's existence.

Existential model The theoretical perspective that human beings are born with the total freedom either to face up to one's existence and give meaning to one's life or to shrink from that responsibility.

Existential therapy A therapy that encourages clients to accept responsibility for their lives and to live with greater meaning and value.

Exorcism The practice in early societies of treating abnormality by coaxing evil spirits to leave the person's body.

Experiment A research procedure in which a variable is manipulated and the effect of the manipulation is observed.

Experimental group In an experiment, the participants who are exposed to the independent variable under investigation.

Exposure and response prevention A behavioral treatment for obsessive-compulsive disorder that exposes a client to anxiety-arousing thoughts or situations and then prevents the client from performing his or her compulsive acts. Also called *exposure and ritual prevention*.

Exposure treatments Behavioral treatments in which persons are exposed to the objects or situations they dread.

Expressed emotion The general level of criticism, disapproval, hostility, and intrusiveness expressed in a family. People recovering from schizophrenia are considered more likely to relapse if their families rate high in expressed emotion.

External validity The degree to which the results of a study may be generalized beyond that study.

Extrapyramidal effects Unwanted movements, such as severe shaking, bizarre grimaces, twisting of the body, and extreme restlessness, sometimes produced by conventional antipsychotic drugs.

Eye movement desensitization and reprocessing (EMDR) An exposure treatment in which clients move their eyes in a rhythmic manner from side to side while flooding their minds with images of objects and situations they ordinarily avoid.

Factitious disorder A disorder in which an individual feigns or induces physical

symptoms, typically for the purpose of assuming the role of a sick person.

Family pedigree study A research design in which investigators determine how many and which relatives of a person with a disorder have the same disorder.

Family systems theory A theory that views the family as a system of interacting parts whose interactions exhibit consistent patterns and unstated rules.

Family therapy A therapy format in which the therapist meets with all members of a family and helps them to change in therapeutic ways.

Fantasy An ego defense mechanism in which a person uses imaginary events to satisfy unacceptable impulses.

Fear The central nervous system's physiological and emotional response to a serious threat to one's well-being.

Fear hierarchy A list of objects or situations that frighten a person, starting with those that are slightly feared and ending with those that are feared greatly; used in systematic desensitization.

Female orgasmic disorder A dysfunction in which a woman persistently fails to reach orgasm, experiences orgasms of very low intensity, or has very delayed orgasms.

Female sexual interest/arousal disorder A female dysfunction marked by a persistent reduction or lack of interest in sex and low sexual activity, as well as, in some cases, limited excitement and few sexual sensations during sexual activity.

Fetal alcohol syndrome A cluster of problems in a child, including low birth weight, irregularities in the hands and face, and intellectual deficits, caused by excessive alcohol intake by the mother during pregnancy.

Fetishistic disorder A paraphilic disorder consisting of recurrent and intense sexual urges, fantasies, or behaviors that involve the use of a nonliving object, often to the exclusion of all other stimuli.

Fixation According to Freud, a condition in which the id, ego, and superego do not mature properly and are frozen at an early stage of development.

Flashback The recurrence of LSD-induced sensory and emotional changes long after the drug has left the body, or, in posttraumatic stress disorder, the reexperiencing of past traumatic events.

Flat affect A symptom of schizophrenia in which the person shows almost no emotion at all.

Flooding A treatment for phobias in which clients are exposed repeatedly and intensively to a feared object and made to see that it is actually harmless.

Forensic psychology The branch of psychology concerned with intersections between psychological practice and research and the judicial system. Also related to the field of *forensic psychiatry*.

Formal thought disorder A disturbance in the production and organization of thought.

Free association A psychodynamic technique in which the patient describes any thought, feeling, or image that comes to mind, even if it seems unimportant.

Free-base A technique for ingesting cocaine in which the pure cocaine basic alkaloid is chemically separated from processed cocaine, vaporized by heat from a flame, and inhaled through a pipe.

Free-floating anxiety Chronic and persistent feelings of anxiety that are not clearly attached to a specific, identifiable threat.

Frotteuristic disorder A paraphilic disorder consisting of repeated and intense sexual urges, fantasies, or behaviors that involve touching and rubbing against a nonconsenting person.

Functional magnetic resonance imaging (fMRI) A neuroimaging technique used to visualize internal functioning of the brain or body.

Fusion The final merging of two or more subpersonalities in multiple personality disorder.

GABA The neurotransmitter gamma-aminobutyric acid, whose low activity has been linked to generalized anxiety disorder.

Gambling disorder A disorder marked by persistent and recurrent gambling behavior, leading to a range of life problems.

Gender dysphoria A disorder in which a person persistently feels extremely uncomfortable about his or her assigned sex and strongly wishes to be a member of the opposite sex. Also known as *transsexualism*.

Gender-sensitive therapies Approaches geared to the pressures of being a woman in Western society. Also called *feminist therapies*.

Gene Chromosome segments that control the characteristics and traits we inherit.

General paresis An irreversible medical disorder whose symptoms include psychological abnormalities, such as delusions of grandeur; caused by syphilis.

Generalized amnesia A loss of memory for events that occurred over a limited period of time as well as for certain events that occurred prior to that period.

Generalized anxiety disorder A disorder marked by persistent and excessive feelings of anxiety and worry about numerous events and activities.

Generic drug A marketed drug that is comparable to a trade-named drug in dosage form, strength, and performance.

Genetic linkage study A research approach in which extended families with high rates of a disorder over several generations are observed in order to determine whether

the disorder closely follows the distribution pattern of other family traits.

Genital stage In Freud's theory, the stage beginning at approximately 12 years old, when the child begins to find sexual pleasure in heterosexual relationships.

Genito-pelvic pain/penetration disorder A sexual dysfunction characterized by significant physical discomfort during intercourse.

Geropsychology The field of psychology concerned with the mental health of elderly people.

Gestalt therapy The humanistic therapy developed by Fritz Perls in which clinicians actively move clients toward self-recognition and self-acceptance by using techniques such as role playing and self-discovery exercises.

Glia Brain cells that support the neurons.

Glutamate A common neurotransmitter that has been linked to memory and to dementia.

Grief The reaction one experiences when a loved one is lost.

Group home A special home where people with disorders or disabilities live and are taught self-help, living, and working skills.

Group therapy A therapy format in which a group of people with similar problems meet together with a therapist to work on those problems.

Guided participation A modeling technique in which a client systematically observes and imitates the therapist while the therapist confronts feared items.

Guilty but mentally ill A verdict stating that defendants are guilty of committing a crime but are also suffering from a mental illness that should be treated during their imprisonment.

Guilty with diminished capacity A legal defense argument that states that because of limitations posed by mental dysfunctioning, a defendant could not have intended to commit a particular crime and thus should be convicted of a lesser crime.

Halfway house A residence for people with schizophrenia or other severe problems, often staffed by paraprofessionals. Also known as a *group home* or *crisis house*.

Hallucination The experiencing of imagined sights, sounds, or other perceptions in the absence of external stimuli.

Hallucinogen A substance that causes powerful changes primarily in sensory perception, including strengthening perceptions and producing illusions and hallucinations. Also called *psychedelic drug*.

Hallucinosis A form of intoxication caused by hallucinogens, consisting of perceptual distortions and hallucinations.

Hardiness A set of positive attitudes and reactions in response to stress.

Health maintenance The principle that young adults should act to promote their physical and mental health to best prepare for the aging process. Also called *wellness*.

Helper T-cell A lymphocyte that identifies foreign invaders and then both multiplies and triggers the production of other kinds of immune cells.

Heroin One of the most addictive substances derived from opium.

High The pleasant feeling of relaxation and euphoria that follows the rush from certain recreational drugs.

Hippocampus A brain area located below the cerebral cortex that is involved in memory.

Histrionic personality disorder A personality disorder in which an individual displays a pattern of excessive emotionality and attention seeking. Once called *hysterical personality disorder*.

Hoarding disorder A disorder in which people persistently feel that they must save items and experience great distress if they try to discard them, resulting in an extreme accumulation of items that clutter their lives and living areas.

Hopelessness A pessimistic belief that one's present circumstances, problems, or mood will not change.

Hormones The chemicals released by endocrine glands into the bloodstream.

Humanistic model The theoretical perspective that human beings are born with a natural inclination to be friendly, cooperative, and constructive and are driven to self-actualize.

Humanistic therapy A system of therapy that tries to help clients look at themselves accurately and acceptingly so that they can fulfill their positive inborn potential.

Humors According to the Greeks and Romans, bodily chemicals that influence mental and physical functioning.

Huntington's disease An inherited disease, characterized by progressive problems in cognition, emotion, and movement, which results in neurocognitive disorder.

Hypertension Chronic high blood pressure.

Hypnosis A sleeplike suggestible state during which a person can be directed to act in unusual ways, to experience unusual sensations, to remember seemingly forgotten events, or to forget remembered events.

Hypnotic amnesia Loss of memory produced by hypnotic suggestion.

Hypnotic therapy A treatment in which the patient undergoes hypnosis and is then guided to recall forgotten events or perform other therapeutic activities. Also known as *hypnotherapy*.

Hypnotism A procedure that places persons in a trancelike mental state during which they become extremely suggestible.

Hypochondriasis A disorder in which people mistakenly fear that minor changes in their physical functioning indicate a serious disease. Now known as *illness anxiety disorder*.

Hypomanic episode An episode of mania in which the symptoms cause relatively little impairment.

Hypomanic pattern A pattern in which a person displays symptoms of mania, but the symptoms are less severe and cause less impairment than those of a manic episode.

Hypothalamic-pituitary-adrenal (HPA) pathway One route by which the brain and body produce arousal and fear.

Hypothalamus A part of the brain that helps maintain various bodily functions, including eating and hunger.

Hypothesis A hunch or prediction that certain variables are related in certain ways.

Hypoxyphilia A pattern in which people strangle or smother themselves, or ask their partners to strangle or smother them, to increase their sexual pleasure.

Hysteria A term once used to describe what are now known as conversion disorder and somatic symptom disorder.

Hysterical disorder A disorder in which physical functioning is changed or lost, without an apparent physical cause.

Iatrogenic Produced or caused inadvertently by a clinician.

Id According to Freud, the psychological force that produces instinctual needs, drives, and impulses.

Ideas of reference Beliefs that unrelated events pertain to oneself in some important way.

Identification Unconsciously incorporating the values and feelings of one's parents and fusing them with one's identity. Also, an ego defense mechanism in which persons take on the values and feelings of a person who is causing them anxiety.

Idiographic understanding An understanding of the behavior of a particular individual.

Illness anxiety disorder A disorder in which persons are chronically anxious about and preoccupied with the notion that they have or are developing a serious medical illness, despite the absence of substantial somatic symptoms. Previously known as *hypochondriasis*.

Illogical thinking According to cognitive theories, illogical ways of thinking that may lead to self-defeating conclusions and psychological problems.

Immune system The body's network of activities and cells that identify and destroy antigens and cancer cells.

Inappropriate affect Display of emotions that are unsuited to the situation; a symptom of schizophrenia.

Incest Sexual relations between close relatives.

Incidence The number of new cases of a disorder occurring in a population over a specific period of time.

Independent variable The variable in an experiment that is manipulated to determine whether it has an effect on another variable.

Individual therapy A therapeutic approach in which a therapist sees a client alone for sessions that may last from 15 minutes to two hours.

Informed consent Requirement that researchers provide sufficient information to participants about the purpose, procedure, risks, and benefits of a study.

Insanity defense A legal defense in which persons charged with a criminal offense claim to be not guilty by reason of insanity at the time of the crime.

Insomnia The most common dyssomnia, characterized by difficulties initiating and maintaining sleep.

Integrity test A test that seeks to measure whether the test taker is generally honest or dishonest.

Intellectual developmental disorder A disorder marked by intellectual functioning and adaptive behavior that are well below average. Also called *intellectual disability*. Previously called *mental retardation*.

Intellectual disability A disorder marked by intellectual functioning and adaptive behavior that are well below average. Also called *intellectual developmental disorder*. Previously called *mental retardation*.

Intelligence quotient (IQ) A score derived from intelligence tests that theoretically represents a person's overall intellectual capacity

Intelligence test A test designed to measure a person's intellectual ability.

Intermittent explosive disorder A disorder in which people periodically fail to resist aggressive impulses and commit serious assaults on other people or destroy property.

Internal validity The accuracy with which a study can pinpoint one of various possible factors as the cause of a phenomenon.

International Classification of Diseases (ICD) The classification system for medical and mental disorders that is used by the World Health Organization.

Internet gaming disorder A disorder marked by persistent, recurrent, and excessive Internet activity, particularly gaming. Recommended for further study for possible inclusion in a future revision of DSM-5. Also called *Internet addiction*.

Interpersonal psychotherapy (IPT) A treatment for unipolar depression that is based on the belief that clarifying and changing one's interpersonal problems will help lead to recovery.

Interrater reliability A measure of the reliability of a test or of research results in which the consistency of evaluations across different judges is assessed. Also called *interjudge reliability*.

Intoxication A temporary drug-induced state in which people display symptoms such as impaired judgment, mood changes, irritability, slurred speech, and loss of coordination.

In vivo desensitization Desensitization that makes use of actual objects or situations, as opposed to imagined ones.

Ion An atom or group of atoms that has a positive or negative electrical charge.

Irresistible impulse test A legal test for insanity that holds people to be insane at the time they committed a crime if they were driven to do so by an uncontrollable "fit of passion."

Isolation An ego defense mechanism in which people unconsciously isolate and disown undesirable and unwanted thoughts, experiencing them as foreign intrusions.

Kleptomania A disorder characterized by the recurrent failure to resist impulses to steal objects not needed for personal use or monetary value.

Korsakoff's syndrome An alcohol-related disorder marked by extreme confusion, memory impairment, and other neurological symptoms.

Latent content The symbolic meaning behind a dream's content.

Lateral hypothalamus (LH) A brain region that produces hunger when activated.

L-dopa A drug used in the treatment of Parkinson's disease, a disease in which dopamine is low.

Learned helplessness The perception, based on past experiences, that one has no control over one's reinforcements.

Libido The sexual energy that fuels the id.

Life change units (LCUs) A system for measuring the stress associated with various life events.

Light therapy A treatment for seasonal affective disorder in which patients are exposed to extra light for several hours. Also called *phototherapy*.

Lithium A metallic element that occurs in nature as a mineral salt and is a highly effective treatment for bipolar disorders.

Lobotomy Psychosurgery in which a surgeon cuts the connections between the brain's frontal lobes and the lower centers of the brain.

Localized amnesia An inability to recall any of the events that occurred over a limited period of time.

Locus ceruleus A small area of the brain that seems to be active in the regulation of emotions. Many of its neurons use norepinephrine.

Long-term care Extended personal and medical support provided to elderly and other persons who may be impaired. It may range from partial support in a supervised apartment to intensive care at a nursing home.

Long-term memory The memory system that contains all the information that a person has stored over the years.

Longitudinal study A study that observes the same participants on many occasions over a long period of time.

Loose associations A common thinking disturbance in schizophrenia, characterized by rapid shifts from one topic of conversation to another. Also known as *derailment*.

LSD (lysergic acid diethylamide) A hallucinogenic drug derived from ergot alkaloids.

Lycanthropy A condition in which persons believe themselves to be possessed by wolves or other animals.

Lymphocytes White blood cells that circulate through the lymph system and bloodstream, helping the body identify and destroy antigens and cancer cells.

Magnetic resonance imaging (MRI) A neuroimaging technique used to visualize internal structures of the brain or body.

Mainstreaming The placement of children with intellectual developmental disorder in regular school classes. Also known as *inclusion*.

Major depressive disorder A severe pattern of unipolar depression that is disabling and is not caused by such factors as drugs or a general medical condition.

Major neurocognitive disorder Neurocognitive disorder in which the decline in cognitive functioning is substantial and interferes with the ability to be independent.

Male hypoactive sexual desire disorder A male dysfunction marked by a persistent reduction or lack of interest in sex and hence a low level of sexual activity.

Malingering Intentionally faking illness to achieve some external gains, such as financial compensation or military deferment.

Malpractice suit A lawsuit charging a therapist with improper conduct or decision making in the course of treatment.

Managed care program An insurance program in which the insurance company decides the cost, method, provider, and length of treatment.

Mania A state or episode of euphoria or frenzied activity in which people may have an exaggerated belief that the world is theirs for the taking.

Manifest content The consciously remembered content of a dream.

Mantra A sound, uttered or thought, used to focus one's attention and to turn away from ordinary thoughts and concerns during meditation.

MAO inhibitor An antidepressant drug that prevents the action of the enzyme monoamine oxidase.

Marijuana One of the cannabis drugs, derived from the buds, leaves, and flowering tops of the hemp plant *Cannabis sativa*.

Marital therapy A therapy approach in which the therapist works with two people who share a long-term relationship. Also known as *couple therapy*.

Masturbation Self-stimulation of the genitals to achieve sexual arousal.

Masturbatory satiation A behavioral treatment in which a client masturbates for a very long period of time while fantasizing in detail about a paraphilic object. The procedure is expected to produce a feeling of boredom that becomes linked to the object.

Mean The average of a group of scores.

Meditation A technique of turning one's concentration inward and achieving a slightly changed state of consciousness.

Melancholia A condition described by early Greek and Roman philosophers and physicians as consisting of unshakable sadness. Today it is known as *depression*.

Melatonin A hormone released by the pineal gland when a person's surroundings are dark.

Memory The faculty for recalling past events and past learning.

Mental incompetence A state of mental instability that leaves defendants unable to understand the legal charges and proceedings they are facing and unable to prepare an adequate defense with their attorneys.

Mental status exam A set of interview questions and observations designed to reveal the degree and nature of a client's abnormal functioning.

Mentally disordered sex offender A legal category that some states apply to certain individuals who are repeatedly found guilty of sex crimes.

Mentally ill chemical abusers (MICAs) Persons suffering from both schizophrenia (or another severe psychological disorder) and a substance-related disorder. Also called *dual diagnosis patients*.

Mesmerism The method employed by Austrian physician F. A. Mesmer to treat hysterical disorders; a precursor of *hypnotism*.

Meta-analysis A statistical method that combines results from multiple independent studies.

Metabolism An organism's chemical and physical breakdown of food and the process of converting it into energy. Also, an organism's biochemical transformation of various substances, as when the liver breaks down alcohol into acetylaldehyde.

Metaworry Worrying about the fact that one is worrying so much.

Methadone A laboratory-made opioid-like drug.

Methadone maintenance program An approach to treating heroin-centered substance use in which clients are given legally and medically supervised doses of a substitute drug, methadone.

Methamphetamine A powerful amphetamine drug that has experienced a surge in popularity in recent years, posing major health and law enforcement problems.

Methylphenidate A stimulant drug, known better by the trade name *Ritalin*, commonly used to treat ADHD.

Migraine headache A very severe headache that occurs on one side of the head, often preceded by a warning sensation and sometimes accompanied by dizziness, nausea, or vomiting.

Mild intellectual developmental disorder (IDD) A level of intellectual developmental disorder (IQ between 50 and 70) at which people can benefit from education and can support themselves as adults.

Mild neurocognitive disorder Neurocognitive disorder in which the decline in cognitive functioning is modest and does not interfere with the ability to be independent.

Milieu therapy A humanistic approach to institutional treatment based on the belief that institutions can help patients recover by creating a climate that promotes self-respect, individual responsible behavior, and meaningful activity.

Mind-body dualism René Descartes's position that the mind is separate from the body.

Mindfulness-based cognitive therapy A type of therapy that teaches clients to be mindful of (just notice and accept) their dysfunctional thoughts or worries.

Mindfulness meditation A type of meditation in which individuals are mindful of (just notice) the various thoughts, emotions, sensations, and other private experiences that pass through their minds and bodies.

Minnesota Multiphasic Personality Inventory (MMPI) A widely used personality inventory consisting of a large number of statements that subjects mark as being true or false for them.

Mixed design A research design in which a correlational method is mixed with an experimental method. Also known as *quasi-experiment*.

M'Naghten test A widely used legal test for insanity that holds people to be insane at the time they committed a crime if, because of a mental disorder, they did not know the nature of the act or did not know right from wrong. Also known as *M'Naghten rule*.

Model A set of assumptions and concepts that help scientists explain and interpret observations. Also called a *paradigm*.

Modeling A process of learning in which an individual acquires responses by observing and imitating others.

Moderate intellectual developmental disorder (IDD) A level of intellectual developmental disorder (IQ between 35 and 49) at which people can learn to care for themselves and can benefit from vocational training.

Monoamine oxidase (MAO) A body chemical that destroys the neurotransmitter norepinephrine.

Monoamine oxidase (MAO) inhibitors Antidepressant drugs that lower MAO activity and thus increase the level of norepinephrine activity in the brain.

Mood disorder A disorder affecting one's emotional state.

Mood stabilizing drugs Psychotropic drugs that help stabilize the moods of people suffering from a bipolar mood disorder.

Moral treatment A nineteenth-century approach to treating people with mental dysfunction that emphasized moral guidance and humane and respectful treatment.

Morphine A highly addictive substance derived from opium that is particularly effective in relieving pain.

Multicultural perspective The view that each culture within a larger society has a particular set of values and beliefs, as well as special external pressures, that help account for the behavior and functioning of its members. Also called *culturally diverse perspective*.

Multicultural psychology The field of psychology that examines the impact of culture, race, ethnicity, gender, and similar factors on our behaviors and thoughts and focuses on how such factors may influence the origin, nature, and treatment of abnormal behavior.

Multidimensional risk perspective A theory that identifies several kinds of risk factors that are thought to combine to help cause a disorder. The more factors present, the greater the risk of developing the disorder.

Munchausen syndrome An extreme and long-term form of factitious disorder in which a person produces symptoms, gains admission to a hospital, and receives treatment.

Munchausen syndrome by proxy A factitious disorder in which parents make up or produce physical illnesses in their children.

Muscle contraction headache A headache caused by the narrowing of muscles surrounding the skull. Also called *tension headache*.

Muscle dysmorphobia Disorder in which individuals become obsessed with the incorrect belief that they are not muscular enough.

Narcissistic personality disorder A personality disorder marked by a broad pattern of grandiosity, need for admiration, and lack of empathy.

Narcolepsy A dyssomnia characterized by sudden onsets of REM sleep during waking hours, generally brought on by strong emotion.

Narcotic Any natural or synthetic opioid-like drug.

Narcotic antagonist A substance that attaches to opioid receptors in the brain and, in turn, blocks the effects of opioids.

National Alliance on Mental Illness (NAMI) A nationwide grass-roots organization that provides support, education, advocacy, and research for people with severe mental disorders and their families.

Natural experiment An experiment in which nature, rather than an experimenter, manipulates an independent variable.

Naturalistic observation A method of observing behavior in which clinicians or researchers observe people in their everyday environments.

Negative correlation A statistical relationship in which the value of one variable increases while the other variable decreases.

Negative symptoms Symptoms of schizophrenia that seem to be deficits of normal thought, emotions, or behaviors.

Neologism A made-up word that has meaning only to the person using it.

Nerve ending The region at the end of a neuron from which an impulse is sent to a neighboring neuron.

Neurocognitive disorder Disorder marked by a significant decline in at least one area of cognitive functioning.

Neurofibrillary tangles Twisted protein fibers that form within certain brain cells as people age. People with Alzheimer's disease have an excessive number of such tangles.

Neuroimaging techniques Neurological tests that provide images of brain structure or activity, such as CT scans, PET scans, and MRIs. Also called *brain scans*.

Neuroleptic drugs An alternative term for conventional antipsychotic drugs, so called because they often produce undesired effects similar to the symptoms of neurological disorders.

Neuroleptic malignant syndrome A severe, potentially fatal reaction to antipsychotic drugs, marked by muscle rigidity, fever, altered consciousness, and autonomic dysfunction.

Neurological Relating to the structure or activity of the brain.

Neurological test A test that directly measures brain structure or activity.

Neuromodulator A neurotransmitter that helps modify or regulate the effect of other neurotransmitters.

Neuron A nerve cell.

Neuropsychological test A test that detects brain impairment by measuring a person's cognitive, perceptual, and motor performances.

Neurosis Freud's term for disorders characterized by intense anxiety, attributed to failure of a person's ego defense mechanisms to cope with unconscious conflicts.

Neurotransmitter A chemical that, released by one neuron, crosses the synaptic space to be received at receptors on the dendrites of neighboring neurons.

Neutralizing Attempting to eliminate thoughts that one finds unacceptable by thinking or behaving in ways that make up for those thoughts and so put matters right internally.

Nicotine An alkaloid (nitrogen-containing chemical) derived from tobacco or produced in the laboratory.

Nicotine patch A patch attached to the skin like a Band-Aid, with nicotine content that is absorbed through the skin, that supposedly eases the withdrawal reaction brought on by quitting cigarette smoking.

Nightmare disorder A parasomnia characterized by chronic distressful, frightening dreams.

Nocturnal penile tumescence (NPT) Erection during sleep.

Nomothetic understanding A general understanding of the nature, causes, and treatments of abnormal psychological functioning in the form of laws or principles.

Non-suicidal self-injury (NSSI) A disorder that is being studied for possible inclusion in a future revision of DSM-5, characterized by persons intentionally injuring themselves on five or more occasions over a one-year period—without the conscious intent of killing themselves.

Norepinephrine A neurotransmitter whose abnormal activity is linked to depression and panic disorder and depression.

Normalization The principle that institutions and community residences should expose persons with intellectual development disorder to living conditions and opportunities similar to those found in the rest of society.

Norms A society's stated and unstated rules for proper conduct.

Not guilty by reason of insanity (NGRI) A verdict stating that defendants are not guilty of committing a crime because they were insane at the time of the crime.

Object relations theory The psychodynamic theory that views the desire for relationships as the key motivating force in human behavior.

Observer drift The tendency of an observer who is rating subjects in an experiment to change criteria gradually and involuntarily, thus making the data unreliable.

Obsession A persistent thought, idea, impulse, or image that is experienced repeatedly, feels intrusive, and causes anxiety.

Obsessive-compulsive disorder A disorder characterized by recurrent and unwanted thoughts and/or a need to perform rigidly repetitive physical or mental actions.

Obsessive-compulsive personality disorder A personality disorder marked by such an intense focus on orderliness, perfectionism, and control that the individual loses flexibility, openness, and efficiency.

Oedipus complex In Freudian theory, the pattern of desires emerging during the phallic stage in which boys become attracted to their mother as a sexual object and see their father as a rival they would like to push aside.

Olanzapine An atypical antipsychotic drug whose brand name is Zyprexa.

Operant conditioning A process of learning in which behavior that leads to satisfying consequences is likely to be repeated.

Opioid Opium or any of the drugs derived from opium, including morphine, heroin, and codeine.

Opium A highly addictive substance made from the sap of the opium poppy seed.

Oppositional defiant disorder A childhood disorder in which children are repeatedly argumentative and defiant, angry and irritable, and, in some cases, vindictive.

Oral stage The earliest developmental stage in Freud's conceptualization of psychosexual development during which the infant's main gratification comes from feeding and from the body parts involved in it.

Orbitofrontal cortex A region of the brain in which impulses involving excretion, sexuality, violence, and other primitive activities normally arise.

Orgasm A peaking of sexual pleasure, consisting of rhythmic muscular contractions in the pelvic region, during which a man's semen is ejaculated and the outer third of a woman's vaginal wall contracts.

Orgasm phase The phase of the sexual response cycle during which an individual's sexual pleasure peaks and sexual tension is released as muscles in the pelvic region contract rhythmically.

Orgasmic reorientation A procedure for treating certain paraphilias by teaching clients to respond to new, more appropriate sources of sexual stimulation.

Outpatient A person who receives diagnosis or treatment in a clinic, hospital, or therapist's office but is not hospitalized overnight.

Panic attacks Periodic, short bouts of panic that occur suddenly, reach a peak within minutes, and gradually pass.

Panic disorder An anxiety disorder marked by recurrent and unpredictable panic attacks.

Paranoid personality disorder A personality disorder marked by a pattern of extreme distrust and suspiciousness of others.

Paraphilias Patterns in which individuals have recurrent and intense sexual urges, fantasies, or behaviors involving nonhuman objects, children, nonconsenting adults, or experiences of suffering or humiliation.

Paraphilic disorder A disorder in which an individual's paraphilia causes great distress, interferes with social or occupational activities, or places the individual or others at risk of harm—either currently or in the past.

Paraprofessional A person without previous professional training who provides services under the supervision of a mental health professional.

Parasomnias Sleep disorders characterized by the occurrence of abnormal events during sleep.

Parasuicide A suicide attempt that does not result in death.

Parasympathetic nervous system The nerve fibers of the autonomic nervous system that help return bodily processes to normal.

Parens patriae The principle by which the state can make decisions to promote the individual's best interests and protect him or her from self-harm or neglect.

Parkinsonian symptoms Symptoms similar to those found in Parkinson's disease. Patients with schizophrenia who take conventional antipsychotic medications may display one or more of these symptoms.

Parkinson's disease A slowly progressive neurological disease, marked by tremors and rigidity, that may also cause dementia.

Participant modeling A behavioral treatment in which people with fears observe a therapist (model) interacting with a feared object and then interact with the object themselves.

Pedophilic disorder A paraphilic disorder in which a person has repeated and intense sexual urges or fantasies about watching, touching, or engaging in sexual acts with prepubescent children and may carry out these urges or fantasies.

Peer review system A system by which clinicians paid by an insurance company may periodically review a patient's progress and recommend the continuation or termination of insurance benefits.

Penile prosthesis A surgical implant consisting of a semi-rigid rod made of rubber and wire that produces an artificial erection.

Performance anxiety The fear of performing inadequately and a related tension experienced during sex.

Perseveration The persistent repetition of words and statements.

Persistent depressive disorder A depressive disorder marked by chronic depression—either chronic major depressive disorder or dysthymia (chronic milder depressive disorder).

Personality A unique and long-term pattern of inner experience and outward behavior that leads to consistent reactions across various situations.

Personality disorder A pattern consisting of abnormal personality traits that repeatedly impair self-functioning and interpersonal functioning.

Personality disorder trait specified A personality disorder, proposed for possible inclusion in future revisions of DSM-5, in which an individual displays significant impairment in personality functioning, characterized by at least one severely maladaptive trait.

Personality inventory A test designed to measure broad personality characteristics, consisting of statements about behaviors, beliefs, and feelings that people evaluate as either characteristic or uncharacteristic of them

Phallic stage In psychoanalytic theory, the period between the third and fourth years when the focus of sexual pleasure shifts to the genitals.

Phalloplasty A surgical procedure designed to create a functional penis.

Phenothiazines A group of antihistamine drugs that became the first group of effective antipsychotic medications.

Phenylketonuria (PKU) A metabolic disorder caused by the body's inability to break down the amino acid phenylalanine, resulting in intellectual developmental disorder and other symptoms.

Phobia A persistent and unreasonable fear of a particular object, activity, or situation.

Pick's disease A neurological disease that affects the frontal and temporal lobes, causing a neurocognitive disorder.

Placebo therapy A sham treatment that the subject in an experiment believes to be genuine.

Play therapy An approach to treating childhood disorders that helps children express their conflicts and feelings indirectly by drawing, playing with toys, and making up stories.

Pleasure principle The pursuit of gratification that characterizes id functioning.

Plethysmograph A device used to measure sexual arousal.

Polygraph A test that seeks to determine whether or not the test taker is telling the truth by measuring physiological responses such as respiration level, perspiration level, and heart rate. Also known as a *lie detector test.*

Polysubstance use The use of two or more substances at the same time.

Positive correlation A statistical relationship in which the values of two variables increase together or decrease together.

Positive psychology The study and enhancement of positive feelings, traits, and abilities.

Positive symptoms Symptoms of schizophrenia that seem to be excesses of or bizarre additions to normal thoughts, emotions, or behaviors.

Positron emission tomography (PET scan) A computer-produced motion picture showing rates of metabolism throughout the brain.

Postpartum depression An episode of depression experienced by some new mothers that begins within four weeks after giving birth.

Postpartum psychosis An episode of psychosis experienced by a small percentage of new mothers that begins within days or weeks after giving birth.

Posttraumatic stress disorder (PTSD) A disorder in which fear and related symptoms continue to be experienced long after a traumatic event.

Poverty of content A lack of meaning in spite of high emotion that is found in the speech of some people with schizophrenia.

Predictive validity The ability of a test or other assessment tool to predict future characteristics or behaviors.

Predisposition An inborn or acquired vulnerability for developing certain symptoms or disorders.

Prefrontal lobes Regions of the brain that play a key role in short-term memory, among other functions.

Premature ejaculation A dysfunction in which a man persistently reaches orgasm and ejaculates within one minute of beginning sexual activity with a partner and before he wishes to. Also called *early ejaculation* and *rapid ejaculation.*

Premenstrual dysphoric disorder A disorder marked by repeated experiences of significant depression and related symptoms during the week before menstruation.

Premenstrual syndrome (PMS) Common and normal cluster of psychological and physical discomforts that precede menses.

Premorbid The period prior to the onset of a disorder.

Preparedness A predisposition to develop certain fears.

Prevalence The total number of cases of a disorder occurring in a population over a specific period of time.

Prevention A key feature of community mental health programs that seek to prevent or minimize psychological disorders.

Primary gain In psychodynamic theory, the gain achieved when somatic symptoms keep internal conflicts out of awareness.

Primary hypersomnia A sleep disorder in which the main problem is excessive sleepiness.

Primary insomnia A sleep disorder in which the main problem is an inability to initiate or maintain sleep.

Primary personality The subpersonality that appears more often than the others in individuals with multiple personality disorder.

Primary prevention Prevention interventions that seek to prevent disorders altogether.

Private psychotherapy An arrangement in which a person directly pays a therapist for counseling services.

Proband The person who is the focus of a genetic study.

Procedural memory Memory of learned skills that a person performs without needing to think about them.

Prodromal phase The period during which the symptoms of schizophrenia are not yet prominent, but the person has begun to deteriorate from previous levels of functioning.

Profound intellectual developmental disorder (IDD) A level of intellectual developmental disorder (IQ below 20) at which individuals need a very structured environment with close supervision.

Projection An ego defense mechanism whereby individuals attribute to other people characteristics or impulses they do not wish to acknowledge in themselves.

Projective test A test consisting of ambiguous material that people interpret or respond to.

Protection and advocacy system The system by which lawyers and advocates who work for patients may investigate the patients' treatment and protect their rights.

Prozac Trade name for fluoxetine, a second-generation antidepressant.

Psychedelic drugs Substances such as LSD that cause profound perceptual changes. Also called *hallucinogenic drugs.*

Psychiatric social worker A mental health specialist who is qualified to conduct psychotherapy upon earning a master's degree or doctorate in social work.

Psychiatrist A physician who in addition to medical school has completed three to four years of residency training in the treatment of abnormal mental functioning.

Psychoanalysis Either the theory or the treatment of abnormal mental functioning that emphasizes unconscious psychological forces as the cause of psychopathology.

Psychodynamic model The theoretical perspective that sees all human functioning as being shaped by dynamic (interacting) psychological forces and explains people's behavior by reference to unconscious internal conflicts.

Psychodynamic therapy A system of therapy whose goals are to help clients uncover past traumatic events and the inner conflicts that have resulted from them, settle those conflicts, and resume personal development.

Psychogenic perspective The view that the chief causes of abnormal functioning are psychological.

Psychological autopsy A procedure used to analyze information about a deceased person, for example, in order to determine whether the person's death was a suicide.

Psychological debriefing A form of crisis intervention in which victims are helped to talk about their feelings and reactions to traumatic incidents. Also called *critical incident stress debriefing.*

Psychological profile A method of suspect identification that seeks to predict an unknown criminal's psychological, emotional, and personality characteristics based on the individual's pattern of criminal behavior and on research into the psychological characteristics of people who have committed similar crimes.

Psychology The study of mental processes and behaviors.

Psychomotor symptoms Disturbances in movement sometimes found in certain disorders such as schizophrenia.

Psychoneuroimmunology The study of the connections among stress, the body's immune system, and illness.

Psychopathology An abnormal pattern of functioning that may be described as deviant, distressful, dysfunctional, and/or dangerous.

Psychopathy *See* Antisocial personality disorder.

Psychopharmacologist A psychiatrist who primarily prescribes medications. Also called *pharmacotherapist*.

Psychophysiological disorders Disorders in which biological, psychological, and sociocultural factors interact to cause or worsen a physical illness. Also known as *psychological factors affecting other medical conditions*.

Psychophysiological test A test that measures physical responses (such as heart rate and muscle tension) as possible indicators of psychological problems.

Psychosexual stages The developmental stages defined by Freud in which the id, ego, and superego interact.

Psychosis A state in which a person loses contact with reality in key ways.

Psychosurgery Brain surgery for mental disorders. Also called *neurosurgery*.

Psychotherapy A treatment system in which words and acts are used by a client (patient) and therapist in order to help the client overcome psychological difficulties.

Psychotropic medications Drugs that mainly affect the brain and reduce many symptoms of mental dysfunctioning.

Quasi-experiment An experiment in which investigators make use of control and experimental groups that already exist in the world at large. Also called a *mixed design*.

Random assignment A selection procedure that ensures that participants are randomly placed either in the control group or in the experimental group.

Rap group A group that meets to talk about and explore members' problems in an atmosphere of mutual support.

Rape Forced sexual intercourse or another sexual act committed against a nonconsenting person or intercourse with an underage person.

Rapid eye movement (REM) sleep The period of the sleep cycle during which the eyes move quickly back and forth, indicating that the person is dreaming.

Rapprochement movement An effort to identify a set of common strategies that run through the work of all effective therapists.

Rational-emotive therapy A cognitive therapy developed by Albert Ellis that helps clients identify and change the irrational assumptions and thinking that help cause their psychological disorder.

Rationalization An ego defense mechanism in which one creates acceptable reasons for unwanted or undesirable behavior.

Reaction formation An ego defense mechanism whereby one counters an unacceptable desire by taking on a lifestyle that directly opposes the unwanted impulse.

Reactive depression A depression that appears to be triggered by clear events. Also known as *exogenous depression*.

Reactivity The extent to which the very presence of an observer affects a person's behavior.

Reality principle The recognition, characterizing ego functioning, that we cannot always express or satisfy our id impulses.

Receptor A site on a neuron that receives a neurotransmitter.

Regression An ego defense mechanism in which a person returns to a more primitive mode of interacting with the world.

Reinforcement The desirable or undesirable stimuli that result from an organism's behavior.

Relapse-prevention training A cognitive-behavioral approach to treating alcohol use disorder in which clients are taught to keep track of their drinking behavior, apply coping strategies in situations that typically trigger excessive drinking, and plan ahead for risky situations and reactions.

Relational psychoanalytic therapy A form of psychodynamic therapy that considers therapists to be active participants in the formation of patients' feelings and reactions and therefore calls for therapists to disclose their own experiences and feelings in discussions with patients.

Relaxation training A treatment procedure that teaches clients to relax at will so they can calm themselves in stressful situations.

Reliability A measure of the consistency of test or research results.

Repression A defense mechanism whereby the ego prevents unacceptable impulses from reaching consciousness.

Residential treatment center A place where formerly addicted persons live, work, and socialize in a drug-free environment. Also called a *therapeutic community*.

Resiliency The ability to avoid or recover from the effects of negative circumstances.

Resistance An unconscious refusal to participate fully in therapy.

Resolution phase The fourth phase in the sexual response cycle, characterized by relaxation and a decline in arousal following orgasm.

Response inventories Tests designed to measure a person's responses in one specific area of functioning, such as affect, social skills, or cognitive processes.

Response prevention *See* Exposure and response prevention.

Response set A particular way of responding to questions or statements on a test, such as always selecting "true," regardless of the actual questions.

Restricting-type anorexia nervosa A type of anorexia nervosa in which people reduce their weight by severely restricting their food intake.

Reticular formation The brain's arousal center, which helps people to be awake, alert, and attentive.

Retrograde amnesia A lack of memory about events that occurred before the event that triggered amnesia.

Retrospective analysis A psychological autopsy in which clinicians and researchers piece together information about a person's suicide from the person's past.

Reversal design A single-subject experimental design in which behavior is measured to provide a baseline (A), then again after the treatment has been applied (B), then again after the conditions during baseline have been reintroduced (A), and then once again after the treatment is reintroduced (B). Also known as *ABAB design*.

Reward A pleasurable stimulus given to an organism that encourages a specific behavior.

Reward center A dopamine-rich pathway in the brain that produces feelings of pleasure when activated.

Reward-deficiency syndrome A condition, suspected to be present in some individuals, in which the brain's reward center is not readily activated by the usual events in their lives.

Right to refuse treatment The legal right of patients to refuse certain forms of treatment.

Right to treatment The legal right of patients, particularly those who are involuntarily committed, to receive adequate treatment.

Risperidone A commonly prescribed atypical antipsychotic drug.

Ritalin Trade name of methylphenidate, a stimulant drug that is helpful in many cases of attention-deficit/hyperactivity disorder (ADHD).

Role play A therapy technique in which clients are instructed to act out roles assigned to them by the therapist.

Rorschach test A projective test, in which a person reacts to inkblots, designed to help reveal psychological features of the person.

Rosenthal effect The general finding that the results of any experiment often conform to the expectations of the experimenter.

Rush A spasm of warmth and ecstasy that occurs when certain drugs, such as heroin, are ingested.

Savant A person with a mental disorder or significant intellectual deficits who has some extraordinary ability despite the disorder or deficits.

Schizoaffective disorder A disorder in which symptoms of both schizophrenia and a mood disorder are prominent.

Schizoid personality disorder A personality disorder in which a person persistently avoids social relationships and shows little emotional expression.

Schizophrenia A psychotic disorder in which personal, social, and occupational functioning deteriorate as a result of strange perceptions, disturbed thought processes, unusual emotions, and motor abnormalities.

Schizophreniform disorder A disorder in which all of the key features of schizophrenia are present but last only between one and six months.

Schizophrenogenic mother A type of mother—supposedly cold, domineering, and uninterested in the needs of others—who was once thought to cause schizophrenia in her child.

Schizotypal personality disorder A personality disorder characterized by extreme discomfort in relationships, odd forms of thinking and perceiving, and behavioral eccentricities.

School phobia A childhood pattern in which children fear going to school and often stay home for a long period of time. Also called *school refusal*.

Scientific method The process of systematically gathering and evaluating information through careful observations to gain an understanding of a phenomenon.

Seasonal affective disorder (SAD) A mood disorder in which mood episodes are related to changes in season.

Second-generation antidepressants New antidepressant drugs that differ structurally from tricyclics and MAO inhibitors.

Second messengers Chemical changes within a neuron just after the neuron receives a neurotransmitter message and just before it responds.

Secondary gain In psychodynamic theory, the gain achieved when somatic symptoms elicit kindness from others or provide an excuse for avoiding unpleasant activities.

Secondary prevention Prevention interventions that seek to address disorders quickly, before they become more serious problems.

Sedative-hypnotic drug A drug used in low doses to reduce anxiety and in higher doses to help people sleep. Also called *anxiolytic drug*.

Selective amnesia An inability to recall some of the events that occurred over a limited period of time.

Selective serotonin reuptake inhibitors (SSRIs) A group of second-generation antidepressant drugs that increase serotonin activity specifically, without affecting other neurotransmitters.

Self-actualization The humanistic process by which people fulfill their potential for goodness and growth.

Self-efficacy The judgment that one can master and perform needed behaviors whenever necessary.

Self-help group A group made up of people with similar problems who help and support one another without the direct leadership of a clinician. Also called a *mutual help group*.

Self-hypnosis The process of hypnotizing oneself, sometimes for the purpose of forgetting unpleasant events.

Self-instruction training A cognitive treatment developed by Donald Meichenbaum that teaches people to use coping self-statements at times of stress or discomfort. Also called *stress inoculation training*.

Self-monitoring Clients' observation of their own behavior.

Self-statements According to some cognitive theorists, statements about oneself, sometimes counterproductive, that come to mind during stressful situations.

Self theory The psychodynamic theory that emphasizes the role of the self—a person's unified personality.

Senile Characteristic of or associated with old age.

Senile plaques Sphere-shaped deposits of beta-amyloid protein that form in the spaces between certain brain cells and in certain blood vessels as people age. People with Alzheimer's disease have an excessive number of such plaques.

Sensate focus A treatment for sexual disorders that instructs couples to take the focus away from orgasm or intercourse and instead spend time concentrating on the pleasure achieved by such acts as kissing, hugging, and mutual massage. Also known as *nondemand pleasuring*.

Separation anxiety disorder A disorder marked by excessive anxiety, even panic, whenever the individual is separated from home, a parent, or another attachment figure.

Serial murders A series of two or more killings carried out separately by the same individual(s) over a period of time—usually a month or more.

Serotonin A neurotransmitter whose abnormal activity is linked to depression, obsessive-compulsive disorder, and eating disorders.

Severe intellectual developmental disorder (IDD) A level of intellectual developmental disorder (IQ between 20 and 34) at which individuals require careful supervision and can learn to perform basic work in structured and sheltered settings.

Sex-change surgery A surgical procedure that changes a person's sex organs, features, and, in turn, sexual identity. Also known as *sexual reassignment surgery*.

Sex offender statute The presumption by some state legislatures that people who are repeatedly found guilty of certain sex crimes have a mental disorder and should be categorized as "mentally disordered sex offenders." Such laws have been changed or abolished by many states over the past two decades.

Sexual dysfunction A disorder marked by a persistent inability to function normally in some area of the human sexual response cycle.

Sexual masochism disorder A paraphilic disorder characterized by repeated and intense sexual urges, fantasies, or behaviors that involve being humiliated, beaten, bound, or otherwise made to suffer.

Sexual response cycle The general sequence of behavior and feelings that occurs during sexual activity, consisting of desire, excitement, orgasm, and resolution.

Sexual sadism disorder A paraphilic disorder characterized by repeated and intense sexual urges, fantasies, or behaviors that involve inflicting suffering on others.

Sexually violent predator laws Laws passed by the federal government and many states that call for certain sex offenders who have been convicted of sex crimes and have served their sentence in prison to be removed from prison before their release and committed involuntarily to a mental hospital for treatment if a court judges them likely to engage in further acts of sexual violence due to a mental or personality abnormality. Also called *sexually dangerous persons laws*.

Shaping A learning procedure in which successive approximations of the desired behavior are rewarded until finally the exact and complete behavior is learned.

Sheltered workshop A supervised workplace for people who are not yet ready for competitive jobs.

Short-term memory The memory system that collects new information. Also known as *working memory*.

Shuttle box A box separated in the middle by a barrier that an animal can jump over in order to escape or avoid shock.

Sildenafil A drug used to treat erectile disorder that helps increase blood flow to the penis during sexual activity. Marketed as *Viagra*.

Single-subject experimental design A research method in which a single participant is observed and measured both before and after the manipulation of an independent variable.

Situation anxiety The various levels of anxiety produced in a person by different situations. Also called *state anxiety*.

Sleep apnea A disorder in which a person frequently stops breathing for up to 30 or more seconds while asleep.

Sleep terror disorder A parasomnia disorder of arousal in which persons awaken suddenly during the first third of sleep, screaming out in extreme fear and agitation.

Sleepwalking disorder A parasomnia disorder of arousal in which people repeatedly leave their beds and walk around without being conscious of the episode or remembering it later.

Social anxiety disorder A severe and persistent fear of social or performance situations in which embarrassment may occur.

Social skills training A therapy approach that helps people learn or improve social skills and assertiveness through role playing and rehearsing of desirable behaviors.

Social therapy An approach to therapy in which the therapist makes practical advice and life adjustment a central focus of treatment for schizophrenia. Therapy also focuses on problem solving, decision making, development of social skills, and management of medications. Also known as *personal therapy*.

Sociocultural model The theoretical perspective that emphasizes the effect of society, culture, and social and family groups on individual behavior.

Sociopathy *See* Antisocial personality disorder.

Sodium amobarbital (Amytal) A drug used to put people into a near-sleep state during which some can better recall forgotten events.

Sodium pentobarbital (Pentothal) *See* Sodium amobarbital.

Somatic symptom disorder A disorder in which persons become excessively distressed, concerned, and anxious about bodily symptoms that they are experiencing, and their lives are greatly and disproportionately disrupted by the symptoms.

Somatogenic perspective The view that abnormal psychological functioning has physical causes.

Special education An approach to educating children with intellectual development disorder in which they are grouped together and given a separate, specially designed education.

Specific learning disorder A developmental disorder marked by impairments in cognitive skills such as reading, writing, arithmetic, or mathematical skills.

Specific phobia A severe and persistent fear of a specific object or situation (other than agoraphobia and social anxiety disorder).

Spectator role A state of mind that some people experience during sex, focusing on their sexual performance to such an extent that their performance and their enjoyment are reduced.

Standardization The process in which a test is administered to a large group of people whose performance then serves as a standard or norm against which any individual's score can be measured.

State-dependent learning Learning that becomes associated with the conditions under which it occurred, so that it is best remembered under the same conditions.

State hospitals Public mental institutions in the United States, run by the individual states.

State school A state-supported institution for individuals with intellectual developmental disorder.

Statistical analysis The application of principles of probability to the findings of a study in order to learn how likely it is that the findings have occurred by chance.

Statistical significance A measure of the probability that a study's findings occurred by chance rather than because of the experimental manipulation.

Stimulant drug A substance that increases the activity of the central nervous system.

Stimulus generalization A phenomenon in which responses to one stimulus are also produced by similar stimuli.

Stress management program An approach to treating generalized and other anxiety disorders that teaches clients techniques for reducing and controlling stress.

Stressor An event that creates a sense of threat by confronting a person with a demand or opportunity for change of some kind.

Stress-reduction and problem-solving seminar A workshop or series of group sessions offered by a business in which mental health professionals teach employees how to cope with and solve problems and reduce stress.

Stress response A person's particular reactions to stress.

Structured interview An interview format in which the clinician asks prepared questions.

Subintentional death A death in which the victim plays an indirect, hidden, partial, or unconscious role.

Subject An individual chosen to participate in a study. Also called a *participant*.

Sublimation In psychoanalytic theory, the rechanneling of id impulses into endeavors that are both socially acceptable and personally gratifying. It can also be used as an ego defense mechanism.

Subpersonalities The two or more distinct personalities found in individuals suffering with dissociative identity disorder. Also known as *alternate personalities*.

Substance use disorder Pattern of maladaptive behaviors and reactions brought about by repeated use of a substance, sometimes also including tolerance for the substance and withdrawal reactions.

Suicidal behavior disorder A classification being studied for possible inclusion in a future revision of DSM-5, in which individuals have tried to commit suicide within the last two years.

Suicide A self-inflicted death in which the person acts intentionally, directly, and consciously.

Suicide prevention program A program that tries to identify people who are at risk of killing themselves and to offer them crisis intervention.

Superego According to Freud, the psychological force that represents a person's values and ideals.

Supportive nursing care A treatment, applied to anorexia nervosa in particular, in which trained nurses conduct a day-to-day hospital program.

Symbolic loss According to Freudian theory, the loss of a valued object (for example, a loss of employment) that is unconsciously interpreted as the loss of a loved one. Also called *imagined loss*.

Sympathetic nervous system The nerve fibers of the autonomic nervous system that quicken the heartbeat and produce other changes experienced as arousal and fear.

Symptom A physical or psychological sign of a disorder.

Synapse The tiny space between the nerve ending of one neuron and the dendrite of another.

Syndrome A cluster of symptoms that usually occur together.

Synergistic effect In pharmacology, an increase of effects that occurs when more than one substance is acting on the body at the same time.

Synesthesia A crossing over of sensory perceptions sometimes caused by LSD and other hallucinogenic drugs. For example, a loud sound may be seen or a color may be felt.

Systematic desensitization A behavioral treatment that uses relaxation training and a fear hierarchy to help clients with phobias react calmly to the objects or situations they dread.

Tarantism A disorder occurring throughout Europe between 900 and 1800 A.D. in which people would suddenly start to jump around, dance, and go into convulsions. Also known as *St. Vitus's dance*.

Tardive dyskinesia Extrapyramidal effects that appear in some patients after they have taken conventional antipsychotic drugs for an extended time.

Tay-Sachs disease A metabolic disorder that causes progressive loss of intellectual functioning, vision, and motor functioning, resulting in death.

Temporal lobes Regions of the brain that play a key role in transforming short-term memory to long-term memory, among other functions.

Tension headache *See* Muscle contraction headache.

Tertiary prevention Prevention interventions that seek to provide effective treatment for moderate or severe disorders as soon as it is needed so that the disorders do not become long-term problems.

Test A device for gathering information about a few aspects of a person's psychological functioning from which broader information about the person can be inferred.

Testosterone The principal male sex hormone.

Tetrahydrocannabinol (THC) The main active ingredient of cannabis.

Thanatos According to the Freudian view, the basic death instinct that functions in opposition to the life instinct.

Thematic Apperception Test (TAT) A projective test consisting of pictures that show people in ambiguous situations that the client is asked to interpret.

Theory of mind Awareness that other people base their behaviors on their own beliefs, intentions, and mental states, not on information they have no way of knowing.

Therapist A professional clinician who applies a system of therapy to help a person overcome psychological difficulties.

Therapy A systematic process for helping persons overcome their psychological problems. It consists of a patient, a trained therapist, and a series of contacts between them.

Token economy program A behavioral program in which a person's desirable behaviors are reinforced systematically throughout the day by the awarding of tokens that can be exchanged for goods or privileges.

Tolerance The adjustment that the brain and the body make to the regular use of certain drugs so that ever larger doses are needed to achieve the earlier effects.

Torture The use of brutal, degrading, and disorienting strategies to reduce victims to a state of utter helplessness.

Trait anxiety The general level of anxiety that a person brings to the various events in his or her life.

Tranquilizer A drug that reduces anxiety.

Transcranial magnetic stimulation (TMS) A treatment procedure for depression in which an electromagnetic coil, which is placed on or above a person's head, sends a current into the individual's brain.

Transference According to psychodynamic theorists, the redirection toward the psychotherapist of feelings associated with important figures in a patient's life, now or in the past.

Transgender experience A sense that one's actual gender identity is different from the gender category to which one

was born physically or that it lies outside the usual male versus female categories.

Transvestic disorder A paraphilic disorder consisting of repeated and intense sexual urges, fantasies, or behaviors that involve dressing in clothes of the opposite sex. Also known as *transvestism* or *cross-dressing*.

Treatment A procedure designed to help change abnormal behavior into more normal behavior. Also called *therapy*.

Trephination An ancient operation in which a stone instrument was used to cut away a circular section of the skull, perhaps to treat abnormal behavior.

Trichotillomania A disorder in which people repeatedly pull at and in some cases yank out their hair, eyelashes, and eyebrows. Also called *hair-pulling disorder*.

Tricyclic An antidepressant drug such as imipramine that has three rings in its molecular structure.

Trisomy A chromosomal abnormality in which an individual has three chromosomes of one kind rather than the usual two.

Tube and intravenous feeding Forced nourishment sometimes provided to sufferers of anorexia nervosa when their condition becomes life-threatening.

Type A personality style A personality pattern characterized by hostility, cynicism, drivenness, impatience, competitiveness, and ambition.

Type B personality style A personality pattern in which persons are more relaxed, less aggressive, and less concerned about time.

Type I schizophrenia According to some theorists, a type of schizophrenia dominated by positive symptoms, such as delusions, hallucinations, and certain formal thought disorders.

Type II schizophrenia According to some theorists, a type of schizophrenia dominated by negative symptoms, such as flat affect, poverty of speech, and loss of volition.

Tyramine A chemical that, if allowed to accumulate, can raise blood pressure dangerously. It is found in many common foods and is broken down by MAO.

Ulcer A lesion that forms in the wall of the stomach or of the duodenum.

Unconditional positive regard Full, warm acceptance of a person regardless of what he or she says, thinks, or feels; a critical component of client-centered therapy.

Unconditioned response (UCR) The natural, automatic response produced by an unconditioned stimulus.

Unconditioned stimulus (UCS) A stimulus that produces an automatic, natural response.

Unconscious The deeply hidden mass of memories, experiences, and impulses that is viewed in Freudian theory as the source of much behavior.

Undoing An ego defense mechanism in which a person unconsciously cancels out an unacceptable desire or act by performing another act.

Unilateral electroconvulsive therapy (ECT) A form of electroconvulsive therapy in which electrodes are attached to the head so that electrical current passes through only one side of the brain.

Unipolar depression Depression without a history of mania.

Unstructured interview An interview format in which the clinician asks spontaneous questions that are based on issues that arise during the interview.

Vagus nerve stimulation A treatment procedure for depression in which an implanted pulse generator sends regular electrical signals to a person's vagus nerve; the nerve, in turn, stimulates the brain.

Validity The accuracy of a test's or study's results; that is, the extent to which the test or study actually measures or shows what it claims.

Valium The trade name of diazepam, an antianxiety drug.

Variable Any characteristic or event that can vary across time, locations, or persons.

Ventromedial hypothalamus (VMH) A brain region that depresses hunger when activated.

Visual hallucinations Hallucinations in which a person may either experience vague visual perceptions, perhaps of colors or clouds, or have distinct visions of people, objects, or scenes that are not there.

Voyeuristic disorder A paraphilic disorder in which a person has repeated and intense sexual desires to observe unsuspecting people in secret as they undress or to spy on couples as they have intercourse and may act upon these desires.

Weight set point The weight level that a person is predisposed to maintain, controlled, in part by the hypothalamus.

Windigo An intense fear of being turned into a cannibal by a flesh-eating monster. The disorder was once found among Algonquin Indian hunters.

Withdrawal Unpleasant, sometimes dangerous reactions that may occur when people who use a drug regularly stop taking or reduce their dosage of the drug.

Working through The psychoanalytic process of facing conflicts, reinterpreting feelings, and overcoming one's problems.

references

AA World Services. (2008). AA fact file. New York: Author.

AA World Services. (2011). AA fact file. New York: Author.

AAIDD (American Association on Intellectual and Developmental Disabilities). (2010). *Intellectual disability: Definition, classification, and system of supports* (11th ed.). Washington, DC: Author.

Aas, M., Steen, N. E., Agartz, I., Aminoff, S. R., Lorentzen, S., Sundet, K., Andreassen, O. A. & Melle, I. (2012). Is cognitive impairment following early life stress in severe mental disorders based on specific or general cognitive functioning? *Psychiatry Research, 198*(3), 495–500.

Abbass, A., Town, J., & Driessen, E. (2011). The efficacy of short-term psychodynamic psychotherapy for depressive disorders with comorbid personality disorder. *Psychiatry: Interpersonal and Biological Processes, 74*(1), 58–71.

Abbey, S. E. (2005). Somatization and somatoform disorders. In J. L. Levenson (Ed.), *The Amerian Psychiatric Publishing textbook of psychosomatic medicine* (pp. 271–296). Washington, DC: American Psychiatric Publishing.

Abdel-Baki, A., Lesage, A., Nicole, L., Cossette, M., Salvat, E., & Lalonde,P. (2011). Schizophrenia, an illness with bad outcomes: Myth or reality? *Canadian Journal of Psychiatry, 56*(2), 92–101.

Abdel-Rahman, E. (Ed.) (2012). *Depression in the elderly.* Hauppauge, NY: Nova Science Publishers.

Abel, G. G., Becker, J. V., & Cunningham-Rathner, J. (1984). Complications, consent, and cognitions in sex between children and adults. *International Journal of Law and Psychiatry, 7,* 89–103.

Abel, G. G., Jordan, A., Hand, C. G., Holland, L. A., & Phipps, A. (2001). Classification models of child molesters utilizing the Abel Assessment for child sexual abuse interest. *Child Abuse and Neglect, 25*(5), 703–718.

Abela, J. R. Z., & Hankin, B. L. (2011). Rumination as a vulnerability factor to depression during the transition from early to middle adolescence: A multiwave longitudinal study. *Journal of Abnormal Psychology, 120*(2), 259–271.

Abercrombie, H. C., Schaefer, S. M., Larson, C. L., Oakes, T. R., Lindgren, K. A., Holden, J. E., et al. (1998). Metabolic rate in the right amygdala predicts negative affect in depressed patients. *NeuroReport, 9,* 3301–3307.

Abi-Dargham, A., & Grace, A. A. (2011). Dopamine and schizophrenia. In D. R. Weinberg & P. Harrison (Eds.), *Schizophrenia* (pp. 413–432). Hoboken, NJ: Wiley-Blackwell.

Abraham, K. (1911). Notes on the psycho-analytic investigation and treatment of manic-depressive insanity and allied conditions. In *Selected papers on psychoanalysis* (pp. 137–156). New York: Basic Books. (Work republished 1960)., 234, 298

Abraham, K. (1916). The first pregenital stage of the libido. In *Selected papers on psychoanalysis* (pp. 248–279). New York: Basic Books. (Work republished 1960)., 234, 298

Abraham, S., & Llewellyn-Jones, D. (1984). *Eating disorders: The facts.* New York: Oxford University Press.

Abramowitz, J. S. (2008). Is nonparaphilic compulsive sexual behavior a variant of OCD? In J. S. Abramowitz, D. McKay, & S. Taylor (Eds.), *Obsessive-compulsive disorder: Subtypes and spectrum conditions.* Oxford, England: Elsevier.

Abramowitz, J. S. (2010). Psychological treatment for obsessive-compulsive disorder. In D. J. Stein, E. Hollander, & B. O. Rothbaum (Eds.), *Textbook of anxiety disorders* (2nd ed., pp. 339–354). Arlington, VA: American Psychiatric Publishing.

Abramowitz, J. S., & Braddock, A. E. (2011). Hypochondriasis and health anxiety. Advances in psychotherapy—Evidence-based practice. Cambridge, MA: Hogrefe Publishing.

Abramowitz, J. S., Deacon, B. J., & Whiteside, S. P. H. (2011). *Exposure therapy for anxiety: Principles and practice.* New York: Guilford Press.

Abramowitz, J. S., McKay, D., & Taylor, S. (Eds.). (2008). *Obsessive-compulsive disorder: Subtypes and spectrum conditions.* Oxford, England: Elsevier.

Abramson, L. Y., Alloy, L. B., Hankin, B. L., Haeffel, G. J., MacCoon, D. G., & Gibb, B. E. (2002). Cognitive vulnerability—Stress models of depression in a self-regulatory and psychobiological context. In I. H. Gotlib & C. L. Hammen (Eds.), *Handbook of depression* (pp. 268–294). New York: Guilford Press.

Abramson, L. Y., Metalsky, G. I., & Alloy, L. B. (1989). Hopelessness depression: A theory-based subtype of depression. *Psychological Review, 96*(2), 358–372.

Abramson, L. Y., Seligman, M. E., & Teasdale, J. D. (1978). Learned helplessness in humans: Critique and reformulation. *Journal of Abnormal Psychology, 87*(1), 49–74.

Acier, D., & Kern, L. (2011). Problematic internet use: Perceptions of addiction counselors. *Computers & Education, 56*(4), 983–989

Acosta, M. C., Haller, D. L., & Schnoll, S. H. (2005). Cocaine and stimulants. In R. J. Frances, A. H. Mack, & S. I. Miller (Eds.), *Clinical textbook of addictive disorders* (3rd ed., pp. 184–218). New York: Guilford Press.

Acosta, M. C., Haller, D. L., & Schnoll, S. H. (2011). Cocaine and stimulants. In R. J. Frances, A. H. Mack, & S. I. Miller (Eds.), *Clinical textbook of addictive disorders* (3rd ed., pp. 184–218). New York: Guilford Press.

Adam, K. S., Bouckoms, A., & Streiner, D. (1982). Parental loss and family stability in attempted suicide. *Archives of General Psychiatry, 39*(9), 1081–1085.

Adams, R. E., & Boscarino, J. A. (2005). Stress and well-being in the aftermath of the World Trade Center attack: The continuing effects of a communitywide disaster. *Journal of Community Psychology, 33*(2), 175–190.

Addington, D., & Addington, J. (2008). First-episode psychosis. In K. T. Mueser & D. V. Jeste (Eds.), *Clinical handbook of schizophrenia* (pp. 367–379). New York: Guilford Press.

Addington, J., & Lewis, S. W. (2011). The prodrome of schizophrenia. In D. R. Weinberg & P. Harrison (Eds.), *Schizophrenia* (pp. 91–103). Hoboken, NJ: Wiley-Blackwell.

Affatati, V., Di Nicola, V., Santoro, M., Bellomo, A., Todarello, G., & Todarello, O. (2004). Psychotherapy of gender identity disorder: Problems and perspectives. *Medica Psicosomatica, 49*(1–2), 57–64.

Agras, W. S., Sylvester, D., & Oliveau, D. (1969). The epidemiology of common fears and phobias. *Comprehensive Psychiatry, 10*(2), 151–156.

Agronin, M. E. (2006). Personality disorders. In D. V. Jeste & J. H. Friedman (Eds.), *Psychiatry for neurologists.* Totowa, NJ: Humana Press.

AHA (American Heart Association). (2011). Heart disease and stroke statistics—2010 update: A report from the American Heart Association. *Circulation, 121,* e-46–e215.

Ahearn, W. H. (2010). What every behavior analyst should know about the "MMR uses autism" hypothesis. *Behavior Analysis in Practice, 3*(1), 46–50.

Ahern, G. L., Herring, A. M., Labiner, D. M., Weinand, M. E., & Hutzler, R. (2000). Affective self-report during the intracarotid sodium amobarbital test: Group differences. *Journal of the International Neuropsychological Society, 6*(6), 659–667.

Ahlers, C. J., Schaefer, G. A., Mundt, I. A., Roll, S., Englert, H., Willich, S. N., & Beier, K. M. (2011). How unusual are the contents of paraphilias? Paraphilia-associated sexual arousal patterns in a community-based sample of men. *Journal of Sexual Medicine, 8*(5), 1362–1370.

Ahmed, S. H. (2011). Escalation of drug use. In M. C. Olmstead (Ed.), *Animal models of drug addiction. Springer protocols: Neuromethods* (pp. 267–292). Totowa, NJ: Humana Press.

Ahrens, C. E., Dean, K., Rozee, P. D., & McKenzie, M. (2008). Understanding and preventing rape. In F. L. Denmark & M. A. Paludi (Eds.), *Psychology of women: A handbook of issues and theories* (2nd ed.). Westport, CT: Praeger Publishers.

AI (Amnesty International). (2000). *Torture worldwide: An affront to human dignity.* New York: Author.

Aiken, C. B. (2010). Neuroprotection in bipolar depression. In M. C. Ritsner (Ed.), *Brain protection in schizophrenia, mood and cognitive disorders* (pp. 451–483). New York: Springer Science + Business Media.

Aiken, L. R. (1985). *Psychological testing and assessment* (5th ed.). Boston: Allyn & Bacon.

Aiken, L. R., & Groth-Marnat, G. (2006). *Psychological testing and assessment* (12th ed.). New York: Pearson/Allyn & Bacon.

Airan, R. D., Meltzer, L. A., Madhuri, R., Gong, Y., Chen, H., & Deisseroth, K. (2007). High-speed imaging reveals neurophysiological links to behavior in an animal model of depression. *Science, 317,* 819–823.

Ajdacic-Gross, V., Ring, M., Gadola, E., Lauber, C., Bopp, M., Gutzwiller, F., et al. (2008). Suicide after bereavement: An overlooked problem. *Psychological Medicine, 38*(5), 673–676.

Akaike, A. (2006). Preclinical evidence of neuroprotection by cholinesterase inhibitors. *Alzheimer's Disease and Associated Disorders, 20*(2, Suppl. 1), S8–S11.

Akhtar, S., Wig, N. H., Verma, V. K., Pershod, D., & Verma, S. K. (1975). A phenomenological analysis of symptoms in obsessive-compulsive neuroses. *British Journal of Psychiatry, 127,* 342–348.

Akinbami, L. J., Moorman, J. E., & Liu, X. (2011, January 12). Asthma prevalence, health care use, and mortality: United States, 2005–2009. *National Health Statistics Report, 32,* 1–14.

Akins, C. K. (2004). The role of Pavlovian conditioning in sexual behavior: A comparative analysis of human and nonhuman animals. *International Journal of Comparative Psychology, 17*(2–3), 241–262.

Akiskal, H. S., & Benazzi, F. (2008). Continuous distribution of atypical depressive symptoms between major depressive and bipolar II disorders: Dose-response relationship with bipolar family history. *Psychopathology, 41*(1), 39–42.

Albala, I., Doyle, M., & Appelbaum, P. S. (2010). The evolution of consent forms for research: A quarter century of changes. *IRB: Ethics & Human Research, 32*(3), 7–11.

Albert, U., Maina, G., Forner, F., & Bogetto, F. (2004). DSM-IV obsessive-compulsive personality disorder: Prevalence in patients with anxiety disorders and in healthy comparison subjects. *Comprehensive Psychiatry, 45*(5), 325–332.

Alcántara, C., & Gone, J. P. (2008). Suicide in Native American communities: A transactional-ecological formulation of the problem. In M. M. Leach & F. T. L. Leong (Eds.), *Suicide among racial and ethnic minority groups: Theory, research, and practice* (pp. 173–199). New York: Routledge/Taylor & Francis Group.

Aldao, A., & Mennin, D. S. (2012). Paradoxical cardiovascular effects of implementing adaptive emotion regulation strategies in generalized anxiety disorder. *Behaviour Research and Therapy, 50*(2), 122–130.

Aldhous, P. (2012). Personality disorder revamp ends in "horrible waste." *New Scientist,* December 3.

Aldwin, C. M., Spiro, A., III, & Park, C. L. (2006). Health, behavior, and optimal aging: A life span developmental perspective. In J. E. Birren & K. W. Schaie (Eds.), *Handbook of the psychology of aging* (6th ed., pp. 85–104). San Diego, CA: Elsevier.

Alegría, A. A., Petry, N. M., Hasin, D. S., Liu, S., Grant, B. F., & Blanco, C. (2009). Disordered gambling among racial and ethnic groups in the US: Results from the national epidemiologic survey on alcohol and related conditions. *CNS Spectrums, 14*(3), 132–142.

Alegria, M., Atkins, M., Farmer, E., Slaton, E., & Stelk, W. (2010). One size does not fit all: Taking diversity, culture and context seriously. *Administration and Policy in Mental Health and Mental Health Service Research, 37*(1-2), 48–60.

Alegria, M., Kessler, R. C., Bijl, R., Lin, E., Heeringa, S. G., Takeuchi, D. T., et al. (2000). Comparing data on mental health service use between countries. In G. Andrews & S. Henderson (Eds.), *Unmet need in psychiatry: Problems, resources, responses* (pp. 97–118). New York: Cambridge University Press.

Alegria, M., Mulvaney-Day, N., Torres, M., Polo, A., Cao, Z., & Canino, G. (2007). Prevalence of psychiatric disorders across Latino subgroups in the United States. *American Journal of Public Health, 97*(1), 68–75.

Alegria, M., Mulvaney-Day, N., Woo, M., & Miruell-Fuentes, E. A. (2012). Psychology of Latino adults: Challenges and an agenda for action. In E. C. Chang & C. A. Downey (Eds.), *Handbook of race and development in mental health* (pp. 279–306). New York: Springer Science 1 Business Media.

Alegria, M., Takeuchi, D., Canino, G., Duan, N., Shrout, P., Meng, X. L., et al. (2004). Considering context, place and culture: The National Latino and Asian American Study. *International Journal of Methods in Psychiatric Research, 13*(4), 208–220.

Alexander, J. F., Sexton, T. L., & Robbins, M. S. (2002). The developmental status of family therapy in family psychology intervention science. In H. A. Liddle, D. A. Santiseban, R. F. Levant, & J. H. Bray (Eds.), *Family psychology: Science-based interventions* (pp. 17–40). Washington, DC: American Psychological Association.

Alfano, C. A., & Beidel, D. C. (Eds.). (2011). *Social anxiety in adolescents and young adults: Translating developmental science into practice.* Washington, DC: American Psychological Association.

Algars, M., Santtila, P., Jern, P., Johansson, A., Westerlund, M., & Sandnabba, N. K. (2011). Sexual body image and its correlates: A population-based study of Finnish women and men. *International Journal of Sexual Health, 23*(1), 26–34.

Algoe, S. B., & Fredrickson, B. L. (2011). Emotional fitness and the movement of affective science from lab to field. *American Psychologist, 66*(1), 35–42.

Ali, M. M., Dwyer, D. S., & Rizzo, J. A. (2011). The social contagion effect of suicidal behavior in adolescents: Does it really exist? *Journal of Mental Health Policy and Economics, 14*(1), 3–12.

Allard, R., Marshall, M., & Plante, M. C. (1992). Intensive follow-up does not decrease the risk of repeat suicide attempts. *Suicide and Life-Threatening Behavior, 22,* 303–314.

Allderidge, P. (1979). Hospitals, madhouses and asylums: Cycles in the care of the insane. *British Journal of Psychiatry, 134,* 321–334.

Allen, B. J., & Gfeller, J. D. (2011). The Immediate Post-Concussion Assessment and Cognitive Testing battery and traditional neuropsychological measures: A construct and concurrent validity study. *Brain Injury, 25*(2), 179–191.

Allen, C. (2005). The links between heroin, crack cocaine and crime: Where does street crime fit in? *British Journal of Criminology, 45*(3), 355–372.

Allen, D. F. (Ed.). (1985). *The cocaine crisis.* Plenum Press: New York.

Allen, G. (2011). The cerebellum in autism spectrum disorders. In E. Hollander, A. Kolevzon & J. T. Coyle (Eds.), *Textbook of autism spectrum disorders.* (pp. 375–381) Arlington, VA: American Psychiatric Publishing, Inc.

Allen, L. A., & Woolfolk, R. L. (2010). Cognitive behavioral therapy for somatoform disorders. *Psychiatric Clinics of North American, 33*(3), 579–593.

Allen, N. B., Gilbert, P., & Semedar, A. (2004). Depressed mood as an interpersonal strategy: The importance of relational models. In N. Haslem (Ed.), *Relational models theory: A contemporary overview* (pp. 309–334). Mahwah, NJ: Lawrence Erlbaum.

Allison, R. (2010). Aligning bodies with minds: The case for medical and surgical treatment of gender dysphoria. *Journal of Gay & Lesbian Mental Health, 14*(2), 139–144.

Allwood, C. M. (2010). Eyewitness confidence. In P. A. Granhag (Ed.), *Forensic psychology in context: Nordic and international approaches* (pp. 291–303). Devon, UK: Willan Publishing.

Almeida, D. M., Stawski, R. S., & Cichy, K. E. (2011). Combining checklist and interview approaches for assessing daily stressors: The Daily Inventory of Stressful Events. In R. J. Contrada & A. Baum (Eds.), *The handbook of stress science: Biology, psychology, and health* (pp. 583–595). New York: Springer Publishing.

Al-Subaie, A., & Alhamad, A. (2000). Psychiatry in Saudi Arabia. In I. Al-Junun (Ed.), *Mental illness in the Islamic world* (pp. 205–233). Madison, CT: International Universities Press.

Altamura, A. C., Lietti, L., Dobrea, C., Benatti, B., Arici, C., & Dell'Osso, B., (2011). Mood sstabilizers for patients with bipolar disorder: The state of the art. *Expert Review of Neurotherapeutics, 11*(1), 85–99.

Althof, S. E. (1995). Pharmacologic treatment of rapid ejaculation. Special issue: Clinical sexuality. *Psychiatric Clinics of North America, 18*(1), 85–94.

Althof, S. E. (2007). Treatment of rapid ejaculation: Psychotherapy, pharmacotherapy, and combined therapy. In S. R. Leiblum, *Principles and practice of sex therapy* (4th ed., pp. 212–240). New York: Guilford Press.

Althouse, R. (2010). Jails are nation's largest institutions for mentally ill. *National Psychologist, 19*(6), 1, 5.

Aly, A., & Green, L. (2010). Fear, anxiety and the state of terror. *Studies in Conflict and Terrorism, 33*(3), 268–281.

Alzheimer's Association. (2007). Care in the U.S. Graph cited in *Newsweek, CXLIX*(25), 56.

Alzheimer's Association. (2011). 2011 Alzheimer's facts and figures. *Alzheimer's & Dementia, 7*(2).

AMA (American Medical Association). (2011). *Physician characteristics and distribution in the U.S.* Chicago, IL: AMA Press.

Aman, M. G., & Farmer, C. A. (2011). Self-injury, aggression, and related problems. In E. Hollander, A. Kolevzon & J. T. Coyle (Eds.), *Textbook of autism spectrum disorders* (pp. 179–187). Arlington, VA: American Psychiatric Publishing, Inc.

American Association of Fundraising Counsel. (2010). *Giving USA: 2009.* Chicago, IL: Author.

American Association on Mental Retardation (AAMR). (1992). *Mental retardation: Definition, classification, and systems of supports* (9th ed.). Washington, DC: Author.

American Psychological Association (APA). (1992). Ethical principles of psychologists and code of conduct. Washington: DC: Author.

American Psychological Association (APA). (2002). Ethical principles of psychologists and code of conduct. Washington: DC: Author.

American Psychological Association (APA). (2009). Report: APA board of scientific affairs, Committee on animal research and ethics. APA Online.

American Psychological Association (APA). (2011, Winter). FYI: Mental health insurance under the Federal Parity Law. *Good Practice,* 19.

Ames, D., Chiu, E., Lindesay, J., & Shulman, K. I. (2010). *Guide to the psychiatry of old age.* New York: Cambridge University Press.

Amianto, F., Abbate-Doga, G., Morando, S., Sobrero, C., & Fassino, S. (2011). Personality development characteristics of women with anorexia nervosa, their healthy siblings, and healthy controls: What prevents and what relates to psychopathology? *Psychiatry Research, 187,* 401–408.

Amianto, F., Abbate-Doga, G., Morando, S., Sobrero, C., & Fassino, S. Personality traits that differentiate individuals with anorexia nervosa and their healthy siblings. *Clinician's Research Digest, 29*(3).

Amini, A. (2008). Interview with J.K. Rowling. Reported by Associated Press.

an der Heiden, W., & Häfner, H. (2011). Course and outcomes. In D. R. Weinberg & P. Harrison (Eds.), *Schizophrenia* (pp. 104–141). Hoboken, NJ: Wiley-Blackwell.

Anderson, D. (1994). *Breaking the tradition on college campuses: Reducing drug and alcohol misuse.* Fairfax, VA: George Mason University Press.

Anderson, K. G., Sankis, L. M., & Widiger, T. A. (2001). Pathology versus statistical infrequency: Potential sources of gender bias in personality disorder criteria. *Journal of Nervous and Mental Disease, 189*(10), 661–668.

Anderson, R. T., Pawaskar, M. D., Camacho, F., & Barkrishnan, R. (2011). Adult diabetes and quality of life, psychosocial issues, and sexual health. In K. M. V. Narayan, D. Williams, E. W. Gregg, & C. C. Cowie (Eds.), *Diabetes public health: From data to policy* (pp. 471–490). New York: Oxford University Press.

Andreasen, N. C., & Black, D. W. (2006). *Introductory textbook of psychiatry* (4th ed.). Washington, DC: American Psychiatric Publishing.

Andresen, J. (2000). Meditation meets behavioral medicine: The story of experimental research on meditation. *Journal of Consciousness Studies, 7*(11–12), 17–73.

Andrews, J. A., & Hops, H. (2010). The influence of peers on substance use. In L. Scheier (Ed.), *Handbook of drug use etiology: Theory, methods, and empirical findings* (pp. 403–420). Washington, DC: American Psychological Association.

Andrews, V. (1998, December 14). Abducted by aliens? Or just a little schizoid? *HealthScout.*

Angst, J., Gamma, A., Endrass, J., Goodwin, R., Ajdacic, V., Eich, D., et al. (2004). Obsessive-compulsive severity spectrum in the community: Prevalence, comorbidity, and course. *European Archives of Psychiatry and Clinical Neuroscience, 254*(3), 156–164.

Annunziato, R. A., Lee, J. N., & Lowe, M. R. (2007). A comparison of weight-control behaviors in African American and Caucasian women. *Ethnicity and Disease, 17,* 262–267.

Anonymous. (1996). First person account: Social, economic, and medical effects of schizophrenia. *Schizophrenia Bulletin, 22*(1), 183.

Anthony, J. C., Arria, A. M., & Johnson, E. O. (1995). Epidemiological and public health issues for tobacco, alcohol, and other drugs. In J. M. Oldham & M. B. Riba (Eds.), *American Psychiatric Press review of psychiatry* (Vol. 14). Washington, DC: American Psychiatric Press.

Antoni, M. H. (2005). Behavioural interventions and psychoneuroimmunology. In K. Vedhara & M. Irwin (Eds.), *Human psychoneuroimmunology.* Oxford, England: Oxford University Press.

Antony, M. M. (2011). Recent advances in the treatment of anxiety disorders. *Canadian Psychology/Psychologie Canadienne, 52*(1), 1–9.

Antony, M. M., & Barlow, D. H. (Eds.). (2004). *Handbook of assessment and treatment planning for psychological disorders.* New York: Guilford Press.

Antony, M. M., & Barlow, D. H. (Eds.). (2010). *Handbook of assessment and treatment planning for psychological disorders* (2nd ed.). New York: Guilford Press.

Antony, M. M., & Roemer, L. (2011). *Behavior therapy.* Washington, DC: American Psychological Association.

APA (American Psychiatric Association). (1992). *Ethical principles of psychologists and code of conduct.* Washington, DC: Author.

APA (American Psychiatric Association). (1993). *Practice guideline for major depressive disorder in adults.* Washington, DC: Author.

APA (American Psychiatric Association). (1994). *Diagnostic and statistical manual of mental disorders* (4th ed.). Washington, DC: Author.

APA (American Psychiatric Association). (2000). *Diagnostic and statistical manual of mental disorders [rom]*(4th ed., text rev.). Washington, DC: Author.

APA (American Psychiatric Association). (2002). *Ethical principles of psychologists and code of conduct.* Washington, DC: Author.

APA (American Psychiatric Association). (2003). Questions and answers on using "insanity" as a legal defense. *HealthyMinds.org.* Arlington, VA: American Psychiatric Association.

APA (American Psychiatric Association). (2005). *Executive summary: Risk factors for meeting the public's need for health service psychologists.* Washington, DC: Author.

APA (American Psychiatric Association). (2010). Ethical principles of psychologists and code of conduct. Washington, DC: Author.

APA (American Psychiatric Association). (2011). Changes to the reformulation of personality disorders for DSM-5. http://www.dsm5.org/ProposedRevision/Pages/PersonalityDisorders.aspx.

APA (American Psychiatric Association). (2011). Mental health insurance under the federal parity law. *Good Practice.* Winter, pp. 19–20.

APA (American Psychiatric Association). (2012). *DSM-5 Draft.* Washington, DC: Author.

APA (American Psychiatric Association). (2013). *Diagnostic and statistical manual of mental disorders* (5th ed.). Washington, DC: Author.

APA (American Psychiatric Association) (2013). *DSM-5 Table of Contents.* Washington, D.C.: American Psychiatric Publishing.

APA (American Psychiatric Association) (2013). *Highlights of Changes from DSM-IV-TR to DSM-5.* Washington, D.C.: American Psychiatric Publishing.

Apfelbaum, B. (2000). Retarded ejaculation: A much misunderstood syndrome. In S. R. Leiblum & R. C. Rosen (Eds.), *Principles and practice of sex therapy* (3rd edition). New York: Guilford Press.

Apostolova, L. G., & Cummings, J. L. (2008). Neuropsychiatric aspects of Alzheimer's disease and other dementing illnesses. In S. C. Yudofsky & R. E. Hales (Eds.), *The American psychiatric publishing textbook of neuropsychiatry and behavioral neurosciences* (5th ed.). Washington, DC: American Psychiatric Publishing.

Apostolova, L. G., Mosconi, L., Thompson, P. M., Green, A. E., Hwang, K. S., Ramirez, A., Mistur, R., Tsui, W. H., & de Leon, M. J. (2010). Subregional hippocampal atrophy predicts Alzheimer's dementia in the cognitively normal. *Neurobiology of Aging, 31*(7), 1077–1088.

Appelbaum, P. S. (2011). Law and psychiatry: Reforming malpractice: The prospects for change. *Psychiatric Services, 62*(1), 6–8.

Appelbaum, P. S. (2011). Law and psychiatry: SSRIs, suicide, and liability for failure to warn of medication risks. *Psychiatric Services, 62*(4), 347–349.

Apter, A., & Wasserman, D. (2007). Suicide in psychiatric disorders during adolescence. In R. Tatarelli, M. Pompili, & P. Girardi (Eds.), *Suicide in psychiatric disorders.* New York: Nova Science Publishers.

Arango, C., & Carpenter, W. T. (2011). The schizophrenia construct: Symptomatic presentation. In D. R. Weinberg & P. Harrison (Eds.), *Schizophrenia* (pp. 9–23). Hoboken, NJ: Wiley-Blackwell.

Arch, J. J., & Craske, M. G. (2011). Addressing relapse in cognitive behavioral therapy for panic disorder: Methods for optimizing long-term treatment outcomes. *Cognitive and Behavioral Practice, 18*(3), 306–315.

Archer, D. (2012, December 15). Reading between the headlines: Another mass murder. *Psychology Today.*

Archer, D., & McDaniel, P. (1995). Violence and gender: Differences and similarities across societies. In R. B. Ruback & N. A. Weiner (Eds.), *Interpersonal violent behaviors: Social and cultural aspects.* New York: Springer.

Arciuli, J., Mallard, D., & Villar, G. (2010). "Um, I can tell you're lying": Linguistic markers of deception versus truth-telling in speech. *Applied Psycholinguistics, 31*(3), 397–411.

Ardjmand, A., Rezayof, A., & Zarrindast, M-R. (2011). Involvement of central amygdala NMDA receptor mechanism in morphine state-dependent memory retrieval. *Neuroscience Research, 69*(1), 25–31.

Ardoin, S. P., Martens, B. K., Wolfe, L. A., Hilt, A. M., & Rosenthal, B. D. (2004). A method for conditioning reinforcer preferences in students with moderate mental retardation. *Journal of Developmental and Physical Disabilities, 16*(1), 33–51.

Arens, E. A., Grabe, H-J., Spitzer, C., & Barnow, S. (2011). Testing the biosocial model of borderline personality disorder: Results of a prospective 5-year longitudinal study. *Personality and Mental Health, 5*(1), 29–42.

Arias, E., Anderson, R. N., Kung, H. C., Murphy, S. L., & Kochanek, K. D. (2003). Deaths: Final data for 2001. *National Vital Statistics Reports, 52.* Hyattsville, MD: National Center for Health Statistics.

Arias, I., Sorlozano, A., Villegas, E., de Dios Luna, J., McKenney, K., Cervilla, J., Gutierrez, B., & Gutierrez, J. (2012). Infectious agents associated with schizophrenia: A meta-analysis. *Schizophrenia Research, 136*(1-3), 128–136.

Arieti, S. (1974). *Interpretation of schizophrenia.* New York: Basic Books.

Arieti, S., & Bemporad, J. (1978). *Severe and mild depression: The psychotherapeutic approach.* New York: Basic Books.

Aring, C. D. (1974). The Gheel experience: Eternal spirit of the chainless mind! *Journal of the American Medical Association, 230*(7), 998–1001.

Aring, C. D. (1975). Gheel: The town that cares. *Family Health, 7*(4), 54–55, 58, 60.

Armitage, R., & Arnedt, J. T. (2011). Sleep and circadian rhythms: An understudied area in treatment resistant depression. In J. F. Greden, M. B. Riba, & M. G. McInnis (Eds.), *Treatment resistant depression: A roadmap for effective care* (pp. 183–192). Arlington, VA: American Psychiatric Publishing.

Armour, S. (2006, August 22). Workplaces quit quietly ignoring mental illness. *USAtoday.com.* Retrieved July 6, 2007, from http://usatoday.com/money/workplace/2006-08-21-depressed-usat_x.htm?csp=N009.

Armstrong, C. (2010). Depression survey: Implications for diverse communities. *NAMI Magazine.* December 10.

Armstrong, M. J. (2001). Ethnic minority women as they age. In J. D. Garner & S. O. Mercer (Eds.), *Women as they age* (2nd ed., pp. 97–114). New York: Haworth.

Arndt, W. B., Hietpas, T., & Kim, J. (2004). Critical characteristics of male serial murderers. *American Journal of Criminal Justice, 29*(1), 117–131.

Arnow, B. A., & Post, L. I. (2010). Depression. In D. McKay, J. S. Abramowitz, & S. Taylor (Eds.), *Cognitive-behavioral therapy for refractory cases: Turning failure into success* (pp. 183–210). Washington, DC: American Psychological Association.

Arntz, A. (2005). Introduction to special issue: Cognition and emotion in borderline personality disorder. *Journal of Behavioral Therapy and Experimental Psychiatry, 36*(3), 167–172.

Arroyos-Jurado, E., Fernández, I. T., & Navarro, R. L. (2010). Multiculturalism and diversity: Implications for the training of school psychologists. In E. Garcia-Vásquez, T. D. Crespi, & C. A. Riccio (Eds.), *Handbook of education, training, and supervision of school psychologists in school and community, Vol. 1: Foundations of professional practice* (pp. 129–147). New York: Routledge/Taylor & Francis.

Arvanites, T. M. (1989). The differential impact of deinstitutionalization on white and nonwhite defendants found incompetent to stand trial. *Bulletin of the American Academy of Psychiatry Law, 17,* 311–320.

Asberg, M., Traskman, L., & Thoren, P. (1976). 5 HIAA in the cerebrospinal fluid: A biochemical suicide predictor? *Archives of General Psychiatry, 33*(10), 1193–1197.

ASCA (American School Counselor Association). (2010). *Report on counseling.* Alexandria, VA: Author.

Ash, R. (1998). *The top 10 of everything 1999.* New York: DK Publishing.

Ash, R. (1999). *Fantastic book of 1001 facts.* New York: DK Publishing.

Ash, R. (2001). *The top 10 of everything 2002* (American ed.). New York: DK Publishing.

Ashcraft, R. (2012). Overcoming participation barriers in workplace wellness. *Good Company Blog,* Feb. 9, 2012.

Ashton, A. K. (2007). The new sexual pharmacology: A guide for the clinician. In S. R. Leiblum (Ed.), *Principles and practice of sex therapy* (4th ed., pp. 509–540). New York: Guilford Press.

Ashton, J. R., & Donnan, S. (1981). Suicide by burning as an epidemic phenomenon: An analysis of 82 deaths and inquests in England and Wales in 1978–9. *Psychological Medicine, 11*(4), 735–739.

Asimov, I. (1997). *Isaac Asimov's book of facts.* New York: Random House (Wings Books).

Asmundson, G. J. G., & Taylor, S. (2008). Health anxiety and its disorders. In M. Hersen & J. Rosqvist (Eds.), *Handbook of psychological assessment, case conceptualization, and treatment, Vol. 1: Adults* (pp. 701–727). Hoboken, NJ: John Wiley & Sons.

Asnis, G. M., Kohn, S. R., Henderson, M., & Brown, N. L. (2004). SSRIs versus non-SSRIs in posttraumatic stress disorder: An update with recommendations. *Drugs, 64*(4), 383–404.

Assal, F. (2011). Neuropsychiatric treatments in Alzheimer's disease. In P. McNamara (Ed.), *Dementia, Vols. 1–3: History and incidence. Science and biology, treatments and developments* (pp. 205–231). Santa Barbara, CA: Praeger/ABC-CLIO.

Astbury, J. (2010). The social causes of women's depression: A question of rights violated? In D. C. Jack & A. Ali (Eds.), *Silencing the self across cultures: Depression and gender in the social world* (pp. 19–45). New York: Oxford University Press.

Astin, J. A. (2004). Mind-body therapies for the management of pain. *Clinical Journal of Pain, 20*(1), 27–32.

Atack, J. R. (2010). GAB(A) receptor α 2/α 3 subtype-selective modulators as potential nonsedating anxiolytics. In M. B. Stein, & T. Steckler (Eds.), *Behavioral neurobiology of anxiety and its treatment* (pp. 331–360). New York: Springer Science + Business Media.

Atanasijevic, T., Jovanovic, A. A., Nikolic, S., Popovic, V., & Jasovic-Gasic, M. (2009). Accidental death due to complete autoerotic asphyxia associated with transvestic festishism and anal self-stimulation—Case report. *Psychiatria Danubina, 21*(2), 246–251.

Aten, J. D., McMinn, M. R., & Worthington, E. L., Jr. (2011). *Spiritually oriented interventions for counseling and psychotherapy.* Washington, DC: American Psychological Association.

Ator, N. A. (2005). Contributions of GABA-sub(A) receptor subtype selectivity to abuse liability and dependence potential of pharmacological treatments for anxiety and sleep disorders. *CNS Spectrums, 10*(1), 31–39.

Ayalon, L., & Huyck, M. H. (2001). Latino caregivers of relatives with Alzheimer's disease. *Clinical Gerontology, 24*(3–4), 93–106.

Ayalon, L., & Young, M. A. (2003). A comparison of depressive symptoms in African Americans and Caucasian Americans. *Journal of Cross-Cultural Psychology 34*(1), 111–124.

Ayd, F. J., Jr. (1956). A clinical evaluation of Frenquel. *Journal of Nervous and Mental Disease, 124,* 507–509.

Ayllon, T. (1963). Intensive treatment of psychotic behavior by stimulus satiation and food reinforcement. *Behavioral Research and Therapy, 1,* 53–62.

Ayllon, T., & Michael, J. (1959). The psychiatric nurse as a behavioural engineer. *Journal of Experimental Analytical Behavior, 2,* 323–334.

Ayoub, C. C. (2006). Munchausen by proxy. In T. G. Plante (Ed.), *Mental disorders of the new millenium: Biology and function* (Vol. 3, pp. 173–193). Westport, CT: Praeger Publishers/Greenwood Publishing.

Ayoub, C. C. (2010). Munchausen by proxy. In J. M. Brown & E. A. Campbell (Eds.), *The Cambridge handbook of forensic psychology* (pp. 690–699). New York: Cambridge University Press.

Ayoub, C. C. (2010). Munchausen by proxy. In R. J. Shaw & D. R. DeMaso (Eds.), *Textbook of pediatric psychosomatic medicine* (pp. 185–198). Arlington, VA: American Psychiatric Publishing.

Ayub, M., Poongan, I., Masood, K., Gul, H., Ali, M., Farrukh, A., Shaheen, A., Chaudhry, H. R., & Naeem, F. (2012). Psychological morbidity in children 18 months after Kashmir earthquake of 2005. *Child Psychiatry and Human Development, 43*(3), 323–336.

Azar, B. (1995). Mental disabilities and the brain-gene link. *APA Monitor, 26*(12), 18.

Azar, B. (2011). Positive psychology advances, with growing pains. *Monitor on Psychology, 42*(4), 32–36.

Baars, B. J. (2010). Spontaneous repetitive thoughts can be adaptive: Postscript on "mind wandering." *Psychological Bulletin, 136*(2), 208–210.

Baca-Garcia, E., Perez-Rodriguez, M. M., Keyes, K. M., Oquendo, M. A., Hasin, D. S., Grant, B. F., & Blanco, C. (2011). Suicidal ideation and suicide attempts among Hispanic subgroups in the United States: 1991–1992 and 2001–2002. *Journal of Psychiatric Research, 45*(4), 512–518.

Bach, A. K., Wincze, J. P., & Barlow, D. H. (2001). Sexual dysfunction. In D. H. Barlow (Ed.), *Clinical handbook of psychological disorders: A step-by-step treatment manual* (3rd ed., pp. 562–608). New York: Guilford Press.

Bach, P. A. (2007). Psychotic disorders. In D. W. Woods & J. W. Kanter (Eds.), *Understanding behavior disorders: A contemporary behavioral perspective.* Reno, NV: Context Press.

Bachevalier, J. (2011). The amygdala in autism spectrum disorders. In E. Hollander, A. Kolevzon & J. T. Coyle (Eds.), *Textbook of autism spectrum disorders.* (pp. 363–374) Arlington, VA: American Psychiatric Publishing, Inc.

Baer, L., & Blais, M. A. (Eds.). (2010). Handbook of clinical rating scales and assessment in psychiatry and mental health. Totowa, NJ: Humana Press.

Baer, L., Platman, S. R., Kassir, S., & Fieve, R. R. (1971). Mechanisms of renal lithium handling and their relationship to mineral corticoids: A dissociation between sodium and lithium ions. *Journal of Psychiatric Research, 8*(2), 91–105.

Bagby, E. (1922). The etiology of phobias. *Journal of Abnormal Psychology, 17,* 16–18.

Baggot, M., & Mendelson, J. (2001). Does MDMA cause brain damage? In J. Holland (Ed.), *Ecstasy: The complete guide; A comprehensive look at the risks and benefits of MDMA* (pp. 110–145). Rochester, VT: Park Street Press.

Bahrick, H. (1996, January). Cited in G. Neimeyer, Anecdotes for education. *Newsletter for Abnormal Psychology.*

Bailer, U. F., & Kaye, W. H. (2011). Serotonin: Imaging findings in eating disorders. In R. A. H. Adan & W. H. Kaye (Eds.), *Behavioral neurobiology of eating disorders. Current topics in behavioral neurosciences* (pp. 59–79). New York: Springer-Verlag Publishing.

Bakalar, N. (2010, May 31) Happiness may come with age, study says. *New York Times, 159*(55,058).

Baker, B. L., Neece, C. L., Fenning, R. M., Crnic, K. A., & Blacher, J. (2010). Mental disorders in five-year-old children with or without developmental delay: Focus on ADHD. *Journal of Clinical Child and Adolescent Psychology, 39*(4), 492–505.

Baker, K. (2010). From "it's not me" to "it was me, after all": A case presentation of a patient diagnosed with dissociative identity disorder. *Psychoanalytic Social Work, 17*(2), 79–98.

Baker, R. (1992). Psychosocial consequences for tortured refugees seeking asylum and refugee status in Europe. In M. Basoglu (Ed.), *Torture and its consequences: Current treatment approaches* (pp. 83–106). Cambridge, England: Cambridge University Press.

Baker, R. (2011). *Understanding panic attacks and overcoming fear* (3rd ed.). Oxford, UK: Lion Hudson.

Balassone, M., (2011). Jails, prisons increasingly taking care of mentally ill. *Washington Post, 134*(49).

Baldessarini, R. J., & Tondo, L. (2007). Psychopharmacology for suicide prevention. In R. Tatarelli, M. Pompili, & P. Girardi (Eds.), *Suicide in psychiatric disorders.* New York: Nova Science Publishers.

Baldessarini, R. J., & Tondo, L. (2011). Psychopharmacology for suicide prevention. In M. Pompili & R. Tatarelli (Eds.), *Evidence-based practice in suicidology: A source book* (pp. 243–264). Cambridge MA: Hogrefe Publishing.

Baldwin, D. S., Ajel, K. I., & Garner, M., (2010). Pharmacological treatment of generalized anxiety disorder. In M. B. Stein & T. Steckler (Eds.), *Behavioral neurobiology of anxiety and its treatment. Current topics in behavioral neurosciences* (pp. 453–467). New York: Springer Science + Business Media.

Baldwin, D. S., Woods, R., Lawson, R., & Taylor, D. (2011, March 19). Efficacy of drug treatments for generalised anxiety disorder: Systematic review and meta-analysis. *British Medical Journal, 342*(7798).

Baldwin, J. S., & Dadds, M. R. (2008). Anxiety disorders. In D. Reitman (Ed.), *Handbook of psychological assessment, case conceptualization, and treatment, Vol. 2: Children and adolescents.* Hoboken, NJ: John Wiley & Sons.

Baldwin, S., & Oxlad, M. (2000). *Electroshock and minors: A fifty-year review.* Westport, CT: Greenwood.

Ballas, C., Benton, T. D., & Evans, D. L. (2010). Pharmacotherapy and relapse prevention for depression. In C. S. Richards & J. G. Perri (Eds.), *Relapse prevention for depression* (pp. 131–153). Washington, DC: American Psychological Association.

Balodis, I. M., Kober, H., Worhunsky, P. D., Stevens, M. C., Pearlson, G. D., & Potenza, M. N. (2012). Diminished frontostriatal activity during processing of monetary rewards and losses in pathological gambling. *Biological Psychiatry, 71*(8), 749–757.

Bancroft, J. (1989). *Human sexuality and its problems.* New York: Churchill-Livingstone.

Bancroft, J., Loftus, J., & Long, J. S. (2003). Distress about sex: A national survey of women in heterosexual relationships. *Archives of Sexual Behavior, 32*(3), 193–208.

Bandelow, B., & Baldwin, D. S. (2010). Pharmacotherapy for panic disorder. In D. J. Stein, E. Hollander, & B. O. Rothbaum (Eds.), *Textbook of anxiety disorders* (2nd ed., pp. 399–416). Arlington, VA: American Psychiatric Publishing.

Bandelow, B., Sher, L., Bunevicius, R., Hollander, E., Kasper, S., Zohar, J., et al. (2012). Guidelines for the pharmacological treatment of anxiety disorders, obsessive–compulsive disorder and post-traumatic stress disorder in primary care. *International Journal of Psychiatry in Clinical Practice, 16*(2), 77–84.

Bandura, A. (1971). Psychotherapy based upon modeling principles. In A. E. Bergin & S. L. Garfield (Eds.), *Handbook of psychotherapy and behavior change.* New York: Wiley.

Bandura, A. (1977). Self-efficacy: Toward a unifying theory of behavioral change. *Psychological Review, 84*(2), 191–215.

Bandura, A. (2004). Swimming against the mainstream: The early years from chilly tributary to transformative mainstream. *Behavioral Research and Therapy, 42*(6), 613–630.

Bandura, A. (2011). But what about that gigantic elephant in the room? In R. M. Arkin (Ed.), *Most underappreciated: 50 prominent social psychologists describe their most unloved work* (pp. 51–59). New York: Oxford University Press.

Bandura, A., & Rosenthal, T. (1966). Vicarious classical conditioning as a function of arousal level. *Journal of Personality and Social Psychology, 3,* 54–62.

Bandura, A., Adams, N. E., & Beyer, J. (1977). Cognitive processes mediating behavioral change. *Journal of Personality and Social Psychology, 35*(3), 125–139.

Bandura, A., Roth, D., & Ross, S. (1963). Imitation of film-mediated aggressive models. *Journal of Abnormal and Social Psychology, 66,* 3–11.

Bankert, E. A., & Madur, R. J. (2006). *Institutional review board: Management and function* (2nd ed.). Boston: Jones and Bartlett Publishers.

Baranski, J. V. (2011). Sleep loss and the ability to self-monitor cognitive performance. In P. L. Ackerman (Ed.), *Cognitive fatigue: Multidisciplinary perspectives on current research and future applications, Decade of Behavior/Science Conference* (pp. 67–82). Washington, DC: American Psychological Association.

Barber, A. (1999, March). HerZines. Some yet-to-be exploited niches in the women's magazine market. *American Demographics.*

Bareggi, S. R., Bianchi, L., Cavallaro, R., Gervasoni, M., Siliprandi, F., & Bellodi, L. (2004). Citalopram concentrations and response in obsessive-compulsive disorder: Preliminary results. *CNS Drugs, 18*(5), 329–335.

Bari, A., Robbins, T. W., & Dalley, J. W. (2011). Impulsivity. In M. C. Olmstead (Ed.), *Animal models of drug addiction. Springer protocols: Neuromethods* (pp. 379–401). Totowa, NJ; Humana Press.

Barkley, R. A. (Ed.). (2002). Taking charge of ADHD: The complete authoritative guide for parents, revised edition. *Journal of the American Academy of Child and Adolescent Psychiatry, 41*(1), 101–102.

Barkley, R. A. (2004). Adolescents with attention-deficit/hyperactivity disorder: An overview of empirically based treatments. *Journal of Psychiatric Practice, 10*(1), 39–56.

Barkley, R. A. (2006). *Attention deficit hyperactivity disorder* (3rd ed.). New York: Guilford Press.

Barkley, R. A., & Benton, C. M. (2010). *Taking charge of adult ADHD.* New York: Guilford Press.

Barlow, M. R. (2011). Memory for complex emotional material in dissociative identity disorder. *Journal of Trauma & Dissociation, 12*(1), 53–66.

Barnard, C. (2007). Ethical regulation and animal science: Why animal behaviour is special. *Animal Behavior, 74*(1), 5–13.

Barnes, A. (2004). Race, schizophrenia, and admission to state psychiatric hospitals. *Administration and Policy in Mental Health, 31*(3), 241–252.

Barnes, D. H. (2010). Suicide. In R. L. Hampton, T. P. Gullotta, & R. L. Crowel (Eds.), *Handbook of African American health* (pp. 444–460). New York: Guilford Press.

Barnes, G. E., & Prosen, H. (1985). Parental death and depression. *Journal of Abnormal Psychology, 94*(1), 64–69.

Barnes, T. R. E., & Marder, S. R. (2011). Principles of pharmacological treatment in schizophrenia. In D. R. Weinberg & P. Harrison (Eds.), *Schizophrenia* (pp. 515–524). Hoboken, NJ: Wiley-Blackwell.

Baron, M. (2002). Manic-depression genes and the new millennium: Poised for discovery. *Molecular Psychiatry, 7*(4), 342–358.

Barr, A. M., Boyda, H. ., & Procysbyn, R. C. (2011). Withdrawal. In M. C. Olmstead (Ed.), *Animal models of drug addiction. Springer protocols: Neuromethods* (pp. 431–459). Totowa, NJ; Humana Press.

Barrera, T. L., Wilson, K. P., & Norton, P. J. (2010). The experience of panic symptoms across racial groups in a student sample. *Journal of Anxiety Disorders, 24*(8), 873–878.

Barrett, N. (2000). Wasting away on the web: Shocking internet sites are encouraging anorexia as a "lifestyle". *Planetgrrl.* Retrieved from http://btinternet.com/~virtuous/planetgrrlbabe/babearticles.

Barron, J. (2008). Working in mental health, the prospect of violence is a part of the job. *New York Times,* February 14, 2008.

Barrowclough, C., & Lobban, F. (2008). Family intervention. In K. T. Mueser & D. V. Jeste (Eds.), *Clinical handbook of schizophrenia* (pp. 214–225). New York: Guilford Press.

Bartholomew, K. (2000). Clinical protocol. *Psychoanalytical Inquiry, 20*(2), 227–248.

Barton, A. (2004). Women and community punishment: The probation hostel as a semipenal institution for female offenders. *Howard J. Criminal Justice, 43*(2), 149–163.

Bartrop, R. W., Lockhurst, E., Lazarus, L., Kiloh, L. G., & Penny, R. (1977). Depressed lymphocyte function after bereavement. *Lancet, 1,* 834–836.

Bartz, J., Kaplan, A., & Hollander, E. (2007). Obsessive-compulsive personality disorder. In W. O'Donohue, K. A. Fowler, S. O. Lilienfeld (Eds.). *Personality disorders: Toward the DSM-V.* Los Angeles: Sage Publications.

Basoglu, M., Jaranson, J. M., Mollica, R., & Kastrup, M. (2001). Torture and mental health: A research overview. In E. Gerrity, T. M. Keane, & F. Tuma (Eds.), *The mental health consequences of torture* (pp. 35–62). New York: Kluwer Academic/Plenum Publishers.

Bass, C., & Jones, D. (2011). Psychopathology of perpetrators of fabricated or induced illness in children: Case series. *British Journal of Psychiatry, 199*(2), 113–118.

Basson, R. (2007). Sexual desire/arousal disorders in women. In S. R. Leiblum (Ed.), *Principles and practice of sex therapy* (4th ed., pp. 25–53). New York: Guilford Press.

Bastien, C. H. (2011). Insomnia: Neurophysiological and neuropsychological approaches. *Neuropsychology Review, 21*(1), 22–40.

Bateman, A. W. (2011). Borderline personality disorder. In J. C. Norcross, G. R. VandenBos, & D. K. Freedheim (Eds.), *History of psychotherapy: Continuity and change* (2nd ed., pp. 588–600). Washington, DC: American Psychological Association.

Bates, G. W., Thompson, J. C., & Flanagan, C. (1999). The effectiveness of individual versus group induction of depressed mood. *Journal of Psychology, 133*(3), 245–252.

Bateson, G. (1974) *Perceval's narrative: A patient's account of his psychosis.* New York: William Morrow.

Bateson, G., Jackson, D., Haley, J., & Weakland, J. (1956). Toward a theory of schizophrenia. *Behavioral Science, 1,* 251–264.

Batki, S. L., & Nathan, K. I. (2008). HIV/AIDS and hepatitis C. In H. D. Kleber & M. Galanter (Eds.), *The American Psychiatric Publishing textbook of substance abuse treatment* (4th ed., pp. 581–593). Arlington, VA: American Psychiatric Publishing.

Baucom, B. R., Atkins, D. C., Simpson, L. E., & Christensen, A. (2009). Prediction of response to treatment in a randomized clinical trial of couple therapy: A 2-year follow-up. *Journal of Consulting and Clinical Psychology, 77*(1), 160–173.

Baucom, D. H., Epstein, N. B., & Gordon, K. C. (2000). Marital therapy: Theory, practice, and empirical status. In C. R. Snyder & R. E. Ingram (Eds.), *Handbook of psychological change: Psychotherapy processes & practices for the 21st century* (pp. 280–308). New York: Wiley.

Baucom, D. H., Epstein, N. B., & Stanton, S. (2006). The treatment of relationship distress: Theoretical perspectives and empirical findings. In A. L. Vangelisti & D. Perlman (Eds.), *The Cambridge* *handbook of personal relationships* (pp. 745–765). New York: Cambridge University Press.

Baucom, D. H., Epstein, N. B., Kirby, J. S., & LaTaillade, J. J. (2010). Cognitive-behavioral couple therapy. In K. S. Dobson (Ed.), *Handbook of cognitive-behavioral therapies* (3rd ed., pp. 411–444). New York: Guilford Press.

Baucom, D. H., Porter, L. S., Kirby, J. S., & Hudepohl, J. (2012). Couple-based interventions for medical problems. *Behavior Therapy, 43*(1), 61–76.

Bauer, M. E. (2005). Stress, glucocorticoids and ageing of the immune system. *Stress: The International Journal of the Biology of Stress, 8*(1), 69–83.

Baum, A., Trevino, L. A., & Dougall, A. L. (2011). Stress and the cancers. In R. J. Contrada & A. Baum (Eds.), *The handbook of stress science: Biology, psychology, and health* (pp. 411–423). New York: Springer Publishing.

Baum, A., Wallander, J. L., Boll, T. J., & Frank, R. G. (Eds.). (2004). *Handbook of clinical health psychology, Vol. 3: Models and perspectives in health psychology.* Washington, DC: American Psychological Association.

Bauman, M. L. (2011). Neuroanatomy of the brain in autism spectrum disorders. In E. Hollander, A. Kolevzon & J. T. Coyle (Eds.), *Textbook of autism spectrum disorder.* (pp. 355–361) Arlington, VA: American Psychiatric Publishing, Inc.

Baxter, L. R., Jr., Ackermann, R. F., Swerdlow, N. R., Brody, A., Saxena, S., Schwartz, J. M., et al. (2000). Specific brain system mediation of obsessive-compulsive disorder responsive to either medication or behavior therapy. In W. K. Goodman, M. V. Rudorfer, & J. D. Maser (Eds.), *Obsessive-compulsive disorder: Contemporary issues in treatment* (pp. 573–609). Mahwah, NJ: Lawrence Erlbaum.

Baxter, L. R., Jr., Clark, E. C., Iqbal, M., & Ackermann, R. F. (2001). Cortical-subcortical systems in the mediation of obsessive–compulsive disorder: Modeling the brain's mediation of a classic "neurosis." In D. G. Lichter & J. L. Cummings (Eds.), *Frontal-subcortical circuits in psychiatric and neurological disorders* (pp. 207–230). New York: Guilford Press.

Baxter, L. R., Phelps, M. E., Mazziotta, J. C., Guze, B. H., et al. (1987). Local cerebral glucose metabolic rates in obsessive-compulsive disorder: A comparison with rates in unipolar depression and in normal controls. *Archives of General Psychiatry, 44*(3), 211–218.

Baxter, L. R., Schwartz, J. M., Bergman, K. S., Szuba, M. P., Guze, B. H., Mazziotta, J. C., et al. (1992). Caudate glucose metabolic rate changes with both drug and behavior therapy for obsessive-compulsive disorder. *Archives of General Psychiatry, 49,* 681–689.

Baxter, L. R., Schwartz, J. M., Guze, B. H., Bergman, K., et al. (1990). PET imaging in obsessive–compulsive disorder with and without depression. Symposium: Serotonin and its effects on human behavior (1989, Atlanta, GA). *Journal of Clinical Psychiatry, 51*(Suppl.), 61–69.

Bazargan, M., Bazargan-Hejazi, S., & Baker, R. S. (2005). Treatment of self-reported depression among Hispanics and African Americans. *Journal of Health Care for the Poor and Underserved, 16,* 328–344.

Bazelon Center. (2008). *Vote: It's your right: A guide to the voting rights of people with mental disabilities.* Washington, DC: Author.

Beals, J., Manson, S. M., Whitesell, N. R., Spicer, P., Novins, D. K., & Mitchell, C. M. (2005). Prevalence of DSM-IV disorders and attendant help-seeking in 2 American Indian reservation populations. *Archives of General Psychiatry, 62*(1), 99–108.

Beals, J., Novins, D., Whitesell, N., Spicer, P., Mitchell, C., & Manson, S. (2005). Prevalence of mental disorders and utilization of mental health services in two American Indian reservation populations: Mental health disparities in a national context. *American Journal of Psychiatry, 162,* 1734–1743.

Bean, A. (2011, January 7). A black president and a falling crime rate: Any correlation? *Friends of Justice.*

Beautrais, A., Joyce, P., & Mulder, R. (2000). Unmet need following serious suicide attempt: Follow-up of 302 individuals for 30 months. In G. Andrews & S. Henderson (Eds.), *Unmet need in psychiatry: Problems, resources, responses.* New York: Cambridge University Press.

Bebbington, P. E., & Kuipers, E. (2011). Schizophrenia and psychosocial stresses. In D. R. Weinberg & P. Harrison (Eds.), *Schizophrenia* (pp. 599–624). Hoboken, NJ: Wiley-Blackwell.

Bebko, J. M., & Weiss, J. A. (2006). Mental retardation. In M. Hersen & J. C. Thomas (Series Eds.) & R. T. Ammerman (Vol. Ed.), *Comprehensive handbook of personality and psychopathology, Vol. 3: Child psychopathology* (pp. 233–253). Hoboken, NJ: Wiley.

Becchetti, L., & Santoro, M. (2007). The income-unhappiness paradox: A relational goods/Baumol disease explanation. In P. L. Porta & L. Bruni (Eds.), *Handbook on the economics of happiness* (pp. 239–262). Northampton, MA: Edward Elgar Publishing.

Beck, A. T. (1967). *Depression: Clinical, experimental and theoretical aspects.* New York: Harper & Row.

Beck, A. T. (1991). Cognitive therapy: A 30-year retrospective. *American Psychologist, 46*(4), 368–375.

Beck, A. T. (2002). Cognitive models of depression. In R. L. Leahy & E. T. Dowd (Eds.), *Clinical advances in cognitive psychotherapy: Theory and application* (pp. 29–61). New York: Springer.

Beck, A. T. (2004). A cognitive model of schizophrenia. *Journal of Cognitive Psychotherapy, 18*(3), 281–288.

Beck, A. T. (2004). Cognitive therapy, behavior therapy, psychoanalysis, and pharmacotherapy: A cognitive continuum. In M. J. Mahoney, P. DeVito, D. Martin, & A. Freeman (Eds.), *Cognition and psychotherapy* (2nd ed., pp. 197–220). New York: Springer Publishing.

Beck, A. T., & Emery, G., with Greenberg, R. L. (1985). Differentiating anxiety and depression: A test of the cognitive content-specificity hypothesis. *Journal of Abnormal Psychology, 96,* 179–183.

Beck, A. T., Freeman, A., Davis, D. D., et al. (2004). *Cognitive therapy of personality disorders* (2nd ed.). New York: Guilford Press

Beck, A. T., & Weishaar, M. (2011). Cognitive therapy. In R. J. Corsini & D. Wedding (Eds.), *Current psychotherapies* (9th ed.). Belmont, CA: Brooks/Cole.

Beck, A. T., Rector, N. A., Stolar, N., & Grant, P. (2011). *Schizophrenia: Cognitive Theory, Research, and Therapy.* New York: Guilford Press.

Beck, A. T., Rush, A. J., Shaw, B. F., & Emery, G. (1979). *Cognitive therapy of depression.* New York: Guilford Press.

Beck, A. T., Ward, C. H., Mendelson, M., Mock, J. E., & Erbaugh, J. (1962). Reliability of psychiatric diagnosis: 2. A study of consistency of clinical judgments and ratings. *American Journal of Psychiatry, 119,* 351–357.

Beck, J. G. (2010). *Interpersonal processes in the anxiety disorders: Implications for understanding psychopathology and treatment.* Washington, DC: American Psychological Association.

Becker, A. E., Burwell, R. A., Gilman, S. E., Herzog, D. B., & Hamburg, P. (2002). Eating behaviors and attitudes following prolonged exposure to television among ethnic Fijian adolescent girls. *British Journal of Psychiatry, 180,* 509–514.

Becker, A. E., Burwell, R. A., Narvara, K., & Gilman, S. E. (2003). Binge eating and binge eating disorder in a small scale indigenous society: The view from Fiji. *International Journal of Eating Disorders, 34,* 423–431.

Becker, A. E., Fay, A., Gilman, S. E., & Stiegel-Moore, R. (2007). Facets of acculturation and their diverse relations to body shape concerns in Fiji. *International Journal of Eating Disorders, 40*(1), 42–50.

Becker, A. E., Grinspoon, S. K., Klibanski, A., & Herzog, D. B . (1999). Eating disorders. *New England Journal of Medicine, 340,* 1092–1098.

Becker, A. E., Roberts, A. L., Perloe, A., Bainivualiku, A., Richards, L. K., Gilman, S. E., & Striegel-Moore R. H. (2010). Youth health-risk behavior assessment in Fiji: The reality of global school-based student health survey content adapted for ethnic Fijian girls. *Ethnicity & Health, 15*(2), 181–197.

Becker, D. R. (2008). Vocational rehabilitation. In K. T. Mueser & D. V. Jeste (Eds.), *Clinical handbook of schizophrenia* (pp. 261–267). New York: Guilford Press.

Becker, J. V., Johnson, B. R., Parthasarathi, U., & Hategan, A. (2012). Gender identity disorders and paraphilias. In J. A. Bourgeois, U. Parthasarathi, & A. Hategan (Eds.), *Psychiatry review and Canadian certification exam preparation guide* (pp. 305–315). Arlington, VA: American Psychiatric Publishing.

Becker, K. D., Ginsburg, G. S., Domingues J., & Tein, J-Y. (2010). Maternal control behavior and locus of control: Examining mechanisms in the relation between maternal anxiety disorders and anxiety symptomatology in children. *Journal of Abnormal Child Psychology: An official publication of the International Society for Research in Child and Adolescent Psychopathology, 38*(4), 533–543.

Becker, K., & Schmidt, M. H. (2004). Internet chat rooms and suicide. *Journal of the American Academy of Child and Adolescent Psychiatry, 43*(3), 246.

Beezhold, J. (2002). Cited in Psychiatrists "driven by fear." *BBC News: Health,* December 17, 2002.

Beidel, D. C., & Turner, S. M. (2005). *Childhood anxiety disorders: A guide to research and treatment.* New York: Routledge/Taylor & Francis.

Beier, E. G., & Young, D. M. (1984). *The silent language of psychotherapy: Social reinforcement of the unconscious processes* (2nd ed.). Hawthorne, New York: Aldine.

Bekkouche, N. S., Holmes, S., Whittaker, K. S., & Krantz, D. S. (2011). Stress and the heart: Psychosocial stress and coronary heart disease. In R. J. Contrada & A. Baum (Eds.), *The handbook of stress science: Biology, psychology, and health* (pp. 385–398). New York: Springer Publishing.

Belkin, L. (1990, June 6). Doctor tells of first death using his suicide device. *New York Times,* A1, p. 3.

Bell, J. (2008, February 6). When anxiety is at the table. *New York Times.*

Bell, K., Lee, J., Foran, S., Kwong, S., & Christopherson, J. (2010). Is there an "ideal cancer" support group? Key findings from a qualitative study of three groups. *Journal of Psychosocial Oncology, 28*(4), 432–449.

Bell, L., Long, S., Garvan, C., & Bussing, R. (2011). The impact of teacher credentials on ADHD stigma perceptions. *Psychology in the Schools, 48*(2), 184–197.

Bell, M. D., Choi, J., & Lysaker, P. (2011). Psychological interventions to improve work outcomes for people with psychiatric disabilities. In R. Hagen, D. Turkington, T. Berge, & R. W. Grawe (Eds.), *CBT for psychosis: A symptom-based approach, International Society for the Psychological Treatments of the Schizophrenias and Other Psychoses* (pp. 210–230). New York: Routledge/Taylor & Francis Group.

Belleville, G., Cousineau, H., Levrier, K., & St-Pierre-Delorme, M-E. (2011). Meta-analytic review of the impact of cognitive-behavior therapy for insomnia on concomitant anxiety. *Clinical Psychology Review, 31*(4), 638–652.

Bellinger, D. L., Madden, K. S., Felten, S. Y., & Felten, D. L. (1994). Neural and endocrine links between the brain and the immune system. In C. S. Lewis, C. O'Sullivan, & J. Barraclough (Eds.), *The psychoimmunology of cancer: Mind and body in the fight for survival.* Oxford, England: Oxford University Press.

Bemporad, J. R. (1992). Psychoanalytically orientated psychotherapy. In E. S. Paykel (Ed.), *Handbook of affective disorders.* New York: Guilford Press.

Benas, J. S., & Gibb, B. E. (2011). Cognitive biases in depression and eating disorders. *Cognitive Therapy and Research, 35*(1), 68–78.

Bender, D. S., & Oldham, J. M. (2005). Psychotherapies for borderline personality disorder. In J. G. Gunderson & P. D. Hoffman (Eds.), *Understanding and treating borderline personality disorder* (pp. 21–41). Washington, DC: American Psychiatric Publishing.

Bender, D. S. (2005). The therapeutic alliance in the treatment of personality disorders. *Journal of Psychiatric Practice, 11*(2), 73–87.

Bender, D. S., Farber, B. A., & Geller, J. D. (2001). Cluster B personality traits and attachment. *Journal of the American Academy of Psychoanalysis, 29*(4), 551–563.

Bender, D. S., Skodol, A. E., Dyck, I. R., Markowitz, J. C., Shea, M. T., Yen, S., et al. (2007). Ethnicity and mental health treatment utilization by patients with personality disorders. *Journal of Consulting and Clinical Psychology, 75*(6), 992–999.

Bender, E. (2006, June 16). APA, AACAP suggest ways to reduce high suicide rates in Native Americans. *Psychiatric News, 41*(12), 6.

Bender, R. E., & Alloy, L. B. (2011). Life stress and kindling in bipolar disorder: Review of the evidence and integration with emerging biopsychosocial theories. *Clinical Psychology Review, 31*(3), 383–398.

Benedict, S., Campbell, M., Doolen, A., Rivera, I., Negussi, T., & Turner-McGrievy, G. (2007). Seeds of HOPE: A model for addressing social and economic determinants of health in a women's obesity prevention project in two rural communities. *Journal of Women's Health, 16*(8), 1117–1124.

Benes, F. M. (2011). The neurobiology of bipolar disorder: From circuits to cells to molecular regulation. In H. K. Manji & C. A. Zarate, Jr. (Eds.), *Behavioral neurobiology of bipolar disorders and its treatment. Current topics in behavioral neurosciences* (pp. 127–138). New York: Springer Science + Business Media.

Benesh, P. (2010). Drug approval process slowing as FDA seeks to stress safety. *Investor's Business Daily.* July, 14. (http://news.investors.com)

Benitez, C. T., & Chamberlain, J. (2008). Methamphetamine-induced psychosis and diminished capacity to form intent to kill: Ultimate issue in expert testimony. *Journal of the American Academy of Psychiatry and the Law, 36*(2), 258–260.

Benjamin, G. A., Kent, L., & Sirikantraporn, S. (2009). A review of duty-to-protect statutes, cases, and procedures for positive practice. In J. L. Werth, Jr., E. R. Welfel, & G. A. H. Benjamin (Eds.), *The duty to protect: Ethical, legal, and professional considerations for mental health professionals* (pp. 9–28). Washington, DC: American Psychological Association.

Bennett, M. D., & Olugbala, F. K. (2010). Don't bother me, I can't cope: Stress, coping, and problem behaviors among young African American males. In W. E. Johnson Jr. (Ed.), *Social work with African American males: Health, mental health, and social policy.* (pp. 179–194) New York: Oxford University Press.

Bennett, M. P. (1998). The effect of mirthful laughter on stress and natural killer cell cytotoxicity. *Dissertation Abstracts International: Section B: The Sciences and Engineering, 58*(7–B), 3553.

Ben-Porath, Y. S. (2012). *Interpreting the MMPI-2-RF.* Minneapolis: University of Minnesota Press.

Berenson, K. R., Downey, G., Rafaeli, E., Coifman, K. G., & Leventhal Paquin, N. (2011). The rejection-rage contingency in borderline personality disorder. *Journal of Abnormal Psychology, 120*(3), 681–690.

Berg, J. E. (2010). Is detoxification or tapering of benzodiazepine abuse advisable in an acute psychiatric clinic? *Clinical Neuropsychiatry: Journal of Treatment Evaluation, 7*(1), 18–21.

Bergler, E. (1951). *Neurotic counterfeit sex.* New York: Grune & Stratton.

Bergquist, K. (2002). "War on crime adversely affects war on terrorism, professor says." http://www.ur.umich.edu/0203/Oct14_02/g_simon.shtml.

Berk, S. N., & Efran, J. S. (1983). Some recent developments in the treatment of neurosis. In C. E. Walker (Ed.), *The handbook of clinical psychology: Theory, research, and practice* (Vol. 2). Homewood, IL: Dow Jones-Irwin.

Berkhof, F., Fox, N. C., Bastos-Leite, A. J., & Scheltens, P. (2011). *Neuroimaging in dementia.* New York: Springer.

Berks, J., & McCormick, R. (2008). Screening for alcohol misuse in elderly primary care patients: A systematic literature review. *International Psychogeriatrics, 20*(6), 1090–1103.

Berman, A. L. (1986). Helping suicidal adolescents: Needs and responses. In C. A. Corr & J. N. McNeil (Eds.), *Adolescence and death.* New York: Springer.

Berner, W., & Briken, P. (2010). Therapy options for men with sexual preference disorders/paraphilias and sexual delinquency. *Forensische Psychiatrie, Psychologie, Kriminologie, 4*(Suppl. 1), S8–S16.

Bernert, R. A., Merrill, K. A., Braithwaite, S. R., Van Orden, K. A., & Joiner, T. E., Jr. (2007). Family life stress and insomnia symptoms in a prospective evaluation of young adults. *Journal of Family Psychology, 21*(1), 58–66.

Berninger, V. W. (2010). Assessing and intervening with children with written language disorders. In D. C. Miller (Ed.), *Best practices in school neuropsychology: Guidelines for effective practice, assessment, and evidence-based intervention* (pp. 507–520). Hoboken, NJ: John Wiley & Sons.

Bernstein, D. P., & Useda, J. D (2007). Paranoid personality disorder. In W. O'Donohue, K. A. Fowler, & S. O. Lilienfeld (Eds.). *Personality disorders: Toward the DSM-V.* Los Angeles: Sage Publications.

Bernstein, H. A. (1981). Survey of threats and assaults directed toward psychotherapists. *American Journal of Psychotherapy, 35,* 542–549.

Berr, C., Wancata, J., & Ritchie, K. (2005). Prevalence of dementia in the elderly in Europe. *European Neuropsychopharmacology, 15*(4), 463–471.

Berrettini, W. (2006). Genetics of bipolar and unipolar disorders. In D. J. Stein, D. J. Kupfer, & A. F. Schatzberg (Eds.), *The American Psychiatric Publishing textbook of mood disorders.* Washington, DC: American Psychiatric Publishing.

Berridge, M. J. (2011). Calcium signaling and Alzheimer's disease. *Neurochemical Research, 36*(7), 1149–1156.

Berrigan, D., Dodd, K., Triano, R. P., Krebs-Smith, S. M., & Barbash, R. B. (2003). Patterns of health behavior in U.S. adults. *Preventive Medicine: An International Journal Devoted to Practice and Theory, 36*(5), 615–623.

Berrigan, D., Troiano, R. P., McNeel, T., DiSogra, C., & Ballard-Barbash, R. (2006). Active transportation increases adherence to activity recommendations. *American Journal of Preventative Medicine, 31*(3), 210–216.

Berthoud, H-R., Shin, A. C., & Zheng, H. (2011). Obesity surgery and gut–brain communication. *Physiology & Behavior, 105*(1), 106–119.

Berti, V., Pupi, A., & Mosconi, L. (2011). PET/CT in diagnosis of dementia. *Annals of the New York Academy of Sciences, 1228*(1), 81–92.

Bertozzi, S., Londero, A. P., Fruscalzo, A., Driul, L., & Marchesoni, D. (2010). Prevalence and risk factors for dyspareunia and unsatisfying sexual relationships in a cohort of primiparous and secondiparous women after 12 months postpartum. *International Journal of Sexual Health, 22*(1), 47–53.

Berzoff, J., Flanagan, L. M., & Hertz, P. (Eds.). (2008). Inside out and outside in: Psychodynamic clinical theory and psychopathology in contemporary multicultural contexts (2nd ed.). Lanham, MD: Jason Aronson.

Beutler, L. E. (2000). David and Goliath: When empirical and clinical standards of practice meet. *American Psychologist, 55*(9), 997–1007.

Beutler, L. E. (2002). The dodo bird is extinct. *Clinical Psychology: Science and Practice, 9*(1), 30–34.

Beutler, L. E., (2011). Prescriptive matching and systematic treatment selection. In J. C. Norcross, G. R. VandenBos, & D. K. Freedheim (Eds.), *History of psychotherapy: Continuity and change* (2nd ed., pp. 402–407). Washington, DC: American Psychological Association.

Beutler, L. E., & Malik, M. L. (Eds.). (2002). *Rethinking the DSM: A psychological perspective. Decade of behavior.* Washington, DC: American Psychological Association.

Beutler, L. E., Clarkin, J. F., & Bongar, B. (2000). *Guidelines for the systematic treatment of the depressed patient.* New York: Oxford University Press.

Beutler, L. E., Harwood, T. M., Kimpara, S., Verdirame, D., & Blau, K. (2011). Coping style. *Journal of Clinical Psychology, 67*(2), 176–183.

Beutler, L. E., Williams, R. E., Wakefield, P. J., & Entwistle, S. R. (1995). Bridging scientist and practitioner perspectives in clinical psychology. *American Psychologist, 50*(12), 984–994.

Bharani, N., & Lantz, M. S. (2008). Newonset agoraphobia in late life. *Clinical Geriatrics,* 1/17/08, 17–20.

Bhattacharya, R., Cross, S., & Bhugra, D. (Eds). (2010). *Clinical topics in cultural psychiatry.* London: Royal College of Psychiatrists.

Bhugra, D., Popelyuk, D., & McMullen, I. (2010). Paraphilias across cultures: Contexts and controversies. *Journal of Sex Research, 47*(2-3), 242–256.

Bhushan, B., & Kumar, J. S. (2007). Emotional distress and posttraumatic stress in children surviving the 2004 tsunami. *Journal of Loss and Trauma, 12*(3), 245–257.

Bickman, L. (2005). A common factors approach to improving mental health services. *Mental Health Services Research, 7*(1), 1–4.

Biddle, S., Akande, D., Armstrong, N., Ashcroft, M., Brooke, R., & Goudes, M. (1996). The self-motivation inventory modified for children: Evidenced on psychometric properties and its use in physical exercise. *International Journal of Sport Psychology, 27*(3), 237–250.

Biederman, J., Mick, E., Faraone, S. V., & Burback, M. (2001). Patterns of remission and symptom decline in conduct disorder: A four-year prospective study of an ADHD sample. *Journal of the American Academy of Child and Adolescent Psychiatry, 40*(3), 290–298.

Biederman, J., Spencer, T., & Wilens, T. (2004). Evidence-based pharmacotherapy for attention-deficit hyperactivity disorder. *International Journal of Neuropsychopharmacology, 7,* 77–97.

Biederman, J., Spencer, T., & Wilens, T. (2005). Evidence-based pharmacotherapy for attention-deficit hyperactivity disorder. In D. J. Stein, B. Lerer, & S. Stahl, *Evidence-based psychopharmacology* (pp. 255–289). New York: Cambridge University Press.

Bigler, E. D. (2009). Traumatic brain injury. In M. F. Weiner & A. M. Lipton (Eds.), *The American Psychiatric Publishing textbook of Alzheimer disease and other dementias* (pp. 229–246) Arlington, VA: American Psychiatric Publishing, Inc.

Bills, C. B., & Li, G. (2005). Correlating homicide and suicide. *International Journal of Epidemiology, 34*(4), 837–845.

Binet, A., & Simon, T. (1916). The development of intelligence in children (The Binet-Simon Scale). Baltimore: Williams & Wilkins.

Binik, Y. M. (2010). The DSM diagnostic criteria for vaginismus. *Archives of Sexual Behavior, 39*(2), 278–291.

Binik, Y. M., Bergeron, S., & Khalifé, S. (2007). Dyspareunia and vaginismus: So-called sexual pain. In S. R. Leiblum (Ed.), *Principles and practice of sex therapy* (4th ed., pp. 157–179). New York: Guilford Press.

Bio, D. S., & Gattaz, W. F. (2011). Vocational rehabilitation improves cognition and negative symptoms in schizophrenia. *Schizophrenia Research, 126*(1-3), 265–269.

Birkett, P., Clegg, J., Bhaker, R., Lee, K-H, Mysore, A., Parks, R., & Woodruff, P. (2011). Schizophrenia impairs phonological speech production: A preliminary report. *Cognitive Neuropsychiatry, 16*(1), 40–49.

Birmingham, C. L. (2011). Physical effects of eating disorders. In J. Alexander & J. Treasure (Eds.), *A collaborative approach to eating disorders* (pp. 93–101). New York: Taylor & Francis.

Birrell, P. (2011). Review of memory matters: Contexts for understanding sexual abuse recollections. *Journal of Trauma & Dissociation, 12*(1), 107–109.

Bisaga, A. (2008). Benzodiazepines and other sedatives and hypnotics. In H. D. Kleber & M. Galanter (Eds.), *The American Psychiatric Publishing textbook of substance abuse treatment* (4th ed., pp. 215–235). Arlington, VA: American Psychiatric Publishing.

Bishop, F. M. (2008). Alcohol abuse. In M. Hersen & J. Rosqvist (Eds.), *Handbook of psychological assessment, case conceptualization and treatment, Vol. 1: Adults.* Hoboken, NJ; John Wiley & Sons.

Bisson, J. I., & Deahl, M. P. (1994). Psychological debriefing and prevention of post-traumatic stress: More research is needed. *British Journal of Psychiatry, 165*(6), 717–720.

Bisson, J. I., Jenkins, P. L., Alexander, J., & Bannister, C. (1997). Randomised controlled trial of psychological debriefing for victims of acute burn trauma. *British Journal of Psychiatry, 171,* 78–81.

Björgvinsson, T., & Hart, J. (2008). Obsessive-compulsive disorder. In M. Hersen & J. Rosqvist (Eds.), *Handbook of psychological assessment, case conceptualization, and treatment, Vol. 1: Adults* (pp. 237–262). Hoboken, NJ: John Wiley & Sons.

Black Youth Project. (2011). *The attitudes and behavior of young Black Americans: Research summary.* Retrieved on May 28, 2011, from www.blackyouthproject.com/survey/findings.

Black, D. W., Gunter, T., Loveless, P., Allen, J., & Sieleni, B. (2010). Antisocial personality disorder in incarcerated offenders: Psychiatric comorbidity and quality of life. *Annals of Clinical Psychiatry, 22*(3), 113–120.

Black, K. J. (2005). Diagnosis. In E. H. Rubin & C. F. Zorumski (Eds.), *Adult psychiatry* (2nd ed.). Oxford, England: Blackwell Publishing.

Blackburn, C., Carpenter, B., & Egerton, J. (2010). Shaping the future for children with foetal alcohol spectrum disorders. *Support for Learning, 25*(3), 139–145.

Blackmore, D. E., Hart, S. L., Albiani, J. J., & Mohr, D. C. (2011). Improvements in partner support predict sexual satisfaction among individuals with multiple sclerosis. *Rehabilitation Psychology, 56*(2), 1176–122.

Blackmore, E. R., Craddock, N., Walters, J., & Jones, I. (2008). Is the perimenopause a time of increased risk of recurrence in women with a history of bipolar affective postpartum psychosis? A case series. *Archives of Women's Mental Health, 11*(1), 75–78.

Blagov, P. S., Fowler K. A., & Lilienfeld, S. O. (2007). Histrionic personality disorder. In W. O'Donohue, K. A. Fowler, & S. O. Lilienfeld (Eds.). *Personality disorders: Toward the DSM-V.* Los Angeles: Sage Publications.

Blair, J., Mitchell, D., & Blair, K. (2005). *The psychopath: Emotion and the brain.* Malden, MA: Blackwell Publishing.

Blais, M. A., & Baer, L. (2010). Understanding rating scales and assessment instruments. In L. Baer & M. A. Blais (Eds.), *Handbook of clinical rating scales and assessment in psychiatry and mental health* (pp. 1–6). Totowa, NJ: Humana Press.

Blais, M. A., Baity, M. R., & Hopwood, C. J. (Eds.). (2010). *Clinical applications of the Personality Assessment Inventory.* New York: Routledge/Taylor & Francis Group.

Blanchard, J. J., Kring, A. M., Horan, W. P., & Gur, R. (2011). Toward the next generation of negative symptom assessments: The Collaboration to Advance Negative Symptom Assessment in Schizophrenia. *Schizophrenia Bulletin, 37*(2), 291–299.

Blanchflower, D. G., & Oswald, A. (2007, February). *Is well-being U-shaped over the life cycle?* (NBER Working Paper No. 12935). Cambridge, MA: National Bureau of Economic Research.

Blanco, C., Davies, C. A., & Nunes, E. V. (2010). Other anxiety disorders in patients with substance use disorders: Panic disorder, agoraphobia, social anxiety disorder, and generalized anxiety disorder. In E. V. Nunes, J. Selzer, P. Levounis, & C. A. Davies (Eds.), *Substance dependence and co-occurring psychiatric disorders: Best practices for diagnosis and treatment* (pp. 4-1–4-36). Kingston, NJ: Civic Research Institute.

Blanco, C., Myers, J., & Kendler, K. S. (2012). Gambling, disordered gambling and their association with major depression and substance use: A web-based cohort and twin-sibling study. *Psychological Medicine, 42*(3), 497–508.

Blanco, C., Schneier, F. R., Vesga-López, O., & Liebowitz, M. R. (2010). Pharmacotherapy for social anxiety disorder. In D. J. Stein, E. Hollander, & B. O. Rothbaum (Eds.), *Textbook of anxiety disorders* (2nd ed., pp. 471–499). Arlington, VA: American Psychiatric Publishing.

Blatt, S. J. (1995). The destructiveness of perfectionism. Implications for the treatment of depression. *American Psychologist., 50*(12), 1003–1020.

Blatt, S. J. (1999). Personality factors in brief treatment of depression: Further analyses of the NIMH-sponsored Treatment for Depression Collaborative Research Program. In D. S. Janowsky (Ed.), *Psychotherapy indications and outcomes.* Washington, DC: American Psychiatric Press.

Blatt, S. J. (2004). Developmental origins (distal antecedents). In S. J. Blatt, *Experiences of depression: Theoretical, clinical, and research perspectives* (pp. 187–229). Washington, DC: American Psychological Association.

Blazer, D. G., & Wu, L-T. (2011). The epidemiology of alcohol use disorders and subthreshold dependence in a middle-aged and elderly community sample. *American Journal of Geriatric Psychiatry, 19*(8), 685–694.

Bliss, E. L. (1980). Multiple personalities: A report of 14 cases with implications for schizophrenia and hysteria. *Archives of General Psychiatry, 37*(12), 1388–1397.

Bliss, E. L. (1980). *Multiple personality, allied disorders and hypnosis.* New York: Oxford University Press.

Bloch, M. H., & McGuire, J. F. (2011). Pharmacological treatment for phobias and anxiety disorders. In D. McKay & E. A. Storch (Eds.), *Handbook of child and adolescent anxiety disorders* (pp. 339–354) New York: Springer Science + Business Media.

Blomstedt, P. O., Sjöberg, R. L., Hansson, M., Bodlund, O., & Hariz, M. I. (2011). Deep brain stimulation in the treatment of depression. *Acta Psychiatrica Scandinavica, 123*(1), 4–11.

Blood, R. W., Pirkis, J., & Holland, K. (2007). Media reporting of suicide methods: An Australian perspective. *Crisis: Journal of Crisis Intervention and Suicide Prevention, 28*(Suppl. 1), 64–69.

Bloom, B. L. (1984). *Community mental health: A general introduction* (2nd ed.). Monterey, CA: Brooks/Cole.

Bloom, J. D. (2004). Thirty-five years of working with civil commitment statutes. *Journal of the American Academy of Psychiatry and the Law, 32*(4), 430–439.

Blow, F. C., Zeber, J. E., McCarthy, J. F., Valenstein, M., Gillon, L., & Bingham, C. R. (2004). Ethnicity and diagnostic patterns in veterans with psychoses. *Social Psychiatry and Psychiatric Epidemiology, 39*(10), 841–851.

Bluglass, K. (2001). Treatment of perpetrators. In G. Adshead & D. Brooke (Eds.), *Munchausen's syndrome by proxy: Current issues in assessment, treatment and research* (pp. 175–184). London: Imperial College Press.

Blum, H. P. (2010). Object relations in clinical psychoanalysis. *International Journal of Psychoanalysis, 91*(4), 973–976.

Blum, K., Braverman, E. R., Holder, J. M., Lubar, J. F., Monastra, V. J., Miller, D., et al. (2000). Reward deficiency syndrome: A biogenetic model for the diagnosis and treatment of impulsive, addictive, and compulsive behaviors. *Journal of Psychoactive Drugs, 32*(Suppl.), 1–68.

Blum, K., Cull, J. G., Braverman, E. R., & Comings, D. E. (1996). Reward deficiency syndrome. *American Scientist, 84*(2), 132–144.

Blum, K., Noble, E. P., Sheridan, P. J., Montgomery, A., Ritchie, T., Jagadeeswaran, P., et al. (1990). Allelic association of human dopamine D2 receptor gene in alcoholism. *Journal of the American Medical Association, 263*(15), 2055–2060.

Blume, J., Douglas, S. D., & Evans, D. L. (2011). Immune suppression and immune activation in depression. *Brain, Behavior, and Immunity, 25*(2), 221–229.

Bock, C., Bukh, J. D., Vinberg, M., Gether, U., & Kessing, L. V. (2010). The influence of comorbid personality disorder and neuroticism on treatment outcome in first episode depression. *Psychopathology, 43*(3), 197–204.

Bockoven, J. S. (1963). *Moral treatment in American psychiatry.* New York: Springer.

Bockting, C. L. H., Spinhoven, P., & Huibers, M. (2010). Cognitive behavior therapy and relapse prevention for depression. In C. S. Richards & J. G. Perri (Eds.), *Relapse prevention for depression* (pp. 53–76). Washington, DC: American Psychological Association.

Bodell, L. P., & Mayer, L. E. S. (2011). Percent body fat is a risk factor for relapse in anorexia nervosa: A replication study. *International Journal of Eating Disorders, 44*(2), 118–123.

Boden, M. T., John, O. P., Goldin, P. R., Werner, K., Heimberg, R. G., & Gross, J. J. (2012). The role of maladaptive beliefs in cognitive-behavioral therapy: Evidence from social anxiety disorder. *Behavior Research and Therapy, 50*(5), 287–291.

Bodfish, J. W. (2011). Restricted repetitive behaviors. In E. Hollander, A. Kolevzon & J. T. Coyle (Eds.), *Textbook of autism spectrum disorders.* (pp. 169–177) Arlington, VA: American Psychiatric Publishing, Inc.

Boeve, B., McCormick, J., Smith, G., Ferman, T., Rummans, T., Carpenter, T., et al. (2003). Mild cognitive impairment in the oldest old. *Neurology, 60*(3), 477–480.

Bogdan, R., & Taylor, S. (1976, January). The judged, not the judges: An insider's view of mental retardation. *American Psychologist., 31*(1), 47–52.

Bohart, A. C., & Tallman, K. (2010). Clients: The neglected common factor in psychotherapy. In B. L. Duncan, S. D. Miller, B. E. Wampold, & M. A. Hubble (Eds.), *The heart and soul of change: Delivering what works in therapy* (2nd ed., pp. 83–111). Washington, DC: American Psychological Association.

Bolgar, H. (1965). The case study method. In B. B. Wolman (Ed.), *Handbook of clinical psychology.* New York: McGraw-Hill.

Bollini, A. M., & Walker, E. F. (2007). Schizotypal personality disorder. In W. O'Donohue, K. A. Fowler, S. O. Lilienfeld (Eds.). *Personality disorders: Toward the DSM-V.* Los Angeles: Sage Publications.

Boltz, M. G., Dyer, R. L., & Miller, A. R. (2010). Are you lying to me? Temporal cues for deception. *Journal of Language and Social Psychology, 29*(4), 458–466.

Bonanno, G. A. (2004). Loss, trauma, and human resilience. *American Psychologist, 59*(1), 20–28.

Bonanno, G. A., & Mancini, A. D. (2010, November 8). Beyond resilience and PTSD: Mapping the heterogeneity of responses to potential trauma. *Psychological Trauma: Theory, Research, Practice, and Policy.*

Bonanno, G. A., & Mancini, A. D. (2012). Beyond resilience and PTSD: Mapping the heterogeneity of responses to potential trauma. *Psychological Trauma: Theory, Research, Practice, and Policy, 4*(1), 74–83.

Bond, C. (2004). International deception. Presentation at congressional briefing: *Detecting deception: Research to secure the homeland.* Washington, DC. March 19, 2004.

Bond, L. A., & Hauf, A. M-C. (2007). Community-based collaboration: An overarching best practice in prevention. *Counseling Psychologist, 35*(4), 567–575.

Bonetta, L. (2010). Study supports methadone maintenance in therapeutic communities. *NIDA Notes, 23*(3).

Boodman, S. G. (2006, April 4). Treat mom, help child. *Washingtonpost.com.* Retrieved July 6, 2007, from http://www.washingtonpost.com.

Boodman, S. G. (2010, March 2). Parity law requires mental health benefits comparable to physical care benefits. *Washington Post, 133*(87).

Boone, K. (2011). Somatoform disorders, factitious disorder, and malingering. In M. R. Schoenberg & J. G. Scott (Eds.), *The little black book of neuropsychology: syndrome-based approach* (pp. 551–565). New York: Springer Science + Business Media.

Borden, L. A., Martens, M. P., McBride, M. A., Sheline, K. T., Bloch, K. K., & Dude, K. (2011). The role of college students' use of protective behavioral strategies in the relation between binge drinking and alcohol-related problems. *Psychology of Addictive Behaviors, 25*(2), 346–351.

Borkovec, T. D., Alcaine, O. M., & Behar, E. (2004). Avoidance theory of worry and generalized anxiety disorder. In R. G. Heimberg, C. L. Turk, & D. S. Mennin (Eds.), *Generalized anxiety disorder: Advances in research and practice* (pp. 77–108). New York: Guilford Press.

Bornstein, R. A., Schwarzkopf, S. B., Olson, S. C., & Nasrallah, H. A. (1992). Third-ventricle enlargement and neuropsychological deficit in schizophrenia. *Biological Psychiatry, 31*(9), 954–961.

Bornstein, R. F. (2005). Psychodynamic theory and personality disorders. In S. Strack (Ed.), *Handbook of personality and psychopathology* (pp. 164–180). Hoboken, NJ: Wiley.

Bornstein, R. F. (2007). Dependent personality disorder. In W. O'Donohue, K. A. Fowler, S. O. Lilienfeld (Eds.). *Personality disorders: Toward the DSM-V.* Los Angeles: Sage Publications.

Bornstein, R. F. (2007). Might the Rorschach be a projective test after all: Social projection of an undesired trait alters Rorschach oral dependency scores. *Journal of Personality Assessment, 88*(3), 354–367.

Borowsky, I. L., Ireland, M., & Resnick M. D. (2001). Adolescent suicide attempts: Risks and protectors. *Pediatrics, 107,* 485–493.

Borrajo, R. H., Zandio, M., Zarzuela, A., Serrano, J. F., Peralta, V., Cuesta, M. J., Rosa, A., & Fananás, L. (2011). Validity of maternal recall of obstetric complications in mothers of patients with schizophrenia spectrum disorders and their healthy siblings. *Schizophrenia Research, 126*(1-3), 308–309.

Borzekowski, D. L. G., Schenk, S., Wilson, J. L., & Peebles, R. (2010). e-Ana and e-Mia: A content analysis of pro-eating disorder web sites. *American Journal of Public Health, 100*(8), 1526–1534.

Bosco, D., Plastino, M., Colica, C., Bosco, F., Arianna, S., Vecchio, A., Galati, F., Cristiano, D., Consoli, A., & Consoli, D. (2012). Opioid antagonist natrexone for the treatment of pathological gambling in Parkinson disease. *Clinical Neuropharmacology, 35*(3), 118–120.

Boss, P. (2011). *Loving someone who has dementia: How to find hope while coping with stress and grief.* San Francisco, CA: Jossey-Bass.

Bott, E. (1928). Teaching of psychology in the medical course. *Bulletin of the Association of American Medical Colleges, 3,* 289–304.

Botvin, G. J.. & Griffin, K. W. (2011). School-based programs. In J. H. Lowinson & P. Ruiz (Eds.), *Substance abuse: A comprehensive textbook, fifth edition.* Philadelphia, PA; Lippincott, Williams, & Wilkins.

Boucsein, W. (2012). *Electrodermal activity* (2nd ed.) New York: Springer Science 1 Business Media.

Bouman, T. K. (2008). Hypochondriasis. In J. S. Abramowitz, D. McKay, & S. Taylor (Eds.), *Obsessive-compulsive disorder: Subtypes and spectrum conditions.* Oxford, England: Elsevier.

Bouman, W. P., Bauer, G. R., Richards, C., & Coleman, E. (2010). World Professional Association for Transgender Health consensus statement on considerations of the role of distress (Criterion D) in the DSM diagnosis of gender identity disorder. *International Journal of Transgenderism, 12*(2), 100–106.

Bouras, N., & Holt, G. (Eds.). (2010). *Mental health services for adults with intellectual disability: Strategies and solutions.* The Maudsley Series. New York: Psychology Press.

Bourin, M., Malinge, M., & Guitton, B. (1995). [Provocative agents in panic disorder.] *Therapie 50*(4), 301–306. [French].

Bourne, E. J., Brownstein, A., & Garano, L. (2004). *Natural relief for anxiety: Complementary strategies for easing fear, panic & worry.* Oakland, CA: New Harbinger Publications.

Bowden, C. L. (2011). Pharmacological treatments for bipolar disorder. In H. K. Manji & C. A. Zarate, Jr. (Eds.), *Behavioral neurobiology of bipolar disorders and its treatment. Current topics in behavioral neurosciences* (pp. 263–283). New York: Springer Science + Business Media.

Bowden, S. C., Saklofske, D. H., & Weiss, L. G. (2011). Invariance of the measurement model underlying the Wechsler Adult Intelligence Scale-IV in the United States and Canada. *Educational and Psychological Measurement, 71*(1), 186–199.

Bowen, D., & Boehmer, U. (2010). The role of behavior in cancer prevention. In J. M. Suls, K. W. Davidson, & R. M. Kaplan (Eds.), *Handbook of health psychology ad behavioral medicine* (pp. 370–380). New York: Guilford Press.

Bower, G. H. (1981). Mood and memory. *American Psychologist, 36*(2), 129–148.

Bowers, T. G., Holmes, E. S., & Rhom, A. (2010). The nature of mass murder and autogenic massacre. *Journal of Police and Criminal Psychology, 25,* 59–66.

Bowman, S. A., Gortmaker, S. L., Ebbeling, C. B., Pereira, M. A., & Ludwig, D. S. (2003). Effects of fast-food consumption on energy intake and diet quality among children in a national household survey. *Pediatrics, 113,* 112–118.

Boxer, P., & Frick, P. J. (2008). Treating conduct problems, aggression, and antisocial behavior in children and adolescents: An integrated view. In R. G. Steele, T. D. Elkin, & M. C. Roberts (Eds.), *Handbook of evidence-based therapies for children and adolescents: Bridging science and practice.* New York: Springer.

Boyd, B. A., Conroy, M. A., Asmus, J., McKenney, E. (2011). Direct observation of peer-related social interaction: Outcomes for young children with autism spectrum disorders. *Exceptionality, 19*(2), 94–108.

Braam, W., Didden, R., Smits, M., & Curfs, L. (2008). Melatonin treatment in individuals with intellectual disability and chronic insomnia: A randomized placebo-controlled study. *Journal of Intellectual Disability Research, 52*(3), 256–264.

Bradford, A., & Meston, C. M. (2011). Behavior and symptom change among women treated with placebo for sexual dysfunction. *Journal of Sexual Medicine, 8*(1), 191–201.

Bradford, J., Booth, B., & Seto, M. C. (2010). Forensic assessment of sex offenders. In R. I. Simon & L. H. Gold (Eds.), *The American Psychiatric Publishing textbook of forensic psychiatry* (2nd ed., pp. 373–394). Arlington, VA: American Psychiatric Publishing.

Bradford, J. M. W., Fedoroff, P., & Firestone, P. (2008). Sexual violence and the clinician. In R. I. Simon & K. Tardiff (Eds.), *Textbook of violence assessment and management* (pp. 441–460). Arlington, VA: American Psychiatric Publishing.

Bradley, R., Conklin, C. Z., & Westen, D. (2005). The borderline personality diagnosis in adolescents: Gender differences and subtypes. *Journal of Child Psychology and Psychiatry, 46,* 1006–1019.

Brady, K. T., & Back, S. E. (2008). Women and addiction. In H. D. Kleber & M. Galanter (Eds.), *The American Psychiatric Publishing textbook of substance abuse treatment* (4th ed. pp. 555–564). Arlington, VA: American Psychiatric Publishing.

Brainerd, C. J., Reyna, V. F., & Ceci, S. J. (2008). Developmental reversals in false memory: A review of data and theory. *Psychological Bulletin, 134*(3), 343–382.

Bram, T., & Björgvinsson, T. (2004). A psychodynamic clinician's foray into cognitive-behavioral therapy utilizing exposure-response prevention for obsessive-compulsive disorder. *American Journal of Psychotherapy, 58,* 304–320.

Brambrink, D. K. (2004). A comparative study for the treatment of anxiety in women using electromyographic biofeedback and progressive relaxation and coping with stress: A manual for women. *Dissertation Abstracts International: Section B: The Sciences and Engineering, 65*(6-B), 3146.

Brandolo, E., ver Halen, N. B., Libby, D., & Pencille, M. (2011). Racism as a psychosocial stressor. In R. J. Contrada & A. Baum (Eds.), *The handbook of stress science: Biology, psychology, and health* (pp. 167–184). New York: Springer Publishing.

Brandon, S. (1981). The history of shock treatment. In Electroconvulsive therapy: An appraisal. Oxford, England: Oxford University Press.

Brandon, T. H., Drobes, D. J., Ditre, J. W., & Elibero, A. (2009). Nicotine. In L. M. Cohen, F. L. Collins, Jr., A. M. Young, D. E. McChargue, T. R. Leffingwell, & K. L. Cook (Eds.), *Pharmacology and treatment of substance abuse: Evidence- and outcome-based perspectives* (pp. 267–293). New York: Routledge/Taylor & Francis Group.

Braun, D. L. (1996, July 28). Interview. In S. Gilbert, More men may seek eating-disorder help. *New York Times.*

Braxton, L. E., Calhoun, P. S., Williams, J. E., & Boggs, C. D. (2007). Validity rates of the Personality Assessment Inventory and the Minnesota Multiphasic Personality Inventory-2 in a VA medical center setting. *Journal of Personality Assessment, 88*(1), 5–15.

Breedlove, L., Decker, C., Lakin, K. C., Prouty, R., & Coucouvanis, K. (2005). Placement of children and youth in state institutions: Forty years after the high point, it is time to just stop. *Mental Retardation, 43*(3), 235–238.

Breitbart, W., Pessin, H., & Kolva, E. (2011). Suicide and desire for hastened death in people with cancer. In D. W. Kossane, M. Maj, & N. Sartorius (Eds.), *Depression and cancer, World Psychiatric Association titles on depression* (pp. 125–150). Hoboken, NJ: Wiley-Blackwell.

Bremner, J. D. (2002). Does stress damage the brain? Understanding trauma-related disorders from a mind-body perspective. New York: Norton.

Bremner, J. D., & Charney, D. S. (2010). Neural circuits in fear and anxiety. In D. J. Stein, E. Hollander & B. O. Rothbaum (Eds.), *Textbook of anxiety disorders* (2nd ed., pp. 55–71). Arlington, VA: American Psychiatric Publishing.

Bremner, J. D., Vythilingam, M., Vermetten, E., Vaccarino, V., & Charney, D. S. (2004). Deficits in hippocampal and anterior cingulate functioning during verbal declarative memory encoding in midlife major depression. *American Journal of Psychiatry, 161*(4), 637–645.

Brendel, R. W., & Glezer, A. (2010). Forensic psychiatry: Opportunities and future challenges. Introduction. *Harvard Review of Psychiatry, 18*(6), 315–316.

Brenot, P. (2011). Can a sexual symptom be fixed without taking account of the couple? *Sexologies: European Journal of Sexology and Sexual Health, 20*(1), 20–22.

Brent, D. A. (2001). Assessment and treatment of the youthful suicidal patient. In H. Hendin & J. J. Mann (Eds.), *The clinical science of suicide prevention* (Vol. 932, pp. 106–131). New York: Annals of the New York Academy of Sciences.

Brent, D. A., & Mann, J. J. (2003). Familial factors in adolescent suicidal behavior. In A. Apter & R. A King (Eds.), *Suicide in children and adolescents* (pp. 86–117). New York: Cambridge University Press.

Breslau, J., Aguilar-Gaxiola, S., Borges, G., Kendler, K. S., Su, M., & Kessler, R. C. (2007). Risk for psychiatric disorder among immigrants and their US-born descendants: Evidence from the National Comorbidity Survey Replication. *Journal of Nervous and Mental Disease, 195*(3), 189–195.

Breslau, J., Aguilar-Gaxiola, S., Kendler, K. S., Su, M., Williams, D., & Kessler, R. C. (2006). Specifying race-ethnic differences in risk for psychiatric disorder in a USA national sample. *Psychological Medicine, 36,* 57–68.

Brewerton, T. D., & Costin, C. (2011). Long-term outcome of residential treatment for anorexia nervosa and bulimia nervosa. *Eating Disorders: The Journal of Treatment & Prevention, 19*(2), 132–144.

Briese, V., Stammwitz, U., Friede, M., & Henneicke von Zepelin, H. H. (2007). Black cohosh with or without St. John's wort for symptom-specific climacteric treatment: Results of a large-scale, controlled, observational study. *Maturitas, 57*(4), 405–414.

Briggs, E. C., Thompson, R., Ostrowski, S., & Lekwauwa, R. (2011). Psychological, health, behavioral, and economic impact of child maltreatment. In E. C. Briggs, M. P. Koss, & A. E. Kazdin (Eds.), *Violence against women and children, Vol. 1: Mapping the terrain* (pp. 99–97). Washington, DC: American Psychological Association.

Britt, R. R. (2005). The odds of dying. *LiveScience. com.* Rape and sexual assault: Reporting to police and medical attention, 1992–2000. Retrieved January 12, 2005, from www.ojp.usdoj.gov/bjs/abstract/rsarp00.htm.

Broadway, J., & Mintzer, J. (2007). The many faces of psychosis in the elderly. *Current Opinions in Psychiatry, 20*(6), 551–558.

Brock, D. W. (2001). Physician-assisted suicide—The worry about abuse. In L. M. Kopelman & K. A. De Ville (Eds.), *Physician-assisted suicide: What are the issues?* (pp. 59–74). Dordrecht, Netherlands: Kluwer Academic.

Brockmann, H., Zobel, A., Schuhmacher, A., Daamen, M., Joe, A., Biermann, K., Schwab, S. G., Biersack, H-J., Maier, W., & Boecker, H. (2011). Influence of 5-HTTLPR polymorphism on resting state perfusion in patients with major depression. *Journal of Psychiatric Research, 45*(4), 442–451.

Brodsky, S., & Poythress, N. (1990). Presentation. American Psychological Association Convention, Boston.

Brody, H. (2000). Better health from your inner pharmacy. *Psychology Today, 32*(4), 60–67.

Broft, A., Berner, L. A., & Walsh, B. T. (2010). Phamacotherapy for bulimia nervosa. In C. M. Grilo & J. E. Mitchell (Eds.), *The treatment of eating disorders: A clinical handbook* (pp. 388–401). New York: Guilford Press.

Brommelhoff, J. A., Conway, K., Merikangas, K., & Levy, B. R. (2004). Higher rates of depression in women: Role of gender bias within the family. *Journal of Women's Health, 13*(1), 69–76.

Bronisch, T., & Lieb, R. (2008). Maternal suicidality and suicide risk in offspring. *Psychiatric Clinics of North America, 31*(2), 213–221.

Brook, D. W. (2008). Group therapy. In H. D. Kleber & M. Galanter (Eds.), *The American Psychiatric Publishing textbook of substance abuse treatment* (4th ed., pp. 413–427). Arlington, VA: American Psychiatric Publishing.

Brook, D. W. (2011). Group therapy. In M. Galanter & H. D. Kleber (Eds.), *Psychotherapy for the treatment of substance abuse* (pp. 277–298). Arlington, VA: American Psychiatric Publishing.

Brooks, G. R., & Richardson, F. C. (1980). Emotional skills training: A treatment program for duodenal ulcer. *Behavior Therapist, 11*(2), 198–207.

Brooks, L., McCabe, P., & Schneiderman, N. (2011). Stress and cardiometabolic syndrome. In R. J. Contrada & A. Baum (Eds.), *The handbook of stress science: Biology, psychology, and health* (pp. 399–409). New York: Springer Publishing.

Brooks, M. K. (2005). Dementia and wandering behavior: Concern for the lost elder. *Social Work Health Care, 41*(2), 95–97.

Brooner, R. K., Disney, E. R., Neufeld, K. J., King, V. L., Kidorf, M., & Stoller, K. B. (2010). Antisocial personality disorder in patients with substance use disorders. In E. V. Nunes, J. Selzer, P. Levounis, & C. A. Davies (Eds.), *Substance dependence and co-occurring psychiatric disorders: Best practices for diagnosis and treatment* (pp. 1–26). Kingston, NJ: Civic Research Institute.

Brophy, M. (2010). Sex, lies, and virtual reality. In D. Monroe (Ed.), *Porn: How to think with kink, Philosophy for everyone* (pp. 204–218). Hoboken, NJ: Wiley-Blackwell.

Brotto, L. A., Petkau, A. J., Labrie, F., & Basson, R. (2011). Predictors of sexual desire disorders in women. *Journal of Sexual Medicine, 8*(3), 742–753.

Brough, P., & Biggs, A. (2010). Occupational stress in police and prison staff. In J. M. Brown & E. A. Campbell (Eds.), *The Cambridge handbook of forensic psychology*. New York: Cambridge University Press.

Brown, A. S. (2012). Maternal infection and schizophrenia. In A. S. Brown & P. H. Patterson (Eds.), *The origins of schizophrenia* (pp. 25–57). New York: Columbia University Press.

Brown, A. S., & Patterson, P. H. (2011). Maternal infection and schizophrenia: Implications for prevention. *Schizophrenia Bulletin, 37*(2), 284–290.

Brown, A. S., & Patterson, P. H. (Eds.). (2012). *The origins of schizophrenia*. New York: Columbia University Press.

Brown, G. K., Stirman, S. W., & Spokas, M. (2010). Relapse prevention of suicide attempts: Application of cognitive therapy. In C. S. Richards & M. G. Perri (Eds.), *Relapse prevention for depression* (pp. 177–198). Washington, DC: American Psychological Association.

Brown, G. K., Wenzel, A., & Rudd, M. D. (2011). Cognitive therapy for suicidal patients. In K. Michel & D. A. Jobes (Eds.), *Building a therapeutic alliance with the suicidal patient* (pp. 273–291). Washington, DC: American Psychological Association.

Brown, G. W. (2002). Social roles, context and evolution in the origins of depression. *Journal of Health and Social Behavior, 43*(3), 255–276.

Brown, G. W. (2010). Psychosocial origins of depressive and anxiety disorder. In D. Goldberg, K. S. Kendler, P. J. Sirovatka, & D. A. Regier (Eds.), *Diagnostic issues in depression and generalized anxiety disorder: Refining the research agenda for DSM-V* (pp. 303–331). Washington, DC: American Psychiatric Association.

Brown, G. W., & Harris, T. O. (1978). Social origins of depression: A study of psychiatric disorder in women. London: Tavistock.

Brown, H. K., Ouellette-Kuntz, H., Bielska, I., & Elliott, D. (2009). Choosing a measure of support need: Implications for research and policy. *Journal of Intellectual Disability Research, 53*(11), 949–954.

Brown, J. H., Henteleff, P., Barakat, S., & Rowe, C. J. (1986). Is it normal for terminally ill patients to desire death? *American Journal of Psychiatry, 143*(2), 208–211.

Brown, J. M. (2010). Ethical practice. In J. M. Brown & E. A. Campbell (Eds.), *The Cambridge handbook of forensic psychology* (pp. 749–757). New York: Cambridge University Press.

Brown, L. S. (2011). Client diversity in psychotherapy. In J. C. Norcross, G. R. VandenBos, & D. K. Freedheim (Eds.), *History of psychotherapy: Continuity and change* (2nd ed., pp. 475–483). Washington, DC: American Psychological Association.

Brown, R. J. (2002). The cognitive psychology of dissociative states. *Cognitive Neuropsychiatry, 7*(3), 221–235.

Brown, R. J., Schrag, A., & Trimble, M. R. (2005). Dissociation, childhood interpersonal trauma, and family functioning in patients with somatization disorder. *American Journal of Psychiatry, 162*(5), 899–905.

Brown, R. T., & McMillan, K. K. (2011). Rett syndrome: A truly pervasive developmental disorder. In S. Goldstein, & C. R. Reynolds (Eds.), *Handbook of neurodevelopmental and genetic disorders in children* (2nd ed., pp. 425–444) New York: Guilford Press.

Brown, T. A. (2010). The boundary between generalized anxiety disorder and the unipolar mood disorders: Diagnostic and psychometric findings in clinical samples. In D. Goldberg, K. S., Kendler, P. J. Sirovatka, & D. A. Regier (Eds.), *Diagnostic issues in depression and generalized anxiety disorder: Refining the research agenda for DSM-V* (pp. 131–138). Washington, DC: American Psychiatric Association.

Brownell, K. D., & O'Neil, P. M. (1993). Obesity. In D. H. Barlow (Ed.), *Clinical handbook of psychological disorders: A step-by-step treatment manual* (2nd ed.). New York: Guilford Press.

Brozovich, F., & Heimberg, R. G. (2011). The relationship of postevent processing to self-evaluation of performance in social anxiety. *Behavior Therapy, 42*(2), 224–235.

Bruch, H. (1962). Perceptual and conceptual disturbances in anorexia nervosa. *Psychosomatic Medicine, 24,* 187–194.

Bruch, H. (1973). *Eating disorders: Obesity, anorexia nervosa and the person within.* New York: Basic Books.

Bruch, H. (1978). *The golden cage: The enigma of anorexia nervosa.* Cambridge, MA: Harvard University Press.

Bruch, H. (1991). The sleeping beauty: Escape from change. In S. I. Greenspan & G. H. Pollock (Eds.), *The course of life, Vol. 4: Adolescence.* Madison, CT: International Universities Press.

Bruch, H. (2001). *The golden cage: The enigma of anorexia nervosa.* Cambridge, MA: Harvard University Press.

Brumberg, J. J. (1988). *Fasting girls: The history of anorexia nervosa.* New York: Penguin Books.

Brunet, K., & Birchwood, M. (2010). Duration of untreated psychosis and pathways to care. In P.

French, J. Smith, D. Shiers, M. Reed, & M. Rayne (Eds.), *Promoting recovery in early psychosis: A practice manual* (pp. 9–16). Hoboken, NJ: Wiley-Blackwell.

Brunette, M. F., Noordsy, D. L., & Green, A. I. (2012). Co-occurring substance use and other psychiatric disorders. In J. A. Lieberman, T. S. Stroup, & D. O. Perkins (Eds.), *Essentials of schizophrenia* (pp. 131–158). Arlington, VA: American Psychiatric Publishing.

Bryan, C. J., & Corso, K. A. (2011). Depression, PTSD, and suicidal ideation among active duty veterans in an integrated primary care clinic. *Psychological Services, 8*(2), 94–103.

Bryant, R. A. (2010). Treating the full range of posttraumatic reactions. In G. M. Rosen, B. C. Frueh (Eds.), *Clinician's guide to posttraumatic stress disorder* (pp. 205–234). Hoboken, NJ: John Wiley & Sons.

Bryant, R. A., Moulds, M. L., Guthrie, R. M., & Nixon, R. D. V. (2005). The additive benefit of hypnosis and cognitive-behavioral therapy in treating acute stress disorder. *Journal of Consulting and Clinical Psychology, 73*(2), 334–340.

Budney, A. J., Vandrey, R. L., & Fearer, S. (2011). Cannabis. In J. H. Lowinson & P. Ruiz (Eds.), *Substance abuse: A comprehensive textbook, fifth edition.* Philadelphia, PA; Lippincott, Williams, & Wilkins.

Buhlmann, U., Glaesmer, H., Mewes, R., Fama, J. M., Wilhelm, S., Brähler, E., & Rief, W. (2010). Updates on the prevalence of body dysmorphic disorder: A population-based survey. *Psychiatry Research, 178*(1), 171–175.

Bunaciu, L., Feldner, M. T., Babson, K. A., Zvolensky, M. J., & Eifert, G. H. (2012). Biological sex and panic-relevant anxious reactivity to abrupt increases in bodily arousal as a function of biological challenge intensity. *Journal of Behavior Therapy and Experimental Psychiatry, 43*(1), 526–531.

Burbach, F. R., Fadden, G., & Smith. J. (2010). Family interventions for first-episode psychosis. In P. French, J. Smith, D. Shiers, M. Reed, & M. Rayne (Eds.), *Promoting recovery in early psychosis: A practice manual* (pp. 210–225). Hoboken, NJ: Wiley-Blackwell.

Burg, M. M., & Pickering, T. G. (2011). The cardiovascular system. In R. J. Contrada & A. Baum (Eds.), *The handbook of stress science: Biology, psychology, and health* (pp. 37–45). New York: Springer Publishing.

Burgess, J. L. (2001). Phosphine exposure from a methamphetamine laboratory investigation. *Journal of Toxicology and Clinical Toxicology, 39,* 165.

Burijon, B. N. (2007). *Biological bases of clinical anxiety.* New York: W. W. Norton & Company

Burke, A. (2011). Pathophysiology of behavioral and psychological disturbances in dementia. In P. McNamara (Ed.), *Dementia, Vols. 1–3: History and incidence. Science and biology, treatments and developments* (pp. 135–158). Santa Barbara, CA: Praeger/ABC-CLIO.

Burke, K., & Riley, J. (2010). Coronary artery disease. In C. Margereson & S. Trenoweth (Eds.), *Developing holistic care for long-term conditions* (pp. 255–273). New York: Routledge/Taylor & Francis Group.

Burlingame, G. M., & Baldwin, S. (2011). Group therapy. In J. C. Norcross, G. R. VandenBos, & D. K. Freedheim (Eds.), *History of psychotherapy: Continuity and change* (2nd ed., pp. 505–515). Washington, DC: American Psychological Association.

Burns, M. K., Scholin, S. E., & Zaslofsky, A. F. (2011). Advances in assessment through research: What have we learned in the past 3 years? *Assessment for Effective Intervention, 36*(2), 107–112.

Burns, T. (2010). Modern community care strategies for schizophrenia care: Impacts on outcome. In W. F. Gattaz & G. Busatto (Eds.), *Advances in schizophrenia research 2009* (pp. 417–427). New York: Springer Science + Business Media.

Burns, T., & Drake, B. (2011). Mental health services and patients with schizophrenia. In D. R. Weinberg & P. Harrison (Eds.), *Schizophrenia* (pp. 625–643). Hoboken, NJ: Wiley-Blackwell.

Burston, D. (2000). The crucible of experience: R. D. Laing and the crisis of psychotherapy. Cambridge, MA: Harvard University Press.

Burt, D. R., Creese, I., & Snyder, S. H. (1977). Anti-schizophrenic drugs: Chronic treatment elevates dopamine receptor binding in brain. *Science, 196*(4287), 326–328.

Burton, V. S. (1990). The consequences of official labels: A research note on rights lost by the mentally ill, mentally incompetent, and convicted felons. *Community Mental Health Journal, 26*(3), 267–276.

Busch, F. N., Milrod, B. L., & Shear, K. (2010). Psychodynamic concepts of anxiety. In D. J. Stein, E. Hollander, & B. O. Rothbaum (Eds.), *Textbook of anxiety disorders* (2nd ed., pp. 117–128). Arlington, VA: American Psychiatric Publishing.

Busch, F. N., Rudden, M. G., & Shapiro, T. (2004). *Psychodynamic treatment of depression*. Washington, DC: American Psychiatric Publishing.

Bushman, B. J., Baumeister, R. F., & Stack, A. D. (1999). Catharsis, aggression, and persuasive influence: Self-fulfilling or self-defeating prophecies? *Journal of Personality and Social Psychology, 76*(3), 367–376.

Buss, D. M. (2000). *The dangerous passion: Why jealousy is as necessary as love and sex*. New York: Free Press.

Bussing, R., Koro-Ljungberg, M. E., Gary, F., Mason, D. M., & Garvan, C. W. (2005). Exploring help-seeking for ADHD symptoms: A mixed-methods approach. *Harvard Review of Psychiatry, 13*(2), 85–101.

Bussing, R., Zima, B. T., & Belin, T. R. (1998). Differential access to care for children with ADHD in special education programs. *Psychiatric Services, 49*(9), 1226–1229.

Bussing, R., Zima, B. T., Gary, F. A., & Garvan, C. W. (2003). Barriers to detection, help-seeking, and service use for children with ADHD symptoms. *Journal of Behavioral Health Services & Research, 30*(2), 176–189.

Butcher, J. N. (2010). Personality assessment from the nineteenth to the early twenty-first century: Past achievements and contemporary challenges. *Annual Review of Clinical Psychology, 6*, 1–20.

Butcher, J. N. (2011). *A beginner's guide to the MMPI-2* (3rd ed.) Washington, DC: American Psychological Association.

Butler, R. N. (2010). Productive aging. In H. M. Fillit, K. Rockwood, K. Woodhouse. (Eds.), *Brocklehurst's textbook of geriatric medicine and gerontology, 7th edition*. Philadelphia, PA: Saunders Publishers.

Butler, T., Andrews, G., Allnutt, S., Sakashita, C., Smith, N. E., & Basson, J. (2006). "Mental disorders in Australian prisoners: A comparison with a community sample": Corrigendum. *Australian and New Zealand Journal of Psychiatry, 40*(8).

Bylsma, L. M., Taylor-Clift, A., & Rottenberg, J. (2011). Emotional reactivity to daily events in major and minor depression. *Journal of Abnormal Psychology, 120*(1), 155–167.

Cachelin, F. M., Phinney, J. S., Schug, R. A., & Striegel-Moore, R. M. (2006). Acculturation and eating disorders in a Mexican American community sample. *Psychological Women Quarterly, 30*(4), 340–347.

Cadge, W., & Fair, B. (2010). Religion, spirituality, health, and medicine: Sociological intersections. In C. E. Bird, P. Conrad, A. M. Fremont, & S. Timmermans (Eds.), *Handbook of medical sociology* (6th ed., pp. 341–362). Nashville, TN: Vanderbilt University Press.

Cadoret, R. J., Yates, W. R., Troughton, E., Woodworth, G., & Stewart, M. A. (1995). Adoption study demonstrating two genetic pathways to drug abuse. *Archives of General Psychiatry, 52*, 42–52.

Cahn, W., Pol, H. E. H., Bongers, M., Schnack, H. G., Mandi, R. C. W., Van Haren, N. E. M., et al. (2002). Brain morphology in antipsychotic-naïve schizophrenia: A study of multiple brain structures. *British Journal of Psychiatry, 181*(Suppl 43), s66–s72.

Cain, D. J. (2007). What every therapist should know, be and do: Contributions from humanistic psychotherapies. *Journal of Contemporary Psychotherapy, 37*(1), 3–10.

Caine, D., Patterson, K., Hodges, J. R., Heard, R., & Haliday, G. (2001). Severe anterograde amnesia with extensive hippocampal degeneration in a case of rapidly progressive frontotemporal dementia. *Neurocase, 7*(1), 57–64.

Caine, E. D. (2010). Preventing suicide is hard to do! *Psychiatric Services, 61*(12), 1171.

Caldeiro, R. M., Meredith, C. W., Saxon, A. J., & Calsyn, D. A. (2009). Pharmacological approaches to the treatment of substance use disorders. In L. M. Cohen, F. L. Collins, Jr., A. M. Young, D. E. McChargue, T. R. Leffingwell, & K. L. Cook (Eds.), *Pharmacology and treatment of substance abuse: Evidence- and outcome-based perspectives* (pp. 529–577). New York: Routledge/Taylor & Francis Group.

Caldwell, S. (2010). Euthanasia cases in Holland rise by 13 percent in a year. *The Telegraph*, June 20.

Caligor, E., & Clarkin, J. F. (2010). An object relations model of personality and personality pathology. In J. F. Clarkin, P. Fonagy, & G. O. Gabbard (Eds.), *Psychodynamic psychotherapy for personality disorders: A clinical handbook* (pp. 3–36). Arlington, VA: American Psychiatric Publishing.

Callahan, L. A., Steadman, H. J., McGreevy, M. A., & Robbins, P. C. (1991). The volume and characteristics of insanity defense pleas: An eight-state study. *Bulletin of the American Academy of Psychiatry Law, 19*(4), 331–338.

Callcott, P., Dudley, R., Standart, S., Freeston, M., & Turkington, D. (2011). Treating trauma in people with first-episode psychosis using cognitive behavioural therapy. In R. Hagen, D. Turkington, T. Berge, & R. W. Grawe (Eds.), *CBT for psychosis: A symptom-based approach, International Society for the Psychological Treatments of the Schizophrenias and Other Psychoses* (pp. 175–192). New York: Routledge/Taylor & Francis Group.

Calogero, R. M., Tantliff-Dunn, S., & Thompson, J. K. (2011). *Self-objectification in women: Causes, consequences, and counteractions.*

Washington, DC: American Psychological Association.

Camacho, E. B., Leon, E. C., & Uribe, M. P. O. (2005). Nature and schizophrenia. *Salud Mental, 28*(2), 59–72.

Cameron, A., Rosen, R. C., & Swindle, R. W. (2005). Sexual and relationship characateristics among an internet-based sample of U.S. men with and without erectile dysfunction. *Journal of Sex and Marital Therapy, 31*(3), 229–242.

Cameron, D. J., Thomas, R. I., Mulvhill, M., & Bronheim, H. (1987). Delirium: A test of the Diagnostic and Statistical Manual III criteria on medical inpatients. *Journal of the American Geriatrics Society, 35*, 1007–1010.

Campbell, D. (2010). Pre-suicide states of mind. In P. Williams (Ed.), *The psychoanalytic therapy of severe disturbance, Psychoanalytic ideas* (pp. 171–183). London, England: Karnac Books.

Campbell, J., Gilmore, L., & Cuskelly, M. (2003). Changing student teachers' attitudes towards disability and inclusion. *Journal of Intellectual and Developmental Disability, 28*, 369–379.

Campbell, M., & Schmidt, U. (2011). Cognitive-behavioral therapy for adolescent bulimia nervosa and binge-eating disorder. In D. Le Grange & J. Lock (Eds.), *Eating disorders in children and adolescents: A clinical handbook*. New York: Guilford Publications.

Campbell, S., Marriott, M., Nahmias, C., & MacQueen, G. M. (2004). Lower hippocampal volume in patients suffering from depression: A meta-analysis. *The American Journal of Psychiatry, 161*(4), 598–607.

Campbell, W. K., & Miller, J. D. (Eds.). (2011). *The handbook of narcissism and narcissistic personality disorder: Theoretical approaches, empirical findings, and treatments*. Hoboken, NJ: John Wiley & Sons.

Cander, J. (2011). Edvard Munch. *Po-Vesti.nl.* http://po-vestinl.clogspot.com/2011/02/edvard-munch.html.

Canetto, S. S. (2003). Older adulthood. In L. Slater, J. H. Daniel, & A. Banks (Eds.) *The complete guide to women and mental health* (pp. 56–64). Boston: Beacon Press.

Canetto, S. S. (2011). Physician-assisted suicide in the United States: Issues, challenges, roles, and implications for clinicians. In S. H. Qualls & J. E. Kasl-Godley (Eds.), *End-of-life issues, grief, and bereavement: What clinicians need to know. Wiley series in clinical geropsychology* (pp. 263–284). Hoboken, NJ: John Wiley & Sons.

Cantor, J. M., Blanchard, R., Christensen, B. K., Dickey, R., Klassen, P. E., Beckstead, A. L., et al. (2004). Intelligence, memory, and handedness in pedophilia. *Neuropsychology, 18*(1), 3–14.

Capuzzi, D., & Gross, D. R. (Eds.). (2008). *Youth at risk: A prevention resource for counselors, teachers, and parents*. Alexandria, VA: American Counseling Association.

Caqueo-Urízar, A., Ferrer-García, M., Toro, J., Gutiérrez-Maldonado, J., Peñaloza, C., Cuadros-Sosa, Y., & Gálvez-Madrid, M. J. (2011). Associations between sociocultural pressures to be thin, body distress, and eating disorder symptomatology among Chilean adolescent girls. *Body Image, 8*(1), 78–81.

Carbonari, J. P., & DiClemente, C. C. (2000). Using transtheoretical model profiles to differentiate levels of alcohol abstinence success. *Journal of Consulting and Clinical Psychology, 68*(5), 810–817.

Cardena, E. (2008). Dissociative disorders measures. In A. J. Rush, Jr., M. B. First, & D. Blacker (Eds.), *Handbook of psychiatric measures* (2nd ed., pp. 587–599). Arlington, VA: American Psychiatric Publishing.

Carducci, B. (2000). Shyness: The new solution. *Psychology Today, 33*(1), 38–45.

Carey, B. (2006). Heart risks with stimulant use? Maybe. Worry? For some. *New York Times,* Feb. 21, section F., p. 1.

Carey, B. (2007, September 4). Bipolar illness soars as a diagnosis for the young. *New York Times Online.* Retrieved September 17, 2007, from http://www.nytimes.com.

Carey, B. (2008, February 10). Making sense of the great suicide debate. *New York Times.* Retrieved February 23, 2008, from www.nytimes.com.

Carey, B. (2010, November 22). In cybertherapy, avatars assist with healing. *New York Times.*

Carey, B. (2011, March 20). Lessons for Japan's survivors: The psychology of recovery. *The New York Times,* March 20. 160(55, 350).

Carey, B. (2011, May 22). Need therapy? A good man is hard to find. *The New York Times,* May 22. 160(55, 413).

Carlin, M. (2010). The psychologist as expert witness in criminal cases. In J. M. Brown & E. A. Campbell (Eds.), *The Cambridge handbook of forensic psychology.* New York: Cambridge University Press.

Carlo, G., Crockett, L. J., & Carranza, M. A. (Eds.). (2011). *Health disparities in youth and families: Research and applications. Nebraska symposium on motivation.* New York: Springer Science + Business Media.

Carlson, G. A., & Fish, B. (2005). Longitudinal course of schizophrenia spectrum symptoms in offspring of psychiatrically hospitalized mothers. *Journal of Child and Adolescent Psychopharmacology, 15*(3), 362–383.

Carlson, J. S., Maupin, A., & Brinkman, T. (2010). Recent advances in the medical management of children with attention deficit/hyperactivity disorder. In P. C. McCabe, & S. R. Shaw (Eds.), *Psychiatric disorders: Current topics and interventions for educators.* (pp. 71–80) Thousand Oaks, CA: Corwin Press.

Carlson, M. (1998, June 22). The best things in life aren't free. *Time, 151,* p. 21.

Carlson, N. R. (2008). *Foundations of physiological psychology* (7th ed.). Boston: Pearson.

Carney, S. M., & Goodwin, G. M. (2005). Lithium—A continuing story in the treatment of bipolar disorder. *Acta Psychiatrica Scandinavica, 111*(Suppl. 426), 7–12.

Caron, J., Julien, M., & Huang, J. H. (2008). Changes in suicide methods in Quebec between 1987 and 2000: The possible impact of Bill C-17 requiring safe storage of firearms. *Suicide and Life-Threatening Behavior, 38*(2), 195–208.

Carr, G. V., & Lucki, I. (2011). The role of serotonin receptor subtypes in treating depression: A review of animal studies. *Psychopharmacology, 213*(2-3), 265–287.

Carr, J. E. (2001). Stress and illness. In D. Wedding (Ed.), *Behavior and medicine* (3rd ed., pp. 231–246). Seattle: Hogrefe & Huber.

Carr, S. N., & Francis, A. J. P. (2010). Do early maladaptive schemas mediate the relationship between childhood experiences and avoidant personality disorder features? A preliminary investigation in a non-clinical sample. *Cognitive Therapy and Research, 34*(4), 343–358.

Carragher, N., & McWilliams, L. A. (2011). A latent class analysis of DSM-IV criteria for pathological gambling: Results from the National Epidemiologic Survey on Alcohol and Related Conditions. *Psychiatry Research, 187*(1-2), 185–192.

Carrard, I., Fernandez-Aranda, F., Lam, T., Nevonen, L., Liwowsky, I., Volkart, A. C., Rouget, P., Golay, A., Van der Linden, M., & Norring. C. (2011). Evaluation of a guided internet self-treatment programme for bulimia nervosa in several European countries. *European Eating Disorders Review, 19*(2), 138–149.

Carrobles, J. A., Gámez-Guadix, M., & Almendros, C. (2011). Sexual functioning, sexual satisfaction, and subjective and psychological well-being in Spanish women. *Anals de Psicologia, 27*(1), 27–34.

Carroll, K. M. (2008). Cognitive-behavioral therapies. In H. D. Kleber & M. Galanter (Eds.), *The American Psychiatric Publishing textbook of substance abuse treatment* (4th ed., pp. 349–360). Arlington, VA: American Psychiatric Publishing.

Carroll, K. M. (2011). Cognitive-behavioral therapies. In M. Galanter & H. D. Kleber (Eds.), *Psychotherapy for the treatment of substance abuse* (pp. 175–192). Arlington, VA: American Psychiatric Publishing.

Carroll, K. M. (2012). Dissemination of evidence-based practices: How far we've come, and how much further we've got to go. *Addiction, 107*(6), 1031–1033.

Carroll, K. M., & Kiluk, B. D. (2012). Integrating psychotherapy and pharmacotherapy in substance abuse treatment. In F. Rotgers, J. Morgenstern, & S. T. Walters (Eds.), *Treating substance abuse: Theory and technique* (3rd ed., pp. 319–354). New York: Guilford Press.

Carroll, M. E., & Meisch, R. A. (2011) Acquisition of drug self-administration. In M. C. Olmstead (Ed.), *Animal models of drug addiction. Springer protocols: Neuromethods* (pp. 237–265). Totowa, NJ: Humana Press.

Carroll, R. A. (2007). Gender dysphoria and transgender experiences. In S. R. Leiblum (Ed.), *Principles and practice of sex therapy* (4th ed., pp. 477–508). New York: Guilford Press.

Carroll, R. A. (2011). Psychological aspects of erectile dysfunction. In K. T. McVary (Ed.), *Contemporary treatment of erectile dysfunction: A clinical guide.* New York: Springer.

Carter, M., Roberts, J., Williams, K., Evans, D., Parmenter, T., Silove, N., Clark, T., & Warren, A. (2011). Interventions used with an Australian sample of preschool children with autism spectrum disorders. *Research in Autism Spectrum Disorders, 5*(3), 1033–1041.

Carter, R. T. (2007). Racism and psychological and emotional injury: Recognizing and assessing race-based traumatic stress. *The Counseling Psychologist, 35*(1), 13–105.

Carvalho, J. P., & Hopko, D. R. (2011). Behavioral theory of depression: Reinforcement as a mediating variable between avoidance and depression. *Journal of Behavior Therapy and Experimental Psychiatry, 42*(2), 154–162.

Carvalho, J., & Nobre, P. (2011). Biopsychosocial determinants of men's sexual desire: Testing an integrative model. *Journal of Sexual Medicine, 8*(3), 754–763.

Carvalho, J., & Nobre, P. (2011). Predictors of men's sexual desire: The role of psychological, cognitive-emotional, relational, and medical factors. *Journal of Sex Research, 48*(2-3), 254–262.

Carver, C. S. (2011). Coping. In R. J. Contrada & A. Baum (Eds.), *The handbook of stress science: Biology, psychology, and health* (pp. 221–229). New York: Springer Publishing.

Casey, D. E. (1995). Motor and mental aspects of EPS. *International Clinical Psychopharmacology, 10,* 105–114.

Casey, E. (2008). Cyberpatterns: Criminal behavior on the internet. In B. E. Turvey (Ed.), *Criminal profiling: An introduction to behavioral evidence analysis* (3rd ed.). San Diego, CA: Elsevier Academic Press.

Casey, P. (2001). Multiple personality disorder. *Primary Care Psychiatry, 7*(1), 7–11.

Cash, T. F., & Henry, P. E. (1995). Women's body images: The results of a national survey in the U. S. A. *Sex Roles, 33*(1/2), 19–28.

Casimir, G. J., & Morrison, B. J. (1993). Rethinking work with "multicultural populations." *Community Mental Health Journal, 29,* 547–559.

Cassells, C. (2010, June 28). New code of conduct formalizes APA's relationship with the pharmaceutical industry. *Medscape Medical News.*

Cassells, C., Paterson, B., Dowding, D., & Morrison, R. (2005). Long- and short-term risk factors in the prediction of inpatient suicide: A review of the literature. *Crisis, 26*(2), 53–63.

Cassidy, F., Weiner, R. D., Cooper, T. B., & Carroll, B. J. (2010). Combined catecholamine and indoleamine depletion following response to ECT. *British Journal of Psychiatry, 196*(6), 493–494.

Castro, Y., Holm-Denoma, J. M., & Buckner, J. D. (2007). Introduction to empirically informed mental health services for diverse populations. In J. D. Buckner, Y. Castro, & J. M. Holm-Denoma (Eds.), *Mental health care for people of diverse backgrounds* (pp. 1–8). Abingdon, England: Radcliffe Publishing.

Castrogiovanni, P., Pieraccini, F., & Di Muro, A. (1998). Suicidality and aggressive behavior. *Acta Psychiatrica Scandinavica, 97*(2), 144–148.

Catalano, R. F., Haggerty, K. P., Hawkins, J. D., & Elgin, J. (2011). Prevention of substance use and substance use disorders: Role of risk and protective factors. In Y. Kaminer & K. C. Winters (Eds.), *Clinical manual of adolescent substance abuse treatment* (pp. 25–63). Arlington, VA: American Psychiatric Publishing.

Catan, T. (2007). Online anorexia sites shut down amid claims they glorify starvation. *TimesOnline* November 22, 2007. Retrieved from http://www.timesonline.uk/tol/life_and_style/health.

Cauli, O., & Morelli, M. (2005). Caffeine and the dopaminergic system. *Behavioral Pharmacology, 16*(2), 63–77.

Cautin, R. L. (2011). A century of psychotherapy, 1860–1960. In J. C. Norcross, G. R. VandenBos, & D. K. Freedheim (Eds.), *History of psychotherapy: Continuity and change* (2nd ed., pp. 3–38). Washington, DC: American Psychological Association.

Cauwels, J. M. (1983). *Bulimia: The binge-purge compulsion.* New York: Doubleday.

Cavett, D. (1992). Goodbye darkness. *People Magazine,* August 3. http://www.people.com/people/archive/article/0,20113244,00.html.

CBC. (2008, May 13). The world's worst natural disasters: Calamities of the 20th and 21st centuries. *CBC News.*

CBS News Poll. (2011, March 18–21). Disaster preparedness and relief. *PollingReport.com.*

CDC (Centers for Disease Control and Prevention). (2005). *Heliobacter pylori* and peptic ulcer disease. *Ulcer Facts.* Atlanta, GA: CDC.

CDC (Centers for Disease Control and Prevention). (2010). *Alzheimer's disease.* Atlanta, GA: Centers for Disease Control and Prevention

CDC (Centers for Disease Control and Prevention). (2010). *Heart disease facts.* Retrieved on May 21, 2011, from www.cdc.gov/heartdisease/facts.htm.

CDC (Centers for Disease Control and Prevention). (2010). *Chronic liver disease or cirrhosis.* Hyattsville, MD: NCHS.

CDC (Centers for Disease Control and Prevention). (2010). *Heliobacter pylori and peptic ulcer disease. Ulcer Facts.* Atlanta, GA: CDC.

CDC (Centers for Disease Control and Prevention). (2010). Suicide rates among persons ages 10 years and older, by race/ethnicity and sex, United States, 2002–2006. *National Suicide Statistics at a Glance.* Atlanta, GA: CDC.

CDC (Centers for Disease Control and Prevention). (2010, December 3). QuickStats: Percentage of adults who had migraines or severe headaches, pain in the neck, lower back, or face/jaw. by sex. National Health Interview Survey, 2009. *Morbidity and Mortality Weekly Report, 59*(47), 1557.

CDC (Centers for Disease Control and Prevention). (2011). Asthma: Data and surveillance. Retrieved on May 21, 2011, from www.cdc.gov/asthma/asthmadata.htm.

CDC (Centers for Disease Control and Prevention). (2011). Cited in NVSS, Deaths: Final Data for 2007. *National Vital Statistics Reports,* 58(19). Hyattsville, MD: National Center for Health Statistics.

CDC (Centers for Disease Control and Prevention). (2011). *Death rates from suicide by selected characteristics: 1990 to 2007.* Suitland, MD: US Department of Commerce, Bureau of the Census.

CDC (Centers for Disease Control and Prevention). (2011). *High blood pressure facts.* Retrieved on May 21, 2011, from www.cdc.gov/bloodpressure/facts.htm.

CDC (Centers for Disease Control and Prevention). (2011). *Key sleep disorders.* Retrieved on May 21, 2011, from www.cdc.gov/sleep/about_sleep/key_disorders.htm.

CDC (Centers for Disease Control and Prevention). (2011). *Suicide prevention.* Atlanta, GA: Centers for Disease Control and Prevention.

CDC (Centers for Disease Control and Prevention). (2011). *United States Life Tables.* Atlanta, GA: National Center for Health Statistics.

CDC (Centers for Disease Control and Prevention). (2011). *Health disparities and inequalities report–United States, 2011.* Atlanta, GA: Author.

CDC (Centers for Disease Control and Prevention). (2012). *Autism spectrum disorders (ASD): Data and statistics.* Atlanta, GA: CDC.

CDC (Centers for Disease Control and Prevention). (2012). *Ten leading causes of death and injury.* Retrieved from http://www.cdc.gov/injury/wisqars/leadingcauses.html.

Cepeda, C. (2010). *Clinical manual for the psychiatric interview of children and adolescents.* Arlington, VA: American Psychiatric Publishing.

Cerletti, U., & Bini, L. (1938). L'elettroshock. *Archives of General Neurology, Psychiatry, and Psychoanalysis, 19,* 266–268.

Cerny, C. A., & Noffsinger, S. (2006). Prisoner rights and suicide. *Journal of the American Academy of Psychiatry and the Law, 34*(4), 549–551.

Chabot, D. R. (2011). Family systems theories of psychotherapy. In J. C. Norcross, G. R. VandenBos, & D. K. Freedheim (Eds), *History of psychotherapy: Continuity and change* (2nd ed., pp. 173–202). Washington, DC: American Psychological Association.

Chacón, F., & Vecina, M. L. (2007). The 2004 Madrid terrorist attack: Organizing a large-scale psychological response. In E. K. Carll (Ed.), *Trauma psychology: Issues in violence, disaster, health, and illness* (Vol. 1). Westport, CT: Praeger Publishers.

Chae, B. J., & Kang, B. J. (2006). Quetiapine for delusional jealousy in a deaf elderly patient. *International Psychogeriatrics, 18*(1), 187–188.

Chaika, E. O. (1990). *Understanding psychotic speech: Beyond Freud and Chomsky.* Springfield, IL: Thomas.

Chalamat, M., Mihalopoulos, C., Carter, R., & Vos, T. (2005). Assessing cost-effectiveness in mental health: Vocational rehabilitation for schizophrenia and related conditions. *Australian and New Zealand Journal of Psychiatry, 39*(8), 693–700.

Chamberlain, S. R., Blackwell, A. D., Fineberg, N. A., Robbins, T. W., & Sahakian, B. J. (2005). The neuropsychology of obsessive compulsive disorder: The importance of failures in cognitive and behavioural inhibition as candidate endopyhenotypic markers. *Neuroscience and Biobehavioral Reviews, 29*(3), 399–419.

Chan, H. C., Heide, K. M., & Beauregard, E. (2011). What propels sexual murderers: A proposed integrated theory of social learning and routine activities theories. *International Journal of Offender Therapy and Comparative Criminology, 55*(2), 228–250.

Chandler, C. (2010). *The science of ADHD: A guide for parents and professionals.* Hoboken, NJ: Wiley-Blackwell.

Chandola, T., & Marmot, M. G. (2011). Socioeconomic status and stress. In R. J. Contrada & A. Baum (Eds.), *The handbook of stress science: Biology, psychology, and health* (pp. 185–193). New York: Springer Publishing.

Chandra, A., Mosher, W.D., & Copen, C. (2011). Sexual behavior, sexual attraction, and sexual identity in the United States: Data from the 2006–2008 national survey of family growth. *National Health Statistics Reports, 36,* March 3.

Chang, K. D., Singh, M. K., Wang, P. W., & Howe, M. (2010). Management of bipolar disorders in children and adolescents. In T. A. Ketter (Ed.), *Handbook of diagnosis and treatment of bipolar disorders* (pp. 389–424). Arlington, VA: American Psychiatric Publishing.

Chang, L., & Krosnick, J. A. (2010). Comparing oral interviewing with self-administered computerized questionnaires: An experiment. *Public Opinion Quarterly, 74*(1). 154–167.

Chaparro, S. (2004). Cited in T. Sauthoff, Professor assigns 48 hours without using cell phone. *The Daily Targum,* April 5, 2004, p. 1.

Chapman, S. (2013). Diagnosis Revision Watch: Monitoring the development of DSM-5, ICD-11, ICD-10-CB. http://dxrevisionwatch.com.

Charland, L. C. (2007). Benevolent theory: Moral treatment at the York Retreat. *History of Psychiatry, 18*(1), 61–80.

Charland, L. C. (2008). A moral line in the sand: Alexander Crichton and Philippe Pinel on the psychopathology of the passions. In L. C. Charland & P. Zachar (Eds.), *Fact and value in emotion* (pp. 15–33). Amsterdam, Netherlands: John Benjamins Publishing Company.

Charles, K. (2011). Social network anxiety disorder? Study cited in *Silicon Valley/San Jose Business Journal,* February 21, 2011.

Charney, D. S., Woods, S. W., Goodman, W. K., & Heninger, G. R. (1987). Neurobiological mechanisms of panic anxiety: Biochemical and behavioral correlates of yohimbine-induced anxiety. *American Journal of Psychiatry, 144*(8), 1030–1036.

Charney, D. S., Woods, S. W., Price, L. H., Goodman, W. K., Glazer, W. M., & Heninger, G. R. (1990). Noradrenergic dys-regulation in panic disorder. In J. C. Ballenger (Ed.), *Neurobiology of panic disorder.* New York: Wiley-Liss.

Charuvastra, A., & Cloitre, M. (2008). Social bonds and posttraumatic stress disorder. In S. Fiske, D. L. Schacter, & R. Sternberg (Eds.), *Annual review of psychology* (Vol. 59). Palo Alto, CA: Annual reviews.

Chase, M. (1993, May 28). Psychiatrists declare severe PMS a depressive disorder. *Wall Street Journal,* pp. B1, B6.

Chassin, L., Collins, R. L., Ritter, J., & Shirley, M. C. (2001). Vulnerability to substance use disorders across the life span. In R. E. Ingram & J. M. Price (Eds.), *Vulnerability to psychopathology: Risk across the lifespan* (pp. 165–172). New York: Guilford Press.

Chaturvedi, S. K., Desai, G., & Shaligram, D. (2010). Dissociative disorders in a psychiatric institute in India—A selected review and patterns over a decade. *International Journal of Social Psychiatry, 56*(5), 533–539.

Chavez, M. L., & Spitzer, M. F. (2002). Herbals and other dietary supplements for premenstrual syndrome and menopause. *Psychiatric Annals, 32*(1), 61–71.

Chavira, D. A., Grilo, C. M., Shea, M. T., Yen, S., Gunderson, J. G., Morey, L. C., et al. (2003). Ethnicity and four personality disorders. *Comprehensive Psychiatry, 44*(6), 483–491.

Chavira, D. A., Stein, M. B., Bailey, K., & Stein, M. T. (2004). Child anxiety in primary care: Prevalent but untreated. *Depression and Anxiety, 20*(4), 155–164.

Chekki, C. (2004, November 10). Treaty 3 cries for help. *The Chronicle Journal* (Thunder Bay, Ontario, Canada), p. A3.

Chemerinski, E., & Siever, L. J. (2011). The schizophrenia spectrum personality disorders. In D.R. Weinberger & P. Harrison (Eds.). *Schizophrenia.* Hoboken, NJ: Wiley-Blackwell.

Chen, C-H., Suckling, J., Lennox, B. R., Ooi, C., & Bullmore, E. T. (2011). A quantitative meta-analysis of fMRI studies in bipolar disorder. *Bipolar Disorders, 13*(1), 1–15.

Chen, C., O'Brien, M. S., & Anthony, J. C. (2005). Who becomes cannabis dependent soon after onset of use? Epidemiological evidence from the United States: 2000–2001. *Drug and Alcohol Dependence, 79*(1), 11–22.

Chen, W., Landau, S., Sham, P., & Fombonne, E. (2004). No evidence for links between autism, MMR and measles virus. *Psychological Medicine: Journal of Research in Psychiatry and the Allied Sciences, 34*(3), 543–553.

Chen, Y., Role, L. W., & Talmage, D. A. (2012). Mutant models of Nrg1 and ErbB4: Abnormalities of brain structures, functions, and behaviors relevant to schizophrenia. In A. S. Brown & P. H. Patterson (Eds.), *The origins of schizophrenia* (pp. 382–411). New York: Columbia University Press.

Cheney, T. (2008, January 13). Take me as I am, whoever I am. *New York Times.* Retrieved from http://www.nytimes.com.

Cheng, A. T. A., Hawton, K., Lee, C. T. C., & Chen, T. H. H. (2007). The influence of media reporting of the suicide of a celebrity on suicide rates: A population-based study. *International Journal of Epidemiology, 36*(6), 1229–1234.

Cherry, K. (2010). 10 facts about Sigmund Freud. *About.com.* Retrieved on April 5, 2011, from http://psychology.about.com/od/sigmundfreud/tp/facts-about-freud.htm.

Cherry, K. (2012). Phobia list—An A to Z list of phobias. *About.com* Retrieved on June 17, 2012, from http://psychology.abouty.com/od/phobias/a/phobialist.htm.

Cherry, K. E., Galea, S., & Silva, J. L. (2007). Successful aging in very old adults: Resiliency in the face of natural disaster. In M. Hersen & A. M. Gross (Eds.), *Handbook of clinical psychology, Vol. 1: Adults.* Hoboken, NJ: Wiley.

Chester, A., & Glass, C. A. (2006). Online counseling: A descriptive analysis of therapy services on the internet. *British Journal of Guidance and Counseling, 34*(2), 145–160.

Chiesa, M., Sharp, R., & Fonagy, P. (2011). Clinical associations of deliberate self-injury and its impact on the outcome of community-based and long-term inpatient treatment for personality disorder. *Psychotherapy and Psychosomatics, 80*(2), 100–109.

Chin, J. H., Ma, L., MacTavish, D., & Jhamandas, J. H. (2007). Amyloid beta protein modulates glutamate-mediated neurotransmission in the rat basal forebrain: Involvement of presynaptic neuronal nicotinic acetylcholine and metabotropic glutamate receptors. *Journal of Neuroscience, 27*(35), 9262–9269.

Chiu, L. H. (1971). Manifested anxiety in Chinese and American children. *Journal of Psychology, 79,* 273–284.

Chrismore, S., Betzelberger, E., Bier, L., & Camacho, T. (2011). Twelve-step recovery in inpatient treatment for internet addiction. In K. S. Young & C. N. de Abreu (Eds.), *Internet addiction: A handbook and guide for evaluation and treatment* (pp. 205–222). Hoboken, NJ: John Wiley & Sons.

Christensen, A., Atkins, D. C., Baucom, B., & Yi, J. (2010). Marital status and satisfaction five years following a randomized clinical trial comparing traditional versus integrative behavioral couple therapy. *Journal of Consulting and Clinical Psychology, 78*(2), 225–235.

Christensen, A., Atkins, D. C., Yi, J., Baucom, D. H., & George, W. H. (2006). Couple and individual adjustment for 2 years following a randomized clinical trial comparing traditional versus integrative behavioral couple therapy. *Journal of Consulting and Clinical Psychology, 74*(6), 1180–1191.

Christensen, B. S., Gronbaek, M., Osler, M., Pedersen, B. V., Graugaard, C., & Frisch, M. (2011). Sexual dysfunctions and difficulties in Denmark: Prevalence and associated sociodemographic factors. *Archives of Sexual Behavior, 40*(1), 121–132.

Christodoulou, M. (2012). Pro-anorexia websites pose public health challenge. *The Lancet, 379,* 110.

Christophersen, E. R., & Friman, P. C. (2010). *Elimination disorders in children and adolescents.* Cambridge, MA: Hogrefe Publishing.

Chudler, E. H. (2007), The power of the full moon. Running on empty? In Della Sala, S. (Ed.), *Tall tales about the mind & brain: Separating fact from fiction* (pp. 401–410). New York: Oxford University Press.

Chung, M. C., Dennis, I., Easthope, Y., Werrett, J., & Farmer, S. (2005). A multiple-indicator multiple-case model for posttraumatic stress reactions: Personality, coping, and maladjustment. *Psychosomatic Medicine, 67*(2), 251–259.

Chung, P. H., Ross, J. D., Wakhlu, S., & Adinoff, B. (2012). Neurobiological bases of addiction treatment. In S. T. Walters & F. Rotgers (Eds.), *Treating substance abuse: Theory and technique* (3rd Ed., pp. 281–318). New York: Guilford Press.

Cigrang, J. A., Rauch, S. A. M., Avila, L. L., Bryan, C. J., Goodie, J. L., Hryshko-Mullen, A., & Peterson, A. L. (2011). Treatment of active-duty military with PTSD in primary care: Early findings. *Psychological Services, 8*(2), 104–113.

Cipani, E., & Schock, K. M. (2012). Functional behavioral assessment, diagnosis, and treatment: A complete system for education and mental health settings (2nd ed.). New York: Springer Publishing Co.

Ciraulo, D. A., Evans, J. A., Qiu, W. Q., Shader, R. I., & Salzman, C. (2010). Antidepressant treatment of geriatric depression. In D. A. Ciraulo & R. I. Shader, *Pharmacotherapy for depression* (2nd ed., pp. 125–183). New York: Springer Science + Business Media.

Ciraulo, D. A., Evans, J. A., Qiu, W. Q., Shader, R. I., & Salzman, C. (2011). Antidepressant treatment of geriatric depression. In D. A. Ciraulo & R. I. Shader, *Pharmacotherapy for depression* (2nd ed., pp. 125–183). New York: Springer Science 1 Business Media.

Ciraulo, D. A., Shader, R. I., & Greenblatt, D. J. (2011). Clinical pharmacology and therapeutics of antidepressants. In D. A. Ciraulo & R. I. Shader (Eds.), *Pharmacotherapy of depression* (2nd ed., pp. 33–124). New York: Springer Science + Business Media.

Claassen, C. A., & Knox, K. L. (2011). Assessment and management of high-risk suicidal states in postdeployment Operation Enduring Freedom and Operation Iraqi Freedom military personnel. In J. I. Ruzek, P. P. Schnurr, J. J. Vasterling, & M. J. Friedman (Eds.), *Caring for veterans with deployment-related stress disorders* (pp. 109–127). Washington, DC: American Psychological Association.

Clabough, R. (2011). Free contraceptives under ObamaCare? HHS says maybe. http://www.thenewamerican.com/usnews/health-care.

Clanton Harpine, E. (2011). *Group-centered prevention programs for at-risk students.* New York: Spring Science.

Clark, D. A., & Beck, A. T. (2010). *Cognitive therapy of anxiety disorders: Science and practice.* New York: Guilford Press.

Clark, D. A., & Beck, A. T. (2012). *The anxiety and worry workbook: The cognitive behavioral solution.* New York: Guilford Press.

Clark, D. A., & Guyitt, B. D. (2008). Pure obsessions: Conceptual misnomer or clinical anomaly? In J. S. Abramowitz, D. McKay, & S. Taylor (Eds.), *Obsessive-compulsive disorder: Subtypes and spectrum conditions.* Oxford, England: Elsevier.

Clark, D. M., & Wells, A. (1995). A cognitive model of social phobia. In R. G. Heimberg, M. R. Liebowitz, D. A. Hope, & F. R. Schneier (Eds.), *Social phobia: Diagnosis, assessment, and treatment* (pp. 69–93). New York: Guilford Press.

Clark, L. A. (2005, November). Dimensional bases of diagnosis. *Clinician's Research Digest, Supplemental Bulletin 33,* 1–2.

Clarke, G. N., & Debar, L. L. (2010). Group cognitive-behavioral treatment for adolescent depression. In J. R. Weisz & A. E. Kazdin (Eds.), *Evidence-based psychotherapies for children and adolescents* (2nd ed., pp. 110–125) New York: Guilford Press.

Clarke, J. C., & Saunders, J. B. (1988). *Alcoholism and problem drinking: Theories and treatment.* Sydney: Pergamon Press.

Clarke, M., Roddy, S., & Cannon, M. (2012). Obstetric complications and schizophrenia: Historical overview and new directions. In A. S. Brown & P. H. Patterson (Eds.), *The origins of schizophrenia* (pp. 96–119). New York: Columbia University Press.

Clarkin, J. F., Foelsch, P. A., Levy, K. N., Hull, J. W., Delaney, J. C., & Kernberg, O. F. (2001). The development of a psychodynamic treatment for patients with borderline personality disorder: A preliminary study of behavioral change. *Journal of Personality Disorders, 15,* 487–495.

Clarkin, J. F., Fonagy, P., & Gabbard, G. O. (Eds.). (2010). *Psychodynamic psychotherapy for personality disorders: A clinical handbook.* Arlington, VA: American Psychiatric Publishing.

Claudino, A. M., & Morgan, C. M. (2011). Unraveling binge eating disorder. In J. Alexander & J. Treasure (Eds.), *A collaborative approach to eating disorders* (pp. 236–248). New York: Taylor & Francis.

Clausen, L., Rosenvinge J. H., Friborg, O., & Rokkedal, K. (2011). Validating the Eating Disorder Inventory-3 (EDI-3): A comparison between 561 female eating disorders patients and 878 females from the general population. *Journal of Psychopathology and Behavioral Assessment, 33*(1), 101–110.

Clay-Warner, J., & Burt, C. H. (2005). Rape reporting after reforms: Have times really changed? *Violence Against Women, 11*(2), 150–176.

Clay, R. A. (2011). A new day for parity. *Monitor on Psychology, 42*(1), 18–19.

Clay, R. A. (2011). Is stress getting to you? *Monitor on Psychology, 42*(1), 58–63.

Clinton, A. B., Fernandez, L., & Alicea, G. (2010, August). *Interviewing, bias, and cultural considerations in Prevention Program Evaluation.* Paper presented at APA 118th Annual Convention, San Diego, California, August 12–15.

Cloak, N. L., & Powers, P. S. (2010). Science or art? Integrating symptom management into psychodynamic treatment of eating disorders. In M. Maine, B. H. McGilley, & D. W. Bunnell (Eds.), *Treatment of eating disorders: Bridging the research-practice gap* (pp. 143–161). San Diego, CA: Elsevier Academic Press.

Cloninger, C. F., & Svrakic, D. M. (2005). Personality disorders. In E. H. Rubin & C. F. Zorumski (Eds.), *Adult psychiatry* (2nd ed., pp. 290–306). Oxford, England: Blackwell Publishing.

CNN. (2008). Girl's suicide leaves dozens ill from fumes. Retrieved on April 24, 2008, at www.CNN.com.

Coccaro, E. F. (2012). Intermittent explosive disorder as a disorder of impulsive aggression for DSM-5. *American Journal of Psychiatry, 169*(6), 577–588.

Coetzer, B. R. (2004). Obsessive-compulsive disorder following brain injury: A review. *International Journal of Psychiatry in Medicine, 34*(4), 363–377.

Coffey, C. E. & Kellner, C. H. (2011). Electroconvulsive therapy. In C.E. Coffey, J.L. Cummings, M.S. George, & D. Weintraub (Eds.), *The American Psychiatric Publishing textbook of geriatric neuropsychiatry.* Arlington, VA: American Psychiatric Publishing, Inc.

Coffey, M. J., & Coffey, C. E. (2011). Mood disorders. In C. E. Coffey, J. L. Cummings, M. S. George, & D. Weintraub (Eds.), *The American Psychiatric Publishing textbook of geriatric neuropsychiatry.* Arlington, VA: American Psychiatric Publishing, Inc.

Coffey, S. F., Schumacher, J. A., Baschnagel, J. S., Hawk, L. W., & Holloman, G. (2011). Impulsivity and risk-taking in borderline personality disorder with and without substance use disorders. *Personality Disorders: Theory, Research, and Treatment, 2*(2), 128–141.

Cogan, J. C., Bhalla, S. K., Sefa-Dedeh, A., & Rothblum, E. D. (1996). A comparison study of United States and African students on perceptions of obesity and thinness. *Journal of Cross-Cultural Psychology, 27,* 98–113.

Cohen-Kettenis, P. T. (2001). Gender identity disorder in DSM? *Journal of the American Academy of Child and Adolescent Psychiatry, 40*(4), 391.

Cohen-Kettenis, P. T., Steensma, T. D., & de Vries, A. L. C. (2011). Treatment of adolescents with gender dysphoria in the Netherlands. *Child and Adolescent Psychiatric Clinics of North America, 20*(4), 689–700.

Cohen, A. S., Najolia, G. M., Brown, L. A., & Minor, K. S. (2011). The state-trait disjunction of anhedonia in schizophrenia: Potential affective, cognitive, and social-based mechanisms. *Clinical Psychology Review, 31*(3), 440–448.

Cohen, D. (2010). Probabilistic epigenesis: An alternative causal model for conduct disorders in children and adolescents. *Neuroscience and Biobehavioral Reviews, 34*(1), 119–129.

Cohen, E. (2007). CDC: Antidepressants most prescribed drugs in U.S. *CNN.* Retrieved July 10, 2007, from http://www.cnn/2007/health/07/09/antidepressants/index.html:cnnSTCTest.

Cohen, L., Ardjoen, R. C., & Sewpersad, K. S. M. (1997). Type A behaviour pattern as a risk factor after myocardial infarction: A review. *Psychology and Health, 12,* 619–632.

Cohen, P. (2008, February 12). Midlife suicide rises, puzzling researchers. *New York Times, 157*(54), 225.

Cohen, S. (2002). Psychosocial stress, social networks, and susceptibility to infection. In H. G. Koenig & H. J. Cohen (Eds.), *The link between religion and health: Psychoneuroimmunology and the faith factor* (pp. 101–123). New York: Oxford University Press.

Cohen, S., Tyrrell, A. D., & Smith, A. P. (1991). Psychological stress and susceptibility to the common cold. *New England Journal of Medicine, 325,* 606–612.

Colburn, D. (1996, November 19). Singer's suicide doesn't lead to "copycat" deaths. *Washington Post Health,* p. 5.

Coldwell, C. M., & Bender, W. S. (2007). The effectiveness of assertive community treatment for homeless populations with severe mental illness: A meta-analysis. *American Journal of Psychiatry, 164*(3), 393–399.

Coleman, L. (1984). The reign of error: Psychiatry, authority, and law. Boston: Beacon.

Coleman, S. L., Pieterefesa, A. S., Holaway, R. M., Coles, M. E., & Heimberg, R. G. (2011). Content and correlates of checking related to symptoms of obsessive compulsive disorder and generalized anxiety disorder. *Journal of Anxiety Disorders, 25*(2), 293–301.

Coles, M. E., Heimberg, R. G., Frost, R. O., & Steketee, G. (2005). Not just right experiences and obsessive-compulsive features: Experimental and self-monitoring perspectives. *Behavioral Research and Therapy, 43,* 153–167.

Coles, M. E., & Pietrefesa, A. S. (2008). Symmetry, ordering, and arranging. In J. S. Abramowitz, D. McKay, & S. Taylor (Eds.), *Obsessive-compulsive disorder: Subtypes and spectrum conditions.* Oxford, England: Elsevier.

Colletti, G., Lynn, S. J., & Laurence, J-R. (2010). Hypnosis and the treatment of dissociative identity disorder. In S. J. Lynn, J.W., Rhue, & I. Kirsch (Eds.), *Handbook of clinical hypnosis* (2nd ed., pp. 433–451). Washington, DC: American Psychological Association.

Comas-Diaz, L. (2006). Cultural variation in the therapeutic relationship. In C. D. Goodheart, A. E. Kazdin, & R. J. Sternberg (Eds.), *Evidence-based psychotherapy: Where practice and research meet* (pp. 81–105). Washington, DC: American Psychological Association.

Comas-Diaz, L. (2011). Multicultural approaches to psychotherapy. In J. C. Norcross, G. R. VandenBos, & D. K. Freedheim (Eds.), *History of psychotherapy: Continuity and change* (2nd ed., pp. 243–267). Washington, DC: American Psychological Association.

Comas-Diaz, L. (2011). Multicultural psychotherapies. In R. J. Corsini & D. Wedding (Eds.), *Current psychotherapies* (9th ed.). Belmont, CA: Brooks/Cole.

Comas-Diaz, L. (2012). *Multicultural care: A clinician's guide to cultural competence. Psychologists in independent practice* (Div. 42). Washington, DC: American Psychological Association.

Comasco, E., Sylvén, S. M., Papadopoulos, F. C., Sundström-Poromaa, I., Oreland, L., & Skalkidou, A. (2011). Postpartum depression symptoms: A case-control study on monoaminergic functional polymorphisms and environmental stressors. *Psychiatric Genetics, 21*(1), 19–28.

Combs, D. R., Basso, M. R., Wanner, J. L., & Ledet, S. N. (2008). Schizophrenia. In M. Hersen & J. Rosqvist (Eds.), *Handbook of psychological assessment, case conceptualization and treatment, Vol. 1: Adults* (pp. 352–402). Hoboken, NJ: John Wiley & Sons.

Comer, J. S., & Kendall, P. C. (2007). Terrorism: The psychological impact on youth. *Clinical Psychology: Science and Practice, 14*(3), 178–212.

Comer, J. S., Mojtabai, R., & Olfson, M. (2011). National trends in the antipsychotic treatment of psychiatric outpatients with anxiety disorders. *American Journal of Psychiatry, 168*(10), 1057–1065.

Comer, J. S., Olfson, M., & Mojtabai, R. (2010). National trends in child and adolescent psychotropic polypharmacy in office-based practice, 1996–2007. *Journal of the American Academy of Child & Adolescent Psychiatry, 49*(10), 1001–1010.

Comer, R. (1973). *Therapy interviews with a schizophrenic patient.* Unpublished manuscript.

Compas, B. E., & Gotlib, I. H. (2002). *Introduction to clinical psychology: Science and practice.* Boston: McGraw-Hill.

Conn, P. M., & Rantin, F. T. (2010). Ethical research as the target of animal extremism: An international problem. *Brazilian Journal of Medical and Biological Research, 43*(2), 124–126.

Conner, K. R., & Weisman, R. L. (2011). Embitterment in suicide and homicide-suicide. In M. Linden & A. Maercker (Eds.), *Embitterment: Societal, psychological, and clinical perspectives* (pp. 240–247). New York: Springer-Verlag Publishing.

Connor, J. P., Young, R. McD., Lawford, B. R., Ritchie, T. L., & Noble, E. P. (2002). D_2 dopamine receptor (DRD2) polymorphism is associated with severity of alcohol dependence. *European Psychiatry, 17*(1), 17–23.

Connor-Greene, P. A. (2007). Observation or interpretation: Demonstrating unintentional subjectivity and interpretive variance. *Teaching of Psychology, 34*(3), 167–171.

Conrad, N. (1992). Stress and knowledge of suicidal others as factors in suicidal behavior of high school adolescents. *Issues in Mental Health Nursing, 13*(2), 95–104.

Constantino, J. N. (2011). Social impairment. In E. Hollander, A. Kolevzon & J. T. Coyle (Eds.), *Textbook of autism spectrum disorders.* (pp. 139–145) Arlington, VA: American Psychiatric Publishing, Inc.

Constantino, M. J., Laws, H. B., Arnow, B. A., Klein, D. N., Rothbaum, B. O., Manber, R. (2012). The relation between changes in patients' interpersonal impact messages and outcome in treatment for chronic depression. *Journal of Consulting and Clinical Psychology, 80*(3), 354–364.

Conus, P., Cotton, S., Schimmelmann, B. G., McGorry, P. D., & Lambert, M. (2007). The first-episode psychosis outcome study: Premorbid and baseline characteristics of an epidemiological cohort of 661 first-episode psychosis patients. *Early Interventions in Psychiatry, 1*(2), 191–200.

Conversano, C., Marazziti, D., Carmassi, C., Baldini, S., Barnabei, G., & Dell'Osso, L. (2012). Pathological gambling: A systematic review of biochemical, neuroimaging, and neuropsychological findings. *Harvard Review of Psychiatry, 20*(3), 130–148.

Conwell, Y., Caine, E. D., & Olsen, K. (1990). Suicide and cancer in late life. *Hospital Community Psychiatry, 43,* 1334–1338.

Cook, C. E., Jeffcoat, A. R., & Perez-Reyes, M. (1985). Pharmacokinetic studies of cocaine and phencyclidine in man. In G. Barnett & C. N. Chiang (Eds.), *Pharmacokinetics and pharmacodynamics of psychoactive drugs.* Foster City, CA: Biomedical Publications.

Cook, I. A., & Leuchter, A. F. (2001). Prefrontal changes and treatment response prediction in depression. *Seminars in Clinical Neuropsychiatry, 6,* 113–120.

Cooke, R., French, D. ., & Sniehotta, F. F. (2010). Wide variation in understanding about what constitutes "binge-drinking." *Drugs: Education, Prevention & Policy, 17*(6), 762–775.

Coon, D., & Mitterer, J. O. (2007). *Introduction to psychology: Gateways to mind and behavior* (11th ed.). Belmont, CA: Wadsworth.

Coons, P. M., & Bowman, E. S. (2001). Ten-year follow-up study of patients with dissociative identity disorder. *Journal of Trauma and Dissociation, 2*(1), 73–89.

Cooper, J. L. (2004). Treatment for children with attention-deficit/hyperactivity disorder. *Dissertation Abstracts International: Section B: The Sciences and Engineering, 65*(5-B), 2338.

Cooper, M. (2011, November 30). 2 Governors asking U.S. to ease rules on marijuana to allow for its medical use. *New York Times.*

Copley, J. (2008, May 8). Psychology of heavy metal music. *Suite101.com.* Retrieved June 14, 2008, from www.suite101.com.

Corey-Bloom, J. (2004). Alzheimer's disease. *Continuum of Lifelong Learning in Neurology, 10,* 29–57.

Corey, G. (2004). *Theory and practice of counseling and psychotherapy* (with web site, chapter quiz booklet, and InfoTrac). Stanford, CT: Wadsworth Publishing., 72

Corey, G. (2008). *Theory and practice of counseling and psychotherapy* (8th ed.). Belmont, CA: Brooks/Cole.

Corey, G. (2012). *Theory and practice of counseling and psychotherapy.* Belmont, CA: Brooks Cole.

Corliss, R., & Lemonick, M. D. (2004, August 30). How to live to be 100. *Time, 164*(9), 40–46.

Cornblatt, B. A., & Keilp, J. G. (1994). Impaired attention, genetics, and the pathophysiology of schizophrenia. *Schizophrenia Bulletin, 20*(1), 31–46.

Cornish, J. W., McNicholas, L. F., & O'Brien, C. P. (1995). Treatment of substance-related disorders. In A. F. Schatzberg & C. B. Nemeroff (Eds.), *The American Psychiatric Press textbook of psychopharmacology.* Washington, DC: American Psychiatric Press.

Cornum, R., Matthews, M. D., & Seligman, M. E. P. (2011). Comprehensive Soldier Fitness: Building resilience in a challenging institutional context. *American Psychologist, 66*(1), 4–9.

Corrie, S., & Callanan, M. M. (2001). Therapists' beliefs about research and the scientist-practitioner model in an evidence-based health care climate? A qualitative study. *British Journal of Medical Psychology, 74*(2), 135–149.

Corsini, R. J., & Wedding, D. (Eds.). (2011). *Current psychotherapies (9th ed.).* Florence, KY: CENGAGE Learning.

Corter, A., & Petrie, K. J. (2011). Expressive writing in patients diagnosed with cancer. In I. Nyklicek, A. Vingerhoets, & M. Zeelenberg (Eds.), *Emotion regulation and well-being* (pp. 297–306). New York: Springer Science + Business Media.

Cosgrove, K. P. (2010). Imaging receptor changes in human drug abusers. In D. W. Self & J. K. Staley (Eds.), *Behavioral neuroscience of drug addiction* (pp. 199–217). New York: Springer Publishing.

Cosmides, L., & Tooby, J. (2000). Evolutionary psychology and the emotions. In M. Lewis & J. M. Haviland (Eds.), *Handbook of emotions* (2nd ed., pp. 91–115). New York: Guilford Press.

Costa, E. (1983). Are benzodiazepine recognition sites functional entities for the action of endogenous effectors or merely drug receptors? *Advances in Biochemistry & Psychopharmacology, 38,* 249–259.

Costa, E. (1985). Benzodiazepine-GABA interactions: A model to investigate the neurobiology of anxiety. In A. H. Tuma & J. Maser (Eds.), *Anxiety and the anxiety disorders.* Hillsdale, NJ: Lawrence Erlbaum.

Costantino, G., Dana, R. H., & Malgady, R. G. (2007). *TEMAS (Tell-Me-A-Story) assessment in multicultural societies.* Mahwah, NJ: Lawrence Erlbaum.

Costello, E. J., Egger, H. L., & Angold, A. (2005). The developmental epidemiology of anxiety disorders: Phenomenology, prevalence, and comorbidity. *Child and Adolescent Psychiatric Clinics of North America, 14*(4), 631–648.

Couturier, J., & Lock, J. (2006). Eating disorders: Anorexia nervosa, bulimia nervosa, and binge eating disorder. In. T. G. Plante (Ed.), *Mental disorders of the new millennium, Vol. 3: Biology and function.* Westport, CT: Praeger Publishers.

Covell, N. H., Essock, S. M., & Frisman, L. K. (2011). Economics of the treatment of schizophrenia. In D. R. Weinberg & P. Harrison (Eds.), *Schizophrenia* (pp. 687–699). Hoboken, NJ: Wiley-Blackwell.

Covell, N. H., Jackson, C. T., Evans, A. C., & Essock, M. S. (2002). Antipsychotic prescribing practices in Connecticut's public mental health system: Rates of changing medications and prescribing styles. *Schizophrenia Bulletin, 28*(1), 17–29.

Covington, M. A., He, C., Brown, C., Naci, L., McClain, J. T., Fjordbak, B. S., et al. (2005). Schizophrenia and the structure of language: The linguist's view. *Schizophrenia Research, 77*(1), 85–98.

Cox, A., Rutter, M., Newman, S., & Bartak, L. (1975). A comparative study of infantile autism and specific developmental receptive language disorder: II. Parental characteristics. *British Journal of Psychiatry, 126,* 146–159.

Cox, B. J., Turnbull, D. L., Robinson, J. A., Grant, B. F., & Stein, M. B. (2011). The effect of avoidant personality disorder on the persistence of generalized social anxiety disorder in the general population: Results from a longitudinal, nationally representative mental health survey. *Depression and Anxiety, 28*(3), 250–255.

Cox, D. J., Morris, J. B., Jr., Borowitz, S. M., & Sutphen, J. L. (2002). Psychological differences between children with and without chronic encopresis. *Journal of Pediatric Psychology, 27*(7), 585–591.

Coyne, J. C. (2001). Depression and the response of others. In W. G. Parrott (Ed.), *Emotions in social psychology: Essential readings* (pp. 231–238). Philadelphia: Psychology Press/Taylor & Francis.

Coyne, J. C., & Calarco, M. M. (1995). Effects of the experience of depression: Application of focus group and survey methodologies. *Psychiatry: Interpersonal and Biological Processes, 58*(2), 149–163.

Craig, K. J., & Chamberlain, S. R. (2010). The neuropsychology of anxiety disorders. In D. J. Stein, E. Hollander, & B. O. Rothbaum (Eds.), *Textbook of anxiety disorders* (2nd ed., pp. 87–102). Arlington, VA: American Psychiatric Publishing.

Craig, T., & Power, P. (2010). Inpatient provision in early psychosis. In P. French, J. Smith, D. Shiers, M. Reed, & M. Rayne (Eds.), *Promoting recovery in early psychosis: A practice manual* (pp. 17–26). Hoboken, NJ: Wiley-Blackwell.

Crandall, C. S., Preisler, J. J., & Aussprung, J. (1992). Measuring life events stress in the lives of college students: The Undergraduate Stress Questionnaire (USQ). *Journal of Behavioral Medicine, 15*(6), 627–662.

Craske, M. G. (2010). *Cognitive–behavioral therapy* Washington, DC: American Psychological Association.

Craske, M. G. (2010). Evaluation. in M. G. Craske, *Cognitive-behavioral therapy: Theories of psychotherapy* (pp. 115–126). Washington, DC: American Psychological Association.

Craske, M. G., & Barlow, D. H. (1993). Panic disorder and agoraphobia. In D. H. Barlow (Ed.), *Clinical handbook of psychological disorders* (2nd Ed., pp. 1–47). New York: Guilford Press.

Craske, M. G., & Barlow, D. H. (2008). Panic disorder and agoraphobia. in D. H. Barlow (Ed.), *Clinical handbook of psychological disorders: A step-by-step treatment manual* (4th ed., pp. 1–64). New York: Guilford Press.

Creese, I., Burt, D. R., & Snyder, S. H. (1977). Dopamine receptor binding enhancement accompanies lesion-induced behavioral supersensitivity. *Science, 197,* 596–598.

Crighton, D. A. (2010). Offender profiling. In G. J. Towl & D. A. Crighton (Eds.), *Forensic psychology* (pp. 148–159). Hoboken, NJ: Wiley-Blackwell.

Crits-Christoph, P., Gibbons, M. B. C., Losardo, D., Narducci, J., Schamberger, M., & Gallop, R. (2004). Who benefits from brief psychodynamic therapy for generalized anxiety disorder? *Canadian Journal of Psychoanalysis, 12*(2), 301–324.

Crits-Christoph, P., Wilson, G. T., & Hollon, S. D. (2005). Empirically supported psychotherapies: Comment on Westen, Novotny, and Thompson-Brenner (2004). *Psychological Bulletin, 131*(3), 412–417.

Crocker, C. B., & Kovera, M. B. (2011). Systematic jury selection. In R. L. Wiener & B. H. Bornstein (Eds.), *Handbook of trial consulting* (pp. 13–31). New York: Springer Science & Business Media.

Croll, J. K. (2010). Nutritional impact on the recovery process. In M. Maine, B. H. McGilley, & D. W. Bunnell (Eds.), *Treatment of eating disorders: Bridging the research-practice gap* (pp. 126–142). San Diego, CA: Elsevier Academic Press.

Crosby, A. E., Espitia-Hardeman, V., Hill, H. A., Ortega, L., & Clavel-Arcas, C. (2009). Alcohol and suicide among racial/ethnic populations—17 states, 2005–2006. *Journal of the American Medical Association, 302*(7), 733–734.

Crow, S. J. (2010). Eating disorders in young adults. In J. E. Grant, & M. N. Potenza (Eds.), *Young adult mental health.* (pp. 397–405) New York: Oxford University Press.

Crow, T. J. (1980). Positive and negative schizophrenic symptoms and the role of dopamine: II. *British Journal of Psychiatry, 137,* 383–386.

Crow, T. J. (1985). The two-syndrome concept: Origins and current status. *Schizophrenia Bulletin, 11*(3), 471–486.

Crow, T. J. (1995). Brain changes and negative symptoms in schizophrenia. *Psychopathology, 28*(1), 18–21.

Crow, T. J. (2008). The "big bang" theory of the origin of psychosis and the faculty of language. *Schizophrenia Research, 102*(1–3), 31–52.

Cruceanu, C., Alda, M., Rouleau, G., & Turecki, G. (2011). Response to treatment in bipolar disorder. *Current Opinion in Psychiatry, 24*(1), 24–28.

Cruikshank, M. (2003). *Learning to be old: Gender, culture, and aging.* Lanham, MD: Rowman & Littlefield.

Crystal, S., Kleinhaus, K., Perrin, M., & Malaspina, D. (2012). Advancing paternal age and the risk of schizophrenia. In A. S. Brown & P. H. Patterson (Eds.), *The origins of schizophrenia* (pp. 140–155). New York: Columbia University Press.

Cuijpers, P., van Straten, A., Hollon, S. D., & Andersson, G. (2010). The contribution of active medication to combined treatments of psychotherapy and pharmacotherapy for adult depression: A meta-analysis. *Acta Psychiatrica Scandinavica, 121*(6), 415–423.

Cukan, A. (2001, March 8). Confronting a culture of cruelty. General feature release. *United Press International.*

Cukrowicz, K. C., Cheavens, J. S., Van Orden, K. A., Ragain, R. M., & Cook, R. L. (2011). Perceived burdensomeness and suicide ideation in older adults. *Psychology and Aging, 26*(2), 331–338.

Culp, A. M., Clyman, M. M., & Culp, R. E. (1995). Adolescent depressed mood, reports of suicide attempts, and asking for help. *Adolescence, 30*(120), 827–837.

Culpepper, L., & Johnson, P. (2011). Managing depression in primary care. In D. A. Ciraulo & R. I. Shader (Eds.), *Pharmacotherapy of depression* (2nd ed., pp. 375–397). New York: Springer Science + Business Media.

Culver, J. L., & Pratchett, L. C. (2010). Adjunctive psychosocial interventions in the management of bipolar disorders. In T. A. Ketter (Ed.), *Handbook of diagnosis and treatment of bipolar disorders* (pp. 661–676). Arlington, VA: American Psychiatric Publishing.

Cummings, C. J., & Fristad, M. A. (2008). Mood disorders in childhood. In R. G. Steele, T. D. Elkin, & M. C. Roberts (Eds.), *Handbook of evidence-based therapies for children and adolescents: Bridging science and practice.* New York: Springer.

Cummings, E. M., & Schatz, J. N. (2012). Family conflict, emotional security, and child development: Translating research findings into a prevention program for community families. *Clinical Child and Family Psychology Review, 15*(1), 14–27.

Cummings, J. L. & Coffey, C. E. (2011). Geriatric neuropsychiatry. In C.E. Coffey, J.L. Cummings, M.S. George, & D. Weintraub (Eds.), *The American Psychiatric Publishing textbook of geriatric neuropsychiatry.* Arlington, VA: American Psychiatric Publishing, Inc.

Cummins, R. A., & Lau, A. L. (2003). Community integration or community exposure? A review and discussion in relation to people with an intellectual disability. *Journal of Applied Research in Intellectual Disabilities, 16,* 145–157.

Cunningham, C. L., Groblewski, P. A., & Voorhees, C. M. (2011). Place conditioning. In M. C. Olmstead (Ed.), *Animal models of drug addiction. Springer protocols: Neuromethods* (pp. 167–189). Totowa, NJ: Humana Press.

Curlin, F. A., Nwodim, C., Vance, J. L., Chin, M. H., & Lantos, J. D. (2008). To die, to sleep: US physicians' religious and other objections to physician-assisted suicide, terminal sedation, and withdrawal of life support. *American Journal of Hospice and Palliative Care, 25*(2), 112–120.

Curry, J. F., & Becker, S. J. (2008). Empirically supported psychotherapies for adolescent depression and mood disorders. In R. G. Steele, T. D. Elkin, & M. C. Roberts (Eds.), *Handbook of evidence-based therapies for children and adolescents: Bridging science and practice.* New York: Springer.

Curtis, V. (2005). Women are not the same as men: Specific clinical issues for female patients with bipolar disorder. *Bipolar Disorders, 7*(Suppl. 1), 16–24.

Curtiss, L. M. (April, 2002). *The marketing of psychotropic drugs: Mind games with mind drugs or meeting the demand for information?* Unpublished thesis, Princeton University.

Cutler, D. M., Glaeser, E. L., & Norberg, K. E. (2001). Explaining the rise in youth suicide. In J. Gruber (Ed.), *Risky behavior among youths: An economic analysis* (pp. 219–269). Chicago: University of Chicago Press.

Cutright, P., & Fernquist, R. M. (2001). The relative gender gap in suicide: Societal integration, the culture of suicide and period effects in 20 developed countries, 1955–1994. *Social Science Research, 30*(1), 76–99.

Cuvelier, M. (2002). Victim, not villain. The mentally ill are six to seven times more likely to be murdered. *Psychology Today, 35*(3), 23.

Cuzin, B. (2011). A cure, to return to a previous sexual state? Developments in the concept of cure in sexology. *Sexologies: European Journal of Sexology and Sexual Health, 20*(1), 3–7.

Cynkar, A. (2007). The changing gender composition of psychology. *The Monitor, 38*(6), 46.

Cytryn, L., & McKnew, D. H., Jr. (1996). *Growing up sad: Childhood depression and its treatment.* New York: Norton.

D'Arienzo, J. A. (2010). Inoculation training for trauma and stress–related disorders. In S. S. Fehr (Ed.), *101 interventions in group therapy* (rev. ed., pp. 431–435). New York: Routledge/Taylor & Francis Group.

Dagan, M., Sanderman, R., Schokker, M. C., Wiggers, T., Baas, P. C., van Haastert, M., & Hagedoorn, M. (2011). Spousal support and changes in distress over time in couples coping with cancer: The role of personal control. *Journal of Family Psychology, 25*(2), 310–318.

Daitch, C. (2011). *Anxiety disorders: The go-to guide for clients and therapists.* New York: W. W. Norton & Co.

Dalby, J. T. (1997). Elizabethan madness: On London's stage. *Psychological Reports, 81,* 1331–1343.

Daley, D. C., Marlatt, G. A., & Douaihy, A. (2011). Relapse prevention. In J. H. Lowinson & P. Ruiz (Eds.), *Substance abuse: A comprehensive textbook, fifth edition.* Philadelphia, PA: Lippincott, Williams, & Wilkins.

Dallery, J., Meredith, S. E., & Budney, A. J. (2012). Contingency management in substance abuse treatment. In S. T. Walters & F. Rotgers (Eds.), *Treating substance abuse: Theory and technique* (3rd ed., pp. 81–112). New York: Guilford Press.

Dallman, M. F., & Hellhammer, D. (2011). Regulation of the hypothalamo-pituitary-adrenal axis, chronic stress, and energy: The role of brain networks. In R. J. Contrada & A. Baum (Eds.), *The handbook of stress science: Biology, psychology, and health* (pp. 11–36). New York: Springer Publishing.

Daly, R. (2010). Shift to community care slowing in many states. *Psychiatric News, 45*(15), 8.

Damasio, A. R. (1994). *Descartes' error: Emotion, reason, and the human brain.* New York: Avon Books.

Dana, R. H. (2000). Culture and methodology in personality assessment. In I. Cuellar & F. A. Paniagua (Eds.), *Handbook of multicultural mental health* (pp. 97–120). San Diego, CA: Academic.

Dana, R. H. (2005). *Multicultural assessment: Principles, applications, and examples.* Mahwah, NJ: Lawrence Erlbaum.

Daniel, M., & Gurczynski, J. (2010). Mental status examination. In D. L. Segal & M. Hersen (Eds.), *Diagnostic interviewing* (pp. 61–88). New York: Springer Publishing.

Daniels, C. W. (2002). Legal aspects of polygraph admissibility in the United States. In M. Klener (Ed.), *The handbook of polygraph testing.* San Diego, CA: Academic.

Dannecker, M. (2010). Gender identity and gender identity disorders. *Zeitschrift für Sexualforschung, 23*(1), 53–62.

Darke, S., Williamson, A., Ross, J., & Teesson, M. (2005). Attempted suicide among heroin users: 12-month outcomes from the Australian Treatment Outcome Study (ATOS). *Drug and Alcohol Dependence, 78*(2), 177–186.

Dattilio, F. M. (2001). Variations in cognitive responses to fear in anxiety disorder subtypes. *Archives of Psychiatry and Psychotherapy, 3*(1), 17–30.

Davey, M. (2010, May 13). Online talk, suicides and a thorny court case. *New York Times.* Retrieved on June 24, 2011, from www.nytimes. com.

Davey, M. (2010, May 14). Did he encourage suicide online? www.ndtv.com.

David, L., Broft, A., & Walsh, B. T. (2011). Pharmacotherapy of eating disorders. In J. Alexander & J. Treasure (Eds.), *A collaborative approach to eating disorders* (pp. 114–124). New York: Taylor & Francis.

Davidson, J. R. T., Connor, K. M., Hertzberg, M. A., Weisler, R. H., Wilson, W. H., & Payne, V. M. (2005). Maintenance therapy with fluoxetine in posttraumatic stress disorder: A placebo-controlled discontinuation study. *Journal of Clinical Psychopharmacology, 25*(2), 166–169.

Davidson, L., Rakfeldt, J., & Strauss, J. (2010). *The roots of the recovery movement in psychiatry: Lessons learned.* Hoboken, NJ: John Wiley & Sons.

Davis, E., Burden, R., & Manning, R. (2010). Early intervention and vocational opportunities. In P. French, J. Smith, D. Shiers, M. Reed, & M. Rayne (Eds.), *Promoting recovery in early psychosis: A practice manual* (pp. 140–146). Hoboken, NJ: Wiley-Blackwell.

Davis, J. O., & Phelps, J. A. (1995). Twins with schizophrenia: Genes or germs? *Schizophrenia Bulletin, 21*(1), 13–18.

Davis, M. (1992). Analysis of aversive memories using the fear potentiated startle paradigm. In N. Butters & L. R. Squire (Eds.), *The neuropsychology of memory* (2nd ed.). New York: Guilford Press.

Davis, R. E., Couper, M. P., Janz, N. K., Caldwell, C. H., & Resnicow, K. (2010). Interviewer effects in public health surveys. *Health Education Research, 25*(1), 14–26.

Davis, T. E., III, & Ollendick, T. H. (2011). Specific phobias. In D McKay & E. A. Storch (Eds.), *Handbook of child and adolescent anxiety disorders* (pp. 231–244). New York: Springer Science & Business Media.

Davison, S. L., & Davis, S. R. (2011). Androgenic hormones and aging—the link with female sexual function. *Hormones and Behavior, 59*(5), 745–753.

Daw, J. (2001). APA's disaster response network: Help on the scene. *Monitor on Psychology, 32*(10), 14–15.

Dawes, R. M., Faust, D., & Meehl, P. E. (2002). Clinical versus actuarial judgment. In D. Kahneman, T. Gilovich, & D. Griffin (Eds.), *Heuristics and biases: The psychology of intuitive judgment* (pp. 716–729). New York: Cambridge University Press.

DAWN (Drug Abuse Warning Network). (2010). National estimates of drug-related emergency department visits, 2004–2009. Retrieved on June 29, 2011, from https:// dawninfo.samhsa.gov/data/report.

Dawson, G. R., Collinson, N., & Atack, J. R. (2005). Development of subtype selective GABA-sub(A) modulators. *CNS Spectrums, 10*(1), 21–27.

Dawson, J. (2010). Compulsory outpatient treatment and the calculus of human rights. In

B. McSherry & P. Weller (Eds.), *Rethinking rights-based mental health law* (pp. 327–354). Portland, OR: Hart Publishing.

Day, D. O., & Moseley, R. L. (2010). Munchausen by proxy syndrome. *Journal of Forensic Psychology Practice, 10*(1), 13–36.

Day, E., & Strang, J. (2011). Outpatient versus inpatient opioid detoxification: A randomized controlled trial. *Journal of Substance Abuse Treatment, 40*(1), 56–66.

Day, J. M. (2010). Religion, spirituality, and positive psychology in adulthood: A developmental view. *Journal of Adult Development, 17*(4), 215–229.

de l'Etoile, S. K. (2002). The effect of musical mood induction procedure on mood state-dependent word retrieval. *Journal of Music Therapy, 39*(2), 145–160.

DeMatteo, D., Heilbrun, K., & Marczyk, G. (2005). Psychopathy, risk of violence, and protective factors in a noninstitutionalized and noncriminal sample. *International Journal of Forensic Mental Health, 4*(2), 147–157.

DEA (Drug Enforcement Administration). (2000, May 16). DEA congressional testimony before the committee on education and the workforce: Subcommittee on early childhood and families.

Dean, A. C., & London, E. D. (2010). Cerebral deficits associated with impaired cognition and regulation of emotion in methamphetamine abuse. In J. D. Kassel (Ed.), *Substance abuse and emotion* (pp. 237–257). Washington, DC: American Psychological Association.

DeAngelis, T. (2008). PTSD treatments grow in evidence, effectiveness. *Monitor on Psychology, 39*(1), 40–43.

Deas, D., Gray, K., & Upadhyaya, H. (2008). Evidence-based treatments for adolescent substance use disorders. In R. G. Steele, T. D. Elkin, & M. C. Roberts (Eds.), *Handbook of evidence-based therapies for children and adolescents* (pp. 429–444). New York: Springer.

Deb, P., Li, C., Trivedi, P. K., & Zimmer, D. M. (2006). The effect of managed care on use of health care services: Results from two contemporary household surveys. *Health Economics, 15*(7), 743–760

Degun-Mather, M. (2002). Hypnosis in the treatment of a case of dissociative amnesia for a 12-year period. *Contemporary Hypnosis, 19*(1), 34–31.

Deitz, S. M. (1977). An analysis of programming DRL schedules in educational settings. *Behavioral Research and Therapy, 15*(1), 103–111.

Delahanty, D. L. (2011). Toward the predeployment detection of risk for PTSD. *American Journal of Psychiatry, 168*(1), 9–11.

Delahanty, D. L., Nugent, N. R., Christopher, N. C., & Walsh, M. (2005). Initial urinary epinephrine and cortisol levels predict acute PTSD symptoms in child trauma victims. *Psychoneuroendocrinology, 30*(2), 121–128.

Delay, J., & Deniker, P. (1952). Le traitment des psychoses par une méthode neurolytique derivée d'hibernothérapie: Le 4560 RP utilisé seul en cure prolongée et continuée. *Congrès des Médicins Aliénistes et Neurologistes de France et des Pays du Langue Francaise, 50,* 503–513.

De Leo, D., & Evans, R. (2004). *International suicide rates and prevention strategies.* Cambridge, MA: Hogrefe & Huber.

de Leon, M. J., Mosconi, L., Blennow, K., De Santi, S., Zinkowski, R., Mehta, P. D.,

et al. (2007). Imaging and CSF studies in the preclinical diagnosis of Alzheimer's disease. In H. Federoff, M. J. de Leon, & D. A. Snider (Eds.), *Imaging and the aging brain* (pp. 114–145). Malden, MA: Blackwell.

Delinsky, S. S. (2011). Body image and anorexia nervosa. In T. F. Cash & L. Smolak, *Body image: A handbook of science, practice, and prevention.* New York: Guilford Press.

Dell, P. F. (2010). Involuntariness in hypnotic responding and dissociative symptoms. *Journal of Trauma & Dissociation, 11*(1), 1–18.

Della Sala, S. (2011). A daguerreotype of Phineas Gage? *Cortex: Journal Devoted to the Study of the Nervous System and Behavior, 47*(4), 415.

DeLuca, N. L., Moser, L. L., & Bond, G. R. (2008). Assertive community treatment. In K. T. Mueser & D. V. Jeste (Eds.), *Clinical handbook of schizophrenia* (pp. 329–338). New York: Guilford Press.

de Maat, S. M., Dekker, J., Schoevers, R. A., & de Jonghe, F. (2007). Relative efficacy of psychotherapy and combined therapy in the treatment of depression: A meta-analysis. *European Psychiatry, 22*(1), 1–8.

DeMatteo, D., Batastini, A., Foster, E., & Hunt, E. (2010). Individualizing risk assessment: Balancing idiographic and nomothetic data. *Journal of Forensic Psychology Practice, 10*(4), 360–371.

Demircin, S., Akkoyun, M., Yilmaz, R., Gökdogan, M. R. (2011). Suicide of elderly persons: Towards a framework for prevention. *Geriatrics & Gerontology International, 11*(1), 107–113.

Dendy, C. A. Z. (2011). *Teaching teens with ADD, ADHD & executive function deficits: A quick reference guide for teachers and parents* (2nd ed.). Bethesda, MD: Woodbine House.

Dennis, J. P., & Brown, G. K. (2011). Suicidal older adults: Suicide risk assessments, safety planning, and cognitive behavioral therapy. In K. H. Sorocco & S. Lauderdale (Eds.), *Cognitive behavior therapy with older adults: Innovations across care settings* (pp. 95–123). New York: Springer Publishing.

Dennison, S. (2007). Criminal responsibility. In D. Carson, R. Milne, F. Pakes, K. Shalev, & A. Shawyer (Eds.), *Applying psychology to criminal justice.* Hoboken, NJ: John Wiley & Sons.

Deplanque, D. (2005). Recreational cannabis use: Not so harmless! *Journal of Neurology and Neurosurgical Psychiatry, 76*(3), 306.

Derenne, J. L., & Beresin, E. V. (2006). Body image, media, and eating disorders. *Academic Psychiatry, 30*(3), 257–261.

Dermitzakis, E. T. (2011). Essays on science and society: Genome-sequencing anniversary-- Gename literacy. *Science, 331*(6018), 689–690.

Dervic, K., Brent, D. A., & Oquendo, M. A. (2008). Completed suicide in childhood. *Psychiatric Clinics of North America, 31*(2), 271–291.

De Sousa, A. A., De Sousa, J. A., & Kapoor, H. (2008). An open randomized trial comparing disulfiram and topiramate in the treatment of alcohol dependence. *Journal of Substance Abuse Treatment, 34*(4), 460–463.

Devanand, D. P. (2011). Psychosis. In C. E. Coffey, J. L. Cummings, M. S. George, & D. Weintraub (Eds.), *The American Psychiatric Publishing textbook*

of geriatric neuropsychiatry. Arlington, VA: American Psychiatric Publishing, Inc.

DeVeaugh-Geiss, J., Moroz, G., Biederman, J., Cantwell, D. P., et al. (1992). Clomipramine hydrochloride in childhood and adolescent obsessive compulsive disorder. A multicenter trial. *Journal of the American Academy of Child and Adolescent Psychiatry, 31*(1), 45–49.

Devineni, T., & Blanchard, E. B. (2005). A randomized controlled trial of an internet-based treatment for chronic headache. *Behavioral Research and Therapy, 43,* 277–292.

deVries, M. W., Müller, N., Möller, H., & Saugstad, L. F. (2008). Emil Kraepelin's legacy: Systematic clinical observation and the categorical classification of psychiatric diseases. *European Archives of Psychiatry and Clinical Neuroscience, 258,* 1–2.

de Wit, H., & Phan, L. (2010). Positive reinforcement theories of drug use. In J. D. Kassel (Ed.), *Substance abuse and emotion* (pp. 43–60). Washington, DC: American Psychological Association.

Dewitte, M., Van Lankveld, J., & Crombez, G. (2011). Understanding sexual pain: A cognitive-motivational account. *Pain, 152*(2), 251–253.

de Zwaan, M. (2010). Obesity treatment for binge-eating disorder in the obese. In C. M. Grilo & J. E. Mitchell (Eds.), *The treatment of eating disorders: A clinical handbook* (pp. 428–436). New York: Guilford Press.

Dhabhar, F. S. (2011). Effects of stress on immune function: Implications for immunoprotection and immunopathology. In R. J. Contrada & A. Baum (Eds.), *The handbook of stress science: Biology, psychology, and health* (pp. 47–63). New York: Springer Publishing.

Dhawan, N., Kunik, M. E., Oldham, J., & Coverdale, J. (2010). Prevalence and treatment of narcissistic personality disorder in the community: A systematic review. *Comprehensive Psychiatry, 51*(4), 333–339.

Dhejne, C., Lichtenstein, P., Boman, M., Johansson, A. L. V., Langström, N., & Landén, M. (2011). Long-term follow-up of transsexual persons undergoing sex reassignment surgery: Cohort study in Sweden. *PLoS ONE, 6*(2), article e16885.

Dhossche, D., van-der-Steen, F., Ferdinand, R. (2002). Somatoform disorders in children and adolescents: A comparison with other internalizing disorders. *Annals of Clinical Psychiatry, 14*(1), 23–31.

Dickens, B. M., Boyle, J. M., Jr., & Ganzini, L. (2008). Euthanasia and assisted suicide. In A. M. Viens & P. A. Singer (Eds.), *The Cambridge textbook of bioethics* (pp. 72–77). New York: Cambridge University Press.

Dickerson, D. (2011). American Indians and Alaskan natives. In J. H. Lowinson & P. Ruiz (Eds.), *Substance abuse: A comprehensive textbook, fifth edition.* Philadelphia, PA: Lippincott, Williams, & Wilkins.

Dickerson, F. B., Tenhula, W. N., & Green-Paden, L. D. (2005). The token economy for schizophrenia: Review of the literature and recommendations for future research. *Schizophrenia Research, 75*(2–3), 405–416.

Dickinson, T., Cook, M., Playle, J., & Hallett, C. (2012). "Queer" treatments: Giving a voice to former patients who received treatments for their "sexual deviations." *Journal of Clinical Nursing, 21*(9-10), 1345–1354.

DiClemente, C. C., Garay, M., & Gemmell, L. (2008). Motivational enhancement. In H. D. Kleber & M. Galanter (Eds.), *The American Psychiatric Publishing textbook of substance abuse treatment* (4th ed., pp. 361–371). Arlington, VA: American Psychiatric Publishing.

Didie, E. R., Kelly, M. M., & Phillips, K. A. (2010). Clinical features of body dysmorphic disorder. *Psychiatric Annals, 40*(7), 310–316.

Diefenbach, M. A., Mohamed, N. E., Turner, G., & Diefenbach, C. S. (2010). Psychosocial interventions for patients with cancer. In J. M. Suls, K. W. Davidson, & R. M. Kaplan (Eds.), *Handbook of health psychology and behavioral medicine* (pp. 462–475). New York: Guilford Press.

Diener, E. (2000, January). Subjective well-being: The science of happiness and a proposal for a national index. *American Psychologist, 55*(1), 34–43.

Diener, E., Gohm, C. L., Suh, E., & Oishi, S. (2000, July). Similarity of the relations between marital status and subjective well-being across cultures. *Journal of Cross-Cultural Psychology, 31*(4), 419–436.

Diener, E., Kahneman, D., Tov, W., & Arora, R. (2010). Income's association with judgments of life versus feelings. In E. Diener, J. F. Helliwell, & D. Kahneman (Eds.), *International differences in well-being*. New York: Oxford University Press.

Diener, E., Ng, W., Harter, J., & Arora, R. (2010). Wealth and happiness across the world: Material prosperity predicts life evaluation, whereas psychosocial prosperity predicts positive feeling. *Journal of Personality and Social Psychology, 99*(1), 52–61.

Dijkstra, B. A. G., De Jong, C. A. J., Wensing, M., Krabbe, P. F. M., & Van Der Staak, C. P. F. (2010). Opioid detoxification: From controlled clinical trial to clinical practice. *American Journal on Addictions, 19*(3), 283–290.

Dike, C. C., Baranoski, M., & Griffith, E. E. H. (2005). Pathological lying revisited. *Journal of the American Academy of Psychiatry and the Law, 33*(3), 342–349.

Dike, C., Baranoski, M., & Griffith, E. E. H. (2006). What is pathological lying? *British Journal of Psychiatry, 189*(1), 86.

Diler, R. S., Birmaher, B., & Miklowitz, D. J. (2010). Clinical presentation and longitudinal course of bipolar disorders in children and adolescents. In D. J. Miklowitz & D. Cichetti (Eds.), *Understanding bipolar disorder: A developmental psychopathology perspective* (pp. 135–165). New York: Guilford Press.

Dilsaver, S. C. (2011). An estimate of the minimum economic burden of bipolar I and II disorders in the United States: 2009. *Journal of Affective Disorders, 129*(1-3), 79–83.

Dilts, S. L., Jr., & Dilts, S. L. (2005). Opioids. In R. J. Frances, S. I. Miller & A. H. Mack (Eds.), *Clinical textbook of addictive disorders* (3rd ed., pp. 138–156). New York: Guilford Publications.

Dilts, S. L., Jr., & Dilts, S. L. (2011) Opioids. In R. J. Frances, S. I. Miller, & A. H. Mack (Eds.), *Clinical textbook of addictive disorders* (3rd ed., Chap. 7). New York: Guilford Press.

Dimsdale, J. E., & Creed, F. H. (2010). The proposed diagnosis of somatic symptom disorders in DSM-V to replace somatoform disorders in DSM-IV—A preliminary report. *Journal of Psychosomatic Research, 68*(1), 99–100.

Dimsdale, J., Sharma, N., & Sharpe, M. (2011). What do physicians think of somatoform disorders? *Psychosomatics: Journal of Consultation Liaison Psychiatry, 52*(2), 154–159.

Dingfelder, S. F. (2010). Time capsule: The first modern psychology study. *Monitor on Psychology, 41*(7).

Di Rosa, M., Kofahl, C., McKee, K., Bien, B., Lamura, G., Prouskas, C., Döhner, H., & Mnich, E. (2011). A typology of caregiving situations and service use in family careers of older people in sex European countries: The EUROFAMCARE study. *GeroPsych: The Journal of Gerontopsychology and Geriatric Psychiatry, 24*(1), 5–18.

Doctor, R. M., & Neff, B. (2001). Sexual disorders. In H. S. Friedman (Ed.), *Specialty articles from the encyclopedia of mental health*. San Diego: Academic Press.

Dodes, L. M., & Khantzian, E. J. (2005). Individual psychodynamic psychotherapy. In R. J. Frances, A. H. Mack, & S. I. Miller (Eds.), *Clinical textbook of addictive disorders* (3rd ed., pp. 457–473). New York: Guilford Press.

Dodes, L. M., & Khantzian, E. J. (2011). Individual psychodynamic psychotherapy. In R. J. Frances, S. I. Miller, & A. H. Mack (Eds.), *Clinical textbook of addictive disorders* (3rd ed., Chap. 21). New York: Guilford Press.

Doering, S., Hörz, S., Rentrop, M., Fischer-Kern, M., Schuster, P., Benecke, C., Buchheim, A., Martius, P., & Buchheim, P. (2010). Transference-focused psychotherapy v. treatment by community psychotherapists for borderline personality disorder: Randomised controlled trial. *British Journal of Psychiatry, 196*(5), 389–395.

Dogu, O., & Pressman, M. R. (2011). Identification of sleepwalking gene(s): Not yet, but soon? *Neurology, 76* (1), 12–13.

Dohrmann, R. J., & Laskin, D. M. (1978). An evaluation of electromyographic feedback in the treatment of myofascial pain-dysfunction syndrome. *Journal of the American Medical Association, 96*, 656–662.

Dolak, K., & Murphy, E. (2012, March 23). Whitney Houston cause of death: How cocaine contributes to heart disease. *ABC News.*

Dolan, E. (2011). Facebook use and social anxiety: Are social behaviors different online and offline? Retrieved February 13, 2011, from www.associatedcontent.com.

Dole, V. P., & Nyswander, M. (1965). A medical treatment for heroin addiction. *Journal of the American Medical Association, 193*, 646–650.

Dole, V. P., & Nyswander, M. (1967). Heroin addiction, a metabolic disease. *Archives of Internal Medicine, 120*, 19–24.

Domino, M. E. (2012). Does managed care affect the diffusion of psychotropic medications? *Health Economics, 21*(4), 428–443.

Domschke, K., & Deckert, J. (2010). Genetics. In M. B. Stein & T. Steckler (Eds.), *Behavioral neurobiology of anxiety and its treatment. Current topics in behavioral neurosciences* (pp. 63–75). New York: Springer Science + Business Media.

Donatelli, J-A. L., Seidman, L. J., Goldstein, J. M., Tsuang, M. T., & Buka, S. L. (2010). Children of parents with affective and nonaffective psychoses: A longitudinal study of behavior problems. *American Journal of Psychiatry, 167*(11), 1331–1338., 35

Dorahy, M. J., & Huntjens, R. J. C. (2007). Memory and attentional processes in dissociative identity disorder: A review of the empirical literature. In D. Spiegel, E. Vermetten, & M. Dorahy (Eds.), *Traumatic dissociation: Neurobiology and treatment* (pp. 55–75). Washington, DC: American Psychiatric Publishing.

dos Reis, S., Butz, A., Lipkin, P. H., Anixt, J. S., Weiner, C. L., & Chernoff, R. (2006). Attitudes about stimulant medication for attention-deficit/hyperactivity disorder among African American families in an inner city community. *Journal of Behavioral Health Services and Research, 33*(4), 423–430.

Doty, R. L. (2008). The olfactory vector hypothesis of neurodegenerative disease: Is it viable? *Annals of Neurology, 63*(1), 7–15.

Doucet, S., Jones, I., Letourneau, N., Dennis C-L., & Blackmore, E. R. (2011). Interventions for the prevention and treatment of postpartum psychosis: A systematic review. *Archives of Women's Mental Health, 14*(2), 89–98.

Dougall, A. L., & Swanson, J. N. (2011). Physical health outcomes of trauma. In R. J. Contrada & A. Baum (Eds.), *The handbook of stress science: Biology, psychology, and health* (pp. 373–384). New York: Springer Publishing.

Douglas, J. (1996). *Mind hunter: Inside the FBI's elite serial crime unit.* New York: Pocket Star.

Dove, E., & Byrne, S. (2011). Obesity and eating disorders. In J. Alexander & J. Treasure (Eds.), *A collaborative approach to eating disorders* (pp. 72–86). New York: Taylor & Francis.

Doweiko, H. E. (2006). *Concepts of chemical dependency* (6th ed.). Belmont, CA: Thomson Brooks/Cole.

Doyle, A. C. (1938). The sign of the four. In *The complete Sherlock Holmes.* Garden City, NY: Doubleday.

Dozier, C. L., Iwata, B. A., & Worsdell, A. S. (2011). Assessment and treatment of foot-shoe fetish displayed by a man with autism. *Journal of Applied Behavior Analysis, 44*(1), 133–137.

Dragowski, E. A., Scharrób-del Rio, M. R., & Sandigorsk, A. L. (2011). Debates surrounding childhood gender identity disorder. In A. M. Bursztyn (Ed.), *Childhood psychological disorders: Current controversies* (pp. 167–186). Santa Barbara, CA: Praeger/ABC-CLIO.

Draguns, J. G. (2006). Culture in psychopathology—psychopathology in culture: Taking a new look at an old problem. In T. G. Plante (Ed.), *Mental disorders of the new millennium: Vol. 2: Public and social problems.* Westport, CT: Praeger Publishers.

Drescher, J. (2010). Queer diagnoses: Parallels and contrasts in the history of homosexuality, gender variance, and the Diagnostic and Statistical Manual. *Archives of Sexual Behavior, 39*(2), 427–460.

Drevets, W. C. (2000). Functional anatomical abnormalities in limbic and prefrontal cortical structures in major depression. *Progress in Brain Research, 126*, 413–431.

Drevets, W. C. (2001). Neuroimaging and neuropathological studies of depression: Implications for the cognitive-emotional features of mood disorders. *Current Opinions in Neurobiology 11*, 240–249.

Drugs.com. (2011). New drug approval process. Retrieved on February 13, 2011 from www.drugs.com/fda-approval-process.html.

Druss, B. G., & Bornemann, T. H. (2010). Improving health and health care for persons with serious mental illness: The window for US Federal policy change. *Journal of the American Medical Association, 303*(19), 1972–1973.

Druss, B. G., Perry, G. S., Presley-Cantrell, L. R., & Dhingra, S. (2010). Mental health promotion in a reformed health care system. *American Journal of Public Health, 100*(12), 1–3.

Druss, B. G., Wang, P. S., Sampson, N. A., Olfson, M., Pincus, H. A., Wells, K. B., & Kessler, R. C. (2007). Understanding mental health treatment in persons without mental diagnoses: Results from the National Comorbidity Survey Replication. *Biological Psychiatry, 64* (10), 1196–1203.

Dubovsky, S. & Dubovsky, A. (2011). Geriatric neuropsychopharmacology: Why does age matter? In C. E. Coffey, J. L. Cummings, M.S. George, & D. Weintraub (Eds.), *The American Psychiatric Publishing textbook of geriatric neuropsychiatry.* Arlington, VA: American Psychiatric Publishing, Inc.

Dubowitz, T., Bates, L. M., & Acevedo-Garcia, D. (2010). The Latino health paradox: Looking at the intersection of sociology and health. In C. E. Bird, P. Conrad, A. M. Fremont, & S. Timmermans (Eds.), *Handbook of medical sociology* (6th ed., pp. 106–123). Nashville, TN: Vanderbilt University Press.

Dudley, R., & Turkington, D. (2011). Using normalising in cognitive behavioural therapy for schizophrenia. In R. Hagen, D. Turkington, T. Berge, & R. W. Grawe (Eds.), *CBT for psychosis: A symptom-based approach, International Society for the Psychological Treatments of the Schizophrenias and Other Psychoses* (pp. 77–85). New York: Routledge/Taylor & Francis Group.

Duenwald, M. (2003, March 18). "Oldest old" still show alertness. *New York Times.* Retrieved August 2, 2008, from www.nytimes.com.

Dugas, M. J., Brillon, P., Savard, P., Turcotte, J., Gaudet, A., Ladouceur, R., Leblanc, R., & Gervais, N. J. (2010). A randomized clinical trial of cognitive-behavioral therapy and applied relaxation for adults with generalized anxiety disorder. *Behavior Therapy, 41*(1), 46–58.

Dugas, M. J., Buhr, K., & Ladouceur, R. (2004). The role of intolerance of uncertainty in etiology and maintenance. In R. G. Heimberg, C. L. Turk, & D. S. Mennin (Eds.)., *Generalized anxiety disorder: Advances in research and practice* (pp. 143–163). New York: Guilford Press.

Duke, D. C., Bodzin, D. K., Tavares, P., Geffken, G. R., & Storch, E. A. (2009). The phenomenology of hair-pulling in a community sample. *Journal of Anxiety Disorders, 23*(8), 1118–1125.

Dulichand, H. D. (2010). New drug approval process: Regulatory view. *Pharmainfo.net, 8*(4). www.pharmainfo.net/reviews.

Dunbar, F. (1948). *Synopsis of psychosomatic diagnosis and treatment.* St. Louis: Mosby.

Dunn, A. L., Trivedi, M. H., Kampert, J. B., Clark, C. G., & Chambliss, H. O. (2005). Exercise treatment for depression: Efficacy and dose response. *American Journal of Preventative Medicine, 28*(1), 1–8.

Dunn, E. F., & Steiner, M. (2000). The functional neurochemistry of mood disorders in women.

In M. Steiner, K. A. Yonkers, & E. Erikson (Eds.), *Mood disorders in women* (pp. 71–82). London: Martin Dunitz.

DuPaul, G. J., & Kern, L. (2011). Assessment and identification of attention-deficit/hyperactivity disorder. In G. J. DuPaul & K. Lee. (Eds.), *Young children with ADHD: Early identification and intervention* (2nd ed., pp. 23–46). Washington, DC: American Psychological Association.

DuPaul, G. J., & Kern, L. (2011). Preschool-based behavioral intervention strategies. In G. J. DuPaul & K. Lee. (Eds.), *Young children with ADHD: Early identification and intervention* (2nd ed., pp. 87–106). Washington, DC: American Psychological Association.

DuPaul, G. J., & Kern, L. (2011). Support for families. In G. J. DuPaul & K. Lee. (Eds.), *Young children with ADHD: Early identification and intervention* (2nd ed., pp. 167–183). Washington, DC: American Psychological Association.

Dupont, R. L., & Dupont, C. M. (2005). Sedatives/hypnotics and benzodiazepines. In R. J. Frances, A. H. Mack, & S. I. Miller (Eds.), *Clinical textbook of addictive disorders* (3rd ed., pp. 219–242). New York: Guilford Press.

Dupont, R. L., & Dupont, C. M. (2011). Sedatives/Hypnotics and benzodiazepines. In R. J. Frances, S. I. Miller, & A. H. Mack (Eds.), *Clinical textbook of addictive disorders* (3rd ed., Chap. 10). New York: Guilford Press.

Durkheim, E. (1951). *Suicide.* New York: Free Press. (Work republished 1951), 299

Durkin, K. F., & Hundersmarck, S. (2008). Pedophiles and child molesters. In E. Goode & D. A. Vail (Eds.), *Extreme deviance.* Los Angeles: Pine Forge Press.

Durkin, M. S., Khan, N. Z., Davidson, L. L., Huq, S., Munir, S., Rasul, I., & Zaman, S. S. (2000). Prenatal and postnatal risk factors for mental retardation among children in Bangladesh. *American Journal of Epidemiology,* 152, 1024–32.

Durso, L. E., Latner, J. D., White, M. A., Masheb, R. M., Blomquist, K. K., Morgan, P. T., & Grilo, C. M. (2012). Internalized weight bias in obese patients with binge eating disorder: Associations with eating disturbances and psychological functioning. *International Journal of Eating Disorders, 45*(3), 423–427.

Durso, S., Bowker, L., Price, J., & Smith, S. (2010). *Oxford American handbook of geriatric medicine.* New York: Oxford University Press.

Duval-Harvey, J., & Rogers, K. M. (2010). Attention-deficit/hyperactivity disorder. In R. L. Hampton, T. P. Gullotta, & R. L. Crowel (Eds.), *Handbook of African American health* (pp. 375–418). New York: Guilford Press.

Dwight-Johnson, M., & Lagomasino, I. T. (2007). Addressing depression treatment preferences of ethnic minority patients. *General Hospital Psychiatry, 29*(3), 179–181.

Dykens, E. M., & Hodapp, R. M. (2001). Research in mental retardation: Toward an etiologic approach. *Journal of Child Psychology and Psychiatry, 42*(1), 49–71.

Easterbrook, G. (2005, January 17). The real truth about money. *Time, 165*(3), A32–A34.

Eaton, W. W., Kalaydjian, A., Scharfstein, D. O., Mezuk, B., & Ding, Y. (2007). Prevalence and incidence of depressive disorder: The Baltimore ECA follow-up, 1981–2004. *Acta Psychiatrica Scandinavica, 116*(3), 182–188.

Eaton, W. W., Shao, H., Nestadt, G., Lee, B. H., Bienvenu, O. J., & Zandi, P. (2008). Population-based study of first onset and chronicity in major depressive disorder. *Archives of General Psychiatry, 65*(5), 513–520.

Eckenrode, J. (2011). Primary prevention of child abuse and maltreatment. In M. P. Koss, J. W. White, & A E. Kazdin (Eds.), *Violence against women and children: Vol. 2. Navigating solutions* (pp. 71–91). Washington, DC: American Psychological Association.

Eddy, K. T., Dutra, L., Bradley, R., & Westen, D. (2004). A multidimensional meta-analysis of psychotherapy and pharmacotherapy for obsessive-compulsive disorder. *Clinical Psychological Review, 24,* 1011–1030.

Edelstein, B. A., Stoner, S. A., & Woodhead, E. (2008). Older adults. In M. Hersen & J. Rosqvist (Eds.), *Handbook of psychological assessment, case conceptualization and treatment: Vol. 1. Adults.* Hoboken, NJ: Wiley.

Edlinger, M., Hofer, A., Rettenbacher, M. A., Baumgartner, S., Widschwendter, C. G., Kemmler, G., Neco, N. A., & Fleischhacker, W. W. (2009). Factors influencing the choice of new generation antipsychotic medication in the treatment of patients with schizophrenia. *Schizophrenia Research, 113*(2–3), 246–251.

Edmunds, J. M., O'Neil, K. A., & Kendall, P. C. (2011). A review of cognitive-behavioral therapy for anxiety disorders in children and adolescents: Current status and future directions. *Tidsskrift for Norsk Psykoilogforening, 48*(1), 26–33.

Edoka, I. P., Petrou, S., & Ramchandani, P. G. (2011). Healthcare costs of paternal depression in the postnatal period. *Journal of Affective Disorders, 133*(1-2), 356–360.

Eeles, E. & Bhat, R. S. (2010). Delirium. In H. M. Fillit, K. Rockwood, K. Woodhouse. (Eds.), *Brocklehurst's textbook of geriatric medicine and gerontology, 7th edition.* Philadelphia, PA: Saunders Publishers.

Egan, M. F., & Cannon, T. D. (2011). Intermediate phenotypes in genetic studies of schizophrenia. In D. R. Weinberg & P. Harrison (Eds.), *Schizophrenia* (pp. 289–310). Hoboken, NJ: Wiley-Blackwell.

Egelko, S., Galanter, M., Dermatis, H., Jurewicz, E., Jamison, A., Dingle, S., et al. (2002). Improved psychological status in a modified therapeutic community for homeless MICA men. *Journal of Addictive Diseases, 21*(1), 75–92.

Ehnvall, A., Parker, G., Hadzi, P. D., & Malhi, G. (2008). Perception of rejecting and neglectful parenting in childhood relates to lifetime suicide attempts for females—but not for males. *Acta Psychiatrica Scandinavica, 117*(1), 50–56.

Eifert, G. H., Greco, L. A., Heffner, M., & Louis, A. (2007). Eating disorders: A new behavioral perspective and acceptance-based treatment approach. In D. W. Woods & J. W. Kanter (Eds.), *Understanding behavior disorders: A contemporary behavioral perspective.* Reno, NV: Context Press.

Eisen, A. R., Sussman, J. M., Schmidt, T., Mason, L., Hausler, L. A., & Hashim, R. (2011). Separation anxiety disorder. In D. McKay & E. A. Storch (Eds.), *Handbook of child and adolescent anxiety disorders* (pp. 245–259). New York: Springer Science & Business Media.

Eisner, B. (1986). *Ecstasy: The MDMA story.* Boston, MA: Little, Brown.

Elder, B. L., & Mosack, V. (2011). Genetics of depression: An overview of the current science. *Issues in Mental Health Nursing, 32*(4), 192–202.

el-Guebaly, N. (2011). Cross-cultural aspects of addiction therapy. In M. Galanter & H. D. Kleber (Eds.), *Psychotherapy for the treatment of substance abuse* (pp. 81–97). Arlington, VA: American Psychiatric Publishing.

Elhai, J. D., Ford, J. D., & Naifeh, J. A. (2010). Assessing trauma exposure and posttraumatic morbidity. In G. M. Rosen, & B. C. Frueh (Eds.), *Clinician's guide to posttraumatic stress disorder* (pp. 119–151). Hoboken, NJ: John Wiley & Sons.

Elias, M. (2006, May 24). Psychiatric drugs fare favorably when companies pay for studies. *USA Today.* Retrieved July 6, 2007, at www.usatoday.com/news/health/2006-05-24-drug-studies_x.htm?csp=34.

Elkin, I. (1994). The NIMH Treatment of Depression Collaborative Research Program: Where we began and where we are. In A. E. Bergin & S. L. Garfield (Eds.), *Handbook of psychotherapy and behavior change* (4th ed.). New York: Wiley.

Elkin, I., Parloff, M. B., Hadley, S. W., & Autry, J. H. (1985). National Institute of Mental Health Treatment of Depression Collaborative Research Program: Background and research plan. *Archives of General Psychiatry, 42,* 305–316.

Elkin, I., Shea, M. T., Watkins, J. T., Imber, S. D., et al. (1989). National Institute of Mental Health Treatment of Depression Collaborative Research Program: General effectiveness of treatments. *Archives of General Psychiatry, 46*(11), 971–982.

Elkins, S. R., & Moore, T. M. (2011). A time-series study of the treatment of panic disorder. *Clinical Case Studies, 10*(1), 3–22.

Ellenberger, H. F. (1970). *The discovery of the unconscious.* New York: Basic Books.

Ellenberger, H. F. (1972). The story of "Anna O.": A critical review with new data. *Journal of the History of the Behavioral Sciences, 8,* 267–279.

Ellenbroek, B. A. (2011). Psychopharmacological treatment of schizophrenia: What do we have, and what could we get? *Neuropharmacology.*

Ellis, A. (1962). *Reason and emotion in psychotherapy.* Secaucus, NJ: Lyle Stuart.

Ellis, A. (2002). The role of irrational beliefs in perfectionism. In G. L. Flett & P. L. Hewitt (Eds.) *Perfectionism: Theory, research, and treatment* (pp. 217–229). Washington, DC: American Psychological Association.

Ellis, A. (2005). Rational-emotive therapy. In R. Corsini & D. Wedding (Eds.), *Current psychotherapies* (7th ed., pp. 166–201). Boston: Thomson/Brooks-Cole.

Ellis, A. (2008). Rational emotive behavior therapy. In R. J. Corsini & D. Wedding (Eds.), *Current psychotherapies* (8th ed.). Belmont, CA: Thomson Brooks/Cole.

Ellis, A. (2011). Rational emotive behavior therapy. In R. J. Corsini & D. Wedding (Eds.), *Current psychotherapies* (9th ed.). Belmont, CA: Brooks/Cole.

Elms, A. C. (2007). Psychobiography and case study methods. In R. F. Krueger, R. W. Robins, & R. C. Fraley (Eds.), *Handbook of research methods in personality psychology* (pp. 97–113). New York: Guilford Press.

Elovainio, M., Merjonen, P., Pulkki-Raback, L., Kivimäki, M., Jokela, M., Mattson, N., Koskinen, T., Viikari, J. S. A., Raitakari, O. T., & Keltikangas-Järvinen, L. (2011). Hostility, metabolic syndrome, inflammation and cardiac control in young adults: The young Finns study. *Biological Psychology, 87*(2), 234–240.

Elwood, C. E., Poythress, N. G., & Douglas, K. S. (2004). Evaluation of the Hare P-SCAN in a non-clinical population. *Personality and Individual Differences, 36*(4), 833–843.

Elwyn, T. S., Tseng, W. S., & Matthews, D. (2010). Cultural competence in child and adolescent forensic mental health. In E. P. Benedek, P. Ash, & C. L. Scott (Eds.), *Principles and practice of child and adolescent forensic mental health* (pp. 91–106). Arlington, VA: American Psychiatric Publishing.

Emanuel, E. J., Crouch, R. A., Arras, J. D., Moreno, J. D., & Grady, C. (Eds.). (2003). *Ethical and regulatory aspects of clinical research: Readings and commentary.* Baltimore: Johns Hopkins University Press.

Emmelkamp, P. M. (1982). Exposure in vivo treatments. In A. Goldstein & D. Chambless (Eds.), *Agoraphobia: Multiple perspectives on theory and treatment.* New York: Wiley.

Emmelkamp, P. M. (1994). Behavior therapy with adults. In A. E. Bergin & S. L. Garfield (Eds.), *Handbook of psychotherapy and behavior change* (4th ed.). New York: Wiley.

Emmons, K. K. (2010). *Black dogs and blue words: Depression and gender in the age of self-care.* Piscataway, NJ: Rutgers University Press.

Endrass, T., Kloft, L., Kaufmann, C., & Kaufmann, N. (2011). Approach and avoidance learning in obsessive-compulsive disorder. *Depression and Anxiety, 28*(2), 166–172.

Engel, G. L. (1968). A life setting conducive to illness: The giving-up-given-up complex. *Annals of Internal Medicine, 69,* 293.

Engel, J. (2009). Migraines/chronic headaches. In W. T. O'Donohue & L. W. Tolle (Eds.), *Behavioral approaches to chronic disease in adolescence: A guide to integrative care* (pp. 155–161). New York: Springer Science + Business Media.

Engel, J. M., Jensen, M. P., & Schwartz, L. (2004). Outcome of biofeedback-assisted relaxation for pain in adults with cerebral palsy: Preliminary findings. *Applied Psychophysiology and Biofeedback, 29*(2), 135–140.

Engman, M., Wijma, K., & Wjima, B. (2010). Long-term coital behaviour in women treated with cognitive behaviour therapy for superficial coital pain and vaginismus. *Cognitive Behaviour Therapy, 39*(3), 193–202.

Engstrom, E. J., Weber, M. M., Burgmair, W. (2006). Emil Wilhelm Magnus Georg Kraepelin (1856–1926). *American Journal of Psychiatry, 163*(10), 1710.

Epstein, D. H., Phillips, K. A., & Preston, K. L. (2011). Opioids. In J. H. Lowinson & P. Ruiz (Eds.), *Substance abuse: A comprehensive textbook, fifth edition.* Philadelphia, PA: Lippincott, Williams, & Wilkins.

Epstein, R. (2001). In her own words. *Psychology Today, 34*(6), 36–37.

Erb, S., & Placenza, F. (2011). Relapse. In M. C. Olmstead (Ed.), *Animal models of drug addiction. Springer protocols: Neuromethods* (pp. 461–479). Totowa, NJ: Humana Press.

Erikson, E. (1963). *Childhood and society.* New York: Norton.

Erlangsen, A., Vach, W., & Jeune, B. (2005). The effect of hospitalization with medical illnesses on the suicide risk in the oldest old: A population-based register study. *Journal of the American Geriatrics Society, 53*(5), 771–776.

Ernsberger, P. (2009). Does social class explain the connection between weight and health? In E. Rothblum & S. Solovay (Eds.), *The fat studies reader* (pp. 25–36). New York: University Press.

ESA (Entertainment Software Association). (2011). 2011 Sales, demographic and usage data. Essential facts about the computer and video game industry. Retrieved on August 7, 2011, from www.theesa.com/facts/m=gameplayer.asp.

Escalante, P. R., Minshew, N. J., & Sweeney, J. A. (2003). Abnormal brain lateralization in high-functioning autism. *Journal of Autism and Development Disorders, 33,* 539–543.

Escobar, J. I. (1995). Transcultural aspects of dissociative and somatoform disorders. *Psychiatric Clinics of North America, 18*(3), 555–569.

Escobar, J. I. (1998). Immigration and mental health: Why are immigrants better off? *Archives of General Psychiatry, 55*(9), 781–782.

Escobar, J. I. (2004, April 15). Transcultural aspects of dissociative and somatoform disorders. *Psychiatric Times, 21*(5), 10.

Escobar, J. I., Canino, G., Rubio-Stipec, M., & Bravo, M. (1992). Somatic symptoms after a natural disaster: A prospective study. *American Journal of Psychiatry, 149*(7), 965–967.

Escobar, J. I., Gara, M., Silver, R. C., Waitzkin, H., Holman, A., & Compton, W. (1998). Somatisation disorder in primary care. *British Journal of Psychiatry, 173,* 262–266.

Escobar, J. I., Randolph, E. T., Puente, G., Spiwak, F., Asamen, J. K., Hill, M., et al. (1983). Posttraumatic stress disorder in Hispanic Vietnam veterans: Clinical phenomenology and sociocultural characteristics. *Journal of Nervous and Mental Disease, 171,* 585–596.

Eser, A. (1981). "Sanctity" and "quality" of life in a historical comparative view. In S. E. Wallace & A. Eser (Eds.), *Suicide and euthanasia: The rights of personhood.* Knoxville: University of Tennessee Press.

Essau, C. A., Lewinsohn, P. M., Seeley, J. R., & Sasagawa. S. (2010). Gender differences in the developmental course of depression. *Journal of Affective Disorders, 127*(1-3), 185–190.

Etaugh, C. (2008). Women in the middle and later years. In F. L. Denmark & M. A. Paludi (Eds.), *Psychology of women: A handbook of issues and theories* (2nd ed.). Westport, CT: Praeger Publishers.

Etkin, A. (2010). Functional neuroanatomy of anxiety: A neural circuit perspective. In M. B. Stein & T. Steckler (Eds.), *Behavioral neurobiology of anxiety and its treatment. Current topics in behavioral neurosciences* (pp. 251–277). New York: Springer Science + Business Media.

Evans, G. W. (2006). Child development and the physical environment. *Annual Review of Psychology, 57,* 423–451.

Evans, J., Heron, J., Lewis, G., Araya, R., & Wolke, D. (2005). Negative self-schemas and the onset of depression in women: Longitudinal study. *British Journal of Psychiatry, 186*(4), 302–307.

Evans, J., & Waller, G. (2012). The therapeutic alliance in cognitive behavioural therapy for adults with eating disorders. In J. Alexander & J. Treasure (Eds.), *A collaborative approach to eating disorders* (pp. 163–176). New York: Routledge/Taylor & Francis.

Evans, M., Donelle, L., & Hume-Loveland, L. (2012). Social support and online postpartum depression discussion groups: A content analysis. *Patient Education and Counseling, 87*(3), 405–410.

Evans, S., & Burghardt, P. (2011). Exercise, nutrition, and treatment resistant depression. In J. F. Greden, M. B. Riba, & M. G. McInnis (Eds.), *Treatment resistant depression: A roadmap for effective care* (pp. 237–252). Arlington, VA: American Psychiatric Publishing.

Everson, S. A., Goldberg, D. E., Kaplan, G. A., Cohen, R. D., et al. (1996). Hopelessness and risk of mortality and incidence of myocardial infarction and cancer. *Psychosomatic Medicine, 58,* 113–121.

Ewen, R. B. (2010). *An introduction to theories of personality* (7th ed.). New York: Psychology Press.

Ewing, C. P. (2011). *Justice perverted: Sex offense law, psychology, and public policy*. New York: Oxford University Press.

Eyler, L. T. (2008). Brain imaging. In K. T. Mueser & D. V. Jeste (Eds.), *Clinical handbook of schizophrenia* (pp. 35–43). New York: Guilford Press.

Faber, R. J. (2011). Diagnosis and epidemiology of compulsive buying. In A. Müller & J. E. Mitchell (Eds.), *Compulsive buying: Clinical foundations and treatment. Practical clinical guidebooks* (pp. 3–17). New York: Routledge/Taylor & Francis Group.

Fabian, J. M. (2011). Paraphilias and predators: The ethical application of psychiatric diagnoses in partisan sexually violent predator civil commitment proceedings. *Journal of Forensic Psychology Practice, 11*(1), 82–98.

Fábrega, H., Jr. (1990). The concept of somatization as a cultural and historical product of Western medicine. *Psychosomatic Medicine, 52*(6), 653–672.

Fábrega, H., Jr. (2002). *Origins of psychopathology: The phylogenetic and cultural basis of mental illness*. New Brunswick, NJ: Rutgers University Press.

Fábrega, H., Jr. (2006). Why psychiatric conditions are special: An evolutionary and cross-cultural perspective. *Perspectives in Biology and Medicine, 49*(4), 586–601.

Fábrega, H., Jr. (2010). Understanding the evolution of medical traditions: Brain/behavior influences, enculturation, and the study of sickness and healing. *Neuropsychoanalysis, 12*(1), 21–27.

Fahrenberg, J., Foerster, F., & Wilmers, F. (1995). Is elevated blood pressure level associated with higher cardiovascular responsiveness in laboratory tasks and with response specificity? *Psychophysiology, 32*(1), 81–91.

Fairbank, J. A., & Keane, T. M. (1982). Flooding for combat-related stress disorders: Assessment of anxiety reduction across traumatic memories. *Behavior Therapist, 13,* 499–510.

Fairburn, C. G. (1985). Cognitive-behavioural treatment for bulimia. In D. M. Garner & P. E. Garfinkel (Eds.), *Handbook of psychotherapy for anorexia nervosa and bulimia*. New York: Guilford Press.

Fairburn, C. G., Agras, W. S., Walsh, B. T., Wilson, G. T., & Stice, E. (2004). Prediction of outcome in bulimia nervosa by early change in treatment. *American Journal of Psychiatry, 161*(12), 2322–2324.

Fairburn, C. G., Cooper, Z., Shafran, R., & Wilson, G. T. (2008). Eating disorders: A transdiagnostic protocol. In D. H. Barlow (Ed.), *Clinical handbook of psychological disorders: A step-by-step treatment manual* (4th ed.). New York: Guilford Press.

Falzer, P. R. (2011). Expertise in assessing and managing risk of violence. The contribution of naturalistic decision making. In K. L. Mosier & U. M. Fischer (Eds.), *Informed by knowledge: Expert performance in complex situations. Expertise: Research and applications* (pp. 313–328). New York: Psychology Press.

Fändrich, M., Schmidt, M., & Grigorieff, N. (2011). Recent progress in understanding Alzheimer's β-amyloid structures. *Trends in Biochemical Sciences, 36*(6), 338–345.

Farberow, N. L., & Litman, R. E. (1970). *A comprehensive suicide prevention program*. Unpublished final report, Suicide Prevention Center of Los Angeles, Los Angeles.

Fareed, A., Vayalapalli, S., Stout, S., Casarella, J., Drexler, K., & Bailey, S. P. (2011). Effect of methadone maintenance treatment on heroin craving, a literature review. *Journal of Addictive Diseases, 30*(1), 27–38.

Farlow, M. R. (2010). Alzheimer's disease. In H. M. Fillit, K. Rockwood, K. Woodhouse. (Eds.), *Brocklehurst's textbook of geriatric medicine and gerontology, 7th edition.* Philadelphia, PA: Saunders Publishers.

Farmer, A. (2011). Antipsychotic medications and their use in first-episode psychosis. In P. French, J. Smith, D. Shiers, M. Reed, & M. Rayne (Eds.), *Promoting recovery in early psychosis: A practice manual* (pp. 73–83). Hoboken, NJ: Wiley-Blackwell.

Farmer, C. A., & Aman, M. G. (2011). Aggressive behavior in a sample of children with autism spectrum disorders. *Research in Autism Spectrum Disorders, 5*(1), 317–323.

Farmer, R. F., & Chapman, A. L. (2008). *Behavioral interventions in cognitive behavior therapy: Practical guidance for putting theory into action*. Washington, DC: American Psychological Association.

Farmer, R. F., & Nelson-Gray, R. O. (2005). Behavioral treatment of personality disorders. In R. F. Farmer & R. O. Nelson-Gray (Eds.), *Personality-guided behavior therapy* (pp. 203–243). Washington, DC: American Psychological Association.

Farrell, C., Lee, M., & Shafran, R. (2005). Assessment of body size estimation: A Review. *European Eating Disorders Review, 13*(2), 75–88.

Fatality Facts. (2004). *Alcohol*. Washington, DC: Insurance Institute for Highway Safety.

Fattal-Valevski, A. (2011). Thiamine (vitamin B₁). *Complementary Health Practice Review, 16*(1), 12–20.

Faust, D., & Ahern, D. C. (2012). Clinical judgment and prediction. In D. Faust (Ed.), *Coping with psychiatric and psychological testimony: Based on the original work by Jay Ziskin* (6th ed., pp. 147–208). New York: Oxford University Press.

Faust, J., Chapman, S., & Stewart, L. M. (2008). Neglected, physically abused, and sexually abused children. In D. Reitman (Ed.), *Handbook of psychological assessment, case conceptualization, and treatment: Vol. 2. Children and adolescents*. Hoboken, NJ: John Wiley & Sons.

Fava, M., Farabaugh, A. H., Sickinger, A. H., Wright, E., Alpert, J. E., Sonawalla, S., et al. (2002). Personality disorders and depression. *Psychological Medicine, 32*(6), 1049–1057.

Fawcett, J. (2007). Comorbid anxiety and suicide in mood disorders. *Psychiatric Annals, 37*(10), 667–671.

Fawcett, J. (2007). What has the "black box" done to reduce suicide? *Psychiatric Annals, 37*(10), 657, 662.

Fawcett, J. (2012, December 27). Bereavement exclusion. In DSM-5: A "living document" that may impact practice, patients' health. *Psychiatric Annals.*

Fawcett, J., Cameron, R. P., & Schatzberg, A. F. (2010). Mixed anxiety-depressive disorder: An undiagnosed and undertreated severity spectrum? In D. J. Stein, E. Hollander, & B. O. Rothbaum (Eds.), *Textbook of anxiety disorders* (2nd ed., pp. 241–257). Arlington, VA: American Psychiatric Publishing.

Fay, B. P. (1995). The individual versus society: The cultural dynamics of criminalizing suicide. *Hastings International and Comparative Law Review, 18,* 591–615.

Fayek, A. (2002). Analysis of a case of psychogenic amnesia: The issue of termination. *Journal of Clinical Psychoanalysis, 11*(4), 586–612.

Fazel, S., & Danesh, J. (2002). Serious mental disorder in 23,000 prisoners: A systematic review of 62 surveys. *Lancet, 359*(9306), 545–550.

Fazel, S., Grann, M., Kling, B., & Hawton, K. (2011). Prison suicide in 12 countries: An ecological study of 861 suicides during 2003–2007. *Social Psychiatry and Psychiatric Epidemiology, 46*(3), 191–195.

FBI (Federal Bureau of Investigation). (2010). Cyber investigations. Retrieved on August 22, 2010 from the Federal Bureau of Investigation: http://www.fbi.gov/cyberinvest/cyberhome.htm.

FDA (Food and Drug Administration). (2011). *FDA drug safety communication: Antipsychotic drug labels updated on use during pregnancy and risk of abnormal muscle movements and withdrawal symptoms in newborns*. Available at *Drugs.com*.

Federoff, J. P., & Marshall, W. L. (2010). Paraphilias. In D. McKay, J. S. Abramowitz, & S. Taylor (Eds.), *Cognitive-behavioral therapy for refractory cases: Turning failure into success* (pp. 369–384). Washington, DC: American Psychological Association.

Feifer, S. G. (2010). Assessing and intervening with children with reading disorders. In D. C. Miller (Ed.), *Best practices in school neuropsychology: Guidelines for effective practice., assessment, and evidence-based intervention* (pp. 483–505). Hoboken, NJ: John Wiley & Sons.

Feigelman, B., & Feigelman, W. (2011). Suicide survivor support groups: Comings and goings, Part I. *Illness, Crisis & Loss, 19*(1), 57–71.

Feigelman, W., & Gorman, B. S. (2008). Assessing the effects of peer suicide on youth suicide. *Suicide and Life-Threatening Behavior, 38*(2), 181–194.

Feldman, M. D. (2004). *Playing sick? Untangling the web of Munchausen syndrome, Munchausen by proxy, malingering and factitious disorder*. New York: Routledge.

Feldman, M. D., & Feldman, J. M. (1995). Tangled in the web: Countertransference in the therapy of factitious disorders. *International Journal of Psychiatry in Medicine, 25,* 389.

Feldman, M. D., Ford, C. V., & Reinhold, T. (1994). *Patient or pretender: Inside the strange world of factitious disorders*. New York: Wiley.

Feldman, S. R., Moritz, S. H., & Benjamin, G. A. H. (2005). Suicide and the law: A practical overview for mental health professionals. *Women and Therapy, 28*(1), 95–103.

Feliciano, L., & Gum, A. M. (2010). Mood disorders. In D. L. Segal & M. Hersen (Eds.), *Diagnostic interviewing* (pp. 153–176). New York: Springer Publishing.

Felix, A., Herman, D., & Susser, E. (2008). Housing instability and homelessness. In K. T. Mueser & D. V. Jeste (Eds.), *Clinical handbook of schizophrenia* (pp. 411–423). New York: Guilford Press.

Felix, E., Hernández, L. A., Bravo, M., Ramirez, R., Cabiya, J., & Canino, G. (2011). Natural disaster and risk of psychiatric disorders in Puerto Rican children. *Journal of Abnormal Child Psychology: An Official Publication of the International Society for Research in Child and Adolescent Psychopathology, 39*(4), 589–600.

Fellenz, M. R. (2007). *The moral menagerie: Philosophy and animal rights.* Champaign, IL: University of Illinois Press.

Fenichel, M. (2011). Online psychotherapy: Technical difficulties, formulations and processes. Retrieved on March 1, 2011, from www.fenichel.com/technical.shtml.

Fennig, S., Fennig, S., & Roe, D. (2002). Cognitive-behavioral therapy for bulimia nervosa: Time course and mechanisms of change. *General Hospital Psychiatry, 24*(2), 87–92.

Ferguson, C. J., Coulson, M., & Barnett, J. (2011). Psychological profiles of school shooters: Positive directions and one big wrong turn. *Journal of Police Crisis Negotiations, 11,*141–158.

Fernbach, P. M., Darlow, A., & Sloman, S. A. (2011, January 10). Asymmetries in predictive and diagnostic reasoning. *Journal of Experimental Psychology: General.*

Fernquist, R. M. (2007). How do Durkheimian variables impact variation in national suicide rates when proxies for depression and alcoholism are controlled? *Archives of Suicide Research, 11*(4), 361–374.

Ferrari, R. (2006). *The whiplash encyclopedia: The facts and myths of whiplash.* Boston: Jones and Bartlett.

Ferrell, G. (2011, November 15). Netherlands looks to expand euthanasia grounds to include lonely, poor. *The Daily Caller.*

Ferreri, F., Lapp, L. K., & Peretti, C-S. (2011). Current research on cognitive aspects of anxiety disorders. *Current Opinion in Psychiatry, 24*(1), 49–54.

Fetissov, S. O., & Meguid, M. M. (2010). Serotonin delivery into the ventromedial nucleus of the hypothalamus affects differently feeding pattern and body weight in obese and lean Zucker rats. *Appetite, 54*(2), 346–353.

Fetto, J. (2001, October 1). Pencil me in. *American Demographics.*

Fetto, J. (2002, April 1). What seems to be the problem? *American Demographics, 64,* 1090.

Fetto, J. (2002, May 1). Drugged out. *American Demographics.*

Fetto, J. (2002, May 1). You never call. *American Demographics, 4*(1), 8–9.

Fichter, M. M., Quadflieg, N., & Hedlund, S. (2008). Long-term course of binge eating disorder and bulimia nervosa: Relevance for nosology and diagnostic criteria. *International Journal of Eating Disorders, 41,* 577–586.

Field, A. P., & Purkis, H. M. (2012). Associative learning and phobias. In M. Haselgrove (Ed.), *Clinical applications of learning theory* (pp. 49–73). New York: Psychology Press.

Fields, J. (2004). *America's families and living arrangements, 2003* (Current Population Reports, P20-553). Washington, DC: U.S. Census Bureau.

Fieve, R. R. (1975). *Moodswing.* New York: Morrow.

Figlewicz, D. P., & Sipols, A. J. (2010). Energy regulatory signals and food reward. *Pharmacology, Biochemistry, and Behavior, 97*(1), 15–24.

Figley, C. R. (1978). Symptoms of delayed combat stress among a college sample of Vietnam veterans. *Military Medicine, 143*(2), 107–110.

Figueira, M. L., & Brissos, S. (2011). Measuring psychosocial outcomes in schizophrenia patients. *Current Opinion in Psychiatry, 24*(2), 91–99.

Finckh, U. (2001). The dopamine D2 receptor gene and alcoholism: Association studies. In D. P. Agarwal & H. K. Seitz (Eds.), *Alcohol in health and disease* (pp. 151–176). New York: Marcel Dekker.

Fine, C. G., & Madden, N. E. (2000). Group psychotherapy in the treatment of dissociative identity disorder and allied dissociative disorders. In R. H. Klein & V. L. Schermer (Eds.), *Group psychotherapy for psychological trauma* (pp. 298–325). New York: Guilford Press.

Fineberg, N. A., & Craig, K. J. (2010). Pharmacotherapy for obsessive-compulsive disorder. In D. J. Stein, E. Hollander, & B. O. Rothbaum (Eds.), *Textbook of anxiety disorders* (2nd ed., pp. 311–337). Arlington, VA: American Psychiatric Publishing.

Finfgeld, D. L. (2002). Anorexia nervosa: Analysis of long-term outcomes and clinical implications. *Archives of Psychiatric Nursing, 16*(4), 176–186.

Fink, G. (2011). Stress controversies: Post-traumatic stress disorder, hippocampal volume, gastroduodenal ulceration. *Journal of Neuroendocrinology, 23*(2), 107–117.

Fink, M. (2001). Convulsive therapy: A review of the first 55 years. *Journal of Affective Disorders, 63*(1–3), 1–15.

Fink, M. (2007). What we learn about continuation treatments from the collaborative electroconvulsive therapy studies. *Journal of ECT, 23*(4), 215–218.

Finkelhor, D., Asdigian, N., & Dziuba-Leatherman, J. (1995). Victimization prevention programs for children: A follow-up. *American Journal of Public Health, 85*(12), 1684–1689.

Finlay, I. G., & George, R. (2011). Legal physician-assisted suicide in Oregon and the Netherlands: Evidence concerning the impact on patients in vulnerable groups—Another perspective on Oregon's data. *Journal of Medical Ethics: Journal of the Institute of Medical Ethics, 37*(3), 171–174.

Finnegan, L. P., & Kandall, S. R. (2008). Perinatal substance abuse. In H. D. Kleber & M. Galanter (Eds.), *The American Psychiatric Publishing textbook of substance abuse treatment* (4th ed., pp. 565–580). Arlington, VA: American Psychiatric Publishing.

Fiori, L. M., Zouk, H., Himmelman, C., & Turecki, G. (2011). X chromosome and suicide. *Molecular Psychiatry, 16*(2), 216–226.

Fischer, B. A., IV, & Carpenter, W. T., Jr. (2008). Remission. In K. T. Mueser & D. V. Jeste (Eds.), *Clinical handbook of schizophrenia* (pp. 559–565). New York: Guilford Press.

Fisher, C. D. (2010) Happiness at work. *International Journal of Management Reviews, 12*(4), 384–412.

Fisher, J. E., Zeiss, A. M., & Carstensen, L. L. (2001). Psychopathology in the aged. In P. B. Sutker & H. E. Adams (Eds.), *Comprehensive handbook of psychopathology* (3rd ed., pp. 921–952). New York: Kluwer Academic/Plenum.

Fisher, P. H., Masia-Warner, C., & Klein, R. G. (2004). Skills for social and academic success: A school-based intervention for social anxiety disorder in adolescents. *Clinical Child and Family Psychology Review, 7*(4), 241–249.

Fisher, P. L., & Wells, A. (2011). Conceptual models of generalized anxiety disorder. *Psychiatric Annals, 41*(2), 127–132.

Fishman, D. B., Rego, S. A., & Müller, K. L. (2011). Behavioral theories of psychotherapy. In J. C. Norcross, G. R. VandenBos, & D. K. Freedheim (Eds.), *History of psychotherapy: Continuity and change* (2nd ed., pp. 101–140). Washington, DC: American Psychological Association.

Fiske, A., Zimmerman, J. A., & Scogin, F. (2011). Geropsychology mentoring: A survey of current practices and perceived needs. *Educational Gerontology, 37*(5), 370–377.

Fitz, A. (1990). Religious and familial factors in the etiology of obsessive-compulsive disorder: A review. *Journal of Psychological Theology, 18*(2), 141–147.

Fitzgerald, P. B., & Daskalakis, Z. J. (2011, April 17). A practical guide to the use of repetitive transcranial magnetic stimulation in the treatment of depression. *Brain Stimulation, 4.*

Flaskerud, J. H. (2009). What do we need to know about the culture-bound syndromes? *Issues in Mental Health Nursing, 30*(6), 406–407.

Flavin, D. K., Franklin, J. E., & Frances, R. J. (1990). Substance abuse and suicidal behavior. In S. J. Blumenthal & D. J. Kupfer (Eds.), *Suicide over the life cycle: Risk factors, assessment, and treatment of suicidal patients.* Washington, DC: American Psychiatry Press.

Fleck, D. E., Keck, P. E., Corey, K. B., & Strakowski, S. M. (2005). Factors associated with medication adherence in African American and white patients with bipolar disorder. *Journal of Clinical Psychiatry, 66*(5), 646–652.

Fletcher, R. J. (Ed.). (2011). *Psychotherapy for individuals with intellectual disability.* Kingston, NY: NADD Press.

Fletcher, T. B. (2000). Primary nocturnal enuresis: A structural and strategic family systems approach. *Journal of Mental Health Counseling, 22*(1), 32–44.

Floyd, A., Dedert, E., Ghate, S., Salmon, P., Weissbecker, I., Studts, J. L., et al. (2011). Depression may mediate the relationship between sense of coherence and quality of life in lung cancer patients. *Journal of Health Psychology, 16*(2), 249–257.

Flynn, H. A., & Himle, J. (2011). Psychotherapy strategies for treatment resistant depression. In J. F. Greden, M. B. Riba, & M. G. McInnis (Eds.), *Treatment resistant depression: A roadmap for effective care* (pp. 193–212). Arlington, VA: American Psychiatric Publishing.

Foa, E. B., Liebowitz, M. R., Kozak, M. J., Davies, S., Campeas, R., Franklin, M. E., et al. (2005). Randomized placebo-controlled trial of exposure and ritual prevention, clomipramine, and their combination in the treatment of obsessive-compulsive disorder. *American Journal of Psychiatry, 162*(1), 151–161.

Folsom, D. P., Fleisher, A. S., & Depp, C. A. (2006). Schizophrenia. In D.V. Jeste & J. H. Friedman (Eds.), *Psychiatry for neurologists* (pp. 59–66). Totowa, NJ: Humana Press.

Forcano, L., Alvarez, E., Santamaría, J. J., Jimenez-Murcia, S., Granero, R., Penelo, E., et al. (2010). Suicide attempts in anorexia nervosa subtypes. *Comprehensive Psychiatry, 52*(4), 352–358.

Ford, D. Y. (2008). Intelligence testing and cultural diversity: The need for alternative instruments, policies, and procedures. In J. L. VanTassel-Baska (Ed.), *Alternative assessments with gifted and talented students* (pp. 107–128). Waco, TX: Prufrock Press.

Ford, E. S., & LaVan, D. (2011, April 26). Death rates among people with high blood pressure falling. *Circulation.*

Ford, L. K., & Zarate, P. (2010). Closing the gaps: The impact of inpatient detoxification and continuity of care on client outcomes. *Journal of Psychoactive Drugs,* (Suppl. 6), 303–314.

Ford, M. R., & Widiger, T. A. (1989). Sex bias in the diagnosis of histrionic and antisocial personality disorders. *Journal of Consulting and Clinical Psychology, 57*(2), 301–305.

Ford, T. (2000). The influence of womanist identity on the development of eating disorders and depression in African American female college students. *Dissertation Abstracts International: Section A: Humanities and Social Sciences, 61,* 2194.

Foreyt, J. P., Poston, W. S. C., & Goodrick, G. K. (1996). Future directions in obesity and eating disorders. *Addictive Behavior, 21*(6), 767–778.

Forgatch, M. S., & Patterson, G. R. (2010). Parent Management Training—Oregon model: An intervention for antisocial behavior in children and adolescents. In J. R. Weisz, & A. E. Kazdin (Eds.), *Evidence-based psychotherapies for children and adolescents* (2nd ed., pp. 159–177) New York: Guilford Press.

Fortune, E. E., & Goodie, A. S. (2012). Cognitive distortions as a component and treatment focus of pathological gambling: A review. *Psychology of Addictive Behaviors, 26*(2), 298–310

Fortune, S. A., & Hawton, K. (2007). Suicide and deliberate self-harm in children and adolescents. *Paediatrics and Child Health, 17*(11), 443–447.

Foster, J. D., Campbell, W. K., & Twenge, J. M. (2003). Individual differences in narcissicm: Inflated self-views across the lifespan and around the world. *Journal of Research in Personality, 37,* 469–486.

Foster, T. (2011). Adverse life events proximal to adult suicide: A synthesis of findings from psychological autopsy studies. *Archives of Suicide Research, 15*(1), 1–15.

Fountaine, E. (2000, June). Stakes are high for overweight jockeys. *New York Thoroughbred Horsemen's Association Newsletter.* Available at www.nytha.com.

Fountoulakis, K. N., & Rihmer, Z. (2011). Suicide prevention programs through education in the community and in the frame of healthcare. In M. Pompili & R. Tatarelli (Eds.), *Evidence-based practice in suicidology: A source book* (pp. 153–169). Cambridge MA: Hogrefe Publishing.

Fowler, J. S., Volkow, N. D., & Wolf, A. P. (1995). PET studies of cocaine in human brain. In A. Biegon & N. D. Volkow (Eds.), *Sites of drug action in the human brain.* Boca Raton, FL: CRC Press.

Fowler, K. A., O'Donohue, W., Lilienfeld, S. O. (2007). Introduction: Personality disorders in perspective. In W. O'Donohue, K. A. Fowler, S. O. Lilienfeld (Eds.). *Personality disorders: Toward the DSM-V.* Los Angeles: Sage Publications.

Fox, D. (2010). The insanity virus. *Discover, 31*(5).

Fox, J. A., & Levin, J. (1999). Serial murder: Myths and realities. In M. D. Smith & M. A. Zahn (Eds.), *Studying and preventing homicide: Issues and challenges* (pp. 79–96). Thousand Oaks, CA: Sage Publications, Inc.

Fox, J. A., & Levin, J. (1999). Serial murder: Popular myths and empirical realities. In M. D. Smith, & M. A. Zahn (Eds.), *Homicide: A sourcebook of social research* (pp. 165–175). Thousand Oaks, CA: Sage Publications, Inc.

Fox, J. A., & Levin, J. (2005). *Extreme killing: Understanding serial and mass murder.* Thousand Oaks, CA: Sage.

Fox, M. D., Buckner, R. L., White, M. P., Greicius, M. D., & Pascual-Leone, A. (2012). Efficacy of transcranial magnetic stimulation targets for depression is related to intrinsic functional connectivity with the subgenual cingulate. *Biological Psychiatry, 72*(7), 595–603.

Foy, D. W., Drescher, K. D., Watson, P. J., & Ritchie, I. (2011). Group therapy. In B. A. Moore & W. E. Penk (Eds.), *Treating PTSD in military personnel: A clinical handbook.* (pp. 125–140). New York: Guilford Press.

Frances, A. J. (2012, February 18). Allen Frances: DSM-5 to the barricades on grief. Defending the Indefensible. *Society for Humanistic Psychology Blog.*

Frances, A. J. (2013, January 16). Bad news: DSM 5 refuses to correct somatic symptom disorder. *Psychology Today.*

Frances, A. J., & Widiger, T. (2012). Psychiatric diagnosis: Lessons from the DSM-IV past and cautions for the DSM-5 future. *Annual Review of Clinical Psychology, 8,* 109–130.

Franchi, S. (2004). Depression and marital discord. *Revista Argentina de Clinica Psicologica, 13*(3), 197–203.

Frank, E. & Levenson, J. C. (2011). Future developments. In E. Frank & J.C. Levenson, (Eds.), *Interpersonal psychotherapy.* (pp. 111–119). Washington, DC: American Psychological Association.

Frank, E., & Levenson, J. C. (2011). *Interpersonal psychotherapy.* Washington, DC: American Psychological Association.

Frank, J. D. (1973). *Persuasion and healing* (rev. ed.). Baltimore: Johns Hopkins University Press.

Franklin, J., & Markarian, M. (2005). Substance abuse in minority populations. In R. J. Frances, A. H. Mack, & S. I. Miller (Eds.), *Clinical textbook of addictive disorders* (3rd ed., pp. 321–339). New York: Guilford Press.

Fraser, G. A. (1993). Special treatment techniques to access the inner personality system of multiple personality disorder patients. *Dissociation: Progress in the Dissociative Disorders, 6*(2–3), 193–198.

Frazier, A. D., & Cross, T. L. (2011). Debunking the myths of suicide in gifted children. In J. L. Jolly, D. J. Treffinger, T. F. Inman, & J. F. Smutny (Eds.), *Parenting gifted children: The authoritative guide from the National Association for Gifted Children* (pp. 517–524). Waco, TX: Prufrock Press.

Frederick, D. A., Forbes, G. B., Grigorian, K. E., & Jarcho, J. M. (2007). The UCLA Body Project. I: Gender and ethnic differences in self-objectification and body satisfaction among 2,206 undergraduates. *Sex Roles, 57,* 317–327.

Freedman, R., Lewis, D.A., Michels, R., Pine, D.S., Schultz, S.K., Tamminga, C.A., Gabbard, G.O., Gau, S.S., Javitt, D.C., Oquendo, M.A., Shrout, P.E., Vieta, E., Yager, J. (2013). The initial field trials of DSM-5: New blooms and old thorns. *The American Journal of Psychiatry, 170,*1–5.

Freking, K. (2007, August 27). Obesity rates show no decline in US. *Yahoo! News.* Retrieved August 27, 2007, from http://news.yahoo.com.

French, A. P., & Berlin, I. N. (1979). *Depression in children and adolescents.* New York: Human Sciences Press.

French, P. (2010). Early detection and treatment opportunities for people at high risk for developing psychosis. In P. French, J. Smith, D. Shiers, M. Reed, & M. Rayne (Eds.), *Promoting recovery in early psychosis: A practice manual* (pp. 93–98). Hoboken, NJ: Wiley-Blackwell.

Frese, F. J., III. (2008). Self-help activities. In D.V. Jeste, & K. T. Mueser (Eds.) *Clinical handbook of schizophrenia* (pp. 298–305). New York: Guilford Press.

Freud, S. (1894). The neuropsychoses of defense. In J. Strachey (Ed.), *The standard edition of the complete psychological works of Sigmund Freud* (Vol. 3). London: Hogarth Press. (Work republished 1962)

Freud, S. (1909). Analysis of a phobia in a five-year-old boy. In *Sigmund Freud: Collected papers* (Vol. 3). New York: Basic Books.

Freud, S. (1914). On narcissism. In *Complete psychological works* (Vol. 14). London: Hogarth Press. (Work republished 1957)

Freud, S. (1915). A case of paranoia counter to psychoanalytic theory. In *Complete psychological works* (Vol. 14). London: Hogarth Press. (Work republished 1957)

Freud, S. (1917). *A general introduction to psychoanalysis* (J. Riviere, Trans.). New York: Liveright. (Work republished 1963).

Freud, S. (1917). Mourning and melancholia. In *Collected papers* (Vol. 4, pp. 152–172). London: Hogarth Press and the Institute of Psychoanalysis. (Work republished 1950).

Freud, S. (1920). Beyond the Pleasure Principle. In J. Strachey (Ed.), (1955), The Standard Edition of the Complete Psychological Works of Sigmund Freud, Volume XVIII (1920–1922): Beyond the Pleasure Principle, Group Psychology and Other Works. London, England: The Hogarth Press and the Institute of Psychoanalysis.

Freud, S. (1924). The loss of reality in neurosis and psychosis. In *Sigmund Freud's collected papers* (Vol. 2, pp. 272–282). London: Hogarth Press.

Freud, S. (1933). New introductory lectures on psychoanalysis. New York: Norton.

Freud, S. (1961). *The future of an illusion.* New York: W. W. Norton.

Freudenreich, O., & Goff, D. C. (2011). Treatment of psychotic disorders. In D. A. Ciraulo & R. I. Shader (Eds.), *Pharmacotherapy of depression* (2nd ed., pp. 185–196). New York: Springer Science + Business Media.

Freyer, T., Klöppel, S., Tüscher, O., Kordon, A., Zurowski, B., Kuelz, A-K., Speck, O., Glauche, V., & Voderholzer, U. (2011). Frontostriatal activation in patients with obsessive-compulsive disorder before and after cognitive behavioral therapy. *Psychological Medicine: A Journal of Research in Psychiatry and the Allied Sciences, 41*(1), 207–216.

Friederich, H-C., & Herzog, W. (2011). Cognitive-behavioral flexibility in anorexia nervosa. In R. A. H. Adan & W. H. Kaye (Eds.), *Behavioral neurobiology of eating disorders. Current topics in behavioral neurosciences* (pp. 111–123). New York: Springer-Verlag Publishing.

Friedman, M., & Rosenman, R. (1959). Association of specific overt behavior pattern with blood and cardiovascular findings. *Journal of the American Medical Association, 169,* 1286.

Friedman, M., & Rosenman, R. (1974). *Type A behavior and your heart.* New York: Knopf.

Friedman, R. A. (2008, February 19). Have you ever been in psychotherapy, doctor? *New York Times.* Retrieved February 25, 2008, from http://www.nytimes.com/2008/02/19/health/19mind.html.

Friman, P. C. (2008). Evidence-based therapies for enuresis and encopresis. In R. G. Steele, T. D. Elkin, & M. C. Roberts (Eds.), *Handbook of evidence-based therapies for children and adolescents: Bridging science and practice.* New York: Springer.

Frith, U. (2000). Cognitive explanations of autism. In K. Lee (Ed.), *Childhood cognitive development: The essential readings. Essential readings in development psychology.* Malden, MA: Blackwell.

Frohman, E. M. (2002). Sexual dysfunction in neurological disease. *Clinical Neuropharmacology, 25*(3), 126–132.

Fromm-Reichmann, F. (1943). Psychotherapy of schizophrenia. *American Journal of Psychiatry, 111,* 410–419.

Fromm-Reichmann, F. (1948). Notes on the development of treatment of schizophrenia by psychoanalytic psychotherapy. *Psychiatry, 11,* 263–273.

Fromm-Reichmann, F. (1950). *Principles of intensive psychotherapy.* Chicago: University of Chicago.

Frosch, W. A., Robbins, E. S., & Stern, M. (1965). Untoward reactions to lysergic acid diethylamide (LSD) resulting in hospitalization. *New England Journal of Medicine, 273,* 1235–1239.

Frost, R. O., & Steketee, G. (2001). Obsessive-compulsive disorder. In H. S. Friedman (Ed.), *Specialty articles from the encyclopedia of mental health.* San Diego: Academic Press.

Frost, R. O., Steketee, G., & Tolin, D. F. (2012). Diagnosis and assessment of hoarding disorder. *Annual Review of Clinical Psychology, 8,* 219–242.

Fu, K. W., Wong, P. W. C., & Yip, P. S. F. (2010) What do internet users seek to know about depression from web searches: A descriptive study of 21 million web queries. *Journal of Clinical Psychiatry, 72*(9), 1246–1247.

Fuller-Thomson, E., & Dalton, A. D. (2011). Suicidal ideation among individuals whose parents have divorced: Findings from a representative Canadian community survey. *Psychiatry Research, 187*(1–2), 150–155.

Furedi, F. (2007, March 20). "The only thing we have to fear is the 'culture of fear' itself." *Spiked.* (Based on a talk at the NY Salon debate.)

Gabbard, G. O. (2001). Psychoanalysis and psychoanalytic psychotherapy. In W. J. Livesley (Ed.), *Handbook of personality disorders: Theory, research, and treatment* (pp. 359–376). New York: Guilford Press.

Gabbard, G. O. (2009). Psychoanalysis and psychodynamic psychotherapy. In J. M. Oldham, A. E. Skodol, & D. S. Bender (Eds.), *Essentials of personality disorders* (pp. 185–207). American Psychiatric Publishing, Inc. Washington, DC.

Gabbard, G. O. (2010). Therapeutic action in the psychoanalytic psychotherapy of borderline personality disorder. In J. F. Clarkin, P. Fonagy, & G. O. Gabbard (Eds.), *Psychodynamic psychotherapy for personality disorders: A clinical handbook.* Arlington, VA: American Psychiatric Publishing, Inc.

Gadalla, T. M. (2009). Eating disorders in men: A community-based study. *International Journal of Men's Health, 8*(1), 72–81.

Gado, M. (2008). The insanity defense: Twinkies as a defense. Retrieved August 17, 2008, from http://www.trutv.com/library/crime/criminal_mind/psychology/insanity.

Galanter, M. (2010). Review of religion and spirituality in psychiatry. *American Journal of Psychiatry, 167*(7), 871–872.

Galanter, M., & Kleber, H. D. (Eds.). (2008). *The American Psychiatric Publishing textbook of substance abuse treatment* (4th ed.). Arlington, VA: American Psychiatric Publishing.

Galea, S., Ahern, J., Resnick, H., Kilpatrick, D., Bucuvalas, M., Gold, J., & Vlahov, D. (2002). Psychological sequelae of the September 11 terrorist attacks in New York City. *New England Journal of Medicine, 13,* 982–987.

Galea, S., Ahern, J., Resnick, H., Kilpatrick, D., Bucuvalas, M., Gold, J., & Vlahov, D. (2007). Psychological sequelae of the September 11 terrorist attacks in New York City. In B. Trappler (Ed.), *Modern terrorism and psychological trauma* (pp. 14–24). New York: Gordian Knot Books/Richard Altschulerr & Associates.

Galea, S., Ahern, J., Resnick, H., & Vlahov, D. (2006). Post-traumatic stress symptoms in the general population after a disaster: Implications for public health. In Y. Neria, R. Gross, R. D. Marshall, & E. S. Susser (Eds.), *9/11: Mental health in the wake of terrorist attacks* (pp. 19–44). New York: Cambridge University Press.

Galimberti, D., & Scarpini, E. (2011). Disease-modifying treatments for Alzheimer's disease. *Therapeutic Advances in Neurological Disorders, 4*(4), 203–216.

Gallagher-Thompson, D., & Thompson, L. W. (1995). Problems of aging. In R. J. Comer (Ed.), *Abnormal psychology.* New York: W. H. Freeman and Company.

Gallo, L. C., Penedo, F. J., de los Monteros, K. E., & Arguelles, W. (2009). Resiliency in the face of disadvantage: Do Hispanic cultural characteristics protect health outcomes? *Journal of Personality, 77*(6), 1707–1746.

Gallup Poll. (2005). Three in four Americans believe in paranormal. *Gallup News Service.* Retrieved from http://www.gallup.com/poll/16915/three-four-americans-believe-paranormal.aspx.

Gallup Poll. (2010). Personal health issues. Retrieved on January 16, 2011, from www.gallup.com/poll/1648.

Gallup Poll. (2010). Work and workplace. Retrieved on January 16, 2011, from www.gallup.com/poll.1720.

Gallup Poll. (2011, March 15). Disaster preparedness and relief. *PollingReport.com.*

Gallup. (2011). Gay and lesbian rights. Retrieved on January 16, 2011, from http://www.gallup.com/poll/1651/Gay-Lesbian-Rights.aspx?version=print.

Gallup. (2011). Marriage. Retrieved on January 16, 2011, from http://www.gallup.com/poll/117328/Marriage.aspx?version=print.

Gallup. (2011). Religion. Retrieved on January 16, 2011, from http://www.gallup.com/poll/1690/Religion.aspx?version=print.

Gallup. (2011). Satisfaction with personal life. Retrieved on January 16, 2011, from http://www.gallup.com/poll/1672/Satisfaction-Personal-Life.aspx?version=print.

Gallup. (2011). Terrorism. Retrieved on January 16, 2011, from http://www.gallup.com/poll/4909/Terrorism-United-States.aspx?version=print.

Gallup/USA Today Poll. (2010, December 23). Satisfaction with leisure time. *USA Today.*

Galvez, J. F., Thommi, S., & Ghaemi, S. N. (2011). Positive aspects of mental illness: A review in bipolar disorder. *Journal of Affective Disorders, 28*(3), 185–190.

Gamble, A. L., Harvey, A. G., & Rapee, R. M. (2010). Specific phobia. In D. J. Stein, E. Hollander, & B. O. Rothbaum (Eds.), *Textbook of anxiety disorders* (2nd ed., pp. 525–541). Arlington, VA: American Psychiatric Publishing.

Gamwell, L., & Tomes, N. (1995). *Madness in America: Cultural and medical perceptions of mental illness before 1914.* Ithaca, NY: Cornell University Press.

Ganasen, K. A., & Stein, D. J. (2010). Pharmacotherapy of social anxiety disorder. In M. B. Stein & T. Steckler (Eds.), *Behavioral neurobiology of anxiety and its treatment. Current topics in behavioral neurosciences* (pp. 487–503). New York: Springer Science + Business Media.

Ganis, G., Rosenfeld, J. P., Meixner, J., Kievit, R. A., & Schendan, H. E. (2011). Lying in the scanner: Covert countermeasures disrupt deception detection by functional magnetic resonance imaging. *NeuroImage, 55*(1), 312–319.

Gao, K., Kemp, D. E., & Calabrese, J. R. (2009). Pharmacological treatment of the maintenance phase of bipolar depression: Focus on relapse prevention studies and the impact of design on generalizability. In C. A. Zarate, Jr. & H. K. Manji (Eds.), *Bipolar depression: Molecular neurobiology, clinical diagnosis and pharmacotherapy. Milestones in drug therapy* (pp. 159–178). Cambridge, MA: Birkhäuser.

Gao, K., Kemp, D. E., Wang, Z., Ganocy, S. J., Conroy, C., Serrano, M. B., et al. (2010). Predictors of non-stabilization during the combination therapy of lithium and divalproex in rapid cycling bipolar disorder: A post-hoc analysis of two studies. *Psychopharmacology Bulletin, 43*(1), 23–38.

Gao, S-F., & Bao, A-M. (2011). Corticotropin-releasing hormone, glutamate, and γ-aminobutyric acid in depression. *The Neuroscientist, 17*(1), 124–144.

Garb, H. N. (2006). The conjunction effect and clinical judgment. *Journal of Social and Clinical Psychology, 25*(9), 1048–1056.

Garb, H. N. (2010). Clinical judgment and the influence of screening on decision making. In A. J. Mitchell & J. C. Coyne (Eds.), *Screening for depression in clinical practice: An evidence-based guide* (pp. 113–121). New York: Oxford University Press.

Garber, K. (2008, January 7). Who's behind the bible of mental illness? *U.S. News & World Report.*

Gard, D. E., Cooper, S., Fisher, M., Genevsky, A., Mikels, J. A., & Vinograddov, S. (2011). Evidence for an emotion maintenance deficit in schizophrenia. *Psychiatry Research, 187*(1-2), 24–29.

Gardner, A., & Boles, R. G. (2011). Beyond the serotonin hypothesis: Mitochondria, inflammation and neurodegeneration in major depression and affective spectrum disorders. *Progress in Neuro-Psychopharmacology & Biological Psychiatry, 35*(3), 730–743.

Gardner, M., Barajas, R. G., & Brooks-Gunn, J. (2010). Neighborhood influences on substance use etiology: Is where you live important? In L. Scheier (Ed.), *Handbook of drug use etiology: Theory, methods, and empirical findings* (pp. 423–441). Washington, DC: American Psychological Association.

Gardner, R. A. (2004). The psychodynamics of patients with False Memory Syndrome (FMS). *Journal of the American Academy of Psychoanalysis and Dynamic Psychiatry, 32*(1), 77–90.

Garlow, S. J. (2002). Age, gender, and ethnicity differences in patterns of cocaine and ethanol use preceding suicide. *American Journal of Psychiatry, 159*(4), 615–619.

Garner, D. M. (1991). *Eating disorder inventory—2: Professional manual.* Odessa, FL: Psychological Assessment Resources.

Garner, D. M. (2005). *Eating Disorder Inventory TM-3 (EDI TM-3).* Lutz, Florida: Psychological Assessment Resources, Inc.

Garner, D. M., Garfinkel, P. E., Schwartz, D., & Thompson, M. (1980). Cultural expectations of thinness in women. *Psychological Reports, 47,* 483–491.

Garner, D. M., Olmsted, M. P., & Polivy, J. (1984). *The EDI.* Odessa, FL: Psychological Assessment Resources.

Garrett, B. L. (2011). *Convicting the innocent: Where criminal prosecutions go wrong.* Cambridge, MA: Harvard University Press.

Gask, L., Aseem, S., Waguas, A., & Waheed, W. (2011). Isolation, feeling "stuck" and loss of control: Understanding persistence of depression in British Pakistani women. *Journal of Affective Disorders, 128*(1-2), 49–55.

Gatchel, R. J., Howard, K., & Haggard, R. (2011). Pain: The biopsychosocial perspective. In R. J. Contrada & A. Baum (Eds.), *The handbook of stress science: Biology, psychology, and health* (pp. 461–473). New York: Springer Publishing.

Gawryluk, J. W., & Young, L. T. (2011). Signal transduction pathways in the pathophysiology of bipolar disorder. In H. K. Manji & C. A. Zarate, Jr. (Eds.), *Behavioral neurobiology of bipolar disorders and its treatment. Current topics in behavioral neurosciences* (pp. 139–165). New York: Springer Science + Business Media.

Gay, P. (1999, March 29). Psychoanalyst Sigmund Freud. *Time,* pp. 66–69.

Gay, P. (2006). *Freud: A life for our time.* New York: W. W. Norton & Co.

Gaynor, S. T., & Baird, S. C. (2007). Personality disorders. In D. W. Woods & J. W. Kanter (Eds.), *Understanding behavior disorders: A contemporary behavioral perspective.* Reno, NV: Context Press.

Geary, J., & DePaulo, B. M. (2007). Issue 7: Can people accurately detect lies? In J. A. Nier, *Taking sides: Clashing views in social psychology* (2nd ed).

Gebhard, P. H. (1965). Situational factors affecting human sexual behavior. In F. Beach (Ed.), *Sex and behavior.* New York: Wiley.

Geddes, J. R., Stroup, S., & Lieberman, J. A. (2011). Comparative efficacy and effectiveness in the drug treatment of schizophrenia. In D. R. Weinberg & P. Harrison (Eds.), *Schizophrenia* (pp. 525–539). Hoboken, NJ: Wiley-Blackwell.

Gelernter, J., & Kranzler, H. R. (2008). Genetics of addiction. In H. D. Kleber & M. Galanter (Eds.), *The American Psychiatric Publishing textbook of substance abuse treatment* (4th ed., pp. 17–27). Arlington, VA: American Psychiatric Publishing.

Gelfand, D. M., Jenson, W. R., & Drew, C. J. (1982). *Understanding child behavior disorders.* New York: Holt, Rinehart & Winston.

George, M. S., Sackeim, H. A., Rush, A. J., Marangell, L. B., Nahas, Z., Husain, M. M., et al. (2000). Vagus nerve stimulation: A new tool for brain research and therapy. *Biological Psychiatry, 47,* 287–295.

George, T. P., & Weinberger, A. H. (2008). Nicotine and tobacco. In H. D. Kleber & M. Galanter (Eds.), *The American Psychiatric Publishing textbook of substance abuse treatment* (4th ed., pp. 201–213). Arlington, VA: American Psychiatric Publishing.

George, W. H., Davis, K. C., Heiman, J. R., Norris, J., Stoner, S. A., Schacht, R. L., et al. (2011). Women's sexual arousal: Effects of high alcohol dosages and self-control instructions. *Hormones and Behavior, 59*(5), 730–738.

Geraerts, E. (2010). Posttraumatic memory. In G. M. Rosen, & B. C. Frueh (Eds.), *Clinician's guide to posttraumatic stress disorder* (pp. 77–95). Hoboken, NJ: John Wiley & Sons.

Geraerts, E., Lindsay, D. S., Merckelbach, H., Jelicic, M., Raymaekers, L., Arnold, M. M., & Schooler, J. W. (2009). Cognitive mechanisms underlying recovered-memory experiences of childhood sexual abuse. *Psychological Science, 20*(1), 92–98.

Gerardi, M., Rothbaum, B. O., Astin, M. C., & Kelley, M. (2010). Cortisol response following exposure treatment for PTSD in rape victims. *Journal of Aggression, Maltreatment & Trauma, 19*(4), 349–356.

Gerbasi, J. B., & Simon, R. I. (2003). Patients' rights and psychiatrists' duties: Discharging patients against medicine advice. *Harvard Review of Psychiatry, 11*(6), 333–343.

Germer, J. (2005). The relationship between acculturation and eating disorders among Mexican American college females: An investigation. *Dissertation Abstracts International: Section B: The Sciences and Engineering, 65*(7-B), 3706.

Gernsbacher, L. M. (1985). *The suicide syndrome.* New York: Human Sciences Press.

Gerrity, E., Keane, T. M., & Tuma, F. (2001). Introduction. In E. Gerrity, T. M. Keane, & F. Tuma (Eds.), *The mental health consequences of torture* (pp. 3–12). New York: Kluwer Academic/ Plenum Publishers.

Gershon, E. S., & Nurnberger, J. I. (1995). Bipolar illness. In J. M. Oldham & M. B. Riba (Eds.), *American Psychiatric Press review of psychiatry* (Vol. 14). Washington, DC: American Psychiatric Press.

Gever, J. (2008, May 7). APA: PTSD may be major combat scar of Iraq vets. Retrieved May 19, 2008, from http://www.medpagetoday.com/ MeetingCoverage/APA/tb/9368.

Ghahramanlou-Holloway, M., Brown, G. K., & Beck, A. T. (2008). Suicide. In M. A. Whisman (Ed.), *Adapting cognitive therapy for depression: Managing complexity and comorbidity* (pp. 159–184). New York: Guilford Press.

Ghahramanlou-Holloway, M., Cox, D. W., & Greene, F. N. (2011). Post-admission cognitive therapy: A brief intervention for psychiatric inpatients admitted after a suicide attempt. *Cognitive and Behavioral Practice.*

Ghazizadeh, S., & Nikzad, M. (2004). Botulinum toxin in the treatment of refractory vaginismus. *Obstetrics and Gynecology., 104*(5, Pt. 1), 922–925.

Gheorghiu, V. A., & Orleanu, P. (1982). Dental implant under hypnosis. *American Journal of Clinical Hypnosis, 25*(1), 68–70.

Ghetti, S., Schaaf, J. M., Qin, J., & Goodman, G. S. (2004). Issues in eyewitness testimony. In W. T. O'Donohue & E. R. Levensky (Eds.), *Handbook of forensic psychology: Resource for mental health and legal professionals* (pp. 513–554). New York: Elsevier Science.

Gianaros, P. J., May, J. C., Siegle, G. J., & Jennings, J. R. (2005). Is there a functional neural correlate of individual differences in cardiovascular reactivity? *Psychosomatic Medicine, 67*(1), 31–39.

Gianaros, P. J., & O'Connor, M-F. (2011). Neuroimaging methods in human stress science. In R. J. Contrada & A. Baum (Eds.), *The handbook of stress science: Biology, psychology, and health* (pp. 543–563). New York: Springer Publishing.

Giesbrecht, T., & Merckelbach, H. (2009). Betrayal trauma theory of dissociative experiences: Stroop and directed forgetting findings. *American Journal of Psychology, 122*(3), 337–348.

Gifford, M., Friedman, S., & Majerus, R. (2010). *Alcoholism.* Santa Barbara, CA: Greenwood Press/ABC-CLIO.

Gilbert, K. L., Quinn, S. C., Ford, A. F., & Thomas, S. B. (2011). The urban context: A place to eliminate health disparities and build organizational capacity. *Journal of Prevention & Intervention in the Community, 39*(1), 77–92.

Gilbert, S. (2011). Eating disorders in women of African descent. In J. Alexander & J. Treasure (Eds.), *A collaborative approach to eating disorders* (pp. 249–261). New York: Taylor & Francis.

Gilbert, S. C., Keery, H., & Thompson, J. K. (2005). The media's role in body image and eating disorders. In J. H. Daniel & E. Cole (Eds.), *Featuring females: Feminist analyses of media* (pp. 41–56). Washington, DC: American Psychological Association.

Gill, A. D. (1982). Vulnerability to suicide. In E. L. Bassuk, S. C. Schoonover, & A. D. Gill (Eds.), *Lifelines: Clinical perspectives on suicide.* New York: Plenum Press.

Gill, R. E. (2006). Psychology enrollment still booming. *National Psychologist, 15*(1), 1–2

Gill, R. E. (2010, January/February). Practice opportunities available despite shrinking mental health dollars. *The National Psychologist,* pp. 1, 3.

Gillam, R. B., & Petersen, D. B. (2011). Language disorders in school-age children. In R. B. Gillam, T. P. Marquardt, & F. N. Martin (Eds.), *Communication sciences and disorders: From science to clinical practice* (2nd ed., pp. 245–270). Boston, MA: Jones and Bartlett Publishers.

Gillig, P. M. (2009). Dissociative identity disorder: A controversial diagnosis. *Psychiatry, 6*(3), 24–29.

Gillis, J. M., & Romanczyk, R. G. (2007). Autism spectrum disorders and related developmental disabilities. In M. Hersen & A. M. Gross (Eds.), *Handbook of clinical psychology* (Vol. 2). Hoboken, NJ: John Wiley & Sons.

Girden, E. R., & Kabacoff, R. I. (2011). *Evaluating research articles: From start to finish* (3rd ed.). Thousand Oaks, CA: Sage Publications.

Gist, R., & Devilly, G. J. (2010). Early intervention in the aftermath of trauma. In G. M. Rosen, B. C. Frueh (Eds.), *Clinician's guide to posttraumatic stress disorder* (pp. 153–175). Hoboken, NJ: John Wiley & Sons.

Gitlin, M. J. (2002). Pharmacological treatment of depression. In I. H. Gotlib & C. L. Hammen (Eds.), *Handbook of depression* (pp. 360–382). New York: Guilford Press.

Glahn, D. C., & Burdick, K. E. (2011). Clinical endophenotypes for bipolar disorder. In H. K. Manji & C. A. Zarate, Jr. (Eds.), *Behavioral neurobiology of bipolar disorder and its treatment. Current topics in behavioral neurosciences* (pp. 51–67). New York: Springer Science + Business Media.

Glass, C. R., & Merluzzi, T. V. (2000). Cognitive and behavioral assessment. In C. E. Watkins, Jr., & V. L. Campbell (Eds.), *Testing and assessment in counseling practice* (2nd ed.). Mahwah, NJ: Lawrence Erlbaum.

Glasser. M. (2010). The history of managed care and the role of the child and adolescent psychiatrist. *Child and Adolescent Psychiatric Clinics of North America, 19*(1), 63–74.

Glazer, M., Baer, R. D., Weller, S. C., de-Alba, J. E. G., & Liebowitz, S. W. (2004). Susto and soul loss in Mexicans and Mexican Americans. *Journal of Comparative Social Science, 38*(3), 270–288.

Glentworth, D., & Reed, M. (2010). Group-based interventions. In P. French, J. Smith, D. Shiers, M. Reed, & M. Rayne (Eds.), *Promoting recovery in early psychosis: A practice manual* (pp. 245–254). Hoboken, NJ: Wiley-Blackwell.

Glidden, L. M., Bamberger, K. T., Draheim, A. R., & Kersh, J. (2011). Parent and athlete perceptions of Special Olympics participation: Utility and danger of proxy responding. *Intellectual and Developmental Disabilities, 49*(1), 37–46.

Gloster, A. T., Wittchen, H-U., Einsle, F., Lang, T., Helbig-Lang, S., Fydrich, T., Fehm, L., Hamm, A. O., Richter, J., Alpers, G. W., Gerlach, A. L., Ströhle, A., Kircher, T., Deckert, J., Zwanzger, P., Höfer, M., & Arolt, V. (2011). Psychological treatment for panic disorder with agoraphobia: A randomized controlled trial to examine the role of therapist-guided exposure in situ in CBT. *Journal of Consulting and Clinical Psychology, 79*(3), 406–420.

Glover, N. G., Crego, C., & Widiger, T. A. (2011, July 4). The clinical utility of the five factor model of personality disorder. *Personality Disorders: Theory, Research, and Treatment.*

Godenzi, A., & DePuy, J. (2001). Overcoming boundaries: A cross-cultural inventory of primary prevention programs against wife abuse and child abuse. *Journal of Primary Prevention, 21*(4), 455–475.

Goisman, R. M., Warshaw, M. G., & Keller, M. B. (1999). Psychosocial treatment prescriptions for generalized anxiety disorder, panic disorder, and social phobia, 1991–1996. *American Journal of Psychiatry, 156*(11), 1819–1821.

Gold, J. H. (1998). Gender differences in psychiatric illness and treatments: A critical review. *Journal of Nervous and Mental Disease, 186*(12), 769–775.

Gold, L. H. (2010). The workplace. In R. I. Simon & L. H. Gold (Eds.), *The American Psychiatric Publishing textbook of forensic psychiatry* (2nd ed., pp. 303–334). Arlington, VA: American Psychiatric Publishing.

Gold, S. N., & Castillo, Y. (2010). Dealing with defenses and defensiveness in interviews. In D. L. Segal & M. Hersen (Eds.), *Diagnostic interviewing* (pp. 89–102). New York: Springer Publishing.

Goldberg, D., Kendler, K. S., Sirovatka, P. J., & Regier, D. A. (Eds.). (2010). *Diagnostic issues in depression and generalized anxiety disorder: Refining the research agenda for DSM-V.* Washington, DC: American Psychiatric Association.

Goldberg, T. E., David, A., & Gold, J. M. (2011). Neurocognitive impairments in schizophrenia: Their character and role in symptom formation. In D. R. Weinberg & P. Harrison (Eds.), *Schizophrenia* (pp. 142–162). Hoboken, NJ: Wiley-Blackwell.

Golden, C. J. (2008). Neurologically impaired children. In D. Reitman (Ed.), *Handbook of psychological assessment, case conceptualization, and treatment, Vol. 2: Children and adolescents.* Hoboken, NJ: John Wiley & Sons.

Goldenberg, I., & Goldenberg, H. (2011). Fanily therapy. In R. J. Corsini & D. Wedding (Eds.), *Current psychotherapies* (9th ed.). Belmont, CA: Brooks/Cole.

Goldiamond, I. (1965). Self-control procedures in personal behavior problems. *Psychological Reports, 17,* 851–868.

Goldin, P. R., Ziv, M., Jazaieri, H., Werner, K., Kraemer, H., Heimberg, R. G., & Gross, J. J. (2012, May 14). Cognitive reappraisal self-efficacy mediates the effects of individual cognitive-behavioral therapy for social anxiety disorder. *Journal of Consulting and Clinical Psychology, 80*(6), 1034–1040.

Goldman, B., Dixon, L. B., Adler, D. A., Berlant, J., Dulit, R. A., Hackman, A., et al. (2010). Rational protection of subjects in research and quality improvement activities. *Psychiatric Services, 61*(2), 180–183.

Goldman, J. G. (1995). A mutual story-telling technique as an aid to integration after abreaction in the treatment of MPD. *Dissociation: Progress in the Dissociative Disorders, 8*(1), 53–60.

Goldman-Rakic, P. S., Castner, S. A., Svensson, T. H., et al. (2004). Targeting the dopamine D1 receptor in schizophrenia: Insights for cognitive dysfunction. *Psychopharmacology, 174,* 3–16.

Goldstein, A. (1994). *Addiction: From biology to drug policy.* New York: W. H. Freeman and Company.

Goldstein, D. J., Potter, W. Z., Ciraulo, D. A., & Shader, R. I. (2011). Biological theories of depression and implications for current and new treatments. In D. A. Ciraulo & R. I. Shader (Eds.), *Pharmacotherapy of depression* (2nd ed., pp. 1–32). New York: Springer Science + Business Media.

Goldstein, K. E., Hazlett, E. A., Savage, K. R., Berlin, H. A., Hamilton, H. K., Zelmanova, Y., Look, A. E., Koenigsberg, H. W., Mitsis, E. M., Tang, C. Y., McNamara, M., Siever, L. J., Cohen, B. H., & New, A. S. (2011). Dorso- and ventro-lateral prefrontal volume and spatial working memory in schziotypal personality disorder. *Behavioural Brain Research, 218*(2), 335–340.

Goldstein, M. J., & Palmer, J. O. (1975). *The experience of anxiety: A casebook.* New York: Oxford University Press.

Goldstein, S. (2011). Attention-Deficit/Hyperactivity disorder. In S. Goldstein, & C. R. Reynolds (Eds.), *Handbook of neurodevelopmental and genetic disorders in children* (2nd ed., pp. 131–150) New York: Guilford Press.

Goldston, D. B., Molock, S. D., Whitbeck, L. B., Murakami, J. L., Zayas, L. H., & Hall, G. C. N. (2008). Cultural considerations in adolescent suicide prevention and psychosocial treatment. *American Psychologist, 63*(1), 14–31.

Gómez-Gil, E., Esteva, I., Almaraz, M. C., Pasaro, E., Segovia, S., & Guillamon, A. (2010). Familiarity of gender identity disorder in non-twin siblings. *Archives of Sexual Behavior, 39*(2), 546–552.

González, H. M., Tarraf, W., Whitfield, K. E., & Vega, W. A. (2010). The epidemiology of major depression and ethnicity in the United States. *Journal of Psychiatric Research, 44,* 1043–1051.

Good, G. E., & Brooks, G. R. (Eds.). (2005). *The new handbook of psychotherapy and counseling with men: A comprehensive guide to settings, problems, and treatment approaches* (Rev. & abridged ed.). San Francisco, CA: Jossey-Bass.

Goode, E., & Vail, D. A. (Eds.). (2008). *Extreme deviance.* Los Angeles: Pine Forge Press.

Goodman, S. H. (2002). Depression and early adverse experiences. In I. H. Gotlib & C. L. Hammen (Eds.), *Handbook of depression* (pp. 245–267). New York: Guilford Press.

Goodman-Brown, T. B., Edelstein, R. S., Goodman, G. S., Jones, D. P. H., & Gordon, D. S. (2003). Why children tell: A model of children's disclosure of sexual abuse. *Child Abuse and Neglect, 27,* 525–540.

Goodwin, C. J. (2011). *Research in psychology: Methods and design,* (6th ed.). Hoboken, NJ: John Wiley & Sons.

Goodwin, F. K., & Jamison, K. R. (1984). The natural course of manic-depressive illness. In R. M. Post & J. C. Ballenger (Eds.), *Neurobiology of mood disorders.* Baltimore: Williams & Wilkins.

Gordon, K. H., Brattole, M. M., Wingate, L. R., & Joiner, T. E., Jr. (2006). The impact of client race on clinician detection of eating disorders. *Behavior Therapy, 37*(4), 319–325.

Gordon, K. H., Perez, M., & Joiner, T. E., Jr. (2002). The impact of racial stereotypes on eating disorder recognition. *International Journal of Eating Disorders, 32,* 219–224.

Goshen, C. E. (1967). *Documentary history of psychiatry: A source book on historical principles.* New York: Philosophy Library.

Goss, K., & Allan, S. (2009). Shame, pride and eating disorders. *Clinical Psychology & Psychotherapy, 16*(4), 303–316.

Goswami, M., Pandi-Perumal, S. R., & Thorpy, M. J. (Eds.). (2010). *Narcolepsy: A clinical guide.* Totowa, NJ: Humana Press.

Goto, S., Terao, T., Hoaki, N., & Wang, Y. (2011). Cyclothymic and hyperthymic temperaments may predict bipolarity in major depressive disorder: A supportive evidence for bipolar II1/2 and IV. *Journal of Affective Disorders, 129*(1-3), 34–38.

Gottesman, I. I. (1991). *Schizophrenia genesis.* New York: W. H. Freeman and Company.

Gottesman, I. I., & Reilly, J. L. (2003). Strengthening the evidence for genetic factors in schizophrenia (without abetting genetic discrimination). In M. F. Lenzenweger & J. M. Hooley (Eds.), *Principles of experimental psychopathology: Essays in honor of Brendan A. Maher* (pp. 31–44). Washington, DC: American Psychological Association.

Gouin, J-P., Glaser, R., Loving, T. J., Malarkey, W. B., Stowell, J., Houts, C., Kiecolt-Glaser, J. K. (2009). Attachment avoidance predicts inflammatory responses to marital conflict. *Brain, Behavior, and Immunity, 23*(7), 898–904.

Gould, M. S., Midle, J. B., Insel, B., & Kleinman, M. (2007). Suicide reporting content analysis: Abstract development and reliability. *Crisis: Journal of Crisis Intervention and Suicide Prevention, 28*(4), 165–174.

Gozlan, O. (2011). Transsexual surgery: A novel reminder and a navel remainder. *International Forum of Psychoanalysis, 20*(1), 45–52.

Grace, S. L., Evindar, A., & Stewart, D. E. (2003). The effect of postpartum depression on child cognitive development and behavior: A review and critical analysis of the literature. *Archives of Women's Mental Health, 6*(4), 263–274.

Graham, J. R. (2006). *MMPI-2: Assessing personality and psychopathology* (4th ed.). New York: Oxford University Press.

Graham, M. (2007). Brain "pacemaker" tickles your happy nerve. Retrieved May 26, 2008, from http://www.wired.com/science/discoveries/news/2007/05/nerve.

Granot, M., Zisman-Ilani, Y., Ram, E., Goldstick, O., & Yovell, Y. (2011). Characteristics of attachment style in women with dyspareunia. *Journal of Sex & Marital Therapy, 37*(1), 1–16.

Grant, J. E., Donahue, C. B., Odlaug, B. L., & Kim, S. W. (2011). A 6-month follow-up of imaginal desensitization plus motivational interviewing in the treatment of pathological gambling. *Annals of Clinical Psychiatry, 23*(1), 3–10.

Grant, J. E., & Odlaug, B. L. (2010). Impulse control disorders. In D. McKay, J. S. Abramowitz & S. Taylor (Eds.), *Cognitive-behavioral therapy for refractory cases: Turning failure into success.* (pp. 231–254). Washington, DC: American Psychological Association.

Grant, J. E., Stein, D. J., Woods, D. W., & Keuthen, N. J. (Eds.), *Trichotillomania, skin picking, and other body-focused repetitive behaviors.* Arlington, VA: American Psychiatric Publishing.

Gratz, K. L., & Tull, M. T. (2011). Borderline personality disorder. In M. J. Zvolensky, A. Bernstein, & A. A. Vujanovic (Eds.), *Distress tolerance: Theory, research, and clinical applications* (pp. 198–220). New York: Guilford Press.

Gray, H. (1959). *Anatomy of the human body* (27th ed.). Philadelphia: Lea & Febiger.

Gray, J. A., & McNaughton, N. (1996). The neuropsychology of anxiety: Reprise. In D. A. Hope (Ed.), *The Nebraska symposium on motivation* (Vol. 43). Lincoln: University of Nebraska Press.

Gray, J., Nielsen, D. R., Wood, L. E., Andresen, M., & Dolce, K. (2000). Academic progress of children who attended a preschool for abused children: A follow-up of the Keepsafe Project. *Child Abuse and Neglect, 24*(1), 25–32.

Gray, N. A., Zhou, R., Du, J., Moore, G. J., & Manji, H. K. (2003). The use of mood stabilizers as plasticity enhancers in the treatment of neuropsychiatric disorders. *Journal of Clinical Psychiatry, 64*(Suppl. 5), 3–17.

Gray, R. M. (2010). Psychopathy and will to power: Ted Bundy and Dennis Rader. In S. Waller (Ed.), *Serial killers: Being and killing. Philosophy for everyone* (pp. 191–205). Hoboken, NJ: Wiley-Blackwell.

Green, K. M., Zebrak, K. A., Fothergill, K. E., Robertson, J. A., & Ensminger, M. E. (2012). Childhood and adolescent risk factors for comorbid depression and substance use disorders in adulthood. *Addictive Behaviors, 37*(11), 1240–1247.

Green, S. A. (1985). *Mind and body: The psychology of physical illness.* Washington, DC: American Psychiatric Press.

Greenberg, G. (2011, December 27). Inside the battle to define mental illness. *Wired Magazine.*

Greene, E., & Ellis, L. (2007). Decision making in criminal justice. In D. Carson, R. Milne, F. Pakes, K. Shalev, & A. Shawyer (Eds.), *Applying psychology to criminal justice.* Hoboken, NJ: John Wiley & Sons.

Greenfield, S. F., Back, S. E., Lawson, K., & Brady, K. T. (2011). Women and addiction. In J. H. Lowinson & P. Ruiz (Eds.), *Substance abuse: A comprehensive textbook, fifth edition.* Philadelphia, PA: Lippincott, Williams, & Wilkins.

Greening, L., Stoppelbein, L., Fite, P., Dhossche, D., Erath, S., Brown, J., et al. (2008). Pathways to suicidal behaviors in childhood. *Suicide and Life-Threatening Behavior, 38*(1), 35–45.

Gregory, R. J. (2004). *Psychological testing: History, principles, and applications.* Needham Heights, MA: Allyn and Bacon.

Gregoski, M. J., Barnes, V. A., Tingen, M. S., Harshfield, G. A., & Treiber, F. A. (2011). Breathing awareness meditation and LifeSkills Training programs influence upon ambulatory blood pressure and sodium excretion among African American adolescents. *Journal of Adolescent Health, 48*(1), 59–64.

Grekin, P. M., Jemelka, R., & Trupin, E. W. (1994). Racial differences in the criminalization of the mentally ill. *Bulletin of the American Academy of Psychiatry Law, 22,* 411–420.

Grier, B. C., Wilkins, M. L., & Jeffords, E. H. (2010). Diagnosis and treatment of pediatric bipolar disorder. In P. C. McCabe, & S. R. Shaw (Eds.), *Psychiatric disorders: Current topics and interventions for educators* (pp. 17–27). Thousand Oaks, CA: Corwin Press.

Griffiths, K. M., & Christensen, H. (2006). Review of randomised controlled trials of Internet interventions for mental disorders and related conditions. *Australian Psychological Society, 10*(1), 16–29.

Griffiths, M. (2006). An overview of pathological gambling. In T. G. Plante (Ed.), *Mental disorders of the new millennium: Vol. 1. Behavioral issues.* Westport, CT: Praeger.

Grigg, J. R. (1988). Imitative suicides in an active duty military population. *Military Medicine, 153*(2), 79–81.

Grilly, D. M. (2002). *Drugs and human behavior* (4th ed.). Boston: Allyn and Bacon.

Grilly, D. M. (2006). *Drugs and human behavior* (5th ed.). Boston: Pearson.

Grilo, C. M. (2006). *Eating and weight disorders.* New York: Psychology Press.

Grilo, C. M., Masheb, R. M., Brody, M., Toth, C., Burke-Martindale, C. H., & Rothschild, B. S. (2005). Childhood maltreatment in extremely obese male and female bariatric surgery candidates. *Obesity Research, 13,* 123–130.

Grilo, C. M., Masheb, R. M., & Crosby, R. D. (2012). Predictors and moderators of response to cognitive behavioral therapy and medication for the treatment of binge eating disorder. *Journal of Consulting and Clinical Psychology, 80*(5), 897–906.

Grilo, C. M. & Mitchell, J.E. (Eds.). (2010). *The treatment of eating disorders: A clinical handbook.* New York: The Guilford Press.

Grimm, J. W. (2011). Craving. In M. C. Olmstead (Ed.), *Animal models of drug addiction. Springer protocols: Neuromethods* (pp. 311–336). Totowa, NJ: Humana Press.

Grob, G. N. (1966). *State and the mentally ill: A history of Worcester State Hospital in Massachusetts, 1830–1920.* Chapel Hill: University of North Carolina Press.

Groër, M., Meagher, M. W., & Kendall-Tackett, K. (2010). An overview of stress and immunity. In K. Kendall-Tackett (Ed.), *The psychoneuroimmunology of chronic disease: Exploring the links between inflammation, stress, and illness* (pp. 9–22). Washington, DC: American Psychological Association.

Grof, P. (2005). Lithium in bipolar disorder. In S. Kasper & R. M. A. Hirschfeld (Eds.), *Handbook of bipolar disorder: Diagnosis and therapeutic approaches* (pp. 267–284). New York: Taylor & Francis.

Grof, P. (2010). Sixty years of lithium responders. *Neuropsychobiology, 62*(1), 8–16.

Grossman, R. (2004). Pharmacotherapy of personality disorders. In J. J. Magnavita (Ed.), *Handbook of personality disorders: Theory and practice.* Hoboken, NJ: Wiley.

Grove, W. M., Zald, D. H., Lebow, B. S., Snitz, B. E., & Nelson, C. (2000). Clinical versus mechanical prediction: A meta-analysis. *Psychological Assessment, 12,* 19–30.

Grover, S. L. (2010). Lying to bosses, subordinates, peers, and the outside world: Motivations and consequences. In J. Greenberg (Ed.), *Insidious workplace behavior. Applied psychology series* (pp. 207–235). New York: Routledge/Taylor & Francis.

Grubin, D. (2010). Polygraphy. In J. M. Brown & E. A. Campbell (Eds.), *The Cambridge handbook of forensic psychology* (pp. 276–282). New York: Cambridge University Press.

Grucza, R. A., Przybeck, T. R., & Cloninger, C. R. (2007). Prevalence and correlates of binge eating disorder in a community sample. *Comprehensive Psychiatry, 48,* 124–131.

Grunhaus, L., Schreiber, S., Dolberg, O. T., Polak, D., & Dannon, P. N. (2003). A randomized controlled comparison of electroconvulsive therapy and repetitive transcranial magnetic stimulation in severe and resistant nonpsychotic major depression. *Biological Psychiatry, 53,* 324–331.

Gruttadaro, D. (2005). Federal leaders call on schools to help. *NAMI Advocate, 3*(1), 7.

GSS (General Social Survey). (2008). A glance: Medical research. Retrieved on May 23, 2011, from www.ropercenter.uconn.edu/data_access/tag/medical_research.html.

Guarnieri, P. (2009). Towards a history of the family care of psychiatric patients. *Epidemiologia e Psichiatria Sociale, 18*(1), 34–39.

Guimón, J. (2010). Prejudice and realities in stigma. *International Journal of Mental Health, 39*(3), 20–43.

Gum, A. M., King-Kallimanis, B., & Kohn, R. (2009). Prevalence of mood, anxiety, and substance-abuse disorders for older Americans in the national comorbidity survey-replication. *The American Journal of Geriatric Psychiatry, 17*(9), 769–781.

Gumley, A. (2011). Staying well after psychosis: A cognitive interpersonal approach to emotional recovery and relapse prevention. In R. Hagen, D. Turkington, T. Berge, & R. W. Grawe (Eds.), *CBT for psychosis: A symptom-based approach, International Society for the Psychological Treatments of the Schizophrenias and Other Psychoses* (pp. 128–143). New York: Routledge/Taylor & Francis Group.

Gunderson, J. G. (2011). Borderline personality disorder. *New England Journal of Medicine, 364*(21), 2037–2042.

Gunter, M. (2005). Individual psychotherapy versus milieu therapy in childhood and adolescence. *Therapeutic Communities, 26*(2), 163–173.

Gunter, T. D. (2010). Forensic telepsychiatry. In E. P. Benedek, P. Ash, & C. L. Scott (Eds.), *Principles and practice of child and adolescent forensic mental health* (pp. 83–90). Arlington, VA: American Psychiatric Publishing.

Günther, T., Konrad, K., De Brito, S. A., Herpertz-Dahlmann, B., Vloet, & T. D. (2011). Attention functions in children and adolescents with ADHD, depressive disorders, and the comorbid condition. *Journal of Child Psychology and Psychiatry, 52*(3), 324–331.

Gupta, M. A., & Levenson, J. L. (2010). Dermatological disorders. In S. J. Ferrando, J. L. Levenson, & J. A. Owen (Eds.), *Clinical manual of psychopharmacology in the medically ill* (pp. 405–429). Arlington, VA: American Psychiatric Publishing.

Gurman, A. S. (2003). Marital therapies. In A. S. Gurman & S. B. Messer (Eds.), *Essential psychotherapies: Theory and practice* (2nd ed.). New York: Guilford Press.

Gurman, A. S. & Snyder, D. K. (2011). Couple therapy. In J. C. Norcross, G. R. VandenBos, & D. K. Freedheim (Eds.), *History of psychotherapy: Continuity and change* (2nd ed., pp. 485–496). Washington, DC: American Psychological Association.

Guterman, J. T., Martin, C. V., & Rudes, J. (2011). A solution-focused approach to frotteurism. *Journal of Systemic Therapies, 30*(1), 59–72.

Gutheil, T. G. (2005). Boundary issues and personality disorders. *Journal of Psychiatric Practice, 11*(2), 88–96.

Gutheil, T. G. (2010). The expert witness. In R. I. Simon & L. H. Gold (Eds.), *The American Psychiatric Publishing textbook of forensic psychiatry* (2nd ed., pp. 93–110). Arlington, VA: American Psychiatric Publishing.

Gutierrez, D. (2010, June 17). Hooked on SSRIs: Antidepressant use doubles in U.S. *Citizens Commission on Human Rights International.* Available at www.cchrint.org.

Gutman, D. A., & Nemeroff, C. B. (2011). Stress and depression. In R. J. Contrada & A. Baum (Eds.), *The handbook of stress science: Biology, psychology, and health* (pp. 345–357). New York: Springer Publishing.

Guttmacher Institute. (2011). *Insurance coverage of contraceptives.* New York: Author.

Haaken, J., & Reavey, P. (Eds.). (2010). *Memory matters: Contexts for understanding sexual abuse recollections.* New York: Routledge/Taylor & Francis Group.

Haberman, C. (2007). It's not the stress, it's how you deal with it. *New York Times, 156*(54), 109.

Haddad, P. M., & Mattay, V. S. (2011). Neurological complications of antipsychotic drugs. In D. R. Weinberg & P. Harrison (Eds.), *Schizophrenia* (pp. 561–576). Hoboken, NJ: Wiley-Blackwell.

Haddock, G., & Spaulding, W. (2011). Psychological treatment of psychosis. In D. R. Weinberg & P. Harrison (Eds.), *Schizophrenia* (pp. 666–686). Hoboken, NJ: Wiley-Blackwell.

Hadley, S. J., Mandel, F. S., & Schweizer, E. (2012). Switching from long-term benzodiazepine therapy to pregabalin in patients with generalized anxiety disorder: A double-blind, placebo-controlled trial. *Journal of Psychopharmacology, 26*(4), 461–470.

Hadley, S. W., & Strupp, H. H. (1976). Contemporary views of negative effects in psychotherapy: An integrated account. *Biological Psychiatry, 33*(1), 1291–1302.

Hafner, H., & an der Heiden, W. (1988). The mental health care system in transition: A study in organization, effectiveness, and costs of complementary care for schizophrenic patients. In C. N. Stefanis & A. D. Rabavilis (Eds.), *Schizophrenia: Recent biosocial developments.* New York: Human Sciences Press.

Hage, S. M., Romano, J. L., Conyne, R. K., Kenny, M., Matthews, C., Schwartz, J. P., et al. (2007). Best practice guidelines on prevention practice, research, training, and social advocacy for psychologists. *Counseling Psychologist, 35*(4), 493–566.

Hagemoser, S. D. (2009). Braking the bandwagon: Scrutinizing the science and politics of empirically supported therapies. *Journal of Psychology: Interdisciplinary and Applied, 143*(6), 601–614.

Hagen, R., Turkingon, D., Berge, T., & Grawe, R. W. (Eds.). (2011). *CBT for psychosis: A synptom-based approach.* International Society for the Psychological Treatments of the Schizophrenias and Other Psychosis. New York: Routledge/Taylor & Francis Group.

Hagerman, R. J. (2011). Fragile X syndrome and fragile X-associated disorders. In S. Goldstein, & C. R. Reynolds (Eds.), *Handbook of neurodevelopmental and genetic disorders in children* (2nd ed., pp. 276–292) New York: Guilford Press.

Haile, C. N. (2012). History, use, and basic pharmacology of stimulants. In T. R. Kosten, T. F. Newton, R. I. De La Garza, & C. N. Haile (Eds.), *Cocaine and methamphetamine dependence: Advances in treatment* (pp. 13–84). Arlington, VA: American Psychiatric Publishing.

Hajjar, E. R. & Hanlon, J. T. (2010). Polypharmacy and other forms of suboptimal drug use in older patients. In L. C. Hutchison & R. B. Sleeper (Eds.), *Fundamentals of geriatric pharmacotherapy: An evidence-based approach.* Bethesda, MD: American Society of Health-Systems Pharmacists.

Hakuhodo Institute of Life and Living. (2001). What price beauty? *From the HILL, 7*(4).

Hale, J. B., Reddy, L. A., Wilcox, G., McLaughlin, A., Hain, L., Stern, A., et al. (2010). In D. C. Miller (Ed.), *Best practices in school neuropsychology: Guidelines for effective practice., assessment, and evidence-based intervention* (pp. 225–279). Hoboken, NJ: John Wiley & Sons.

Haliburn, J. (2005). Australian and New Zealand clinical practice guidelines for the treatment of anorexia nervosa. *Australian and New Zealand Journal of Psychiatry, 39*(7), 639–640.

Haliburn, J. (2010). Adolescent suicide and SSRI antidepressants. *Australasian Psychiatry, 18*(6), 587.

Hall-Flavin, D. K. (2011). *Nervous breakdown: What does it mean?* Rochester, MN: Mayo Foundation for Medical Education and Research.

Hall, C. W., & Webster, R. E. (2002). Traumatic symptomatology characteristics of adult children of alcoholics. *Journal of Drug Education, 32*(3), 195–211.

Hall, J., Olabi, B., Lawrie, S. M., & Mcintosh, A. M. (2010). Hippocampal and amygdala volumes in borderline personality disorder: A meta-analysis of magnetic resonance imaging studies. *Personality and Mental Health, 4*(3), 172–179.

Hall, K. (2007). Sexual dysfunction and childhood sexual abuse: Gender differences and treatment implications. In S. R. Leiblum (Ed.), *Principles and practice of sex therapy* (4th ed., pp. 350–370). New York: Guilford Press.

Hall, K. (2010). The canary in the coal mine: Reviving sexual desire in long-term relationships. In S. R. Leiblum (Ed.), *Treating sexual desire disorders: A clinical casebook* (pp. 61–74). New York: Guilford Press.

Hall, L. (2012). *Bulimia: A guide to recovery* (completely revised and updated). Buchanan, NY: ReadHowYouWant Publishers.

Hall, L., with Cohn, L. (1980). *Eat without fear.* Santa Barbara, CA: Gurze.

Halloway, J. D. (2004). California psychologists prepare for hospital privileges battle. *APA Monitor on Psychology, 35*(1), 28–29.

Hallquist, M. N., Deming, A., Matthews, A., & Chaves, J. F. (2010). Hypnosis for medically unexplained symptoms and somatoform disorders. In S. J. Lynn, J. W. Rhue, & I. Kirsch (Eds.), *Handbook of clinical hypnosis* (2nd ed., pp. 615–639). Washington, DC: American Psychological Association.

Halmi, K. A. (2010). Psychological comorbidity of eating disorders. In W. S. Agras (Ed.), *The Oxford handbook of eating disorders. Oxford library of psychology* (pp. 282–303). New York: Oxford University Press.

Halpern, J. H. (2003). Hallucinogens: An update. *Current Psychiatry Report, 5*(5), 347–354.

Hamani, C., Mayberg, H., Stone, S., Laxton, A., Haber, S., & Lozano, A. M. (2011). The subcallosal singulate gyrus in the context of major depression. *Biological Psychiatry, 69*(4), 301–308.

Hammar, A., Strand, M., Ardal, G., Schmid, M., Lund, A., & Elliot, R. (2011). Testing the cognitive effort hypothesis of cognitive impairment in major depression. *Nordic Journal of Psychiatry, 65*(1), 74–80.

Hammen, C. L., & Glass, D. R. (1975). Expression, activity, and evaluation of reinforcement. *Journal of Abnormal Psychology, 84*(6), 718–721.

Hammen, C. L., & Krantz, S. (1976). Effect of success and failure on depressive cognitions. *Journal of Abnormal Psychology, 85*(8), 577–588.

Hampton, K., Goulet, L.S., Rainie, L., & Purcell, K. (2011). Social networking sites and our lives. *Report: Communities, social network, web 2.0.* Washington, DC: Pew Internet & American Life Project.

Haney, M. (2008). Neurobiology of stimulants. In H. D. Kleber & M. Galanter (Eds.), *The American Psychiatric Publishing textbook of substance abuse treatment* (4th ed., pp. 143–155). Arlington, VA: American Psychiatric Publishing.

Hankin, B. L., Grant, K. E., Cheeley, C., Wetter, E., Farahmand, F. K., & Westerholm, R. I. (2008). Depressive disorders. In D. Reitman (Ed.), *Handbook of psychological assessment, case conceptualization, and treatment: Vol. 2. Children and adolescents.* Hoboken, NJ: John Wiley & Sons.

Hanna, D., Kershaw, K., & Chaplin, R. (2009). How specialist ECT consultants inform patients about memory loss. *Psychiatric Bulletin, 33*(11), 412–415.

Hansen, W. B., Derzon, J., Dusenbury, L., Bishop, D., Campbell, K., & Alford, A. (2010). Operating characteristics of prevention programs: Connections to drug use etiology. In L. Scheier (Ed.), *Handbook of drug use etiology: Theory, methods, and empirical findings* (pp. 597–616). Washington, DC: American Psychological Association.

Hansson, L., Middelboe, T., Sorgaard, K. W., Bengtsson, T. A., Bjarnason, O., Merinder, L., et al. (2002). Living situation, subjective quality of life and social network among individuals with schizophrenia living in community settings. *Acta Pyschiatrica Scandinavica, 106*(5), 343–350.

Hardin, S. B., Weinrich, S., Weinrich, M., Garrison, C., Addy, C., & Hardin, T. L. (2002). Effects of a long-term psychosocial nursing intervention on adolescents exposed to catastrophic stress. *Issues in Mental Health Nursing, 23*(6), 537–551.

Hardman, M. L., Drew, C. J., & Egan, M. W. (2002). *Human exceptionality: Society, school and family.* Boston: Allyn & Bacon.

Hare, R. D. (1993). *Without conscience: The disturbing world of the psychopaths among us.* New York: Pocket Books.

Harenski, C. L., Thornton, D. M., Harenski, K. A., Decety, J., & Kiehl, K. A. (2012). Increased frontotemporal activation during pain observation in sexual sadism: Preliminary findings. *Archives of General Psychiatry, 69*(3), 283–292.

Harklute, A. (2010, July 26). Computer uses in clinical psychology. Retrieved on March 1, 2011, from www.ehow.com/print/list_6775537_computer-uses-clinical-psychology.html.

Harkness, K. L., & Lumley, M. N. (2008). Child abuse and neglect and the development of depression in children and adolescents. In J. R. Z. Abela & B. L. Hankin (Eds.), *Handbook of depression in children and adolescents.* New York: Guilford Press.

Harlapur, M., Abraham, D., & Shimbo, D. (2010). Cardiology. In J. M. Suls, K. W. Davidson, & R. M. Kaplan, (Eds.), *Handbook of health psychology and behavioral medicine* (pp. 411–425). New York: Guilford Press.

Harlow, H. F., & Harlow, M. K. (1965). The affectional systems. In A. Schrier, H. Harlow, & F. Stollnitz (Eds.), *Behavior of nonhuman primates* (Vol. 2). New York: Academic Press.

Harlow, H. F., & Zimmermann, R. R. (1996). Affectional responses in the infant monkey. In L. C. Drickamer & L. D. Houck (Eds.), *Foundations of animal behavior: Classic papers with commentaries* (pp. 376–387). Chicago, IL: University of Chicago Press.

Haroules, B. (2007). Involuntary commitment is unconstitutional. In A. Quigley (Ed.), *Current controversies: Mental health.* Detroit: Greenhaven Press/Thomson Gale.

Harper, K. N., & Brown, A. S. (2012). Prenatal nutrition and the etiology of schizophrenia. In A. S. Brown & P. H. Patterson (Eds.), *The origins of schizophrenia* (pp. 58–95). New York: Columbia University Press.

Harris Poll. (2004). Number of cyberchondriacs. *Harris Interactive.* Available at http://www.harrisinteractive.com/harrispoll.

Harris Poll. (2005, April 27). *Majorities of U.S. adults favor euthanasia and physician-assisted suicide by more than two-to-one* (Harris Poll, No. 32). Retrieved June 9, 2008, from www.harrisinteractive.com.harris_poll.

Harris Poll. (2006, August 8). *Doctors and teachers most trusted among 22 occupations and professions: Fewer adults trust the president to tell the truth* (Harris Poll, No. 61). Retrieved June 9, 2008, from http://www.harrisinteractive.com/harris_poll.

Harris Poll. (2007, July 31). Harris Poll shows number of "cyberchondriacs"—adults who have ever gone online for health information—increases to an estimated 160 million nationwide (Harris Poll No. 76). New York: Harris Interactive.

Harris Poll. (2008, February 8). Three in ten Americans with a tattoo say having one makes them feel sexier. (Harris Poll No. 15). New York: Harris Interactive.

Harris Poll. (2010). Annual happiness index finds one-third of Americans are very happy. *Harris Interactive.* Available at http://www.harrisinteractive.com/NewsRoom/HarrisPolls/tabid/447.

Harris, A., Ayers, T., & Leek, M. R. (1985). Auditory span of apprehension deficits in schizophrenia. *Journal of Nervous and Mental Disease, 173*(11), 650–657.

Harris, G. (2008, January 24). F.D.A. requiring suicide studies in drug trials. *New York Times.* Retrieved January 24, 2008, from www.nytimes.com.

Harris, G. T., & Rice, M. E. (2006). Treatment of psychopathy: A review of empirical findings. In C. J. Patrick (Ed.), *Handbook of psychopathy.* New York: Guilford Press.

Harris, J. C. (2010). Intellectual disability: A guide for families and professionals. New York: Oxford University Press.

Harrison, E. & Petrakis, I. (2011). Naltrexone pharmacotherapy. In J. H. Lowinson & P. Ruiz (Eds.), *Substance abuse: A comprehensive textbook, fifth edition.* Philadelphia, PA: Lippincott, Williams, & Wilkins.

Harrison, P. J., Lewis, D. A., & Kleinman, J. E. (2011). Neuropathology of schizophrenia. In D. R. Weinberg & P. Harrison (Eds.), *Schizophrenia* (pp. 372–392). Hoboken, NJ: Wiley-Blackwell.

Hart, C., Ksir, C., & Ray, O. (2010). *Drugs, society, and human behavior.* New York: McGraw-Hill Humanities.

Hart, S., Russell, J., & Abraham, S. (2011). Nutrition and dietetic practice in eating disorder management. *Journal of Human Nutrition and Dietetics, 24*(2), 144–153.

Hartberg, C. B., Sundet, K., Rimol, L. M., Haukvik, U. K., Lange, E. H., Nesvag, R., Melle, I., Andreassen, O. A., & Agartz, I. (2011). Subcortical brain volumes relate to neurocognition in schizophrenia and bipolar disorder and healthy controls. *Progress in Neuro-Psychopharmacology & Biological Psychiatry, 35*(4), 1122–1130.

Hartford, D., & Marcus, L. M. (2011). Educational approaches. In E. Hollander, A. Kolevzon & J. T. Coyle (Eds.), *Textbook of autism spectrum disorders.* (pp. 537–553). Arlington, VA: American Psychiatric Publishing, Inc.

Hartley, T. A., Violanti, J. M., Fekedulegn, D., Andrew, M. E., & Burchfield, C. M. (2007). Associations between major life events, traumatic incidents, and depression among Buffalo police officers. *International Journal of Emergency Mental Health, 9*(1), 25–35.

Hartmann, U., & Waldinger, M. D. (2007). Treatment of delayed ejaculation. In S. R. Leiblum (Ed.), *Principles and practice of sex therapy* (4th ed., pp. 241–276). New York: Guilford Press.

Harway, M. (Ed.). (2005). *Handbook of couples therapy.* New York: Wiley.

Hastings, R. P. (2008). Stress in parents of children with autism. In E. McGregor, M. Núñez, K. Cebula, & J. C. Gómez (Eds.), *Autism: An integrated view from neurocognitive, clinical, and intervention research.* Malden, MA: Blackwell Publishing.

Hausman, A. (2008). Direct-to-consumer advertising and its effect on prescription requests. *Journal of Advertising Research, 48*(1), 42–56.

Hawkins, J. R. (2004). The role of emotional repression in chronic back pain: A study of chronic back pain patients undergoing psychodynamically oriented group psychotherapy as treatment for their pain. *Dissertation Abstracts International: Section B: The Sciences and Engineering, 64*(8-B), 4038.

Hawkley, L. C., Thisted, R. A., Masi, C. M., & Cacioppo, J. T. (2010). Loneliness predicts blood pressure: 5-year cross-lagged analyses in middle-aged and older adults. *Psychology and Aging, 25*(1), 132–141.

Hawkrigg, J. J. (1975). Agoraphobia. *Nursing Times, 71,* 1280–1282.

Hawks, E., Blumenthal, H., Feldner, M. T., Leen-Feldner, E. W., & Jones, R. (2011). An examination of the relation between traumatic event exposure and panic-relevant biological challenge responding among adolescents. *Behavior Therapy, 42*(3), 427–438.

Hayaki, J., Friedman, M. A., & Brownell, K. D. (2002). Shame and severity of bulimic symptoms. *Eating Behaviors, 3*(1), 73–83.

Hayden, L. A. (1998). Gender discrimination within the reproductive health care system: Viagra v. birth control. *Journal of Law and Health, 13,* 171–198.

Hayes, R. D. (2011). Circular and linear modeling of female sexual desire and arousal. *Journal of Sex Research, 48*(2-3), 130–141.

Hayes, S. C. (2002). Acceptance, mindfulness, and science. *Clinical Psychology: Science and Practice, 9,* 101–106.

Hayes, S. C., Follette, V. M., & Linehan, M. M. (Eds.). (2004). *Mindfulness and acceptance: Expanding the cognitive-behavioral tradition.* New York: Guilford Press.

Hayes, S. C., & Lillis, J. (2012). *Acceptance and commitment therapy: Theories of psychotherapy series.* Washington, DC: American Psychological Association.

Hayes, S. C., Luoma, J. B., Bond, F. W., Masuda, A., & Lillis, J. (2006). Acceptance and commitment therapy: Model, processes and outcomes. *Behavioral Research and Therapy, 44,* 1–25.

Haynes, S. G., Feinleib, M., & Kannel, W. B. (1980). The relationship of psychosocial factors to coronary heart disease in the Framingham study: III. Eight-year incidence of coronary heart disease. *American Journal of Epidemiology, 111,* 37–58.

Haynes, S. N. (2001). Clinical applications of analog behavioral observations: Dimensions of psychometric evaluations. *Psychological Assessment, 13*(1), 73–85.

Hayward, M. D., & Taylor, J. E. (1965). A schizophrenic patient describes the action of intensive psychotherapy. *Psychiatric Quarterly, 30.*

Hazlett, E. A., Goldstein, K. E., Tajima-Pozo, K., Speidel, E. R., Zelmanova, Y., Entis, J. J., Silverman, J. M., New, A. S., Koenigsberg, H. W., Haznedar, M. M., Byne, W., & Siever, L. J. (2011). Cingulate and temporal lobe fractional anisotropy in schizotypal personality disorder. *NeuroImage, 55*(3), 900–908.

HBIGDA (Harry Benjamin International Gender Dysphoria Association). (2001). The standards of care for gender identity disorders (6th version). *International Journal of Transgenderism, 5*(1).

Healy, D., Whitaker, C., & LaPierre, Y. D. (2010). Does taking antidepressants lead to suicide? In B. Slife (Ed.), *Clashing views on psychological issues* (16th ed., 272–291). New York: McGraw-Hill.

Heard-Davison, A., Heiman, J. R., & Briggs, B. (2004). Sexual disorders affecting women. In L. J. Haas (Ed.), *Handbook of primary care psychology* (pp. 495–509). New York: Oxford University Press.

Heavey, L., Pring, L., & Hermelin, B. (1999). A date to remember: The nature of memory in savant calendrical calculators. *Psychological Medicine, 29*(1), 145–160.

Heffernan, T., Clark, T., Bartholomew, J., & Stephens, S. (2010). Does binge drinking in teenagers affect their everyday prospective memory? *Drug and Alcohol Dependence, 109*(1-3), 73–78.

Hegerl, U., Schönknecht, P., & Mergl, R. (2012). "Are antidepressants useful in the treatment of minor depression: A critical update of the current literature": Erratum. *Current Opinion* in Psychiatry, 25(2), 163.

Heilbrun, K., & Erickson, J. (2007). A behavioural science perspective on identifying and managing hindsight bias and unstructured judgement: Implications for legal decision making. In D. Carson, R. Milne, F. Pakes, K. Shalev, & A. Shawyer (Eds.), *Applying psychology to criminal justice*. Hoboken, NJ: John Wiley & Sons.

Heilbrun, K., Goldstein, N. E. S, & Redding, R. E. (Eds.). (2005). *Juvenile delinquency: Prevention, assessment, and intervention* (pp. 85–110). New York: Oxford University Press.

Heiman, J. R. (2000). Organic disorders in women. In S. R. Leiblum & R. C. Rosen (Eds.), *Principles and practice of sex therapy* (3rd ed., pp. 118–153). New York: Guilford Press.

Heiman, J. R. (2002). Psychologic treatments for female sexual dysfunction: Are they effective and do we need them? *Archives of Sexual Behavior, 31,* 445–450.

Heiman, J. R. (2002). Sexual dysfunction: Overview of prevalence, etiological factors, and treatments. *Journal of Sex Research, 39*(1), 73–78.

Heiman, J. R. (2007). Orgasmic disorders in women. In S. R. Leiblum (Ed.), *Principles and practice of sex therapy* (4th ed., pp. 84–123). New York: Guilford Press.

Heiman, J. R., Gladue, B. A., Roberts, C. W., & LoPiccolo, J. (1986). Historical and current factors discriminating sexually functional from sexually dysfunctional married couples. *Journal of Marital and Family Therapy, 12*(2), 163–174.

Heiman, J. R., Rupp, H., Janssen, E., Newhouse, S. K., Brauer, M., & Laan, E. (2011). Sexual desire, sexual arousal and hormonal differences in premenopausal US and Dutch women with and without low sexual desire. *Hormones and Behavior, 59*(5), 772–779.

Heimberg, R. G., Brozovich, F. A., & Rapee, R. M. (2010). A cognitive-behavioral model of social anxiety disorder: Update and extension. In S.G. Hofmann & P.M. DiBartolo (Eds.), *Social anxiety: Clinical, developmental, and social perspectives*. New York: Academic Press.

Heinrichs, D. W., & Carpenter, W. T., Jr. (1983). The coordination of family therapy with other treatment modalities for schizophrenia. In W. McFarlane (Ed.), *Family therapy in schizophrenia*. New York: Guilford Press.

Heir, T., Piatigorsky, A., & Weisaeth, L. (2010). Posttraumatic stress symptom clusters associations with psychopathology and functional impairment. *Journal of Anxiety Disorders, 24*(8), 936–940.

Heitman, D., Schmuhl, M., Reinisch, A., & Bauer, U. (2012). Primary prevention for children of mentally ill parents: The Kanu-program. *Journal of Public Health, 20*(2), 125–130.

Helder, S. G., & Collier, D. A. (2011). The genetics of eating disorders. In R. A. H. Adan & W. H. Kaye (Eds.), *Behavioral neurobiology of eating disorders. Current topics in behavioral neurosciences* (pp. 157–175). New York: Springer-Verlag Publishing.

Hellings, J. A., Cardona, A. M., & Schroeder, S. R. (2010). Long-term safety and adverse events of resperidone in children, adolescents, and adults with pervasive developmental disorders. *Journal of Mental Health Research in Intellectual Disabilities, 3*(3), 132–144.

Hembree, E. A., & Foa, E. B. (2010). Cognitive behavioral treatments for PTSD. In G. M. Rosen & B. C. Frueh (Eds.), *Clinician's guide to posttraumatic stress disorder* (pp. 177–203). Hoboken, NJ: John Wiley & Sons.

Hemmings, C. (2010). Service use and outcomes. In N. Bouras (Ed.), *Mental health services for adults with intellectual disability: Strategies and solutions. The Maudsley Series* (pp. 75–88). New York: Psychology Press.

Henderson, V. (2010). Diminishing dissociative experiences for war veterans in group therapy. In S. S. Fehr (Ed.), *101 interventions in group therapy* (rev. ed., pp. 217–220). New York: Routledge/Taylor & Francis Group.

Hendin, H. (2002). The Dutch experience. In K. Foley & H. Hendin (Eds.), *The case against assisted suicide: For the right to end-of-life care* (pp. 97–121). Baltimore, MD: The John Hopkins University Press.

Henley, T. C., & Thorne, B. M. (2005). The lost millennium: Psychology during the Middle Ages. *Psychological Record, 55*(1), 103–113.

Henry, A. (2011). *Cell phone use is up, but brain cancer rates are down*. Available at http://www.extremetech.com/mobile/24862-23752.

Herbeck, D. M., West, J. C., Ruditis, I., Duffy, F. F., Fitek, D. J., Bell, C. C., et al. (2004). Variations in use of second-generation antipsychotic medication by race among adult psychiatric patients. *Psychiatric Services, 55*(6), 677–684.

Herbert, J. D. (2007). Avoidant personality disorder. In W. O'Donohue, K. A. Fowler, & S. O. Lilienfeld (Eds.). *Personality disorders: Toward the DSM-V.* Los Angeles: Sage Publications.

Herbert, J. D., Gaudiano, B. A., Rheingold, A., Harwell, V., Dalrymple, K., & Nolan, E. M. (2005). Social skills training augments the effectiveness of cognitive behavior group therapy for social anxiety disorder. *Behavior Therapy, 36,* 125–138.

Herholz, K., & Ebmeier, K. (2011). Clinical amyloid imaging in Alzheimer's disease. *Lancet Neurology, 10*(7), 667–670.

Herman, N. J. (1999). Road rage: An exploratory analysis. *Michigan Sociological Review, 13,* 65–79.

Hernandez-Avila, C. A. & Kranzler, H. R. (2011). Alcohol use disorders. In J. H. Lowinson & P. Ruiz (Eds.), *Substance abuse: A comprehensive textbook, fifth edition.* Philadelphia, PA: Lippincott, Williams, & Wilkins.

Herning, R. I., Better, W. E., Tate, K., & Cadet, J. L. (2005). Cerebrovascular perfusion in marijuana users during a month of monitored abstinence. *Neurology, 64,* 488–493.

Herpertz, S. C. (2011). Contribution of neurobiology to our knowledge of borderline personality disorder. *Der Nervenarzt, 82*(1), 9–15.

Herrick, A. L., Marshal, M. P., Smith, H. A., Sucato, G., & Stall, R. D. (2011). Sex while intoxicated: A meta-analysis comparing heterosexual and sexual minority youth. *Journal of Adolescent Health, 48*(4), 306–309.

Hersen, M., Bellack, A. S., Himmelhoch, J. M., & Thase, M. E. (1984). Effects of social skill training, amitriptyline, and psychotherapy in unipolar depressed women. *Behavior Therapist, 15,* 21–40.

Hertzman, M. (2010). Do antidepressants cause suicide? In M. Hertzman & L. Adler (Eds.), *Clinical trials in psychopharmacology: A better brain* (2nd ed., pp. 31–41). Hoboken, NJ: Wiley-Blackwell.

Herzig, H. (2004). *Medical information.* Somerset, England: Somerset and Wessex Eating Disorders Association.

Herzog, T., Zeeck, A., Hartmann, A., & Nickel, T. (2004). Lower targets for weekly weight gain lead to better results in inpatient treatment of anorexia nervosa: A pilot study. *European Eating Disorders Review, 12*(3), 164–168.

Hess, A. (2009 June 16). *Huffington Post:* Sometimes a cigar is just a nipple is just sexist. *Washington City Paper.*

Hess, N. (1995). Cancer as a defence against depressive pain. University College Hospital/Middlesex Hospital Psychotherapy Department. *Psychoanalytic Psychotherapy, 9*(2), 175–184.

Heston, L. L. (1992). *Mending minds: A guide to the new psychiatry of depression, anxiety, and other serious mental disorders.* New York: W. H. Freeman and Company.

Heylens, G., De Cuyper, G., Zucker, K. J., Schelfaut, C., Elaut, E., Vanden Bossche, H., De Baere, E., & T'Sjoen, G. (2012). Gender identity disorder in twins: A review of the case report literature. *Journal of Sexual Medicine, 9*(3), 751–757.

Heyman, R. E., & Slep, A. M. S. (2002). Do child abuse and interparental violence lead to adulthood family violence? *Journal of Marriage and Family, 64*(4), 864–870.

HHS (Department of Health & Human Services). (2009). *Mental health and African Americans.* Washington, DC: Office of Minority Health.

Hibbs, E. D., & Jensen, P. S. (2005). Analyzing the research. In E. D. Hibbs & P. S. Jensen (Eds.), *Psychosocial treatments for child and adolescent disorders: Empirically based strategies for clinical practice* (2nd ed., pp. 3–8). Washington, DC: American Psychological Association.

Hickey, E. (2002). *Serial murderers and their victims* (3rd ed.). Belmont: Wadsworth.

Hickling, E. J., & Blanchard, E. B. (2007). Motor vehicle accidents and psychological trauma. In E. K. Carll (Ed.), *Trauma psychology: Issues in violence, disaster, health, and illness* (Vol. 2). Westport, CT: Praeger Publishers.

Hiday, V. A. (2006). Putting community risk in perspective: A look at correlations, causes and controls. *International Journal of Law and Psychiatry 29*(4), 316–331.

Hiday, V. A., & Burns, P. J. (2010). Mental illness and the criminal justice system. In T. L. Scheid & T. N. Brown (Eds.), *A handbook for the study of mental health: Social contexts, theories, and systems* (2nd ed., pp. 478–498). New York: Cambridge University Press.

Hiday, V. A., & Wales, H. W. (2003). Civil commitment and arrests. *Current Opinions in Psychiatry, 16*(5), 575–580.

Higgins, E. S., & George, M. S. (2007). *The neuroscience of clinical psychiatry: The pathophysiology of behavior and mental illness.* Philadelphia: Wolters Kluwer/Lippincott Williams & Wilkins.

Higgins, S. T., Budney, A. J., Bickel, W. K., Hughes, J., Foerg, F., & Badger, G. (1993).

Achieving cocaine abstinence with a behavioral approach. *American Journal of Psychiatry, 150*(5), 763–769.

Higgins, S. T., Silverman, K., Washio, Y. (011). Contingency management. In M. Galanter & H. D. Kleber (Eds.), *Psychotherapy for the treatment of substance abuse* (pp. 192–218). Arlington, VA: American Psychiatric Publishing.

Highet, N., Thompson, M., & McNair, B. (2005). Identifying depression in a family member: The carers' experience. *Journal of Affective Disorders, 87*(1), 25–33.

Hildebrand, K. M., Johnson, D. J., Dewayne, J., & Bogle, K. (2001). Comparison of patterns of alcohol use between high school and college athletes and non-athletes. *College Student Journal, 35,* 358–365.

Hildebrandt, T., & Alfano, L. (2009). A review of eating disorders in males: Working towards an improved diagnostic system. *International Journal of Child and Adolescent Health, 2*(2), 185–196.

Hill, A. J. (2006). Body dissatisfaction and dieting in children. In P. J. Cooper & A. Stein (Eds.), *Childhood feeding problems and adolescent eating disorders.* London: Routledge/Taylor & Francis Group.

Hill, K. P., & Weiss, R. D. (2011). Amphetamines and other stimulants. In J. H. Lowinson & P. Ruiz (Eds.), *Substance abuse: A comprehensive textbook, fifth edition.* Philadelphia, PA: Lippincott, Williams, & Wilkins.

Hillemeier M. M., Foster, E. M., Heinrichs, B., & Heier, B. (2007). Racial differences in parental reports of attention-deficit/hyperactivity disorder behaviors. *Journal of Developmental and Behavioral Pediatrics, 28*(5), 353–361.

Hinchliff, S., & Gott, M. (2011). Seeking medical help for sexual concerns in mid- and later life: A review of the literature. *Journal of Sex Research, 48*(2-3), 106–117.

Hingson, R., Heeren, T., Zakocs, R., Kopstein, A., & Wechsler, H. (2002). Magnitude of alcohol-related morbidity, mortality, and alcohol dependence among U.S. college students age 18–24. *Journal of Studies on Alcohol, 63*(2), 136–144.

Hingson, R. W., & White, A. M. (2010). Magnitude and prevention of college alcohol and drug misuse: US college students aged 18–24. In J. Kay & V. Schwartz (Eds.), *Mental health care in the college community* (pp. 289–324). Hoboken, NJ: Wiley-Blackwell.

Hinrichsen, G. A. (1999). Interpersonal psychotherapy for late-life depression In M. Duffy (Ed.), *Handbook of counseling and psychotherapy with older adults.* New York: Wiley.

Hinrichsen, G. A. (2010). Public policy and the provision of psychological services to older adults. *Professional Psychology: Research and Practice, 41*(2), 97–103.

Hinshelwood, R. D. (2010). Psychoanalytic research: Is clinical material any use? *Psychoanalytic Psychotherapy, 24*(4), 362–379.

Hiroeh, U., Appleby, L., Mortensen, P.-B., & Dunn, G. (2001). Death by homicide, suicide, and other unnatural causes in people with mental illness: A population-based study. *Lancet, 358*(9299), 2110–2112.

Hirsch, J. K., Duberstein, P. R., & Unützer, J. (2009). Chronic medical problems and distressful thoughts of suicide in primary care patients: Mitigating role of happiness. *International Journal of Geriatric Psychiatry, 24*(7), 671–679.

Hirschfeld, R. M., Lewis, L., & Vornik, L. A. (2003). Perceptions and impact of bipolar-disorder: How far have we really come? Results of the National Depressive and Manic-Depressive Associations 2000 Survey of Individuals with Bipolar Disorder. *Journal of Clinical Psychiatry, 64*(2), 161–174.

Hirstein, W. (2011). Confabulations about personal memories, normal and abnormal. In S. Nalbantian, P. M. Matthews, & J. L. McClelland (Eds.), *The memory process: Neuroscientific and humanistic perspectives* (pp. 217–232). Cambridge, MA: MIT Press.

Hitti, M. (2004). Brain chemicals suggest marijuana's effects. Retrieved September 24, 2004, from my.webmd.com/content/-Article/94/102660.htm.

Hoaas, L. E. C., Lindholm, S. E., Berge, T., & Hagen, R. (2011). The therapeutic alliance in cognitive behavioral therapy for psychosis. In R. Hagen, D. Turkington, T. Berge, & R. W. Grawe (Eds.), *CBT for psychosis: A symptom-based approach, International Society for the Psychological Treatments of the Schizophrenias and Other Psychoses* (pp. 59–76). New York: Routledge/Taylor & Francis Group.

Hoagwood, K., Kelleher, K. J., Feil, M., & Comer, D. M. (2000). Treatment services for children with ADHD: A national perspective. *Journal of the American Academy of Child and Adolescent Psychiatry, 39*(2), 198–206.

Hobbs, F. B. (1997). The elderly population. *U.S. Census Bureau: The official statistics.* Washington, DC: U.S. Census Bureau.

Hobson-West, P. (2010). The role of "public opinion" in the UK animal research debate. *Journal of Medical Ethics: Journal of the Institute of Medical Ethics, 36*(1), 46–49.

Hochman, S. (2011, May 5). Victorino's positive spirit has helped him deal with ADD. *Philadelphia Daily News.*

Hodapp, R. M., & Dykens, E. M. (2003). Mental retardation (intellectual disabilities). In E. J. Mash & R. A. Barkley (Eds.), *Child psychopathology* (2nd ed.). New York: Guilford Press.

Hodges, S. (2003). Borderline personality disorder and posttraumatic stress disorder: Time for integration? *Journal of Counseling & Development, 81*(4), 409–417.

Hodgson, R. J., & Rachman, S. (1972). The effects of contamination and washing in obsessional patients. *Behavioral Research and Therapy, 10,* 111–117.

Hofer , M. A. (2010). Evolutionary concepts of anxiety. In D. J. Stein, E. Hollander, & B. O. Rothbaum (Eds.), *Textbook of anxiety disorders* (2nd ed., pp. 129–145). Arlington, VA: American Psychiatric Publishing.

Hoffman, J. (2011, September 25). When your therapist is only a click away. *New York Times.*

Hoffman, K. B. (2007, May 26). Kevorkian's cause founders as he's freed. Retrieved May 26, 2007, from http://news.yahoo.com.

Hoffman, R. E. (2010). Revisiting Arieti's "listening attitude" and hallucinated voices. *Schizophrenia Bulletin, 36*(3), 440–442.

Hoffman, R. E., Boutros, N. N., Hu, S., et al. (2000). Transcranial magnetic stimulation and auditory hallucinations in schizophrenia [Letter]. *Lancet, 355*(9209), 1073–1075.

Hoffman, R. E., Hampson, M., Wu, K., Anderson, A. W., Gore, J. C., Buchanan, R. J., et al. (2007, February 13). Probing the pathophysiology of auditory/verbal hallucinations by combining functional magnetic resonance imaging and transcranial magnetic stimulation. *Cerebral Cortex.* Retrieved August 5, 2008, from http://cercor.oxfordjournals.org/cgi/content/abstractbhl183.

Hofmann, S. G. (2007). Cognitive factors that maintain social anxiety disorder: A comprehensive model and its treatment implications. *Cognitive Behaviour Therapy, 36*(4), 193–209.

Hofmann, S. G., Rief, W., & Spiegel, D. A. (2010). Psychotherapy for panic disorder. In D. J. Stein, E. Hollander, & B. O. Rothbaum (Eds.), *Textbook of anxiety disorders* (2nd ed., pp. 417–433). Arlington, VA: American Psychiatric Publishing.

Hogan, R. A. (1968). The implosive technique. *Behavioral Research and Therapy, 6,* 423–431.

Hogarty, G. E. (2002). *Personal therapy for schizophrenia and related disorders: A guide to individualized treatment.* New York: Guilford Press.

Hogarty, G. E., Anderson, C. M., Reiss, D. J., Kornblith, S. J., Greenwald, D. P., Javna, C. D., et al. (1986). Family psychoeducation, social skills training, and maintenance chemotherapy in the aftercare treatment of schizophrenia: I. One-year effects of a controlled study on relapse and expressed emotion. *Archives of General Psychiatry, 43*(7), 633–642.

Hogarty, G. E., et al. (1974). Drug and sociotherapy in the aftercare of schizophrenic patients: II. Two-year relapse rates. *Archives of General Psychiatry, 31*(5), 603–608.

Hogarty, G. E., et al. (1974). Drug and sociotherapy in the aftercare of schizophrenic patients: III. Adjustment of nonrelapsed patients. *Archives of General Psychiatry, 31*(5), 609–618.

Hogarty, G. E., Greenwald, D. P., & Eack, S. M. (2006). Durability and mechanism of effects of cognitive enhancement therapy. *Psychiatric Services, 57*(12), 1751–1757.

Hohagen, F., Winkelmann, G., Rasche-Raeuchle, H., Hand, I., Koenig, A., Muenchau, N., et al. (1998). Combination of behaviour therapy with fluvoxamine in comparison with behaviour therapy and placebo: Results of a multicentre study. *British Journal of Psychiatry, 173*(Suppl. 35), 71–78.

Holder, M. D., & Klassen, A. (2010). Temperament and happiness in children. *Journal of Happiness Studies, 11*(4), 419–439.

Holifield, C., Goodman, J., Hazelkorn, M., & Heflin, L. J. (2010). Using self-monitoring to increase attending to task and academic accuracy in children with autism. *Focus on Autism and Other Developmental Disabilities, 25*(4), 230–238.

Holinger, P. C., & Offer, D. (1982). Prediction of adolescent suicide: A population model. *American Journal of Psychiatry, 139,* 302–307.

Holinger, P. C., & Offer, D. (1991). Sociodemographic, epidemiologic, and individual attributes. In L. Davidson & M. Linnoila (Eds.), *Risk factors for youth suicide.* New York: Hemisphere.

Holinger, P. C., & Offer, D. (1993). *Adolescent suicide.* New York: Guilford Press.

Hollander, E., & Simeon, D. (2011). Anxiety disorders. In R. E. Hales, S. C. Yudofsky, & G. O. Gabbard (Eds.), *Essentials of psychiatry* (3rd ed., pp. 185–228). Arlington, VA: American Psychiatric Publishing.

Hollander, E., Zohar, J., Sirovatka, P. J., & Regier, D. A. (2011). *Obsessive-compulsive spectrum disorders: Refining the research agenda for DSM-V.* Washington, DC: American Psychiatric Association.

Hollingworth, P., Harold, D., Jones, L., Owen, M. J., & Williams, J. (2011). Alzheimer's disease genetics: Current knowledge and future challenges. *International Journal of Geriatric Psychiatry, 26*(8), 793–802.

Hollon, S. D., DeRubeis, R. J., Shelton, R. C., Amsterdam, J. D., Salomon, R. M., O'Reardon, J. P., et al. (2005). Prevention of relapse following cognitive therapy v. medications in moderate to severe depression. *Archives of General Psychiatry, 62,* 417–422.

Hollon, S. D., & DiGiuseppe, R. (2011). Cognitive theories of psychotherapy. In J. C. Norcross, G. R. VandenBos, & D. K. Freedheim (Eds.), *History of psychotherapy: Continuity and change* (2nd ed., pp. 203–241). Washington, DC: American Psychological Association.

Hollon, S. D., Haman, K. L., & Brown, L. L. (2002). Cognitive behavioral treatment of depression. In I. H. Gotlib & C. L. Hammen (Eds.), *Handbook of depression* (pp. 383–403). New York: Guilford Press.

Hollon, S. D., & Ponniah, K. (2010). A review of empirically supported psychological therapies for mood disorders in adults. *Depression and Anxiety, 27*(10), 891–932.

Hollon, S. D., Stewart, M. O., & Strunk D. (2006). Enduring effects for cognitive behavior therapy in the treatment of depression and anxiety. *Annual Review of Psychology, 57,* 285–315.

Hollway, J. A., & Aman, M. G. (2011). Pharmacological treatment of sleep disturbance in developmental disabilities: A review of the literature. *Research in Developmental Disabilities, 32*(3), 939–962.

Holm, H. J., & Kawagoe, T. (2010). Face-to-face lying—An experimental study in Sweden and Japan. *Journal of Economic Psychology, 31*(3), 310–321.

Holmes, T. H., & Rahe, R. H. (1967). The Social Readjustment Rating Scale. *Journal of Psychosomatic Research, 11,* 213–218.

Holmes, T. H., & Rahe, R. H. (1989). The Social Readjustment Rating Scale. In T. H. Holmes & E. M. David (Eds.), *Life change, life events, and illness: Selected papers.* New York: Praeger.

Holstein, J. A. (1993). Court-ordered insanity: Interpretive practice and involuntary commitment. New York: Aldine de Gruyter.

Holwerda, T. J., Schoevers, R. A., Dekker, J., Deeg, D. J. H., Jonker, C., & Beekman, A. T. F. (2007). The relationship between generalized anxiety disorder, depression and mortality in old age. *International Journal of Geriatric Psychiatry, 22*(3), 241–249.

Hölzel, L., Härter, M., Reese, C., & Kriston, L. (2011). Risk factors for chronic depression—A systematic review. *Journal of Affective Disorders, 129*(1-3), 1–13.

Homant, R. J., & Kennedy, D. B. (2006). Serial murder: A biopsychosocial approach. In W. Petherick (Ed.), *Serial crime: Theoretical and practical issues in behavioral profiling* (pp. 189–228). San Diego, CA: Elsevier.

Honberg, R. (2005). Decriminalizing mental illness. *NAMI Advocate, 3*(1), 4–5.

Hong, J. P., Samuels, J., Bienvenu, O. J., III, Cannistraro, P., Grados, M., Riddle, M. A., et al. (2004). Clinical correlates of recurrent major depression in obsessive-compulsive disorder. *Depression and Anxiety, 20*(2), 86–91.

Hooper, J. F., McLearen, A. M., & Barnett, M. E. (2005). The Alabama structured assessment of treatment completion for insanity acquittees (The AlaSATcom). *International Journal of Law and Psychiatry, 28*(6), 604–612.

Hope, L. (2010). Eyewitness testimony. In G. J. Towl & D. A. Crighton (Eds.), *Forensic psychology* (pp. 160–177). Hoboken, NJ: Wiley-Blackwell.

Hopfer, C. (2011). Club drug, prescription drug, and over-the-counter medication abuse: Description, diagnosis, and intervention. In Y. Kaminer & K. C. Winters (Eds.), *Clinical manual of adolescent substance abuse treatment* (pp. 187–212). Arlington, VA: American Psychiatric Publishing.

Hopko, D. R., Robertson, S. M. C., Widman, L., & Lejuez, C. W. (2008). Specific phobias. In M. Hersen & J. Rosqvist (Eds.), *Handbook of psychological assessment, case conceptualization, and treatment: Vol. 1. Adults* (pp. 139–170). Hoboken, NJ: John Wiley & Sons.

Horney, K. (1937). *The neurotic personality of our time.* New York: Norton.

Hornyak, L. M., & Green, J. P. (Eds.). (2000). *Healing from within: The use of hypnosis in women's health care.* Washington, DC: American Psychological Association.

Horowitz, J. A., Damato, E. G., Duffy, M. E., & Solon, L. (2005). The relationship of maternal attributes, resources, and perceptions of postpartum experiences to depression. *Research in Nursing and Health, 28*(2), 159–171.

Horowitz, J. A., Damato, E., Solon, L., Metzsch, G., & Gill, V. (1995). Postpartum depression: Issues in clinical assessment. *Journal of Perinatal Medicine, 15*(4), 268–278.

Horowitz, M. J. (2011). *Stress response syndromes: PTSD, grief, adjustment, and dissociative disorders* (5th ed.). Lanham, MD: Jason Aronson.

Horowitz, M. J., & Lerner, U. (2010). Treatment of histrionic personality disorder. In J. F. Clarkin, P. Fonagy, & G. O. Gabbard (Eds.), *Psychodynamic psychotherapy for personality disorders: A clinical handbook.* Arlington, VA: American Psychiatric Publishing.

Horton, M. A. (2008, September). The incidence and prevalence of SRS among US residents, Out & Equal Workplace Summit. Retrieved from http://www.gender.net/taw/thbcost.html:prevalence.

Horwitz, A. V., & Wakefield, J. C. (2007, December 9). Sadness is not a disorder. *The Philadelphia Inquirer,* pp. C1, C5.

Hoshiai, M., Matsumoto, Y., Sato, T., Ohnishi, M., Okabe, N., Kishimoto, Y., et al. (2010). Psychiatric comorbidity among patients with gender identity disorder. *Psychiatry and Clinical Neurosciences, 64*(5), 514–519.

Hoste, R. R., Doyle, A. C., & Le Grange, D. (2012). Families as an integral part of the treatment team: Treatment culture and standard of care challenges. In J. Alexander & J. Treasure (Eds.). *A collaborative approach to eating disorders* (pp. 136–143). New York: Routledge/Taylor & Francis.

Hou, C., Miller, B. L., Cummings, J. L., Goldberg, M., Mychack, P., Bottino, V., et al. (2000). Artistic savants. *Neuropsychiatry, Neuropsychology, and Behavioral Neurology, 13*(1), 29–38.

Houts, A. C. (2010). Behavioral treatment for enuresis. In J. R. Weisz & A. E. Kazdin (Eds.), *Evidence-based psychotherapies for children and adolescents* (2nd ed., pp. 359–374) New York: Guilford Press.

Howell, E. F. (2011). *Understanding and treating dissociative identity disorder: A rational approach.* New York: Routledge/Taylor & Francis Group.

Howes, R. (2008, April 16). Fundamentals of Therapy: Who goes? *Psychology Today.*

Howland, J., Rohsenow, D. J., Greece, J. A., Littlefield, C. A., Almeida, A., Heeren, T., et al. (2010). The effects of binge drinking on college students' next-day academic test-taking performance and mood state. *Addiction, 105*(4), 655–665.

Howland, R. H. (2011). Sleep interventions for the treatment of depression. *Journal of Psychosocial Nursing and Mental Health Services, 49*(1), 17–20.

Howland, R. H., Shutt, L. S., Berman, S. R., Spotts, C. R., & Denko, T. (2011). The emerging use of technology for the treatment of depression and other neuropsychiatric disorders. *Annals of Clinical Psychiatry, 23*(1), 48–62.

Hoyer, J., van der Heiden, C., & Portman, M. E. (2011). Psychotherapy for generalized anxiety disorder. *Psychiatric Annals, 41*(2), 987–94.

Hoyer, M., & Heath, B. (2012, December 19) A mass killing in U.S. occurs every 2 weeks. *USA Today.*

Hoza, B., Kaiser, N., & Hurt, E. (2008). Evidence-based treatments for attention-deficit/hyperactivity disorder (ADHD). In R. G. Steele, T. D. Elkin, & M. C. Roberts (Eds.), *Handbook of evidence-based therapies for children and adolescents: Bridging science and practice.* New York: Springer.

Hróbjartsson, A., & Gøtzsche, P. C. (2001). Is the placebo powerless? An analysis of clinical trials comparing placebo with no treatment. *New England Journal of Medicine, 344*(21), 1594–1602.

Hróbjartsson, A., & Gøtzsche, P. C. (2006). Unsubstantiated claims of large effects of placebo on pain: Serious errors in meta-analysis of placebo analgesia mechanism studies. *Journal of Clinical Epidemiology, 59,* 336–338.

Hróbjartsson, A., & Gøtzsche, P. C. (2007). Powerful spin in the conclusion of Wampold et al.'s re analysis of placebo versus no-treatment trials despite similar results as in original review. *Journal of Clinical Psychology, 63*(4), 373–377.

Hróbjartsson, A., & Gøtzsche, P. C. (2007). Wampold et al. reiterate spin in the conclusion of a re-analysis of placebo versus no-treatment trials despite similar results as in original review. *Journal of Clinical Psychology, 63*(4), 405–408.

Hsu, M. C., Schubiner, H., Lumley, M. A., Stracks, J. S., Clauw, D. J., & Williams, D. A. (2010). Sustained pain reduction through affective self-awareness in fibromyalgia: A randomized controlled trial. *Journal of General Internal Medicine, 25*(10) 1064–1070.

Hu, W., Ranaivo, H. R., Craft, J. M., Van Eldik, L. J., & Watterson, D. M. (2005). Validation of the neuroinflammation cycle as a drug discovery target using integrative chemical biology and lead compound development with an Alzheimer's disease-related mouse model. *Current Alzheimer Research, 2*(2), 197–205.

Huang, J-J., Yang, Y-P., & Wu, J. (2010). Relationships of borderline personality disorder and childhood trauma. *Chinese Journal of Clinical Psychology, 18*(6), 769–771.

Hucker, S. J. (2008). Sexual masochism: Psychopathology and theory. In D. R. Laws & W. T. O'Donohue (Eds.), *Sexual deviance: Theory, assessment, and treatment* (2nd ed., pp. 250–263). New York: Guilford Press.

Hucker, S. J. (2011). Hypoxyphilia. *Archives of Sexual Behavior, 40*(6), 1323–1326.

Hudd, S., Dumlao, J., Erdmann-Sager, D., Murray, D., Phan, E., Soukas, N., et al. (2000). Stress at college: Effects on health habits, health status and self-esteem. *College Student Journal, 34*(2), 217–227.

Hudson, J. I., Hiripi, E., Pope, H. G., Jr., & Kessler, R. C. (2007). The prevalence and correlates of eating disorders in the National Comorbidity Survey Replication. *Biological Psychiatry, 61*(3), 348–358.

Hudson, J. L., & Rapee, R. M. (2004). From anxious temperament to disorder: An etiological model of generalized anxiety disorder. In R. G. Heimberg, C. L. Turk, & D. S. Mennin (Eds.), *Generalized anxiety disorder: Advances in research and practice* (pp. 51–74). New York: Guilford Press.

Hudson-Allez, G. (2006). The stalking of psychotherapists by current or former clients: Beware of the insecurely attached! *Psychodynamic Practice, 12*(3), 249–260.

Hugdahl, K. (1995). *Psychophysiology: The mind-body perspective.* Cambridge, MA: Harvard University Press.

Hughes, S. (2011). Untangling Alzheimer's. *The Pennsylvania Gazette, 109*(4), 30–41.

Huijding, J., Borg, C., Weijmar-Schultz, W., & de Jong, P. J. (2011). Automatic affective appraisal of sexual penetration stimuli in women with vaginismus or dyspareunia. *Journal of Sexual Medicine, 8*(3), 806–813.

Humphrey, J. A. (2006). *Deviant behavior.* Upper Saddle River, NJ: Pearson/Prentice Hall.

Humphreys, K. (1996). Clinical psychologists as psychotherapists. History, future, and alternatives. *American Psychologist, 51*(3), 190–197.

Humphry, D., & Wickett, A. (1986). *The right to die: Understanding euthanasia.* New York: Harper & Row.

Hunt, C., & Andrews, G. (1995). Comorbidity in the anxiety disorders: The use of a life-chart approach. *Journal of Psychiatric Research, 29*(6), 467–480.

Huprich, S. K. (Ed.). (2006). *Rorschach assessment to the personality disorders.* Mahwah, NJ: Lawrence Erlbaum.

Hurlbert, D. F. (1991). The role of assertiveness in female sexuality: A comparative study between sexually assertive and sexually nonassertive women. *Journal of Sex and Marital Therapy, 17*(3), 183–190.

Hurlbert, D. F. (1993). A comparative study using orgasm consistency training in the treatment of women reporting hypoactive sexual desire. *Journal of Sex and Marital Therapy, 19,* 41–55.

Hurlbert, D. F., Apt, C., & Rabehl, S. M. (1993). Key variables to understanding female sexual satisfaction: An examination of women in non-distressed marriages. *Journal of Sex and Marital Therapy, 19,* 154–165.

Hurt, S., & Oltmanns, T. F. (2002). Personality traits and pathology in older and younger incarcerated women. *Journal of Clinical Psychology, 58*(4), 457–464.

Hyde, J. S. (1990). *Understanding human sexuality* (4th ed.). New York: McGraw-Hill.

Hyde, J. S. (2005). The genetics of sexual orientation. In J. S. Hyde (Ed.), *Biological substrates of human sexuality.* Washington, DC: American Psychological Association.

Hyman, S. E. (2011). Diagnosis of mental disorders in light of modern genetics. In D. A. Regier, W. E. Narrow, E. A. Kuhl, & D. J. Kupfer (Eds.), *The conceptual evolution of DSM-5* (pp. 3–17). Arlington, VA: American Psychiatric Publishing.

Hymowitz, N. (2005). Tobacco. In R. J. Frances, A. H. Mack, & S. I. Miller (Eds.), *Clinical textbook of addictive disorders* (3rd ed., pp. 105–137). New York: Guilford Press.

Iacono, T. (2006, Sept.). Ethical challenges and complexities of including people with intellectual disability as participants in research. *Journal of Intellectual and Developmental Disability, 31*(3), 173–179.

Iacono, W. G. (2008). Effective policing: Understanding how polygraph tests work and are used. *Criminal Justice and Behavior, 35*(10), 1295–1308.

Iantaffi, A., & Bockting, W. O. (2011). Views from both sides of the bridge? Gender, sexual legitimacy and transgender people's experiences of relationships. *Culture, Health & Sexuality, 13*(3), 355–370.

Ihle, W., Jahnke, D., Heerwagen, A., & Neuperdt, C. (2005). Depression, anxiety, and eating disorders and recalled parental rearing behavior. *Kindheit Entwicklung, 14*(1), 30–38.

Ikeda, M., Aleksic, B., Kinoshita, Y., Okochi, T., Kawashima, K., Kushima, I., Ito, Y., Nakamura, Y., Kishi, T., Okumura, T., Fukuo, Y., Williams, H. J., Hamshere, M. L., Ivanov, D., Inada, T., Suzuki, M., Hashimoto, R., Ujike, H., Takeda, M., Craddock, N., Kaibuchi, K., Owen, M. J., Ozaki, N., O'Donovan, M. C., & Iwata, N. (2011). Genome-wide association study of schizophrenia in a Japanese population. *Biological Psychiatry, 69*(5), 472–478.

Infurna, F. J., Gerstorf, D., & Zarit, S. H. (2011). Examining dynamic links between perceived control and health. Longitudinal evidence for differential effects in midlife and old age. *Developmental Psychology, 47*(1), 9–18.

Ingram, R. E., Nelson, T., Steidtmann, D. K., & Bistricky, S. L. (2007). Comparative data on child and adolescent cognitive measures associated with depression. *Journal of Consulting and Clinical Psychology, 75*(3), 390–403.

Innamorati, M., Pompili, M., Amore, M., Vittorio, C. D., Serafini, G., Tatarelli, R., & Lester, D. (2011). Suicide prevention in late life: Is there sound evidence for practice? In M. Pompili & R. Tatarelli (Eds.), *Evidence-based practice in suicidology: A source book* (pp. 211–232). Cambridge MA: Hogrefe Publishing.

Inouye, S. K. (2006). Delirium in older persons. *New England Journal of Medicine, 354*(11), 1157–1165.

Inouye, S. K., Bogardus, S. T., Jr., Williams, C. S., et al. (2003). The role of adherence on the effectiveness of nonpharmacologic interventions: Evidence from the delirium prevention trial. *Archives of Internal Medicine, 163,* 958–964.

Isacsson, G., & Adler, M. (2012). Randomized clinical trials underestimate the efficacy of antidepressants in less severe depression. *Acta Psychiatrica Scandinavica, 125*(6), 453–459.

Isacsson, G., Reutfors, J., Papadopoulos, F. C., Ösby, U. & Ahlner, J. (2010). Antidepressant medication prevents suicide in depression. *Acta Psychiatrica Scandinavica, 122*(6), 454–460.

Iskowitz, M. (2011, April 22). As brand revenue shrinks, so does brand promotion. Retrieved from *Mmm-online.com.*

Iverson, K. M., Lester, K. M., & Resick, P. A. (2011). Psychosocial treatments. In D. M. Benedek & G. H. Wynn (Eds.), *Clinical manual for management of PTSD* (pp. 157–203). Arlington, VA: American Psychiatric Publishing.

IWS (Internet World Stats). (2011). Top 20 countries with the highest number of internet users. Retrieved on May 27, 2011, from www.interneworldstats.com/top20.htm.

Jablensky, A. (2000). Epidemiology of schizophrenia: The global burden of disease and disability. *European Archives of Psychiatry and Clinical Neuroscience, 250,* 274–285.

Jablensky, A., Kirkbride, J. B., & Jones, P. B. (2011). The secondary schizophrenias. In D. R. Weinberg & P. Harrison (Eds.), *Schizophrenia* (pp. 185–225). Hoboken, NJ: Wiley-Blackwell.

Jackson, B. R., & Bergeman, C. S. (2011). How does religiosity enhance well being? The role of perceived control. *Psychology of Religion and Spirituality, 3*(2), 149–161.

Jackson, J. S., Knight, K. M., & Rafferty, J. A. (2010). Race and unhealthy behaviors: Chronic stress, the HPA axis, and physical and mental health disparities over the life course. *American Journal of Public Health, 100*(5), 933–939.

Jackson, Y. (Ed.). (2006) *Encyclopedia of multicultural psychology.* Thousand Oaks, CA: Sage Publications.

Jacob, K. S., Prince, M., & Goldberg, D. (2010). Confirmatory factor analysis of common mental disorders across cultures. In D. Goldberg, K. S. Kendler, P. J. Sirovatka, & D. A. Regier (Eds.), *Diagnostic issues in depression and generalized anxiety disorder: Refining the research agenda for DSM-V* (pp. 191–210). Washington, DC: American Psychiatric Association.

Jacobi, C., & Fittig, E. (2010). "Psychosocial risk factors in eating disorders." In W. S. Agras (Ed.), *The Oxford handbook of eating disorders. Oxford library of psychology* (pp. 123–136). New York: Oxford University Press.

Jacobs, A. K. (2008). Components of evidence-based interventions for bullying and peer victimization. In R. G. Steele, T. D. Elkin, & M. C. Roberts (Eds.), *Handbook of evidence-based therapies for children and adolescents: Bridging science and practice.* New York: Springer.

Jacobs, D. (2011). *Analyzing criminal minds: Forensic investigative science for the 21st century. Brain, behavior, and evolution.* Santa Barbara, CA: Praeger/ABC-CLIO.

Jacobs, M. (2003). *Sigmund Freud.* London: Sage.

Jacobson, C. M., & Mufson, L. (2010). Treating adolescent depression using interpersonal psychotherapy. In J. R. Weisz, & A. E. Kazdin (Eds.), *Evidence-based psychotherapies for children and adolescents* (2nd ed., pp. 140–155) New York: Guilford Press.

Jacobson, G. (1999). The inpatient management of suicidality. In D. G. Jacobs (Ed.), *The Harvard Medical School guide to suicide assessment and intervention.* San Francisco: Jossey-Bass.

Jacobson, N. S., Dobson, K. S., Truax, P. A., Addis, M. E., et al. (1996). A component analysis of cognitive-behavioral treatment for depression. *Journal of Consulting and Clinical Psychology, 64*(2), 295–304.

Jacobson, N. S., Martell, C. R., & Dimidjian, S. (2001). Behavioral activation treatment for depression: Returning to contextual roots. *Clinical Psychology: Science and Practice, 8,* 255–270.

Jacofsky, M. D, Santos, M. T., Khemlani-Patel, S., Neziroglu, F. (2010, June 28). The biopsychosocial model: Causes of pathological anxiety. Retrieved from *MentaHelp.net.*

Jaffe, S. L., & Kelly, J. F. (2011). Twelve-step mutual-help programs for adolescents. In Y. Kaminer & K. C. Winters (Eds.), *Clinical manual of adolescent substance abuse treatment* (pp. 269–282). Arlington, VA: American Psychiatric Publishing.

Jaffe, S. L., & Klein, M. (2010). Medical marijuana and adolescent treatment. *American Journal on Addictions, 19*(5), 460–461.

Jahn, D. R., Cukrowicz, K. C., Linton, K., & Prabhu, F. (2011). The mediating effect of perceived burdensomeness on the relation between depressive symptoms and suicide ideation in a community sample of older adults. *Aging & Mental Health, 15*(2), 214–220.

Jakupcak, M., & Varra, E. M. (2011). Treating Iraq and Afghanistan war veterans with PTSD who are at high risk for suicide. *Cognitive and Behavioral Practice, 18*(1), 85–97.

James, W. (1890). *Principles of psychology* (Vol. 1). New York: Holt, Rinehart & Winston.

Jamison, K. R. (1995, February). Manic-depressive illness and creativity. *Scientific American*, pp. 63–67.

Jamison, K. R. (1995). *An unquiet mind.* New York: Vintage Books.

Jan, J. E., Reiter, R. J., Wong, P. K. H., Bax, M. C. O., Ribary, U., & Wasdell, M. B. (2011). Melatonin has membrane receptor-independent hypnotic action on neurons: An hypothesis. *Journal of Pineal Research: Molecular, Biological, Physiological and Clinical Aspects of Melatonin, 50*(3), 33–240.

Janicak, P. G., Davis, J. M., Preskorn, S. H., & Ayd, F. J. (2001). *Principles and practice of psychopharmacotherapy* (3rd ed.). Philadelphia: Lippincott Williams & Wilkin.

Jannini, E., & Lenzi, A. (2005). Ejaculatory disorders: Epidemiology and current approaches to definition, classification and subtyping. *World Journal of Urology, 23,* 68–75.

Janowsky, D. S., El-Yousef, M. K., Davis, J. M., & Sekerke, H. J. (1973). Provocation of schizophrenic symptoms by intravenous administration of methylphenidate. *Archives of General Psychiatry, 28,* 185–191.

Janus, S. S., & Janus, C. L. (1993). *The Janus report on sexual behavior.* New York: Wiley.

Janzen, R., Pancer, S. M., Nelson, G., Loomis, C., & Hasford, J. (2010). Evaluating community participation as prevention: Life narratives of youth. *Journal of Community Psychology, 38*(8), 992–1006.

Jardri, R., Pouchet, A., Pins, D., & Thomas, P. (2011). Cortical activations during auditory verbal hallucinations in schizophrenia: A coordinate-based meta-analysis. *American Journal of Psychiatry, 168*(1), 73–81.

Jaussent, I., Dauvilliers, Y., Ancelin, M-L., Dartigues, J-F., Tavernier, B., Touchon, J., et al. (2011). Insomnia symptoms in older adults: Associated factors and gender differences. *American Journal of Geriatric Psychiatry, 19*(1), 88–97.

Jefferson, D. J. (2005, August 8). America's most dangerous drug. *Newsweek, 146*(6), 40–48.

Jeglic, E. L., & Murphy-Eberenz, K. (2012). Women and depression. In E. L Jeglic & K. Murphy-Eberenz (Eds.), *Women and mental disorders (Vols. 1–4). Women's psychology* (pp. 209–228). Santa Barbara, CA: Praeger/ABC-CLIO.

Jenike, M. A. (1992). New developments in treatment of obsessive-compulsive disorder. In A. Tasman & M. B. Riba (Eds.), *Review of psychiatry* (Vol. 11). Washington, DC: American Psychiatric Press.

Jenkins, R. L. (1968). The varieties of children's behavioral problems and family dynamics. *American Journal of Psychiatry, 124*(10), 1440–1445.

Jensen, M. P., Ehde, D. M., Gertz, K. J., Stoelb, B. L., Dillworth, T. M., Hirsh, A. T., et al. (2011). Effects of self-hypnosis training and cognitive restructuring on daily pain intensity and catastrophizing in individuals with multiple sclerosis and chronic pain. *International Journal of Clinical and Experimental Hypnosis, 59*(1), 45–63.

Jeste, D. (2012, December 4). A message from APA President Dilip Jeste, MD on *DSM-5. Psychiatric News.*

Jeste, D.V., Blazer, D. G., & First, M. (2005). Aging-related diagnostic variations: Need for diagnostic criteria appropriate for elderly psychiatric patients. *Biological Psychiatry, 58*(4), 265–271.

Jiang, W., & Krishnan, K. R-R. (2011). Treatment of depression in the medically ill. In D. A. Ciraulo & R. I. Shader (Eds.), *Pharmacotherapy of depression* (2nd ed., pp. 399–414). New York: Springer Science + Business Media.

Jiang, Y., Haxby J. V., Martin, A., Ungerleider, L. G., & Parasuraman R. (2000). Complementary neural mechanisms for tracking items in human working memory. *Science, 287*(5453), 643–646.

Jimenez, D. E., Alegria, M., Chen, C-N., Chan, D., & Laderman, M. (2010). Prevalence of psychiatric illnesses in older ethnic minority adults. *Journal of the American Geriatrics Society, 38*(2), 256–264.

Jimerson S. R., Swearer S. M., & Espelage D. L. (Eds.). (2010). *Handbook of bullying in schools: An international perspective.* New York: Routledge/Taylor & Francis Group.

Jimerson S. R., Swearer S. M., & Espelage D. L. (Eds.). (2010). International scholarship advances science and practice addressing bullying in schools. In S. R. Jimerson, S. M. Swearer, & D. L. Espelage (Eds.), *Handbook of bullying in schools: An international perspective.* (pp. 1–6) New York: Routledge/Taylor & Francis Group.

Jiron, C. (2010). Assessing and intervening with children with externalizing disorders. In D. C. Miller (Ed.), *Best practices in school neuropsychology: Guidelines for effective practice., assessment, and evidence-based intervention* (pp. 359–386). Hoboken, NJ: John Wiley & Sons.

Johansson, A., Sundborn, E., Höjerback, T., & Bodlund, O. (2010). A five-year follow-up study of Swedish adults with gender identity disorder. *Archives of Sexual Behavior, 39*(6), 1429–1437.

Johnson, C. (1995, February 8). National Collegiate Athletic Association study. *The Hartford Courant.*

Johnson, L. A. (2005, July 21). Lobotomy back in spotlight after 30 years. *Netscape News.*

Johnson, S., Hollis, C., Kochhar, P., Hennessy, E., Wolke, D., & Marlow, N. (2010). Psychiatric disorders in extremely preterm children: Longitudinal finding at age 11 years in the EPICure study. *Journal of the American Academy of Child and Adolescent Psychiatry, 49*(5), 453–63.e1.

Johnson, W. E., Jr. (Ed.). (2010). *Social work with African American males: Health, mental health, and social policy.* New York,: Oxford University Press.

Johnston, C. A., & Tyler, C. (2008). Evidence-based therapies for pediatric overweight. In R. G. Steele, T. D. Elkin, & M. C. Roberts (Eds.), *Handbook of evidence-based therapies for children and adolescents: Bridging science and practice.* New York: Springer.

Johnston, J. M. (2004). Eating disorders and childhood obesity: Who are the real gluttons? *Canadian Medical Association Journal, 171*(12), 1459–1460.

Johnston, L. D., O'Malley, P. M., & Bachman, J. G. (1993). *National survey results on drug use from the Monitoring the Future Study, 1975–1992.* Rockville, MD: National Institute on Drug Abuse.

Johnston, L. D., O'Malley, P. M., Bachman, J. G., & Schulenberg, J. E. (2007). *Monitoring the future national results on adolescent drug use: Overview of key findings, 2006* (NIH Publication No. 07-6202). Bethesda, MD: National Institute on Drug Abuse.

Johnston, L. D., O'Malley, P. M., Bachman, J. G., & Schulenberg, J. E. (2011). *Monitoring the future national results on adolescent drug use: Overview of key findings, 2010.* Ann Arbor, MI: Institute for Social Research.

Johnston, M.V., & Smith, R. O. (2010). Single subject designs: Current methodologies and future directions. *OTJR: Occupation, Participation and Health, 30*(1), 4–10.

Joiner, T. E., Jr. (2002). Depression in its interpersonal context. In I. H. Gotlib & C. L. Hammen (Eds.), *Handbook of depression* (pp. 295–313). New York: Guilford Press.

Jolley, S., & Garety, P. (2011). Cognitive behavioural interventions. In W. Gaebel (Ed.), *Schizophrenia: Current science and clinical practice World Psychiatric Association evidence and experience in psychiatry series* (pp. 185–215). Hoboken, NJ: Wiley-Blackwell.

Jones, G., & Jordan, R. (2008). Research base for intervention in autism spectrum disorders. In E. McGregor, M. Núñez, K. Cebula, & J. C. Gómez (Eds.), *Autism: An integrated view from neurocognitive, clinical, and intervention research.* Malden, MA: Blackwell Publishing.

Jones, M. C. (1968). Personality correlates and antecedents of drinking patterns in males. *Journal of Consulting and Clinical Psychology, 32,* 2–12.

Jones, M. C. (1971). Personality antecedents and correlates of drinking patterns in women. *Journal of Consulting and Clinical Psychology, 36,* 61–69.

Jones, M. T. (2010). Mediated exhibitionism: The naked body in performance and virtual space. *Sexuality & Culture: An Interdisciplinary Quarterly, 14*(4), 253–269.

Juan, W., Ziao-Juan, D., Jia-Ji, W., Xin-Wang, W., & Liang, X. (2011). How do risk-taking behaviors relate to suicide ideation and attempts in adolescents? *Clinician's Research Digest, 29*(1).

Judd, L. L., Akiskal, H. S., & Paulus, M. P. (1997). The role and clinical significance of subsyndromal depressive symptoms (SSD) in unipolar major depressive disorder. *Journal of Affective Disorders, 45*(1–2), 5–17.

Judd, L. L., Rapaport, M. H., Yonkers, K. A., Rush, A. J., Frank, E., Thase, M. E., et al. (2004). Randomized, placebo-controlled trial of fluoxetine for acute treatment of minor depressive disorder. *American Journal of Psychiatry, 161*(10), 1864–1871.

Judelson, D. A., Armstrong, L. E., Sokmen, B., Roti, M. W., Casa, D. J., & Kellogg, M. D. (2005). Effect of chronic caffeine intake on choice reaction time, mood, and visual vigilance. *Physiology and Behavior, 85*(5), 629–634.

Juel-Nielsen, N., & Videbech, T. (1970). A twin study of suicide. *Acta Geneticae Medicae et Gemellologiae, 19,* 307–310.

Juhnke, G. A., Granello, D. H., & Granello, P. F. (2011). *Suicide, self-injury, and violence in the schools: Assessment, prevention, and intervention strategies.* Hoboken, NJ: John Wiley & Sons.

Juliano, L. M., Anderson, B. L., & Griffiths, R. R. (2011). Caffeine. In J. H. Lowinson & P. Ruiz (Eds.), *Substance abuse: A comprehensive textbook, fifth edition.* Philadelphia, PA: Lippincott, Williams, & Wilkins.

Julien, R. M., Advokat, C. D., & Comaty, J. (2011). *Primer of drug action* (12th ed.). New York: Bedford, Freeman, & Worth.

Kabat-Zinn, J. (2005). *Wherever you go, there you are: Mindfulness meditation in everyday life.* New York: Hyperion.

Kafka, M. P. (2000). The paraphilia-related disorders: Nonparaphilic hypersexuality and sexual compulsivity/addiction. In S. R. Leiblum & R. C. Raymond (Eds.), *Principles and practice of sex therapy* (3rd ed., pp. 471–503). New York: Guilford Press.

Kafka, M. P. (2007). Paraphilia-related disorders: The evaluation and treatment of nonparaphilic hypersexuality. In S. R. Leiblum (Ed.), *Principles and practice of sex therapy* (4th ed., pp. 442–476). New York: Guilford Press.

Kagan, J. (2003). Biology, context and developmental inquiry. *Annual Review of Psychology, 54,* 1–23.

Kagan, J. (2007). The limitations of concepts in developmental psychology. In G. W. Ladd (Ed.), *Appraising the human developmental sciences: Essays in honor of Merrill-Palmer Quarterly* (pp. 30–37). Detroit, MI: Wayne State University Press.

Kagan, J., & Snidman, N. (1991). Infant predictors of inhibited and uninhibited profiles. *Psychological Science, 2,* 40–44.

Kagan, J., & Snidman, N. (1999). Early childhood predictors of adult anxiety disorders. *Biological Psychiatry, 46*(11), 1536–1541.

Kahn, A. P., & Fawcett, J. (1993). *The encyclopedia of mental health.* New York: Facts on File.

Kaij, L. (1960). *Alcoholism in twins: Studies on the etiology and sequels of abuse of alcohol.* Stockholm: Almquist & Wiksell.

Kaiser Family Foundation. (2001, November). *Understanding the effects of direct-to-consumer prescription drug advertising.* Menlo Park, CA: The Health Care Marketplace Project Publications.

Kaiser Family Foundation. (2010). *Distribution of U.S. population by race/ethnicity, 2010 and 2050.* Menlo Park, CA: author.

Kalb, C. (2000, January 31). Coping with the darkness: Revolutionary new approaches in providing care for helping people with Alzheimer's stay active and feel productive. *Newsweek,* pp. 52–54.

Kalin, N. H. (1993, May). The neurobiology of fear. *Scientific American,* pp. 94–101.

Kalodner, C. R., & Coughlin, J. W. (2004). Psychoeducational and counseling groups to prevent and treat eating disorders and disturbances. In J. L. DeLucia-Waack, D. A. Gerrity, C. R. Kalodner, & M. T. Riva (Eds.), *Handbook of group counseling and psychotherapy* (pp. 481–496). Thousand Oaks, CA: Sage.

Kamali, M., & McInnis, M. G. (2011). Genetics of mood disorders: General principles and potential applications for treatment resistant

depression. In J. F. Greden, M. B. Riba, & M. G. McInnis (Eds.), *Treatment resistant depression: A roadmap for effective care* (pp. 293–308). Arlington, VA: American Psychiatric Publishing.

Kambam, P., & Benedek, E. P. (2010). Testifying: The expert witness in court. In E. P. Benedek, P. Ash, & C. L. Scott (Eds.), *Principles and practice of child and adolescent forensic mental health* (pp. 41–51). Arlington, VA: American Psychiatric Publishing.

Kaminer, Y., Spirito, A., & Lewander, W. (2011). Brief motivational interventions, cognitive-behavioral therapy, and contingency management for youth substance use disorders. In Y. Kaminer & K. C. Winters (Eds.), *Clinical manual of adolescent substance abuse treatment* (pp. 213–237). Arlington, VA: American Psychiatric Publishing.

Kangelaris, K. N., Vittinghoff, E., Otte, C., Na, B., Auerbach, A. D., & Whooley, M. A. (2010). Association between a serotonin transporter gene variant and hopelessness among men in the Heart and Soul Study. *Journal of General Internal Medicine, 25*(10). 1030–1037.

Kanner, B. (1995). *Are you normal?: Do you behave like everyone else?* New York: St. Martin's Press.

Kanner, B. (1998, February). Are you normal? Turning the other cheek. *American Demographics.*

Kanner, B. (1998, May). Are you normal? Creatures of habit. *American Demographics.*

Kanner, B. (2004). *Are you normal about sex, love, and relationships?* New York: St. Martin's Press.

Kanner, B. (2005). *Are you normal about sex, love, and relationships?* New York: St. Martin's Press.

Kanner, L. (1943). Autistic disturbances of affective contact. *Nervous Child, 2,* 217.

Kanner, L. (1954). To what extent is early infantile autism determined by constitutional inadequacies? In *Genetics and the inheritance of integrated neurological and psychiatric patterns.* Baltimore: Williams and Wilkins.

Kantor, M. (2006). The psychopathy of everyday life. In T. G. Plante (Ed.), *Mental disorders of the new millennium: Vol. 1. Behavioral issues.* Westport, CT: Praeger Publishers.

Kantor, M. (2010). *The essential guide to overcoming avoidant personality disorder.* Santa Barbara, CA: Praeger/ABC-CLIO.

Kantrowitz, B., & Springen, K. (2004, August 9). What dreams are made of. *Newsweek, 144*(6), 40–47.

Kantrowitz, B., & Springen, K. (2007). Confronting Alzheimer's. *Newsweek, 149*(25), 54–61.

Kapardis, A. (2010). *Psychology and law: A critical introduction* (3rd ed.) New York: Cambridge University Press.

Kaplan, H. S. (1974). *The new sex therapy: Active treatment of sexual dysfunction.* New York: Brunner/Mazel.

Kaplan, R. M. (2010). Syphilis, sex and psychiatry, 1789–1925: Part 1. *Australasian Psychiatry, 18*(1), 17–21.

Karlin, B. E., Ruzek, J. I., Chad, K. M., Eftekhari, A., Monson, C. M., Hembree, E. A., et al. (2010). Dissemination of evidence-based psychological treatments for posttraumatic stress disorder in the Veterans Health Administration. *Journal of Traumatic Stress, 23*(6), 663–673.

Karon, B. P. (1985). Omission in review of treatment interactions. *Schizophrenia Bulletin, 11*(1), 16–17.

Kasckow, J., Felmet, K., & Zisook, S. (2011). Managing suicide risk in patients with schizophrenia. *CNS Drugs, 25*(2), 129–143.

Kashdan, T. B., Adams, L., Savostyanova, A., Ferssizidis, P., McKnight, P. E., & Nezlek, J. B. (2011). Effects of social anxiety and depressive symptoms on the frequency and quality of sexual activity: A daily process approach. *Behaviour Research and Therapy, 49*(5), 352–360.

Kasl, S. V., & Jones, B. A. (2011). An epidemiological perspective on research design, measurement, and surveillance strategies. In J. C. Quick & L. E. Tetrick (Eds.), *Handbook of occupational health psychology* (2nd ed., pp. 375–394). Washington, DC: American Psychological Association.

Kaslow, F. W. (2011). Family therapy. In J. C. Norcross, G. R. VandenBos, & D. K. Freedheim (Eds.), *History of psychotherapy: Continuity and change* (2nd ed., pp. 497–504). Washington, DC: American Psychological Association.

Kassel, J. D., Hussong, A. M., Wardle, M. C., Veilleux, J. C., Heinz, A., Greenstein, J. E., & Evatt, D. P. (2010). Affective influences in drug use etiology. In L. Scheier (Ed.), *Handbook of drug use etiology: Theory, methods, and empirical findings* (pp. 183–205). Washington, DC: American Psychological Association.

Kassel, J. D., Wardle, M. C., Heinz, A. J., & Greenstein, J. E. (2010). Cognitive theories of drug effects on emotion. In J. D. Kassel (Ed.), *Substance abuse and emotion* (pp. 61–82). Washington, DC: American Psychological Association.

Katel, P., & Beck, M. (1996, March 29). Sick kid or sick Mom? *Newsweek,* p. 73.

Kavanagh, D. J. (2008). Management of co-occurring substance use disorders. In K. T. Mueser & D. V. Jeste (Eds.), *Clinical handbook of schizophrenia* (pp. 459–470). New York: Guilford Press.

Kavanagh, D. J., & Mueser, K. T. (2011). The treatment of substance misuse in people with serious mental disorders. In R. Hagen, D. Turkington, T. Berge, & R. W. Grawe (Eds.), *CBT for psychosis: A symptom-based approach, International Society for the Psychological Treatments of the Schizophrenias and Other Psychoses* (pp. 161–174). New York: Routledge/Taylor & Francis Group.

Kawas, C., Resnick, S., Morrison, A., Brookmeyer, R., Corrada, M., Zonderman, A., et al. (1997). A prospective study of estrogen replacement therapy and the risk of developing Alzheimer's disease: The Baltimore Longtitudinal Study of Aging. *Neurology, 48*(6), 1517–1521.

Kaye, W. H. (2011). Neurobiology of anorexia nervosa. In D. Le Grange & J. Lock (Eds.), *Eating disorders in children and adolescents: A clinical handbook.* New York: Guilford Publications.

Kaye, W. H., Bailer, U. F., & Klabunde, M. (2012). Neurobiology explanations for puzzling behaviours. In J. Alexander & J. Treasure (Eds.), *A collaborative approach to eating disorders* (pp. 35–51). New York: Routledge/Taylor & Francis.

Kaye, W. H., Frank, G. K., Bailer, U. F., Henry, S. E., Meltzer, C. C., Price, J. C., et al. (2005). Serotonin alterations in anorexia and bulimia nervosa: New insights from imaging studies. *Physiological Behavior, 85*(1), 73–81.

Kaye, W. H., Gendall, K. A., Fernstrom, M. H., Fernstrom, J. D., McConaha, C. W., & Weltzin, T. E. (2000). Effects of acute tryptophan depletion on mood in bulimia nervosa. *Biological Psychiatry, 47*(2), 151–157.

Kaye, W. H., Strober, M., & Rhodes, L. (2002). Body image disturbance and other core symptoms in anorexia and bulimia nervosa. In

D. J. Castle & K. A. Phillips (Eds.), *Disorders of body image* (pp. 67–82). Petersfield, England: Wrightson Biomedical.

Kaye, W. H., Wagner, A., Fudge, J. L., & Paulus, M. (2011). Neurocircuitry of eating disorders. In R. A. H. Adan & W. H. Kaye (Eds.), *Behavioral neurobiology of eating disorders. Current topics in behavioral neurosciences* (pp. 37–57). New York: Springer-Verlag Publishing.

Kazdin, A. E. (1994). Methodology, design, and evaluation in psychotherapy research. In A. E. Bergin & S. L. Garfield (Eds.), *Handbook of psychotherapy and behavior change* (4th ed.). New York: Wiley.

Kazdin, A. E. (2002). Psychosocial treatments for conduct disorder in children and adolescents. In P. E. Nathan & J. M. Gorman (Eds.), *A guide to treatments that work* (2nd ed., pp. 57–85). London: Oxford University Press.

Kazdin, A. E. (2003). Problem-solving skills training and parent management training for conduct disorder. In A. E. Kazdin & J. R. Weisz (Eds.), *Evidence-based psychotherapies for children and adolescents.* New York: Guilford Press.

Kazdin, A. E. (2004). Evidence-based treatments: Challenges and priorities for practice and research. *Child and Adolescent Psychiatric Clinics of North America, 13*(4), 923–940.

Kazdin, A. E. (2005). *Parent management training: Treatment for oppositional, aggressive, and antisocial behavior in children and adolescents.* New York: Oxford University Press.

Kazdin, A. E. (2006). Assessment and evaluation in clinical practice. In R. J. Sternberg, C. D. Goodheart, & A. E. Kazdin (Eds.), *Evidence-based psychotherapy: Where practice and research meet* (pp. 153–177). Washington, DC: American Psychological Association.

Kazdin, A. E. (2007). Psychosocial treatments for conduct disorder in children and adolescents. In P. E. Nathan & J. M. Gorman (Eds.), *A guide to treatments that work* (3rd ed., pp. 71–104). New York: Oxford University Press.

Kazdin, A. E. (2010). Problem-solving skills training and parent management training for oppositional defiant disorder and conduct disorder. In J. R. Weisz, & A. E. Kazdin (Eds.), *Evidence-based psychotherapies for children and adolescents* (2nd ed., pp. 211–226) New York: Guilford Press.

Kazdin, A. E. (2011). Establishing the effectiveness of animal-assisted therapies: Methodological standards, issues, and strategies. In P. McCardle, S. McCune, J. A. Griffin, & V. Maholmes (Eds.), *How animals affect us: Examining the influences of human–animal interaction on child development and human health* (pp. 35–51). Washington, DC: American Psychological Association.

Kazdin, A. E. (2011). *Single-case research designs: Methods for clinical and applied settings* (2nd ed.). New York: Oxford University Press.

Kearney, C. A. (1999). *Casebook in child behavior disorders.* Belmont, CA: Wadsworth.

Kearney, C. A., & Steichen-Asch, P. (1990). Men, body image, and eating disorders. In A. E. Andersen (Ed.), *Males with eating disorders.* New York: Brunner/Mazel.

Keefe, R. S. E., & Eesley, C. E. (2012) Neurocognitive impairments. In J. A. Lieberman, T. S. Stroup, & D. O. Perkins (Eds.), *Essentials of schizophrenia* (pp. 73–92). Arlington, VA: American Psychiatric Publishing.

Keel, P. K., Gravener, J. A., Joiner, T. E., Jr., & Haedt, A. A. (2010). Twenty-year follow-up of bulimia nervosa and related eating disorders not otherwise specified. *International Journal of Eating Disorders, 43*(6), 492–497.

Keel, P. K., & McCormick, L. (2010). Diagnosis, assessment, and treatment planning for anorexia nervosa. In C. M. Grilo & J. E. Mitchell (Eds.), *The treatment of eating disorders: A clinical handbook* (pp. 3–27). New York: Guilford Press.

Keel, P. K., Mitchell, J. E., Davis, T. L., & Crow, S. J. (2002). Long-term impact of treatment in women diagnosed with bulimia nervosa. *International Journal of Eating Disorders, 31*(2), 151–158.

Keel, P. K., Mitchell, J. E., Miller, K. B., Davis, T. L., & Crow, S. J. (2000). Social adjustment over 10 years following diagnosis with bulimia nervosa. *International Journal of Eating Disorders, 27*(1), 21–28.

Keen, E. (1970). *Three faces of being: Toward an existential clinical psychology.* New York: Meredith Corp. (Reprinted by permission of Irvington Publishers.)

Keenan, K., Wroblewski, K., Hipwell, A., Loeber, R., & Stouthamer-Loeber, M. (2010). Age of onset, symptom threshold, and expansion of the nosology of conduct disorder for girls. *Journal of Abnormal Psychology, 119*(4), 689–698.

Keith, S. J., Regier, D. A., & Rae, D. S. (1991). Schizophrenic disorders. In L. N. Robins & D. S. Regier (Eds.), *Psychiatric disorders in America: The Epidemiological Catchment Area Study.* New York: Free Press.

Kelleher, E., & Campbell, A. (2011). A study of consultant psychiatrists' response to patients' suicide. *Irish Journal of Psychological Medicine, 28*(1), 35–37.

Kellerman, H., & Burry, A. (2007). *Handbook of psychodiagnostic testing: Analysis of personality in the psychological report.* New York: Springer Publishing.

Kelly, M. A., & Barry, L. M. (2010). Identifying and alleviating the stresses of college students through journal writing. In K. M. T. Collins, A. J. Onwuegbuzie, & Q. G. Jiao (Eds.), *Toward a broader understanding of stress and coping: Mixed methods approaches. Research on stress and coping in education* (pp. 343–370). Greenwich, VT: IAP Information Age Publishing.

Kelly, M. P., Strassberg, D. S., & Kircher, J. R. (1990). Attitudinal and experimental correlates of anorgasmia. *Archives of Sexual Behavior, 19,* 165–172.

Kelm, M. K., Criswell, H. E., & Breese, G. R. (2011). Ethanol-enhanced GABA release: A focus on G protein-coupled receptors. *Brain Research Reviews, 65*(2), 113–123.

Kemp, C. G., & Collings, S. C. (2011). Hyperlinked suicide: Assessing the prominence and accessibility of suicide websites. *Crisis: Journal of Crisis Intervention and Suicide Prevention, 32*(3), 143–151.

Kemp, D. R. (1994). *Mental health in the workplace: An employer's and manager's guide.* Westport, CT: Quorum Books.

Kendall-Tackett, K. A. (2010). *Depression in new mothers: Causes, consequences, and treatment alternatives* (2nd ed.). New York: Routledge/ Taylor & Francis Group.

Kendall-Tackett, K. A. (Ed.). (2010). *The psychoneuroimmunology of chronic disease: Exploring the links between inflammation, stress, and illness.* Washington, DC: American Psychological Association.

Kendall, J., & Hatton, D. (2002). Racism as a source of health disparity in families with children with attention deficit hyperactivity disorder. *Advances in Nursing Science, 25*(2), 22–39.

Kendall, P. C., Furr, J. M., & Podell, J. L. (2010). Child-focused treatment of anxiety. In J. R. Weisz, & A. E. Kazdin (Eds.), *Evidence-based psychotherapies for children and adolescents* (2nd ed., pp. 45–60) New York: Guilford Press.

Kendler, K. S., Heath, A., & Martin, N. G. (1987). A genetic epidemiologic study of self-report suspiciousness. *Comprehensive Psychiatry, 28*(3), 187–196.

Kendler, K. S., Myers, J., & Prescott, C. A. (2005). Sex differences in the relationship between social support and risk for major depression: A longitudinal study of opposite-sex twin pairs. *American Journal of Psychiatry, 162*(2), 250–256.

Kendler, K. S., Neale, M. C., Kessler, R. C., Heath, A. C., & Eaves, L. J. (1993). Panic disorder in women: A population-based twin study. *Psychological Medicine, 23,* 397–406.

Kendler, K. S., Ochs, A. L., Gorman, A. M., Hewitt, J. K., Ross, D. E., & Mirsky, A. F. (1991). The structure of schizotypy: A pilot multitrait twin study. *Psychiatry Research, 36*(1), 19–36.

Kendler, K. S., Walters, E. E., Neale, M. C., Kessler, R. C., et al. (1995). The structure of the genetic and environmental risk factors for six major psychiatric disorders in women: Phobia, generalized anxiety disorder, panic disorder, bulimia, major depression, and alcoholism. *Archives of General Psychiatry, 52*(5), 374–383.

Kennedy, D. P., & Squire, L. R. (2007). An analysis of calendar performance in two autistic calendar savants. *Learning & Memory, 14*(8), 533–538.

Kerber, K., Taylor, K., & Riba, M. B. (2011). Treatment resistant depression and comorbid medical problems: Cardiovascular disease and cancer. In J. F. Greden, M. B. Riba, & M. G. McInnis (Eds.), *Treatment resistant depression: A roadmap for effective care* (pp. 137–156). Arlington, VA: American Psychiatric Publishing.

Kern, M. L., & Friedman, H. S. (2011). Personality and pathways of influence on physical health. *Social and Personality Psychology Compass, 5*(1), 76–87.

Kern, M. L., & Friedman, H. S. (2010). Why do some people thrive while others succumb to disease and stagnation? In P. S. Fry & C. L. M. Keyes (Eds.), *New frontiers in resilient aging: Life-strengths and well-being in late life* (pp. 162–184). New York: Cambridge University Press.

Kernberg, O. F. (1989). Narcissistic personality disorder in childhood. *Psychiatric Clinics of North America, 12*(3), 671–694.

Kernberg, O. F. (1992). *Aggression in personality disorders and its perversions.* New Haven, CT: Yale University Press.

Kernberg, O. F. (1997). Convergences and divergences in contemporary psychoanalytic technique and psychoanalytic psychotherapy. In J. K. Zeig (Ed.), *The evolution of psychotherapy: The third conference.* New York: Brunner/Mazel.

Kernberg, O. F. (2001). The concept of libido in the light of contemporary psychoanalytic theorizing. In P. Hartocollis (Ed.), *Mankind's Oedipal destiny: Libidinal and aggressive aspects of sexuality* (pp. 95–111). Madison, CT: International Universities Press.

Kernberg, O. F. (2005). Object relations theories and technique. In E. S. Person, A. M. Cooper, & G. O. Gabbard (Eds.), *The American Psychiatric Publishing textbook of psychoanalysis* (pp. 57–75). Washington, DC: American Psychiatric Publishing.

Kernberg, O. F. (2010). Narcissistic personality disorder. In J. F. Clarkin, P. Fonagy, & G. O. Gabbard (Eds.), *Psychodynamic psychotherapy for personality disorders: A clinical handbook* (pp. 257–287). Arlington, VA: American Psychiatric Publishing.

Kernberg, O. F., & Caligor, E. (2005). A psychoanalytic theory of personality disorders. In M. F. Lenzenweger & J. F. Clarkin (Eds.), *Major theories of personality disorder* (2nd ed., pp. 114–156). New York: Guilford Press.

Kerr, J. H., Lindner, K. J., & Blaydon, M. (2007). *Exercise dependence.* London: Routledge.

Kessler, D. A., & Pines, W. L. (1990). The federal regulation of prescription drug advertising and promotion. *Journal of the American Medical Association, 264*(18), 2409–2415.

Kessler, R. C. (2002). Epidemiology of depression. In I. H. Gotlib & C. L. Hammen (Eds.), *Handbook of depression* (pp. 23–42). New York: Guilford Press.

Kessler, R. C., Adler, L. A., Barkley, R., Biederman, J., Conners, C. K., Faraone, S. V., et al. (2005). Patterns and predictors of attention-deficit/hyperactivity disorder persistence into adulthood: Results from the National Comorbidity Survey Replication. *Biological Psychiatry, 57*(11), 1442–1451.

Kessler, R. C., Akiskal, H. S., Ames, M., Birnbaum, H., Greenberg, P., Hirschfeld, R. M. A., Wang, P. S. (2006). Prevalence and effects of mood disorders on work performance in a nationally representative sample of U.S. workers. *The American Journal of Psychiatry, 163*(9), 1561–1568.

Kessler, R. C., Amminger, G. P., Aguilar-Gaxiola, S., Alongo, J., & Lee, S. (2007). Age of onset of mental disorders: A review of recent literature. *Current Opinions in Psychiatry, 20*(4), 359–364.

Kessler, R. C., Avenevoli, S., Green, J., Gruber, M. J., Guyer, M., He, Y., et al. (2009). National comorbidity survey replication adolescent supplement (NCS-A): III. Concordance of DSM-IV/CIDI diagnoses with clinical reassessments. *Journal of the American Academy of Child & Adolescent Psychiatry, 48*(4), 386–399.

Kessler, R. C., Berglund, P., Demler, O., Jin, R., Merikangas, K. R., & Walters, E. E. (2005). Lifetime prevalence and age-of-onset distributions of DSM-IV disorders in the national comorbidity survey replication. *Archives of General Psychiatry, 62*(6), 593–602.

Kessler, R. C., Chiu, W. T., Demler, O., & Walters, E. E. (2005). Prevalence, severity, and comorbidity of 12-month DSM-IV disorders in the National Comorbidity Survey Replication. *Archives of General Psychiatry, 62,* 617–627.

Kessler, R. C., Chiu, W. T., Jin, R., Ruscio, A. M., Shear, K., & Walters, E. E. (2006). The epidemiology of panic attacks, panic disorder, and agoraphobia in the National Comorbidity Survey Replication. *Archives of General Psychiatry, 63,* 415–424.

Kessler, R. C., Coccaro, E. F., Fava, M., Jaeger, S., Jin, R., & Walters, E. (2006). The prevalence and correlates of DSM-IV intermittent explosive disorder in the national comorbidity survey replication. *Archives of General Psychiatry, 63*(6), 669–678.

Kessler, R. C., Demier, O., Frank, R. G., Olfson, M., Pincus, H. A., Walters, E. E., et al. (2005). Prevalence and treatment of mental disorders, 1990 to 2003. *The New England Journal of Medicine, 352*(24), 2515–2523.

Kessler, R. C., DuPont, R. L., Berglund, P., & Wittchen, H. U. (1999). Impairment in pure and comorbid generalized anxiety disorder and major depression at 12 months in two national surveys. *American Journal of Psychiatry, 156*(12), 1915–1923.

Kessler, R. C., Gruber, M., Hettema, J. M., Hwang, I., Sampson, N., Yonkers, K. A. (2010). Major depression and generalized anxiety disorder in the National Comorbidity Survey follow-up survey. In D. Goldberg, K. S. Kendler, P. J. Sirovatka, & D. A. Regier (Eds.), *Diagnostic issues in depression and generalized anxiety disorder: Refining the research agenda for DSM-V* (pp. 139–170). Washington, DC: American Psychiatric Association.

Kessler, R. C., McGonagle, K. A., Zhao, S., Nelson, C. B., Hughes, M., Eshleman, S., et al. (1994). Lifetime and 12-month prevalence of DSM-III-R psychiatric disorders among persons aged 15–54 in the United States: Results from the National Comorbidity Survey. *Archives of General Psychiatry, 51*(1), 8–19.

Kessler, R. C., Ruscio, A. M., Shear, K., & Wittchen, H-U. (2010). Epidemiology of anxiety disorders. In M. B. Stein & T. Steckler (Eds.), *Behavioral neurobiology of anxiety and its treatment. Current topics in behavioral neurosciences* (pp. 21–35). New York: Springer Science + Business Media.

Kessler, R. C., & Stang, P. E. (Eds.). (2006). *Health and work productivity: Making the business case for quality health care.* Chicago, IL: University of Chicago Press.

Kessler, R. C., & Wang, P. S. (2009). Epidemiology of depression. In I. H. Gotlib & C. L. Hammen (Eds.), *Handbook of depression* (2nd ed., pp. 5–22). New York: Guilford Press.

Kessler, R. C., & Zhao, S. (1999). The prevalence of mental illness. In A. V. Horwitz & T. L. Scheid (Eds.), *A handbook for the study of mental health: Social contexts, theories, and systems.* Cambridge, England: Cambridge University Press.

Ketter, T. A. (2010). Principles of assessment and treatment of bipolar disorders. In T. A. Ketter (Ed.), *Handbook of diagnosis and treatment of bipolar disorders* (pp. 1–9). Arlington, VA: American Psychiatric Publishing.

Ketter, T. A. (Ed.). (2010). *Handbook of diagnosis and treatment of bipolar disorders.* Arlington, VA: American Psychiatric Publishing.

Ketter, T. A., & Wang, P. W. (2010). Management of acute manic and mixed episodes in bipolar disorders. In T. A. Ketter (Ed.), *Handbook of diagnosis and treatment of bipolar disorders* (pp. 107–164). Arlington, VA: American Psychiatric Publishing.

Ketter, T. A., & Wang, P. W. (2010). Mood stabilizers and antipsychotics: Pharmacokiunetics, drug interactions, adverse effects, and administration. In T. A. Ketter (Ed.), *Handbook of diagnosis and treatment of bipolar disorders* (pp. 499–609). Arlington, VA: American Psychiatric Publishing.

Ketter, T. A., & Wang, P. W. (2010). Overview of pharmacotherapy for bipolar disorders. In T. A. Ketter (Ed.), *Handbook of diagnosis and treatment of bipolar disorders* (pp. 83–106). Arlington, VA: American Psychiatric Publishing.

Kety, S. S. (1988). Schizophrenic illness in the families of schizophrenic adoptees: Findings from the Danish national sample. *Schizophrenia Bulletin, 14*(2), 217–222.

Kety, S. S., Rosenthal, D., Wender, P. H., et al. (1968). The types and prevalence of mental illness in the biological and adoptive families of schizophrenics. *Journal of Psychiatric Research, 6,* 345–362.

Keuthen, N. J., Koran, L. M., Aboujaoude, E., Large, M. D., Serpe, R. T. (2010). The prevalence of pathologic skin picking in US adults. *Comprehensive Psychiatry, 51*(2), 183–186.

Keuthen, N. J., Rothbaum, B. O., Welch, S. S., Taylor, C., Falkenstein, M., Heekin, M., et al. (2010). Pilot trial of dialectical behavior therapy-enhanced habit reversal for trichotillomania. *Depression and Anxiety, 27*(10), 953–959.

Keuthen, N. J., Siev, J., & Reese, H. (2012). Assessment of trichotillomania, pathological skin picking, and stereotypic movement disorder. In J. E. Grant, D. J. Stein, D. W. Woods, & N. J. Keuthen (Eds.), *Trichotillomania, skin picking, and other body-focused repetitive behaviors* (pp. 129–150). Arlington, VA: American Psychiatric Publishing.

Keyes, C. L. M., & Goodman, S. H. (Eds.). (2006). *Women and depression: A handbook for the social, behavioral, and biomedical sciences.* New York: Cambridge University Press.

Keys, A., Brozek, J., Henschel, A., Mickelson, O., & Taylor, H. L. (1950). *The biology of human starvation.* Minneapolis: University of Minnesota Press.

Khare, T., Pal, M., & Petronis, A. (2011). Understanding bipolar disorder: The epigenetic perspective. In H. K. Manji & C. A. Zarate, Jr. (Eds.), *Behavioral neurobiology of bipolar disorder and its treatment. Current topics in behavioral neurosciences* (pp. 31–49). New York: Springer Science + Business Media.

Kibler, J. L., Joshi, K., & Hughes, E. E. (2010). Cognitive and behavioral reactions to stress among adults with PTSD: Implications for immunity and health. In K. Kendall-Tackett (Ed.), *The psychoneuroimmunology of chronic disease: Exploring the links between inflammation, stress, and illness* (pp. 133–158). Washington, DC: American Psychological Association.

Kiecolt-Glaser, J. K., Garner, W., Speicher, C., Penn, G. M., Holliday, J., & Glaser, R. (1984). Psychosocial modifiers of immunocompetence in medical students. *Psychosomatic Medicine, 46,* 7–14.

Kiecolt-Glaser, J. K., Glaser, R., Gravenstein, S., Malarkey, W. B., & Sheridan, J. (1996). Chronic stress alters the immune response to influenza virus vaccine in older adults. *Proceedings of the National Academy of Science, 93,* 3043–3047.

Kiecolt-Glaser, J. K., McGuire, L., Robles, T. F., & Glaser, R. (2002). Psychoneuroimmunology: Psychological influences on immune function and health. *Journal of Consulting and Clinical Psychology, 70*(3), 537–547.

Kiernan, W. (2000). Where we are now: Perspectives on employment of persons with mental retardation. *Focus on Autism and Other Developmental Disabilities, 15*(2), 90–96.

Kiesler, C. A. (2000). The next wave of change for psychology and mental health services in the health care revolution. *American Psychologist, 55*(5), 481–487.

Kiesler, D. J. (1966). Some myths of psychotherapy research and the search for a paradigm. *Psychological Bulletin, 65,* 110–136.

Kiesler, D. J. (1995). Research classic: "Some myths of psychotherapy research and the search for a paradigm": Revisited. *Psychotherapy Research, 5*(2), 91–101.

Kiev, A. (1989). Suicide in adults. In J. G. Howells (Ed.), *Modern perspectives in the psychiatry of the affective disorders.* New York: Brunner/Mazel.

Kikuchi, H., Fujii, T., Abe, N., Suzuki, M., Takagi, M., Mugikura, S., Takahashi, S., & Mori, E. (2010). Memory repression: Brain mechanisms underlying dissociative amnesia. *Journal of Cognitive Neuroscience, 22*(3), 602–613.

Kim, J., Han, J. Y., Shaw, B., McTavish, F., & Gustafson, D. (2010). The roles of social support and coping strategies in predicting breast cancer patients' emotional well-being: Testing mediation and moderation models. *Journal of Health Psychology, 15*(4), 543–552.

Kim, K. L., Parr, A. F., & Alfano, C. A. (2011). Behavioral and cognitive behavioral treatments for social anxiety disorder in adolescents and young adults. In C. A. Alfano & D. C. Beidel (Eds.), *Social anxiety in adolescents and young adults: Translating developmental science into practice* (pp. 245–264). Washington, DC: American Psychological Association.

Kim, K-H., Lee, S-M., Paik, J-W., & Kim, N-S. (2011). The effects of continuous antidepressant treatment during the first 6 months on relapse or recurrence of depression. *Journal of Affective Disorders, 132*(1), 121–129.

Kim, P., & Evans, G. W. (2011). Family resources, genes, and human development. In A. Booth, S. M. McHale, & N. S. Landale (Eds.), *Biosocial foundations of family processes, National symposium on family issues* (pp. 221–230). New York: Springer Science + Business Media.

Kim, S. M., Han, D. H., Lee, Y. S., & Renshaw, P. F. (2012). Combined cognitive behavioral therapy and bupropion for the treatment of problematic on-line game play in adolescents with major depressive disorder. *Computers in Human Behavior, 28*(5), 1954–1959.

Kim, Y. H., Kim, S. M., Kim, J. J., Cho, I. S., Jeon, M. J. (2011). Does metabolic syndrome impair sexual function in middle- to old-aged women? *Journal of Sexual Medicine, 8*(4), 1123–1130.

Kimball, A. (1993). Nipping and tucking. In Skin deep: Our national obsession with looks. *Psychology Today, 26*(3), 96.

King, L. (2002, March 19). Interview with Russell Yates. *Larry King Live.* Atlanta, GA: CNN.

King, N. S., & Kirwilliam, S. (2011). Permanent post-concussion symptoms after mild head injury. *Brain Injury, 25*(5), 462–470.

King, R. A. (2003). Psychodynamic approaches to youth suicide. In R. A. King & A. Apter (Eds.), *Suicide in children and adolescents* (pp. 150–169). New York: Cambridge University Press.

Kinzie, J., Leung, P., Boehnlein, J., & Matsunaga, D. (1992). Psychiatric epidemiology of an Indian village: A 19-year replication study. *Journal of Nervous and Mental Disease, 180*(1), 33–39.

Kirby, J. B., Hudson, J., & Miller, G. E. (2010). Explaining racial and ethnic differences in antidepressant use among adolescents. *Medical Care Research and Review, 67*(3), 342–363.

Kirby, M. (2000). Psychiatry, psychology, law and homosexuality—Uncomfortable bedfellows. *Psychiatry, Psychology and Law, 7*(2), 139–149.

Kirkcaldy, B. D., Richardson, R., & Merrick, J. (2010). Suicide risk. In J. M. Brown & E. A. Campbell (Eds.), *Cambridge Handbook of Forensic Psychology.* Cambridge: Cambridge University Press.

Kirkpatrick, M. E., & Clark, A. S. (2011). Androgen inhibition of sexual receptivity is modulated by estrogen. *Physiology & Behavior, 102*(3–4), 361–366.

Kirmayer, L. J. (2001). Cultural variations in the clinical presentation of depression and anxiety: Implications for diagnosis and treatment. *Journal of Clinical Psychiatry, 62*(Suppl. 13), 22–28.

Kirmayer, L. J. (2002). The refugee's predicament. *Evolution Psychiatrique, 67*(4), 724–742.

Kirmayer, L. J. (2003). Failures of imagination: The refugee's narrative in psychiatry. *Anthropology and Medicine, 10*(2), 167–185.

Kirmayer, L. J., & Looper, K. J. (2007). Somatoform disorders. In M. Hersen, S. M. Turner, & D. C. Beidel (Eds.), *Adult psychopathology and diagnosis* (5th ed., pp. 410–472). Hoboken, NJ: Wiley.

Kisker, G. W. (1977). *The disorganized personality.* New York: McGraw-Hill.

Kleespies, P. M., Van Orden, K. A., Bongar, B., Bridgeman, D., Bufka, L. F., Galper, D. I., et al. (2011). Psychologist suicide: Incidence, impact, and suggestions for prevention, intervention, and postvention. *Professional Psychology: Research and Practice, 42*(3), 244–251.

Klein, B., Meyer, D., Austin, D. W., & Kyrios, M. (2011). Anxiety online—A virtual clinic: Preliminary outcomes following completion of five fully automated treatment programs for anxiety disorders and symptoms. *Journal of Medical Internet Research, 13*(4), 353–372.

Klein, C., & Gorzalka, B. B. (2009). Sexual functioning in transsexuals following hormone therapy and genital surgery: A review. *Journal of Sexual Medicine, 6*(11), 2922–2939.

Klein, D. A., & Miller, A. L. (2011). Dialectical behavior therapy for suicidal adolescents with borderline personality disorder. *Child and Adolescent Psychiatric Clinics of North America, 20*(2), 205–216.

Klein, D. F. (1964). Delineation of two drug-responsive anxiety syndromes. *Psychopharmacologia, 5,* 397–408.

Klein, D. F., & Fink, M. (1962). Psychiatric reaction patterns to imipramine. *American Journal of Psychiatry, 119,* 432–438.

Klein, W. C., & Jess, C. (2002). One last pleasure? Alcohol use among elderly people in nursing homes. *Health and Social Work, 27*(3), 193–203.

Kleinman, A. (1987). Anthropology and psychiatry: The role of culture in cross-cultural research on illness. *British Journal of Psychiatry, 151,* 447–454.

Kleinman, A. (2004). Culture and depression. *New England Journal of Medicine, 351*(10), 951–953.

Kleinplatz, P. J. (2010). "Desire disorders" or opportunities for optimal erotic intimacy? In S. R. Leiblum (Ed.), *Treating sexual desire disorders: A clinical casebook* (pp. 92–113). New York: Guilford Press.

Kliem, S., Kröger, C., & Kosfelder, J. (2010). Dialectical behavior therapy for borderline personality disorder: A meta-analysis using mixed-effects modeling. *Journal of Consulting and Clinical Psychology, 78*(6), 936–951.

Kliewer, W. (2010). Family processes in drug use etiology. In L. Scheier (Ed.), *Handbook of drug use etiology: Theory, methods, and empirical findings* (pp. 365–381). Washington, DC: American Psychological Association.

Kline, N. S. (1958). Clinical experience with iproniazid (Marsilid). *Journal of Clinical and Experimental Psychopathology, 19*(1, Suppl.), 72–78.

Klitzman, R. (2008). *When doctors become patients.* New York: Oxford University Press.

Kluft, R. P. (1985). Hypnotherapy of childhood multiple personality disorder. *American Journal of Clinical Hypnosis, 27*(4), 201–210.

Kluft, R. P. (1987). The simulation and dissimulation of multiple personality disorder. *American Journal of Clinical Hypnosis, 30*(2), 104–118.

Kluft, R. P. (1988). The dissociative disorders. In J. Talbott, R. Hales, & S. Yudofsky (Eds.), *Textbook of psychiatry.* Washington, DC: American Psychiatric Press.

Kluft, R. P. (1991). Multiple personality disorder. In A. Tasman & S. M. Goldfinger (Eds.), *American Psychiatric Press review of psychiatry* (Vol. 10). Washington, DC: American Psychiatric Press.

Kluft, R. P. (1999). An overview of the psychotherapy of dissociative identity disorder. *American Journal of Psychotherapy, 53*(3), 289–319.

Kluft, R. P. (2000). The psychoanalytic psychotherapy of dissociative identity disorder in the context of trauma therapy. *Psychoanalytical Inquiry, 20*(2), 259–286.

Kluft, R. P. (2001). Dissociative disorders. In H. S. Friedman (Ed.), *Specialty articles from the encyclopedia of mental health.* San Diego: Academic Press.

Kluger, J. (2004, December 6). Blowing a gasket. *Time, 164*(23), . 72–80.

Knight, B. G., Kaskie, B., Shurgot, G. R., & Dave, J. (2006). Improving the mental health of older adults. In J. E. Birren & K. W. Schaie (Eds.), *Handbook of the psychology of aging* (6th ed., pp. 408–425). San Diego, CA: Elsevier.

Knight, B. G., & McCallum, T. J. (2011). Older adults. In J. C. Norcross, G. R. VandenBos, & D. K. Freedheim (Eds.), *History of psychotherapy: Continuity and change* (2nd ed., pp. 458–466). Washington, DC: American Psychological Association.

Knight, S. C., Meyer, R. G., & Goldstein, A. M. (2007). Forensic hypnosis. In A. M. Goldstein (Ed.), *Forensic psychology: Emerging topics and expanding roles* (pp. 734–763). Hoboken, NJ: Wiley.

Knoll, J. L. (2010). The "pseudocommando" mass murderer: Part I. The psychology of revenge and obliteration. *Journal of the American Academy of Psychiatry and the Law, 38,* 87–94.

Knudson, R. M. (2006). Anorexia dreaming: A case study. *Dreaming, 16*(1), 43–52.

Knutson, B., Wolkowitz, O. M., Cole, S. W., Chan, T., Moore, E. A., Johnson, R. C., et al. (1998). Selective alteration of personality and social behavior by serotonergic intervention. *American Journal of Psychiatry, 155,* 373–379.

Kobeissi, J., Aloysi, A., Tobias, K., Popeo, D., & Kellner, C. H. (2011). Resolution of severe suicidality with a single electroconvulsive therapy. *The Journal of ECT, 27*(1), 86–88.

Koch, W. J., & Haring, M. (2008). Posttraumatic stress disorder. In M. Hersen & J. Rosqvist (Eds.), *Handbook of psychological assessment, case conceptualization, and treatment: Vol. 1. Adults* (pp. 263–290). Hoboken, NJ: John Wiley & Sons.

Kocsis, R. N. (2008). *Serial murder and the psychology of violent crimes.* Totowa, NJ: Humana Press.

Kodituwakku, P. W., & Kodituwakku, E. L. (2011). From research to practice: An integrative framework for the development of interventions for children with fetal alcohol spectrum disorders. *Neuropsychology Review, 21*(2), 204–223.

Koegel, L. K., Koegel, R. L., & Brookman, L. I. (2005). Child-initiated interactions that are pivotal in intervention for children with autism. In E. D. Hibbs & P. S. Jensen (Eds.), *Psychosocial treatments for child and adolescent disorders: Empirically based strategies for clinical practice* (2nd ed., pp. 633–657). Washington, DC: American Psychological Association.

Koegel, R. L., Koegel, L. K., Vernon, T. W., & Brookman-Frazee, L. (2010). Empirically supported pivotal response treatment for children with autism spectrum disorders. In J. R. Weisz, & A. E. Kazdin (Eds.), *Evidence-based psychotherapies for children and adolescents* (2nd ed., pp. 327–344) New York: Guilford Press.

Koenen, K. C., Lyons, M. J., Goldberg, J., Simpson, J., Williams, W. M., Toomey, R., et al. (2003). Co-twin control study of relationships among combat exposure, combat-related PTSD, and other mental disorders. *Journal of Traumatic Stress, 16*(5), 433–438.

Koenig, H. G. (2002). The connection between psychoneuroimmunology and religion. In H. G. Koenig & H. J. Cohen (Eds.), *The link between religion and health: Psychoneuroimmunology and the faith factor.* New York: Oxford University Press.

Koenigsberg, H. W., Harvey, P. D., Mitropoulou, V., Schmeidler, J., New, A. S., Goodman, M., et al. (2002). Characterizing affective instability in borderline personality disorder. *American Journal of Psychiatry, 159*(5), 784–788.

Koenigsberg, H. W., Harvey, P., Mitropoulou, V., New, A. Goodman, M., Silverman, J., et al. (2001). Are the interpersonal and identity disturbances in the borderline personality disorder criteria linked to the traits of affectivity and impulsivity? *Journal of Personality Disorders, 15,* 358–370.

Koenigsberg, H. W., Reynolds, D., Goodman, M., New, A. S., Mitropoulou, V., Trestman, R. L., et al. (2003). Risperidone in the treatment of schizotypal personality disorder. *Journal of Clinical Psychiatry, 64*(6), 628–634.

Koerner, B. I. (2007). Drug makers find new markets by publicizing "hidden epidemics" of mental illness. In A. Quigley (Ed.), *Current controversies: Mental health.* Detroit: Greenhaven Press/Thomson Gale.

Koh, K. B., Kim, D. K., Kim, S. Y., & Park, J. K. (2005). The relation between anger expression, depression, and somatic symptoms in depressive disorders and somatoform disorders. *Journal of Clinical Psychiatry, 66*(4), 485–491.

Koh, M., Nishimatsu, Y., & Endo, S. (2000). Dissociative disorder. *Journal of International Society of Life Information Science, 18*(2), 495–498.

Kohen, D. P., & Olness, K. (2011). *Hypnosis and hypnotherapy with children* (4th ed.). New York: Routledge/Taylor & Francis Group.

Kohler, F. W., Strain, P. S., & Goldstein, H. (2005). Learning experiences . . . An alternative program for preschoolers and parents: Peer-mediated interventions for young children with autism. In E. D. Hibbs & P. S. Jensen (Eds.),

Psychosocial treatments for child and adolescent disorders: Empirically based strategies for clinical practice (2nd ed., pp. 659–687). Washington, DC: American Psychological Association.

Kohut, H. (1977). *The restoration of the self.* New York: International Universities Press.

Kohut, H. (2001). On empathy. *European Journal for Psychoanalytic Therapy and Research, 2*(2), 139–146.

Kokish, R., Levenson, J. S., & Blasingame, G. D. (2005). Post-conviction sex offender polygraph examination: Client-reported perceptions of utility and accuracy. *Sexual Abuse Journal of Research and Treatment, 17*(2), 211–221.

Kolassa, I-T., Ertl, V., Eckart, C., Kolassa, S., Onyut, L. P., & Elbert, T. (2010). Spontaneous remission from PTSD depends on the number of traumatic event types experienced. *Psychological Trauma: Theory, Research, Practice, and Policy, 2*(3), 169–174.

Komaroff, A. L., Masuda, M., & Holmes, T. H. (1986). The Social Readjustment Rating Scale: A comparative study of Negro, White, and Mexican Americans. *Journal of Psychosomatic Research, 12,* 121–128.

Komaroff, A. L., Masuda, M., & Holmes, T. H. (1989). The Social Readjustment Rating Scale: A comparative study of Black, White, and Mexican Americans. In T. H. Holmes & E. M. David (Eds.), *Life change, life events, and illness.* New York: Praeger.

Kong, D. (1998, November 18). Still no solution in the struggle on safeguards—Doing harm: Research on the mentally ill. *Boston Globe,* p. A1.

Konstantellou, A., Campbell, M., & Eisler, I. (2012). The family context: Cause, effect or resource. In J. Alexander & J. Treasure (Eds.), *A collaborative approach to eating disorders* (pp. 5–18). New York: Routledge/Taylor & Francis.

Koob, G. F. (2008). Neurobiology of addiction. In H. D. Kleber & M. Galanter (Eds.), *The American Psychiatric Publishing textbook of substance abuse treatment* (4th ed., pp. 3–16). Arlington, VA: American Psychiatric Publishing.

Koob, G. F., & LeMoal, M. (2008). Addiction and the brain antireward system. *Annual review of psychology, 59,* 29–53.

Koocher, G. P., & Keith-Spiegel, P. (2008). *Ethics in psychology and the mental health professions: Standards and cases* (3rd ed.). Oxford, England: Oxford University Press.

Koopman, C., Palesh, O., Marten, B., Thompson, B., Ismailji, T., Holmes, D. D., et al. (2004). Child abuse and adult interpersonal trauma as predictors of posttraumatic stress disorder symptoms among women seeking treatment for intimate partner violence. In T. A. Corales (Ed.), *Focus on posttraumatic stress disorder research* (pp. 1–16). Hauppauge, NY: Nova Science.

Kooyman, I., & Walsh, E. (2011). Societal outcomes in schizophrenia. In D. R. Weinberg & P. Harrison (Eds.), *Schizophrenia* (pp. 644–665). Hoboken, NJ: Wiley-Blackwell.

Kopelowicz, A., Liberman, R. P., & Zarate, R. (2007). Psychosocial treatments for schizophrenia. In P. E. Nathan & J. M. Gorman (Eds.), *A guide to treatments that work* (3rd ed., pp. 243–269). New York: Oxford University Press.

Kopelowicz, A., Liberman, R. P., & Zarate, R. (2008). Psychosocial treatments for schizophrenia. In K. T. Mueser & D. V. Jeste (Eds.), *Clinical handbook of schizophrenia* (pp. 243–269). New York: Guilford Press.

Korda, J. B., Goldstein, S. W., & Goldstein, I. (2010). The role of androgens in the treatment of hypoactive sexual desire disorder in women. In S. R. Leiblum (Ed.), *Treating sexual desire disorders: A clinical casebook* (pp. 201–218). New York: Guilford Press.

Korda, J. B., & Sommer, F. (2010). Anti-androgen treatment of paraphilias from the urologist's perspective. *Forensische Psychiatrie, Psychologie, Kriminologie, 4*(Suppl. 1), S17–S21.

Koren, D., Norman, D., Cohen, A., Berman, J., & Klein, E. M. (2005). Increased PTSD risk with combat-related injury: A matched comparison study of injured and uninjured soldiers experiencing the same combat events. *American Journal of Psychiatry, 162*(2), 276–282.

Kosel, M., Brockmann, H., Frick, C., Zobel, A., & Schlaepfer, T. E. (2011). Chronic vagus nerve stimulation for treatment-resistant depression increases regional cerebral blood flow in the dorsolateral prefrontal cortex. *Psychiatry Research: Neuroimaging, 191*(3), 153–159.

Koss, M. P. (1993). Rape: Scope, impact, interventions, and public policy responses. *American Psychologist, 48*(10), 1062–1069.

Koss, M. P. (2005). Empirically enhanced reflections on 20 years of rape research. *Journal of Interpersonal Violence, 20*(1), 100–107.

Koss, M. P., Abbey, A., Campbell, R., Cook, S., Norris, J., Testa, M., et al. (2007). Revising the SES: A collaborative process to improve assessment of sexual aggression and victimization. *Psychology of Women Quarterly, 31*(4), 357–370.

Koss, M. P., Abbey, A., Campbell, R., Cook, S., Norris, J., Testa, M., et al. (2008). Revising the SES: A collaborative process to improve assessment of sexual aggression and victimization: Erratum. *Psychology of Women Quarterly, 32*(4), 493.

Koss, M. P., & Heslet, L. (1992). Somatic consequences of violence against women. *Archives of Family Medicine, 1*(1), 53–59.

Koss, M. P., White, J. W., & Kazdin, A. E. (2011). Violence against women and children: Perspectives and next steps. In M. P. Koss, J. W. White, & A. E. Kazdin (Eds.), *Violence against women and children: Vol. 2. Navigating solutions* (pp. 261–305). Washington, DC: American Psychological Association.

Koss, M. P., White, J. W., & Kazdin, A. E. (Eds.). (2011). *Violence against women and children: Vol. 2. Navigating solutions.* Washington, DC: American Psychological Association.

Kosten, T. R., George, T. P., & Kleber, H. D. (2005). The neurobiology of substance dependence: Implications for treatment. In R. J. Frances, A. H. Mack, & S. I. Miller (Eds.), *Clinical textbook of addictive disorders* (3rd ed., pp. 3–15). New York: Guilford Press.

Kosten, T. R., George, T. P., & Kleber, H. D. (2011). The neurobiology of substance dependence: Implications for treatment. In R. J. Frances, S. I. Miller, & A. H. Mack (Eds.), *Clinical textbook of addictive disorders* (3rd ed.). New York: Guilford Press.

Kosten, T. R., Sofuoglu, M., & Gardner, T. J. (2008). Clinical management: Cocaine. In H. D. Kleber & M. Galanter (Eds.), *The American Psychiatric Publishing textbook of substance abuse treatment* (4th ed., pp. 157–168). Arlington, VA: American Psychiatric Publishing.

Kouimtsidis, C., & Drummond, C. (2010). Cognitive behaviour therapy for opiate misusers in methadone maintenance treatment. In S. MacGregor (Ed.), *Responding to drug misuse: Research and policy priorities in health and social care* (pp. 114–127). New York

Kposowa, A. J., McElvain, J. P., & Breault, K. D. (2008). Immigration and suicide: The role of marital status, duration of residence, and social integration. *Archives of Suicide Research, 12*(1), 82–92.

Krack, P., Hariz, M. I., Baunez, C., Guridi, J., & Obeso, J. A. (2010). Deep brain stimulation: From neurology to psychiatry? *Trends in Neurosciences, 33*(10), 474–484.

Kraft, D., & Kraft, T. (2010). Use of in vivo desensitization in the treatment of mouse phobia: Review and case study. *Contemporary Hypnosis, 27*(3), 184–194.

Kraines, S. H., & Thetford, E. S. (1972). *Help for the depressed.* Springfield, IL: Thomas.

Krakauer, S. Y. (2001). *Treating dissociative identity disorder: The power of the collective heart.* Philadelphia: Brunner-Routledge.

Kral, M. J., Garcia, J. I. R., Aber, M. S., Masood, N., Duta, U., & Todd, N. R. (2011). Culture and community psychology: Toward a renewed and reimagined vision. *American Journal of Community Psychology, 47*(1–2), 46–57.

Kramer, U., & Meystre, C. (2010). Assimilation process in a psychotherapy with a client presenting schizoid personality disorder. *Schweizer Archiv für Neurologie und Psychiatrie, 161*(4), 128–134.

Krantz, J. H. (2011). Psychological research on the net. Retrieved April 6, 2011, from htpp://psych.hanover.edu/research/exponnet.html.

Krapohl, D. J. (2002). The polygraph in personnel screening. In M. Kleiner (Ed.), *The handbook of polygraph testing.* San Diego, CA: Academic.

Kravitz, R. L., Epstein, R. M., Feldman, M. D., Franz, C. E., Azari, R., Wilkes, M. S., et al. (2005). Influence of patients' requests for direct-to-consumer advertised antidepressants. *Journal of the American Medical Association, 293*(16), 1905–2002.

Kreek, M. J. (2008). Neurobiology of opiates and opioids. In H. D. Kleber & M. Galanter (Eds.), *The American Psychiatric Publishing textbook of substance abuse treatment* (4th ed., pp. 247–264). Arlington, VA: American Psychiatric Publishing.

Kring, A. M., & Neale, J. M. (1996). Do schizophrenic patients show a disjunctive relationship among expressive, experiential, and psychophysiological components of emotion? *Journal of Abnormal Psychology, 105*(2), 249–257.

Krippner, S., & Paulson, C. M. (2006). Posttraumatic stress disorder among U.S. combat veterans. In T. G. Plante (Ed.), *Mental disorders of the new millennium: Vol. 2. Public and social problems.* Westport, CT: Praeger Publishers.

Krueger, R. B. (2010). The DSM diagnostic criteria for sexual masochism. *Archives of Sexual Behavior, 39*(2), 346–356.

Krueger, R. G., & Kaplan, M. S. (2002). Behavioral and psychopharmacological treatment of the paraphilic and hypersexual disorders. *Journal of Psychiatric Practice, 8*(1), 21–32.

Krueger, R. B., & Kaplan, M. S. (2008). Frotteurism: Assessment and treatment. In D. R. Laws & W. T. O'Donohue (Eds.), *Sexual deviance: Theory, assessment, and treatment* (2nd ed., pp. 150–163). New York: Guilford Press.

Krüger, A., Schmidt, A., & Müller, J. (2010). Technological and research perspectives of old-age ubiquitous computing. *GeroPsych, 23*(2), 99–105.

Kruger, S., Young, L. T., & Braunig, P. (2005). Pharmacotherapy of bipolar mixed states. *Bipolar Disorders, 7*(3), 205–215.

Kruger, T. H. C., Burri, A., & Schedlowski, M. (2011). Melatonin plasma levels during sexual arousal and orgasm in males. *Journal of Sexual Medicine, 8*(4), 1255–1256.

Krystal, J. H., & Moghaddam, B. (2011). Contributions of glutamate and GABA systems to the neurobiology and treatment of schizophrenia. In D. R. Weinberg & P. Harrison (Eds.), *Schizophrenia* (pp. 433–461). Hoboken, NJ: Wiley-Blackwell.

Kubera, M., Obuchowicz, E., Goehler, L., Brzeszcz, J., & Maes, M. (2011). In animal models, psychosocial stress-induced (neuro) inflammation, apoptosis and reduced neurogenesis are associated to the onset of depression. *Progress in Neuro-Psychopharmacology & Biological Psychiatry, 35*(3), 744–759.

Kubler, A., Murphy, K., & Garavan, H. (2005). Cocaine dependence and attention switching within and between verbal and visuospatial working memory. *European Journal of Neuroscience, 21*(7), 1984–1992.

Kuhn, R. (1958). The treatment of depressive states with G-22355 (imipramine hydrochloride). *American Journal of Psychiatry, 115,* 459–464.

Kuhn, T. S. (1962). *The structure of scientific revolutions.* Chicago: University of Chicago Press.

Kulka, R. A., Schlesenger, W. E., Fairbank, J. A., Hough. R. L., Jordan, B. K., Marmar, C. R., et al. (1990). *Trauma and the Vietnam War generation: Report of findings from the National Vietnam Veterans Readjustment Study.* New York: Brunner/Mazel.

Kukla, L., Selesova, P., Okrajek, P., & Tulak, J. (2010). Somatoform dissociation and symptoms of traumatic stress in adolescents. *Activitas Nervosa Superior, 52*(1), 29–31.

Kunst, M. J. J. (2011). Affective personality type, post-traumatic stress disorder symptom severity and post-traumatic growth in victims of violence. *Stress and Health: Journal of the International Society for the Investigation of Stress, 27*(1), 42–51.

Kuo, J. R., Goldin, P. R., Werner, K., Heimberg, R. G., & Gross, J. J. (2011). Childhood trauma and current psychological functioning in adults with social anxiety disorder. *Journal of Anxiety Disorders, 25*(4), 467–473.

Kuo, W., Gallo, J. J., & Eaton, W. W. (2004). Hopelessness, depression, substance disorder, and suicidality. *Social Psychiatry and Psychiatric Epidemiology, 39,* 497–501.

Kuroki, M. (2010). Suicide and unemployment in Japan: Evidence from municipal level suicide rates and age-specific suicide rates. *Journal of Socio-Economics, 39*(6), 683–691.

Kurtz, J. E. (2010). Assessment of outpatients using the PAI. In M. A. Blais, M. R. Baity, & C. J. Hopwood (Eds.), *Clinical applications of the Personality Assessment Inventory* (pp. 13–33). New York: Routledge/Taylor & Francis Group.

Kurtz, M. M., & Mueser, K. T. (2008). A meta-analysis of controlled research on social skills training for schizophrenia. *Journal of Consulting and Clinical Psychology, 76*(3), 491–504.

Kutcher, S., & Gardner, D. M. (2008). Use of selective serotonin reuptake inhibitors and youth suicide: Making sense from a confusing story. *Current Opinions in Psychiatry, 21*(1), 65–69.

Kutscher, E. C. (2008). Antipsychotics. In K. T. Mueser & D. V. Jeste (Eds.), *Clinical handbook of schizophrenia* (pp. 159–167). New York: Guilford Press.

Kwag, K. H., Jang, Y., Rhew, S. H., & Chiriboga, D. A. (2011). Neighborhood effects on physical and mental health: A study of Korean American older adults. *Asian American Journal of Psychology, 2*(2), 91–100.

La Greca, A. M., & Silverman, W. K. (2009). Treatment and prevention of posttraumatic stress reactions in children and adolescents exposed to disasters and terrorism: What is the evidence? *Child Development Perspectives, 3*(1), 4–10.

Labbé, E. E. (2011). *Psychology moment by moment: A guide to enhancing your clinical practice with mindfulness and meditation.* Oakland, CA: New Harbinger Publications.

Lagger, G., Pataky, Z., & Golay, A. (2010). Efficacy of therapeutic patient education in chronic diseases and obesity. *Patient Education and Counseling, 79*(3), 283–286.

Lagnado, L. (2007, December 4). Prescription abuse seen in U.S. nursing homes. *Wall Street Journal Online.* Retrieved January 21, 2008, from http://online.wsj.com/article/SB119672919018312521.html.

Lahey, B. B. (2008). Oppositional defiant disorder, conduct disorder, and juvenile delinquency. In S. P. Hinshaw & T. P. Beauchaine (Eds.), *Child and adolescent psychopathology* (pp. 335–369). Hoboken, NJ: Wiley.

Lahey, B. B., Loeber, R., Burke, J. D., & Applegate, B. (2005). Predicting future antisocial personality disorder in males from a clinical assessment in childhood. *Journal of Consulting and Clinical Psychology, 73*(3), 389–399.

Lahmann, C., Henningsen, P., & Noll-Hussong, M. (2010). Somatoform pain disorder—Overview. *Psychiatria Danubina, 22*(3), 453–458.

Lai, C-H. (2011). Major depressive disorder: Gender differences in symptoms, life quality, and sexual function. *Journal of Clinical Psychopharmacology, 31*(1), 39–44.

Laing, R. D. (1959). *The divided self: An existential study in sanity and madness.* London: Tavistock.

Laing, R. D. (1964). *The divided self* (2nd ed.). London: Pelican.

Laing, R. D. (1967). *The politics of experience.* New York: Pantheon.

Lake, C. R. (2012). *Schizophrenia is a misdiagnosis: Implications for the DSM-5 and ICD-11.* New York: Springer Science 1 Business Media.

Lalonde, J. K., Hudson, J. I., Gigante, R. A., & Pope, H. G., Jr. (2001). Canadian and American psychiatrists' attitudes toward dissociative disorders diagnoses. *Canadian Journal of Psychiatry, 46*(5), 407–412.

Lalonde, J. K., Hudson, J. I., & Pope, H. G., Jr. (2002). Canadian and American psychiatrists' attitudes toward dissociative disorder diagnoses: The authors reply. *Canadian Journal of Psychiatry, 47*(3), 1.

Lamar M., Foy, C. M. L., Beacher, F.., Daly, E., Poppe, M., Archer, N., et al. (2011). Down syndrome with and without dementia: An in vivo proton magnetic resonance spectroscope study with implications for Alzheimer's disease. *NeuroImage, 57*(1), 63–68.

Lamb, D. H., Catanzaro, S. J., & Moorman, A. S. (2003). Psychologists reflect on their sexual relationships with clients, supervisees, and students: Occurrence, impact, rationales and collegial intervention. *Professional Psychologist, 34,* 102–107.

Lambert, K., & Kinsley, C. H. (2005). *Clinical neuroscience: The neurobiological foundations of mental health*. New York: Worth Publishers.

Lambert, M. J. (2010). Using outcome data to improve the effects of psychotherapy: Some illustrations. In M. J. Lambert (Ed.), *Prevention of treatment failure: The use of measuring, monitoring, and feedback in clinical practice* (pp. 203–242). Washington, DC: American Psychological Association.

Lambert, M. J., Shapiro, D. A., & Bergin, A. E. (1986). The effectiveness of psychotherapy. In S. L. Garfield & A. E. Bergin (Eds.), *Handbook of psychotherapy and behavioral change* (3rd ed.). New York: Wiley.

Lambert, M. J., Weber, F. D., & Sykes, J. D. (1993, April). *Psychotherapy versus placebo*. Poster presented at the annual meeting of the Western Psychological Association, Phoenix, AZ.

Lambert, M. T. (2003). Suicide risk assessment and management: Focus on personality disorders. *Current Opinions in Psychiatry, 16*(1), 71–76.

Lamprecht, F., Kohnke, C., Lempa, W., Sack, M., Matzke, M., & Munte, T. F. (2004). Event-related potentials and EMDR treatment of posttraumatic stress disorder. *Neuroscience Research, 49*(2), 267–272.

Lancet. (2010, February 2). Retraction—Ileal-lymphoidnodular hyperplasia, non-specific colitis, and pervasive developmental disorder in children. *The Lancet.*

Lancioni, G. E., Singh, N. N., O'Reilly, M. F., Sigafoos, J., Bosco, A., Zonno, N., & Badagliacca, F. (2011). Persons with mild or moderate Alzheimer's disease learn to use urine alarms and prompts to avoid large urinary accidents. *Research in Developmental Disabilities, 32*(5), 1998–2004.

Landrigan, P. (2007, January 27). Cited in M. Ritter, Lead linked to aging in older brains. *YAHOO! News.*

Landrigan, P. J. (2011). Environment and autism. In E. Hollander, A. Kolevzon & J. T. Coyle (Eds.), *Textbook of autism spectrum disorders.* (pp. 247–264) Arlington, VA: American Psychiatric Publishing, Inc.

Landreth, G. L. (2012). *Play therapy: The art of relationship* (3rd ed.). New York: Routledge/ Taylor & Francis Group.

Landry, M. J. (1994). *Understanding drugs of abuse: The processes of addiction, treatment, and recovery.* Washington, DC: American Psychiatric Press.

Landsbergis, P. A., Schnall, P. L., Belkic, K. L., Baker, D., Schwartz, J. E., & Pickering, T. G. (2011). Workplace and cardiovascular disease: Relevance and potential role for occupational health psychology. In J. C. Quick, & L. E. Tetrick (Eds.), *Handbook of occupational health psychology* (2nd ed., pp. 243–264) Washington, DC: American Psychological Association.

Lane, K. L., Menzies, H. M., Bruhn, A. L., & Crnobori, M. (2011). *Managing challenging behaviors in school: Research-based strategies that work. What works for special-needs learners.* New York: Guilford Press.

Laney, C., & Loftus, E. F. (2010). False memory. In J. M. Brown & E. A. Campbell (Eds.), *The Cambridge handbook of forensic psychology* (pp. 187–194). New York: Cambridge University Press.

Lang, A. J. (2004). Treating generalized anxiety disorder with cognitive-behavioral therapy. *Journal of Clinical Psychiatry, 65*(Suppl. 13), 14–19.

Lang, E. V. (2010). Procedural hypnosis. In A. F. Barabasz, K. Olness, R. Boland, & S. Kahn (Eds.), *Medical hypnosis primer: Clinical and research evidence* (pp. 87–90). New York: Routledge/Taylor & Francis Group.

Lang, J. (1999, April 16). Local jails dumping grounds for mentally ill. *Detroit News.*

Lange, A., van de Ven, J. P., Schrieken, B., & Smit, M. (2004). "Interapy" burnout: Prevention and therapy of burnout via the Internet. *Verhaltenstherapie, 14*(3), 190–199.

Långström, N., & Seto, M. C. (2006). Exhibitionist and voyeuristic behavior in a Swedish national population survey. *Archives of Sexual Behavior, 35,* 427–435.

Långström, N., & Zucker, K. J. (2005). Transvestic fetishism in the general population: Prevalence and correlates. *Journal of Sex and Marital Therapy, 31*(2), 87–95.

Lanier, C. (2010). Structure, culture, and lethality: An integrated model approach to American Indian suicide and homicide. *Homicide Studies: An Interdisciplinary & International Journal, 14*(1), 72–89.

Lanigan, J. D. (2011). The substance and sources of young children's healthy eating and physical activity knowledge: Implications for obesity prevention efforts. *Child: Care, Health and Development, 37*(3), 368–376.

Lanning, K. V. (2001). *Child molesters: A behavioral analysis* (4th ed.). Washington, DC: National Center for Missing and Exploited Children.

Lanska, D. J., & Lanska, J., T. (2007). Franz Anton Mesmer and the rise and fall of animal magnetism: Dramatic cures, controversy, and ultimately a triumph for the scientific method. In D. J. Whitaker, C. U. M. Smith, & S. Finger (Eds.), *Brain, mind and medicine: Essays in eighteenth century neuroscience* (pp. 301–320). New York: Springer Science + Business Media.

Lanyon, R. I. (2007). Utility of the psychological screening inventory: A review. *Journal of Clinical Psychology, 63*(3), 283–307.

Lapierre, S., Erlangsen, A., Waern, M., De Leo, D., Oyama, H., Scocco, P., et al. (2011). A systematic review of elderly suicide prevention programs. *Crisis: Journal of Crisis Intervention and Suicide Prevention, 32*(2), 88–98.

Large, M. M., Nielssen, O., Ryan, C. J., & Hayes, R. (2008). Mental health laws that require dangerousness for involuntary admission may delay the initial treatment of schizophrenia. *Social Psychiatry and Psychiatric Epidemiology, 43*(3), 251–256.

Larimer, M. E., Neighbors, C., Lostutter, T. W., Whiteside, U., Cronce, J. M., Kaysen, D., & Walker, D. D. (2012). Brief motivational feedback and cognitive behavioral interventions for prevention of disordered gambling: A randomized clinical trial. *Addiction, 107*(6), 1148–1158.

Larsen, A., Boggild, H., Mortensen, J. T., Foldager, L., Hansen, J., Christensen, A., et al. (2010). Mental health in the workforce: An occupational psychiatric study. *International Journal of Social Psychiatry, 56*(6), 578–592.

Larsson, B., & Ivarsson, T. (1998). Clinical characteristics of adolescent psychiatric inpatients who have attempted suicide. *European Child and Adolescent Psychiatry, 7*(4), 201–208.

Lask, B., & Bryant-Waugh, R. (Eds.). (2000). *Anorexia nervosa and related eating disorders in childhood and adolescence* (2nd ed.). Hove, England: Psychology Press/Taylor & Francis.

Lasker Foundation. (2000). *Exceptional returns: The economic value of America's investment in biomedical research, 2000.* Retrieved from http://www.laskerfoundation.org/reports/pdf/ exceptional.pdf.

Latzer, Y., Katz, R., & Spivak, Z. (2011). Facebook users more prone to eating disorders. Retrieved from http://newmedia-eng.haifa. ac.il/.

Laumann, E. O., Gagnon, J. H., Michael, R. T., & Michaels, S. (1994). *The social organization of sexuality.* Chicago: University of Chicago Press.

Laumann, E. O., Nicolosi, A., Glasser, D. B., Paik, A., Gingell, C., Moreira, E., et al. (2005). Sexual problems among women and men aged 40–80 years: Prevalence and correlates identified in the Global Study of Sexual Attitudes and Behaviors. *International Journal of Impotence Research, 17,* 39–57.

Laumann, E. O., Paik, A., & Rosen, R. C. (1999). Sexual dysfunction in the United States: Prevalence and predictors. *Journal of the American Medical Association, 281*(13), 1174.

Lavin, M. (2008). Voyeurism: Psychopathology and theory. In D. R. Laws & W. T. O'Donohue (Eds.), *Sexual deviance: Theory, assessment, and treatment* (2nd ed., pp. 305–319). New York: Guilford Press.

Lawlor, B. A., McCarron, M., Wilson, G., & McLoughlin, M. (2001). Temporal lobe-oriented CT scanning and dementia in Down's syndrome. *International Journal of Geriatric Psychiatry, 16*(4), 427–429.

Lawrence, P. J., & Williams, T. I. (2011). Pathways to inflated responsibility beliefs in adolescent obsessive-compulsive disorder: A preliminary investigation. *Behavioral and Cognitive Psychotherapy, 39*(2), 229–234.

Lawrie, S. M., & Pantelis, C. (2011). Structural brain imaging in schizophrenia and related populations. In D. R. Weinberg & P. Harrison (Eds.), *Schizophrenia* (pp. 334–352). Hoboken, NJ: Wiley-Blackwell.

Laws, D. R., & Ward, T. (2011). *Desistance from sex offending: Alternatives to throwing away the keys.* New York: Guilford Press.

Lawson, W. B. (2008). Schizophrenia in African Americans. In K. T. Mueser & D. V. Jeste (Eds.), *Clinical handbook of schizophrenia* (pp. 616–623). New York: Guilford Press.

Lawson, W. B., Herrera, J., & Lawson, R. G. (2011). African Americans: Alcohol and substance. In J. H. Lowinson & P. Ruiz (Eds.), *Substance abuse: A comprehensive textbook, fifth edition.* Philadelphia, PA: Lippincott, Williams, & Wilkins.

Lawton, E. M., Shields, A. J., & Oltmanns, T. F. (2011). Five-factor model personality disorder prototypes in a community sample: Self- and informant-reports predicting interview-based DSM diagnoses. *Personality Disorders.*

Lazarov, O., Robinson, J., Tang, Y. P., Hairston, I. S., Korade-Mirnics, Z., Lee, V. M., et al. (2005). Environmental enrichment reduces Abeta levels and amyloid deposition in transgenic mice. *Cell, 120*(5), 572–574.

Lazarus, A. A. (1965). The treatment of a sexually inadequate man. In L. P. Ullman & L. Krasner (Eds.), *Case studies in behavior modification.* New York: Holt, Rinehart & Winston.

Lazarus, R. S., & Folkman, S. (1984). *Stress, appraisal, and coping.* New York: Springer Publishing.

Lazzari, C., Egan, S. J., & Rees, C. S. (2011). Behavioral activation treatment for depression in older adults delivered via videoconferencing: A pilot study. *Cognitive and Behavioral Practice, 18*(4), 555–565.

Leach, M. M., & Leong, F. T. L. (Eds.). (2008). *Suicide among racial and ethnic minority groups: Theory, research, and practice. Series in death, dying, and bereavement.* New York: Routledge/Taylor & Francis Group.

Leahy, R. L. (2004). Cognitive-behavioral therapy. In R. G. Heimberg, C. J. Turk, & D. S. Mennin (Eds.), *Generalized anxiety disorder: Advances in research and practice.* New York: Guilford Press.

Leahy, R. L., Beck, J., & Beck, A. T. (2005). Cognitive therapy for the personality disorders. In S. Strack (Ed.), *Handbook of personality and psychopathology* (pp. 442–461). Hoboken, NJ: Wiley.

Lebow, J. L., & Uliaszek, A. A. (2010). Couples and family therapy for personality disorders. In J. J. Magnavita (Ed.), *Evidence-based treatment of personality dysfunction: Principles, methods, and processes.* (pp. 193–221) Washington, DC: American Psychological Association.

LeBuffe, P. A., Robison, S., & Chamberlin-Elliott, D. J. (2010). Residential treatment centers for children and adolescents with conduct disorders. In R. C. Murrihy, A. D. Kidman, & T. H. Ollendick (Eds.), *Clinical handbook of assessing and treating conduct problems in youth* (pp. 333–364). New York: Springer Science + Business Media.

Ledoux, S., Miller, P., Choquet, M., & Plant, M. (2002). Family structure, parent-child relationships, and alcohol and other drug use among teenagers in France and the United Kingdom. *Alcohol Alcoholism, 37*(1), 52–60.

Lee, A. M. R., Simeon, D., Cohen, L. J., Samuel, J., Steele, A., & Galynker, I. I. (2011). Predictors of patient and caregiver distress in an adult sample with bipolar disorder seeking family treatment. *Journal of Nervous and Mental Disease, 199*(1), 18–24.

Lee, D. E. (1985). Alternative self-destruction. *Perceptual and Motor Skills, 61*(3, Part 2), 1065–1066.

Lee, E., Mishna, F., & Brennerstuhl, S. (2010). How to critically evaluate case studies in social work. *Research on Social Work Practice, 20*(6), 682–689.

Lee, T. (2011). A review on thirty days to hope & freedom from sexual addiction: The essential guide to beginning recovery and relapse prevention. *Sexual Addiction & Compulsivity, 18*(1), 52–55.

Lee, T., & Seeman, P. (1980). Elevation of brain neuroleptic/dopamine receptors in schizophrenia. *American Journal of Psychiatry, 137,* 191–197.

Leenaars, A. A. (2004). Altruistic suicide: A few reflections. *Archives of Suicide Research, 8*(1), 1–7.

Leenaars, A. A. (2007). Gun-control legislation and the impact of suicide. *Journal of Crisis Intervention and Suicide Prevention, 28*(Suppl. 1), 50–57.

Leenaars, A. A. (2011). Evidence-based psychotherapy with suicidal people: A systematic review. In M. Pompii & R. Tatarelli (Eds.), *Evidence-based practice in suicidology: A source book* (pp. 89–123). Cambridge MA: Hogrefe Publishing.

Leenaars, A. A. (2011). Psychotherapy with suicidal people: Some common implications for response. In K. Michel & D. A. Jobes (Eds.), *Building a therapeutic alliance with the suicidal patient* (pp. 231–254). Washington, DC: American Psychological Association.

Leenaars, L. S., & Leenaars, A. A. (2011). Suicide postvention programs in colleges and universities. In D. A. Lamis & D. Lester (Eds.), *Understanding and preventing college student suicide* (pp. 273–290). Springfield, IL: Charles C Thomas Publisher.

Leenaars, A. A., & Lester, D. (2004). The impact of suicide prevention centers on the suicide rate in the Canadian provinces. *Crisis, 25*(2), 65–68.

le Grange, D. (2011). Family-based treatment for bulimia nervosa: Theoretical model, key tenets, and evidence base. In D. Le Grange & J. Lock (Eds.), *Eating disorders in children and adolescents: A clinical handbook.* New York: Guilford Publications.

le Grange, D., & Lock, J. (Eds.). (2011). *Eating disorders in children and adolescents: A clinical handbook.* New York: Guilford Publications.

le Grange, D., & Rienecke Hoste, R. (2010). Family therapy. In W. S. Agras (Ed.), *The Oxford handbook of eating disorders. Oxford library of psychology* (pp. 373–385). New York: Oxford University Press.

Legrand, L. N., Iacono, W. G., & McGue, M. (2005). Predicting addiction: Behavioral genetics uses twins and time to decipher the origins of addiction and learn who is most vulnerable. *American Scientist, 93*(2), 140–147.

Lehman, A. F., Kreyenbuhl, J., Buchanan, R. W., Dickerson, F. B., Dixon, L. B., Goldberg, R., et al. (2004). The schizophrenia Patient Outcomes Research Team (PORT): Updated treatment recommendations 2003. *Schizophrenia Bulletin, 30,* 193–217.

Leiblum, S. R. (2007). Sex therapy today: Current issues and future perspectives. In S. R. Leiblum (Ed.), *Principles and practice of sex therapy* (4th ed., pp. 3–22). New York: Guilford Press.

Leiblum, S. R. (2010). Introduction and overview: Clinical perspectives on and treatment for sexual desire disorders. In S. R. Leiblum (Ed.), *Treating sexual desire disorders: A clinical casebook* (pp. 1–22). New York: Guilford Press.

Leichsenring, F., Leibing, E., Kruse, J., New, A. S., & Leweke, F. (2011). Borderline personality disorder. *Lancet, 377*(9759), 74–84.

Leichsenring, F., & Rabung, S. (2008). Effectiveness of long-term psychodynamic psychotherapy: A meta-analysis. *Journal of the American Medical Association, 300*(13), 1551–1565.

Leichsenring, F., & Rabung, S. (2010). On the efficacy of long-term psychodynamic psychotherapy for complex psychological disorders. *Verhaltenstherapie & Psychosoziale Praxis, 42*(1), 111–126.

Leichsenring, F., & Rabung, S. (2011). Long-term psychodynamic psychotherapy in complex mental disorders: Update of a meta-analysis. *British Journal of Psychiatry, 199*(1), 15–22.

Leiknes, K. A., Arnstein, F., & Moum, T. (2010). Commonalities and differences between the diagnostic groups: Current somatoform disorders, anxiety and/or depression, and musculoskeletal disorders. *Journal of Psychosomatic Research, 58*(5), 439–446.

Leis-Newman, E. (2011). Unhappy: There's an app for that. *Monitor on Psychology, 42*(6), 30–31.

Lekander, M. (2002). Ecological immunology: The role of the immune system in psychology and neuroscience. *European Psychiatry, 7*(2), 98–115.

Lemma, A., Target, M., & Fonagy, P. (2011). The development of a brief psychodynamic intervention (dynamic interpersonal therapy) and its application to depression: A pilot study. *Psychiatry: Interpersonal and Biological Processes, 74*(1), 41–48.

Lemogne, C., Mayberg, H., Bergouignan, L., Volle, E., Delaveau, P., Lehéricy, S., et al. (2010). Self-referential processing and the prefrontal cortex over the course of depression: A pilot study. *Journal of Affective Disorders, 124*(1-2), 196–201.

Lencer, R., Harris, M. S. H., Weiden, P. J., Stieglitz, R-D., & Vauth, R. (2011). *When psychopharmacology is not enough: Using cognitive behavioral therapy techniques for persons with persistent psychosis.* Cambridge MA: Hogrefe Publishing.

Lenhart, A., Jones, S., & Macgill, A. (2008). Adults and video games. *Report: Gaming, families, teens.* Washington, DC: Pew Internet & American Life Project.

Lenhart, A., Kahne, J., Middaugh, E., Macgill, A., Evans, C., Vitak, J. (2008). Teens, video games and civics. *Report: Teens, gaming, politics, families, communities.* Washington, DC: Pew Internet & American Life Project.

Lenhart, A., Purcell, K., Smith, A., & Zickuhr, K. (2010). Social media and young adults. *Report: Teens, social networking, mobile, generations, blogs, web 2.0.* Washington, DC: Pew Internet & American Life Project.

Lentz, V., Robinson, J., & Bolton, J. M. (2010). Childhood adversity, mental disorder comorbidity, and suicidal behavior in schizotypal personality disorder. *Journal of Nervous and Mental Disease, 198*(11), 795–801.

Lenze, E. J., Wetherell, J. L., & Andreescu, C. (2011). Anxiety disorders. In C.E. Coffey, J.L. Cummings, M.S. George, & D. Weintraub (Eds.), *The American Psychiatric Publishing textbook of geriatric neuropsychiatry.* Arlington, VA: American Psychiatric Publishing, Inc.

Lenzenweger, M. F., Lane, M. C., Loranger, A. W., & Kessler, R. C. (2007). DSM-IV personality disorders in the National Comorbidity Survey Replication. *Biological Psychiatry, 62*(6), 553–564.

Leon, G. R. (1984). *Case histories of deviant behavior* (3rd ed.). Boston: Allyn & Bacon.

Leon, G. R. (1991). *Case histories of psychopathology.* Upper Saddle River, NJ: Pearson Education.

Leonardo, E. D., & Hen, R. (2006). Genetics of affective and anxiety disorders. *Annual Review of Psychology, 57,* 117–137.

Leong, G. B. (2000). Diminished capacity and insanity in Washington State: The battle shifts to admissibility. *Journal of the American Academy of Psychiatry and the Law, 28*(1), 77–81.

Leor, J., Poole, W. K., & Kloner, R. A. (1996) Sudden cardiac death triggered by an earthquake. *New England Journal of Medicine, 334*(7), 413–419.

Lepore, S. J., Revenson, T. A., Weinberger, S. L., Weston, P., Frisina, P. G., Robertson, R., et al. (2006). Effects of social stresses on cardiovascular reactivity in black and white women. *Annals of Behavioral Medicine, 31*(2), 120–127.

Lester, D. (1972). Myth of suicide prevention. *Comprehensive Psychiatry, 13*(6), 555–560.

Lester, D. (1985). The quality of life in modern America and suicide and homicide rates. *Journal of Social Psychology, 125*(6), 779–780.

Lester, D. (1989). *Can we prevent suicide?* New York: AMS Press.

Lester, D. (2000). *Why people kill themselves: A 2000 summary of research on suicide.* Springfield, IL: Charles C. Thomas.

Lester, D. (2011). Evidence-based suicide prevention by helplines: A meta-analysis. In M. Pompili & R. Tatarelli (Eds.), *Evidence-based practice in suicidology: A source book* (pp. 139–151). Cambridge MA: Hogrefe Publishing.

Lester, D. (2011). Evidence-based suicide prevention by lethal methods restriction. In M. Pompili & R. Tatarelli (Eds.), *Evidence-based practice in suicidology: A source book* (pp. 233–241). Cambridge MA: Hogrefe Publishing.

Lester, D., Innamorati, M., & Pompili, M. (2007). Psychotherapy for preventing suicide. In R. Tatarelli, M. Pompili, & P. Girardi (Eds.), *Suicide in psychiatric disorders.* New York: Nova Science Publishers.

Leucht, S., Correll, C. U., & Kane, J. M. (2011). Approaches to treatment-resistant patients. In D. R. Weinberg & P. Harrison (Eds.), *Schizophrenia* (pp. 540–560). Hoboken, NJ: Wiley-Blackwell.

Leucht, S., Heres, S., Kissling, W., & Davis, J. M. (2011). Evidence-based pharmacotherapy of schizophrenia. *International Journal of Neuropsychopharmacology, 14*(2), 269–284.

Le Unes, A. D., Nation, J. R., & Turley, N. M. (1980). Male-female performance in learned helplessness. *Journal of Psychology, 104,* 255–258.

Leutwyler, K. (1996). Paying attention: The controversy over ADHD and the drug Ritalin is obscuring a real look at the disorder and its underpinnings. *Scientific American, 272*(2), 12–13.

Levavi, E. E., Schneider, F. J., & McCabe, P. C. (2010). Parental control and separation anxiety disorder. In P. C. McCabe, & S. R. Shaw (Eds.), *Psychiatric disorders: Current topics and interventions for educators.* (pp. 28–40) Thousand Oaks, CA: Corwin Press.

Levesque, R. J. R. (2002). *Dangerous adolescents, model adolescents: Shaping the role and promise of education.* New York: Kluwer Academic/Plenum Publishers.

Levi, F., LaVecchia, C., Lucchini, F., Negri, E., Saxena, S., Maulik, P. K., et al. (2003). Trends in mortality from suicide, 1965–99. *Acta Psychiatrica Scandinavica, 108*(5), 341–349.

Levin, B. E. (2010). Developmental gene x environment interactions affecting systems regulating energy homeostasis and obesity. *Frontiers in Neuroendocrinology, 31*(3), 270–283.

Levin, B. E. (2010). Interaction of perinatal and pre-pubertal factors with genetic predisposition in the development of neural pathways involved in the regulation of energy homeostasis. *Brain Research, 1350,* 10–17.

Levine, M. P., & Maine, M. (2010). Are media an important medium for clinicians? Mass media, eating disorders, and the bolder model of treatment, prevention, and advocacy. In M. Maine, B. H. McGilley, & D. W. Bunnell (Eds.), *Treatment of eating disorders: Bridging the research-practice gap* (pp. 53–67). San Diego, CA: Elsevier Academic Press.

Levine, M. P., & Smolak, L. (2010) Cultural influences on body image and the eating disorders.

In W. S. Agras (Ed.), *The Oxford handbook of eating disorders. Oxford library of psychology* (pp. 223–246). New York: Oxford University Press.

Levy, E., Shefler, G., Loewenthal, U., Umansky, R., Bar, G., & Heresco-Levy, U. (2005). Characteristics of schizophrenia residents and staff rejection in community mental health hostels. *Israel Journal of Psychiatry and Related Sciences, 42*(1), 23–32.

Levy, K. N., Reynoso, J. S., Wasserman, R. H., & Clarkin, J. F. (2007). Narcissistic personality disorder. In W. O'Donohue, K. A. Fowler, S. O. Lilienfeld (Eds.), *Personality disorders: Toward the DSM-V.* Los Angeles: Sage Publications.

Levy, T. B., Barak, Y., Sigler, M., & Aizenberg, D. (2011). Suicide attempts and burden of physical illness among depressed elderly inpatients. *Archives of Gerontology and Geriatrics, 52*(1), 115–117.

Leweke, F. M., Gerth, C. W., Koethe, D., Klosterkotter, J., Ruslanova, I., Krivogorsky, B., et al. (2004). Antibodies to infectious agents in individuals with recent onset schizophrenia. *European Archives of Psychiatry and Clinical Neuroscience, 254*(1), 4–8.

Lewin, A. B. (2011). Parent training for childhood anxiety. In D McKay & E. A. Storch (Eds.), *Handbook of child and adolescent anxiety disorders* (pp. 405–417). New York: Springer Science & Business Media.

Lewin, B. D. (1950). *The psychoanalysis of elation.* New York: Norton.

Lewinsohn, P. M., Antonuccio, D. O., Steinmetz, J. L., & Teri, L. (1984). *The coping with depression course.* Eugene, OR: Castalia.

Lewinsohn, P. M., Clarke, G. N., Hops, H., & Andrews, J. (1990). Cognitive-behavioral treatment for depressed adolescents. *Behavior Therapist, 21,* 385–401.

Lewinsohn, P. M., Hoberman, H. M., Rosenbaum, M. (1988). A prospective study of risk factors for unipolar depression. *Journal of Abnormal Psycholology, 97*(3), 251–264.

Lewinsohn, P. M., Youngren, M. A., & Grosscup, S. J. (1979). Reinforcement and depression. In R. A. Depue (Ed.), *The psychobiology of the depressive disorders.* New York: Academic Press.

Li, R., & El-Mallakh, R. S. (2004). Differential response of bipolar and normal control lymphoblastoid cell sodium pump to ethacrynic acid. *Journal of Affective Disorders, 80*(1), 1–17.

Liberman, R. P., & Raskin, D. E. (1971). Depression: A behavioral formulation. *Archives of General Psychiatry, 24,* 515–523.

Libow, J. A., & Schreier, H. A. (1998) Factitious disorder by proxy. In R. T. Ammerman & J. V. Campo (Eds.), *Handbook of pediatric psychology and psychiatry: Vol. 1. Psychological and psychiatric issues in the pediatric setting.* Boston: Allyn & Bacon.

Lichtenstein, E., Zu, S-H, & Tedeschi, G. J. (2010). Smoking cessation quitlines: An underrecognized intervention success story. *American Psychologist, 65*(4), 252–261.

Lickey, M. E., & Gordon, B. (1991). *Medicine and mental illness: The use of drugs in psychiatry.* New York: W. H. Freeman and Company.

Lieberman, J. A. (2010). Psychiatric care shortage: What the future holds. *Medscape Psychiatry and Mental Health.* Retrieved from www://www.medscape.com/viewarticle/727435.

Lieberman, J. A., Chakos, M., Wu, H., Alvir, J., Hoffman, E., Robinson, D., et al. (2001). Longitudinal study of brain morphology in first episode schizophrenia. *Biological Psychiatry, 49*(6), 487–499.

Lieberman, J. D., & Olson, J. (2009). The psychology of jury selection. In J. D. Lieberman & D. A. Krauss (Eds.), *Jury psychology: Social aspects of trial processes: Psychology in the courtroom,* (Vol. 1, pp. 97–128). Burlington, VT: Ashgate Publishing Co.

Liebman, J. I., McKinley-Pace, M. J., Leonard, A. M., Sheesley, L. A., Gallant, C. L., Renkey, M. E., & Lehman, E. B. (2002). Cognitive and psychosocial correlates of adults' eyewitness accuracy and suggestibility. *Personality and Individual Differences, 33*(1), 49–66.

Lifton, R. J. (2005). *Home from the war: Learning from Vietnam veterans: With a new preface by the author on the war in Iraq.* New York: Other Press.

Lightdale, H. A., Mach, A. H., & Frances, R. J. (2008). Psychodynamics. In H. D. Kleber & M. Galanter (Eds.), *The American Psychiatric Publishing textbook of substance abuse treatment* (4th ed., pp. 333–347). Arlington, VA: American Psychiatric Publishing.

Lightdale, H. A., Mack, A. H., & Frances, R. J. (2011). Psychodynamic psychotherapy. In M. Galanter & H. D. Kleber (Eds.), *Psychotherapy for the treatment of substance abuse* (pp. 219–247). Arlington, VA: American Psychiatric Publishing.

Lilenfeld, L. R. R. (2011). Personality and temperament. In R. A. H. Adan & W. H. Kaye (Eds.), *Behavioral neurobiology of eating disorders. Current topics in behavioral neurosciences* (pp. 3–16). New York: Springer-Verlag Publishing.

Lim, L. W., Tan, S. K. H., Groenewegen, H. J., & Temel, Y. (2011). Electrical brain stimulation in depression: Which target(s)? *Biological Psychiatry, 69*(4), e5–e6.

Lin, C-H, Lane, H-Y., & Tsai, G. E. (2011, April 1). Glutamate signaling in the pathophysiology and therapy of schizophrenia. *Pharmacology, Biochemistry and Behavior.*

Lindau, S. T., Schumm, L. P., Laumann, E. O., Levinson, W., O'Muircheartaigh, C. A., & Waite, L. J. (2007). A study of sexuality and health among older adults in the United States. *New England Journal of Medicine, 357,* 762–774.

Lindenmayer, J. P., & Khan, A. (2012). Psychopathology. In J. A. Lieberman, T. S. Stroup, & D. O. Perkins (Eds.), *Essentials of schizophrenia* (pp. 11–54). Arlington, VA: American Psychiatric Publishing.

Lindheim, O., Bernard, K., & Dozier, M. (2011). Maternal sensitivity: Within-person variability and the utility of multiple assessments. *Child Maltreatment, 16*(1), 41–50.

Lindholm, C., & Lindholm C. (1981). World's strangest mental illnesses. *Science Digest,* 52–58.

Lindner, M. (1968). *Hereditary and environmental influences upon resistance to stress.* Unpublished doctoral dissertation, University of Pennsylvania, Philadelphia.

Lindsay, J., Sykes, E., McDowell, I., Verreault, R., & Laurin, D. (2004). More than the epidemiology of Alzheimer's disease: Contributions of the Canadian Study of Health and Aging. *Canadian Journal of Psychiatry, 49*(2), 83–91.

Lindsey, P. (2011). Managing behavioral and psychological symptoms of dementia. In P. McNamara (Ed.), *Dementia: Vols. 1–3. History and incidence. Science and biology, treatments and developments* (pp. 73–91). Santa Barbara, CA: Praeger/ABC-CLIO.

Linehan, M. M. (1993). *Skills training manual for treating borderline personality disorder.* New York: Guilford Press.

Linehan, M. M., Cochran, B. N., & Kehrer, C. A. (2001). Dialectical behavior therapy for borderline personality disorder. In D. H. Barlow (Ed.), *Clinical handbook of psychological disorders* (3rd ed., pp. 470–522). New York: Guilford Press.

Linehan, M. M., Comtois, K. A., Murray, A., Brown, M. Z., Gallop, R. J., Heard, H. L., et al. (2006). Two-year randomized trial + follow-up of dialectical behavior therapy vs. therapy by experts for suicidal behaviors and borderline personality disorder. *Archives of General Psychiatry, 63,* 757–766.

Linehan, M. M., Dimeff, L. A., Reynolds, S. K., Comtois, K. A., Welch, S. S., Heagerty, P., & Kivlahan, D. R. (2002). Dialectical behavior therapy versus comprehensive validation therapy plus 12-step for the treatment of opioid dependent women meeting criteria for borderline personality disorder. *Drug and Alcohol Dependence, 67*(1), 13–26.

Ling, S., Zhou, J., Rudd, J. A., Hu, Z., & Fang, M. (2011). The recent updates of therapeutic approaches against aβ for the treatment of Alzheimer's disease. *Anatomical Record, 294*(8), 1307–1318.

Link, B. G., Struening, E. L., Neese-Todd, S., Asmussen, S., & Phelan, J. C. (2001). Stigma as a barrier to recovery: The consequences of stigma for the self-esteem of people with mental illness. *Psychiatric Services, 52*(12), 1621–1626.

Link, B. G., Yang, L. H., Phelan, J. C., & Collins, P. Y. (2004). Measuring mental illness stigma. *Schizophrenia Bulletin, 30*(3), 511–541.

Linnet, J., Moller, A., Peterson, E., Giedde, A., & Doudet, D. (2011). Dopamine release in ventral striatum during Iowa Gambling Task performance is associated with increased excitement levels in pathological gambling. *Addiction, 106*(2), 383–390.

Liotti, M., Mayberg, H. S., McGinnis, S., Brannan, S. L., & Jerabek, P. (2002). Unmasking disease-specific cerebral blood flow abnormalities: Mood challenge in patients with remitted unipolar depression. *American Journal of Psychiatry, 159,* 1830–1840.

Lipkin, P. H., Cozen, M. A., Thompson, R. E., & Mostofsky, S. H. (2005). Stimulant dosage and age, race, and insurance type in a sample of children with attention-deficit/hyperactivity disorder. *Journal of Child and Adolescent Psychopharmacology, 15*(2), 240–248.

Lipton, A. A., & Simon, F. S. (1985). Psychiatric diagnosis in a state hospital: Manhattan State revisited. *Hospital Community Psychiatry, 36*(4), 368–373.

Litman, R. E., & Farberow, N. L. (1994). Pop-rock music as precipitating cause in youth suicide. *Journal of Forensic Sciences, 39,* 494–499.

Litwack, T., Zapf, P. A., Groscup, J. L., & Hart, S. D. (2006). Violence risk assessment: Research, legal, and clinical considerations. In A. K. Hess & I. B. Weiner (Eds.), *Handbook of forensic psychology* (3rd ed., pp. 487–533). New York: Wiley.

Liu, A. (2007). *Gaining: The truth about life after eating disorders.* New York: Warner Books.

Loas, G., Cormier, J., & Perez-Dias, F. (2011). Dependent personality disorder and physical abuse. *Psychiatry Research, 185*(1–2), 167–170.

Lochman, J. E., Barry, T., Powell, N., & Young, L. (2010). Anger and aggression. In D. W. Nangle, D. J. Hansen, C. A. Erdley & P. J. Norton (Eds.), *Practitioner's guide to empirically based measures of*

social skills (pp. 155–166). New York: Springer Publishing Co.

Lochman, J. E., Boxmeyer, C. L., Powell, N. P., Barry, T. D., & Pardini, D. A. (2010). Anger control training for aggressive youths. In J. R. Weisz, & A. E. Kazdin (Eds.), *Evidence-based psychotherapies for children and adolescents* (2nd ed., pp. 227–242) New York: Guilford Press.

Lochman, J. E., Powell, N. P., Boxmeyer, C. L., & Jimenez-Camargo, L. (2011). Cognitive-behavioral therapy for externalizing disorders in children and adolescents. *Child and Adolescent Psychiatric Clinics of North America, 20*(2), 3095–318.

Lochner, C., Serebro, P., van der Merwe, L, Hemmings, S., Kinnear, C., Seedat, S., & Stein, D. J. (2011). Comorbid obsessive-compulsive personality disorder in obsessive-compulsive disorder (OCD): A marker of severity. *Progress in Neuro-Psychopharmacology & Biological Psychiatry, 35*(4), 1087–1092.

Lock, J. (2011). Family-based treatment for anorexia nervosa: Evolution, evidence base, and treatment approach. In D. Le Grange & J. Lock (Eds.), *Eating disorders in children and adolescents: A clinical handbook.* New York: Guilford Publications.

Loewenstein, R. J. (1991). Psychogenic amnesia and psychogenic fugue: A comprehensive review. In A. Tasman & S. M. Goldfinger (Eds.), *American Psychiatric Press review of psychiatry* (Vol. 10). Washington, DC: American Psychiatric Press.

Loewenthal, K. (2007). *Religion, culture and mental health.* New York: Cambridge University Press.

Loftus, E. F. (1993). The reality of repressed memories. *American Psychologist, 48,* 518–537.

Loftus, E. F. (2001). Imagining the past. *Psychologist, 14*(11), 584–587.

Loftus, E. F. (2003). Make-believe memories. *American Psychologist, 58*(11), 867–873.

Loftus, E. F. (2003). Our changeable memories: Legal and practical implications. *Nature Reviews Neuroscience, 4,* 231–234.

Loftus, E. F., & Cahill, L. (2007). Memory distortion: From misinformation to rich false memory. In J. S. Nairne (Ed.), *The foundations of remembering: Essays in honor of Henry L. Roediger, III.* New York: Psychology Press.

Logue, A. W. (1991). *The psychology of eating and drinking.* New York: W. H. Freeman and Company.

Lombardi, G., Celso, M., Bartelli, M., Cilotti, A., & Del Popolo, G. (2011. Female sexual dysfunction and hormonal status in multiple sclerosis patients. *Journal of Sexual Medicine, 8*(4), 1138–1146.

Loo, C. (2010). ECT in the 21st century: Optimizing treatment: State of the art in the 21st century. *The Journal of ECT, 26*(3), 157.

Loomer, H. P., Saunders, J. C., & Kline, N. S. (1957). A clinical and pharmacodynamic evaluation of iproniazid as a psychic energizer. *America Psychiatric Association Research Report, 8,* 129.

López, S. R., & Guarnaccia, P. J. (2000). Cultural psychopathology: Uncovering the social world of mental illness. *Annual Review of Psychology, 51,* 571–598.

López, S. R., & Guarnaccia, P. J. (2005). Cultural dimensions of psychopathology: The social world's impact on mental illness. In B. A. Winstead & J. E. Maddux, *Psychopathology: Foundations for a contemporary understanding* (pp. 19–37). Mahwah, NJ: Lawrence Erlbaum.

López, S. R., & Guarnaccia, P. J. (2008). Cultural dimensions of psychopathology: The

social world's impact on mental disorders. In J. E. Maddux & B. A. Winstead (Eds.), *Psychopathology: Foundations for a contemporary understanding* (2nd ed., pp. 19–38). New York: Routledge/Taylor & Francis Group.

Lopez-Duran, N. (2011, October 18). Fifty percent (50%) of teens have experienced a psychiatric condition by their 18th birthday. *Child Psychology Research.* Retrieved January 19, 2011, from http://www.child-psych.org.

LoPiccolo, J. (1991). Post-modern sex therapy for erectile failure. In R. C. Rosen & S. R. Leiblum (Eds.), *Erectile failure: Diagnosis and treatment.* New York: Guilford Press.

LoPiccolo, J. (1995). Sexual disorders and gender identity disorders. In R. J. Comer, *Abnormal psychology* (2nd ed.). New York: W. H. Freeman and Company.

LoPiccolo, J. (1997). Sex therapy: A post-modern model. In S. J. Lynn & J. P. Garske (Eds.), *Contemporary psychotherapies: Models and methods* (2nd ed.). Columbus, OH: Merrill.

LoPiccolo, J. (2002). Postmodern sex therapy. In F. W. Kaslow (Ed.), *Comprehensive handbook of psychotherapy: Integrative/eclectic* (Vol. 4, pp. 411–435). New York: Wiley.

LoPiccolo, J. (2004). Sexual disorders affecting men. In L. J. Haas (Ed.), *Handbook of primary care psychology* (pp. 485–494). New York: Oxford University Press.

LoPiccolo, J., & Stock, W. E. (1987). Sexual function, dysfunction, and counseling in gynecological practice. In Z. Rosenwaks, F. Benjamin, & M. L. Stone (Eds.), *Gynecology.* New York: Macmillan.

LoPiccolo, J., & Van Male, L. M. (2000). Sexual dysfunction. In A. E. Kazdin (Ed.), *Encyclopedia of psychology* (Vol. 7, pp. 246–251). Washington, DC: Oxford University Press/American Psychological Association.

Lorand, S. (1968). Dynamics and therapy of depressive states. In W. Gaylin (Ed.), *The meaning of despair.* New York: Jason Aronson.

Lourenco, M., Azevedo, L. P., & Gouveia, J. L. (2011). Depression and sexual desire: An explanatory study in psychiatric patients. *Journal of Sex & Marital Therapy, 37*(1), 32–44.

Lovaas, O. I. (1987). Behavioral treatment and normal educational/intellectual functioning in young autistic children. *Journal of Consulting and Clinical Psychology, 55,* 3–9.

Lovaas, O. I. (2003). *Teaching individuals with developmental delays: Basic intervention techniques.* Austin, TX: Pro-Ed.

Lovejoy, M. (1982). Expectations and the recovery process. *Schizophrenia Bulletin, 8*(4), 605–609.

Lovejoy, M. (2001). Disturbances in the social body: Differences in body image and eating problems among African-American and white women. *Gender and Society, 15*(2), 239–261.

Lovell, B., & Wetherell, M. A. (2011). The cost of caregiving: Endocrine and immune implications in elderly and non elderly caregivers. *Neuroscience and Biobehavioral Reviews, 35*(6), 1342–1352.

Löwe, B., Mundt, C., Wolfgang, H., Brunner, R., Backenstrass, M., Kronmüller, K., et al. (2008). Validity of current somatoform disorder diagnoses: Perspectives for classification in DSM-V and ICD-11. *Psychopathology, 41*(1), 4–9.

Lowe, C., & Cohen, B. M. (2010). *Living with someone who's living with bipolar disorder: A practical guide for family, friends, and coworkers.* San Francisco, CA: Jossey-Bass.

Loweth, J. A., & Vezina, P. (2011). Sensitization. In M. C. Olmstead (Ed.), *Animal models of drug addiction. Springer protocols: Neuromethods* (pp. 191–205). Totowa, NJ: Humana Press.

Luber, M. (Ed.). (2009). *Eye movement desensitization and reprocessing (EMDR) scripted protocols: Basics and special situations*. New York: Springer Publishing.

Luborsky, L. (1973). Forgetting and remembering (momentary forgetting) during psychotherapy. In M. Mayman (Ed.), *Psychoanalytic research and psychological issues* (Monograph 30). New York: International Universities Press.

Luborsky, L. (2004). Helen Sargent's 1961 paper: Both a classic and still current. *Psychiatry: Interpersonal and Biological Processes, 67*(1), 23–25.

Luborsky, L. B., Barrett, M. S., Antonuccio, D. O., Shoenberger, D., & Stricker, G. (2006). What else materially influences what is represented and published as evidence? In J. C. Norcross, L. E. Beutler, & R. F. Levant (Eds.), *Evidence-based practices in mental health: Debate and dialogue on the fundamental questions* (pp. 257–298). Washington, DC: American Psychological Association.

Luborsky, E. B., O'Reilly-Landry, M., & Arlow, J. A. (2011). Psychoanalysis. In R. J. Corsini & D. Wedding (Eds.), *Current psychotherapies* (9th ed.). Belmont, CA: Brooks/Cole.

Luborsky, L., Rosenthal, R., Diguer, L., Andrusyna, T. P., Berman, J. S., Levitt, J. T., et al. (2002). The dodo bird verdict is alive and well—mostly. *Clinical Psychology: Science and Practice, 9*(1), 2–12.

Luborsky, L., Rosenthal, R., Diguer, L., Andrusyna. T. P., Levitt, J. T., Seligman, D. A., et al. (2003). Are some psychotherapies much more effective than others? *Journal of Applied Psychoanalytic Studies, 5*(4), 455–460.

Luborsky, L., Singer, B., & Luborsky, L. (1975). Comparative studies of psychotherapies. *Biological Psychiatry, 32,* 995–1008.

Lucas, G. (2006). Object relations and child psychoanalysis (French). *Revue Française de Psychanalyse, 70*(5), 1435–1473.

Ludwig, A. M. (1995). *The price of greatness: Resolving the creativity and madness controversy*. New York: Guilford Press.

Lumley, V. A., & Scotti, J. R. (2001). Supporting the sexuality of adults with mental retardation: Current status and future directions. *Journal of Positive Behavior Interventions, 3*(2), 109–119.

Lundberg, U. (2011). Neuroendocrine measures. In R. J. Contrada & A. Baum (Eds.), *The handbook of stress science: Biology, psychology, and health* (pp. 531–542). New York: Springer Publishing.

Lundqvist, D., & Ohman, A. (2005). Emotion regulates attention: The relation between facial configurations, facial emotion, and visual attention. *Visual Cognition., 12*(1), 51–84.

Lundqvist, T. (2005). Cognitive consequences of cannabis use: Comparison with abuse of stimulants and heroin with regard to attention, memory and executive functions. *Pharmacology, Biochemistry and Behavior, 81,* 391–330.

Lundqvist, T. (2010). Imaging cognitive deficits in drug abuse. In D. W. Self & J. K. Staley (Eds.), *Behavioral neuroscience of drug addiction* (pp. 247–275). New York: Springer Publishing.

Luyten, P., & Blatt, S. J. (2011). Psychodynamic approaches to depression: Whither shall we go? *Psychiatry: Interpersonal and Biological Processes, 74*(1), 1–3.

Lyche, P., Jonassen, R., Stiles, T. C., Ulleberg, P., & Landro, N. I. (2011). Verbal memory functions in unipolar major depression with and without co-morbid anxiety. *Clinical Neuropsychologist, 25*(3), 359–375.

Lyman, B. (1982). The nutritional values and food group characteristics of foods preferred during various emotions. *Journal of Psychology, 112,* 121–127.

Lynn, S. J., & Deming, A. (2010). The "Sybil tapes": Exposing the myth of dissociative identity disorder. *Theory & Psychology, 20*(2), 289–291.

Lynn, S. J., Rhue, J. W., & Kirsch, I. (Eds.). (2010). *Handbook of clinical hypnosis* (2nd ed.) Washington, DC: America Psychological Association.

Lyon, G. J., Abi-Dargham, A., Moore, H., Lieberman, J. A., Javitch, J. A., & Sulzer, D. (2011). Presynaptic regulation of dopamine transmission in schizophrenia. *Schizophrenia Bulletin, 37*(1), 108–117.

Lysaker, P. H., & Hermans, H. J. M. (2007). The dialogical self in psychotherapy for persons with schizophrenia: A case study. *Journal of Clinical Psychology, 63*(2), 129–139.

Maack, D. J., Lyons, J. A., Connolly, K. M., & Ritter, M. (2011). Couple and family therapy. In B. A. Moore & W. E. Penk (Eds.), *Treating PTSD in military personnel: A clinical handbook* (pp. 141–154). New York: Guilford Press.

MacDonald, W. L. (1998). The difference between blacks' and whites' attitudes toward voluntary euthanasia. *Journal for the Scientific Study of Religion, 37*(3), 411–426.

Mack, A., & Joy, J. (2001). *Marijuana as medicine? The science beyond the controversy*. Washington, DC: National Academy Press.

MacLaren, V. V. (2001). A qualitative review of the Guilty Knowledge Test. *Journal of Applied Psychology, 86*(4), 674–683.

MacLean, J., Kinley, D. J., Jacobi, F., Bolton, J. M., & Sareen, J. (2011). The relationship between physical conditions and suicidal behavior among those with mood disorders. *Journal of Affective Disorders, 130*(1-2), 245–250.

Macleod, S. H., Elliott, L., & Brown, R. (2011). What support can community mental health nurses deliver to carers of people diagnosed with schizophrenia? Findings from a review of the literature. *International Journal of Nursing Studies, 48*(1), 100–120.

Magee, C. L. (2007). The use of herbal and other dietary supplements and the potential for drug interactions in palliative care. *Palliative Medicine, 21*(6), 547–548.

Magiati, I., Moss, J., Charman, T., & Howlin, P. (2011). Patterns of change in children with autism spectrum disorders who received community based comprehensive interventions in their pre-school years: A seven year follow-up study. *Research in Autism Spectrum Disorders, 5*(3), 1016–1027.

Maher, W. B., & Maher, B. A. (1985). Psychopathology: I. From ancient times to the eighteenth century. In G. A. Kimble & K. Schlesinger (Eds.), *Topics in the history of psychology* (Vol. 2). Hillsdale, NJ: Lawrence Erlbaum.

Maher, W. B., & Maher, B. A. (2003). Abnormal psychology. In D. K. Freedheim (Ed.), *Handbook of psychology: History of psychology* (Vol. 1, pp. 303–336). New York: Wiley.

Maheu, M. M. (2010). The ehealth, telehealth and telemedicine blog. *Telehealth.net*. Retrieved on March 2, 2011, from http://telehealth.net/blog/email-chat-rooms-or-skype-for-mental-health-what about-mandated-reporting.

Mak, T. (2012, June 15). Rahm Emanuel: Reduce pot penalties. *Politico.*

Malberg, J. E., & Bonson, K. R. (2001). How MDMA works in the brain. In J. Holland (Ed.), *Ecstasy: The complete guide: A comprehension look at the risks and benefits of MDMA* (pp. 29–38). Rochester, VT: Park Street Press.

Malberg, J. E., & Schechter, L. E. (2005). Increasing hippocampal neurogenesis: A novel mechanism for antidepressant drugs. *Current Pharmaceutical Design, 11,* 145–155.

Malcolm, A. H. (1990, June 9). Giving death a hand. *New York Times*, p. A6.

Maldonado, J. R., & Spiegel, D. (2003). Dissociative disorders. In S. C. Yudofsky & R. E. Hales (Eds.), *The American Psychiatric Publishing textbook of clinical psychiatry* (4th ed., pp. 709–742). Washington, DC: American Psychiatric Publishing.

Maldonado, J. R., & Spiegel, D. (2007). Dissociative disorders. In S. C. Yudofsky, J. A. Bourgeois, & R. E. Hales (Eds.), *The American Psychiatric Publishing Board prep and review guide for psychiatry* (pp. 251–258). Washington, DC: American Psychiatric Publishing.

Malik, M. L., & Beutler, L. E. (2002). The emergence of dissatisfaction with the DSM. In L. E. Beutler & M. L. Malik (Eds.), *Rethinking the DSM: A psychological perspective. Decade of behavior.* Washington, DC: American Psychological Association.

Malik, V., Schulze, M., & Hu, F. (2006). Intake of sugar-sweetened beverages and weight gain: A systematic review. *American Journal of Clinical Nutrition, 84,* 274–288.

Maller, R. G., & Reiss, S. (1992). Anxiety sensitivity in 1984 and panic attacks in 1987. *Journal of Anxiety Disorders, 6*(3), 241–247.

Mammen, O. K., Kolk, D. J., & Pilkonis, P. A. (2002). Negative affect and parental aggression in child physical abuse. *Child Abuse and Neglect, 26,* 407–424.

Manfredi, C., Caselli, G., Rovetto, F., Rebecchi, D., Ruggiero, G. M., Sassaroli, S., & Spada, M. M. (2011). Temperament and parental styles as predictors of ruminative brooding and worry. *Personality and Individual Differences, 50*(2), 186–191.

Manicavasgar, V., Parker, G., & Perich, T. (2011). Mindfulness-based cognitive therapy vs cognitive behaviour therapy as a treatment for non-melancholic depression. *Journal of Affective Disorders, 130*(1-2), 138–144.

Manji, H. K., & Zarate, C. A., Jr. (Eds.). (2011). *Behavioral neurobiology of bipolar disorder and its treatment. Current Topics in behavioral neurosciences.* New York: Springer Science + Business Media.

Mankad, M. V., Beyer, J. L., Weiner, R. D., & Krystal, A. D. (2010). *Clinical manual of electroconvulsive therapy*. Arlington, VA: American Psychiatric Publishing.

Mann, D. (2004, June 28). Born to lie? *WebMD*.

Mann, J. J., & Currier, D. (2007). Neurobiology of suicidal behavior. In R. Tatarelli, M. Pompili, & P. Girardi (Eds.), *Suicide in psychiatric disorders.* New York: Nova Science Publishers.

Mann, J. J., & Currier, D. (2011). Evidence-based suicide prevention strategies in suicidology: A source book. In M. Pompili & R. Tatarelli (Eds.), *Evidence-based practice in* *suicidology: A source book* (pp. 67–87). Cambridge MA: Hogrefe Publishing.

Mann, R. E., Ainsworth, F., Al-Attar, Z., & Davies, M. (2008). Voyeurism: Assessment and treatment. In D. R. Laws & W. T. O'Donohue (Eds.), *Sexual deviance: Theory, assessment, and treatment* (2nd ed., pp. 320–335). New York: Guilford Press.

Mann, T., Tomiyama, A. J., Westling, E., Lew, A.-M., Samuels, B., & Chatman, J. (2007). Medicare's search for effective obesity treatments: Diets are not the answer. *American Psychologist, 62,* 220–233.

Manson, J. E., Skerrett, P. J., & Willett, W. C. (2004). Obesity as a risk factor for major health outcomes. In G. A. Bray & C. Bouchard (Eds.), *Handbook of obesity: Etiology and pathophysiology* (2nd ed.). New York: Marcel Dekker.

Manson, J. E., Willett, W. C., Stampfer, M. J., Colditz, G. A., et al. (1995). Body weight and mortality among women. *New England Journal of Medicine, 333*(11), 677–685.

Mansueto, C. S., & Rogers, K. E. (2012). Trichotillomania: Epidemiology and clinical characteristics. In J. E. Grant, D. J. Stein, D. W. Woods, & N. J. Keuthen (Eds.), *Trichotillomania, skin picking, and other body-focused repetitive behaviors* (pp. 3–20). Arlington, VA: American Psychiatric Publishing, Inc.

Marceaux, J. C., & Melville, C. L. (2011). Twelve-step facilitated versus mapping-enhanced cognitive-behavioral therapy for pathological gambling: A controlled study. *Journal of Gambling Studies, 27*(1), 171–190.

Marchione, M. (2007, September 10). Thousands of GIs cope with brain damage. *Yahoo! News.* Retrieved September 10, 2008, from http://news.yahoo.com., 577

Margo, J. L. (1985). Anorexia nervosa in adolescents. *British Journal of Medical Psychology, 58*(2), 193–195.

Margolis, R. D., & Zweben, J. E. (2011). Determining appropriate treatment. In R. D. Margolis & J. E. Zweben (Eds.), *Treating patients with alcohol and other drug problems: An integrated approach* (2nd ed., pp. 83–116). Washington, DC: American Psychological Association.

Margolis, R. D., & Zweben, J. E. (2011). Relapse prevention. In R. D. Margolis & J. E. Zweben (Eds.), *Treating patients with alcohol and other drug problems: An integrated approach* (2nd ed., pp. 199–224). Washington, DC: American Psychological Association.

Maris, R. W. (2001). Suicide. In H. S. Friedman (Ed.), *Specialty articles from the encyclopedia of mental health.* San Diego: Academic Press.

Mark, R. L., Coffey, R. M., Vandivort-Warren, R., Harwood, H. J., King, E. C., et al. (2005, March 29). U.S. spending for mental health and substance treatment, 1991–2001. *Health Affairs* (Web exclusive).

Mark, T. L., Dirani, R., Slade, E., & Russo, P. A. (2002). Access to new medications to treat schizophrenia. *Journal of Behavioral Health Services & Research, 29*(1), 15–29.

Mark, T. L., Harwood, H. J., McKusick, D. C., King, E. D., Vandivort-Warren, R., & Buck, J. A. (2008). Mental health and substance abuse spending by age, 2003. *Journal of Behavioral Health Services & Research, 35*(3), 279–289.

Mark, T. L., Palmer, L. A., Russo, P. A., & Vasey, J. (2003). Examination of treatment pattern differences by race. *Mental Health Services Research, 5*(4), 241–250.

Markin, R. D., & Kivlighan, D. M., Jr. (2007). Bias in psychotherapist ratings of client transference and insight. *Psychotherapy: Theory, Research, Practice, Training, 44*(3), 300–315

Markle-Reid, M. F., Keller, H. H., & Browne, G. (2010). Health promotion for the community-living older adult. In H. M. Fillit, K. Rockwood, & K. Woodhouse. (Eds.), *Brocklehurst's textbook of geriatric medicine and gerontology, 7th edition.* Philadelphia, PA: Saunders Publishers.

Markovitz, P. J. (2001). Pharmacotherapy. In W. J. Livesley (Ed.), *Handbook of personality disorders: Theory, research, and treatment* (pp. 475–494). New York: Guilford Press.

Markovitz, P. J. (2004). Recent trends in the pharmacotherapy of personality disorders. *Journal of Personality Disorders, 18*(1), 90–101.

Marks, B., Sisirak, J., Heller, T., & Wagner, M. (2010). Evaluation of community-based health promotion programs for Special Olympics athletes. *Journal of Policy and Practice in Intellectual Disabilities, 7*(2), 119–129.

Marks, I. M. (1977). Phobias and obsessions: Clinical phenomena in search of a laboratory model. In J. Maser & M. Seligman (Eds.), *Psychopathology: Experimental models.* San Francisco: W. H. Freeman and Company..

Marks, I. M. (1987). *Fears, phobias and rituals: Panic, anxiety and their disorders.* New York: Oxford University Press.

Marks, I. M., & Gelder, M. G. (1967). Transvestism and fetishism: Clinical and psychological changes during faradic aversion. *British Journal of Psychiatry, 113,* 711–730.

Marlatt, G. A. (1985). *Relapse prevention.* New York: Guilford Press.

Marlatt, G. A. (2007). *Cognitive-behavioral relapse prevention for addictions: Specific treatments for specific populations.* Washington, DC: American Psychological Association.

Marlatt, G. A., Kosturn, C. F., & Lang, A. R. (1975). Provocation to anger and opportunity for retaliation as determinants of alcohol consumption in social drinkers. *Journal of Abnormal Psychology, 84*(6), 652–659.

Marques, L., LeBlanc, N., Weingarden, H., Greenberg, J. L., Traeger, L. N., Keshaviah, A., & Wilhelm, S. (2011). Body dysmorphic symptoms: Phenomenology and ethnicity. *Body Image, 8*(2), 163–167.

Marques, L., Robinaugh, D. J., LeBlanc, N. J., & Hinton, D. (2011). Cross-cultural variations in the prevalence and presentation of anxiety disorders. *Expert Review of Neurotherapeutics, 11*(2), 313–322.

Marshall, J. J. (1997). Personal communication.

Marshall, T., Jones, D. P. H., Ramchandani, P. G., Stein, A., & Bass, C. (2007). Intergenerational transmission of health benefits in somatoform disorders. *British Journal of Psychiatry, 191*(4), 449–450.

Marshall, W. L., Marshall, L. E., Serran, G. A., & O'Brien, M. D. (2011). *Rehabilitating sexual offenders: A strength-based approach.* Washington, DC: American Psychological Association.

Marshall, W. L., Serran, G. A., Marshall, L. E., & O'Brien, M. D. (2008). Sexual deviation. In M. Hersen & J. Rosqvist (Eds.), *Handbook of psychological assessment, case conceptualization and treatment: Vol. 1. Adults.* Hoboken, NJ: John Wiley & Sons.

Marsiglia, F. F., & Smith, S. J. (2010). An exploration of ethnicity and race in the etiology of substance use: A health disparities approach.

In L. Scheier (Ed.), *Handbook of drug use etiology: Theory, methods, and empirical findings* (pp. 289–304). Washington, DC: American Psychological Association.

Marston, W. M. (1917). Systolic blood pressure changes in deception. *Journal of Experimental Psychology, 2,* 117–163.

Martell, C. R., Dimidjian, S., & Herman-Dunn, R. (2010). *Behavioral activation for depression: A clinician's guide.* New York: Guilford Press.

Martens, W. H. J. (2005). Multidimensional model of trauma and correlated antisocial personality disorder. *Journal of Loss and Trauma, 10*(2), 115–129.

Martin, A. R., Nieto, J. M. M., Ruiz, J. P. N., & Jimenez, L. E. (2008). Overweight and obesity: The role of education, employment and income in Spanish adults. *Appetite, 51*(2), 266–272.

Martin, E. I., & Nemeroff, C. B. (2010). The biology of generalized anxiety disorder and major depressive disorder: Commonalities and distinguishing features. In D. Goldberg, K. S. Kendler, & P. J. Sirovatka (Eds.), *Diagnostic issues in depression and generalized anxiety disorder: Refining the research agenda for DSM-V* (pp. 45–70). Washington, DC: American Psychiatric Association.

Martin, G., Bergen, H. A., Roeger, L., & Allison, S. (2004). Depression in young adolescents: Investigations using 2 and 3 factor versions of the Parental Bonding Instrument. *Journal of Nervous and Mental Disease, 192*(10), 650–657.

Martin, H. (2009). A bright future for psychological assessment. *Psychotherapy Bulletin, 44*(4).

Martin, P., Baenziger, J., MacDonald, M., Siegler, I. C., & Poon, L. W. (2009). Engaged lifestyle, personality, and mental status among centenarians. *Journal of Adult Development, 16*(4), 199–208.

Martin, P., MacDonald, M., Margrett, J., & Poon, L. W. (2010). Resilience and longevity: Expert survivorship of centenarians. In P. S. Fry & L. M. Corey (Eds.), *New frontiers in resilient aging: Life-strengths and well-being in late life* (pp. 213–238). New York: Cambridge University Press.

Martin, P. L. (2000). Potency and pregnancy in Japan: Did Viagra push the pill? *Tulsa Lawyers Journal, 35,* 651–677.

Martin, S. (2002). Easing migraine pain. *Monitor on Psychology, 33*(4), 71.

Marx, B. P., & Sloan, D. M. (2005). Peritraumatic dissociation and experimental avoidance as predictors of posttraumatic stress symptomatology. *Behavioral Research and Therapy, 43*(5), 569–583.

Masdrakis, V. G., & Papakostas, I. G. (2004). The role of challenges in the research for the etiology of panic disorder. *Psychiatriki, 15*(2), 129–142.

Mash, E. J., & Wolfe, D. A. (2010). *Abnormal child psychology* (4th ed.). Stamford, CT: Wadsworth/ Cengage Learning.

Maslow, A. H. (1970). *Motivation and personality* (2nd ed.). New York: Harper & Row.

Masters, W. H., & Johnson, V. E. (1966). *Human sexual response.* Boston: Little, Brown.

Masters, W. H., & Johnson, V. E. (1970). *Human sexual inadequacy.* Boston: Little, Brown.

Mataix-Cols, D., & Pertusa, A. (2012). Annual research review: Hoarding disorder: Potential benefits and pitfalls of a new mental disorder. *Journal of Child Psychology and Psychiatry, 53*(5), 608–618.

Mathew, J., & McGrath, J. (2002). Readability of consent forms in schizophrenia research. *Australian and New Zealand Journal of Psychiatry, 36*(4), 564–565.

Mathews, D. M., & Wang, M. (2007). Anesthesia awareness and trauma. In E. K. Carll (Ed.), *Trauma psychology: Issues in violence, disaster, health, and illness* (Vol. 2). Westport, CT: Praeger Publishers.

Mathys, M., & Belgeri, M. T. (2010). Psychiatric disorders. In L. C. Hutchison & R. B. Sleeper (Eds.), *Fundamentals of geriatric pharmacotherapy: An evidence-based approach.* Bethesda, MD: American Society of Health-Systems Pharmacists.

Matsumoto, D. (Ed.). (2001). *The handbook of culture and psychology.* New York: Oxford University Press.

Matsumoto, D. (2007). Culture, context, and behavior. *Journal of Personality, 75*(6), 1285–1320.

Matsumoto, D., & Hwang, H. S. (2011). Culture, emotion, and expression. In M. J. Gelfand, C-Y Chiu, & Y-Y. Hong (Eds.), *Advances in culture and psychology (Vol. 1), Advances in culture and psychology* (pp. 53–98). New York: Oxford University Press.

Matsumoto, D., & Hwang, H. S. (2012). Culture and emotion: The integration of biological and cultural contributions. *Journal of Cross-Cultural Psychology, 43*(1), 91–118.

Matsumoto, D., & Juang, L. (2008). *Culture and psychology* (4th ed.). Australia: Thomson Wadsworth.

Matsumoto, D., & van de Vijver, F. J. R. (Eds.). (2011). *Cross-cultural research methods in psychology. Culture and psychology.* New York: Cambridge University Press.

Matsunaga, H., & Seedat, S. (2011). Obsessive-compulsive spectrum disorders: Cross-national and ethnic issues. In E. Hollander, J. Zohar, P. J. Sirovatka, & D. A. Regier (Eds.), *Obsessive-compulsive spectrum disorders: Refining the research agenda for DSM-V* (pp. 205–221). Washington, DC: American Psychiatric Association.

Mattia, J. I., & Zimmerman, M. (2001). Epidemiology. In W. J. Livesley (Ed.), *Handbook of personality disorders: Theory, research, and treatment* (pp. 107–123). New York: Guilford Press.

Maulik, P. K., Eaton, W. W., & Bradshaw, C. P. (2010). Mediating effect of mental disorders in the pathway between life events and mental health services use: Results from the Baltimore Epidemiologic Catchment Area Study. *Journal of Nervous and Mental Disease, 198*(3), 187–193.

Maulik, P. K., Eaton, W. W., & Bradshaw, C. P. (2010). The effect of social networks and social support on common mental disorders following specific life events. *Acta Psychiatrica Scandinavica, 122*(2), 118–128.

Maurice, W. L. (2007). Sexual desire disorders in men. In S. R. Leiblum (Ed.), *Principles and practice of sex therapy* (4th ed., pp. 181–210). New York: Guilford Press.

Mauthner, N. S. (2010). "I wasn't being true to myself": Women's narratives of postpartum depression. In D. C. Jack & A. Ali (Eds.), *Silencing the self across cultures: Depression and gender in the social world* (pp. 459–484). New York: Oxford University Press.

Mayahara, K., & Ito, H. (2002). Readmission of discharged schizophrenic patients with and without day care in Japan. *International Medical Journal, 9*(2), 121–123.

Mayberg, H. S., Brannan, S. K., Mahurin, R. K., Jerabek, P. A., Brickman, J. S., Tekell, J. L., et al. (1997). Cingulate function in depression: A potential predictor of treatment response. *NeuroReport, 8,* 1057–1061.

Mayberg, H. S., Brannan, S. K., Mahurin, R. K., & McGinnin, S. (2000). Regional metabolic effects of fluoxetine in major depression: Serial changes and relationship to clinical response. *Biological Psychiatry, 48,* 830–843.

Mayberg, H. S., Lozano, A. M., Voon, V., McNeely, H. E., Seminowicz, D., Hamani, C., et al. (2005). Deep brain stimulation for treatment-resistant depression. *Neuron, 45,* 651–660.

Mayr, U. (2007, June 14). Cited in J. Steenhuysen, Brain gets a thrill from charity: Study. *YAHOO! News.*

Mazza, M., Mandelli, L., Zaninotto, L., Nicola, M. D., Martinotti, G., Harnic, D., et al. (2012). Bipolar disorder: "Pure" versus mixed depression over a 1-year follow-up. *International Journal of Psychiatry in Clinical Practice, 16*(2), 113–120.

McAnulty, R. D. (2006). Pedophilia. In R. D. McAnulty & M. M. Burnette (Eds.), *Sex and sexuality: Vol. 3. Sexual deviation and sexual offenses.* Westport, CT: Praeger Publishers.

McCabe, R. E., & Antony, M. M. (2005). Panic disorder and agoraphobia. In M. M. Antony, D. R. Ledley, & R. G. Heimberg (Eds.), *Improving outcomes and preventing relapse in cognitive-behavioral therapy* (pp. 1–37). New York: Guilford Press.

McCaffery, J. M. (2011). Genetic epidemiology of stress and gene by stress interaction. In R. J. Contrada & A. Baum (Eds.), *The handbook of stress science: Biology, psychology, and health* (pp. 77–85). New York: Springer Publishing.

McCaghy, C. H., Capron, T. A., Jamieson, J. D., & Carey, S. H. (2006). *Deviant behavior: Crime, conflict, and interest groups* (7th ed.). New York: Pearson/Allyn & Bacon.

McCance, D. (2011). *Critical animal studies: An introduction.* Basingstoke, UK: Palgrave Macmillan.

McCance-Katz, E. F. (2010). Drug interactions in the pharmacological treatment of substance use disorders. In E. V. Nunes, J. Selzer, P. Levounis, & C. A. Davies (Eds.), *Substance dependence and co-occurring psychiatric disorders: Best practices for diagnosis and treatment* (pp. 18-1–18-36). Kingston, NJ: Civic Research Institute.

McCance-Katz, E. F., & Kosten, T. R. (2005). Psychopharmacological treatments. In R. J. Frances, A. H. Mack, & S. I. Miller (Eds.), *Clinical textbook of addictive disorders* (3rd ed., pp. 688–614). New York: Guilford Press.

McCarthy, B., & Breetz, A. (2010). Confronting male hypoactive sexual desire disorder: Secrets, variant arousal, and good-enough sex. In S. R. Leiblum (Ed.), *Treating sexual desire disorders: A clinical casebook* (pp. 75–91). New York: Guilford Press.

McCarthy, B., & McCarthy, E. (2012). *Sexual awareness: Your guide to healthy couple sexuality* (5th ed.). New York: Routledge/Taylor & Francis Group.

McCarthy, D. E., Curtin, J. J., Piper, M. E., & Baker, T. B. (2010). Negative reinforcement: Possible clinical implications of an integrative model. In J. D. Kassel (Ed.), *Substance abuse and emotion* (pp. 15–42). Washington, DC: American Psychological Association.

McCauley, J. L., Calhoun, K. S., & Gidycz, C. A. (2010). Binge drinking and rape: A prospective examination of college women with a history of previous sexual victimization. *Journal of Interpersonal Violence, 25*(9), 1655–1668.

McClelland, S. (1998, September 21). Grief crisis counsellors under fire: Trauma teams were quick to descend on Peggy's Cove. Susan McClelland asks whether they do more harm than good. *Ottawa Citizen,* p. A4.

McCloud, A., Barnaby, B., Omu, N., Drummond, C., & Aboud, A. (2004). Relationship between alcohol use disorders and suicidality in a psychiatric population: In-patient prevalence study. *British Journal of Psychiatry, 184*(5), 439–445.

McClure, E. B., Monk, C. S., Nelson, E. E., Parrish, J. M., Adler, A., Blair, R. J., et al. (2007). Abnormal attention modulation of fear circuit function in pediatric generalized anxiety disorder. *Archives of General Psychiatry, 64,* 97–106.

McConaghy, N. (2005). Sexual dysfunctions and disorders. In B. A. Winstead & J. E. Maddux (Eds.), *Psychopathology: Foundations for a contemporary understanding* (pp. 255–280). Mahwah, NJ: Lawrence Erlbaum.

McConnaughey, J. (2007, May 31). NFL study links concussions, depression. *San Francisco Chronicle.* Retrieved May 31, 2007, from http://www.sfgate.com/cgi-bin/article.cgi?f=/n/a/2007/05/31/sports/s135640D10.DTL.

McCoy, S. A. (1976). Clinical judgments of normal childhood behavior. *Journal of Consulting and Clinical Psychology, 44*(5), 710–714.

McCullumsmith, C. B., & Ford, C. V. (2011). Simulated illness: The factitious disorders and malingering. *Psychiatric Clinics of North America, 34*(3), 621–641.

McDermott, B. M., & Jaffa, T. (2005). Eating disorders in children and adolescents: An update. *Current Opinions in Psychiatry, 18*(4), 407–410.

McDowell, D. (2005). Marijuana, hallucinogens, and club drugs. In R. J. Frances, A. H. Mack, & S. I. Miller (Eds.), *Clinical textbook of addictive disorders* (3rd ed., pp. 157–183). New York: Guilford Press.

McDowell, D. (2011). Hallucinogens and club drugs. In R. J. Frances, S. I. Miller, & A. H. Mack (Eds.), *Clinical textbook of addictive disorders* (3rd ed.). New York: Guilford Press.

McEachin, J. J., Smith, T., & Lovaas, O. I. (1993). Long-term outcome for children with autism who received early intensive behavioral treatment. *American Journal of Mental Retardation, 97*(4), 359–372.

MCEER. (2010). Haiti earthquake 2010: Facts, engineering, images and maps. Retrieved January 19, 2011, from http://mceer.buffalo.edu/infoservice/disassters/Haiti-earthquake-2010.asp.

McElroy, S. L., Guerdjikova, A. I., O'Melia, A. M., Mori, N., & Keck, P. E., Jr. (2010). Pharmacotherapy of the eating disorders. In W. S. Agras (Ed.), *The Oxford handbook of eating disorders. Oxford library of psychology* (pp. 417–451). New York: Oxford University Press.

McEvoy, P. M. (2007). Effectiveness of cognitive behavioural group therapy for social phobia in a community clinic: A benchmarking study. *Behavioral Research and Therapy, 45*(12), 3030–3040.

McEvoy, P. M., & Richards, D. (2007). Gatekeeping access to community mental health teams: A qualitative study. *International Journal of Nursing Studies, 44*(3), 387–395.

McFarlane, W. R. (2011). Integrating the family in the treatment of psychotic disorders. In R. Hagen, D. Turkington, T. Berge, & R. W. Grawe (Eds.), *CBT for psychosis: A symptom-based approach, International Society for the Psychological Treatments of the Schizophrenias and Other Psychoses* (pp. 193–209). New York: Routledge/Taylor & Francis Group.

McGhie, A., & Chapman, J. S. (1961). Disorders of attention and perception in early schizophrenia. *British Journal of Medical Psychology, 34,* 103–116.

McGilloway, A., Hall, R. E., Lee, T., & Bhui, K. S. (2010). A systematic review of personality disorder, race and ethnicity: Prevalence, aetiology and treatment. *BMC Psychiatry, 10,* Article 33.

McGlothlin, J. M. (2008). *Developing clinical skills in suicide assessment, prevention, and treatment.* Alexandria, VA: American Counseling Association.

McGoldrick, M., Loonan, R., & Wohlsifer, D. (2007). Sexuality and culture. In S. R. Leiblum (Ed.), *Principles and practice of sex therapy* (4th ed., pp. 416–441). New York: Guilford Press.

McGrath, J. (2011). Why are antidepressants the most prescribed drug in the U.S.? *Discovery Health.*

McGrath, J. (2012). Understanding panic attacks. *Discovery Health.* Retrieved from http: //health. howstuffworks.com/mental-health/anxiety/ panic-attack.htm.

McGrath, J. J., & Murray, R. M. (2011). Environmental risk factors for schizophrenia. In D. R. Weinberg & P. Harrison (Eds.), *Schizophrenia* (pp. 226–244). Hoboken, NJ: Wiley-Blackwell.

McGrath, R. E., & Carroll, E. J. (2012). The current status of "projective tests." In H. Cooper, P. M. Camic, D. L. Long, A. T. Panter, D. Rindskopf, & K. J. Sher (Eds.), *APA handbook of research methods in psychology. Vol. 1: Foundations, planning, measures, and psychometrics* (pp. 329–348). Washington, DC: American Psychological Association.

McGrath, R. E., & Moore, B. A. (Eds.). (2010). *Pharmacotherapy for psychologists: Prescribing and collaborative roles.* Washington, DC: American Psychological Association.

McGuffin, P., Katz, R., Watkins, S., & Rutherford, J. (1996). A hospital-based twin register of the heritability of DSM-IV unipolar depression. *Archives of General Psychiatry, 53,* 129–136.

McGuire, P. A. (2000, February). New hope for people with schizophrenia. *Monitor on Psychology, 31*(2), 24–28.

McGuire, P. K., Silbersweig, D. A., Wright, I., Murray, R. M., Frackowiak, R. S., & Frith, C. D. (1996). The neural correlates of inner speech and auditory verbal imagery in schizophrenia: Relationship to auditory verbal hallucinations. *British Journal of Psychiatry, 169*(2), 148–159.

McIntosh, K., & Kleiman, A. M. (2007). *"Natural" alternatives to antidepressants: St. John's wort, kava kava, and others.* Broomall, PA: Mason Crest Publishers.

McKay, D., Gosselin, J. T., & Gupta, S. (2008). Body dysmorphic disorder. In J. S. Abramowitz, D. McKay, & S. Taylor (Eds.), *Obsessive-compulsive disorder: Subtypes and spectrum conditions.* Oxford, England: Elsevier.

McKay, D., & Storch, E. A. (Eds.). (2011). *Handbook of child and adolescent anxiety disorders.* New York: Springer Science & Business Media.

McKay, D., Taylor, S., & Abramowitz, J. S. (2010). Cognitive-behavioral therapy and refractory cases: What factors lead to limited treatment response? In D. McKay, J. S. Abramowitz & S. Taylor (Eds.), *Cognitive-behavioral therapy for refractory cases: Turning failure into success.* (pp. 3–10) Washington, DC: American Psychological Association.

McKay, D., Taylor, S., & Abramowitz, J. S. (2010). Obsessive-compulsive disorder. In D. McKay, J. S. Abramowitz & S. Taylor (Eds.), *Cognitive-behavioral therapy for refractory cases: Turning failure into success.* (pp. 89–109) Washington, DC: American Psychological Association.

McKendrick, K., Sullivan, C., Banks, S., & Sacks, S. (2007). Modified therapeutic community treatment for offenders with MICA disorders: Antisocial personality disorder and treatment outcomes. *Journal of Offender Rehabilitation, 44*(2–3), 133–159.

McKenna, K. E. (2001). Neural circuitry involved in sexual function. *The Journal of Spinal Cord Medicine, 24*(3), 148–154.

McKenzie, G. & Teri, L. (2011). Psychosocial therapies. In C. E. Coffey, J. L. Cummings, M. S. George, & D. Weintraub (Eds.), *The American Psychiatric Publishing textbook of geriatric neuropsychiatry.* Arlington, VA: American Psychiatric Publishing, Inc.

McLaughlin, K. A., & Nolen-Hoeksema, S. (2011). Rumination as a transdiagnostic factor in depression and anxiety. *Behaviour Research and Therapy, 49*(3), 186–193.

McLay, R. N., Daylo, A. A., & Hammer, P. S. (2006). No effect of lunar cycle on psychiatric admissions or emergency evaluations. *Military Medicine, 17*(12), 1239–1242.

McMahon, R. J., & Frick, P. J. (2005). Evidence-based assessment of conduct problems in children and adolescents. *Journal of Clinical Child and Adolescent Psychology, 34,* 477–505.

McMahon, R. J., & Frick, P. J. (2007). Conduct and oppositional disorders. In E. J. Mash, & R. A. Barkley (Eds.), *Assessment of childhood disorders* (4th ed., pp. 132–183) New York: Guilford Press.

McMahon, R. J., & Kotler, J. S. (2008). Evidence-based therapies for oppositional behavior in young children. In R. G. Steele, T. D. Elkin, & M. C. Roberts (Eds.), *Handbook of evidence-based therapies for children and adolescents: Bridging science and practice.* New York: Springer.

McNally, R. J. (2004, April 1). Psychological debriefing does not prevent posttraumatic stress disorder. *Psychiatric Times,* p. 71.

McNally, R. J., Clancy, S. A., Barrett, H. M., & Parker, H. A. (2005). Reality monitoring in adults reporting repressed, recovered, or continuous memories of childhood sexual abuse. *Journal of Abnormal Psychology, 114*(1), 147–152.

McNally, R. J., & Geraerts, E. (2009). A new solution to the recovered memory debate. *Perspectives on Psychological Science, 4*(2), 126–134.

McNeal, E. T., & Cimbolic, P. (1986). Antidepressants and biochemical theories of depression. *Psychological Bulletin, 99*(3), 361–374.

McNeely, H. E., Mayberg, H. S., Lozano, A. M., & Kennedy, S. H. (2008). Neuropsychological impact of Cg25 deep brain stimulation for treatment-resistant depression: Preliminary results over 12 months. *Journal of Nervous and Mental Disease, 196*(5), 405–410.

McNeil, E. B. (1967). *The quiet furies.* Englewood Cliffs, NJ: Prentice Hall.

McPherson, M., Smith-Lovin, L., & Brashears, M. (2006). Social isolation in America: Changes in core discussion networks over two decades. *American Sociological Review, 71,* 353–375.

McShane, K. M. (2011). Mental Health in Haiti: A resident's perspective. *Academic Psychiatry, 35*(1), 8–10.

McSherry, B., & Weller, P. (2010). *Rethinking rights-based mental health law.* Portland, OR: Hart Publishing.

McSweeney, S. (2004). Depression in women. In L. Cosgrove & P. J. Caplan (Eds.), *Bias in psychiatric diagnosis* (pp. 183–188). Northvale, NJ: Jason Aronson.

Meaden, A., & Hacker, D. (2011). *Problematic and risk behaviours in psychosis: A shared formulation approach.* New York: Routledge/Taylor & Francis Group.

Meader, N. (2010). A comparison of methadone, buprenorphine, and alpha$_2$ adrenergic agonists for opioid detoxification: A mixed treatment comparison meta-analysis. *Drug and Alcohol Dependence, 108*(1-2), 110–114.

Mealy, M., Stephan, W., & Urrutia, I. C. (2007). The acceptability of lies: A comparison of Ecuadorians and Euro-Americans. *International Journal of Intercultural Relations, 31*(6), 689–702.

Meana, M. (2012). *Sexual dysfunction in women. Advances in psychotherapy—Evidence-based practice.* Cambridge, MA: Hogrefe Publishing.

Meares, R., Gerull, F., Stevenson, J., & Korner, A. (2011). Is self disturbance the core of borderline personality disorder: An outcome study of borderline personality factors. *Australian and New Zealand Journal of Psychiatry, 45*(3), 214–222.

Mednick, S. A. (1971). Birth defects and schizophrenia. *Psychology Today, 4,* 48–50.

Meehl, P. E. (1960). The cognitive activity of the clinician. *American Psychologist, 15,* 19–27.

Meehl, P. E. (1996). *Clinical versus statistical prediction: A theoretical analysis and a review of the evidence.* Northvale, NJ: Jason Aronson.

Meeks, T. W., & Jeste, D. V. (2008). Older individuals. In K. T. Mueser & D.V. Jeste (Eds.), *Clinical handboook of schizophrenia* (pp. 390–397). New York: Guilford Press.

Meersand, P. (2011). Psychological testing and the analytically trained child psychologist. *Psychoanalytic Psychology, 28*(1), 117–131.

Meichenbaum, D. H. (1975). A self-instructional approach to stress management: A proposal for stress inoculation training. In I. Sarason & C. D. Spielberger (Eds.), *Stress and anxiety* (Vol. 2). New York: Wiley.

Meichenbaum, D. H. (1977). *Cognitive-behavior modification: An integrative approach.* New York: Plenum Press.

Meichenbaum, D. H. (1993). Stress inoculation training: A 20-year update. In P. M. Lehrer & R. L. Woolfolk (Eds.), *Principles and practice of stress management* (2nd ed.). New York: Guilford Press.

Meichenbaum, D. H. (1997). The evolution of a cognitive-behavior therapist. In J. K. Zeig (Ed.), *The evolution of psychotherapy: The third conference.* New York: Brunner/Mazel.

Meijer, E. H., & Verschuere, B. (2010). The polygraph and the detection of deception. *Journal of Forensic Psychology Practice, 10*(4), 325–338.

Melfi, C. A., Croghan, T. W., Hanna, M. P., & Robinson, R. L. (2000). Racial variation in antidepressant treatment in a Medicaid population. *Journal of Clinical Psychiatry, 61*(1), 16–21.

Mellon, M. W., & Houts, A. C. (2006). Nocturnal enuresis. In J. E. Fisher & W. T. O'Donohue (Eds.), *Practitioner's guide to evidence-based psychotherapy.* (pp. 432–441). New York: Springer Science + Business Media.

Melón, L. C., & Boehm, S. L., II. (2011). GABAA receptors in the posterior, but not anterior, ventral tegmental area mediate Ro15-4513-induced attenuation of binge-like ethanol consumption in C57BL/6J female mice. *Behavioural Brain Research, 220*(1), 230–237.

Meloy, J. R., & Yakeley, J. (2010). Psychodynamic treatment of antisocial personality disorder:

Psychodynamic psychotherapy for personality disorders: A clinical handbook. In J. F. Clarkin, P. Fonagy, & G. O. Gabbard (Eds.), *Psychodynamic psychotherapy for personality disorders: A clinical handbook* (pp. 311–336). Arlington, VA: American Psychiatric Publishing.

Meltzer, H. Y. (2011). Evidence-based treatment for reducing suicide risk in schizophrenia. In M. Pompili & R. Tatarelli (Eds.), *Evidence-based practice in suicidology: A source book* (pp. 317–328). Cambridge MA: Hogrefe Publishing.

Melville, J. (1978). *Phobias and obsessions.* New York: Penguin.

Mendels, J. (1970). *Concepts of depression.* New York: Wiley.

Mendes, E. (2010). Uptick in high cholesterol and high blood pressure in U.S. Retrieved on April 13, 2011, from www.gallup.com/poll/127055.

Mendlewicz, J., Linkowski, P., & Wilmotte, J. (1980). Linkage between glucose-6–phosphate dehydrogenase deficiency in manic depressive psychosis. *British Journal of Psychiatry, 137,* 337–342.

Mendlewicz, J., Simon, P., Sevy, S., Charon, F., Brocas, H., Legros, S., et al. (1987). Polymorphic DNA marker on X chromosome and manic depression. *Lancet, 1,* 1230–1232.

Mennin, D. S., Heimberg, R. G., Turk, C. L., & Fresco, D. M. (2002). Applying an emotion regulation framework to integrative approaches to generalized anxiety disorder. *Clinical Psychology: Science and Practice, 9,* 85–90.

Mennin, D. S., Heimberg, R. G., Turk, C. L., & Fresco, D. M. (2005). Preliminary evidence for an emotion dysregulation model of generalized anxiety disorder. *Behavioral Research and Therapy, 43*(10), 1281–1310.

Mennin, D. S., Turk, C. L., Heimberg, R. G., & Carmin, C. (2004). Regulation of emotion in generalized anxiety disorder. In M. A. Reinecke & D. A. Clark (Eds.), *Cognitive therapy over the lifespan: Theory, research, and practice* (pp. 60–89). New York: Wiley.

Merenda, R. R. (2008). The posttraumatic and sociocognitive etiologies of dissociative identity disorder: A survey of clinical psychologists. *Dissertation Abstracts International: Section B: The Sciences and Engineering, 68*(8-B), 55–84.

Merikangas, K. R., He, J-P., Brody, D., Fisher, P. W., Bourdon, K., & Koretz, D. (2010). Prevalence and treatment of mental disorders among US children in the 2001–2004 NHANES. *Pediatrics, 125*(1), 75–81.

Merikangas, K. R., Jin, R., He, J-P., Kessler, R. C., Lee, S., Sampson, N. A., et al. (2011). Prevalence and correlates of bipolar spectrum disorder in the World Mental Health Survey Initiative. *Archives of General Psychiatry, 68*(3), 241–251.

Merikangas, K. R., & Swanson, S. A. (2010). Comorbidity in anxiety disorders. In M. B. Stein & T. Steckler (Eds.), *Behavioral neurobiology of anxiety and its treatment. Current topics in behavioral neurosciences* (pp. 37–59). New York: Springer Science + Business Media.

Merkl, A., Schubert, F., Quante, A., Luborzewski, A., Brakemeier, E-L., Grimm, S., et al. (2011). Abnormal cingulate and prefrontal cortical neurochemistry in major depression after electroconvulsive therapy. *Biological Psychiatry, 69*(8), 772–779.

Merrick, E. L., & Reif, S. (2010). Services in an era of managed care. In B. L. Levin, & M. A. Becker (Eds.), *A public health perspective of women's mental health.* New York: Springer Science + Business Media.

Merrick, E. S., Hodgkin, D., Hiatt, D., Horgan, C. M., Greenfield, S. F., & McCann, B. (2011). Integrated employee assistance program: Managed behavioral health plan utilization by persons with substance use disorders. *Journal of Substance Abuse Treatment, 40*(3), 299–306.

Merz, E. L., & Roesch, S. C. (2011). Modeling trait and state variation using multilevel factor analysis with PANAS daily dairy data. *Journal of Research in Personality, 45*(1), 2–9.

Messer, S. B., & Abbass, A. A. (2010). Evidence-based psychodynamic therapy with personality disorders. In J. J. Magnavita (Ed.), *Evidence-based treatment of personality dysfunction: Principles, methods, and processes.* (pp. 79–111) Washington, DC: American Psychological Association.

Messias, E., & Dixon, L. (2012). Medical comorbidities. In J. A. Lieberman, T. S. Stroup, & D. O. Perkins (Eds.), *Essentials of schizophrenia* (pp. 159–171). Arlington, VA: American Psychiatric Publishing.

Messinger, J. W., Trémeau, F., Antonius, D., Mendelsohn, E., Prudent, V., Stanford, A. D., & Malaspina, D. (2011). Avolition and expressive deficits capture negative symptom phenomenology: Implications for DSM-5 and schizophrenia research. *Clinical Psychology Review, 31*(1), 161–168.

Metzl, J. M. (2004). Voyeur nation? Changing definitions of voyeurism, 1950–2004. *Harvard Review of Psychiatry, 12*(q), 127–131.

Metzner, J. L., & Dvoskin, J. A. (2010). Correctional psychiatry. In R. I. Simon & L. H. Gold (Eds.), *The American Psychiatric Publishing textbook of forensic psychiatry* (2nd ed., pp. 395–411). Arlington, VA: American Psychiatric Publishing.

Meuleman, E. J. H. (2011). Men's sexual health and the metabolic syndrome. *Journal of Sex Research, 48*(2-3), 142–148.

Meuret, A. E., Ritz, T., Wilhelm, F. H., & Roth, W. T. (2005). Voluntary hyperventilation in the treatment of panic disorder—functions of hyperventilation, their implications for breathing training, and recommendations for standardization. *Clinical Psychological Review, 25*(3), 285–306.

Meyer, G. J., Finn, S. E., Eyde, L. D., Kay, G. G., Moreland, K. L., Dies, R. R., et al. (2003). Psychological testing and psychological assessment: A review of evidence and issues. In A. E. Kazdin (Ed.), *Methodological issues and strategies in clinical research* (3rd ed., pp. 265–345). Washington, DC: American Psychological Association.

Meyer, J. S., & Quenzer, L. F. (2005). *Psychopharmacology: Drugs, the brain, and behavior.* Sunderland, MA: Sinauer Associates.

Meyer, R. G. (2005). *Case studies in Abnormal Behavior.* Needham Heights, MA: Allyn & Bacon.

Meyer, V. (1966). Modification of expectations in cases with obsessional rituals. *Behavioral Research and Therapy, 4,* 273–280.

Meyer-Lindenberg, A., & Bullmore, E. T. (2011). Functional brain imaging in schizophrenia. In D. R. Weinberg & P. Harrison (Eds.), *Schizophrenia* (pp. 353–371). Hoboken, NJ: Wiley-Blackwell.

Meyers, L. (2008). Warding off dementia. *Monitor on Psychology, 39*(3), 22–23.

MHA (Mental Health America). (2004, March 7). *NMHA policy positions: In support of the insanity defense.* National Mental Health Association.

MHA (Mental Health America). (2007). The insanity defense is a legitimate legal approach. In A. Quigley (Ed.), *Current controversies: Mental health.* Detroit: Greenhaven Press/Thomson Gale.

MHA (Mental Health America). (2008). *Americans reveal top stressors, how they cope.* Alexandria, VA: Author.

MHA (Mental Health America). (2010). *Americans Reveal Top Stressors.* New Mexico Health Association.

Michal, M. (2011). Review of depersonalization: A new look at a neglected syndrome. *Journal of Psychosomatic Research, 70*(2), 199.

Miklowitz, D. J. & Cichetti, D. (Eds.). (2010). *Understanding bipolar disorder: A developmental psychopathology perspective.* New York: Guilford Press.

Miller, A. L., McEvoy, J. P., Jeste, D. V., & Marder, S. R. (2012). Treatment of chronic schizophrenia. In J. A. Lieberman, T. S. Stroup, & D. O. Perkins (Eds.), *Essentials of schizophrenia* (pp. 225–243). Arlington, VA: American Psychiatric Publishing.

Miller D. C. (Ed.). (2010). *Best practices in school neuropsychology: Guidelines for effective practice, assessment, and evidence-based intervention.* Hoboken, NJ: John Wiley & Sons.

Miller, D. N. (2011). *Child and adolescent suicidal behavior: School-based prevention, assessment, and intervention. the Guilford practical Intervention in the schools series.* New York: Guilford Press.

Miller, J. A. (2010). Sex offender civil commitment: The treatment paradox. *California Law Review, 98,* 2093-2092128.

Miller, J. S., & Ozonoff, S. (2011). Asperger's syndrome. In E. Hollander, A. Kolevzon & J. T. Coyle (Eds.), *Textbook of autism spectrum disorders.* (pp. 77–88) Arlington, VA: American Psychiatric Publishing, Inc.

Miller, L. J., & LaRusso, E. M. (2011). Preventing postpartum depression. *Psychiatric Clinics of North America, 34*(1), 53–65.

Miller, M., & Kantrowitz, B. (1999, January 25). Unmasking Sybil: A re-examination of the most famous psychiatric patient in history. *Newsweek,* pp. 66–68.

Miller, M. A., & Rahe, R. H. (1997). Life changes scaling for the 1990s. *Journal of Psychosomatic Research, 43*(3), 279–292.

Miller, M. C. (2004, July 1). Hypochondria. *Harvard Mental Health Letter.*

Miller, M. C. (2005, January 1). Falling apart: Dissociation and its disorders. *Harvard Mental Health Letter.*

Miller, M. C. (2005, July 1). What is body dysmorphic disorder? *Harvard Mental Health Letter.*

Miller, N. E. (1948). Studies of fear as an acquirable drive: I. Fear as motivation and fear-reduction as reinforcement in the learning of new responses. *Journal of Experimental Psychology, 38,* 89–101.

Miller, P. M., Ingham, J. G., & Davidson, S. (1976). Life events, symptoms, and social support. *Journal of Psychiatric Research, 20*(6), 514–522.

Miller, S. G. (1994). Borderline personality disorder from the patient's perspective. *Hospital Community Psychiatry, 45*(12), 1215–1219.

Miller, S. G. (1999). Borderline personality disorder in cultural context: Commentary on Paris. *Psychiatry, 59*(2), 193–195.

Miller, W. D., Sadegh-Nobari, T., & Lillie-Blanton, M. (2011). Healthy starts for all: Policy prescriptions. *American Journal of Preventive Medicine, 40*(1, Suppl 1), S19–S37.

Miller, W. R., & Seligman, M. E. (1975). Depression and learned helplessness in man. *Journal of Abnormal Psychology, 84*(3), 228–238.

Millichap, J. G. (2010). *Attention deficit hyperactivity disorder handbook: A physician's guide to ADHD* (2nd ed.). New York: Springer Science + Business Media.

Millon, T. (1969). *Modern psychopathology: A biosocial approach to maladaptive learning and functioning.* Philadelphia: Saunders.

Millon, T. (2011). *Disorders of personality: Introducing a DSM/ICD spectrum from normal to abnormal* (3rd ed.). Hoboken, NJ: John Wiley Sons.

Millon, T., Davis, R., Millon, C., Escovar, L., & Meagher, S. (2000). *Personality disorders in modern life.* New York: Wiley.

Millon, T., & Grossman, S. (2007). *Moderating severe personality disorders: A personalized psychotherapy approach.* Hoboken, NJ: Wiley.

Mills, J. F., Kroner, D. F., & Morgan, R. D. (2011). *Clinician's guide to violence risk assessment.* New York: Guilford Press.

Milner, B. (2010). Reflections on the field of brain and memory: A tribute to H.M. *NARSAD Research Quarterly, 3*(1).

Miner, I. D., & Feldman, M. D. (1998). Factitious deafblindness: An imperceptible variant of factitious disorder. *General Hospital Psychiatry, 20,* 48–51.

Minuchin, S. (1974). *Families and family therapy.* Cambridge, MA: Harvard University Press.

Minuchin, S. (1987). My many voices. In J. K. Zeig (Ed.), *The evolution of psychotherapy.* New York: Brunner/Mazel.

Minuchin, S. (1997). The leap to complexity: Supervision in family therapy. In J. K. Zeig (Ed.), *The evolution of psychotherapy: The third conference.* New York: Brunner/Mazel.

Minuchin, S. (2007). Jay Haley: My teacher. *Family Process, 46*(3), 413–414.

Minuchin, S., Lee, W-Y., & Simon, G. M. (2006). *Mastering family therapy: Journeys of growth and transformation* (2nd ed.). Hoboken, NJ: John Wiley & Sons.

Minzenberg, M. J., Yoon, J. H., & Carter, C. S. (2011). Schizophrenia. In R. E. Hales, S. C. Yudofsky, & G. O. Gabbard (Eds.), *Essentials of psychiatry* (3rd ed., pp. 111–150). Arlington, VA: American Psychiatric Publishing.

Miranda, J., Siddique, J., Belin, T. R., & Kohn-Wood, L. P. (2005). Depression prevalence in disadvantaged young black women: African and Caribbean immigrants compared to US-born African Americans. *Social Psychiatry and Psychiatric Epidemiology, 40*(4), 253–258.

Miret, M., Nuevo, R., & Ayuso-Mateos, J. (2009). Documentation of suicide risk assessment in clinical records. *Psychiatric Services, 60*(7), 994.

Miret, M., Nuevo, R., Morant, C., Sainz-Cortón, E., Jiménez-Arriero, M. A., López-Ibor, J. J., et al. (2011). The role of suicide risk in the decision for psychiatric hospitalization after a suicide attempt. *Crisis: Journal of Crisis Intervention and Suicide Prevention, 32*(2, 65–73.

Mirone, V., Longo, N., Fusco, F., Mangiapia, F., Granata, A. M., & Perretti, A. (2001). Can the BC reflex evaluation be useful for the diagnosis primary premature ejaculation? *International Journal of Impotence Research, 13,* S47.

Mishara, B. L. (1999). Conceptions of death and suicide in children ages 6–12 and their implications for suicide prevention. *Suicide and Life-Threatening Behavior, 29*(2), 105–118.

Mitchell, A. J. (2010). Overview of depression scales and tools. In J. Mitchell & J. C. Coyne (Eds.), *Screening for depression in clinical practice:*

An evidence-based guide (pp. 29–56). New York: Oxford University Press.

Mitchell, A. J. (2010). Why do clinicians have difficulty detecting depression? In A. J. Mitchell & J. C. Coyne (Eds.), *Screening for depression in clinical practice: An evidence-based guide* (pp. 57–82). New York: Oxford University Press.

Mitchell, A. J., Rao, S., & Vaze, A. (2011). Can general practitioners identify people with distress and mild depression? A meta-analysis of clinical accuracy. *Journal of Affective Disorders, 130*(1-2), 26–36.

Mitchell, I. (2001). Treatment and outcome for victims. In G. Adshead & D. Brooke (Eds.), *Munchausen's syndrome by proxy: Current issues in assessment, treatment and research* (pp. 185–196). London: Imperial College Press.

Mitchell, J. E., & Crow, S. J. Medical comorbidities of eating disorders. In W. S. Agras (Ed.), *The Oxford handbook of eating disorders. Oxford library of psychology* (pp. 259–266). New York: Oxford University Press.

Mitchell, J. E., Devlin, M. J., de Zwaan, M., Crow, S. J., & Peterson, C. B. (2008). *Binge-eating disorder: Clinical foundations and treatment.* New York: Guilford Press.

Mitchell, J. T. (1983). When disaster strikes. . . the critical incident stress debriefing process. *Journal of Emergency Medical Services, 8,* 36–39.

Mitchell, J. T. (2003). Crisis intervention & CISM: A research summary. Retrieved from www.icisf.org/articles/cism_research_summary.pdf.

Mitka, M. (2011). Study looks at PTSD among workers in Twin Towers during 9/11 attack. *Journal of the American Medical Association, 305*(9), 874–875.

Mitropoulou, V., Friedman, L., Zegarelli, G., Wainberg, S., Meshberg, J., Silverman, J. M., & Siever, L. J. (2011). Eye tracking performance and the boundaries of the schizophrenia spectrum. *Psychiatry Research, 186*(1), 18–22.

Mittal, V. A., Kalus, O., Bernstein, D. P., & Siever, L. J. (2007). Schizoid personality disorder. In W. O'Donohue, K. A. Fowler, & S. O. Lilienfeld (Eds.). *Personality disorders: Toward the DSM-V.* Los Angeles: Sage Publications.

MMG (Miniwatts Marketing Group). (2011). *Internet world statistics.* Bogota, Colombia, SA: International Division of Miniwatts de Colombia Ltd. (www.miniwatts.com).

Moberg, T., Nordström, P., Forslund, K., Kristiansson, M., Asberg, M., & Jokinen, J. (2011). Csf 5-hiaa and exposure to and expression of interpersonal violence in suicide attempters. *Journal of Affective Disorders, 125*(1-3), 388–392.

MobiThinking. (2011). *Global mobile statistics 2011: All quality mobile marketing research, mobile Web stats, subscribers, ad revenue, usage, trends.* Retrieved August 7, 2011, from http://mobithinking.com/mobile-marketing-tools/latest-mobile-stats.

Mockus, D. S., Macera, C. A., Wingard, D. L., Peddecord, M., Thomas, R. G., & Wilfrey, D. E. (2011). Dietary self-monitoring and its impact on weight loss in overweight children. *International Journal of Pediatric Obesity, 6*(3-4), 197–205.

Modlin, T. (2002). Sleep disorders and hypnosis: To cope or cure? *Sleep and Hypnosis, 4*(1), 39–46.

Modrow, T. (1992). *How to become a schizophrenic: The case against biological psychiatry.* Everett, WA: Apollyon Press.

Moffatt, F. W., Hodnett, E., Esplen, M. J., & Watt-Watson, J. (2010). Effects of guided imagery on blood pressure in pregnant women

with hypertension: A pilot randomized controlled trial. *Birth: Issues in Perinatal Care, 37*(4), 296–306.

Mohler, H., & Okada, T. (1977). Benzodiazepine receptor: Demonstration in the central nervous system. *Science, 198*(4319), 849–851.

Mohler, H., Richards, J. G., & Wu, J-Y. (1981). Autoradiographic localization of benzodiazepine receptors in immunocytochemically identified Y-aminobutyric synapses. *Proceedings of the National Academy of Science, 78,* 1935–1938.

Mohlman, J., Sirota, K. G., Papp, L. A., Staples, A. M., King, A., & Gorenstein, E. E. (2012). Clinical interviewing with older adults. *Cognitive and Behavioral Practice, 19*(1), 89–100.

Mokros, A., Osterheider, M., Hucker, S. J., & Nitschke, J. (2011). Psychopathy and sexual sadism. *Law and Human Behavior, 35*(3), 188–199.

Moldavsky, D. (2004, June 1). Transcultural psychiatry for clinical practice. *Psychiatric Times, 21*(7), p. 36.

Möller, J., Björkenstam, E., Liung, R., Yngwe, M. A. (2011). Widowhood and the risk of psychiatric care, psychotropic medication and all-cause mortality: A cohort study of 658,022 elderly people in Sweden. *Aging & Mental Health, 15*(2), 259–266.

Monahan, J. (1992). Mental disorder and violent behavior: Perceptions and evidence. *American Psychologist, 47*(4), 511–521.

Monahan, J. (1993). Limiting therapist exposure to Tarasoff liability: Guidelines for risk containment. *American Psychologist, 48*(3), 242–250.

Monahan, J. (2001). Major mental disorder and violence: Epidemiology and risk assessment. In G. F. Pinard & L. Pagani (Eds.), *Clinical assessment of dangerousness: Empirical contributions* (pp. 89–102). New York: Cambridge University Press.

Monahan, J. (2010). The classification of violence risk. In R. K. Otto, & K. S. Douglas (Eds.), *Handbook of violence risk assessment* (pp. 187–198). New York: Routledge/Taylor & Francis Group.

Monroe, S. M. (2010). Recurrence in major depression: Assessing risk indicators in the context of risk estimates. In C. S. Richards & M. C. Perri (Eds.), *Relapse prevention for depression* (pp. 27–49). Washington, DC: American Psychological Association.

Monson, C. M., Fredman, S. J., & Taft, C. T. (2011). Couple and family issues and interventions for veterans of the Iraq and Afghanistan wars. In J. I. Ruzek, P. P. Schnurr, J. J. Vasterling, & M. J. Friedman (Eds.), *Caring for veterans with deployment-related stress disorders* (pp. 151–169). Washington, DC: American Psychological Association.

Montejo, A-L, Perahia, D. G. S., Spann, M. E., Wang, F., Walker, D. J., Yang, C. R., & Detke, M. J. (2011). Sexual function during long-term duloxetine treatment in patients with recurrent major depressive disorder. *Journal of Sexual Medicine, 8*(3), 773–782.

Monteleone, P. (2011). New frontiers in endocrinology of eating disorders. In R. A. H. Adan & W. H. Kaye (Eds.), *Behavioral neurobiology of eating disorders. Current topics in behavioral neurosciences* (pp. 189–208). New York: Springer-Verlag Publishing.

Monti, F., Agostini, F., & Martini, A. (2004). Postpartum depression and mother-infant interaction. *Eta Evolutiva, 78,* 77–84.

Moore, P. S., March, J. S., Albno, A. M., & Thienemann, M. (2010). Anxiety disorders in children and adolescents. In D. J. Stein, E. Hollander, & B. O. Rothbaum (Eds.), *Textbook of anxiety disorders* (2nd ed., pp. 629–649). Arlington, VA: American Psychiatric Publishing.

Moorhouse, P. A. & Rockwood, K. (2010). Vascular cognitive impairment. In H. M. Fillit, K. Rockwood, & K. Woodhouse. (Eds.), *Brocklehurst's textbook of geriatric medicine and gerontology, 7th edition.* Philadelphia, PA: Saunders Publishers.

Moos, R. H., & Timko, C. (2008). Outcome research on 12-step and other self-help programs. In H. D. Kleber & M. Galanter (Eds.), *The American Psychiatric Publishing textbook of substance abuse treatment* (4th ed., pp. 511–521). Arlington, VA: American Psychiatric Publishing.

Moreno, C. (2007). National trends in the outpatient diagnosis and treatment of bipolar disorder in youth. *Archives of General Psychiatry, 64,* 1032–1039.

Moreno, C., Laje, G., Blanco, C., Jiang, H., Schmidt, A. B., & Olfson, M. (2007). National trends in the outpatient diagnosis and treatment of bipolar disorder in youth. *Archives of General Psychiatry, 64*(9), 1032–1039.

Morgan, A. B., & Lilienfeld, S. O. (2000). A meta-analytic review of the relation between antisocial behavior and neuropsychological measures of executive function. *Clinical Psychology Review, 20,* 113–136.

Morgan, A. H., & Hilgard, E. R. (1973). Age differences in susceptibility to hypnosis. *International Journal of Clinical and Experimental Hypnosis, 21,* 78–85.

Morgan, C. D., & Murray, H. A. (1935). A method of investigating fantasies: The Thematic Apperception Test. *Archives of Neurological Psychiatry, 34,* 289–306.

Morgan, J. F. (2011). Male eating disorders. In J. Alexander & J. Treasure (Eds.), *A collaborative approach to eating disorders* (pp. 272–278). New York: Taylor & Francis.

MORI (Market Opinion Research International). (1999, May 22). Poll on animal experimentation. *New Scientist.*

MORI (Market Opinion Research International). (2005, January). *Use of animals in medical research for Coalition for Medical Progress.* London: Author.

Morokoff, P. J., & Gillilland, R. (1993). Stress, sexual functioning, and marital satisfaction. *Journal of Sex Research, 30*(1), 43–53.

Morrall, P., Marshall, P., Pattison, S., & MacDonald, G. (2010). Crime and health: A preliminary study into the effects of crime on the mental health of UK university students. *Journal of Psychiatric and Mental Health Nursing, 17*(9), 821–828.

Morris, T. L., & Ale, C. M. (2011). Social anxiety. In D. McKay & E. A. Storch (Eds.), *Handbook of child and adolescent anxiety disorders* (pp. 289–301). New York: Springer Science & Business Media.

Morrissey, J. P., & Cuddeback, G. S. (2008). Jail diversion. In K. T. Mueser & D. V. Jeste (Eds.), *Clinical handbook of schizophrenia* (pp. 524–532). New York: Guilford Press.

Morse, S. J. (1982). A preference for liberty: The case against involuntary commitment of the mentally disordered. *California Law Review, 70,* 55–106.

Mosconi, L., Berti, V., Glodzik, L., Pupi, A., De Santi, S., & de Leon, M. J. (2010). Pre-clinical detection of Alzheimer's disease using FDG-PET, with or without amyloid imaging. *Journal of Alzheimer's Disease, 20*(3), 843–854.

Mosconi, L., De Santi, S., Li, J., Tsui, W. H., Li, Y., Boppana, M., et al. (2008). Hippocampal hypometabolism predicts cognitive decline from normal aging. *Neurobiology of Aging, 29*(5), 676–692.

Moscovitch, D. A. (2009). What is the core fear in social phobia? A new model to facilitate individualized case conceptualization and treatment. *Cognitive and Behavioral Practice, 16*(2), 123–134.

Moskowitz, E. S. (2001). *In therapy we trust: America's obsession with self-fulfillment.* Baltimore: Johns Hopkins University Press.

Moskowitz, E. S. (2008). *In therapy we trust: America's obsession with self-fulfillment.* Baltimore, MD: Johns Hopkins University Press.

Moss, D. (2002). Biofeedback. In S. Shannon (Ed.), *Handbook of complementary and alternative therapies in mental health* (pp. 135–158). San Diego, CA: Academic Press.

Mouilso, E. R., Calhoun, K. S., & Gidycz, C. A. (2011). Effects of participation in a sexual assault risk reduction program on psychological distress following revictimization. *Journal of Interpersonal Violence, 26*(4), 769–788.

Mowery, J. M., Miltenberger, R. G., & Weil, T. M. (2010). Evaluating the effects of reactivity to supervisor presence on staff response to factile prompts and self-monitoring in a group home setting. *Behavioral Interventions, 25*(1), 21–35.

Mowrer, O. H. (1939). A stimulus-response analysis of anxiety and its role as a reinforcing agent. *Psychological Review, 46,* 553–566.

Mowrer, O. H. (1947). On the dual nature of learning: A reinterpretation of "conditioning" and "problem-solving." *Harvard Education Review, 17,* 102–148.

Mowrer, O. H., & Mowrer, W. M. (1938). Enuresis: A method for its study and treatment. *American Journal of Orthopsychiatry, 8,* 436–459.

Moyano, O. (2010). A case of depersonalization-derealization in adolescence: Clinical study of dissociative disorders. *Neuropsychiatrie de l'Enfance et de l'Adolescence, 58*(3), 126–131.

Mueller, S. E., Petitjean, S., Boening, J., & Wiesbeck, G. A. (2007). The impact of self-help group attendance on relapse rates after alcohol detoxification in a controlled study. *Alcohol Alcoholism, 42*(2), 108–112.

Mueser, K. T., & VandenBos, G. R. (2011). Schizophrenia. In J. C. Norcross, G. R. VandenBos, & D. K. Freedheim (Eds.), *History of psychotherapy: Continuity and change* (2nd ed., pp. 601–611). Washington, DC: American Psychological Association.

Mulder, R. T. (2010). Antidepressants and suicide: Population benefit vs. individual risk. *Acta Psychiatrica Scandinavica, 122*(6), 442–443.

Mulhauser, G. (2010). Disadvantages of counselling or therapy by email. Retrieved on March 2, 2011, from http://counsellingresource.com/counselling-service/online-disadvantages.html.

Mulhern, B. (1990, December 15–18). Everyone's problem, no one's priority. *Capital Times.*

Mulholland, C. (2010). Depression and suicide in men. Retrieved on June 18, 2011, from http://www.netdoctor.co.uk/menshealth/facts/depressionsuicide.htm.

Mullen, P. E. (2004). The autogenic (self-generated) massacre. *Behavioral Sciences and the Law, 22*(3), 311–323.

Müller, C. A., Banas, R., Heinz, A., & Hein, J. (2011). Treatment of pathological gambling with disulfiram: A report of 2 cases. *Pharmacopsychiatry, 44*(2), 81–84.

Müller, C. A., Schäfer, M., Schneider, S.., Heimann, H. M., Hinzpeter, A., Volkmar, K., et al. (2010). Efficacy and safety of levetiracetam for outpatient alcohol detoxification. *Pharmacopsychiatry, 43*(5), 184–189.

Müller, D. J., Likhodi, O., & Heinz, A. (2010). Neural markers of genetic vulnerability to drug addiction. In D. W. Self & J. K. Staley (Eds.), *Behavioral neuroscience of drug addiction* (pp. 277–299). New York: Springer Publishing.

Munsey, C. (2010). Medicine or menace? *Monitor on Psychology, 41*(6), 50–55.

Munsey, C. (2010). The kids aren't all right. *Monitor on Psychology, 41*(1), 22–25.

Muran, J. C., Eubanks-Carter, C., & Safran, J. D. (2010). A relational approach to the treatment of personality dysfunction. In J. J. Magnavita (Ed.), *Evidence-based treatment of personality dysfunction: Principles, methods, and processes.* (pp. 167–192) Washington, DC: American Psychological Association.

Murdock, S. G., O'Neill, R. E., & Cunningham, E. (2005). A comparison of results and acceptability of functional behavioral assessment procedures with a group of middle school students with emotional/behavioral disorders (E/BD). *Journal of Behavioral Education, 14*(1), 5–18.

Murphy, J. G., McDevitt-Murphy, M. E., & Barnett, N. P. (2005). Drink and be merry? Gender, life satisfaction, and alcohol consumption among college students. *Psychology of Addictive Behavior, 19,* 184–191.

Murphy, R., Straebler, S., Cooper, Z., & Fairburn, C. G. (2010). Cognitive behavioral therapy for eating disorders. *Psychiatric Clinics of North America, 33*(3), 611–627.

Murphy, W. D., & Page, I. J. (2006). Exhibitionism. In R. D. McAnulty & M. M. Burnette (Eds.), *Sex and sexuality: Vol. 3. Sexual deviation and sexual offenses.* Westport, CT: Praeger Publishers.

Murray, K. E., & Nyp, S. S. (2011). Postpartum depression. *Journal of Developmental and Behavioral Pediatrics, 32*(2), 175.

Musiat, P., & Schmidt, U. (2010). Self-help and stepped care in eating disorders. In W. S. Agras (Ed.), *The Oxford handbook of eating disorders.* (pp. 386–401) New York: Oxford University Press.

Musikantow, R. (2011). Thinking in circles: Power and responsibility in hypnosis. *American Journal of Clinical Hypnosis, 54*(2), 83–85.

Mydans, S. (1996, October 19). New Thai tourist sight: Burmese "giraffe women." *New York Times,* p. C1.

Myers, D. G. (2000). The funds, friends, and faith of happy people. *American Psychologist, 55*(1), 56–67.

Myers, D. G., & Diener, E. (1996, May). The pursuit of happiness. *Scientific American,* pp. 70–72.

Myers, L. B. (2010). The importance of the repressive coping style: Findings from 30 years of research. *Anxiety, Stress and Coping: An International Journal, 23*(1), 3–17.

Myrick, H., & Wright, T. (2008). Clinical management of alcohol abuse and dependence. In H. D. Kleber & M. Galanter (Eds.), *The American Psychiatric Publishing textbook of substance abuse treatment* (4th ed., pp. 129–142). Arlington, VA: American Psychiatric Publishing.

Myrtek, M. (2007). Type A behavior and hostility as independent risk factors for coronary heart disease. In J. Jordan, B. Bardé, & A. M. Andreas (Eds.), *Contributions toward evidence-based psychocardiology: A systematic review of the literature* (pp. 159–183). Washington, DC: American Psychological Association.

Nace, E. P. (2005). Alcohol. In R. J. Frances, A. H. Mack, & S. I. Miller (Eds.), *Clinical textbook of addictive disorders* (3rd ed., pp. 75–104). New York: Guilford Press.

Nace, E. P. (2008). The history of Alcoholics Anonymous and the experiences of patients. In H. D. Kleber & M. Galanter (Eds.), *The American Psychiatric Publishing textbook of substance abuse treatment* (4th ed., pp. 499–509). Arlington, VA: American Psychiatric Publishing.

Nace, E. P. (2011). Alcohol. In R. J. Frances, S. I. Miller, & A. H. Mack (Eds.), *Clinical textbook of addictive disorders* (3rd ed.). New York: Guilford Press.

Nace, E. P. (2011). The history of Alcoholics Anonymous and the experiences of patients. In M. Galanter & H. D. Kleber (Eds.), *Psychotherapy for the treatment of substance abuse* (pp. 351–373). Arlington, VA: American Psychiatric Publishing.

Nagy, T. F. (2011) Avoiding harm and exploitation. In T. F. Nagy, *Essential ethics for psychologists: A primer for understanding and mastering core issues* (pp. 127–144). Washington, DC: American Psychological Association.

Nagy, T. F. (Ed.). (2011). *Essential ethics for psychologists: A primer for understanding and mastering core issues.* Washington, DC: American Psychological Association.

Nagy, T. F. (Ed.). (2011). Ethics in research and publication. In T. F. Nagy, *Essential ethics for psychologists: A primer for understanding and mastering core issues* (pp. 199–216). Washington, DC: American Psychological Association.

Nahas, Z., Marangell, L. B., Husain, M. M., Rush, A. J., Sackeim, H. A., Lisanby, S. H., et al. (2005). Two-year-outcome of vagus nerve stimulation (VNS) for treatment of major depressive episodes. *Journal of Clinical Psychiatry, 66*(9), 1097–1104.

NAHIC (National Adolescent Health Information Center). (2006). *Fact sheet on suicide: Adolescents & young adults.* San Francisco: University of California.

Nairn, S. (2012). A critical realistic approach to knowledge: Implications for evidence-based practice in and beyond nursing *Nursing Inquiry, 19*(1), 6–17.

NAMI (National Alliance on Mental Illness). (2011). *Mental health care gets my vote! State Voting Laws.* Arlington, VA: Author.

Naninck, E. F. G., Lucassen, P. J., & Bakker, J. (2011). Sex differences in adolescent depression: Do sex hormones determine vulnerability? *Journal of Neuroendocrinology, 23*(5), 383–392.

Naquin, C. E., Kurtzberg, T. R., & Belkin, L. Y. (2010). The finer points of lying online: E-mail versus pen and paper. *Journal of Applied Psychology, 95*(2), 387–394.

Nardi, A. E., Valenca, A. M., Nascimento, I., & Zin, W. A. (2001). Hyperventilation challenge test in panic disorder and depression with panic attacks. *Psychiatry Research, 105,* 57–65.

Narrow, W. E., Rae, D. S., Robins, L. N., & Regier, D. A. (2002). Revised prevalence based estimates of mental disorders in the United States: Using a clinical significance criterion to reconcile 2 surveys' estimates. *Biological Psychiatry, 59*(2), 115–123.

Nash, M. R. (2001, July). The truth and the hype of hypnosis. *Scientific American,* pp. 47–55.

Nash, M. R. (2004). Salient findings: Pivotal reviews and research on hypnosis, soma, and cognition. *International Journal of Clinical and Experimental Hypnosis, 52*(1), 82–88.

Nash, M. R. (2005). Salient findings: A potentially groundbreaking study on the neuroscience of hypnotizability, a critical review of hypnosis' efficacy, and the neurophysiology of conversion disorder. *International Journal of Clinical and Experimental Hypnosis, 53*(1), 87–93.

Nash, M. R. (2006). Salient findings: Identifying the building blocks of hypnotizability, and the neural underpinnings of subjective pain. *International Journal of Clinical and Experimental Hypnosis, 54*(3), 360–365.

Nathan, D. (2010). *Sybil exposed: The extraordinary story behind the famous multiple personality case.* New York: Free Press.

Nation, D. A., Hong, S., Jak, A. J., Delano-Wood, L., Mills, P. J., Bondi, M. W., & Dimsdale, J. E. (2011). Stress, exercise, and Alzheimer's disease: A neurovascular pathway. *Medical Hypotheses, 76*(6), 847–854.

National Center for PTSD. (2008). Appendix A. Case examples from Operation Iraqi Freedom. *Iraq War Clinician Guide.* Washington, DC: Department of Veteran Affairs.

National Crime Victimization Survey (NCVS). (1993). *Highlights from 20 years of surveying crime victims: The National Crime Victimization Survey, 1973–1992.* Washington, DC: Bureau of Justice Statistics.

National Crime Victimization Survey (NCVS). (1996). Washington, DC: Bureau of Justice Statistics.

National Crime Victimization Survey (NCVS). (1997). Washington, DC: Bureau of Justice Statistics.

National Crime Victimization Survey (NCVS). (2006). Washington, DC: Bureau of Justice Statistics.

National Highway Traffic Safety Administration. (2010). Early estimate of motor vehicle traffic fatalities for the first half (January-June) of 2010. *Traffic Safety Facts.* Washington, DC: U.S. Department of Transportation.

National Highway Traffic Safety Administration. (2010). Fatality analysis reporting system (FARS). http://www.nhtsa.gov/FARS.

Nawata, H., Ogomori, K., Tanaka, M., Nishimura, R., Urashima, H., Yano, R., et al. (2010). Regional cerebral blood flow changes in female to male gender identity disorder. *Psychiatry and clinical Neurosciences, 64*(2), 157–161.

Nazarian, M., & Craske, M. G. (2008). Panic and agoraphobia. In M. Hersen & J. Rosqvist (Eds.), *Handbook of psychological assessment, case conceptualization, and treatment: Vol. 1. Adults* (pp. 171–203). Hoboken, NJ: John Wiley & Sons.

NCASA (National Center on Addiction and Substance Abuse at Columbia University). (2007, March). *Wasting the best and the brightest: Substance abuse at America's colleges and universities.* Washington, DC: Author.

NCPG (National Council on Problem Gambling). (2012). *Facts and figures.* Washington, DC: Author.

Neeleman, J., Wessely, S., & Lewis, G. (1998). Suicide acceptability in African- and White Americans: The role of religion. *Journal of Nervous and Mental Disease, 186*(1), 12–16.

Neergaard, L. (2007, August 13). Helping find lost Alzheimer's patients. Retrieved August 15, 2007, from http://news.yahoo.com.

Neider, M. B., Gaspar, J. G., McCarley, J. S., Crowell, J. A., Kaczmarski, H., & Kramer, A. F. (2011). Walking and talking: Dual-task effects on street crossing behavior in older adults. *Psychology and Aging, 26*(2), 260–268.

Neisser, U., Boodoo, G., Bouchard, T. J., Jr., Boykin, A. W., et al. (1996). Intelligence: Knowns and unknowns. *American Psychologist, 51*(2), 77–101.

Nelson, T. D. (2006). *The psychology of prejudice* (2nd ed.). New York: Pearson/Allyn & Bacon.

Nelson, T. F., & Wechsler, H. (2001). Alcohol and college athletes. *Medicine and Science in Sports and Exercise, 33*(1), 43–47.

Nemecek, S. (1996, September). Mysterious maladies. *Scientific American,* 24–26.

Nenadic-Sviglin, K., Nedic, G., Nikolac, M., Kozaric-Kovacic, D., Stipcevic, T., Seler, D. M., & Pivac, N. (3022). Suicide attempt, smoking, comorbid depression, and platelet serotonin in alcohol dependence. *Alcohol, 45*(3), 209–216.

Neugroschi, J., & Wang, S. (2011). Alzheimer's disease: Diagnosis and treatment across the spectrum of disease severity. *Mount Sinai Journal of Medicine, 78*(4), 596–612.

Neumark-Sztainer, D. R., Wall, M. M., Haines, J. I., Story, M. T., Sherwood, N. E., & van den Berg, P. A. (2007). Shared risk and protective factors for overweight and disordered eating in adolescents. *American Journal of Preventative Medicine, 33*(5), 359–369.

New, A. S., Hazlett, E. A., Buchsbaum, M. S., Goodman, M., Reynolds, D., Mitropoulou, V., et al. (2002). Blunted prefrontal cortical 18fluorodeoxyglucose positron emission tomography response to meta-chlorophenylpiperazine in impulse aggression. *Archives of General Psychiatry, 59,* 621–629.

New, A. S., Trestman, R. F., Mitropoulou, V., Goodman, M., Koenigsberg, H. H., Silverman, J., et al. (2004). Low prolactin response to fenfluramine in impulsive aggression. *Journal of Psychiatric Research, 38,* 223–230.

Newcomer, J. W., & Leucht, S. (2011). Metabolic adverse effects associated with antipsychotic medications. In D. R. Weinberg & P. Harrison (Eds.), *Schizophrenia* (pp. 577–597). Hoboken, NJ: Wiley-Blackwell.

Newcomer, R., Fox, P. J., & Harrington, C. A. (2001). Health and long-term care for people with Alzheimer's disease and related dementias: Policy research issues. *Aging and Mental Health, 5*(Suppl. 1), S124–S137.

Newman, M. G., Castonguay, L. G., Borkovec, T. D., Fisher, A. J., Boswell, J. F., Szkodny, L. E., & Nordberg, S. S. (2011). A randomized controlled trial of cognitive-behavioral therapy for generalized anxiety disorder with integrated techniques from emotion-focused and interpersonal therapies. *Journal of Consulting and Clinical Psychology, 79*(2), 171–181.

Neziroglu, F., McKay, D., Todaro, J., & Yaryura-Tobias, J. A. (1996). Effect of cognitive behavior therapy on persons with body dysmorphic disorder and comorbid Axis II diagnoses. *Behavior Therapist, 27,* 67–77.

Neziroglu, F., Roberts, M., & Yaryura-Tobias, J. A. (2004). A behavioral model for body dysmorphic disorder. *Psychiatric Annals, 34*(12), 915–920.

Nezlek, J. B., Hampton, C. P., & Shean, G. D. (2000). Clinical depression and day-to-day social interaction in a community sample. *Journal of Abnormal Psychology, 109*(1), 11–19.

Nezu, A. M., Nezu, C. M., & Xanthopoulos, M. S. (2011). Stress reduction in chronically ill patients.

In R. J. Contrada & A. Baum (Eds.), *The handbook of stress science: Biology, psychology, and health* (pp. 475–485). New York: Springer Publishing.

Ni, H., & Cohen, R. (2004). Trends in health insurance coverage by race/ethnicity among persons under 65 years of age: United States 1997–2001. National Center for Health Statistics. Retrieved from www.cdc.gov/nchs/-products/pubs/pubd/hestats/healthinsur.htm.

Ni, X., Chan, K., Bulgin, N., Sicard, T., Bismil, R., McMain, S., et al. (2006). Association between serotonin transporter gene and borderline personality disorder. *Journal of Psychiatric Research, 40,* 448–453.

Nichols, M., & Shernoff, M. (2007). Therapy with sexual minorities: Queering practice. In S. R. Leiblum (Ed.), *Principles and practice of sex therapy* (4th ed., pp. 379–414). New York: Guilford Press.

Nichols, W. C. (2004). Integrative marital and family treatment of dependent personality disorders. In M. M. MacFarlane (Ed.), *Family treatment of personality disorders: Advances in clinical practice* (pp. 173–204). Binghamton, NY: Haworth Clinical Practice Press.

Nickel, R., Ademmer, K., & Egle, U. T. (2010). Manualized psychodynamic-interactional group therapy for the treatment of somatoform pain disorders. *Bulletin of the Menninger Clinic, 74*(3), 219–237.

Nicolini, H., Arnold, P., Nestadt, G., Lanzagorta, N., & Kennedy, J. L. (2011). Overview of genetics and obsessive-compulsive disorder. In E. Hollander, J. Zohar, P. J. Sirovatka, & D. A. Regier (Eds.), *Obsessive-compulsive spectrum disorders: Refining the research agenda for DSM-V* (pp. 141–159). Washington, DC: American Psychiatric Association.

NIDA (National Institute on Drug Abuse). (2002). New research report presents marijuana facts. *NIDA Notes, 17*(3), 1–2.

NIDA (National Institute on Drug Abuse). (2011, March). *DrugFacts: Understanding drug abuse and addiction.* Bethesda, MA: Author.

Nieder, T. O., Herff, M., Cerwenka, S., Preuss, W. F., Cohen-Kettenis, P. T., De Cuypere, G., et al. (2011). Age of onset and sexual orientation in transsexual males and females. *Journal of Sexual Medicine, 8*(3), 783–791.

Nielsen Company. (2010). *Report: Heavy drug ad spending doesn't pay off.* http://www.marketingcharts.com/television.

Nierenberg, A. A., Akiskal, H. S., Angst, J., Hirschfeld, R. M., Merikangas, K. R., Petukhova, M., & Kessler, R. C. (2010). Bipolar disorder with frequent mood episodes in the national comorbidity survey replication (NCS-R0). *Molecular Psychiatry, 15*(11), 1075–1087.

Nietzel, M. T., Bernstein, D. A., Milich, R. S., & Kramer, G. (2003). *Introduction to clinical psychology* (6th ed.). Upper Saddle River, NJ: Pearson Education.

NIH (National Institutes of Health). (2011). Herbal medicine. Retrieved on June 18, 2011 from http://www.nlm.nih.gov/medlineplus.herbalmedicine.html.

Nijinsky, V. (1936). *The diary of Vaslav Nijinsky.* New York: Simon & Schuster.

Nillni, Y. I., Rohan, K. J., & Zvolensky, M. J. (2012, August 25). The role of menstrual cycle phase and anxiety sensitivity in catastrophic misinterpretation of physical symptoms during a CO_2 challenge. *Archives of Women's Mental Health,* pp. 1–10.

NIMH (National Institute of Mental Health). (2004). *Depression and Cancer.* Bethesda, MD: Author.

NIMH (National Institute of Mental Health). (2004). *Depression and Heart Disease.* Bethesda, MD: Author.

NIMH (National Institute of Mental Health). (2004). *Depression and Stroke.* Bethesda, MD: Author.

NIMH (National Institute of Mental Health). (2010). *Questions and answers about the NIMH Treatment for Adolescents with Depression Study (TADS).* Retrieved on June 18, 2011, from www.nimh.nih.gov/trials/pracatical/tads/questions-and-answers.shtml.

NIMH (National Institute of Mental Health). (2010). *Schizophrenia.* Retrieved on July 28, 2011, from http://www.nimh/nih/gov/statistics/1SCHIZ.shtml.

NIMH (National Institute of Mental Health). (2010). *Use of mental health services and treatment among adults.* Retrieved January 19, 2011, from http://www.nimh.nih, gov/statistics/3USE_MT_ADULT.shtml.

NIMH (National Institute of Mental Health). (2011). *Agoraphobia among adults.* Bethesda, MD: Author.

NIMH (National Institute of Mental Health). (2011). *Army study to assess risk and resilience in servicee members: A partnership between NIMH and the U.S. Army.* Retrieved January 19, 2011, from http://www.nimh/nih/gov/index.shtml.

NIMH (National Institute for Mental Health). (2011, February 11). *Treatment for Adolescents with Depression Study (TADS).* www.nimh.nih.gov/trials/practical/tads.index.shtml.

NIMH (National Institute of Mental Heath). (2012). *Percentage of Americans with phobias.* Bethesda: MD: Author.

Ninan, P. T., & Dunlop, B. W. (2005). Neurobiology and ethiology of panic disorder. *Journal of Clinical Psychiatry, 66*(Suppl. 4), 3–7.

NINDS (National Institute of Neurological Disorders and Stroke) (2010). *Narcolepsy Fact Sheet.* Bethesda, MD: National Institutes of Health.

Niv, N., Shatkin, J. P., Hamilton, A. B., Unützer, J., Klap, R., & Young, A. S. (2010). The use of herbal medications and dietary supplements by people with mental illness. *Community Mental Health Journal, 46*(6), 563–569.

Nivoli, A. M. A., Colom, F., Murru, A., Pacchiarotti, I., Castro-Loli, P., González-Pinto, A., et al. (2011). New treatment guidelines for acute bipolar depression: A systematic review. *Journal of Affective Disorders, 129*(1-3), 14–26.

NMHA (National Mental Health Association). (1999, June 5). Poll. *U.S. Newswire.*

Nock, M. K., Kazdin, A. E., Hiripi, E., & Kessler, R. C. (2006). Prevalence, subtypes, and correlates of DSM-IV conduct disorder in the National Comorbidity Survey Replication. *Psychological Medicine, 36*(5), 699–710.

Noeker, M. (2004). Factitious disorder and factitious disorder by proxy. *Praxis der Kinderpsychologie und Kinderpsychiatrie, 53*(7), 449–467.

Noh, Y. (2009). Does unemployment increase suicide rates? the OECD panel evidence. *Journal of Economic Psychology, 30*(4), 575–582.

Nolen-Hoeksema, S. (1990). *Sex differences in depression.* Stanford, CA: Stanford University Press.

Nolen-Hoeksema, S. (2000). The role of rumination in depressive disorders and mixed anxiety/depressive symptoms. *Journal of Abnormal Psychology, 109,* 504–511.

Nolen-Hoeksema, S. (2002). Gender differences in depression. In I. H. Gotlib & C. L. Hammen (Eds.), *Handbook of depression* (pp. 492–509). New York: Guilford Press.

Nolen-Hoeksema, S., & Corte, C. (2004). Gender and self-regulation. In K. D. Vohs & R. F. Baumeister (Eds.), *Handbook of self-regulation: Research, theory, and applications* (pp. 411–421). New York: Guilford Press.

Nolen-Hoeksema, S., & Girgus, J. (1995). Explanatory style and achievement, depression, and gender differences in childhood and early adolescence. In G. Buchanan & M. Seligman (Eds.), *Explanatory style.* Hillsdale, NJ: Lawrence Erlbaum.

Nonacs, R. M. (2002, March 12). Postpartum psychiatric illness. *eMedicine Journal, 3*(3).

Nonacs, R. M. (2007). Postpartum depression. *eMedicine Clinical Reference.* Retrieved July 30, 2008, from http: /www.emedicine.com/med/topic 3408.htm.

Noonan, D. (2003, June 16). A healthy heart. *Newsweek, 141*(24), 48–52.

Norcross, J. C., & Beutler, L. (2011). Integrative psychotherapies. In R. J. Corsini & D. Wedding (Eds.), *Current psychotherapies* (9th ed.). Belmont, CA: Brooks/Cole.

Norcross, J. C., & Goldfried, M. R. (Eds.). (2005). *Handbook of psychotherapy integration* (2nd ed.). New York: Oxford University Press.

Nord, M., & Farde, L. (2011). Antipsychotic occupancy of dopamine receptors in schizophrenia. *CNS Neuroscience & Therapeutics, 17*(2), 97–103.

Nordal, K. (2010, January–February). Interview with R. Gill. Practice opportunities available despite shrinking dollars. *National Psychologist,* pp. 1–3.

Nordstrom, P., Samuelsson, M., & Asberg, M. (1995). Survival analysis of suicide risk after attempted suicide. *Acta Psychiatrica Scandinavica, 91*(5), 336–340.

Norko, M. A., & Baranoski, M. V. (2008). The prediction of violence: Detection of dangerousness. *Brief Treatment and Crisis Intervention, 8*(1), 73–91.

Norman, G. R., & Eva, K. W. (2010). Diagnostic error and clinical reasoning. *Medical Education, 44*(1), 94–100.

North, C. S. (2005). Somatoform disorders. In E. H. Rubin & C. F. Zorumski (Eds.), *Adult psychiatry* (2nd ed., pp. 261–274). Oxford, England: Blackwell Publishing.

North, C. S. (2010). A tale of two studies of two disasters: Comparing Psychological responses to disaster among Oklahoma City bombing survivors and Hurricane Katrina evacuees. *Rehabilitation Psychology, 55*(3), 241–246.

North, C. S., & Yutzy, S. H. (2005). Dissociative disorders, factitious disorders, and malingering. In E. H. Rubin & C. F. Zorumski (Eds.), *Adult psychiatry* (2nd ed., pp. 275–289). Oxford, England: Blackwell Publishing.

Norton, P. J., Paukert, A. L., & Sears, K. C. (2010). Adult measures. In D. W. Nangle, D. J. Hansen, C. A. Erdley, & P. J. Norton (Eds.), *Practitioner's guide to empirically based measures of social skills* (pp. 383–418). New York: Springer Publishing.

Novak, B., McDermott, B. E., Scott, C. L., & Guillory, S. (2007). Sex offenders and insanity: An examination of 42 individuals found not guilty by reason of insanity. *Journal of the American Academy of Psychiatry and the Law, 35*(4), 444–450.

NPD Group. (2008). Entertainment Trends Report. Cited by Mike Antonucci in *San Jose Mercury News,* April 3, 2008.

NSDUH (National Survey on Drug Use and Health). (2008). *National survey on drug use.* Washington, DC: Department of Health and Human Services, Substance Abuse and Mental Health Services Administration, Office of Applied Studies.

NSDUH (National Survey on Drug Use and Health). (2009, October 8). *Mental health support and self-help groups.* Retrieved on March 2, 2011, from www.oas.samhsa. gov/2k9/161/161MHSupportGroup.htm.

NSDUH (National Survey on Drug Use and Health). (2010). *Results from the 2009 National Survey on Drug Use and Health: Volume 1. Summary of national findings.* (Office of Applied Studies, NSDUH Series H-38a.) Rockville, MD: Substance Abuse and Mental Health Services Administration.

Nunes, E. V., Hennessy, G., & Selzer, J. (2010). Depression in patients with substance use disorders. In E. V. Nunes, J. Selzer, P. Levounis, & C. A. Davies (Eds.), *Substance dependence and co-occurring psychiatric disorders: Best practices for diagnosis and treatment* (pp. 1-1–1-36). Kingston, NJ: Civic Research Institute.

Nussbaum, R. L., & Ellis, C. E. (2003). Alzheimer's disease and Parkinson's disease. *New England Journal of Medicine, 348,* 1356–1364.

NVSR (National Vital Statistics Reports). (2010, August 9). *Births: Final data for 2007, 58*(24). Hyattsville, MD: National Center for Health Statistics.

NVSR (National Vital Statistics Reports). (2010). *Deaths: Final Data for 2007. National vital statistics reports, 58*(19). Hyattsville, MD: National Center for Health Statistics.

NVSR (National Vital Statistics Reports). (2011). *Deaths: Preliminary data for 2009. National vital statistics reports, 59*(4). Hyattsville, MD: National Center for Health Statistics.

Nwokike, J. (2005). Federal insanity acquittees. *Journal of the American Academy of Psychiatry and the Law, 33*(1), 126–128.

Nydegger, R. V., & Paludi, M. (2006). Obsessive-compulsive disorder: Diagnostic, treatment, gender, and cultural issues. In T. Plante (Ed.) *Mental disorders of the new millennium* (Vol. 3). New York: Praeger.

O'Brien, C., & Kampman, K. M. (2008). Antagonists of opioids. In H. D. Kleber & M. Galanter (Eds.), *The American Psychiatric Publishing textbook of substance abuse treatment* (4th ed., pp. 325–329). Arlington, VA: American Psychiatric Publishing.

O'Brien, C. P., & Lyons, F. (2000). Alcohol and the athlete. *Sports Medicine, 29,* 295–300.

O'Brien, C. P., O'Brien, T. J., Mintz, J., & Brady, J. P. (1975). Conditioning of narcotic abstinence symptoms in human subjects. *Drug and Alcohol Dependence, 1,* 115–123.

O'Brien, W. B., Piedrahita, J. G., & Bacatan, F. P., Jr. (2011). The therapeutic community. In J. H. Lowinson & P. Ruiz (Eds.), *Substance abuse: A comprehensive textbook, fifth edition.* Philadelphia, PA: Lippincott, Williams, & Wilkins.

O'Brien, W. H., & Carhart, V. (2011). Functional analysis in behavioral medicine. *European Journal of Psychological Assessment, 27*(1), 4–16.

Obulesu, M., Venu, R., & Somashekhar, R. (2011). Tau mediated neurodegeneration: An insight into Alzheimer's disease pathology. *Neurochemical Research, 36*(8), 1329–1335.

O'Connor, B. P. (2008). Other personality disorders. In M. Hersen & J. Rosqvist (Eds.), *Handbook of psychological assessment, case conceptualization and treatment: Vol. 1: Adults* (pp. 438–462). Hoboken, NJ: John Wiley & Sons.

Odlaug, B. L., & Grant, J. E. (2010). Pathologic skin picking. *The American Journal of Drug and Alcohol Abuse, 36*(5), 296–303.

Odlaug, B. L., & Grant, J. E. (2012). Pathological skin picking. In J. E. Grant, D. J. Stein, D. W. Woods & N. J. Keuthen (Eds.), *Trichotillomania, skin picking, and other body-focused repetitive behaviors* (pp. 21–41). Arlington, VA: American Psychiatric Publishing, Inc.

Odlaug, B. L. & Grant, J. E. (2012). Two cases of obsessive-compulsive disorder. *Psychiatric Times.*

O'Donohue, W., Fowler, K. A., & Lilienfeld, S. O. (Eds.). (2007). *Personality disorders: Toward the DSM-V.* Los Angeles: Sage Publications.

O'Donovan, M. C., & Owen, M. J. (2011). Genetic associations in schizophrenia. In D. R. Weinberg & P. Harrison (Eds.), *Schizophrenia* (pp. 269–288). Hoboken, NJ: Wiley-Blackwell.

OFWW. (2004, December 25). Drivers admit to experiencing road rage. *Obesity, Fitness & Wellness Week,* 1209.

Ogloff, J. R. P., Schweighofer, A., Turnbull, S. D., & Whittemore, K. (1992). Empirical research regarding the insanity defense: How much do we really know? In J. R. P. Ogloff (Ed.), *Law and psychology: The broadening of the discipline* (pp. 171–210). Durham, NC: Carolina Academic Press.

O'Hanlon, L. (2010, August 31). Chilean miners "suffering like soldiers." *Discovery News.*

O'Hara, M. W. (2003). Postpartum depression. *Clinician's Research Digest,* (Supp. Bulletin 29).

O'Hara, M. W., Schiller, C. E., & Stuart, S. (2010). Interpersonal psychotherapy and relapse prevention for depression. In C. S. Richards & J. G. Perri (Eds.), *Relapse prevention for depression* (pp. 77–97). Washington, DC: American Psychological Association.

Ohayon, M. M., Lemoine, P., Arnaud-Briant, V., & Dreyfus, M. (2002). Prevalence and consequenstes of sleep disorders in a shift worker population. *Journal of Psychosomatic Research, 53*(1), 577–583.

Ohman, A., & Mineka, S. (2003). The malicious serpent: Snakes as a prototypical stimulus for an evolved module of fear. *Current Directions in Psychological Science, 12*(1), 5–9.

Oinas-Kukkonen, H. & Mantila, L. (2009). Lisa, Lisa the machine says I have performed an illegal action. Should I tell the police? A survey and observations of inexperienced elderly internet users. Proceedings of the Southern Association for Information Systems Conference. Georgia Southern University, 146-151.

OJJDP (Office of Juvenile Justice and Delinquency Prevention). (2010). *SMART office coordinates nation's efforts to register and monitor sex offenders.* Retrieved on July 3, 2011, from http://psycnet.apa.org/index.

Okawa, J. B., & Hauss, R. B. (2007). The trauma of politically motivated torture. In E. K. Carll (Ed.), *Trauma psychology: Issues in violence, disaster, health, and illness* (Vol. 1). Westport, CT: Praeger Publishers.

Okello, E. S., & Ekblad, S. (2006). Lay concepts of depression among the Baganda of Uganda: A pilot study. *Transcultural Psychiatry, 43*(2), 287–313.

Oksenberg, J. R., & Hauser, S. L. (2010). Mapping the human genome with newfound precision. *Annals of Neurology, 67*(6), A8–A10.

Olatunji, B. O., Huijding, J., de Jong, P. J., & Smits, J. A. J. (2011). The relative contributions of fear and disgust reductions to improvements in spider phobia following exposure-based treatment. *Journal of Behavior Therapy and Experimental Psychiatry, 42*(1), 117–121.

Olivarez-Giles, N. (2011). Twitter, launched five years ago, delivers 350 billion tweets a day. *Media Mentions.* Washington, DC: Pew Internet & American Life Project.

Oliver, R. J., Spilsbury, J. C., Osiecki, S. S., Denihan, W. M., & Zureick. J. L. (2008). Brief report: Preliminary results of a suicide awareness mass media campaign in Cuyahoga County, Ohio. *Suicide and Life-Threatening Behavior, 38*(2), 245–249.

Olmsted, M. P., Kaplan, A. S., & Rockert, W. (1994). Rate and prediction of relapse in bulimia nervosa. *American Journal of Psychiatry, 151*(5), 738–743.

Olmsted, M. P., Kaplan, A. S., & Rockert, W. (2005). Defining remission and relapse in bulimia nervosa. *International Journal of Eating Disorders, 38*(1), 1–6.

Olmsted, M. P., McFarlane, T. L., Carter, J. C., Trottier, K., Woodside, D. B., & Dimitropoulos, G. (2010). Inpatient and day hospital treatment for anorexia nervosa. In C. M. Grilo & J. E. Mitchell (Eds.), *The treatment of eating disorders: A clinical handbook* (pp. 198–211). New York: Guilford Press.

Olson, D. (2011). FACES IV and the Circumplex Model: Validation study. *Journal of Marital and Family Therapy, 37*(1), 64–80.

Olson, S. L., & Sameroff A. J. (Eds.). (2009). *Biopsychosocial regulatory processes in the development of childhood behavioral problems.* New York: Cambridge University Press.

Olsson, S. E., & Moller, A. R. (2003). On the incidence and sex ratio of transsexualism in Sweden. *Archives of Sexual Behavior, 32*(4), 381–386.

O'Malley, S. S., Jaffe, A. J., Chang, G., Schottenfeld, R., Meyer, R., & Rounsaville, B. (1992). Naltrexone and coping skills therapy for alcohol dependence. *Archives of General Psychiatry, 49,* 881–888.

O'Malley, S. S., Jaffe, A. J., Rode, S., & Rounsaville, B. J. (1996). Experience of a "slip" among alcoholics treated with naltrexone or placebo. *American Journal of Psychiatry, 153,* 281–283.

O'Malley, S. S., Krishnan-Sarin, S., Farren, C., & O'Connor, P. G. (2000). Naltrexone-induced nausea in patients treated for alcohol dependence: Clinical predictors and evidence for opioid-mediated effects. *Journal of Clinical Psychopharmacology, 20*(1), 69–76.

Öncü, F., Türkcan, S., Canbek, Ö., Yessilbursa, D., & Uygur, N. (2009). Fetishism and kleptomania: A case report in forensic psychiatry. *Nöropsikiyatri Arsivi/Archives of Neuropsychiatry, 46*(3), 125–128.

O'Neill, H. (2012, December 15). No rise in mass killings, but their impact is huge. *Associated Press.*

ONDCP (Office of National Drug Control Policy). (2008). *Drug facts.*

Onen, S. H., Onen, F., Mangeon, J. P., Abidi, H., Courpron, P., & Schmidt, J. (2005). Alcohol abuse and dependence in elderly emergency department patients. *Archives of Gerontology and Geriatrics, 41*(2), 191–200.

Opinion Research Corporation. (2004, May 17). National Survey Press Release.

Opinion Research Corporation Poll/CNN. (2011, March 18–20). Disaster preparedness and relief. *PollingReport.com.*

Oquendo, M. A., Dragatsi, D., Harkavy-Friedman, J., Dervic, K., Currier, D., Burke, A. K., et al. (2005). Protective factors against suicidal behavior in Latinos. *Journal of Nervous and Mental Disease, 193*(7), 438–443.

Oquendo, M. A., Lizardi, D., Greenwald. S., Weissman, M. M., & Mann, J. J. (2004). Rates of lifetime suicide attempt and rates of lifetime major depression in different ethnic groups in the United States. *Acta Psychiatrica Scandinavica, 110*(6), 446–451.

Oquendo, M. A., Placidi, G. P. A., Malone, K. M., Campbell, C., Keilp, J., Brodsky, B., et al. (2003). Positron emission tomography of regional brain metabolic responses to a serotonergic challenge and lethality of suicide attempts in major depression. *Archives of General Psychiatry, 60*(1), 14–22.

Oquendo, M. A., Russo, S. A., Underwood, M. D., Kassir, S. A., Ellis, S. P., Mann, J. J., & Arango, V. (2006). Higher post mortem prefrontal 5-HT2A receptor binding correlates with lifetime aggression in suicide. *Biological Psychiatry, 59,* 235–243.

Orbach, I., & Iohan, M. (2007). Stress, distress, emotional regulation and suicide attempts in female adolescents. In R. Tatarelli, M. Pompili, & P. Girardi (Eds.), *Suicide in psychiatric disorders.* New York: Nova Science Publishers.

ORR (Office of Refugee Resettlement). (2006). *Office of Refugee Resettlement (ORR) Services for Survivors of Torture Program: Program description.* Retrieved October 5, 2006, from http://www.acf.hhs.gov/programs/orr/programs/services_survivors_torture.htm.

ORR (Office of Refugee Resettlement). (2011). *Services for survivors of torture.* Retrieved on May 28, 2011, from www.acf.hhs.gov/programs/orr/programs/services_survivors_torture.htm.

Orsillo, S. M., & Roemer, L. (2011). *The mindful way through anxiety: Break free from chronic worry and reclaim your life.* New York: Guilford Press.

Oshima, I., Mino, Y., & Inomata, Y. (2005). Effects of environmental deprivation on negative symptoms of schizophrenia: A nationwide survey in Japan's psychiatric hospitals. *Psychiatry Research, 136*(2–3), 163–171.

Osman, A., Bagge, C. L., Freedenthal, S., Gutierrez, P. M., & Emmerich, A. (2011). Development and evaluation of the Social Anxiety and Depression Life Interference-24 (SADLI-24) inventory. *Journal of Clinical Psychology, 67*(1), 82–98.

Osman, A., Barrios, F. X., Gutierrez, P. M., Williams, J. E., & Bailey, J. (2008). Psychometric properties of the Beck Depression Inventory-II in nonclinical adolescent samples. *Journal of Clinical Psychology, 64*(10), 83–102.

Ostrove, N. M. (2001, July 24). Statement before the subcommittee on consumer affairs, foreign commerce, and tourism, Senate committee on commerce, science, and transportation. Retrieved from www.fda.gov.

Ott, J., van Trotsenburg, M., Kaufmann, U., Schrögendorfer, K., Haslik, W., Huber, J. C., & Wenzl, R. (2010). Combined hysterectomy/salpingo-oophorectomy and mastectomy is a safe and valuable procedure for female-to-male transsexuals. *Journal of Sexual Medicine, 7*(6), 2130–2138.

Otten, K. L. (2004). An analysis of a classwide self-monitoring approach to improve the behavior of elementary students with severe emotional and behavioral disorders. *Dissertation Abstracts International: Section A: Humanities and Social Sciences, 65*(3-A), 893.

Otto, R. K. & Douglas, K. S. (Eds.). (2010). *Handbook of violence risk assessment.* New York: Routledge/Taylor & Francis Group.

Ouellette, S. C., & DiPlacido, J. (2001). Personality's role in the protection and enhancement of health: Where the research has been, where it is stuck, how it might move. In A. Baum, T. A. Revenson, & J. E. Singer (Eds.), *Handbook of health psychology.* Mahwah, NJ: Lawrence Erlbaum.

Overton, D. (1964). State-dependent or "dissociated" learning produced with pentobarbital. *Journal of Comparative Physiology and Psychology, 57,* 3–12.

Overton, D. (1966). State-dependent learning produced by depressant and atropine-like drugs. *Psychopharmacologia, 10,* 6–31.

Ovsiew, F. (2006). Hysteria in neurological practice: The somatoform and dissociative disorders. In D. V. Jeste & J. H. Friedman (Eds.), *Psychiatry for neurologists* (pp. 67–80). Totowa, NJ: Humana Press.

Owen, F., Crow, T. J., & Poulter, M. (1987). Central dopaminergic mechanisms in schizophrenia. *Acta Psychiatrica Belgium, 87*(5), 552–565.

Owen, F., Crow, T. J., Poulter, M., & et al. (1978). Increased dopamine receptor sensitivity in schizophrenia. *Lancet, 2,* 223–226.

Owen-Howard, M. (2001). Pharmacological aversion treatment of alcohol dependence. I. Production and prediction of conditioned alcohol aversion. *American Journal of Drug and Alcohol Abuse, 27*(3), 561–585.

Oyama, H., Sakashita, T., Hojo, K., Ono, Y., Watanabe, N., Takizawa, T., et al. (2010). A community-based survey and screening for depression in the elderly: The short-term effect on suicide risk in Japan. *Crisis: The Journal of Crisis Intervention and Suicide Prevention, 31*(2), 100–108.

Ozden, A., & Canat, S. (1999). Factitious hemoptysis. *Journal of American Child and Adolescent Psychiatry*, 38, 356–357.

Ozer, E. J. (2005). The impact of violence on urban adolescents: Longitudinal effects of perceived school connection and family support. *Journal of Adolescent Research, 20*(2), 167–192.

Pacala, J. T. (2010). Preventive and anticipatory care. In H. M. Fillit, K. Rockwood, & K. Woodhouse. (Eds.), *Brocklehurst's textbook of geriatric medicine and gerontology, 7th edition.* Philadelphia, PA: Saunders Publishers.

Pace, T. W. W., & Heim, C. M. (2011). A short review on the psychoneuroimmunology of posttraumatic stress disorder: From risk factors to medical comorbidities. *Brain, Behavior, and Immunity, 25*(1), 6–13.

Paczynski, R. P., & Gold, M. S. (2011). Cocaine and crack. In J. H. Lowinson & P. Ruiz (Eds.), *Substance abuse: A comprehensive textbook, fifth edition.* Philadelphia, PA: Lippincott, Williams, & Wilkins.

Padwa, L. (1996). *Everything you pretend to know and are afraid someone will ask.* New York: Penguin.

Palermo, G. B., Kocsis, R. N., & Slovenko, R. (Eds.). (2005). *Offender profiling: An introduction to the sociopsychological analysis of violent crime.* Springfield, IL: Charles C. Thomas.

Palijan, T. Z., Radeljak, S., Kovac, M., & Kovacevic, D. (2010). Relationship between comorbidity and violence risk assessment in forensic psychiatry—The implication of neuroimaging studies. *Psychiatria Danubina, 22*(2), 253–256.

Pallanti, S., Bernardi, S., Allen, A., & Hollander, E. (2010). Serotonin function in pathological gambling: Blunted growth hormone response to sumatriptan. *Journal of Psychopharmacology, 24*(12), 1802–1809.

Pallanti, S., Haznedar, M. M., Hollander, E., LiCalzi, E. M., Bernardi, S., Newmark, R., & Buchsbaum, M. S. (2010). Basal ganglia activity in pathological gambling: A fluorodeoxyglucose-positron emission tomography study. *Neuropsychobiology, 62*(2), 132–138.

Pandina, R. J., Johnson, V. L., & White, H. R. (2010). Peer influences on substance use during adolescence and emerging adulthood. In L. Scheier (Ed.), *Handbook of drug use etiology: Theory, methods, and empirical findings* (pp. 383–401). Washington, DC: American Psychological Association.

Panjari M., Bell, R. J., & Davis, S. R. (2011). Sexual function after breast cancer. *Journal of Sexual Medicine, 8*(1), 294–302.

Pankevich, D. E., Teegarden, S. L., Hedin, A. D., Jensen, C. L., & Bale, T. L. (2010). Caloric restriction experience reprograms stress and orexigenic pathways and promotes binge eating. *Journal of Neuroscience, 30*(48). 16399–16407.

Papadimitriou, G. N., Calabrese, J. R., Dikeos, D. G., & Christodoulou, G. N. (2005). Rapid cycling bipolar disorder: Biology and pathogenesis. *International Journal of Neuropsychopharmacology, 89*(2), 281–292.

Papastavrou, E., Kalokerinou, A., Papacostas, S. S., Tsangari, H., & Sourtzi, P. (2007). Caring for a relative with dementia: Family caregiver burden. *Journal of Advanced Nursing, 58*(5), 446–457.

Papolos, D., Hennen, J., & Cockerham, M. S. (2005). Factors associated with parent-reported suicide threats by children and adolescents with community-diagnosed bipolar disorder. *Journal of Affective Disorders, 86*(2–3), 267–275.

Paris, J. (1991). Personality disorders, parasuicide, and culture. *Transcultural Psychiatry Research and Review, 28*(1), 25–39.

Paris, J. (2001). Cultural risk factors in personality disorders. In J. F. Schumaker & T. Ward (Eds.), *Cultural cognition and psychopathology.* Westport, CT: Praeger.

Paris, J. (2001). Psychosocial adversity. In W. J. Livesley (Ed.), *Handbook of personality disorders: Theory, research, and treatment* (pp. 231–241). New York: Guilford Press.

Paris, J. (2005). Borderline personality disorder. *Canadian Medical Association Journal, 172*(12), 1579–1583.

Paris, J. (2010). Estimating the prevalence of personality disorders in the community. *Journal of Personality Disorders, 24*(4), 405–411.

Paris, J. (2010). *Treatment of borderline personality disorder: A guide to evidence-based practice.* New York: Guilford Press.

Paris, J. (2011). Reducing suicide risk in personality disorders: The state of current evidence. In M. Pompili & R. Tatarelli (Eds.), *Evidence-based* *practice in suicidology: A source book* (pp. 339–347). Cambridge MA: Hogrefe Publishing.

Parish, B. S., & Yutsy, S. H. (2011). Somatoform disorders. In R. E. Hales, S. C. Yudofsky, & G. O. Gabbard, *Essentials of psychiatry* (3rd ed., pp. 229–254). Arlington, VA: American Psychiatric Publishing.

Park, S-H., Kim, J-J., Kim, C-H., Kim, J-H., & Lee, K-H. (2011). Sustained attention in the context of emotional processing in patients with schizophrenia. *Psychiatry Research, 187*(1-2), 18–23.

Parker, G. (1992). Early environment. In E. S. Paykel (Ed.), *Handbook of affective disorders.* New York: Guilford Press.

Parker, G. B., & Brotchie, H. L. (2004). From diathesis to dimorphism: The biology of gender differences in depression. *Journal of Nervous and Mental Disease, 192*(3), 210–216.

Parker, G., Hadzi-Pavlovic, D., Greenwald, S., & Weissman, M. (1995). Low parental care as a risk factor to lifetime depression in a community sample. *Journal of Affective Disorders, 33*(3), 173–180.

Parker, G., & Hyett, M. (2010). Screening for depression in medical settings: Are specific scales useful? In A. J. Mitchell & J. C. Coyne (Eds.), *Screening for depression in clinical practice: An evidence-based guide* (pp. 191–201). New York: Oxford University Press.

Parker, S., Nichter, M., Vuckovic, N., Sims, C., & Ritenbaugh, C. (1995). Body image and weight concerns among African American and white adolescent females: Differences that make a difference. *Human Organization, 54*(2), 103–114.

Patel, D. R., & Greydanus, D. E. (2010). Pharmacotherapy of anxiety disorders in children and adolescents. *International Journal of Child and Adolescent Health, 3*(2), 197–205.

Patel, L., & Grossberg, G. T. (2011). Combination therapy for Alzheimer's disease. *Drugs & Aging, 28*(7), 539–546.

Paton, C., & Beer, D. (2001). Caffeine: The forgotten variable. *International Journal of Psychiatry in Clinical Practice, 5*(4), 231–236.

Patrick, C. J. (2007). Antisocial personality disorder and psychopathy. In W. O'Donohue, K. A. Fowler, & S. O. Lilienfeld (Eds.). *Personality disorders: Toward the DSM-V.* Los Angeles: Sage Publications.

Patterson, D. (2011). The linkage between secondary victimization by law enforcement and rape case outcomes. *Journal of Interpersonal Violence, 26*(2), 328–347.

Patterson, P. H. (2012). Animal models of the maternal infection risk factor for schizophrenia. In A. S. Brown & P. H. Patterson (Eds.), *The origins of schizophrenia* (pp. 255–281). New York: Columbia University Press.

Patton, J. R., Polloway, E. A., & Smith, T. E. C. (2000). Educating students with mild mental retardation. *Focus on Autism and Other Developmental Disabilities, 15*(2), 80–89.

Paul, G. L. (1967). The strategy of outcome research in psychotherapy. *Journal of Counseling Psychology, 31,* 109–118.

Paul, G. L. (2000). Milieu therapy. In A. E. Kazdin (Ed.), *Encyclopedia of psychology* (Vol. 5, pp. 250–252). New York: Oxford University Press.

Paul, G. L., & Lentz, R. (1977). *Psychosocial treatment of the chronic mental patient.* Cambridge, MA: Harvard University Press.

Paul, R., & Gilbert, K. (2011). Development of language and communication. In E. Hollander, A. Kolevzon & J. T. Coyle (Eds.), *Textbook of autism*

spectrum disorders. (pp. 147–157) Arlington, VA: American Psychiatric Publishing, Inc.

Pauls, C. A., & Stemmler, G. (2003). Repressive and defensive coping during fear and anger. *Emotion, 3*(3), 284–302.

Paxton, S. J., & McLean, S. A. (2010). Treatment for body-image disturbances. In C. M. Grilo & J. E. Mitchell (Eds.), *The treatment of eating disorders: A clinical handbook* (pp. 471–486). New York: Guilford Press.

Paykel, E. S. (2003). Life events and affective disorders. *Acta Psychiatrica Scandinavica, 108*(Suppl. 418), 61–66.

Paykel, E. S. (2003). Life events: Effects and genesis. *Psychological Medicine, 33*(7), 1145–1148.

Paykel, E. S. (2006). Editorials: Depression: Major problem for public health. *Epidemiologia e Psichiatria Sociale, 15*(1), 4–10.

Paykel, E. S., & Cooper, Z. (1992). Life events and social stress. In E. S. Paykel (Ed.), *Handbook of affective disorders.* New York: Guilford Press.

Payne, A. F. (1928). *Sentence completion.* New York: New York Guidance Clinics.

Pechnick, R. N., & Cunningham, K. A. (2011). Hallucinogens. In J. H. Lowinson & P. Ruiz (Eds.), *Substance abuse: A comprehensive textbook, fifth edition.* Philadelphia, PA: Lippincott, Williams, & Wilkins.

Pekkanen, J. (2002, July). Dangerous minds. *Washingtonian.*

Pekkanen, J. (2007). Involuntary commitment is essential. In A. Quigley (Ed.), *Current controversies: Mental health.* Detroit: Greenhaven Press/ Thomson Gale.

Pellegrini, A. D. (2011). "In the eye of the beholder": Sex bias in observations and ratings of children's aggression. *Educational Researcher, 40*(6), 281–286.

Pendery, M. L., Maltzman, I. M., & West, L. J. (1982). Controlled drinking by alcoholics? New findings and a reevaluation of a major affirmative study. *Science, 217*(4555), 169–175.

Penn, D. L., & Nowlin-Drummond, A. (2001). Politically correct labels and schizophrenia: A rose by any other name? *Schizophrenia Bulletin, 27*(2), 197–203.

Perdeci, Z., Gulsun, M., Celik, C., Erdem, M., Ozdemir, B., Ozdag, F., & Kilic, S. (2010). Aggression and the event-related potentials in antisocial personality disorder. *Bulletin of Clinical Psychopharmacology, 20*(4), 300–306.

Perez-Alvarez, M., Garcia-Montes, J. M., Perona-Garcelan, S., & Vallina-Fernandez, O. (2008). Changing relationships with voices: New therapeutic perspectives for treating hallucinations. *Clinical Psychology and Psychotherapy, 15,* 75–85.

Perilla, J. L., Norris, F. H., & Lavizzo, E. A. (2002). Ethnicity, culture, and disaster response: Identifying and explaining ethnic differences in PTSD six months after Hurricane Andrew. *Journal of Social and Clinical Psychology, 21,* 20–45.

Perkins, D. O., & Lieberman, J. A. (2012). Prodrome and first episode. In J. A. Lieberman, T. S. Stroup, & D. O. Perkins (Eds.), *Essentials of schizophrenia* (pp. 57–71). Arlington, VA: American Psychiatric Publishing.

Perkins, H. W. (2002). Surveying the damage: A review of research on consequences of alcohol misuse in college populations. *Journal of Alcohol Studies,* (Suppl. 14), 91–100.

Perlin, M. L. (2000). *The hidden prejudice: Mental disability on trial.* Washington, DC: American Psychological Association.

Perlin, M. L. (2004). "Salvation" or a "lethal dose"? Attitudes and advocacy in right to refuse treatment cases. *Journal of Forensic Psychology Practice, 4*(4), 51–69.

Perls, T. T. (2010). Successful aging: The centenarians. In H. M. Fillit, K. Rockwood, & K. Woodhouse. (Eds.), *Brocklehurst's textbook of geriatric medicine and gerontology, 7th edition.* Philadelphia, PA: Saunders Publishers.

Perry, J. C. (2005). Dependent personality disorder. In G. O. Gabbard, J. S. Beck & J. Holmes (Eds.), *Oxford textbook of psychotherapy* (pp. 321–328). New York: Oxford University Press.

Perry, J. D. C., & Perry, J. C. (2004). Conflicts, defenses and the stability of narcissistic personality features. *Psychiatry: Interpersonal and Biological Processes, 67*(4), 310–330.

Perugi, G., Medda, P., Zanello, S., Toni, C., & Cassano, G. B. (2012). Episode length and mixed features as predictors of ECT nonresponse in patients with medication-resistant major depression. *Brain Stimulation, 5*(1), 18–24.

Perugi, G., Medda, P., Zanello, S., Toni, C., & Cassano, G. B. (2011, March 21). Episode length and mixed features as predictors of ect nonresponse in patients with medication-resistant major depression. *Brain Stimulation.*

Peteet, J. R., Lu, F. G., & Narrow, W. E. (Eds.). (2011). *Religious and spiritual issues in psychiatric diagnosis: A research agenda for DSM-V.* Washington, DC: American Psychiatric Association.

Peterlin, B. L., Rosso, A. L., Sheftell, F. D., Libon, D. J., Mossey, J. M., Merikangas, K. R. (2011). Post-traumatic stress disorder, drug abuse and migraine: New findings from the National Comorbidity Survey Replication (NCS-R). *Cephalalgia, 31*(2), 235–244.

Peters, R. H., Sherman, P. B., & Osher, F. C. (2008). Treatment in jails and prisons. In K. T. Mueser & D. V. Jeste (Eds.), *Clinical handbook of schizophrenia* (pp. 354–364). New York: Guilford Press.

Peters-Scheffer, N., Didden, R., Korzilius, H., & Sturmey, P. (2011). A meta-analytic study on the effectiveness of comprehensive ABA-based early intervention programs for children with autism spectrum disorders. *Research in Autism Spectrum Disorders, 5*(1), 60–69.

Petersen, J. L., & Hyde, J. S. (2011). Gender differences in sexual attitudes and behaviors: A review of meta-analytic results and large datasets. *Journal of Sex Research, 48*(2-3), 149–165.

Petersen, L., Mortensen, P. B., & Pedersen, C. B. (2011). Paternal age at birth of first child and risk of schizophrenia. *American Journal of Psychiatry, 168*(1), 82–88.

Peterson, C., Ruch, W., Beermann, U., Park, N., & Seligman, M. E. P. (2007). Strengths of character, orientations to happiness, and life satisfaction. *Journal of Positive Psychology, 2*(3), 149–156.

Peterson, E., Moller, A., Doudet, D. J., Bailey, C. J., Hansen, K. V., Rodell, A., Linnet, J., & Giedde, A. (2010). Pathological gambling: Relation of skin conductance response to dopaminergic neurotransmission and sensation-seeking. *European Neuropsychopharmacology, 20*(11), 766–775.

Peterson, L., & Roberts, M. C. (1991). Treatment of children's problems. In C. E. Walker (Ed.), *Clinical psychology: Historical and research foundations.* New York: Plenum Press.

Peterson, R. L., & Pennington, B. F. (2010). Reading disability. In K. O. Yeates, M. D. Ris,

H. G. Taylor & B. F. Pennington (Eds.), *Pediatric neuropsychology: Research, theory, and practice* (2nd ed., pp. 324–362) New York: Guilford Press.

Petrie, K. J., Fontanilla, I., Thomas, M. G., Booth, R. J., & Pennebaker, J. W. (2004). Effect of written emotional expression on immune function in patients with human immunodeficiency virus infection: A ran-domized trial. *Psychosomatic Medicine, 66*(2), 272–275.

Petrila, J. (2010). Rights-based legalism and the limits of mental health law: The United States of America's experience. In B. McSherry & P. Weller (Eds.), *Rethinking rights-based mental health law* (pp. 357–378). Portland, OR: Hart Publishing.

Petrocelli, J. V. (2002). Effectiveness of group cognitive-behavioral therapy for general symptomatology: A meta-analysis. *Journal for Specialists in Group Work, 27*(1), 92–115.

Petrovich, G. D. (2011). Learning and the motivation to eat: Forebrain circuitry. *Physiology & Behavior, 104*(4), 582–589.

Pew Internet. (2010). Most teens text friends daily: The % of teens who contact their friends daily by different methods, by age. *Project surveys.* Washington, DC: Pew Internet & American Life Project.

Pew Research Center. (2009). The harried life of the working mother. *Pew Social & Demographic Trends.* Retrieved from http://www.pewsocialtrends.org/2009/10/09.

Pew Research Center. (2010). *8% of online Americans use Twitter.* Washington, DC: author.

Pew Research Center. (2010). *Mobile Access 2010.* Washington, DC: author.

Pew Research Center. (2011). Twitter, launched five years ago, delivers 350 billion tweets a day. *Media Mentions.* Washington, DC: Pew Internet & American Life Project.

Pfeffer, C. R. (1986). *The suicidal child.* New York: Guilford Press.

Pfeffer, C. R. (2003). Assessing suicidal behavior in children and adolescents. In R. A. King & A. Apter (Eds.), *Suicide in children and adolescents* (pp. 211–226). Cambridge, England: Cambridge University Press.

Pfeiffer, P. N., Valenstein, M., Hoggatt, K. J., Ganoczy, D., Maixner, D., Miller, E. M., & Zivin, K. (2011). Electroconvulsive therapy for major depression within the Veterans Health Administration. *Journal of Affective Disorders, 130*(1-2), 21–25.

Pham, A. V., Carlson, J. S., & Koschiulek, J. F. (2010). Ethnic differences in parental beliefs of attention-deficit/hyperactivity disorder and treatment. *Journal of Attention Disorders, 13*(6), 584–591.

Phillips, D. P. (1974). The influence of suggestion on suicide: Substantive and theoretical implications of the *Werther* effect. *American Sociological Review, 39,* 340–354.

Phillips, D. P., & Ruth, T. E. (1993). Adequacy of official suicide statistics for scientific research and public policy. *Suicide and Life-Threatening Behavior, 23*(4), 307–319.

Phillips, K. A. (2005). Olanzapine augmentation of fluoxetine in body dysmorphic disorder. *American Journal of Psychiatry, 162*(5), 1022.

Phillips, K. A. (2005). Placebo-controlled study of pimozide augmentation of fluoxetine in body dysmorphic disorder. *American Journal of Psychiatry, 162*(2), 377–379.

Phillips, K. A. (2010). Pharmacotherapy for body dysmorphic disorder. *Psychiatric Annals, 40*(7), 325–332.

Phillips, K. A., & Castle, D. J. (2002). Body dysmorphic disorder. In D. J. Castle & K. A. Phillips (Eds.), *Disorders of body image.* Petersfield, England: Wrightson Biomedical Publishing, Ltd.

Phillips, K. A., Fallon, B. A., & King, T. (2008). Somatoform and factitious disorders and malingering measures. In A. J. Rush, Jr., M. B. First, & D. Blacker (Eds.), *Handbook of psychiatric measures* (2nd ed., pp. 559–585). Arlington, VA: American Psychiatric Publishing.

Phillips, K. A., McElroy, S. L., Keck, P. E., Pope, H. G., et al. (1993). Body dysmorphic disorder: 30 cases of imagined ugliness. *American Journal of Psychiatry, 150*(2), 302–308.

Phillips, K. A., & Rogers, J. (2011). Cognitive-behavioral therapy for youth with body dysmorphic disorder: Current status and future directions. *Child and Adolescent Psychiatric Clinics of North America, 20*(2), 287–304.

Phillips, M. L. (2011). Treating postpartum depression. *Monitor on Psychology, 42*(2).

Pickel, K. L. (2004). When a lie becomes the truth: The effects of self-generated misinformation on eyewitness memory. *Memory, 12*(1), 14–26.

Pickover, C. A. (1999). *Strange brains and genius: The secret lives of eccentric scientists and madmen.* New York: HarperCollins/Quill.

Pierce, K., & Courchesne, E. (2001). Evidence for a cerebellar role in reduced exploration and stereotyped behavior in autism. *Biological Psychiatry, 49*(8), 655–664.

Pierce, K., & Courchesne, E. (2002). "A further support to the hypothesis of a link between serotonin, autism and the cerebellum": Reply. *Biological Psychiatry, 52*(2), 143.

Pierre, J. M. (2010). The borders of mental disorder in psychiatry and the DSM: Past, present, and future. *Journal of Psychiatric Practice, 16*(6), 375–386.

Pigott, H. E., Leventhal, A. M., Alter, G. S., & Boren, J. J. (2010). Efficacy and effectiveness of antidepressants: Current status of research. *Psychotherapy and Psychosomatics, 79*(5), 267–279.

Pike, K. M., Carter, J. C., & Olmsted, M. P. (2010). Cognitive-behavioral therapy for anorexia nervosa. In C. M. Grilo & J. E. Mitchell (Eds.), *The treatment of eating disorders: A clinical handbook* (pp. 83–107). New York: Guilford Press.

Pilecki, B., & McKay, D. (2011). Cognitive behavioral models of phobias and pervasive anxiety. In D McKay & E. A. Storch (Eds.), *Handbook of child and adolescent anxiety disorders* (pp. 39–48). New York: Springer Science & Business Media.

Pinals, D. A., & Mossman, D. (2012). *Evaluation for civil commitment: Best practices in forensic mental health assessment.* New York: Oxford University Press.

Pinals, D. A., Packer, I., Fisher, B., & Roy, K. (2004). Relationship between race and ethnicity and forensic clinical triage dispositions. *Psychiatric Services 55,* 873–878.

Pincus, D. (2012). *Complex biopsychosocial dynamics, behavioral medicine, and psychotherapy.* Abstracts to the International Nonlinear Science Conference, University of Barcelona Spain.

Pines, W. L. (1999). A history and perspective on direct-to-consumer promotion. *Food and Drug Law Journal, 54,* 489–518.

Pinkham, A. E., Mueser, K. T., Penn, D., Glynn, S. M., McGurk, S. R., & Addington, J. (2012). Social and functional impairments. In J. A. Lieberman, T. S. Stroup, & D. O. Perkins (Eds.), *Essentials of schizophrenia* (pp. 93–130). Arlington, VA: American Psychiatric Publishing.

Pinquart, M., & Sörensen, S. (2011). Spouses, adult children, and children-in-law as caregivers of older adults: A meta-analytic comparison. *Psychology and Aging, 26*(1), 1–14.

Pinto, A., Eisen, J. L., Mancebo, M. C., & Rasmussen, S. A. (2008). Obsessive-compulsive personality disorder. In J. S. Abramowitz, D. McKay, & S. Taylor (Eds.), *Obsessive-compulsive disorder: Subtypes and spectrum conditions.* Oxford, England: Elsevier.

Pipe, R. T. (2010). Something for everyone: Busty Latin anal nurses in leather and glasses. In D. Monroe (Ed.), *Porn: How to think with kink. Philosophy for everyone* (pp. 193–203). Hoboken, NJ: Wiley-Blackwell.

Piper, A., & Merskey, H. (2004a). The persistence of folly: A critical examination of dissociative identity disorder. Part I. The excesses of an improbable concept. *Canadian Journal of Psychiatry, 49*(9), 592–600.

Piper, A., & Merskey, H. (2004b). The persistence of folly: Critical examination of dissociative identity disorder. Part II: The defence and decline of multiple personality or dissociative identity disorder. *Canadian Journal of Psychiatry, 49*(10), 678–683.

Piper, A., & Merskey, H. (2005). Reply: The persistence of folly: A critical examination of dissociative identity disorder. *The Canadian Journal of Psychiatry, 50*(12), 814.

Piper, W. E., & Joyce, A. S. (2001). Psychosocial treatment outcome. In W. J. Livesley (Ed.), *Handbook of personality disorders: Theory, research, and treatment* (pp. 323–343). New York: Guilford Press.

Pirkl, J. J. (2009). The demographics of aging. *Transgenerational Design Matters.* http://transgenerational.org/aging/demographics.htm.

Pisula, E. (2010). The autistic mind in the light of neuropsychological studies. *Acta Neurobiologiae Experimentalis, 70*(2), 119–130.

Plante, T. (2006). How can we prevent abnormal behavior from occurring and developing? In T. Plante (Ed.) *Mental disorders of the new millennium.* New York: Praeger.

Planty, M., Hussar, W., Snyder, T., Provasnik, S., Kena, G., Dinkes, R., et al. (2008). *The condition of education 2008.* Washington, DC: National Center for Education Statistics.

Plaud, J. J. (2007). Sexual disorders. In P. Sturmey (Ed.), *Functional analysis in clinical treatment. Practical resources for the mental health professional* (pp. 357–377). San Diego, CA: Elsevier Academic Press.

Plaze, M., Paillere-Martinot, M-L., Penttilä, J., Januel, D., de Beaurepaire, R., Bellivier F., et al. (2011). "Where do auditory hallucinations come from"—A brain morphometry study of schizophrenia patients with inner or outer space hallucinations. *Schizophrenia Bulletin, 37*(1), 212–221.

Pliszka, S. R. (2011). Anxiety disorders. In S. Goldstein, & C. R. Reynolds (Eds), *Handbook of neurodevelopmental and genetic disorders in children* (2nd ed.). (pp. 188–208) New York: Guilford Press.

Poeppl, T. B., Nitschke, J., Dombert, B., Santtila, P., Greenlee, M. W., Osterheider, M., & Mokros, A. (2011). Functional cortical and subcortical abnormalities in pedophilia: A combined study using a choice reaction time task and fMRI. *Journal of Sexual Medicine, 8*(6), 1660–1674.

Pole, N., Best, S. R., Weiss, D. S., Metzler, T., Liberman, A. J., & Fagan, J. (2001). Effects of gender and ethnicity on duty-related posttraumatic stress symptoms among urban police officers. *Journal of Nervous and Mental Disease, 189*(7), 442–448.

Pollack, M. H. (2005). The pharmacotherapy of panic disorder. *Journal of Clinical Psychiatry, 66*(Suppl. 4), 23–27.

Polo, A. J., Alegria, M., Chen, C-N., & Blanco, C. (2011). The prevalence and comorbidity of social anxiety disorder among United States Latinos: A retrospective analysis of data from 2 national surveys. *Journal of Clinical Psychiatry, 72*(8), 1096–1105.

Pomaki, G., Franche, R-L., Murray, E., Khushrushahi, N., & Lampinen, T. M. (2012). Workplace-based work disability prevention interventions for workers with common mental health conditions: A review of the literature. *Journal of Occupational Rehabilitation, 22*(2), 182–195.

Pompili, M., Innamorati, M., Girardi, P., Tatarelli, R., & Lester, D. (2011). Evidence-based interventions for preventing suicide in youths. In M. Pompili & R. Tatarelli (Eds.), *Evidence-based practice in suicidology: A source book* (pp. 171–209). Cambridge MA: Hogrefe Publishing.

Pompili, M., & Lester, D. (2007). Suicide risk in schizophrenia. In R. Tatarelli, M. Pompili, & P. Girardi (Eds.), *Suicide in psychiatric disorders.* New York: Nova Science Publishers.

Pompili, M., Lester, D., Grispini, A., Calandro, F., De Pisa, E., & Innamorati, M. (2007). Suicide and attempted suicide in anorexia nervosa, bulimia nervosa, obesity and weight-image concern. In R. Tatarelli, M. Pompili, & P. Girardi (Eds.), *Suicide in psychiatric disorders.* New York: Nova Science Publishers.

Pompili, M., Lester, D., Leenaars, A. A., Tatarelli, R., & Girardi, P. (2008). Psychache and suicide: A preliminary investigation. *Suicide and Life-Threatening Behavior, 38*(1), 116–121.

Pompili, M., Serafini, G., Innamorati, M., Möller-Leimhühler, A. M., Giupponi, G., Girardi, P., et al. (2010). The hypothalamic-pituitary-adrenal axis and serotonin abnormalities: A selective overview for the implications of suicide prevention. *European Archives of Psychiatry and Clinical Neuroscience, 280*(8), 583–600.

Pontoski, K. E., Heimberg, R. G., Turk, C. L., & Coles, M. E. (2010). Psychotherapy for social anxiety disorder. In D. J. Stein, E. Hollander, & B. O. Rothbaum (Eds.), *Textbook of anxiety disorders* (2nd ed., pp. 501–521). Arlington, VA: American Psychiatric Publishing.

Poon, L. W., Martin, P., & Margrett, J. (2010). Cognition and emotion in centenarians. In C. A. Depp & D. V. Jeste (Eds.), *Successful cognitive and emotional aging* (pp. 115–133). Arlington, VA: American Psychiatric Publishing.

Pope, H. G., Jr., Poliakoff, M. B., Parker, M. P., Boynes, M., & Hudson, J. I. (2007). Is dissociative amnesia a culture-bound syndrome? Findings from a survey of historical literature: Reply. *Psychological Medicine, 37*(7), 1065–1067.

Pope, K. S., Keith-Spiegel, P., & Tabachnick, B. G. (2006). Sexual attraction to clients: The human therapist and the (sometimes) inhuman training system. *Training and Education in Professional Psychology, 5*(2), 96–111.

Pope, K. S., Sonne, J. L., & Greene, B. (2006). *What therapists don't talk about and why: Understanding taboos that hurt us and our clients.* Washington, DC: American Psychological Association.

Pope, K. S., & Tabachnick, B. G. (1993). Therapists' anger, hate, fear, and sexual feelings:

National survey of therapist responses, client characteristics, critical events, formal complaints, and training. *Professional Psychology: Research and Practice, 24*(2), 142–152.

Pope, K. S. & Tabachnick, B. G. (1994). Therapists as patients: A national survey of psychologists' experience, problems, and beliefs. *Professional Psychology: Research and Practice, 25*, 247–258.

Pope, K. S., & Vasquez, M. J. T. (2007). *Ethics in psychotherapy and counseling.* Hoboken, NJ: Wiley.

Pope, K. S., & Vasquez, M. J. T. (2011). *Ethics in psychotherapy and counseling: A practical guide* (4th ed.). Hoboken, NJ: John Wiley & Sons.

Pope, K. S., & Wedding, D. (2008). Contemporary challenges and controversies. In R. J. Corsini & D. Wedding (Eds.), *Current psychotherapies* (8th ed.). Belmont, CA: Thomson Brooks/Cole.

Pope, K., & Wedding, D. (2011). Contemporary challenges and controversies. In R. J. Corsini & D. Wedding (Eds.), *Current psychotherapies* (9th ed.). Belmont, CA: Brooks/Cole.

Porcerelli, J., Dauphin, B., Ablon, J. S., et al. (2007). Psychoanalysis of avoidant personality disorder: A systematic case study. *Psychotherapy: Theory, Research, Practice, Training, 44*, 1–13.

Poretz, M., & Sinrod, B. (1991). *Do you do it with the lights on?* New York: Ballantine Books.

Porter, S., & ten Brinke, L. (2008). Reading between the lies: Identifying concealed and falsified emotions in universal facial expressions. *Psychological Science, 19*(5), 508–514.

Posmontier, B. (2010). The role of midwives in facilitating recovery in postpartum psychosis. *Journal of Midwifery & Women's Health, 55*(5), 430–437.

Post, R. M. (2005). The impact of bipolar depression. *Journal of Clinical Psychiatry, 66*(Suppl. 5), 5–10.

Post, R. M. (2011). Treatment of bipolar depression. In D. A. Ciraulo & R. I. Shader (Eds.), *Pharmacotherapy of depression* (2nd ed., pp. 197–237). New York: Springer Science + Business Media.

Post, R. M., Ballenger, J. C., & Goodwin, F. K. (1980). Cerebrospinal fluid studies of neurotransmitter function in manic and depressive illness. In J. H. Wood (Ed.), *The neurobiology of cerebrospinal fluid* (Vol. 1). New York: Plenum Press.

Post, R. M., Lake, C. R., Jimerson, D. C., Bunney, J. H., Ziegler, M. G., & Goodwin, F. K. (1978). Cerebrospinal fluid norepinephrine in affective illness. *American Journal of Psychiatry, 135*(8), 907–912.

Post, R. M., & Miklowitz, D. J. (2010). The role of stress in the onset, course, and progression of bipolar illness and its comorbidities: Implications for therapeutics. In D. J. Miklowitz & D. Cichetti (Eds.), *Understanding bipolar disorder: A developmental psychopathology perspective* (pp. 370–413). New York: Guilford Press.

Potvin, S., Stip, E., Lipp, O., Roy, M. A., Demers, M. F., Bouchard, R. H., et al. (2008). Anhedonia and social adaptation predict substance abuse evolution in dual diagnosis schizophrenia. *American Journal of Drug and Alcohol Abuse, 34*(1), 75–82.

Poulos, C. X., Le, A. D., & Parker, J. L. (1995). Impulsivity predicts individual susceptibility to high levels of alcohol self-administration. *Behavioral Pharmacology, 6*(8), 810–814.

Pouncey, C. L., & Lukens, J. M. (2010). Madness versus badness: The ethical tension between the

recovery movement and forensic psychiatry. *Theoretical Medicine and Bioethics, 31*(1), 93–105.

Powers, M. B., Halpern, J. M., Ferenschak, M. P., Gillihan, S. J., & Foa, E. B. (2010). A meta-analytic review of prolonged exposure for posttraumatic stress disorder. *Clinical Psychology Review, 30*(6), 635–641.

Practice Update. (2011, February). Few Americans aware of mental health parity law. *Practice Update, 8*(3).

Prelock, P. A., Paul, R., & Allen, E. M. (2011). Evidence-based treatments in communication for children with autism spectrum disorders. In B. Reichow, P. Doehring, D. V. Cicchetti, & F. R. Volkmar (Eds.), *Evidence-based practices and treatments for children with autism* (pp. 93–169). New York: Springer Science + Business Media.

Present, J., Crits-Christoph, P., Gibbons, M. B. C., Hearon, B., Ring-Kurtz, S., Worley, M., et al. (2008). Sudden gains in the treatment of generalized anxiety disorder. *Journal of Clinical Psychology, 64*(1), 119–126.

Preti, A. (2011). Animal model and neurobiology of suicide. *Progress in Neuro-Psychopharmacology & Biological Psychiatry, 35*(4), 818–830.

Preti, A. (2011). Do animals commit suicide? Does it matter? *Crisis: Journal of Crisis Intervention and Suicide Prevention, 32*(1), 1–4.

Price, D. D., Finniss, D. G., & Benedetti, F. (2008). A comprehensive review of the placebo effect: Recent advances and current thought. *Annual Review of Psychology, 59*, 565–590.

Price, M. (2011). Upfront: Marijuana addiction a growing risk as society grows more tolerant. *Monitor on Psychology, 42*(5).

Princeton Survey Research Associates. (1996). *Healthy steps for young children: Survey of parents.* Princeton, NJ: Author.

Prochaska, J. O., & Norcross, J. C. (2003). *Systems of psychotherapy: A transtheoretical analysis* (5th ed.). Pacific Grove, CA: Brooks/Cole.

Prochaska, J. O., & Norcross, J. C. (2006). *Systems of psychotherapy: A transtheoretical analysis.* Pacific Grove, CA: Brooks/Cole.

Prochaska, J. O., & Norcross, J. C. (2007). *Systems of psychotherapy: A transtheoretical analysis* (6th ed.). Pacific Grove, CA: Brooks/Cole.

Prochaska, J. O., & Norcross, J. C. (2010). *Systems of psychotherapy: A transtheoretical analysis* (7th ed.). Pacific Grove, CA: Brooks/Cole.

Protopopescu, X., Pan, H., Tuesher, O., Cloitre, M., Goldstein, M., Engelien, W., et al. (2005). Differential time courses and specificity of amygdala activity in posttraumatic stress disorder subjects and normal control subjects. *Biological Psychiatry, 57*(5), 464–473.

Prudic, J., & Sackeim, H. A. (1999). Electroconvulsive therapy and suicide risk. *Journal of Clinical Psychiatry, 60*(Suppl. 2), 104–110.

Prusiner, S. B. (1991). Molecular biology of prion diseases. *Science, 252*, 1515–1522.

Pryce, C. R., Ruedi-Bettschen, D., Dettling, A. C., Weston, A., Russig, H., Ferger, B., et al. (2005). Long-term effects of early-life environmental manipulations in rodents and primates: Potential animal models in depression research. *Neuroscience and Biobehavioral Reviews, 29*(4–5), 649–674.

Pugno, M. (2007). The subjective well-being paradox: A suggested solution based on relational goods. In P. L. Porta & L. Bruni (Eds.), *Handbook on the economics of happiness* (pp. 263–289). Northampton, MA: Edward Elgar Publishing.

Punamäki, R., Qouta, S. R., & El Sarraj, E. (2010). Nature of torture, PTSD, and somatic symptoms among political ex-prisoners. *Journal of Traumatic Stress, 23*(4), 532–536.

Pungello, E. P., Kainz, K., Burchinal, M., Wasik, B. H., Sparling, J. J., Ramey, C. T., & Campbell, F. A. (2010). Early educational intervention, early cumulative risk, and the early home environmental as predictors of young adult outcomes within a high-risk sample. *Child Development, 81*(1), 410–426.

Punkanen, M., Eerola, T., & Erkkilä. (2011). Biased emotional recognition in depression: Perception of emotions in music by depressed patients. *Journal of Affective Disorders, 130*(1-2), 118–126.

Putnam, F. W. (1984). The psychophysiologic investigation of multiple personality disorder. *Psychiatric Clinics of North America, 7,* 31–40.

Putnam, F. W. (2000). Dissociative disorders. In A. J. Sameroff, M. Lewis et al. (Eds.), *Handbook of developmental psychopathology* (2nd ed., pp. 739–754). New York: Kluwer Academic/Plenum Press.

Putnam, F. W. (2006). Dissociative disorders. In D. Cicchetti & D. J. Cohen (Eds.), *Developmental psychopathology: Vol. 3. Risk, disorder, and adaptation* (2nd ed., pp. 657–695). Hoboken, NJ: John Wiley & Sons.

Putnam, F. W., Zahn, T. P., & Post, R. M. (1990). Differential autonomic nervous system activity in multiple personality disorder. *Journal of Psychiatric Research, 31*(3), 251–260.

Quas, J. A., Malloy, L. C., Melinder, A., Goodman, G. S., D-Mello, M., & Schaaf, J. (2007). Developmental differences in the effects of repeated interviews and interviewer bias on young children's event memory and false reports. *Developmental Psychology, 43*(4), 823–837.

Quayle, E. (2011). Pedophilia, child porn, and cyberpredators. In C. D. Bryant (Ed.), *The Routledge handbook of deviant behavior. Routledge international handbooks* (pp. 390–396). New York: Routledge/Taylor & Francis Group

Queinec, R., Beitz, C., Contrad, B., Jougla, E., Leffondré, K., Lagarde, E., & Encrenaz, G. (2011). Copycat effect after celebrity suicides: Results from the French national death register. *Psychological Medicine: Journal of Research in Psychiatry and the Allied Siences, 41*(3), 668–671.

Querido, J. G., & Eyberg, S. M. (2005). Parent-child interaction therapy: Maintaining treatment gains of preschoolers with disruptive behavior disorders. In E. D. Hibbs & P. S. Jensen (Eds.), *Psychosocial treatments for child and adolescent disorders: Empirically based strategies for clinical practice* (2nd ed., pp. 575–97). Washington, DC: American Psychological Association.

Quillian, L., & Pager, D. (2010). Estimating risk: Stereotype amplification and the perceived risk of criminal victimization. *Social Psychology Quarterly, 73*(1), 79–104.

Raad, R., & Makari, G. (2010). Samuel Tuke's description of the retreat. *The American Journal of Psychiatry, 167*(8), 898.

Raboch, J., & Raboch, J. (1992). Infrequent orgasm in women. *Journal of Sex and Marital Therapy, 18*(2), 114–120.

Rachman, S. (1966). Sexual fetishism: An experimental analog. *Psychological Record, 18,* 25–27.

Rachman, S. (1993). Obsessions, responsibility and guilt. *Behavioral Research and Therapy, 31*(2), 149–154.

Racine, S. E., Root, T. L., Klump, K. L., & Bulik, C. M. (2011). Environmental and genetic risk factors for eating disorders: A developmental perspective. In D. Le Grange & J. Lock (Eds.), *Eating disorders in children and adolescents: A clinical handbook.* New York: Guilford Publications.

Radcliffe, P., & Stevens, A. (2010). Early exit: Estimating and explaining early exit from drug treatment. In S. MacGregor (Ed.), *Responding to drug misuse: Research and policy priorities in health and social care* (pp. 79–85). New York: Routledge/Taylor & Francis Group.

Rainie, L., Purcell, K., & Smith, A. (2011). The social side of the internet. *Report: Communities, religion, social networking.* Washington, DC: Pew Internet & American Life Project.

Rajkowska, G. (2000). Postmortem studies in mood disorders indicate altered numbers of neurons and glial cells. *Biological Psychiatry, 48,* 766–777.

Raley, J. A. (2011). Etiology of exhibitionism in adolescence: A case example of countershame theory. *Adolescent Psychiatry, 1*(2), 179–183.

Ramaekers, J. G., Kauert, G., van Ruitenbeek, P., Theunissen, E. L., Schneider, E., & Moeller, M. R. (2006). High-potency marijuana impairs executive function and inhibitory motor control. *Neuropsychopharmacology, 31*(10), 2296–2303.

Ramchand, R., Schell, T. L., Jaycox, L. H., & Tanielian, T. (2011). Epidemiology of trauma events and mental health outcomes among service members deployed to Iraq and Afghanistan. In J. I. Ruzek, P. P. Schnurr, J. J. Vasterling, & M. J. Friedman (Eds.), *Caring for veterans with deployment-related stress disorders* (pp. 13–34). Washington, DC: American Psychological Association.

Ramchandani, P., Stein, A., Evans, J., O'Connor, T. G., & ALSPAC Study Team. (2005). Paternal depression in the postnatal period and child development: A prospective population study. *Lancet, 365*(9478), 2201–2205.

Ramdoss, S., Lang, R., Mulloy, A., Franco, J., O'Reilly, M., Didden, R., & Lancioni, G. (2011). Use of computer-based interventions to teach communication skills to children with autism spectrum disorders: A systematic review. *Journal of Behavioral Education, 20*(1), 55–76.

Rametti, G., Carrillo, B., Gómez-Gil, E., Jungue, C., Segovia, S., Gomez, A., & Guillamon, A. (2011). White matter microstructure in female to male transsexuals before cross-sex hormonal treatment. A diffusion tensor imaging study. *Journal of Psychiatric Research, 45*(2), 199–204.

Ramey, C. T., & Ramey, S. L. (1992). Effective early intervention. *Mental Retardation, 30*(6), 337–345.

Ramey, C. T., & Ramey, S. L. (2004). Early learning and school readiness: Can early intervention make a difference? *Merrill-Palmer Quarterly, 50*(4), 471–491.

Ramey, C. T., & Ramey, S. L. (2007). Early learning and school readiness: Can early intervention make a difference? In G. W. Ladd, (Ed.), *Appraising the human developmental sciences: Essays in honor of Merrill-Palmer Quarterly, Landscapes of childhood* (pp. 329–350). Detroit, MI: Wayne State University Press.

Ramey, S. L., Ramey, C. T., & Lanzi, R. G. (2007). Early intervention: Background, research findings, and future directions. In J. W. Jacobson,

J. A. Mulick, & J. Rojahn (Eds.), *Handbook of intellectual and developmental disabilities. Issues in clinical child psychology* (pp. 445–463). New York: Springer Publishing.

Ramsay, J. R. (2010). *Nonmedication treatments for adult ADHD: Evaluating impact on daily functioning and well-being.* Washington, DC: American Psychological Association.

Ramsland, K. & Kuter, R. (2011). Eve and Sybil. *Multiple Personalities: Crime and Defense.* Crime Library on truTV.com. http://www.trutv.com/library/crime/criminal_mind/psychology/multiples/3.html.

Ramsland, K. & Kuter, R. (2011). *Multiple personalities: Crime and defense.* Atlanta, GA: Turner Entertainment Networks, Inc.

RAND Corporation. (2008, April 17). 1 in 5 Iraq, Afghanistan vets has PTSD, major depression. *Science Blog.* Retrieved May 19, 2008, from http://www.scienceblog.com/cms/1-5-iraq-afghanistan-vet-has-ptsd-major-depression-rand-15954.html.

RAND Corporation. (2010). Studies' estimate of PTSD prevalence rates for returning service members vary widely. Retrieved on May 19, 2011, from www.rand.org/pubs/research_briefs/RB9509.html.

Rapp, C. A., & Goscha, R. J. (2008). Strengths-based case management. In K. T. Mueser & D.V. Jeste (Eds.), *Clinical handbook of schizophrenia* (pp. 319–328). New York: Guilford Press.

Rapport, M. D., Kofler, M. J., Alderson, R. M., & Raiker, J. S. (2008). Attention-deficit/hyperactivity disorder. In D. Reitman (Ed.), *Handbook of psychological assessment, case conceptualization, and treatment: Vol. 2. Children and adolescents.* Hoboken, NJ: John Wiley & Sons.

Raskin, D. C., & Honts, C. R. (2002). The comparison question test. In M. Kleiner (Ed.), *The handbook of polygraph testing.* San Diego, CA: Academic.

Raskin, N. J., Rogers, C., & Witty, M. (2011). Person-centered therapy. In R. J. Corsini & D. Wedding (Eds.), *Current psychotherapies* (9th ed.). Belmont, CA: Brooks/Cole.

Rasmussen, K. G. (2011). Some considerations in choosing electroconvulsive therapy versus transcranial magnetic stimulation for depression. *The Journal of ECT, 27*(1), 51–54.

Rathbone, J. (2001). *Anatomy of masochism.* New York: Kluwer Academic/Plenum.

Ravindran, L. N., & Stein, M. B. (2011). Pharmacotherapy for social anxiety disorder in adolescents and young adults. In C. A. Alfano & D. C. Beidel (Eds.), *Social anxiety in adolescents and young adults: Translating developmental science into practice* (pp. 265–279). Washington, DC: American Psychological Association.

Ray, M. J. (2010, April 30). Mental needs of Haitian earthquake victims not in sync with Western medicine. *Mental Health News.*

Raymond, K. B. (1997). The effect of race and gender on the identification of children with attention deficit hyperactivity disorder. *Dissertation Abstracts International: Section A: Humanities and Social Sciences, 57*(12-A), 5052.

Read, K., & Purse, M. (2007, March 22). Postpartum psychosis: Linked to bipolar disorder. *About.com.* Retrieved July 30, 2008, from http://bipolar.about.com/od/relateddisorders/a/postpartumpsych.htm.

Redick, R. W., Witkin, M. J., Atay, J. E., & Manderscheid, R. W. (1992). Specialty mental health system characteristics. In R. W. Manderscheid & M. A. Sonnenschein (Eds.), *Mental health, United States, 1992*. Washington, DC: U.S. Department of Health and Human Services.

Redmond, D. E. (1977). Alterations in the function of the nucleus locus coeruleus: A possible model for studies of anxiety. In I. Hanin & E. Usdin (Eds.), *Animal models in psychiatry and neurology*. New York: Pergamon Press.

Redmond, D. E. (1979). New and old evidence for the involvement of a brain norepinephrine system in anxiety. In W. E. Fann, I. Karacan, A. D. Pokorny, & R. L. Williams (Eds.), *Phemenology and treatment of anxiety*. New York: Spectrum.

Redmond, D. E. (1981). Clonidine and the primate locus coeruleus: Evidence suggesting anxiolytic and anti-withdrawal effects. In H. Lal & S. Fielding (Eds.), *Psychopharmacology of clonidine*. New York: Alan R. Liss.

Redmond, D. E. (1985). Neurochemical basis for anxiety and anxiety disorders: Evidence from drugs which decrease human fear or anxiety. In A. H. Tuma & J. Maser (Eds.), *Anxiety and the anxiety disorders*. Hillsdale, NJ: Lawrence Erlbaum.

Reeb, R. N. (2000). Classification and diagnosis of psychopathology: Conceptual foundations. *Journal of Psychological Practice, 6*(1), 3–18.

Rees, W. D., & Lutkin, S. G. (1967). Mortality of bereavement. *British Medical Journal, 4*, 13–16.

Reese, J., Kraschewski, A., Anghelescu, I., Winterer, G., Schmidt, L. G., Gallinat, J., Rüschendorf, F., Rommelspacher, H., & Wernicke, C. (2010). Haplotypes of dopamine and serotonin transporter genes are associated with antisocial personality disorder in alcoholics. *Psychiatric Genetics, 20*(4), 140–152.

Regier, D. A., Narrow, W. E., Kuhl, E. A., & Kupfer, D. J. (Eds.). (2011). *The conceptual evolution of DSM-5*. Arlington, VA: American Psychiatric Publishing.

Regier, D. A., Narrow, W. E., Rae, D. S., Manderscheid, R. W., Locke, B. Z., & Goodwin, F. K. (1993). The de facto U.S. Mental and Addictive Disorders Service System: Epidemiologic Catchment Area prospective 1-year prevalence rates of disorders in services. *Archives of General Psychiatry, 50*, 85–94.

Rehm, L. P. (2010). *Depression. Advances in psychotherapy—Evidence-based practice*. Cambridge, MA: Hogrefe Publishing.

Reichenberg, A., Gross, R., Kolevzon, A., & Susser, E. S. (2011). Parental and perinatal risk factors for autism. In E. Hollander, A. Kolevzon & J. T. Coyle (Eds.), *Textbook of autism spectrum disorders*. (pp. 239–246) Arlington, VA: American Psychiatric Publishing, Inc.

Reinecke, A., Cooper, M., Favaron, E., Massey-Case, R., & Harmer, C. (2011). Attentional bias in untreated panic disorder. *Psychiatry Research, 185*(3), 387–393.

Reisch, T., Seifritz, E., Esposito, F., Wiest, R., Valach, L., & Michel, K. (2010). An fMRI study on mental pain and suicidal behavior. *Journal of Affective Disorders, 126*(1-2), 321–325.

Reissing, E. D., Binik, Y. M., Khalife, S., Cohen, D., & Amsel, R. (2003). Etiological correlates of vaginismus: Sexual and physical abuse, sexual knowledge, sexual self-schema and relationship adjustment. *Journal of Sex and Marital Therapy, 29*(1), 47–59.

Reitan, R. M., & Wolfson, D. (1996). Theoretical, methodological, and validational bases of the Halstead-Reitan neuropsychological test battery. In I. Grant & K. M. Adams (Eds.), *Neuropsychological assessment of neuropsychiatric disorders* (2nd ed., pp. 3–42). New York: Oxford University Press.

Reitan, R. M., & Wolfson, D. (2005). The effect of age and education transformations on neuropsychological test scores of persons with diffuse or bilateral brain damage. *Applied Neuropsychology, 12*(4), 181–189.

Reivich, K. J., Seligman, M. E. P., & McBride, S. (2011). Master resilience training in the U.S. Army. *American Psychologist, 66*(1), 25–34.

Remington, G. J., Agid, O., & Foussias, G. (2011). Schizophrenia as a disorder of too little dopamine: Implications for symptoms and treatment. *Expert Review of Neurotherapeutics, 11*(4), 589–607.

Remler, D. K., & Van Ryzin, G. G. (2011). *Research methods in practice: Strategies for description and causation*. Thousand Oaks, CA: Sage Publications.

Renaud, J., Berlim, M. T., McGirr, A., Tousignant, M., & Turecki, G. (2008). Current psychiatric morbidity, aggression/impulsivity, and personality dimensions in child and adolescent suicide: A case-control study. *Journal of Affective Disorders, 105*(1–3), 221–228.

Rennison, C. M. (2002, August). Rape and sexual assault: Reporting to police and medical attention, 1992–2000 (NCJ 194530). Washington, DC: U.S. Department of Justice Statistics Selected Findings.

Report of the Surgeon General. (1988). *The health consequences of smoking: Nicotine addiction: A report of the surgeon general. (*DHHS Publication No. CDC 88-8406). Bethesda, MD: National Institutes of Health, Center for Health Promotion and Education.

Resnick, P. H. J., & Harris, M. R. (2002). Retrospective assessment of malingering in insanity defense cases. In R. I. Simon & D. W. Schuman (Eds.), *Retrospective assessment of mental states in litigation: Predicting the past* (pp. 101–134) Washington, DC: American Psychiatric Publishing.

Ressler, K., & Davis, M. (2003). Genetics of childhood disorders: Learning and memory. Part 3: Fear conditioning. *Journal of the American Academy of Child and Adolescent Psychiatry, 42*(5), 612–615.

Reutens, S., Nielsen, O., & Sachdev, P. (2010). Depersonalization disorder. *Current Opinion in Psychiatry, 23*(3), 278–283.

Reuters. (2004, September 7). It's a bumper-to-bumper life. *Reuters (Washington)/Yahoo!News)*.

Reuters. (2010, April 8). *They walk among us: 1 in 5 believe in aliens?* Retrieved from http://www.reuters.com/assets/print?aid.

Rich, E. (2011). "I see her being obesed!": Public pedagogy, reality media and the obesity crisis. *Health: Ana Interdisciplinary Journal for the Social Study of Health, Illness and Medicine, 15*(1), 3–21.

Richard, I. H., & Lyness, J. M. (2006). An overview of depression. In D. V. Jeste & J. H. Friedman (Eds.), *Psychiatry for neurologists* (pp. 33–42). Totowa, NJ: Humana Press.

Richard, M. (2005). Effective treatment of eating disorders in Europe: Treatment outcome and its predictors. *European Eating Disorders Review, 13*(3), 169–179.

Richards, H., & Jackson, R. L. (2011). Behavioral discriminators of sexual sadism and Paraphilia Nonconsent in a sample of civilly committed sexual offenders. *International Journal of Offender Therapy and Comparative Criminology, 55*(2), 207–227.

Richtel, M. (2010, November 21). Growing up digital, wired for distraction. *New York Times*.

Retrieved on December 30, 2010, from www.nytimes.com.

Ridgway, P. (2008). Supported housing. In K. T. Mueser & D. V. Jeste (Eds.), *Clinical handbook of schizophrenia* (pp. 287–297). New York: Guilford Press.

Rieber, R. W. (1999, March). Hypnosis, false memory, and multiple personality: A trinity of affinity. *History of Psychiatry, 10*(37), 3–11.

Rieber, R. W. (2002). The duality of the brain and the multiplicity of minds: Can you have it both ways? *History of Psychiatry 13*(49, pt1), 3–18.

Rieber, R. W. (2006). *The bifurcation of the self: The history and theory of dissociation and its disorders*. New York, NY: Springer Science + Business Media.

Riemann, D., Spiegelhalder, K., Espie, C., Pollmächer, T., Léger, D., Bassetti, C., & van Someren, E. (2011). Chronic insomnia: Clinical and research challenges—An agenda. *Pharmacopsychiatry, 44*(1), 1–14.

Ries, R. K. (2010). Suicide and substance abuse. In E. V. Nunes, J. Selzer, P. Levounis, & C. A. Davies (Eds.), *Substance dependence and co-occurring psychiatric disorders: Best practices for diagnosis and treatment* (pp. 1–14). Kingston, NJ: Civic Research Institute.

Riesch, S. K., Jacobson, G., Sawdey, L., Anderson, J., & Henriques, J. (2008). Suicide ideation among later elementary school-aged youth. *Journal of Psychiatric and Mental Health Nursing, 15*(4), 263–277.

Riess, H. (2002). Integrative time-limited group therapy for bulimia nervosa. *International Journal of Group Psychotherapy, 52*(1), 1–26.

Rihmer, Z., Rutz, W., & Pihlgren, H. (1995). Depression and suicide on Gotland. An intensive study of all suicides before and after a depression-training programme for general practitioners. *Journal of Affective Disorders, 35*, 147–152.

Riley, B., & Kendler, K. S. (2011). Classical genetic studies of schizophrenia. In D. R. Weinberg & P. Harrison (Eds.), *Schizophrenia* (pp. 245–268). Hoboken, NJ: Wiley-Blackwell.

Ringman, J. M., & Vinters, H. V. (2011). Alzheimer's disease and the frontotemporal dementia syndromes. In C. E. Coffey, J. L. Cummings, M. S. George, & D. Weintraub (Eds.), *The American Psychiatric Publishing textbook of geriatric neuropsychiatry*. Arlington, VA: American Psychiatric Publishing, Inc.

Ringuette, E., & Kennedy, T. (1966). An experimental study of the double bind hypothesis. *Journal of Abnormal Psychology, 71*, 136–141.

Ristow, A., Westphal, A., & Scahill, L. (2011). Treating hyperactivity in children with pervasive developmental disorders. In E. Hollander, A. Kolevzon, & J. T. Coyle (Eds.)., *Textbook of autism spectrum disorders* (pp. 479–486). Arlington, VA: American Psychiatric Publishing.

Ritsner, M. S., & Gibel, A. (2007). Quality of life impairment syndrome in schizophrenia. In M. S. Ritsner & A. G. Awad (Eds.), *Quality of life impairment in schizophrenia, mood and anxiety disorders: New perspectives on research and treatment*. Amsterdam, The Netherlands: Springer Publishing.

Ritter, K., Dziobek, I., Preissler, S., Rüter, A., Vater, A., Fydrich, T., et al. (2011). Lack of empathy in patients with narcissistic personality disorder. *Psychiatry Research, 187*(1-2), 241–247.

Ritter, M. (2008, January 27). Lead linked to aging in older brains. *YAHOO! News*.

Ritter, M. R., Blackmore, M. A., & Heimberg, R. G. (2010). Generalized anxiety disorder. In

D. McKay, J. S. Abramowitz, & S. Taylor (Eds.), *Cognitive-behavioral therapy for refractory cases: Turning failure into success* (pp. 111–137). Washington, DC: American Psychological Association.

Rivett, M. (2011). Embracing change in clinical practice. *Journal of Family Therapy, 33*(1), 1–2.

Rizvi, S. L., Dimeff, L. A., Skutch, J., Carroll, D., Linehan, M. M. (2011). A pilot study of the DBT coach: An interactive mobile phone application for individuals with borderline personality disorder and substance use disorder. *Behavior Therapy, 42*, 589–600.

Robbins, B. (2012, Jan. 24). Allen Frances: Defenses from DSM-5 Get "curioser and curioser." Society for Humanistic Psychology Blog.

Roberts, C. M., Kane, R., Bishop, B., Cross, D., Fenton, J., & Hart, B. (2010). The prevention of anxiety and depression in children from disadvantaged schools. *Behaviour Research and Therapy, 48*(1), 68–73.

Robinson, M. S., & Alloy, L. B. (2003). Negative cognitive styles and stress-reactive rumination interact to predict depression: A prospective study. *Cognitive Therapy and Research, 27*(3), 275–292.

Rocca, P., Aimetti, M., Giugiario, M., Pigella, E., Romano, F., Crivelli, B., et al. (2010). The complaint of oral malodour: Psychopathological and personality profiles. *Psychotherapy and Psychosomatics, 79*(6), 392–394.

Roche, B., & Quayle, E. (2007). Sexual disorders. In D. W. Woods & J. W. Kanter (Eds.), *Understanding behavior disorders: A contemporary behavioral perspective.* Reno, NV: Context Press.

Roche, T. (2002, January 20). The Yates odyssey. *TIME.com: Nation.*

Roddenberry, A., & Renk, K. (2010). Locus of control and self-efficacy: Potential mediators of stress, illness, and utilization of health services in college students. *Child Psychiatry and Human Development, 41*(4), 353–370.

Rodebaugh, T. L., Gianoli, M. O., Turkheimer, E., & Oltmanns, T. F. (2010). What kinds of interpersonal problems are unique to avoidant personality disorder when self-report and peer ratings are considered? *Clinician's Research Digest, 28*(8).

Rodewald, F., Wilhelm-Gößling, C., Emrich, H. M., Reddemann, L., & Gast, U. (2011). Axis-I comorbidity in female patients with dissociative identity disorder and dissociative identity disorder not otherwise specified. *Journal of Nervous and Mental Disease, 199*(2), 122–131.

Rodriguez, B. F., Weisberg, R. B., Pagano, M. E., Machan, J. T., Culpepper, L., & Keller, M. B. (2004). Frequency and patterns of psychiatric comorbidity in a sample of primary care patients with anxiety disorders. *Comprehensive Psychiatry, 45*(2), 129–137.

Rodriguez-Ruiz, S., Guerra, P. M., Moreno, S., Fernández, M. C., & Vila, J. (2012). Heart rate variability modulates eyeblink startle in women with bulimic symptoms. *Journal of Psychophysiology, 26*(1), 10–19.

Roelofs, K., Hoogduin, K. A. L., Keijsers, G. P. J., Naering, G. W. B., Moene, F. C., & Sandijck, P. (2002). Hypnotic susceptibility in patients with conversion disorder. *Journal of Abnormal Psychology, 111*(2), 390–395.

Roemer, L., Salters, K., Raffa, S. D., & Orsillo, S. M. (2005). Fear and avoidance of internal experiences in GAD: Preliminary tests of a conceptual model. *Cognitive Therapy and Research, 29*(1), 71–88.

Roepke, S., Schröder-Abé, M., Schütz, A., Jacob, G., Dams, A., Vater, A., Rüter, A., Merkl, A., Heuser, I., Lammers, C-H. (2011). Dialectic behavioural therapy has an impact on self-concept clarity and facets of self-esteem in women with borderline personality disorder. *Clinical Psychology & Psychotherapy, 18*(2), 148–158.

Roesch, R. (1991). *The encyclopedia of depression.* New York: Facts on File.

Roesch, R., Zapf, P. A., Golding, S. L., & Skeem, J. L. (1999). Defining and assessing competence to stand trial. In A. K. Hess, I. B. Weiner, et al. (Eds.), *The handbook of forensic psychology* (2nd ed.). New York: Wiley.

Roesch, R., Zapf, P. A., & Hart, S. D. (2010). *Forensic psychology and law.* Hoboken, NJ: John Wiley & Sons.

Roesler, T. A., & McKenzie, N. (1994). Effects of childhood trauma on psychological functioning of adults sexually abused as children. *Journal of Nervous and Mental Disease, 182*(3), 145–150.

Rogers, C. R. (1951). *Client-centered therapy.* Boston: Houghton Mifflin.

Rogers, C. R. (1954). The case of Mrs. Oak: A research analysis. In C. R. Rogers & R. F. Dymond (Eds.), *Psychotherapy and personality change* (pp. 259–269). Chicago: University of Chicago Press.

Rogers, C. R. (1987). Rogers, Kohut, and Erickson: A personal perspective on some similarities and differences. In J. K. Zeig (Ed.), *The evolution of psychotherapy.* New York: Brunner/Mazel.

Rogers, C. R. (2000). Interview with Carl Rogers on the use of the self in therapy. In M. Baldwin (Ed.), *The use of self in therapy* (2nd ed., pp. 29–38). Binghamton, NY: Haworth.

Rogers, J. R., Madura, T. L., & Hardy, J. L. (2011). Evidence-based psychosocial interventions for suicidal behavior: What is the evidence? In M. Pompili & R. Tatarelli (Eds.), *Evidence-based practice in suicidology: A source book* (pp. 125–138). Cambridge MA: Hogrefe Publishing.

Rogers, R. (2008). Insanity evaluations. In R. Jackson (Ed.), *Learning forensic assessment* (pp. 109–128). New York: Routledge/Taylor & Francis Group.

Rogler, L. H., Malgady, R. G., & Rodriguez, O. (1989). *Hispanics and mental health: A framework for research.* Malabar, FL: Krieger Publishing.

Roisko, R., Wahlberg, K-E., Hakko, H., Wynne, L., Tienari, P. (2011). Communication deviance in parents of families with adoptees at a high or low risk of schizophrenia-spectrum disorders and its associations with attributes of the adoptee and the adoptive parents. *Psychiatry Research, 185*(1-2), 66–71.

Rollin, H. R. (1980). *Coping with schizophrenia.* London: Burnett.

Rolon, Y. M., & Jones, J. C. W. (2008). Right to refuse treatment. *Journal of the American Academy of Psychiatry and the Law, 36*(2), 252–255.

Romito, S., Bottanelli, M., Pellegrini, M., Vicentini, S., Rizzuto, N., & Bertolasi, L. (2004). Botulinum toxin for the treatment of genital pain syndromes. *Gynecologic and Obstetric Investigation, 58*(3), 164–167.

Ronningstam, E. (2011). Narcissistic personality disorder: A clinical perspective. *Journal of Psychiatric Practice, 17*(2), 89–99.

Rook, K. S., August, K. J., & Sorkin, D. H. (2011). Social network functions and health. In R. J. Contrada & A. Baum (Eds.), *The handbook of stress science: Biology, psychology, and health* (pp. 123–135). New York: Springer Publishing.

Rose, T., Joe, S., & Lindsey, M. (2011). Perceived stigma and depression among black adolescents in outpatient treatment. *Children and Youth Services Review, 33*(1), 161–166.

Rosen, E. F., Anthony, D. L., Booker, K. M., Brown, T. L., et al. (1991). A comparison of eating disorder scores among African American and white college females. *Bulletin of Psychosomatic Society, 29*(1), 65–66.

Rosen, G. M., Lilienfeld, S. O., & Orr, S. P. (2010). Searching for PTSD's biological signature. In G. M. Rosen, B. C. Frueh (Eds.), *Clinician's guide to posttraumatic stress disorder* (pp. 97–116). Hoboken, NJ: John Wiley & Sons.

Rosen, L. W., & Hough, D. O. (1988). Pathogenic weight-control behaviors of female college gymnasts. *Physician Sports Medicine, 16*(9), 141–144.

Rosen, L. W., McKeag, D. B., Hough, D. O., & Curley, V. (1986). Pathogenic weight--control behavior in female athletes. *Physician Sports Medicine, 14*(1), 79–86.

Rosen, R. C. (2007). Erectile dysfunction: Integration of medical and psychological approaches. In S. R. Leiblum (Ed.), *Principles and practice of sex therapy* (4th ed., pp. 277–310). New York: Guilford Press.

Rosen, R. C., & Rosen, L. R. (1981). *Human sexuality.* New York: Knopf.

Rosenbaum, T. Y. (2007). Physical therapy management and treatment of sexual pain disorders. In S. R. Leiblum (Ed.), *Principles and practice of sex therapy* (4th ed., pp. 157–177). New York: Guilford Press.

Rosenbaum, T. Y. (2011). Addressing anxiety in vivo in physiotherapy treatment of women with severe vaginismus: A clinical approach. *Journal of Sex & Marital Therapy, 37*(2), 89–93.

Rosenberg, A., Ledley, D. R., & Heimberg, R. G. (2010). Social anxiety disorder. In D. McKay, J. S. Abramowitz, & S. Taylor (Eds.), *Cognitive-behavioral therapy for refractory cases: Turning failure into success* (pp. 65–88). Washington, DC: American Psychological Association.

Rosenberg, J., & Rosenberg, S. (Eds.). (2006). *Community mental health: Challenges for the 21st century.* New York: Routledge.

Rosenberg, L. (2011). Seeing the person not the illness. *Journal of Behavioral Health Services & Research, 38*(1), 1–2.

Rosenberg, O., Isserles, M., Levkovitz, Y., Kotler, M., Zangen, A., & Dannon, P. N. (2011). Effectiveness of a second deep TMS in depression: A brief report. *Progress in Neuro-Psychopharmacology & Biological Psychiatry, 35*(4), 1041–1044.

Rosenberg, T., & Pace, M. (2006). Burnout among mental health professionals: Special considerations for the marriage and family therapist. *Journal of Marital and Family Therapy, 32*(1), 87–99.

Rosenfeld, B. (2004). Influence of depression and psychosocial factors on physician-assisted suicide. In B. Rosenfeld (Ed.), *Assisted suicide and the right to die: The interface of social science, public policy, and medical ethics* (pp. 77–93). Washington, DC: American Psychological Association.

Rosenhan, D. L. (1973). On being sane in insane places. *Science, 179*(4070), 250–258.

Rosenthal, M. B., Berndt, E. R., Donohue, J. M., Frank, R. G., & Epstein, A. M. (2002). Promotion of prescription drugs to consumers. *New England Journal of Medicine, 346*(7), 498–505.

Rosenthal, R. (1966). *Experimenter effects in behavioral research.* New York: Appleton--Century-Crofts.

Rosenthal, R. N. (2011). Alcohol abstinence management. In J. H. Lowinson & P. Ruiz (Eds.), *Substance abuse: A comprehensive textbook, fifth edition*. Philadelphia, PA: Lippincott, Williams, & Wilkins.

Rosenthal, R. N., & Levounis, P. (2005). Polysubstance use, abuse, and dependence. In R. J. Frances, A. H. Mack, & S. I. Miller (Eds.), *Clinical textbook of addictive disorders* (3rd ed., pp. 245–270). New York: Guilford Press.

Rosenthal, R. N., & Levounis, P. (2011). Polysubstance use, abuse, and dependence. In R. J. Frances, S. I. Miller, & A. H. Mack (Eds.), *Clinical textbook of addictive disorders* (3rd ed.). New York: Guilford Press.

Roskar, S., Podlesek, A., Kuzmanic, M., Demsar, L. O., Zaletel, M., & Marusic, A. (2011). Suicide risk and its relationship to change in marital status. *Crisis: Journal of Crisis Intervention and Suicide Prevention, 32*(1), 24–30.

Ross, C. A., & Gahan, P. (1988). Techniques in the treatment of multiple personality disorder. *American Journal of Psychotherapy, 42*(1), 40–52.

Ross, C. A., & Ness, L. (2010). Symptom patterns in dissociative identity disorder patients and the general population. *Journal of Trauma & Dissociation, 11*(4), 458–468.

Rotge, J-Y., Grabot, D., Aouizerate, B., Pélissolo, A., Lépine, J-P, & Tignol, J. (2011). Childhood history of behavioral inhibition and comorbidity status in 256 adults with social phobia. *Journal of Affective Disorders, 129*(1-3), 338–341.

Rotgers, F. (2012). Cognitive-behavioral theories of substance abuse. In S. T. Walters & F. Rotgers (Eds.), *Treating substance abuse: Theory and technique* (3rd ed, pp. 113–137). New York: Guilford Press.

Roth, A., & Fonagy, P. (2005). *What works for whom? A critical review of psychotherapy research* (2nd ed.). New York: Guilford Press.

Rothbaum, B. O., Foa, E. B., Riggs, D. S., Murdock, T., & Walsh, W. (1992). A prospective examination of posttraumatic stress disorder in rape victims. *Journal of Traumatic Stress, 5*(3), 455–475.

Rothbaum, B. O., Gerardi, M., Bradley, B., & Friedman, M. J. (2011). Evidence-based treatments for posttraumatic stress disorder in Operation Enduring Freedom and Operation Iraqi Freedom military personnel. In J. I. Ruzek, P. P. Schnurr, J. J. Vasterling, & M. J. Friedman (Eds.), *Caring for veterans with deployment-related stress disorders* (pp. 215–239). Washington, DC: American Psychological Association.

Rothschild, A. J. (2010). Major depressive disorder, severe with psychotic features. In C. B. Taylor (Ed.), *How to practice evidence-based psychiatry: Basic principles and case studies*. (pp. 195–202). Arlington, VA: American Psychiatric Publishing.

Rothschild, D. (2009). On becoming one-self: Reflections on the concept of integration as seen through a case of dissociative identity disorder. *Psychoanalytic Dialogues, 19*(2), 175–187.

Rotter, M. (2011). Embitterment and personality disorder. In M. Linden & A. Maercker (Eds.), *Embitterment: Societal, psychological, and clinical perspectives* (pp. 177–186). New York: Springer-Verlag Publishing.

Rowan, P. (2005, July 31). Cited in J. Thompson, "Hungry for love": Why 11 million of us have serious issues with food. *Independent on Sunday.*

Rowe, S. L., Jordan, J., McIntosh, V. V. W., Carter, F. A., Frampton, C., Bulik, C. M., Joyce, P. R. (2010). Complex personality disorder in bulimia nervosa. *Comprehensive Psychiatry, 51*(6), 592–598.

Rowe, S., Jordan, J., McIntosh, V. V. M., Carter, F., Frampton, C., Bulik, C., & Joyce, P. (2011). Dimensional measures of personality as a predictor of outcome at 5-year follow-up in women with bulimia nervosa. *Psychiatry Research, 185*(3), 414–420.

Rowland, D. L. (2012). *Sexual dysfunction in men. Advances in psychotherapy—Evidence-based practice.* Cambridge, MA: Hogrefe Publishing

Rowland, D. L., Georgoff, V. L., & Burnett, A. L. (2011). Psychoaffective differences between sexually functioning and dysfunctional men in response to a sexual experience. *Journal of Sexual Medicine, 8*(1), 132–139.

Roy, A. (1992). Genetics, biology, and suicide in the family. In R. W. Maris, A. L. Berman, et al. (Eds.), *Assessment and prediction of suicide* (pp. xxii, 697). New York: Guilford Press.

Roy, A. (2011). Combination of family history of suicidal behavior and childhood trauma may represent correlate of increased suicide risk. *Journal of Affective Disorders, 130*(1-2), 205–208.

Roy, M. J., Rizzo, A., Difede, J., & Rothbaum, B. O. (2011). Emerging and alternative therapies. In D. M. Benedek & G. H. Wynn (Eds.), *Clinical manual for management of PTSD* (pp. 227–253). Arlington, VA: American Psychiatric Publishing.

Roy-Byrne, P. P. (2005). The GABA-benzodiazepine receptor complex: Structure, function, and role in anxiety. *Journal of Clinical Psychiatry, 66*(Suppl. 2), 14–20.

Roy-Byrne, P., Arguelles, L., Vitek, M. E., Goldberg, J., Keane, T. M., True, W. R., et al. (2004). Persistence and change of PTSD symptomatology: A longitudinal co-twin control analysis of the Vietnam Era Twin Registry. *Social Psychiatry and Psychiatric Epidemiology, 39*(9), 681–685.

Rubin, E. H. (2005). Psychiatry and old age. In E. H. Rubin & C. F. Zorumski (Eds.), *Adult psychiatry* (2nd ed.). Oxford, England: Blackwell Publishing.

Rubinstein, S., & Caballero, B. (2000). Is Miss America an undernourished role model? *Journal of the American Medical Association, 283*(12), 1569.

Rudd, M. D., Berman, L., Joiner, T. E., Nock, M., Mandrusiak, M., Van Orden, K., et al. (2006). Warning signs for suicide: Theory, research, and clinical application. *Suicide and Life-Threatening Behavior, 36*, 255–262.

Rudd, M. D., & Brown, G. K. (2011). A cognitive theory of suicide: Building hope in treatment and strengthening the therapeutic relationship. In K. Michel & D. A. Jobes (Eds.), *Building a therapeutic alliance with the suicidal patient* (pp. 169–181). Washington, DC: American Psychological Association.

Rufer, M., Hand, I., Alsleben, H., Braatz, A., Ortmann, J., Katenkamp, B., et al. (2005). Long-term course and outcome of obsessive-compulsive patients after cognitive-behavioral therapy in combination with either fluvoxamine or placebo: A 7-year follow-up of a randomized double-blind trial. *European Archives of Psychiatry and Clinical Neuroscience, 255*(2), 121–128.

Ruijs, C. D. M., Kerkhof, A. J. F. M., van der Wal, G., & Onwuteaka-Philipsen, B. (2011). Depression and explicit requests for euthanasia in end-of-life cancer patients in primary care in the Netherlands: A longitudinal, prospective study. *Family Practice, 28*(4), 393–399.

Ruiz, P. (2011). Hispanic Americans. In J. H. Lowinson & P. Ruiz (Eds.), *Substance abuse: A comprehensive textbook, fifth edition*. Philadelphia, PA: Lippincott, Williams, & Wilkins.

Ruscio, A. M., Chiu, W. T., Roy-Byrne, P. Stang, P. E., Stein, D. J., Wittchen, H. U., & Kessler, R. C. (2007). Broadening the definition of generalized anxiety disorder: Effects on prevalence and associations with other disorders in the National Comorbidity Survey Replication. *Journal of Anxiety Disorders, 21*(5), 662–676.

Rush, B. (2010). Selected writings of Benjamin Rush. In A. J. Milson, C. H. Bohan, P. L. Glanzer, & J. W. Null (Eds.), *American educational thought: Essays from 1640–1940* (2nd ed., pp. 53–70).

Russell, M. C., Lipke, H., & Figley, C. (2011). Eye movement desensitization and reprocessing. In B. A. Moore & W. E. Penk (Eds.), *Treating PTSD in military personnel: A clinical handbook* (pp. 74–89). New York: Guilford Press.

Russell, T. (2007). Reducing stress at work. [Electronic version]. *Human Resources,* May 1, 2007.

Russo, N. F., & Tartaro, J. (2008). Women and mental health. In F. L. Denmark & M. A. Paludi (Eds.), *Psychology of women: A handbook of issues and theories* (2nd ed., pp. 440–483). Westport, CT: Praeger Publishers.

Ruta, N., & Cohen, L. S. (1998). Postpartum mood disorders: Diagnosis and treatment guidelines. *Journal of Clinical Psychiatry, 59*(Suppl 2), 34–40.

Ruzek, J. I., & Batten, S. V. (2011). Enhancing systems of care for posttraumatic stress disorder: From private practice to large health care systems. In J. I. Ruzek, P. P. Schnurr, J. J. Vasterling, & M. J. Friedman (Eds.), *Caring for veterans with deployment-related stress disorders* (pp. 261–282). Washington, DC: American Psychological Association.

Ruzek, J. I., Schnurr, P. P., Vasterling, J. J., & Friedman, J. (Eds.). (2011). *Caring for veterans with deployment-related stress disorders.* Washington, DC: American Psychological Association.

Sacks, O. (2000, May). *An anthropologist on Mars: Some personal perspectives on autism* (Keynote address). Eden Institute Foundation's Sixth Annual Princeton Lecture Series on Autism, Princeton, NJ.

Sadoff, R. L. (2011). Expert psychiatric testimony. In R. L. Sadoff, J. A. Baird, S. M. Bertoglia, E. Valenti, & D. L. Vanderpool (Eds.), *Ethical issues in forensic psychiatry: Minimizing harm* (pp. 97–110). Hoboken, NJ: Wiley-Blackwell.

Sadoff, R. L., Baird, J. A., Bertoglia, S. M., Valenti, E., & Vanderpool, D. L. (Eds.). (2011). *Ethical issues in forensic psychiatry: Minimizing harm.* Hoboken, NJ: Wiley-Blackwell.

Safer, D. (1994). The impact of recent lawsuits on methylphenidates sales. *Clinical Pediatrics, 33*(3), 166–168.

Safren, S. A., Gershuny, B. S., Marzol, P., Otto, M. W., & Pollack, M. H. (2002). History of childhood abuse in panic disorder, social phobia, and generalized anxiety disorder. *Journal of Nervous and Mental Disease, 190*(7), 453–456.

Sahoo, F. M., Sahoo, K., & Harichandan, S. (2005). Five big factors of personality and human happiness. *Social Science International, 21*(1), 20–28.

Sakinofsky, I. (2011). Evidence-based approaches for reducing suicide risk in major affective disorders. In M. Pompili & R. Tatarelli (Eds.), *Evidence-based practice in suicidology: A source book* (pp. 275–315). Cambridge, MA: Hogrefe Publishing.

Sakurai, T., Cai, G., Grice, D. E., & Buxbaum, J. D. (2011). Genomic architecture of autism spectrum disorders. In E. Hollander, A. Kolevzon & J. T. Coyle (Eds.), *Textbook of autism spectrum disorders.* (pp. 281–298) Arlington, VA: American Psychiatric Publishing, Inc.

Salekin, R. T., & Rogers, R. (2001). Treating patients found not guilty by reason of insanity. In J. B. Ashford, B. D. Sales, & W. H. Reid (Eds.) *Treating adult and juvenile offenders with special needs* (pp. 171–195). Washington, DC: American Psychological Association.

Sales, B. D., & Shuman, D. W. (2005). *Experts in court: Reconciling law, science, and professional knowledge.* Washington, DC: American Psychological Association.

Salfati, C. G. (2011). Criminal profiling. In B. Rosenfeld & S. D. Penrod (Eds.), *Research methods in forensic psychology* (pp. 122–134). Hoboken, NJ: John Wiley & Sons.

Salkovskis, P. M. (1985). Obsessional-compulsive problems: A cognitive-behavioural analysis. *Behavioral Research and Therapy, 23,* 571–584.

Salkovskis, P. M. (1999). Understanding and treating obsessive-compulsive disorder. *Behavioral Research and Therapy, 37*(Suppl. 1), S29–S52.

Salkovskis, P. M., Thorpe, S. J., Wahl, K., Wroe, A. L., & Forrester, E. (2003). Neutralizing increases discomfort associated with obsessional thoughts: An experimental study with obsessional patients. *Journal of Abnormal Psychology, 112*(4), 709–715.

Salvatore, G., Nicolo, G., & Dimaggio, G. (2005). Impoverished dialogical relationship patterns in paranoid personality disorder. *American Journal of Psychotherapy, 59*(3), 247–265.

Salzer, S., Winkelbach, C., Leweke, F., Leibing, E., & Leichsenring, F. (2011). Long-term effects of short-term psychodynamic psychotherapy and cognitive-behavioral therapy in generalized anxiety disorder: 12-month follow-up. *Canadian Journal of Psychiatry, 56*(8), 503–508.

SAMHSA. (2007, March 13). *Emergency room visits climb for misuse of prescription and over-the-counter drugs.* Washington DC: Department of Health and Human Services.

SAMHSA. (2008, June 16). *Racial and ethnic groups: Reports and data.* Washington DC: Department of Health and Human Services.

Samorodnitzky-Naveh, G., Geiger, S. B., & Levin, L. (2007). Patients' satisfaction with dental esthetics. *Journal of the American Dental Association, 138*(6), 805–808.

Samos, L. F., Aguilar, E., & Ouslander, J. G. (2010). Institutional long-term care in the United States. In H. M. Fillit, K. Rockwood, & K. Woodhouse (Eds.), *Brocklehurst's textbook of geriatric medicine and gerontology, 7th edition.* Philadelphia, PA: Saunders Publishers.

Sampath, G., Shah, A., Kraska, J., & Soni, S. D. (1992). Neuroleptic discontinuation in the very stable schizophrenic patient: Relapse rates and serum neuroleptic levels. *Human Psychopharmacology: Clinical and Experimental, 7*(4), 255–264.

Sample, I. (2005, November 30). Mental illness link to art and sex. *Guardian.* Retrieved July 6, 2007, from http://www.guardian.co.uk.

Samuel, D. B., & Widiger, T. A. (2011). Conscientiousness and obsessive-compulsive personality disorder. *Personality Disorders: Theory, Research, and Treatment, 2,* 161–174.

Samuel, V. J., Curtis, S., Thornell, A., George, P., Taylor, A., Brome, D. R., et al. (1997).

The unexplored void of ADHD and African-American research: A review of the literature. *Journal of Attention Disorders, 1*(4), 197–207.

Sánchez Bravo, C., Meléndez, J. C., Ayala, N. P. C., & Ruiz, B. E. T. (2010). Profiles and psychological indicators related to dyspareunias and vaginismus: Qualitative study, Part two. *Salud Mental, 33*(5), 437–449.

Sanders, A. R., Duan, J., & Gejman, P. V. (2012). Schizophrenia genetics: What have we learned from genomewide association studies? In A. S. Brown & P. H. Patterson (Eds.), *The origins of schizophrenia* (pp. 175–209). New York: Columbia University Press.

Sandler, M. (1990). Monoamine oxidase inhibitors in depression: History and mythology. *Journal of Psychopharmacology, 4*(3), 136–139.

Sanftner, J. L., & Tantillo, M. (2011). Body image and eating disorders: A compelling source of shame for women. In R. L. Dearing & J. P. Tangney (Eds.), *Shame in the therapy hour* (pp. 277–303). Washington, DC: American Psychological Association.

Sano, M. (2003). Noncholinergic treatment options for Alzheimer's disease. *Journal of Clinical Psychiatry, 64*(Suppl. 9), 23–28.

Santa-Cruz, N. (2010, June 10). Minority population growing in the United States, census estimates show. *Los Angeles Times.*

Santiseban, D. A., Muir-Malcolm, J. A., Mitrani, V. B., & Szapocznik, J. (2001). Chapter 16: Integrating the study of ethnic culture and family psychology intervention science. In H. A. Liddle, D. A. Santiseban, R. F. Levant, & J. H. Bray (Eds.), *Family psychology: Science-based interventions* (pp. 331–352). Washington, DC: American Psychological Association.

Santtila, P., Sandnabba, N. K., Alison, L., & Nordling, N. (2002). Investigating the underlying structure in sadomasochistically oriented behavior. *Archives of Sexual Behavior, 31*(2), 185–196.

Santtila, P., Sandnabba, N. K., & Nordling, N. (2006). Sadomasochism. In R. D. McAnulty & M. M. Burnette (Eds.), *Sex and sexuality: Vol. 3. Sexual deviation and sexual offenses.* Westport, CT: Praeger Publishers.

Sar, V., Akyuz, G., & Dogan, O. (2007). Prevalence of dissociative disorders among women in the general population. *Psychiatry Research, 149*(1–3), 169–176.

Sareen, J., Afifi, T. O., McMillan, K. A., & Asmundson, G. J. G. (2011). Relationship between household income and mental disorders: Findings from a population-based longitudinal study. *Archives of General Psychiatry, 68*(4), 419–426.

Sareen, J., Enns, M. W., & Cox, B. J. (2004). Potential for misuse of sedatives. *American Journal of Psychiatry, 161,* 1722–1723.

Sargalska, J., Miranda, R., & Marroquin, B. (2011). Being certain about an absence of the positive: Specificity in relation to hopelessness and suicidal ideation. *International Journal of Cognitive Therapy, 4*(1), 104–116.

Sassi, R. B., & Soares, J. C. (2002). Neural circuitry and signaling in bipolar disorder. In G. B. Kaplan & Hammer, R. P. (Eds.), *Brain circuitry and signaling in psychiatry: Basic science and clinical implications.* Washington, DC: American Psychiatric Publishing.

Satir, V. (1964). *Conjoint family therapy: A guide to therapy and technique.* Palo Alto, CA: Science & Behavior Books.

Satir, V. (1967). *Conjoint family therapy* (Rev. ed.). Palo Alto, CA: Science & Behavior Books.

Satir, V. (1987). Going behind the obvious: The psychotherapeutic journey. In J. K. Zeig (Ed.), *The evolution of psychotherapy.* New York: Brunner/Mazel.

Sauvé, W. M., & Stahl, S. M. (2011). Psychopharmacological treatment. In B. A. Moore & W. E. Penk (Eds.), *Treating PTSD in military personnel: A clinical handbook* (pp. 155–172). New York: Guilford Press.

Savitz, J., & Drevets, W. C. (2011). Neuroimaging and neuropathological findings in bipolar disorder. In C. A. Zarate, Jr. & H. K. Manji (Eds.), *Bipolar depression: Molecular neurobiology, clinical diagnosis and pharmacotherapy. Milestones in drug therapy* (pp. 201–225). Cambridge, MA: Birkhäuser.

Saxon, A. J. & Miotto, K. (2011). Methadone maintenance. In J. H. Lowinson & P. Ruiz (Eds.), *Substance abuse: A comprehensive textbook, fifth edition.* Philadelphia, PA: Lippincott, Williams, & Wilkins.

Scarborough, B. K., Like-Haislip, T. Z., Novak, K. J., Lucas, W. L., & Alarid, L. F. (2010). Assessing the relationship between individual characteristics, neighborhood context, and fear of crime. *Journal of Criminal Justice, 38*(4), 819–826.

Scelfo, J. (2005, June 13). Bad girls go wild. *Newsweek,* 66–67.

Schafer, J. A., Varano, S. P., Jarvis, J. P., & Cancino, J. M. (2010, July-August). Bad moon on the rise? Lunar cycles and incidents of crime. *Journal of Criminal Justice, 38*(4), 359–367.

Schechter, D., Singer, T. M., Kuperman, J., & Endicott, J. (1998). Selection of "normal" control subjects for psychiatric research: Update on a model for centralized recruitment. *Psychiatry Research, 79*(2), 175–185.

Scheffler, R. M., Hinshaw, S. P., Modrek, S., & Levine, P. (2007). The global market for ADHD medications. *Health Affairs (Project Hope), 26*(2), 450–457.

Scheid, T. L. (2010). Consequences of managed care for mental health providers. In T. L., Scheid & T. N. Brown (Eds.), *A handbook for the study of mental health: Social contexts, theories, and systems* (2nd ed., pp. 529–547). New York: Cambridge University Press.

Scher, C. D., Steidtmann, D., Luxton, D., & Ingram, R. E. (2006). Specific phobia: A common problem, rarely treated. In T. G. Plante (Ed.), *Mental disorders of the new millennium: Vol. 1. Behavioral issues.* Westport, CT: Praeger Publishers.

Scheuermann, B., Webber, J., Boutot, E. A., & Goodwin, M. (2003). Problems with personnel preparation in autism spectrum disorders. *Focus on Autism and Other Developmental Disabilities, 18,* 197–206.

Scheuffgen, K., Happe, F., Anderson, M., & Frith, U. (2000). High "intelligence," low "IQ"? Speed of processing and measured IQ in children with autism. *Development and Psychopathology, 12*(1), 83–90.

Schienle, A., Hettema, J. M., Cáceda, R., & Nemeroff, C. B. (2011). Neurobiology and genetics of generalized anxiety disorder. *Psychiatric Annals, 41*(2), 133–123.

Schiffer, B., Peschel, T., Paul, T., Gizewski, E., Forsting, M., Levgraf, N., et al. (2007). Structural brain abnormalities in the frontostriatal system and cerebellum in pedophilia. *Journal of Psychiatric Research, 41*(9), 753–762.

Schiffman, J., Abrahamson, A., Cannon, T., LaBrie, J., Parnas, J. Schulsinger, F., et al. (2001). Early rearing factors in schizophrenia. *International Journal of Mental Health, 30*(1), 3–16.

Schiffman, J., LaBrie, J., Carter, J., Cannon, T., Schulsinger, F., Parnas, J., et al. (2002). Perception of parent-child relationships in high-risk families, and adult schizophrenia outcome of offspring. *Journal of Psychiatric Research, 36*(1), 41–47.

Schiffman, J., Maeda, J. A., Hayashi, K., Michelsen, N., Sorensen, H. J., Ekstrom, M., et al. (2006). Premorbid childhood ocular alignment abnormalities and adult schizophrenia-spectrum disorder. *Schizophrenia Research, 81*(2–3), 253–260.

Schildkraut, J. J. (1965). The catecholamine hypothesis of affective disorders: A review of supporting evidence. *American Journal of Psychiatry, 122*(5), 509–522.

Schlesinger, J., & Ismail, H. (Eds.). (2004). Heroic, not disordered: Creativity and mental illness revisited: Comment. *British Journal of Psychiatry, 184*(4), 363–364.

Schmidt, H. D., Vassoler, F. M., & Pierce, C. (2011). Neurobiological factors of drug dependence. In J. H. Lowinson & P. Ruiz (Eds.), *Substance abuse: A comprehensive textbook, fifth edition.* Philadelphia, PA: Lippincott, Williams, & Wilkins.

Schmidtke, A., & Häfner, H. (1988). The Werther effect after television films: New evidence for an old hypothesis. *Psychological Medicine, 18,* 665–676.

Schmiedek, F., Bauer, C., Lövdén, M., Brose, A., & Lindenberger, U. (2010). Cognitive enrichment in old age: Web-based training programs. *GeroPsych: The Journal of Gerontopsychology and Geriatric Psychiatry, 23*(2), 59–67.

Schmitz, J. M. & Stotts, A. L. (2011). Nicotine. In J. H. Lowinson & P. Ruiz (Eds.), *Substance abuse: A comprehensive textbook, fifth edition.* Philadelphia, PA: Lippincott, Williams, & Wilkins.

Schneider, K. J., & Krug, O. T. (2010). *Existential–humanistic therapy. Theories of psychotherapy.* Washington, DC: American Psychological Association.

Schneider, K. L., & Shenassa, E. (2008). Correlates of suicide ideation in a population-based sample of cancer patients. *Journal of Psychosocial Oncology, 26*(2) 49–62.

Schöning, S., Engelien, A., Bauer, C., Kugel, H., Kersting, A., Roestel, C., et al. (2010). Neuroimaging differences in spatial cognition between men and male-to-female transsexuals before and during hormone therapy. *Journal of Sexual Medicine, 7*(5), 1858–1867.

Schopp, R., Wiener, R. L., Bornstein, B. H., & Willborn, S. L. (Eds.). *Mental disorder and criminal law: Responsibility, punishment and competence.* New York: Springer Publishing.

Schottenfeld, R. S. (2008). Opioid maintenance treatment. In H. D. Kleber & M. Galanter (Eds.), *The American Psychiatric Publishing textbook of substance abuse treatment* (4th ed., pp. 289–308). Arlington, VA: American Psychiatric Publishing.

Schrag, M., Mueller, C., Oyoyo, U., Smith, M. A., & Kirsch, W. M. (2011). Iron, zinc and copper in the Alzheimer's disease brain: A quantitative meta-analysis. some insight on the influence of citation bias on scientific opinion. *Progress in Neurobiology, 94*(3), 296–306.

Schreiber, C. (2011). Social skills interventions for children with high-functioning autism spectrum disorders. *Journal of Positive Behavior Interventions, 13*(1), 49–62.

Schreiber, F. R. (1973). *Sybil.* Chicago: Regnery.

Schreibman, L., & Koegel, R. L. (2005). Training for parents of children with autism: Pivotal responses, generalization, and individualization of interventions. In E. D. Hibbs & P. S. Jensen (Eds.), *Psychosocial treatments for child and adolescent disorders: Empirically based strategies for clinical practice* (2nd ed., pp. 605–631). Washington, DC: American Psychological Association.

Schreier, H. A., Ayoub, C. C., & Bursch, B. (2010). Forensic issues in Munchausen by Proxy. In E. P. Benedek, P. Ash, & C. L. Scott (Eds.), *Principles and practice of child and adolescent forensic mental health* (pp. 241–252). Arlington, VA: American Psychiatric Publishing.

Schuel, H., Burkman, L. J., Lippes, J. Crickard, K., Mahony, M. C., Guiffrida, A., et al. (2002). Evidence that anandamide-signalling regulates human sperm functions required for fertilization. *Molecular Reproduction and Development, 63,* 376–387.

Schulte, I. E., & Petermann, F. (2011). Somatoform disorders: 30 years of debate about criteria! What about children and adolescents? *Journal of Psychosomatic Research, 70*(3), 218–228.

Schultz, G. (2007, May 24). Marital breakdown and divorce increases rates of depression, StatCan study finds. *LifeSiteNews.com.*

Schultz, L. T., Heimberg, R. G., & Rodebaugh, T. L. (2008). Social anxiety disorder. In M. Hersen & J. Rosqvist (Eds.), *Handbook of psychological assessment, case conceptualization, and treatment: Vol. 1. Adults* (pp. 204–236). Hoboken, NJ: John Wiley & Sons.

Schultz, L. T., Heimberg, R. G., Rodebaugh, T. L., Schneier, F. R., Liebowitz, M. R., & Telch, M. J. (2006). The Appraisal of Social Concerns scale: Psychometric validation with a clinical sample of patients with social anxiety disorder. *Behavior Therapist, 37*(4), 393–405.

Schulz, S., & Laessle, R. G. (2012). Stress-induced laboratory eating behavior in obese women with binge eating disorder. *Appetite, 58*(2), 457–461.

Schuster, J-P., Hoertel, N., & Limosin, F. (2011). The man behind Philippe Pinel: Jean-Baptiste Pussin (1746–1811)—Psychiatry in pictures. *British Journal of Psychiatry, 198*(3), 241.

Schuster, J-P., Hoertel, N., & Limosin, F. (2011). "The man behind Philippe Pinel: Jean- Baptiste Pussin (1746–1811)—Psychiatry in Pictures": Correction. *British Journal of Psychiatry, 198*(4), 327.

Schuster, M. A., Stein, B. D., Jaycox, L. H., Collins, R. L., Marshall, G. N., Elliot, M. N., et al. (2001). A national survey of stress reactions after the September 11, 2001, terrorist attacks. *New England Journal of Medicine, 20,* 1507–1512.

Schwalb, M. (1999). Interviewed in M. S. Baum, Autism: Locked in a solitary world. *HealthState, 17*(2), 18–22.

Schwartz, B. S., & Stewart, W. F. (2007). Lead and cognitive function in adults: A questions and answers approach to a review of the evidence for cause, treatment, and prevention. *International Review of Psychiatry, 19*(6), 671–692.

Schwartz, J. (2010, October 2). Bullying, suicide, punishment. *New York Times, 160,* 55, 182.

Schwartz, M. (2011). The retrospective profile and the facilitated family retreat. In J. R. Jordan & J. L.

McIntosh (Eds.), *Grief after suicide: Understanding the consequences and caring for the survivors. Series in death, dying and bereavement* (pp. 371–379). New York: Routledge/Taylor & Francis Group.

Schwartz, S. (1993). *Classic studies in abnormal psychology.* Mountain View, CA: Mayfield Publishing.

Schwartz, S., & Johnson, J. J. (1985). *Psychopathology of childhood.* New York: Pergamon Press.

Schwarz, A. (2010, October 20). As injuries rise, scant oversight of helmet safety. *New York Times.*

Scott, G. G. (2010). *Playing the lying game: Detecting and dealing with lies and liars, from occasional fibbers to frequent fabricators.* Santa Barbara, CA: Praeger/ABC-CLIO.

Seeman, P. (2011). All roads to schizophrenia lead to dopamine supersensitivity and elevated dopamine D2High receptors. *CNS Neuroscience & Therapeutics, 17*(2), 118–132.

Seeman, P. (2011). Schizophrenia diagnosis and treatment. *CNS Neuroscience & Therapeutics, 17*(2), 81–82.

Segal, D. L., & Hersen, M. (Eds.). (2010). *Diagnostic interviewing.* New York: Springer Publishing.

Segal, D. L., June, A., & Marty, M. A. (2010). Basic issues in interviewing and the interview process. In D. L. Segal & M. Hersen (Eds.), *Diagnostic interviewing* (pp. 1–21). New York: Springer Publishing.

Segal, R. (2008). *The national association for retarded citizens.* Silver Spring, MD: The Arc.

Segraves, T., & Althof, S. (2002). Psychotherapy and pharmacotherapy for sexual dysfunctions. In P. E. Nathan & J. M. Gorman (Eds.), *A guide to treatments that work* (2nd ed., pp. 497–524). London: Oxford University Press.

Segrin, C. (2000). Social skills deficits associated with depression. *Clinical Psychology Review, 20*(3), 379–403.

Seiden, R. H. (1981). Mellowing with age: Factors influencing the nonwhite suicide rate. *International Journal of Aging and Human Development, 13,* 265–284.

Seitz, D., Purandare, N., & Conn, D. (2010). Prevalence of psychiatric disorders among older adults in long-term care homes: A systematic review. *International Psychogeriatrics, 22*(7), 1025–1039.

Seligman, M. E. P. (1971). Phobias and preparedness. *Behavior Therapist, 2,* 307–320.

Seligman, M. E. P. (1975). *Helplessness.* San Francisco: Freeman.

Seligman, M. E. P., Castellon, C., Cacciola, J., Schulman, P., et al. (1988). Explanatory style change during cognitive therapy for unipolar depression. *Journal of Abnormal Psychology, 97*(1), 13–18.

Seligman, M. E. P., & Fowler, R. D. (2011). Comprehensive soldier fitness and the future of psychology. *American Psychologist, 66*(1), 82–86.

Selkoe, D. J. (1991). Amyloid protein and Alzheimer's disease. *Scientific American, 265,* 68–78.

Selkoe, D. J. (1992). Alzheimer's disease: New insights into an emerging epidemic. *Journal of Geriatric Psychiatry, 25*(2), 211–227.

Selkoe, D. J. (2000). The origins of Alzheimer's disease: A is for amyloid. *Journal of the American Medical Association, 283*(12), 1615–1617.

Selkoe, D. J. (2011). Alzheimer's disease. *Cold Spring Harbor Perspectives in Biology, 3*(7).

Selling, L. S. (1940). *Men against madness.* New York: Greenberg.

Selvaraj, S., Murthy, N. V., Bhagwagar, Z., Bose, S. K., Hinz, R., Grasby, P. M., &

Cowen, P. J. (2011). Diminished brain 5-HT transporter binding in major depression: A positron emission tomography study with [¹¹C] DASB. *Psychopharmacology, 213*(2-3), 555–562.

Semmler, C., & Brewer, N. (2010). Eyewitness memory. In J. M. Brown & E. A. Campbell (Eds.), *The Cambridge handbook of forensic psychology.* New York: Cambridge University Press.

Senior, J., Hayes, A. J., Pratt, D., Thomas, S. D., Fahy, T., Leese, M., et al. (2007). The identification and management of suicide risk in local prisons. *Journal of Forensic Psychiatry and Psychology, 18*(3), 368–380.

Sennott, S. L. (2011). Gender disorder as gender oppression: A transfeminist approach to rethinking the pathologization of gender non-conformity. *Women & Therapy, 34*(1-2), 93–113.

Serby, M. J., Yhap, C., & Landron, E. Y. (2010). A study of herbal remedies for memory complaints. *Journal of Neuropsychiatry and Clinical Neurosciences, 22*(3), 345–347.

Serpell, L., & Treasure, J. (2002). Bulimia nervosa: Friend or foe? The pros and cons of bulimia nervosa. *International Journal of Eating Disorders, 32*(2), 164–170.

Seto, M. C. (2008). *Pedophilia and sexual offending against children: Theory, assessment, and intervention.* Washington, DC: American Psychological Association.

Seto, M. C., Lalumiere, M. L., Harris, G. T., & Chivers, M. L. (2012). The sexual responses of sexual sadists. *Journal of Abnormal Psychology, 121*(3), 739–753.

Seto, M. C., Maric, A., & Barbaree, H. E. (2001). The role of pornography in the etiology of sexual aggression. *Aggression and Violent Behavior, 6*(1), 35–53.

Shafran, R. (2005). Cognitive-behavioral models of OCD. In J. S. Abramowitz & A. C. Houts (Eds.), *Concepts and controversies in obsessive-compulsive disorder.* New York: Springer Science + Business Media.

Shain, B. N. (2007). Suicide and suicide attempts in adolescents. *Pediatrics, 120*(3), 669–678.

Shamloul, R., & Bella, A. J. (2011). Impact of cannabis use on male sexual health. *Journal of Sexual Medicine, 8*(4), 971–975.

Shamoo, A. E. (2002). *Moral and compliance issues in clinical research, Part 1: Where we are today, RAPS RA interactive* (pp. 1–2). Retrieved from http://www.raps.org/rainteractive/articleCT.cfm?article_ID=63.

Shankar, A., McMunn, A., Banks, J., & Steptoe, A. (2011). Loneliness, social isolation, and behavioral and biological health indicators in older adults. *Health Psychology, 30*(4), 377–385.

Shapiro, D. L., & Smith, S. R. (2011). Other areas of liability in practice. In D. L. Shapiro & S. R. Smith (Eds.), *Malpractice in psychology: A practical resource for clinicians* (pp. 119–137). Washington, DC: American Psychological Association.

Shapiro, E. R. (2004). Discussion of Ernst Prelinger's "Thoughts on hate and aggression." *Psychoanalytic Study of the Child, 39,* 44–51.

Shapiro, J. L., & Bernadett-Shapiro, S. (2006). Narcissism: Greek tragedy, psychological syndrome, cultural norm. In T. G. Plante (Ed.), *Mental disorders of the new millennium: Vol. 1. Behavioral issues.* Westport, CT: Praeger Publishers.

Shapiro, J. R., Bauer, S., Andrews, E., Pisetsky, E., Bulik-Sullivan, B., Hamer, R. M., & Bulik, C. M. (2010). Text messaging in the treatment of bulimia nervosa. *Clinician's Research Digest, 28*(12).

Sharf, R. S. (2012). *Theories of psychotherapy & counseling: Concepts and cases* (5th ed.). Pacific Grove, CA: Brooks/Cole.

Sharma, B. R. (2009). Is attempted suicide an offense? *Aggression and Violent Behavior, 14*(2), 139–145.

Sharma, M. (Ed.). (2005). Editorial: Improving interventions for prevention and control of alcohol use in college students. *Journal of Alcohol and Drug Education, 49*(2), 3–6.

Shastry, B. S. (2005). Bipolar disorder: An update. *Neurochemistry International, 46*(4), 273–279.

Shaw, K. (2004). *Oddballs and eccentrics.* Edison, NJ: Castle Books.

Shaw, L., Descarreaux, M., Bryans, R., Duranleau, M., Marcoux, H., Potter, B., et al. (2010). A systematic review of chiropractic management of adults with whiplash-associated disorders: Recommendations for advancing evidence-based practice and research. *Journal of Prevention, Assessment & Rehabilitation, 35*(3), 369–394.

Shaw, R. J., Spratt, E. G., Bernard, R. S., & DeMaso, D. R. (2010). Somatoform disorders. In R. J. Shaw & D. R. DeMaso (Eds.), *Textbook of pediatric psychosomatic medicine* (pp. 121–139). Arlington, VA: American Psychiatric Publishing.

Shaw, S. R., & Dawkins, T. (2010). Atypical antipsychotic use in children and adolescents with autism spectrum disorders: A review for educators. In P. C. McCabe & S. R. Shaw (Eds.), *Psychiatric disorders: Current topics and interventions for educators* (pp. 51–59). Thousand Oaks, CA: Corwin Press, National Association of School Psychologists.

Shcherbatykh, I., & Carpenter, D. O. (2007). The role of metals in the etiology of Alzheimer's disease. *Journal of Alzheimer's Disease, 11*, 191–205.

Shedler, J., & Westen, D. (2004). Dimensions of personality pathology: An alternative to the five-factor model. *American Journal of Psychiatry, 161,* 1743–1754.

Shedler, J., & Westen, D. D. (2010). The Shedler-Westen assessment procedure: Making personality diagnosis clinically meaningful. In J. F. Clarkin, P. Fonagy & G. O. Gabbard (Eds.), *Psychodynamic psychotherapy for personality disorders: A clinical handbook.* (pp. 125–161) Arlington, VA: American Psychiatric Publishing, Inc.

Sheldon, P. (2008). The relationship between unwillingness-to-communicate and student's facebook use. *Journal of Media Psychology, 20*(2), 67–75.

Shenk, D. (2001). *The forgetting: Alzheimer's: Portrait of an epidemic.* New York: Doubleday.

Sher, L., Oquendo, M. A., Falgalvy, H. C., Grunebaum, M. F., Burke, A. K., Zalsman, G., et al. (2005). The relationship of aggression to suicidal behavior in depressed patients with a history of alcoholism. *Addictive Behavior, 30*(6), 1144–1153.

Sheras, P., & Worchel, S. (1979). *Clinical psychology: A social psychological approach.* New York: Van Nostrand.

Sherlock, R. (1983). Suicide and public policy: A critique of the "new consensus." *Bioethics, 4,* 58–70.

Sherrer, M. V., & O'Hare, T. (2008). Clinical case management. In K. T. Mueser & D. V. Jeste (Eds.), *Clinical handbook of schizophrenia* (pp. 309–318). New York: Guilford Press.

Sherry, A., & Whilde, M. R. (2008). Borderline personality disorder. In M. Hersen & J. Rosqvist (Eds.), *Handbook of psychological assessment, case*

conceptualization and treatment: Vol. 1. Adults (pp. 403–437). Hoboken, NJ: John Wiley & Sons.

Shields, B. (2010). The advantages of animal testing. *eHOW.* www.ehow.com/print/list_5996753_advantages-animal-testing.html.

Shneidman, E. S. (1963). Orientations toward death: Subintentioned death and indirect suicide. In R. W. White (Ed.), *The study of lives.* New York: Atherton.

Shneidman, E. S. (1979). An overview: Personality, motivation, and behavior theories. In L. D. Hankoff & B. Einsidler (Eds.), *Suicide: Theory and clinical aspects.* Littleton, MA: PSG Publishing.

Shneidman, E. S. (1981). Suicide. *Suicide and Life-Threatening Behavior, 11*(4), 198–220.

Shneidman, E. S. (1985). *Definition of suicide.* New York: Wiley.

Shneidman, E. S. (1987, March). At the point of no return. *Psychology Today.*

Shneidman, E. S. (1993). *Suicide as psychache: A clinical approach to self-destructive behavior.* Northvale, NJ: Jason Aronson.

Shneidman, E. S. (2001). *Comprehending suicide: Landmarks in 20th-century suicidology.* Washington, DC: American Psychological Association.

Shneidman, E. S. (2005). Anodyne psychotherapy for suicide: A psychological view of suicide. *Clinical Neuropsychiatry: Journal of Treatment Evaluation, 2*(1), 7–12.

Shneidman, E. S., & Farberow, N. (1968). The Suicide Prevention Center of Los Angeles. In H. L. P. Resnick (Ed.), *Suicidal behaviors: Diagnosis and management.* Boston: Little, Brown.

Shneidman, E. S., & Mandelkorn, P. (1983, 1967). How to prevent suicide. *Public Affairs Pamphlets,* New York City.

Shriver, M. (2011). *Alzheimer's in America: The Shriver Report on women and Alzheimer's.* New York: Free Press.

Sieberg, C. B., Huguet, A., von Baeyer, C. L., & Seshia, S. S. (2012). Psychological interventions for headache in children and adolescents. *Canadian Journal of Neurological Sciences, 39*(1), 26–34.

Siegel, B., & Ficcaglia, M. (2006). Pervasive developmental disorders. In M. Hersen & J. C. Thomas (Series Eds.) & R. T. Ammerman (Vol. Ed.), *Comprehensive handbook of personality and psychopathology: Vol. 3. Child psychopathology* (pp. 254–71). Hoboken, NJ: Wiley.

Siegel, R. K. (1990). In J. Sherlock, Getting high—Animals do it, too. *USA Today,* p. 1A.

Siep, N., Jansen, A., Havermans, R., & Roefs, A. (2011). Cognitions and emotions in eating disorders. In R. A. H. Adan & W. H. Kaye (Eds.), *Behavioral neurobiology of eating disorders. Current topics in behavioral neurosciences* (pp. 17–33). New York: Springer-Verlag Publishing.

Sierra, M., & David, A. S. (2011). Depersonalization: A selective impairment of self-awareness. *Consciousness and Cognition: An International Journal, 20*(1), 99–108.

Sigerist, H. E. (1943). *Civilization and disease.* Ithaca, NY: Cornell University Press.

Silbersweig, D. A., Stern, E., Frith, C., Cahill, C., et al. (1995). A functional neuroanatomy of hallucinations in schizophrenia. *Nature, 378,* 176–179.

Silk, K. R., & Jibson, M. D. (2010). Personality disorders. In M. D. Rothschild & J. Anthony (Eds.), *The evidence-based guide to antipsychotic medications* (pp. 101–124). Arlington, VA: American Psychiatric Publishing.

Silverman, K., Evans, S. M., Strain, E. C., & Griffiths, R. R. (1992). Withdrawal syndrome after the double-blind cessation of caffeine consumption. *New England Journal of Medicine, 327*(16), 1109–1114.

Silverstein, M. L. (2007). Descriptive psychopathology and theoretical viewpoints: Paranoid, obsessive-compulsive, and borderline personality disorders. In M. L. Silverstein, *Disorders of the self: A personality-guided approach* (pp. 97–113). Washington, DC: American Psychological Association.

Simard, V., Nielsen, T. A., Tremblay, R. E., Boivin, M., & Montplaisir, J. Y. (2008). Longitudinal study of bad dreams in preschool-aged children: Prevalence, demographic correlates, risk and protective factors. *Sleep, 31*(1), 62–70.

Simeon, D., Knutelska, M., Nelson, D., & Guralnik, O. (2003). Feeling unreal: A depersonalization disorder update of 117 cases. *Journal of Clinical Psychiatry, 64*(9), 990–997.

Simmon, J. (1990). Media and market study. In skin deep: Our national obsession with looks. *Psychology Today, 26*(3), 96.

Simon, R. (Ed.). (2011). *Psychotherapy Networker.* www.psychotherapynetworker.org.

Simon, R. I. (2011). Suicide. In R. E. Hales, S. C. Yudofsky, & G. O. Gabbard (Eds.), *Essentials of psychiatry* (3rd ed., pp. 699–717). Arlington, VA: American Psychiatric Publishing.

Simon, R. I., & Gold, L. H. (2010). Psychiatric diagnosis in litigation. In R. I. Simon & L. H. Gold (Eds.), *The American Psychiatric Publishing textbook of forensic psychiatry* (2nd ed., pp. 151–173). Arlington, VA: American Psychiatric Publishing.

Simon, R. I., & Shuman, D. W. (2011). Psychiatry and the law. In R. E. Hales, S. C. Yudofsky & G. O. Gabbard (Eds.), *Essentials of psychiatry* (3rd ed., pp. 661–697). Arlington, VA: American Psychiatric Publishing, Inc.

Simonton, D. K. (2010). So you want to become a creative genius? You must be crazy! In D. H. Cropley, A. J. Cropley, J. C. Kaufman, & M. A. Runco (Eds.), *The dark side of creativity* (pp. 218–234). New York: Cambridge University Press.

Simpson, H. B. (2010). Pharmacological treatment of obsessive-compulsive disorder. In M. B. Stein & T. Steckler (Eds.), *Behavioral neurobiology of anxiety and its treatment. Current topics in behavioral neurosciences* (pp. 527–543). New York: Springer Science + Business Media.

Simpson, H. B., Maher, M. J., Wang, Y., Bao, Y., Foa, E. B., & Franklin, M. (2011). Patient adherence predicts outcome from cognitive behavioral therapy in obsessive-compulsive disorder. *Journal of Consulting and Clinical Psychology, 79*(2), 247–252.

Simpson, S. G. (1996, January 17). Cited in W. Leary, As fellow traveler of other illness, depression often goes in disguise. *New York Times,* p. C9.

Sinclair, J. (2011, February 24). Significant changes in attitudes towards psychotherapy. *Changing Attitudes Towards Psychotherapy and Counselling.* www.cavendishpsychotherapy.co.uk. psychotherapycounsellingnotes/2011/02.

Singh, D., Deogracias, J. J., Johnson, L. L., Bradley, S. J., Kibblewhite, S. J., Owen-Anderson, A., et al. (2010). The Gender Identity/Gender Dysphoria Questionnaire for Adolescents and Adults: Further validity evidence. *Journal of Sex Research, 47*(1), 49–58.

Singh, D., McMain, S., & Zucker, K. J. (2011). Gender identity and sexual orientation in women with borderline personality disorder. *Journal of Sexual Medicine, 8*(2), 447–454.

Singh, S. P., & Kunar, S. S. (2010). Cultural diversity in early psychosis. In P. French, J. Smith, D. Shiers, M. Reed, & M. Rayne (Eds.), *Promoting recovery in early psychosis: A practice manual* (pp. 66–72). Hoboken, NJ: Wiley-Blackwell.

Sinton, M. M., & Taylor, C. B. (2010). Prevention: Current status and underlying theory. In W. S. Agras (Ed.), *The Oxford handbook of eating disorders. Oxford library of psychology* (pp. 307–330). New York: Oxford University Press.

Sit, D., Rothschild, A. J., & Wisner, K. L. (2006). A review of postpartum psychosis. *Journal of Women's Health, 15*(4), 352–368.

Sizemore, C. C. (1991). *A mind of my own: The woman who was known as "Eve" tells the story of her triumph over multiple personality disorder.* New York: William Morrow.

Sizemore, C. C., & Pittillo, E. S. (1977). *I'm Eve.* Garden City, NY: Doubleday.

Sjolie, I. I. (2002). A logotherapist's view of somatization disorder and a protocol. *International Forum for Logotherapy, 25*(1), 24–29.

Skegg, K., Firth, H., Gray, A., & Cox, B. (2010). Suicide by occupation: Does access to means increase the risk? *Australian and New Zealand Journal of Psychiatry, 44*(5), 429–434.

Skodol, A. E. (2005). The borderline diagnosis: Concepts, criteria, and controversies. In J. G. Gunderson & P. D. Hoffman (Eds.), *Understanding and treating borderline personality disorder* (pp. 3–19). Washington, DC: American Psychiatric Publishing.

Skodol, A. E. (2010). Dimensionalizing existing personality disorder categories. In T. Millon, R. F. Krueger, & E. Simonsen (Eds.), *Contemporary directions in psychopathology: Scientific foundations of the DSM-V and ICD-11* (pp. 362–373). New York: Guilford Press.

Skodol, A. E., Gunderson, J. G., McGlashan, T. H., Dyck, I. R., Stout, R. L., Bender, D. S., et al. (2002). Functional impairment in patients with schizotypal, borderline, avoidant, or obsessive-compulsive personality disorder. *American Journal of Psychiatry, 159*(2), 276–283.

Slater, M. D., Kelly, K. J., Lawrence, F. R., Stanley, L. R., & Comello, M. L. G. (2011). Assessing media campaigns linking marijuana non-use with autonomy and aspirations: "Be under your own influence" and ONDCP's "above the influence." *Prevention Science, 12*(1), 12–22.

Sleeper, R. B. (2010). Adverse drug events in elderly patients. In L. C. Hutchison & R. B. Sleeper (Eds.), *Fundamentals of geriatric pharmacotherapy: An evidence-based approach.* Bethesda, MD: American Society of Health-Systems Pharmacists.

Sloan, D. M. (2002). Does warm weather climate affect eating disorder pathology? *International Journal of Eating Disorders, 32,* 240–244.

Slovenko, R. (1992). Is diminished capacity really dead? *Psychiatric Annals, 22*(11), 566–570.

Slovenko, R. (1995). *Psychiatry and criminal culpability.* Oxford, England: John Wiley & Sons.

Slovenko, R. (2002a). *Psychiatry in law/Law in psychiatry.* New York: Brunner-Routledge.

Slovenko, R. (2002b). The role of psychiatric diagnosis in the law. *Journal of Psychiatry and Law, 30*(3), 421–444.

Slovenko, R. (2004). A history of the intermix of psychiatry and law. *Journal of Psychiatry and Law, 32*(4), 561–592.

Slovenko, R. (2006). Editorial: Patients who deceive. *International Journal of Offender Therapy and Comparative Criminology, 50*(3), 241–244.

Slovenko, R. (2009). *Psychiatry in law/Law in psychiatry (2nd ed.).* New York: Routledge/Taylor & Francis Group.

Slovenko, R. (2011, March 23a). *Psychotherapy testimonial privilege in criminal cases.* Presentation at American College of Forensic Psychiatry conference, San Diego, CA.

Slovenko, R. (2011b). The DSM in litigation and legislation. *Journal of the American Academy of Psychiatry and the Law, 39*(1).

Sluhovsky, M. (2007). *Believe not every spirit: Possession, mysticism, & discernment in early modern Catholicism.* Chicago: University of Chicago Press.

Sluhovsky, M. (2011). Spirit possession and other alterations of consciousness in the Christian Western tradition. In E. Cardeña & M. Winkelman (Eds.), *Altering consciousness: Multidisciplinary perspectives (Vols. 1 and 2): History, culture, and the humanities: Biological and psychological perspectives* (pp. 73–88). Santa Barbara, CA: Praeger/ABC-CLIO.

Slutske, W. S., Moffitt, T. E., Poulton, R., & Caspi, A. (2012). Undercontrolled temperament at age 3 predicts disordered gambling at age 32: A longitudinal study of a complete birth cohort. *Psychological Science, 23*(5), 510–516.

Smart-Richman, L., Pek, J., Pascoe, E., & Bauer, D. J. (2010). Discrimination is bad for your health. *Clinician's Research Digest, 28*(11).

Smith, A. (2010). *Americans and their gadgets.* Washington, DC: Pew Internet & American Life Project.

Smith, A. (2011). *Twitter update 2011.* Washington, DC: Pew Internet & American Life Project.

Smith, C. A., & Kirby, L. D. (2011). The role of appraisal and emotion in coping and adaptation. In R. J. Contrada & A. Baum (Eds.), *The handbook of stress science: Biology, psychology, and health* (pp. 195–208). New York: Springer Publishing.

Smith, M. L., & Glass, G. V. (1977). Meta analysis of psychotherapy outcome studies. *American Psychologist, 32*(9), 752–760.

Smith, M. L., Glass, G. V., & Miller, T. I. (1980). *The benefits of psychotherapy.* Baltimore: Johns Hopkins University Press.

Smith, P. K. (2010). Bullying in primary and secondary schools: Psychological and organizational comparisons. In S. R. Jimerson, S. M. Swearer & D. L. Espelage (Eds.), *Handbook of bullying in schools: An international perspective.* (pp. 137–150) New York: Routledge/Taylor & Francis Group.

Smith, P. K. (2011). Bullying in schools: Thirty years of research. In C. P. Monks, & I. Coyne (Eds.), *Bullying in different contexts.* (pp. 36–60) New York: Cambridge University Press.

Smith, P. K., & Slonje, R. (2010). Cyberbullying: The nature and extent of a new kind of bullying, in and out of school. In S. R. Jimerson, S. M. Swearer & D. L. Espelage (Eds.), *Handbook of bullying in schools: An international perspective.* (pp. 249–262) New York: Routledge/Taylor & Francis Group.

Smith, P., Perrin, S., Yule, W., & Clark, D. M. (2010). *Post traumatic stress disorder: Cognitive therapy with children and young people. CBT with children, adolescents and families.* New York: Routledge/Taylor & Francis Group.

Smith, T. (2010). Early and intensive behavioral intervention in autism. In J. R. Weisz, & A. E. Kazdin (Eds.), *Evidence-based psychotherapies for children and adolescents* (2nd ed., pp. 312–326) New York: Guilford Press.

Smith, T., Lovaas, N. W., & Lovaas, O. I. (2002). Behaviors of children with high-functioning autism when paired with typically developing versus delayed peers: A preliminary study. *Behavioral Interventions, 17*(3), 129–143.

Smyth, J. M., & Pennebaker, J. W. (2001). What are the health effects of disclosure? In A. Baum, T. A. Revenson, & J. E. Singer (Eds.), *Handbook of health psychology* (pp. 339–348). Mahwah, NJ: Lawrence Erlbaum.

Snipes, J. B., & Maguire, E. R. (1995). Country music, suicide, and spuriousness. *Social Forces, 74,* 327–329.

Snoeren, E. M. S., Chan, J. S. W., de Jong, T. R., Waldinger, M. D., Olivier, B., & Oosting, R. S. (2011). A new female rat animal model for hypoactive sexual desire disorder: Behavioral and pharmacological evidence. *Journal of Sexual Medicine, 8*(1), 44–56.

Snow, E. (1976, December). In the snow. *Texas Monthly Magazine.*

Snow, M. S., Wolff, L., Hudspeth, E. F., & Etheridge, L. (2009). The practitioner as researcher: Qualitative case studies in play therapy. *International Journal of Play Therapy, 18*(4), 240–250.

Snowdon, J., Pertusa, A., & Mataix-Cols, D. (2012). On hoarding and squalor: A few considerations for DSM-5. *Depression and Anxiety, 29*(5), 417–424.

Snyder, S. (1980). *Biological aspects of mental disorder.* New York: Oxford University Press.

Snyder, W. V. (1947). *Casebook of non-directive counseling.* Boston: Houghton Mifflin.

So, J. K. (2008). Somatization as cultural idiom of distress: Rethinking mind and body in a multicultural society. *Counselling Psychology Quarterly, 21*(2), 167–174.

Soares, J. C., Mallinger, A. G., Dippold, C. S., Frank, E., & Kupfer, D. J. (1999). Platelet membrane phospholipids in euthymic bipolar disorder patients: Are they affected by lithium treatment? *Biological Psychiatry, 45*(4), 453–457.

Soban, C. (2006). What about the boys? Addressing issues of masculinity within male anorexia nervosa in a feminist therapeutic environment. *International Journal of Men's Health, 5*(3), 251–267.

Sobczak, S., Honig, A., van Duinen, M. A., & Riedel, W. J. (2002). Serotonergic dysregulation in bipolar disorders: A literature review of serotonergic challenge studies. *Bipolar Disorders, 4*(6), 347–356.

Sobell, M. B., & Sobell, L. C. (1973). Individualized behavior therapy for alcoholics. *Behavior Therapist, 4*(1), 49–72.

Sobell, M. B., & Sobell, L. C. (1984). The after-math of heresy: A response to Pendery et al.'s (1982) critique of "Individualized Behavior Therapy for Alcoholics." *Behavioral Research and Therapy, 22*(4), 413–440.

Sobell, M. B., & Sobell, L. C. (1984). Under the microscope yet again: A commentary on Walker and Roach's critique of the Dickens Committee's enquiry into our research. *British Journal of Addiction, 79*(2), 157–168.

Sohn, A., & Grayson, C. (2005). *Parenting your Asperger child.* New York: Perigree.

Solar, A. (2011). Supported employment can reduce social exclusion and improve schizophrenia. *Australasian Psychiatry, 19*(1), 78–80.

Soliman, M., Santos, A. M., & Lohr, J. B. (2008). Emergency, inpatient, and residential treatment. In K. T. Mueser & D. V. Jeste (Eds.), *Clinical handbook of schizophrenia* (pp. 339–353). New York: Guilford Press.

Soloff, P. H. (2005). Pharmacotherapy in borderline personality disorder. In J. G. Gunderson & P. D. Hoffman (Eds.), *Understanding and treating borderline personality disorder: A guide for professionals and families.* Washington, DC: American Psychiatric Publishing.

Solomon, D., Ford, E., Adams, J., & Graves, N. (2011). Potential of St. John's wort for the treatment of depression: The economic perspective. *Australian and New Zealand Journal of Psychiatry, 45*(2), 123–130.

Solter, V., Thaller, V., Bagaric, A., Karlovic, D., Crnkovic, D., & Potkonjak, J. (2004). Study of schizophrenia comorbid with alcohol addiction. *European Journal of Psychiatry, 18*(1), 15–22.

Somers, J. M., Goldner, E. M., Waraich, P., & Hsu, L. (2004). Prevalence studies of substance-related disorders: A systematic review of the literature. *Canadian Journal of Psychiatry, 49*(6).

Sonne, J. L. (2012). Duty to protect: Reporting client threat of harm to another. In J. L. Sonne, *PsycEssentials: A pocket resource for mental health practitioners* (pp. 151–161). Washington, DC: American Psychological Association.

Sookman, D., & Leahy, R. L. (Eds.). (2010). *Treatment resistant anxiety disorders: Resolving impasses to symptom remission.* New York: Routledge/Taylor & Francis Group.

Sookman, D., & Steketee, G. (2010). Specialized cognitive behavior therapy for treatment resistant obsessive compulsive disorder. In D. Sookman & R. L. Leahy (Eds.), *Treatment resistant anxiety disorders: Resolving impasses to symptom remission* (pp. 31–74). New York: Routledge/Taylor & Francis Group.

Soorya, L. V., Carpenter, L. A., & Romanczyk, R. G. (2011). Applied behavior analysis. In E. Hollander, A. Kolevzon & J. T. Coyle (Eds.), *Textbook of autism spectrum disorders.* (pp. 525–535) Arlington, VA: American Psychiatric Publishing, Inc.

Sorensen, J. L., & Copeland, A. L. (2000). Drug abuse treatment as an HIV prevention strategy: A review. *Drug and Alcohol Review, 59*(1) 17–31.

Sorge, R. E., & Clarke, P. B. S. (2011). Nicotine self-administration. In M. C. Olmstead (Ed.), *Animal models of drug addiction. Springer protocols: Neuromethods* (pp. 101–132). Totowa, NJ: Humana Press.

Sorocco, K. H., & Lauderdale, S. (2011). *Cognitive behavior therapy with older adults: Innovations across care settings.* New York: Springer Publishing.

Sorrentino, D., Mucca, A., Merlotti, E., Galderisi, S., & Maj, M. (2005). Modified nutritional counseling to increase motivation to treatment in anorexia nervosa. *European Psychiatry, 20*(2), 186–187.

Soto, J. A., Dawson-Andoh, N. A., & BeLue, R. (2011). The relationship between perceived discrimination and Generalized Anxiety Disorder among African Americans, Afro Caribbeans, and non-Hispanic Whites. *Journal of Anxiety Disorders, 25*(2), 258–265.

Soukup, J. E. (2006). Alzheimer's disease: New concepts in diagnosis, treatment, and management. In T. G. Plante (Ed.), *Mental disorders of the new millennium: Vol. 3. Biology and function.* Westport, CT: Praeger Publishers.

Sowislo, J. F., & Orth, U. (2012, June 25). Does low self-esteem predict depression and anxiety? A meta-analysis of longitudinal studies. *Psychological Bulletin.*

Spanos, N. P., & Coe, W. C. (1992). A social-psychological approach to hypnosis. In E. Fromm & M. R. Nash (Eds.), *Contemporary hypnosis research.* New York: Guilford Press.

Spanton, T. (2008, July 28). UFOs: We believe. *The Sun.* Retrieved August 2008 from http://www.thesun.co.uk/sol/homepage/news/ufos/article1477122.ece.

Speaking of Research. (2011). *Facts.* http://speakingofresearch.com/facts/

Speaking of Research. (2011). *Statistics.* http://speakingofresearch.com/facts/statistics/.

Sperry, L. (2003). *Handbook of diagnosis and treatment of DSM-IV-TR personality disorders* (2nd ed.). New York: Brunner-Routledge.

Spiegel, D. (2009). Coming apart: Trauma and the fragmentation of the self. In D. Gordon (Ed.), *Cerebrum 2009: Emerging ideas in brain science* (pp. 1–11). Washington, DC: Dana Press.

Spiegel, D., & Fawzy, F. I. (2002). Psychosocial interventions and prognosis in cancer. In H. G. Koenig & H. J. Cohen (Eds.), *The link between religion and health: Psychoneuroimmunology and the faith factor* (pp. 84–100). New York: Oxford University Press.

Spiegler, M. D., & Guevremont, D. C. (2003). *Contemporary behavior therapy.* Belmont, CA: Thomson/Wadsworth.

Spielberger, C. D. (1966). Theory and research on anxiety. In C. D. Spielberger (Ed.), *Anxiety and behavior.* New York: Academic Press.

Spielberger, C. D. (1972). Anxiety as an emotional state. In C. D. Spielberger (Ed.), *Anxiety: Current trends in theory and research* (Vol. 1). New York: Academic Press.

Spielberger, C. D. (1985). Anxiety, cognition, and affect: A state-trait perspective. In A. H. Tuma & J. Maser (Eds.), *Anxiety and the anxiety disorders.* Hillsdale, NJ: Lawrence Erlbaum.

Spirito, A., & Esposito-Smythers, C. (2008). Evidence-based therapies for adolescent suicidal behavior. In R. G. Steele, T. D. Elkin, & M. C. Roberts (Eds.), *Handbook of evidence-based therapies for children and adolescents: Bridging science and practice.* New York: Springer.

Spirito, A., Simon, V., Cancilliere, M. K., Stein, R., Norcott, C., Loranger, K., & Prinstein, M. J. (2011). Outpatient psychotherapy practice with adolescents following psychiatric hospitalization for suicide ideation or a suicide attempt. *Clinical Child Psychology and Psychiatry, 16*(1), 53–64.

Spitz, R. A. (1945). Hospitalization: An inquiry into the genesis of psychiatric conditions of early childhood. In R. S. Eissler, A. Freud, H. Hartman, & E. Kris (Eds.), *The psychoanalytic study of the child* (Vol. 1). New York: International Universities Press.

Spitz, R. A. (1946). Anaclitic depression. *The psychoanalytic study of the child* (Vol. 2). New York: International Universities Press.

Spitzer, R. L., Gibbon, M., Skodol, A. E., Williams, J. B. W., & First, M. B. (Eds.). (1994). *DSM-IV casebook: A learning companion to the diagnostic and statistical manual of mental disorders* (4th ed.). Washington, DC: American Psychiatric Press.

Spitzer, R. L., Gibbon, M., Skodol, A. E., Williams, J. B. W., & First, M. B. (2002). *DSM-IV-TR casebook: A learning companion to the diagnostic and statistical manual of mental disorders,*

Fourth Edition, Text Revision. Arlington, VA: American Psychiatric Publishing.

Spitzer, R. L., Skodol, A., Gibbon, M., & Williams, J. B. W. (1981). *DSM-III case book* (1st ed.). Washington, DC: American Psychiatric Press.

Spitzer, R. L., Skodol, A., Gibbon, M., & Williams, J. B. W. (1983). *Psychopathology: A case book.* New York: McGraw-Hill.

Splevins, K., Mireskandari, S., Clayton, K., & Blaszczynski, A. (2010). Prevalence of adolescent problem gambling, related harms and help-seeking behaviours among an Australian population. *Journal of Gambling Studies, 26*(2), 189–204.

Spoletini, I., Cherubini, A., Banfi, G., Rubino, I. A., Peran, P., Caltagirone, C., & Spalletta, G. (2011). Hippocampi, thalami, and accumbens microstructural damage in schizophrenia: A volumetry, diffusivity, and neuropsychological study. *Schizophrenia Bulletin, 37*(1), 118–130.

Spooren, W., Lesage, A., Lavreysen, H., Gasparini, F., & Steckler, T. (2010). Metabotropic glutamate receptors: Their therapeutic potential in anxiety. In M. B. Stein & T. Steckler (Eds.), *Behavioral neurobiology of anxiety and its treatment. Current topics in behavioral neurosciences* (pp. 391–413). New York: Springer Science + Business Media.

Sprecher, S., & Hatfield, E. (1996). Premarital sexual standards among U. S. college students: Comparison with Russian and Japanese students. *Archives of Sexual Behavior, 25*(3), 261–288.

Springman, R. E., Wherry, J. N., & Notaro, P. C. (2006). The effects of interviewer race and child race on sexual abuse disclosures in forensic interviews. *Journal of Child Sexual Abuse, 15*(3), 99–116.

Squire, L. R. (1977). ECT and memory loss. *American Journal of Psychiatry, 134,* 997–1001.

Sreenivasan, S., Weinberger, L. E., & Garrick, T. (2003). Expert testimony in sexually violent predator commitments: Conceptualizing legal standards of "mental disorder" and "likely to reoffend." *Journal of the American Academy of Psychiatry and the Law, 31*(4), 471–485.

Srisurapanont, M., Arunpongpaisal, S., Wada, K., Marsden, J., Ali, R., & Kongsakon, R. (2011). Comparisons of methamphetamine psychotic and schizophrenic symptoms: A differential item functioning analysis. *Progress in Neuro-Psychopharmacology & Biological Psychiatry, 35*(4), 959–964.

Stacciarini, J. M. R., O'Keeffe, M., & Mathews, M. (2007). Group therapy as treatment for depressed Latino women: A review of the literature. *Issues in Mental Health Nursing, 28*(5), 473–488.

Stack, S. (2004). Emile Durkheim and altruistic suicide. *Archives of Suicide Research, 8*(1), 9–22.

Stack, S., Gundlach, J., & Reeves, J. L. (1994). The heavy metal subculture and suicide. *Suicide and Life-Threatening Behavior, 24,* 15–23.

Stack, S., & Kposowa, A. J. (2008). The association of suicide rates with individual-level suicide attitudes: A cross-national analysis. *Social Science Quarterly, 89*(1), 39–59.

Stack, S., & Wasserman, I. (2009). Gender and suicide risk: The role of wound site. *Suicide and Life-Threatening Behavior, 39*(1), 13–20.

Stagnitti, M. N. (2005, May). *Antidepressant use in the U.S. civilian noninstitutionalized population, 2002* (MEPS-HC, Statistical Brief No. 77). Rockville, MD: AHRQ/NCHS.

Stahl, S. M., Sommer, B., & Allers, K. A. (2011). Multifunctional pharmacology of flibanserin: Possible mechanism of therapeutic action in hypoactive sexual desire disorder. *Journal of Sexual Medicine, 8*(1), 15–27.

Stahlberg, O., Anckarsater, H., & Nilsson, T. (2010). Mental health problems in youths committed to juvenile institutions: Prevalences and treatment needs. *European Child & Adolescent Psychiatry, 19*(12), 893–903.

Staller, K. M., & Faller, K. C. (Eds.). (2010). *Seeking justice in child sexual abuse: Shifting burdens and sharing responsibilities.* New York: Columbia University Press.

Stanford, M. S. (2007). Demon or disorder: A survey of attitudes toward mental illness in the Christian church. *Mental Health, Religion and Culture, 1*(5), 445–449.

Stanley, B., & Brodsky, B. S. (2005). Suicidal and self-injurious behavior in borderline personality disorder: A self-regulation model. In J. G. Gunderson & P. D. Hoffman (Eds.), *Understanding and treating borderline personality disorder: A guide for professionals and families* (pp. 43–63). Washington, DC: American Psychiatric Publishing.

Stanley, B., Molcho, A., Stanley, M., Winchel, R., Gameroff, M. J., Parsons, B., et al. (2000). Association of aggressive behavior with altered serotonergic function in patients who are not suicidal. *American Journal of Psychiatry, 157*(4), 609–614.

Stanley, M., Stanley, B., Traskman-Bendz, L., Mann, J. J., & Meyendorff, E. (1986). Neurochemical findings in suicide completers and suicide attempters. In R. W. Maris (Ed.), *Biology of suicide.* New York: Guilford Press.

Stanley, M., Virgilio, J., & Gershon, S. (1982). Tritiated imipramine binding sites are decreased in the frontal cortex of suicides. *Science, 216,* 1337–1339.

Stares, J. (2005, November). Einstein, eccentric genius, smoked butts picked up off street. *The Telegraph.*

Steadman, H. J., Monahan, J., Robbins, P. C., Appelbaum, P., Grisso, T., Klassen, D., et al. (1993). From dangerousness to risk assessment: Implications for appropriate research strategies. In S. Hodgins (Ed.), *Mental disorder and crime.* New York: Sage.

Stearns, P. N. (2006). Far and contemporary history: A review essay. *Journal of Social History, 40*(2), 477–484.

Steele, H. (2011). Multiplicity revealed in the Adult Attachment Interview: When integration and coherence means death. In V. Sinason (Ed.), *Attachment, trauma and multiplicity: Working with dissociative identity disorder* (2nd ed., pp. 37–46). New York: Routledge/Taylor & Francis Group.

Steele, R. G., Roberts, M. C., & Elkin, T. D. (2008). Evidence-based therapies for children and adolescents: Problems and prospects. In R. G. Steele, T. D. Elkin & M. C. Roberts (Eds.), *Handbook of evidence-based therapies for children and adolescents: Bridging science and practice.* New York: Springer.

Steiger, H., Bruce, K. R., & Groleau, P. (2011). Neural circuits, neurotransmitters, and behavior: Serotonin and temperament in bulimic syndromes. In R. A. H. Adan & W. H. Kaye (Eds.), *Behavioral neurobiology of eating disorders. Current topics in behavioral neurosciences* (pp. 125–138). New York: Springer-Verlag Publishing.

Steiger, H., & Israel, M. (2010). Treatment of psychiatric comorbidities. In C. M. Grilo & J. E. Mitchell (Eds.), *The treatment of eating disorders: A clinical handbook* (pp. 447–457). New York: Guilford Press.

Stein, D., Kaye, W. H., Matsunaga, H., Orbach, I., Har-Evan, D., Frank, G., et al. (2002). Eating-related concerns, mood, and personality traits in recovered bulimia nervosa subjects: A replication study. *International Journal of Eating Disorders, 32*(2), 225–229.

Stein, D. J., & Fineberg, N. A. (2007). *Obsessive-compulsive disorder.* Oxford, England: Oxford University Press.

Stein, D. J., Hollander, E., & Rothbaum, B. O. (2010). *Textbook of anxiety disorders* (2nd ed.). Arlington, VA: American Psychiatric Publishing.

Stein, D. J., & Williams, D. (2010). Cultural and social aspects of anxiety disorders. In D. J. Stein, E. Hollander, & B. O. Rothbaum (Eds.), *Textbook of anxiety disorders* (2nd ed., pp. 717–729). Arlington, VA: American Psychiatric Publishing.

Stein, J. (2003, August 4). Just say Om. *Time, 162*(5), pp. 48–56.

Stein, M. B., & Steckler, T. (Eds.). (2010). *Behavioral neurobiology of anxiety and its treatment. Current topics in behavioral neurosciences.* New York: Springer Science + Business Media.

Stein, M. B., Steckler, T., Lightfoot, J. D., Hay, E., & Goddard, A. W. (2010). Pharmacologic treatment of panic disorder. In M. B. Stein & T. Steckler (Eds.), *Behavioral neurobiology of anxiety and its treatment. Current topics in behavioral neurosciences* (pp. 469–485). New York: Springer Science + Business Media.

Steiner, H., Smith, C., Rosenkranz, R. T., & Litt, I. (1991). The early care and feeding of anorexics. *Child Psychiatry and Human Development, 21*(3), 163–167.

Steinhausen, H. C. (2002). The outcome of anorexia nervosa in the 20th century. *American Journal of Psychiatry, 159*(8), 1284–1293.

Steinhausen, H. C. (2009). Outcome of eating disorders. *Child and Adolescent Psychiatric Clinics of North America, 18*(1), 225–242.

Steinhausen, H. C., Boyadjieva, S., Grigoroiu-Serbanescu, M., Seidel, R., & Winkler-Metzke, C. (2000). A transcultural outcome study of adolescent eating disorders. *Acta Psychiatrica Scandinavica, 101*(1), 60–66.

Steinhausen, H. C., & Weber, S. (2009). The outcome of bulimia nervosa: Findings from one-quarter century of research. *American Journal of Psychiatry, 166*(12), 1331–1341.

Stekel, W. (2010). *Sadism and masochism: The psychopathology of sexual cruelty.* Chicago, IL: Solar Books/Solar Asylum.

Steketee, G., Frost, R., Bhar, S., Bouvard, M., Clamari, J., Carmin, C., et al. (2003). Psychometric validation of the obsessive beliefs questionnaire and the interpretation of intrusions inventory. Part I. *Behavioral Research and Therapy, 41*(8), 863–878.

Stephens, R., Atkins, J., & Kingston, A. (2009). Swearing as a response to pain. *NeuroReport, 20*(12). 1056–1060.

Stern, A. (1938). Psychoanalytic investigation and therapy in the borderline group of neuroses. *Psychoanalytical Quarterly, 7,* 467–489.

Sternberg, R. J., Grigorenko, E. L., & Bundy, D. A. (2001). The predictive value of IQ. *Merrill-Palmer Quarterly, 47*(1), 1–41.

Stetter, F., & Kupper, S. (2002). Autogenic training: A meta-analysis of clinical outcome studies. *Applied Psychophysiology and Biofeedback, 27*(1), 45–98.

Stevens, J., Harman, J. S., & Kelleher, K. J. (2005). Race/ethnicity and insurance status as factors associated with ADHD treatment patterns. *Journal of Child and Adolescent Psychopharmacology, 15*(1), 88–96.

Stevens, J., & Ward-Estes, J. (2006). Attention-deficit/hyperactivity disorder. In M. Hersen & J. C. Thomas (Series Eds.) & R. T. Ammerman (Vol. Ed.), *Comprehensive handbook of personality and psychopathology: Vol. 3. Child psychopathology* (pp. 316–329). Hoboken, NJ: Wiley.

Stevens, L. M., Lynm, C., & Glass, R. M. (2002). Postpartum depression. *Journal of the American Medical Association, 287*(6), 802.

Stevenson, R. J., Langdon, R., & McGuire, J. (2011). Olfactory hallucinations in schizophrenia and schizoaffective disorder: A phenomenological survey. *Psychiatry Research, 185*(3), 321–327.

Stevenson, R. W. D., & Elliott, S. L. (2007). Sexuality and illness. In S. R. Leiblum (Ed.), *Principles and practice of sex therapy* (4th ed., pp. 313–349). New York: Guilford Press.

Steward, S., & Worley, P. (2002). Local synthesis of proteins at synaptic sites on dendrites: Role in synaptic plasticity and memory consolidation? *Neurobiology of Learning and Memory, 78*(3), 508–527.

Stewart, A. (2004). Prevention of eating disorders. In P. B. Harper & K. N. Dwivedi (Eds.), *Promoting the emotional well-being of children and adolescents and preventing their mental ill health: A handbook* (pp. 173–197). Philadelphia: Jessica Kingsley Publishers.

Stewart, R. E., & Chambless, D. L. (2007). Does psychotherapy research inform treatment decisions in private practice? *Journal of Clinical Psychology, 63*(3), 267–281.

Stewart, T. M., & Williamson, D. A. (2008). Bulimia nervosa. In M. Hersen & J. Rosqvist (Eds.), *Handbook of psychological assessment, case conceptualization and treatment: Vol. 1. Adults.* Hoboken, NJ: John Wiley & Sons.

Stice, E., Hayward, C., Cameron, R. P., Killen, J. D., & Taylor, C. B. (2000). Body-image and eating disturbances predict onset of depression among female adolescents: A longitudinal study. *Journal of Abnormal Psychology, 109*(3), 438–444.

Stice, E., & Presnell, K. (2010). Dieting and the eating disorders. In W. S. Agras (Ed.), *The Oxford handbook of eating disorders.* (pp. 148–179) New York: Oxford University Press.

Stice, E., Yokum, S., Zald, D., & Dagher, A. (2011). Dopamine-based reward circuitry responsivity, genetics, and overeating. In R. A. H. Adan & W. H. Kaye (Eds.), *Behavioral neurobiology of eating disorders.* (pp. 81–93). New York: Springer-Verlag Publishing.

Stokes, D., & Lappin, M. (2010). Neurofeedback and biofeedback with 37 migraineurs: A clinical outcome study. *Behavioral and Brain Functions, 6*(2), Article 9.

Stolberg, R. A., Clark, D. C., & Bongar, B. (2002). Epidemiology, assessment, and management of suicide in depressed patients. In I. H. Gotlib & C. L. Hammen (Eds.), *Handbook of depression* (pp. 581–601). New York: Guilford Press.

Stone, M. H. (2010). Sexual sadism: A portrait of evil. *Journal of the American Academy of Psychoanalysis & Dynamic Psychiatry, 38*(1), 133–157.

Stotland, N. (2010). DSM5: The debate continues. *Psychiatric Times.* http://www.psychiatrictimes.com/bipolar-ii-disorder/content/article/10168/1583072.

Strachan, E. (2008). Civil commitment evaluations. In R. Jackson (Ed.), *Learning forensic assessment* (pp. 509–535). New York: Routledge/Taylor & Francis Group.

Strate, J. M., Zalman, M., & Hunter, D. J. (2005). Physician-assisted suicide and the politics of problem definition. *Mortality, 10*(1), 23–41.

Streatfield, D. (2007). *Brainwash: The secret history of mind control.* New York, NY: Thomas Dunne Books.

Street, A. E., Bell, M. E., & Ready, C. B. (2011). Sexual assault. In D. M. Benedek, & G. H. Wynn (Eds.), *Clinical manual for management of PTSD.* (pp. 325–348) Arlington, VA: American Psychiatric Publishing.

Stricker, G., & Trierweiler, S. J. (1995). The local clinical scientist. A bridge between science and practice. *American Psychologist, 50*(12), 995–1002.

Strickland, B. R., Hale, W. D., & Anderson, L. K. (1975). Effect of induced mood states on activity and self-reported affect. *Journal of Consulting and Clinical Psychology, 43*(4), 587.

Striegel-Moore, R. H., Fairburn, C. G., Wilfley, D. E., Pike, K. M., Dohm, F-A., & Kraemer, H. C. (2005). Toward an understanding of risk factors for binge-eating disorder in black and white women: A community-based case-control study. *Psychological Medicine, 35*(6), 907–917.

Strober, M., Freeman, R., Lampert, C., Diamond, J., & Kaye, W. (2000). Controlled family study of anorexia nervosa and bulimia nervosa: Evidence of shared liability and transmission of partial syndromes. *American Journal of Psychiatry, 157*(3), 393–401.

Strober, M., Freeman, R., Lampert, C., Diamond, J., & Kaye, W. (2001). Males with anorexia nervosa: A controlled study of eating disorders in first-degree relatives. *International Journal of Eating Disorders, 29*(3), 264–269.

Strober, M., & Yager, J. (1985). A developmental perspective on the treatment of anorexia nervosa in adolescents. In D. M. Garner & P. E. Garfinkel (Eds.), *Handbook of psychotherapy for anorexia nervosa and bulimia.* New York: Guilford Press.

Stromme, P., & Magnus, P. (2000). Correlations between socioeconomic status, IQ and aetiology in mental retardation: A population-based study of Norwegian children. *Social Psychiatry and Psychiatric Epidemiology, 35*(1), 12–18.

Strong, P. (2010, July 30). The mindfulness approach: Therapeutic techniques that work. *Psychology Today.*

Strothers, H. S., Rust, G., Minor, P., et al. (2005). Prescription of pharmacotherapy for depression in elderly people varies with age, race, gender, and length of care. *Journal of the American Geriatrics Society, 53,* 456–461.

Stroup, T. S., Marder, S. R., & Lieberman, J. A. (2012). Pharmacotherapies. In J. A. Lieberman, T. S. Stroup, & D. O. Perkins (Eds.), *Essentials of schizophrenia* (pp. 173–206). Arlington, VA: American Psychiatric Publishing.

Strümpfel, U. (2004). Research on gestalt therapy. *International Gestalt Journal, 27*(1), 9–54.

Strümpfel, U. (2006). *Therapie der gefühle: Forschungsbefunde zur gestalttherapie.* Cologne, Germany: Edition Huanistiche Psychologie.

Stuart, S., Noyes, R., Jr., Starcevic, V., & Barsky, A. (2008). An integrative approach to somatoform disorders combining interpersonal and cognitive-behavioral theory and techniques. *Journal of Contemporary Psychotherapy, 38*(1), 45–53.

Stunkard, A. J. (1959). Eating patterns and obesity. *Psychiatric Quarterly,* 33, 284–295.

Stunkard, A. J. (1975). From explanation to action in psychosomatic medicine: The case of obesity. *Psychosomatic Medicine, 37,* 195–236.

Sturmey, P. (2008). Adults with intellectual disabilities. In M. Hersen & J. Rosqvist (Eds.), *Handbook of psychological assessment, case conceptualization, and treatment: Vol. 1. Adults.* Hoboken, NJ: John Wiley & Sons.

Styron, W. (1990). *Darkness visible: A memoir of madness.* New York: Random House.

Sue, D. W., & Sue, D. (2003) *Counseling the culturally diverse: Theory and practice* (4th ed.). New York: Wiley.

Suhail, K., & Nisa, Z. (2002). Prevalence of eating disorders in Pakistan: Relationship with depression and body shape. *Eating and Weight Disorders, 7*(2), 131–138.

Sullivan, C. J., McKendrick, K., Sacks, S., & Banks, S. (2007). Modified therapeutic community treatment for offenders with MICA disorders: Substance use outcomes. *American Journal of Drug and Alcohol Abuse, 33*(6), 823–832.

Sullivan, E. L., Smith, M. S., & Grove, K. L. (2011). Perinatal exposure to high-fat diet programs energy balance, metabolism and behavior in adulthood. *Neuroendocrinology, 93*(1), 1–8.

Sullivan, H. S. (1953). *The interpersonal theory of psychiatry.* New York: Norton.

Sullivan, H. S. (1962). *Schizophrenia as a human process.* New York: Norton.

Summers, M. J., & Saunders, N. L. J. (2012). Neuropsychological measures predict decline to Alzheimer's dementia from mild cognitive impairment. *Neuropsychology, 26*(4), 498–508.

Sundgot-Borgen, J., & Bratland-Sanda, S. (2012). Eating disorders and athletes. In J. Alexander & J. Treasure (Eds.), *A collaborative approach to eating disorders* (pp. 262–271). New York: Taylor & Francis.

Suppes, T., Baldessarini, R. J., Faedda, G. L., & Tohen, M. (1991). Risk of recurrence following discontinuation of lithium treatment in bipolar disorder. *Archives of General Psychiatry, 48*(12), 1082–1088.

Sussman, S. (2010). Cognitive misperceptions and drug misuse. In L. Scheier (Ed.), *Handbook of drug use etiology: Theory, methods, and empirical findings* (pp. 617–629). Washington, DC: American Psychological Association.

Svartberg, M., & McCullough, L. (2010). Cluster C personality disorders: Prevalence, phenomenology, treatment effects, and principles of treatment. In J. F. Clarkin, P. Fonagy, & G. O. Gabbard (Eds.), *Psychodynamic psychotherapy for personality disorders: A clinical handbook* (pp. 337–367). Arlington, VA: American Psychiatric Publishing.

Svartberg, M., & Stiles, T. C. (1991). Comparative effects of short-term psychodynamic psychotherapy: A meta-analysis. *Journal of Consulting and Clinical Psychology, 59,* 704–714.

Svartberg, M., Stiles, T. C., & Seltzer, M. H. (2004). Randomized, controlled trial of the effectiveness of short-term dynamic psychotherapy and cognitive therapy for Cluster C personality disorders. *American Journal of Psychiatry, 161,* 810–817.

Swann, A. C., Lijffijt, M., Lane, S. D., Kjome, K. L., Steinberg, J. L., & Moeller, F. G. (2011). Criminal conviction, impulsivity, and course of illness in bipolar disorder. *Bipolar Disorders, 13*(2), 173–181.

Swanson, H. L. (2011). Learning disabilities: Assessment, identification, and treatment. In M. A. Bray & T. J. Kehle (Eds.), *The Oxford handbook of school psychology* (pp. 334–350). New York: Oxford University Press.

Swanson, J. W. (2010, March 6). Cited by Tony Leys, Crimes Distort Reality of schizophrenia. *Des Moines Register.*

Swartz, M. S., Frohberg, N. R., Drake, R. E., & Lauriello, J. (2012).Psychosocial therapies. In J. A. Lieberman, T. S. Stroup, & D. O. Perkins (Eds.), *Essentials of schizophrenia* (pp. 207–224). Arlington, VA: American Psychiatric Publishing.

Swartz, M. S., Wagner, H. R., Swanson, J. W., Hiday, V. A., & Burns, B. J. (2002). The perceived coerciveness of involuntary outpatient commitment: Findings from an experimental study. *Journal of the American Academy of Psychiatry and the Law, 30*(2), 207–217.

Swearer, S. M., Wang, C., Givens, J., Berry, B., & Reinemann, D. (2011). Mood disorders. In S. Goldstein, & C. R. Reynolds (Eds.), *Handbook of neurodevelopmental and genetic disorders in children* (2nd ed., pp. 209–227) New York: Guilford Press.

Swonger, A. K., & Constantine, L. L. (1983). *Drugs and therapy: A handbook of psychotropic drugs* (2nd ed.). Boston: Little, Brown.

Szabo, A. N., McAuley, E., Erickson, K. I., Voss, M., Prakash, R. S., Mailey, E. L., et al. (2011). Cardiorespiratory fitness, hippocampal volume, and frequency in older adults. *Neuropsychology, 25*(5), 545–553.

Szabo, M., & Lovibond, P. F. (2004). The cognitive content of thought-listed worry episodes in clinic-referred anxious and nonreferred children. *Journal of Cinical Child and Adolescent Psychology, 33*(3), 613–622.

Szasz, T. S. (1960). The myth of mental illness. *American Psychologist, 15,* 113–118.

Szasz, T. S. (1963*). The manufacture of madness.* New York: Harper & Row.

Szasz, T. S. (1977). *Psychiatric slavery.* New York: Free Press.

Szasz, T. S. (2006). The pretense of psychology as science: The myth of mental illness in *statu nascendi. Current Psychology: Developmental, Learning, Personality, Social, 25*(1), 42–49.

Szasz, T. S. (2007). *Coercion as cure: A critical history of psychiatry.* New Brunswick, NJ: Transaction.

Szasz, T. S. (2010). Psychiatry, anti-psychiatry, critical psychiatry: What do these terms mean? *Philosophy, Psychiatry, & Psychology, 17*(3), 229–232.

Szasz, T. S. (2011). The myth of mental illness: 50 years later. *The Psychiatrist, 35*(5), 179–182.

Szasz, T. (2012) *Primum non coercere*: Private personal services and public social services. *Journal of Humanistic Psychology, 52*(2), 154–164.

Szumilas, M., Wei, Y., & Kutcher, S. (2010). Psychological debriefing in schools. *Canadian Medical Association Journal, 182*(9), 883–884.

Tacon, A., & Caldera, Y. (2001). Behavior modification. In R. McComb & J. Jacalyn (Eds.), *Eating disorders in women and children: Prevention, stress management, and treatment* (pp. 263–272). Boca Raton, FL: CRC Press.

TADS (Treatment for Adolescents with Depression Study Team, U.S.). (2004). Fluoxetine, cognitive behavioral therapy, and their combination for adolescents with depression: Treatment for Adolescents with Depression Study (TADS) randomized controlled trial. *Journal of the American Medical Association, 292*(7), 807–820.

TADS (Treatment for Adolescents with Depression Study Team, U.S.). (2007). The Treatment for Adolescents with Depression Study (TADS): Long-term effectiveness and safety outcomes. *Archives of General Psychiatry, 64*(10), 1132–1144.

TADS (Treatment for Adolescents with Depression Study Team, U.S.). (2010). *Treatment for Adolescents with Depression Study.* http://www.nimh.nih.gov/trials/practical/tads/index.shtml.

Takei, Y., Shimada, H., & Suzuki, S. (2011). Cognitive and behavioral features on the recovery process of loss. *Japanese Journal of Counseling Science, 44*(1), 50–59.

Tallis, F., Davey, G., & Capuzzo, N. (1994). The phenomenology of non-pathological worry: A preliminary investigation. In G. Davey & F. Tallis (Eds.), *Worrying: Perspectives on theory, assessment and treatment* (pp. 61–89). Chichester, England: John Wiley.

Tamminga, C. A., Shad, M. U., & Ghose, S. (2008). Neuropsychiatric aspects of schizophrenia. In S. C. Yudofsky & R. E. Hales (Eds.), *The American Psychiatric Publishing textbook of neuropsychiatry and behavioral neurosciences* (5th ed.). Washington, DC: American Psychiatric Publishing.

Tang, C. S-K. (2006). Positive and negative post-disaster psychological adjustment among adult survivors of the Southeast Asian earthquake-tsunami. *Journal of Psychosomatic Research, 61*(5), 699–705.

Tang, C. S-K. (2007). Trajectory of traumatic stress symptoms in the aftermath of extreme natural disaster: A study of adult Thai survivors of the 2004 Southeast Asian earthquake and tsunami. *Journal of Nervous and Mental Disease, 195*(1), 54–59.

Tanofsky-Kraff, M., & Wilfley, D. E. (2010). Interpersonal psychotherapy for bulimia nervosa and binge-eating disorder. In C. M. Grilo & J. E. Mitchell (Eds.), *The treatment of eating disorders: A clinical handbook* (pp. 271–293). New York: Guilford Press.

Tantam, D. (2006). The machine as psychotherapist: Impersonal communication with a machine. *Advances in Psychiatric Treatment, 12,* 416–426.

Tanzer, N. K., Hof, J., & Jackson, J. (2010, August). *Culturally incongruent items: A case of bias in nonverbal intelligence tests?* Paper presented at 118th Annual Convention of the American Psychological Association, San Diego, CA.

Tarrier, N. (2008). Schizophrenia and other psychotic disorders. In D. H. Barlow (Ed.), *Clinical handbook of psychological disorders: A step-by-step treatment manual* (4th ed.). New York: Guilford Press.

Tarrier, N., Taylor, K., & Gooding, P. (2008). Cognitive-behavioral interventions to reduce suicide behavior: A systematic review and meta-analysis. *Behavior Modification, 32*(1), 77–108.

Tashakova, O. (2011, March 25). Am I too fat? *Khaleej Times.*

Tashkin, D. P. (2001). Airway effects of marijuana, cocaine, and other inhaled illicit agents. *Current Opinions in Pulmonary Medicine, 7*(2), 43–61.

Taube-Schiff, M., & Lau, M. A. (2008). Major depressive disorder. In M. Hersen & J. Rosqvist (Eds.), *Handbook of psychological assessment, case conceptualization, and treatment: Vol. 1. Adults* (pp. 319–351). Hoboken, NJ: John Wiley & Sons.

Taylor, G. M., & Ste. Marie, D. M. (2001). Eating disorders symptoms in Canadian female pair and dance figure skaters. *International Journal of Sport Psychology, 32*(1), 21–28.

Taylor, M., & Quayle, E. (2010). Internet sexual offending. In J. M. Brown & E. A. Campbell (Eds.), *The Cambridge handbook of forensic psychology.* New York: Cambridge University Press.

Taylor, R. (1975). Electroconvulsive treatment (ECT): The control of therapeutic power. Exchange.

Taylor, S. E. (2006). *Health psychology* (6th ed.). New York: McGraw Hill.

Taylor, S. E. (2010). Health psychology. In R. F. Baumeister & E. J. Finkel (Eds.), *Advanced social psychology: The state of the science* (pp. 697–731). New York: Oxford University Press.

Taylor, S. E. (2010). Health. In S. T. Fiske, D. T. Gilbert, & G. Lindzey (Eds.), *Handbook of social psychology,* (Vol. 1, 5th ed., pp. 698–723). Hoboken, NJ: John Wiley & Sons.

Taylor, S. E. (2011). *Health psychology* (8th ed.). New York: McGraw-Hill.

Teachman, B. A. (2011). Treatment-induced change in misinterpretations of bodily sensations are critical to outcomes in panic control treatment. *Clinician's Research Digest, 29*(2).

Teglasi, H. (2010). *Essentials of TAT and other storytelling assessments* (2nd ed., Essentials of psychological assessment series) Hoboken, NJ: John Wiley & Sons.

Teicher, M. H., Andersen, S. L., Navalta, C. P., Tomoda, A., Polcari, A., & Kim, D. (2008). Neuropsychiatric disorders of childhood and adolescence. In S. C. Yudofsky & R. E. Hales (Eds.), *The American Psychiatric Publishing textbook of neuropsychiatry and behavioral neurosciences* (5th ed.). Washington, DC: American Psychiatric Publishing.

Telner, J. I., Lapierre, Y. D., Horn, E., & Browne, M. (1986). Rapid reduction of mania by means of reserpine therapy. *American Journal of Psychiatry, 143*(8), 1058.

Teplin, L. A., Abram, K. M., & McClelland, G. M. (1994). Does psychiatric disorder predict violent crime among released jail detainees? *American Psychologist, 49*(4), 335–342.

Terhune, D. B., Cardena, E., & Lindgren, M. (2011). Dissociative tendencies and individual differences in high hypnotic suggestibility. *Cognitive Neuropsychiatry, 16*(2), 113–135.

ter Kuile, M. M., Bulté, I., Weijenborg, P. T. M., Beekman, A., Melles, R., & Onghena, P. (2009). Therapist-aided exposure for women with lifelong vaginismus: A replicated single-case design. *Journal of Consulting and Clinical Psychology, 77*(1), 149–159.

Thakker, J., & Ward, T. (1998). Culture and classification: The cross-cultural application of the DSM-IV. *Clinical Psychology Review, 18,* 501–529.

Thase, M. E. (2006). The failure of evidence-based medicine to guide treatment of antidepressant nonresponders. *Journal of Clinical Psychiatry, 67*(12), 1833–1835.

Thase, M. E. (2010). Pharmacotherapy for adults with bipolar depression. In D. J. Miklowitz & D. Cichetti (Eds.), *Understanding bipolar disorder: A developmental psychopathology perspective* (pp. 445–465). New York: Guilford Press.

Thase, M. E., Trivedi, M. H., & Rush, A. J. (1995). MAOIs in the contemporary treatment of depression. *Neuropsychopharmacology, 12*(3), 185–219.

Theodorou, S., & Haber, P. S. (2005). The medical complications of heroin use. *Current Opinions in Psychiatry, 18*(3), 257–263.

Thibaut, F., De LaBarra, F., Gordon, H., Cosyns, P., & Bradford, J. M. W. (2010). The World Federation of Societies of Biological Psychiatry (WRSBP) guidelines for the biological treatment of paraphilias. *World Journal of Biological Psychiatry, 11*(3-4), 604–655.

Thigpen, C. H., & Cleckley, H. M. (1957). *The three faces of Eve.* New York: McGraw-Hill.

Thomas, J. (2004). Firewall needed between marketing and science. *The National Psychologist, 13*(5), pp. 1, 5.

Thomas, J. (2005). Expansion of Tarasoff "duty to warn" headed to trial in California. *The National Psychologist, 14*(1), pp. 1, 3.

Thomas, S. P. (2011). From the editor—Advances in cybertherapy. *Issues in Mental Health Nursing, 32*(3), 145.

Thompson, A. H., Stuart, H., Bland, R. C., Arboleda-Florez, J., Warner, R., & Dickson, R. A. (2002). Attitudes about schizophrenia from the pilot site of the WPA worldwide campaign against the stigma of schizophrenia. *Social Psychiatry and Psychiatric Epidemiology, 37*(10), 475–482.

Thompson, R. A., & Sherman, R. T. (2010). *Eating disorders in sport.* New York: Routledge/Taylor & Francis Group.

Thornton, L. M., Mazzeo, S. E., & Bulik, C. M. (2011). The heritability of eating disorders: Methods and current findings. In R. A. H. Adan & W. H. Kaye (Eds.), *Behavioral neurobiology of eating disorders. Current topics in behavioral neurosciences* (pp. 141–156). New York: Springer-Verlag Publishing.

Thurston, C. (2008, April). Dietary supplements: The latest trends and issues. *Nutraceuticals World.* Retrieved May 2008 from http://www.nutraceuticalsworld.com/articles/2008/04/dietary-supplements-the-latest-trends-issues.

Tierney, A. J. (2000). Egas Moniz and the origins of psychosurgery: A review commemorating the 50th anniversary of Moniz's Nobel Prize. *Journal of the History of the Neurosciences, 9*(1), 22–36.

Time. (1982, Oct. 25). The 27 Faces of Charles, p. 70.

Time. (1983, September 5). Child abuse: The ultimate betrayal. (By Ed Magnuson).

Tjaden, P., & Thoennes, N. (2000). Prevalence and consequences of male-to-female and female-to-male intimate partner violence as measured by the National Violence Against Women Survey. *Violence Against Women, 6*(2), 142–161.

Tolan, P., Gorman-Smith, D., & Henry, D. (2006). Family violence. *Annual Review of Psychology, 57,* 557–583.

Tolin, D. F., & Meunier, S. A. (2008). Contamination and decontamination. In J. S. Abramowitz, D. McKay, & S. Taylor (Eds.), *Obsessive-compulsive disorder: Subtypes and spectrum conditions.* Oxford, England: Elsevier.

Tonioni, F., D'Alessandris, L., Lai, C., Martinelli, D., Corvino, S., Vasale, M., et al. (2012). Internet addiction: Hours spent online, behaviors and psychological symptoms. *General Hospital Psychiatry, 34*(1), 80–87.

Torgersen, S. (1983). Genetic factors in anxiety disorders. *Archives of General Psychiatry, 40,* 1085–1089.

Torgersen, S. (1984). Genetic and nosological aspects of schizotypal and borderline personality disorders: A twin study. *Archives of General Psychiatry, 41,* 546–554.

Torgersen, S. (1990). Comorbidity of major depression and anxiety disorders in twin pairs. *American Journal of Psychiatry, 147,* 1199–1202.

Torgersen, S. (2000). Genetics of patients with borderline personality disorder. *Psychiatric Clinics of North America, 23*(1), 1–9.

Toro, J., Gila, A., Castro, J., Pombo, C., & Guete, O. (2005). Body image, risk factors for eating disorders and sociocultural influences in Spanish adolescents. *Eating and Weight Disorders, 10*(2), 91–97.

Torrey, E. F. (1991). A viral-anatomical explanation of schizophrenia. *Schizophrenia Bulletin, 17*(1), 15–18.

Torrey, E. F. (2001). *Surviving schizophrenia: A manual for families, consumers, and providers* (4th ed.). New York: HarperCollins.

Torrey, E. F., Bowler, A. E., Taylor, E. H., & Gottesman, I. I. (1994). *Schizophrenia and manic-depressive disorder.* New York: Basic Books.

Torrey, E. F., Buka, S., Cannon, T. D., Goldstein, J. M., Seidman, L. J., Liu, T., et al. (2009). Paternal age as a risk factor for schizophrenia: How important is it? *Schizophrenia Research, 114*(1-3), 1–5.

Touchette, E., Henegar, A., Godart, N. T., Pryor, L., Falissard, B., Tremblay, R. E., & Côté, S. M. (2011). Subclinical eating disorders and their comorbidity with mood and anxiety disorders in adolescent girls. *Psychiatry Research, 185*(1-2), 185–192.

Touyz, S. W., & Carney, T. (2010). Compulsory (involuntary) treatment for anorexia nervosa. In C. M. Grilo & J. E. Mitchell (Eds.), *The treatment of eating disorders: A clinical handbook* (pp. 212–224). New York: Guilford Press.

Traish, A. M., & Gooren, L. J. (2010). Safety of physiological testosterone therapy in women: Lessons from female-to-male transsexuals (FMT) treated with pharmacological testosterone therapy. *Journal of Sexual Medicine, 7*(11), 3758–3764.

Tramontin, M., & Halpern, J. (2007). The psychological aftermath of terrorism: The 2001 World Trade Center attack. In E. K. Carll (Ed.), *Trauma psychology: Issues in violence, disaster, health, and illness* (Vol. 1). Westport, CT: Praeger Publishers.

Tran, T. T., Srivareerat, M., & Alkadhi, K. A. (2011). Chronic psychosocial stress accelerates impairment of long-term memory and late-phase long-term potential in an at-risk model of Alzheimer's disease. *Hippocampus, 21*(7), 724–732.

Travis, C. B., & Meltzer, A. L. (2008). Women's health: Biological and social systems. In F. L. Denmark & M. A. Paludi (Eds.), *Psychology of women: A handbook of issues and theories* (2nd ed., pp. 353–399). Westport, CT: Praeger Publishers.

Treanor, M. (2011). The potential impact of mindfulness on exposure and extinction learning in anxiety disorders. *Clinical Psychology Review, 31*(4), 617–625.

Treasure, J., Williams, C., & Schmidt, U. (2010). Family processes as maintaining factors for eating disorders. In J. Treasure, U. Schmidt, & P. MacDonald (Eds.), *The clinician's guide to collaborative caring in eating disorders: The new Maudsley method* (pp. 60–83). New York: Routledge/Taylor & Francis Group.

Treatment Advocacy Center. (2007). *Briefing paper: Criminalization of individuals with severe psychiatric disorders.* Retrieved from www.Treatmentadvocacycenter.org.

Trefis Team. (2011, February 22). After torrid growth, Facebook user count likely to taper. *Forbes.*

Treit, D., Engin, E., & McEown, K. (2010). Animal models of anxiety and anxiolytic drug action In M. B. Stein & T. Steckler (Eds.), *Behavioral neurobiology of anxiety and its treatment, Current topics in behavioral neurosciences* (pp. 121–160). New York: Springer Science + Business Media.

Trevino, K., McClintock, S. M., & Husain, M. M. (2010). A review of continuation electroconvulsive therapy: Application, safety, and efficacy. *Journal of ECT, 26*(3), 186–195.

Trierweiler, S. J., Neighbors, H. W., Munday, C., Thompson, S. E., Binion, V. J., & Gomez, J. P. (2000). Clinician attribution associated with diagnosis of schizophrenia in African American and non-African American patients. *Journal of Consulting and Clinical Psychology, 68,* 171–175.

Tripoli, T. M., Sato, H., Sartori, M. G., de Arauio, F. F., Girao, M. J. B. C., & Schor, E. (2011). Evaluation of quality of life and sexual satisfaction in women suffering from chronic pelvic pain with or without endometriosis. *Journal of Sexual Medicine, 8*(2), 497–503.

Troiano, R. P., Frongillo, E. A., Sobal, J., & Levitsky, D. A. (1996). The relationship between body weight and mortality: A quantitative analysis of combined information from existing studies. *International Journal of Obesity, 20,* 63–75.

True, W. R., & Lyons, M. J. (1999). Genetic risk factors for PTSD: A twin study. In R. Yehuda (Ed.), *Risk factors for posttraumatic stress disorder.* Washington, DC: American Psychiatric Press.

Trull, T. J., & Widiger, T. A. (2003). Personality disorders. In G. Stricker, T. A. Widiger, & I. B. Wiener (Eds.), *Handbook of psychology: Clinical psychology.* New York: Wiley.

Tryon, G. (1987). Abuse of therapist by patient. *Professional Psychologist, 17,* 357–363.

Trzepacz, P. T., & Meagher, D. J. (2008). Neuropsychiatric aspects of delirium. In S. C. Yudofsky & R. E. Hales (Eds.), *The American psychiatric publishing textbook of neuropsychiatry and behavioral neurosciences* (5th ed.). Washington, DC: American Psychiatric Publishing.

Tsai, J., Stroup, T. S., & Rosenheck, R. A. (2011). Housing arrangements among a national sample of adults with chronic schizophrenia living in the United States: A descriptive study. *Journal of Community Psychology, 39*(1), 76–88.

Tsai, J. L., Ying, Y. W., & Lee, P. A. (2001). Cultural predictors of self-esteem: A study of Chinese American female and male young adults. *Cultural Diversity and Ethnic Minority Psychology, 7,* 284–297.

Tschöke, S., & Steinert, T. (2010). Dissociative identity disorder or schizophrenia: Schneiderian first rank symptoms as a problem for differential diagnosis. *Fortschritte der Neurologie, Psychiatrie, 78*(1), 33–37.

Tsuang, M. T., Bar, J. L., Harley, R. M., & Lyons, M. J. (2001). The Harvard twin study of substance abuse: What we have learned. *Harvard Review of Psychiatry, 9*(6), 267–279.

Tsuang, M., Domschke, K., Jerkey, B. A., & Lyons, M. J. (2004). Agoraphobic behavior and panic attack: A study of male twins. *Journal of Anxiety Disorders, 18*(6), 799–807.

Tsuang, J. W. & Pi, E. H. (2011). Asian Americans and Pacific Islanders. In J. H. Lowinson & P. Ruiz (Eds.), *Substance abuse: A comprehensive textbook, fifth edition.* Philadelphia, PA: Lippincott, Williams, & Wilkins.

Tsuchiya, K. J., Agerbo, E., & Mortensen, P. B. (2005). Parental death and bipolar disorder: A robust association was found in early maternal suicide. *Journal of Affective Disorders, 86*(2–3), 151–159.

Tuber, S., Goudsmit, N., Ferst, A., Shagrin, S., & Wolitzky, R. (2008). A review of projective tests for children: Recent developments. In C. Coulacoglou (Ed.), *Exploring the child's personality: Developmental, clinical and cross-cultural applications of the fairy tale test* (pp. 5–28). Springfield, IL: Charles C. Thomas Publisher.

Tucker, E. (2007, April 22). Advocates for mentally ill say restrictions on voting unfair. *Boston.com*. Retrieved August 19, 2008, from http://www.boston.com.

Tucker, J. (2010). If I had a billion dollars. *The Monkey Cage,* September 16. http://themonkeycage.org/blog/2010/09/16.

Tucker-Drob, E. M. (2011). Neurocognitive functions and everyday functions change together in old age. *Neuropsychology, 25*(3), 368–377.

Tune, L. E. & DeWitt, M. A. (2011). Delirium. In C. E. Coffey, J. L. Cummings, M. S. George, & D. Weintraub (Eds.), *The American Psychiatric Publishing textbook of geriatric neuropsychiatry.* Arlington, VA: American Psychiatric Publishing, Inc.

Turk, C. L., & Mennin, D. S. (2011). Phenomenology of generalized anxiety disorder. *Psychiatric Annals, 41*(2), 72–78.

Turkat, I. D., Keane, S. P., & Thompson-Pope, S. K. (1990). Social processing errors among paranoid personalities. *Journal of Psychopathology and Behavioral Assessment, 12*(3), 263–269.

Turkington, C., & Harris, J. R. (2001). *The encyclopedia of memory and memory disorders* (2nd ed.). New York: Facts on File.

Turkington, C., & Harris, J. R. (2009). *The encyclopedia of the brain and brain disorders* (3rd ed.). New York: Facts On File, Inc.

Turner, E. H., Matthews, A. M., Linardatos, E., Tell, R. A., & Rosenthal, R. (2008). Selective publication of antidepressant trials and its influence on apparent efficacy. *New England Journal of Medicine, 358,* 252–260.

Turner, S. M., Beidel, D. C., & Frueh, B. C. (2005). Multicomponent behavioral treatment of chronic combat-related posttraumatic stress disorder: Trauma management therapy. *Behavior Modification, 29*(1), 39–69.

Turney, K. (2011). Chronic and proximate depression among mothers: Implications for child well-being. *Journal of Marriage and Family, 73*(1), 149–163.

Turton, M. D., O'Shea, D., Gunn, I., Beak, S. A., et al. (1996, January 4). A role for glucagon-like peptide-1 in the central regulation of feeding. *Nature, 379,* 69–72.

Turvey, B. E. (2008). A history of criminal profiling. In B. E. Turvey (Ed.), *Criminal profiling: An introduction to behavioral evidence analysis* (3rd ed., pp. 1–42). San Diego, CA: Elsevier.

Turvey, B. E. (2008). Ethics and the criminal profiler. In B. E. Turvey (Ed.), *Criminal profiling: An introduction to behavioral evidence analysis* (3rd ed., pp. 717–744). San Diego, CA: Elsevier.

Twain, M. (1884). *The adventures of Huckleberry Finn.*

Tyre, P. (2005, December 5). Fighting anorexia: No one to blame. *Newsweek, 146*(23), 50–59.

Tyrer, P., Mitchard, S., Methuen, C., & Ranger, M. (2003). Treatment rejecting and treatment seeking personality disorders: Type R and type S. *Journal of Personality Disorders, 17*(3), 263–268.

Tyson, A. S. (2006, December 20). Repeat Iraq tours raise risk of PTSD, Army finds. *Washington Post.* Retrieved July 6, 2007, from www.washingtonpost.com.

U.S. Bureau of Justice Statistics (BJS). (2011). Victims. http://bjs.ojp.usdoj.gov/index.

U. S. Bureau of Labor Statistics (BLS). (2002a). Counselors. In Bureau of Labor Statistics, *Occupational outlook handbook* (2004–05 ed.). Washington, DC: Author.

U.S. Bureau of Labor Statistics (BLS). (2002b). Social workers. In Bureau of Labor Statistics, *Occupational outlook handbook* (2004–05 ed.). Washington, DC: Author.

U.S. Bureau of Labor Statistics (BLS). (2009). *American Time Use Survey (ATUS).* Washington, DC: Author.

U.S. Bureau of Labor Statistics (BLS). (2010). *American Time Use Survey (ATUS).* Washington, DC: Author.

U.S. Bureau of Labor Statistics (BLS). (2011). *BLS Spotlight on statistics: Women at work.* (www.bls.gov/spotlight).

U.S. Bureau of Labor Statistics (BLS). (2011). *Occupational Outlook Handbook, 2010-11 Edition,* Counselors. Retrieved January 19, 2011, from http://www.bls.gov/oco/ocos067.htm.

U.S. Bureau of Labor Statistics (BLS). (2011). *Occupational Outlook Handbook, 2010-11 Edition,* Psychologists. Retrieved January 19, 2011, from http://www.bls.gov/oco/ocos056.htm.

U.S. Bureau of Labor Statistics (BLS). (2011). *Occupational Outlook Handbook, 2010-11 Edition,* Social Workers. Retrieved January 19, 2011, from http://www.bls.gov/oco/ocos060.htm.

U.S. Census Bureau. (2005). *Statistical abstract of the United States, 2006* (125th ed.). Washington, DC: Government Printing Office.

U.S. Census Bureau. (2010). 2010 *Census data: Redistricting data.* Retrieved on February 13, 2011, from http://2010.census.gov/2010census/data.

U.S. Census Bureau. (2010). Race and ethnicity. *American FactFinder.* Retrieved from http://factfinder.census.gov/servlet/ACSSAFFPeople?

U.S. Census Bureau. (2011). *2011 statistical abstract: International statistics.* Retrieved on February 13, 2011 from www.census.gov/compendia/statab/cats/international–statistics.html.

U.S. Census Bureau. (2011). Death rates from suicide by selected characteristics: 1990 to 2007. *Statistical Abstract of the United States: 2011.* Suitland, MD: US Department of Commerce, Bureau of the Census.

U.S. Census Bureau. (2011). *The statistical abstract: The National Data Book 2011 Population.* Suitland, MD: US Department of Commerce, Bureau of the Census.

U.S. Department of Justice, Federal Bureau of Investigation. (2010). About hate crime statistics, 2010. *Uniform crime reports.* http://www.fbi.gov/about-us/cjis/ucr/hate-crime/2010/index.

U.S. Department of Justice. (1994). *Violence between inmates: Domestic violence.* Annapolis Junction, MD: Bureau of Justice Statistics Clearinghouse.

U.S. Department of Justice. (2006, September 10). *Teens and young adults experience the highest rates of violent crime.* Bureau of Justice Statistics. Retrieved August 11, 2008, from http://ojp.usdoj.gov/ bjs/glance/vage.html.

U.S. Department of Justice. (2008). *Report: Girls study group, 2008.* Washington, DC: Author.

U.S. Department of Justice. (2010). Arrests. *Crime in the United States 2009.* http://www2.fbi.gov/ucr/cius2009/arrests/index.html.

U.S. Department of Justice. (2010, February 10). Girls delinquency. *OJJDP in Focus.,* p.1.

U.S. Department of Justice. (2010). *National study of jail suicide: 20 years later.* Washington, DC: National Institute of Corrections.

Uchino, B. N., & Birmingham, W. (2011). Stress and support processes. In R. J. Contrada & A. Baum (Eds.), *The handbook of stress science: Biology, psychology, and health* (pp. 111–121). New York: Springer Publishing.

Uchiyama, T., Kurosawa, M., & Inaba, Y. (2007). MMR-vaccine and regression in autism spectrum disorders: Negative results presented from Japan. *Journal of Autism and Developmental Disorders, 3*(2), 210–217.

Uher, R., Dernovsek, M. Z., Mors, O., Hauser, J., Souery, D., Zobel, A., et al. (2011). Melancholic, atypical and anxious depression subtypes and outcome of treatment with escitalopram and nortriptyline. *Journal of Affective Disorders, 132*(1-2), 112–120.

Uher, R., Mors, O., Hauser, J., Rietschel, M., Maier, W., Kozel, D., et al. (2011). Changes in body weight during pharmacological treatment of depression. *International Journal of Neuropsychopharmacology, 14*(3), 367–375.

Ulrich, R. S. (1984). View from a window may influence recovery from surgery. *Science, 224,* 420–421.

Ungar, W. J., Mirabelli, C., Cousins, M., & Boydell, K. M. (2006). A qualitative analysis of a dyad approach to health-related quality of life measurement in children with asthma. *Social Science and Medicine, 63*(9), 2354–2366.

Urban Mobility Report. (2010). *Annual Urban Mobility Report.* College Station: Texas Transportation Institute.

Urcuyo, K. R., Boyers, A. E., Carver, C. S., & Antoni, M. H. (2005). Finding benefit in breast cancer: Relations with personality, coping, and concurrent well-being. *Psychology and Health, 20*(2), 175–192.

Uretsky, S. (1999, June 25). Clear as mud: They call it informed consent. HeathScott.

Ursache, A., Blair, C., Stifter, C., & Voegtline, K. (2012, May 7). Emotional reactivity and regulation in infancy interact to predict executive functioning in early childhood. *Developmental Psychology, 7.*

Ursano, R. J., Boydstun, J. A., & Wheatley, R. D. (1981). Psychiatric illness in U.S. Air Force Vietnam prisoners of war: A five-year follow-up. *American Journal of Psychiatry, 138*(3), 310–314.

Ursano, R. J., McCarroll, J. E., & Fullerton, C. S. (2003). Traumatic death in terrorism and disasters: The effects of posttraumatic stress and behavior. In R. J. Ursano, C. S. Fullerton, & A. E. Norwood (Eds.), *Terrorism and disaster: Individual and community mental health interventions* (pp. 308–332). New York: Cambridge University Press.

USGS (U.S. Geological Survey). (2011, April 14). *Earthquakes with 1000 or more deaths since 1900.* Retrieved from http://earthquake.usgs/gov/earthquakes/world/world_deaths.php.

Utsey, S. O., Payne, Y. A., Jackson, E. S., & Jones, A. M. (2002). Race-related stress, quality of life indicators, and life satisfaction among elderly African Americans. *Cultural Diversity and Ethnic Minority Psychology, 8*(3), 224–233.

Utsey, S. O., Stanard, P., & Hook, J. N. (2008). Understanding the role of cultural factors in relation to suicide among African Americans: Implications for research and practice. In M. M. Leach & F. T. L. Leong (Eds.), *Suicide among racial and ethnic minority groups: Theory, research, and* *practice* (pp. 57–79). New York: Routledge/-Taylor & Francis Group.

Vahia, V. N., & Vahia, I. V. (2008). Schizophrenia in developing countries. In K. T. Mueser & D.V. Jeste (Eds.), *Clinical handbook of schizophrenia* (pp. 549–555). New York: Guilford Press.

Valbak, K. (2001). Good outcome for bulimic patients in long-term group analysis: A single-group study. *European Eating Disorders Review, 9*(1), 19–32.

Valenstein, E. S. (1986). *Great and desperate cures.* New York: Basic Books.

Van Ameringen, M., Mancini, C., Paterson, B., Simpson, W., & Truong, C. (2010). Pharmacotherapy for generalized anxiety disorder. In D. J. Stein, E. Hollander, & B. O. Rothbaum (Eds.), *Textbook of anxiety disorders* (2nd ed., pp. 193–218). Arlington, VA: American Psychiatric Publishing.

Van Buskirk, E. (2009, December 1). All posts tagged "e-stop." Thousands of NY sex offenders booted from Facebook, MySpace. *Wired Magazine.*

van der Flier, W. M., van der Vlies, A. E., Weverling-Rijnsburger, A. W. E., de Boer, N. L., Admiraal-Behloul, F., Bollen, E. L. E. M., et al. (2005). MRI measures and progression of cognitive decline in nondemented elderly attending a memory clinic. *International Journal of Geriatric Psychiatry, 20*(11), 1060–1066.

Vanderschuren, L. J. M. J., & Pierce, R. C. (2010). Sensitization processes in drug addiction. In D. W. Self & J. K. Staley (Eds.), *Behavioral neuroscience of drug addiction* (pp. 179–195). New York: Springer Publishing.

van Duijl, M., Nijenhuis, E., Komproe, I. H., Gernaat, H. B. P. E., & de Jong, J. T. (2010). Dissociative symptoms and reported trauma among patients with spirit possession and matched healthy controls in Uganda. *Culture, Medicine and Psychiatry, 34*(2), 380–400.

Van Dusen, A. (2007, February 16). How depressed is your country? *Forbes.com.*

Van Dyke, C. J., Regan, J., & Albano, A. M. (2009). Separation anxiety disorder. In D. McKay & E. A. Storch (Eds.), *Cognitive-behavior therapy for children: Treating complex and refractory cases* (pp. 115–140). New York: Springer Publishing Co.

Van Orden, K. A., Witte, T. K., Selby, E. A., Bender, T. W., & Joiner, T. E., Jr. (2008). Suicidal behavior in youth. In J. R. Z. Abela & B. L. Hankin (Eds.), *Handbook of depression in children and adolescents.* New York: Guilford Press.

van Os, J., Faòanas, L., Cannon, M., Macdonald, A., & Murray, R. (1997). Dermatoglyphic abnormalities in psychosis: A twin study. *Biological Psychiatry, 41,* 624–626.

Van Praag, H. M. (2011). Commentary 4A on "Religious and spiritual issues in anxiety and adjustment disorders": A new psychiatric frontier? In J. R. Peteet, F. G. Lu, & W/ E. Narrow (Eds.), *Religious and spiritual issues in psychiatric diagnosis: A research agenda for DSM-V* (pp. 97–99). Washington, DC: American Psychiatric Association.

van Son, G. E., van Koeken, D., van Furth, E. F., Donker, G. A., & Hoek, H. W. (2010). Course and outcome of eating disorders in a primary care-based cohort. *International Journal of Eating Disorders, 43*(2), 130–138.

van Stralen, M. M., de Vries, H., Mudde, A. N., Bolman, C., & Lechner, L. (2011). The long-term efficacy of two computer-tailored physical activity interventions for older adults: Main effects and mediators. *Health Psychology, 30*(4), 442–452.

Van Wagner, K. (2007). Phobia list: An A to Z list of phobias. *About.com.* Retrieved July 22, 2008, from http://psychology.about.com/od/. phobias/a/phobialist.htm.

Vasquez, M. J. T. (2007, Nov.). Cultural difference and the therapeutic alliance: An evidence-based analysis. *American Psychologist, 62*(8), 878–885.

Vazquez, G., Tondo, L., & Baldessarini, R. J. (2011). Comparison of antidepressant responses in patients with bipolar vs. unipolar depression: A meta-analytic review. *Pharmacopsychiatry, 44*(1), 21–26.

Vedantam, S. (2005, June 26). Patients' diversity is often discounted: Alternatives to mainstream medical treatment call for recognizing ethic, social differences. *Washington Post,* p. A01.

Veen, G., van Vliet, I. M., DeRijk, R. H., Giltay, E. J., van Pelt, J., & Zitman, F. G. (2011). Basal cortisol levels in relation to dimensions and DSM-IV categories of depression and anxiety. *Psychiatry Research, 185*(1-2), 121–128.

Vega, W. A., Ang, A., Rodriguez, M. A., & Finch, B. K. (2011). Neighborhood protective effects on depression in Latinos. *American Journal of Community Psychology, 47*(1-2), 114–126.

Veiga-Martinez, C., Perez-Alvarez, M., & Garcia-Montes, J. M. (2008). Acceptance and commitment therapy applied to treatment of auditory hallucinations. *Clinical Case Studies, 7,* 118–135.

Vela, R. M., Glod, C. A., Rivinus, T. M., & Johnson, R. (2011). Antidepressant treatment of pediatric depression. In D. A. Ciraulo & R. I. Shader, *Pharmacotherapy for depression* (2nd ed., pp. 355–374). New York: Springer Science + Business Media.

Vermote, R., Lowyck, B., Luyten, P., Vertommen, H., Corveleyn, J., Verhaest, Y., Stroobants, R., Vandeneede, B., Vansteelandt, K., & Peuskens, J. (2010). Process and outcome in psychodynamic hospitalization-based treatment for patients with a personality disorder. *Journal of Nervous and Mental Disease, 198*(2), 110–115.

Vetter, H. J. (1969). *Language behavior and psychopathology.* Chicago: Rand McNally.

Vickrey, B. G., Samuels, M. A., & Ropper, A. H. (2010). How neurologists think: A cognitive psychology perspective on missed diagnoses. *Annals of Neurology, 67*(4), 425–433.

Vierck, E., & Silverman, J. M. (2011). Family studies of autism. In E. Hollander, A. Kolevzon & J. T. Coyle (Eds.), *Textbook of autism spectrum disorders.* (pp. 299–312) Arlington, VA: American Psychiatric Publishing, Inc.

Villarreal, C. (2010). Black Swan—A cinematic portrayal of schizophrenia? *Examiner.com.* (www. examiner.com).

Visser, M. (2003). Gregory Bateson on deutero-learning and double bind: A brief conceptual history. *Journal of the History of the Behavioral Sciences, 39*(3), 269–278.

Voelker, R. (2010). Memories of Katrina continue to hinder mental health recovery in New Orleans. *Journal of the American Medical Association, 304*(8), 841–843.

Vögele, C., & Gibson, E. L. (2010). Mood, emotions, and eating disorders. In W. S. Agras (Ed.), *The Oxford handbook of eating disorders. Oxford library of psychology* (pp. 180–205). New York: Oxford University Press.

Vogt, D. S., Dutra, L., Reardon, A., Zisserson, R., & Miller, M. W. (2011). Assessment of trauma, posttraumatic stress disorder, and related mental health outcomes. In J. I. Ruzek, P. P. Schnurr, J. J.Vasterling, & M. J. Friedman (Eds.), *Caring for veterans with deployment-related stress disorders* (pp. 59–85). Washington, DC: American Psychological Association.

Voida, A., Grinter, R. E., Ducheneaut, N., Edwards, W. K., Newman, M. W. (2005). Listening in: Practices surrounding iTunes music sharing. *Proceedings of ACM CHI 2005* (Association for Computing Machinery), 191–200.

Volfson, E. & Oslin, D. (2011). Addiction. In C. E. Coffey, J. L. Cummings, M. S. George, & D. Weintraub (Eds.), *The American Psychiatric Publishing textbook of geriatric neuropsychiatry.* Arlington, VA: American Psychiatric Publishing, Inc.

Volkow, N. D., Fowler, J. S., & Wang, G. J. (2002). Role of dopamine in drug reinforcement and addiction in humans: Results from imaging studies. *Behavioral Pharmacology, 13,* 355–366.

Volkow, N. D., Fowler, J. S., & Wang, G. J. (2004). The addicted human brain viewed in the light of imaging studies: Brain circuits and treatment strategies. *Neuropharmacology, 47*(Suppl. 1), 3–13.

Volkow, N. D., Fowler, J. S., Wang., G. J., & Swanson, J. M. (2004). Dopamine in drug abuse and addiction: Results from imaging studies and treatment implications. *Molecular Psychiatry, 9*(6), 557–569.

Vonnegut, M. (1974, April). Why I want to bite R. D. Laing. *Harper's, 248*(1478), 80–92.

Vosburgh, B. (2011, May 27). Herbal supplement sales gain. *WHRefresh.* Retrieved on June 18, 2011, from http://whrefresh.com/2011/05/27/ herbal-supplement-sales.gain.

Vrij, A. (2004). The polygraph and lie detection. *Howard Journal of Criminal Justice, 43*(1), 108–110.

Vrij, A. (2008). *Detecting lies and deceit: Pitfalls and opportunities.* (2nd ed.) New York: John Wiley.

Waddington, J. L., O'Tuathaigh, C. M. P., & Remington, G. J. (2011). Pharmacology and neuroscience of antipsychotic drugs. In D. R. Weinberg & P. Harrison (Eds.), *Schizophrenia* (pp. 483–514). Hoboken, NJ: Wiley-Blackwell.

Wade, T. D., & Watson, H. J. (2011). Psychotherapies in eating disorders. In J. Alexander & J. Treasure (Eds.), *A collaborative approach to eating disorders* (pp. 125–135). New York: Taylor & Francis.

Wain, H., Kneebone, I. I., & Cropley, M., (2011). Attributional intervention for depression in two people with multiple sclerosis (MS): Single case design. *Behavioural and Cognitive Psychotherapy, 39*(1), 115–121.

Waisbren, S. E. (2011). Phenylketonuria. In S. Goldstein, & C. R. Reynolds (Eds.), *Handbook of neurodevelopmental and genetic disorders in children* (2nd ed., pp. 398–424) New York: Guilford Press.

Wakefield, A. J., Murch, S. H., Anthony, A., Linnell, J., Casson, D. M., Malik, M., et al. (1998). Retracted: Ileal-lymphoid-nodular hyperplasia, non-specific colitis, and pervasive developmental disorder in children. *The Lancet, 351*(9103), 637–641.

Wakefield, J. C., & Horwitz, A. V. (2010). Normal reactions to adversity or symptoms of disorder? In G. M. Rosen & B. C. Frueh (Eds.), *Clinician's guide to post-traumatic stress disorder* (pp. 33–49). Hoboken, NJ: John Wiley & Sons.

Walderhaug, E., Varga, M., San Pedro, M., Hu, J., & Neumeister, A. (2011). The role of the aminergic systems in the pathophysiology of bipolar disorder. In C. A. Zarate, Jr. & H. K. Manji (Eds.), *Bipolar depression: Molecular neurobiology, clinical diagnosis and pharmacotherapy. Milestones in drug therapy* (pp. 107–126). Cambridge, MA: Birkhäuser.

Waldinger, M. D., Berendsen, H., Blok, B., Olivier, B., & Holstege, B. (1998). Premature ejaculation and serotonergic antidepressants-induced delayed ejaculation: The involvement of the serotonergic system. *Behavior, Brain and Research, 92*(2), 111–118.

Walker, L. E., & Shapiro, D. L. (2010). Parental alienation disorder: Why label children with a mental diagnosis? *Journal of Child Custody: Research, Issues, and Practices, 7*(4), 266–286.

Waller, J. (2009). A forgotten plague: Making sense of dancing mania. *Lancet, 373*(9664), 624–625.

Waller, S. (Ed.). (2010). *Serial killers: Being and killing. Philosophy for everyone.* Hoboken, NJ: Wiley-Blackwell.

Wallis, C. (2005, January 17). The new science of happiness. *Time, 165*(3), A2–A9., 18

Walters, G. D. (2002). The heritability of alcohol abuse and dependence: A meta-analysis of behavior genetic research. *American Journal of Drug and Alcohol Abuse, 28*(3), 557–584.

Walther, S., Federspiel, A., Horn, H., Razavi, N., Wiest, R., Dierks, T., et al. (2011). Resting state cerebral blood flow and objective motor activity reveal basal ganglia dysfunction in schizophrenia. *Psychiatry Research: Neuroimaging, 192*(2), 117–124.

Waltz, T. J., & Hayes, S. C. (2010). Acceptance and commitment therapy. In N. Kazantzis, M. A. Reinecke, & A. Freeman (Eds.), *Cognitive and behavioral theories in clinical practice.* New York: Guilford Press.

Wampold, B. E., Hollon, S. D., & Hill, C. E. (2011). Unresolved questions and future directions in psychotherapy research. In J. C. Norcross, G. R. VandenBos, & D. K. Freedheim (Eds.), *History of psychotherapy: Continuity and change* (2nd ed., pp. 333–356). Washington, DC: American Psychological Association.

Wang, J., Korczykowski, M., Rao, H., Fan, Y., Pluta, J., Gur, R. C., et al. (2007). Gender difference in neural response to psychological stress. *Social Cognitive and Affective Neuroscience, 2*(3), 227–239.

Wang, J. L., Smailes, E., Sareen, J., Fick, G. H., Schmitz, N., & Patten, S. B. (2010). The prevalence of mental disorders in the working population over the period of global economic crisis. *Canadian Journal of Psychiatry, 55*(9), 598–605.

Wang, M., & Jiang, G-R. (2007). Psychopathological mechanisms and clinical assessment of dissociative identity disorder. *Chinese Journal of Clinical Psychology, 15*(4), 426–429.

Wang, P. S., Berglund, P., Olfson, M., Pincus, H. A., Wells, K. B., & Kessler, R. C. (2005). Failure and delay in initial treatment contact after first onset of mental disorders in the National Comorbidity Survey Replication. *Archives of General Psychiatry, 62*, 603–613.

Wang, P. S., Demler, O., & Kessler, R. C. (2002). Adequacy of treatment for serious mental illness in the United States. *American Journal of Public Health, 92*(1), 92–98.

Wang, P. S., Demler, O., Olfson, M., Pincus, H. A., Wells, K. B., & Kessler, R. C. (2006).

Changing profiles of service sectors used for mental health care in the United States. *American Journal of Psychiatry, 163*(7), 1187–1198.

Wang, P. S., Lane, M., Olfson, M., Pincus, H. A., Wells, K. B., & Kessler, R. C. (2005). Twelve-month use of mental health services in the United States. *Archives of General Psychiatry, 62*, 629–640.

Wang, S. S. (2007, December 4). The graying of shock therapy. *Wall Street Journal Online.* Retrieved August 14, 2008, from http://online.wsg.com/public/article_print/SB119673737406312767.html.

Wang, S. S. (2007, September 25). Depression care: The business case. *Wall Street Journal Online.* Retrieved October 19, 2007, from http://blogs.wsj.com/health.

Wang, T., Xiao, S., Li, X., Wang, H., Liu, Y., Su, N., & Fang, Y. (2012). Reliability and validity of the Chinese version of the neuropsychiatric inventory in mainland China. *International Journal of Geriatric Psychiatry, 27*(5), 539–544.

Wang Ping. (2000). *Aching for beauty: Footbinding in China.* Minneapolis: University of Minnesota Press.

Ward, E. C. (2007). Examining differential treatment effects for depression in racial and ethnic minority women: A qualitative systematic review. *Journal of the American Medical Association, 99*(3), 265–274.

Warner, J. (2004, June 25). Alien abduction tales offer clues on memory: Study: Distress doesn't necessarily validate traumatic memories. *WebMD Health.*

Warner, J. (2004, April 2). How Americans rank at spotting a liar. *WebMD.*

Waschbusch, D. A. (2002). A meta-analytic examination of comorbid hyperactive--impulsive--attention problems and conduct problems. *Psychological Bulletin, 128*, 118–150.

Wass, H., Miller, M. D., & Redditt, C. A. (1991). Adolescents and destructive themes in rock music: A follow-up. *Omega: Journal of Death and Dying, 23*, 199–206.

Waters, F. A. V., Badcock, J. C., & Maybery, M. T. (2007). Hearing voices: What are they telling us? In J. E. Pletson (Ed.), *Psychology and schizophrenia.* New York: Nova Science Publishers.

Watson, D. (2012). Objective tests as instruments of psychological theory and research. In H. Cooper, P. M. Camic, D. L. Long, A. T. Panter, D. Rindskopf, & K. J. Sher (Eds.), *APA handbook of research methods in psychology. Vol. 1: Foundations, planning, measures, and psychometrics* (pp. 349–369). Washington, DC: American Psychological Association.

Watson, H. J. (2011). Combined psychological and pharmacological treatment of pediatric anxiety disorders. In D McKay & E. A. Storch (Eds.), *Handbook of child and adolescent anxiety disorders* (pp. 379–402). New York: Springer Science & Business Media.

Watson, J. B., & Rayner, R. (1920). Conditioned emotional reaction. *Journal of Experimental Psychology, 3*, 1–14.

Watson, J. C., Goldman, R. N., & Greenberg, L. S. (2011). Humanistic and experiential theories of psychotherapy. In J. C. Norcross, G. R. VandenBos, & D. K. Freedheim (Eds.), *History of psychotherapy: Continuity and change* (2nd ed., pp. 141–172). Washington, DC: American Psychological Association.

Watson, P. J., & Shalev, A. Y. (2005). Assessment and treatment of adult acute responses to traumatic stress following mass traumatic events. *CNS Spectrums, 10*(2), 123–131.

Watson, T. S., Watson, T. S., & Ret, J. (2008). Learning, motor, and communication disorders. In D. Reitman (Ed.), *Handbook of psychological assessment, case conceptualization, and treatment: Vol. 2. Children and adolescents.* Hoboken, NJ: John Wiley & Sons.

Watt, T. T. (2002). Marital and cohabiting relationships of adult children of alcoholics: Evidence from the National Survey of Family and Households. *Journal of Family Issues, 23*(2), 246–265.

Watts, G., & Nettle, D. (2010). The role of anxiety in vaginismus: A case-control study. *Journal of Sexual Medicine 7*(1, Pt. 1), 143–148.

Weaver, M. F., & Schnoll, S. H. (2008). Hallucinogens and club drugs. In H. D. Kleber & M. Galanter (Eds.), *The American Psychiatric Publishing textbook of substance abuse treatment* (4th ed., pp. 191–200). Arlington, VA: American Psychiatric Publishing.

Webster-Stratton, C. (2005). Early intervention with videotype modeling: Programs for families of children with oppositional defiant disorder or conduct disorder. In E. D. Hibbs & P. S. Jensen (Eds.), *Psychosocial treatments for child and adolescent disorders: Empirically based strategies for clinical practice* (2nd ed., pp. 507–555). Washington, DC: American Psychological Association.

Webster-Stratton, C., & Reid, M. J. (2010). The Incredible Years parents, teachers, and children training series: A multifaceted treatment approach for young children with conduct disorders. In J. R. Weisz & A. E. Kazdin (Eds.), *Evidence-based psychotherapies for children and adolescents* (2nd ed., pp. 194–210). New York: Guilford Press.

Wechsler, H., Davenport, A., Dowdall, G., Moeykens, B., & Castillo, S. (1994). Health and behavioral consequences of binge drinking in college. *Journal of the American Medical Association, 272*(21), 1672–1677.

Wechsler, H., Dowdell, G. W., Davenport, A., & Castillo, S. (1995). Correlates of college student binge drinking. *American Journal of Public Health, 85*(7), 921–926.

Wechsler, H., Lee, J. E., Kuo, M., & Lee, H. (2000). College binge drinking in the 1990s: A continuing problem: Results of the Harvard School of Public Health 1999 College Alcohol Study. *Journal of American College Health, 48*(5), 199–210.

Wechsler, H., Lee, J. E., Kuo, M., Seibring, M., Nelson, T. F., & Lee, H. (2002). Trends in alcohol use, related problems and experience of prevention efforts among US college students 1993 to 2001: Results from the 2001 Harvard School of Public Health college alcohol study. *Journal of American College Health, 50*, 203–217.

Wechsler, H., & Nelson, T. F. (2008). What we have learned from the Harvard School of Public Health College Alcohol Study: Focusing attention on college student alcohol consumption and the environmental conditions that promote it. *Journal of Studies on Alcohol and Drugs, 69*, 481–490.

Wechsler, H., Seibring, M., Liu, I. C., & Ahl, M. (2004). Colleges respond to student binge drinking: Reducing student demand or limiting access. *Journal of American College Health, 52*(4), 159–168.

Wechsler, H., & Wuethrich, B. (2002). *Dying to drink: Confronting binge drinking on college campuses.* Emmaus, PA: Rodale Press.

Wedding, D. (Ed.) (2010, July 6). Barriers to Personality Assessment. PsychCRITIQUES Blog.

Weder, N. D., Muralee, S., Penland, H., & Tampi, R. R. (2008). Catatonia: A review. *Annals of Clinical Psychiatry, 20*(2), 97–107.

Week, F., Ritter, V., & Stangier, U. (2012). Variants of exposure in body dysmorphic disorder and hypochondriasis. In P. Neudeck & H-U. Wittchen (Eds.), *Exposure therapy: Rethinking the model—Refining the method.* New York: Springer Science 1 Business Media.

Weeks, D., & James, J. (1995). *Eccentrics: A study of sanity and strangeness.* New York: Villard.

Weems, C. F., & Varela, R. E. (2011). Generalized anxiety disorder: Handbook of child and adolescent anxiety disorders. In D. McKay & E. A. Storch (Eds.), *Handbook of child and adolescent anxiety disorders* (pp. 261–274). New York: Springer Science & Business Media.

Wei, Y., Szumilas, M., & Kutcheer, S. (2010). Effectiveness on mental health of psychological debriefing for crisis intervention in schools. *Educational Psychology Review, 22*(3), 339–347.

Weidner, G., & Kendel, F. (2010). Prevention of coronary heart disease. In J. M. Suls, K. W. Davidson, & R. M. Kaplan (Eds.), *Handbook of health psychology ad behavioral medicine* (pp. 354–369). New York: Guilford Press.

Weinberger, J., & Rasco, C. (2007). Empirically supported common factors. In J. Weinberger & S. G. Hofmann (Eds.), *The art and science of psychotherapy* (pp. 103–129). New York: Routledge/Taylor & Francis Group.

Weiner, I. B., & Greene, R. L. (2008). *Handbook of personality assessment.* Hoboken, NJ: John Wiley & Sons.

Weiner, M., Warren, L., & Fiedorowicz, J. G. (2011). Cardiovascular morbidity and mortality in bipolar disorder. *Annals of Clinical Psychiatry, 23*(1), 40–47.

Weinstein, Y., Shanks, D. R. (2010). Rapid induction of false memory for pictures. *Memory, 18*(5), 533–542.

Weis, R., & Smenner, L. (2007). Construct validity of the Behavior Assessment system for Children (BASC) Self-Report of Personality: Evidence from adolescents referred to residential treatment. *Journal of Psychoeducational Assessment, 25*(2), 111–126.

Weishaar, M. E., & Beck, A. T. (2006). Cognitive theory of personality and personality disorders. In S. Strack (Ed.), *Differentiating normal and abnormal personality* (2nd ed., pp. 113–135) New York: Springer Publishing Co.

Weisman, R. L. (Ed.). (2004). Introduction to the special section on integrating community mental health and the criminal justice systems for adults with severe mental illness: Bridges and barriers. *Psychiatric Quarterly, 75*(2), 105–106.

Weiss, D. E. (1991). *The great divide.* New York: Poseidon Press/Simon & Schuster.

Weiss, D. S., Marmar, C. R., Schlenger, W. E., Fairbank, J. A., Jordan, B. K., Hough, R. L., et al. (1992). The prevalence of lifetime and partial posttraumatic stress disorder in Vietnam theater veterans *Journal of Traumatic Stress, 5*(3), 365–376.

Weiss, F. (2011). Alcohol self-administration. In M. C. Olmstead (Ed.), *Animal models of drug addiction. Springer protocols: Neuromethods* (pp. 133–165). Totowa, NJ: Humana Press.

Weissman, M. M. (2000). Social functioning and the treatment of depression. *Journal of Clinical Psychiatry, 61*(Suppl.), 33–38.

Weissman, M. M., & Markowitz, J. C. (2002). Interpersonal psychotherapy for depression. In I. H. Gotlib & C. L. Hammen (Eds.), *Handbook of depression* (pp. 404–421). New York: Guilford Press.

Weissman, M. M., & Verdeli, H. (2011). Interpersonal psychotherapy. In R. J. Corsini & D. Wedding (Eds.), *Current psychotherapies* (9th ed.). Belmont, CA: Brooks/Cole.

Weissman, M. M., et al. (1992). The changing rate of major depression: Cross-national comparisons. Cross-national collaborative group. *Journal of the American Medical Association, 268*(21), 3098–3105.

Weissman, M. M., Livingston, B. M., Leaf, P. J., Florio, L. P., & Holzer, C., III. (1991). Affective disorders. In L. N. Robins & D. A. Regier (Eds.), *Psychiatric disorders in America: The Epidemiologic Catchment Area Study.* New York: Free Press.

Weissman, S. W. (2000). America's psychiatric work force. *Psychiatric Times, 17*(11).

Wekerle, C., MacMillan, H. L., Leung, E., & Jamieson, E. (2007). Child maltreatment. In M. Hersen & A. M. Gross (Eds.), *Handbook of clinical psychology* (Vol. 2). Hoboken, NJ: John Wiley & Sons.

Welburn, K. R., Fraser, G. A., Jordan, S. A., Cameron, C., Webb, L. M., & Raine, D. (2003). Discriminating dissociative identity disorder from schizophrenia and feigned dissociation on psychological tests and structured interview. *Journal of Trauma and Dissociation, 4*(2), 109–130.

Welch, W. M. (2007). Post-traumatic stress disorder is a serious problem for Iraq War veterans. In A. Quigley (Ed.), *Current controversies: Mental health.* Detroit: Greenhaven Press/Thomson Gale.

Weller, P. (2010). Lost in translation: Human rights and mental health law. In B. McSherry & P. Weller (Eds.), *Rethinking rights-based mental health law.* (pp. 51–72). Portland, OR: Hart Publishing.

Wells, A. (2005). The metacognitive model of GAD: Assessment of meta-worry and relationship with DSM-IV generalized anxiety disorder. *Cognitive Therapy and Research, 29*(1), 107–121.

Wells, A. (2009). *Metacognitive therapy for anxiety and depression.* New York: Guilford Press.

Wells, A. (2010). Metacognitive therapy: Application to generalized anxiety disorder. In D. Sookman & R. L. Leahy (Eds.), *Treatment resistant anxiety disorders: Resolving impasses to symptom remission* (pp. 1–29). New York: Routledge/Taylor & Francis Group.

Wells, A. (2011). Metacognitive therapy. In J. D. Herbert & E. M. Forman (Eds.), *Acceptance and mindfulness in cognitive behavior therapy: Understanding and applying the new therapies.* (pp. 83–108). Hoboken, NJ: John Wiley & Sons Inc.

Wells, A. (2012, March 5). Interview in G. Caselli, Metacognitive Therapy (MCT): An interview with Prof. Adrian Wells. *State of Mind, 14*(39).

Wells, A., Fisher, P., Myers, S., Wheatley, J., Patel, T., & Brewin, C. R. (2012). Metacognitive therapy in treatment-resistant depression: A platform trial. *Behaviour Research and Therapy, 50*(6), 367–373.

Wells, G. L. (2008). Field experiments on eyewitness identification: Towards a better understanding of pitfalls and prospects. *Law and Human Behavior, 32*(1), 6–10.

Welsh, C. J., & Liberto, J. (2001). The use of medication for relapse prevention in substance dependence disorders. *Journal of Psychiatric Practice, 7*(1), 15–31.

Wender, P. H., Reimherr, F. W., Marchant, B. K., Sanford, M. E., Czajkowski, L. A., & Tomb, D. A. (2011). A one year trial of methylphenidate in the treatment of ADHD. *Journal of Attention Disorders, 15*(1), 36–45.

Wendland, J. R., & McMahon, F. J. (2011). Genetics of bipolar disorder. In C. A. Zarate, Jr. & H. K. Manji (Eds.), *Bipolar depression: Molecular neurobiology, clinical diagnosis and pharmacotherapy. Milestones in drug therapy* (pp. 19–30). Cambridge, MA: Birkhäuser.

Weng, X., Odouli, R., & Li, D. K. (2008). Maternal caffeine consumption during pregnancy and the risk of miscarriage: A prospective cohort study. *American Journal of Obstetrics and Gynecology, 198*(3), 297.e1–8.

Wenzel, A. (2011). Obsessions and compulsions. In *Anxiety in childbearing women: Diagnosis and treatment.* (pp. 55–71). Washington, DC: American Psychological Association.

Wenzel, A. (2011). Panic attacks. In *Anxiety in childbearing women: Diagnosis and treatment.* (pp. 73–90). Washington, DC: American Psychological Association.

Wenzel, A. (2011). Social anxiety. In *Anxiety in childbearing women: Diagnosis and treatment.* (pp. 91–102). Washington, DC: American Psychological Association.

Wenzel, A. (2011). Worry and generalized anxiety. In *Anxiety in childbearing women: Diagnosis and treatment.* (pp. 37–53). Washington, DC: American Psychological Association.

Werth, J. L., Jr. (1996). *Rational suicide? Implications for mental health professionals.* Washington, DC: Taylor & Francis.

Werth, J. L., Jr. (Ed.). (1999). *Contemporary perspectives on rational suicide.* Philadelphia, PA: Brunner/Mazel.

Werth, J. L., Jr. (2000). Recent developments in the debate over physician-assisted death. In R. W. Maris, S. S. Canetto, J. L. McIntosh, & M. M. Silverman (Eds.), *Review of suicidology, 2000.* New York: Guilford Press.

Werth, J. L., Jr. (2001). Policy and psychosocial considerations associated with non-physician assisted suicide: A commentary on Ogden. *International Journal of Eating Disorders, 25*(5), 403–411.

Werth, J. L., Jr. (2004). The relationships among clinical depression, suicide, and other actions that may hasten death. *Behavioral Sciences and the Law, 22*(5), 627–649.

Wertheimer, A. (2001). *A special scar: The experiences of people bereaved by suicide* (2nd ed.). East Sussex, England: Brunner-Routledge.

Wesson, D. W., Nixon, R. A., Levy, E., & Wilson, D. A. (2011). Mechanisms of neural and behavioral dysfunction in Alzheimer's disease. *Molecular Neurobiology, 43*(3), 163–179.

Westen, D. (2007). Discovering what works in the community: Toward a genuine partnership of clinicians and researchers. In S. G. Hofmann & J. Weinberger (Eds.), *The art and science of psychotherapy* (pp. 3–29). New York: Routledge/Taylor & Francis Group.

Westen, D., Betan, E., & Defife, J. A. (2011). Identity disturbance in adolescence: Associations with borderline personality disorder. *Development and Psychopathology, 23*(1), 305–313.

Westen, D., Dutra, L., & Shedler, J. (2005). Assessing adolescent personality pathology: Quantifying clinical judgment. *British Journal of Psychiatry, 186*(3), 227–238.

Westermeyer, J. (1993). Substance use disorders among young minority refugees: Common themes in a clinical sample. *NIDA Research Monograph, 130,* 308–320.

Westermeyer, J. (2001). Alcoholism and co-morbid psychiatric disorders among American

Indians. *American Indian and Alaska Native Mental Health Research, 10,* 27–51.

Westermeyer, J. (2004). Acculturation: Advances in theory, measurement, and applied research. *Journal of Nervous and Mental Disease, 192*(5), 391–392.

Westheimer, R. K., & Lopater, S. (2005). *Human sexuality: A psychosocial perspective* (2nd ed.). Baltimore, MD: Lippincott Williams & Wilkins.

Wetherell, J. L., Lang, A. J., & Stein, M. B. (2006). Anxiety disorders. In D.V. Jeste & J. H. Friedman (Eds.), *Psychiatry for neurologists* (pp. 43–58). Totowa, NJ: Humana Press.

Wetterling, T. (2005). Somatic diseases in elderly patients with delirium. *Zeitschrift für Gerontopsychologie und Psychiatrie, 18*(1), 3–7.

Wetzel, R. D., & Murphy, G. E. (2005). Suicide. In E. H. Rubin & C. F. Zorumski (Eds.), *Adult psychiatry* (2nd ed., pp. 409–419). Oxford, England: Blackwell Publishing.

Weyandt, L. L. (2006). *The physiological basis of cognitive and behavioral disorders.* Mahwah, NJ: Lawrence Erlbaum.

Weyandt, L. L., Verdi, G., & Swentosky, A. (2011). Oppositional, conduct, and aggressive disorders. In S. Goldstein, & C. R. Reynolds (Eds.), *Handbook of neurodevelopmental and genetic disorders in children* (2nd ed., pp. 151–170) New York: Guilford Press.

Wheatley, D. (2004). Triple-blind, placebo-controlled trial of ginkgo biloba in sexual dysfunction due to antidepressant drugs. *Human Psychopharmacology: Clinical and Experimental, 19*(8), 545–548.

Wheeler, B. W., Gunnell, D., Metcalfe, C., Stephens, P., & Martin, R. M. (2008). The population impact on incidence of suicide and non-fatal self harm of regulatory action against the use of selective serotonin reuptake inhibitors in under 18s in the United Kingdom: Ecological study. *British Medical Journal, 336*(7643), 542.

WHF (Women's Heart Foundation). (2011). *Women and heart disease facts.* Retrieved on May 27, 2011, from www.womensheart.org/content/heartdisease/heart_disease_facts.asp.

Whiffen, V. E., & Demidenko, N. (2006). Mood disturbance across the life span. In J. Worell & C. D. Goodheart (Eds.), *Handbook of girls' and women's psychological health* (pp. 51–59). New York: Oxford University Press.

Whipple, R., & Fowler, J. C. (2011). Affect, relationship, schemas, and social cognition: Self-injuring borderline personality disorder inpatients. *Psychoanalytic Psychology, 28*(2), 183–195.

Whisman, M. A. (2001). The association between depression and marital dissatisfaction. In S. R. H. Beach (Ed.), *Marital and family processes in depression: A scientific foundation for clinical practice* (pp. 3–24). Washington, DC: American Psychological Association.

Whisman, M. A. (2010). Loneliness and the metabolic syndrome in a population-based sample of middle-aged and older adults. *Health Psychology, 29*(5), 550–554.

Whisman, M. A., & Bruce, M. L. (1999). Marital dissatisfaction and incidence of major depressive episode in a community sample. *Journal of Abnormal Psychology, 108*(4), 674–678.

Whisman, M. A., & Schonbrun, Y. C. (2010). Marital distress and relapse prevention for depression. In C. S. Richards & J. G. Perri (Eds.), *Relapse prevention for depression* (pp. 251–269). Washington, DC: American Psychological Association.

Whitaker, R. (2002). *Mad in America: Bad science, bad medicine, and the enduring mistreatment of the mentally ill.* Cambridge, MA: Perseus.

Whitaker, R. (2010). *Anatomy of an epidemic: Magic bullets, psychiatric drugs, and the astonishing rise of mental illness in America.* Norwalk, CT: Crown House Publishing Limited.

White, B. J., & Madara, E. J. (Eds.). (2010). *Self-help group sourcebook online.* Retrieved March 2, 2011, on www.mentalhelp.net/selfhelp.

Whiteside, M. (1983, September 12). A bedeviling new hysteria. *Newsweek.*

Whitman, T. A., & Akutagawa, D. (2004). Riddles in serial murder: A synthesis. *Aggression and Violent Behavior, 9*(6), 693–703.

Whitney, S. D., Renner, L. M., Pate, C. M., & Jacobs, K. A. (2011). Principals' perceptions of benefits and barriers to school-based suicide prevention programs. *Children and Youth Services Review, 33*(6), 869–877.

Whitten, L. (2010). Marijuana linked with testicular cancer. *NIDA Notes, 23*(3).

Whittle, A. (2010). Computer identity theft—Modern day confidence tricksters. *Legal Expert ON-LINE.* Retrieved April 6, 2011, at http://legal.03893.com/htm/computer-identity-theft-modern-day-confidence-tricksters.html.

Whitty, M. T., & Carville, S. E. (2008). Would I lie to you? Self-serving lies and other-oriented lies told across different media. *Computers in Human Behavior, 24*(3), 1021–1031.

WHO (World Health Organization). (2004). Prevalence, severity, and unmet need for treatment of mental disorders in the World Health Organization World Mental Health Surveys. *Journal of the American Medical Association, 291*(21), 2581–2590.

WHO (World Health Organization). (2006). *Depression.* Retrieved from http://www.who.int/mental_health/management/depression/definition/en.

WHO (World Health Organization). (2010). *Mental health: Depression.* http://www.who.int/mental_health/management/depression/definition/en/.

WHO (World Health Organization). (2010). *Targeting people with mental health conditions as a vulnerable group.* http://www.who.int/mediacentre/news/releasess/2010/mental_disabilities_20100916/en/index.html.

WHO (World Health Organization). (2011). Suicide rates per 100,000 by country, year and sex (Table). http://www.who.int/mental_health/prevention/suicide_rates/en/.

Wickwire, E. M., Jr., Roland, M. M. S., Elkin, T. D., & Schumacher, J. A. (2008). Sleep disorders. In D. Reitman (Ed.), *Handbook of psychological assessment, case conceptualization, and treatment: Vol. 2. Children and adolescents.* Hoboken, NJ: Wiley.

Widiger, T. A. (2006). Understanding personality disorders. In S. K. Huprich, (Ed.), *Rorschach assessment of the personality disorders.* Mahwah, NJ: Lawrence Erlbaum.

Widiger, T. A. (2007a). Alternatives to DSM-IV: Axis II. In S. O. Lilienfeld, W. O'Donohue, & K. A. Fowler (Eds.), *Personality disorders: Toward the DSM-V* (pp. 21–40). Thousand Oaks, CA: Sage Publications.

Widiger, T. A. (2007b). Current controversies in nosology and diagnosis of personality disorders. *Psychiatric Annals, 37*(2), 93–99.

Widiger, T. A., & Mullins-Sweatt, S. N. (2010). Clinical utility of a dimensional model of personality disorder. *Professional Psychology: Research and Practice, 41*(6), 488–494.

Widom, C. S. (2001). Child abuse and neglect. In S. O. White (Ed.), *Handbook of youth and justice* (pp. 31–47). New York: Kluwer Academic/Plenum Press.

Wiederman, M. W. (2001). "Don't look now": The role of self-focus in sexual dysfunction. *Family Journal: Counseling and Therapy for Couples and Families, 9*(2), 210–214.

Wiegand, T., Thai, D., & Benowitz, N. (2008). Medical consequences of the use of hallucinogens: LSD, mescaline, PCP, and MDM ("ecstasy"). In J. Brick (Ed.), *Handbook of the medical consequences of alcohol and drug abuse* (2nd ed., pp. 461–490). New York: Haworth Press/Taylor & Francis Group.

Wilczynski, S. M., Fisher, L., Sutro, L., Bass, J., Mudgal, D., Zeiger, V., et al. (2011). Evidence-based practice and autism spectrum disorders. In M. A. Bray & T. J. Kehle (Eds.), *The Oxford handbook of school psychology.* (pp. 567–592) New York: Oxford University Press.

Wilder-Smith, O. H. G. (2005). Opioid use in the elderly. *European Journal of Pain, 9*(2), 137–140.

Wiley-Exley, E. (2007). Evaluations of community mental health care in low- and middle-income countries: A 10-year review of the literature. *Social Science and Medicine, 64*(6), 1231–1241.

Wilkes, M. S., Bell, R. A., & Kravitz, R. L. (2000). Direct-to-consumer prescription drug advertising: Trends, impact, and implications. *Health Affairs, 19*(2), 110–128.

Wilkinson, P., & Goodyer, I. (2011). Non-suicidal self-injury: *European Child & Adolescent Psychiatry, 20*(2), 103–108.

Wilkinson, T. (2011, January 12). Haiti still mired in post-quake problems. *Los Angeles Times.*

Will, O. A. (1961). Paranoid development and the concept of self: Psychotherapeutic intervention. *Psychiatry, 24*(2), 516–530.

Will, O. A. (1967). Psychological treatment of schizophrenia. In A. M. Freedman & H. I. Kaplan (Eds.), *Comprehensive textbook of psychiatry.* Baltimore: Williams & Wilkins.

Williams, A., While, D., Windfuhr, K., Bickley, H., Hunt, I. M., Shaw, J., et al. (2011). Birthday blues: Examining the association between birthday and suicide in a national sample. *Crisis: Journal of Crisis Intervention and Suicide Prevention, 32*(3), 134–142.

Williams, A. D., Grisham, J. R., Erskine, A., & Cassedy, E. (2012). Deficits in emotion regulation associated with pathological gambling. *British Journal of Clinical Psychology, 51*(2), 223–238.

Williams, C. L., & Butcher, J. N. (2011). *A beginner's guide to the MMPI-A.* Washington, DC: American Psychological Association.

Williams, M. T., Cahill, S. P., & Foa, E. B. (2010). Psychotherapy for posttraumatic stress disorder. In D. J. Stein, E. Hollander, & B. O. Rothbaum (Eds.), *Textbook of anxiety disorders* (2nd ed., pp. 603–626). Arlington, VA: American Psychiatric Publishing.

Williams, P. (2010). Psychotherapeutic treatment of Cluster A personality disorders. In J. F. Clarkin, P. Fonagy, G. O. Gabbard (Eds.), *Psychodynamic psychotherapy for personality disorders: A clinical handbook.* Arlington, VA: American Psychiatric Publishing, Inc.

Williams, P. (2012). Object relations. In G. O. Gabbard, B. E. Litowitz, & P. Williams (Eds.). (2012). *Textbook of psychoanalysis* (2nd ed., pp. 171–183). Arlington, VA: American Psychiatric Publishing.

Williams, P. G. (2004). The psychopathology of self-assessed health: A cognitive approach to health anxiety and hypochondriasis. *Cognitive Therapy and Research, 28,* 629–644.

Williams, P. G., Smith, T. W., Gunn, H. E., & Uchino, B. N. (2011). Personality and stress: individual differences in exposure, reactivity, recovery, and restoration. In R. J. Contrada & A. Baum (Eds.), *The handbook of stress science: Biology, psychology, and health* (pp. 231–245). New York: Springer Publishing.

Williams, S., & Reid, M. (2010). Understanding the experience of ambivalence in anorexia nervosa: The maintainer's perspective. *Psychology & Health, 25*(5), 551–567.

Williams, T. M. (2008). *Black pain: It just looks like we're not hurting.* New York: Scribner.

Williamson, D. A., White, M. A., York-Crowe, E., & Stewart, T. M. (2004). Cognitive-behavioral theories of eating disorders. *Behavior Modification, 28*(6), 711–738.

Willick, M. S. (2001). Psychoanalysis and schizophrenia: A cautionary tale. *Journal of the American Psychoanalytical Association, 49*(1), 27–56.

Willick, M. S., Milrod, D., & Karush, R. K. (1998). Psychoanalysis and the psychoses. In M. Furer, E. Nersessian, & C. Perri (Eds.), *Controversies in contemporary psychoanalysis: Lectures from the faculty of the New York Psychoanalytic Institute.* Madison, CT: International Universities Press.

Wills, T. A., & Ainette, M. G. (2010). Temperament, self-control, and adolescent substance use: A two-factor model of etiological processes. In L. Scheier (Ed.), *Handbook of drug use etiology: Theory, methods, and empirical findings* (pp. 127–146). Washington, DC.

Willuhn, I., Wanat, M. J., Clark, J. J., & Phillips, P. E. M. (2010). Dopamine signaling in the nucleus accumbens of animals self-administering drugs of abuse. In D. W. Self & J. K. Staley (Eds.), *Behavioral neuroscience of drug addiction* (pp. 29–71). New York: Springer Publlishing.

Wilson, C. J., & Deane, F. P. (2010). Help-negation and suicidal ideation: The role of depression, anxiety and hopelessness. *Journal of Youth and Adolescence, 39*(3), 291–305.

Wilson, G. T. (2005). Psychological treatment of eating disorders. *Annual Review of Clinical Psychology, 1*(1), 439–465.

Wilson, G. T. (2010). Cognitive behavioral therapy for eating disorders. In W. S. Agras (Ed.), *The Oxford handbook of eating disorders. Oxford library of psychology* (pp. 331–347). New York: Oxford University Press.

Wilson, G. T. (2010). What treatment research is needed for bulimia nervosa? In C. M. Grilo & J. E. Mitchell (Eds.), *The treatment of eating disorders: A clinical handbook* (pp. 544–553). New York: Guilford Press.

Wilson, G. T. (2011). Behavior therapy. In R. J. Corsini & D. Wedding (Eds.), *Current psychotherapies* (9th ed.). Belmont, CA: Brooks/Cole.

Wilson, G. T. (2011). Treatment of binge eating disorder. *Psychiatric Clinics of North America, 34*(4), 773–783.

Wilson, G. T., Becker, C. B., & Heffernan, K. (2003). Eating disorders. In E. J. Mash & R. A. Barkley (Eds.), *Child psychopathology* (2nd ed., pp. 687–715). New York: Guilford Press.

Wilson, G. T., Heffernan, K., & Black, C. M. D. (1996). Eating disorders. In E. J. Mash & R. A. Barkley (Eds.), *Developmental psychopathology.* New York: Guilford Press.

Wilson, I. (2010). Substance misuse in first-episode psychosis. In P. French, J. Smith, D. Shiers, M.

Reed, & M. Rayne (Eds.), *Promoting recovery in early psychosis: A practice manual* (pp. 147–156). Hoboken, NJ: Wiley-Blackwell.

Wilson, J., & Kimball, R. (2010, October 19). Our cell phone use, by the numbers. *CNN.*

Wilson, J. J. (2010). Substance abuse during adolescence. In E. V. Nunes, J. Selzer, P. Levounis, & C. A. Davies (Eds.), *Substance dependence and co-occurring psychiatric disorders: Best practices for diagnosis and treatment.* Kingston, NJ: Civic Research Institute.

Wilson, K. A., & Hayward, C. (2005). A prospective evaluation of agoraphobia and depression symptoms following panic attacks in a community sample of adolescents. *Journal of Anxiety Disorders, 19*(1), 87–103.

Wilson, K. R., Jordan, J. A., Kras, A. M., Tavkar, P., Bruhn, S., Asawa, L. E., et al. (2010). Adolescent measures: practitioner's guide to empirically based measure of social skills. In D. W. Nangle, D. J. Hansen, C. A. Erdley, & P. J. Norton (Eds.), *Practitioner's guide to empirically based measures of social skills* (pp. 327–381). New York: Springer Publishing.

Wilson, R. S., Scherr, P. A., Schneider, J. A., Tang, Y., & Bennett, D. A. (2007). Relation of cognitive activity to risk of developing Alzheimer disease. *Neurology, 69*(20), 1911–1920.

Wincze, J. P., Bach, A. K., & Barlow, D. H. (2008). Sexual dysfunction. In D. H. Barlow (Ed.), *Clinical handbook of psychological disorders: A step-by-step treatment manual* (4th ed.). New York: Guilford Press.

Windsor, T. D., & Anstey, K. J. (2011). "Age differences in psychosocial predictors of positive and negative affect: A longitudinal investigation of young, midlife, and older adults": Correction to Windsor and Anstey (2010). *Psychology and Aging, 26*(2), 350.

Wing, L. (1976). *Early childhood autism.* Oxford, England: Pergamon Press.

Winick, B. J. (2008). A therapeutic jurisprudence approach to dealing with coercion in the mental health system. *Psychiatric and Psychological Law, 15*(1), 25–39.

Winslade, W. J., & Ross, J. (1983). *The insanity plea.* New York: Scribner's.

Winstock, A. R., Lintzeris, N., & Lea, T. (2011). "Should I stay or should I go?" Coming off methadone and buprenorphine treatment. *International Journal of Drug Policy, 22*(1), 77–81.

Winter, E. C., & Bienvenu, O. J. (2011). Temperament and anxiety disorders. In D. McKay & E. A. Storch (Eds.), *Handbook of child and adolescent anxiety disorders* (pp. 203–212). New York: Springer Science & Business Media.

Winterer, G., & McCarley, R. W. (2011). Electrophysiology of schizophrenia. In D. R. Weinberg & P. Harrison (Eds.), *Schizophrenia* (pp. 311–333). Hoboken, NJ: Wiley-Blackwell.

Witkiewitz, K. A., & Marlatt, G. A. (2004). Relapse prevention for alcohol and drug problems: That was zen, this is tao. *American Psychologist, 59*(4), 224–235.

Witkiewitz, K. A., & Marlatt, G. A. (Eds.). (2007). *Therapist's guide to evidence-based relapse prevention.* San Diego, CA: Elsevier.

Witkiewitz, K., & Wu, J. (2010). Emotions and relapse in substance use: Evidence for a complex interaction among psychological, social, and biological processes. In J. D. Kassel (Ed.), *Substance abuse and emotion* (pp. 171–187). Washington, DC: American Psychological Association.

Witte, T. K., Merrill, K. A., Stellrecht, N. E., Bernert, R. A., Hollar, D. L., Schatschneider, C., et al. (2008). "Impulsive" youth suicide attempters are not necessarily all that impulsive. *Journal of Affective Disorders, 107*(1–3), 107–116.

Witthöft, M., & Hiller, W. (2010). Psychological approaches to origins and treatments of somatoform disorders. *Annual Review of Clinical Psychology, 6,* 257–283.

Wittstein, I. S., Thiemann, D. R., Lima, J. A. C., Baughman, K. L., Schulman, S. P., Gerstenblith, G., et al. (2005). Neurohumoral features of myocardial stunning due to sudden emotional stress. *New England Journal of Medicine, 352*(6), 539–548.

Wolberg, L. R. (1967). *The technique of psychotherapy.* New York: Grune & Stratton.

Wolberg, L. R. (2005). *The technique of psychotherapy.* Lanham, MD: Jason Aronson.

Wolfe, B. E. (2005). The application of the integrative model to specific anxiety disorders. In B. E. Wolfe, *Understanding and treating anxiety disorders: An integrative approach to healing the wounded self* (pp. 125–153). Washington, DC: American Psychological Association.

Wolfe, D. A., Edwards, B., Manion, I., & Koverola, C. (1988). Early intervention for parents at risk for child abuse and neglect: A preliminary investigation. *Journal of Consulting and Clinical Psychology, 56,* 40–47.

Wolff, S. (1991). Schizoid personality in childhood and adult life I: The vagaries of diagnostic labeling. *British Journal of Psychiatry, 159,* 615–620.

Wolff, S. (2000). Schizoid personality in childhood and Asperger syndrome. In S. S. Sparrow, A. Klin, & F. R. Volkmar (Eds.), *Asperger syndrome* (pp. 278–305). New York: Guilford Press.

Wolitzky, D. L., (2011). Psychoanalytic theories of psychotherapy. In J. C. Norcross, G. R. VandenBos, & D. K. Freedheim (Eds.), *History of psychotherapy: Continuity and change* (2nd ed., pp. 65–100). Washington, DC: American Psychological Association.

Wolitzky-Taylor, K. B., Resnick, H. S., McCauley, J. L., Amstadter, A. B., Kilpatrick, D. G., & Ruggiero, K. J. (2011). Is reporting of rape on the rise? A comparison of women with reported versus unreported rape experiences in the National Women's Study-Replication. *Journal of Interpersonal Violence, 26*(4), 807–832.

Wolpe, J. (1958). *Psychotherapy by reciprocal inhibition.* Stanford, CA: Stanford University Press.

Wolpe, J. (1969). *The practice of behavior therapy.* Oxford, England: Pergamon Press.

Wolpe, J. (1987). The promotion of scientific psychotherapy: A long voyage. In J. K. Zeig (Ed.), *The evolution of psychotherapy.* New York: Brunner/Mazel.

Wolpe, J. (1990). *The practice of behavior therapy* (4th ed.). Elmsford, NY: Pergamon Press.

Wolpe, J. (1995). Reciprocal inhibition: Major agent of behavior change. In W. T. O'Donohue & L. Krasner (Eds.), *Theories of behavior therapy: Exploring behavior change.* Washington, DC: American Psychological Association.

Wolpe, J. (1997). From psychoanalytic to behavioral methods in anxiety disorders: A continuing evolution. In J. K. Zeig (Ed.), *The evolution of psychotherapy: The third conference.* New York: Brunner/Mazel.

Wolrich, M. K. (2011). Body dysmorphic disorder and its significance to social work. *Clinical Social Work Journal, 39*(1), 101–110.

Wong, J. P. S., Stewart, S. M., Claassen, C., Lee, P. W. H., Rao, U., & Lam, T. H. (2008). Repeat suicide attempts in Hong Kong community adolescents. *Social Science and Medicine, 66*(2), 232–241.

Wong, M. M., Brower, K. J., & Zucker, R. A. (2011). Sleep problems, suicidal ideation, and self-harm behaviors in adolescence. *Journal of Psychiatric Research, 45*(4), 505–511.

Wong, P. W. C., Yeung, A. W. M., Chan, W. S. C., Yip, P. S. F., & Tang, A. K. H. (2009). Suicide notes in Hong Kong in 2000. *Death Studies, 33*(4), 372–381.

Wong, Y., & Huang, Y. (2000). Obesity concerns, weight satisfaction and characteristics of female dieters: A study on female Taiwanese college students. *Journal of American College Nutrition, 18*(2), 194–199.

Wood, J. M., Garb, H. N., Lilienfeld, S. O., & Nezworski, M. T. (2002). Clinical assessment. *Annual Review of Psychology, 53,* 519–543.

Woodall, A. (2011). Nation's first transgender trial judge overcome discrimination. *Washington Post, 134*(63).

Woodside, D. B., Bulid, C. M., Halmi, K. A., Fichter, M. M., Kaplan, A., Berrettini, W. H., et al. (2002). Personality, perfectionism, and attitudes towards eating in parent of individuals with eating disorders. *International Journal of Eating Disorders, 31*(3), 290–299.

Woodward, J. (2008, June 12). Bullies blamed after suicide of "Emo" music fan. *The Independent.* Retrieved June 14, 2008, from www.Independent.co.uk.

Worley, L. L. M. (2010). Review of understanding postpartum psychosis: A temporary madness. *Psychosomatics: Journal of Consultation Liaison Psychiatry, 51*(2), 181.

Worthington, E. L., Jr. (2011). Integration of spirituality and religion into psychotherapy. In J. C. Norcross, G. R. VandenBos, & D. K. Freedheim (Eds.), *History of psychotherapy: Continuity and change* (2nd ed., pp. 533–543). Washington, DC: American Psychological Association.

Wortman, C. M., Wolff, K., & Bonanno, G. A. (2004). Loss of an intimate partner through death. In D. J. Mashek & A. Aron (Eds.), *Handbook of closeness and intimacy* (pp. 305–320). Mahwah, NJ: Lawrence Erlbaum.

Wriedt, E., Wiberg, A., Sakar, V., & Noterdaeme, M. (2010). Psychiatric disorders and neurological comorbidity in children with intellectual disability. *Zeitschrift für Kinder- und Jugendpsychiatrie und Psychotherapie, 38*(3), 201–209.

Wright, J. H., Thase, M. E., & Beck, A. T. (2011). Cognitive therapy. In R. E. Hales, S. C. Yudofsky, & G. O. Gabbard (Eds.), *Essentials of psychiatry* (3rd ed., pp. 559–587). Arlington, VA: American Psychiatric Publishing.

Wright, L. W., Jr., & Hatcher, A. P. (2006). Treatment of sex offenders. In R. D. McAnulty & M. M. Burnette (Eds.), *Sex and sexuality: Vol. 3. Sexual deviation and sexual offenses.* Westport, CT: Praeger Publishers.

Wright, L. W., Jr., Hatcher, A. P., & Willerick, M. S. (2006). Violent sex crimes. In R. D. McAnulty & M. M. Burnette (Eds.), *Sex and sexuality: Vol. 3. Sexual deviation and sexual offenses.* Westport, CT: Praeger Publishers.

Wright, S. (2010). Depathologizing consensual sexual sadism, sexual masochism, transvestic fetishism, and fetishism. *Archives of Sexual Behavior, 39*(6), 1229–1230.

Wright, S., & Truax, P. (2008). Behavioral conceptualization. In M. Hersen & J. Rosqvist (Eds.), *Handbook of psychological assessment, case conceptualization, and treatment: Vol. 1. Adults* (pp. 53–75). Hoboken, NJ: John Wiley & Sons.

Wroble, M. C., & Baum, A. (2002). Toxic waste spills and nuclear accidents. In A. M. La Greca, W. K. Silverman, E. M. Vernberg, & M. C. Roberts (Eds.). *Helping children cope with disasters and terrorism* (pp. 207–221). Washington, DC: American Psychological Association.

Wu, D., Loke, I. C., Xu, F., & Lee, K. (2011). Neural correlates of evaluations of lying and truth-telling in different social contexts. *Brain Research, 1389,* 115–142.

Wu, D. M., Lu, J., Zheng, Y. L., Zhou, Z., Shan, Q., & Ma, D. F. (2008). Purple sweet potato color repairs D-galactose-induced spatial learning and memory impairment by regulating the expression of synaptic proteins. *Neurobiology of Learning and Memory, 90*(1), 19–27.

Wu, G., & Shi, J. (2005). The problem of AIM and countermeasure for improvement in interviews. *Psychological Science (China), 28*(4), 952–955.

Wu, J., Kramer, G. L., Kram, M., Steciuk, M., Crawford, I. L., & Petty, F. (1999). Serotonin and learned helplessness: A regional study of 5–HT-sub(1A), 5–HT-sub(2A) receptors and the serotonin transport site in rat brain. *Journal of Psychiatric Research, 33*(1), 17–22.

Wurman, R. S., Leifer, L., & Sume, D. (2000). *Information anxiety 2.* Indianapolis, IN: Que.

Wurst, F. M., Kunz, I., Skipper, G., Wolfersdorf, M., Beine, K. H., & Thon, N. (2011). The therapist's reaction to a patient's suicide: Results of a survey and implications for health care professionals' well-being. *Crisis: Journal of Crisis Intervention and Suicide Prevention, 32*(2), 99–105.

Wyatt, G. W., & Parham, W. D. (2007). The inclusion of culturally sensitive course materials in graduate school and training programs. *Psychotherapy: Theory, Research, Practice, Training, 22*(2, Suppl.) Sum 1985, 461–468.

Yalom, I., & Josselson, R. (2011). Existential psychotherapy. In R. J. Corsini & D. Wedding (Eds.), *Current psychotherapies* (9th ed.). Belmont, CA: Brooks/Cole.

Yalom, I. D. (1960). Aggression and forbiddenness in voyeurism. *Archives of General Psychiatry, 3,* 305–319.

Yamasaki, T., Muranaka, H., Kaseda, Y., Mimori, Y., & Tobimatsu, S. (2012). Understanding the pathophysiology of Alzheimer's disease and mild cognitive impairment: A mini review on fMRI and ERP studies. *Neurology Research International, 2012,* 719056.

Yeates, K. O., Ris, M. D., Taylor H. G. & Pennington B. F. (Eds.). (2010). *Pediatric neuropsychology: Research, theory, and practice* (2nd ed.) New York: Guilford Press.

Yehuda, R., & Bierer, L. M. (2007). Transgenerational transmission of cortisol and PTSD risk. *Progress in Brain Research, 167,* 121–135.

Yehuda, R., Flory, J. D., Pratchett, L. C., Buxbaum, J., Ising, M., & Holsboer, F. (2010). Putative biological mechanisms for the association between early life adversity and the subsequent development of PTSD. *Psychopharmacologia, 212*(3), 405–417.

Yehuda, R., Golier, J. A., Bierer, L. M., Mikhno, A., Pratchett, L. C., Burton, C. L., et al. (2010). Hydrocortisone responsiveness in Gulf War veterans with PTSD: Effects on ACTH, declarative memory hippocampal [^{18}F]FDG uptake on PET. *Psychiatry Research: Neuroimaging, 184*(2), 117–127.

Yen, H. (2012, August 7) Minority birth rate: Racial and ethnic minorities surpass whites in U.S. births for first time, Census reports. *Huffington Post.*

Yeomans, F. W., & Diamond, D. (2010). Transference-focused psychotherapy and borderline personality disorder. In J. F. Clarkin, P. Fonagy, & G. O. Gabbard (Eds.), *Psychodynamic psychotherapy for personality disorders: A clinical handbook.* Arlington, VA: American Psychiatric Publishing, Inc.

Yewchuk, C. (1999). Savant syndrome: Intuitive excellence amidst general deficit. *Developmental Disabilities Bulletin, 27*(1), 58–76.

Yin, S. (2002, May 1). Coming up short. *American Demographics.*

Yonkers, K. A., & Clarke, D. E. (2011). Gender and gender-related issues in DSM-5. In D. A. Regier, W. E. Narrow, E. A. Kuhl, & D. J. Kupfer (Eds.), *The conceptual evolution of DSM-5* (pp. 287–301). Arlington, VA: American Psychiatric Publishing.

Yontef, G., & Jacobs, L. (2011). Gestalt therapy. In R. J. Corsini & D. Wedding (Eds.), *Current psychotherapies* (9th ed.). Belmont, CA: Brooks/Cole.

Yoon, H-K., Kim, Y-K., Lee, H-J., Kwon, D-Y. & Kim, L. (2012). Role of cytokines in atypical depression. *Nordic Journal of Psychiatry, 66*(3), 183–188.

Yoon, J. H., Fintzy, R., & Dodril, C. L. (2012). Behavioral interventions. In T. R. Kosten, T. F. Newton, R. De La Garza II, & C. N. Haile (Eds.), *Cocaine and methamphetamine dependence: Advances in treatment* (pp. 105–142). Arlington, VA: American Psychiatric Publishing.

Yoshimasu, K., Kiyohara, C., & Ohkuma, K. (2002). Efficacy of day care treatment against readmission in patients with schizophrenia: A comparison between out-patients with and without day care treatment. *Psychiatry and Clinical Neurosciences, 56*(4), 397–401.

You, S., Van Orden, K. A., & Conner, K. R. (2011). Social connections and suicidal thoughts and behavior. *Psychology of Addictive Behaviors, 25*(1), 180–184.

Young, C., & Skorga, P. (2011). Aspirin with or without an anti-emetic for migraine headaches in adults. *International Journal of Evidence-Based Healthcare, 9*(1), 74–75.

Young, K. S. (2011). CBT-IA: The first treatment model for internet addiction. *Journal of Cognitive Psychotherapy, 25*(4), 304–312.

Young, K. S., & de Abreu, C. N. (Eds.). (2011). *Internet addiction: A handbook and guide to evaluation and treatment.* Hoboken, NJ: John Wiley & Sons.

Young, K. S., Yue, S. D., & Ying, L. (2011). Prevalence estimates and etiologic models of internet addiction. In K. S. Young & C. N. de Abreu (Eds.), *Internet addiction: A handbook and guide for evaluation and treatment* (pp. 3–17). Hoboken, NJ: John Wiley & Sons.

Young, M., Benjamin, B., & Wallis, C. (1963). Mortality of widowers. *Lancet, 2,* 454–456.

Yusko, D. (2008). At home, but locked in war. Retrieved from: *Times-Union (Albany) Online.*

Yutzy, S. H. (2007). Somatoform disorders. In S. C. Yudofsky, J. A. Bourgeois, & R. E. Hales (Eds.), *The*

American Psychiatric Publishing Board prep and review guide for psychiatry (pp. 235–243). Washington, DC: American Psychiatric Publishing.

Zagrosek, A., Messroghli, D., Schulz, O., Dietz, R., & Schulz-Menger, J. (2010). Effect of binge drinking on the heart as assessed by cardiac magnetic resonance imaging. Journal of the American Medical Association, 304(12), 1328–1330.

Zakzanis, K. K., Campbell, Z., & Jovanovski, D. (2007). The neuropsychology of ecstasy (MDMA) use: A quantitative review. Human Psychopharmacology: Clinical and Experimental, 22(7), 427–435.

Zanarini, M. C., Reichman, C. A., Frankenburg, F. R., Reich, D. B., & Fitzmaurice, G. (2010). The course of eating disorders in patients with borderline personality disorder: A 10-year follow-up study. International Journal of Eating Disorders, 43(3), 226–232.

Zapf, P. A., & Roesch, R. (2006). Competency to stand trial: A guide for evaluators. In A. K. Hess & I. B. Weiner (Eds.), Handbook of forensic psychology (3rd ed., pp. 305–331). New York: Wiley.

Zapf, P. A., & Roesch, R. (2009). Evaluation of competence to stand trial. New York: Oxford University Press.

ZDNet. (2005). Got playlist anxiety? You're not alone. April, 6. Accessed from: http://www.zdnet.com/news/got-playlist-anxiety-youre-not-alone/142180.

Zeckey, C., Hildebrand, F., Pape, H-C., Mommsen, P., Panzica, M., Zelle, B. A., et al. (2011). Head injury in polytrauma—Is there an effect on outcome more than 10 years after the injury? Brain Injury, 25(6), 551–559.

Zeeck, A., Stelzer, N., Linster, H. W., Joos, A., & Hartmann, A. (2011). Emotion and eating in binge eating disorder and obesity. European Eating Disorders Review, 19(5), 426–437.

Zeeck, A., Weber, S., Sandholz, A., Joos, A., & Hartmann, A. (2011). Stability of long-term outcome in bulimia nervosa: A 3-year follow-up. Journal of Clinical Psychology, 67(3), 318–327.

Zelkowitz, P., Paris, J., Guzder, J., & Feldman, R. (2001). Diathesis and stressors in borderline pathology of childhood: The role of neuropsychological risk and trauma. Journal of the American Academy of Child and Adolescent Psychiatry, 40, 100–105.

Zerbe, K. J. (2001). The crucial role of psychodynamic understanding in the treatment of eating disorders. Psychiatric Clinics of North America, 24(2), 305–313.

Zerbe, K. J. (2001). When the self starves: Alliance and outcome in the treatment of eating disorders.

In J. Petrucelli, & C. Stuart (Eds.), Hungers and compulsions: The psychodynamic treatment of eating disorders and addictions. (pp. 183–206) Lanham, MD: Jason Aronson.

Zerbe, K. J. (2008). Integrated treatment of eating disorders beyond the body betrayed. New York: W. W. Norton.

Zerbe, K. J. (2010). Psycodynamic therapy for eating disorders. In C. M. Grilo & J. E. Mitchell (Eds.), The treatment of eating disorders: A clinical handbook (pp. 339–358). New York: Guilford Press.

Zetsche, U., D'Avanzato, C., & Joormann, J. (2012). Depression and rumination: Relation to components of inhibition. Cognition and Emotion, 26 (4), 758–767.

Zhou, J. N., Hofman, M. A., Gooren, L. J. G., & Swaab, D. F. (1995). A sex difference in the human brain and its relation to transsexuality. Nature, 378, 68–70.

Zhou, J. N., Hofman M. A, Gooren L. J. G., & Swaab D. F. (1997). A sex difference in the human brain and its relation to transsexuality. International Journal of Transgenderism, 1(1), http://www.symposion.com/ijt/ijtc0106.htm.

Zhou, Y., Flaherty, J. H., Huang, C., Lu, Z., & Dong, B. (2011). Association between body mass index and cognitive function among Chinese nonagenarians/centenarians. Dementia and Geriatric Cognitive Disorders, 30(6), 517–524.

Zhuo, J. (2010, November 29). Where anonymity breeds contempt. New York Times. Retrieved on June 24, 2011, from www.nytimes.com.

Zilboorg, G., & Henry, G. W. (1941). A history of medical psychology. New York: Norton.

Zimbardo, P. (1976). Rational paths to madness. Presentation at Princeton University, Princeton, NJ.

Zipp, F., & Aktas, O. (2006). The brain as a target of inflammation: Common pathways link inflammatory and neurodegenerative diseases. Trends in Neuroscience, 29(9), 518–527.

Zisser, A., & Eyberg, S. M. (2010). Parent-child interaction therapy and the treatment of disruptive behavior disorders. In J. R. Weisz, & A. E. Kazdin (Eds.), Evidence-based psychotherapies for children and adolescents (2nd ed., pp. 179–193) New York: Guilford Press.

Ziv, I., Leiser, D., & Levine, J. (2011). Social cognition in schizophrenia: Cognitive and affective factors. Cognitive Neuropsychiatry, 16(1), 71–91.

Zivanovic, O., & Nedic, A. (2012). Kraepelin's concept of manic-depressive insanity: One hundred years later. Journal of Affective Disorders, 137(1-3), 15–24.

Zoellner, T. (2000, November). "Don't get even, get mad." Men's Health, 15(9), 56.

Zonana, H., Roth, J. A., & Coric, V. (2004). Forensic assessment of sex offenders. In R. I. Simon & L. H. Gold (Eds.), The American Psychiatric Publishing textbook of forensic psychiatry (pp. 349–376). Washington, DC: American Psychiatric Publishing.

Zubeidat, I., Sierra, J. C., Salinas, J. M., & Rojas-Garcia, A. (2011). Reliability and validity of the Spanish version of the Minnesota Multiphasic Personality Inventory-Adolescent (MMPI-A). Journal of Personality Assessment, 93(1), 26–32.

Zucker, K. J. (2010). Gender identity and sexual orientation. In M. K. Dulcan (Ed.), Dulcan's textbook of child and adolescent psychiatry (pp. 543–552). Arlington, VA: American Psychiatric Publishing.

Zucker, K. J., & Bradley, S. J. (1995). Gender identity disorder and psychosexual problems in children and adolescents. New York: Guilford Press.

Zucker, K. J., Bradley, S. J., Owen-Anderson, A., Kibblewhite, S. J., Wood, H., Singh, D., & Choi, K. (2012). Demographics, behavior problems, and psychosexual characteristics of adolescents with gender identity disorder or transvestic fetishism. Journal of Sex & Marital Therapy, 38(2), 151–189.

Zucker, N. L., Loeb, K. L., Patel, S., & Shafer, A. (2011). Parent groups in the treatment of eating disorders. In D. Le Grange & J. Lock (Eds.), Eating disorders in children and adolescents: A clinical handbook. New York: Guilford Publications.

Zuckerman, M. (2011). Psychodynamic approaches. In M. Zuckerman, Personality science: Three approaches to the causes and treatment of depression (pp. 11–45). Washington, DC: American Psychological Association.

Zuckerman, M. (2011). Trait and psychobiological approaches. In M. Zuckerman (Ed.), Personality Science: Three approaches and their applications to the causes and treatment of depression (pp. 47–77). Washington, DC: American Psychological Association.

Zurolo, A., & Napolitano, S. (2008). Il feticcio e la maschera [The fetishism and the mask]. Psicoterapia Psicoanalitica, 15(2), 179–196.

Zweig, R. D., & Leahy, R. L. (2012). Treatment plans and interventions for bulimia and binge eating disorder. Treatment plans and interventions for evidence-based psychotherapy. New York: Guilford Press.

Zwickl, S., & Merriman, G. (2011). The association between childhood sexual abuse and adult female sexual difficulties. Sexual and Relationship Therapy, 26(1), 16–32.

name index

Abbass, A. A., 476, 494, 501, 503, 508
Abbey, S. E., 194
Abdel-Baki, A., 472
Abdel-Rahman, E., 563, 570
Abdul, P., 343
Abel, G. G., 411
Abela, J. R. Z., 238
Abercrombie, H. C., 233
Abi-Dargham, A., 437, 438
Abraham, K., 234, 235, 298
Abraham, S., 336, 343
Abramowitz, J., 199, 200
Abramowitz, J. S., 36, 129, 134, 142, 144, 147, 407
Abramson, L. Y., 240
Acevedo-Garcia, D., 176
Acier, D., 383
Acosta, M. C., 358, 359, 361, 362
Adam, K. S., 298
Adams, R. E., 161
Addington, D., 466
Addington, J., 433, 466
Adkins, J., 308
Adler, A., 53, 55
Affatati, V., 418
Agronin, M. E., 481, 489, 496
Ahearn, W. H., 543
Ahern, G. L., 104, 214
Ahlers, C. J., 406
Ahmed, S. H., 357
Ahrens, C. E., 160
Aiken, C. B., 280, 281
Aiken, L. R., 88, 97
Ainette, M. G., 371
Airan, R. D., 233
Ajdacic-Gross, V., 307
Ajel, K. I., 125
Akaike, A., 574
Akhtar, S., 142
Akinbami, L. J., 170
Akins, C. K., 414, 415
Akiskal, H. S., 102
Aktas, O., 575
Akutagawa, D., 608
Alba, J., 343
Albala, I., 37
Albert ("Little"), 128
Albert, U., 507
Alcaine, O. M., 121
Alcantara, C., 305, 307
Aldao, A., 121
Alder, 272
Aldhous, P., 512
Aldwin, C. M., 563
Ale, C. M., 520
Alegria, A. A., 76
Alegria, M., 19, 35, 76
Alexander, J. F., 74
Alfano, C. A., 133, 135
Alfano, L., 335
Algars, M., 421
Algoe, S. B., 164
Alhamad, A., 333

Ali, M., 575, 578
Ali, M. M., 296, 297
Alicea, G., 87
Allan, C., 454
Allan, S., 322
Allard, R., 309
Allderidge, P., 11
Allen, A., 542
Allen, B. J., 96
Allen, C., 357
Allen, D., 63
Allen, D. F., 359
Allen, G., 543
Allen, N. B., 200, 235
Allen, W., 51
Allers, K. A., 403
Allman, G., 358
Alloy, L. B., 240, 253
Allwood, C. M., 607
Almeida, D. M., 154
Alonzo, T., 584, 585
Al-Subaie, A., 333
Altamura, A. C., 280
Althof, S. E., 395, 396, 403, 404, 405
Althouse, R., 16, 76, 466, 603, 617
Alvarez, L., 167
Aly, A., 8
Alzheimer, A., 570, 571
Aman, M. G., 267, 541
Ames, D., 567, 569, 570, 572, 575, 577, 581
Amiant, F., 326, 340
Amini, A., 257
an der Heiden, W., 426, 433, 451
Anderson, B. L., 362
Anderson, D., 352
Anderson, K. G., 497
Anderson, L. K., 238
Anderson, R. T., 390, 393
Andreasen, N. C., 420, 435
Andresen, J., 183
Andrews, G., 114
Andrews, J. A., 371
Andrews, V., 443
Angle, J., 342
Angst, J., 141
Aniston, J., 151
Anna O., 29, 53, 195
Annunziato, R. A., 333
Anstey, K. J., 562
Anthony, J. C., 362
Antoni, M. H., 184
Antony, M. M., 122, 130, 131, 134, 140, 399
Apfelbaum, B., 397
Apostolova, L. G., 570, 575, 576, 580
Appelbaum, P. S., 37, 605, 606
Apple, F., 343
Apter, A., 303
Arango, C., 427, 432
Archer, D., 487, 489
Arciuli, J., 511

Ardjmand, A., 211
Ardoin, S. P., 553
Arens, E. A., 493
Arias, E., 51, 302
Arieti, S., 235, 425, 426
Aring, C. D., 11
Aristotle, 10, 25, 393, 441
Armitage, R., 226, 245
Armour, S., 611
Armstrong, C., 258
Armstrong, M. J., 582
Arndt, W. B., 608
Arnedt, J. T., 226, 245
Arnow, B. A., 228
Arntz, A., 491
Arroyos-Jurado, E., 19
Arvanites, T. M., 597
Asberg, M., 300
Ash, R., 159, 586
Ashcraft, R., 611
Ashton, A. K., 396, 402, 403, 405
Ashton, J. R., 297
Asimov, I., 6, 11, 43, 145, 514
Asnis, G. M., 165
Asperger, H., 540
Assal, F., 578
Astbury, J., 224, 242, 243
Astin, J. A., 126
Atack, J. R., 123
Atanasijevic, T., 414
Aten, J. D., 68
Ator, N. A., 123
August, K. J., 178
Auguste D., 570
Avrin, A., 325
Avrin, J., 325
Avrin, M., 325
Avrin, W., 325
Ayalon, L., 244, 582
Ayd, F. J., Jr., 231
Ayers, N., 16
Ayllon, T., 452
Ayoub, C. C., 191, 192
Azar, B., 18

Baars, B. J., 213
Baca-Garcia, E., 291, 305
Bach, A. K., 389, 405
Bach, P. A., 441, 461
Bachevalier, J., 542
Back, S. E., 381
Badger, R., 308
Baer, L., 84, 88, 92, 96, 281
Bagby, E., 127
Baggot, M., 365
Bahrick, H., 85
Bailer, U. F., 327
Baird, S. C., 488, 489
Bakalar, N., 18
Baker, B. L., 553
Baker, K., 210, 215, 216
Baker, R., 140, 162
Balassone, M., 471, 473
Baldessarini, R. J., 309
Baldwin, D. S., 125, 138
Baldwin, J. S., 519
Baldwin, S., 72, 73, 604
Ballas, C., 270, 276

Balodis, I. M., 382
Bancroft, J., 394, 397
Bandelow, B., 138
Bandura, A., 61, 62, 128, 129, 130
Bankert, E. A., 42
Banks, J., 164
Bao, A.-M., 232
Baranoski, M. V., 601
Baranski, J. V., 98
Barbaree, H. E., 415
Barber, A., 20
Barber, C., 616
Barber, R., 50
Barber, T., 50, 236
Bareggi, S. R., 147
Bari, A., 371
Barkley, R. A., 532, 534
Barlow, D. H., 389, 399
Barlow, M. R., 132, 212
Barnard, C., 40
Barnes, A., 442
Barnes, C. A., 207
Barnes, D. H., 291, 292, 305, 307
Barnes, G. E., 235
Barnes, T. R. E., 455, 456, 458
Baron, M., 252
Baron-Cohen, S., 481
Barr, A. M., 359, 362
Barrera, T. L., 136
Barrett, N., 108
Barron, J., 599
Barrowclough, C., 444, 462, 464, 469
Barry, B., 84
Barry, L. M., 184
Barrymore, D., 358
Bartholomew, K., 214
Barton, A., 11
Bartrop, R. W., 180
Bartz, J., 507, 508
Basoglu, M., 160, 162
Bass, C., 191, 192
Basson, R., 390, 392, 402
Bastien, C. H., 171, 173
Bateman, A. W., 493
Bates, G. W., 238
Bates, L. M., 176
Bateson, G., 430, 444
Batki, S. L., 358
Batten, S. V., 168
Baucom, D. H., 75
Bauer, M. E., 181
Baum, A., 115, 178, 182
Bauman, M. L., 542
Baxter, L. R., 146
Baxter, L. R., Jr., 146, 148
Bazargan, M., 244
Beals, J., 77
Bean, A., 8
Beatrice of Nazareth, 341
Beauregard, E., 414
Beautrais, A., 309
Bebbington, P. E., 433, 440, 444, 463
Bebko, J. M., 551, 553
Becchetti, L., 18

subject index

Milestones in Abnormal Psychology

Stone Age Mental disorders treated by trephination. *p. 9*

430–377 B.C. Hippocrates cites brain as source of mental disorders. *pp. 9–10*

500–1450 Middle Ages adopts demonological explanations and treatments. *pp. 10–11*

1547 Bethlehem Hospital in London converted into asylum. *pp. 11–12*

1693 Witch-hunting trials peak in Salem, Massachusetts. *p. 10*

1773 First American hospital exclusively for mental patients opens in Williamsburg, Virginia. *pp. 12–13*

1793 Phillipe Pinel frees asylum patients at LaBicêtre in Paris. *pp. 12–13*

1812 Benjamin Rush writes first American textbook on psychiatry. *pp. 12–13*

1842 Dorothea Dix begins campaign to reform mental hospitals in the United States. *pp. 12–13*

1865 Gregor Mendel publishes theories of genetics. *p. 50*

1879 German professor Wilhelm Wundt establishes first laboratory for experimental study of psychology. *p. 26*

1883 Emil Kraepelin publishes textbook on psychiatry, likening mental disorders to physical diseases. *pp. 13, 99*

1892 American Psychological Association founded. *pp. 20–21*

1893 Sigmund Freud, with Josef Breuer, publishes first chapters of *On the Psychical Mechanisms of Hysterical Phenomena*, launching psychoanalysis. *pp. 15, 53*

1896 Lightner Witmer establishes first psychological clinic in the U.S. at University of Pennsylvania. *pp. 15, 20*

1897 General paresis linked to physical cause, syphilis. *pp. 13–14*

1900 Freud publishes *The Interpretation of Dreams*. *pp. 56–57*

1900 Morton Prince uses hypnosis to treat multiple personality disorder. *pp. 214–216*

1901 Ivan Pavlov demonstrates classical conditioning. *pp. 59–60*

1905 First intelligence test published. *pp. 96–97*

1907 Alzheimer's disease identified by Dr. Alois Alzheimer. *pp. 570–571*

1908 Clifford Beers writes autobiography *A Mind That Found Itself*, launching Mental Hygiene Movement in the United States. *p. 452*

1909 Freud makes his only visit to America and lectures at Clark University. *pp. 15, 53*

1913 Behaviorist John Watson argues that psychology should abandon study of consciousness. *pp. 58–59, 128*

1917 The U.S. Congress declares all nonmedical opioids illegal. *p. 356*

1921 Rorschach Test published. *p. 88*

1923 Freud publishes *The Ego and the Id*. *pp. 53–54*

1929 EEG developed. *p. 94, 96*

1935 Alcoholics Anonymous founded. *pp. 379–380*

1935 First use of lobotomy for mental disorders. *pp. 451, 453*

1937 Marijuana made illegal in the United States. *p. 368*

1938 Electroconvulsive therapy introduced in Rome. *p. 268*

1938 B. F. Skinner proposes operant conditioning. *p. 59*

1939 The Wechsler-Bellevue Intelligence Scale published. *pp. 96–97*

1943 LSD's hallucinogenic effects discovered. *pp. 363–364, 366*

1943 Minnesota Multiphasic Personality Test (MMPI) published. *pp. 90–92*

1943 Jean-Paul Sartre's existential book *Being and Nothingness* published. *p. 65*

1949 Lithium salts first used for bipolar disorder. *pp. 278–279*

1951 Chlorpromazine, first antipsychotic drug, tested. *pp. 455–456*

1951 Carl Rogers publishes *Client-Centered Therapy*. *pp. 65–67*

1952 First edition of DSM published by the American Psychiatric Association. *p. 99*

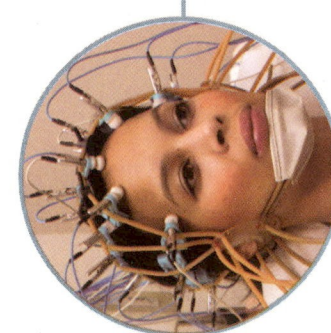